# DISCOVERING SOUTHERN AFRICA

**Other books by T. V. Bulpin**

*Natal and the Zulu Country*
*Lost Trails of the Transvaal*
*To the Banks of the Zambezi*
*Islands in a Forgotten Sea*
*The Ivory Trail*
*The Hunter is Death*
*Trail of the Copper King*
*The White Whirlwind*
*Tickey, the Story of a Clown*
*Southern Africa, Land of Beauty and Splendour*

# DISCOVERING

# SOUTHERN AFRICA

## T.V. BULPIN.

*Creative Assistant: Hilary Rennie*

T. V. Bulpin Publications (Pty) Ltd
1004 Cape of Good Hope Savings Bank Building
St George's Street
Cape Town
P.O. Box 1516
8000

© T. V. Bulpin 1980
First Edition 1970
(Six Impressions)
Second Edition (enlarged and revised) 1980

ISBN 0 949956 17 1

Photosetting by McManus Bros (Pty) Ltd
Colour separations by Hirt & Carter (Pty) Ltd
Printed and bound by Creda Press (Pty) Ltd

*To the excitement of discovery;*
*the long views;*
*the other side of the horizon;*
*the surprise around the corner and the song of the wind.*
*To the fun of having a companion and the pleasure of experiences that are shared.*

# EXPLANATION

*Discovering Southern Africa* is intended to be a well-informed, loquacious and opinionated guide to the various territories comprising Southern Africa.

There are no advertisements or sponsorship. The opinions expressed in the text are entirely those of the author. Each successive edition of the book is revised and updated. In this connection the author will be happy to receive from readers any suggestions, corrections or criticisms which might lead to improvement of the book. The desire of the author and publisher is that this book be regarded as a completely dependable guide to the pleasures and excitement of travel, the wealth of fascinating discoveries to be explored, and the joy of life to be found in the sunshine of the great spaces of Southern Africa.

Every place of tourist accommodation – hotel, motel, caravan park, camping ground, holiday camp, youth hostel, etc. – has a free listing, and every effort is made to ensure that this listing is comprehensive. Rates for accommodation are correct only at time of publication. They are subject to rapid changes. Assessments of accommodation and of tourist attractions are those of the author. In making assessments, the opinions and experiences of travellers are invaluable, as are readers' suggestions for innovations, new facilities and developments.

The gradings given are very simple, based on the traditional star system which refers to available facilities. One * means good; ** means very good; *** means excellent; **** means outstanding; ***** means superlative. An ® means a special personal recommendation for pleasant, relaxed atmosphere, courteous, hospitable staff or idyllic settings. This recommendation can be given, for example, to a camping spot which has no facilities to grade but is uniquely situated.

The spelling of place names in Southern Africa is inconsistent. With names originating from so many different language groups, and many of them containing odd sounds such as clicks, these inconsistencies are unavoidable. Only in recent times have efforts been made to at least impose uniformity of spelling, but a great deal of work has still to be done in this direction.

The reader will also no doubt be confused by the way in which African names are spelt out, often with the initial letter being small, and followed by a capital. African grammar is composed of classes of words, each class identifiable by a particular prefix, which often simply means 'the'. Where possible in this book, the English form of 'the' has been left out when referring to an African word already containing the prefix (i.e. a river known as *uMzimkulu*, the great home). Conversely, where the English form of 'the' has been used, the prefix has been omitted (i.e. the *Mzimkulu* River). In certain instances, where the prefix has been incorporated into the word due to Anglicisation (i.e. *Usutu* River instead of *uSuthu*), the use of both forms of 'the' is unavoidable – the Usutu River, which would really be translated as, the the Suthu River.

# CONTENTS

# ABBREVIATIONS

| | |
|---|---|
| B/B | bed and breakfast |
| D | daily |
| D/B/B | dinner, bed and breakfast |
| km | kilometres |
| m | metres |
| mm | millimetres |
| ℓ | litres |
| ha | hectares |
| E | Emalangeni (Swazi currency) |
| P | Pula (Botswana currency) |
| R | Rand (South African currency) |
| $ | Dollar (Zimbabwe currency) |

# DISTANCES

| | |
|---|---|
| 1 foot | = 30,48 centimetres |
| 39,37 inches | = 1 metre |
| 1 mile | = 1,6 kilometres |
| 37 miles | = 60 kilometres |
| 74 miles | = 120 kilometres |

An easy, quick conversion: 5 miles = 8 kilometres.

## Prelude

# THE HIGHWAYS OF SOUTHERN AFRICA

It is axiomatic that the extent of a country's development can be measured by its orderliness: that a man or his wife may take a stroll around the corner at night without considerable danger of assault; that a letter they might post will have every prospect of reaching its destination speedily and without interference; that the cities be free of smells; that the water from a tap be pure and palatable; and that the roads be open, convenient, reliably surfaced, graded and located so that the traveller along them feels himself secure, within reach of competent aid should he meet with accident, and always free to go anywhere without bureaucratic, legal or military impedence as long as he behaves himself according to the accepted, reasonable laws of the land and conforms to the premise that democratic rights are based on the golden rule of 'do unto others as you would have them do unto you'.

In Southern Africa the above conditions prevail in nearly every particular when it comes to travel. The network of roads, in relation to the scattered population, vast area, and geographical configuration, is a credit to the wisdom of the various governments who financed them, and to the genius and labour of the men who planned and made them. If the quality of roads may be used as a gauge of a country's degree of civilisation, then the ultimate measure should be made against the extent of their beautification apart from their function: whereas a railway is essentially for mass transportation, a road or pathway is for personal transportation. In addition to being made well, roads must be pleasant and beautiful, and acceptance of this obligation by engineers is the ultimate test of perfection.

There is a romantic flavour to the story of the building of Southern Africa's great highways. In the beginning there were simply game trails. Great herds of antelope wandering backwards and forwards between their winter and summer grazing, blazed the first tracks over the Drakensberg range, destined to be used by the Voortrekkers; the elephants finding their way to reliable water, trampled passages through the densest bush which explorers and hunters subsequently followed on their ventures into the distant interior.

When the man apes came, they tramped pathways to caves and waterholes, and these were trodden in turn by Stone Age Bushmen and Hottentots, and Iron Age African tribes who migrated down from the north in the years after the birth of Christ. Trade began – there were miners and pedlars among the tribal people and arterial pathways came into use which linked the tribal areas and provided routes from the interior to coastal ports established by Arab traders.

Along these paths tramped raiding bands and war parties, safari traders and slavers, pedlars of beads and bangles, porters carrying gold dust and copper bars, innumerable refugees from tribal wars. The network of pathways became so complete that it is said that one could have walked from the Cape to Cairo or from the east to the west coast of Africa without encountering a break in well-defined routes.

Many of these ancient pathways are still in use and the tribespeople who use them consider them every bit as vital to their way of life as the tarmac dual carriageways are to modern, built-up areas. For those who like to sit and marvel at the passing show, the human beings to be seen tramping along these pathways have a variegated individuality which is not easily observable on a busy, traffic-laden road.

*Overleaf: As old as the presence of man; the pathways of Africa and the custom of travellers dropping a stone for luck on a wayside pile.*

In *The Ivory Trail* the celebrated poacher, Stephanus Barnard, describes how, on the ancient pathway leading from Crooks Corner in the Northern Transvaal into the wilds of Moçambique, he once encountered a man struggling along that lonely trail carrying a heavy grandfather clock. To Barnard's incredulous question, the man answered with simple gravity that he was returning from contract labour on the Witwatersrand gold mines and, if he eventually managed to reach home with his load (a souvenir of civilisation), the chimes of the clock would tell his wives when to feed him!

On the ancient pathway of the Ndawu people, which finds its way over the heights of the Chimanimani Mountains between Zimbabwe and Moçambique, an endless stream of foot travellers may still be encountered making their way backwards and forwards between the two countries in search of trade or work. With a meagre blanket roll for covering at night, a couple of fowls in a wicker basket to provide food, a roll of tobacco to barter, and a fund of gossip about scenes and experiences to exchange on the long journey, they tramp along a pathway ascending a scenic heaven which, to a sick, weary or frightened man, must become an interminable hell of steep climbs and descents.

Beside many of these ancient pathways can be seen 'luck' heaps made of pebbles or plaits of grass, deposited at strategic points by travellers hoping for good fortune or seeking to propitiate the spirits. In Zululand some of these luck heaps or *isiVivane* reach impressive proportions, especially at the approaches to former royal courts of Shaka, Dingane and other Zulu kings. How many of those who deposited a stone on these cairns with a prayer for luck passed on and never returned is an unwritten story.

In Swaziland, where the great arterial pathway known as *iNdhlelakayomi* (the path never empty), meanders across the full width of that beautiful little country, plaits of grass are still deposited on the side of the path by travellers hoping that this will ensure good luck. The Karanga people favoured tapping lines across the paths (still extant at the approaches to Great Zimbabwe) where travellers paused in their journey, picked up a pebble, and tapped it across the pathway to propitiate the spirits.

When Europeans came with their ox wagons – surely the most rugged form of wheeled transport ever devised – they converted many of these footpaths into trails. There was no road construction: the wheels of wagons, the boots of pioneers, the hooves of draught animals simply widened the paths, wagon men only occasionally used a shovel to facilitate the crossing of a ford or the ascent of a slippery slope. The pioneers moved far ahead of civilisation and government. It took years for authority, tax collectors and professional road-makers to catch up with the drift of population. In Southern Africa over 300 000 km of unplanned, haphazard trails developed.

The rule of the Dutch East India Company over the Cape Colony saw no expenditure of public money on roads. It was a momentous day indeed when the first government authority in Southern Africa undertook the earliest road construction and expended public money on improving a gradient or making a proper surface. The first step towards official responsibility came with the British in 1812 when the *landdros* of the newly established town of George, Adrianus van Kervel, secured funds from the government for the making of the Cradock Kloof Pass over the Outeniqua Mountains. This pass was built, and while it did not prove to be a practical success, its construction by a local authority using government funds set a precedent, and it served as the pioneer forerunner to the building of the modern highway from George to the interior.

In 1823 the construction of a second mountain pass, the Franschhoek Pass, was undertaken by the government. The Franschhoek Pass was built to replace an old trail which had become practically impassable. The pass was completed in 1825 by soldiers working as labourers, supervised by a competent officer of the Royal Engineers, Major Holloway. This was the first professionally located, designed and constructed stretch of highway in Southern Africa.

Popular clamour now increased: something had to be done about other mountain passes, which were in so deplorable a state that all traffic between Cape Town and the interior was hazardous. The pass over the Hottentots Holland mountains, carrying some of the heaviest traffic in the Cape Colony and the only way of crossing what were known as the Mountains of Africa on the way up the east coast, was particularly urgently in need of repair. Known as the *Gantouw* (elands path), it had originated as a game trail; man had done nothing to prepare it for excessive use and it was badly rutted and damaged.

The new Governor, Sir Lowry Cole, realising the urgent need for reconstruction of the pass, authorised expenditure. When this news reached the British Colonial Office, outraged at the expense, they ordered the immediate cessation of the work. The people of the Cape offered to indemnify Governor and State, and the British Government relented: times were hard, but the pass could be properly built on official funds. In 1830 Sir Lowry's Pass was opened, professionally designed and built by Major Charles Michell, surveyor-general and civil engineer of the Cape Colony.

This was the beginning of proper road construction in Southern Africa. The government of the Cape Colony was thoroughly aware of the need for systematic road construction, and only shortage of funds impeded the work. For ten years little could be done, but with what money was available Major Michell did what he could to improve existing passes, and he built a permanent road across the shifting sand dunes of the Cape Flats.

The financial picture changed radically in the 1840s when a first-class colonial secretary was appointed to the Cape. This man, John Montagu, cleared up the public debt and put the Colony on a sound financial footing. He also understood the essential nature of good roads and together with Michell he commenced the first major programme of road construction, solving in part the shortage of finance by the use of convicts who, instead of being left to rot in chains, were given a chance to reform through work on productive, rewarding and stimulating tasks.

To assist the two great leaders, Andrew Geddes Bain applied for a post as a road builder. The three names of Montagu, Michell and Bain will always be linked. They were the classic road builders of Southern Africa and in their time one great mountain pass after the other was completed – Michell's Pass, Gydo Pass, Bain's Kloof, Karoo Poort.

After the completion of these passes Andrew Geddes Bain was sent to the Eastern Cape, while his brilliant son, Thomas Bain, continued work in the Western Cape, building the road from Karoo Poort to Beaufort West; Grey's Pass; the complex passes between George and Knysna; Prince Alfred's Pass; Tradouw Pass; Garcia's Pass; Cogmans Kloof; Pakhuis Pass; Swartberg Pass; the wonderful Victoria Road from Sea Point to Hout Bay. All these major works and many more were completed in this golden age of road building.

From then on there was no cessation in road construction in Southern Africa. The Voortrekkers in the Transvaal blazed trails to reach the coast at Lourenço Marques; the prospectors and transport men who rushed to the Eastern Transvaal goldfields blazed the romantic trails known as the Jock of the Bushveld Road and Pettigrew's Road. Hunters tramped the first trail up to the Ndebele country in Zimbabwe, and Rhodes in 1890 sent Frederick Selous and Frank Johnson at the head of 400 men to blaze the Pioneer Road from Palapye to Salisbury. And meanwhile, the great discoveries of diamonds and gold in the interior were luring properly made highways from the Cape further and further northwards to feed from the coastal ports the new industries and volatile population.

In the Cape, over the years, laws were made concerning roads, the disposal of carcasses of transport animals (formerly left to rot by the wayside) and the maintenance and construction of new routes which would be financed from tolls.

In 1834, John Montagu devised an ordinance establishing divisional road boards into whose care government-made roads were committed for maintenance. This was the forerunner of the Divisional Council system introduced to the Cape in 1855, after the granting of responsible government. These boards controlled the entire administration of the roads of the Cape; construction, however, remained the responsibility of the government, with funds voted by Parliament and much influenced by the persuasiveness of individual members from particular parts of the country.

Under this system the Cape roads developed tremendously. The Cape was divided into 93 divisional councils, each one in turn divided into elective wards. Rates were levied on immovable property and the funds were used for road maintenance and expansion in the division, embracing public health, extermination of vermin and noxious weeds, building of recreational resorts and other worthwhile local projects. With care and planning lavished on them, the roads flourished; the pride of a council in developing its own area served as an additional stimulant. Each year the councils held a congress and comparative reports on developments stimulated further activity.

It was at this stage that the petrol-driven vehicle appeared on the scene and, soon after the Anglo-Boer War, started to make known its particular requirements. Infinitely more fragile than the hardy old wagons and carts, and able to travel at far higher speeds, the new vehicles demanded radical improvements in road surfaces and locations. As they grew faster, these vehicles introduced special problems, such as the curious phenomenon of 'corrugations' – parallel ridges in the surface of a gravel road which could make travelling insufferable. The faster and heavier the traffic, the worse the corrugations, and for years there was great controversy over the exact cause. With a crest-to-crest width of 46 cm to 61 cm, penetrating a road surface by as much as 0,3 m, these corrugations were apparently caused by the harmonic frequency of the springs of a vehicle. Empty vehicles, especially, would start the obnoxious rhythm by bouncing on an uneven surface; the motion would continue, compacting the road surface beneath the wheels into corrugations which, once fully developed, could literally shake a vehicle to pieces.

Many experiments were made all over the world to find an answer to corrugations. Dragging, sweeping, grading, mixing of soils and gravels were tried; mixing ant heap soil with gravel definitely reduced corrugations but was not a permanent solution. When the roads were wet there were no corrugations, but mud and potholes instead. As soon as the roads dried, corrugations reappeared. The only answer to these problems was a permanent hard-top layer. But to the old-timers, this development meant expansions in technology and finance which were staggering. Such road surfaces could not be made in a haphazard, unskilled way by convict gangs and overseers working on relief; road building would have to be accorded the full dignity of science, involving specialised chemistry, laboratory-controlled techniques, and elaborate machinery. To find the men and the money for such development presented obstacles so great as to seem insurmountable.

The extent of the problem was amply demonstrated in Zimbabwe in October 1925, in the midst of the mounting crisis about roads, Stuart Chandler was appointed chief road engineer. On investigation of his department he found that its resources comprised six lorries, 326 Scotchcarts, 2 262 oxen and 126 mules. Nothing else. The roads were little more than tracks without a single bridge or culvert, wandering through the bush to serve a country 375 830 square kilometres in extent and only sparsely populated, with taxpaying individuals singularly elusive, and practically every problem ever confronted by a road engineer clamouring for immediate solution.

Man, however, always seems to be at his best in times of adversity, and Southern Africa produced a remarkable set of individuals to launch its revolutionary age of massive road construction. In Stuart Chandler, Zimbabwe found an individual versatile and resilient enough to face difficulties which would have daunted more conventional engineers.

Roads Zimbabwe had to have, but there was hardly any money. Materials, too, were scarce and expensive, but labour, fortunately, was cheap. The answer to the problem was to orientate road design towards construction methods which required labour rather than material. Chandler had worked on roads in the Cape and had observed experiments with strip roads there. In the Cape, where materials were cheaper and labour more expensive, strip roads were not found to be very economical, and the idea had been discarded. Chandler revived these roads and developed them to the limits of perfection possible with this type of construction. Despite all their defects, the strip roads opened Zimbabwe to development and provided an immediate answer to a difficult set of circumstances. The scattered population needed good roads, but they could barely finance even gravel roads. In addition, to make permanent gravel roads in Zimbabwe was exceedingly difficult: much of the country consists of a granite sand surface on top of clay, and in the wet season this sand surface simply becomes saturated. Only hard-surface roads seemed to offer a solution, but where was the money to pay for them?

The strips were made of concrete or asphalt, whichever material was available. When made of concrete they were 15 cm thick and laid down in 10-m lengths separated by 1,2 cm expansion joints. The two parallel strips were each 0,6 m wide and 0,8 m apart to suit the standard motor vehicle wheel track of 1,4 m. The strips could accommodate traffic densities of 250 to 400 vehicles a day, with a maximum speed limit of 60 km an hour. Anybody driving along them at a high speed would be a menace, for all traffic on the strips was of necessity travelling in the centre of the road and passing vehicles had to move sideways, so that each had two wheels on one strip only and the other two in the mud, dust or gravel. A vehicle travelling at speed was in considerable danger of a skid if its driver had to hastily move off the strips.

In 1930 the first concrete strip in Zimbabwe was built: an experimental 366 m on the Gwelo-Selukwe road. The cost worked out at £400 per 1,6 km and everybody in Zimbabwe was optimistic about the project. Strip roads were the answer for Zimbabwe.

Another problem Stuart Chandler had to contend with was the complete absence of bridges. The Beit Trust came to the rescue with finance for 91 bridges, including such key structures as the Birchenough Bridge over the Save River (£120 000), the Beit Bridge over the Limpopo (£126 000), and the great Otto Beit Bridge over the Zambezi at Chirundu. These were spectacular bridges over majestic rivers, but the smaller rivers also had to be bridged and for these Chandler perfected the low-level bridge which, though temporarily inundated in times of flood, still provided a secure crossing for most of the year was was very economical to build.

Vigorous road construction continued in Zimbabwe. With European labour under an unemployment relief scheme, concrete strips were built on the Salisbury-Enkeldoorn, Bulawayo-Matopos and Bulawayo-Lonely Mine roads. The European labour raised the cost of the strips to about £1 000 per 1,6 km and, in order to reduce construction costs, experiments were made with asphalt instead of concrete. The first asphalt strips were laid down in 1932 on the Salisbury-Sinoia road, which carried heavy traffic. The experiment proved satisfactory and asphalt construction was generally adopted.

By the end of 1937, 2 074 km of strip roads had been constructed at a cost of £350 per 1,6 km compared with £200 per 1,6 km for gravel surface. But it was calculated that mainte-nance costs over a period of 20 years would total £1 000 per 1,6 km for asphalt strips and £3 028 for gravel. There was no sure means of knowing the increase in traffic volume during this period, however; between 1932 and 1937 traffic in Zimbabwe increased by 467 per cent and the demands of speed were increasingly felt.

When Stuart Chandler retired in 1943 he had supervised the construction of 13 high-level bridges, 366 low-level bridges and 5 742 culverts. He had directed the re-alignment of 4 828 km of road, and seen the completion of 4 023 km of gravel roads and 3 416 km of strips, including the Sinoia-Chirundu section on the Great North Road in 1930. He had arranged for the commencement of a ferry across the Zambezi River in 1931, and on 24 May 1939 he saw the opening of the great bridge at Chirundu to replace the ferry. The opening of the Birchenough

Bridge over the Great Save River on 20 December 1935 had completed the road from Umtali to Fort Victoria. At the end of 1938 it was possible to drive from Umtali through Salisbury and Bulawayo to Beit Bridge on continuous strips, the longest paved stretch of road in Africa; in 1941 the Bulawayo-Victoria Falls road was completed in strips. Parts of this road consisted of abandoned stretches of railway track complete with bridges. Altogether no small achievement for the indefatigable Stuart Chandler! The low-level bridges were the particular brainchild of Mr Chandler, imitated in other parts of the world, only imperfectly.

Meanwhile, what had been happening in South Africa? There, the demand for major highway construction of hard-top, full-width mat-surfaced roads had reached an overwhelming pitch. In 1927 the contract was given to Griffiths and Raw for the tarmac surfacing of the road from Bellville to Paarl, and from this beginning arose the dream of an all-tarmac surface along the romantic old Cape-to-Cairo road. There was no other tarmac surface along its entire length outside the municipal areas of big cities such as Johannesburg.

The amount of planning, finance and labour necessary to convert the main roads of South Africa to tarmac surfaces was obviously going to be prodigious. In 1925 the government had already appointed the Holmswood Committee to enquire into the matter but despite this body's far-reaching recommendations nothing was done. The man for the occasion was found in the person of H. J. Raubenheimer, an attorney in the town of George where, it will be remembered, the first magistrate, Adrianus van Kervel, had undertaken the earliest major road construction using public money.

Raubenheimer was born on *Klipdrift* farm in the Long Kloof. He was a member of the George Divisional Council and a great champion of roads. At the Divisional Council's congress at George in 1926, he proposed a petrol tax of 3d a gallon to finance roadmaking on a national scale. There was a great outcry and the motion was thrown out, but at every succeeding congress he raised the matter again.

In 1932 Raubenheimer became president of the Association of Divisional Councils of the Cape Province and in this high office in every possible way he promoted progress in general and roads in particular, again proposing the idea of the petrol tax to raise finance.

In 1935 the Government of South Africa passed the National Road Fund and created a national road board to finance and plan a great network of roads, leaving construction to each of the four provinces of the country. Finance was to come from a duty of 3d per gallon on all petrol sold in South Africa.

Mr Raubenheimer was appointed to the National Roads Board and remained its guiding spirit throughout its existence. On the board with him were G. S. Burt-Andrews, the city engineer of Johannesburg, F. C. Hollander, M. E. C. of Natal, C. V. Botha, of the Orange Free State, J. A. Harris, assistant general manager, commercial, of the South African Railways, and as chairman C. F. Schmidt, controller and auditor-general. Mr W. F. Murray, head of the Orange Free State roads department, was appointed chief technical adviser.

While Murray concentrated on solving the difficult problem of the almost complete absence of engineers by recruiting staff from every possible source, the board set to work selecting routes. This became something of a nightmare task. Every kilometre of the location of a road is, understandably, of vital importance to some vested interest: a road can enrich an owner whose property was formerly inaccessible, and it can ruin somebody else by bypassing some comfortable little business – hotel, garage or café – that had previously flourished on passing traffic.

There were no tarmac roads at the time in South Africa outside of urban areas and the board members were forced to swallow not only a prodigious amount of string-pulling, rivalry, outright attempts at bribery and all manner of emotional persuasions, but also clouds of dust from the thousands of kilometres they had to travel to select routes. They interviewed 192 deputations, many so totally contradictory that if the board had yielded to everybody, the national roads network of South Africa would have resembled a regular cat's cradle!

It was impossible for the board to avoid antagonising many influential vested interests. Nearly every decision they reached produced a clamour accusing members of favouritism, prejudice or incompetence. Particularly bitter arguments came from municipalities who found themselves bypassed. Eventually a programme of 14 national roads was planned embracing 8 683 km of trunk road construction to be financed out of the National Roads Fund. The 14 roads were as follows:

N1. *The Road of South Africa* George to Beit Bridge. This was to be the backbone of the network, from which ribs radiated to Durban, East London, Port Elizabeth, Cape Town etc.

N2. *The Garden Route* The base connecting Cape Town to Durban.

N3. *Durban-Johannesburg.*

N4. *Pretoria-Lourenço Marques.*

N5. *Winburg-Ladysmith.*

N6. *East London-Reddersburg.*

N7. *Port Elizabeth-Middelburg.*

N8. *Bloemfontein-Kimberley.*

N9. *Cape Town-Colesberg.*

N10. *Kokstad-Pietermaritzburg.*

N11. *Cape Town-Viooslsdrif.*

N12. *Outeniqua Pass-Oudtshoorn-Beaufort West.*

N13. *Three Sisters-Kimberley-Johannesburg.*

N14. *Durban-Zululand-Ermelo.*

From these 14 basic trunk roads, numerous subsidiary roads would, in due course, be constructed. The announcement of the basic routes produced a storm of criticism and complaint. Fraserburg, which had always been on the road to the north (via Ceres), now found itself left literally in the cold; Oudtshoorn was enraged at being left on a spur. They had wanted N1 to start at Mossel Bay, climb the mountains by means of Robinson Pass, and then traverse the entire Little Karoo. Cape Town, in turn, was infuriated that N1 did not start in the mother city of Southern Africa, which was the traditional beginning of the Cape-to-Cairo road.

The route from East London to the north had provided the board with considerable difficulties, and members had been split on the issue. The various towns concerned had presented most resolute arguments for their case. The route had either to lead through Molteno or Queenstown, and finally only a casting vote on the board made it Queenstown.

Vituperative attacks on the Board reached a frenzied pitch. Raubenheimer came in for particularly virulent criticism, especially by various interests in the Cape who disagreed with routes.

The start of construction produced a fresh rush of squabbles. To launch the national roads, the government had made a special vote of £500 000. The 3d a gallon on petrol was adopted from 31 March 1935, an estimated £1 250 000 a year which had to be used entirely on construction. This was not a fortune and it was immediately evident that priority would have to be given to certain routes. Cape Town and Johannesburg were already well connected by train and air through Kimberley, so this route was left almost to the last. There was tremendous ill-feeling from Kimberley over this decision.

The five-year plan of the Board was presented to the government on 22 February 1939, by far the biggest single development concept ever undertaken in Southern Africa. The railway network had been built piecemeal, but the national roads were a concentrated effort. In the teeth of bitter argument, with costs always rising in a frightening manner above estimates, it is pleasing to know that successive ministers of finance always supported the Board and complied with pleas for additional funds.

The Second World War delayed the entire project while men and machinery were absorbed by the army. Continuing dissension also tended to hamstring the Board, especially in the Cape and the Transvaal where jealousies and, in the Transvaal, an ineffective provincial road department perpetuated endless carping and bickering without producing any concrete achievement.

The entire programme of the National Roads Board was particularly vulnerable to friction in its connection with the provincial authorities. The Board had to plan routes, lay down standards, provide finance and supervise construction, but the provincial authorities had to do the actual building of the roads. This arrangement resulted in no little wastage of time and money, and innumerable petty jealousies and squabbles. The Board had to contend with all manner of vexations and complaints. One amusing complaint was that the 800 Italian prisoners-of-war employed on the construction of the Outeniqua Pass were indulging in fun and games with the Coloured girls of the Blanco area. A touch of humanity is indicated here. The minutes of the Board testify that they were not prepared to do anything about this – 'men would be men' and besides, there would be possible compensations in an improvement to the musical talents of the Coloured people and a more plentiful supply of caddies to the George golf course in six or seven years' time!

The really important thing, however, was that despite all these difficulties the national roads network – the pride and joy of transport in South Africa – came to fruition, largely owing to the men who designed and constructed these superb highways. Among many, certain names stand out: Bryan Shannon, first chief engineer of the National Roads Board and (after he was lost on active service), his successor Johan Durr; and P. A. de Villiers, the location engineer, a supreme road engineer who deserves his place with classic old-timers such as the Bain family. He was responsible for Du Toit's Kloof Pass, most of the Garden Route, and the great Outeniqua Pass, one of the boldest and most majestically conceived of all the roads of Southern Africa.

In 1948 the National Roads Board was absorbed into the National Transport Commission. This change saw the passing of several familiar faces, among them H. J. Raubenheimer, who had been the focus of too much criticism and invective to survive South Africa's post-war change of government, with its accompanying spasm of witch-hunting and vendettas. Another man to depart was Johan Durr. Offered an inferior post in the new organisation, he preferred to accept an appointment as Chief Engineer of the Zimbabwean roads. Durr's departure was certainly South Africa's loss and Zimbabwe's gain, as he became the father of modern roads in Zimbabwe.

It is interesting to examine transport developments in that part of Southern Africa at this time. The great upsurge in progress and the economic and population changes at the end of the Second World War produced a crisis on Zimbabwean roads. The famous strip roads of Stuart Chandler had become not only antique but a menace. High speeds and heavy traffic demands had caused them to deteriorate to such an extent that they were no longer economical to maintain. Circumstances, too, had changed so much that labour had now become expensive and materials cheap – a complete reversal of the old conditions which had given rise to the construction of strip roads and low-level bridges. It was now actually cheaper to make a narrow mat rather than a strip road. Modern machinery, in fact, could not cope with strips, which had to be handmade. Sharp edges and potholes on the strips made travelling unpleasant, while the confinement of all traffic to the exact centre of roads was a major factor contributing to one of the highest accident rates in the world.

In 1949, the figures for fatal accidents in Zimbabwe stood at 0,35 per million vehicle kilometres travelled, compared to 0,27 in South Africa, 0,08 in Britain and 0,056 in America. There were many reasons for this high figure: paramount among them was the combination of loaded vehicles and speed in a land where transport confronted hazards such as wild animals, cyclists, loose stones, dust, blind corners, rises, narrow bridges, grids; and all these with every vehicle in the middle of the road and a high proportion of unserviceable vehicles extremely badly driven. To complicate matters increasingly powerful vehicles were being marketed and driven by owners – often fools or drunkards – who used public highways as

8

missile tracks, hurtling along through all hazards at uncontrolled speeds.

Something drastic had to be done. Stuart Chandler had retired in 1943, and his two successors, E. Greenshields (1943 to 1945) and C. Brown (1945 to 1949) were both confronted with massive problems whose solution required a political, economic and engineering virtuosity which it was not really fair to expect from men who were purely engineers. In Johan Durr Zimbabwe found the organisational man so sorely lacking.

Mat roads were already being made to replace strips in areas of heavy traffic and a ten-year programme had been planned to allow for full-width asphalt roads, high-level bridges and expanded local roads. A soil-testing laboratory, heavy roadmaking equipment and skilled labour had to be organised, along with the money to pay for such spectacular progress.

A ministry of roads and road traffic was formed by the Zimbabwean Government and Johan Durr became the first Commissioner of Roads and Road Traffic. His first task was to re-orientate an already launched programme of off-main road construction: the initial plan had been to leave the main roads to the strips while secondary roads were improved.

The constructional capacity of the roads department had to be radically improved. There was a prodigious backlog of roadwork to be done; disintegration of roads had reached such a pass that there were frequent traffic hold-ups. The wet season of 1951-1952 saw the roads in chaos. Rural traffic was in imminent danger of complete breakdown. Massive funds would have to be spent but the existing road organisation was so antiquated that to transmute money into roads was beyond its ability. In 1949 it only utilised £319 000 of a modest road vote of £1 100 000 for capital works.

Durr improvised an emergency operation to replace the now thoroughly discredited strips with narrow (2,8 m-wide) mats. He steadily built up his organisation until by 1956 he had a department which could transmute a vote of £7 000 000 into successful road construction. This was no mean achievement, but Johan Durr was not only an engineer; he was also a born organiser, planner and 'go-getter'.

The main road from Beit Bridge through Bulawayo, Gwelo and Que Que to Salisbury and Umtali was the transport and strategic backbone of Zimbabwe and this was given priority in the conversion to a wide-mat, high-level bridge highway. The stretch of the Great North Road from Salisbury to Chirundu also required urgent attention in view of the heavy transport demands on it as a result of the construction of Kariba. This fine road, completed in 1962 to Chirundu (as with many others in Zimbabwe), will always be associated with the name of Jack Fogarty, the location engineer; the superb pass down the Zambezi escarpment, designed in harmony with natural contours, is his finest memorial.

The Gwayi River-Wankie and the Umtali-Inyanga roads are also superlative examples of road location in Zimbabwe. The Umtali-Inyanga road, built by Zanen Contractors & Engineers (Pty) Ltd, a South African offshoot of a Dutch company, was the first contractor-financed road in South Africa.

Johan Durr always paid great attention to the beautification of roads. He fought long battles with post office engineers to force them to discontinue the wholesale destruction of wayside trees because they interfered with unsightly communication cables. Post office and radio engineers have made a great nuisance of themselves in many parts of the world – notably in South Africa, where they have disfigured many beautiful mountains and landmarks by erecting hideous towers of micro-wave communication or F.M. transmitters. Justifying insensitive vandalism by pure functional requirements, these individuals consider landscape or urban areas satisfactory only if they consist of a world of unobstructed pipes, wires, drainpipes and gutters.

Zimbabwean main roads are today well signposted and aesthetically pleasing, by blending with their environment and graced by many pleasant lay-bys and resting places. They are a credit to their country and will not rapidly become obsolete. During their creation, Johan Durr enjoyed the satisfaction of several major technical breakthroughs, among them, notably, mastery of the problem of construction over granite sand veld country where the sand, overlying clay, becomes saturated in the rainy season and makes the roads unstable; complex and carefully devised drainage was the answer. Another problem he solved concerned construction in Kalahari sand country, where the sand would not compact. Watering it artificially proved a failure, but the answer lay in waiting for the rains, and then working fast.

Johan Durr retired in 1964 and was succeeded by A. D. Harris who, in the years after the collapse of the Federation of Rhodesia and Nyasaland, had to contend with shortage of funds in the face of heavy demands for entirely new roads to rapidly developing areas such as the Hippo Valley. The roads of Zimbabwe today are numbered clockwise from Salisbury and then from Bulawayo. With their fine locations, superb surfacing, more than 180 lay-bys and 100 picnic places, they make travelling through the diverse and beautiful countryside a delight.

Today, the roads of Southern Africa are generally as good as those anywhere else in the world. The establishment of the basic framework of the road network has permitted the construction of elaborate modern improvements such as dual carriageways, freeways, flyovers, traffic interchanges, the elimination of mountain pass gradients and ravines by means of tunnels and spectacular bridges, and the increasing use of concrete surfaces in place of tarmac.

The safety factor still remains a blot on the reputation of these magnificent highways. Statistics reveal that the drivers of Southern Africa are the worst in the civilised world, making nonsense of the arguments of the 'goon squad' that their democratic birthright is to be allowed to do very much as they please on public highways. As roads improve, so the control of drivers – for their own good – must become increasingly severe. Roads are made by man and their abuse is purely a manmade problem, like that of overpopulation.

Extensive research by the South African Road Safety Council has shown that in fact the accident rate in South Africa for every one million vehicular kilometres travelled is not higher than that of other countries, but the death rate is twice that of Britain and seven times that of the United States. The principal reason for this discrepancy in the proportion of deaths is the higher average speed travelled in South Africa as compared with Britain and the United States. The faster a vehicle travels the worse the impact and the more catastrophic the consequences of any accident.

The South African Council for Scientific and Industrial Research has found that half the vehicles using rural roads travel at speeds in excess of 100 km an hour. As a result, although there are 15 times as many accidents in cities as in rural areas, the number of deaths is about the same because the density of traffic in the former forces drivers to travel at slower speeds.

It is frequently suggested that speed is not in itself the cause of accidents, and that a good driver will not necessarily be more susceptible to accidents at a higher speed. According to this syllogistic argument, then, the only interpretation of South African accident statistics is that there must be a great number of bad drivers using the highways. In fact, even at the risk of penalising the good drivers, the only effective way of preventing motorists from killing people is to discipline them into speeds which are not potentially lethal. In the final analysis, zero speeds would mean zero accidents, therefore a speed must be set at which motorists can do as little damage as a reasonable amount of motion allows. When the happy day comes that accident statistics at lower speeds become acceptable, then the driver could perhaps be rewarded with the privilege of faster travel.

The South African open road speed limit before the oil crisis was 112 km an hour. Few other countries have ever allowed such a speed on public highways. In America the general speed limits were 104 km an hour in daylight and 88 km an hour at night. At speeds above 100 km an hour the chances of surviving an accident are slim and the distance required to stop a car too great to allow effective avoiding action. Moderation on the part of drivers is the answer to road fatalities, but speed, bad manners and drunkenness are frequently the rules of the road in South Africa. As a result, what is known as 'South African Confetti' (broken glass from collisions) is a common sight on local roads, especially after pay nights on Fridays and at the end of each month.

Why so many South Africans should want to travel so fast is uncertain. They do nothing very notable with the time they save. It has been suggested that they suffer from a disease known as *gatkanker* (cancer of the rectum): from the moment they sit in a car they are in agony. They drive as fast as possible in order to terminate the discomfort; under the stress of pain they are understandably irritable and bad-mannered. Many of them try to relieve the weight on their behinds by holding on to the roof of the vehicle with one hand, or leaning out of the window. Driving in the middle of the road is also a palliative as the vehicle is less tilted and, oddly enough, the passage immediately underneath of the white centre line is said to be soothing, something like a massage. This belief, however, may stem from the realm of faith healing . . .

The South African National Road Safety Council and the various traffic law enforcement bodies have been notably ineffectual in coping with the accident rate. It took the petrol crisis of 1974 to have a beneficial effect, and an excellent suggestion has been made: that all personnel in the Road Safety Council should be dismissed as redundant and a representative of the oil sheiks be invited to preside over South African road safety. Indeed, by reducing the amount of petrol available, the sheiks have been the only authority ever to succeed in reducing the South African accident rate. They forced a prudence and discipline on drivers which, alas, was shortlived. Drivers soon slipped back into their old ways and up went the casualty figures. Apart from an endless stream of pious hopes, the road safety authorities failed to use the opportunity for the imposition of a lasting discipline. Statistics were made available in plenty; South African authorities are excellent at over-management, detailed statistics and pseudo-scientific gobbledegook. The National Institute for Road Research published figures to show that the average reduction of 27 per cent in speed as a result of the petrol shortage produced a 23 per cent reduction in road traffic accidents. They then happily recommended that when the petrol crisis came to an end, new speed limits on ordinary roads should be 100 km an hour and on freeways (of which at present there are only 600 km in the country) the speed limit should be 120 km an hour!!!

A great lobby for undisciplined road use is the vested interest of panel beaters, garages, breakdown truck operators and undertakers. When the oil crisis forced speeds to be reduced to 80 km (60 km in urban areas) these interests made a great fuss, claiming that they were being forced out of business. Motoring writers in the press published drivel about the deleterious effect on engines of slow driving. Editorials to similar effect were even published in leader pages. Much of the blood and misery of road casualties is attributable in part to such irresponsible people. But for the surgeons, nurses, ambulance drivers, and policemen who have the miserable task of clearing up the mess, the speed limits produced telling results: empty beds in the casualty wards and empty slabs in the mortuaries.

This book is dedicated to the wonderful roads of Southern Africa. To enjoy them, the driver needs only to be sensible about speed, considerate to others, to remain sober, to see that his vehicle is not overloaded and is in a good state of repair and, when he feels tired, to pull off the road and rest at one of the numerous lay-bys considerately provided for him by the road engineers. Abide by these few elementary requirements and you will enjoy a travel experience in Southern Africa which cannot be bettered anywhere else on earth.

# Chapter One

# CAPE TOWN

Cape Town, with its population of 892 190, lies in one of the most spectacular scenic settings of any of the world's principal cities. The massive sandstone bulk of Table Mountain, flanked by Devil's Peak, Lion's Head and Signal Hill, provides not only a monumental approach to Southern Africa from the sea; this mountain also actually fathered the city, and decisively influenced its growth, climate, layout and general development.

Table Mountain, although no giant as world peaks go (1 086 m), is certainly one of the best known of all mountains. It is visible to approaching ships from over 150 km away. Its distinctive table shape makes it immediately identifiable even to a stranger, and it serves as an unmistakable beacon and a major landfall on one of the great shipping routes of the world.

From the time of the first discovery of the southern end of Africa, seafarers looked forward eagerly to the sight of this renowned mountain. It was comparable to a gigantic sign of an inn promising hospitality, and Cape Town became known as the tavern of the seas. Fresh water from mountain streams could always be obtained there, along with provisions such as meat, fresh vegetables and fruit, which are essential to counter hazards of long voyages such as scurvy. Ships from many countries habitually sheltered in the bay, repairing, refreshing and revictualling, and crews rested and exercised ashore. Postal matter was left under inscribed stones for other ships to find and carry forward. These so-called post-office stones are still found in excavations for modern buildings, and there is an interesting collection of them in the South African Museum.

Several nations considered establishing some form of settlement at the foot of Table Mountain. The British made the first attempt in 1615 when they left a party of eight convicts on the shores of the bay. These men later crossed to the small island known as *Robben* (place of seals) at the entrance to Table Bay. There they remained for some months until a passing ship took them away. This was an abortive attempt at settlement, although strangely enough, Robben Island is today a convict station for maximum security prisoners.

In 1652, the Dutch East India Company established a permanent settlement. They sent three small ships from Holland under the command of Jan Antony van Riebeeck, whose instructions were to build a stronghold on the shores of Table Bay and commence the growing of vegetables, systematic bartering of livestock from nomadic Hottentot tribes, the building of a hospital, and a sanctuary for the repair of ships. Van Riebeeck thus laid the foundations of Cape Town, and his first fort, subsequently reconstructed as the present castle, was its first building.

The shoreline and landing beach were then totally different from today. A stream of fresh water from the mountain reached the sea at what was known as *Roggebaai* (rocky bay). Shipping anchored in a roadstead off this bay, and small boats plied between ships and the shore, with many wrecks occurring when storms, especially during the winter months, sent great rollers into Table Bay. The bustle in Table Bay and the coming and going of fleets of sailing ships trading between Europe and the East were a source of inspiration for many artists, not all of whom actually visited the place. Some very imaginative impressions of the scene were painted, with Table Mountain distorted into extraordinary shapes, but exhibitions of these paintings did serve to familiarise people in many faraway lands with the sight of the mountain and the port at its foot.

The modern harbour is completely manmade and is continuously being expanded and developed. It consists of the older Victoria Basin and Alfred Dock, the Duncan Dock completed during the Second World War, and a new dock with 22 berths, especially designed for container ships. The solid rock which forms the bottom of Table Bay inhibits dredging. The maximum harbour depth is 12 m at low water, with 141,5 ha of enclosed docking area and 35 berths for ocean-going ships.

Table Bay is the principal passenger and mail harbour of Southern Africa, the third largest fruit exporting harbour in the world, a major fishing base and a haven for repairing, revictualling and refuelling passing ships. The Sturrock Graving Dock, the largest in the Southern Hemisphere, has a length of 360 m, a width of 47,5 m and a depth on the entrance sill of 13,7 m. The smaller Robinson Dock has a length of 161,2 m and there is a floating dock capable of lifting 1 016 tons.

The pre-cooling stores have space for 29 100 tons of deciduous and citrus fruit, and during the export season, from January to July, there is considerable activity, with refrigerated trains and ships carrying cases of fruit expertly cooled to a temperature suiting their variety and stage of ripeness.

There is also a grain elevator, with a capacity of 27 220 tons and a yacht harbour, presided over by the Royal Cape Yacht Club. Many international yachting events are staged from this harbour and it is the starting place of several races, including the famous Cape to Rio yacht race held biennially in January (politics permitting).

The Table Bay fishing industry is enormous, as nine-tenths of the fish eaten in South Africa are landed, processed and railed from Cape Town. From the harbour, South African trawlers work the Agulhas Banks, while fishing fleets from many foreign countries, far outnumbering the local ships, use Table Bay as a base, transhipping their catches on to refrigerated vessels for transport to their home countries, replenishing their own stores and fuel, and allowing their crews spells of shore leave.

Hake, or stock fish, is the principal export fish, with rock lobster, many of which are flown alive to supply the epicures of America and Europe. Kingklip, sole, snoek, silver fish, hottentot, kabeljou and yellowtail are also main local varieties and there are many less numerous species. In the winter snoek season the fishing wharves are particularly busy, with the long, handsome, silver-coloured fish being landed by the hundreds of thousands, providing particularly delicious eating for those who care to go to the harbour personally and purchase the fish absolutely fresh. With abalone, oysters, mussels, crabs and prawns also landed in Cape Town, its seafoods are justly renowned. In fact, a seafood supper at the Harbour Café, situated on the waterfront of the small boat harbour in Victoria Basin, and then an evening trip on one of the launches which take visitors on excursions can be a very pleasant way of exploring the harbour. On a warm, windless, moonlit night in summer, such an outing can be memorable. In the old clock tower of Victoria Basin there is a small museum of interest to ship lovers. It is open on Saturday afternoons.

The two main dock gates both face Table Mountain from slightly different angles, and take the traveller on to what is known as the Foreshore. This is a 145-ha, level area which was reclaimed from the sea during the vast dredging operations which were necessary for the construction of the Duncan Dock. The spoil from this dredging was pumped on to the landward side of the new harbour, and completely buried the original shoreline of Roggebaai.

When the dredging and pumping were over, Cape Town found itself separated from its harbour by a wide open, windswept Foreshore, which, once the dust had settled, had great potential to provide the city, already compressed between mountain and sea, with a unique facelift – a new approach and a new building area with exciting architectural possibilities. There is a legend originating from those days of wide open spaces that currency notes of various denominations and countries were often blown from the persons of sailors returning to their ships after late night revelries. After a really powerful summer south-easter, these notes could be found the next morning adorning the dock security fence, and a number of local vagrants scavenged the fences daily in search of this treasure of the Foreshore.

The Foreshore of today yields few such items of value. A grid of roads and a hotchpotch of buildings have settled the dust and partially broken the wind. The original anchorage of *Roggebaai* (rocky bay) is buried deep beneath the modern reclamation and the site is traversed by the main thoroughfare known as the *Heerengracht* (gentleman's canal), the name given in former years to the canalised lower section of the river. The traffic junction of this thoroughfare, outside the dock gates, is the unmarked beginning of one of the most romantic highways in the world, the Cape-to-Cairo road, taken by countless travellers using many different forms of transport.

Further up the Heerengracht, there is a traffic circle around a fountain and ornamental pools where a happy and garrulous squawk of sea birds habitually disport themselves. The site of the pools roughly marks the original shoreline, and growing in the vicinity are a few palm trees, displaced relics of a once handsome line of palms standing along a vanished marine promenade.

Looking across the pools at the mountain is a graceful bronze statue of Jan Antony van Riebeeck, created by the sculptor John Tweed and presented to Cape Town in 1899 by Cecil Rhodes. The statue stands very near the spot where this founder of Cape Town must have landed on 7 April 1652. Near to him is a second statue, that of his wife Maria de la Queillerie, presented to Cape Town in 1952 by the Van Riebeeck Committee of Holland. This statue is the work of the Dutch sculptor, Dirk Wolbers. It is slightly larger in scale than that of her spouse, but the two make a benevolent pair, appearing to watch with parental interest the changing city they founded.

The statues and pools mark the end of the Foreshore. Among the various buildings standing on it, there is the Nico Malan, containing an opera house and theatre, both very well equipped, with excellent acoustics and seating accommodation. Each year many worthwhile performances of ballet, opera, music, drama and other theatrical entertainments take place at these two venues. Under the management of CAPAB (Cape Performing Arts Board), the Nico Malan is one of Cape Town's principal cultural assets. Connected to this entertainment complex is the civic centre, a large municipal administrative building, erected partly over the dividing thoroughfare, and acting as a good buffer for the south-easter, as well as housing numerous officials. Cape Town became a municipality in 1861 and a city in 1913.

Beyond the statues of Van Riebeeck and his wife is the main street of Cape Town, *Adderley Street*. This street is named after C. B. Adderley, a member of the British House of Commons, who, in 1850, gave considerable support to the people of the Cape Colony in their struggle to dissuade the British Government from turning the colony into a convict settlement. At the beginning of Adderley Street is an imposing bronze monument to those who fell in the two World Wars and the Korean War. It was done by Vernon March, who modelled it on the famous Winged Victory (the Nike of Samothrace) in the Louvre. On the right-hand side of the street, in front of the Medical Centre, just before the war memorial, there is a small bronze ship mounted on a pedestal, erected in memory of Robert Falcon Scott, the explorer of the Antarctic. On the left-hand side of the street, opposite the monument, is the extensive building housing Cape Town railway station, airways terminal and railway bus depot. An attractive and well-maintained garden sets this modern building off to advantage. It is the terminal station of the whole railway network of Southern Africa, which reaches northwards without a break to places throughout South Africa, Zimbabwe, Moçambique, Zambia, South West Africa and as far away as Dar-es-Salaam in Tanzania and Benguela in Angola. The concourse of the main line section of the station displays the first locomotive to work from Cape Town after construction was commenced in 1859.

Adderley Street, lined with commercial buildings, continues for nine blocks towards the mountain. It is the main shopping street of the central city area and is an animated scene during the week. New arrivals from overseas are immediately aware that there is a peculiar quality to the air in Southern Africa that seems to make everything a little brighter than it really is. Certainly Adderley Street on a clear morning has an attractive sparkle, with everybody on the run, and fast-moving pedestrians and traffic showing an alarming tendency to ignore each other. Smartly-dressed women drift at will through moving streams of vehicles, casually pushing prams laden with infants and shopping bags, quite undaunted by the proximity of noisy buses and cars and the hooting of exasperated drivers. Fashions in Southern Africa generally follow Europe and America, with a slight delay to cover shipping and handling. There is much of the same mindless adherence to the same fads. The pedestrian traffic is, however, interestingly cosmopolitan: a many-hued throng presenting a well-dressed, amiable, perhaps somewhat overfed picture, with black ladies flaunting bright colours to particular advantage.

Shopping hours are from 08h30 until 17h30 on weekdays, with a half-holiday from 13h00 on Saturdays. After commercial hours the city area is practically lifeless save for a few window shoppers. Cafés with open doors become hard to find and there is little night life. A few third-rate night clubs cater for sailors, providing overloud music and the usual sailors' fare in women as entertainment, mainly teenagers chewing gum with their mouths open. Capetonians, however, abandon the city area for homes and entertainment in the suburbs. Much of the basic household shopping is also done in the suburbs and, as with most cities, the centre of Cape Town is becoming increasingly a place for the offices of financial institutions, lawyers and accountants.

The buildings of Adderley Street are attractive, without any particularly noteworthy examples of architecture. The railway station is connected to the opposite side of Adderley Street by an underground shopping mall. Between the General Post Office and the railway station there is an extensive so-called Golden Acre development; this is a massive construction on the site of Cape Town's first railway station, which used to be the site of an early reservoir, the walls of which were salvaged, carefully removed, and preserved in the precincts of the new building. At this reservoir, old-time seafarers filled their water casks and bartered for food, and most of the post office stones in the museum were found in excavations between this point and Darling Street. The Grand Parade Centre, just beyond the Golden Acre, was the site of Cape Town's first post office. The modern post office, on the corner of Darling and Parliament streets, displays one of the post office stones in its entrance foyer.

Just off Adderley Street, in a roofed alley known as Trafalgar Place, is the centre of Cape Town's flowersellers where loquacious ladies and some men of varied temperament and masculinity offer wonderful flowers for sale, and combine any transaction with a colourful commentary of life in general.

The Grand Parade Centre and the post office were both built on what was originally part of the military parade ground in front of the Castle. The remaining portion of the parade north of the post office has remained open, and is mostly used as a parking ground, but occasionally some military occasion or public meeting takes place there. Religious fanatics and political groups also hold meetings here, and on Wednesdays and Saturday mornings there is an open-air market displaying plants, books and second-hand bric-à-brac for sale. A line of fruit kiosks stands on the south side. By day and night, the Grand Parade is colourful and lively, haunted by people of all creeds and colours, as well as some expert pickpockets intent on fleecing the unwary.

The first earthwork fort was built somewhere on the present open section of the parade. The Castle of Good Hope, regarded as the first bastion of civilisation in Southern Africa, was built on its present site, at the northern end of the Parade, between 1666 and 1679. It is in the shape of a pentagon, with walls over 10 m high and each side of the pentagon is 175 m long, leading to a bastion at the angle. The five bastions were named after the titles of the Prince of Orange: Leerdam contained the kitchens and pay office; Buren contained officers' quarters; Oranje contained the arsenal and workshops, and Nassau the powder magazine; Catzenellenbogen provided accommodation for the garrison, while below sea level were the dark dungeons, with graffiti, pathetic memorials of the inmates, carved and written on the walls and doors of the cells. The gateway has a pediment containing the arms of the six chambers of the Dutch East India Company. A defensive cross wall (the Kat) was built across the interior grounds of the castle in 1691. The Kat contained the official quarters of the Governor and his staff. Today it houses a fine collection of paintings and antiques of the old Cape, and a collection of paintings by the renowned wildlife artist, Edmund Caldwell. The collection, known as the William Fehr Collection, is open weekdays 09h30 to 16h00 and on weekends during the summer holiday period. The ornamental balcony in front of the Kat was the scene of important proclamations and the swearing-in of new governors. There is an interesting military and a maritime museum containing uniforms, medals, ship and aircraft models, as well as other items of martial interest. The Castle is still in use as the military headquarters of the Western Cape Command. It is open to the public with tours at hourly intervals from 10h00. It is closed on Saturday afternoons and Sundays.

Originally, around the walls of this Castle of Good Hope there was a moat filled with water from a canal known as the Keizersgracht, connected to the Fresh River. The route of this canal is now followed by Darling Street, named after C. H. Darling, Lieutenant-Governor of the Cape from 1852 to 1854. Across this street, overlooking the Grand Parade, is the city hall, a massive sandstone building in the Italian style, completed in 1905. The clock tower contains, apart from an excellent clock, the first, and largest carillon in South Africa (44 bells). The hall is the home of the Cape Town Symphony Orchestra, a body of professional musicians giving concerts of a first-class standard under the baton of various international guest conductors, generally on Thursday and Sunday evenings. Further along Darling Street, beyond the walls of the Castle, stands the impressive exhibition hall, completed in 1977 and designed by Dr Antonio Nervi of Rome. The main hall seats 8 000 people and has the world's largest freespanning cross-vault concrete roof. It is known as the Good Hope Centre.

Above the intersection with Darling Street, Adderley Street continues towards the mountain. On the left-hand side stands one of its most notable buildings, the Groote Kerk (great church). This, the mother church of the Dutch Reformed Church in Southern Africa, is also the oldest surviving church, completed in 1704 and enlarged twice since. It contains a magnificent pulpit carved by Anton Anreith, and the original bell tower contains a clock with a pleasantly distinctive two-tone stroke. The organ is superb.

Beyond the Groote Kerk, on the same side of Adderley Street, stands the Old Lodge, originally the quarters for slaves employed in the great vegetable garden founded by Van Riebeeck and maintained by the Dutch East India Company to provide fresh food for ships. In later years, when slavery came to an end, the lodge became the building housing the Supreme Court. Today it is a well-maintained cultural museum, containing an interesting collection of furniture and articles from Cape Town's past. The customs and art of the Malay people in the Cape are well represented. The museum is open Mondays to Saturdays 10h00 to 17h00; Sundays 10h00 to 17h00. Adderley Street ends with the cultural museum. A sharp right-hand turn takes traffic into the beginning of Wale Street (Waale or Walloon Street, where two individuals of that nationality used to live). A hospital maintained by the Dutch East India Company once stood on the corner opposite the cultural museum. Up Wale Street, on the left-hand side, stands the substantial concrete pile of the Cape Provincial Council's administration buildings. The archway under it leads to Keerom Street, where, among other buildings, stands the modern Supreme Court. Past the provincial council building, Wale Street climbs the lower slopes of Signal Hill to reach what is known as the Malay Quarter, an interesting area largely inhabited by Moslems. Many of the neat little cottages here have been recently restored; there are several pretty mosques and the call to prayer can be heard at all proper hours. The various annual festivals, such as the Feast of the Orange Leaves held on the

sexton's house adjoining this Lutheran church was built in 1787 and is now occupied by the Netherlands Consulate. On the south side of the church is the Martin Melck House, a fine specimen of an 18th century Cape-Dutch house, actually built just after Melck's death in 1781 but named in his honour.

On the opposite side of Strand Street stands another graceful old house, built in 1702 and named the Koopmans de Wet House after the family who acquired it at the beginning of the 19th century. It is now an historical monument and museum, containing an interesting collection of period furniture, antiques and prints. It is open to the public from 10h00 to 16h30 daily except Sundays.

Between the top of Government Avenue and the slopes of Table Mountain lie the oldest residential suburbs of Cape Town. Gardens is a great place for boarding houses and rooms for business people; *Vredehoek* (peaceful corner) and *Kloof* (cleft) are also populated by working and business people of the city; *Oranjezicht* (orange view), originally a farm, was so named because the farmhouse had a view of the Oranje bastion of the Castle of Good Hope; *Tamboerskloof* (drummer's ravine) is further west, against the slopes of Lion's Head; Devil's Peak, University Estate and what used to be a picturesquely decrepit slum area, District Six, all lie on the slopes of Devil's Peak. District Six, now demolished, once enjoyed an atmosphere of great vitality and gaiety, despite its slum conditions. 'This is fairyland' was the claim of graffiti carelessly scrawled on a dingy wall.

On 1 and 2 January each year, the Coloured people staged their Coon Carnival in the city centre; this was a series of parades through the streets of vividly dressed groups of singing and dancing men, women and children, all belonging to several dozen different troupes competing with one another for the best and most novel costumes, music and dancing. This was one of the few carnival parades in the world in which men played the violoncello on the march. Competitions are still held in the outlying dormitory suburbs where the inhabitants of District Six have been relocated, but the spirit of the occasion belongs to the streets of Cape Town. The Coon Carnival was, and one day may be again, the most colourful occasion in the social calendar of South Africa.

The eastern boundaries of the farm on which the suburb of Oranjezicht now stands were along the banks of the Fresh River. Although this river has been forced underground in the lower reaches of its flow through the modern city, the stream in its upper reaches remains on the surface and, in the winter rainy season when there is a flow of water, it is pleasant to walk along its shady banks and find lingering there something of the atmosphere of Cape Town long ago.

To reach the beginning of this still unspoilt upper valley of the Fresh River, go up what was once the outlying street of Cape Town, *Buitenkant* (outer side) Street. This street passes the lovely old rococo house, *Rust-en-Vreugd* (rest and gladness). This house is now a national monument and a gallery for the fine water colours collected by William Fehr. It is open daily 10h00 to 16h00.

Beyond *Rust-en-Vreugd,* the street reaches the imposing building and grounds of the Jewish Old Aged Home. It is here that the Fresh River is freed from its conduit, and flows merrily down the mountain slopes through a beautiful, tree-filled valley, nowadays called the Van Riebeeck Park, and attractively laid out with paths, picnic spots and shady glades. Many lovely, perfectly maintained homes, such as *Rheezicht,* nestle among the trees on both sides of the valley. In former years a cobbled pathway, known as the 'slave walk', made its way up this portion of the valley to wash-houses where the clothes of Cape Town were laundered.

About 90 m above the ruins of these wash-houses stand a pair of cottages which were once a watermill. In former times at least five such mills ground corn from the power of the passing river, but nothing is left of them today. The growth of the town demanded a less haphazard water supply than filling pails from the passing stream, and the watermills were a luxury that the river could no longer support. In 1868 the municipality bought them all out, and they were closed down. A weir was built across the river at the point where it was joined by one of its principal tributaries from the mountain, the Silverstream. From here the water was filtered and piped to the population of Cape Town.

Above this weir, on a steep slope of the tongue of land between the two streams, stood a house, whose ruins, more than half buried in shrubbery, still overlook the valley through a tangle of oak and fir trees; the view stretches as far as the distant waters of Table Bay. There are many legends about this house, which was called *De Grendel van de Platteklip Kloof* (the bolt of the flat stone cleft), because it blocked access to the upper reaches of the river. Its isolated situation, the shadows of the trees, the tumbling rush of a waterfall beside it, certainly make it an ideal home for ghosts. Here, legend has it, lived Antjie Somers, the favourite bogeyman or woman of the Cape Coloureds. Antjie Somers is a mystical character who appears in many rhymes and tales, especially those told by mothers to frighten naughty children. In this area too, according to folklore, stood *Verlatenbosch* (abandoned bush), where the leprous son of a former Governor lived in solitude. He had apparently been infected by playing a flute he had picked up once owned by a leper and deliberately placed by an enemy of the Governor where his son could find it. The sound of the flute is said to still haunt the area.

Just above the ruins of the abode of Antjie Somers the Fresh River comes racing down over a series of flat rock surfaces which give the name of *Platteklip* (flat stones) to the higher reaches of the river and the great diagonal gorge which cleaves the front of Table Mountain, providing the easiest (but dullest) scramble up to the summit, where the busy little river has its source.

Climbers have found over 350 separate routes, ranging from easy to very difficult, to the summit of Table Mountain. This great pile of sandstone, a mountain playground in the backyard of a city, is also a national monument and recreational area belonging to all, with wild flowers in astonishing profusion, sizes and colours, ranging from the giant protea to the fragile disa, to be seen somewhere on the mountain throughout the year.

The level but rough and rocky summit has many points of interest. It is 3 km long, east to west, with its highest point the 1 086-m Maclear's Beacon (Sir T. Maclear was a one-time Astronomer Royal), lying on the eastern end. The western end of the narrow table plateau supports the distinctive concrete 'pimple' of the upper cable station, where the engines are housed which safely lift some 250 000 people each year up 1 220 m of cable to the summit. The cableway was built in 1929, the brainchild of a Norwegian engineer named T. Strömsoe. Climbing the mountain should not be attempted without expert advice, as several people are killed on it each year. The Mountain Club of South Africa, at 97 Hatfield Street, will be pleased to advise prospective climbers. This club also publishes an excellent guide and map for walkers and climbers, with all climbs rated. The Table Mountain aerial cableway works daily (weather permitting) from 08h30 to 18h00, and up to 22h30 on summer evenings. Phone 43-0866.

The narrow table top falls away sharply into the back table, a walker's rugged paradise, with gorges, wild flowers, pine forests, and a set of reservoirs supplying water to Cape Town. This back table eventually ends precipitately in the south, in Orange Kloof. Its eastern precipices, beautifully wooded, overlook the southern suburbs of Cape Town. The 12 sun-drenched and bare buttresses of its western precipices, known as the Twelve Apostles, dominate the Atlantic Ocean suburbs such as Camps Bay.

The actual western edge of the table, with the upper cable station and tearoom on its tip, falls away almost alarmingly to the saddle of land known as Kloof Nek. This saddle links Table Mountain to one of its satellites, 669-m-high Lion's Head. This striking sugarloaf-shaped peak is connected by a long body to a rump known as Signal Hill, which overlooks the docks and has on it the ceremonial cannons of Lion's Battery which each day cause the pigeons of Cape Town to take fright by firing a shot at noon. Lion's Head was once known as the Sugarloaf. The reason for the change of name is apparently owing either to its shape, or the shooting there of the last Cape lion. For many years a lookout man was stationed on its summit to warn Cape Town with a small signal cannon and flags of the approach and identity of ships. A well-trodden pathway spirals to the summit through sparkling groves of silver trees and lovely spring displays of watsonias, its final stretch up steep rocks facilitated by chains.

The climb is not unduly demanding and the 360-degree panorama is, if anything, aesthetically superior to the higher but more directional view from the top of Table Mountain. The road which climbs the slopes of Lion's Head runs past the domed *kramat* (tomb) of Mohamed Gasan Gaibie Shah, a Moslem holy man, and leads to the summit of Signal Hill. There is a barbecue and picnic site near the tomb, on top of the saddle of land linking Lion's Head to Signal Hill. A pair of old signal cannons are mounted on a lookout just above the tomb. Countless sightseers have travelled this road to view the scene at night, when the whole city lies glittering like a fairyland necklace elegantly suspended around the smoothly curved neck of Table Bay. Midnight on the last day of the year is a memorable time to be on this wonderful vantage point. The glow of the lights, firing of rockets, distant sounds of revelry, hooting of ships, whistling trains, the sound of bells, all rising from the city and echoing and reflecting from the watching face of Table Mountain, provide an almost dreamlike prelude to the coming year.

From the Signal Hill observation point it is pleasant to drive back to Kloof Nek and then along Tafelberg Road, which starts at Kloof Nek, and, with constantly changing views, lovely by day and night, follows the 350-m contour below the rock face of Table Mountain, past the lower cable station and several picnic sites, to the pine-covered slopes of the 1 001-m-high Devil's Peak, which stands guard on the flank of Table Mountain opposite to Lion's Head.

Devil's Peak was originally known as the Wind Mountain, and the reason for its two names is not only interesting but also explains several local weather peculiarities. An oft-told local legend introduces us to a certain retired pirate named Van Hunks. This rugged character, it appears, was accustomed to spend his days sitting beneath a clump of trees at what is known as Breakfast Rock on the saddle of land connecting Devil's Peak to Table Mountain. There he passed his time smoking a potent mixture of rum-soaked tobacco and viewing the shipping in the bay, speculating on the wealth of their cargoes. One day, the devil visited Van Hunks and the two began a smoking contest. This contest continues throughout the summer months. (In winter Van Hunks has rheumatism and cannot climb the mountain.) Proof of the competition is the marvellous, billowing, smoke-like cloud which, in the summer, seems to begin at the clump of trees, grows, expands, and then rolls over the summit of Table Mountain to produce the phenomenon of the tablecloth. Penny Miller's delightful book for children, *The Story of Rory*, and her *Myths and Legends of Southern Africa,* provides us with an amusing account of Van Hunks, the last lion of Lion's Head, and the tablecloth.

The scientific explanation for the tablecloth is equally fascinating, and from it we learn something of Cape Town's famous south-east wind. This wind is as much a part of the Cape as Table Mountain and it has had a definite influence on the development of the city. It is the prevailing wind during the summer, appearing towards the end of October and petering out in February, leaving before the most idyllic months at the Cape, March and April. In May the north-west wind appears, far less venomous in impact, but the bringer of cool weather and up to 1 524 mm of rain during winter, turning the Cape into a green garden.

The famous south-easter, the 'Cape Doctor', which blows away insects, miasmas, smogs and pollution from the atmosphere of the Cape, is, in fact, not originally a south-east wind at all. It is born in the high-pressure areas (the anti-cyclones) which, in the southern summer, girdle the earth between latitudes of 35 degrees and 40 degrees south. Cape Town's latitude is only 34 degrees south, but the whirling masses of air, rotating in an anti-clockwise direction on account of the rotation of the earth, throw out tongues of air and these reach the southern end of Africa travelling from the south or south-west. The long line of mountains which lies just inland from the southern coast of Africa forces this air to pile up and move along it with compressed vigour. At Cape Hangklip the air suddenly finds itself released from this imprisonment. It howls around Cape Hangklip with what is known as 'corner effect' and, like a wild beast run amuck, goes swirling across the waters of False Bay, picking up a high moisture content. It then collides head-on with the mountains of the Cape Peninsula. A number of interesting things now take place.

The mountains force the wind to rise sharply and what is known as 'orographic condensation' occurs. The moisture in the wind is suddenly condensed to a thick white cloud as soon as it reaches the cooler altitude of the mountain tops. The summit of Table Mountain, ideally placed and the highest point of the range, catches the bulk of this cloud and, with its thickness determined by the height of the wind, the cloud rolls over the mountain as the famous tablecloth, and drapes itself over the edge like a tumbling waterfall which abruptly disappears in an almost straight line where the mist dissolves in the warmer air of a lower altitude.

Lower reaches of the wind, meanwhile, have rushed along the eastern precipices of the mountain chain. Devil's Peak, the wind mountain, acts as a cornerstone, and here the stream of air whips around in another corner effect. It pours down into the city area of Cape Town, the Table Valley of the Fresh River, and here, coming at last from a truly south-easterly direction and compressed between rows of buildings, it can play havoc, reaching speeds of 130 km per hour (hurricane force) on occasions, and from time to time breaking records with a speed of 150 km per hour and more. Unlike the north-wester of winter, which blows in spurts, the south-easter can maintain its force for days, but as a rule it slackens in the early hours, allowing people some relaxation in the mornings, and reappears about noon.

The south-easter normally is a shallow wind about 610 m in height. Signal Hill and Lion's Head are high enough to buffer it and drive it out to sea, leaving the suburbs on the Atlantic coast – Green Point, Sea Point, Clifton and Camps Bay – sun-tanning in almost breathless warmth. But if the wind reaches a certain height (fortunately not often) it not only provides a howling gale for the city, but also produces a thick, dark cloud on the mountains (a black south-easter), with some drizzle over the southern suburbs. This wind sneaks over the top of Lion's Rump, driving the sunbathers of Sea Point off the beach. The south-easter, unlike the north-wester of winter, does not bring rain to the Cape, but rather drives it far inland to the regions of summer rainfall. To visitors the south-easter can be something of a shock, especially if their stay in Cape Town coincides with a really big blow and they still insist on taking their family to the beach. For the Capetonian, the south-easter has its blessings. Like the vegetation (trees are seldom blown over), Capetonians have learned to live with the wind. They know that if nobody can beat it there are ways of avoiding it. To one who knows the Peninsula, the wind can be appreciated with some detachment – after all, it not only makes Cape Town one of the healthiest ports and cities on earth, but, by laying the tablecloth on the mountain top, it also provides the world with one of its greatest natural wonders and scenic spectacles.

## Accommodation

★ Café Royal Hotel, Church Street, 10 rooms, 3 with baths. R4 - R6 B/B. Phone 22-9047.

★★★★ Capetonian Hotel, Pier Place, Foreshore, 170 rooms, all with baths. R25 room only. Phone 47-1030.

★★ Carlton Heights Hotel, Queen Victoria Street, 66 rooms, all with baths. R10 - R18 B/B. Phone 22-0131.

★ Castle Hotel, Canterbury Street, 13 rooms, 4 with baths. R4,50 - R6 B/B. Phone 22-9227.

★ City Hall Hotel, Darling Street, 10 rooms, 6 with baths. R5 - R8 B/B. Phone 22-3771.

★★★★ ® De Waal Hotel, Mill Street, 134 rooms, all with baths. R24 - R34 room only. Phone 45-1311.

★ Good Hope Hotel, Loop Street, 11 rooms, 3 with baths. R5 - R8 B/B. Phone 22-3369.

★ Green Hansom Hotel, Long Street, 10 rooms, 4 with baths. R5,50 - R7 B/B. Phone 22-6667.

★★★★★ ® Heerengracht Hotel, St George's Street, 210 rooms, all with baths. R34 - R52 room only. Phone 41-3151.

★ Helmsley Green Park Hotel, Hof Street, 82 rooms, 31 with baths. R9,25 - R10,25 B/B. Phone 22-6516.

★★★ Holiday Inn, Melbourne Road, 214 rooms, all with baths. R25 - R32 room only. Phone 47-4060.

★ Kimberley Hotel, Roeland Street, 11 rooms, 3 with baths. R9 B/B. Phone 46-5572.

★★★ Metropole Hotel, Long Street, 50 rooms, all with baths. R9 - R17 B/B. Phone 22-9737.

★ Mountain View Hotel, Long Street, 10 rooms, 3 with baths. R6 B/B. Phone 22-2251.

★★★★★ ® Mount Nelson Hotel, Orange Street, 196 rooms, all with baths. R24 - R89 room only. Phone 22-0012.

★ Oranje Hotel, Union Street, 50 rooms, 32 with baths. R7 - R9 B/B. Phone 41-0525.

★★ Pleinpark Travel Lodge, Barrack/Corporation streets, 28 rooms, all with baths. R12 - R16 B/B. Phone 45-7563.

★ Queens Hotel, Dock Road, 10 rooms, 3 with baths. R5,50 B/B. Phone 22-4630.

★ Red Lion Hotel, Longmarket Street, 10 rooms, 3 with baths. R6,50 - R7,25 B/B. Phone 22-0247.

★★ Skyway Hotel, Strand/Bree streets, 84 rooms, all with baths. R9,90 B/B. Phone 22-4756.

★ Southfield Hotel, Victoria Road, 17 rooms, 12 with baths. R6,50 - R7 B/B. Phone 71-5067.

★ Stags Head Hotel, 10 rooms, 4 with baths. R5 - R7 B/B. Phone 45-4918.

★ Stardust Hotel, Hope Street, 10 rooms, 4 with baths. R5 - R5,50 B/B. Phone 45-4918.

★★★ ® Town House Hotel, Corporation Street, 103 rooms, all with baths. R13 - R22 B/B. Phone 45-7050.

★ Tudor Hotel, Greenmarket Square, 44 rooms, 20 with baths. R7 - R8 B/B. Phone 41-0196.

★★★ Tulbagh Hotel, Tulbagh Square, 56 rooms, all with baths. R15 - R17 B/B. Phone 41-2903.

## Chapter Two

# THE CAPE PENINSULA

The drive around the Cape Peninsula is one of the most famous scenic experiences in the world. It is strikingly varied, combining scenery that is both dramatic and charming with a piquant atmosphere. From the time of its first discovery, the serenely beautiful Cape Peninsula, with its interesting ocean currents, its marine fauna, and its unique scents and flavours, was accepted as a merging place of East and West. Man has also made great changes here, and a vital maelstrom of human history, cultures, activities, emotions and aspirations has coloured the majestic ambiance of this most renowned and strategic cape.

Luis de Camões, the poet genius of Portugal, tells us of the legendary origin of the Cape Peninsula in the majestic verse of his *Lusiads*. The monstrous Adamastor was one of the 100 giants who rebelled against the gods of ancient Greece and attempted to take Mount Olympus by storm. Defeated by Hercules and Vulcan at the head of all the gods, the giants were condemned to eternal punishment. They were banished to the far places of the earth and buried there beneath volcanoes and mountains.

Adamastor, the personification of the barbarism of ancient Africa, was condemned to a special transmutation. It is his body, 'turned to rocks all rough and strange', which forms the peninsula of the Cape of Good Hope. His pagan spirit forever haunts this tomb. With Table Mountain as his workshop for storms and thunderbolts, he roams the surrounding seas in the form of howling gales and dark storm clouds, raving dire vengeance on the men who disturb his seclusion. The pioneer Portuguese explorers were the sailors who first dared this rage of Adamastor, and the vengeance which he cursed upon them still persists, as we shall see in the strange tale of the Flying Dutchman.

The geological origin of the Cape Peninsula is as interesting as the legend. Underlying the Peninsula there is a basement of granite. In several parts of the Peninsula this granite is revealed. One of these parts is the very tip of the Peninsula, known as Cape Point. Here the granite is exposed to a force quite as relentless as the rage of Adamastor. Surging in upon the Cape of Good Hope comes the full weight of the enormous rollers created in the welter and disturbance of the meeting of two great ocean currents, the Benguela and the Moçambique-Agulhas, at the end of the vast land mass of Africa. The coast of the whole Peninsula takes a heavy pounding, especially on the western side. Steep cliffs, detached rocks and oddly shaped pinnacles have been eroded by the restless water. In the granite beneath Cape Point itself there are sea caves, one of them 51 m deep with a mouth 12 m in diameter. It is only approachable from the sea.

On top of the granite basement, the higher levels of the Peninsula consist of sedimentary sandstone and quartzite laid down beneath the sea in comparatively recent geological times, about 300 million years ago. In a series of great convulsions this sedimentary mass was elevated above the sea to form part of the Cape System which, with its three related series of sedimentary deposits laid down under water in different conditions at different times, provides the spectacular valley and mountain scenery of the Cape coastal area and Natal.

The sandstone is a coarse rock composed of large grains of sand stained red and brown with iron. At times this iron content cements the sand grains together to form ferricrete. Manganese is also present in dark layers or, at places such as Bordjiesrif, it gives the rocks a generally darker hue. At various parts of the Peninsula attempts have been made to mine manganese but it is too erratic to be profitably worked.

To the eye, the surface of the southern end of the Peninsula consists of a line of hills on the eastern side, the highest points being Paulsberg (367 m), Judas Peak (328 m) and Vasco da Gama (268 m). On the western side of these hills lies a gently undulating plateau averaging 61 m above the sea and topped with a thin layer of very acid soil, containing little organic matter but chemically replenished by constant disintegration of the sandstone. Nature makes this unpromising-looking soil a paradise for the ancient macchia-type vegetation known as Cape schlerophyll, with no less than 1 800 species of plants lustily competing on the Cape Peninsula for existence in conditions which would be regarded by any gardener as hopeless.

To further complicate all forms of life on the Cape Peninsula, there are obvious signs of several former variations in the sea level. Old sea cliffs, marine terraces, wave-polished boulders, shell deposits inland: all record variations in the sea level which were so substantial that the Peninsula was often fragmented into two islands when the sea flooded across the valley of Fish Hoek and inundated the Cape Flats.

Primitive men might easily have been marooned on these islands. The signs of their middens and artefacts certainly indicate that they were present in the area at a remote period, when it is difficult even to guess the precise nature of the weather and other natural conditions prevailing at the time. It is unlikely, however, that the southern portion of the Peninsula was ever an area particularly salubrious to early man. The tip of the Peninsula probes southwards as far as 34,22° of south latitude. This is getting close to the Roaring Forties with their interminable gales, and the Cape of Good Hope is noted for its winds.

In the dry summer months (November to March) the south-east wind is persistent, averaging 17 km to 40 km per hour but having periodic tantrums which reach 120 km per hour. This is a peculiarly relentless and unavoidable wind. It influences the direction of the growth of trees (which all grow away from it), and exasperates man into defensive concepts of architecture and outdoor activity, but it also provides the Peninsula as a whole with a significant service. The south-east wind, also known as the 'Cape Doctor', disperses smog and stench, clears visibility, and makes life so difficult for insects that such pests as flies, mosquitoes and gnats are not a health problem to man on the Peninsula.

In winter (May to August) a north-west wind replaces the south-easter. This wind, however, is far less persistent. It does blow periodic gales of great violence and brings rain to the southern Peninsula (averaging 35 cm at Cape Point), but it lacks the venom of the south-easter. The carrier of rain is the bringer of life, and the north-wester alternates its 'blows' with days of sunny calm when the Peninsula, green, clean and fresh from its shower, is at its best.

The average temperature of the southern Peninsula is 20,3°C in summer and 15,5°C in winter. The long, narrow Peninsula is three-quarters surrounded by sea. As such it is very much influenced by oceanic conditions which, to complicate matters further, vary from side to side. In summer there is usually a difference of at least 6°C between sea temperatures on the eastern and western sides. In winter the difference is slight, but still there at around 0,5°C, with the eastern side always the warmer of the two. This temperature variation influences the species of marine life, as well as recreational and commercial fishing.

At this stage it is perhaps necessary to clarify a persistent controversy about the waters washing the two sides of the Cape Peninsula. Are these waters those of the Indian Ocean or those of the Atlantic Ocean? In actual fact, the sea knows no oceans. Man, for the sake of geographical convenience, has applied a variety of names to portions of the sea, but the straight lines he draws between them are just as imaginary as the thread stretched across the lens of a telescope by sailors and shown as the equator to gullible people when they first cross the famous 'line'.

The sea knows only the differences of temperature and currents in its various parts, and these are the decisive influences affecting all forms of marine life. When the first sailors came down the west coast searching for an end to Africa and a sea route to the east, they discovered that the peninsula of the Cape of Good Hope was the most south-westerly point. It was not the most southerly point – this is Cape Agulhas 170 km eastwards – but it was to them the most important point, for on doubling it, they not only commenced the great swing eastwards, but changes in water temperature and marine life confirmed for them that they were entering a new world. No such significant changes were discernible on either side of Cape Agulhas at any season of the year. It was the Cape of Good Hope which marked the blending of the cultures of East and West. It is there that two powerful currents of this part of the sea, the warm Moçambique Current coming down the east coast, and the cold Antarctic drift which forms the Benguela Current running up the west coast of Africa, have their collision course. The warm waters of the east finally lose themselves, but, by their pressure, ensure that the cold waters sweep on up the west coast and do not penetrate eastwards.

Modern geographers have drawn a straight line south from Cape Agulhas and marked this as the division of the Atlantic and Indian oceans. But this is purely a manmade convenience. The actual point of impact of the prevailing currents could never be a straight line; as with the cultures of East and West, so the sea currents with their different temperatures experience an erratic and varying blending. The cold Antarctic Current surges up from the south and collides with the south-western coast from Cape Point westwards. In summer the pressure of the warm Moçambique Current holds it roughly in that position and it sweeps northwards as the Benguela Current. In winter the Moçambique Current is weaker and the meeting place is slightly further east.

However, the Cape of Good Hope is always the beacon; it is one of the great landmarks of the world, proclaiming that this is where the two halves of the world merge, where two ways of life have their frontiers, and where two major ocean currents, each with an enormous influence on all forms of life and scenery in their proximity, have a rendezvous and, simultaneously, a parting of ways.

Apart from leaving a few middens – kitchen refuse of marine shells, game animal skeletons, etc, – prehistoric man played no significant part in the story of the Cape Peninsula. His ancient garbage dumps may still be seen at places such as Batsata Cove, Cape Maclear, Bonteberg and Rooikrans, where there was some natural shelter from the winds, and drinking water was available from springs.

The early men in these areas collected shellfish and lobsters, trapped other fish species, foraged for bulbs, roots and any edible vegetation, and hunted and trapped game in close competition with other resident predators, such as the now extinct Cape lion and the lynx. There were probably not many game animals. The winds made life unpleasant and the absence in the soil of such essentials to animal welfare as copper traces made the grazing unpalatable, except for migrating animals who wandered about at will. Such migrants could have included Cape buffaloes, elephants, black rhinos and various antelope. Baboons were always present and are today a feature of amusement for all visitors, and of interest to scientists in that they scavenge the beaches in search of seafoods in similar fashion to prehistoric man.

It is illegal to feed baboons. By handfeeding baboons, well-meaning visitors actually do them considerable harm. They turn these animals into panhandlers who quite lose their normal feeding habits and become dangerous, aggressive and demanding in their approach to human beings.

Bird life was moderately varied, with about 150 species resident at different seasons of the year. A variety of sea birds was the principal feature. Jackass penguins landed on the beaches, while albatrosses, giant petrels, gannets, black-backed gulls, Hartlaub's gulls and cormorants were all common around the coast. Of the land birds, the malachite and orange-breasted sunbird was probably the most striking.

In the surrounding sea, Cape sea lions, whales, porpoises, sharks, tunny, yellowtail and snoek were in abundance. On land, tortoises have always been common, and the Cape of Good Hope is, in fact, one of their great breeding grounds. A few Cape cobras, *boomslang*, mole snakes, puffadders and other snakes also made their homes in the southern Peninsula.

The modern history of the Cape of Good Hope began in a howling gale which blew in the last three weeks of January 1488. Concealed in this gale was the sullen fury of the giant Adamastor and the termination of the age of legends. Down the west coast, probing, searching and inquiring, came the illustrious Portuguese explorer, Bartholomew Dias. In a cramped cockleshell of a ship, with his crew sick and frightened, he persisted in sailing southwards, hoping to find an end to the continent of Africa.

On 6 January 1488, off the south-west coast, they saw the lovely Cedarberg range and named it 'Mountains of the Three Magi Kings'. Then a storm enveloped them. The tiny ship was blown far from land, with Dias pitting his own resolution against the full force of nature. At last the storm abated. The sailors looked for land and found to the east nothing save the swirling sea. They swung northwards. In the storm, they had unknowingly doubled the end of Africa. Only on 3 February 1488 did they reach land, at what is known as Mossel Bay. The unseen Cape around which they had found their way they named the *Cabo Tormentoso* (the Cape of Storms).

Dias went on, with his crew in a mutinous and sulky mood. Beyond Algoa Bay, off the mouth of the Chalumna River, Dias was forced to turn back, leaving a stone pillar erected on a lonely headland known as the 'Rock of the Fountains'. But at least the weather was fine. Keeping close to the coast they discovered Cape Agulhas, naming it 'Cape St Brendan', as it was on his feast day, 16 May 1488, that they passed it. A few days later they passed Cape Hangklip, looked into the spacious and lovely 'Gulf within the Mountains' (False Bay) and then, in fair and gentle weather at last, as the Portuguese historian Barros writes, 'they beheld that great and remarkable Cape hidden for so many centuries, which when discovered revealed not itself alone, but another world of lands'.

To this cape Dias gave the name of Cape of Good Hope. The name was applied to the whole Cape, not simply to some minor point upon it. Dias spent a month anchored somewhere off its shores, probably in Table Bay resting his crew, writing his reports and perfecting a map of his voyage. Then, leaving another stone cross (no trace has ever been found of it), he sailed for home to report his finding to his king.

In naming the Cape of Good Hope, Dias conveniently forgot his earlier 'Cape of Storms' but it – and the vengeance of Adamastor – did not forget him. In 1500 Dias once again set out to double the Cape of Good Hope. Again he encountered a terrible storm, and this time his ship was overwhelmed. It lies somewhere in the deep waters off the Cape. Legend has it that in this disaster Adamastor had his revenge; and so the tale arose of a phantom sea captain and his ship, condemned forever to attempt the doubling of the Cape of Good Hope, but always frustrated by violent storms. The nationality of the unfortunate individual has varied with the telling through the years. Wagner, in his opera *The Flying Dutchman*, gave particular renown to the Dutch version, with Captain Van der Decken as the central character whose fate was redeemed by the constancy of a woman. But fundamentally the tale is rooted in the curse of Adamastor's fury and his vengeance on Bartholomew Dias, and this feud continues forever. It is in fact astonishing how many sailors navigating these waters have made serious reports about a sighting of the phantom ship.

Since the time of its discovery, the Cape of Good Hope has remained a point of great interest to all voyagers. East- and west-bound travellers alike regard it as the halfway mark on their voyages. To double it in a storm is an achievement comparable to doubling Cape Horn; to sail around it in fair weather is a delightful experience. From the tiny 100-ton *Golden Hind*, Sir Francis Drake, in the course of his round-the-world journey (1577 to 1580), described it as 'the fairest cape and the most stately thing we saw in the whole circumference of the globe'. Few disagree with his enthusiasm.

Let us start our own exploration of the Cape Peninsula in the centre of Cape Town, at the intersection of Adderley and Strand streets. There are several variants to the route we shall follow, but it has been planned, in the course of going completely around the Peninsula, to include all major places of interest and to follow the most pleasant scenic route, keeping to the east on the outward journey, and to the west on the return journey to our starting point.

With the railway station on the left, and Table Mountain looming on the right, the road passes the Castle and the exhibition hall known as the Good Hope Centre, and then climbs the traffic interchange to turn left into the elevated Eastern Boulevard. With the city now beneath it, the road (supported on tall concrete legs) strides over the rooftops, treating the traveller to fine panoramic views of the harbour, commercial centre, and the dominant bulk of Table Mountain and its companions – Devil's Peak on the left, and Lion's Head and Signal Hill on the right.

After 3 km there is a turnoff leading to the first of the southern suburbs of Cape Town.

## WOODSTOCK

The heavily built-up suburb of Woodstock was once a fashionable residential area known as *Papendorp* from a well-known inhabitant of those parts named Pieter van Papendorp. In 1881, when the place became a municipality, the majority of its inhabitants, who were all satisfied customers of the local pub, the Woodstock, arranged a change of name in honour of their favourite place of recreation. Whether the social downfall of the neighbourhood dated from this change of name is unknown, but nonetheless Woodstock became substantially less select and far more congested.

In former years, a tollgate stood on the main road, and the property of the headquarters of Cape Tramways (Cape Town's transport company) is still known as Toll Gate.

### Accommodation
* Altona Hotel, 11 rooms, 3 with baths. R5 – R6,50 B/B. Phone 47-5655.
* Beach Hotel, 10 rooms, 4 with baths. R6,50 B/B. Phone 55-5736.
*** Holiday Inn, 214 rooms, all with baths. R25 – R32 room only. Phone 47-4060.
* Lord Milner Hotel, 11 rooms, 5 with baths. R6,50 B/B. Phone 47-4726.

Beyond the turnoff to Woodstock, the Eastern Boulevard continues its gentle climb up the slopes of Devil's Peak. On both sides of the road lie the suburbs of Devil's Peak, University Estate and the partly cleared former slum of District Six, once beloved by artists (if not by its inhabitants) for its picturesquely decayed buildings, but now with little of interest remaining save a few mosques.

Passing the Holiday Inn on the right, the Eastern Boulevard continues under a major traffic flyover and then, at what is known as Hospital Bend, joins De Waal Drive, which has come around the slopes of Devil's Peak from the upper portion of the city.

At this junction, our route has reached its highest level on the slopes of Devil's Peak. From this point onwards there is generally a distinct reduction in the temperature (especially in summer). The road also leaves the built-up area below, and on the left there is a fine view over the Cape Flats towards the mountain ranges on the near horizon. On the right, the beautifully wooded slopes of Devil's Peak rise upwards to the mountain's impressive, jagged summit. Standing beside the road here is a small pillar erected as a memorial to those who died during the First World War.

*De Waal Drive*, which we have now joined, is named after Sir Frederick de Waal, first administrator of the Cape Province, who conceived the original route. It is cut into the slopes of Devil's Peak in finely graded curves, with its verges and grade separations planted with indigenous, flowering plants which provide many visitors with their first sight of the wonderful flora of Southern Africa.

The combined roads now take on the name of Rhodes Drive. The drive sweeps down the slopes of what is known as Hospital Bend. On the left is the vast complex of Groote Schuur Hospital, the buildings of the medical school, an old-aged home lower down in the built-up area, and, in perhaps unfortunate if convenient proximity, a cemetery. This coincidental grouping of interrelated human activities and inactivities should provide motorists with food for thought, but it seems to have little noticeable effect on the local brand of demon drivers. Hospital Bend is a favourite area for accidents. Perhaps speed goons or those suffering beyond endurance with the agonies of the type of cancer mentioned in the prelude to this book are in fact tempted into driving excesses by the convenient locations of the above-mentioned facilities!

Groote Schuur Hospital was founded in 1932 and became world famous when Professor Chris Barnard performed the first heart transplant operation there on 3 December 1967. Visiting hours at the hospital are: 14h30 to 17h30 and 19h00 to 19h30 daily.

Below the hospital and cemetery lies Main Road, a principal (and very congested) commercial thoroughfare, and the suburbs of Salt River and . . .

## OBSERVATORY

In 1821 the British Admiralty established in Cape Town a Southern Hemisphere branch of the Royal Observatory. The site selected, on the banks of the Liesbeek River, was then pleasantly rural and free from the glare of modern electric lighting. Many important research tasks were given to this observatory and many distinguished scientists worked in it. Its principal instruments were the 101-cm Elizabeth reflecting telescope and the 60-cm Victoria refracting telescope. Apart from its observations, the observatory was given the task of setting standard time for Southern Africa and, by remote electrical control, it fired the noon gun on Signal Hill.

In modern times, the steady encroachment of urban areas, atmospheric pollution and floodlighting on nearby roads such as Black River Parkway made work in the observatory increasingly difficult. Most astronomical work in Southern Africa is now done in the clear air of the Karoo at Sutherland, but much routine and analytical activity, as well as the measurement of stellar distances, continues in the old Royal Observatory, now known as the South African Astronomical Observatory. Visitors are welcome each month on the second Saturday evening at 20h00, weather permitting. Admission is free. There is a guided tour.

The buildings to the right of the observatory house the principal mental hospital of the Western Cape, *Valkenberg,* once the private home of Cornelis Valk. The football grounds of Hartleyvale are also near by.

Back to Hospital Bend, just past the turnoff to Groote Schuur Hospital, and 5 km from the start of our journey, there is a major traffic intersection where the main east coastal road, Settlers Way, starts its long journey through the Garden Route to Port Elizabeth and Durban. On the right-hand side of what is now Rhodes Drive, the pine plantations on the slopes of Devil's Peak give way at this point to a series of large, smoothly grassed paddocks. In these paddocks, against a handsome background of rugged mountain heights, there are antelope dotted about: bontebok, eland, wildebeest, zebra, Chinese deer and others, all graze peacefully in a semi-natural state of freedom.

This beautiful land was originally the farm *Welgelegen* of the Van Reenen family. In 1891, the renowned Cecil Rhodes acquired the property, and on his death he bequeathed it to the South African nation, to be preserved for all time as an area of scenic beauty. It is so full of interesting sights and attractive scenes that a walk through it is thoroughly worthwhile.

A convenient point to start such a walk is 5,5 km from the start of our journey: here Rhodes Drive reaches a turnoff to the suburb of Mowbray, immediately in front of Mosterts Mill. This well-preserved windmill was built in 1796 and worked by the miller, Sybrandt Mostert, from whom the place takes its name. The mill, with its adjoining threshing floor, is open, free to the public, daily from 09h00 to 17h00. Close to it, a gracefully designed footbridge crosses Rhodes Drive and takes walkers to a path leading through a shady plantation of stone pines, favourite trees of Cecil Rhodes.

In the plantation are picnic and barbecue sites. In one of the paddocks, the walled cemetery of the original owners of the farm can be seen. There is also a path winding up in easy gradients to the superbly situated Rhodes Memorial. Built in 1912 on a site particularly beloved by Rhodes for its enchanting view over the Cape Flats, the memorial is a most impressive and vital piece of work. It was designed by F. Masey and Sir Herbert Baker, and its centrepiece is a copy of the famous bronze by G. F. Watts – *Physical Energy;* this is a cast of the original which stands in Hyde Park, London and was completed in 1870. Silver trees and proteas flourish around the memorial, and a tearoom behind it provides refreshment. Paths lead upwards through the pines to join the contour path, which wanders through the trees high up on the slopes of the mountains. Among the trees on the slopes of Devil's Peak lie the remnants of three blockhouses and their cumbersome period cannon, erected there with great effort by the British army during the time of the first occupation of the Cape in 1795.

From the seats below Rhodes Memorial, where Rhodes himself was fond of sitting, the outlook is sweeping, revealing the whole of the Cape Flats from Table Bay to False Bay, and a glorious vista stretching from the built-up suburbs below, as far as the lovely mountain ranges on the northern horizon. Below us are the suburbs of . . .

## MOWBRAY, ROSEBANK AND RONDEBOSCH

Mowbray and Rosebank were both named after the estates on which they have developed. *Rondebosch* (round bush) is a fashionable suburb, noted for its trees, gardens and schools. Rustenburg School for girls has on its grounds the original summer residence of the later Dutch governors of the Cape. The open space of Rondebosch Common, where several species of flowers still find a sanctuary, lies in the middle distance with, on its far side, the buildings of the Red Cross War Memorial Children's Hospital. In Cecil Road, Rosebank, is situated the Irma Stern Museum devoted to the works of this artist. The museum is open daily except Mondays, 10h00 to 13h00 and 14h00 to 17h00.

### Accommodation
★ Mowbray Hotel (Mowbray), 12 rooms, 3 with baths. R6,25 B/B. Phone 66-3766.
★ Royal Standard Hotel, 12 rooms, 3 with baths. R7,50 – R8 B/B. Phone 69-2001.
★★ Glendower Hotel (Rosebank), 100 rooms, 85 with baths. R9,50 – R12,50 B/B. Phone 69-9621.
★★ Fairmead Hotel (Rondebosch), 100 rooms, all with baths. R12 B/B Phone 69-4741.
★ Randalls Hotel, 15 rooms, 4 with baths. R7,50 – R8 B/B. Phone 69-9794.
★ Westerford Arms Hotel, 10 rooms, 6 with baths. R6,50 – R8 B/B. Phone 69-5051.

Rhodes Drive continues from Mosterts Mill, immediately reaching a turnoff leading down Woolsack Road, past the administrative and some faculty buildings of the University of Cape Town and then joins the Main Road through the suburbs of Rosebank and Rondebosch. The attractive complex of the Baxter Theatre stands at this junction.

The main cluster of buildings of the University of Cape Town lies on the right-hand side of Rhodes Drive 6 km from the city centre, where our journey began. The situation of the university is magnificent, with the serrated summit of Devil's Peak and the rugged cliffs of the back of Table Mountain forming a spectacular backdrop. A statue of Rhodes, great benefactor of the place, sits on the steps in front of the university, looking in pensive mood at the creeper-covered buildings and the playing fields.

The University of Cape Town is the oldest in the Southern Hemisphere. It began in 1829 as a private enterprise named the South African College, housed in the city area proper, with buildings including what are now the archives in Queen Victoria Street. The private college became a public venture in 1837 and then, as a university, was transferred to its present situation in 1925, when the foundation stone of the first building was laid by the Prince of Wales. The imposing site is on Rhodes's great gift of his Groote Schuur estate. Over 9 000 students study each year in the ten faculties of this university.

Rhodes Drive passes below the creeper-covered walls of the university. On the left stands the white, one-time summer house of British governors known as the *Belvedere*. Beyond it the dual carriageway curves around the end of the university campus and passes between the grounds of the small zoo founded by Rhodes (open to the public daily from 09h00 to 17h00) and, on the left, the gateway leading to the lovely homestead of *Groote Schuur* (the great barn). This was originally built by Van Riebeeck as a grain store. It was converted by later English owners into a residence called *The Grange,* and then purchased by Rhodes as the nucleus of his great estate along the slopes of the back of Table Mountain and Devil's Peak. A disastrous fire practically destroyed the place in 1896. It was then remodelled for Rhodes in the Cape-Dutch style by the famous architect, Sir Herbert Baker. It is full of treasures, for Rhodes was a great collector of antiques and curiosities. The garden outside became famous for its hydrangeas, passion flowers and plumbago (Rhodes's favourite flower), all planted in great banked masses which he felt were appropriate to the prodigious scale of the African continent. A pleasant tradition was that each Christmas the hydrangeas were cut, and – literally by the truck-load – taken to decorate the wards of Groote Schuur and other hospitals.

Rhodes bequeathed his wonderful home as the official residence of the Prime Minister of the Cape (now of South Africa). A second house on the estate, the *Woolsack* was originally built by Rhodes as a summer home for his friend, Rudyard Kipling, and later became the official residence of the Deputy Prime Minister. It is now part of the university. Across the way from *Groote Schuur* is *Westbrooke,* originally bought in 1800 by Judge William Westbrooke Burton, and today the country residence of the State President of the Republic of South Africa.

Immediately beyond the gateway to *Groote Schuur,* 7,5 km from the start of our journey there is a turnoff leading to the zoo, to Rhodes Memorial and to the suburb of . . .

## NEWLANDS

Newlands is the area of Cape Town with the heaviest winter rainfall (over 1 500 mm) and its consequent greenery is very delightful to the eye. The suburb was originally a logging area and farm, *Nieuwland* (new land), on the banks of the upper reaches of the Liesbeek River. In 1700, Willem van der Stel, the then Governor, discovered the beauty of the area and built a country house there. This made the area distinctly upper class, and it is still considered to be one of the choicest residential suburbs of Cape Town. Even the Liesbeek River rises to the occasion in these parts, and carries a fair population of those aristocrats of freshwater fish – trout! The houses along the shallow river valley include some particularly handsome buildings. The cottage named *Paradise,* where the loquacious letterist, Lady Anne Barnard, once lived, lay among the oaks on the right-hand side of the double carriageway on the farm of *Paradijs* granted to W. ten Damme in 1706. Today only ruins of the foundations of the dream cottage remain, but pleasant pathways meander past the site and enter the cool shadows of the beautiful Newlands forests. Bird lovers will be interested to see a small population of the European chaffinch, introduced by Cecil Rhodes, nesting in these trees.

Lower down the course of the Liesbeek River, the second home of Lady Anne, *The Vineyard,* remains in the form of a well-known hotel. *Newlands House* still stands in Newlands Avenue with its stately lines of oak trees. There is an interesting walk up and down the course of the river. In its lower reaches the stream passes the magnificent Newlands swimming bath, bubbles merrily under the lower Main Road at Westerford, passes the picturesque, disused Josephine watermill standing at the approach to the Newlands rugby ground, flows close to the cricket fields, and then gurgles off towards the sea.

## Accommodation
**** Newlands Hotel, 144 rooms, all with baths, R24 – R34 room only. Phone 65-4180.
*** Vineyard Hotel, 30 rooms, all with baths. R19 – R30 B/B. Phone 69-5731.

The section of the Rhodes Drive double carriageway from the Groote Schuur gateway to the intersection of Newlands Avenue is known as Union Avenue, and is a real scenic delight. On the right-hand side, forest-covered mountain slopes dominate the Avenue. Indigenous flowers turn the verges and grade separations of the road into a long garden, while on the left-hand side the attractive houses of the suburb of Newlands doze in the shade of trees.

The forestry station and municipal waterworks lie among the trees on the right. The reservoir there is fed by three pipelines 51,5 km in length from the main reservoir of Steenbras in the Hottentots Holland mountains. There is a parking area beneath the trees just above the turnoff to Rhodes Memorial and the zoo, and from here paths lead into the forest, where wild blackberries and many silver trees grow among the pines.

Union Avenue ends at the junction with Newlands Avenue 9,5 km from the start of our journey. This is an important junction on the route. To the left, Newlands Avenue stretches off to the lower Main Road through a notable avenue of oaks. Straight ahead, the double carriageway continues down Paradise Road, crosses the Liesbeek River and, 10 km from its start in the city centre, reaches a turnoff leading to the busy suburb of . . .

# CLAREMONT

Claremont, which has an important commercial centre, is still sometimes referred to as 'the village' and its rugby team is known as the Villagers. It is today more like an infant city, with a major shopping centre and one of the most beautiful public parks in Southern Africa, the Arderne Gardens. This garden was originally part of the estate known as *The Hill* in the halcyon days when Claremont was still a village in the centre of a quiet rural area. In 1840 an English immigrant, Ralph Arderne, acquired this estate. He was a lover of trees, and on the site he planted one of the finest tree collections in Southern Africa. From all over the world, he acquired about 325 species of trees, including magnificent Norfolk Island pines, Indian rubber trees, Atlas mountain cedars, North American swamp cypresses and many others. All flourished in Ralph Arderne's garden. The Black River has its source in this garden and the spring was converted by Arderne into a delightful Japanese garden, with bridges, ferns and waterfowl. Azaleas, rhododendrons and roses grow to perfection in the park, and it is always a colourful scene.

In 1927, after hard economic times and the unfortunate death of Arderne's son and heir, Henry, had forced the family to dispose of the fine estate, 4,5 ha were acquired by the municipality and, saved from the mercies of property developers, converted into the public gardens of today.

Harfield Road, leading off from the park, was named after *Harfield Cottage*, famous in the annals of missionary work in Africa as the transit quarters of the staff of the London Missionary Society. In this cottage, eminent men such as Moffat and Livingstone stayed when they were in Cape Town.

## Accommodation
* Lansdowne Drop Inn, 10 rooms, 3 with baths. R,750 – R11 B/B. Phone 81-5124.

--------

At the important intersection of Union Avenue with Newlands Avenue and Paradise Road (9,5 km from the city), let us turn sharp right off the double carriageway and follow the continuation of Rhodes Drive up the avenue along the bottom of the slopes of the back of Table Mountain. The road is a scenic delight, and leads us through what is without doubt one of the most attractive residential areas to be found anywhere in the world – the green and fertile expanse of the lands of Van Riebeeck's old farm of *Boschheuwel* (bushy slope), now known more generally as *Bishopscourt,* from the offical residence there of the Anglican archbishop of Cape Town.

*Boschheuwel* was laid out in the sheltered valley of the upper Liesbeek River. The south-eastern rise took the name of Wynberg from the farm vineyard. The valley is now covered with lovely homes and a drive through the estate is a thoroughly enjoyable diversion from the main route of Rhodes Drive. A very pleasant little road to explore is Boshoff Avenue, the first turnoff to the right down Paradise Road. This road passes through the gates of the old Boshoff Estate. Shaded by a fine avenue of oaks, it continues past many a handsome home including, on the right, the original Boshoff homestead with the date 1776 on its gable and, further on, the beautiful and secluded *Fernwood* (now simply the pavilion of the Parliamentary Sports Club), in whose commodious grounds lies what is surely one of the most splendid cricket fields to be found anywhere in the world where the game is played.

After 2 km, just beyond the point where Boshoff Avenue rejoins Rhodes Drive, the drive passes the entrance to Kirstenbosch, one of the most famous of the world's botanical gardens. In this garden some 4 000 of the 18 000 species of the plants of Southern Africa are cultivated. The garden covers an area of 560 ha including the entire overlooking slopes and back of Table Mountain right up to its highest point, Maclears Beacon. Apparently named after J. F. Kirsten, an official of the old Dutch Government, the area became the property of Henry Alexander, Colonial Secretary in the British administration in 1811. He was something of a character: he had the first homestead built with windowless bedrooms, as he considered these rooms would only be used at night. This interesting establishment was unfortunately burned down; it was later replaced by the present tearoom. Another of Alexander's construc-tions was the exquisite little sunken bath – for some reason erroneously known as Lady Anne Barnard's Bath – in one of the springs of the Liesbeek. Cecil Rhodes bought the whole property in 1895 and presented it to the nation as the ideal site for a botanical garden. In 1913 it was proclaimed as the National Botanic Garden of South Africa with Professor Pearson as first director. He set to work to make Kirstenbosch pre-eminently a home for the collection, preservation and study of the indigenous flora of Southern Africa. The success of his pioneer efforts is gloriously self-evident in the all-year-round display of wild flowers and the magnifi-cent collection of cycads, silver trees and other shrubs, plants and trees. Professor Pearson's grave in the garden has a fitting epitaph: 'All ye who seek his monument, look around.'

Lectures and exhibitions are arranged in halls in the gardens. The Compton Herbarium, named after one of the directors of the garden, contains more than 200 000 specimens of the indigenous plants of Southern Africa. A tearoom provides refreshment and the Botanical Society of South Africa who have their headquarters in the gardens, offer an interesting variety of books and other items for sale. Kirstenbosch is open to the public daily, 07h30 to 19h00.

From Kirstenbosch, Rhodes Avenue climbs the southern slopes of the Liesbeek valley, providing many views of fashionable Bishopscourt; then the avenue swings sharply right to reach the summit of the rise at the junction with Klaasen Road, which if we follow it, would take us off to Wynberg. Along the Kirstenbosch side of the road there is a still flourishing stretch of the hedge of wild almonds planted in Van Riebeeck's time to mark the boundary between the first European settlement and the wilderness of Africa.

Rhodes Avenue winds off through avenues of chestnut trees planted by Rhodes, and beneath lovely tunnels of oak trees. This whole area was acquired by Cecil Rhodes with the express dream of preserving its beauty and building a scenic drive around the mountain slopes above the estates of Southern Cross and *Witteboomen* (silver trees) to Constantia Nek. The forest above the road is called *Cecilia* after Rhodes, and through it wind many paths and tracks leading to beauty spots such as the Cecilia waterfall, and right up to the reservoirs on the back of Table Mountain.

At Constantia Nek, 5 km from Kirstenbosch, where artists are wont to exhibit pictures for sale in the open air, the road divides. To the right it descends by a winding route through an entrancing succession of oak tree avenues and eventually reaches the marine drive at Hout Bay, where we will join it later.

To the left the road descends into the famous wine-producing valley of Constantia and 3 km away we reach, via a short approach drive, the historic homestead of *Groot Constantia*. This magnificent building, the prototype of the Cape-Dutch style, was built in 1685 by the Governor, Simon van der Stel. The reason for its name is somewhat obscure. The young daughter of the Commissioner, Baron van Rheede, was named Constantia and, as her father granted this spacious farm to Van der Stel, it is likely that he named the place after the little girl in order to please the family. The great house he built was a perfect blending of Dutch-German design, with those odd touches which skilled Malay craftsmen used so successfully with the available building materials at the Cape – lime-washed walls and black thatch. It harmonises with its environment to perfection. The furnishings are all suited to the period.

The vineyards of Constantia were at one time the most famous in the Cape, if only because they were, in the early years of the local wine industry, the largest producers and also the most accessible to tourists. For many years, in fact, Constantia wine was synonymous with Cape wine. The district specialised in muscatel wines, for it was here, in the local soil and climatic conditions, that the muscatel variety of grape introduced from Spain in Van Riebeeck's time grew to particular perfection. Known with the earthy humour of the old farmers as the *hanepoot* (rooster's testicle) from the shape of its berries, this delicious golden, musk-flavoured grape not only yielded a fine wine, but, with its mutation, the red hanepoot – said to have been first discovered in the Cape by Van der Stel while he was inspecting his vineyard – is certainly one of the sweetest and most delicately flavoured of all table grapes.

When Simon van der Stel died, on 24 June 1712, he bequeathed his property to his five surviving children, none of whom lived in the Cape. Constantia was therefore sold. It was divided into two portions: *Groot* (great) and *Klein* (little) *Constantia. Groot Constantia* passed through the hands of several owners, and was finally purchased by Hendrik Cloete in 1778. Cloete developed the production of wine, and built handsome cellars designed for him by the French architect, Louis Thibault, with the pediments sculpted by Anton Anreith. In the cellars, he carefully blended grapes grown on the estate. Cloete offered for sale, and exported to many overseas countries, a range of wines of such excellent reputation that his regular customers included the monarchs of several countries, and many other illustrious personalities, including wine connoisseurs from East and West. Authors and poets such as Jane Austen, Alexandre Dumas, Longfellow and others wrote fondly of the vintages of Constantia.

Hendrik Cloete was a master of the subtle art of winemaking, and the soils and climate of *Groot Constantia* provided him with grapes from which unique estate wines were made. The grapes were leisurely crushed by the bare feet of his slaves, to the rhythms of soft music; then they were crushed again, to faster music; they were then passed through a fine sieve, and the skins were left with the juice just long enough to enhance colour and flavour. The ultimate skill of the winemaster was in blending the various pressings; these were tested on the palate of Hendrik Cloete, who alone knew the secret of his Constantia wines, which today, alas, are the pleasure of a bygone age.

Wine is still produced on what is left of the estate. Unfortunately no attempt has been made in modern times to duplicate the subtle blends of Hendrik Cloete, although the intention now is to produce a late harvest wine similar to the Edelkeur of Nederburg. Cloete's descendants and successors continued making wine on *Groot Constantia* and on a neighbouring estate,

*High Constantia. Groot Constantia* was eventually acquired by the government, and thus was protected from avid land developers. The other vineyards of the area have been divided into housing estates; today only fragments of them remain.

In the late 1920s, R. F. Bertram purchased the estate of *High Constantia* and developed winemaking there with some interesting results. In 1939, the business was acquired by G. N. Maskell, a man of considerable international experience in the wine trade. He retained the well-established name of Bertrams Wines, introduced a complete range of wines and spirits, built handsome new cellars near *Groot Constantia,* and expanded the company's landhold-ings until he controlled much of the remaining part of the Constantia area that was productive. In 1943, Maskell acquired control of the *Groot Constantia* estates, which held a lease of the famous vineyards. In 1959, Bertrams Wines was acquired by Simeon Blumberg of Devon Valley near Stellenbosch and the head office of the company was moved to the seat of the new owner. The South African Government then took over *Groot Constantia* and the buildings housing Bertrams cellars. A control board now manages the estate. Grapes grown there are crushed and a series of estate wines are produced; they are sold directly to the public in the two cellars from 09h30 to 12h45 daily. Cabernet, Shiraz, Pinotage and Steen are produced on the estate, and the bottles bear the Groot Constantia label. The quality is superlative. The Cabernet, Shiraz and Pinotage in different vintages have been classified as estate wines of origin superior, the highest possible classification. In 1977 two new cultivars were introduced: Pinot Noir and Riesling. Quantities are limited and rationed. A Rosé is also produced and a sweet red. *Groot Constantia* is open Mondays to Fridays from 10h00 to 17h30. Tours of the cellars are conducted at 11h00 and 15h00. In one of the outbuildings is a restaurant known as the Jonkershuis where the wines of Constantia may be bought as a pleasant accompaniment to good food.

Although no descendants of Simon van der Stel remain in the Constantia area today, some descendants of Hendrik Cloete still live there. A grandson of Cloete acquired the farm *Alphen,* close to Constantia, on which stood a beautiful homestead and substantial wine cellars. For many years, wine was produced on this estate, but today the vineyards have largely van-ished, swallowed by urban development. The homestead on *Alphen* was converted into a hotel and a bottle store in 1963, and the winery has been converted by the Cape Divisional Council into a library. The Cloete family still produce wine under the *Alphen* name, but nowadays it is produced on an estate which they own on the slopes of the Helderberg, overlooking Stellenbosch.

One kilometre from the driveway to *Groot Constantia* the road we are following reaches another parting of the ways. The left-hand road would take us on for 3 km past the Alphen Hotel to join the Simon van der Stel Freeway (see further on) and on to Wynberg and the suburbs of Plumstead and Heathfield with their shopping and built-up areas.

The right-hand turn in the road from Constantia takes us through a pleasant world of vineyards and country homes. At an intersection leading across the Simon van der Stel freeway to the residential suburbs of *Bergvliet* (mountain brook), Meadowridge and Sweet Valley, our scenic road bears sharp right down the Spaanschemat Road. A pleasant drive brings us to the Tokai Forest with its shady picnic places and beautiful manor house dating back to 1792, when the estate was first granted and named after the hills in Hungary, where the decorative and subtly flavoured Tokai grape had its original home. The manor house is now a national monument and the abode of the principal of the Porter Reformatory for Coloured youths which is situated in the forest. The house is one of the reputedly haunted places of the Cape. The story is that for a wager, a wild son of a former owner, Petrus Eksteen, once rode his horse up the steep steps into the manor and around the guests seated at dinner. On the way out the horse stumbled and young Eksteen was killed. His ghost is said to ride again on certain nights.

The Tokai Forest was the foundation forest for the South African policy of reafforestation commenced in 1883. Trees of many different kinds were experimentally planted here in ideal climatic conditions for growth. The forest today covers a substantial area of the slopes of the 927-m-high Constantiaberg which dominates this area, and has a tall radio mast on its summit. In the cliffs of this mountain, overlooking the forest, the entrance to a cave may be seen. Nowadays it is known as the Elephant's Eye, but according to legend it was once the retreat of a princess of one of the early Hottentot tribes. Its old name was the *Prinseskasteel* (castle of the princess).

In the winter months of decreased fire hazard, permits may be obtained from the forester to enter the main area of the forest. The walk up the track leading to the radio mast on Constantiaberg is one of the finest excursions in the Cape. From Tokai the spectacular road known as the Ou Kaapse Weg climbs to the top of the Silvermine plateau and thence to Fish Hoek (see further on). The portion of the Tokai Forest on the right-hand side of the road is open to the public until sunset each day. Sheltered from all winds, it is one of the best and most spacious of all the picnic spots of the Cape.

---

Back at the turnoff to Claremont, 10 km on the main double carriageway from the city centre, let us continue our tour of the Peninsula. At this stage of its journey the road is known as Edinburgh Drive and it leads through the fine residential area of Upper Claremont (here with a truly 'clear view' of the back of Table Mountain and Devil's Peak), and past, on the right, the fashionable area of the old estate known as the *Hen and Chickens* from a landmark of granite rocks shaped like a hen and her brood. At this stage the road climbs the slopes of what Van Riebeeck named the *Wynberg* (wine mountain) and, as it tops the rise of this hill, there is a fine view over the Cape Flats and towards False Bay, with a first glimpse in the distance of the tip of the Cape Peninsula, which is our principal objective on this pleasant journey. A vineyard still flourishes on the slopes of the old wine mountain and this provides a fitting foreground to the panoramic view.

Just over the summit of the hill 12 km from the city centre, there is a turnoff leading past the stone pines, oaks and silver trees of Wynberg Park, and by turning left after passing the second traffic lights, we enter the suburb of . . .

## WYNBERG

Wynberg, with its substantial and very congested commercial centre, is the largest suburb of Cape Town. Its military oamp and hospital, established by the British when they occupied the Cape, have always tended to dominate the suburb and provide it with a particular atmosphere. In modern times, many of the old cottages have been restored in what is known locally as 'Chelsea' style, and in them a sprinkling of artists and would-be artists have made their homes and studios. The park and open-air theatre of Maynardville is also in this area.

James Maynard, after whom the lovely park is named, was a timber merchant and member of the Cape Legislative Assembly. He acquired the estate in 1844. His grandson (through his daughter), William Maynard Farmer, inherited the estate in 1874. Having accumulated wealth in the exciting days of the diamond rushes, he lived in style, and employed a gardener trained at Kew who created a colourful, ornamental garden of oleanders, hydrangeas, fountains and lawns. In 1949, the property was offered to the Cape Town municipality, and became a park and open-air theatre. The original homestead has been demolished, but several ghosts of its grand days reputedly linger on. Included among them are such supernatural bric-à-brac as a cast-off, unwed daughter with babe in arms, and rapidly receding horse's hooves, said to be either the culprit fleeing or the father in pursuit.

Also in Wynberg, in magnificent grounds, is *Hawthorndene,* the home of the late Sir J. B.

*Overleaf: The Cape of Good Hope, meeting place of two ocean currents and the cultures of Africa, the East and the West.*

Robinson, and his son-in-law, Count Labia. In 1976 this residence was donated to the Cape Provincial Council to be maintained as a cultural museum. It was built in 1880 and contains many fine late Victorian paintings and statuary. The Robinson and Labia family mausoleum is in the grounds and in the garages are two superb vintage cars.

## Accommodation
* ★ Royal Hotel, 19 rooms, 6 with baths.R7,60 B/B. Phone 77-1344.
* ★ Wynberg Hotel, 12 rooms, 3 with baths. R7 B/B. Phone 71-2618.

# KENILWORTH

Kenilworth is the suburb between Wynberg and Claremont. It grew as a residential area around the original homestead of *Stellenburg* farm. It was in this area that the Dutch governors had the kennels of their hunting hounds. The name Kenilworth was first applied to the estate and then to the railway station. The Kenilworth Race Course, scene of the principal horse race of the Cape, the Metropolitan Handicap, is in the lower part of the suburb adjoining the military base of Youngsfield.

## Accommodation
★★★ Palace Hotel, 75 rooms, all with baths. R18 room only. Phone 71-1161.

---

From the turnoff to Wynberg and Kenilworth, 12 km from the city centre, the main double carriageway continues down the southern slopes of Wynberg Hill. It crosses Wynberg Park by means of a bridge and, with a splendid view of the farming and residential area of Constantia, descends until, at a point 14 km from the city centre, it reaches a turnoff leading to the suburbs of Wynberg, Plumstead, Constantia, and over Constantia Nek to Hout Bay. This turnoff is the road we followed past Kirstenbosch.

The double carriageway continues southwards across an undulating, green and pleasant landscape. There are turnoffs to suburbs such as Diep River (via Kendal Road), Bergvliet and Meadowridge (via Ladies Mile Road) and, 20 km from the city, a turnoff left leading for 1 km to the suburb of Retreat, and the lovely forest area of Tokai.

## Accommodation
* ★★★ Alphen Hotel (Constantia), 29 rooms, all with baths. R22,50 – R45 room only. Phone 74-1011.
* ★ Constantia Berg Drop Inn (Diep River), 15 rooms, 6 with baths. R7,50 – R11 B/B. Phone 72-9230.
* ★★ Hohenort Hotel, 27 rooms, 12 with baths. R9,90 – R17 B/B. Phone 74-1027.

## Caravans and camping
* ★★ Sweet Valley Caravan Park, 100 sites. R2 D plus 50c D per person, Oct. – Feb. R1,50 D plus 25c D per person, March – Sept. Phone 74-3010.

# RETREAT, TOKAI AND THE OU KAAPSE WEG

The suburb of *Retreat* was named for its connections with the British army, which established there two camps, Pollsmoor and Westlake, both used as marshalling and resting places for troops in transit to Asia or Europe, especially during the First and Second World Wars. With the interminable movement of manpower during these war years, countless numbers of men found themselves quartered in Retreat, and it remains an address remembered by many.

From the turnoff to Retreat and Tokai (21,5 km from the city), the Simon van der Stel freeway continues 1,5 km and then reaches an intersection. To the left, the turnoff leads to Steenberg, Lakeside and Muizenberg. To the right is the scenic *Ou Kaapse Weg* (Old Cape Way), which is a superb drive.

Passing the important naval communications centre on the left, securely constructed in the depths of the mountain, the Ou Kaapse Weg commences a steady climb up the *Steenberg* (stony mountain). At a point 4 km from the intersection the road reaches a viewsite on the summit, with a turnoff leading to a parking area, and further on, to a tollgate providing admittance during the day to pine forests and an old reservoir which once supplied drinking water to the residential areas below the mountains. The whole area is known as the Silvermine Nature Reserve, and it is rich in indigenous flora. Even the verges of the road are gardens of wild flowers, brilliant with colour, especially in the months of spring.

There are many pleasant picnic places in the area of the nature reserve, and the walks are delightful, notably the circular walk up the forest road which leads from the reservoir to the summit of the mountain and then down to the other side of the reservoir. Near the highest point of the road, a short walk away, the stone beacon on top of the Noordhoek Peak (756 m above sea level) may be seen. From this beacon there is a tremendous view of Hout Bay and the Atlantic Ocean.

One kilometre further along the Ou Kaapse Weg, beyond the turnoff to the summit viewsite and tollgate, there is another turnoff: this one is on the left-hand side of the road and is signposted 'Waterfall'. A tollgate, open during daylight hours, allows access to another popular picnic area close to a waterfall which, in wet winter months, is an attractive spectacle. From this site there are walks to the Kalk Bay and Muizenberg mountains with their caves, wild flowers and glorious views over False Bay (see further on).

Beyond the waterfall turnoff the Ou Kaapse Weg descends into the Fish Hoek Valley. After 2,5 km the road passes on the right-hand side the original pit sunk in 1687 by prospectors searching for silver in the area. This was the first mining activity in Southern Africa undertaken by Europeans. No silver was found, only traces of manganese, but even these in quite unpayable quantities. The name 'Silvermine' clings to the area, a reminder of a long-past disappointment.

One kilometre beyond the shaft, the road reaches a crossroads. The right-hand turn leads to Noordhoek and the left-hand turn (gravel) leads to Clovelly. The Ou Kaapse Weg continues southwards, and after another 3 km reaches the Sun Valley township, where it joins the main road running along the western side of the Peninsula from Cape Town to Cape Point (page 52).

---

At the turnoff to Steenberg, Lakeside and the Ou Kaapse Weg, the main double carriageway of the Simon van der Stel freeway comes to an end, its eventual route still uncertain – either a tunnel through the mountains or to continue for a further half-kilometre to join Boyes Drive cut into the mountains overlooking False Bay. *Boyes Drive* takes its name from George Boyes, a magistrate of Simons Town whose enthusiasm for the road largely stimulated its construction in the 1920s. It is cut high into the slopes of the Muizenberg and Kalk Bay mountains. On the left-hand side there are superlative views over False Bay. On the right-hand side there are several pathways leading climbers into the same lovely area of wild flowers, caves and extensive views as that which is reached from the waterfall turnoff on the Ou Kaapse Weg, described earlier. Below us lies the seaside suburb of Muizenberg, which can be reached by taking the turnoff left from the present end of the Simon van der Stel freeway. Muizenberg is 26 km from the city.

# MUIZENBERG, FALSE BAY AND THE LAKES

Muizenberg is justly ranked as one of the world's most famous seaside resorts, although in modern times it became much neglected by public authority. The suburb itself is a nondescript, congested collection of hotels, boarding houses, and private residences. The greatest asset of the place is its beach, which is the finest and most spacious in Southern Africa, and one of the safest and liveliest bathing beaches in the world. The whole area, including the lake known as Sandvlei, is a major recreational and holiday area for the people of the Cape Peninsula and for many visitors from other parts of Southern Africa.

Muizenberg lies on the north-western end of False Bay, a 29-km-wide by 30-km-deep inlet of sparkling blue water contained within the mountainous arms of the Cape Peninsula and the Hottentots Holland range projecting into the sea at Cape Hangklip. The name *False Bay* was given to it because ships coming from the East often confused Cape Hangklip with the Cape of Good Hope. By turning in error into False Bay instead of doubling the Cape of Good Hope, they suffered great inconvenience, and usually had no little difficulty in extricating themselves.

During the summer months, when the prevailing wind is the powerful south-easter, the warm Moçambique Current from the Indian Ocean is deflected into False Bay. This is the beautifully blue water of holiday time, with a temperature of around 22° C. From November to April, False Bay is at its best for swimming.

In the winter months the north-west wind takes over. The driving pressure of the south-east wind is relaxed, and the warm water in False Bay is displaced by the greenish-coloured, plankton-rich flow of the Benguela Current from the Atlantic Ocean. The water temperature drops to around 15°C. This is not so pleasant for swimmers, but surfing conditions are at their best at this time, with a heavy swell and an offshore wind. During the months of April and May, nautilus shells are washed ashore on the False Bay coast and make fine prizes for collectors.

Muizenberg is cradled between sea and high mountains. Its magnificent beach stretches off eastwards for 35 km to the mountain range of the Hottentots Holland. From the traffic circle at Sunrise Beach, Muizenberg, the Baden-Powell Drive follows the shoreline, providing an attractive panorama of glistening beaches, restless surf and serene mountain ranges on both sides of the great bay. There are kilometres of safe and enjoyable bathing, surfing and fishing stretches such as those at *Strandfontein* (beach fountain), 6,8 km from Muizenberg, *Mnandi* (pleasant place) and *Swartklip* (black rock), 18 km from Muizenberg. From Swartklip the road veers inland to join Settlers Way (24,5 km from Muizenberg).

Close to the shores of False Bay lie several small lakes. These are fed by streams which have sources mainly in the mountains of Constantia and Tokai. Among these streams are the *Spaanschemat* (Spanish rushes), *Keysers* (after Johannes Keyser who was drowned there), and the *Diep* (deep). These streams meander seawards across built-up areas which were once fertile farmlands producing, among other things, some of the most delectable table grapes of South Africa.

On reaching the level ground of the Cape Flats, these streams half lose themselves in the sandy, former sea bed in depressions which trap their flow. The streams become shallow lakelets such as the *Sandvlei* (sandy marsh), beloved by canoeists, owners of small yachts and numerous birds. This expanse of water is fed by the Spaanschemat, Keysers and other streams. On its northern, western and eastern verge, the *Marina da Gama,* named in memory of the Portuguese navigator, Vasco da Gama, was constructed. This is an extensive luxury housing project with waterside sites opening on to a series of artificial canals leading from Sandvlei. It is an imaginative residential concept, first conceived in 1969 by David Jack of the Cape Town Planning Department, and built on what was originally a garbage dump and wasteland. The land was systematically acquired over several years, and involved more than 1 000 separate land transactions by the project's principal motivator, John Bridgeman. It was opened in 1974.

The Diep River supplies water for the two connected lakelets known as Little and Big Princess vleis. The name comes from a Hottentot princess who was reputedly held captive in the Elephant's Eye cave at Tokai by Portuguese sailors. Her tears are said to have formed the two little lakes, famed for the size and number of the carp living in their waters, and for their reflecting qualities on calm days.

Two other lakelets fed by water from the mountains that is trapped by the sands are *Zeekoevlei* (hippopotamus marsh), the largest of them all and a favourite haunt of yachtsmen, and *Rondevlei* (round marsh), a famous bird sanctuary established on 1 January 1952 as the first ornithological field station in South Africa. In this 105-ha sanctuary some 200 bird species make their home, or are occasional visitors. These birds include flamingos and pelicans. They are systematically studied in relation to one another, to food and to climatic conditions. Midsummer sees the vlei with its densest population. There are observation towers and a hide open to the public, and an interesting museum. Close to Rondevlei lie the extensive artificial lakes of the Strandfontein Sewage Disposal Area. In these nutrient-rich lakes live an array of water birds rivalling any of the world's famous bird sanctuaries. Flamingos, both the greater and the lesser species, pelicans, avocets, stilts, innumerable ducks and other birds visit the area seasonally or live there permanently.

Rondevlei is open to the public daily from 1 January to 31 July. On weekends, entry is unrestricted. For visits during the week, a permit must be obtained from the offices of the Divisional Council of the Cape, 44 Wale Street, Cape Town.

---

It was on the shores of Sandvlei, in 1743, that a sergeant by the name of Wynand Muys was placed in charge of a cattle post and strongpoint on the road from Cape Town to Simonstown. The post became known after its commander as *Muysenburg* (Muys's stronghold) and this name was later corrupted to the Muizenberg of today.

Muizenberg really became fashionable as a holiday resort in 1899, when Cecil Rhodes, then at the height of his personal and financial power, bought *Barkly Cottage* there from the estate of J. R. Reid. His love for the place (he used it to recuperate from the effects of his experiences in the siege of Kimberley) attracted the attention of many other well-to-do individuals. The area became the prototype of the South African coastal township, where inland residents build a seaside house which they occupy for a short holiday season and then leave boarded up for the rest of the year. Such absentee owners have little community interest, and improvement or change is resented. Muizenberg therefore tended to stagnate in the Edwardian state in which it was originally built in the first rush of enthusiasm during Rhodes's time.

On 26 March 1902, Rhodes died in his unpretentious little cottage. It is nowadays maintained as a museum, containing many interesting personal possessions and photographs concerned with the eventful life of a remarkable man. The cottage is open to the public daily except Mondays from 10h00 to 17h00.

Muizenberg, with False Bay and its lakes, remains the main recreational area of Cape Town and a major holiday resort for Southern Africa. False Bay itself is one of the world's principal angling areas. As the terminal point of the Moçambique-Agulhas Current it is of great value and significance to marine biologists. Its eventual proclamation as a marine national park is most desirable. With an ever increasing demand for recreational space, it is essential that the whole False Bay coastal area be carefully maintained, so as to preserve unspoilt all its striking assets – pure, warm water, fresh air, wide, clean beaches, safe swimming, delightful lakelets and ubiquitous scenic beauty. Its marine fauna is astonishingly rich, while bird life is magnificent.

## Accommodation

★ Balmoral Hotel, 82 rooms, 46 with baths. R9,50 – R10,50 B/B. Phone 88-4141.
★★ Marine Hotel, 50 rooms, 25 with baths. R8,50 B/B out of season, R25 D in season. Phone 88-1162.
Abe Bailey Youth Hostel, Maynard Road. 60 beds, R1,20 D for members. Phone 88-4283.

## Caravans and camping

★★★®Sandvlei Caravan Park, 108 sites. R3 D, Feb. – Nov. R5 D, Dec. – Jan. 12 cottages (4 and 6 berth) R7,50 – R19, seasonal.

Rhodes's cottage lies on the southern outskirts of Muizenberg where the narrow and (on holidays and weekends) badly congested coastal main road twists around the foot of the mountains, with the sea on the left and a line of imposing villas on the right. After 1,5 km the road passes the suburb of . . .

# ST JAMES

*St James* was named after the first church that was built there. This suburb is well sheltered from the wind, has a pleasant little beach and tidal swimming pool, and has always been popular with visitors from overseas.

## Accommodation

★ Robin Gordon Hotel, 50 rooms, 18 with baths. R8,50 – R13,50 B/B. Phone 88-1141.
★★★ St James Hotel, 54 rooms, 39 with baths. R12,85 – R24,50 B/B. Phone 88-8931

Beyond St James, the coastal road continues for a further 1,5 km and then joins the turnoff coming down the slopes from Boyes Drive at the fishing harbour and suburb of . . .

# KALK BAY

*Kalk Bay* (lime bay) takes its name from former years when a kiln was burned there in order to produce lime for painting buildings. Quite a number of the white-walled homes of the Cape owed their smart appearance to the lime from this kiln. The harbour is always a busy scene, but around June and July, the peak of the snoek season in False Bay, it is especially bustling. Catches of 40 000 snoek landed in one day in this compact little harbour are not uncommon.

Kalk Bay harbour is also a seaside resort for the Coloured community. On weekends and public holidays it is crowded with vivacious and loquacious people, swimming, gossiping and taking boat trips out into the bay.

Seal Island in False Bay is visited by a passenger launch from Kalk Bay, leaving at 10h00 and 15h15 daily, weather and boat permitting; this trip provides visitors with an interesting spectacle, for the rocky little island is densely populated with seals, and has an impressive setting in False Bay.

The mountain massif dominating the Muizenberg to Kalk Bay stretch of the False Bay coast is a superb recreational area for the energetic walker, cave explorer and nature lover. It is like a gigantic rock garden, ingeniously devised by nature to shelter a vast variety of flowering plants, displaying their lovely blooms against a background of views across False Bay.

There are paths to most places of interest in these mountains. Perhaps the most intriguing places to explore are the many remarkable caves, about which there is a fascinating story.

In 1924 a schoolmaster by the name of Johannes B. Meyer spent a holiday at Kalk Bay.

Hearing that there were caves in the mountains, he spent some of his time following the paths meandering up to the heights. His experiences entranced him; his holiday became a period of joyful discovery. The paths which made their way upwards, some steep and direct, others gradual and diagonal, rewarded him with memorable views. At his feet were gaily coloured wild flowers – heaths, proteas, everlastings, watsonias, scarlet coloured flames and countless other lovely shrubs.

The caves added a touch of drama and adventure to this natural beauty. Several caves were already well known in the 1920s. Muizenberg Cave, with its enchanting moss-grown entrance, its low caverns and deep, mysterious well, had not yet been totally disfigured by morons with their idiotic name painting, but the process had started, with a first date as early as 1873.

Clovelly Cave with its labyrinth of passages and chambers was sufficiently known as to be considered haunted by the local Coloured folk. Apparently a half-demented old mountain hermit had once made his home there, and had amused himself by stealthily approaching visitors on the mountains and scaring them out of their wits with his sudden chuckle close behind them. Eventually he was found dead in his cave. The sinister echo of his chuckle is reputed to linger on in the cave, and it is said that a cold hand touches any interloper's shoulder the moment his light goes out.

The amazing Boomslang Cave, penetrating right through a ridge for 146 m, was discovered in 1911 by Arderne and Sampson, and it was here that Meyer met a fellow explorer. It was an amusing chance meeting. Meyer started his cave journey from the low northern entrance, wriggling in on his stomach. At the same time, J. C. W. Moore started from the southern side, where the entrance is high and overlooks the Fish Hoek Valley. The two men met in one of the high chambers in the middle reaches of the cave and, with a candle burning on a ledge of rock, they enjoyed a chat about the mountains and the wonders of the secret caverns. Moore was a Kalk Bay man who knew the area well, and his knowledge stimulated Meyer to learn more about this fascinating place.

As a result of his explorations during his holiday, he was privileged to discover two new caves, which he named Central Grotto and Johles Cave, the latter a combination of his own name and that of a companion, Leslie van Blerk. He never forgot the pleasure of these pioneer explorations.

In 1935 Meyer retired. He was a sick man, but he returned to Kalk Bay and made his home there, determined to devote what time he had left to a study of the mountains and to the discovery of more caves.

During the following months he wandered over the heights, and the more he explored, the more caves he found; the exercise and the fresh air gave him a new lease of life.

A small band of friends gathered around Meyer, for he was a most amiable companion on the mountains – knowledgeable, communicative, humorous; he knew many good yarns and was a fine hand at brewing coffee or grilling a chop. Through their activities, Meyer and his friends became known as the Moles. Meyer was recognised as First Mole; a certificate was awarded to his companions who had explored at least the dozen principal caves of the 95 assorted grottoes, caverns, pits and other exciting places mostly discovered and named by Meyer on the Kalk Bay mountains.

Alvin Meyer, Phillip Hitchcock, Anne Hefere, Leslie van Blerk, Horatio Nelson, Basil Harris, Arthur Pratten and J. W. Hurlingh were some of the Moles, and something of the pleasure they had in their various outings is reflected in the names they and the First Mole attached to their discoveries: Rest-a-Bit, Light and Gloom, Six Moles Cave, Moss and Diamonds, Drip-Drop, Sunbeam Cave, Noonday Rest, Mirth Parlour and many more. Some of these names have vanished from modern maps but most remain, many painted on to the rock walls of the caves by Meyer and the Moles. Countless later visitors have enjoyed pleasant days of adventurous exercise and relaxation in rediscovering these interesting places.

43

The heights of this sandstone mass consist of a number of parallel ridges. The ceaseless dripping and washing of water during the wet months of winter has eroded the rocks into curious shapes (such as the remarkable head, overlooking Devil's Pit, which resembles that of a latter-day South African Prime Minister) and modelled numerous caverns.

Of the caverns, the most extensive so far found is Ronan's Well. This cave was known before Meyer's time, but for many years it was thought to be only 68 m long. Then a modern cave explorer (or speleologist), Michael McAdam, followed a draught of air coming through a narrow crack and, with some difficult scrambling and a tight 2,5-m-long squeeze, opened the way into an involved series of underground chambers, halls and crevices stretching for 365 m into the depth of what is known as Ridge Peak and thence out through two other caves, Aladdin and Robin Hood. Ronan's Well is not a cave for a beginner to explore. Even the entrance is tricky: a rather sinister-looking grotto with a dark hole 5,5 m up its inner wall which takes the explorer into the heart of the mountain.

Boomslang Cave, the second most extensive cave so far found, is a safe, exciting 146-m passage through the ridge known as Cave Peak. There are several impressive chambers, a 9-m crawl at the northern end, and an imposing southern exit high over Fish Hoek. It was at the pool on the floor of this exit that the original discoverers disturbed a boomslang quenching its thirst – hence the name.

The third largest cave in these mountains was found by Meyer in 1941. The exploration of this cave must have given its discoverer many a thrill, as the first entrance that was found was a narrow 9,5-m deep pit to descend which a rope ladder was necessary.

At the bottom end of this pit the cave stretches out in a succession of holes and chambers for 132 m. At the south-eastern end an easier entrance was subsequently found: a chimney 3,6 m deep connected through a low cavern and a narrow passageway with Annie's Hall, the first of the large caverns. Meyer, who named several of his cave discoveries after figures in Greek mythology, named this whole remarkable cave sequence Oread Hall after the Oreads, the nymphs of caverns and mountains in Greek legend. The 13,7-m-deep Devil's Pit was another cave first explored by Meyer by means of a rope ladder; now it is usually entered from a hole in the ravine below it which leads through Creepy Corridor and Herripilation Chamber for 36,5 m, and then into the pit.

Among the numerous parties which Meyer conducted through the caves was one consisting of 20 women teachers. Getting them through the section of Boomslang Cave where explorers are forced to crawl must have taken some coaxing, but generally he seems to have enjoyed having ladies accompany him on explorations; several of his cave discoveries carry names such as Pollie's Cave, Beatrice Cave, Bettie's Cave, Martha's Cave, Nellie's Pool and Dolly's Doorway.

The last cave found by Meyer and his Moles was a small cavern rather wistfully named Me Too. The First Mole sickened after that, and in 1951 his health broke down completely. He recovered partially, made two more climbs, and then died of lung cancer on 9 September 1952. He was 78 years old and the mountains had given him the gift of 19 healthy years during which his diary records 1 700 climbs into the Kalk Bay mountains. Memories of him will always linger over the mountains; in later days José Burman and S. MacPherson found a cave on the Red Afrikaner Ridge (named from the watsonias there) and fittingly named it Meyer's Memorial.

---

From Kalk Bay, the coast road continues past the entrance to the harbour and curves around the slopes of the mountains. After 1,5 km, a fine view of Fish Hoek and its valley is revealed, with, on the northern side, the small residential suburb of . . .

# CLOVELLY

Few railway stations have ever displayed signs such as those of Clovelly station, prohibiting angling from the platform. At Clovelly the sea washes against the station buildings, and if the railway administration was not so firmly set against it this little station could easily provide good fishing for travellers! Clovelly station was originally known as *Trappies* (steps) because of the steep flight of stairs leading from the station to the houses.

The area of Clovelly was once a farm named *Klein Tuin* (little garden) owned by the De Kock family. An Englishwoman, a guest of the De Kocks, is said to have been responsible for the name of Clovelly, because she fancied the place resembled her native Devon. At Clovelly, the Silvermine stream (when it flows during the winter months) reaches the sea. A road to the right leads up the banks of this stream through the wind-sheltered residential area to the Clovelly Country Club, and then, as a country lane, eventually joins the Ou Kaapse Weg and carries on to Noordhoek.

The municipal area of the City of Cape Town ends at the Silvermine stream. Across the stream, the road enters the municipal area of Fish Hoek, with its centre 1,5 km from Clovelly.

# FISH HOEK

The municipality of Fish Hoek, with its population of 7 560, is unique in Southern Africa. The original grant of the farm *Vischhoek* (fish glen) was made by the Governor, Lord Charles Somerset, to Andries Bruins in 1818. There were conditions to this grant. The farm lay directly on the road to the naval station of Simonstown and some very thirsty sailors on shore leave. The prudent Lord Somerset therefore stipulated that no public wine house be kept on the farm. This condition was perpetuated in the township laid out in 1919 and the modern municipality is therefore the only teetotal town in Southern Africa.

With bottle stores and bars absent, Fish Hoek boasts a minimal crime rate. It is a residential area connected by electric railway to Cape Town and despite being rather congested and haphazardly laid out, it is a relaxed, self-contained little town with a fine, safe bathing beach.

The glen in which Fish Hoek lies cuts right across the Cape Peninsula. In comparatively recent geological times (Cretaceous), the sea washed through the glen, leaving the southern portion of the Peninsula an island. The present floor of the glen is the sandy former sea bed. In a great rock shelter overlooking this glen, prehistoric man once lived and dined on marine shells, fish and other tidal life which teemed in the waters. The rock shelter became known as the *Schildersgat* (painters' cave) but is now more generally known as Peers Cave after Victor Peers and his son Bertram who, in 1927, commenced a painstaking exploration of the place which resulted in the excavation of the skull of Fish Hoek Man, a representative of the people who inhabited this part of Southern Africa 15 000 years ago.

Peers Cave may be reached by following the road which leads from Fish Hoek through the glen to the other side of the Peninsula. Just before the Robinvale Caravan Park, 3,5 km from the centre of Fish Hoek, take the road that turns off to the Fish Hoek Squash Club and Brakkloof Forest and Fire Station. At the end of this road there is an interesting walk over glistening, white sand dunes and up the slopes of a rocky ridge which contains the cave. The path to the cave continues to the summit of the ridge where there is another remarkable cave, Tunnel Cave, in which interesting discoveries of artefacts have been made. The path ends at a beacon just above this cave, and from this vantage point a fine view of the whole glen may be enjoyed.

## Accommodation
* Avenue Private Hotel, 35 rooms, 8 with baths. R7,50 – R11,50 B/B. Phone 82-1814.
* Outspan Private Hotel, 46 rooms, 16 with baths. R11,50 – R13,50 D/B/B. Phone 82-1140.

45

### Caravans and camping
® Municipal caravan park (on beach), 24 sites R1 – R2,20 D.
★ Robinvale Caravan Park, 40 sites. R1,50 – R2 D plus 50c D per person. 10 rondawels, R4 – R8D.

# GLENCAIRN

From Fish Hoek the main road continues along the coàst around the slopes of the 303-m-high Elsie's Peak, passes Sunnycove railway station and enters the valley of the *Elserivier* (river of *els* or alder trees). A branch road leads up this valley past many residences, the Rotary, Moth and Gordons camps, and the buildings of the farms *Welcome* and *Oaklands*, originally granted in the early 19th century to the well-known Brand family, whose sons have played so distinguished a part in the administration of South Africa (Johannes Brand was President of the Orange Free State from 1864 to 1889). The road continues up to the modern Da Gama Park, a housing estate built for members of the South African Navy and named after the Portuguese navigator, Vasco da Gama.

The inlet at the mouth of the stream, marked on the maps as Elsiesbaai, has a small beach and a tidal swimming pool. The residential area is known as *Glencairn*, so named, it is said, by a Scot who came from the original Glen Cairn and was in the habit of wandering about this little valley, playing his bagpipes. Glencairn is administered as part of Simons Town, which is reached by the main coast road 6 km from Fish Hoek (36,6 km from Cape Town).

In the breakers between Glencairn and Simons Town the tops of engine cylinders can be seen, all that remains of the *Clan Stuart,* a naval collier which was blown ashore there on 20 November 1914. The ship had been at anchor with her engines off when a south-easter carried her gently ashore. The crew ended the day playing billiards and drinking beer in the Glencairn Hotel. The ship settled in the sand and refused to budge.

When the south-east wind is not blowing, Glencairn beach can be very pleasant. In 1939, it was reported that a large number of people on this beach saw the spectral Flying Dutchman.

### Accommodation
★ Glencairn Hotel, 12 rooms, 5 with baths. R8,50 – R9 B/B. Phone 82-1081.

# SIMONS TOWN

The municipality of Simons Town has 5 945 inhabitants and is spectacularly situated beneath a 678-m-high ridge of mountains. The bay of Simons Town was originally known as *Isselsteijn Bay* from a Dutch East Indiaman of that name which, in 1671, sheltered there from contrary winds. The crew of this ship found the bay so much to their liking that their reports eventually stimulated its development as an alternate winter sanctuary to Table Bay, which was exposed to north-westerly storms. The bay was renamed in honour of the Governor, Simon van der Stel, and a stone pier and two small forts were built there. In 1814 the British converted Simons Town into a naval base for the South Atlantic Squadron, and substantial workshops and a dry dock were constructed. It is from this time that Simons Town acquired something of the special naval atmosphere of a small English seafaring town, with narrow twisting streets. The handsome Admiralty House and St George's Church, the oldest Anglican church in Southern Africa, both date from this period. The local cemetery records on its tombstones a colourful story of sea fights, cuttings-out and escapades of the period.

On 2 April 1957 the South African Navy took over Simons Town, and the coming and going of ships and the great activity of small craft in the fishing harbour create a real seafaring atmosphere in the port. Apart from commercial fishing boats, Simons Town is the home port for over 200 ocean-going yachts and power boats, used by their wealthy owners to pursue big game fish – tunny and marlin – during the summer season off the Cape of Good Hope. The South African Marlin and Tuna Club has its quarters close to the harbour. The South African record bluefin tunny stands at 361 kg and was caught by Brian Cohen in December 1968.

Simons Town is the terminus of the suburban railway from Cape Town. It is worthwhile strolling down its main street. There are several reminders of the past, and an interesting and well-arranged little museum housed in an old Martello Tower, open from 10h00 to 16h00 Mondays to Fridays.

The Martello Tower was erected in 1796 by the British who, after seizing the Cape, wished to prevent possible attempts by Napoleon to occupy it. Unfortunately the tower was allowed to fall into a ruinous state. Finally, in 1966, after 30 years of efforts to have it restored, the South African Defence Force created a museum section in the tower. For the first time, defence funds were spent on non-military objectives; the tower was restored, and opened as a maritime museum in April 1973. It is thought to be one of the oldest surviving constructions of the Corsican pattern anywhere. Certainly the 73 similar towers strung along the south-eastern shores of England were not built until 1803.

The ground floor of the museum is devoted to a series of dioramas of Simons Town over the years, with ancillary items to add interest and verisimilitude. There are some early photographs of the development of the naval base, and a series of portraits of the Commanders-in-chief of the South Atlantic Station of the Royal Navy (which until 1957 was Simons Town). Upstairs are uniforms of the South African Navy and the Royal Navy, with historical information, and relics of the two world wars in which the Cape played a significant role. A curiosity which is worth inspecting is a copy of *The Times* of 7 November 1805, in which the news of Nelson's death and the victory of Trafalgar are recorded. Also upstairs is a most delightful iron firegate, lovingly restored, with GR IV on each side.

To find the museum, drive right through the town, past the second gate into the dockyard, and follow the yellow sandstone wall to its end. Then, still by the wall, turn sharply left into a narrow road leading to the sports ground. Turn left again, with the wall, to the car park. A wire fence with a gate surrounds the tower which houses the museum.

Just before the main coastal road enters Simons Town, there is a branch to the right which climbs Red Hill. From its summit a sweeping view of the whole of False Bay is revealed, with Simons Town below looking like a three-dimensional model of itself. Branching off this road are turnoffs to the Lewis Gay Dam in the Elserivier and left, to the naval radio transmitters. Straight ahead is a drive across the Peninsula to the Atlantic coast.

## Accommodation
★ Lord Nelson Hotel, 11 rooms, 3 with baths. R7 B/B. Phone 86-1386.

## Caravans and camping
★★® Oatlands Caravan Park, 90 sites. R2,10 – R4,50 D, seasonal. 20 rondawels and 7 cottages, R5 – R20 D.

The main coastal road leaves Simons Town (and the last petrol point for 55 km) and continues to the end of the Peninsula along a stretch of coast that is best described as one long ocean playground. Here are delectable little bathing places such as Seaforth and Boulders, which are sheltered from the winds of summer and provide wonderful sport for the canoeist, underwater fisherman and swimmer. *Seaforth* was named by an early settler, Captain Harington, whose wife was a niece of the Earl of Seaforth.

## MILLER'S POINT
The climax of this stretch of coast comes 8 km from Simons Town, at Miller's Point. In 1828 this

beautiful locality was acquired by Edmund Miller who built a seaside cottage there called *Elsmere*. Until 1850 his family had the whole place to themselves, and he conducted whaling operations in False Bay. Then the estate passed into other hands. Today Miller's Point is one of the finest coastal resort developments in Southern Africa. In this superb setting, the present owner, the Cape Divisional Council, has imaginatively created a caravan park, with vehicles deployed on terraces that enjoy a view of sea and distant mountain which no luxury hotel could equal.

Playgrounds, a restaurant, a large tidal swimming pool, green lawns, innumerable picnic spots and a profusion of wild flowers are among the attractions of this recreational area. For the canoeist and underwater swimmer there is a glorious garden beneath the ocean, with anemones and sea urchins of brilliant hues set in waving forests of seaweed where shoals of lively fish wander like butterflies living in a magical world.

### Caravans and camping
★★★® Miller's Point Caravan Park, 40 sites. R3 – R3,50 D plus 50c D per person, seasonal. Phone 86-1142.

## SMITSWINKEL BAY

From Miller's Point the road continues south along the coast for a further 5 km, passing many picnic and viewsites until, gaining steadily in height, it climbs diagonally along the cliffs 91 m above the bay known as *Smitswinkel* (the blacksmith's shop), a name suggested by a pair of rocks, one shaped like an anvil, the other like a bellows. Smitswinkel Bay is a favourite fishing spot, with a cluster of informal shacks built on the water's edge where their owners enjoy a happy privacy.

The road now swings away from the coast and, after 8 km, reaches a junction, with a turnoff to the left taking the traveller for the final 13 km southwards to the end of the road at Cape Point. These final 13 km lead through the Cape of Good Hope Nature Reserve.

## THE CAPE OF GOOD HOPE NATURE RESERVE

A visit to the Cape of Good Hope Nature Reserve at the tip of the Cape Peninsula is a most fascinating outing. The area has excellent roads and is easily accessible at all seasons of the year. The summer months (November to March) are inclined to be windy. The winter months (May to August) are pleasant, as the rainfall is hardly sufficient to disturb visitors for more than a few days in each year. Spring (September and October), when the countryside is colourfully strewn with wild flowers, is particularly lovely. The reserve has a tearoom and a refreshment kiosk. At Buffels Bay there are enclosed tidal swimming pools and launching ramps for boats. There are several picnic spots in the reserve. Behind the restaurant there is a field museum dealing with the area. Admission to it is free.

In the early years, the southern part of the Cape Peninsula remained a windswept wilderness of wild flowers. A few fishermen and runaways from justice occasionally made their way down to the tip of the Cape, but there were no roads and no settlement in the area until the first quarter of the 19th century, when the British took control of the Cape and Simons Town was developed as a naval base.

Farms were then allocated in the area and on 1 July 1816, John Osmond was granted the farm *Buffelsfontein*, also known as *Uiterstehoek*, which included the tip of the Peninsula. A condition of the grant was that the Naval Department would retain the right to erect a lighthouse on any part of the farm which might be judged best for such a purpose. Access to this lighthouse was also to be permanently available.

Nothing was done about a lighthouse for some years, although the need for a beacon became increasingly urgent as the volume of shipping around the Cape increased. In 1823, the coastline was properly surveyed by Royal Navy chartists such as Captain Owen, and names were given to the various outlying rocks, including Bellows (the dangerous outlying rock always covered in foam), Anvil, Whittle (in False Bay) and Dias Reef. Captain Owen, incidentally, also reported sighting the Flying Dutchman.

The first lighthouse, a prefabricated iron tower painted white, was erected in May 1860 on the summit of Cape Point, 210 m above sea level. The first lighthouse keepers, J. Coe and his assistant H. Franks, soon found that their light was too high. When the mists swept in, the light was often well above the clouds and quite invisible to any shipping. This was a dangerous situation but for some time nothing was done to rectify matters.

Apart from the lightkeepers, a few farmers established themselves on land in the southern Peninsula, but little is remembered of them. With bad roads, thin soil and incessant wind, they were forced to live on a subsistence economy. Horses flourished in the area, the farmers managed to grow some barley and wheat, and milk and vegetables were produced for the shipping at Simons Town. A few homesteads were built of local sandstone cemented with lime made from shells in kilns at Buffels Bay and Bordjiesrif, and in these buildings the farmers passed their days. Remnants of the homesteads may still be seen, but memories of the personalities who lived in them and events which took place have long since been blown away with the winds.

Occasionally a shipwreck occurred somewhere around the coast, or there were sightings of the Flying Dutchman. One of the most famous of these was logged in 1881 by King George V, when he was a midshipman on *HMS Bacchante*. The lightkeepers also reported sightings of odd vessels, with all sails set even in the worst weather, persistently trying to double the Cape. Even the coming of steamships did not end these rumours of sea ghosts.

On the night of 18 April 1911, a major disaster occurred when a 5 557-ton Portuguese liner *Lusitania* struck Bellows Rock. The lighthouse of Cape Point was completely obscured by the mist. The ship was a total loss, although fortunately only four out of the 774 people aboard were drowned. This disaster tragically emphasised the urgency of a change to the lighthouse.

A new site was selected, lower down on the tip of Cape Point, only 87 m above the sea and overlooking Dias Rock. On 25 April 1914 the foundation was laid for the new lighthouse. In this construction, a 500 000 candlepower paraffin lamp was installed. In 1936 this lamp was converted to electricity, with a giant reflector and lens providing 19 000 000 candlepower, making the lighthouse the most powerful in the world.

The light at Cape Point can justly be described as one of the greatest shipping beacons in the world, and countless sailors have been guided by its tremendous beam. The giant tankers which make their way around the Cape, rusty freighters, trim ocean liners, pugnacious warships, sneaky submarines on the prowl – all regard it as a massive landmark. During the Second World War, German submarines lurked by day beneath the waters, and by night lay on the restless surface just beyond the beam of light, waiting patiently for prey. Several of these nocturnal prowlers reported sightings of the Flying Dutchman, and just before the war, early in 1939, crowds of holidaymakers on False Bay beaches reported a weird-looking battered old sailing ship making its way towards Muizenberg and then vanishing in a cloud of mist. This intriguing legend persists into modern times, a colourful part of the character and romantic atmosphere of the Cape of Good Hope, whose commanding presence dominates one of the great strategic trade routes of the world.

The idea of preserving the southern portion of the Cape Peninsula as a nature reserve originated in 1928, when the whole area was threatened with development into seaside resorts, complete with 'Trespassers will be prosecuted' signs and forlorn, dilapidated shacks deserted by owners who used them only during holiday periods.

Fortunately at this time several public-spirited and influential Capetonians became interested in the area. Brian Mansergh, a Cape Town architect, had known the area since his youth, and had often discussed its conservation with local farmers. In November 1928 he wrote to the Minister of Lands pleading for the establishment of a nature reserve, but his plea was rejected on grounds of cost. Mansergh continued to promote the idea of a reserve, supported by a number of friends who gathered for a weekly informal lunch during which they discussed affairs in general. News of the formation of a syndicate to develop townships in the southern Peninsula particularly disturbed them, and a patient spell of propaganda and systematic agitation followed. Dr Stacy Skaife, Dr Leonard Gill, Anthony Leyds and Henry Hope concerned themselves with arousing public interest. The key property in the area was *Smith's Farm*, owned by Norman Smith and his family. This was actually the farm *Buffelsfontein* or *Uiterstehoek* originally granted to John Osmond, containing the end of the Peninsula. The Smith family was approached and, approving the idea of conservation, agreed to sell to the conservationists rather than to land speculators.

The Cape Town City Council was then approached, but the area was well outside their boundaries and individual councillors were not enthusiastic. One of the councillors, A. Z. Berman, summed up resistance to the idea by stating flatly that he would be against spending council money on an area where 'there was not enough vegetation to keep a scorpion alive'. Another councillor, W. F. Fish, described it as 'wasteland, waterless and treeless'.

The enthusiasts were not dismayed. They started to make plans for raising the money to buy *Smith's Farm*, fence it in, and make it pay for its maintenance as a nature reserve by erecting a tollgate on the road leading across it to the lighthouse and resorts such as Buffels Bay and the famous fishing ledges at Rooikrans, places already much frequented by visitors.

At this stage Will and Percy Hare, owners of the farm *Bloubergvlei*, which was also in the area, offered their property to the projected nature reserve providing that it would be maintained as a wilderness, and that they would be allowed to live undisturbed in their seaside cottage at Brightwater; also, no road was ever to be built across what had been their land.

The whole concept of a nature reserve gained in stature. The Simons Town municipality supported the idea, and its mayor, L. C. Gay, was particularly enthusiastic. The local morning newspaper, *Cape Times,* gave it considerable editorial support. One memorable leader (23 November 1938) was amusingly specific:

*'It seems almost treasonable to this stately peninsula of ours to think that its extreme end, now the only unspoilt part of our heritage, should fall into the hands of men who will cause it to pimple into a bungaloid acne.'*

The city council, however, remained hostile to the establishment of a nature reserve, although a poll of the people of Cape Town revealed overwhelming support. Charles Duminy, chairman of the Divisional Council of the Cape, and Jerwyn Owen, its secretary, had fortunately also been interested in the project for some time. They put it to their council and the idea was at last officially accepted. On 11 April 1939, a special meeting of the council approved the purchase of *Smith's Farm,* and the Cape of Good Hope Nature Reserve came into being, with the specific object of preserving for all time the 'fairest Cape', in the state in which it must have been seen by Bartholomew Dias. Norman Smith was appointed first warden with £250 a year as salary and free occupation of his farmhouse.

The Divisional Council spent R32 000 in purchasing *Smith's Farm* with its homestead and three privately owned bungalows. Crown land was added by the State. In 1941 the farms *Olifantbos, Theefontein* and *Krommerivier* were bought from the estate of D. C. de Villiers, as well as the Minicki family farm, *Klaasjagers*. Other land was acquired to consolidate the area. The last property to be purchased (in 1965) was, oddly enough, a portion of *Wildschutsbrand* owned by Mrs Jacoba Malherbe. This farm had been the first to be granted in the southern Peninsula and originally it was the home of the first Field-Cornet (district officer) appointed over the area. The homesteads of all these farms have vanished, including, unfortunately, the one known locally as *Die Spookhuis* (the haunted house), a building with quite a selection of tales about its unorthodox residents. A picnic spot on the site of the house still bears its name.

With this acquisition, the Cape of Good Hope Nature Reserve attained its present dimension of 7 680 ha, acquired by the Divisional Council of the Cape at a total cost of R127 000. Completely protected and carefully maintained, this nature reserve is a scenic and botanical delight. Game animals of the type which once roamed freely over the Southern Cape (eland, bontebok, etc) have been introduced and these, together with descendants of the indigenous population of rhebok, grysbok, baboons, marine life, birds, tortoises and other wild creatures, live their natural lives in a setting which is peaceful, beautiful and quite unique.

The gates to the reserve are open at the following times:
06h00 to 20h00 1 November to 31 January.
07h00 to 19h00 1 February to 30 April.
08h00 to 18h00 1 May to 31 July.
07h00 to 19h00 1 August to 31 October.

---

From the turnoff leading into the Cape of Good Hope Nature Reserve, the main road commences its journey back up the west coast of the Peninsula. There are pleasant picnic sites beneath the trees on either side of the road, while 8,5 km towards Cape Town, just after the junction with the road coming from Simons Town over Red Hill, the Divisional Council has converted *Perdekloof* (horse ravine) farm into a free recreational area, with shady trees and green grass.

A further 3 km takes the road past . . .

## SCARBOROUGH, SOETWATER AND SLANGKOP

Scarborough consists of a cluster of weekend cottages close to the oddly shaped roadside landmark known as Camel Rock. There is a pretty beach and, when the wind is not blowing, the picnic and camping sites are pleasant. For 7,5 km beyond Scarborough the country is wild and bush-covered, with sandy bays such as *Witsands* (white sands), and many picnic sites and camping grounds in sheltered places along the way. After 5 km there is a crossroads with a turnoff left which leads to the recreational area of *Soetwater* (sweet water), much used by the Coloured community. A right turn provides a short cut through the Coloured housing estate of Oceanview to Fish Hoek. The main road now climbs the face of a cliff and reveals below a large stretch of coast with tidal pools and a recreation area dominated by the graceful steel tower of *Slangkop* (snake peak) lighthouse which, with a lamp of 16 750 000 candlepower, was the second most powerful in Africa to be commissioned after Cape Point.

### Caravans and camping
★★★® Soetwater Caravan Park, phone 8-3747. Divided into 3 areas:
★★ Medusa Caravan Park, 66 sites. R2,70 D plus 55c D per person in excess of 5.
★ Die Anker camping ground, 60c D.
Soetwater and Sandkop camping ground, 2 000 camping sites. 30c D.
Witsands camping ground, 25c D.

The road now descends into the little resort known as . . .

## KOMMETJIE

*Kommetjie* (the little basin) takes its name from a natural inlet in the rocks which has been developed into a large tidal pool. This inlet is a favourite place for surf riders, as is Long Beach, especially in the summer months when the south-easter is blowing. The view north towards Chapman's Peak and Hout Bay is particularly impressive from here. Swimming in the tidal pool is safe and the water is relatively warm.

## Accommodation
★ Kommetjie Hotel, 7 rooms, 2 with baths. R7,50 – R10,50 B/B. Phone 83-1706.

## Caravans and camping
★★★® Imhoff Park, 120 sites. R1,90 – R2,70 D, seasonal. Phone Kommetjie 7976.
★★ Sunnyacres Caravan Park, 50 sites. R2 D plus 50c D per person, seasonal. Phone 82-2913.

North of Kommetjie the road leads through an avenue of flowering gums. After 1 km a road turns off to the left and leads down to the Imhoff Park caravan park and to the beach at *Klein-Slangkoppunt* (little snake peak point) from where there is a good walk up the beach of Chapman's Bay to the wreck, more than half buried in the sands, of the *Kakapo*. The *Kakapo* was 1 500 tons brand new on delivery voyage from British builders to the Union Steamship Co. of New Zealand. On 25 May 1900 in a fresh north-westerly wind she ran aground. Her crew of 24 simply walked ashore. All attempts to refloat her were a failure. The railways used portions of her steel plating to flank the line at Fish Hoek and stop sand drift. Local residents had free coal for some time as the ship carried ample bunkers for the long voyage to Australia. In later times she was used as a set in the film *Ryans Daughter*.

Seven kilometres from Kommetjie the main road reaches the junction with the road which crosses the waist of the Peninsula to Fish Hoek. The road bears left from this junction. After 1 km the road reaches a junction with the *Ou Kaapse Weg* (already described). Continuing left through the Sun Valley township, the main coast road reaches . . .

# NOORDHOEK

*Noordhoek* (north glen) is a rural settlement, shaded by oak trees, situated just below Chapman's Peak. From the main road a side road turns off through the trees, passes the Chapman's Peak tearoom and leads down to the beach. When the south-easter blows this is a windy spot, but there are superb surfing waves at *De Hoek* (the corner), where the beach ends on the steep slopes of Chapman's Peak. There is some fine walking along the great beach which skirts Chapman's Bay all the way up to Kommetjie. The name 'Chapman' applied to the bay and the dominant peak on the north side originated on 29 July 1607 when the *Consort* under Captain David Middleton anchored off this coast. The master's mate, John Chapman, was sent in a boat to see if there was any anchorage. His name was thenceforth attached to the peak and the bay. The estate and home of the late Sir Drummond Chaplin lies on the slopes east of the road.

## Caravans and camping
Shady Oaks Caravan Park, 50 sites. R2,50 D.

# CHAPMAN'S PEAK

For the next 11 km from Noordhoek the main road follows one of the world's most spectacular marine drives, cut into the cliffs around the 650-m-high Chapman's Peak. This famous scenic road was the brainchild of Sir Frederick de Waal, the same energetic first administrator of the Cape Province after whom De Waal Drive is named. Stimulated by his enthusiasm, the road was built between 1915 and 1922 and still remains an engineering feat of the first magnitude. On the grave of the engineer responsible, Robert Glenday, in the Woltemade Cemetery, a stone quarried from Chapman's Peak was erected by his colleagues as a fitting memorial to a magnificent piece of work. From this road, with its numerous lookout points and (on the far side) picnic places, there are incomparable views back over the great beach of Chapman's Bay, and north across the handsome sweep of Hout Bay to the 331-m-high Sentinel which looms over the busy fishing harbour. The road itself, for most of its journey around Chapman's Peak, has been cut into the junction line of the Cape granite and the sedimentary Table Mountain sandstone laid down on top of the granite and brilliantly coloured in layers of red, orange and yellow silt. Dark lines of manganese may also be noticed. Many picnic sites have been created by the roadside in the descent to Hout Bay.

At the end of this great drive the road descends with a grand sweep into the residential and fishing village of Hout Bay.

## HOUT BAY

Soon after his arrival in the Cape in 1652, Jan van Riebeeck sent a party to explore the bay behind Table Mountain. The explorers found it to be a beautiful bay scenically, but dangerously exposed for shipping. In the valley there were rare fir trees and from their presence the bay was named *Houtbaai* (wood bay).

Over the years the trees were cut down to supply timber for ships. In 1681 a lease was given over the area. A sawmill was built and a wagon track made to the bay over Constantia Nek. A community of woodcutters settled at Hout Bay. The last two elephants there were shot in 1689. A few fishermen started to work from the bay and the area became regarded as an interesting expansion of the settlement at Cape Town.

During the American War of Independence, the French troops who garrisoned the Cape built a battery on the western end of Hout Bay harbour to defend the place from any possible British invasion. A second battery was built on the eastern side of the bay in 1799. Two years later the British troops occupied the Cape and built a blockhouse above the eastern battery. To these varied military constructions the Batavians contributed, in 1804, also building a battery. The ruins of these various structures still stand.

No invading force ever did threaten Hout Bay, but at least, during the Napoleonic wars, a French corsair captain Malo le Nouvel was driven into the bay by a great storm. He and his ship were taken prisoner there by the British garrison.

A particularly beautiful architectural survival from this period is the homestead of *Kronendal* farm, built in 1800 and now a national monument. The building is used as a restaurant of very high standard.

The fishing industry of Hout Bay really got started about 1867 when a German immigrant, Jacob Trautman, settled at the bay and began catching and salting snoek for export to such places as Mauritius.

The presence in the area of vast numbers of rock lobsters was also noticed. In 1903 the hulk of a British barge, *R. Morrow*, wrecked at Mouille Point, was bought, towed to Hout Bay, beached, and converted into a canning factory. This factory continued until 1914 when an explosion in its refrigeration killed seven people. The remnants of the hulk remained in Hout Bay until after the Second World War when they were removed to make way for the substantial fishing harbour of today with two large factories on the shore.

Manganese was also produced in Hout Bay from a mine, and shipped out by means of a jetty which still partly survives the battering of the sea. The deposit proved too patchy to be profitable and work ceased.

The bronze leopard mounted on the rocks overlooking the bay is the work of the late sculptor Ivan Mitford-Barberton, who lived in Hout Bay. There are boat trips around the bay and to the seals on weekends.

## Accommodation
* Chapman's Peak Hotel, 5 rooms, all with baths. R6,50 – R8 B/B. Phone 70-4141.
* Hout Bay Hotel, 19 rooms, all with baths. R12 – R15 B/B. Phone 70-4142.

There are some fine walks around Hout Bay. From the harbour area it is interesting to walk over the saddle of land connecting the Sentinel to the mainland. Duyker Island with its resident population of seals may be viewed from this walk. From the harbour a disused road climbs steeply to the old radio station built during the Second World War on top of the 653-m-high Karbonkelberg. The views are stunning. For the really hardy there is a rough and surprisingly long walk around the coast to Llandudno. With its crevices and hard going, this is a day-long outing, so be warned, even though it looks short on the map.

Immediately out of Hout Bay village the marine drive reaches a junction with the road which comes down through shady avenues of oaks from Constantia Nek. The main road veers left, bridges the course of the Disa River, makes its way through an avenue of plane trees, and then reaches a junction where a short road branches off left and leads to the fishing harbour. The main road veers sharp right and climbs the slopes of the 436-m-high mountain known from pronounced similarities in shape as Little Lion's Head. To the right there are fine views of the valley of the Disa River, while silver trees and many indigenous flowering shrubs ornament the estates on either side of the road.

At its highest point, the road passes over the saddle of land connecting Little Lion's Head to the Twelve Apostles (the back of Table Mountain), and an entirely new vista of sea and mountain opens up. Immediately below lies the attractive little beach and residential area of Llandudno, with a road branching off left to provide access. The main marine drive, now known as Victoria Road, descends the face of the cliffs diagonally, with the sea on its left and the twelve great buttresses of the back of Table Mountain glowering down its right. From Llandudno there is a short walk south to Sandy Bay, a secluded area much liked by sunbathers. The wreck of a tanker, the *Romelia*, lies on the rocks where it came to grief in 1977 while being towed to a Far Eastern scrapyard. The tow rope snapped and the single tug lost control.

Three kilometres from the Llandudno turnoff the road sweeps around a bend and reveals, especially on a sunny day, one of the finest views of the Cape. Across a sparkling stretch of sea, Lion's Head can be seen at its most handsome aspect with the houses of Camps Bay and Bakoven in pleasingly multi-coloured disarray beneath it. The whole stretch of the Twelve Apostles (originally called the Gable Mountains but given their present name by the British Governor, Sir Rufane Donkin) provides a panorama on the right, while on the left the sea rolls in through a mass of granite boulders, with many little coves and inlets, frequented by holidaymakers and fishermen. One of these places, *Hottentots Huisie* (Hottentots shack) developed over the years into a curious community of permanent cave dwellers. Remnants of the wreck of the coaster *Bluff* lie on the rocks where it ran aground in 1965. The tanker *Antipolis* also lies on the rocks here. It was wrecked in 1977 while being towed with the *Romelia* to shipbreakers in the Far East.

Three kilometres along this interesting stretch of coast, past the tomb of a Malay holy man, Nureel Mobeek, and the imposing *Oudekraal* farmhouse of the Van Bredas, the road enters the municipal area of Cape Town at what is known as *Bakoven* (the bake oven) from the shape of a large rock on the coast. It is now a little seaside area of bungalows built down to the water's edge and through it the main road leads directly into the suburb of Camps Bay.

# CAMPS BAY

*Camps Bay* was named after Frederick von Kamptz, an invalid sailor who, in 1778, landed in the Cape, married the widow of the owner of the original farm at Camps Bay, *Ravensteyn,* and made his home in the farmhouse which stood on the site of the former Rotunda Hotel. Camps Bay, today, is a well-to-do suburb built on the slopes of the Twelve Apostles and overlooking a spacious beach, much used by sunbathers and picnickers, with a large tidal pool. Surfers find sport in a cove (Glen Beach) on the north side of Camps Bay, but swimming is marred by very cold water and a frequent backwash.

From Camps Bay two roads lead up the slopes of the mountain, join at Kloof Nek, and finally enter the city area. One of these roads, Geneva Drive, branches right from Victoria Road just after it passes the pavilion. The other road, Kloof Road, branches right as Victoria Road leaves Camps Bay. This is a pleasant route around the slopes of Lion's Head past the Round House Inn (an old shooting box of the British Governors) and the Glen picnic area, with fine views of Camps Bay through the trees.

**Accommodation**
Youth Hostel, Stans Halt, The Glen. 30 beds, R1,20 D. Phone 48-9039.

# CLIFTON

On the coastal side, Camps Bay ends in a small headland preserved as a scenic and botanical reserve. Beyond this lies Clifton with its four famous beaches, all ideal for sunbathing and a display of feminine pulchritude, the coldness of the Atlantic Ocean providing bikini beauties with an excellent excuse not to swim. Informal (but expensive) little cottages (some not so little) are built on the cliffs overlooking the beach, and are today very fashionable places in which to live. Several of these cottages were originally built as emergency housing after the First World War!

At Clifton, Lion's Head is much closer to the sea, and many of the houses along Victoria Road are built on stilts and piles. Rooftop parking is common.

# BANTRY BAY

From Clifton, Victoria Road cuts into the cliffs, winds tortuously around a mountain spur, and passes through the heavily built-up area of Bantry Bay. Here, groups of apartment buildings cluster at the edge of a turbulent little bay. *Bantry* (botany) Bay was a botanical garden in the 19th century, planted in terraces long since overwhelmed by houses and flats.

At the end of Bantry Bay the road enters the suburb of . . .

# SEA POINT

Sea Point, which has the advantage of skirting the beachfront, is unfortunately an overcrowded, unplanned suburb with narrow, densely built-up streets. At the earliest opportunity a traveller should turn left out of Main Road into Beach Road, a far more relaxing route which follows the coast, with, however, an almost continuous cliff of nondescript apartment buildings on the landward side of the road. Sea Point is Cape Town's most populous residential area. Some startlingly high rentals are paid for apartments whose principal asset seems to be what is free anyway – an elevated view of some very lovely sunsets.

Sea Point beachfront is laid out as a promenade, with lawns, gardens and tidal swimming pools, including Graaff's Pool where men may swim in the nude, named after Sir Jacobus

*Overleaf: False Bay at dawn, with the silver sands of Muizenberg reaching towards the sun as it rises over the range of the Hottentots Holland.*

Graaff who once had his mansion opposite, where a great block of flats stands today. This pool was originally a quarry from which stone was blasted to provide ballast for the suburban railway which once connected the city area with Sea Point. A concrete causeway carried a trolley from the quarry to the railway line. Along the beachfront there are children's playgrounds, and amenities such as the largest saltwater swimming bath in the Southern Hemisphere. A great variety of hotels and restaurants flourish in the area. The ocean promenade is a favourite walk for people and their dogs taking the air on summer evenings. There are public conveniences for man and dog. The shoreline is rocky, making swimming difficult in places other than the tidal and swimming pools provided.

There is one place of particular interest to geologists. On the sea front opposite the President Hotel there is a plaque with the following inscription:

*'The rocks between this plaque and the sea reveal an impressive contact zone of dark slate with pale intrusive granite. This interesting example of contact between a sedimentary and an igneous rock was first recorded by Clarke Abel in 1818. Since its discovery it has had an inspiring influence on the historical development of geology. Notable amongst those who have described it is Charles Darwin who visited it in 1836.'*

## Accommodation

★★★ Ambassador by the Sea Hotel, 65 rooms, all with baths. R20 – R37 B/B. Phone 49-6170.

★★★ Arthur's Seat Hotel, 120 rooms, all with baths. R14,50 – R19 B/B. Phone 44-3344.

★★ Atlantis Hotel, 102 rooms, all with baths. R10,95 – R14,95 B/B. Phone 44-8932.

★★Belmont Hotel, 47 rooms, all with baths. R12 B/B. Phone 49-1155.

★★★ Century Hotel, 123 rooms, all with baths. R14,95 B/B. Phone 49-1181.

★★ Elizabeth Hotel, 83 rooms, 44 with baths. R15 – R25 B/B. Phone 44-9321.

★ Kings Hotel, 29 rooms, all with baths. R8,50 – R10,50 B/B. Phone 49-6040.

★★★★★® President Hotel, Beach Road, 147 rooms, all with baths. R27 – R80 room only. Phone 44-1121.

★★ Regency Hotel, 46 rooms, all with baths. R10 – R17 B/B. Phone 49-6101.

★★★ Ritz Plaza Hotel, 227 rooms, all with baths. R15,25 – R23,25 B/B. Phone 49-6010.

★★ Silver Sands Hotel, 90 rooms, all with baths. R9,50 – R13,50 B/B. Phone 44-9531.

★★ Surfcrest Hotel, 63 rooms, all with baths. R8 – R14,50 B/B. Phone 44-8721.

★★★ Winchester Mansions Hotel, 36 rooms, all with baths. R20 – R30 B/B. Phone 44-1620.


# THREE ANCHOR BAY

The small inlet, which marks the end of Sea Point, is known as Three Anchor Bay and is named after three anchors originally used to hold a defensive chain across the inlet. It is a base for the operations of private fishermen working along the coast.

## Accommodation

★ Carnaby Hotel, 40 rooms, 12 with baths. R7,50 - R12,50 B/B. Phone 44-3361.


# MOUILLE POINT

Beach Road follows the coast beyond Three Anchor Bay past the old *Mouille* (mole) built in an early effort to construct a breakwater in Table Bay. A promenade lined with lawns and rockeries leads along the beachfront, and the lighthouse, with its 850 000 candlepower lamp and a foghorn of even greater potency, is a prominent landmark.

Large, luxury apartment buildings interspersed with old, weatherbeaten houses and small blocks of flats line Beach Road. At the city end of this road is the New Somerset Hospital, a modern building side by side with the original Somerset Hospital, which is still in use. Further on, past the entrance to the docks, the road curves and passes an old prison where hard-labour convicts were employed in the construction of the early docks and breakwater. The so-called Breakwater Prison is often mentioned by Edgar Wallace in his crime stories.

## GREEN POINT

Green Point, situated between Mouille Point and the slopes of Signal Hill, is crowded with houses and flats, especially along the High Level Road. Though not particularly attractive, it is a convenient suburb in which to live, providing speedy access to the city. The Green Point Common, once a grazing area for cattle, is today a well-known recreational centre, encompassing various sportsfields, a municipal stadium, golf course and athletic tracks and the buildings housing the Cape Town Art Centre and the South Atlantic Underwater Club.

### Accommodation

** Claridges International Hotel, Main Road, 150 rooms, all with baths. R11,90 – R18,50 B/B. Phone 44-1171.

Beyond Green Point, the main road enters the city area of Cape Town, and the circular drive around the Cape Peninsula comes to an end 143 km from where it began.

## Chapter Three

# THE CAPE FLATS AND THE SANDVELD

It was not so long ago (geologically speaking) that Table Mountain loomed as a precipitous island, separated from the mainland of Africa by a shallow expanse of sea. This was during Cretaceous times, 60 million years ago. When the sea receded, or the land was elevated, the sandy former sea bed was left to dry and, through the combined efforts of man and nature, was covered with trees, shrubs and grass. This former sea bed is a sandy, gently undulating area today, not very high above the level of the sea. It is known as the Cape Flats to the east and south-east of Cape Town, and as the sandveld in the north, where it merges along the banks of the Olifants River with the outlying dunes of the Namib Desert and the arid area of Namaqualand.

The Cape Flats provides the built-up Cape Peninsula with generous space for expansion into a level and open area which all cities would regard with delight as the perfect answer to their problems of congestion. The northern suburbs and most of the satellite towns of Cape Town have been built in this area. Some of these satellite towns are growing at a pace which makes them substantial centres themselves, and most new township developments in the vicinity of Cape Town are taking place in the area of the Cape Flats. It is a pity that, given the available level space, some of these developments do not result in something better than the characterless hotchpotches of congested, nondescript buildings which abound, and pass as smart and modern. Private enterprise has little interest in devising a pleasant, warm environment. Gardens, boulevards and attractive buildings are not as profitable as concrete boxes jammed against one another in narrow streets. Public authorities and town planning are usually so ineffectual as to be non-existent. It seems that such authorities confine their activities to discreetly turning their backs on the venality of private developers. Here, architecture is often judged simply by height, the tallest building being the most admired. For the tourist, therefore, these satellite towns of Cape Town on the Cape Flats are dull and sometimes downright hideous; however, the scenery and atmosphere of the sandveld and the outlying areas up to Saldanha and St Helena Bay are extremely interesting.

The northern suburbs and satellite towns are linked to Cape Town by an electrified railway (the main line to the north), and by a badly congested highway known as Voortrekker Road. To reach this road from the centre of the city, let us (as we did for the trip around the Cape Peninsula) drive up Strand Street from its intersection with Adderley Street. Passing the walls of the Castle, the road continues under the traffic interchange where the Peninsula road turned off. Its name becoming first Newmarket and then Albert Road, the route leads through a congestion of warehouses, dingy shops and residences until, 3,5 km from the start, it reaches a busy traffic circle in the centre of the suburb known as Salt River. A left turn at this circle leads into Voortrekker Road, which rises over the railway tracks at Salt River station, continues through a densely built-up area, and then, 5 km from the centre of Cape Town, enters the suburb of *Maitland*, named after Sir Peregrine Maitland, Governor of the Cape in the 1840s.

### Accommodation
* Goodwins Hotel, Albert Road, 12 rooms, 4 with baths. R5,20 – R5,72 B/B. Phone 55-8898.
* Junction Hotel, Voortrekker Road, 10 rooms, 3 with baths. R4–R4,50 D/B/B. Phone 55-8658.

* Locomotive Hotel, Durham Avenue, 12 rooms, 3 with baths. R4,50 – R5 B/B. Phone 55-3483.
* Standard Hotel, Camp Road, 12 rooms, 4 with baths. R5 – R5,50 B/B. Phone 51-2833.
* Voortrekker Hotel, Voortrekker Road, 23 rooms, 4 with baths.R7,50 B/B. Phone 51-6176.
* Welcome Hotel, Voortrekker Road, 21 rooms, 7 with baths. R6,24 – R6,76 D/B/B. Phone 51-6126.

Light industrial and commercial establishments line the road until, on the left, we find the open space of the Wingfield military aerodrome and on the right, the seemingly endless wall marking the confines of Cape Town's principal cemetery. This is known as *Woltemade* after Wolraad Woltemade, a keeper of the menagerie in the Company's gardens who, in 1773, heroically lost his life while rescuing men from a shipwreck at the mouth of the Salt River.

## GOODWOOD

Eleven kilometres along the way we enter the municipal area of Goodwood with a population of 29 090, a volatile housing development and a busy cluster of industries. The place was originally a horse-racing track (hence the name, after the English race course), but this sporty beginning has long since been forgotten. Today its growth is such that it has suburbs of its own, notably *Vasco* (after Vasco da Gama, the first Portuguese navigator to reach the East), and *Elsies River* (after Elsie van Suurwaarde, who farmed on the banks of the river in the 1690s). The Goodwood showground is the scene of the Western Cape Province Agricultural Society's show, held at the end of February each year.

### Accommodation
** Goodwood Hotel, Voortrekker Road, 28 rooms, 12 with baths. R5,50 – R6,50 room only. Phone 98-3671.
* Reo Hotel (Elsies River), 17 rooms, 3 with baths. R4,68 – R5,20 B/B. Phone 98-3606.
* Vasco Hotel, Voortrekker Road, 16 rooms, 4 with baths. R5 – R6 B/B. Phone 98-3478.

## PAROW

The houses of Goodwood merge with the buildings of the next municipality, *Parow*, named after Johann Parow, a German sea captain who was wrecked in Table Bay in 1865 and settled in the area. Parow, with a population of 69 050, is another busy industrial and commercial area with a handsome civic centre, extensive housing estates, such as *Tiervlei* (leopard swamp), and a huge hospital. Eighteen kilometres from Cape Town, Parow merges with the buildings of Bellville.

### Accommodation
* Central Hotel, Voortrekker Road, 12 rooms, 5 with baths. R7 B/B. Phone 92-4115.
** New National Hotel, Voortrekker Road, 22 rooms, all with baths. R11,95 B/B. Phone 92-7140.

### Caravans and camping
** ® Parow Caravan Park (at Platteklip Kloof, on slopes of Tygerberg), 38 sites. Each site with private bath and toilet. R4,50 D. Phone 92-1913.

## BELLVILLE

*Bellville* (named after Charles Bell, a one-time surveyor-general of the Cape) is the third of the outlying northern municipalities of Cape Town. It is a modern but hardly a garden town with a population of 73 193, many handsome buildings, including a magnificent civic centre and theatre, but a congested layout. The occasionally flowing Elsies River meanders through the town, and a pleasant park has been created in its valley. Overlooking Bellville is the 415-m-high Tygerberg, and a very worthwhile and not too strenuous walk of 4 km leads up a gravel track to the air navigation beacon on its summit. The track starts from the upper end of Bellville's suburb of Welgemoed and leads to one of the finest viewsites in the Cape, with a magnificent panorama of the whole of the Cape Flats, from Table Mountain right up to the slopes of the mountain ranges of the interior. The immense development of the Cape Flats is perfectly revealed, as is the way in which the problem of the drifting sands was solved.

After endless difficulty with the sand which blew over all the early roads, John Montagu, Secretary to the Cape Government in 1845, imported a variety of exceptionally hardy, sand-loving shrubs from Australia, including the wattle, Port Jackson, and hakea. These were planted on the Cape Flats, along with Hottentot figs, and within an astonishingly short time they completely overwhelmed the sand. In a place where even grass had never before taken root, the exotic vegetation simply smothered the sand in greenery, making the Cape Flats habitable to man and, by binding the sand, also bringing out its true fertility – a fact amply demonstrated by the luxuriance of modern flower and vegetable gardens. The modern suburbs and townships have developed on ground reclaimed from the sand and wind by this alien vegetation which, despite its tendency to run riot at times and become a pest, has performed an invaluable function. Bellville became a municipality in 1940 and a city in 1979.

## Accommodation
** Boston Hotel, Voortrekker Road, 120 rooms, all with baths. R14 – R21 room only. Phone 97-0911.
* Drop Inn, Durban Road, 22 rooms, 6 with baths. R7,50 – R10 B/B. Phone 97-3941.
** Holiday Inn, Cross Street, 144 rooms, all with baths. R21 – R31 room only. Phone 97-8111.
* Outspan Hotel, Strand Street, 28 rooms, 7 with baths. R6 – R6,50 B/B. Phone 97-2631.

## Caravans and camping
*** Hardekraaltjie Caravan Park, Voortrekker Road, 120 sites. R3 – R3,50 D, seasonal. Phone 97-1084.
** ® Gypsey Caravan Park, Exit 10 National Road, 50 sites. R3,50 D. Phone 97-2828.

# DURBANVILLE

Bellville was originally known as Durban Road, for it was once merely a railway convenience for the pleasant rural town of *Durbanville*, 8 km away. Originally known by the rather naïve name of *Pampoenkraal* (pumpkin corral) this little town was renamed in 1836 after the Governor, Sir Benjamin D'Urban. With a population of 12 910, Durbanville has become a fashionable dormitory town, but it still retains something of its original country charm, while its former railway station, now Bellville, has long outgrown its early, lowly position and has become the bustling and ambitious centre of today. Durbanville became a municipality in 1901. Horse races are periodically held there.

## Accommodation
* Oxford Hotel, 13 rooms, 5 with baths. R8 – R8,50 B/B. Phone 9-6441.

From Bellville, the road divides at a point 21 km from Cape Town. One branch swings north-eastwards towards Paarl, the other passes through Stikland and on to the small municipality of Kuilsrivier 25 km from Cape Town.

# KUILSRIVIER

*Kuilsrivier* (river of pools), with its population of 12 435, was started in the 17th century as a cattle corral of the Dutch East India Company. Today it is a busy little industrial town, and the centre of the pioneer school for the care and education of epileptic children.

## Accommodation
★ De Kuile Hotel, 10 rooms, all with baths. R8,50 room only. Phone 33-1105.

## Caravans and camping
★★ ® Kuilsrivier Caravan Park, 90 sites. R2,60 - R3,50 D. Phone 33-3113.

The road now runs through a pleasantly rural landscape dotted with vegetable gardens, poultry farms and vineyards, and with a good view of the mountains to the north. Passing the Kuilsrivier Caravan Park, and the small industrial centres of Blackheath and Eersterivier, the road reaches a junction at Faure (13,5 km from Kuilsrivier, 38,5 km from Cape Town) with the main road connecting Cape Town to Stellenbosch. If we turn south at this junction, the route joins the main coastal highway, the Settlers Way, after another 3,5 km, and along it we can return to Cape Town, or go off to Port Elizabeth. However, if we continue straight ahead, we can enjoy a pleasant journey of 4 km to the shores of False Bay at Swartklip, a favourite area for fishermen, and a sanctuary for southern black-backed gulls. Their nesting colony is protected. From there, a fine marine drive leads westwards along the shores of the bay for 13,5 km to Strandfontein and then, after another 7,5 km, to Muizenberg. From here it is 26 km back to the centre of Cape Town along the Simon van der Stel freeway described in the section on the Cape Peninsula.

―――――――――――

There is a choice of several interesting routes which can be taken to explore the sandveld of the Western Cape. Perhaps the most beautiful and varied is the one starting at the beginning of the Cape-to-Cairo road at the entrance to Table Bay harbour (foot of the Heerengracht). Follow this road, known here as Table Bay Boulevard. After 2 km, turn left on the road marked Paarden Eiland and Milnerton. The road leads north up the shores of Table Bay, with the sombre pile of the Salt River power station on the right. After 3 km the road reaches an intersection leading left to the Ben Schoeman Container Dock and right into the light industrial area known as *Paarden Eiland* (the island of horses), from its original use as a grazing ground for those animals. On the left-hand side, there is an impressive view over Table Bay; the shipping and the mighty pile of Table Mountain are seen to great advantage. Unfortunately, the beach is grubby, as is usually the case on the verges of a busy harbour, but the area is much used by surf riders.

After 8 km the road crosses the *Liesbeek* (reedy) River and reaches the lagoon at the mouth of the Salt River (sometimes known as the Dieprivier). In former years this river formed something of a delta. One of its channels reached the sea at the present mouth of the Liesbeek River, and the segment of land enclosed in this delta was Paarden Eiland. Modern reclamation of the land has changed the landscape, and the river now finds its way to the sea through a narrow lagoon much beloved by bird life, canoeists and aquaplaners.

# MILNERTON
On the right, meanwhile, the industrialisation of Paarden Eiland has given way to the munici-

pality of *Milnerton,* named in 1902 after Sir Alfred Milner (then Governor of the Cape) and converted into a municipality in 1955. This is a pleasant, if slightly airy, part of the Cape, with a population of 23 180. The beauty of cultivated gardens prepares us for the spectacular wild flower area just ahead. There is a golf course between the lagoon and the beach and 11 km from the start of the road, the Ascot Race Track of the Cape Turf Club is situated.

## Accommodation

★★ Cambridge Hotel, 28 rooms, all with baths. R7,50 – R10,50 B/B. Phone 52-3110.

★ Killarney Hotel, 10 rooms, all with baths. R9 B/B. Phone 52-5454.

After 11 km, just after the turnoff to the Ascot Race Track, the road crosses a bridge over the seasonally flowing Salt River and sweeps close to the beach, passing on the right the old water bird paradise of *Rietvlei* (reedy swamp) abortively planned as a new fishing harbour. In spring this portion of the drive is graced by a blaze of wild flowers: white Cape daisies (*Dimorphotheca pluvialis*), golden *gousblom* (*Arctotis acaulis*) and many others carpet the sandy ground. But at any time of the year the drive is memorable, especially after the first 16 km, where, at a crossroads, the road reaches the Table View Hotel and Inn. It is from here that the oft-painted, endlessly photographed view of Table Mountain and its companions, Devil's Peak and Lion's Head, is to be seen 10 km away across the restless waters of Table Bay. A walk along this lovely spacious beach with this world-famous view before one is an experience to remember, and although the Atlantic Ocean hereabouts is slightly on the cold side for bathing (15°C in summer), it is a most popular area for fishermen, picnickers, sunbathers and all who love life in the sunshine.

## Accommodation

★ Tableview Hotel, 18 rooms, all with baths. R9 – R14,80 B/B. Phone 57-1141.

At the crossroads, there is a turn (right) leading to Table View township and, left, leading for 2 km along the shore to . . .

# BLOUBERGSTRAND

The seaside village of *Bloubergstrand* (blue mountain beach) is named from the 331-m-high hill which rises near by. Seen from the sea, this hill has a tendency for some reason to take on a particularly blue appearance. The village itself is an informal little place of weekend and seaside cottages; many of the older houses have actually partly been built with timber that has washed up on to the beach. Surf riders are fond of the great rollers which sweep in from the Atlantic Ocean. Shells are numerous, and in spite of the cold water, there are hardy people who even enjoy swimming. *Robben* (seal) Island with its numerous buildings and lighthouse, lies due west across the Atlantic Ocean.

## Accommodation

★★ Blue Peter Inn, 6 rooms, all with baths. R13 – R15 B/B. Phone 56-1956.

From Bloubergstrand there is a road running along the sand dunes of the coast, with many stopping places favoured by fishermen and picnickers, many glimpses of wild flowers, and intermittent views over a sparkling beach to the now receding bulk of Table Mountain. The Blouberg looms on the right with, on its summit, the ruins of a war-time radar and observation post.

# MELKBOSSTRAND

Eleven kilometres from Bloubergstrand, the coast road reaches another seaside resort, *Melkbosstrand* (beach of milkwood trees). This is another informal little place, particularly favoured by farmers who, each summer holiday season, stage there a day of *boeresport* (farmers' sports), when burly and sunbronzed rustic characters may be seen at tug-of-war and a variety of other antics. It is a favourite picnicking place for Cape Town people. The beach, rich in Atlantic Ocean shells, is a favourite haunt of walkers, but should definitely be avoided when the south-east wind is blowing during the summer months. The bay itself, known as Losperds Bay, was the scene of the British landing on 6 January 1806. After a minor battle around the slopes of Blouberg, the Dutch of Cape Town surrendered to the British. From the village a tarmac road leads for 2 km to the Ou Skip Caravan Park. A further 2 km along the road leads to the grounds of the nuclear power station of the Electricity Supply Commission.

### Accommodation
★ Miramar Hotel, 16 rooms, 5 with baths. R6 – R7 B/B. Phone 2344.

### Caravans and camping
★★★® Ou Skip Caravan Park, 260 sites. R3,20 D plus 50c D per person. Phone 2058.
★ Zonnekus Holiday Resort, 100 sites. R2,60 D plus 50c D per person. Phone 632.

The main Cape Town-Saldanha road, from the turnoff to Bloubergstrand 16 km from Cape Town, has continued more inland on a straighter, less interesting course. Passing close to Blouberg, at 27 km there is a crossroads with a left turn to Melkbosstrand and a right turn leading for 10 km to the Cape Town-Namaqualand main road.

At 32,5 km there is a turnoff to the Koeberg Nuclear Power Station and at 37,5 km a turnoff to the residential and industrial township of Atlantis built in the first half of the 1970s.

At 41,5 km there is a crossroads with a left turn leading for 3,5 km to the lovely beach known as Silwerstroomstrand, developed as a camping resort for Coloured people, and a right turn leading for 11 km to the mission station of . . . .

# MAMRE

This mission was established in March 1808 as a result of an invitation extended to the Moravians by the then Governor, Lord Caledon. He invited them to create in the area a work similar to their highly successful activity at Genadendal. Known as *Groenkloof* (green ravine), the area had long been regarded as something of a sanctuary for the remnants of a few Hottentot tribes which had once grazed their herds at the Cape. In 1701 a barracks had been built there for a garrison of ten men and a sergeant, whose duty was to defend the area against stock thieves. This barracks fell into disuse, and the Moravians found the old building half forgotten amidst a clump of oak trees. They named the place *Mamre* (amid the oaks) for it was there that Joseph had lived in the holy land. On the site they erected a church, a school and a watermill, and laid out the present picturesque settlement of white-walled, black-thatched cottages. With fertile and well-watered fields available for cultivation, Mamre in due course attracted a population of over 2 000 resident Coloured people. Today it remains the home of many families whose offspring work in Cape Town and return on weekends; with advancing years they eventually settle permanently. The place is a favourite resort for artists and photographers. The cottages, gardens, parsonage and church (this last with a primly-plain interior) retain their original charm, and it is pleasant to walk through the lanes and streets. The watermill has been beautifully restored by the Rembrandt Company, and is open to the public on weekdays from 09h00 to 17h00 and on Sundays from 14h00 to 17h00. Easter particularly is a time of reunion for the people of Mamre, and they gather from far and wide to attend a succession of services in the church, to sing and to listen to the music of their brass band. In 1789, in this Groenkloof area, the first four merino ewes and two rams were put to breed by their importer, Colonel Robert Gordon; thus beginning the wool industry in Southern Africa.

From Mamre a road leads for 17 km to Darling and for 21 km through a superb avenue of eucalyptus trees to intersect a road from Melkbosstrand to the main Cape Town-Namaqualand road.

## DARLING

The main Cape Town-Saldanha road continues north beyond the turnoff to Mamre for another 29 km of rather dull scrub country and is then intersected (70,5 km from Cape Town) by a tarmac road linking Darling (15 km right), to the coastal resort of Ysterfontein (8 km left).

*Darling*, with its population of 2 152, was laid out in 1853 and named in honour of the then Lieutenant-Governor, Charles Henry Darling. It became a municipality in 1955 and is the centre for prosperous farming activities: it is particularly noted for its dairy produce, peas, wool, export lupins and chincherinchees. Its spring flowers are renowned, and an annual flower show is held in the third week of September. The Tinie Versfeldt Wild Flower Reserve lies 12,5 km from the town, on the tarmac road to Ysterfontein. Seven kilometres north on the gravel road at Platteklip siding there is a memorial to Field-Cornet C. P. Hildebrand of the Maritz Commando. He was killed there on 12 November 1901 when the Boers raided deep into the Cape Colony during the Anglo-Boer War. This was the most southerly scene of fighting during the war.

### Accommodation
* Commercial Hotel, 12 rooms, 4 with baths. R7,90 B/B. Phone 522.
* Nemesia Hotel, 12 rooms, 4 with baths. R8,90 B/B. Phone 263.

From Darling, the traveller has a choice of three routes: one road leads eastwards for 32 km to Malmesbury, where it joins the main Cape Town-Namaqualand road, thus providing a circular drive back to Cape Town (total 175 km); the second road from Darling leads north-eastwards for 24 km across flat, wheat-producing country, and then joins the main road connecting Malmesbury with Saldanha; the third road from Darling leads westwards past the Tinie Versfeldt Wild Flower Reserve and across the main Cape Town-Saldanha road for 23 km until it reaches the coast at the seaside resort of Ysterfontein (iron fountain).

## YSTERFONTEIN

This is an exposed bay, windy in summer, and always washed by the cold water of the Benguela Current; however, it has a fine beach and great rollers beloved by surfers. Near by are the ruins of an ill-fated fish-canning factory (built just after the Second World War), with a 150-m-long jetty which now provides a lee for surf riders and a vantage point for fishermen. There are several rock promontories along the coast which are also used by fishermen. Dassen Island lies 10 km south-west, and in the bay is the rocky islet known as *Meeurots* (gull rock), the nesting place for a large colony of sea birds. For many years, a derelict thatched cottage, a forlorn reminder of an old mystery, stood on the shore. In about 1910, two men, Matthys Schreuder and Johannes Genade, were murdered by an unknown assailant while they were fishing on a rock. For a long time afterwards their cottage was regarded as being haunted. Ysterfontein is now built up with weekend and vacation cottages of a very pleasant kind.

## Caravans and camping
* ® Ysterfontein Caravan Park, 50 sites. R2,50 D.

---

The whole length of the road from Darling to Ysterfontein is lined with wild flowers, and leads through sheep and dairy farming country. Kilns, used to burn shells for lime-making, can be seen by the roadside. At 18,5 km from Darling there is a gravel turnoff to Donkergat, on the extreme northern tip of the narrow isthmus of land separating Langebaan Lagoon from the sea. This is an interesting drive, leading across country so unspoilt that numerous wild creatures can still be seen – steenbok, grysbok, hares, bat-eared foxes, ostriches and numerous birds. Puffadders and mole snakes are also common.

Fourteen and a half kilometres along this road, at the point where it reaches the southern end of Langebaan Lagoon, there is a junction. To the right there is an interesting drive up the east shores of the lagoon with many fine views and passing several old farmhouses. After 14,5 km this road reaches the village of Langebaan. To the left, the road continues up the isthmus to Donkergat, passing on the way pleasant little fishing settlements such as Churchhaven (at 22,5 km) and Schryvershoek (at 25 km). In 1666, a garrison of 12 men was sent from the Cape to occupy this area, because the French were making a claim to Saldanha Bay and the lagoon, and were sealing on the islands. In those days, ships watered at a spring on the isthmus beneath what is today known as Posberg. For some years the Dutch and the French occupied the area alternately, but the Dutch were eventually left in possession. Ensign Izaak Schryver was once in command of the outpost, and one of the small settlements of fishermen bears his name.

## Caravans and camping
* Flamingo Farm (Churchhaven), 40 sites. R2 D. 9 Rondawels, 4 beds each, R5 D. Phone Somerset West 2-2704.

The road leads above a beautiful beach, with cliffs providing a lee from the south-easters of summer. The bay is a favourite anchorage for yachts and houseboats. At a point 30 km along this road, it enters the Posberg Private Nature Reserve. The original Dutch garrison was established in the grounds of this private property, at the freshwater spring near the shore.

At 39 km the road reaches the site of the Donkergat Whaling Station, now a disused jumble of ruins and remnants. One kilometre further on, the road (now just a track) ends at Salaman- der Bay, where the ruins of several former fishing, whaling and other concerns which came to grief there, may be viewed. The wrecks of several whale catchers and other derelict vessels lie in the bay. There is also a rather pathetic little sailors' cemetery, with tombstones dating back as far as the last century. There is an added touch of melancholy about this isolated cemetery: the tombstones record the deaths of very young sailors, who had to be buried far away from their homes in Norway and other parts of Europe. The navy now uses the area for training purposes.

The name of the bay comes from the Dutch ship *Salamander,* which once sheltered there with its crew stricken with scurvy. From this northern point of the isthmus, there is a broad, splendid view over the entrance to Saldanha Bay, with the modern harbour development on the opposite shore, the five bird islands, and Langebaan village on the eastern shore. Saldanha Bay is one of the great natural harbours of the world. It is a magnificent spread of sheltered water: on a still day or a calm evening it has a tranquillity and quietness which is dreamlike; the diminutive waves seem to sigh as they come to rest on the beach; the lights of Saldanha and Langebaan trail glittering pathways across the water; the only sounds are the distant murmur of the surf, the calling of birds, and perhaps the 'putt-putt' of some fishing boat.

From the intersection with the Darling-Ysterfontein road, the main Cape Town-Saldanha road (70,5 km from Cape Town) continues northwards across scrub-covered country and then, 108,5 km from Cape Town, is intersected by the tarmac road linking Langebaan (11 km left) to the Malmesbury-Saldanha road (6 km right). The main road is still to be constructed north of this intersection.

## LANGEBAAN

Langebaan, founded in 1922, has a pleasant beach and is a characteristic lagoon-side holiday resort, with a collection of cottages, fishing boats, an anchorage for yachts, an airforce crash boat station, shops, a hotel, a caravan park, and the base of Pearl Oyster Shell Industries (Pty) Ltd, which dredges shells from the lagoon. The population is 1 310. The town lies at the head of the lagoon, where it joins Saldanha Bay proper. The connection is half blocked by Skaap and Meeu islands. Yachting, fishing and aquaplaning are favourite pastimes at Langebaan. Swimming is good but the water is cold. Wild flowers make a colourful display in spring.

### Accommodation
★ Panoramic Hotel, 32 rooms, 23 with baths. R11 – R16,50 B/B. Phone 712.

### Caravans and camping
Municipal caravan park, 110 sites. R3,64 D. Phone 615.

---

Where the Cape Town-Saldanha road joins the Langebaan intersection, a right turn leads for 6 km to the Malmesbury-Saldanha road at the air force station and flying school of Langebaan Road. From this point a right turn (southwards) leads for 24 km to . . .

## HOPEFIELD

*Hopefield* has a population of 3 496 and was named after two surveyors, Messrs Hope and Field, who originally laid out the town on the farm *Langekuil* when it was anticipated that a trunk road would be built linking Cape Town with Saldanha Bay. It is a small farming and railway centre with the usual cluster of stores, garages and houses built in the valley of the generally dry *Soutrivier* (salt river). It is the principal centre of what is known as the *Voorbaai* (before the bay), the area immediately east of Saldanha Bay.

Despite the unspectacular nature of this little town, it is a fact that the name of Hopefield is perhaps as widely known among international scientists as is Johannesburg. The reason for this is that in May 1951, Dr Ronald Singer, palaeontologist of the South African Museum, visited the farm *Elandsfontein* in the Hopefield district. Seven years previously Dr J. G. Smit of Wynberg had found a few fossils there while on a hunting trip, and had reported to Dr Singer.

As soon as Dr Singer reached the eroded, sand dune area of *Elandsfontein,* he realised the tremendous significance of the place. It is, in fact, one of the world's most important sites for the prehistorian. Originally a small lake in arid surroundings, it attracted to its shores a considerable variety of ancient life. Consistent work there has so far rewarded archaeologists with 6 000 important fossil bones and 3 000 manmade stone implements. The fossils include bone fragments of an extinct Neanderthal-type human, Saldanha Man. Remains of two extinct giraffe species, extinct buffaloes, lions, baboons, sabretoothed tigers, zebrine horses, wild pigs, giant boars, elephants, cave hyenas and representatives of numerous modern game animals – rhinos, hippos and antelope – have been found as well.

The fossils date from a period ranging from 75 000 years to 150 000 years ago. The stone implements found fall into three major groups: the first group, and the most primitive, is a hand-axe industry known as the Cape Coastal Fauresmith; the second group belongs to the Middle Stone Age (Still Bay Culture); the third group belongs to the Later Stone Age (Bushmen and Hottentots). Several other minor fossil sites have been found in the area.

## Accommodation
★ Commercial Hotel, 14 rooms, 11 with baths. R7,95 B/B. Phone 106.

From Hopefield, the tarmac road continues southwards through flat sand country, which is attractive in August and September because of the wild flowers, but remains dull for the rest of the year. After 64 km the road joins the main Cape Town-Namaqualand road 4,5 km north of Malmesbury.

---

From the Langebaan intersection, the main tarmac road continues north past the Langebaan phosphate quarries; a deposit thought to be fossilised guano lying on top of a former island. The road then crosses the railway line connecting Saldanha Bay with the iron-mining areas of the northern Cape at Sishen, and climbs a long slope to reach (after 16 km) the most important town and administrative centre of what is known as the *Agterbaai* (the rear bay), the area north of Saldanha Bay.

# VREDENBURG-SALDANHA

*Vredenburg* (town of peace), with its population of 28 300, had a beginning somewhat less peaceful than its name. The best spring of fresh water in the area bubbles to the surface here on the boundary line separating the two farms *Heuningklip* and *Witteklip*. The original owners of these two farms, W. Baard and C. Loubser respectively, quarrelled so much over water rights that the spring was first known as *Twisfontein* (fountain of strife), and later as *Prosesfontein* (lawsuit fountain). In 1875, when it was decided to create a centre for the area, the site of this contentious spring was selected; a church was built there, and the name was changed to the present Vredenburg. Today it is the seat of a magistracy and the communications centre for the area. Numerous shops and garages grace the principal street. In 1975 Vredenburg and Saldanha were united as Vredenburg-Saldanha. The combined area of 67 208 ha makes it the largest municipality (space-wise) in South Africa.

## Accommodation
★ North Western Hotel, 12 rooms, 4 with baths. R6,75 – R8,50 B/B. Phone 3-1291.
★ Vredenburg Hotel, 13 rooms, 5 with baths. R6,75 – R8,50 B/B. Phone 3-1446.
★ West Coast Inn, 10 rooms, 4 with baths. R7,50 B/B. Phone 31513.

From Vredenburg, the main tarmac road swings south-westwards, sweeps down past the great granite boulders of *Witteklip* farm, and off through wheat fields for 12 km to . . . .

# SALDANHA

The port of Saldanha is now part of the Vredenburg-Saldanha municipality with a combined population of 28 300. Saldanha originally consisted of only a few shacks, erected by impoverished fishermen who earned a living by catching mullet and mackerel, drying them to make what are known as *bokkems* (kippers) and selling them to the local farmers as rations for labourers. Then, early in the 1900s, a partnership, Holland & Hinchliffe, shipped up from Cape Town the machinery from a small factory which French interests had set up in Table Bay for the canning of rock lobsters. This venture had gone bankrupt. The new owners set the machinery going on the shores of Saldanha Bay, and, with a 'fleet' consisting of two ancient fishing boats, commenced an industry.

This North Bay Cannery Company (as it was called) was the start of the present great fishing and processing industry in Saldanha Bay. The settlement, originally known as *Hoetjies Bay* from the Hottentot word *houtee* (seal), began to grow steadily. The shortage of fresh water which had handicapped Saldanha Bay since its discovery was alleviated by a filtration plant which was built during the Second World War on the Berg River. From here the water was piped to the area, allowing Saldanha Bay to be utilised as a naval base, a sanctuary for damaged ships, and a laying-up anchorage.

After the war, the naval facilities were converted into a training settlement which eventually developed into the modern naval gymnasium. Three fish processing and canning factories also began operating at Saldanha after the war: the Saldanha Bay Canning Co (Pty) Ltd; Southern Sea Fishing Enterprises (Pty) Ltd; and the Spanish Pescanova Fishing Co. Gelatine-rich seaweed is harvested in the bay. The islands yield guano and eggs, and shoals of mullet are netted from the beach, especially at night.

In 1970 the government decided to develop Saldanha as the export town for iron, manganese and other ores mined in the Northern Cape. A direct railway was built to carry this ore from Sishen to Saldanha. The line was opened in 1976, and vast harbour operations were undertaken which developed Saldanha Bay into a major port for the use of large bulk carriers.

### Accommodation
** Hoedjies Bay Hotel, 16 rooms, all with baths. R11,25 B/B. Phone 4-1271.
** Saldanha Hotel, 34 rooms, 21 with baths. R8,25 – R12,45 B/B. Phone 4-1201.

### Caravans and camping
** Municipal holiday resort, 80 sites. R1,50 –R2,50 D plus 50c D per person. 42 cottages, R6,50 – R12 D.

## SALDANHA BAY

The name *Saldanha Bay* comes from the Portuguese admiral, Antonio de Saldanha, although, oddly enough, he never actually visited the place. In 1503, as commodore of a Portuguese fleet, he anchored below Table Mountain and for nearly 100 years thereafter, the name Saldanha Bay was applied to what is now called Table Bay. It was the Dutch who changed the name: in 1601 they gave Table Bay its modern name and transferred the name of Saldanha to its present situation.

All the early visitors to Saldanha Bay were immediately impressed by the abundance of marine life in the area. Sea birds and seals frequented the islands in immense numbers, and their plumpness was visual proof of the presence of huge shoals of fish on which they fed. Early in the 17th century the French started sealing operations in the bay, regarding the area as their proper possession.

Very shortly after Van Riebeeck settled at the Cape, he despatched a yacht, the *Goede Hoop*, on an exploration up the coast. The crew of this vessel paid particular attention to the various islands, for rumours of the great profits made by French fur sealers had penetrated to the Dutch. Immediately south of the entrance to Saldanha Bay the Dutch sailors found an island occupied by such a large number of seals that the animals sported in the sea in huge shoals, like porpoises. It was an incredible spectacle, and the Dutch named the island *Vondeling* (foundling). When they landed there, they found it covered with a bitter asparagus, reeds and thorny shrubs. Tortoises were numerous and an occasional snake startled them.

In the bay they found five other islets, which they named *Jutten* (Joyce's); *Malgas* (gannets); *Meeu* (after the sound of the gulls); *Marcus* (after Corporal Marcus Robbeljaert, commander of Robben Island); and *Skaap* (sheep) because they left two sheep there as food for future shipwrecked sailors in distress. Rabbits were later left on this island to replace the sheep and their descendants still flourish. Gannets, penguins, cormorants and seals covered all the islands of Saldanha Bay. On Skaap Island the Dutch found a pile of 2 733 seal skins neatly stacked by French sealers to await shipment. Thanking the Lord for such a gift and keeping a watchful eye over their shoulders, the Dutch loaded the skins on to their yacht and gleefully sailed off to Cape Town.

For some time after that there was a comedy of rivalries between the French and Dutch over the possession of Saldanha Bay and its islets. The French erected beacons of possession; the Dutch engraved the initials (V. O. C.) of their company on to outstanding rocks on the islands; the French sealers promptly defaced them. The Dutch, however, had to win: they were occupying the Cape and were nearest to Saldanha Bay. In 1666 they established a small garrison at the principal fountain of drinking water on the western shore of the Langebaan lagoon. After a few changes of ownership over the next five years, with the French periodically chasing out the Dutch and the latter returning as soon as the French were gone, the area of Saldanha Bay eventually came under the control of the Dutch East India Company.

Drinking water was always the great problem of Saldanha Bay. With so magnificent and sheltered a harbour, a perennial supply of good water would certainly have made it the site of Cape Town. Instead, for many years, it served only as an occasional anchorage for ships, as a resort of sealers, and as a lair for pirates. In 1693 one of these adventurers, Captain George Dew of the *Amy,* had the misfortune to be caught there by a Dutch warship while his vessel lay careened on the beach. He and his crew were taken to Europe to stand trial.

The Dutch were also occasionally surprised in Saldanha Bay. On 21 July 1781, the *Middelburg* and five other Dutch ships were caught in the bay by an English squadron. The *Middelburg* was put to fire and sunk by her own crew, but her five consorts were captured. Many other ships have been sunk or scuttled in the bay and the bottom of it is liberally littered with relics of these vessels. One of the most famous was the *Meerestyn,* wrecked on 3 April 1707 off Jutten Island. Twenty years after this disaster, John Lethbridge, using a wooden barrel as a diving apparatus, salvaged R500 000 worth of silver bars and ducatoons from this wreck. Odd coins and fragments of china can still be found in the sands and pools.

Perhaps the most extraordinary event in the early history of Saldanha Bay was the guano rush. In the mid 1830s, Europe discovered the value of guano as a fertilizer. The greatest deposits known, off the Peruvian coast, were all in the hands of monopolies. There were searches for other sources of supply, and attention was directed to the various islands off the coast of South West Africa and the Cape. At first Ichaboe Island, off the south west African coast, was the scene of a great rush, but then the deposits on the islands of Saldanha Bay were discovered.

It is recorded that in August 1844 there were over 300 ships in Saldanha Bay loading guano from the islands. Several of the islands (particularly Malgas) were found to be covered with guano to a depth of 10 m. A flagstaff was planted in the centre of Malgas Island. From the staff, lines were marked partitioning the island into something like slices of a huge cake. Each slice was apportioned to a different vessel.

For some time Malgas Island presented the aspect of a fair, with tents, scaffolding and a boisterous crowd of men. Grog vendors and young ladies from the Cape hurried there to make their share of profits. Tent houses of business were erected, each sporting some flag with a fanciful name such as 'Wapping', 'Sheerness' or 'London Docks'. Brawls and riots became commonplace and a warship had to be sent up from Cape Town to restore order. A tax of £1 per ton was levied on all guano removed, and the government accumulated over

£200 000 from this source. With guano selling in Europe at £6 per ton, the profits were enormous, and these little islands rank as true treasure islands of the world. Preserved by the ammonium content of the guano were countless carcasses of birds and on Malgas Island, the body of a French sealer named l'Ecluse. This mummy was shipped to Europe and for years was a famous exhibit in sideshows.

The southern end of Saldanha Bay consists of the lagoon known as *Langebaan* (the long channel), 16 km by 4,5 km in extent, and seldom more than about 6 m in depth. The lagoon is fed by water from the bay; it is cold at the northern end, but the water is progressively warmed by the sun until, at the shallow bottom end, the water is generally 10°C warmer than the sea.

Flamingos, as well as many other waders and sea birds frequent the lagoon, and beneath the surface lies a deposit of oyster shells so enormous that it is rivalled in all the world only by the deposit in Chesapeake Bay in the United States. The origin of this deposit is a mystery. The shells (of the species *Cabria*) lie in huge, flat beds 3 m to 7 m thick and intersected by the tidal flow. In an area of about 6 square kilometres the deposit amounts to about 30 million tons.

The oysters probably died as a result of one of the following three causes: in the successive elevations and submergences to which this part of the coast was subject during Cretaceous times (60 million years ago), the lagoon seems to have been the estuary of the Berg River for a while; silt discharged by this river could have caused the death of the oysters; alternately, the oyster beds may have been elevated above the sea, and the molluscs killed by exposure to the air; or perhaps a change in the prevailing temperature of the sea could have brought about their end. Whatever the case, the beds were left for man to discover in modern times; from them an industry for the making of lime and poultry food has developed. Oysters have not been able to re-establish themselves in the lagoon. Perhaps this area will be artificially restocked in the future.

Saldanha is the terminus of the road and railway from Cape Town. From Vredenburg, however, a road leads northwards on an interesting journey through a countryside of wheat fields and oddly shaped outcrops of granite boulders. After 16 km this road reaches the sea at the pleasant little fishing village of . . .

# PATERNOSTER

The source of the name *Paternoster* (Our Father) remains unknown. This part of the coast was mapped in the 1790s by Captain Francis Renier Duminy, with the Dutch East India Company ship *De Meermin*. Duminy Point bears his name – perhaps he said a prayer at Paternoster and then named it, although, more likely, it takes its name from the fishing tackle known as the paternoster. Today it is a place of white-walled fishermen's cottages, with a fine beach washed by a cold sea. There is considerable activity in the catching and processing of rock lobster, with a factory run by Paternoster Fisheries. This part of the coast is rich in lobsters, perlemoen and other seafoods. The rock lobster fishing season is from 1 October to 31 May.

**Accommodation**
* Paternoster Hotel, 10 rooms, all with baths. R7,80 B/B. Phone 703.

From Paternoster, a track runs south for 3 km along a rugged coastline to the lighthouse at *Cape Columbine* (cape of doves). This 9 million candlepower lighthouse and radio beacon is a major navigational point for shipping approaching the coast of Southern Africa from Europe and America. The lighthouse stands in an area noted for its spring flowers. The track continues for some kilometres along the coast, and is used by line fishermen finding their way to the numerous promontories and bays. One kilometre beyond the lighthouse this track passes the rocky little bay named *Titties* or *Titus Bay* from a Coloured fisherman who had the misfortune to be drowned there. There are many fine camping sites along this coast, but there are no facilities other than toilets. Wild flowers, fresh air and a rugged seascape make up the beauty of this part of the world.

---

North-west of Paternoster, a gravel road runs for 16 km to *Stompneusbaai* (bay of stumpnose fish) on the shores of St Helena Bay.

## ST HELENA BAY

This great bay received its name, St Helena, from the Portuguese navigator, Vasco da Gama. He discovered the bay on the day of that saint (7 November 1497) while on his pioneer voyage from Europe to the East. There is a memorial to this event consisting of three marble pedestals erected close to the main road at Stompneusbaai. On the beach somewhere here or near the mouth of the Berg River (which the Portuguese called the River of St James), the Portuguese explorers careened their four ships and relaxed for a week after their four-month ocean voyage. It was there, too, that a foolish brawl developed between one of the sailors and a group of Hottentots – the first clash on the shores of Southern Africa between Europeans and Africans. Nobody was killed.

St Helena Bay is one of the world's principal fishing centres. The cold Benguela Current surges upwards along this part of the coast and brings to the surface large concentrations of nutrient salts. Huge shoals of pilchards and anchovies feed in the area on the plankton which flourish on the nutrient salts and the number of fish-processing factories built along the southern shore of the bay is such that a visitor might be pardoned for thinking that the area is an industrial suburb of a city.

Twelve busy fish-processing factories are established along the 21-km curve of the shore from Stompneusbaai to the mouth of the Berg River. The scene is quite extraordinary, especially during the pilchard season (1 January to 31 July). Wheat fields reach down almost to the water's edge, and only a tarmac road running along the coast provides a boundary line between agriculture and fishing; the factories stand between the road and the sea, with their jetty 'feet' in the water to receive the catches of one fishing boat after the other.

### Accommodation
★ Steenberg's Cove Hotel, 12 rooms, 5 with baths. R6 – R7 B/B. Phone 710.

From Stompneusbaai, a tarmac road leads along the southern shores of St Helena Bay for 17 km and then joins the tarmac road from Vredenburg (right turn, 10 km) to Velddrif (left turn, 12 km).

## VELDDRIF-LAAIPLEK

As the road crosses the Berg River, it enters the river mouth harbour of the combined municipality of Velddrif-Laaiplek, a major fishing centre, with a population of 4 200.

*Velddrif,* as its name indicates, was originally a fording place across the river for the road traversing the sandveld from Cape Town to the north. Inevitably, a store, blacksmith's shop and hotel came into being to serve travellers. *Laaiplek* (the loading place), lower down at the mouth of the Berg River, was formerly a shipping point for the wheat grown in the area. In 1871, an enterprising Cape Town merchant, Johann Carel Stephan, patched up the hulk of a sailing ship, the *Nerie,* wrecked in Table Bay, and sailed it up to Laaiplek. There it was permanently anchored, and for years it served as a home, store and place of business for Stephan, who became known as the so-called *Koring Koning* (corn king) of St Helena Bay. As the general factotum of the area, he bought wheat in bulk, stored it in the holds of his anchored hulk, shipped produce to Cape Town, brought in assorted goods and managed an export trade in salted snoek to the island of Mauritius and to Natal – where this fish was in favour as standard rations for workers on the sugar estates.

For nearly 30 years, the tall, gaunt-faced Johann Stephan was the trading baron of the coast, and his influence and that of his family will never quite vanish from the great bays of Saldanha and St Helena. The Stephans built stores, started fisheries and attracted to their employ a whole community of Italian and Portuguese fishermen – the Colombos, Carosinis, Sienis, Seras, Canessas, Violos, Pharos, Depoalas, Donighis and many others whose descendants still fish and work in the area; they regard the wild and windswept waters of the Benguela Current as the source of their prosperity, and they speak of what we might call the Cannery Coast as their permanent home.

Beginning in desperate poverty, the area has risen to affluence. The first factory of the Berg River mouth was opened in 1944 and, two years later, Velddrif became a local authority, with municipal status attained in September 1960.

A new and deeper artificial harbour entrance was built in 1966 to bypass the silting river mouth. The future of the area seems assured for as long as there are fish in this most productive pocket of the Atlantic Ocean.

## Accommodation

★ Laaiplek Hotel, 14 rooms, 10 with baths. R9 – R10 B/B. Phone 15.
★ Riviera Hotel, 16 rooms, 5 with baths. R9 – R10 B/B. Phone 37.

## Caravans and camping

★ Stywe Lyne Caravan Park (Laaiplek), 50 sites. R2,50 D plus 20c D per person. Phone 12.

From Velddrif there is a road leading eastwards for 65 km to Piketberg on the main Cape Town-Namaqualand road. A second road follows the left bank of the Berg River, past the water filtration and pumping plant for Saldanha Bay (24 km), and then returns to Hopefield (total 40 km) and the tarmac road to Cape Town.

Chapter Four

# THE GARDEN OF THE WESTERN CAPE

Nature has created a garden of great splendour in the folded sandstone mountain ranges of the Western Cape. In this scenic setting of vividly coloured mountains and deep valleys, the green fingers of Pan have lavished an overwhelming number of flowering plants, all flourishing in an area of winter rainfall and a mild Mediterranean-like climate. Protected for the last 200 million years by singularly stable climatic and topographical conditions, these plants have had the leisure necessary to produce their vast variety of species; many colours, shapes and sizes proliferate, forming the unique domain of flowers known to botanists as the Cape Sclerophyll, an area of ancient macchia-like vegetation, and a veritable kingdom of wild flowers, unmatched anywhere else in the world.

The mountain ranges act as watersheds for the valleys. These ranges are preserved in their natural state mainly by the Forestry Department and serve as sanctuaries for plants and wildlife. The mountains also provide magnificent recreational areas for climbers, hikers, trout fishermen, campers and all those who appreciate fresh, clear air, glorious views, the fragrance of aromatic plants, and the taste of pure, amber-coloured stream water, tinted only by the natural chemistry of the soil.

During the crisp winter months, from May to September, the mountain ranges receive about 1 000 mm of rainfall. Their peaks are just high enough to gather a mantle of snow from the passing north-westerly winds. 'The dam is full today,' the farmers in the Hex River Valley say with satisfaction when they awake in the cold dawn to find a good snowfall covering the peaks. And indeed, it is the pure water from winter rains and the melted snow percolating into the sandstone mountains which are part of the secret of the agricultural wealth of the Western Cape. The snow and rain are stored in the mountains for a while, then they replenish the water table of the valley, and gush in streams to fill the dams which irrigate the farmlands during the dry, warm summers, when the orchards and vineyards revel in the sunshine but also need plentiful supplies of cool water to quench their thirst.

Fruit and wine in great variety and considerable quantities are produced in these spacious valleys. Patient experimental work by nurserymen such as the pioneer, Harry Pickstone, and the modern government research stations, has succeeded in bringing into South Africa, fruit varieties from all over the world. These are tested in local conditions, varieties are bred, and the most suitable are established commercially as *cultivars* (cultivated varieties) in the valleys of the Western Cape. It is fascinating to know something of the origin of these beautiful and tasty immigrants from foreign parts.

In the royal family of fruit, the apple is king. Its lineage is ancient; it has played a part in the human story since the days of Adam and Eve. No fruit, other than the grape, the queen of fruits, has featured more in history and legend. The apple, whose natural home is on the southern slopes of the Caucasian mountains, has been planted all over the world and today there are 450 million apple trees bearing fruit. America has become the great home of this fruit: over 7 000 varieties are listed there for the apple does not grow true to seed, and varieties are common.

Five main varieties of apples are grown in the Western Cape. The earliest bearing of these cultivars is harvested in February and is known as the *Ohinimuri* a New Zealand selected mutation of *Dunn's Seedling,* a chance seedling found in the 19th century by a Mr Dunn of

*Overleaf: Dassen Island, home of the jackass penguin and regarded by naturalists as one of the wonders of the world.*

South Australia. The Ohinimuri (misspelt in South Africa Ohenimuri) takes its Maori name from the Ohinimuri county on the Thames River in the north island of New Zealand. It is an apple with the advantage of early ripening, but the local disadvantage of a tendency to crack.

In March, three main cultivars come into bearing: *Golden Delicious, Starking* and the *White Winter Pearmain*. The *White Winter Pearmain* is one of the oldest of all commercially cultivated apples, originating in the Parma area of Italy (hence the name). This apple was a standard feature in the orchards of medieval monasteries. It found its way to Britain and the Pilgrim Fathers carried it with them to America where it is regarded as one of the classic varieties. It was introduced to South Africa by Harry Pickstone. In modern times it seems to have lost some of its favour with consumers, which is a pity for it has a piquant flavour all its own.

The *Golden Delicious* cultivar is one of the world's great commercial apple varieties. It originated in about 1890 as a chance seedling on the farm of Anderson Mullins of West Virginia in the United States. The great nursery of Stark Bros. introduced it commercially in 1916. It was brought to South Africa in 1934 by six members of the Elgin Fruit Growers Co-operative (the Moltenos, Col. Cunningham, H. Blackburn, Miss K. Murray, G. Thomas and J. Green) who shared the cost of importation. Each received four trees with which to commence cultivation. Miss Murray sent the first consignment of 400 single-layer trays of fruit from the trees to London where they were enthusiastically received. It is a magnificent apple, highly popular with producers and consumers. A bud mutation known as *Starkspur Golden Delicious* was discovered in America in 1959 by Philip Jenkins in Yakima, Washington. It was commercially introduced in 1961 by the Stark Bros. nursery and brought to South Africa in 1963 by the Department of Agricultural Technical Services.

The *Granny Smith* originated in 1867 as a seed planted by Mrs Maria Ann Smith, wife of the mayor of Parramatta in New South Wales, Australia. It seems to have been introduced to South Africa in 1919 by Professor O. S. H. Reinecke. Notable for its tangy flavour, handsome size, rich green appearance and excellent keeping qualities, it is in firm demand in the world fruit markets.

The *Starking* cultivar is one of the most beautiful and tasty of all apples. It originated from the famous *Hawkeye* apple discovered in 1872 by Jesse Hiatt in Iowa, America. The parent was introduced commercially in 1895 by the Stark Bros. and by them given the name of *Delicious*, for the specimens sent to them by Hiatt for exhibition had arrived minus the original name. Only in the following year, when Hiatt sent more specimens for exhibition, did the Stark Bros. learn the original name given by Hiatt. This magnificent apple quickly became the most popular cultivar in America, providing one-fifth of the total apple production. In 1921 an all-red bud mutation of *Delicious* was found in Munroeville, New Jersey by Lewis Mood. It was commercially introduced in 1924 by the Stark Bros. and named the *Starking Delicious*. Well over 100 million trees of this beautiful apple have been propagated since then and, notwithstanding some tendency to mealyness in cold storage, it is deservedly one of the world's most popular varieties. A bud mutation known as *Starkrimson Delicious* was found in 1953 by a Mr Bisbee of Hood River, Oregon. This was introduced commercially in 1956 by the Stark Bros. and brought to South Africa in 1963 by the Herold Nurseries of Magaliesburg. It has a brilliant crimson colour and a delicious flavour.

May sees the end of the apple harvesting in the Western Cape with the ripening of the *York Imperial*. This apple originated in the early 19th century on a farm near York in Pennsylvania. A farmer named Johnson was attracted to the tree by the attention given to it by small boys who visited it in early spring to eat the apples which had passed the winter covered by leaves on the ground. The excellent condition in which the fruit survived the winter months impressed the farmer. Jessop, a local nurseryman, propagated the variety before 1830 under the name of *Johnsons Fine Winter*. In about 1850 Charles Downing pronounced it to be the 'imperial of keepers' and suggested the name of *York Imperial*. A pretty little apple with a most distinctive flavour and excellent keeping qualities, it has the disadvantage of small and irregular size. In a world which prefers large things, the *York Imperial* has unfortunately lost much of its saleability although its late ripening is still of great value to growers. It was introduced to South Africa in about 1906 by Pickstone.

Apart from the preceding five main cultivars there are twelve other apple varieties grown in the Western Cape although not on any considerable commercial scale. These varieties are the following:

*Austin,* a South African variety bred early this century by a Mr Smith of Pietermaritzburg who named it after his son, Austin. *Baldwin,* one of the leading varieties in the United States. It first appeared in about 1740 as a chance seedling on the farm of John Ball in Massachusetts. At first grown only as a local variety, it was taken up by Colonel Baldwin of Woburn who propagated and gave his name to it. A monument stands on the site of the original tree. *Barnack Beauty,* the earliest ripener in the Western Cape, was bred in about 1845 by a Mr Charles in Barnack, Lincoln, United States. *Cox's Orange Pippin,* the famous old English apple, was bred in 1830 by Mr M. R. Cox at Colnbrook Lawn, Buckinghamshire. It was introduced commercially in 1850 by Charles Turner. *Jonathan,* originated as a chance seedling early in the 19th century on the farm of Philip Rick of Ulster County, New York. It was named after Jonathan Hasbrouck who first directed attention to it. It was introduced to South Africa by Pickstone. *McIntosh* was found by John McIntosh in Canada. Clearing land for a new farm in 1811 he found a clump of about 20 trees which had apparently all sprung from the core of an apple dropped there by some unknown person. McIntosh replanted the trees, but they all died except for one. This bore fruit of such flavour and aroma that the variety became famous. *Rokewood* originated as a chance seedling found in the 1890s on a farm in New South Wales, Australia. *Rome Beauty* originated as a chance seedling raised by H. N. Gillet in 1848 on his farm near the town of Rome in Ohio. Pickstone introduced it to South Africa. *Wemmershoek,* another South African variety, originated from seed taken from an imported apple and first grown in Grahamstown in 1890. *Winter Banana* originated in about 1876 on the farm of David Flory in Cass County, Indiana. Commercially introduced in 1890 by the Greening Bros., it was brought to South Africa in 1917 by Mr M. J. Smith of Gezina, Transvaal. *Zoba* or *Lobo* was bred in 1966 in Ottawa, Canada by the Canadian Division of Horticulture.

There is an endless search for better varieties and for varieties with ripening times which would extend the harvesting period both earlier and later. Over 130 varieties of the *Starking* alone have been bred, with one of them, *Top Red,* a likely apple for future cultivation on account of its brilliant colour.

It is impossible to visualise the apples of the future. Perhaps they will be the same varieties of today; perhaps by careful breeding or the chance discovery of mutations they will change in appearance, improve in flavour, extend in harvesting times, be superior in keeping qualities and approach the farmer's dream of perfection which may still be within his grasp in the apple which Eve gave man and which he has never tired of eating.

The apple-producing areas of the Cape are Grabouw, Elgin, the Long Kloof and Ceres. About 776 000 tons are exported each year, and considerable numbers are also sold on the domestic market.

If the apple is the king of fruits and the grape the queen, then the peach is undoubtedly the princess. Delicately coloured and exquisitely flavoured, it originates from China; from there it was brought to Persia and then to Europe, where it took its name from the old French *pesche,* derived from the Latin *persicum* (Persian apple). Jan van Riebeeck introduced the first peaches to South Africa. He imported trees of the common yellow peach from St Helena, where they had been planted by the Portuguese. Harry Pickstone established the basic commercial varieties, and today the most widely grown kind is the *Peregrine* (foreign), which was first bred in England by that master nurseryman, Thomas Rivers. Several other types, such as the luscious *Rhodes* peach, are popular early in the season, and the *Boland* peach is a magnificent mid-season fruit. In the Western Cape the peach areas are situated around

Elgin, Ceres, Piketberg and the upper Berg River Valley. About 400 tons of peaches are exported each year from a production of over 2 125 tons.

The apricot takes its name from the Latin *praecox* (early ripe). The old French variety known as the *Royal* is the most popular commercial type grown in the Western Cape – over 25 000 double-layer trays are exported annually. An interesting new local variety, the *Peeka* (named after the initials of Mr P. K. le Roux, former Minister of Technical Services), is now being introduced on a large scale. The main apricot-growing areas are situated around Barrydale, Ladismith, Ceres, Montagu and Piketberg. About 110 tons of apricots are exported each season.

The plum comes from the East, and its commercial establishment in the Western world was largely owing to the work of the famous Luther Burbank, of Santa Rosa in the United States. In the Western Cape, the most popular types grown are the *Gaviota*, bred by Luther Burbank from a cross between Japanese and native American types; the *Kelsey*, propagated by John Kelsey of Berkeley, United States, from trees imported from Japan in 1870; and the *Santa Rosa* another of Luther Burbank's products. The largest plum-producing areas of the Western Cape are the upper Berg River Valley, Paarl, Stellenbosch, Wolseley and Ceres. Over 4 000 tons of plums are exported each season.

The pear is indigenous to Europe, and grows wild in England. The most popular varieties grown in the Western Cape are *Packham's Triumph*, an Australian pear introduced into South Africa in 1904, and Williams's *Bon Chretien* (good Christian), first propagated in England in the 1760s by a nurseryman named Williams working on stock bred by a schoolmaster named Wheeler. In America this pear was introduced by Enoch Bartlett in 1799, and what became known as the Bartlett pear is the most widely grown in the world today. Other popular pears grown in the Western Cape include the *Beurre Bosc* (butter pear) from Belgium, the *Winter Nelis*, the *Beurre Hardy* and the *Keiffer,* which originated in 1873 in America, in the garden of Peter Keiffer of Roxborough. In the Western Cape, about 42 000 tons of pears are exported each season. The principal areas of production are Ceres and Elgin.

Minor fruits grown in the Western Cape include the greengage, a plum mutation introduced from France into Britain in the early 1800s by Sir Thomas Gage; the smooth-skinned mutation of the peach known as the nectarine from the nectar-like flavour of its firm flesh; the loquat or rush orange; the South American guava; and berries such as the loganberry, the piquantly flavoured cross between a blackberry and a raspberry which was a result of the work of Judge Logan in California in 1881.

The orchards of the Western Cape are beautiful and productive, but it is the vineyards and the wild flowers which give the region its greatest renown. The grape, delectable to the palate and heady to the senses, has brought both joy and tragedy to man ever since he first sampled its flesh and drank its fermented juice. The vines, attractive to the eye and sensitive to the moods of nature, undergo seasonal colour changes which provide the Western Cape with a striking spectacle. The Barlinka vine leaves in the Hex River Valley are particularly spectacular in autumn, when they change from green to a brilliant scarlet. In this beautiful setting, when the mountains are sprinkled with early snow, the grape, royalty against a majestic backdrop, sumptuously, regally and graciously holds her last court of the season, and then retires gracefully to sleep until the warmth of spring, like the kiss of a young prince, revives her to begin the cycle of life and productivity once again. Some 350 million vines grow in the Western Cape, producing 60 000 tons of dessert fruit each season. About half of the crop is exported. Approximately 310 million of these vines grow in an area 104 154 ha in extent, and over 5 million litres (909 998 leaguers) of wine are produced. South Africa is the fourteenth largest wine producer in the world; France is the largest, with a production of 60 million litres followed by Italy, Algeria, Spain, Portugal, Rumania, the Argentine, Yugoslavia, Russia, Greece, Germany, Hungary, the United States of America and South Africa.

The English name, grape, is rather a curious misnomer: it is really a confusion of the French name for the fruit. The French call the grape *raisin;* a bunch of grapes is *une grappe de raisins.*

In English, the French name, *raisin,* is only applied to the dried fruit – and the word *grappe* (bunch), anglicised to grape, is applied to the fresh fruit. It is anomalies such as this that cause the French to shrug their shoulders at the English.

Traditionally, the natural home of the cultured grape is said to be northern Persia. The ideal climate for vines is a long, warm summer and autumn, with little rain from the time the grapes start to ripen. Rain during this critical ripening period promotes the development of disease, cracking of the skin and watery fruit. Heavy rain is only necessary during the winter when the vines are dormant. The colder it is during the rainy season, the safer and more sound asleep the vines will be.

The quality of the grape is largely dependent on these climatic conditions, as well as on deep, cool soil, not very rich, but well drained. In northern Persia all these conditions prevail, and man has brought the grape to similar areas in many distant parts of the world. Wine was made in Egypt as far back as 6 000 years ago. Since then, the demand for the grape and its juice has always been so great that suitable growing areas have continuously been sought all over the world.

The father of South African viticulture is Jan van Riebeeck. He brought the first vines to the Cape and on 2 February 1659, he recorded in his diary his thanks to the Lord for the taste of the first wine produced in Southern Africa.

There is no way of knowing what varieties of grape Van Riebeeck introduced. The only hint he gives us is when he states that the 'Spanish' grapes were not yet ripe. From this, we can probably assume that the first vines grown in the Cape originated from Spain. The first vines, wherever they came from, were almost certainly all varieties that were selected for winemaking rather than eating. The still ubiquitous *green grape* probably produced the white wines, and *Hermitage* probably produced the red wines. Almost certain to have been among these pioneer varieties was the grape called by the Spaniards *Moscatel gordo blanco* (the fat, white muscatel), by the French *Muscat d'Alexandrie,* and known to South Africans (from its shape) as *Hanepoot* (rooster's testicle). This variety produced not only muscatel wines, but also muscatel raisins. It is, in addition, a magnificent dessert grape, with a sweet and piquantly musky flavour.

For 250 years after Van Riebeeck's time the Hanepoot grape remained the standard dessert grape. When the export market developed at the end of the 1880s, the search for new varieties began. The Hanepoot always remained the favourite local eating grape, but its skin is far too delicate to allow it to travel well. In spite of every care taken in packing, entire shipments were often useless by the time they reached overseas markets.

Varieties of dessert grapes with tougher skins and good keeping qualities had to be found, and today, the stars of many of the prosperous vineyards are the export varieties of grapes. It is interesting to know something of the work of the men who found or bred these varieties.

Far and away the most popular of all export grape varieties grown in the Western Cape is the *Barlinka,* which provides half of the total grape crop. This handsome black grape was found by Professor A. I. Perold of Stellenbosch University who observed it growing on the farm of Leon Roseau, near the village of Novi, 80 km west of Algiers. Roseau had obtained the grape from the natives of Algeria and the cuttings sent by Perold to South Africa produced the Barlinka vines of today.

The second most popular export grape is the *Waltham Cross,* which supplies about one-fifth of the total crop. This large yellow grape was bred in England by William Paul, a grower in the area of Waltham Cross. He developed it from the Turkish variety known as *Razaki Sari,* and in 1871 he received a first-class certificate for the grape from the Royal Horticultural Society. Waltham Cross was introduced into South Africa at the beginning of the 20th century.

The third most popular export grape is the black *Alphonse Lavalle,* which supplies 10 per cent of the crop. This grape, of the same stock as the *Rivier,* was named after the well-known

French viticulturist and author of the standard *Histoire Statistique de la Vigne et des Grands Vins de la Côte d'Or,* published in 1885. In 1925, Major E. G. Munro, of the Covent Garden firm of George Munro Ltd, strongly recommended the Alphonse Lavalle to one of his South African suppliers, J. R. Frater of Paarl; the grape, which ripens early, was being imported to Britain from the Argentine, and was fetching excellent prices. Mr Frater's son, Gerard, wrote to a Buenos Aires nurseryman and arranged for him to place some vine cuttings in the care of the steward of a Japanese boat leaving for Cape Town. From the steward's pantry, the cuttings were handed to the Fraters, and the Alphonse Lavalle was introduced into South Africa. The Rivier was imported in the same year by Durban Cloete.

The fourth export variety is the *New Cross,* which makes up 9,9 per cent of the total crop. This type, and the related, late ripening, white *Almeria* (the fifth export variety, supplying 2,8 per cent of the crop) were introduced into South Africa by L. M. Dicey, one of the best known farmers in the Hex River Valley. In 1898, six years after he had settled in the valley and founded the Cape Orchard Company, Dicey imported the Almeria, an ancient grape favourite, from Spain. By chance, Dicey found among the cuttings the variety he named the *New Cross.*

The sixth export variety of grape, supplying 1 per cent of the total crop, is the *Queen of the Vineyard,* an early ripening cross of the *Pearl of Csaba* and *Queen Elizabeth* varieties. The Queen of the Vineyard was introduced into South Africa from Austria in the mid 1930s.

The seventh and youngest export variety, the *Golden Hill,* had an unusual beginning. In 1940, Douglas Hill, of Sandhills in the Hex River Valley, visited John Heatlie of *Orange Grove* farm. While wandering about the place, Hill noticed a strange looking vine, whose fruit was ripening at an unusual time. Grape farmers were always on the lookout for varieties with different ripening times, and so Hill asked for details. Heatlie told him that on the veranda of the *Orange Grove* homestead, there was a tin of geraniums. Among the flowers, a vine had appeared, which had seeded there by chance. The Heatlies watched with some amusement as the little vine struggled for life. When the geraniums were discarded, the vine narrowly escaped destruction. Somebody, however, took compassion on it and transplanted it. When Hill saw it, it was bearing its first fruit, and not at the usual bearing time. The fruit itself was not particularly impressive, but its ripening time was certainly interesting. Douglas Hill took cuttings of the vine, and on his own farm he grafted these cuttings on to old Hanepoot stock. The result was the tasty handsome Golden Hill grape, with its valuable ripening time, which is between that of established varieties.

These are the principal stars of the dessert grape industry in the Western Cape; they all ripen during a lengthy season extending from December to July, and yield table grapes of superlative quality and flavour. About 37 000 tons of grapes are exported each year to many foreign countries, and the high profits, together with profits from mass sales on the local market, as well as the proceeds from the wine industry, provide the finance for the beautiful homesteads, the high land values and the congenial way of life of farmers in the mountain valleys of the Western Cape. The Hex River Valley produces the great bulk of the dessert grapes of Southern Africa (75 per cent), and the Paarl area also produces substantial amounts.

The export of deciduous fruit is controlled by the Deciduous Fruit Board, which was established in Cape Town in 1939. Fruit is shipped by this body through the largest precooling store in the world, built in Table Bay docks. The production and export of wines and spirits are controlled by the Co-operative Wine Growers' Association of South Africa (the famous KWV – the *Kooperatiewe Wijnbouwers Vereniging van Zuid Afrika*) founded in 1918, with headquarters and cellars – gigantic cathedrals of wine – at Paarl.

---

# THE WINES OF THE CAPE

Since Van Riebeeck's time, the viticulture or wine industry of the Western Cape has developed considerably. Vines, visually beautiful, having a romantic history, and fascinating in their subtlety and variety, are influenced by local conditions in the different natural areas of the mountain valleys where they grow. These areas differ from one another slightly but decisively. Each is influenced by various climatic and topographical factors, such as the blend of winds from moist coast and arid interior; temperature; and the chemistry of the soils – sandstones, shales and granites.

Van Riebeeck first planted small experimental vineyards in the Company's Garden near the Castle. He then planted over 1 000 vines on *Wynberg* (wine mountain), and gradually, vines were planted further and further away. A great variety of cultivars were planted. On *Constantia* estate in the Cape Peninsula, first Simon van der Stel, and then Hendrik Cloete produced the earliest, truly superior South African wines: these were the famous Constantia wines, one a highly regarded red, and the other a less popular white. They were sweet wines, apparently made from late harvest grapes, or what the Germans call *Trockenbeerenauslese* (selected overripe grapes). They were skilfully blended by a master winemaker, who used mainly white and red muscatel (Hanepoot) grapes, mixed perhaps with Pontac and red Muscat d'Frontignac. They were classed as natural wines, but they do seem to have been slightly fortified with brandy and aged in wood for a few years. The red had an alcoholic content of 13,42 per cent and the white 15,01 per cent with a sugar content of 218 grams per litre.

As pioneers moved into the interior, one river valley after the other was settled, and each farm had its vineyard alongside its orchards, meadows and wheat fields. The first river valley to be settled and cultivated was that of the *Eerste* (first) River. Then the *Berg* (mountain) River Valley, the *Breë* or *Breede* (broad) River Valley and the *Olifants* (elephants) River Valley were each in turn settled and cultivated. Each river had its tributaries flowing through valleys of their own, and each valley had a distinct character. The valleys were the mothers and the human cultivators were the fathers of a family of crops. To their family, the parents bequeathed something of the chemistry of the soil, something of the essence of the winds and rain, some of the effects of altitude and orientation, and a great deal which was owing to the farmers' skill and empathy with the soil.

There is no crop more sensitive to its inheritance than the grape; and wine is its essence and its offspring. In the making of wine, many delicate factors are involved: subtleties of environment, cultivation, and ultimately, the skill and fine instinct of the winemaker, the artist who blends and refines the juice of the grape to a liquid of delicate perfection, and then carefully nurses this infant in the womb-like security of his cellar.

Man introduced most of the standard wine grapes of Europe and the Middle East to the river valleys of the Western Cape. He learned by experience which varieties adapted best to the new setting. About 100 different varieties are cultivated in the Cape. The white grapes which adapted best are the Chenin Blanc (also known in South Africa as the Steen or Stein); the Palomino (French White) good for eating as well as for wine; the Green Grape (Semillon), which produces in France the fine, sweet, white wines of Sauternes and Graves; the Pedro Luis; the Clairette Blanche; the Colombar; Muscat d'Alexandrie (known in South Africa as the Hanepoot); St Emilion; and the Riesling, the principal German variety, producer of the moselles, the Spätlesen, Auslesen and Trockenbeerenauslese wines. The red varieties which adapted best include the Cinsaut, formerly known as the Hermitage from the hill overlooking the town of Tain-l'Hermitage, where a famous hermit, Gaspard de Steinburg, a knight who wearied of the crusades settled to grow grapes and to meditate. This is the most widely grown red grape. Other red varieties include the Pinot Noir; the very successful local hybrid of Hermitage and Pinot called Pinotage, developed in 1928 by Professor A. I. Perold; Tinta Barocca (the Portuguese 'tinted grape of the gorge'); Shiraz, the Persian grape taken to Europe from the town of Shiraz in Iran; the famous French Cabernet Sauvignon, a shy bearer, but the producer of superlative wine; and the Red Muscatel or muscat (red Hanepoot) which grows to such perfection in the Robertson area and the Little Karoo. This is a marvellous table grape and the producer of such excellent wines as Moscato and Marsala. This was the great grape of Arabia, of the Saracens and romantic Muscat.

Distinctly separate areas of cultivation in the river valleys of the Cape emerged with the years, each area having its own characteristics. On 16 June 1972, official recognition was accorded these areas of origin. They are the Boberg (the upper valley of the Berg River), Breë River Valley, Caledon, Constantia, Durbanville, Little Karoo, Swartland, Olifants River, Paarl, Piketberg, Robertson, Stellenbosch, Swellendam, Tulbagh and Worcester. An additional area, known as the Coastal was officially recognised on 17 February 1978.

Five wards have also been demarcated for the production of wines of origin: McGregor, Goudini, Vinkrivier, Goree, Riverside and Eilandia. They are all in the Breë River Valley.

Forty individual estates have been demarcated for the production of estate wines. Of these, 24 estates are in the Eerste River Valley in the Stellenbosch area.

In the beginning, the production and marketing of wines in South Africa was controlled by private enterprise. During this time, some fine wines were produced, but by the First World War there was hopeless overproduction, and uneconomic returns from chaotic marketing. To save the industry from ruin, the *Kooperatiewe Wijnbouwers Vereniging van Zuid Afrika Beperk* (KWV) was established in 1918 under the chairmanship of C. W. H. Kohler, a great champion and organising genius of the industry.

The purposes of the co-operative were to regulate the industry, to promote the consumption of wine, to provide the industry with a recognised corporate voice for negotiation, and to improve standards of production. Marketing within South Africa was left to private enterprise in order to ensure that fair prices were returned to producers. The organisation was also to ensure absorption of surplus production, and to use any surplus of high quality wines and spirits to expand overseas markets, particularly in Britain and Canada, and even in Europe. As a result of thorough marketing, the Scandinavian countries, Finland and even France, the great home of wines, have developed an appreciation of the subtleties of South African wines.

The wine grapes are harvested in the Cape from January to March. This is a time of great activity in the vineyards. The scene is little changed from the time when man first began to cultivate the vine in the lost years of antiquity. A perfect machine to harvest grapes has only recently been devised and on most farms each bunch must still be picked by hand, placed in containers, and conveyed in bulk to the presses.

The estates of origin have their own presses. The other producers (supplying about 80 per cent of the total crop) send their fruit to one of the 58 co-operative wine cellars scattered throughout the wine areas. Impatient queues of trucks and trailers form outside these cellars, waiting their turn to be weighed with their loads. The weight of the grapes is written up to the credit of the supplier, as is also the nature of the grapes; their variety, quality and sugar content. Some wines, such as the late harvest ones, demand special delayed harvesting in order to ensure high sugar content and piquancy of flavour.

The grapes are unloaded into containers and winemaking begins. This is an entirely natural process. Man expedites and improves it, but no part of it is synthetic. A grape crushed underfoot would automatically produce wine, providing the juice was not lost through evaporation or saturation into the ground. Man is there to provide the ideal conditions and, like a parent discreetly promoting a good match for a favoured child, he expedites and influences events in order to achieve a desired end.

The grapes are fed into a mill, which extracts and discards the stems, and crushes the berries to produce a mixture of husks (skins) and juice, known as must. The juice of all grapes would produce a white wine; it is the skins or husks which affect the colour, and it is the bloom on the skins which contains the yeast, the living unicellular organisms of microscopic size which mingle with the juice, feed on the sugar, and by a process of fermentation, convert it into alcohol, carbon dioxide and other byproducts. Yeasts, however, have different strains, which produce different effects. It is at this stage, therefore, that man intervenes in the natural process and directs it along predetermined lines by cultivating special yeasts. The skill of the winemaster now comes into full play and this is the science of oenerology.

If a white wine is being produced, the husks are separated from the juice very soon after pressing. In the making of certain wines, the husks are left long enough to influence the acidity and piquancy of the wine. Once separated, the husks are re-pressed, and the juice extracted is used in general winemaking, or it can be added to the main body of juice in carefully measured quantities in order to influence its flavour. Then, after being left to ferment slightly, the husks are pressed for the third time. The juice from this final pressing is distilled into spirits. The dry husks are used for compost.

The must, freed from the husks and all pips and flesh (which have been filtered out in many ingenious ways), is poured into stainless steel tanks for fermentation. To ensure that fermentation occurs in the desired way, quantities of specially cultured grape yeast are added. Fermentation then proceeds, generating considerable heat. As this heat can be detrimental to the wine, the must is cooled by refrigeration, and a temperature of 15° C to 18° C is maintained. The carbon dioxide escapes into the air and the sugar in the must is steadily converted into alcohol. If not controlled and influenced, fermentation would eventually cause the disappearance of all the sugar; the resultant wine would be a completely natural light wine, which would be very dry (or sugarless) to the taste. However, fermentation can be artificially arrested by subjecting the wine to low temperatures or high pressure. The yeasts become paralysed and are prevented from further action, and the wines have some sweetness, the amount of which depends on the stage when fermentation was arrested.

Such delicate, light, white table wines are known in Germany as Moselles if they are very light, and as Hocks if they are slightly stronger in flavour. In France, these wines are the Chablis and the Graves.

If all the carbon dioxide is allowed to escape, the wine will be a still one; if some of the gas is left, then the wine will be a perlé. Sparkling wines, such as French champagnes, are made from carefully selected natural wines, and they are then subjected to a second fermentation, either in their bottles, or in sealed containers. Carbon dioxide is retained in the wine, and this constitutes the sparkle and fizz. Depending on the amount of sugar, sparkling wines can be *brut* (exceptionally dry); *extra-sec* (extra dry); *demi-sec* (medium dry); or *doux* (sweet).

Another method of retaining sugar in the wine is by fortification: at a carefully chosen moment in fermentation, pure wine spirit is added to the must. This spirit paralyses the action of the yeast and fermentation is arrested, leaving the desired amount of sugar in the wine. The fortified wines are heavy, with a stronger alcoholic content than the light natural wines; this is because of the artificial addition of pure spirits. The alcohol content of the fortified wines ranges from 17 per cent to 20 per cent; the natural wines have an alcohol content of 11 per cent to 14 per cent.

The sweetest wines are the jerepigos; this is because the fortifying wine spirit is added to the must before any natural fermentation has taken place. This means that all the natural sugar remains in the wine, and the alcohol content, though pure in itself, is artificially added by the winemaker. Sherries, port, marsalas and muscatels are all fortified wines.

For the production of red wines, the husks are left with the must, yeast is added, and fermentation takes place either in open vats or tanks or in closed steel tanks. The husks rise to the surface and form a head which is so solid that it can support the weight of a man. Under the direction of the winemaker, this head is periodically broken up and pushed down into the must. From this mixing comes the colour, flavour, and tannin of red wines. The husks are eventually removed from the must at the discretion of the winemaker. Fermentation is allowed to proceed until the sugar content has been reduced to about 4 per cent. The wine is then pumped into wooden vats. The separated husks are pressed and all residual juice is extracted; some is returned to the fermenting must. In the wooden vats, fermentation continues until all the sugar content has vanished and the wine is completely dry. Small quantities of gases such as oxygen slowly percolate through the wood into the maturing wine. As these intruding gases gently work on the tannin and mineral salts which the wine has absorbed from its husks, the wine steadily mellows. Time is the only aid in the process of maturation. Man, always impatient, has tried methods of forcing wine to age quickly, but wine is curiously alive in its foibles – it clings to its raw, astringent and crude youth. It settles down only in its own good time, and begins to mellow; but it traditionally needs to enjoy at least three undisturbed years in the oak casks, and a reflective five-year period in bottles lying in a cool, dark, quiet cellar. Some of the fortified wines, such as ports, only reach their best after 100 years of maturation; sherries need 20 years of tranquillity in order to attain the really rich, nutty flavour and piquant aftertaste which they inherit from grapes such as the Palomino (or French grape), from which they are made, and from the all-important Flor.

Sherries, which range from very dry to very sweet, start off as white wines. They undergo a second, very special fermentation, in which the peculiar wine yeast called *Flor* is used. This yeast was originally thought to be found only in Spain, but its discovery in the bloom of a locally grown grape made the production of sherry possible in the Cape. All the principal varieties are produced: *Fino* (dry); *Amontillado* (slightly sweet); *Oloroso* (sweet); and *Old Brown* (very sweet and full – almost a banquet of grape syrup and raisins).

Port wines, ruby, tawny and small quantities of the aristocrat Vintage Port, are produced from grape varieties such as Tinta Barocca; Hermitage; Souzao; and Tinta Roriz. They are fortified during fermentation when the sugar content is 12 per cent, receiving an alcohol content of up to 20 per cent. They demand a combination of loving care and delicate skill from the winemaker.

Rosé wines, which are among the lightest of all wines, can be made in various ways: red and white wines can be mixed, but the best rosé wines are produced from grape varieties with red to light black skins. The skins are left in the must just long enough for the fermenting juice to absorb from them colour, flavour and aromatic substance.

Brandy, which takes the English name from the Dutch *brandewijn* (burnt wine), is distilled wine. Grape varieties such as the Palomino and Colombard are pressed at 21 per cent sugar content and the husks are immediately removed from the must. After fermentation, samples of these distilling wines are tested by the government. When approved, they are distilled by heat, and the vapours are collected and condensed; they are then distilled a second time, and the first and last runnings are cut off; the middle run, or heart, is preserved. From this, a rebate brandy is made by maturing the spirit in oak casks for at least three years. It is stipulated by law that South African brandies must contain a minimum of 25 per cent of this rebate brandy.

Herbal brandies and wines of several different types are also produced; these have a wide variety of flavours, aromas and effects. Vermouth demands approximately 30 different herbs and plants in its production. Liqueurs also require considerable subtlety in their blending. Van der Hum, a peculiarly South African liqueur with a tangerine flavour, was first blended in the early days at the Cape. It seems to embody something of the essence of past years, when pirates and East Indiamen anchored side by side in Table Bay. One can almost imagine, as one sips this liqueur, the glowering faces of rival captains as they gossiped over liqueurs or downed rum or savoured the sweet, rich wines of Constantia, acquired in the inns of the old tavern of the seas.

---

# THE LABELLING, CERTIFICATION AND CLASSIFICATION OF WINE

Most wine-producing countries apply strict controls to the standards of wine and the claims made on the labels by the producers. The South African Government applies a stringent discipline on winemakers. On 1 September 1973 the South African Wine of Origin Legislation became law. From thence on seals of certification were issued to wines attaining standards prescribed by the Government Wine and Spirit Board. This Board consists of a chairman and six members, all experts: two appointed from the liquor trade, two from the Government Research Institute of Nietvoorbij, and two from the KWV (Co-operative Wine Farmers' Union). Every Wednesday morning the Board meets at the laboratory of the Government Research Institute at Nietvoorbij, near Stellenbosch. Each member retires to a cubicle and the wines to be tested are passed to him one at a time. Each member has three switches in his cubicle: green (approved); amber (passed with reservations); and red (denied). He cannot see or hear his fellow members. His decision about the wine is transmitted electrically from his switches.

The seal of certification which the wine will carry if it is approved by the Board guarantees the correctness of the information contained in the main descriptive label of the bottle. The seal is affixed to the top of the neck of each bottle. If the word 'estate' appears on the certificate, then 100 per cent of the wine in the bottle must originate from the estate mentioned on the label. If the world 'origin' in a blue band is on the certificate, then at least 80 per cent of the wine in the bottle must come from the specific geographical area claimed on the label.

If the word 'vintage' appears in a red band on the certificate, then the vintage claimed on the label is correct, with at least 75 per cent of the wine from that vintage.

If the word 'cultivar' appears in a green band on the certificate, then 75 per cent of the wine in the bottle must originate from the type of grape described on the label. With certain varieties, this discipline is relaxed until specific dates when it must be met in full. An identification number is also given to each wine and is printed on the certificate.

Finally comes the magic word 'Superior'. To achieve this high honour, the wine must be of superlative quality, a real aristocrat of its kind and subject to the most stringent tests of the Board.

The following is a roll of honour of the wines granted the Superior seal up to the end of 1979:

### Aan-De-Doorns Koöp Wynmakery
Worcester Muscat d' Alexandrie – 1977

### Allesverloren Estate
Swartland Cabernet sauvignon – 1974, 1976
Swartland Tinta Barocca – 1975
Swartland Port – 1974

### Alto Estate
Stellenbosch Cabernet sauvignon – 1967, 1969, 1970, 1971
Stellenbosch Alto Rouge – 1975

### Backsberg Estate
Paarl Cabernet sauvignon – 1969, 1971, 1972, 1973, 1974, 1975, 1976, 1977
Paarl Shiraz – 1974, 1976
Paarl Chenin blanc – 1978

**Badsberg Koöp Wynkelder Bpk**
Worcester Hanepoot – 1974
Goudini Hanepoot – 1976, 1977, 1978

**P M E Barlow**
Stellenbosch Rustehburg Cabernet sauvignon – 1971, 1972, 1973, 1975
Stellenbosch Rustenburg Dry Red – 1973, 1974, 1975, 1976

**Bertrams Wines Ltd**
Stellenbosch Cabernet sauvignon – 1973, 1974, 1975, 1976
Stellenbosch Shiraz – 1973, 1975, 1976

**Boschendal Estate**
Paarl Steen – 1979
Paarl Chenin blanc – 1979

**Delheim Wines**
Stellenbosch Goldspatz Steen – 1973, 1975
Stellenbosch Steen – 1974
Stellenbosch Demi-Sec Riesling – 1975
Stellenbosch Spatzendreck Chenin blanc Late Harvest – 1976
Stellenbosch Pinotage – 1974
Stellenbosch Shiraz – 1974, 1976
Stellenbosch Cabernet sauvignon – 1975, 1976
Stellenbosch Pinotage Rosé – 1979

**De Wetshof Estate**
Robertson Riesling – 1975

**Distillers Corporation**
Tulbagh Drostdy Pale Dry Sherry
Tulbagh Drostdy Full Cream Sherry
Tulbagh Drostdy Medium Cream Sherry
Fleur du Cap Shiraz – 1970
Kusstreek Fleur du Cap Riesling – 1979
Kusstreek Fleur du Cap Late Harvest – 1979
Kusstreek Fleur du Cap Emerald Stein – 1979
Kusstreek Fleur du Cap Golden Harvest – 1979
Stellenbosch Stellenryck Riesling – 1976, 1979
Stellenbosch Stellenryck Chenin blanc – 1979
Stellenbosch Stellenryck Cabernet sauvignon – 1975

**Goede Hoop Estate**
Stellenbosch Droë Rooi – 1974

**Groot Constantia Estate**
Constantia Cabernet sauvignon – 1970, 1971, 1972, 1973, 1974, 1975, 1976
Constantia Pinotage – 1971, 1972, 1973, 1974
Constantia Heerenrood – 1976
Constantia Shiraz – 1972, 1973, 1974, 1975, 1976
Constantia Weisser Riesling – 1979

**Hazendal Estate**
Stellenbosch Steen – 1975, 1977, 1978

**Huguenot Wynboere Bpk**
Boberg Aspen Extra Dry Sherry
Boberg Aspen Dry Cape Sherry
Boberg Aspen Medium Sherry
Boberg Aspen Full Cream Sherry

**Jacobsdal Estate**
Stellenbosch Pinotage – 1974

**Johann Graue Estate**
Paarl Cabernet sauvignon – 1970, 1971
Paarl Riesling – 1973, 1974
Paarl Private Bin S312 – 1973, 1974
Paarl Private Bin S311 – 1973
Paarl Edelkeur – 1973, 1974
Paarl Steen – 1974

**Klawer Koöp Wynkelder Bpk**
Olifantsrivier Hanepoot – 1977

**K W V**
Boberg Tawny Likeurwyn – 1929
Boberg Ruby Likeurwyn – 1949, 1960
Boberg Bleek Likeurwyn (V O Sherry)
Paarl Cabernet sauvignon – 1973
Kusstreek Weisser Riesling – 1978
Kusstreek Special Late Harvest – 1975

**Lebensraum Estate**
Goudini Soet Hanepoot – 1978

**Louwshoek-Voorsorg Koöp Wynkelder Bpk**
Goudini Muscat d' Alexandrie – 1977

**Meerendal Estate**
Durbanville Pinotage – 1971, 1972, 1973, 1974
Durbanville Shiraz – 1971, 1972, 1973, 1974,1976

**Meerlust Estate**
Stellenbosch Cabernet sauvignon – 1975, 1976

**Merwida Koöp Wynkelders Bpk**
Worcester Colombard – 1978

**Montagne Estate**
Stellenbosch Cabernet sauvignon – 1971,. 1972, 1974, 1975
Stellenbosch Riesling – 1974

**Mont Blois Estate**
Robertson Muskadel – 1974, 1976, 1977
Robertson Wit Muskadel – 1975

**Montpellier Estate**
Tulbagh Riesling – 1971, 1972
Tulbagh Gewürztraminer – 1973

**Nederburg Wines Ltd**
Paarl Cabernet sauvignon – 1970, 1971, 1972, 1973
Paarl Riesling – 1974, 1976
Paarl Private Bin S312 – 1974, 1977, 1978
Paarl Private Bin S311 – 1975, 1976, 1977, 1978
Paarl Private Bin S333 – 1974, 1977
Paarl Baronne – 1974
Paarl Private Bin R103 – 1975, 1976
Paarl Edelkeur – 1969, 1973, 1974, 1975, 1976, 1977, 1978
Paarl Steen – 1974
Paarl Pinotage – 1974
Paarl Shiraz – 1974, 1975
Paarl Kerner – 1977
Paarl Bukettraube – 1977
Paarl Late Harvest – 1973, 1974, 1975, 1976, 1977, 1978, 1979
Paarl Golden Harvest – 1976, 1977, 1978, 1979

**Nuwehoop Wynkelder Bpk**
Goudini Semi-Soet – 1977
Goudini Laat Oes – 1979

**Nuy Koöp Wynkelder Bpk**
Nuy Colombard (Effe-soet) – 1979

**Overgaauw Estate**
Stellenbosch Cabernet sauvignon – 1972, 1973

**Rietvallei Estate**
Robertson Muskadel – 1978

**Roodezandt Koöp Wynmakery Bpk**
Robertson Soet Hanepoot – 1978, 1979
Robertson Wit Muskadel – 1979

**Rooibergse Koöp Wynmakery Bpk**
Eilandia Hanepoot – 1977
Vinkrivier Muskadel – 1976
Vinkrivier Chenin blanc – 1977, 1979
Vinkrivier Late Vintage – 1977, 1979
Vinkrivier Colombard – 1978

**S F W**
Stellenbosch Oude Libertas Cabernet sauvignon – 1976, 1977

Kusstreek Zonnebloem Cabernet sauvignon – 1976, 1977, 1978
Kusstreek Zonnebloem Late Harvest – 1979

**Simonsig Estate**
Stellenbosch Pinotage – 1972
Stellenbosch Private Reserve – 1973
Stellenbosch Colombard – 1975
Stellenbosch Gewürztraminer – 1977
Stellenbosch Cabernet sauvignon – 1977
Stellenbosch Weisser Riesling – 1977, 1978

**Simonsvlei Koöp Wynkelder Bpk**
Paarl Cabernet sauvignon – 1973
Paarl Chenin blanc – 1977

**Slanghoek Koöp Wynkelder Bpk**
Slanghoek Chenin blanc ← 1979
Slanghoek Colombard – 1979

**Spier Estate**
Stellenbosch Edelsteen Late Harvest – 1978
Stellenbosch Pinotage – 1974

**Swartland Koöp Wynkelder Bpk**
Swartland Pinotage – 1971

**Theuniskraal Estate**
Tulbagh Late Harvest Steen – 1977
Tulbagh Gewürztraminer – 1976, 1978

**Uiterwyk Estate**
Stellenbosch Cabernet sauvignon – 1973, 1974, 1975, 1976, 1977

**Uitkyk Estate**
Stellenbosch Carlonet Cabernet sauvignon – 1973, 1974, 1975
Stellenbosch Shiraz – 1973

**Vergenoegd Estate**
Stellenbosch Cabernet sauvignon – 1971, 1972, 1973, 1974, 1975, 1976
Stellenbosch Shiraz – 1971, 1972, 1973, 1974, 1975

**Vlottenburg Koöp Wynkelder Bpk**
Stellenbosch Riesling – 1976

**Weltevrede Estate**
Bonnievale Privé – 1979
Robertson Rooi Muskadel – 1977
Robertson Muscat de Hambourg – 1977

**Zandvliet Estate**
Robertson Shiraz – 1975, 1976

The list of superior wines on the previous pages is not meant to infer that all other wines are less tasty. One of the fascinations of wine is the variety, quality, aroma and flavour obtained from many odd little vintages. The choosing of wines is a matter of personal taste. Whatever the opinion is of some poohbah, the drinker is no fool if he has his own preference, red or white, sweet or dry. Exploring country cellars and wine estates is an absorbing pastime.

In the space below record your own preferences or recommendations given to you by others, as well as the discoveries you have made during pleasant occasions of tasting, and amiable discussion.

———

## Chapter Five

# THE VALLEY OF THE EERSTE RIVER

It is a delightful experience in travel to explore the wine and fruit-producing valleys of the *Boland* (upland) areas of the Western Cape Province. The principal valleys are those of the Berg, Breë and Eerste rivers, with their various tributaries. Each is beautiful, full of charming scenes and rich in fragments of history. The valley of the *Eerste* River, as its name (first) indicates, was the first of the inland valleys to be settled by farmers from the Cape, and it deserves to be the first to be explored by any traveller. Scenically it is superb. Stellenbosch, which lies at its upper end, is without doubt the prettiest of all the small towns in Southern Africa, while the wines, wild flowers and fruits of the valley are among the finest in the world.

## STELLENBOSCH

*Stellenbosch,* with its population of 34 197, has a situation, atmosphere, architecture and general appearance which all contribute to a unique charm. Essentially an academic and farming centre, it is largely free of the relentless pressures of industry and excessive population growth. Here, man has a chance to live in a more relaxed atmosphere, to take stock of the good things around him, conserve and beautify, and learn that it is more pleasant by far to live in the shade of a tree rather than that of a lamp post. If developers, town planners, civil engineers and traffic authorities claim that old buildings, trees and open spaces are contrary to modern planning, then it is best that these gentlemen are transferred or removed to the Sahara Desert and for the good things to be left where they are.

The nature of Stellenbosch becomes immediately apparent as one enters it by road or railway at its southern end. Overlooking it are the forested slopes of the *Papegaaiberg* (parrot mountain) with the rather humbly named stream, the *Plankenbrugrivier* (plank bridge river) bustling through the valley at its foot to join the Eerste as a tributary. At the point where the main road from Cape Town crosses the railway and river by means of the Adam Tas Bridge there is a small monument on the left-hand side marking the site of a borrow-pit in which, in 1899, Louis Peringuey discovered stone implements which proved the great antiquity of man in this part of Southern Africa.

Across the Adam Tas Bridge the traveller is welcomed into Stellenbosch by flowers and oaks. During all the seasons the town is colourful and beautiful. The main road, Dorp Street, leads right from just beyond the bridge and finds a way beneath cool shadows of oaks; many pleasant vistas of white-walled buildings are revealed, dappled with patterns of sunshine playing through the leaves and branches.

Furrows of clear water gurgle on either side of the road and one beautifully framed picture after the other appears down each intersecting street. Stellenbosch should be walked through; it is not a place to view from the window of a car. It requires leisure. A promenade along the full length of Dorp Street is very rewarding. Although it has several unfortunate gaps, it is by far the best preserved old-time street in South Africa.

On the right, immediately across the main road which branches off to Somerset West, is the beautifully restored *Libertas Parva,* with its gables dating from 1783. These buildings now house the Rembrandt van Rijn Art Gallery and the Oude Meester Stellenryck Wine Museum, both open to the public Mondays to Fridays from 09h00 to 12h45 and 14h00 to 17h00; on Saturdays from 10h00 to 13h00 and 14h00 to 17h00.

Just up Dorp Street stands *Vredelust* and above it two interesting streets branch off left: first Market, and then Herte, which eventually curve and converge to provide a pleasant return walk. Both these streets are lined with delightful old buildings which have been carefully restored and are a joy to the eye. Where the two streets converge, Market Street turns sharp right and leads past the walled garden of the Rhenish Parsonage with the Mill Stream running in front of it, and on to the open space known as the *Braak* (fallow area), a true village green. This was originally used, amongst other things, as a military parade ground, and the *Kruithuis* (powder house or arsenal) still stands at the point where Market Street reaches the Braak. It is now maintained as a military museum, and is open Tuesdays to Fridays 10h00 to 13h00; 14h30 to 17h00. Saturdays, Sundays and public holidays, 14h00 to 17h00. Closed Mondays. Around the Braak are several handsome buildings: the Burger House, now a museum; the coachman's cottage; the pretty little Anglican church, St Mary's-on-the-Braak; the Rhenish Mission Church; and other interesting places.

Dorp Street itself continues on its pleasant way. On the left-hand side there is a long row of beautiful old houses, numbered 102 to 122; all were converted into double-storeys in Victorian times, but they still retain their former character. Opposite them is what was once the parsonage of the Reverend Meent Borcherds, who built this lovely home, *La Gratitude,* in 1798, and placed in its gable an 'all-seeing eye'. How many passers-by have felt a trifle uneasy as they met its unflinching stare? It is now the home of the Winshaw family who founded the Stellenbosch Farmers' Winery and the name of the house is the name of one of their most popular white wines.

Meul Street, turning left, provides a direct access to the Braak and commercial streets such as Plein which contains, among other buildings, the modern town hall. Above Meul Street, Dorp Street continues past interesting buildings in the Cape Georgian style such as Nos 125, 133 and 135. Opposite them stands the original Lutheran Church built in 1851 and now the University art gallery.

Van Ryneveld Street, branching left, contains some attractive little homes which are worth seeing. The oldest town house surviving in South Africa is Schreuder House, in Van Ryneveld Street. It was built in 1709 and is an interesting and atmospheric little cottage. It is open to the public Tuesdays to Saturdays 10h00 to 13h00; 14h30 to 17h00. Sundays and holidays 14h00 to 17h00. It is closed on Mondays. Dorp Street continues past a row of gabled houses and then reaches on the right-hand side the imposing Theological Seminary, built upon the walls of the original *drostdy* (magistracy). Opposite this building, Drostdy Street branches left, a short street and with an east side which is quite superb. First is *Utopia,* the offices of the handsome Dutch Reformed Mother Church which stands next to it and dominates the street. Above the church is *Grosvenor House,* now the Stellenbosch museum, with the former slave quarters on its left and the original coach house on the right. It is the only remaining perfect specimen in Stellenbosch of a town house with two storeys and a flat roof. It had its beginning in 1782 as the home of Christian Neethling. Subsequent owners, the Collins family, named it *Grosvenor House.*

The Stellenbosch museum is open to the public daily from 09h00 to 17h00 and 14h00 to 17h00 on Sundays. It contains a good collection of furniture, dolls, and domestic utensils of the past years. There is a stable containing vehicles used by the fire brigade, an early ambulance, a penny-farthing bicycle and some carts. The garden behind the museum is beautiful.

Of all South African towns, Stellenbosch is fortunate in retaining so much of its original character. Its history started on the afternoon of 6 November 1679. It was then that the recently appointed Governor of the Cape, Simon van der Stel, in the course of a first tour of inspection of his new responsibility, rode into what he described as the most charming valley he had yet seen. The diversity of the hills, the richness of the grass, the patches of evergreen forest trees, the river of sweet water, all delighted his eye and mind. In part of its course the Eerste River divides into two channels, forming a finely wooded island, and it was there, under a handsome tree, that Van der Stel made his camp. He called the site *Stellenbosch* (Van der Stel's bush) and determined on founding a settlement in an area so obviously suited to the habitation of man. Within a month the first settler arrived and in May of the following year eight families removed from Cape Town and were given the right of selecting for themselves as much ground in the valley as they could cultivate, with unlimited use of the surrounding grazing.

Stellenbosch grew rapidly. In 1682 it received its first local authority and in 1685 it became the seat of a magistrate whose authority extended over no less than 25 000 square kilometres of the whole inland area of the Cape. For over a century, Stellenbosch remained the seat of this frontier magistracy.

Simon van der Stel always retained a particular love for the town he had founded. It became his habit to spend his birthdays there and the occasions became regular holiday galas for the inhabitants of the valley of the Eerste River. There were sports, feasts and shooting competitions at a target made in the shape of a *papegaai* or parrot (hence the name *Papegaaiberg* for the hill overlooking the town). Van der Stel also ordered the planting of oak trees in the town, making of the place a regular *eikestad* (city of oaks). Several of the original trees are still standing but just as pleasing are the young trees which are the sign of the care and determination of the inhabitants to preserve the original charm of their town. The Jan Marais Nature Reserve near the centre of the town is a botanical sanctuary for the rich flora which must have covered the site of the town before its founding. The reserve is open daily from 07h30 to sunset. The University of Stellenbosch has a superb Botanical Garden in Van Riebeeck Street. It is notable for its collection of ferns, orchids, bonsai trees and succulents, including such rarities as welwitschias from the Namib Desert. The Garden is open weekdays 09h00 to 17h00; Saturdays 09h00 to 11h00.

Stellenbosch received its first school in 1683. In 1881 the Victoria College was established, and in 1918 it was granted higher status and became the University of Stellenbosch which today, with its 10 000 students, dominates the town, not only physically with its impressive complex of buildings, but also culturally and socially with its atmosphere of learning, varsity life and sport. To sit in some pleasant little café – such as the Südwest Stube in Plein Street – and watch the passing show is to savour something of the atmosphere of a Continental university town. This could almost be a part of Holland, with its neatness, scrupulous cleanliness, and a particular polish to all the windows.

The quality of food in Stellenbosch is justly renowned. The Südwest Stube in Plein Street offers superb venison. Along the Somerset West road there is the *Volkskombuis aan de Wagenweg,* featuring traditional Cape dishes, and the beautifully restored *Doornbosch,* where the K.W.V. maintains a taphouse, restaurant and cellar. The wines of the Eerste River Valley may be purchased here.

### Accommodation
★★ Coetzenberg Hotel, 25 rooms, 15 with baths. R10,50 – R11,50 B/B. Phone 7-2930.
★ Drostdy Herberg, 18 rooms, 6 with baths. R11 – R13,50 B/B. Phone 7-0220.
★★★® Lanzerac Hotel, 35 rooms, all with baths. R19,50 – R27,90 room only. Phone 5020.

Stellenbosch is the centre for a considerable industry in the production of wine, gin and brandy. The three principal commercial producers and distributors of wines and spirits in Southern Africa all have their headquarters in the immediate vicinity of the town. Visitors are welcome to inspect the cellars and sample some of their wares. Each offers a guided tour and interesting explanations of the process of winemaking.

The largest of the 'big three' of the wine merchants is The Stellenbosch Farmers' Winery Ltd, whose extensive cellars are situated 1 km from Stellenbosch on the road to Cape Town down the shallow valley of the Eerste River. This company was the child of an American, William

*Overleaf: Dorp Street, Stellenbosch; cold winter shadows and the lovely architecture of years long past.*

Charles Winshaw, who came to South Africa in 1900 with a cargo of 4 000 mules destined for the British army. He was a qualified doctor, born in Kentucky in 1871. He served with the British army, then settled in South Africa, practising medicine until he decided to turn farmer, renting *Patrys Vallei* (partridge valley now *Brown Hills*) for £6 a month and starting to make wine in his kitchen.

From the beginning Winshaw managed to produce good wine. In 1909 he founded the Stellenbosch Grape Juice Works but it was a difficult time in which to establish a wine industry. There was overproduction and little demand. In 1921 he went insolvent but his faith in wine remained unshaken. Two years later, he joined J. G. Krige in a new venture based on Krige's farm. This fine farm, named *Libertas* (liberty), had first been granted by Simon van der Stel in 1689 to Jan van Oud-Beyerland, who transferred it in 1690 to Hans Grimpe. On his death, his widow married a well-known character in the history of the Cape, Adam Tas. It was purely coincidental that his name was part of the farm name, but the cellar of the farm, built in 1706, is named after him and several of the modern company's wines, such as the Taskelder and Oude Libertas ranges and Oom Tas, are reminders of a stalwart defender of civil liberties.

In 1869 Gideon Krige purchased the northern section of *Libertas* and founded a business as a distiller and wine merchant. In 1924 William Winshaw rehabilitated his estate, bought the farm and business from Krige, and founded the Stellenbosch Farmers' Winery Ltd. Winshaw remained as managing director of this company until 1962 when, aged 92, he retired. All his life he insisted on high standards of production and the healthiness of natural wine. He died at the fine age of 96 and his enthusiasm for the qualities of good wine had obviously served him well. His son, also William, succeeded him and in 1950 became chairman of the Stellenbosch Farmers' Wine Trust Ltd which incorporated the original Stellenbosch Farmers' Winery and the wine firm of V. H. Matherson and Son Ltd. In 1960 the company merged with the South African Breweries Ltd by means of a share exchange. The Winshaw family continued management and the company expanded, in 1966 absorbing the Paarl firm of Monis Wineries and being renamed as The Stellenbosch Wine Trust Ltd. The magnificent *Nederburg* estate at Paarl, owned by Monis, was brought into the group at the same time, and in 1970 Sedgwick Taylor was also acquired.

The company today markets well over 50 per cent of all wines sold in Southern Africa, employing over 6 000 people and with a turnover in excess of R200 million. Visitors are taken by appointment through the cellars at 10h30 and 14h30 from Monday to Thursday and at 10h30 on Fridays.

Opposite their cellars, on the farm *Oude Libertas,* the company has a very impressive reception and training complex, the Oude Libertas Centre. This includes a restaurant, an amphitheatre and the restored homestead of *Mon Repos*. Concerts, ballet and other entertainments are staged in the amphitheatre. The restaurant is connected to a cellar containing 11 000 bottles of red wine laid down for maturing. The Cape Town firm of architects, Mallows, Louw, Hoffe and Orme, designed this very attractive complex of buildings. The lighting effects at night are romantic and a concert or stage performance beneath the stars has given many audiences a very deep pleasure. The setting lends itself particularly well to Spanish dancing.

The second of the big three of the wine business is the Distillers Corporation (S.A.) Ltd, founded in 1945 as part of the Oude Meester group of companies controlled by Anton Rupert and his associates. This group has its magnificent *Bergkelder* (mountain cellar) on the slopes of the Papegaaiberg, just behind the Stellenbosch railway station. Visitors are welcome and conducted tours take place at 15h00 on Mondays; at 10h00 and 15h00 on Tuesdays to Thursdays; and at 10h00 on Fridays. Wine may be tasted but is not sold at the cellars.

The Bergkelder is notable for magnificent vats, carved in 1968 by the artist, Karl Wilhelm. Brought out from Germany to do the work, he completed all the vats in less than a year and then decided to settle in the Cape where his talents are a considerable asset and his work may be seen in many forms.

In 1979 Cape Wine and Distillers Ltd was formed to combine financial control of The Stellenbosch Wine Trust Ltd and Distillers Corporation of Southern Africa Ltd. In this huge combine the South African Breweries retain a 30 per cent interest, the Oude Meester group 30 per cent, the K.W.V. 30 per cent, and independent producers 10 per cent.

The third of the big three wine and spirit producers of Southern Africa is Gilbey Distillers and Vintners (Pty) Ltd, who have their headquarters on the right bank of the Plankenbrug River, below the slopes of the Papegaaiberg. This concern had its origin in Britain where W. and A. Gilbey, already well established, started importing and distributing Cape wines in 1857. In 1950 they opened a gin distillery in Pietermaritzburg and in 1962 acquired the wine and brandy company of Rene Santhagens, whose seat of operations was the *Oude Molen* (old mill) at Stellenbosch. This became the headquarters in South Africa of Gilbey Distillers and Vintners (Pty) Ltd. A working replica of the original watermill, first built in 1710, was constructed and the place, already a handsome centre of production, very considerably expanded.

In 1972 the company acquired Bertrams Wines, a company with an established reputation in the wine trade. R. F. Bertram had in the late 1900s purchased the *High Constantia* estate, adjoining the famous *Groot Constantia,* built a cellar and produced fine wine from grapes grown on both estates. In 1939 Bertram's company was bought by G. N. Maskell, who expanded the concern and then sold it in 1959 to Simeon Blumberg, owner of the wine estate, *Kleine Zalze,* near Stellenbosch. He moved the entire company to the Devon Valley near Stellenbosch and in 1972 sold it to Gilbeys who, by this acquisition, became number three wine and spirit producers and distributors of Southern Africa.

Visitors are welcome to the Gilbey works. The Oude Molen complex is a distillery and maturation cellar. No wine is sold there but it provides an interesting tour. The main cellars are at the head of the Devon Valley 7 km from Stellenbosch. Guided tours and wine tasting take place at 10h30 and 15h00 Mondays to Fridays, but not on holidays or weekends. Wine is sold in a shop at the main cellars during normal trading hours.

The Devon Valley, in which Gilbeys have their estate and cellars, is reached after a pleasant, short drive from Stellenbosch. The road branches off from the main Stellenbosch-Cape Town road at a point 1 km from the Adam Tas Bridge over the Plankenbrug River. Handsomely laid out vineyards lie on either side of the road. After 4,5 km there is a turnoff right leading to *Protea Heights,* the famous private wild flower farm founded by Frank and Ivy Batchelor. The story of this farm is particularly interesting.

In 1920 Frank Batchelor, then a twenty-one-year-old bookkeeper, purchased on very easy terms from two uncles, a 46-ha piece of their farm *Craighall.* This section of the farm he named *The Firs* and there he made a living by growing strawberries and gladioli. The venture was a success but at the same time he became aware of an unfortunate sequence of events. The Devon Valley had always been a paradise for wild flowers. The rare *Gladiolus blandus* (painted ladies) had the valley as their natural home while proteas, erica and pincushions provided such dazzling displays that the spectacle was almost fatal to themselves. Vandals descended on the flowers with a frightening determination to utterly destroy them by means of shovels and picking hands. The spread of cultivation in the valley and the building of roads threatened the flowers with complete destruction. The dismal sight of all this change gave Frank Batchelor the idea of conserving the last of the valley's wild flowers by propagating them in a sanctuary of his own where visitors could see, but not harm them. With this object, in 1944, he bought 24 ha of the farm *Nooitgedacht* and on this he laid out what became *Protea Heights,* a vast garden designed to look as the Western Cape could have looked if all its scattered flower varieties had ever grown together in one place.

In 1953 *Protea Heights* was first opened to the public and thenceforth it became one of the major botanical attractions of the Cape each spring. An enormous number of proteas of many varieties flourish in the sanctuary. *Leucospermum* sp. (pincushions) grow there to perfection while many of the wonderful *Serruria* genera have made the place their home. Amongst them is *Serruria florida*, the delicate blushing bride flower whose original home was in so restricted a part of the Franschhoek mountains that only careful cultivation in gardens such as *Protea Heights* has saved them from extinction. Even with this cultivation, the seed of the blushing bride has a marketable value of over R1 000 for 1 kg and it remains a rare treasure. On *Protea Heights* it not only grows in profusion but, in 1947, with *Serruria aemula* produced a red-tinted hybrid which Mrs Batchelor named the Maid of Honour. In 1976 the Batchelors presented *Protea Heights* to the South African Wild Life Foundation.

Just beyond the turn to *Protea Heights* the tarmac road leading up the valley passes the Devon Valley Hotel.

## Accommodation

★★® Devon Valley Hotel, 21 rooms, all with baths. R12 – R14 B/B. Phone 3814.

One kilometre beyond the turn to the Devon Valley Hotel takes the road into the Devon Valley estate of Bertrams Winery where there is a pleasant picnic ground for visitors.

The grounds of the estate are closed to the public from 13h00 on Saturdays to Monday morning. For the rest of the week, visitors may drive through the estate. Beyond the turnoff to the cellars, the private road continues through a grove of olive trees. At the end of this grove, turn right. The road climbs up the hill slope, revealing a fine panorama of vineyards and mountains. Over the summit, 9 km from the start of the journey, the estate road joins the tarmac Bottelary road from Stellenbosch. A right turn leads for 7,5 km of pleasant travelling back to Stellenbosch. The views from this road of the bulky, magnificent massif of Simonsberg are very fine. A left turn from the junction of the estate road takes the traveller on another pleasant drive along the Bottelary road. The road is so named because it leads along the north slopes of the *Bottelaryberg*, itself named from the farm *Bottelary* (the bottlery or pantry). For 21 km the road leads past several handsome farms, the pleasantly named area of *Koelenhof* (cool garden) and eventually joins the main Bellville-Faure road.

There are three notable farms along this road. At 6,5 km from Stellenbosch there is a turnoff right leading through the rural centre of Koelenhof, and, just across the railway, passing the entrance to the *Simonsig* (Simon's View) estate owned by Frans Malan. This estate combines two adjoining farms, *De Hoop* and *Simonsig*. Visitors are welcome to the cellars at 10h00 and 15h00 on weekdays and at 10h00 on Saturdays. The wines of the estate, including the only bottle-fermented sparkling wine produced in South Africa (Kaapse Vonkel) may be purchased at the cellars during normal daily trading hours.

Along the main Bottelary road, 2 km beyond the turn to Koelenhof, there is a turn left leading to the *Hartenberg* estate of Dr M. Finlayson where the outstanding Montagne range of wines are produced. Tours of the cellar are conducted on Mondays to Saturdays at 10h30; 11h30; 14h30 and 15h45. The wines of the estate may be purchased during normal trading hours.

A half-kilometre beyond the turnoff to *Hartenberg*, takes the road past the cellars of the Bottelary Co-operative Winemakers. Cellar tours can be arranged and the wines made there may be purchased during normal trading hours.

Four kilometres beyond this co-operative, the main road passes a turnoff leading to the estate of *Koopmanskloof* (merchant's ravine), owned by S. Smit. The cellar is open to visitors on Thursdays between 14h00 and 17h00. The wines of the estate may be purchased during normal trading hours.

From Stellenbosch, there is a road leading up the valley of the Eerste River to Jonkershoek, where the river nestles in a most lovely womb of mountains. The drive is not a long one, but leads all the way through superlative scenery, which is beautiful at all seasons, but is especially striking in autumn, when the green leaves of the vines and trees turn the most delicate shades of red, yellow and brown.

*Jonkershoek* apparently takes its name from an early settler in the area, Jan de Jonker. Several of the original graceful old farmhouses built in the glen by the pioneers may still be seen, although suburban development has enveloped much of the land.

After 3 km, there is a turnoff right leading to *Lanzerac*, a handsome cluster of farm buildings erected in 1830 and converted in modern times to one of the most unique hotels in the Western Cape. The same turnoff leads on to the banks of the Eerste River where, amid a forest of oaks, there is a park and picnic area.

The main tarmac road continues up the valley, lined with trees and revealing many pleasant views of farmlands and the towering mountains of Jonkershoek. After 7,5 km the road passes on the left the homestead of *Old Nectar.* This lovely old place was built in 1780 and designed by the famous architect, Louis Thibault. Its present gable was added in 1815. It is a delightful example of a Cape-Dutch farmhouse, complete with the inevitable ghost; this one a conservative character who is never seen but always makes its disapproving presence felt when building alterations, no matter how slight, are made. At such times, loud knockings and irate groanings are said to be heard, and workmen are frightened away. The house, originally named *Nektar,* is now the home of Major-General K. R. van der Spuy, the great authority on the cultivation of roses, and his wife Una, a well-known author of gardening books. The house is a national monument.

Less than 1 km beyond *Old Nectar,* just before the entrance to the grounds of the Department of Nature Conservation, there is a turnoff right leading to a splendid municipal picnicking ground extending for nearly 1 km beneath the trees growing on the right bank of the Eerste River. This picnic ground is one of the loveliest in Southern Africa, and in autumn, when the leaves are falling, as richly coloured as the amber water of the fast-flowing river, the scene is unforgettable.

The main tarmac road enters the grounds of the Department of Nature Conservation 7,5 km from Stellenbosch. This is sacred ground for all lovers of trout and freshwater fishing. In 1893, the Cape Government first rented part of the farm *Jonkershoek,* and a professional pisciculturist, Ernest Latour, was employed there in the construction of ponds for breeding trout. From that time, Jonkershoek became the principal fish hatchery in Africa and one of the best known in the world. From this mother hatchery, many of the streams and rivers of Southern and East Africa received their trout populations. The Eerste River itself, flowing through the grounds of the hatchery, is one of the best trout streams in Southern Africa, and offers particularly excellent sport during spring and autumn. The hatcheries may be visited by arrangement with the officials. There is an aquarium open on weekdays 08h30 to 16h30 from 1 October to the end of February each year.

Adjoining the fish hatcheries are the premises of the Division of Fauna and Flora, which house some interesting exhibits for the public. The road ends at the gate to the grounds of the Forestry Department, and a free permit is necessary in order to proceed further up the valley. These permits are more readily available during the winter (1 April to 31 October) because of the reduced fire hazard, but at no time are cooking fires permitted. The permits give the holder the privilege of proceeding around a superb circular drive, leading for 6 km up the valley and then down the other side to the entrance gate. Despite the gravel road, the drive is delightful. At the bridge where the road crosses the river and turns back is the start of a path which meanders up the left bank of the river, providing a fine walk.

Masses of wild flowers (especially proteas) throng on both sides of the path. It passes what is known as First Waterfall on the right, and then, after 4 km, reaches the gorge of the Second Waterfall on the right. At this point, the path branches. One branch fords the stream and continues to the head of the valley, over the divide, and then down into the valley of the Riviersonderend. This is a strenuous two-day walk, which eventually ends at the Highlands Forestry Station and the road to Elgin. It forms the Hottentots Holland Wilderness Trail.

The right-hand branch leads up the gorge to the Second Waterfall. Here the scenery is exquisite with a succession of pools, waterfalls and masses of ferns. The course of the path is complicated, and some simple climbing is necessary to avoid several cascades. Perseverance is well rewarded when the path reaches the head of the gorge in an amphitheatre where the superb Second Waterfall plummets for 100 m. When the author first visited this fall in 1957, there was a deep pool at its foot, into which he dived and swam. However, on a return visit one year later, he found that a landslide had completely entombed the pool, filling it with boulders. The waterfall, however, is still beautiful, and fine contra-light photographs may be taken of it from the slopes above the landslide to the left. The morning is the best time to take these.

The whole Jonkershoek area is superb for walkers and climbers. The 1 495-m-high Jonkershoek Twins are the dominant heights, providing some complex climbing for mountaineers and fine scenery for photographers.

---

Another very interesting drive from Stellenbosch is along the tarmac road leading for 12 km to Klapmuts and the main road, which links Cape Town to Paarl and the north. This road makes its way through some of the very best Cape scenery, passing many neat farmlands on the slopes of the 1 390-m-high Simonsberg, whose classic shape provides this part of the world with a great landmark.

Two kilometres from Stellenbosch, there is a turn right leading to the buildings of the Nietvoorbij Research Institute for Viticulture and Oenology. This is the principal centre for study and research on the culture of the grape and the production of wine in South Africa. Quality, standards and certification are done from here. The national wine museum is housed in the Institute.

Three and a half kilometres from Stellenbosch the road passes the Beverley Hills Hotel, and after 7 km there is a turn right into the foothills of Simonsberg and the outlying peak known as *Kanonkop* (cannon summit), once used as a signal point. Along the road there are several fine wine estates, whose owners welcome visitors and sell wines directly from the cellars. *Muratie* (ruins) is one of these estates. Paul Canitz, the artist, acquired this place, and on his death his daughter continued to produce a range of excellent wines there. The cellars can be visited on Thursdays from 14h00 to 17h00, or by appointment. Wine may be bought during normal trading hours, but not on holidays or Sundays.

Just beyond *Muratie* lies the *Driesprongh* (three forks of the river) estate of Delheim Wines (Pty) Ltd, owned by Hans Hoheisen and his nephew, the well-known winemaker, 'Spatz' Sperling. Mrs Hoheisen was the 'Dela' of *Delheim,* the *'heim'* meaning 'home'. The range of wines is outstanding. Guided tours through the cellars take place on Saturdays at 11h00 and daily during the December and January holiday season. Wine may be bought on the estate during normal daily trading hours, but not on holidays or Sundays.

Back again on the main road to Klapmuts, very shortly after the turnoff just followed, there is a turnoff left which leads to the Elsenberg Agricultural College, *Simonsig* wine estate, the rural centre of Koelenhof, and then after 3,5 km, it joins the Bottelary road to Stellenbosch.

Eight and a half kilometres from Stellenbosch on the Klapmuts road a turnoff stretches left to Muldersvlei and Elsenburg. The road then climbs through a lovely vale and reaches the summit of the saddle of land connecting Simonsberg massif to the outlying 522-m-high point known from its shape as *Klapmutskop.* A *klapmuts* was a type of cap worn by Dutch sailors in former years. The road descends over this saddle into the valley of the Berg River, passing estates such as *Wiesenhof* with its range of wine and a game park, and the turnoff (12 km from Stellenbosch) to *Backsberg* wine estate and Simondium. After a further 1,5 km the road reaches the rural centre of Klapmuts and joins the main road from Cape Town to Paarl. This area is described in the chapter on the Berg River Valley.

## Accommodation
★ Beverley Hills Hotel, 25 rooms, all with baths. R10,50 B/B. Phone 7-0145.

From Stellenbosch, there is another tarmac road leading into the Berg River Valley; this one leads over the pass known as *Helshoogte* (precipitous heights). The drive along this road is one of the great scenic routes of the Cape, and part of what is known as the Four Passes circular drive from Cape Town to Stellenbosch, over the Helshoogte Pass to the Berg River Valley, then over the Franschhoek Pass to the upper Riviersonderend Valley, then over the Viljoen Pass to Elgin, and finally back to Cape Town down Sir Lowry's Pass.

The road over Helshoogte starts climbing as it leaves Stellenbosch, at the point where another road branches off left and leads for 4 km up what is known as Ida's Valley, after one of the farms there. This road, a short but pleasant drive, ends at *Rustenburg* farm.

The main road climbs through the Coloured township of Ida's Valley and passes the Bergplaas Holiday Resort. Four and a half kilometres from Stellenbosch, there is a gravel road branching left which leads for a short distance to a locked gate. From this point there is a walk of nearly 1 km up to the Ida's Valley reservoir, from where some very impressive views of Simonsberg can be seen, especially from across the water.

The summit of the Helshoogte Pass is reached 7,5 km from Stellenbosch. From here there is a fine view of Simonsberg, the Berg River Valley, the magnificent pile of the Groot Drakenstein mountains on the right and, directly ahead, across the valley, the flat summit of the Wemmershoek table mountain. After pausing to admire the scenery, the traveller begins the descent into the fertile valley of the Berg River, to which a separate chapter is devoted.

## Caravans and camping
★★ Bergplaas Holiday Resort, 40 sites. R4,50 D.

From Stellenbosch, two tarmac roads lead down the shallow valley of the Eerste River: one road keeps to the right-hand side and leads to Cape Town, and the other leads down the left-hand side to Somerset West. The tremendous fertility of the valley is evident from both roads, and they pass the grounds of several famous vineyards and estates.

The road to Somerset West leads southwards from its intersection with Dorp Street, in the centre of Stellenbosch. After 4 km there is a turn left, leading for 1 km to the Coloured township of Webers Valley. Just beyond this turnoff, there is another one, leading to the estate of *Blaauwklippen* (blue stones), which boasts an imposing Cape-Dutch farmhouse, built in an 'H'-shape, with some very graceful gables. The present owner, Graham Boonzaier, maintains the homestead in an immaculate state. He has built up an interesting private museum, and runs a cheese factory, producing 'Country Blue' cheese. Visitors are welcome from Mondays to Fridays from 09h30 to 12h00 and 14h30 to 17h00. Wine and cheese are sold on the estate.

Beyond *Blaauwklippen,* the branch gravel road continues to several other farms, notably *Stellenrust* and, after 4 km, the new *Alphen* estate, developed by the Cloete family to replace their old wine producing farmlands now buried beneath housing estates on the Cape Peninsula. Just before *Alphen,* there is a road known as the Stellenrust road, which leads directly back to the main tarmac road to Somerset West.

Less than 1 km further along this main road, there is another branch road turning left; this is known as the Annandale road. It is only 2 km long but provides access to several great estates, including *Alto,* one of the most prestigious of all the red wine-producing estates. *Alto* is not open to the public except by special arrangement with the owner, Mr Piet du Toit. The homestead is Edwardian, and the estate, high (as the name implies) on the slopes of the Helderberg, is superb.

Opposite the Annandale turnoff to *Alto*, there is a turn right leading across the valley of the Eerste River and linking with the main road to Cape Town along the right bank of the river, at Lynedoch. Three and a half kilometres beyond this turn, there is another turn right to Firgrove rural centre; after 1,5 km this turn passes the co-operative wine cellars of De Helderberg, one of the oldest of the co-operative wine cellars, established in 1907. De Helderberg produces a range of very good red and white wines. Wine is sold at the cellars during normal business hours, but not on Sundays or holidays. The cellars can be inspected by arrangement with the manager.

Five kilometres beyond this turn, the main tarmac road reaches a crossroads: ahead lies the main road from Cape Town to Port Elizabeth; to the right lies Firgrove; and 3 km to the left is the town of Somerset West.

––––––––––

The main road from Stellenbosch to Cape Town leads south-west from the town, across the railway line and the Plankenbrug River. Half a kilometre from the Adam Tas Bridge over the river, there is a turnoff right which goes to *Middelvlei*, the imposing estate owned by Mr J. H. Momberg. On this estate, the traditional parrot shoot was held in the days of Simon van der Stel. Today *Middelvlei* is a leading producer of light-bodied red and white wines. It is not open to the public.

Beyond the turn to *Middelvlei*, on the left-hand side, stands the vast complex of cellars belonging to the Stellenbosch Farmers' Wineries. The turnoff right to Devon Valley is opposite the cellars.

Two kilometres from Stellenbosch stand the buildings of the Plant Protection Research Institute, and just beyond, there is a turn right to the wine estate of *Verdun*, owned by J. F. and Kosie Roux. This estate boasts a charming homestead with a notable garden, and produces an excellent range of red and white wines which are sold to the public during normal trading hours, but not on Sundays or holidays. The cellars can be visited at 14h00 and 16h00 on Wednesdays, and 10h00 and 12h00 on Saturdays.

Beyond *Verdun*, 3 km from Stellenbosch, the Cape Town road turns left. Directly ahead is what is known as the *Polkadraai* road, from its sweeping bends. This road leads to Kuils River, passing on the way well-known wine estates such as *Neethlingshof*, named after a quaint local character from the past, 'Lord' Neethling. Today the estate, with its handsome Cape-Dutch farmhouse, is owned by Mr J. Momberg. It produces excellent white and red wines which are sold at the cellars from November to January during normal business hours. For the rest of the year, wine is sold only on Wednesdays during normal business hours. There are no organised tours of the cellar.

Next on the Polkadraai road is a turnoff to the estate of *Overgaauw*, owned by David van Velden, a descendant of Elizabeth Overgaauw, who gave the place its name. A varied range of excellent to outstanding wines is produced on the estate. Wines are sold at the cellars, and visitors are welcome on Wednesdays from 14h00 to 17h00.

Further up the branch road to *Overgaauw* lies the estate of *Uiterwyk*, which has a superb Cape-Dutch farmhouse. The estate is owned by D. de Waal. Wine is sold, and the cellar can be visited from 09h00 to 12h00 on Saturdays. Still further along the Polkadraai road is the estate of *Goedgeloof*, the cellar of which may be visited from Mondays to Fridays at 11h00.

––––––––––

From the junction with the Polkadraai road, the main road to Cape Town continues south-westwards down the valley of the Eerste River. Vineyards and fruit orchards cover the floor of the shallow valley, and several Cape-Dutch farmhouses grace the area. There are two large co-operatives, the Vlottenburg and the Eersterivier, where visitors are welcome. The cellars can be viewed by arrangement, and wine is sold during normal business hours.

The original slave quarters on the estate of *Spier* have been converted into a pleasant licensed restaurant, open Tuesdays to Saturdays from 11h00 to 23h30 and on Sundays from 12h00 to 17h00. *Spier* was originally granted to Arnold Janz, who named it after his home town, Speyer, in Germany. It is now owned by Mr Niel Joubert, who produces some very good wine there which is on sale to the public during normal business hours, and is always available in the restaurant. A second restaurant has also been created in the main farmhouse, known as Jonkershuis. This is open daily from 09h00 to 17h00.

The main road passes the station of Lynedoch with its hotel, and the turnoff which leads across the valley to join the Somerset West road on the east side of the river.

### Accommodation
* Drie Gewels Hotel, 5 rooms, all with baths. R9 B/B. Phone 207.

### Caravans and camping
* Drie Gewels Caravan Park (at hotel), 25 sites. R3 D. 22 cottages, R8 D.

The road continues past the hotel down this fertile and pleasant valley. On the left-hand side of the road lies the magnificent farm of *Meerlust* (sea longing) owned by the Myburgh family who produce outstanding wine there. The homestead is dated 1776 and is said to be haunted by the wistful ghost of a young woman occasionally seen arranging cut flowers in the early mornings or standing at the windows looking at the view. The pigeon loft is a national monument. The dam on the farm attracts a considerable variety of water birds at all seasons.

At 13,5 km from Stellenbosch, the road crosses the Bellville-Somerset West railway and road. Two kilometres further on, the road passes the farm of *Vergenoegd* (far enough) owned by the Faure family whose winemaking is renowned. The homestead was built in 1773. It is said that the artisan who put the name of the farm on the gable could not spell, making it *Vergenoegt*. The slave bell and outbuildings are notably beautiful.

Beyond *Vergenoegd* the road joins the main Cape Town-Port Elizabeth road at a point 30,5 km from its start near Groote Schuur Hospital in Cape Town. Across the junction point with this major highway a tarmac road continues to Swartklip (5,5 km) on the shores of False Bay, and from there a beautiful scenic drive follows the coast to Muizenberg, 19 km away.

## Chapter Six

# THE BERG RIVER VALLEY

It was in the year 1687 that the renowned Governor of the Cape, Simon van der Stel, decided it was time to effect a settlement in the valley where the Berg River has its headwaters in the superb cluster of mountains north of Stellenbosch. For this purpose, 23 men who fancied themselves as pioneers were gathered in Stellenbosch. At daybreak on 16 October, accompanied on horseback by Van der Stel and his attendants, the party made its way up the slopes of Helshoogte, probably following much the same route as the present road does to the summit. And it was at the summit that they paused and looked down, as modern travellers do, at a scene which has stopped (for a little while) the hearts of countless people, in the course of their journey over this same road.

It was early one lovely spring morning that Van der Stel and his men first saw this valley. It must have seemed like a dream; richly covered in vegetation, with proteas, erica, everlastings, and the delicate blushing brides waving a welcome in the wind; waterfalls tumbling down from the surrounding heights, while the Berg River, its water the colour of amber wine stained by the soil of the Cape, meandering along the floor of the valley, ornamenting it with many deep pools and calm reflections.

Flowing down to the Berg River from the Helshoogte summit was a tributary, the Dwars. It was along the banks of this tributary and the Berg River that the fortunate 23 pioneers secured their farms. Each farm was about 50 ha in extent, fronted by the river. To these farms the settlers brought their families and began the task of building homes, planting trees and laying out lands.

To the area, never before tilled by the hand of man, Van der Stel applied the name of *Drakenstein* (dragon rock) after the great estate in Holland of the lords of Mydrecht.

During the following year (1688) the 23 pioneers of the valley were joined by a band of 176 French Huguenot refugees who had fled from religious persecution in their own country. To the lovely Drakenstein Valley these newcomers added a subtle French atmosphere and their skill in winemaking soon gave the area a particular renown.

Some of the most romantically beautiful farmhouses in the world were built in this valley: *Bien Donné* (well bestowed); *La Rhône; Boschendal* (bush and dale); *Languedoc; La Motte; De Goede Hoop; Bellingham; Terre de Luc* (land of Luke); *L'Ormarins; Bethlehem; Champagne; Lekkerwyn; Delta; Werda; Zondernaam; Weltevreden; La Paris; L'Arc D'Orleans; La Provence; La Brie; Bourgogne; La Dauphine;* and many other serene pieces of pastoral architecture. In these homesteads lived the forebears of some of the most numerous families in Southern Africa today: the Lombards, Fouchés, De Villiers, Du Plessis, Jouberts, Rousseaus, Nels, Rouxs, Malans and others whose present numbers are proof of the virility of their ancestors.

At the time of the first settlement of the Drakenstein Valley the area around the head of the Helshoogte Pass was a rugged mountain wilderness, dangerous for its wild animals as well as its heights. It was known as *Banghoek* (fearful corner) but its old terrors have long since vanished. The modern road twists down through scenery which is peaceful and lovely at any time of the year but is especially spectacular in spring and autumn.

One and a half kilometres below the summit of the pass there is a turnoff right (opposite the Banghoek Garage) which leads for just over a kilometre to the fine old farmhouse of *Zeven*

*Rivieren* (seven rivers). Immediately before reaching the farmhouse, the tarmac divides into two gravel roads. The branch to the left leads through the trees for 3 km before ending at *Wentworth* farm. The branch to the right leads for 4,5 km up the valley of the Banghoek River to farms such as *Rainbow* (the highest farm) and *Pear Tree* (the furthest farm up the valley). This is a mixed farming area. In spring the spectacle of the fruit trees (mainly plum, pear and peach) in blossom is superb. In autumn the late grape varieties – barlinka and prune de cazoul – turn the slopes scarlet with the colour of their leaves while the almeria vines (especially on *Wentworth)* are golden. Against the blue background of the Groot Drakenstein mountains to the right and the Simonsberg to the left, these colours are sensational.

The main road descending into the Drakenstein Valley leads for 4 km beyond the Banghoek turnoff, passes the wayside Samburgh Inn and then reaches the Dutch Reformed Church mission of *Pniel* (the face of God), established in 1843. This is now a substantial settlement of Coloured people who work on the many great fruit farms in the vicinity. Next to the mission church, on the left-hand side of the road, is a short tarmac drive leading to the beautiful homestead of *De Goede Hoop* and its finely preserved cluster of Cape-Dutch style buildings, outhouses and original slave bell.

The signs at the turnoffs to various farms – *Bethlehem, Rhône, Languedoc, Boschendal* – all indicate they are now part of the Rhodes Fruit Farms Ltd. At 17 km from Stellenbosch, the road crosses the railway line at Groot Drakenstein station and joins the main road running the length of the valley, passing at the intersection the central fruit-packing sheds of this substantial and historic organisation.

## Accommodation

★ Samburgh Inn, 5 rooms, all with baths. R10 B/B. Phone Stellenbosch 2548.

# THE DRAKENSTEIN VALLEY

The Drakenstein Valley was the actual birthplace of the deciduous fruit export industry in Southern Africa. From the time of the first settlement in the Cape, fruit was produced and eaten with relish, but the only way in which such products could be exported was in dried form (principally raisins) or bottled as wine and brandy.

Refrigeration was not even a dream in the minds of inventors. Only one method of preserving grapes was devised. Some farmer (perhaps a man excessively fond of that delicately flavoured muscatel, the hanepoot) discovered that this grape could be preserved for several months if bunches with long stems full of sap were cut. The tips of the stems were sealed with pitch or beeswax and the bunches were hung in the cool attics beneath the thatched roofs of the farmhouses. In such conditions the grapes would preserve their deliciously sweet and slightly musky flavour.

This ingenious dodge was actually the basis of the export fruit industry of Southern Africa. In the year 1886, at a time when the volume of fruit grown in the Cape so far exceeded the local demand that it was hardly worth the trouble of picking, somebody, writing under the *nom-de-plume* of 'Old Salt', suggested in a letter to the *Cape Times* that the original idea of preserving grapes could surely be used to achieve their export. The letter produced rapid results. Two months later, in April 1886, the *Cape Times* reported that a Dr Smuts had successfully transported to London several boxes of grapes with the stems of the bunches sealed with beeswax. The flavour of the grapes was superb and with prices in London reaching 15s. per lb compared to the 1d. per lb (roughly R1,50 compared to 1c) on the Cape Town market, this successful experiment was like a glimpse of heaven to the fruit growers of Southern Africa.

There was a great stirring in the farmhouses of the Cape. Many experiments were made and two years later the Reverend Mr Legg made the first attempt to export a consignment of peaches in the cramped cold store of the *Grantully Castle*. The attempt was a failure but the idea was fascinating to ship owners as well as to farmers. What a profitable new high-tariff cargo could be found for their ships if peaches, pears, plums, apricots, apples and citrus, as well as grapes, could be made to survive the lengthy voyages of the day.

Brilliant confirmation of the whole idea came on 2 February 1892. Percy Molteno, manager of the Castle Steamship Company, contrived, by means of the cold store of the *Drummond Castle,* to land in Britain, the first Cape peaches to be successfully exported. Fourteen trays of beautiful peaches survived the long journey to perfection. The peaches received such an ovation on the Covent Garden market, selling for 2s. 3d. (about 25c) each, that they might have been prima donnas in the nearby opera, with the applause being the merry tinkle of the cash register echoing all the way back to the farming valleys of the Cape.

But there were many heartbreaks to come. The cold stores on ships were hopelessly small and quite unsuitable for preserving fruit. Everything had yet to be learned about the delicate art of selective picking, pre-cooling and handling. Worst of all, the available fruit varieties were not very suitable for the highly competitive export trade. Pernickety palates overseas had their special preferences and few of the local varieties produced in carefree fashion in the Cape quite measured up to international standards.

In the midst of these tentative ventures into the export markets, disaster struck the grape farmers. A bacterial disease known as phylloxera reached the Cape. This bacteria had first attacked the vineyards of the United States in 1854, then spread to France in 1863, and, notwithstanding stringent controls, appeared in the Cape vineyards in 1886. The grape farmers were ruined. There was just no answer to the disease apart from the total replacement of all vines by phylloxera-immune American stocks.

Fate, however, produced a man for the occasion. In 1889 a young Englishman, Harry Ernest Pickstone, came to South Africa for military service. He liked what he saw of the country – its space, sunshine and opportunity – and decided to make the place his home. However, on his return to England at the end of his military service, he was attracted to California by the gold rush but finding no gold, worked instead as a nurseryman in a climate and landscape which irresistibly reminded him of his first love, South Africa.

In 1892, therefore, Pickstone returned to the Cape as a man of destiny. He had an introduction to Cecil Rhodes and to that renowned individual the young man expounded a particular dream which was close to his heart. It was a dream of planting in the waiting soil of Southern Africa, the finest fruit gathered from all over the world. With these varieties he would experiment to find those most suited to local conditions. He would search for, and systematically breed, new types perfectly adapted to this land and, while the engineers solved the problems of pre-cooling, cold storage and transport, he would find the ideal fruit.

Supported by Rhodes, Harry Pickstone and his brother Horace settled in the Drakenstein Valley and began the famous nursery which has mothered so many of the great commercial varieties of export fruit of Southern Africa. By 1896 Pickstone's trees were flourishing and Rhodes entered the fruit business with spectacular enthusiasm. He instructed Pickstone to buy up, if possible, the whole of the Drakenstein Valley. It was an order which must have staggered the young nurseryman but he set to work. Within a year, 29 of the magnificent Drakenstein Valley farms had been acquired. They were moulded together to form the block of the Rhodes Fruit Farms, with nearly every unit of the group preserving on its grounds, in immaculate condition, the original Cape-Dutch style homestead. Around these farmhouses stretch the great orchards of pear, plum and peach trees whose luscious fruit, carried each summer season to many far countries by refrigerated train and ship, will always remind us in their perfection of the painstaking work of Harry Pickstone and the faith of Cecil Rhodes.

The formation of Rhodes Fruit Farms as a company was only achieved on 25 March 1902, with the formalities concluded by Rhodes's partners in the project, Leander Starr Jameson, Sir Charles Metcalfe and E. R. Syfret, gathered around his sick bed in his Muizenberg cottage. It was the last project of Rhodes to reach fulfilment, for he died the following day.

Rhodes's holding company, De Beers, managed the farms, commissioned the first canning factory in time for the 1905-1906 season, and in 1911 made the first profit from the enterprise. During the depression years of the late 1920s several of the farms were sold. Amongst these was *Bien Donné,* which was acquired by the government as a research farm. In 1936, Sir Abe Bailey bought Rhodes Fruit Farms but he died in 1941 and the company was then acquired by a syndicate of four men, E. J. Crean, A. B. M. McDonald, S. J. Richards and G. H. Starck. In 1969, however, a majority shareholding in the company was acquired by the Anglo American Corporation, in conjunction with De Beers and Rand Selection Corporation Ltd. Once again the farms were under the control of the financial interests directly descended from Rhodes.

Rhodes Fruit Farms now consists of a 3 000-ha block of 17 farms, all united in the production of fresh and canned fruit, jams, fresh juice concentrates and wine under the Boschendal label. Pigs and cows are also kept. Their ham, bacon and the milk from a magnificent herd of Ayrshires is a rich product of the company while the manure fertilises the agricultural lands. The whole complex industry, its details controlled by a computer, produces 10 000 tons of fruit and grapes each year, of which 60 per cent are exported. The canning and juice concentrate plants take in still more fruit bought from neighbouring areas and process over 11 000 tons each year. From November to March harvesting is in full swing with about 1 400 people employed in picking, packing and processing. An interesting feature of the estate is the housing of the workers. A village of 110 cottages was designed by the celebrated architect, Sir Herbert Baker, and named Languedoc, with a modern extension added, known as New Languedoc. This village is worth seeing, for compared with the usual dreadful municipal sub-economic housing estates, it is a delight.

The historic homesteads of *De Goede Hoop, Weltevreden, Boschendal, La Rhône* and *Bethlehem,* are all immaculately maintained and each seems to be lovelier than the other. *Boschendal* has been completely renovated together with all the outbuildings, including a most fascinating poultry house (a real palace for aristocratic birds), and the whole place declared a national monument in 1976. The superb interior of this homestead is notable for its friezes adorned with acorn patterns, and the graceful gable. It was built in 1812 by Paul de Villiers and remained in the possession of the De Villiers family until it was bought by Rhodes. Like most of these old Cape homesteads, it has its ghost. The *Boschendal* ghost is a wire-haired terrier puppy who joyfully scampers in at the front of the house and out through the back, in complete silence, except for the patter of its feet on the floor. People have often reported seeing it, generally just after midnight.

Boschendal is now a restaurant, while the neighbouring homestead of *La Rhône* has in its outbuildings the cellar for Boschendal wines and a taphouse where wines can be tasted and bought by the public. The public is invited to join an association known as *Die Geselskap van Vrye Wynburgers van Boschendal,* which offers preferential buying rights to wine, and the privilege of attending various social functions on the estate. The Boschendal restaurant is open daily for lunch. It is closed at night. Phone 0251-4252.

---

The upper (eastern) reaches of the Drakenstein Valley have many interesting and beautiful farms, scenes and places. From the intersection where the road from Stellenbosch joins it, the main road up the valley leads through a fine avenue of trees. On either side there are vineyards and orchards, while the towering, red-coloured sandstone cliffs of the Groot Drakenstein mountains dominate the valley from the western side.

After 1,5 km the road crosses the Dwars River tributary of the Berg. The entrances to several handsome farms lead off from the road. One of the most interesting, 3 km beyond the bridge, is the wine estate of *Bellingham,* the proud possession of Captain J. B. Podlashuk, who acquired the property just after the Second World War. By careful development, much personal enthusiasm and shrewd promotion, he created on this estate a range of wines of considerable renown. Wines are not sold from the cellar but the products are widely distributed. Visitors must make an appointment (phone Wellington 31001) if they wish to visit the estate.

The *Bellingham* estate is the producer of a vast quantity of deciduous and citrus fruit, especially lemons. Captain Podlashuk has bequeathed his estate to the Huguenot Society of South Africa, thereby ensuring its preservation, with its farming operation maintaining the homestead and contributing to the funds of various universities.

A little over 1 km beyond the entrance to *Bellingham* there is a turnoff left leading to the Waterval caravan and camping site laid out beneath wattle trees growing on the banks of the Berg River, where there is river swimming and fishing.

### Caravans and camping
Waterval Caravan Park, 150 sites. R2 D.

The main road crosses the Berg River just beyond the caravan park and less than 1 km further on reaches the entrance to a spacious and beautiful picnic ground maintained by the Forestry Department. This resort, laid out under the shade of trees on the banks of a stretch of the Berg River, is open from 10h00 to sunset on weekends and public holidays, and daily during school holiday periods. Admission is 20c per person. No overnight camping is allowed.

Half a kilometre beyond this picnic ground, the main road reaches a junction with a tarmac road coming from Paarl past the Wemmershoek Dam. This road is described on page 106.

The main road continues up the valley and 2 km beyond the Wemmershoek junction it passes the farm, store and butchery of La Motte. Another kilometre takes the road past the buildings of the La Motte Forestry Station, the centre for an extensive afforestation of the upper catchment area of the Berg River in what is known as the *Assegaibosch Kloof* (assegai bush ravine).

There is a 13-km drive up the right bank of the river through this beautiful cleft in the mountains. A permit must be obtained from the forestry office for this worthwhile drive. The Berg River has its birth high up where the Groot Drakenstein mountains meet the Jonkershoek range in country so wild and broken that few men have even drunk from the cold spring at the river's source. The vigorous young river leaps down in a spectacular fall, and during the rainy season, what seem to be dozens of tributary streams all race to join it in its course through this lovely valley.

The river swells rapidly in size. Overlooked by the gaunt cliffs of the Franschhoek mountains, with dense stands of trees crowding its banks, the river tumbles off, leapfrogging a long chain of pools which lie like a necklace of amber beads, each linked on the thread made by the flurry of white-water cascades. Ferns, orchids and wild flowers galore all find sanctuary here, while fat trout lurk in the pools.

---

From the turnoff to this forestry area, the main road continues its own way up the valley of a tributary of the Berg River, past the farm *La Provence* and the hamlet of La Roux Dorp and then, 15 km from the point where the Stellenbosch road joins it at Groot Drakenstein railway station, it reaches the town of . . .

# FRANSCHHOEK

Named after the Huguenot settlers who pioneered this valley, *Franschhoek* (French glen) is a straggling little town with a population of 2 656. It became a municipality in 1881. After the beauty of Stellenbosch and the drive up the Drakenstein Valley, Franschhoek is something of an anti-climax with its one nondescript street denuded of trees. There are the usual shops, garages, an imposing church, a public park and swimming pool and, at the far end of the road, the *pièce de resistance* of the town, the impressive Huguenot Memorial and museum. The monument was erected to mark the 250th year (1938) of the Huguenots' arrival in the valley. The central figure is a woman standing with a Bible in her right hand and a broken chain in her left hand symbolising freedom from religious oppression. This is the work of the sculptor, Coert Steynberg. The three arches behind her represent the trinity and the globe at her feet leaves her poised in the regions of the spirit. Above the arches shines the sun of righteousness tipped by the cross. The reflection pool below expresses tranquillity experienced after great strife. Against the handsome background of the mountains the monument is effective and beautiful. The adjoining museum was opened in 1965. The building housing it is an exact reconstruction of the homestead, *Saasveld,* the Cape Town house belonging to Baron van Reede van Oudtshoorn, built in 1791. This house was demolished and as much of the material as possible was bodily removed to its present site, when property development in Cape Town made its destruction inevitable. The museum contains items concerned with the history of the Huguenots. The Huguenot Memorial and museum stands in a very lovely garden, especially notable for its roses which bloom during the summer months. Entrance is free except on Saturdays, Sundays and public holidays when 20c per person is charged for admission to the museum, which is open Mondays to Saturdays 09h00 to 17h00; Sundays 14h00 to 17h00. There is an extension to the museum housed in an elegant example of modern construction situated across the road from the original building.

The Franschhoek Wine Cellars Co-operative Ltd has its cellars in Franschhoek. Wine is sold to the public Mondays to Fridays, 08h00 to 17h00.

## Accommodation
★ Huguenot Hotel, 12 rooms, 6 with baths. R7,30 – R7,80 B/B. Phone 2092.

Immediately before the Huguenot Memorial the main road divides. The right turn leads for 3 km to several farms such as *La Dauphine* and *Burgundy* in the southern cul-de-sac of the valley. The tarmac road ends at the handsome Swiss-style building of the Swiss Farm Excelsior Hotel, with its swimming bath and fine garden. A 5-km gravel road branch from the tarmac road leads past estates such as *Champagne* (well known for its honey) and ends at *Robertsvlei* farm which is situated in a handsome bowl in the mountains.

## Accommodation
★★ Swiss Farm Excelsior Hotel, 46 rooms, 30 with baths. R13,50 – R16 D. Phone 2071/2.

The main road turns left at the Huguenot Memorial and begins climbing the Franschhoek Pass. This fine pass is justifiably famous for the beauty of its views as well as for the skill involved in its construction. It was originally a trail known as the *Oliphantspad* (elephant's path) and used from time immemorial by migrating herds of game. This was the start which many of the mountain passes of Southern Africa had. The game animals unerringly found the line of least resistance across the mountains and man simply followed in their tracks. In 1819 one of the settlers of the Drakenstein Valley, by the name of Cats, received a government contract to convert the old game trail into a proper road open to wagons. Four years later the Catspad (as it was called) was improved by a military party under Major Holloway and this remained the route until the 1930s when a new road with an easier gradient was built. In 1965 work was completed on relocating and bituminising the pass and today it provides a magnificent 6-km drive from the Huguenot Memorial to the summit, 520 m above the level of Franschhoek.

On the summit of the pass there is a track leading left for a short distance to an old forestry cottage. From there a path climbs northwards into the mountains and provides walkers and mountaineers with access to the Wemmershoek range of mountains. Wild flowers are very numerous here in spring.

The Franschhoek Pass descends for 7,5 twisting kilometres on its eastern side, bridges the stream at the foot of the pass, and then enters the basin in the mountains in which the *Riviersonderend* (river without end) has its headwaters. This basin in the mountains lacks the fertility of the Drakenstein Valley and by comparison appears arid although it is improved by the presence of the Teewaterskloof Dam. The road skirts its north-eastern fringes, passing the picnic grounds at the old toll and, 10 km from the bottom of the pass, reaches a junction; a left turn leads to Villiersdorp; a right turn crosses the Riviersonderend, divides again, with a left-hand branch wandering off towards Caledon, and a right-hand branch crossing the floor of the bowl passing many pleasant sheep runs and fruit orchards, and eventually leading to Elgin and back to Cape Town down Sir Lowry's Pass. This area is described on page 261.

---

Back in the Drakenstein Valley, it is interesting to explore the road which leads down the northern side of the valley to Paarl. From its branch 8 km from Franschhoek, this tarmac road first passes a state sawmill and then, after 1 km, the entrance to the recreational resort named *De Hollandsche Molen* (The Dutch Mill), much frequented by Capetonians during summer as a refuge from the south-easter. This resort is extensive with a large river-fed swimming pool. The place was founded just before the Second World War when a Dutch master builder, A. W. Diepering, discovered the site and built a tearoom there in the form of a windmill. The sails of this structure have long since been blown away but the odd building remains and provides an unusual restaurant decorated with a collection of Dutch prints and oddments.

**Caravans and camping**
* De Hollandsche Molen, 200 sites. R4 D plus 20c D per person. 20 flats, R9 D. Phone Franschhoek 2704.

Less than 1 km beyond De Hollandsche Molen, there is a turnoff leading to the Wemmershoek Dam which is one of the principal suppliers of pure mountain water to Cape Town and other parts of the Western Cape Province. The dam was opened in January 1958 and is notable for a 518-m-long earth wall made watertight with a thick clay core. The dam, 52 m deep in places, covers 308 ha. Across the water, fine views may be seen of the various peaks of the Wemmershoek mountains, particularly impressive in winter when covered with snow.

A permit obtainable in Cape Town from the municipal booking office is required to visit Wemmershoek Dam. There are picnic sites below the wall of the dam and trout fishing is allowed in the river.

From the turn to the Wemmershoek Dam, the road continues through well-wooded and fertile farming country. Passing the lovely old homesteads of *L'Arc D'orleans* and *La Paris,* and the unlovely Victor Verster Prison, the road, 7,5 km from its start, reaches the turnoff to Safariland, a game park and holiday resort. A further 4 km takes the road past the Paarl municipal caravan park of Wateruintjiesvlei (see page 112). At 12,5 km the road passes under the main Cape Town-Johannesburg road and enters the municipal area of Paarl.

**Accommodation**
Safariland Game Park, 12 cottages, R15 – R20 D.

The main road down the Drakenstein Valley, which the road from Stellenbosch joined at Groot

Drakenstein station 15 km from Franschhoek, leads down the southern side of the valley, the floor of which is covered with pine plantations, vineyards and orchards, while the pleasant scene is dominated from the south by the great bulk of Simonsberg.

Less than 1 km along the road there is a gravel turnoff leading to one of the most beautiful of all the homesteads of the Cape, *Bien Donné,* now the experimental farm of the Fruit and Food Technology Research Institute. Visitors may view the homestead but entrance to the experimental orchards and vineyards requires special permission.

After 2 km of travel the main tarmac road reaches the hamlet of *Simondium,* named after Pierre Simond, the minister and head of the original Huguenot community. The place comprises a huddle of shops, post office, garage, church and hotel.

### Accommodation
★ Simondium Hotel, 8 rooms, 3 with baths. R5 – R5,50 B/B. Phone Paarl 4382.

From Simondiurn there is a tarmac road turning off to *Bien Donné* 3 km away. Less than 1 km after leaving Simondium, there is a turnoff left leading for 8,5 km to join the Klapmuts-Stellenbosch road. At 3 km along this road there stands the lovely farmhouse of *Babylonstoren,* the possession of the Louw family for several generations. Just beyond this farmhouse, there is a turnoff to the wine estate of *Backsberg,* one of the finest vineyards in the Cape.

# BACKSBERG

The farm *Klein Babylonstoren* (little tower of Babylon) was named after the hillock which dominates it. In 1916, Charles Back acquired this estate. With an expert manager, John Martin, he and his son Sydney developed it skilfully until its 162 ha of vines (55 per cent red varieties) became one of the most notable producers of fine quality wine in the Cape. Drip irrigation, with each vine receiving 9 l of water twice a week, is used on the farm and incessant care and labour has produced superb vineyards, a modern cellar and an outstanding range of wines whose quality reflects something of the pleasant atmosphere of the estate. There is an interesting little museum containing winemaking implements and a very amusing series of cartoons featuring 'Bull'. Visitors are welcome. Guided tours are conducted through the cellar, with the process of winemaking illustrated throughout the year by means of closed-circuit television.

Wine is sold on the estate Mondays to Fridays 08h00 to 18h00 and Saturdays 08h00 to 13h00, public holidays included. With over 40 000 people visiting the estate each year, and many sending orders through the post, almost the entire production of *Backsberg* is sold direct to the public.

The road from Simondium, which leads past the entrance to *Backsberg,* joins the Klapmuts-Stellenbosch road after another 5 km. The hamlet of Klapmuts and the junction with the main Cape Town-Johannesburg road lies less than a kilometre to the right. On the left is the beautiful 12-km drive to Stellenbosch. The Stellenbosch side of the road has been described on page 96. On the Klapmuts side, as the road climbs the saddle of land connecting Simonsberg to the outlying Klapmuts hill, the entrance to the estate of *Natte Valleij,* owned by Mr R. A. Külenkampff is passed. On this estate the Wiesenhof Wild Park has been developed on 280 ha of land with a collection of free-roaming game animals, numerous viewsites and drives, a large spring-fed swimming pool, roller skating facilities, a restaurant and a winery selling a number of palatable wines, brandies and other drinks, carrying the Wiesenhof, Natte Valleij, and other labels.

Wiesenhof is open 10h00 to 18h00 daily but closed Wednesdays, Christmas and New Year's Day. The winery maintains normal daily trading hours.

Back on the main road which runs down the Drakenstein Valley, at less than a kilometre beyond the turnoff to Klapmuts, there is a turnoff right leading to the famous nursery of H. E. V. Pickstone & Brother. This nursery is still a very active producer of fruit trees and, as already described, is the true mother of countless orchards scattered all over Southern Africa. Beyond the turnoff to this nursery, the main road passes first the Drakenstein Co-operative Winery and then a series of vineyards, fruit orchards and nurseries, most of whom specialise in roses. In spring this area is particularly beautiful. At 9 km from Groot Drakenstein station, the road passes the turnoff to the riverside resort of Campers Paradise and then leads under the main railway to the north and joins the old main road which enters Paarl.

### Caravans and camping
★★ Campers Paradise, 400 sites. R1 D plus 50c D per person. 21 cottages, flats and rondawels, R5,50 – R8,50 D.

# PAARL

The municipality of *Paarl* (pearl) with its population of 60 051, lies on the banks of the Berg River at the foot of a cluster of giant granite domes which surge 654 m into the sky and provide a remarkable contrasting landmark in a countryside generally dominated by folded ranges of reddish-coloured sandstone.

It was in October 1657 that Abraham Gabbema, a pioneer explorer from the settlement at the Cape, became the first European to reach the valley of the Berg River. The cluster of granite domes, moistened by rain, glistened so much in the sunlight that he named them the *paarl* (pearl) and *diamandt* (diamond) mountains, while the valley in which the town was destined to grow became known as the *Paarlvallei* (pearl valley).

In 1687 the first farms were granted to settlers in the area. *Laborie, Picardie, Goede Hoop, La Concorde* and *Nancy* were settled by French Huguenots in the following year. *Laborie,* on the slopes of the Paarl mountains, is now owned by the K.W.V. who run it as a model wine estate. The restored homestead is used to house guests of the great wine farmers' co-operative and its period furniture is magnificent. With Paarl converting many of the farmlands which formerly surrounded it into housing estates (productive rather of children than of food and drink), it is commendable that an estate such as *Laborie* with its homestead and farmyard facing directly on to the main street of the town, should be preserved as a living reminder of the past.

The town of Paarl had its start in 1720 when a church was built, the long main street laid out and oak trees planted. Several beautiful buildings were erected in this period. One of the best of these to survive is the *Oude Pastorie* (old parsonage) built in 1787. In 1937 the building was bought by the municipality, restored and converted into a cultural museum containing a fine collection of antique furniture, Cape silver, glass, copper and brassware. An interesting curiosity is a lacemaking machine. Visitors should note the lock, handle and bolt on the door at the back of the main room. The museum is open weekdays 09h00 to 12h00 and 14h00 to 17h00. Saturdays 09h00 to 12h00. Closed Sundays and public holidays.

Another interesting old building is the homestead of *Vergenoegd* situated at 188 Main Street. This building is now owned by the Historical Homes of South Africa and is used as a home for the aged. The original yellowwood and stinkwood doors and windows, and the well in the backyard, are features of this place.

Also facing Main Street is the Dutch Reformed *Strooidak* (thatched roof) Church, conse-crated on 28 April 1805 and still in use. The church stands in a spacious, shady churchyard, amid flowerbeds, smooth lawns and cypress trees. The interior, cruciform in shape, is severe in the Calvinist manner but impressive, and contains a fine pulpit, galleries, and a sounding board which must have amplified the words of many sermons. The place is deliciously cool during summers which are notably hot in this town. The famous architect, Thibault, is said to have designed the church and its gables are superb. The rather sunbaked little graveyard contains gabled vaults and some interesting tombstones.

The church is kept locked but visits may be made by request to the church office. There is often somebody working in the grounds or building who will open the door.

A walk through Paarl will reveal several other examples of architecture which survive from different periods. Zeederberg Square contains a variety of buildings in different stages of maintenance, which are worth seeing. Zeederberg House is a two-storeyed brick-built home, with tall, shuttered windows. The *Toringkerk* (tower church) in Main Street is another fine building while, of the various buildings erected in modern times, *La Concorde,* the administrative offices of the K.W.V. and headquarters of the South African Wine Industry, is elegantly beautiful, with a fine entrance graced by some magnificent vines whose leaves turn blood-red in autumn.

One very extraordinary construction in Paarl, unfortunately no longer remains. A miller named Blake had a watermill with a wheel so enormous that it resembled something from the famous Vienna amusement park. Harry Lime might well have taken a turn in it!

Paarl became a municipality on 9 October 1840 and, with the railway reaching the place in 1859, it developed into a substantial and prosperous town, a farming centre, and the home of some specialised industries, notably the working of granite into building stone and tombstones, and the building of wagons and Cape carts. Paarl wagons were renowned and they played a major part in the exploration and development of the whole of Southern Africa. The middle reaches of the Berg River Valley were often known as the *Val du Charron* (valley of wagons) or the *Wagenmakers valleij* (wagon makers' valley) and Paarl inherited this reputation as it grew as a centre for the industry.

Culturally, Paarl played a major part in the establishment of the Afrikaans language. A man from Holland, Arnoldus Pannevis, who taught classical languages at the Paarl Gymnasium, became increasingly aware in the 1870s that, while Dutch was the established language, the vast majority of people could hardly comprehend it. Over the years the common people had lost touch with High Dutch to such an extent, that they had created not simply a dialect, but a new language, Afrikaans.

Pannevis discussed the matter with several of his colleagues and on 14 August 1875, at a meeting in the homestead of Gideon Malherbe (a farmer who was married to the daughter of Dr G. W. van der Lingen, the principal of the Gymnasium) the *Genootskap van Regte Afrikaners* (Institute of True Afrikaners) was formed with the purpose of establishing Afrikaans as a written and accepted language.

With his colleagues, Pannevis worked on the grammar and vocabulary of the language. On 15 January 1876 they launched the first Afrikaans newspaper *Die Patriot,* printed on a simple little press in Malherbe's house. This press was from then on responsible for the production of many books in Afrikaans. It was in Paarl, in January 1896, that the first congress on the language was held and the ultimately successful campaign commenced to establish Afrikaans as an official language of South Africa.

The residence of Gideon Malherbe is now an Afrikaans language museum. It has been perfectly restored, the seven rooms of the upper floor displaying the history of the language while the five rooms on the ground floor are maintained as they were when the Malherbes were in residence from 1860 to 1921. It is a fascinating collection which should be seen by every visitor to Paarl. The Gideon Malherbe Museum is open weekdays 09h00 to 12h00 and 14h00 to 16h30. Saturdays 09h00 to 12h00. Sundays 15h30 to 17h30.

On a commanding viewsite high on the slopes of the Paarl mountains an impressive monument to the Afrikaans language has been erected and is visible for a considerable distance. It is reached by a tarmac road, 5 km long, leading from Main Street just after it passes under the main Cape Town-Johannesburg road at the southern entrance to Paarl.

*Overleaf: A serene example of Cape-Dutch architecture; the white gable of the cellar on Rhône estate in perfect harmony with its surroundings.*

The language monument was designed by Jan van Wijk. It is built of concrete made of local granite and stands in a handsome setting of granite boulders and indigenous trees. The monument has several distinct features: three linked columns symbolise the contribution of the enlightened west; three rounded shapes represent the magic, mystery and tradition of Africa; a low wall depicts the cultural contribution of the Malayan people to Afrikaans; a rising wall merges into a covered corridor leading to a 57-m-high pillar which soars upwards from a spring of clear water at its base. This pillar is hollow, and light from the top pours down to illuminate the water at its base. A second pillar, parallel and close to the language pillar, symbolises the political growth of the Republic of South Africa. The monument was inaugurated on 10 October 1975. The *Taalmonument* (language monument) is open May to October from 09h00 to 18h00. November to April from 08h00 to 20h00.

Today Paarl consists of an amiable mixture of assorted homes, vineyards, old oaks and young jacaranda trees, all gathered along the pivot of a 6-km-long main street which stretches beneath the shade of trees until it loses itself with a sharp right-hand turn into the nondescript, commercial Lady Grey Street.

One kilometre from the start of this main street at the turnoff from the main road to Cape Town, there is a turn left marked Jan Phillips Drive. Jan Phillips was one of the most successful wagonmakers of Paarl. When the project of this fine scenic drive was first mooted, he contributed £5 000 out of the £9 000 used for the construction. The gravel road, opened in 1928, with its 10 km of shady driving and spectacular views of the Berg River Valley, is, in its way, an admirable memorial to the wagons and carts which, built at Paarl, left the tracks of their wheels on countless thousands of kilometres of the pioneer trails of Southern Africa.

Six kilometres along this road lies the camping ground and entrance to the mountain reserve and wild flower garden situated in the sheltered valley of the *Meulwater* (mill water), the stream which once provided power for the watermill. The garden, dedicated to Lil de Villiers, who founded the Paarl Town Beautifying Society in 1931, is one of the finest wild flower reserves in the Cape. Spectacularly positioned on the mountain slopes, its collection of pincushions and proteas is particularly impressive (especially *Leucospermum reflexum*), and in the late spring the masses of red, orange and yellow flowers provide the colour photographer with superlative opportunities.

Just beyond the entrance to the garden the road forks. The right-hand fork is the continuation of the Jan Phillips Drive, leading for a further 4 km along the mountain slopes and yielding magnificent views over the vineyards before it descends to join the tarmac road from Paarl to Malmesbury.

The left-hand fork (after the wild flower reserve) climbs past the camping ground known as Pienaarskamp, and then reaches a fork. The left-hand side leads onwards around the top of the garden and past what is still known as Breakfast Rocks where, in the energetic old days, walkers on what was then only a path, paused to refresh themselves. The habit has for so long been abandoned that the site is now simply and rather unromantically marked by a sign warning visitors not to light fires or pollute water.

Past Breakfast Rocks the road continues climbing and after a total of 3 km reaches a sharp turn at a clump of fir trees. From this point a footpath leads to the top of the granite dome known today as Paarl Rock. There is no means of knowing precisely to what points Gabbema applied his names of *Diamandt and Paarl*. Some speculate that the names apply to the mass of rock known today as *Gladdeklip* (slippery stone) which lies to the left of Paarl Rock (as seen from Paarl), which certainly has a pronounced glitter in wet weather. Others are of the opinion that the names apply to the two high twin domes, nowadays known as Britannia and Gordon's rocks.

The modern Paarl Rock, although substantially lower than the twins behind it, nevertheless dominates the town of Paarl. On the top is a beacon and an old ship's cannon which originally stood on Kanonkop and was used to inform farmers of the *Agter Paarl* (behind Paarl) that shipping had arrived in Table Bay and required fresh provisions. The summit of Paarl Rock is littered with an extraordinary assembly of giant boulders. To the left of the beacon stands a strange, vaulted and hollowed boulder, reputedly once used by a runaway murderer as his hiding place. The smoke from his cooking fires eventually betrayed his retreat. He was arrested and hanged, but his curious hideaway is still haunted by his presence, for the wisp of smoke which betrayed him is said to be occasionally seen rising into the clear air at dawn. Passing beneath this boulder the footpath finds its way to a truly colossal rock, easily visible from all around. The base of this rock is riddled with caves, niches and hollows in which one half expects to find standing a few petrified sentries. The acoustics of the main caves are remarkable – a whisper at the narrow end is augmented and penetrates the full length of the cave. The atmosphere of Paarl Rock is very reminiscent of the Matobo hills in Zimbabwe.

From the parking place at Paarl Rock, the road makes a sharp turn to the right and for a final half kilometre climbs to its terminus at the foot of the two giant granite domes, Britannia (left) and Gordon's (right). A footpath leads to the top of Britannia with chains to provide help on the steeper portions. The view from the summit is impressive and the climb is easy and worthwhile. A very clear echo reflects from the face of Gordon's Rock (which is more difficult to climb). Just beyond the parking area, the footpath to Britannia Rock passes the great leaning rock shelter with its natural rock table (about which there is a legend that poltergeists have been observed playing cards there). At this point, a less-used path branches right and takes the climber up a steep slope, eventually leading to the summit of Gordon's Rock through a narrow cleft with a chimney rather awkward for stout people. A fine view of Britannia Rock, however, rewards the climber. The origin of the name Gordon is obscure; it is said that a young man of that name slipped and was killed on this rock.

From the top of these two granite domes the nature of the surrounding highlands of the Paarl mountains may be seen. Gravel roads provide access to most parts of this highland. It is a catchment area for the Paarl municipal water supply. Wild flowers and small game are numerous in the area and there are several popular camping and picnic grounds such as Tredoux Camp, Christmas Camp, Renosterkop (from a tree stump shaped like a rhino); Oulapklip (where the Oukraal Club of athletic types who walk or run up the mountain have their meeting place); and Waboomkop, the highest point in the Paarl mountains, from whose summit may be seen a tremendous panoramic view. The reservoirs, Nantes and Bethel, built in the valleys leading down to the farms of those names, are stocked with black bass and trout.

Paarl is the headquarters of the K.W.V. (Ko-operatiewe Wijnbouwers Vereniging), founded in 1918 as the great central co-operative of the wine producers of South Africa. Their administrative office, La Concorde, is a notably attractive modern building in the Cape-Dutch style. The frieze over the main entrance, the gateway, gardens, interior, and the vines growing on trellises, all contribute to a sensitive piece of design. Also in Paarl are the cellars of the organisation – colossal temples of Bacchus, heady with the aroma of about 150 million litres of wine, spirits, and Eau de Cologne. From here the export wine and spirit industry of South Africa is controlled.

The K.W.V. has a permanent exhibition devoted to the wine industry. Lectures and wine tastings are presented, and there are conducted tours from Mondays to Fridays at 09h30, 11h00, 14h30 and 15h45. Weekends and public holidays excluded. The homestead of Laborie has been converted into a restaurant and taphouse on traditional lines. A cellar is stocked with the wines of the Berg River Valley which may be purchased.

## Accommodation
★ Adelaar Hotel, 10 rooms, 3 with baths. R6 – R7 B/B. Phone 2-4995.
★ Central Hotel, 18 rooms, 7 with baths. R13 – R28 B/B. Phone 2-2135.
★ International Hotel, 12 rooms, 3 with baths. R5,50 – R6,50 B/B. Phone 2-9188.
★ Picardie Hotel, 38 rooms, 18 with baths. R9 – R11 B/B. Phone 2-3118.

* Ronnies Hotel, 10 rooms, 3 with baths. R8,50 – R9,50 B/B. Phone 2-8011.
* Station Hotel, 11 rooms, 2 with baths. R5,50 – R6,50 B/B. Phone 2-2490.

### Caravans and camping
**® Wateruintjiesvlei Caravan Park, 130 sites. R2 D plus 10c D per person. Phone 2-7552.

From Paarl there are two main tarmac roads running down the valley of the Berg River to Wellington. The road on the western side of the valley branches off from the top of Lady Grey Street and provides a pleasant drive through the northern residential area of Paarl and after 3 km, passes the turnoff to the Jan Phillips mountain road. A further half kilometre takes the road to the branch leading behind the granite mountain to Agter Paarl, and then for 5 km past several fine vineyards and farms. At 8,8 km the road crosses the Durbanville-Wellington road and by turning right over the Berg River bridge, immediately enters Wellington. Continuing down the western side of the valley, the original road also leads into Wellington after 5,5 km (a total of 14 km from Paarl).

The second road to Wellington, travelling down the eastern side of the valley, leads from the bridge over the river at Huguenot station at the bottom end of Lady Grey Street. This road proceeds through the industrial area of *Daljosefat* (dale of Joseph) and reaches Wellington after 10 km of travel. Two kilometres along this road from Paarl, is a turnoff leading to the great wine estate of . . .

# NEDERBURG

The most prestigious wine estate in Southern Africa, *Nederburg,* had its origin in 1792. Sebastiaan Cornelis Nederburgh, chief advocate of the Dutch East India Company, was in that year engaged in the investigation of various complaints, irregularities, abuses and problems in the administration of the Cape. In the course of his inquiry, the chief advocate was aided by Philip Wolvaart, to whom was subsequently granted an estate which he named after Mr Nederburgh. Nowadays the name is spelled without the 'h'.

The homestead of *Nederburg* was built in 1800 and farming commenced on the estate, but a succession of owners failed to raise the place to a position of any considerable eminence. The right man to appreciate the potential of the estate only came in 1937. In that year, a brewer from Bremen in Germany, Johann Georg Graue, acquired *Nederburg.* He was a dedicated, intuitive and eager winemaster and the possibilities of *Nederburg* excited him: lying on the eastern side of the Berg River Valley, the lands of the estate covered part of the foothills of the Klein Drakenstein mountains. There was considerable variation in altitude, soils (sandstone, shale, granite) and directional slopes. The Berg River Valley is a notably hot area in summer but the directional variations influence amounts of sunshine and exposure to the seasonal south-east wind; this wind – warm, unpolluted, healthy and locally rain-free – could vitally influence vine diseases and fungi.

Johann Graue began a detailed study of the estate in all its different parts. He replanted *Nederburg* with the finest vine varieties, especially cabernet sauvignon and riesling. The latest German innovations of control and cellar technique were also introduced, including cold fermentation. Aided by his wife, Ilse and his only son, Arnold, Johann Graue made spectacular progress. By 1953, *Nederburg* had won eight gold medals, 158 first prizes and 104 trophies for excellent wines.

Unfortunately a sad disaster occurred. On 12 September 1953, at Youngsfield aerodrome in Cape Town, a military training plane accidentally landed on top of a light plane taxiing along the runway. The pilot of the light plane was Arnold Graue, then 28 years of age. He was killed and the effect on *Nederburg* was traumatic. For some time Johann Graue thought of letting the whole place go for it was inextricably tied up with memories of his son.

At the time of the accident, the great estate was looking its best at the beginning of spring. Father and son had recently added to it a new farm, high in the foothills. This acquisition they had named *Hochheim* after the area in the Rhineland where the famous Hocks of German wines were produced. The two men had planned many innovative experiments on this high vineyard. Johann Graue could not simply abandon everything.

In 1955, two years after the accident, Werner Thielscher, one of Johann Graue's associates, went to Germany on business. In Weinsberg he found a young man named Günter Brözel working as a cellar and research assistant in the State Research and Training Institute for the wine industry. Born on 3 April 1934, Günter Brözel came from a family of winemakers and coopers. He was an articulate and sensitive individual, greatly dedicated to his career as winemaker. Brözel accepted the offer of a position as assistant to Horst Saalwaechter, who was then the winemaster of *Nederburg* estate.

Brözel reached *Nederburg* on 6 February 1956 and found the estate on the threshold of a great change. Johann Graue had decided to gradually withdraw from actual management, but to do so in such a way that *Nederburg* would live, progress and not be harmed by the change. In July 1956 he sold 50 per cent of the shares to the firm of Monis, producers of high-grade sherries and sweet dessert wines in the Italian style, such as Marsala and Moscato. Roberto Moni, the founder of this firm, had immigrated to South Africa from Italy in 1905 and had created in Paarl a substantial business of high reputation.

The winemaster of Monis, Dr E. N. Costa, was regarded as a man of superlative skill. He took over the direction of *Nederburg* with Günter Brözel becoming his principal technician. When Johann Graue died on 12 April 1959, he was comforted by the knowledge that his beloved *Nederburg* was in excellent hands.

By the end of 1978, *Nederburg* had produced no less than 23 wines which had been awarded the ultimate certification of Superior. The estate remains a great innovator, ceaselessly experimenting with new cultivars and techniques. Apart from the aristocratic estate wines of origin Superior, *Nederburg* has produced several non-vintage wines which reflect the skill, taste and subtle blending of their creators. *Edelrood* (noble red) is one of these wines of non-specific vintage. *Fonternel* (fountain of Nel), so named from a vineyard where a pleasant little fountain bubbles to life, is an aromatic wine personally created by Günter Brözel. Introduced in 1972, it is blended by a master winemaker with the particular intention of creating a subtle drink which he is happy to think has been the start of quite a number of romances. Into this wine, the alchemist blended such cultivars as Muscat d'Alexandre, with its punchy sensuous touch; Muscat de Canelli with its delicate feminine fragrance; Riesling for elegance; and a touch of Chenin Blanc to add body. The result is something which would make even enemies become acquainted – not too sweet, not too dry, something to make friends laugh and lovers sigh!

The production of a late harvest wine, the first in South Africa to receive Superior certification, led the winemakers of *Nederburg* to achieve their ultimate goal – the creation of an *Edelkeur* (noble choice) – the pride of the estate and the first of its kind to be produced in South Africa.

For such a wine to be produced, the South African wine law itself had to be changed. This law excluded the production in South Africa of wines similar to the Sauternes of France, the Trockenbeerenauslese of Germany and the Tokai essences of Hungary. The winemasters of *Nederburg* sensed, however, that conditions in the Cape were near ideal for the production of this type of royal wine, and they longed to be allowed the opportunity to do so by law.

The technique of creating this type of wine had been pioneered by the Benedictine Abbey of Fulda in Germany. Carefully selected, specially cultivated noble grapes are used. Even before the first budding in spring, the vines are carefully watched – pruning, amount of rain, amount of sunshine, soil chemistry, humidity – all are regularly checked and studied. If conditions are considered suitable, the grapes are left to ripen to perfection in the sun.

At this critical stage a fungus, *Botrytis cinerea,* plays a vital part. This little spore lurks in the soil and on the leaves of the vines, hungry for sugar, filled with the overwhelming desire to consummate a union with the good things contained in the berries. Within the ripening time, nature must intervene with a very light drizzle providing 100 per cent humidity for at least 24 hours. A film of water forms over the sun-ripened grape, just before it turns into a raisin. In this water film, the spore develops two fins. Aided by these fins it swims over the surface of the grape and as the skin is softened by the water and loses its resistance, the spore finds a weak spot and enters the berry, roots itself and starts to feed on the sugar.

As it feeds the fungus extracts water at a faster rate than it does the sugar. The sugar content within the grape therefore rises in proportion to the volume of water. The grape shrinks, shrivels and becomes a raisin. The wind, now welcome, must blow away the exuded moisture until the sugar concentration is as near to the winemaker's ideal of a luscious 50 per cent as possible. Throughout this process, the winemaker – a voyeur with a magnifying glass – is testing and watching the love affair of berry and spore, picking a couple of berries here and there, putting them into a breeding disk under simulated conditions to see what will happen to the 'lovers' in the vineyard under possible climatic changes.

If the mists are insufficient, the soil must be saturated to provide moisture by evaporation. Weather conditions are decisive, the exact day of harvest must be selected, just before the berries are in any danger of turning sour. Picking can only be done by hand for it is selective. Normally a wine grape yield is 8 to 12 tons per hectare. From the royal grapes 2 to 4 tons at most are produced. Even the harvesting is done under government scrutiny and discipline. With the harvest in, the winemaker turns midwife, the wine is the infant. Starting in 1962, two vintages were obtained but could not be sold, then in 1969, the wine law was changed to allow marketing of a royal wine and more knowledgeable production commenced. Edelkeur can only be marketed if it is certified as Superior. An inferior vintage of an Edelkeur could only be used as an enrichment for other wines. Analysis of the 1976 vintage showed that the wine contained 10,1 per cent alcohol and 218 grams of sugar per litre.

*Nederburg* is the scene of the annual South African wine auction, the principal social event of the local wine industry. In 1975 Sotheby's introduced this auction, which takes place in February or March. All the great estates of the Cape offer their finest wines for sampling by international buyers. Amid a lovely scene of sunshine, coloured tents, brightly dressed women and serious wine authorities, quality is assessed and bids made. The public may watch but only the trade may bid. Aided by the balmy weather (usual for this time of year), generous sample tastings and vivacious company, the animated scene (becoming, perhaps, a little jollier towards the end) proceeds under the serene and benevolent gaze of the gracious old homestead. In 1979 a permanent hall, restaurant and other buildings, collectively known as the Johann Graue Centre, were built at Nederburg for use in these auctions and for exhibitions and functions.

---

# WELLINGTON

The traveller arrives in Wellington expecting to find something exciting and characteristic of the Western Cape, but instead he is confronted by two rather dreary main streets which – devoid of trees – are baking hot in summer and which possess few outstanding buildings apart from the Dutch Reformed Church with its fine tower.

The town was founded in 1837 as the centre for a farming community living in what was known as the *Limiet Vallei* (limit or frontier valley) or the *Wagenmakers Vallei* (Wagonmakers' Valley) after a considerable industry in the area in the manufacture of carts and wagons. A committee, elected by the local inhabitants with Richard Addey, a local justice of the peace, as chairman, laid out the town on the farm *Champagne*. On 27 June 1838 the foundation of the church was laid. In the following year the first erven were sold and the Governor of the Cape, Sir George Napier, was asked to give the new town a name. His reply was forthright: 'Call it Wellington. It is a disgrace that in this colony no town bears that name. On 26 March 1840 the name of Wellington was gazetted.

The original homestead of *Champagne* farm still survives. It is known today as *Twistniet* and is a fine example of the Cape-Dutch style. The gable bears the date 1811. The house stands at 31 Burg Street and although hemmed in badly by modern buildings it is still worth seeing.

The growth of Wellington (its population now stands at 19 703), was substantial after the opening of Bain's Kloof Pass in 1853 (see page 116) and the opening on 4 November 1863 of the Cape Town-Wellington railway, the first step of the long railway journey into the interior.

Scholastically, the importance of Wellington had its start in December 1872 when Dr Andrew Murray, a renowned minister of the Dutch Reformed Church, went on holiday to Kalk Bay on the Cape Peninsula. While there he happened to read a book describing the founding in America of the Mount Holyoke College, a famous centre of church-inspired education. The account so impressed Murray that he resolved to establish a similar institution in Wellington where devout young women could be trained as teachers for evangelical and mission work.

Murray wrote to the principal of the Mount Holyoke College and asked if a teacher could be spared to come to South Africa. The appeal reached Miss Abbie Ferguson and, with Miss Anna Bliss, she sailed for the Cape in September 1873. On 19 January 1874, the Huguenot Seminary was opened in Wellington with 40 pupils. This was the beginning of the Huguenot University College which continued until 1950 and then closed down, when its premises were taken over by the Huguenot College of the Dutch Reformed Church which concentrates on the training of social and missionary workers, and on bible study.

Dr Andrew Murray is suitably remembered in Wellington by a seated statue erected outside the church, and the preservation of his home, *Clairvaux*, situated opposite the town hall. Surrounding this house are the buildings belonging to the Huguenot College, of which the Samuel Hall, approached over a shady green lawn, is one of Wellington's most impressive buildings. The town is also the home of a teachers' training college, high and primary schools, and the Hugo Rust Practising School (kindergarten).

Industrially, Wellington is the centre of the South African dried fruit industry, where the Dried Fruit Board and the South African Fruit Co-operative Ltd have their head offices. The fourth largest of the liquor distributors in Southern Africa, Union Wine Corporation, also has its headquarters in the town while there are three co-operative wineries in the district: Bovlei, Wamakersvlei, and Wellington Wine Farmers' Co-operative. Wine is not sold to the public from these co-operatives but visitors are welcome during the harvest season.

There are many fine private gardens in the town and Victoria Park is notable for its roses. The coronation arch commemorates the coronation of King Edward VII in 1902. Also carried out in the town is an industry unique to South Africa, that of piano making.

In the vicinity of the town are situated several superb examples of Cape-Dutch architecture. *Versailles*, on the main road, is a classic illustration of the H-shape structure common to these houses. A former owner, Pieter Malan, donated land as a site for the Wellington railway station on condition that all passenger trains should stop there.

A cluster of these lovely old houses may be seen in the Bovlei area between Wellington and the foot of the dominant Groenberg massif. *Groenfontein, Leliefontein* and *Welvanpas* are three of these homesteads. *Welvanpas* was granted in 1704 to Pierre Mooij whose 15-year-old daughter married Francois Retief in 1719. This couple were the grandparents of the famous Voortrekker leader, Pieter Retief, who was born in the Wellington district in 1780 and grew up at *Welvanpas*. *Hexenberg, De Fortuin* and *Leeuwen Vallei* are other fine old houses. Jacaranda trees flourish in the Wellington area and flower in November.

## Accommodation
* Commercial Hotel, 15 rooms, 5 with baths. R8 – R9 B/B. Phone 3-2253.
* Railway Hotel, 10 rooms, 3 with baths. R5,50 – R6 B/B. Phone 3-2065.

## Caravans and camping
** Katruintjiesdrif camping area, 300 sites. R1 D plus 40c D per person.
*** Pinnie Joubert Caravan Park, 64 sites. R2 D.

The scenic pride and joy of the Wellington district is the magnificent Limietberg range of mountains and the spectacular Bain's Kloof Pass which carries the road to Ceres and the Breë River Valley over its heights. This mountain pass provides one of the most glorious scenic drives in Southern Africa.

# BAIN'S KLOOF PASS

South Africans often do not realise how fortunate they are to live in a country which is not only beautiful, with an exciting atmosphere of unspoilt wilderness, but also accessible. The lovely mountain country above Wellington is a superb example of a scenic playground – a world of swimming, fishing, climbing, camping, walking and most pleasant recreation – all brought within the convenient reach of motorists, cyclists and walkers by an excellent road.

History books tell us that Bain's Kloof Pass was first explored in 1846 by Andrew Geddes Bain, best known of all South African road engineers. At the time, this busy young engineer was working on the construction of Michell's Pass, which was to lead through the mountain barrier from the Breë River Valley to Ceres. From his construction camp at the southern entrance to this pass, Bain faced the Elandskloof and Slanghoek ranges which provided so formidable a barrier between the valleys of the Breë and the Berg rivers. He was intrigued by what appeared to be a natural gap in the obstacle which hindered easy transport to Cape Town. At that time the only roads from Cape Town to the interior went through Tulbagh Kloof (where the main railway line passes today) and the tortuous way round over the Franschhoek Pass.

At the first opportunity, Bain explored the apparent cleft through the mountains. Starting from the Wellington side, he set out before dawn one morning, climbed to the summit of the opening and spent a fascinating day scrambling along the boulder-strewn course of the Witte River whose erosive action has made this spectacular pass. By evening Bain had proved to his own satisfaction the practicability of the pass. After traversing the full length of the future road route, he arrived back safely at his construction camp at the entrance to Michell's Pass. The report he gave to his superiors reflected his excitement and pleasure at the discovery of a mountain passage at once so useful and beautiful.

As soon as Michell's Pass was completed, Bain set to work on the new pass. It was eventually opened in September 1853 with a cheerful little ceremony and from then on, the 16-km-long pass became the established route through the mountains to the interior.

Many of the place names originally given to remarkable portions of the pass survive as reminders of the pleasant, leisurely days of travel 100 years ago, when surveyors could afford to leave a deliberate twist in a road, or a tree or an overhanging rock, simply because their removal would scar the beauty of the scene. The names Montagu Rocks, Bell Rocks, Pilkington Bridge, and Dacres Pulpit are still attached to features along the pass. Dacres Pulpit was the name applied to the rock overhanging the road with an unmistakable resemblance to the sounding board of a pulpit. The Reverend Mr Dacres delivered a sermon there at the opening of the pass.

Such was the early history of Bain's Kloof Pass. Now let us take a journey along this most interesting scenic way. From Wellington the road to Ceres leaves the northern end of the jacaranda-lined Church Street and climbs steadily up the slopes of the Limietberg. The constant change of views is spectacular and the pass has a singular air of the pioneer days when wagons laboured up the gradients and every foot gained seemed an achievement for the early travellers. Oak trees, gnarled and battered by the weather and mountain fires, line the route, inducing the wish that modern road engineers would plant more trees.

After 13 km of climbing, the road reaches the summit, where a tremendous view to the left (the west) may be seen and on the right a gravel track leads into the valley of the upper *Witte* (white) River. A chain prevents vehicles from using this track. Permission to use this track (and a key to the lock) must be obtained from the forester at the Bainsberg Forestry Station further down the main pass.

The track is worth exploring. The Witte River, whose erosive activity has produced this great natural pass through the mountains, is so named because its waters are comparatively free of the dark-amber colour common to most of the peat-stained mountain streams of the Cape. It is one of the principal upper tributaries of the Breë River and anyone who has followed the Witte to its source will agree that the valley through which it flows is one of the most beautiful in this world of mountains. In late winter and in spring Paradise Valley, as it is called, is a blaze of flowers. A succession of pools provide fine swimming and interesting fishing for brown trout. The mountains which hem in the valley provide endless attractions for climbers.

There are many interesting stories about this valley. On the left-hand side of the road stands a concrete memorial with these words engraved upon it:

*'Ter Gedagtenis Aan die Durf en Heldemoed van L. van Dyk; F. van Dyk; C. Krynauw; Lettie de Jager. Witrivier Kamp. 23 Mei, 1895.'*

This memorial refers to a most poignant tragedy which occurred in the last century. A party of 13 young girls from the Huguenot Seminary in Wellington set out to climb the 1 689-m Sneeukop on 22 May. They were caught in heavy rain and made the classic climbing mistake of dividing the party into two sections, with the stronger going on, and the weaker lagging behind.

The first party got back to the seminary at 20h50 but the others failed to arrive. A search party with the aid of lanterns set out to find them. The searchers reached the stream and found that it had suddenly come down in flood, marooning the second party on the opposite bank. More rescuers with ropes were obtained from Wellington. At dawn one of them, C. Krynauw, swam across the river with a rope and food and drink were taken across. Then four of the rescuers set out to ferry Miss De Jager back across the stream. The current and the icy water of early winter proved too much for them. They managed to lift the girl on to a projecting rock but the normally happy little stream seemed to be intent on claiming human victims that day. As the people on the bank stood watching in horror, the flood rose sharply. Three of the men and the girl were carried away and drowned, with nobody able to do the slightest thing to help them. The rest of the party were eventually rescued by being carried over in a basket manoeuvred along the rope like a miniature aerial cableway.

The relic of a much more recent disaster may be seen on the saddle of land over which the track passes at the entrance to Paradise Valley. At this wonderful viewsite stands the melancholy ruin of the great Hugo mansion which was burned down on 22 February 1949, when a bush fire fanned by a strong gale swept across the mountains and set the place alight. The house had been built by the late P. J. Hugo, the Wellington jam manufacturer. He died before he could achieve his ambition of retiring to the place. His estate sold it together with a large tract of surrounding ground to the Paarl municipality for use in a projected water scheme. At the time of the fire only a caretaker was in residence.

In the process of creating his dream home, Mr Hugo effected one really curious modification to the topography. In order to feed his swimming pool he blasted out a deep furrow diverting water from the Witte River through the grounds of his house and then releasing it to flow down the mountains on the Wellington side. By means of this furrow he redirected a portion of the normal flow of the river from one side of its watershed to the other. The regular course of the river is a tributary of the Breë leading to the Indian Ocean on the east coast. But the furrow carries its flow to join the Pombers stream, itself a tributary of the Berg River which flows to the Atlantic Ocean on the west coast. The ruins of the house are reputedly haunted and in 1979 a nasty murder took place when an escaped convict found camped there a young couple and their dog. They were innocently hiking through the mountains but were most brutally killed.

The succession of lovely swimming and fishing pools on the upper reaches of the Witte River are all worth visiting. Mountaineers who care to follow the river to its very end, will be delighted to find some fine cascades, each with magnificent fern-girt pools lying at their feet. The ultimate springs of the stream lie on the slopes of the great Slanghoek Peak, from whose summit may be seen a fabulous view overlooking the Breë Valley into the heart of the Hex River Mountains. In winter it is almost as though one was viewing the snow-covered Himalayas.

---

On the summit of Bain's Kloof Pass, just beyond the gravel turnoff up Paradise Valley, the main road enters a pleasant thicket of wattle trees and here the Divisional Council has created an attractive camping ground. A cluster of private holiday cottages have also been erected here. Various paths descend to swimming pools in the Witte River. A hotel, the Hotel in the Mountains, once stood at the summit of the pass but was burned down in 1976.

From the end of the path on the Ceres side of the old hotel site across the river, another path climbs up the banks and then veers downstream. This is the start of a fine walk. The path climbs steadily up a mountain slope rich in wild flowers and for 6 km finds a way into the Baviaanskloof. This is a handsome valley, hemmed in by high peaks and a perennial stream – full of fine swimming pools – courses down its floor. Near the head of the valley a path branches to the left and leads down to a camping ground where a waterfall tumbles into a deep swimming pool. The main path continues to the head of the valley where cliffs close in and the stream falls a sheer 25 m, rushing off through a series of rapids, pools and a jumble of mighty boulders. Care is needed in climbing through this gorge but the scenery and the deep pools are magnificent.

The walk to the head of the valley and back to the hotel site takes three hours. It is a delight at any season of the year. It is essential to obtain permission from the forester at Bainsberg Forestry Station.

### Caravans and camping
Divisonal Council camping ground, 50 sites. Entrance free. Water and w.c.'s available.

Beyond the camping ground the main road begins its tortuous descent down the precipitous valley of the Witte River. This is one of the most celebrated road passes in Africa, where strange rock formations and numerous wild flowers abound. Incessantly twisting, the pass descends, providing a succession of memorable views.

After 8 km of descent the road reaches *Wolvenkloof* (ravine of the hyenas) where, on the site of the original toll house, there is a popular camping ground, a series of deep swimming pools and a short turnoff left leading to the Bainsberg Forestry Station. From this forestry station there is a magnificent 13-km-long circular path which leads the walker past waterfalls, wild flowers, indigenous forest and high up to the summit of the Limietberg before returning to its starting point via another route. The best time to do this walk is on a winter's morning when the Hex River Mountains, covered in snow, provide spectacular, photogenic views. In February, however, disas may be seen, especially growing on the rock faces around one high waterfall, while wild flowers bloom at all times of the year. The walk is best done in an anti-clockwise direction. It is essential to obtain permission from the forester.

## Caravans and camping
Toll House (Forestry Department), 10c D per person. Water and flush toilets available.

Beyond Wolvenkloof, the main road tends to level off and keeps to the alluvial floor of the river valley. It passes Sebastiankloof, where a locked gate provides access to a mountain club hut. After 8 km the main road reaches the Darling bridge across the Breë River, a favourite camping area for the Coloured community. One kilometre beyond the river there is a turnoff right leading eastwards to Worcester (see page 126).

---

From Wellington the main road northwards crosses the railway and passes several industrial sites. After 3 km, it reaches a small fort built by the British during the Anglo-Boer War. This fort whose position was the most southerly, was one of a series erected to guard all major railway bridges. Smaller blockhouses, each garrisoned by about seven men of the South African Constabulary, were built at intervals of 3 000 m from one another all along the main lines of rail.

Beyond the fort, the country changes, vineyards giving way to wheat fields and sheep runs. After 23,5 km the road reaches the rural centre of *Hermon,* named after the Biblical place name meaning 'exalted'.

## Accommodation
★ Hermon Hotel, 12 rooms, 2 with baths. R7,50 – R8 B/B. Phone 533.

From Hermon a road branches north-westwards and leads across wheat fields for 10 km to the village of Riebeek-Kasteel, lying in the centre of large vineyards on the slopes of the isolated 946-m-high mountain formerly known as Van Riebeeks-Kasteel but now called Kasteelberg.

Six kilometres beyond Riebeek-Kasteel, the road reaches another village on the slopes of the mountain. This is Riebeek-West, a rural centre notable for its vineyards and the fact that two of South Africa's Prime Ministers were born in the district: General J. C. Smuts on the farm *Ongegund* and Dr D. F. Malan on *Allesverloren.*

---

The main road from Hermon crosses the railway line and continues northwards across wheat fields for 10 km and then passes the dam of *Voëlvlei* (bird marsh), one of the major water supplies for the Western Cape.

Voëlvlei was originally a natural lake but had a small catchment area allowing it to collect little more than 1 m in depth of water. During the Second World War the military authorities were compelled to find a solution to the problem of supplying water to the harbour of Saldanha. A water scheme was hurriedly devised, feeding to the area water pumped from the Berg River. After the war this supply was extended to such places as Vredenburg and Velddrif but the erratic seasonal flow of the Berg River proved a great problem.

To solve this difficulty, a storage dam was built at Voëlvlei in 1952. The dam is 8 km long and 1,5 km wide, impounding 171 500 ml of water behind a rock and earth fill embankment, 9,8 m high. Water is fed into this dam from weirs in the Little Berg River where it flows through the Nuwekloof from Tulbagh, and from the Leeu River and the group of streams known as the Twenty-four Rivers. From these sources 82 500 ml of water a year is fed into Voëlvlei and stored there. During the dry summer months when the flow of the Berg River becomes very sluggish, water is fed into it from Voëlvlei and supplies are maintained to users as far away as Cape Town in the south and Velddrif in the north. The dam is also used by yachtsmen for recreation and is stocked with bass. Permits to enter the area may be obtained at the gate. No camping is allowed.

Eight kilometres north of Voëlvlei the road reaches a junction. Straight ahead the road leads to the Nuwekloof and the upper valley of the Little Berg River (see page 121). A left turn leads for 2 km to the village of *Gouda,* which, built on a farm named after Gouda in Holland, had its own start as a railway station at first called Porterville Road. About the village still lingers a true corn-country atmosphere although the grand days have passed when 300 ox wagons a day could be seen bringing wheat to the railway, and the hotels were crowded with thirsty men.

### Accommodation
⋆ Gouda Hotel, 11 rooms, 5 with baths. R7,50 – R8,50 B/B. Phone 4.

The country around Gouda shelters such celebrated estates as *Lorelei* and *La Bonne Esperanza,* and their products of wheat, wine and wool are of superlative quality. Five kilometres from Gouda there is a left turn to Riebeek-West (22 km), while 8,5 km further on is a right turn (east) leading for 3 km to the mission station of *Saron* (after the Biblical name meaning 'on the plains'), maintained for the Coloured community by the Dutch Reformed Church. The mission – a great place for the making of *velskoen* – lies under the 1 499-m-high Saronsberg which dominates this part of the country.

Five kilometres north of the Saron turnoff, the main tarmac road reaches the first of a series of bridges spanning what is known as the Twenty-four Rivers, a succession of stony-bedded mountain torrents rushing down to feed the Berg River. Eighteen kilometres further on the road passes through a fine avenue of gum trees and, 30 km from Gouda, reaches the town of . . .

# PORTERVILLE

Founded in 1863 when F. J. Owen, an 1820 Settler, divided a portion of his *Pomona* farm into erven, *Porterville* was named after William Porter, the popular Attorney-General of those days. As the centre for a prosperous industry in the production of sheep, cattle, fruit and wheat, Porterville grew into a pleasant little town and today the population has reached 6 600. It attained municipal status on 24 September 1881, and became a magistracy in 1908. Outside the magistrate's court, next to the flagstaff, stands an old naval gun originally found on the farm *Dammetjies* where it had been erected by the Dutch East India Company as one of their signal guns.

### Accommodation
⋆ Porterville Hotel, 14 rooms, 8 with baths. R8 – R9 B/B. Phone 183.

The *Olifantsrivierberge* (elephant's river mountains) which overlook Porterville from the east, are renowned for their wild flowers, rock formations and Bushman paintings. A spectacular drive climbs to the top of this mountain range. Continuing north from Porterville, past a turnoff left leading westwards to Piketberg (23 km away), the main road travels north towards Citrusdal (46 km away). Four kilometres out of Porterville there is a gravel turnoff right (east) marked Cardouw. The *Kardouw* (narrow pass) was an old route used by the Hottentot tribes to cross the mountain range. It is now disused, but after 9 km of travel on this road – which runs along the foot of the mountains – there is another turn to the right which takes the road 7 km up the spectacular *Dasklip* (coney rock) pass to the summit of the range.

Several farmers have settled along the top of the range and a rough road finds a way over the plateau summit, through a high world of striking rock formations, wild flowers and forests of waboom. The scenery is spectacular and in winter the high peaks of the Groot Winterhoek-berge (2 076 m) are well covered in snow.

On the highest point of the pass there is a turn to the private Beaverlac Nature Reserve. After a further 4 km there is a fork, with the left-hand road leading to farms such as *Rockhaven* and *Phoenix Rock*. The right-hand turn continues for 2 km to the Groot Winterhoek Forestry Station. Permits to continue are now required and the rough road (after a further 6 km), ends at a fork leading to two locked gates beyond which only walking is allowed. The views, grotesque rock formations and flowers are superb.

There are several dozen caves in this mountain area decorated with galleries of Bushman paintings. There is a well-ornamented cave on the farm *Driebos*. The farm *Eselfontein*, on the top of Dasklip pass, has some unusual abstract paintings which may be seen about 8 km along the road on a large rock standing on the marshy flats known as the Zuurvlakte. Further along the road towards the old *Winterhoek* farm, in a deep canyon known as Die Hel, there is a large cave close to a 9-m-high waterfall. This was an important Bushman centre, for it was a source of ochre-white, off-white and pink, with a lower cave yielding red. The walls of the caves are adorned with scenes of hunters and elephants.

Among the several other Bushman cave galleries in this area there is one on the farm *Noordbron*, 2 km south-east of the summit of Dasklip pass, which contains a picture of a sailing ship with flags flying. The winds must have been rather contrary for the flags are all flying in different directions!

---

At Gouda, where the road to Porterville branches off, the right-hand road continues in company with the main railway line, passing the mass of rock known as Bushman's Rock, and twisting easily into the ravine through the mountains washed by the Little Berg River, the principal tributary of the Berg.

## TULBAGH PASS OR NUWEKLOOF

In the entire length of what the pioneers at the Cape called the mountain range of Africa, the passage forced by the Little Berg River is the only easy and level way through the mountains into the interior. In March 1658, when Van Riebeeck sent out a party under Sergeant Jan van Harwarden on a journey of exploration, they found this natural pass. The surveyor, Pieter Potter, partly explored it, then continued north along the ridge known as the *Roodezandberg* (red sand mountain). From the summit of what is known as the *Oude Kloof* (old ravine) he was the first European to look down into the inner valley of the mountains which, in 1699, Willem van der Stel named the *Land of Waveren* in honour of an illustrious Amsterdam family with which he was connected.

For many years the Oudekloof of the Roodezandberg was the accepted way through the mountains. Then the more natural pass up the valley of the Little Berg River (Tulbagh Kloof) gradually came into use, with the road swinging in past Bushman's Rock, crossing and re-crossing the bed of the river and then emerging into the Land of Waveren. About 1850 a proper road was constructed up this ravine and it became known as the *Nuwekloof* to distinguish it from the old mountain passage. The modern tarmac road keeps to the side of the river opposite to the old road and 8 km from the Gouda turnoff it enters the Land of Waveren at the railway station of *Tulbaghweg* (Tulbagh road). The view of the fertile valley is impressive, with the high peaks of the Winterhoekberge lying to the north and the beautiful range of the *Witsenberg* (named by Van der Stel after Nicolaas Witsen, a director of the Dutch East India Company) providing a seemingly impassable wall to the east.

The Little Berg River has its watershed in a superb basin in the mountains with the Winterhoek Valley forming the northern cul-de-sac, dominated by peaks such as the Kleinberg (1 551 m), Klein Winterhoek (1 957 m), and the Groot Winterhoek (2 076 m). In the centre of this basin, 4 km from the way out of the Nuwekloof, stands the town of . . .

# TULBAGH

When the first settlers came to the basin of the Little Berg River on 31 July 1700 Tulbagh, with its present population of 2 580, had its beginning. At first these pioneers were only interested in establishing farms but a centre for their area had to be created, with a church being built and a village being laid out in 1795. In 1804 a magistrate was appointed for the district named in honour of Ryk Tulbagh, one of the best Governors of the Cape.

The magistracy (the *drostdy*) was built on the farm *Rietvlei*, 4 km north of the church, and is a fine, if slightly severe, example of Cape-Dutch architecture. It was designed by the famous Louis Thibault and is open to the public Mondays to Saturdays 10h00 to 13h00. Closed religious holidays. The original church is now a museum housing an interesting collection of furniture, and things such as a large patent penny-in-the-slot symphonium, a sort of deep-toned musical-cum-juke-box which played (and still plays) a large selection of the hit tunes of Victorian times. This museum is open 09h00 to 13h00, 14h00 to 17h00 daily except religious holidays. 15h00 to 17h00 on Sundays. Both building and collections are worth seeing.

A severe earthquake devastated Tulbagh on 29 September 1969, killing nine people and causing considerable damage to property. A second minor quake occurred on 14 April 1970. After the disaster, however, some magnificent restoration work was begun. The main commercial street remains a rather drab stretch of sunbaked shops, but Kerk Street is a sheer delight with its long line of carefully restored buildings and pretty gardens which perfectly emphasise the pleasure of living if man blends with his environment without wantonly destroying it for the sake of venality.

One of the restored buildings, set in a spacious garden, is run by the K.W.V. as a restaurant under the name of the *Paddagang Taphuis*.

## Accommodation
* Tulbagh Hotel, 10 rooms, 3 with baths. R8 – R8,80 B/B. Phone 9903.
* Witsenberg Hotel, 19 rooms, 4 with baths. R7,30 – R8,20 B/B. Phone 159.

## Caravans and camping
* Municipal caravan park, 20 sites. R2 D.

No visitor to Tulbagh should fail to explore the upper valley of the Little Berg River, which is a beautiful area at all seasons. Two main farm roads lead from Tulbagh up the valley. The one road passes the modern Dutch Reformed Church, leads for 4 km to the drostdy, then passes the Drostdy Wine Cellars and travels off into one of the major wine-producing areas of the Western Cape.

At 6,5 km from Tulbagh there is a turnoff to the vineyard of *Theuniskraal*, home of the Jordaan family and a producer of some excellent estate wines, especially the dry whites for which this upper valley of the Little Berg River is so notable.

Beyond the turn to *Theuniskraal*, the tarmac road continues across lovely farming country for a further 6,5 km before ending in the grounds of *Remhoogte*, the farm of Mr J. N. Theron, a great producer of prunes, pears and apples. This is one of the finest estates in the Winterhoek Valley of the upper Berg River. Its homestead is modern but the whitewashed stone-walled corrals, the flowers and the trees – especially beautiful during autumn – give it considerable charm.

The second farm road from Tulbagh branches off to the left from the road to the drostdy at the Dutch Reformed Church, passes the parsonage and after 2,5 km reaches a turnoff to the wine estate of *Montpellier*, home of the De Wet Theron family. From this estate comes the Vlottenheimer range of wines and many other good products of the Winterhoek Valley.

Four kilometres beyond this turnoff, the road reaches the immaculate estate of *Twee Jonge Gezellen* (two young companions) where the well-known Mr N. C. Krone produces an excellent range of estate wines of origin. In the days when the Dutch East India Company first allocated farms in the land of Waveren, this estate was granted, so the story goes, to two young bachelors – great friends – who named it *Twee Jongegezellen* (two young bachelors). Years later, when the Theron family acquired the estate, they subtly changed the name to the present form of *Twee Jonge Gezellen* (two young companions) because they were sensitive to local jokes insinuating that the Therons were descendants of bachelors. The Krones are related to the Therons on the female side. The family is notable for its dedication to quality, innovation and high skill in the complex creation of white wines of subtle delicacy in flavour and bouquet. The estate, with its homestead, flowering creepers and trees, in a setting of vineyards and mountains, is a classic example of the Cape-Dutch style of domestic architecture, of which there is nothing more serene or beautiful to be seen anywhere in the world.

The road continues past this glorious farm for a further 5 km and then ends at the *Roodezand* farm of Mr J. Lombard where prunes, peaches and grapes cover many hectares of the foothills of the Winterhoek mountains. In spring, when the orchards are in blossom, in autumn when the leaves turn golden to red and the blue mountains are touched with snow, this area is unforgettable – a joy to the eye, a delight to any visitor, and an inspiration to any artist, writer or composer.

# Chapter Seven

# THE VALLEY OF THE BREË RIVER

The river known as the *Breë* (formerly Breede) or broad, has its source in a basin held in the palm of the half-open hand of the Western Cape mountains. It is a basin so fertile that it is often likened to the open end of the horn of Ceres, the goddess of agriculture. Nature has graced this great basin with bountiful supplies of water, wild flowers, a crisp, sunny climate and fertile soil. Man has seized the opportunity to fill it to overflowing with fruit, wheat, dairy products and wool, and topped it with congenial living places in a beautiful environment.

The basin is known as the *Warmbokkeveld* (warm buck veld) to distinguish it from the higher land to the north called the *Kouebokkeveld* (cold buck veld). The mountain ranges enclosing the basin consist of the Hex River Mountains to the east and south, the Witsenberg to the west, and the Skurweberg, Gydoberg and Waboomberg to the north. These massive piles of sedimentary material collect and store pure water from winter rains and snows and this seeps into the basin below in the form of innumerable springs. The springs feed streams, which in turn fill dams that irrigate the farmlands and then unite to form two main rivulets: the Dwars and the Titus. After flowing down many cascades, rapids and waterfalls, broadening into pools and resting in tranquil, tree-shaded stretches where trout play among the dapples of sunshine, the two rivulets eventually unite. With its new-found strength the young river shoulders its way through the south-western rim of the basin, tumbles down a waterfall into a boiling pool known as the 'Coffee Pot' and, now known as the 'Breë', finds a tortuous way through the mountains out into the great valley which carries the river south-eastwards to the sea.

The basin where the Breë River has its headwaters was used by Bushmen as a hunting ground from early times. In the middle of the 18th century a handful of European pastoralists found their way into the area, but the mountains held the basin in an iron grip and the only link to the outside world was an atrocious track which followed the river through the mountains and was passable only by pack animals. Wagons had to be pulled to pieces, carried bodily through the pass, and then reassembled, not a profitable way of conveying produce to a market.

In 1765, the situation improved. Jan Mostert, whose farm *Wolvenkloof* was situated where the river found its way out of the mountains, built a road at his own expense, criss-crossing the bed of the river into the basin through what became known as Mostertshoek (Mostert's glen). The name of this enterprising farmer is commemorated by the 2 031-m-high twin peak, which looms above the eastern side of the pass and is the beginning of the Hex River range. The oak trees planted by Mostert still shade the *Wolvenkloof* farmhouse but the road he made has long since been claimed by nature.

By the 1840s a permanent road into the basin became essential in order to provide a gateway to the Karoo in the north. Work started in October 1846. Andrew Geddes Bain was the engineer in charge and he built the pass with the aid of 240 convicts. Opened on 1 December 1848, the pass was named in honour of the surveyor-general of the Cape, Colonel Charles Michell. The popular Governor, Sir Harry Smith, performed the opening ceremony, during which at least half the local population rode through the pass in procession.

The route of the modern road, concreted in 1946, is substantially the same as that of the pass made by Bain, and the original toll house is maintained as a monument in the middle of the 8-km-long route. The scenery of the pass is majestic: high peaks, strange rock shapes

124

and, winding their way down the slopes to join the young river, bustling mountain torrents. One of these tributary streams is the *Witels* (white alder), renowned among climbers and trout fishermen for its complex upper course, which comprises 14 'swims' at points where the containing ravine is so narrow that explorers can only proceed by swimming, pushing their impedimenta ahead on inflatable mattresses. There are camping, picnicking and viewsites at various points along the pass.

With the opening of Michell's Pass, the basin in the mountains was at last easily accessible, and development was rapid. In 1849, shortly after the opening of the pass, a town was laid out on the banks of the Dwars River just before it entered the mountains.

# CERES

This town, named after the goddess of agriculture, has a population of 9 000. Its location is admirable: apart from the Dwars River, several streams such as the Koekedouw flow from the mountains on to town lands and in the past there was little danger of any shortage of water to inhibit growth, irrigation, the generation of power and recreation in the form of swimming and angling. In order for the town to be beautiful, all that was needed was sensible gardening, and an appreciation of the potential of such a well-endowed situation. In both these respects Ceres was very fortunate in its people.

In 1864 Ceres became a municipality under the chairmanship of its magistrate, J. A. Munnik. Planting trees to shade the streets was a municipal priority and for this purpose Mr Munnik obtained a number of young oaks from Stellenbosch and Paarl. Eucalyptus trees, introduced into the Cape from Australia in 1827 by Sir Lowry Cole, the Governor, had already been planted and what is reputedly the largest specimen of its kind in South Africa stands on the banks of the Dwars River watching the traffic cross the main bridge. The trunk of this tree is 10 m in circumference and the crown 45 m off the ground.

Pin oaks and poplars were also planted and forests of pine trees (*dennebosse*) grew on the outskirts. Constantine William Carson served Ceres as chairman of its municipal management committee for nearly 30 years. A great gardener, he supervised the planting of many trees and flowers, laid out walks and paths and created recreational parks which are the green heritage of the town today. The autumn spectacle of poplar trees losing their leaves along the banks of the Dwars River is a superb reward for all the work of planting and conservation.

On 18 May 1912 the branch railway from Wolseley to Ceres through Michell's Pass was opened, and three special trains carried sightseers on a scenic journey. In 1929 the line was extended to the terminus at Prince Alfred's Hamlet. Today this railway route with its tunnels, cuttings and gradients is still a traveller's delight.

Ceres is now a prosperous town. A busy agricultural centre and a great resort for holidaymakers, it is warm in summer while in winter the snows on the mountains provide a fine spectacle and limited opportunities for winter sports. The numerous pools and rapids of the Dwars, Titus and Koekedouw rivers offer good trout fishing.

## Accommodation
★★ ® Belmont Hotel, 51 rooms, all with baths. R10,50 – R18 B/B. Phone 230.

## Caravans and camping
★★★ ® Pine Forest Holiday Camp, 350 sites. R2,60 D. 75 cottages and rondawels, R2,60 – R13,40 D.

From Ceres the old main road to the north leads through Karoo Poort. This route is described on page 221. Another drive is along a 10-km-long tarmac road leading through orchards and past packing houses to the small agricultural centre of . . .

# PRINCE ALFRED HAMLET

Established by proclamation on 8 December 1874, this little place was laid out on the farm *Wagenboomsrivier,* owned by J. G. Goosen. It became the terminus of the branch railway from Wolseley in 1929 and is now a centre for the despatch of fruit and other agricultural products to the markets of the world.

The hamlet lies 3 km from the beginning of the *Gydo* (euphorbia) Pass which climbs for a spectacular winding 7 km up the slopes of the *Skurweberge* (scaly mountains) to reach the farming area of the Kouebokkeveld. The pass is famous for its views of the basin of the Warmbokkeveld and the encompassing mountains, which are especially lovely during the snows of winter, when the pass itself is occasionally closed. Wild flowers of many species abound on the mountain slopes. The displays of erica are particularly dazzling, and in autumn the yellow-flowered *Protea repens* blooms in vast quantities.

From the top of the pass the road leads on to Citrusdal and the Cedarberg.

### Accommodation
★ Hamlet Hotel, 5 rooms, all with baths. R8 B/B. Phone 65.

From the western end of Michell's Pass, the Breë River and the road follow a wide bend into the valley which leads south-eastwards to the Indian Ocean. The upper end of this seemingly uninterrupted valley is finally separated by a divide and forms part of the watershed of the Little Berg River which drains through the mountain at Tulbagh Kloof and then joins the Berg River which flows to the Atlantic Ocean on the west coast. The divide occurs in the middle of the town of Wolseley which lies 7 km from the entrance to Michell's Pass.

# WOLSELEY

On 3 October 1893, a village was established named after Sir Garnet Wolseley, the renowned British general who saw service in South Africa. Today the town has a population of 2 410 and is a railway and agricultural centre which bustles with fruit canning, packing and despatching in summer.

Water flows down the streets in furrows, but the citizens seem unaware of the benefits of trees and the town bakes and blinks bareheaded in the hot summer months.

### Accommodation
★ Waverley Hotel, 15 rooms, 4 with baths. R7,50 – R8 B/B. Phone 113.
★ Wolseley Hotel, 12 rooms, 3 with baths. R7,50 – R8 B/B. Phone 240.

Wolseley is 4,5 km north of the Breë River. The tarmac road crosses the river over a bridge guarded by two well-preserved blockhouses built by the British during the Anglo-Boer War. Both blockhouses have recently served as residences and they have a homely appearance in their serene rural setting of orchards and vineyards. One and a half kilometres away from the blockhouses and bridge, the road joins the route descending the east bank of the river from Michell's Pass and leads across vineyards, past the station and wine cellars at Romans River, to the west of the valley, where the Witte River flows out of the mountains to join the Breë. Here the road reaches a fork, and one branch follows the course of the Witte River, crossing the mountains by means of Bain's Kloof Pass.

The tarmac road along the valley of the Breë continues south-eastwards. To the north the Hex River Mountains are a grand sight and a complex mass of high peaks to the south and west seem to enclose the valley entirely. Orchards, vineyards, cellars and homesteads cover the level floor of the valley. The soil is a sandy alluvial deposit eroded by streams from the folded mountains of the Cape System and distributed over the floor of the valley, which needs only irrigation for the cultivation of fruit and grapes. Rainfall occurs in winter: about 720 mm fall in the western end of the long valley, decreasing to a skimpy 210 mm in the east. Little rain falls in summer and during this season conservation, artificial distribution and irrigation form the backbone of farming. Efficient utilisation of available water supplies makes this middle part of the Breë River Valley the largest grape producing area – mainly for wine and brandy – in the Cape. There are 31 co-operative cellars in the valley and several private cellars on estates.

The main road continues south-eastwards down the valley in close company with the railway line. At a point 38 km from Wolseley this road joins the Cape-to-Cairo road, but leaves it again after a short union and, 5 km further on, reaches the principal town of the Breë River Valley.

## WORCESTER

Named after the Marquis of Worcester, the oldest brother of Lord Charles Somerset, Governor of the Cape at the time, the town was founded in 1820. Before then, Tulbagh was the administrative centre for the frontier areas of the Western Cape. The development of agriculture and the importance of communications to the Hex River Valley and the eastern valley of the Breë necessitated the establishment of a new sub-magistracy, and at the end of 1818 two farms, *Roodedraai* and *Langerug,* were bought from the brothers Du Toit. On these farms the new town was laid out and on 28 February 1820 the first building plots were sold. Today, Worcester has a population of 46 218.

The centre of the new town was a sumptuous and elegant *drostdy* (magistracy) built to the order of Lord Charles Somerset in such a way that it could serve as a shooting box and residence when the Governor was on official visits to the inland areas. Captain Charles Trappes was the first *landdros* (magistrate) of Worcester and he supervised the construction of the residence in 1825, ensuring that it would be a building of lasting value. Now part of the Drostdy Technical High School, it is an historical monument and regarded as the finest Regency building in South Africa. Captain Trappes died on 5 September 1828; his grave lies in the grounds of the drostdy.

Several other buildings from early Worcester still survive and one, the homestead of *Kleinplasie,* was built in 1800. This pleasingly austere-looking farmhouse is now a taproom and restaurant run by the K.W.V. One of the original outbuildings serves as a shop which offers for sale most of the wines produced by the various co-operative cellars in the Breë River Valley. The collector, connoisseur and bargain-hunter will find this wine shop a convenient and pleasant introduction to many novelties of vintage which would be difficult to find without visiting out-of-the-way cellars. Part of the original farmland of *Kleinplasie* is now the showground of the Worcester Agricultural Society, which holds its annual show in February; it is also the site of an agricultural museum.

The oldest surviving residence in Worcester stands at 3 Trappes Street. The original gaol, later converted into a residence, is now a school for the blind. Church Street contains several fine buildings, most of them dating from 1840 to 1855. One of these buildings, on the corner of Church and Baring streets, facing Church Square, has been restored and is now the Worcester Museum. In the garden behind the museum is a bathing house fed by a stream and beyond it, facing Church Street, a delightful cottage houses the Afrikaner Museum, which displays a doctor's surgery, a dentist's surgery and a lawyer's office dating from the early days of Worcester. Next to the Worcester Museum, in Baring Street, is an art gallery contain-

*Overleaf: The Cape mountains, born as sandstone layers deposited beneath the sea, became twisted and folded as they rose to bask in the sun.*

ing a collection of works of two well-known local artists, Hugo Naudé and Jean Welz. From 1919 until the place was bought by the municipality, the museum was the home of a mayor of Worcester, Attorney J. E. J. Krige. Built in 1841, it is now maintained in its original state: a gentleman's home, complete with stable and coach house containing a smart Cape cart and ensemble. The Afrikaner and Worcester museums and the art gallery are open Mondays to Fridays 08h00 to 13h00 and 14h00 to 17h00. Saturdays 09h00 to 12h00.

The Dutch Reformed Church, a fine example of the Gothic style, dominates Church Square. Completed in 1832, its first minister was the Reverend Henry Sutherland from Scotland, a renowned churchman of the period. The original spire was squat, and in 1927 was replaced by the present graceful spire. The pulpit was the work of a local craftsman, Wouter de Vos. The square in front of the church contains a garden of remembrance with several monuments and memorials.

In Church Street, next to the Afrikaner Museum, stands the Congregational Church, built in 1948 in classic Cape-Dutch style. In a beautiful garden setting, it is very photogenic, and contains furnishings of outstanding craftsmanship.

Worcester became a municipality in 1842. The advent of the railway in 1877 and the building of good roads to Cape Town and on into the interior made the town a place of consequence and the main street, High Street, became lined with places of business. Unfortunately in modern times this street was robbed of the trees that once shaded it, and little remains to remind one of past years except for furrows on both sides of the street which are still filled with running water from streams.

The mountains overlooking the town provide a spectacular setting and are the recreational areas of an active local branch of the Mountain Club of South Africa. Climbers such as Izak Meiring and Dr Auden have left their names on high peaks which they were the first to climb. Several great gorges in the mountains, especially Jan du Toit's Kloof in the Hex River range, are famous for their scenic beauty.

An attractive feature of Worcester is the Karoo Garden, established in 1921 at Whitehill, near Matjiesfontein in the Karoo. This situation proved rather inaccessible to the public and the National Botanic Garden requested a site from the Worcester municipality. Land was granted which encompassed the foothills of the Brandwag Mountain, where conditions of soil and climate were ideally 'Karoo'. A well-known local farmer, Charles Heatlie, donated additional land, and the garden was brought to a total area of 119 ha.

In July 1946 the original plants were transferred from Whitehill to Worcester and under the skilful control of Jacques Thudichum, the first director of the new garden, the Karoo Botanic Garden was opened in September 1948 in Worcester. The garden specialises in plant species from the arid areas of Southern Africa and its collection of succulents is considerable. Stapelias bloom from January to mid-March; June is a good month for aloes; August, September and October see dazzling displays of many flowering plants. Stone plants, euphorbias, cycads, stem succulents, desert grapes, spekboom and brilliantly-flowering mesembryanthemums are all plentiful. The garden is open daily until sunset.

A notable feature of Worcester are the schools for the blind and the deaf founded by the Dutch Reformed Church in 1881. A braille printing press produces a weekly magazine as well as books in several languages. There are also homes and workshops for the blind, and a special department in the school for deaf-blind children.

### Accommodation
* ★ Brandwacht Hotel, 20 rooms, 6 with baths. R8,50 – R9,50 B/B. Phone 4162.
* ★ Cumberland Hotel, 44 rooms, 14 with baths. R9 – R10 B/B. Phone 5641.

### Caravans and camping
★★ ® Burger Park, 54 sites. R2 – R3 D.

# STETTYNSKLOOF AND BRANDVLEI

Worcester and much of the highly productive area of the middle Breë River Valley depend for water on Lake Marais, a dam built over a marsh known as *Brandvlei* (burning marsh) from the hot springs which fed it. This artificial lake, used for yachting, feeds water through canals to the middle reaches of the valley of the Breë River. The lake in turn is fed by two streams: the *Smalblaar*, named from the smalblaar trees which grow in the area, and produce a blossom which imparts a bitter taste to wild honey; and the more important of the two streams, the *Goudini*, which takes its Hottentot name (*Kgo dani*, bitter honey), from this taste. In recent times the latter stream has been prosaically renamed the Holsloot. Its source lies at the head of Stettynskloof, a narrow, rugged gorge where, in 1952, the Worcester municipality built a dam which supplies the town's water. The remaining flow of the Holsloot reaches Lake Marais. The entire course of the stream is notable for its swimming pools and trout.

From Worcester a tarmac road leads south-westwards for 3,5 km to the Breë River. Immediately across the river there is a fork. The left turn leads to Villiersdorp (see page 130); the right (west) turn stretches for 11 km to the town of Rawsonville. From the latter road are two turnoffs at 7 km and 10 km; both are marked Louwshoek and climb for 22 km up Stettynskloof to the dam.

# RAWSONVILLE

Founded in 1858 as a centre for the area known as Goudini, after the stream, this town was named after William Rawson, one of the members of the first legislative council of the Cape Colony.

In former years Rawsonville was the centre for a considerable raisin-making industry. Today it still produces vast quantities of grapes but these are mainly dessert species, and species used for the making of wine in several local co-operative cellars. There is a fine church and some of the streets are lined with jacarandas.

## Accommodation
★ Rawsonville Hotel, 12 rooms, 7 with baths. R8 – R9 B/B. Phone Worcester 9-1080.

# GOUDINI SPA

Six kilometres north-west of Rawsonville, across the main road from Cape Town to the north, there is a resort built at a hot spring known as Goudini Spa. The spring is situated at the south-eastern base of a range of sandstone hills. The water surfaces at 40° C, and is very pure, containing only 32,8 mg silica per litre; 13 mg magnesium carbonate; 11 mg sodium chloride; and 8,8 mg potassium chloride. There is some radio activity. The Rondalia organisation has created a resort at the springs which offers two enclosed swimming baths, an open pool, a restaurant, hotel and shop, bungalows and a caravan park.

## Accommodation
★ Hotel, 20 rooms, all with baths. R8 – R20,70 room only. Phone Worcester 9-1100.

## Caravans and camping
★★★ Caravan park, 50 sites. R3,60 – R5,30 D, seasonal. 50 flats (2 beds and double divan), R10 – R17 D, seasonal. 100 bungalows (4 beds), R11 – R20,70 D, seasonal.

From the Goudini Spa stretch two roads, which link up with the Ceres-Worcester road. One of the routes is a fine scenic drive of 18 km through the Slanghoek Valley with its vineyards and cellars.

From the bridge across the Breë River, 3,5 km from Worcester, at the same point where the road to Rawsonville branches off, the left-hand road follows the shores of Lake Marais. At 11 km from Worcester there is a turnoff to Brandvlei Prison and at 18 km a turnoff to the Kwaggaskloof Dam. The tarmac road continues through a pleasant rural landscape with the high mass of the Stettynsberg range looming on the western side. At 35 km from Worcester the road passes the Stettyn Co-operative Wine Cellars and at 49 km there is a turnoff into the mountains leading for 5 km to the estate of . . .

## HIGH NOON

In 1952 Douglas Ovenstone bought a farm in the spectacular valley of the Elands River, a tributary of the Riviersonderend. He named the farm *High Noon* because it was exactly at noon that he first drove into the valley. At first he farmed in the area, gradually acquiring most of the other properties in the valley, but later the block of farms was developed as a wildlife sanctuary with over 100 km of scenic drives, many exotic and indigenous animals displayed in enclosures, picnic places, a restaurant, a farm shop, stables of Palomino stud-horses which were displayed to the public in an arena, a profusion of wild flowers, continued farming activity, forests, swimming pools and many other diverting scenes and occupations. High Noon was closed to the public and reverted to farming from 1 March 1980.

At 1,5 km beyond the turn to High Noon lies . . .

## VILLIERSDORP

This town was named after Pieter de Villiers, a local farmer who established the place in 1843. As with the Du Toits in the Worcester area, so the De Villiers family in the Villiersdorp district have played a major part in the development of the area. Sir David de Villiers Graaff provided the money and ground for the construction of a school in 1901 and this, in 1907, became the well-known De Villiers Graaff High School, one of the best in Southern Africa. The town has a population of 2 808.

Villiersdorp is pleasantly shaded with oaks. There is an interesting Veteran Motor Museum and a protea garden where 60 varieties of proteas grow, including those that are claimed to be the largest in the world, the giant king proteas, with pink and cream coloured flowers more than 0,5 m in diameter. Watsonias and ericas also flourish in great profusion. The mountain rose, *Cedro montana*, is indigenous to this area.

### Accommodation
* Boland Hotel, 18 rooms, 6 with baths. R5,50 – R7,50 B/B. Phone 52.
** Keerom Hotel, 10 rooms, all with baths. R10,50 B/B. Phone 63.

### Caravans and camping
* Municipal caravan park, 30 sites. R2,50 D.

From Villiersdorp the road continues for 9 km then reaches a junction: the left turn cuts through the rural centre of Vyeboom to Elgin (see page 263); the right turn goes to the Franschhoek Pass and the Berg River Valley (see page 105). The Teewaterskloof Dam covers part of the basin in the hills beside the road, and stores water from one of the principal tributaries of the Breë, the Riviersonderend, feeding it out for irrigation.

---

From Worcester, the main tarmac road down the valley of the Breë River turns south-eastwards in close company with the railway line. The landscape is semi-arid; agricultural activity only occurs north of the road on the slopes of the better-watered Langeberg range, or south along the course of the Breë River. After 14 km there is a tarmac turn to Nuy which leads to the slopes of the mountains and then onwards for 22 km through many fine farmlands to join the main road to the north at De Wet.

The road down the valley of the Breë continues, passing the Cape Lime Company works at 31 km from Worcester, the Rooiberg Co-operative Wine Cellars after another 2,5 km, and, at 41 km from Worcester, a cul-de-sac turns to the farming areas of Gorrie and Riverside. The road then makes a handsome approach to the rich farming area around Robertson, with a turnoff to the riverside holiday resort of Silwerstrand, 1,5 km before the road (at 46 km from Worcester), enters the town of . . .

# ROBERTSON

A handsomely situated town, notable for its fine jacaranda trees, flower gardens and an impressive Dutch Reformed Church. The place was named in honour of Dr W. Robertson, pastor of the Swellendam congregation in 1852 when the town was founded. At that time the Dutch Reformed Church purchased the farm *Roode Zand* from its owner J. van Zyl and established a new community centre which held its first sale of plots on 4 May 1853.

The town became a municipality in 1902, and today has a population of 10 820. It is the centre for a considerable industry in the production of wine and brandy. Muscatel grapes do particularly well in the area and it has been claimed with some justification that Robertson is the capital of muscatel country; both the red and white species of the sweet, musk-flavoured grape do better here than anywhere else in the world, and the dessert wine produced from this grape in the local cellars is of superlative quality. Lovers of this type of wine find it tremendously rewarding to visit the nine local co-operative wine cellars and the six estates which produce their own wine for sale. Another estate, the beautiful *Mont Blois,* produces a muscatel wine of origin certified as Superior and distributed through the trade. Colombard grapes grow to perfection in the area and also yield a delectable wine. Jerepigos and sherries, too, are produced, and the town has the largest brandy distillery in South Africa, holding 128 stills in the K.W.V.'s potstill house.

Yellow peaches, apricots and lucerne are grown in the fertile alluvial soil along the river, and the horses bred in this region have raced on many race tracks in Southern Africa.

On the banks of the Breë River at Silwerstrand the Robertson municipality has developed a fine inland holiday resort offering superb swimming, boating and aquaplaning along a long, deep stretch of the river.

The K.W.V. runs a restaurant and taphouse called Branewynsdraai. The restaurant features traditional South African dishes. It is open from 12h00 to 14h30 daily except Mondays and from 19h00 Tuesdays to Saturdays. A range of wines produced in the Robertson area are available for sale at the taphouse.

## Accommodation
* Commercial Hotel, 23 rooms, 8 with baths. R8,50 – R9 B/B. Phone 353.
* Grand Hotel, 12 rooms, 5 with baths. R9 – R10 B/B. Phone 603.
* Masonic Hotel, 16 rooms, 8 with baths. R7,50 B/B. Phone 159.

**Caravans and camping**

★★★® Silwerstrand Resort, 170 sites. R2– R3 D, seasonal. 18 rondawels, R4– R6 D, seasonal. 6 cottages, R6 – R10 D, seasonal. 12 flats, R6 – R15 D, seasonal. Phone 627.

From Robertson, there are several very interesting drives, and for the lover of scenery, fruit, wine and cheese an exploration of these routes is recommended. A short 11-km-long road stretches to the foothills of the Langeberg as far as De Hoop, passing estates such as *Mont Blois* and culminating in a shady cul-de-sac where mountaineers can begin their climbs up slopes adorned with the rare, beautifully flowering nerina. Another road into the foothills of the Langeberg leads to Dassieshoek, where climbers start the long path up Donkerkloof to the summit of the range.

South of Robertson a tarmac road enters a fine avenue of giant eucalyptus trees, crosses the Breë River and then forks. The right-hand road leads for 22 km through the farming areas of Le Chasseur and Agterkliphoogte, passing a succession of wine, fruit and other estates in an alluvial valley watered by a tributary of the Breë named the Poesjenels. The left turn at the fork also passes many fine farms and after 17 km reaches the charming little town of . . .

# McGREGOR

The Reverend Andrew McGregor, one of the Scots ministers who served the Dutch Reformed Church, gave his name to this place, founded in 1861 in a situation and environment strangely reminiscent of a village in Scotland. The architecture, however, is pure Cape-Dutch, and the inhabitants have taken pride in carefully maintaining a delightful assembly of buildings. The church stands in the centre of a garden of flowers, and all the houses are so immaculately whitewashed and topped with black thatched roofs that they almost appear to have gathered to listen to an open-air service by the estimable Dr McGregor! The housing estate for the Coloured community, too, has been carefully laid out with neat little cottages in Cape-Dutch style which are far more attractive than the dreary rows of buildings which pass for modern sub-economic housing estates in many other towns. McGregor is an agricultural centre with a population of 1 300. It has a co-operative wine cellar.

There is an interesting continuation of the road directly through the town and then for 16,5 km up the slopes of the Riviersonderend mountains to the head of Boesmanskloof, a renowned area for wild flowers. The road reaches a sudden and disconsolate end at a precipice known as *Die Galg* (the gallows). Originally it was planned to continue right through Boesmanskloof to Greyton and then to Caledon on the southern side of the mountains, but a sad story of financial muddle and incompetence aborted the project.

From McGregor another road leads for 32 km to the foot of the pass which climbs from Bonnievale through the Riviersonderend mountains to Stormsvlei.

---

A tarmac road from Robertson stretches for 30 km to Bonnievale. This is a very rewarding drive for photographers, revealing fine views of the valley of the Breë, the Langeberg range and many wine, fruit and horse-breeding estates.

# BONNIEVALE

At one time serving as a halfway railway crossing point between Robertson and Swellendam, this place was simply named 'Vale'. In 1917 it became Bonnievale, in 1922 it became a village, and in 1953 a town which today has a population of 2 469. Water flows in canals all the way from Lake Marais to the fertile alluvial soil of the valley and the area is renowned for its production of muscatel wines and sherries. Cognac-type grapes yield fine brandy, and there are four co-operative cellars and several private wine-producing estates in the area. Peaches and apricots are also grown in large quantities while Gouda and Cheddar cheese, produced under the 'Bonnita' label by a local cheese co-operative, Die Boesmansrivierse Ko-op Kaasfabriek Bpk, are outstanding in a country which is not really renowned for producing cheeses much better than 'mouse trap' quality. The yellow clingstone peaches of Bonnievale are also of superlative quality. There is a museum in the charming little Myrtle Rigg church.

### Accommodation
* Bonnievale Hotel, 20 rooms, 5 with baths. R7 – R7,75 B/B. Phone 37.

From Bonnievale a tarmac road crosses the Breë River (where there is a camping ground and ramps for launching boats), passes the cheese co-operative and then leads for 20 km over the Riviersonderend mountains to Stormsvlei (see page 269). Another road, 3 km long, connects the town to the main road from Robertson to Swellendam.

---

The main road from Robertson down the Breë River Valley goes in an easterly direction from the town and, after 18 km of pleasant travelling past many productive farms, reaches the town of . . .

## ASHTON

This town has grown around the giant canning and food-processing plant established there in 1940 by the Langeberg Koöperasie Bpk, today the largest factory of its kind in the Southern Hemisphere. *Ashton* is named after a managing director of the private company which built the railway line from Worcester in 1887. The town achieved municipal status on 1 January 1956, and now has a population of 4 900. Apart from the factory and some colourful gardens, the principal object of note in Ashton is an extraordinary building in the shape of an aeroplane, complete with propeller. This architectural curiosity was built to house the Aero Co-operative, a local trading concern.

### Accommodation
* Olympic Hotel, 15 rooms, 6 with baths. R8,25 – R8,75 B/B. Phone 3.

One kilometre east of Ashton, the road divides. Straight ahead it goes to Montagu and the Little Karoo (see page 256); a right turn snakes south-eastwards down the valley, passes two turnoffs to Bonnievale, and then, at 48,5 km from Ashton, reaches the town of . . .

## SWELLENDAM

In a well-watered valley beneath the most spectacular peaks of the Langeberg range lies this attractive town of 6 603 people. It is said that from the shadow fall of some of these peaks – the Clock Peaks, individually known (from east to west) from the hours as seven, eight, nine, ten, eleven, twelve, one – it is possible to estimate the time of day.

Swellendam has experienced an eventful past. The area was once famous for its game animals. Lion, rhino, hippo, elephant and ostrich abounded, as well as antelope in great number and variety, including eland, zebra, hartebeest, the now rare bontebok and the now extinct kwagga and bluebuck. The concentration of game and the congenial nature of the countryside attracted the Hessekwa Hottentot tribe, who erected their principal kraals in areas such as Bontebokskloof where the graves of their last leaders, Klaas and Markus Sababa, may still be seen.

With the advent of Europeans many fine farms were established along the slopes of the mountains where perennial streams provided ample water, and along the banks of the Breë River: *Grootvadersbosch,* home of Captain Benjamin Moodie, descendant of the wild lairds of Melsetter and a great coloniser whose grandson led the Moodie trek into Zimbabwe; *Rhenosterfontein,* the fine farm of the Van Reenens; *Bruintjiesrivier; The Glen; Rietvlei* (Oude Post); *Klip River,* home of the famous F. W. Reitz, politician and man of progress whose son Frank became President of the Orange Free State; *Somerset Gift;* and *Rotterdam,* home of the renowned landdros, Anthonie Faure. All these and several other farms still have their original homesteads, many of which are characterised by interesting architectural features. Cattle, horses, sheep and wheat were farmed in the area and in order to provide it with an administrative centre, the Dutch East India Company authorities decided in 1743 to establish civil authority over this remote frontier portion of the unwieldy district of Stellenbosch.

Johannes Rhenius was appointed as the first landdros and, together with his councillors, he selected for his seat a particularly charming locality in the valley of one of the streams known as the Cornlands River, tumbling down from the Clock Peaks of the Langeberg range. A residency (*drostdy*) was built in this pleasant situation and in the same year that it was completed – 1747 – the new district was named *Swellendam,* in honour of Governor Hendrik Swellengrebel and his wife Helena ten Damme.

The original drostdy was substantially renovated in later years. Beautifully preserved as a national monument, it is today one of the architectural gems of Southern Africa and houses a museum containing an interesting collection of period furniture and household bric-à-brac dating back over the years since the place was built. The Drostdy Museum is open weekdays from 08h00 to 13h00 and from 14h00 to 17h00; closed Sundays, Christmas Day and Good Friday.

Swellendam has been the scene of lively and varied human activity. For a short while it was even one of the capitals of the world! On 17 June 1795 the citizens of the town, enraged by the misrule of the Dutch East India Company, gathered at the drostdy, dismissed the landdros and declared an independent republic with a local resident, Hermanus Steyn, as President. The pocket republic lasted only three months: the first British occupation of the Cape provided a new regime and the little republic quietly expired.

In 1798 Swellendam consisted of 20 houses scattered along the river valley. It was not until 1802 that the place acquired even a church; for years it was simply the eastern frontier village on what was known as the *Kaapse Wapad* (the wagon road to the Cape), the pioneer road to the east blazed by cattle traders, hunters and explorers. The drostdy was regarded by these people as something of an inn and many celebrated travellers found hospitality there in the course of their travels.

As the years of the first half of the 19th century passed, Swellendam steadily developed into the prosperous administrative and commercial capital of what was known as the *Overberg* (over the mountain) area. The wool industry of Southern Africa was first established commercially in the Overberg with Swellendam as the centre. Wool farming provided the stimulus for the town's development, and its long main street – running up the right bank of the Cornlands River – became lined with a varied collection of buildings, including the warehouse and trading headquarters of the merchant prince of the Overberg, Joseph Barry. It is worth walking along the main street preferably towards evening when it is cool, for no trees have been left to fend off the daytime heat and glare. Odd gables, gateways, relics and fragments of many interesting old buildings survive and it is easy to visualise this street in the 1850s, when traders, farmers, travellers and wagon builders lent to the place a bustle and importance.

In 1864 the Great Western Agricultural Exhibition was held in Swellendam, and this was the peak year of the old order. A newspaper, the *Overberg Courant,* had appeared in 1859, and there were amenities such as a race track, library and literary society. The Barrys had organised a shipping service and a coaster connected the mouth of the Breë River to Cape Town. The district anticipated a brilliant future. Unfortunately, 1865 proved a disastrous year for Swellendam: on 17 May a spark from a baker's oven started a fire that practically gutted the town. The flames, carried by a powerful wind from one thatched roof to the next, destroyed 40 of the fine old houses. Even more destructive to the prosperity of the town was a persistent drought. Little money remained in the district and many of the ventures of the Barrys (Barry and Nephews) fell on evil times. After 45 years of prominence in the Overberg, the Barry concerns went bankrupt in 1866, leaving a huge void in the commerce of the Overberg.

Many memories of the 'golden years' when the town was a hub of commerce still linger in Swellendam. The old jingle *As jy lekker wil lewe koop by Barry en Newe* (if you want to live nicely, purchase at Barry and Nephews) is still occasionally hummed by children playing beside the long main street. Today Swellendam remains a picturesque little town, an important rail and road centre and an interesting stopover for those journeying along the modern highway which has replaced the old 'wagon road to the Cape'.

Opposite the Drostdy Museum is a craft centre containing restorations of a blacksmith's shop, a shoe maker's, a charcoal burner's, a coppersmith's, a cooper's, and a working watermill where stone ground flour may be bought.

### Accommodation
* Carlton Hotel, 28 rooms, 9 with baths. R8,50 – R9,50 B/B. Phone 8.
** Swellengrebel Hotel, 22 rooms, 11 with baths. R9,75 – R13 B/B. Phone 712.
* Ten Damme Hotel, 29 rooms, 23 with baths. R9,75 – R10,75 B/B. Phone 42.

### Caravans and camping
** ® Municipal caravan park, 100 sites. R2,50 D. 4 chalets (4 beds), R10,50 D.

## THE BONTEBOK NATIONAL PARK

One and a half kilometres from Swellendam, just off the main road east of the town, is the entrance to a 2 586-ha wilderness area preserving a handsome expanse of the old Overberg in something of its original state when man first discovered it. Dominated by the tall peaks of the Langeberg and fronting on some fine stretches of the Breë River, this national park provides a sanctuary for many species of game animals that once roamed this part of the world as their natural home. Chief among these animals is the rare bontebok, a species of antelope peculiar to the sandy flat country of the southern end of Africa and, until a handful of local farmers granted them protection, almost on the point of extinction. In 1931 the Parks Board established a sanctuary for bontebok near Bredasdorp, but the area provided poor grazing and the animals failed to flourish.

In 1960 the Bontebok National Park at Swellendam was established and the animals in the old Bredasdorp sanctuary were captured and translocated to a new and ideal home where, according to old records, they were originally present in great numbers. Grey rhebuck, steenbok, grysbok and duiker were already in the area and, in addition to bontebok, the Parks Board reintroduced eland, red hartebeest, and springbok. In the healthy environment these animals have all thrived and the park today is an attractive and interesting place, with beautiful aloes flowering in winter and many trees, including *Acacia karoo,* wild olive, milkwood, yellowwood and candlewood. Gravel roads lead motorists to all parts of the park. A pleasant picnic site and caravan park are situated among a grove of acacia trees on the banks of the Breë River. There is a tearoom and curio shop at the park entrance. A visit to the Bontebok National Park – so conveniently situated to Swellendam and the national road – is thoroughly recommended. The park is open throughout the year from 08h30 to 17h30. The entrance fee is R2 per vehicle with five passengers plus 20 cents for each extra person.

## Caravans and camping
★★ ® 25 sites. R2,60 D.

The Breë River forms the southern boundary of the Bontebok National Park. Beyond the park, the river flows across an undulating coastal terrace, meandering around the hills and falling gently towards the sea. This is wheat country, dotted with flowering aloes in winter, and great flocks of sheep grazing in the meadowlands.

From the Buffelsjag River, 10 km along the main road east of Swellendam, a gravel road winds its way southwards parallel to the river and feeds various farms lining the riverbanks. After 29 km this road reaches the quaint little former river port named *Malgas* from the gannet sea birds. From here a pont, the last of its kind working in South Africa, conveys traffic across the river. From the west bank a road stretches for 60 km to Bredasdorp. The pont charge is 50c per vehicle and it operates from 06h00 to 18h00 daily. This is a picturesque and enjoyable means of crossing the river which, at this point, is sufficiently broad and deep to allow the penetration of coasters in former years from the mouth, 40 km away.

The shipping service, alas, no longer works. In the 1850s, when the merchant house of Barry and Nephews dominated trade in the Overberg area, it was found that three full weeks were needed for wagons to transport goods to Cape Town. The Breë River was obviously perfectly navigable in its lower reaches, and the enterprising firm acquired a fleet of small sailing vessels and built a store at Malgas.

The Breë River mouth is in St Sebastian Bay, with Cape Infanta on its south side. The bay offers little protection from the prevailing south-easterly winds, which can be violent. The river mouth is wide but blocked by the sandbanks usual in rivers, and sailing vessels had a tricky time entering what was called Port Beaufort. Once across the bar into the river, navigation was more simple but if the wind was in a treacherous mood a sailing vessel could suddenly find itself becalmed at an awkward point, and would end up on the beach.

To overcome this problem, the Barrys had a special steamer built on the Clyde. Named the *Kadie*, this perky little 150-ton coaster arrived at the mouth of the river on her maiden voyage on 26 September 1859. She steamed across the bar without difficulty and from the banks of Port Beaufort picked up practically everybody of importance in the district. With flags flying and all on board very merry on good wine and brandy from the Breë River Valley, the ship steamed upriver to Malgas and there unloaded a cargo and those passengers who could find their way home. It was a very happy occasion on the Breë River.

For the next six years the *Kadie* carried to Cape Town cargoes of butter, bitter aloes, wool, sheep and grain valued at over R300 000, and brought back trade goods to stock the Barry stores. The *Kadie* crossed the bar on 240 voyages, then, on 17 November 1865, she struck the rocks on the west bank of the river and was totally wrecked. The ship's bell and some salvaged furniture are in the Barry home in Swellendam, *The Auld House*.

Other coasters continued the trade to Port Beaufort. The last was a famous little ship named the *Chubb*, 172 tons with a draft a little over a metre. Built originally as a waterboat for Simonstown, she was bought in 1933 by Dart and Howes for £100. The new owners removed the watertanks and put the ship on the Breë River run carrying fuels, oils and other cargoes for the farmers and traders. The railways soon complained that the trade was 'unfair' competition and the *Chubb* was transferred to the run to Port Nolloth. She ended up on the shore at Paternoster.

Nowadays only pleasure craft and fishermen sail across the bar of the Breë River. From Malgas a road leads for 20 km down to Witsands, at the mouth of the river, where there is a holiday resort, launching ramps, a fine beach and a small harbour for fishing and sporting boats. Many fine fish, among them giant grunter and cob, are caught in the river mouth and bay. Boating on the river is superb but always dangerous as a result of unpredictable winds. Oysters flourish in the warm waters and there is an old jingle that 'in St Sebastian's Bay you can find pearls'. The hint of their presence at the mouth of the Breë provides a fitting culmination to a river which, along its entire course, brings man so much pleasure and prosperity.

## Accommodation
⋆ Lucky Strike Botel, 14 rooms, all with baths. R10,50 B/B. Phone 31.

## Caravans and camping
⋆⋆ Witsands Caravan Park, 90 sites. R2 D.

Chapter Eight

# THE COAST OF FLOWERS

The rugged coastline from False Bay around Cape Hangklip, past Hermanus, Danger Point and off to Cape Agulhas and Arniston is one of the most beautiful in the world. Its waters, rich in fish, attract thousands of sea birds, and its rocky promontories and cliffs are full of vantage points for anglers. Reefs and islets and capes are enriched by memories of shipwrecks and disasters. There are sandy beaches for swimming and sheltered bays where the waves seem far too lazy even to break. There are caves and pleasant camping grounds, handsome mountains crowd close to the shore and above all there are the wild flowers, dazzling in quantity, variety and brilliance of colour.

The road which follows the coast of flowers begins at Muizenberg, where the beach of silver-coloured sand which forms the northern cul-de-sac of False Bay reaches its western end in the afternoon shadow of the mountains of the Cape Peninsula. From the traffic circle where Prince George's Drive reaches Sunrise Beach, the marine route known as Baden-Powell Drive leads eastwards close to the shore, providing access to an uninterrupted 30 km of beach where swimmers, anglers, surfers and sunbathers find superlative recreation on a sandy coast gently sloping beneath a sea which is warm in summer, cool in winter, safe and always beautiful.

At 3 km the road passes an enclosed area much loved by bird watchers. Invisible from the road, behind low sand dunes, lie a series of artificial lakes which are home to a vast and diverse population of aquatic birds – pelicans, flamingos, terns, cormorants and many others – who find life pleasant in purified water, which is at the end of the cycle of the Cape Town sewage disposal system. To visit this great bird sanctuary a day permit costing 50c must be obtained from the municipal offices.

Beyond these manmade lakes, the road bridges over a stream, which drains the largest of the natural lakes of the Cape Flats, *Zeekoevlei* (hippopotamus marsh), once the home of hippos but now a venue for yachtsmen, aquaplaners and, along its banks, picnickers. Access to Zeekoevlei and to the artificial lakes is along a road which joins the coast road at Strandfontein 8 km from Muizenberg.

Strandfontein has been developed by the Cape Town municipality as a holiday resort for the Coloured community. Adjacent to it inland is the housing estate of Mitchell's Plain, named after Colonel Charles Michell, surveyor general of the Cape in the 1840s, and builder of Michell's Pass. The reason for the addition of a 't' in the name of the estate is unknown. For several kilometres the coast road forms the divide between residential and recreational areas; among the latter is the beach euphemistically named *Mnandi* (the pleasant place), much used by residents of the nearby townships of Guguletu and Langa.

### Caravans and camping
★ Caravan and camping sites. R3 – R5 D, seasonal.
Holiday cabins, 54 with 4 bunks in each. R4 – R6,25 D, seasonal.

The coast road continues eastwards, revealing splendid views over False Bay and across to the Hottentots Holland mountains. Seal Island lies 6 km from the coastline, its rocky shore crowded with seals and birds; gulls squabble and make up in nesting crevices and ledges of the cliffs overlooking the sea 16 km from Muizenberg.

Two kilometres beyond the gull sanctuary, the coast road passes a turnoff leading inland to the main coastal road, and then reaches the swimming and angling area of Swartklip. Beyond this rocky cliff lies the sweeping stretch of Macassar Beach. The coastal road has still to be built along this section; the tarmac road makes a temporary turn inland to join the main 'Settlers Way' Cape Town-Port Elizabeth road at a point 24,5 km from Muizenberg, leaving a 12-km roadless gap along the coast. Along this highway the coast is bypassed until the turnoff to Strand, which leads back to the coast. The intervening stretch of roadless coast is served by a track, which is much used by fishermen and walkers exploring Macassar Beach and the estuary of the Eerste River.

## MACASSAR BEACH

Sheik Yussuf of Macassar was a prince of Bantam and a religious leader who was exiled to the Cape by the Dutch in 1694. Accompanied by 49 followers, two wives and 12 children, he was obliged to reside at an outpost on the farm *Zandvliet.* When he died, on 23 May 1699 at the age of 73, he was buried on a hilltop there. Since that time, his gravesite has been regarded as a holy place by all Moslems. The *kramat* (tomb) was built over the grave in 1925 by Hadji Sullaiman Shah Mohomed. It is an impressive little memorial: the perfumed and beflagged tomb shelters within a domed chamber and is visited by many pilgrims who cover the tomb with thank-offerings of brilliantly coloured silken quilts which are periodically removed by the guardian.

Old cannon guard the kramat and overlook a grand panorama stretching from Table Mountain to the end of the Hottentots Holland mountains. Sheik Yussuf's kramat is the most important of six holy tombs, all built over the graves of religious leaders. The other five kramats are on Signal Hill, at Oudekraal, on Robben Island and two are in Constantia. All attract pilgrims. It is said that a line joins together all these kramats, making a holy circle which encloses Cape Town and brings peace and blessings to true believers who reside there.

Sheik Yussuf's kramat is close to the beach of Macassar, where a seaside resort has been developed mainly for the Moslem community. A gravel road 4,5 km long connects the area to the main road between Cape Town and Somerset West.

Macassar Beach ends at the estuary of the Eerste River. East of this the coast is part of the well-wooded grounds of African Explosives and Chemical Industries, whose Capex fertilizer and explosives factory buildings stand among the trees. Where the company ground ends the shoreline continues along what is known as Milk Bay. On this broad and gently shelving beach, one of the safest bathing beaches in Africa, stands the resort of . . .

## STRAND

This holiday resort stretches for 3 km along the beach of Milk Bay. Originally intended as a seaside suburb for Somerset West, the place soon outgrew its parent and became a municipality of its own on 15 June 1896. Its original name was Somerset Strand, later abbreviated to the simpler form of Strand. Today the town has a population of 30 800 and is an extremely popular summer holiday resort offering excellent swimming, surfing, boating and the pleasure of an almost limitless beach.

### Accommodation
** Aroma Sands Hotel, 47 rooms, 39 with baths. R12 – R18 B/B. Phone 3-3303.
** Metropole Hotel, 33 rooms, 18 with baths. R9 – R10,50 B/B. Phone 3-1501.

**Caravans and camping**

★★ Kays Caravan Park, 95 sites. R2,50 – R4 D.
★★ Voortrekker Park, 320 sites. R2,60 – R4,20 D, seasonal.

From Strand the road continues for 5 km parallel to what is known as the Harmony Coast and then reaches the resort of . . .

# GORDON'S BAY

An attractive seaside resort lying immediately below the Hottentots Holland mountains, the town's namesake was Captain Robert Gordon, an officer of the Dutch East India Company who explored the area in 1778. Gordon's Bay became a municipality on 1 February 1961 and now has a population of 1 670.

Though swimming is somewhat complicated by a rocky shore and large numbers of sea urchins, Gordon's Bay is well protected from the winds and in summer its waters are warm. In winter, too, the climate can be delightful: False Bay is often calmer than an inland lake and the cottages of Gordon's Bay send shimmering reflections of themselves across the surface of the sea. At this time fishing boats and yachts in the harbour sleep easily on tranquil water so clear that, until you see the shoals of fish moving lazily beneath them, the boats seem to be touching bottom.

Adjacent to the harbour at Gordon's Bay are the buildings of the naval college for cadet officers. The letters G. B. and an anchor laid out in white stones on the mountain slopes above Gordon's Bay refer to the original name of this training school, when it was known as the General Botha Training College for merchant navy officers.

**Accommodation**

★ Gordonia Hotel, 21 rooms, 11 with baths. R8 – R10 B/B. Phone 4-1231.
★★ Van Riebeeck Hotel, 69 rooms, 42 with baths. R7 – R16 B/B. Phone 4-1441.

**Caravans and camping**

★★ Apple Farmer Caravan Park, Steenbras River Mouth, 250 sites. R4 D.
★★ Panorama Caravan Park, 100 sites. R4,50 D.
★★ Sea Breeze Caravan Park, 200 sites. R3 – R4,50 D.

At Gordon's Bay the mountains crowd close to the sea and the famous marine drive cuts into their slopes. Two kilometres out of Gordon's Bay a turnoff left provides a spectacular route to the summit of the range where the imposing buildings of the Steenbras filtration plant stand. This plant supplies water to the Cape Peninsula and the towns of the Cape Flats. The 4-km-long road up to the filtration plant reveals some magnificent views. At the plant there is a gate and a permit to continue the journey is essential. Permits are available from the municipal offices of Cape Town, Strand and Gordon's Bay. From the gate the road crosses the summit of the Hottentots Holland and then descends into the beautiful valley of the Steenbras River, now completely flooded by the waters of the Steenbras Dam.

Steenbras Dam, which has a surface of 380 ha, is one of the scenic showpieces of the Western Cape. Built in 1921, and later enlarged by raising the wall to a height of 22,1 m, it supplies the Western Cape with drinking water fed through three pipelines, 52 km in length, which end at Newlands reservoir in Cape Town. The dam has also been developed as a major recreational area. One thousand two hundred and fourteen hectares of pines have been planted around the reservoir and a magnificent garden of wild flowers (especially of the protea family) has been laid out. There is also a picnic site beneath the pines. When the dam overflows during the winter rainy season (around August) the spillway makes a spectacular picture and a short way down the course of the river, there is a fine natural waterfall. From the

Steenbras Dam the road continues for 5 km, then joins the main Cape Town-Port Elizabeth road on the Grabouw side of Sir Lowry's Pass.

## Accommodation
Municipal bungalows, 14 for Europeans and 7 for Non-Europeans. Four beds in each bungalow. Mon to Fri R4 D, weekends R5,50 D.

Back to the marine drive which, as it continues along the mountain slopes from Gordon's Bay, overlooks a stretch of precipitous and rocky coast, one of the finest fishing areas in Southern Africa. Innumerable great catches of the teeming fish life of False Bay have been made here. But the coast has also claimed a toll of human lives, for it is an excessively dangerous area and many an unwary or overzealous fisherman has slipped on the cliffs or been caught on an exposed rock by a sudden wave and been catapulted to join the fish he was so eager to catch.

At 3 km from Gordon's Bay the road reaches the mouth of the Steenbras River (named after the steenbras fish species). Beyond the river is the Clarence Drive and, 8 km from Gordon's Bay, a memorial, dated 1 January 1950 to G. J. V. (Jack) Clarence 'whose vision, faith and determination helped to bring the road into being'. Clarence was one of the directors of the Cape Hangklip Beach Estate Company, an organisation which planned ambitious real estate projects.

At this point the drive enters its most spectacular stretch. It climbs around the cliffs and then, 3 km beyond the Clarence memorial, drops down to the beautiful (but dangerous) beach of *Koeëlbaai* (bullet bay) backed by the dominant pile of the 1 268-m-high *Koeëlberg* (bullet mountain). The scenery is superb but the sea is treacherous and unsafe for swimming. At the southern end of the bay is the *Blousteenberg* (blue stone or manganese mountain), where once a small mine was worked; the ruins of the jetty may still be seen. There is a caravan and camping ground (R2 D) run by the Cape Town municipality, especially for the Coloured community.

Nineteen kilometres from Gordon's Bay the road reaches the mouth of the *Rooi-els* River, named from the red alder trees growing there. A pretty beach is marred by a tricky backwash.

Across this river the road swings inland and climbs steeply, entering the area of the original Cape Hangklip Beach Estate Company. This region is renowned for its wild flowers and for their sake it is perhaps fortunate that the original grandiose township schemes for this area have produced only a scattering of rather dismal fishermen's cottages. The everlastings, the watsonias and, above all, the proteas have always flourished best in this environment of sweeping mountains and interminable winds.

Five kilometres from the Rooi-els River is a right turn which leads to *Pringle Bay* – Rear-Admiral Thomas Pringle was in command of the Cape station in 1796 – and to the 452,6-m-high landmark of *Hangklip* (overhanging rock), the leaning mountain from which the cape – the eastern end of False Bay – takes its name. An automatic lighthouse, a few cottages and a hotel, are at the cape.

## Accommodation
★ Hangklip Hotel, 10 rooms, 2 with baths. R6,50 – R7,90 B/B. Phone Betty's Bay 1331.

## Caravans and camping
★ Hangklip Caravan Park, 18 sites. R2,50 D.

The main road proceeds for a further 6 km beyond the Hangklip turnoff. Wild flowers and several lakelets (stocked with black bass) make the drive both interesting and attractive. At 32 km from Gordon's Bay the road reaches a turnoff right, which leads to the ruins of the old whaling station at Stony Point. Founded in 1907 by a Captain Cook, it was called the Southern

Cross Whaling Station. In those days it was a lonely place served by no roads; only the comings and goings of the four little ships stationed there provided any link with the outside world.

Over the years other companies took over the running of the station: first the Shepstone Whaling Company under Captain Berntsen, and then in 1916 Irvin and Johnson took over and ran the place until it closed down in 1928. Its rough and ready staff of whalermen wandered away to adventures in other parts, and the buildings were left to rust. The hulk of one of the whalers, the *Balena,* still lies next to the remains of the jetty. West of Stony Point, in Silver Sands Bay, the swimming is good, and there is fishing all along the coast, which is strewn with many interesting shells.

After the turnoff to Stony Point the main road continues, passing a turnoff to Betty's Bay beach and picnic area, and, after 1,5 km, the Betty's Bay store; it then enters the village area of . . .

# BETTY'S BAY

Named after Betty Youlden, the daughter of the managing director of the first company to attempt development of the Cape Hangklip area, the whole area of the village was once a great retreat for runaway slaves, who sought sanctuary in the mountains from the oppression of their owners. Many tales are still told of pursuit and desperate defiance in the caves and hidden valleys of these mountains, where much human blood was shed in the course of this unhappy chapter of man's inhumanity to man.

In later years the area became a ranch, owned by John Walsh of Caledon, who ran livestock there and organised a small fishing enterprise at Holbaai, sending fish across to the Kalk Bay market. He also exported everlasting flowers to Germany and Russia, where they have always been in demand for the making of wreaths. A reminder of those past days is the place named *Dawidskraal* (David's kraal), where for many years a Coloured shepherd lived in the shelter of the milkbush trees.

On the death of Walsh the property passed into the hands of Youlden first and then, in 1938, after the stock-exchange crash of Black Friday, into the possession of the Cape Hangklip Beach Estate Company, whose 'guiding geniuses' were Jack Clarence and Harold Porter. Their grandiose schemes of massive development proved abortive, but Betty's Bay grew into an informal little village of weekend and holiday cottages with one particularly beautiful asset, the Harold Porter Botanic Reserve, bequeathed by Porter in February 1958 to the National Botanic Gardens of South Africa. This reserve is now the permanent home for the magnificent wild flowers of the area. Pleasant paths have been made which lead visitors through the reserve, up the slopes of the mountains and as far as the waterfall in Disa Kloof, where indigenous trees, identified by tags, provide a shady walk.

Forty-six kilometres from Gordon's Bay the road leaves the Cape Hangklip area proper and passes through *Elephant Rock Estate,* a protea farm named after an unusually-shaped rock high up on the mountain, near the waterfall on the left-hand side of the road. Three kilometres further on, the road crosses the Palmiet River just above a lagoon which has popular picnic and camping grounds along its banks. There is a forestry track going up the river, but the entrance gate is locked; a permit must be obtained to explore this beautiful area.

# KLEINMOND

Three kilometres beyond the Palmiet River (51 km from Gordon's Bay) the road reaches this holiday resort which, as its name implies, is built at the 'small mouth' of a lagoon. With a permanent population of 1 502, Kleinmond is a great centre in summer for caravanners and campers, especially from inland farming areas. Despite the fact that the lagoon at the river mouth is considerably polluted, people swim in it, and there is a fishing harbour. The long beach of Sandown Bay, spacious but steeply sloping, is rather dangerous for swimming, but well liked by fishermen. A superb mountain backdrop is enhanced in springtime by magnificently blooming proteas.

## Accommodation
★ Sandown Hotel, 12 rooms, 9 with baths. R8 – R9 B/B. Phone 17.
Brightwood, 9 bungalows, 4 - 8 beds in each. R9 – R12,50 D.

## Caravans and camping
★ Fairy Glen Caravan Park, 40 sites. R1,20 D plus 20c D per person.
★ Kleinmond Caravan Park, 300 sites. R2 – R3 D plus 20c D per person.
★ Palmiet River Mouth, 300 sites. R3 D plus 25c D per person.

From Kleinmond the tarmac road continues through a countryside full of flowers and strange rock shapes. Directly ahead looms the great 1 168-m-high Babylon's Tower, on whose precipitous peaks grow many rare flowers. June is a good month for proteas along this road; October to November is the time for everlastings, watsonias and chincherinchees. At 11 km a turnoff left leads for 5,5 km to the Highlands Forestry Station; a fine drive up a rough road with steep gradients. From the forestry station the road continues to Grabouw. Immense concentrations of wild flowers carpet the area.

Back at the main road: after 5 km a junction with the Bot River-Hermanus road is reached. A left turn leads for 3 km to a junction with the Cape Town to Port Elizabeth road; a right turn goes south, down the left-hand side of the Bot River lagoon, through wheat, onion and potato fields. At 13 km there is a turnoff to Lake Marina township and at 14 km a turnoff to Sonesta Holiday Resort. At 16 km the road reaches . . .

# HAWSTON

Mr Haw was a one-time civil commissioner of the Caledon district and his namesake is now a favourite camping ground and holiday resort for the Coloured community. A gravel road leads for 3 km to a beach at Harry's Bay and to a rocky inlet now developed into what is known as the 'New Harbour', with a slipway for fishing boats.

## Accommodation
★★★® Sonesta Holiday Resort, 15 luxury bungalows (6 persons), R18,70 D, in season. 30 rondawels (4 persons), R13,75 D, in season. Caravan Park, 190 sites. R4,50 D, in season.

The Sonesta resort is one of the finest in the country, managed and administered by an associate company of the Coloured Development Corporation. Attractively situated, it has its own swimming and paddling pool, children's playground and various indoor and outdoor sporting facilities, including a beach and a lagoon for angling, surfing and yachting. Other amenities are a restaurant, snack bar, shop, etc. Phone bookings can be made from March (for Christmas) to November (for Easter). Phone 5740 or 5790.

## Caravans and camping
★ Divisional Council caravan park, 500 sites. R1 D.

Three kilometres beyond Hawston the road reaches the seaside resort and village of . . .

# ONRUS

The first Europeans to visit this place named it *Onrus* (restless) because of the 'everlasting droning of the sea'. The coast here is rockbound, with heavy surf, a small beach and a lagoon at the mouth of the Onrus River; a natural swimming pool lies among in the rocks. Well wooded, green and with the fresh, clear air of this part of the coast, Onrus is a particular haunt of campers, especially those who are gregarious by nature, for the undoubtedly fine camping ground becomes a jam-packed tent town over the Christmas holidays. Regular devotees of the place book the same sites year after year, enjoying the fishing, bowls and relaxation in the pure air.

## Caravans and camping
* Municipal camping ground, 260 sites. R3,20 D.
* Paradise Caravan Park, 36 sites. R2,50 D. Rondawels, R6 D.
* Seaview Caravan Park, 28 sites. R2,50 – R3,50 D plus R1,50 D per person.
** Sherwood Caravan Park, 70 sites. R2 – R3,50 D, plus R1 – R1,50 D per person, seasonal.

Behind Onrus the mountains cluster close to the sea; only a green and pleasant terrace separates them from the surf. For 7 km beyond Onrus the tarmac road leads through thickly wooded and attractive country, dotted with pretty homesteads, diverse scenery and myriad flowers. Then the trees suddenly divide, disclosing a vista of the immaculate and obviously prosperous resort of Hermanus, lined with cottages, seaside mansions, hotels, and various retreats for tired millionaires, jaded businessmen and many ordinary people who appreciate one of the world's finest areas for relaxation. Crisp air, rugged coast and mountains richly ornamented with wild flowers, waterfalls, ravines and grottoes create a restful and attractive atmosphere.

# HERMANUS

This town has had a curiously romantic history. Back in the 1830s a certain Hermanus Pieters wandered through the Caledon district. A man of some slight education, who earned his living by selling his services to the farmers as a combined shepherd and teacher, he never remained in one place for long, but drifted from one farm to the other.

One dry summer he passed through the valley of *Hemel-en-Aarde* (heaven and earth) which lies behind the mountains overlooking Hermanus. A leper station had been established in this secluded valley in 1814 and from that time until the end of 1845, when the patients were transferred to Robben Island, it was a retreat of the abandoned.

Hermanus Pieters heard from the lepers that there was a path, known as *Olifants Pad* (elephant's way) which climbed over the mountains to the coast and was used by an occasional individual who wanted to fish. Curiosity led Hermanus Pieters along this path. He reached the summit of the range and looked down in admiration at the beautiful landscape beneath him. Intensely green, streaked with rivulets tumbling down to the sea as eagerly as small boys, and no sign of human habitation.

Following the path down to the shore, Hermanus Pieters found a congenial campsite at a spring almost in reach of the spray of the great rollers which pounded incessantly on the rocky coast. To a restless child of nature, this unspoilt wilderness was a terrestrial heaven and each summer it became Hermanus's habit to camp at the place which later became known as *Hermanus Pietersfontein* (the spring of Hermanus Pieters). There he tended his flocks and herds, fished and wandered as free as the winds among the wild flowers and the heath. The fountain of Hermanus Pieters is marked by a plaque next to the present Marine Drive.

In due course other people discovered the potential of Hermanus Pieters's fountain, among them a German, Michael Henn, with his wife Henrietta, five sons, five daughters and, inevitably (for the young Henn girls were reputedly comely), five young men to marry the girls. They were Thomas Montgomery, a ship's carpenter who turned up at Hawston and was gathered into the flock; James Warrington, from Cape Town who was also added to the brood; John (Scotty) Paterson, formerly of the Royal Navy, who found his way to this little Henn house; Thomas Leff, a wandering Pole, joined the clutch; and Harry Plumridge, a deserter from the Royal Navy who cheerfully found a roost for himself with the youngest of the Henn girls.

In addition to fishing at Harry's Bay, the Henns burned shells to make lime. There were huge and ancient deposits of shells strewn along the various beaches and in numerous kitchen middens left by prehistoric man. While making their way to one of these shell deposits, at Skilphoek, the Henns explored the area of Hermanus Pieters's fountain and, liking what they saw, decided to move there. Packing their belongings into ox wagons and into their boat, the *Nellie* (originally the gig used by Dr Culhave, ship's doctor of the ill-fated *Birkenhead,* to reach Harry's Bay after the shipwreck) they made their way to the present site of Hermanus, where Michael Henn built the first house. His sons and sons-in-law followed suit. Other people were attracted to the area and a hamlet grew. The first church, St Peter's, and a school, opened in 1868.

In June 1891 the place became a village with its own management board, and in the same year Walter MacFarlane built the first hotel, the Victoria (now the Astoria); it would have been fitting if the ghost of old Hermanus Pieters could have been the first guest . . .

Fishing developed along with the holiday trade. The old *Nellie* and all the first fishing boats worked from the unique natural harbour, which was a rocky cove with a precarious entrance – a most unreliable shelter from what Kipling called 'the dread Agulhas roll'. Damage to the fishing vessels and even a number of wreckages occurred before public agitation brought about the construction of a better harbour. In September 1904, by which time its name had been abbreviated (the postal authorities had quietly dropped the 'Pietersfontein' in 1902), Hermanus was made a municipality. The place became renowned for its excellent fishing, especially the kabeljou run from November to March. Prominent people such as Sir William Hoy, then general manager of South African Railways, were attracted and Hermanus became a fashionable resort for the wealthy and the wise. Today the town boasts a population of 5 378. Sir William Hoy and his wife are buried on a hillock in the centre of Hermanus; a path leads to the summit, and a good view.

Some exciting catches have been made at Hermanus. On 28 April 1922 after five and a half hours of battle, W. R. Selkirk landed the greatest catch ever made with rod and line up to that date anywhere in the world: a 4-m-long shark weighing 986 kg. Another record catch was a 50-kg kabeljou caught by the Hon. W. P. Schreiner, and many other tremendous fish have been landed. Today Hermanus is a flourishing holiday resort. Yachting and aquaplaning take place in the great lagoon; a spectacular 6-km-long scenic road (Rotary Way) carves up the mountain slopes to a viewsite on the summit; Fernkloof Nature Reserve, opened in January 1960, is a 171-ha sanctuary for flowers, birds and game, with 17 km of carefully graded footpaths which take even the elderly to many beautiful settings where wild flowers grow in their natural element; a fine golf course, bowling greens and other sporting facilities, as well as two superb bathing beaches (Voëlklip and Grotto), are additional attractions. A 12-km-long footpath runs along the cliffs from the new harbour to the mouth of the lagoon; this track reaches all fishing points and is a fine walk, embellished by many types of wild flowers and entrancing views. A magnetic survey station is located in Hermanus; visitors are allowed on Wednesdays by appointment.

## Accommodation

★★ Astoria Hotel, 12 rooms, all with baths. R9,50 – R12,50 B/B. Phone 159.
★★ Bay View Hotel, 83 rooms, 63 with baths. R11,45 – R22,75 B/B. Phone 2-1100.

*Overleaf: In the sandstone soils of the Western Cape blooms one of nature's most exquisite gardens with flowers more diverse and numerous than anywhere on earth.*

★★ Birkenhead Hotel, 45 rooms, 29 with baths. R10 – R19,50 B/B. Phone 651.
★★ Riviera Hotel, 42 rooms, 40 with baths. R8,50 – R12,50 B/B. Phone 2-1153.
★ Royal Hotel, 18 rooms, 4 with baths. R8 – R8,50 B/B. Phone 184.
★ Windsor Hotel, 48 rooms, 14 with baths. R7 – R10 D/B/B. Phone 236.

**Caravans and camping**
★★ De Mond Caravan Park, 220 sites. R2,50 – R3,50 D plus 25c D per person.

From Hermanus the tarmac road runs for 18 km along the verge of the spacious lagoon of the *Kleinrivier* (little river). This is a particularly fine drive: the mountains crowd close to the road and in the winter months sparkling white necklaces of waterfalls adorn the slopes, whispering through the air like a sigh.

# STANFORD

Twenty-four kilometres from Hermanus is a small farming and road centre named after Captain Robert Stanford who owned the *Klein River* farm on which it was laid out in 1856. Stanford became a village in 1892 and a municipality on 22 December 1919. It has a population of 1 023.

**Accommodation**
★ Stanford Hotel, 10 rooms, 3 with baths. R7 – R7,50 B/B. Phone 24.

From Stanford there is a 17-km drive to the 834-ha Salmondsdam Nature Reserve, created in 1962 by the Divisional Council of Caledon. Named, it is said, in memory of Captain Robert Salmond, commander of the ill-fated *Birkenhead,* it contains specimens of most of the game animals indigenous to these parts and a vast variety of flowering plants. Spring is the best time to visit this reserve but there are always flowers in bloom. A mountain drive takes visitors to a high viewpoint. Entrance fee to the reserve is R1 per car.

**Accommodation**
Cottages, R4 – R8 D.

**Caravans and camping**
★ 20 sites, R1 D.

Beyond Stanford the main tarmac coast road continues south across undeveloped, bush-covered country, frequented by small antelope and a fine area for flowering plants. After 17 km the road approaches the coast once more and a short gravel turnoff leads to . . .

# DE KELDERS

Consisting of a handful of cottages and a hotel, this place takes its name, which means 'the cellars', from a curious underground cavern. There is a superb view over the great sweep of Walker Bay, where whales flirt and laze in early summer and white sand dunes rise in strange contrast to the blue mountains of the coastal range. The natural cavern (the cellars) has a cool stream flowing through it and a swim underground in the crystal-clear water is an interesting experience. Lady Anne Barnard visited the place in 1798 and left an amusing description of her journey to what was then called the *Drupkelder* – a lair of hyenas full of bones, stalactites, stalagmites and other dripstone formations. Entrance to the cave is 30c.

### Accommodation
★ De Kelders Hotel, 16 rooms, 4 with baths. R8 – R9 B/B. Phone 80.

Three kilometres from De Kelders the tarmac road reaches the fishing harbour of . . . .

## GANSBAAI

Built around the largest fishing harbour along this part of the coast, the village of *Gansbaai* (goose bay) is nondescript, but the harbour, with its fish-processing factory, is photogenic, and the views from the breakwater of Walker Bay and the coastal mountains are sweeping. Walker, of *Walker Bay* was a master in the Royal Navy and he must have been well pleased to have so handsome a stretch of coast named after him. A huge swell often shoulders its way into the bay, bringing tremendous waves.

### Accommodation
Sea View Hotel, 10 rooms, 4 with baths. R11 D. Phone 27.

### Caravans and camping
★ ® Municipal caravan park, R3,50 D.

## DANGER POINT

From Gansbaai the road continues in a south-westerly direction for 2 km and then reaches a turnoff leading for 8 km to the lighthouse at Danger Point. This is a worthwhile journey, for Danger Point, menacing and rocky, is very atmospheric, and the Birkenhead rock of sorrowful memory lies less than a kilometre off the point.

The wreck of the *Birkenhead* is one of the most celebrated of all maritime disasters. The *Birkenhead* was a steam transport conveying reinforcements from Simon's Bay to serve in the Eighth Kaffir War. The ship struck the submerged rock off Danger Point at 02h00 on 26 February 1852. It practically tore open at the bottom and many soldiers were drowned as they lay asleep in their hammocks. The rest rushed on deck and were drawn up in good order. Two boats were launched, which took the seven women and 13 children on board, along with as many men as the boats could hold. The gig was also launched with nine men. Within 20 minutes of striking the rock the *Birkenhead* went down, leaving part of the hull with the mainmast precariously balanced on the rock.

The gig reached the coast near Hawston. The two other lifeboats met a coasting schooner which rescued them and then proceeded to the scene of the disaster. About 50 men were found clinging to the remnants of the ship. They were taken aboard the coaster and, carrying a total of 116 survivors, the little boat made its way to Simonstown with news of the wreck. Sixty-eight men and eight horses survived a final buffeting by the surf and rocks and managed to reach the shore. Nine officers, 349 men of other rank and 87 of the crew were drowned.

Set in the base of the Danger Point lighthouse is a plaque commemorating the wreck of the *Birkenhead*. The lighthouse, with a 4 750 000 candlepower light, makes a fine picture as it stands guard over this point of dramatic memories. The gravel road ends at the lighthouse gate but a fishermen's track winds around the fence to the actual point, where there is a blowhole linked to the sea by an underground chasm. At times of very high tide the great powerhouse rollers which pound upon Danger Point roar their way up this cavern and force a jet of water through the blowhole. Fishermen have reported that the jet has been seen to reach a height of more than 10 m.

## UILENSKRAAL

After the turnoff to Danger Point the coast road continues through scrub and flower country. Five kilometres on there is a short turnoff leading to the coast at the mouth of the *Uilenskraal* (owl's kraal) *River*. There is a fine beach and lagoon at this point and the area is popular for camping and caravanning, offering excellent bathing and fishing. To the south-east of this resort are the guano and seal islands of *Dyer* (Sampson Dyer was an American negro who once worked guano on this island) and Geyser, where fur seals are hunted each year.

**Caravans and camping**
Divisional Council caravan park, 650 sites. R3,50 D. 14 cottages (6 beds), R8,50 – R10 D, seasonal.

Beyond the Uilenskraal turnoff the gravel road continues through undulating, bushy country. After 10 km the road climbs a good vantage point which reveals a sweeping view of the coast and its rocky islands. Twelve kilometres further on the road passes through a diminutive settlement with the odd name of *Baardskeerdersbos* (beard shaver's bush) and a kilometre beyond that point is a turnoff to . . .

## PEARLY BEACH

The 3-km gravel road taking travellers to this beach passes through magnificent wild flower country. In early summer yellow, white and pink everlastings, as well as numerous pincushions are in flower. The summit of a rise along the way gives a fine view of the coast with a line of very elegant sand dunes looming steeply against the blue of the sea. Swimming, fishing and hiking are pleasant pastimes for holidaymakers at Pearly Beach.

**Caravans and camping**
★ Pearly Beach, 25 sites. R3 D plus 50c D per person. Bungalows: 4 beds, R5,50 – R8 D; 5 beds, R12,50; 7 beds, R15,50.

The main gravel road continues from the Pearly Beach turnoff through hilly wild flower country. After 10 km there is a turnoff over the hills back to Stanford; six kilometres further on a turn leads to Napier. Twenty-six kilometres from the Pearly Beach turnoff the road reaches . . .

## ELIM

Until recently this was the most attractive and picturesque old-time South African mission station surviving from the past. It shelters in a well-watered hollow in an undulating plain noted for its spring everlastings. Houses, church and watermill are all still there but now somewhat forlorn, for the former spirit of the place, along with the fruit trees which once lined the streets, seems to have vanished.

On 12 May 1824 Bishop Hallbeck of the Moravian Church acquired the 2 570-ha farm *Vogelfontein* from Johannes Schonken. On Ascension Thursday, 12 May 1825, the name was changed to *Elim* and a mission was established around the original farmhouse, built in 1796 by a Huguenot named Louis du Toit. Neat little cottages were built to house the Coloured community and a substantial church (severely plain as with all Moravian churches) became the pivot of the settlement.

An interesting later addition to this church was its clock. Just before the First World War, the Reverend Mr Will, the then encumbent of Elim, went to Germany on furlough. He heard about a clock built in 1764 in Zittau, Saxony, by a renowned watchmaker named Prasse. This clock had been installed in the church at Herrenhut and for 140 years had kept time for the congregation. In 1905 the clock had been pensioned off and was now lying in store. Mr Will secured the clock and shipped it to Elim, where, in 1914, it started work again. With a slow, deliberate pendulum swing and a deep resolute tick, it still keeps excellent time.

In Elim is one of the last of the watermills of the Cape, built in 1828 to replace an earlier mill. Its machinery was made entirely of wood, but in 1881, the mill was re-equipped with 5 442 kg of iron machinery and today only the waterwheel is of wood. The mill once had a curiously graceful air of old-fashioned elegance. Its great, slow-turning grindstones produced flour of superb aroma and taste and the whirr of its racks, the rumbling of the grinding stones and the merry splashing of the water created an atmosphere of honest work and pride in its production. Like the rest of the mission, this mill is nowadays dilapidated. Elim badly needs to be restored to its former state; only a few years back it was the scene of considerable activity, involving production of sausages, salami, cigars, and the export of everlastings to wreath-makers in Germany. There was a small boarding house, a lovely old-world garden and a charming elegance to the whole mission.

The main gravel road continues eastwards from Elim for 12 km to *Voëlvlei* (bird marsh) where there is a junction. The left-hand turn leads for 19 km to Bredasdorp; the right-hand turn leads through flat farmland, sprinkled with numerous lakelets, marshes and dried-out beds of former lakelets. Aquatic birds are numerous and flamingos breed here. The road skirts the verges of the large *Zoetendalvlei* (a marsh and farm named after the wreck of the *Zoetendal* in 1673 and renowned as one of the principal breeding grounds of the first woolled sheep in South Africa) and, 23 km from the Voëlvlei junction, joins the tarmac road connecting Bredasdorp (left turn, 19 km) to Cape Agulhas.

Turning right, this tarmac road leads for 4 km to a cluster of fishermen's cottages, which often features in the paintings of South African artists. The unusual name of this little place – *Hotagterklip* (left behind the stone) – comes from the days of the first wagon track, when a stone outcrop imposed a sharp detour on all travellers. Unfortunately most of the old cottages have been allowed to fall into ruin and the fishermen are now housed in the usual drab modern abodes.

## STRUISBAAI

Two kilometres beyond Hotagterklip the tarmac road reaches the village and holiday resort of *Struisbaai* (straw bay), named, it is said, after fishermen's cottages built there in the past of straw. Another version of the name is that it used to be *Vogelstruis* (ostrich) *Bay*. Whatever the origin of its name, this handsome bay has a fine beach for swimming, fishing and shell collecting.

### Accommodation
★ Struisbaai Motel, 32 double bungalows. R3,50 – R4,25 room only. Phone 4422.

### Caravans and camping
★ Divisional Council caravan park, 280 sites. R3,64 D. 16 bungalows, R8,32 – R10,40 D.

The tarmac road continues along the coast beyond Struisbaai for 8 km and then ends at the village, holiday resort and lighthouse at the most southerly point of Africa . . .

# CAPE AGULHAS

Originally named Cape Saint Brendan because on the day of that saint – 16 May – Bartholomew Dias passed by on his homeward voyage in 1488. The name *Agulhas* was originally
applied to Struisbaai (*Golfo das Agulhas* – gulf of the needles) but later applied to the cape as
well. According to De Castro in his *Roteiro*, the etymology of the name is interesting: it was at
this cape that a remarkable change in magnetic forces occurred:

'It is an axiom with the pilots,' wrote De Castro, 'that here there is no variation in the
needles of their compasses, which bear directly upon the true poles of the earth. Hence
they call it the Cape of the Needles.'

To the men of the sailing ships, who lived close to the sea, the Cape of Good Hope was
indisputably the meeting place of the Indian and Atlantic oceans while Agulhas, with its
tremendous rollers and rocky bottoms, was a place of magnetic change. To the eye Cape
Agulhas is not a dramatic point: a range of hills forms a wall separating the sea from the flat
inland and a 12 million candlepower lighthouse and radio beacon stand permanent watch
over the end of Africa. The land peters out into a flat and rocky projection which, at a depth of
60 fathoms, continues under the sea for 250 km before falling steeply into the 1 800 fathom
depths of the southern ocean.

The holiday resort of Agulhas consists of a few stores and a rather unlovely cluster of
cottages thrown up in modern times. Fishing is good and tidal swimming pools have been
made along the rocky shore.

## Accommodation

★ Suidpunt Hotel, 45 rooms, 9 with baths. R6 – R6,50 B/B. Phone 4211.

## Caravans and camping

★ Municipal caravan park, 100 sites. R2,50 – R3,25 D. 16 bungalows (2 bedrooms and living
room in each), R7 – R10 D.

The tarmac road ends at Cape Agulhas. Retracing the road past Struisbaai to Bredasdorp,
the spacious farm *Zoetendals Vallei* belonging to the Van Bredas is passed. Seven and a half
kilometres beyond that point there is a gravel turnoff right to Arniston. This road leads across a
fine stretch of level farming country (wheat and stock). At the immaculate *Prinskraal* farm
belonging to Patrick Swart (7 km) there is a crossroads connecting the small coastal resort of
De Mond to Bredasdorp. The principal road continues east for 7 km and then joins the tarmac
connecting Bredasdorp to Arniston. A right turn leads down this road for 7,5 km, curving
around an impressive line of giant sand dunes, and then reaches the sea at the attractive little
fishing harbour and resort of . . .

# ARNISTON

This place takes its name from the disastrous wreck of the transport ship, *Arniston*, in the bay.
On the afternoon of 30 May 1815, homeward bound from Ceylon, the *Arniston* ran ashore
under the influence of wind and a powerful current. It is difficult to understand exactly what
happened after this event, for no boat appears to have been launched. Night came and some
time before midnight the ship went to pieces. A carpenter and five sailors reached the shore
alive but 372 other people were drowned, including 14 women, 25 children and Lord and
Lady Molesworth.

Arniston started off as a fishing village generally known as *Waenhuiskrans* (wagon house
cliff) from an enormous cavern eroded into the cliffs about 2 km south of the present village.
The entire coastline in this region is notable for its bizarre marine erosion: arches, caverns and

all manner of odd shapes are modelled into the long line of rocky cliffs. Near Arniston there is a magnificent natural archway. The great cavern of Waenhuiskrans is accessible only at low tide. If the Waenhuiskrans cavern could be entered from the land it could certainly contain about six wagons complete with their spans of oxen. It is curious that interesting shells and seaweeds are often found on the floor of this cavern as well as the beans of *Entada gigas*, the so-called 'seabean'. This creeper grows in the tropics and produces an enormous bean pod about 1 m long. The seed beans are distributed by the sea to many distant shores and those found in the great cavern have travelled down with the Agulhas current from the shores of East Africa. These tough, brown, much-travelled beans may also be found along the beach, together with a multitude of beautiful shells. A worthwhile but long walk up the coast leads to Ryspunt, where parts of the wreck of the *Clan McGregor* may still be seen although it ran aground as far back as 1902. Swimming, surfing and fishing are all good at Arniston, providing that the wind isn't blowing. The fishing village itself has been attractively restored and is a treat for artists and photographers.

## Accommodation
★ Arniston Hotel, 16 rooms, 4 with baths. R6,24 – R9,36 B/B. Phone Bredasdorp 6204.

## Caravans and camping
★ Arniston Caravan Park, 100 sites. R3,50 D. Bungalows, R8 – R10 D.

Arniston is at the end of the 25-km-long tarmac road from Bredasdorp. The road runs straight across exceptionally level but very attractive farming country with handsome and historic estates such as *Nacht Wacht* (night watch) to provide interest to the journey.

At 7 km from Arniston there is a gravel turnoff leading for 16 km to the rather dreary fishermen's resort of Ryspunt, a place of cottages half collapsing from the onslaught of the wind. There is a firm, fine beach with rocky shallows in which lie numerous prehistoric stone fish kraals. At 12 km from Arniston there is another gravel turnoff stretching for 27 km to the fishing resort of Skipskop, somewhat less dreary than Ryspunt. One kilometre further on there is a turn to the as yet undeveloped township of Skihaven. Six kilometres on lies the provincial game farm of *De Hoop* which has a large pan much frequented by waterfowl. Tortoises are numerous in *De Hoop* and the Southern Cape generally. With the Cape Province being the principal home in the world for these little creatures, nine different species are found in the area, including the very rare geometric tortoise, so named from the striking pattern on its shell.

Beyond the turnoff to Skipskop and *De Hoop*, the main tarmac road continues for another 12 km and then, 24 km from Arniston, reaches . . .

# BREDASDORP

With a population of 6 208, this town is the administrative centre for the southern end of Africa. It originated in 1837 when the farm *Langefontein* was sold to the Dutch Reformed Church and laid out as a town. On 16 May 1838, the first erven were sold and the place was named in honour of Michiel van Breda, a leading member of the local community and church. Bredasdorp became a municipality in 1917. Wheat, wool and wild flowers are the principal products of the district. The town is clean and pleasant, situated on the slopes of a 368-m-high hill, on the ridges of which grows a profusion of giant proteas. There is a nature reserve and a first-class small museum with a fascinating hall devoted to the theme of shipwrecks; another room houses a collection of ancient vehicles and furniture. The museum is open Tuesdays to Fridays 09h00 to 12h30 and 14h00 to 16h00. Saturdays 09h00 to 12h00.

### Accommodation

* Standard Hotel, 30 rooms, 18 with baths. R7 – R8 B/B. Phone 49.
* Victoria Hotel, 31 rooms, 16 with baths. R7 – R8,50 B/B. Phone 88.

### Caravans and camping

* Municipal caravan park, 30 sites. R2 D plus 50c D per person.

Seventeen kilometres from Bredasdorp the tarmac road reaches the small town of . . .

# NAPIER

Founded on 12 April 1838, when the first erven were sold, this place was named after the then Governor, Sir George Napier and is today the centre of a prosperous wheat and wool farming area. The town has a population of 1 500 and possesses a substantial church and a street lined with stores and places of business. Considerable quantities of strawberries are grown in the district.

### Accommodation

* Napier Hotel, 10 rooms, 3 with baths. R7 – R7,75 B/B. Phone 64.

From Napier the tarmac road winds through a sun-soaked, mellow and gently undulating land of wheat and sheep sprinkled with many fine farms such as *Fairfield*, owned by the Van der Byl family. After 56 km of pleasant travelling the road reaches Caledon and joins the main road to Cape Town, 114 km away.

## Chapter Nine

# THE COPPER WAY TO NAMAQUALAND

The Copper Way which traverses the entire length of the north-western Cape might well be described as the way of citrus, gemstones and flowers. It begins at a traffic interchange on the Cape-to-Cairo road, 11 km from the entrance to Table Bay harbour, the start of the latter highway.

From the traffic interchange, the double carriageway tarmac leads northwards, passing the housing estates of Bothasig and Bosmansdam, and impressive-looking chemical and refining plants with clusters of huge storage tanks.

There are turnoffs east to Milnerton (3,5 km from the start of the road) and to Durbanville (after 7 km), lying in the hills behind the *Tygerberg* (leopard mountain); and west to Melkbos and Atlantis (after 14,8 km). After crossing the Diep River the road points almost straight north-east, through a pleasant, gently undulating, rural landscape of wheat fields, with extended views to the east of the lovely mountain ranges of Groot Drakenstein and the Wellington area. Then, after a final 5 km of minor twists and 51 km from its start, the road reaches the town of . . .

## MALMESBURY

The principal centre of the wheat-producing area named by Van Riebeeck *Het Zwarte Land,* the *Swartland* (black country) from the colour of its brackish but rich soil. At the site of the town, in the shallow valley of the Diep River, there is a tepid (32° C) sulphur chloride spring, similar in its rich mineral content to the famous medicinal bath of Aachen in Europe. By 1805 this spring was already in use by a Dr Hassner, and bore a reputation of curing sufferers of rheumatism. As early as 1744 a few people had settled around this spring and permission had been granted for them to establish a church and school at the site. At first simply known as Swartland's Kerk, this was the beginning of the present town. The name of *Malmesbury* was given to it in 1829 when the British Governor, Sir Lowry Cole, visited the site and renamed the place in honour of his father-in-law, the Earl of Malmesbury. The town became a municipality in 1896, and today has a population of 12 282. A congenial, if rather awkwardly laid-out little place, it is the centre for the production of wheat, oats and milk, with huge storage silos, flour mills, and the largest grain distributer in Southern Africa.

There is a good swimming bath but the medicinal spring (near by the swimming bath in the centre of the town) has not been developed, which is a pity for its potential is considerable.

### Accommodation
* Swartland Hotel, 11 rooms, 4 with baths. R7 – R9 B/B. Phone 2-1141.

From Malmesbury, the Copper Way continues north over undulating wheat fields, with spacious views of the mountain ranges in the east. After 5 km there is a turnoff north-west to Hopefield and Saldanha. Another 16 km takes the road past the Langgewens Experimental Farm, where wheat research takes place, and 11 km further on (32 km from Malmesbury) the road reaches a turnoff leading for 3 km to the rural and rail centre of . . .

# MOORREESBURG

A wheat, oats and wool centre which likes to claim that its district holds the densest population of sheep in the world. Founded as a church centre on the farm *Hooikraal* by the Dutch Reformed Church in 1882, the place was named after the Reverend H. A. Moorrees, and it became a municipality in 1909. Today there are 8 750 people living there. Wheat is the principal product and storage silos and mills predominate. The railway, built in 1902, carries from the district a substantial amount of the total wheat production of Southern Africa, and Moorreesburg can be accurately described as an inhabited island in a sea of wheat.

There is an interesting wheat museum, open on Mondays, Tuesdays, Thursdays and Fridays from 09h00 to 17h00 and on Wednesdays from 09h00 to 13h00.

## Accommodation
* ★ International Hotel, 24 rooms, 2 with baths. R7,40 – R9 B/B. Phone X03.
* ★ Samoa Hotel, 17 rooms, 6 with baths. R7,50 – R9 B/B. Phone 201.

The Copper Way continues its easy route north from Moorreesburg across fields of wheat and lupins. After 22,5 km the road bridges across the Berg River, climbs over a foothill spur of the Piketberg, and passes (after 5 km) the factory of the Cape Portland Cement Company at De Hoek. The limestone quarry of this factory is the third largest manmade hole in Southern Africa and the biggest open-cast limestone mine in Africa. It is the only quarry where limestone is being won at depth instead of from hills or surface workings. Just beyond the cement factory is a turnoff west leading to Velddrift (63 km), while 3 km from the factory (30,5 km from Moorreesburg) the road reaches the town of . . .

# PIKETBERG

This little place lies at the foot of sandstone cliffs of the Piketberg range, which towers above the wheatlands to the maximum height of the 1 459-m Zebrakop.

In former years the impressive mass of the Piketberg served as a stronghold for the Bushmen and many well-preserved galleries of their paintings, mainly monochromes in red, are still to be seen in the rock shelters on farms such as *Bushman's Hollow, Langberg, Bangkop* and *Stawelklip,* up in the heights. Around the base of the mountains the Kogikwa Hottentots roamed with their herds. Their leader, Gonnema, featured prominently in records of the founding of the settlement at the Cape. It was during the various brawls between Gonnema's followers and the European settlers that the name of the *Piketberg* (outpost mountain) was first used. A small military post was established there to check the cattle rustling activities of the Hottentots.

European settlers began to establish themselves on farms around the Piketberg in the first quarter of the 18th century. The great herds of game which once frequented the area were steadily destroyed (in 1868 there were still 12 zebra grazing on Zebrakop) and the Bushmen were driven back into the wilderness of the north.

On 31 December 1835 the government granted to the district the farm *Grootfontein* and here, on the mountain slopes, a church was built. Beneath it, like a congregation of buildings gradually attracted to listen to a discourse, the town grew. With the coming of the railway in 1902, Piketberg became the centre of a prosperous agricultural area, producing wheat, fruit, maize and a variety of other crops. The town now has 4 924 inhabitants.

Of particular interest to visitors, is the agricultural activity atop the Piketberg massif. It is said that the first European inhabitants of this mountain land were two sailors – one Dutch, the other English – who had deserted their ships and found sanctuary in these remote heights. Then, in about 1868, Mr J. Versfeld bought the farm *Langberg* on top of the mountains for £300, and started to grow tobacco. Conveying crops to market from the isolated farm in the clouds was at first a problem; in 1889, Mr Versfeld built the spectacular *Versfeld Pass*, made famous by three loops designed to allow the ascent of ox wagons.

Versfeld Pass opened the mountain summit to others – settlers who had formerly thought Versfeld mad to have settled there. A prosperous community soon made their homes on the heights, finding the area ideal for the growing of crops such as apples, pears and peaches. Frank Versfeld planted the first deciduous fruit orchard there in 1907. Buchu was also produced after the forester of Algeria (in the Cedarberg), George Bath, started the industry, promoting a boom in the sale of leaves in 1918.

A fine new road built up the pass in 1943 rewards the traveller with a delightful exploration of a surprisingly beautiful rural area. The road reaches the summit 10 km from Piketberg, continues as a tarmac surface for a further 10 km, then ends after 3 km of gravel at a cul-de-sac 22,5 km from Piketberg. From the summit there are wide views of fine avenues, beautiful orchards, wild flowers, pleasant farms; Bushman paintings can be seen on the rocks.

### Accommodation
★ Boland Hotel, 12 rooms, 4 with baths. R9,60 – R10,20 B/B. Phone 99.
★ Neederberg Hotel, 16 rooms, 5 with baths. R11,40 – R12,60 B/B. Phone 116.

At 32 km from Piketberg is the small rail centre of Eendekuil, renowned for the quality of cheese produced in the local factory. Cheese in South Africa tends to be erratic in quality, so the Eendekuil cheese is worth sampling.

### Accommodation
★ Eendekuil Hotel, 11 rooms, 4 with baths. R8 – R8,50 B/B. Phone 10.

The Copper Way leads north-eastwards from Piketberg across the pool-studded, level floor of a broad valley between the Piketberg and the Olifants River Mountains. Completely covered in fields of wheat, oats and lupins, this valley is a fine spectacle in winter, when it is delightfully green, or spring, when the wheat turns golden. Mountain ranges hem the valley in from all sides.

After 32 km the road reaches the foot of the Olifants River Mountains and starts to climb what is known as the *Piekeniers Kloof Pass* (pass of the pikemen). The name comes from the conflict with Gonnema and his Hottentots in 1675. After his people had carried out a raid, they were pursued by a party of European soldiers, including pikemen. The Hottentots escaped into the mountains, and the ravine originally climbed by the road was given the name which commemorates the disappointed pikemen who made the weary journey in vain.

This old pass served as the early gateway between the settled areas of the Western Cape and the wilder lands of the Nama tribe. It marked, too, a dramatic change in the landscape, and many early explorers travelled this way in search of mythical cities in the wilderness and the famed copper mountains of the north. On 7 December 1660, guided by Bushmen, Jan Danckert crossed the mountains here – the first European to do so. In February of the following year a second party of explorers made their way up this pass and one of the leaders, Pieter van Meerhof, left his name on the rounded, 962-m-high mountain overlooking the pass, *Van Meerhoff's Castle*. Simon van der Stel also made his way up the original pass on his classic journey to discover the source of the copper traded by the Nama Hottentots and, with all the wagons and escorting soldiers, it must have made quite a cavalcade.

On 17 November 1858 a new pass was opened, built by the renowned Thomas Bain and named after Sir George Grey, the Governor. This pass began at the foot of Van Meerhoff's Castle, at a small hostelry known as 'The Rest', built in the shade of tall gum trees. Its route up the mountain slopes can still be seen below the line of the present pass built in the late 1950s. The latter was once more named the Piekeniers Kloof Pass – although the original pass of that name is really up the gorge which reaches the present road only at the summit.

After 6 km of climbing the road reaches the summit of the pass at a fine viewsite, 518 m above sea level. On the summit there are citrus groves, and oranges are sold by the wayside during the winter. Then the road descends for 5 km on the eastern side of the mountain into the handsome valley of the Olifants River. Backed by a superb mass of mountain ranges, neat groves of citrus grow to perfection on the warm alluvial valley floor. In 1660, on the slopes of the mountains east of the river, the first European explorers under Jan Danckert saw a vast herd of 200 to 300 elephants, and named the river the *Olifants* (elephants).

As the road reaches the floor of this fertile valley, 43,5 km from Piketberg, there is a turnoff east, which crosses the Olifants River to the small town of . . .

# CITRUSDAL

Aptly named 'the dale of citrus', in this little town the orange is king. Beautiful citrus groves cover the landscape and a vast pack house marshals and dispatches the golden fruit to many customers all over the world. The town was founded by the Dutch Reformed Church in 1916 and became a municipality on 1 March 1957. Its population is 2 102. Its superlative situation makes it a fine centre from which to explore the surrounding world of mountains, valleys, farmlands and wild flowers. During the citrus packing season (May to October) a great bustle overtakes the town, and a visit to the pack house, opened in 1946, is worthwhile. It exports over 56 thousand tons of citrus each year.

The lovely old farmhouse of *Karnmelkvlei*, 19 km from Citrusdal, was built in 1767 and is worth seeing. Some interesting Bushman paintings may be seen near Citrusdal on the farm *Vlaksrug* and up the Olifants Valley, where a series of paintings depict European men and women in costumes worn 250 years ago; there are also wagons and scenes of European hunters pursuing a lion.

### Accommodation
\* Citrusdal Hotel, 34 rooms, 12 with baths. R10,50 – R12 B/B. Phone 82.

### Caravans and camping
\*\*® Municipal caravan park, 50 sites. R2,50 D.

Several interesting and spectacular roads lead from Citrusdal into most diverse scenery. Two roads follow the valley on either side of the Olifants River and take the traveller through kilometres of orange groves and fertile farmland until they culminate in cul-de-sacs. The road up the left bank of the river reaches the hot spring known simply as The Baths after 16 km of interesting travelling. These springs, 45° C in temperature, are claimed to be radio-active. They lie in a well-wooded ravine which enters the main valley. Amenities include a swimming bath and several private baths, a shop, restaurant, and varied accommodation. Admission to swimming baths is 20c for adults, 10c for children. Private baths, 20c. Accommodation at the baths is R2 - R3,50 D per person in rooms, flats or bungalows; caravans R2 D.

Eastwards from Citrusdal the Buffels Hoek Pass finds a spectacular route over the mountains. For the first 7 km the road is tarmac, then it becomes an adequate gravel surface leading through entrancing scenery, passing many amazing rock shapes and, 8 km from Citrusdal, a pretty 24-m-high waterfall with a natural swimming pool at its base. At 28 km a turnoff leads for 6 km to *Sandfontein* farm, a popular base for mountaineers visiting natural wonders such as the Sandfontein Arch. The main road penetrates a narrow ravine (at 32 km) and then emerges onto what is known as the *Kouebokkeveld* (cold buck veld), a fine, rugged mountain plateau studded with many beautiful farms, which are dominated by a set of wild-looking mountains such as the Skurweberge on the west, whose slopes, scarred by strange rock shapes, seem like an ancient battlefield where men once fought with such bestiality that the gods were offended and punished the warriors by petrifying them into weird rock formations.

At 55 km the road has a tarmac surface. A further 14 km takes the road through the hamlet of *Op De Berg* (on the mountain). Five kilometres on (74 km from Citrusdal) a rough road from Wuppertal and the Cedarberg comes in from the north. At 93 km there is a tarmac turnoff west into the fruit farming valley of the *Achterwitsenberg* (behind the Witsenberg). This is a very beautiful drive which ends in a cul-de-sac. The tarmac road first leads for 5 km through a pass; then there is a gravel turnoff, signposted 'Witsenberg Vlakte', which stretches for 26,5 km past many fruit farms and comes to an end at the great pool known as Visgat, where the Olifants River tumbles into the head of its upper gorge. For the adventurous there is a six-hour journey – swimming and on lilos – through this gorge with a one and a half hour walk back; an exciting experience and superb scenery.

The main Citrusdal road (after the turnoff to the Achterwitsenberg) descends via the spectacular *Gydo* (euphorbia) Pass into the Ceres valley, reaching Prince Alfred's Hamlet (101 km from Citrusdal), and Ceres (110 km). This route completes a fine circular drive – Cape Town-Citrusdal-Ceres-Cape Town – and is highly recommended, especially in September or October, when the orchards are in blossom.

## THE CITRUS INDUSTRY

If the Caucasian apple is the king of fruits and the Persian grape the queen, then their royal relative from Asia is a true Chinese mandarin – the citrus, replendent with luxuriant deep green leaves and fruit so rich in colour that it sometimes seems to be made of solid gold.

How the citrus family left its home in the tropical rain forests of southern China and the Malay archipelago and found its way around the world into pleasant sanctuaries such as the Olifants River Valley is a historical romance, featuring the Arabs and the Portuguese in principal roles as carriers and cultivators of the golden fruit of the sun.

In the beginning the Arabs carried the sour orange, the lime and the lemon from their Asian home and planted them throughout the Middle East ,along the north coast of Africa, into Spain and down the east coast of Africa as far as modern Zimbabwe, where the first British settlers were surprised to find lemon trees of the common Indian *Jamburi* variety growing along the banks of the Mazowe River.

The Crusaders, in turn, among other good things adopted from the Arab culture, introduced the apricot, sour orange, lime and lemon to the more northerly parts of Europe. The sweet orange only followed later, sometime in the 15th century, and precisely how it was introduced is an interesting speculation. When Vasco da Gama doubled the Cape of Good Hope in 1498 and made his way up the east coast of Africa, the Arab ruler of Mombasa received him with a boatload of the produce of the place, including 'citrons, lemons and large sweet oranges'. Some writers think that Da Gama took the sweet orange back with him to Europe; certainly the Portuguese claim the honour of growing the first sweet oranges in Europe. They say that the first sweet orange tree of the Western world grew in Lisbon, in the garden of the Count St Laurent; and that this tree, if not actually brought by Vasco da Gama, was certainly introduced at about the time of his return from his visit to the East. However the sweet orange came to grow in Europe, it became known as *Portugal Orange* and was popularly believed to have originated from the voyage of Vasco da Gama.

There is no doubt at all, however, about precisely when and how the sweet orange was introduced into Southern Africa. On 11 June 1654, the yacht *Tulp* brought the first trees to Cape Town from the island of St Helena, where they had been planted by the Portuguese for the enjoyment of sick sailormen. In Cape Town the trees were planted in the Company's garden and on 26 July 1661, the first fruits were plucked by Jan van Riebeeck and pronounced 'very good'.

Other sweet orange trees (the familiar old seedling type) were also imported from India. At the time the St Helena trees bore their first fruit, Van Riebeeck had 1 162 young citrus trees growing in his garden – the first South African orchard, containing an interesting assortment of seedling oranges, lemons and the *Citrus maxima* known as *bombolmoes* in Tamil, *pampelmoes* in Dutch, and known to the British as the *pummelo* or the *Shaddock,* after Captain Shaddock who introduced it to the West Indies where its bud mutation, the grapefruit, first developed.

From Van Riebeeck's pioneer citrus orchard, trees became dispersed over the expanding settlement of the Cape. In the latter half of the 18th century, when the Olifants River Valley was first portioned out to settlers, the citrus family reached *Hexrivier* when this farm was granted to Mr C. J. Mouton. The Moutons later married into the Visser family and today Dirk Visser is the owner of this fine estate, proud of showing visitors one of the original seedling orange trees planted in the valley by the first Mouton. The old tree still bears a palatable and juicy fruit after more than 200 years of changing seasons! It is now an historical monument.

The famous *Washington Navel* is the real backbone of orange production. This delectable fruit originated in the early 19th century at Bahia, in Brazil, where it was possibly a mutation of the earlier *Selecta* orange. In 1869, the Reverend F. I. Schneider, the first Presbyterian missionary in Bahia, sent a eulogistic report about the orange to the United States Commissioner of Agriculture. In reply, the missionary was asked to send a few trees to Washington for testing, which he did in the following year, 1870. This proved to be a momentous date in the history of orange growing.

In Washington the trees were propagated by the Department of Agriculture and in 1873 the first budded specimens were sent to various parts of the United States to see how they would grow. Two of the trees were sent to Mrs L. C. Tibbets, in California, who planted them in her yard. There they flourished, and from these two trees arose the entire navel orange industry, not only of the United States but also of most of the world. One of the parent trees is still alive. Its offspring, all grown from cuttings, must run into many million. Think of that next time you cut a juicy navel orange!

The *Washington Navel* was introduced into South Africa in 1903 by that indefatigable nurseryman, H. Pickstone, who also introduced into this country the second great commercial variety, the *Valencia Late*. This orange came into being at almost the same time as the *Washington Navel*. In 1876 an assorted, unlabelled package of orange trees was shipped by the famous British nurseryman, Thomas Rivers, to the Californian grower, Mr. A. Chapman. Chapman cultivated the trees but only one proved of any value. This single tree, however, was worth a fortune, for its fruit, although it bore seeds, ripened well after the *Washington Navel*.

Chapman named the orange, the *Rivers' Late*. Later, however, a Spanish grower identified it as a variety grown in Spain under the name of *Naranja Tarde de Valencia.* Chapman accordingly changed the name of his tree to the *Valencia Late,* and under this name it was introduced to massive commercial growing. Chapman's single tree, probably a chance find of Thomas Rivers somewhere in southern Europe, became the parent of a prodigious number of offspring.

As in America, the two varieties of orange described above contributed the great bulk of the 665 844 tons of citrus fruit grown in South Africa in 1979. Both varieties do exceptionally well in South Africa and on the highly competitive world markets the fruit is well regarded.

Of the three main orange growing areas of South Africa (Transvaal, Sundays River Valley and Olifants River Valley) the Olifants River Valley is the smallest producer (56 549 tons in 1979) but its product is of supreme standard – for a very good reason. The valley of the

158

Olifants lies in a winter rainfall area of very low humidity and the hot summer and crisp but frostless winter make it a particularly congenial home for the citrus family. Soil chemistry and climate combine naturally to produce a fruit with thickish skin but a 'rag' or tissue far finer than, for instance, the Transvaal lowveld orange, produced in an area of summer rainfall and high humidity. Palatability of the fruit depends on a delicate balance between acidity and solids, or sugar. This balance must be fine, or the end result will be either too tart or too insipid. It is generally considered that the Olifants River Valley product is almost ideal in flavour and tissue.

All industries have their problems. With citrus production most of the basic difficulties – pests and parasites – have yielded to science. One practical problem that remains is the propagation of a really satisfactory mid-season orange. At present there is an awkward gap of about three weeks between the last of *Washington Navel* and the first *Valencia Late*. This gap seriously embarrasses the entire industry, particularly the pack houses, which have to employ numerous staff for the season, who during those weeks remain idle in their homes and hostels.

There have been many attempts to breed a satisfactory mid-season orange. The famous Dr P. Nortjie of Clanwilliam found a bud mutation on an old seedling orange tree which has come into some favour among local growers in the Olifants River Valley. This mid-season tree is, paradoxically, a seedless seedling. Known as the *Clanor* (a combination of the names of Clanwilliam and Nortjie) it has not yet been grown in sufficient quanitity to have discernible commercial impact. Constant research continues to find an ideal mid-season orange variety, as well as early and late-season fruit.

## CITRUSDAL TO CLANWILLIAM

The Copper Way continues from the turnoff to Citrusdal northwards, down the left bank of the Olifants River. This is a beautiful drive down a magnificent river valley, noted for its wild flowers and fine mountain scenery. At 27 km there is a turnoff east to the Algeria Forestry Station, and 22,5 km further on the road reaches the great dam in the Olifants River. This dam, completed in 1935 to a capacity of 67 million cubic metres, was expanded in 1968 by raising the height of the wall. It supplies water to the town of Clanwilliam and to the Bulshoek Barrage, which feeds water to 12 140 ha of irrigated farmland. The dam is popular for recreation and across its surface are spacious views of the Cedarberg and other peaks. The Olifants River is excellent for canoeing, with good rapids, especially from below the dam wall to the road bridge and then down to the junction with the Jan Dissels stream. Reeds, narrow channels and various obstacles combine with strong currents to make this an exciting ride for canoers. Anglers will find seven varieties of fish in the river and dam. The yellow fish *(Barbus capensis)* can reach more than 11 kg in mass.

One and a half kilometres beyond the dam (51,5 km from Citrusdal) there is a crossroads leading to Lamberts Bay (west) and east to the pleasant little town of . . . .

## CLANWILLIAM

This little place lies in the well-watered valley of the Jan Dissels stream, where most things seem to grow well: sub-tropical and deciduous fruit trees, and many vividly coloured flowers, notably red-hot pokers.

In the early years Clanwilliam was known as Jan Dissels Vlei, but in 1814 this name was changed by the Governor, Sir John Cradock, in honour of his father-in-law, the Earl of Clanwilliam. At the time of the arrival of the 1820 Settlers, five Irish parties were sent to settle in this area but they did not find the valley of the Jan Dissels stream to their liking and most of them went off to the Eastern Cape. A handful, however, remained; one man, Captain W. Synnot, became deputy-landdrost of the district. A descendant of one of these settler families, Charles Fryer, became the first mayor of the town when it acquired municipal status on 12 July 1900.

Clanwilliam today has a population of 3 902 and is a prosperous agricultural centre serving a district which produces citrus, rooibos tea, vegetables, tobacco and cereals. A convenient tourist centre, it is much frequented during the spring by visitors admiring the profusion of wild flowers which covers the countryside. The *rooibos* (red bush) tea plant grows wild on the mountains. Dr P le Fras Nortier, a bosom friend of Louis Leipoldt, was the father of the industry. This tea is now cultivated, packed in Clanwilliam and widely exported. A wild flower garden, recreational area and caravan park are situated on the shores of the Olifants River dam at Ramskop.

## Accommodation
★ Clanwilliam Hotel, 21 rooms, 8 with baths. R8,50 – R11,50 B/B. Phone 2.

## Caravans and camping
★ Ramskop, 30 sites. R2– R3 D.

# THE CLANWILLIAM DISTRICT

Several interesting branch roads from Clanwilliam penetrate the surrounding countryside and the Cedarberg. One road crosses the mountains to Calvinia (153 km) and from this route tourists can turn off to view the wild flowers in the Bidouw Valley, and to visit the picturesque Rhenish mission station of *Wuppertal,* named after a town in Germany.

The road heads east from Clanwilliam and climbs the *Pakhuis* (pack house) Pass, passing an extraordinary collection of rock shapes. After 14,5 km the grave of the renowned writer and individualist Dr C. Louis Leipoldt is reached (28 December 1880 to 12 April 1947). This grave, in a Bushman rock shelter complete with a gallery of faded paintings, is worth visiting. The rock containing the shelter is made up of a pile of sandstone boulders, a veritable Bushman's castle. To the left of the grave a path passes through a cave to a perennial stream which flows through a rugged valley choked with giant rocks and guarded by dassies (coneys.)

A parking and picnicking area is next to the grave and a great deal of fine walking and scrambling about can be done in the vicinity. The site was a favourite haunt of Louis Leipoldt. Such was the amiable nature of the man that visitors may be sure that he shares in the pleasure of their outing and is present, a silent and happy ghost, at their camp fire.

Five kilometres beyond the grave, the road reaches the summit of the pass. Eighteen kilometres further on (37 km from Clanwilliam) is a turnoff south to Bidouw and Wuppertal. After 14,5 km on this road there is a turn east to Bidouw. The main road continues its sharp descent for another 18 km and then reaches Wuppertal (69 km from Clanwilliam), a most attractive little oasis in a very rugged wilderness. The western slopes of the Cedarberg are arid but from the mountains spurt beautiful streams, nature's kiss of life to the area.

Among these streams is the *Tra-Tra* (bushy). Where it tumbles from the high Cedarberg it gouges a deep valley, narrow and hemmed in by harsh peaks. The valley floor, however, is fertile, and green, producing all manner of vegetables and fruits, excellent corn and tobacco.

Rooibos tea flourishes on the slopes; grapes, figs, quinces, peaches, pomegranates and blackberries all thrive. At Wuppertal there is a spruce Rhenish mission founded in 1830. The rest of the village consists of a store, three terraces of neat, photogenic little cottages – each with garden and plot – and a meandering street with water flowing in furrows as well as coursing down a natural bed in the valley floor.

In the village, excellent *velskoen* (a type of shoe) are made, tobacco is dried and worked into rolls, rooibos tea is sorted and packed; in short, a great deal of productive activity takes place, which is surprising to any traveller descending the steep pass into the isolated valley. At Christmas time there is a festival of carol singing at the mission and the mountains echo to the voices of the people of Wuppertal.

The village is dominated by the *Vaalheuningberge* (tawny, honey mountains) to the south and the *Krakadouw* (women's pass) range to the west. The original 'women's pass', an old Hottentot and Bushman pathway, penetrates the mountains from Wuppertal to Clanwilliam and is a spectacular but strenuous walk. From Wuppertal a gravel road leads south through rugged and sandy country and eventually, at Matjiesrivier, joins the road from Algeria to Ceres.

From the Bidouw turnoff (18 km before Wuppertal), the branch road leads eastwards down the valley of the Bidouw stream, whose slopes are renowned for their spring flowers, at their best in August and September. After 29 km (rather rough, with numerous gates) the road reaches a ford over the Doring River at Uitspankraal – deep when the river is in spate. After it crosses the river, the road deteriorates into a rough but passable track which finds a rather solitary way across a harsh stretch of arid Karoo country, watched over from the western horizon by the summits of the Cedarberg. After 51,5 km of travelling from the river crossing, the road reaches the main gravel road from Calvinia (56 km) to Ceres (209 km).

## CLANWILLIAM TO LAMBERT'S BAY

A tarmac road leads westwards from Clanwilliam to the coast. After 29 km this road reaches the railway centre of Graafwater, notable for the fact that 32 km north of it, on the Vredendal road, there is an interesting old cave (now an historical monument) known as the *Heeren-logement* (gentlemen's lodging), where the initials written and carved on the walls by about 170 different early travellers reveal that the place was used as a shelter in the 18th century.

**Accommodation**
★ Spoorweg Hotel (Graafwater), 13 rooms, 3 with baths. R7,80 – R8,80 B/B. Phone 124.

The gravel road continues from Graafwater westwards for 30,5 km and then (59,5 km from Clanwilliam) enters the fishing harbour of . . .

## LAMBERT'S BAY

Essentially a fishing village with two fish and crayfish processing and canning factories, this town was named after Rear-Admiral Sir Robert Lambert, commander of the Cape Station in 1820. Bird Island, with its great colony of gannets, lies in the harbour and yields about 286 metric tons of guano each year. Anglers find Lambert's Bay a productive area and bird watchers have a fascinating time. Eight kilometres south of Lambert's Bay, on the road to Leipoldtville, a series of pans at Steenbokfontein and Wagendrift are frequented by countless aquatic birds, including flamingos.

**Accommodation**
★ Marine Hotel, 38 rooms, 18 with baths. R8 – R8,50 B/B. Phone 49.

**Caravans and camping**
★ Municipal caravan park, 200 sites. R2,50 D.

# THE ROCK WILDERNESS OF THE CEDARBERG

This mighty rock wilderness is a superb recreational area. The walker, climber, lover of nature, photographer and artist finds himself in a realm of inexhaustible scenic beauty: novel rock shapes, rich flora, clear atmosphere and challenges to adventure through strange caverns and ravines, and climbs to the summits of many high peaks.

Access to the Cedarberg is easy. From the Copper Way there is a gravel turnoff 27 km from Citrusdal on the way to Clanwilliam. This turnoff crosses the Olifants River by means of a low-level concrete causeway; then, for 16 km it finds a rugged route with steep gradients through the *Kriedouw* (difficult passage) over the Nieuwoudt Pass. From the summit of this pass there is an impressive view of the Cedarberg. The valley of the *Rondegat* (round hole) River lies below the pass. To the left is the 1 745-m-high *Krakadouw* (women's pass) mountain, while in front towers the 1 513-m-high Middelberg ridge.

In the valley below is the forestry station of Algeria, founded in 1904 by George Bath, the first forester of the Cedarberg. The gnarled old cedar trees growing on the mountains and the general appearance of the area reminded Bath of the Atlas Mountains of North Africa, and for this reason he named the new station *Algeria*. Bath blazed the paths which penetrate the range, built the first mountain hut at Middelberg, and gave such names as *Crystal Pools* to the lovely swimming pools in the heart of the range, where he decided to build a second hut. He also established the plantation of cedar trees which preserved this variety of cyprus for all time.

Today the Cedarberg range is a proclaimed wilderness area. Intriguing paths meander through the mountains, taking the walker to all manner of remarkable places. There are caves, waterfalls, stupendous viewsites and astonishing formations such as the Wolfberg Arch and the Maltese Cross, a rock pillar standing 9 m high, like an ancient totem pole in an eerie setting of rock shapes reminiscent of the petrified forms of worshippers of some forgotten religion. These bizarre rock shapes are a feature of the Cedarberg, masquerading as myriad different things – faces, animals, bridges, archways. The fiery colours of sandstone formations, the heady clarity of the air, the magnificence of the wild flowers make the atmosphere of the range unique.

In the trees around the Algeria Forestry Station a fine camping ground is enhanced by the river, which forms a natural swimming pool. This is the base camp for many excursions into the range. The main path leads up through the plantation of cedar trees, past a beautiful cascade, to the first hut at Middelberg. Guides and donkeys may be hired through the forester. From the Middelberg hut paths take visitors for days of wonderful walking and climbing to places such as Crystal Pools, Sneeuwkop (1 931 m), the strange Wolfberg Arch and Cracks, as well as to many other interesting places. The pride of the Cedarberg is the lovely snow protea, which grows only above the snowline and is pure white; it blooms around March. A close second to this flower is the blood-red Cedarberg pincushion.

## Caravans and camping
** Cedarberg Recreational Area, 50 sites. R2 D.

From Algeria roads lead up and down the valley of the Rondegat River. Downriver, the road passes through fine scenery for 30,5 km to Clanwilliam; upriver the road begins a spectacular climb over the *Uitkyk* (lookout) Pass, past farms and forestry centres such as *Driehoek* (14,5 km); *Eikeboom* (16 km); *Rypvlei* and *Paardekloof* (19 km); *Dwarsrivier* and *Sandrif* (27 km); and *Kromrivier* (35 km).

*Dwarsrivier, Sandrif* and *Kromrivier* (crooked river) are farms belonging to members of the Nieuwoudt family, who have lived in the Cedarberg for many years. The first Gerrit Nieuwoudt got himself into a rather awkward situation when he killed Coenraad Fiet, the magistrate of Clanwilliam, in a duel. Sentenced to life imprisonment, he was reprieved and on his release retired deep into the mountains to what was then (and still is) a very isolated farming area. Today there are three Nieuwoudt families in the Cedarberg and all are renowned individualists. Nieuwoudt Pass is named in their honour.

At *Sandrif* the Nieuwoudts maintain a camping ground next to the Sand River (R1 D per site). This is the starting point of many walks and climbs to places such as the Wolfberg Arch and Cracks.

At *Kromrivier* the Nieuwoudts maintain bungalows and a caravan park for the use of mountaineers. There is an interesting little museum and a shop supplying fresh milk, homebaked bread and fresh fruit in season. This farm makes an excellent base for walks to the Maltese Cross, the 2 027-m-high Sneeuberg, and many other spectacular parts of the range.

**Accommodation**
Bungalows, 4 beds, with baths, R12 – R16 D. Without baths, R10 D.

**Caravans and camping**
★ R2 D per site plus 25c D per person.

Beyond the turnoff to *Kromrivier,* the main road from Algeria continues. After 4 km a track to the right leads to a massive rock (1,5 km) on which there are Bushman paintings of elephants and men; then (1,5 km further) the track ends at a marvellous honeycomb of caves and weird rock formations known as the *Stadsaal* (town hall).

Three kilometres beyond the turnoff to the Stadsaal, the main road from Algeria joins the road coming south from Wuppertal at Matjiesrivier. The gravel road is reasonably surfaced and provides a spectacular route to Ceres, 110 km away. On the way this road crosses the Kouebokkeveld, bridges over the Grootrivier (19 km from Matjiesrivier), joins the tarmac Ceres-Citrusdal road (53 km from Grootrivier) and then continues for another 38 km down the Gydo Pass to Ceres. This is a true scenic switchback ride. The gravel road is in fair condition but demands cautious driving.

## CLANWILLIAM TO NAMAQUALAND

After Clanwilliam, the main tarmac road continues north down the left bank of the Olifants River. The country becomes more arid, but there are kilometres of irrigated farmland along the banks of the river, and many fine views. The canal carrying irrigation water keeps close company with the road. At 47 km from Clanwilliam the road bridges the Olifants River and 6 km further on there is a tarmac turnoff west to the railway centre of Klawer (3 km) and Vredendal (27 km). Twenty-one kilometres further on (74 km from Clanwilliam), the Copper Way reaches the sunbaked little town of . . .

## VANRHYNSDORP

At the entrance to Namaqualand, this place is named after Petrus Benjamin van Rhyn, first member for Namaqualand in the old Cape Legislative Council, and a leading public figure in the district.

First explored by Europeans in 1662 (Pieter Crythoff), then in 1682 (Oloff Bergh), and in 1685 (Van der Stel), the area around Vanrhynsdorp was finally settled in the 1740s. The farm on which Vanrhynsdorp stands, *Troe-Troe,* received its unusual name from a Hottentot war cry *Toru-Toro* meaning 'return, return'. Lying on the verge of Namaqualand, to the north of the *Matsikama* (mountains that yield water), the farm was a good site for a town. In 1850 a Namaqualand congregation was established and on 8 September 1866, at a meeting of male

*Overleaf: The rocky wilderness of the Cedarberg looks down on the Olifants River Valley, carpeted with flowers and groves of citrus.*

church members, Petrus van Rhyn offered to provide a church building for ten years on condition that each member paid one shilling a year towards maintenance.

This church was the beginning of Vanrhynsdorp. A township was laid out in 1880 and this became a village management board in 1904 and a municipality in modern times. The town is a rural centre with a population of 2 928. It lies at a crossroads leading to several interesting parts of the north-west Cape.

## Accommodation
★ North Western Hotel, 24 rooms, 9 with baths. R9 – R9,50 B/B. Phone 3.

## THE WILD FLOWERS OF NAMAQUALAND

Namaqualand has always been a Cinderella area of the most extraordinary contrasts. With only 120 mm of rain a year, the arid countryside presents the world's most spectacular display of flowers. A paradox of drought counterpoised by a treasury of diamonds, copper and untapped mineral wealth, this is a land bitten by relentless summer heat and frozen by cold in winter; but over all, there rests a brooding, intangible essence – something akin to the siren spirit of the Transvaal lowveld – which lures the traveller back time and again to a wilderness both strange and lovely.

The reason for Namaqualand's aridity is the cold Benguela Current sweeping up the coast: too cold to provide any moisture through evaporation, it leaves the hinterland with dry, crisp air and scarcely a cloud. Water (especially along the coast) is often scarcer than diamonds . . .

The famous wild flowers make their appearance in spring, and the display depends on at least some rainfall in the winter, and an absence of searing winds. The season lasts from mid-July to mid-September. Among the earliest species to bloom are the white daisies (*Dimorphotheca*), and the *Oxalis* in numerous forms and shades. Mid-August sees the light-purple wild cineraria (*Senecio*), the dark purple everlastings (*Lackenalia*) and, particularly on sandy soil, the red and orange Namaqualand daisies (*Ursina*). Growing along with these are the hazy-blue flax (*Heliophilia*).

The height of the season sees in full bloom the yellow *vetkousies (Carpanthea)*, the *duikerwortel (Grielum grandiflorum)*, the vari-coloured *weeskindertjies (Nemesia versicolor)*, the dark-red *Lapeyrousea*, and the yellow *aandblommetjies (Sutera tristis)*.

Towards the end of the season, at the beginning of September, the yellow *blindevlieg-blommetjies (Relhania pumila)* appear, together with the dark-orange *Gortevia personata* with their three characteristic black spots on the inside of the petals; the purple bush *vygies (Lampranthus)*, especially around Mauwerskop on the rural road to the Matsikama; the dark-orange *botterblomme (Gazanias);* the almost fluorescent-coloured *vygies (Mesembryanthema);* and numerous succulents along the national road north of Vanrhynsdorp.

It is not possible to be too precise about the best localities for wild flowers as these vary considerably each year according to local rainfall. From Vanrhynsdorp, however, visitors will seldom be disappointed if they take the rural road south-east through Raskraal and Urionskraal to Bottervlei, visiting the 121-m-high waterfall on the east side of the Matsikama mountains (at Ouberg). They can then return north from Bonteheuvel along the road running parallel to the Bokkeveldberge escarpment, passing Lion Head and the entrance to the *Kobee* (flow away) Valley, and on to the tarmac road back to Vanrhynsdorp from Nieuwoudtville. There are many pleasant picnic spots in the mountain ravines along this circular drive. The flowers are always at their best on sunny days from noon till 14h00. Local residents, garage attendants, hotel and tearoom staff will all advise as to the whereabouts of the best displays at any given time.

---

In addition to the rural road described above, which explores the wild flower country in the great basin between the eastern escarpment and the Matsikama mountains, there is another sensational rural road which climbs to the summit of the latter range by means of a rugged pass. The summit is a great area for chincherinchees, which bloom in August. Lethal to livestock, it is from them that this bulky height takes its European name – *Gifberg* (poison mountain). The road serves several farms on the summit and then reaches a cul-de-sac. The red sandstone cliffs of the Matsikama overlook magnificent patches of wild flowers during spring.

From Vanrhynsdorp, a tarmac road stretches west to areas irrigated by the Olifants River. This road penetrates spectacular wild flower country and after 24 km reaches the town of . . .

## VREDENDAL

With a population of 4 268, *Vredendal* (the dale of peace) is the principal centre of the irrigated area and is surrounded by kilometres of vineyards and fruit orchards. There is a wine cellar near the railway station. The town was established in 1945 and acquired municipal status on 1 March 1963.

### Accommodation
⋆ Maskam Hotel, 22 rooms, 14 with baths. R10,50 – R13,50 B/B. Phone 288.
⋆ Vredendal Hotel, 21 rooms, 14 with baths. R10 – R11,50 B/B. Phone 513.

The tarmac road continues from Vredendal down the irrigated valley, and after 21 km reaches a gravel turnoff leading for 32 km to the coast at Strandfontein, a holiday resort frequented by the farmers of Namaqualand. The main tarmac road crosses the Olifants River, passes the small centre of Lutzville and (30,5 km from Vredendal) reaches Koekenaap, composed of a cluster of shops and garages loitering around a railway station. Here the tarmac ends, but the road continues with a good gravel surface, passing through wild flower country for 51,5 km until it joins the Copper Way, at the hamlet of Nuwerus; from here the traveller can complete a circular drive back to Vanrhynsdorp.

### Accommodation
⋆ Lutzville Hotel, 10 rooms, 5 with baths. R9,50 – R10,60 B/B. Phone 35.

### Caravans and camping
⋆ Strandfontein Caravan and Camping Park, 300 sites. R2,50 – R4,50 D.

## VANRHYNSDORP TO THE NORTH

From Vanrhynsdorp, the main tarmac road continues north through fine wild flower and succulent country, arid and searing hot for much of the year and a typical piece of Namaqualand scenery – an immense, gently undulating plain, covered in low scrub and rocks, with a long ridge of mountains on the horizon to the east. The water is brackish and the stream beds are saline. Gypsum is mined in the area. At 22 km, there is a turnoff to the strangely named *Douse the Glim*. Despite the size of the sign, this is simply a farm whose name, it is said, was given it by a tired surveyor who, in his tent one weary night, irately told his assistant to *'douse the glim'* ('put out the light') and go to sleep!

After 66 km the tarmac road enters more rugged country and skirts the rural hamlet of *Nuwerus* (new rest), perched on a hill slope known as *Erdvarkgat* (antbear hole). The road passes it by and continues over low, rocky hills for a further 14,5 km to the railhead of Bitterfontein. Here, in a shallow valley, the 465-km-long railway from Cape Town comes to a sudden and disconsolate end at a pile of coal and a drab cluster of corrugated iron sheds and railwaymen's houses. The line to the place was opened in 1927 but north of this point Namaqualand was left to the mercies of road transport. Only vehicles are encountered from now on, engaged on an endless shuttle service between the railhead and points far and wide.

### Accommodation
★ Railway Hotel, 10 rooms, 3 with baths. R8 – R8,50 B/B. Phone 42.

The tarmac road bypasses Bitterfontein and continues north for 63 km through increasingly rugged country until it reaches the village of . . .

## GARIES

This little place is simply one long street consisting of church, houses and shops built along the banks of the stream named by the Hottentots *Th'aries* (Garies) because of the queek grass growing there. The place has a population of 1 270.

### Accommodation
★ Garies Hotel, 13 rooms, 4 with baths. R7,50 – R8 B/B. Phone 42.
Caravan sites in high school sports ground, R1 D.

The valley of Garies is hemmed in by a rocky and wild-looking assembly of mountains. The road climbs steeply out of the valley up heavy cuttings, and makes its way north through rugged country. After 5 km a gravel turnoff west leads to Hondeklip Bay (85 km) and 35 km further on another turnoff leads to the same fishing and seaside resort.

## HONDEKLIP BAY

This little coastal resort and fishing harbour has a crayfish processing factory. There are camping grounds, and the place is a holiday resort for local farmers. In former years Hondeklip Bay was used as a port of shipment for copper. Limited accommodation at the two restaurants is available.

---

Five kilometres north of the turnoff to Hondeklip Bay (45 km from Garies) the Copper Way passes the hamlet of . . .

## KAMIESKROON

This little village is locked in by the huge granite masses of the range known as the *Kamiesberg* from the Hottentot name *Th'amies,* aptly meaning 'a jumble'. The *kroon* (crown) of Kamieskroon, about 1,5 km from the village, is a prominent height with a huge cleft rock on the summit.

### Accommodation
★ Kamieskroon Hotel, 10 rooms, 3 with baths. R8,75 – R9,75 B/B. Phone 14.

Kamieskroon is in fact the descendant of an earlier town. Six kilometres to the north, the Copper Way twists its way through heavy granite country shadowed all around by great domes and whalebacks, and then descends into the narrow valley of the Wilgenhouts Kloof.

166

Here are the ruins of an abandoned settlement, founded in 1864 by the Dutch Reformed Church as the site of the first church in Namaqualand. Known as *Bowesdorp* after the district-surgeon, Dr Henry Bowe, the town could not develop in the narrow ravine and in 1924 the church, school, police station, post office and shops were all transferred to the present site of Kamieskroon. The ruins of the earlier place provide a melancholy, ghostly touch in the ancient granite landscape.

Between Kamieskroon and Bowesdorp, the Copper Way passes near by the site of the early Leliefontein Mission, founded in 1816 by the Reverend Barnabas Shaw and named after the *Lanticeschia aethiopica* lilies which flourish in the area. Close to the mission site is an old Hottentot settlement with, in this arid setting, the lovely, liquid Hottentot name of *Ouss* (a fountain).

The main road continues northwards through massive granite country, the route taking many twists, climbs and descents. This is Namaqualand at its most rugged – a difficult land in which to live, populated by some weatherbeaten characters working hard for their livelihood.

The first *kokerbooms* (quiver trees) – *Aloe dichotoma* – appear on the granite slopes. The kokerboom, an aloe species, is extremely slow growing and lives for more than 100 years. The Bushmen made pincushion-type quivers for their arrows from the fibrous core. At 45 km from Kamieskroon the road passes the small rural centre of Mesklip and 21 km further on (66 km from Kamieskroon), the Copper Way reaches the curiously wild-west little town of . . . .

## SPRINGBOK

The area of this town was once a favourite haunt of springbok and these entrancing little antelope gave the place its original name – *Springbokfontein* (springbok fountain). The story of Springbok is essentially the story of copper mining in Namaqualand (described further on). Suffice to say here that the town was laid out in 1862 by the copper mining concern of Messrs Phillips and King, which had purchased the land (a farm named *Melkboschkuil*) from its owners, the Cloete family, in 1850.

The first sale of plots took place on 28 October 1862. The town is situated in a narrow valley between high granite domes of the *Klein Koperberge* (small copper mountains); an odd little hillock stands in the middle of the valley as though on sentry duty. The town developed around this hillock but suffered a grievous setback in the late 1870s, when rich copper was found at O'Okiep: nearly every inhabitant moved off to the scene of the new discovery.

The fountain of Springbok continued to supply good drinking water, however, and as other copper deposits were located the town was established as a communications, administrative, school and commercial centre for the miners. On 27 June 1922 it became a village management board and on 26 June 1933 a municipality. Today, with a population of 7 450, it is one of the most important points on the trunk road between Cape Town and South West Africa, and a centre for tourists visiting the many wild flower regions and other interesting areas of Namaqualand and the north-west Cape. The place retains much of the atmosphere of the rugged early days of the copper boom. Just beyond the airport is a nature reserve named after Hester Malan, wife of a former provincial administrator. On ground presented in 1965 by the O'Okiep Copper Company, this interesting sanctuary preserves the flora and fauna of the area, including gemsbok and other antelope.

### Accommodation
★ Masonic Hotel, 29 rooms, 19 with baths. R8,50 – R9,50 B/B. Phone 48.
★ Springbok Hotel, 30 rooms, 18 with baths. R9,50 – R10,50 B/B. Phone 115.

### Caravans and camping
★★ ® Little Rock Caravan Park, 25 sites. R2,50 D. 30 rooms, all with baths. R4,50 – R7,50 D.

# THE COPPER MINES OF NAMAQUALAND

Copper mining in Namaqualand dates back to a period long before the advent of the European in South Africa. The Nama Hottentot tribe worked the metal, producing tools, weapons and ornaments, and used these items to barter with neighbouring tribes.

In December 1681, a party of these early miners visited the settlement at the Cape and presented the Governor, Simon van der Stel, with such excellent samples of copper that he immediately sent the metal off to Holland for inspection by the directors of the Dutch East India Company. The result was an instruction that the source of the ore be found and the first major prospecting expeditions ever organised in South Africa were sent off, one after the other, to try and locate the copper mountains of Namaqualand.

Each expedition managed to penetrate further into the north than the one before it. Eventually, in August 1685, Van der Stel himself led a major expedition on the copper trail, equipped with 15 wagons, a boat for crossing rivers, two small cannon to impress local tribes, 56 Europeans and a great camp following of Hottentots and slaves. The assembly must have made a picturesque and colourful cavalcade as it moved through the lovely mountainous countryside of what is now the granary of South Africa.

It had been an excellent winter in the Cape. Good rains had fallen and the exploring party travelled for kilometres across a multicoloured mosaic of flowers – few ventures into unknown country could have been as delightful and fascinating. To top it all, the expedition was successful: on 21 October, Simon van der Stel reached the fabled *Koperberg* (what is known today as Copper Mountain West) and the three shallow prospect shafts sunk by his men yielded quantities of ore of impressive richness.

Two hundred years were to pass, however, before this discovery was worked by Europeans. Its remote location precluded earlier attempts at working the ore, for the cost of primitive transport and the limited value of copper in the old days made it unprofitable to develop such far-off mines.

The 19th century saw world industrialisation and a steady rise in the value of copper. In 1936, James Alexander became the father of Namaqualand copper mining: he re-examined Van der Stel's old prospect shafts and other outcrops in the Richtersveld at places such as Numees and Kodas, and then formed a company in London to promote a mining venture.

The difficulties of opening up mines in so remote and rugged a territory were formidable. Men had to be found who were prepared to work in complete isolation from the outside world, their only form of communication a laborious ox wagon transport system which carried the ore to the Orange River. From there it was floated in barges down to Alexander Bay, and then shipped to Swansea in Wales, where it was milled, smelted and refined.

Despite the problems associated with mining, other companies became interested in Namaqualand copper. The 1850s, in fact, brought a rush to the area: mushroom companies and syndicates were established, even in some of the smallest towns of the Cape Province, and men poured into the copper area brainwashed with fallacies that copper lay thick and pure on the ground like overripe apples in an orchard.

The 'copper rush' collapsed as soon as the newcomers found that both hard work and substantial capital were needed in order to extract copper from its mother reef. Two companies remained: the Concordia Company, and two Welshmen, Messrs Phillips and King. The latter partnership sold out to the Cape Copper Mining Company in 1880. These two companies were both energetic and successful, and also fortunate in that the ore they were working was astonishingly rich, producing upwards of 31,5 per cent copper from the parent load. In the 1870s the O'Okiep Mine ranked as the richest copper mine in the world and by 1904 had produced some one million tons of ore.

The mines constructed their own narrow-gauge railway between Port Nolloth and O'Okiep. This was opened on 1 January 1876, although at first mule and horse traction was used until steam engines could be obtained. This private railway served as the principal outlet to the sea for 68 years. Only in 1942 were running operations abandoned in favour of road transport. The last engine in use, the *Clara,* is preserved at Nababeep.

In 1937 the two working companies merged to become the O'Okiep Copper Company which operates the mines today. A major economic factor in the life of Namaqualand, the mines have an annual output of some one million tons of ore from three principal mines – Nababeep, O'Okiep, Carolusberg – and several smaller workings.

A visit to the modern mines is a fascinating experience. The first impression the visitor receives is of the high degree of mechanisation. However, the old-time miners, especially those from Cornwall, were magnificent craftsmen, who devised a technique of mining which is still in use today; the difference is that the tools of the modern miners have become infinitely more efficient and powerful. In the old days, too, ore had to bear a tremendous concentration of metal in order to be profitably mined. Nowadays mechanisation and modern flotation and smelting processes have reduced working costs to such an extent that ore which the early miners discarded as unprofitably lean can be quite payably worked.

The milling and concentrating of the copper ore make a particularly interesting spectacle. The company has three mills, at Nababeep, Carolusberg and O'Okiep; each capable of handling more than 2 000 tons of ore every day. In these mills the ore is ground fine and converted into a pulp which flows into flotation machines. Here the copper separates from the waste matter by attaching itself to bubbles formed in the machines from the addition of detergents. These bubbles are collected and pumped to a thickener where the heavy copper settles and, after passing through a filter, emerges from the process as a damp concentrate.

The concentrate is dried and then taken to the smelting plant, where it is exposed to carefully controlled heat in a reverberatory furnace with a working temperature rising to 1 600° C; this reduces it to a molten matte containing about 50 per cent copper. The process of smelting is a fireworks display, especially at night. The waste material (slag) provides a particularly awesome spectacle: after being trammed away by an electric locomotive, it is poured down the side of a waste dump in a vivid burst of colour, like a waterfall of fire.

The matte is carried off in huge steel ladles to what is known as a converter. By means of compressed air, which is blown through the molten matte, the converter oxidises unwanted sulphur to a gas and removes iron by turning it into a silicate which is skimmed off. What remains is molten copper, 99 per cent pure. This is carried off, also in ladles, and poured into moulds fitted onto a huge wheel, 6,7 m in diameter. Each mould contains 159 kg of blister copper and by the time the wheel has turned full circle the copper has cooled. These bars are the finished product of the mine, and a fleet of heavy transport vehicles take them down to the railhead at Bitterfontein, from where they are entrained to Cape Town to be included among South Africa's varied exports. The blister copper is refined overseas.

Visitors to Namaqualand are struck by the effects of the copper mining industry on the arid countryside. Well-kept houses, recreation centres, tarmac roads and other signs of civilisation flourish in an environment which, without copper, would be solitary and bare. Just as rain can touch this barren land with magical fingers and turn it into an amazing garden of wild flowers, so copper has blessed the wastelands with wealth which has lasted through 150 years of intensive mining activity. From geological signs and discoveries, mining will continue to be a major factor in the economy of Namaqualand for many years to come.

The prospecting shafts from the original Van der Stel expedition and the smelter smoke-stack of the original Springbokfontein Mine are preserved as national monuments. Many interesting relics of early mining are to be seen at O'Okiep, and the abandoned stations, embankments and culverts of the old narrow-gauge railway run alongside the Copper Way, between Springbok and Steinkopf, and then close to the road to Port Nolloth.

# SPRINGBOK TO VIOOLSDRIF

After Springbok, the main road passes the old smelter stack of the original Springbokfontein Mine, crosses high granite hills and after 6 km reaches a turnoff west leading for 13 km to the substantial modern copper mining town of *Nababeep* (the water behind the little hill). With a population of 8 960, this town is managed by the O'Okiep Copper Company.

### Accommodation
★ Nababeep Hotel, 28 rooms, 19 with baths. R10,50 – R11,50 B/B. Phone 19.

The main road continues north and after 1,5 km (8 km from Springbok) passes the outskirts of the copper mining centre at the fountain known as O'Okiep from the Hottentot *U-gieb* (the great brack). Here the old smelter stack, built in 1880, still stands, a reminder of the early boom years of copper mining. In a stone building near the hotel there is also a remarkable pump, built in Cornwall in 1882. The mine at O'Okiep is still very active and a mining community of 5 750 people live in the town today.

### Accommodation
★ O'Okiep Hotel, 10 rooms, 6 with baths. R9 – R10 B/B. Phone 8.

At O'Okiep a gravel road branches north-westwards and leads via the drift at Goodhouse to South West Africa. The main tarmac road continues northwards among huge piles of granite. Many kokerbooms grow on the slopes and relics of early mining activity may be seen. The embankments of the abandoned narrow-gauge railway keep company with the road through the hills.

The landscape levels off into an arid plain, notable for its spring displays of wild flowers. At 48 km from Springbok, the tarmac road reaches the mission station of *Steinkopf,* originally founded for the Nama Hottentots by the Rhenish Mission Society, but now run by the Dutch Reformed Church at Steinkopf. Named after the Reverend Mr Steinkopf, the mission is an interesting place for in it still stand the curious, round 'matjie and sack' houses built by the Nama people in a world where shelter from the sun is of greater importance than protection from an insignificant rainfall. From Steinkopf, a gravel road branches west to Port Nolloth (see further on).

Still in a northerly direction, the main road crosses arid plains dotted with rocky hillocks. After 13 km a turnoff right takes travellers for 39 km to the date plantations at Henkries. Straight ahead looms a mass of mountains and 51 km from Steinkopf the road commences a gradual descent among huge piles of boulders gathered together as though swept from the plains by giant charladies. At the bottom of this 14-km descent, 114 km from Springbok, the road reaches the Orange River at the fording place known as *Vioolsdrif* from a Coloured shepherd, Viool, who once lived there. A modern bridge across the Orange takes the road on into South West Africa. At the bridge the Orange River is dominated by a spectacularly coloured line of high cliffs, and the area is rich in the beautiful decorative Vioolsdrif Stone. Relentless summer heat blankets the valley, but irrigation from the river allows successful production of tropical fruit, dates, citrus, lucerne, vegetables, corn and other crops. A cluster of farmhouses, a police post and a garage are at the bridge. This sunbaked but dramatic frontier post of the Cape Province is also the terminal point of the Copper Way.

---

From Steinkopf (48 km from Springbok) the gravel road to what is known as the Diamond Coast branches westwards from the Copper Way and stretches to the edge of the Namaqualand plain. After 10 km the road passes the abandoned railway station of Klipfontein, where a couple of kokerbooms grow on the old platform, as though waiting hopefully for a train.

The road now descends through successive terraces, each more arid than the one before. At 18 km from Steinkopf the road reaches the bottom of the Anenous Pass. There is a turnoff south to Spektakel at 59,5 km from Steinkopf; thirteen kilometres further on the road passes the works of the Diamant-Quartzite Industries and the Namaqualand Quartzite Company, which produces an attractive building stone. At 79 km from Steinkopf there is a turnoff south to Kleinsee (45 km), where Consolidated Diamond Mines have a mine in a prohibited area. Just before the gate of the mine, at Grootmis, a road stretches for 96,5 km to Springbok, crossing the interesting *Spektakel* (spectacle) Pass – a fascinating drive on a gravel road. Fourteen and a half kilometres beyond the turnoff to Kleinsee, on the main route at 93 km from Steinkopf, the road reaches the coast at . . .

# PORT NOLLOTH

This cluster of houses confronts a diminutive harbour protectively enclosed in the arms of a reef of rock. A pretty stretch of beach and calm water within the reef are visually inviting to the holidaymaker, but the Benguela Current sweeping up the coast is bitterly cold and the little port is plagued by contradictory weather conditions. The cold sea (16° C maximum) resists evaporation, with the result that the coastal terrace on which Port Nolloth lies is an unprepossessing semi-desert, level, sandy and scrub covered, with a rainfall of 45 mm a year mainly from great, clammy banks of mist which blanket the place intermittently between February and June and precipitate about 2 mm of moisture in 24 hours. From October to March the southerly wind tends to blow at gale force. February can be oven hot, July ranges from cool to cold; but the latter month, together with August and September, is the best time to visit the Diamond Coast.

Port Nolloth is an odd, isolated little desert port, but despite its weather problems it has a distinctive atmosphere: a hardy character, memories of past things, tough men and forgotten adventures, make the Diamond Coast unique.

Port Nolloth goes back to the time of the copper boom, long before diamonds were found. Originally known as *Robbebaai* (bay of seals), it was surveyed in 1854 by Captain M. S. Nolloth and proved to be the most practical harbour on the Namaqualand coast for the shipment of copper ore. In March 1855 the proposed harbour was named after its surveyor by the Governor, Sir George Grey, and Port Nolloth was established.

At first copper ore was laboriously conveyed to the place by wagon and the draught animals suffered badly on the tortuous old road. In 1876, however, the narrow-gauge railway was opened to the copper mines and, after a preliminary spell of animal-drawn trains, a stream of puffing billies worked their way backwards and forwards along the line, taking trucks of ore to the port.

A town was laid out at the port, destined to be dominated for years by enterprises such as the Cape Copper Company, the South African Copper Company, and the O'Okiep Copper Company.

Nobody was very satisfied with Port Nolloth. The opening in the reef allowed only small vessels of the coastal type to enter the harbour, while the cost of imported coal made the narrow-gauge railway an expensive enterprise. When the railway was opened from Cape Town to Bitterfontein, and the development of heavy trucks made road transport practical, the narrow-gauge railway fell into disuse and was eventually rooted up, leaving only a chain of 'ghost' stations and remnants of culverts and cuttings. Left in operation was an 8-km stretch from Port Nolloth to some freshwater springs from which the O'Okiep Copper Company railed water to the town at 1d per 18ℓ. Only in 1949 did the town secure its own water supply from boreholes.

171

After being abandoned by the copper companies, Port Nolloth went into a decline. Then commercial fishing developed in the area. Three crayfish factories – John Ovenstone Ltd, Hicksons Canning Co. and Port Nolloth Visserye – were established. In 1930 Port Nolloth became a village management board and on 1 July 1945, a municipality. Today 3 050 people live in the town. What really got the place going again, however, was the spectacular discovery of diamonds. Port Nolloth is the only holiday resort on an otherwise prohibited entry diamond-mining coast, and *McDougall's Bay* (named after a pioneer trader, miner and fisherman Donald McDougall, who settled here in the early years) has a picturesque cluster of shacks on ground leased from the municipality.

## Accommodation
★ Scotia Inn, 23 rooms, 8 with baths. R8 – R9 B/B. Phone 14.

## Caravans and camping
★ McDougall Bay, 10 sites. R1,50 D. 3 bungalows, R2,50 D.

-----------

# THE DIAMOND COAST

It is difficult for man to comprehend the mood of nature in the creation of the Diamond Coast. Harsh and grim? Cynical and ruthless? The icy seas, oven-baked land, freezing nights, barrenness and solitude, the thirst – even the few springs callously salty to torment what life there is – would certainly suggest a savage fury. And yet, when all was done and nature had relieved her mood, the power of creation looked down on the deformed landscape and compassion came: in a way which no man has ever convincingly explained, diamonds appeared in the marine terraces along the beach, making this Cinderella land one of the richest places on earth.

Why man took so long to find these diamonds is yet another mystery. Rumours of their existence circulated for many years, but the great discovery only occurred in June 1926.

Captain Jack Carstens, son of William Carstens, a storekeeper in Port Nolloth, was home on leave from service in the Indian army. He took to prospecting, abandoned his military career, and with his cousin, Percy Hughes, pegged claims 10 km south of Port Nolloth. There Carstens found the first diamonds, and the news, quickly reported by Carstens senior, the local correspondent for Reuters, attracted a rush of prospectors.

A partnership consisting of Kennedy, Misdall and J. P. White went up to Alexander Bay but had no luck. On his way back, Kennedy stopped at what was known as the Cliffs, where he had noticed red soil and traces of gravel when on the way north. Within a few days Kennedy found 14 small diamonds. This, the second discovery, stimulated tremendous local excitement, and a little later a storekeeper from Steinkopf named Rabinowitz found 334 diamonds at Buchuberg, north of the Cliffs.

In the midst of the excitement, another Steinkopf storekeeper, Mick Caplan, went to Alexander Bay with a small party of workmen. They pegged 20 claims and found some magnificent diamonds.

Now prospectors, option hunters and diamond buyers flocked to the Diamond Coast. Namaqualand seethed with excitement and rumours. Company promoters and mining experts such as the famed Hans Merensky hastened to the area. One of the most discerning of all geologists, Merensky soon noted that diamonds were invariably found in association with beds of gravel interspersed with fossilised shells of *Ostrea prismatica*, an extinct warmwater oyster. He looked for a place which had concentrations of these shells and took options on claims pegged by Caplan's party at Alexander Bay. All his instincts told him that this was the richest area, and he set out to secure control of the entire so-called 'oyster line' around the shores of the bay. For a total of £17 000 (about R35 000) Merensky gained control of what became one of the world's richest natural treasure chests. Under a single flat stone, the prospector found 487 diamonds and, within a month, 2 762 diamonds totalling 4 308,9 carats had been found at Alexander Bay.

Hans Merensky hastened to Cape Town and saw the Prime Minister, warning him that the sensational finds would certainly incite a stampede of fortune-seekers to the Diamond Coast and in the harsh conditions most of the hopefuls would simply die of thirst or hunger. There could be no repetition of the wild rush to Lichtenburg; most of the diamondiferous coastline was, in any event, already in the hands of big companies.

The government took rapid action. On 22 February 1927 all further prospecting for diamonds along the Namaqualand coast was prohibited. This measure, drastic but essential, brought the entire coast under tight control. As it was, when the so-called Hans Merensky Association halted operations in accordance with the government ban they had, in one month's work, already found 6 890 diamonds weighing 12 549 carats and valued at £153 000. Further unlimited exploitation of these fields could only bring about a collapse in the market value of diamonds.

At this point the Diamond Syndicate, guided by Ernest Oppenheimer, intervened, undertaking to buy the entire output of the Namaqualand fields, and to place the stones on the world market in an orderly fashion to maintain prices. Oppenheimer also bought his way into Merensky's association; by July 1927 he had obtained £500 000 worth of shares and had become the dominant personality on the Diamond Coast.

The problem of operating the coastal alluvial fields was comprehensively solved by the government: the coast would become a state digging, with the exception of discoverers' rights on distinct geological deposits, of which there were six altogether. Of these the 'Oyster Line' and the 'River Gravel areas' went to Merensky; the 'Pebbly Limestone Line' at the Cliffs to Kennedy; the Buchuberg area to Rabinowitz; and the 'Operculum Beds' went to the Gelgorcap Syndicate. After some legal wrangling, the sixth deposit, the 'Extension of the Oyster Line', also went to Merensky and his association. By wheeling and dealing Merensky and Oppenheimer then bought up the other discoverers' rights, and made themselves sole controllers of Alexander Bay, obliged, however, to sell their production to the government.

On 1 May 1928 work was resumed along the Diamond Coast in areas controlled by the Merensky Association and on the state diggings, controlled by the government. The strictest security precautions were enforced on the fields. Barbed wire and guards kept unauthorised persons out, but the very severity of the restrictions became a challenge to many ingenious thieves who, over the years, used every possible scheme to smuggle diamonds through the security screen.

Public resentment, especially by the people of Namaqualand, of government preclusion of their hopes for fortune, and of the exclusive monopoly of the Merensky Association was considerable and understandable. It seemed that the newly discovered riches of the area, like the oil of the Middle East, would be looted for the benefit of only a few individuals, and Namaqualand would be left to its poverty. Successful diamond smugglers were applauded as poor Robin Hoods robbing the rich.

Port Nolloth was bursting at the seams with an influx of would-be diggers, many from as far away as Lichtenburg; all were disgruntled, and existing in appalling conditions of squalor. Among them moved I.D.B.s (illicit diamond buyers) and all manner of adventurers waiting for the main chance. Among this community it was not considered a crime to rob the state or Merensky's diggings, and simply a misfortune, but no disgrace, to be caught. The atmosphere became electric with open talk that the restricted areas should be rushed by force.

In December 1928 an abortive effort was made to rush Buchuberg. This was restrained only by vigorous police action, but when the men involved were taken back to Port Nolloth in handcuffs, an angry crowd demanded, and secured, their release. This was the beginning of what became known as the Namaqualand Rebellion.

The crowd threatened to storm Merensky's monopoly at Alexander Bay unless the government made some land available for public working. More policemen were rushed in by the authorities and money was voted for the relief of would-be diggers, whose condition was becoming deplorable. Port Nolloth was reminiscent of a dead-end town of lost souls; starvation and frustration were etched on the faces of nearly everyone.

A stormy meeting was held by the diggers and an ultimatum was sent to the government: unless some ground was made available as a public diggings by 28 December, they would storm Alexander Bay. The government reply was to send in still more policemen, vote funds for the relief of poverty among the would-be diggers, and offer employment on roadworks and the railways in various parts of South Africa.

The offer was shouted down at a meeting and a fresh ultimatum was sent: Alexander Bay would be stormed on 7 January 1929 unless public diggings were proclaimed. The atmosphere at Port Nolloth became even more electric; scores of policemen arrived and diggers were increasingly truculent; bars and tearooms were crowded with men holding meetings while police patrols marched up and down the two sandy streets of the town.

Diggers were also squabbling among themselves. Considerable friction existed between local men and those who had rushed to Namaqualand, mainly from the Lichtenburg diamond fields. Both groups tended to work separately, and this weakened their cause. The general plan was to hold a mass meeting on 7 January and then drive out in trucks to Alexander Bay, where they would establish themselves around the outer fence, and lay siege to the place for three days to allow for further negotiations. After that there would be serious trouble.

At Alexander Bay, police mounted machine guns and preparations were made to resist attack. Truckloads of police reinforcements arrived. January 6 passed with a great bustle of opposing sides preparing for the climax. The squabble between the Namaqualanders and the Lichtenburgers (as they were known) mounted; only the leadership of the renowned Manie Maritz, of Anglo-Boer War and 1914 rebellion fame, kept the two sides to a single purpose.

January 7 found Port Nolloth seething with excitement and frustration. Committees of Namaqualanders and Lichtenburgers met to organise proceedings, but simply squabbled for five weary hours while 2 000 impatient would-be rebels clamoured for leadership outside. At 15h00 a mass meeting was called. Two thousand men gathered for the occasion but Manie Maritz counselled caution and the rebellion fizzled out. A deputation was appointed to interview the Minister of Mines on 25 January.

For the next 48 hours a howling south-west wind swept over the Diamond Coast and even the most militant men lay low for shelter. The spirit of rebellion was scattered by the winds, and when calm returned, only poverty and despondency remained. Manie Maritz was appointed by the government as a welfare officer for the area, and poor relief would be given to the would-be diggers. But no diamond areas on the coast would ever be available for public working – they were to be a prohibited zone for all time.

Diamonds found along the Namaqualand coast are gemstones of particularly fine quality, recovered along the line of an ancient beach (hence the association with fossil oysters) and by marine dredging from deposits beneath the sea north of Oranjemund. Alexander Bay (84 km north of Port Nolloth) and Kleinsee (56 km south of Port Nolloth) are the two principal areas of coastal recovery, but there are substantial deposits on the coast which are kept in reserve. Outside the area of the original discoverers' claims, the Diamond Coast of Namaqualand is operated as a state diggings; casual visitors to the fenced areas, unless they are vouched for by persons employed on the fields and issued with a permit, are unwelcome. Of the total of R445 million worth of diamonds produced in South Africa in 1978, the Cape Alluvial Diggings yielded R65 million. The output is restricted and co-ordinated so as not to depress the market value of gemstones.

## Chapter Ten

# CAPE TOWN TO THE ORANGE RIVER

The Great North Road – the Cape-to-Cairo road – is the great trunk route of Africa. It begins, unmarked by sign or monument, at the foot of the Heerengracht, just in front of the entrance to Cape Town docks. Also known as N1, this is the trunk road from Cape Town through Bloemfontein to Johannesburg and Zimbabwe, then continuing northwards across the Zambezi, through the interminable brachystegia forests of Zambia, the nyika wilderness of Tanzania, the game plains of East Africa and down the Nile to Egypt and the Mediterranean.

This has always been a road of adventure, hope and romance. From the time of the first settlement of the Cape, Van Riebeeck and his pioneers looked wistfully at the mountains of the north and east, wondering what lay beyond – what riches, strange tribes and natural marvels. As the road was blazed stage by stage into the interior, it became a pathway for explorers, hunters, missionaries, traders, prospectors and farmers. Fortune-seekers, too, poured by the thousands up the trail to reach the gold and diamond areas. Tented wagons, bicycles with sails, stylish and outlandish carts, rickety old motor vehicles, footsloggers and hitchhikers, record breakers, freaks, runaways from law and escapists from society – all have helped to beat this great road into the ground. Stories rich enough to fill a thousand books have originated along this road and built up to a climax of human comedy or drama whose ending is often lost in mystery.

From its start at the foot of the Heerengracht the road keeps below the concrete Eastern Boulevard and follows the fence of Cape Town docks for 1,5 km, keeping to the verge of Table Bay; the bulk of Table Mountain on the right, the great beacon heralding the southern end of Africa, is also the gateway of the route into the interior.

After 1,5 km, where there is a branch left to Milnerton, the shores of Table Bay swing north-westwards. The road continues as a handsome dual carriageway, passing (at 7 km) the cloverleaf Koeberg Road interchange which takes traffic off to Muizenberg and Milnerton, and then along the verges of the Ysterplaat air station, where fledgling helicopter pilots train in their odd insect-like machines.

On the right is the modern housing estate, *Kensington*, for Coloured people; on the left, in the near distance, are the refineries and chemical works of organisations such as Caltex and Fisons. After 14 km, at a traffic interchange, there is the road to Namaqualand and Namibia. Modern housing estates crowd close to the verges.

For 7 km the road climbs along the slopes of the Tygerberg, providing the traveller with spectacular views of the great housing development of the Cape Flats and the city of Cape Town – a particularly magnificent spectacle at the end of each day, when the lights are coming on and Table Mountain is silhouetted in the fiery glow of sunset.

At 19 km from Cape Town the road reaches the turnoff to Parow and at 24 km the turnoff to Bellville. Housing developments abound, and each dwelling is so close to its neighbour that borrowings of foodstuffs and utility items may be made by means of outstretched arms through windows! The entire area is, in fact, a congested 'night' industrial site (baby-producing factories) with little of beauty save the view of Table Mountain.

The residential area of Brackenfell, where there is a motel and caravan park by the roadside, is reached via a turnoff 29 km from Cape Town.

### Accommodation

★ Aroma Inn, 20 rooms, 15 with baths. R10 – R14 B/B. Phone 901-2171.

### Caravans and camping

★® Gypsy Caravan Park, 50 sites. R3,50 D.

For the next 30 km the double carriageway crosses the Cape Flats, heading towards Paarl and the mountain ranges. The 1 390-m-high bulk of Simonsberg – among the handsomest of Cape mountains – dominates the scene on the right while to the left a cluster of granite domes looks down from the heights of Paarl.

Flyover bridges cross the road: to Kraaifontein at 32 km from Cape Town and to Stellenbosch at 40 km. Just off the road, 48 km from Cape Town at the little centre of *Klapmuts* (so named from the overlooking hill whose shape resembles the Dutch sailor's hat of that name) there is a cluster of garages, wayside cafés and a hotel.

### Accommodation

★ Klapmuts Hotel, 8 rooms, 2 with baths. R8,50 B/B. Phone 5315.
★ Kraaifontein Hotel, 14 rooms, 5 with baths. R5,50 – R6 B/B. Phone 32-1532.

Roads to Agter Paarl and Franschhoek lead off left and right while 56 km from Cape Town a major turnoff left takes travellers into the town of Paarl (see page 108).

The road now burrows under the main railway line, bridges across the Berg River and, 60 km from Cape Town, after shedding turnoffs to Wellington and Franschhoek, starts to climb one of the finest scenic mountain passes in Southern Africa . . .

## DU TOIT'S KLOOF PASS

A French Huguenot by the name of Francois du Toit gave his name to this fine mountain pass. He secured from the Governor, Simon van der Stel, the farm *De Kleyne Bos*, lying at the foot of the Drakenstein mountains just below the saddle allowing access to the gorge which carries the road today.

The need for a road through this gorge was apparent from an early period, for it would provide a direct link between the valleys of the Berg and Breë rivers. In 1824 the first attempt at building a pass was made by Detlef Schönfeldt, a former lieutenant in the 45th Würtemburg Hussars. Using £1 527 raised by himself and the public, he made a rough track, of little use other than to walkers; wagons crossed it at their peril. Schönfeldt had such faith in the future of the pass, however, that he purchased most of the gorge and planned to finance road construction by means of tolls. He died with his project unfulfilled, but several others became interested in the pass. In 1846 it was surveyed by Colonel Michell and the road inspector, Andrew Geddes Bain, but their estimated cost of £340 000 made construction prohibitive. For nearly 100 years nothing further was done to the pass, other than the construction in the 1920s of a private track up the Drakenstein slopes and over the saddle into the gorge, where a Paarl farmer, J. le Roux, had a buchu-producing farm.

Finally, in 1935, with the establishment of the National Road Board, the project of this pass was re-examined. P. A. de Villiers, one of the great roadmakers of South Africa, was then an engineer of the board and he surveyed the route. His report, made in 1940, estimated construction costs at £260 000. Building commenced in 1943 with 500 Italian prisoners-of-war as labourers. The 40-km-long pass climbed to 820 m above sea level and traversed a 223-m-long tunnel through Kleigat. It was opened on 26 March 1949 by the then Prime Minister, the Honourable D. F. Malan. The final cost of construction was £750 000.

The summit of the pass is reached 77 km from Cape Town. Here many travellers pause awhile for a last look (or a first if they are coming down from the north) at Table Mountain in the distance, across the valley of the Berg River; the towns of Paarl and Wellington lie directly below. This is a superb view and viewpoint. The mountain slopes are rich in wild flowers, and from the summit of the pass a footpath and also a private road on the left (north) side lead to a telecommunications tower and to the beautiful Krom River with its swimming pools and Mountain Club hut – the base for many fine climbs and walks up the surrounding high peaks.

In the 5 km from the head of the pass down to the tunnel, the traveller is treated to spectacular views of the great bulk of the 1 655-m-high Du Toit's Kloof Peak. In winter, when the peaks are covered in snow, many beautiful waterfalls grace the left (north) side of the pass. Wild flowers are sold at a farm just before the tunnel entrance.

Beyond the tunnel – a favourite rendezvous for baboons – the road bridges the Elandspad River, up whose valley there are fine walks and famous trout-fishing pools. The Mountain Club of South Africa has a hut just beyond the river and the entire area of the pass offers wonderful recreation for climbers, hikers and fishermen. At the 85-km point from Cape Town there is a hotel and a garage.

### Accommodation
* Protea Park, 15 rooms, 9 with baths. R9,50 – R18 B/B. Phone Worcester 9-1092.

For 9 km beyond the hotel the road descends through the valley of the *Molenaars* (miller's) River, overlooked on both sides by towering cliffs and peaks. At 94 km from Cape Town the road crosses this mountain torrent and emerges from Du Toit's Kloof Pass into the broad, alluvial and stony valley of the Breë River. Ahead (north and north-east) lies the handsome sandstone range of the Hex River mountains with the Mostert's Hoek Twins on the left and the *Brandwag* (sentry) mountain (1 809 m) straight ahead.

The valley of the Breë River (see pages 124 to 137) is one of the principal grape and deciduous fruit farming valleys of the Western Cape, and the road passes through neat vineyards where some of the sweetest grapes (notably hanepoot) in Southern Africa are grown. During the season, January to April, grapes are sold at several farm stalls by the wayside. After 8 km of vineyards a crossroads leads right to the small village of Rawsonville and left to Goudini Baths (page 129).

On the far side of the valley of the Breë River, 24 km from the exit of Du Toit's Kloof Pass, and 118 km from Cape Town, a turnoff left goes to Wolseley and, shortly ahead, a turnoff right enters the principal centre of the valley, the town of Worcester (see page 127).

The main highway to the north passes the outskirts of Worcester and the Bergsig Garage, Café and Caravan Park 124 km from Cape Town, just after the turn to the Karoo Botanical Gardens (page 128). Three kilometres further on stand the wine cellars at *De Wet*. The road crosses the Hex River and enters the lower end of the famous Hex River Mountain Pass where the Hex River finds a narrow passage between the Kwadouw and the Hex River mountain range. The passage is so tortuous that the pioneer wagon track was forced to ford the river nine times and from this the river was first named the *Ekse* (criss-cross). The name later became corrupted to *Hexe* and then to *Hex*.

Just before the road crosses the railway there is a fruit kiosk on *Glen Heatlie* farm, which is noted for its fruit, and a parking ground for caravans with shade, toilets and water.

## HEX RIVER VALLEY

The river passage of the Hex is a spectacular entrance way to the wealthy grape-producing valley which lies along the south-east face of the Hex River mountains. From the Bushman paintings in the caves of these sandstone mountains it is apparent that the valley was once the sanctuary of various antelope, as well as giraffe and lion. On migrations backwards and forwards through the river passage, these animals blazed the first trails, which were later followed by Bushman hunters.

It is not known who the earliest European to follow this ancient trail was, but on 21 December 1709 Roelof Jantz van Hoeting was the first person to receive licence to graze his livestock 'under the mountains of Red Sand above the Rock of the Lions'. This was an auspicious date for the valley – the beginning of its modern agricultural history and the advent of European settlement in an area which, until then, had belonged only to the Bushmen and the wild animals, which they hunted for their food.

Other cattle keepers followed Van Hoeting to the valley. Official names of farms began to feature in the records: on 8 December 1723, for instance, *Vendutie Kraal* (the sale pen) was granted to Jacob van der Merwe and the name of the farm hints at an established industry in cattle breeding and auction. In view of the value of land in the valley today it is interesting to note that Mr Van der Merwe paid 24 rixdollars (R12) for his grant and agreed to deliver one-tenth of his grain crop each year to the landdros of Stellenbosch; the latter part of the deal he could quite easily evade by not growing any grain at all.

By the end of the 18th century six farms had been granted, covering all the best reaches of the valley. *Kanetvlei* (named after the type of reeds in the marsh there) was in the hands of the Stofberg family; *Roodesand* was owned by the Jourdans and noted for the quality of its Madeira-type wines; *Vendutie Kraal* belonged to the Van der Merwes; *Modderdrif* was owned by the Conradies; *De Doorns* (the thorns) was the home of the De Vos family, whose hospitable home was already recognised as the natural community centre of the valley; and *Buffelskraal,* a farm at the upper end of the valley, was owned by another branch of the same De Vos family.

Each farm had a handsome Cape-Dutch style farmhouse and it is in one of these, on *Buffelskraal,* that the tradition was born of the fair ghost (the *hex* or witch) who is supposed to haunt the Hex River mountains. It is said that in the year 1768, just after the house had been built, one of its occupants was a beautiful girl named Eliza Meiring. She was so popular with the local young bloods that she set any would-be suitor the initial task of bringing her a disa from the inaccessible precipices of the 2 249-m Matroosberg, highest peak of the range.

The very difficulty of the task was intended to deter unwanted suitors. Unknown to Eliza, however, the one young man she really favoured set out to surprise her by securing a disa. In the attempt he fell and was killed. The shock deranged the fair Eliza and she had to be locked in an upper room of the house. One night she contrived to force a window open but in trying to reach the ground she slipped and was killed. It is said to be her spirit, lamenting the death of her lover, which wanders along the windswept peaks at night. The date, 1768, and the initials E. M. were once carved into the windowsill but later removed by renovators; these graffiti were thought to commemorate the tragedy. Now, when moonlight glitters on the first sprinkling of winter snows someone living on the valley floor is sure to remark 'the witch is on the mountains tonight'.

Eliza suffered a tragic end, but most of her fellows in the valley at the time were a carefree lot, with few worries save the effects on their figures of hearty eating, good wine, and a pleasant life in the sunshine and crisp Karoo air. Today, of the six original farms of the Hex River Valley, there are nearly 150 subdivisions. The value of any single subdivision is so greatly in excess of the original combined value of the first six farms, that the comparison is ludicrous. In contrast to the quiet economic conditions of the cattle-grazing past, an economic revolution has come to the valley in comparatively recent times.

The change began in 1875, when the Hex River railway pass was surveyed by Wells Hood and built, at a cost of R1 million, to carry the main railway line from Cape Town to the north and the diamond fields of Kimberley. Before the construction of the railway most of the traffic to the north had followed the early road route through Ceres and Sutherland, but now the Hex River Valley became accepted as the principal route to the interior. The early wagon trail over the criss-cross river was gradually improved until it became the Great North Road we know today and the valley at last gained the advantage of first-class communications.

Seven years after the opening of this great railway pass – certainly the most famous in Southern Africa – the first tentative export of table grapes was made to Britain. In 1886 the grapes (red and white hanepoot) were privately dispatched to Dr Smuts in London. Carefully packed in cork and charcoal dust, with their stems sealed in beeswax, and without any refrigeration, they arrived in excellent condition. This was the auspicious beginning of the great export grape trade of today. The Hex River Valley is the principal centre and producer of dessert grapes of international quality and renown. To understand the remarkable rise of the valley from past obscurity to its present affluent position, it is necessary to know something of the fascinating background to grape cultivation in the Cape. For this information, the reader should turn to page 77.

The railway to the north brought the first increase in the demand for table fruit and the Hex River Valley farmers found that they had a slight advantage in the competition for new markets on the diamond and goldfields. The railway station and locomotive depot built on *De Doorns* farm was, by rail, 200 km nearer the northern markets than Cape Town. Freight costs were therefore slightly cheaper and the fruit was subjected to some 20 hours less of buffeting and heat from constant stoppages at sidings and crossing points – common in goods railage in those days.

From this period the Hex River Valley farmers started to become seriously interested in table grapes. They soon made a significant discovery: that the ideal climate for vines is a long, warm summer and autumn, with little rain from the time the grapes start to ripen; rain during the critical ripening period promotes disease, cracking of skin and watery grapes. Only when the vine is dormant in winter must heavy rain fall, and the colder it is then, the safer and more sound asleep the plant will be.

The quality of the grape is therefore largely dependent on the prevalence of the critical conditions described above; in addition, vines must be grown in deep, cool, well-drained soil. All these conditions prevail in the traditional home of the vine, northern Persia. Since earliest times man has carried the fruit to many parts of the world (wine was made in Egypt 6 000 years ago), but no area is a greater paradise for grapes than the Hex River Valley. Not only do grapes grow superbly there, free of most diseases and blemishes, but the lengthy, dry autumn allows the fruit to remain on the vines until the very end of the season, when prices are excellent.

In the developing local market the hanepoot remained the ideal grape variety for production not only in the Hex River Valley but in most areas of the Cape hot enough to allow for good ripening. After the opening of the export market to Britain, however, the hanepoot was found to have a serious weakness: its skin was too soft for it to travel really well. Despite care and ingenuity in packing, the first 20 years of the struggling export grape industry were seriously handicapped by this weakness of the hanepoot; entire shipments were often useless by the time the grapes reached the overseas markets.

The answer was to find or breed other varieties of grape with tougher skins which made them keep better.

The most popular of the varieties subsequently grown is the barlinka, introduced from Algeria in 1909. This large, luscious, black grape grows to perfection in the Hex River Valley and today the area produces the bulk of South Africa's export grape harvest. The productivity of the valley has been substantially increased by a complex irrigation project: a storage dam has been built in the upper Hex and water is fed into the valley by means of a tunnel through the mountains.

Late autumn and early winter (around the month of June) see the Hex River Valley aflame with one of the world's great botanical spectacles, for it is then that the leaves of the barlinka vines turn an almost unbelievable shade of scarlet.

The principal centre in the valley of the Hex River, 150 km by road from Cape Town, is . . .

# DE DOORNS

Built on the farm *De Doorns* (the thorns), this town with a population of 4 500, started as a railway station in 1875. It is now the principal commercial, administrative and educational centre for the Hex River Valley.

**Accommodation**
★ Hex Valley Hotel, 19 rooms, 8 with baths. R7 – R8 B/B. Phone 2090.

The main road continues from the turnoff left to De Doorns. The 2 249-m-high rounded dome of the *Matroosberg* (named after Klaas Matroos, a shepherd who once lived there) dominates the upper end of the valley. After 4,5 km the road passes the Bonny Brand Fruit Stall and soon starts to climb out of the valley along a serpentine pass up the edge of the escarpment of South Africa to the 965-m level, 173 km from Cape Town; here the traveller finds himself on the fringe of the high central plateau of Southern Africa.

## THE HEX RIVER VALLEY RAILWAY PASS

The Hex River Railway Pass is one of the best known and most dramatic feats of railway engineering in Africa. From De Doorns, at 477 m above sea level, the railway in 25 km climbs to Matroosberg station, 959 m above sea level. The pass was built in 1875 at a cost of £500 000 and modern engineers agree that the surveyor who located the line, Wells Hood, did a magnificent job. To find an easier gradient through this complex mass of mountains has involved modern planners in a project of prodigious tunnelling, including one tunnel 12 km long.

The ruling gradient in the pass is 1-in-40 uncompensated at curves. If put together, all the curves in the pass would take a train into 16 complete circuits. The pass is a great scenic thrill for countless passengers and many will miss it when the new pass is eventually completed. The new pass will decrease the ruling gradient to an easy 1-in-66, shorten the pass by 7 km and eliminate most of the curves, but passengers will be treated to little more than the inside view of a series of long, dark tunnels.

The great Hex River Railway Pass has a fine safety record, which speaks for the care and attention in its maintenance. All manner of specialist railwaymen play a part in keeping this pass in operation: gangers, patrolmen, men who recharge the nine automatic greasers which lubricate the flanges of the wheels of passing trains, men who grease the sides of the rails at curves to ease friction, signalmen, drivers and many others. Only one serious accident has taken place in the pass since its construction. On 10 September 1914, at 18h00, a troop train conveying 500 men of the Kaffrarian Rifles was derailed on the way down the pass. Ten coaches rolled over the side at the point marked by a monument midway between the stations of Tunnel and Matroosberg. By a miracle only ten men were killed, although 40 were injured.

From the summit of the Hex River road pass (173 km from Cape Town) the main road passes the turn right to Montagu and the turn left to Ceres. Over undulating and increasingly arid country the road continues until (194 km from Cape Town) it reaches the town of . . .

## TOUWS RIVER

On 7 November 1877, a station named Montagu Road was opened on the newly-built railway from Cape Town. On 1 January 1883 its name was changed to *Touws River* (river of the pass).

Essentially a railway town, Touws River is a major staging post on the way to the north, a

*Overleaf: When the snow witch roams the Hex River Mountains the barlinka vines turn scarlet in a supreme autumn spectacle.*

junction for the branch line to Ladismith, and was a great coaling depot until the line was electrified on 14 May 1954. Touws River became a municipality on 1 January 1962 and is now inhabited by 7 700 people.

## Accommodation
* Loganda Hotel, 15 rooms, all with baths. R8,50 – R10,50 B/B. Phone 130.

## Caravans and camping
* Loots Caravan Park, 50 sites. R2,80 D. 30 rooms and rondawels, R2,60 – R3,12 D.

The main road leads from Touws River in an easterly direction, passing through a complex of semi-arid hills and valleys made of tillite and shales. It is a curious landscape, and as the road passes Tweedside (32 km from Touws River) with its wrought-iron gates and rows of gum trees, the military graveyard, 11 km further on, and, 250 km from Cape Town, the turnoff right to Matjiesfontein, one can sense an unusual story about the area . . .

# MATJIESFONTEIN

*Matjiesfontein* (the fountain of matrushes) is the 'capital' of this area, and it is worth turning off the main road for at least an inspection. The story began when a Scot, James Douglas Logan, destined to be known as the 'Laird of Matjiesfontein', was on his way to Australia in 1877 at the age of 20. Instead of continuing on his journey, he left the ship at Simonstown on the Cape Peninsula. In somewhat straitened circumstances, Logan became a porter on Cape Town railway station, and from this position he literally worked his way up the line to become district superintendent of the Touws River-Prince Albert Road section of the railway.

He took a liking to the wild landscape of that part of the world. It suited his health and he felt that he could make his fortune there. He resigned from the railway and opened a hotel in Touws River, where his name is still retained by the Loganda Hotel. Matjiesfontein, however, was the place which appealed to him most. Little was there other than a few rough buildings and the surrounding wilderness, but he saw hidden virtues. He paid £400 for a 2 998-ha farm which he named *Tweedside* and built a homestead, bought handsome wrought-iron gates, and planted thousands of hardy eucalyptus trees. Gradually he bought up neighbouring properties until he owned 51 390 ha of ground.

Logan sank innumerable boreholes, planted huge orchards of fruit trees, built a handsome shooting lodge and made *Tweedside* one of the model farms of Southern Africa. At the same time he developed Matjiesfontein. He imported real London lamp posts and built a large windmill to crush wheat and used its power to generate electricity – his house was the first private residence in South Africa with electric lighting. He also pioneered water-borne sewerage and piped water to Matjiesfontein from a 50 000-l-a-day spring on his farm. He made money by selling the water to the railways: a train consumed 250 000 l of water on the journey across the arid Karoo from Touws River to De Aar and any dependable supply on the wayside was invaluable. The thirst of the locomotives was curbed in modern times, first by condenser tenders, which re-converted steam into water, and later by electrification.

Logan suffered from a weak chest and his liking for his adopted home was connected with the beneficial effects of its dry, crisp air on his health. He set out to develop Matjiesfontein as an international health resort. His success was astonishing. He built a substantial hotel complete with fountains playing in the bright sunlight. Lady Sprigg, wife of the Cape Prime Minister, opened the place by turning on the fountains and thereafter it became a resort of the élite. Aristocrats all the way from Europe came by sea to enjoy the life-giving air of Matjiesfontein. Lord Randolph Churchill, the Duke of Hamilton, the Sultan of Zanzibar, Cecil Rhodes and many other notables visited the place.

A keen sportsman, Logan twice brought out Lord Hawke's cricket team, who actually played in Matjiesfontein. When the health of George Lohmann, the great English cricketer, broke down, Logan prolonged his life by many years by employing him in the warm sunshine and keen air of Matjiesfontein. Lohmann died in Matjiesfontein on 1 December 1901 and was buried in the cemetery at Monument, beneath a handsome tombstone which records him as one of the cricketing greats of all time.

On Matjiesfontein railway station Logan maintained a magnificent dining room for the refreshment of railway passengers (there were no dining cars in those days). He also opened a mineral water factory in Matjiesfontein, managed a chain of restaurants on other railway stations, and entered the Cape parliament as Progressive member of the Legislative Assembly for Worcester. His home remained at the elegant *Tweedside Lodge* he built at Matjiesfontein. Among his many other activities, he was an expert photographer and amateur magician.

With the outbreak of the Anglo-Boer War, Matjiesfontein became the headquarters of the Cape Command and many of the crack British regiments of the day came there, among them the Coldstream Guards and the 17th Lancers; other visitors were men such as Douglas Haig and Edgar Wallace, both of whom later became famous.

The Matjiesfontein Hotel was used as a military hospital, and its turret became a lookout post. The hotel still stands in its original state, and London lamp posts still light the main street. Logan died in Matjiesfontein on 30 July 1920. His son James continued to run his father's interests. A keen botanist, he made a study of the rich flora in the area between Matjiesfontein and Sutherland. The collection of game animals' heads in the hotel was also acquired by young Logan, who lived in *Tweedside Lodge,* planting succulents in the garden and becoming almost as well known in his way as his father. He died in Matjiesfontein in 1960. His sister had married Colonel Buist and they continued to reside in *Tweedside Lodge.* Their son, Major John Buist, eventually succeeded to the management of the extensive family interests in the area. However, the village of Matjiesfontein, together with the Lord Milner Hotel, was sold by Major Buist to Mr David Rawdon in 1969.

The new owner was proprietor of the well-known Nottingham Road Hotel in Natal and had recently converted the historic farm of *Lanzerac* in Stellenbosch to a hotel showpiece. He set out to restore Matjiesfontein to all its former Victorian glory and the village was opened in mid-1970, a unique resort offering a museum, a fine hotel, a superlative menu, a traditional *losieshuis* (boarding house), and swimming, riding, shooting, and relaxation in the pure air of the Karoo. *Tweedside Lodge,* with its 12 rooms and 13 cellars, is a wonderfully atmospheric museum-piece depicting a remarkable family lifestyle. The village is an entertaining, worthwhile and tasteful restoration. It would be apt if the railways would restore the original dining room in the station building, where the staff, with commendable enthusiasm, have started a railway museum on their own.

Fittingly, Matjiesfontein is reported to be one of the most richly haunted areas in Southern Africa. The ghosts of the hotel are all jovial: they can afford to be since they don't have to pay the hotel bills. The clicks of billiards and cues are heard when there is nobody in the billiard room; glasses clink and laughter and whispered conversation linger in empty rooms. A great number of people from all walks of life passed through the place; convalescents wounded during the Anglo-Boer War, chest sufferers, unusual visitors from overseas, soldiers and sailors, and such was the hospitality of Matjiesfontein that many felt welcome to return – albeit discreetly.

The Logan family entertained living visitors so frequently that they were always tolerant of unseen residents. The family have a delightful story of one invisible resident who caused no trouble except that he (or she) could not open doors, and would rattle doorknobs until a member of the family obliged by opening the door. Although the ghost appeared to be well-mannered, however, it was also rather touchy . . .

On one occasion, after Jennifer Buist's marriage, she was busy packing presents when there was a great rattling at the door. For a while she was too engrossed in her packing to oblige the ghost and the rattling mounted to an impatient crescendo. Rather crossly, she flung open the door, saying, 'Oh come on in if you must, but don't make such a damn noise about it!' A puff of cold air rushed past her, rattled its way irritably through the window – and was never heard or felt again!

Jean du Plooy, the housekeeper, relates another account of touchy ghosts in Matjiesfontein. She was alone in the hotel while it was being refitted. The night after the workmen had finished laying new wall-to-wall carpets, Jean was awakened by a ringing at the door. She clambered out of bed and went downstairs, expecting to have to turn away some would-be guests. She opened the door and was confronted by five rather peculiar travellers – all she could see of them was their upper bodies! In her astonishment, she blurted out the thought uppermost in her mind: 'For God's sake don't make a mess of the new carpets!' The ghosts stared at her blankly, looked down at their invisible feet, and vanished . . .

James Douglas Logan, the founder of Matjiesfontein, is buried in a little graveyard next to the Cape-to-Cairo road, 10 km before it reaches the turnoff to the hotel and railway station. Born in Reston in Scotland on 26 November 1857, he died at Matjiesfontein on 30 July 1920. His wife, Emma, died on 29 March 1938 and is buried close to her husband, as is their son, James, who was born in 1880 and died in 1960 and was known in his lifetime as 'Daddy Jim'.

Also in this atmospheric cemetery is the grave of George Alfred Lohmann, the great cricketer; born on 2 June 1865, he died on 1 December 1901. There is the grave with monument of Major-General Andrew Waughope, born in Scotland on 5 July 1846 and killed in action at the battle of Magersfontein on 11 December 1899. Several other graves lie in this cemetery, some are nameless, others record names of soldiers and visitors who died at Matjiesfontein. There is also a celebrated ghost – a British soldier in the uniform worn during the Anglo-Boer War. His arm is in a sling, and he has a bloodied bandage around his head. It has been reported that he is often seen standing beside the road at the turnoff to the cemetery. Motorists stop, thinking that there has been an accident and that he needs help, or a lift, but he vanishes instantly. It is interesting how often he has been clearly described by people of widely different origin who know nothing of Matjiesfontein and its band of ghosts.

## Accommodation
★★ ® Lord Milner Hotel, 45 rooms, all with baths. R14,80 B/B. Phone 3.

The main road continues from Matjiesfontein through harsh, dramatic hills of shale and tillite for 28 km and then (278 km from Cape Town) bridges the Buffels River and enters the town of . . .

# LAINGSBURG

This little town stands on a 10 278-ha farm once known as *Vischkuil-aan-de-Buffelsrivier*. The farm was bought for £800 by Stephanus Greeft, who planned to develop a township there. By 1879, however, this project had fared so poorly that only a single residence existed on the place. Then the railway came and a cluster of corrugated iron shacks was erected around a siding named *Buffelsrivier*. The name conflicted with Buffalo River at East London, so the name was changed, first to *Nassau* and then to *Laingsburg* in honour of John Laing, the Commissioner of Crown lands in the Cape. The town was properly laid out in 1881 and became a municipality in 1904; today 3 106 people live there.

Laingsburg lies more or less on the junction point of the winter rainfall (west) and summer rainfall (east) areas. Its own rainfall is negligible – about 50 mm a year. Despite this, goats and sheep flourish, and wheat, lucerne and fruit are grown along the Buffels River. Between 1953 and 1956 an irrigation dam with a wall 28 m high was built in this river at Floriskraal, 24 km south of Laingsburg, and supplies water for considerable farming activity.

A typical little town of the Great Karoo, Laingsburg has a unique Victorian atmosphere easy to sense if one takes a stroll down its side streets at sunset. The architecture is quaint, and some of the houses have involved wrought-iron embellishments. Windpumps draw water from the depths of the seemingly dry river course, and gardens are spectacular: quinces, figs, pomegranates, grapes and many colourful creepers and flowering shrubs flourish in the soil and climate. There are odd little corner shops and *losieshuise* (lodging houses), the latter invariably draped with some character lolling on the veranda regarding strangers with an open stare, while his old woman peeps out through a window.

The skies are generally aflame at this hour, and there are no more spectacular sunsets to be seen in the world. Strangely shaped hills loom close by, long trains incessantly come and go; headlights of cars move over the deep spaces of the Karoo, and drivers stop in Laingsburg for fuel and refreshments. The little town – an oasis in the wilderness – hardly heeds them. It seems to be part of a bygone world where, at sunset, travellers can step back 50 years simply by wandering off the main street.

### Accommodation
* Grand Hotel, 13 rooms, all with baths. R9,25 B/B. Phone 38.
** Laingsburg Hotel, 14 rooms, all with baths. R10,25 B/B. Phone 9.

### Caravans and camping
* Pepper Tree Caravan Park, 20 sites. R2,75 D.
* Sit-en-Rus Caravan Park, 10 sites. R2,80 D.

From Laingsburg the main road climbs over the hills. At 14 km east of the town the road bridges over the Geelbek's River. A well-preserved example of an Anglo-Boer War block-house stands guard on the right bank of the river. Twenty-seven kilometres further on the road passes Koup station where the Divisional Council maintains free of charge, a caravan, camping and resting place with water, shade, barbecue sites and pit toilets. Across the railway line, 4,5 km on, the road enters as 'howling' a stretch of wilderness as any would-be recluse could desire: if 10 mm of rain a year fall on this area the few inhabitants consider themselves well served. To the eye the scene has an eerie fascination, especially in the long shadows and colours of sunset. The mountain wall of the Swartberg range acts as a great barrier in the south, preventing rain clouds from penetrating to this parched rock-strewn wilderness, which seems to undulate gently, like the petrified surface of an ancient lunar sea . . .

## THE KAROO

The Hottentot name *Karoo* (a thirstland) describes perfectly this area of minimal rainfall, scanty soil, coarse surface rubble and numerous outcrops of rock concealed by little vegetation other than clumps of the hardy renosterbos.

This landscape is part of what is known to geologists as the Karoo System, which occupies fully one half of the entire area of Southern Africa. It consists of an enormous, high-lying, shallow basin, arid in the south; but where it forms the highveld of the well-watered Orange Free State and Transvaal, it is covered with grass. The Karoo System is a sedimentary system, laid down in a series of shales and sandstones on a base of glacial tillite and, in parts, with a roof of basaltic lava.

The Karoo and its extraordinary landscape is described in a chapter of its own (see pages 219 to 241). To many travellers the landscape is boring and seemingly interminable, especially during the hot hours of the day. However many interesting scenes and surprising places are hidden away in odd corners.

Providing some rain has fallen, spring (September to October) sees even the most arid areas of the Karoo transformed into a garden with a multitude of flowers carpeting the ground and the smell of pollen heavy on the warm air. Particularly striking are the glowing, iridescent mesembryanthemums (*vygies*) with their masses of mauve, magenta, pink and white flowers.

Eighty-six kilometres from Laingsburg, the road reaches the railway station of Prince Albert Road. A garage, some shops and a hotel stand at the point where a tarmac road branches off east, stretching for 42 km to the town of . . .

## PRINCE ALBERT

A picturesque little Karoo municipality which has a population of 4 490. Lying at the entrance to the spectacular Swartberg Pass (see page 250), it was founded in 1842 as a church centre on the farm *Kweekvallei* and, on 31 July 1845, named *Prince Albert* in honour of the infant British prince. Watered by perennial mountain streams, it is famous for its fruit, especially the peaches in January and grapes in March. One of the last working watermills in Southern Africa may be seen grinding corn in the town.

### Accommodation
* Karoo Hotel (Prince Albert Road), 10 rooms, 4 with baths. R8 B/B. Phone 2.
* Swartberg Hotel (Prince Albert), 18 rooms, 13 with baths. R9,05 – R10,35 B/B. Phone 74.

### Caravans and camping
* Hanet Caravan Park, 15 sites. R2 D.
* Rap-Skrap Rest Camp (Prince Albert), 8 sites. R2,50 D. 6 rondawels, 1 cottage R6 D.

Beyond Prince Albert Road, the Cape-to-Cairo road continues its journey north-east across the Great Karoo. After 25 km water and shade can be found at the national road camp at Palmiet siding and at 48 km the road reaches the small railway centre of . . .

## LEEU-GAMKA

An unlovely modern name combines the Afrikaans and the Hottentot word for lion. Once called Fraserburg Road, this little place consists of a cluster of commercial buildings standing at the junction of the road to the small, isolated town of Fraserburg, 115 km away (see page 222).

### Accommodation
* Leeu-Gamka Hotel, 9 rooms, 3 with baths. R7,95 B/B. Phone 1.

Past Leeu-Gamka the national road continues across the Karoo for 77 km, passes a turnoff to Oudtshoorn, then bridges over the railway and (501 km from Cape Town) reaches the principal town in this part of the Great Karoo . . .

## BEAUFORT WEST

People like to style this town as the 'oasis in the Karoo' and although local rainfall only averages 200 mm a year, this figure is far higher than the rainfall in much of the surrounding country. In addition, the situation of Beaufort West – below the southern heights of the Nuweveld range – provides it with a dependable supply of good mountain water. The town is built on the banks of the *Gamka* (lion) River which, although usually dry, occasionally floods its banks; in 1877 it completely overflowed the town.

In the second half of the 18th century farmers first started to penetrate the Karoo settling in what was known as the *Nuweveld* (new veld), and the *Koup* (or *Gouph*), a Hottentot name which means caul fat and refers to the fat sheep grazing in the area. Scarcity of surface water confined the human population to areas with springs, and the relatively well-watered site of the present town was once the haunt of nomadic Hottentots and Bushmen; the latter's paintings of horses, ostriches and game can still be seen in rock shelters at places such as Grootplaat on the town commonage. With the advent of Europeans the site of Beaufort West became a farm, *Hooivlakte in de Carro* (high flats in the Karoo) and its owner, Abraham de Klerk, the local *field-cornet* (district officer), nurtured a place which became known for the quality of its stock and produce – sheep, cattle, horses, corn, barley and fruit – and for its hospitality.

More settlers arrived in the area, especially after the ill-fated Slagtersnek Rebellion, when a number of the men implicated were banished to the Karoo. On 27 November 1818 the district was proclaimed and the farms *Hooivlakte in de Carro* and the adjacent *Boesjemansberg* were bought for £1 025, destined to be the site of a proposed town. The new district and town were named *Beaufort,* as the Governor of the Cape, Lord Charles Somerset, was the son of the Duke of Beaufort. The *West* part was added later in order to distinguish the place from Fort Beaufort and Port Beaufort in other parts of the Cape.

The town was laid out in 1820 and the first erven were sold in March of the following year. The government offices were the pivot of the growing town and the first *landdros,* J. Baird, made the furrows which still channel water along the sides of the streets; he also planted pear trees that shade the streets, today a pleasing feature of the town.

In 1836 Beaufort West became a municipality, the first in the Cape under a new ordinance which permitted the formation of elective municipal councils. The town hall was the first in the Karoo. It was designed by James Bisset in 1864 and opened in 1866. It is now a national monument.

Great changes took place in the area. Arthur Kinnear introduced the first merino wool sheep; the drought of 1849 precipitated the disappearance of the huge herds of plains game, killing off countless thousands of animals which once grazed in the area. A description of this event, recorded by Sir John Fraser, son of Reverend Colin Fraser, the Beaufort West pastor, is worth quoting:

'One day a travelling *smous* (pedlar) came to Beaufort and brought the tidings that thousands of *trekbokken* (migrating antelope) were coming from the north, devouring everything before them. About a week after the *smous* had left Beaufort West, we were awakened one morning by a sound as of a strong wind before a thunderstorm, followed by the trampling of thousands of all kinds of game – wildebeest, blesboks, springboks, quaggas, elands, antelope of all kinds – which filled the streets and gardens and, as far as one could see, covered the whole country, grazing off everything eatable before them, drinking up the waters in the furrows, fountains and dams wherever they could get at them; and, as the poor creatures were all in a more or less impoverished condition, the people killed them in numbers in their gardens. It took about three days before the whole of the *trekbokken* had passed, and it left our country as if a fire had raged over it. It was indeed a wonderful sight.'

The passing of game animals marked in a tragic way the end of old times in that part of the Karoo. Huge flocks of merino sheep replaced the game and Beaufort West developed as a commercial centre. Mr J. C. Molteno floated the first bank in the town in 1854 and a newspaper, the *Courier*, was founded in 1869. The railway from Cape Town reached Beaufort West in 1880 and it became a major locomotive depot and marshalling yard on the way to the north. A great dam, with a retaining wall 63 m high, was built in 1955 in the Gamka River high up in the Nuweveld mountains, and provides copious water. Beaufort West is now a bustling centre with a population of 21 335. It offers the traveller along the Cape-to-Cairo road a cluster of hotels, garages, restaurants and other amenities. There is a modern airport. The Dutch Reformed Church with its 46-m-high tower is a notable landmark, and a museum in the town is open Mondays to Fridays from 11h00 to 12h00 and from 15h30 to 16h30.

## Accommodation
* ⋆ Karoo Hotel, 15 rooms, 3 with baths. R9,50 – R10 B/B. Phone 3011.
* ⋆ Masonic Hotel, 20 rooms, 7 with baths. R9 – R9,50 B/B. Phone 2332.
* ⋆⋆ Oasis Hotel, 46 rooms, 38 with baths. R8,25 – R11,50 B/B. Phone 3221.
* ⋆ Queens Hotel, 12 rooms, 3 with baths. R7,50 – R8 B/B. Phone 2717.
* ⋆ Royal Hotel, 33 rooms, 14 with baths. R8,50 – R10,50 B/B. Phone 3241.
* ⋆ Wagon Wheel Motel, 48 rooms, 40 with baths. R12,50 room only. Phone 2801.

## Caravans and camping
* ⋆⋆ Bly of Gly Holiday Farm (18 km from Beaufort West), 36 sites. R2 D plus 50c D per person. 7 rooms, R3,50 D.
* ⋆⋆ Municipal caravan park, 250 sites. R2 D.
* ⋆⋆ Wagon Wheel, 40 sites. R3,50 D.

# THE KAROO NATIONAL PARK

Proclaimed on 12 September 1979, the Karoo National Park consists of 7 200 ha of the former commonage of Beaufort West, and the area of the farms *Stolshoek* and *Buttersvlei*, making a combined 20 000 ha of varied Karoo country. The purpose of the park is to conserve typical Karoo flora and fauna. Animals such as black wildebeest, springbok, mountain zebra, red hartebeest, and gemsbok have been reintroduced. The warden has his headquarters at *Stolshoek* from where a hiking trail, the Springbok Trail, leads on a three-day walk. Two overnight huts provide accommodation. The park is still being developed with various facilities planned for the future.

---

The road continues from Beaufort West in a north-easterly direction, crossing a level plain at the foot of the Nuweveld mountains. After 40 km the road climbs a spur of the mountains and then swings northwards past the railway station (50 km from Beaufort West) of . . .

# NELSPOORT

As far back as the 1850s, David Livingstone wrote about the beneficial qualities of the South African climate for all patients suffering from pulmonary complaints. In 1889 Dr E. Symes Thompson of the Royal Colonial Institute in London said of the Karoo:

'We find the region characterised by excessive dryness of air and soil, where, at a level of less than 1 000 m above the sea, remarkable purity and coolness of air are secured with an almost complete absence of floating matter; great intensity of light and solar influence; great stillness in winter; a large amount of ozone, and a degree of rarefaction of proved value in cases of phthisis.'

Many chest sufferers began visiting South Africa. Consumption, or as it is now called, tuberculosis, was a common complaint in the damp, smoggy climate of Europe, but the illness was rife even in sunny South Africa, where living conditions in slums such as District Six in Cape Town were the breeding grounds of many fearsome diseases.

In 1891, Dr Alfred Anderson became medical officer of health for Cape Town. He was immediately confronted with the disgraceful conditions in slum areas, where people were dying of many different diseases, largely deprived of care and medication. The government and the affluent section of the population simply pretended that the situation did not exist. To make matters worse, during the Anglo-Boer War plague broke out and much of the slum areas had to be destroyed, with the result that there was increasing congestion in remaining areas.

Tuberculosis became so rampant that Dr Anderson established the Society for the Prevention of Consumption but he received little government money or support. Then, in 1911, John Garlick, founder of the merchant house which bears his name and very much a public-spirited individual, joined Anderson's society. Garlick was appalled at the inroads made by tuberculosis, particularly on the Coloured people. He had also recently read Thomas Mann's novel *The Magic Mountain* which told of a sanatorium in the Alps where victims of the disease were nursed back to normal life.

In 1918, John Garlick offered Dr Anderson a donation of £25 000 to be used to set up an institution for consumptives. It was estimated that this establishment would require £75 000 and Garlick's generous offer influenced the Cape parliament and the public to give additional support. The total sum collected was £108 000.

A search was made for a suitable site for a sanatorium. The attention of the committee was drawn to a farm near Nelspoort named *Salt River*. The Salt River flowed through a valley in the Nuweveld mountains and there was ample water for drinking and irrigation with well-nigh perfect climatic conditions for a sanatorium.

The farm was bought and Dr Peter Allan, a Scottish doctor with experience in pulmonary complaints, was appointed as director. By the end of 1920 the sanatorium had been planned. Several Cape municipalities contributed additional funds and on 24 July 1925 the Prince of Wales conducted the official opening of the Nelspoort Farm Sanatorium for Tuberculosis. The first patient had already been admitted on 5 May of the previous year.

The sanatorium was steadily enlarged over the years and additional facilities were provided, such as an X-ray theatre, and new techniques introduced, such as Pneumo-Thorax lung collapsing. In 1947 the British Royal Family visited the hospital, which then had 460 patients. In 1969 psychiatric patients were admitted and for a while Nelspoort treated both tuberculous and mental cases. Today, however, Nelspoort is entirely devoted to mental patients; tuberculosis, no longer the disastrous scourge of old, is now a socio-economic problem, breeding still in poverty and malnutrition but treatable by curative drugs in the patient's own home.

Passing the turnoff to the sanatorium, the Cape-to-Cairo road continues through thickets of acacia trees which provide shady resting places. After 27 km (79 km from Beaufort West) the road reaches a major junction at a well-known landmark – the three dolerite-capped hillocks known as the Three Sisters. To the left the Diamond Way branches off northwards to Kimberley and the Northern Cape (see pages 196 to 218). The right turn of the road crosses the railway line and swings in a north-easterly direction around the slopes of the Three Sisters. Twisting and turning around the hillocks of the Karoo, the road makes its way across a landscape which, though essentially arid, can be green and pleasant in a summer of good rains. At each watercourse or fountain stands a cluster of homestead and farm buildings surrounded by willow trees, busy windpumps and sheep corrals. Many are fine modern Karoo farms such as *Skietkuil,* which belongs to P. van der Merwe, and is well watered by Gabriel's Stream.

At 104 km from Three Sisters the road reaches the typical Karoo town of . . .

# RICHMOND

A town founded on 11 October 1843, when the presbytery of Graaff-Reinet formed a new congregation for that region of the Karoo. A portion of the farm *Driefontein* was bought and erven were sold there on 19 April 1845 during the course of a gathering for *nagmaal* (communion). The town was named after the Duke of Richmond, the father of Lady Sarah Maitland, the wife of the then Governor of the Cape, Sir Peregrine Maitland.

*Driefontein* farm was well watered and a great game haunt. The three fountains from which the place originally took its name still bubble to life in the Wilgersloot and the banks of the Ongers River which flows through the town once provided cover for numerous lions. In this setting Richmond grew slowly, its history marked by lengthy droughts and occasional violent floods. During the Anglo-Boer War it was twice attacked by the Boers and eight little forts were erected on the surrounding hills. Today Richmond is a clean and pleasant Karoo town, inhabited by 3 900 people. Gardens are full of flowers and streets shady beneath eucalyptus trees.

### Accommodation
⋆ Belsana Hotel, 11 rooms, 7 with baths. R8 – R8,50 B/B. Phone 36.
⋆ Richmond Hotel, 12 rooms, 5 with baths. R8 – R8,50 B/B. Phone 61.

### Caravans and camping
⋆ Municipal caravan park, 50 sites. R2 D.

From Richmond the main road continues north-east across the Karoo plains. Three kilometres from the town, at the branch right to Middelburg, there is a shady resting place with water. At 62 km from Richmond the road reaches the town of . . .

# HANOVER

Like Richmond, this town was formerly a part of the Graaff-Reinet district and was known simply as *Bo-Zeekoeirivier* (upper hippopotamus river). As the farming population of the area grew, a community centre became necessary and in 1854 the 8 656-ha farm *Petrusvallei* belonging to G. Gous was bought for 33 333 rixdollars (R5 000). The vendor requested that the proposed town be named *Hanover,* as his ancestors had come from that town in Germany.

The site of the town lay at the source of a powerful spring (204 570 l a day) at the foot of a cluster of hillocks. Thus, well watered and the centre for a famous merino sheep area (the world record price at the time was paid for a locally-bred merino ram) the town grew steadily. Today it has a population of 2 460. Hanover's first magistrate, C. R. Beere, came in October 1876, and laid the streets out around a handsome Dutch Reformed Church. He had trees planted and built a footpath to the summit of *Trappieskoppie* (hillock of little steps), from which point there is a commanding view of the town and countryside. A stone pyramid was erected on top of this hillock in memory of Mr Beere and his good works. He died in Hanover on 9 November 1881. Hanover's first minister, the Reverend T. F. Burgers, became the second President of the Transvaal.

### Accommodation
⋆ Grand Hotel, 12 rooms, 5 with baths. R7,50 – R8 B/B. Phone 19.

### Caravans and camping
⋆ Municipal caravan park, 60 sites. R1,50 D.

The main road continues from Hanover north-eastwards across the Karoo plains, becoming perceptibly better covered with vegetation as rainfall increases to an average of about 250 mm a year. At 3 km from Hanover there is a tarmac turnoff to Philipstown and the P. K. le

Roux Dam (see page 194). At 22 km from the town the road crosses the railway line from De Aar to Noupoort; fifty-one kilometres further on, it joins the main road coming from George and Port Elizabeth, and then reaches the town of . . .

# COLESBERG

An important junction on the road to the north, it is fittingly beaconed by one of the most conspicuous landmarks along the entire length of the southern section of the Cape-to-Cairo road. This is the 1 707-m-high, remarkably symmetrical hillock, known as *Coleskop*, which is discernible from all directions for a deceptively long distance.

Pioneer travellers in the area called this landmark *Tooverberg* (towering mountain). At its foot was a marsh which provided water for a host of game animals. In 1814 a mission station was established there in the hope of bringing peace to what was a very unruly frontier area of the Cape Colony. A second mission station, *Hepzibah,* was established a few kilometres away, and the two stations soon attracted 1 700 Bushmen causing great alarm among frontier settlers who felt their security was threatened. In 1818 the Cape Government intervened, putting an end to the mission work.

In 1822 the farmers petitioned for a town to be established in the area, and this was granted by Lord Charles Somerset, the Governor. A 15 417-ha extent of ground in the area was presented by the government to the community, to be administered on their behalf by the local church council. In November 1830 the first erven were sold, and the town was named after Sir Lowry Cole, the Cape Governor at the time.

As a frontier town, Colesberg flourished on trade with the interior. Gunpowder and alcohol passed through the place in such quantities that in 1837 a magistrate, Fleetwood Rawstone, was stationed there to impose order in the place.

On 19 June 1840 Colesberg was made a municipality and in the face of all the disturbances of frontier life, became the centre of a considerable stockbreeding area: horses, sheep and cattle flourish in the crisp air.

Nowadays Colesberg is inhabited by 10 950 people. Though it is slightly off the main road, it is worth turning aside and driving through the streets, which have a distinct atmosphere of 100 years ago. A rather higgledy-piggledy jumble of Victorian buildings is built around a cluster of hillocks and the churches in the town are worth inspecting. The fine Dutch Reformed Church with its white walls dominates the main street; Christ Church, the Anglican church, contains many notable objects. Its first rector, Dr C. Orpen, was a considerable scholar who presented his library, which included many rare books, to form a nucleus for the town's library. His wife was a titled lady and, through the good offices of her family connections, the church was beautifully decorated with a stained glass east window, a carved oak lectern, an oak pulpit and font and many other handsome items.

In the town clerk's office the original windowpane can be seen; scratched into it are the letters *D. P.,* made by the first diamond found in South Africa. When John O'Reilly brought a mysterious white pebble into the town early in 1867, the acting Civil Commissioner of Colesberg, Lorenzo Boyes, tested the stone (found on the farm *De Kalk* in the Hopetown area) by scratching on the windowpane of his office. He then looked at the two letters and declared to the anxious O'Reilly, 'I believe it to be a diamond.' (See page 199 for details of this discovery.)

## Accommodation
★★ Central Hotel, 54 rooms, 27 with baths. R9,50 – R10,50 B/B. Phone 90.
★★ Merino Inn, 41 rooms, all with baths. R8,25 – R11 room only. Phone 265.
★ Torenberg Hotel, 19 rooms, 7 with baths. R8 – R9 B/B. Phone 315.
★ Van Zyl's Vlei Motel, 19 rooms, 15 with baths. R5,60 – R7,60 room only. Phone 1513.

**Caravans and camping**
* Municipal caravan park, 100 sites. R2,50 D.
* Van Zyl's Vlei Motel, 20 sites. R5 D plus 50c D per person.

Beyond Colesberg the main road continues northwards through the northern limit of the Great Karoo. After 30 km the road reaches the Orange River at Bothasdrif, now spanned by the handsome Serfontein bridge. Across the river the road enters the Orange Free State, and this part of the northwards journey is covered in Chapter 25 (from page 502 to 522). At this point it is interesting to know something about the most important river of South Africa . . .

# THE ORANGE RIVER AND ITS DAMS

The source of this great river is more than 3 000 m above sea level, on the mountain plateau of Lesotho just behind the Drakensberg peak known as *Mnweni* (the place of the fingers), or The Rockeries. Its course, 2 000 km long, ends in the Atlantic Ocean at the diamond-mining centres of Alexander Bay and Oranjemund. Named on 17 August 1779 in honour of the Prince of Orange by Captain Gordon, who explored its lower reaches, the river was known to Hottentot and Bushman tribes as the *Nu Gariep* (great river).

The Orange carries 23 per cent of the total water run-off of South Africa to the sea. At flood periods 11 330 cubic metres (1 875 000 gallons) of water per second flow down the river. The two principal tributaries of the Orange – the Vaal and the Caledon – together supply half of the total discharge of the river.

The Vaal River has already been thoroughly harnessed by man (see page 521), but the Orange and the Caledon are only now starting to play a major role in modern development, irrigating 29 400 ha of dry Karoo land, supplying 455 million litres of potable water per day, and generating 177 000 kw of continuous power from 20 hydro-electric sites.

Heavy rains in the highlands of Lesotho – at least 2 000 mm per year – as well as heavy snowfalls feed the river prodigious volumes of water. In summer the flow reaches its peak; in winter the river is often reduced to little more than a series of deep pools linked by a trickle of water.

At all times, the water of the Orange is free of the blight of bilharzia. The winter freshets of melted snow effectively destroy the snails which carry bilharzia in tropical rivers. Even mosquitoes are no great problem along its course: the abundant fish eat the larvae, and the type of mosquito that breeds there is not a malaria carrier.

Along its middle and lower reaches, the Orange flows through the most arid country in South Africa: at its mouth the rainfall does not exceed 50 mm a year, and the river is the bringer of life to the northern areas of the Karoo, Bushmanland and the north-west Cape. As with the Nile, there is a startling contrast between the green islets and banks of the river, and the surrounding desert landscape. The shallow river valley has many areas suitable for irrigation, and the water and silt carried by the Orange nourish a variety of crops.

The engineering achievement in harnessing the Orange is impressive. The Hendrik Verwoerd Dam is the central storage dam, covering 374 square kilometres and containing 5 958,3 million cubic metres of water behind a wall 947,9 m long and at present 90,5 m high; but eventually this wall is to be raised to 118 m.

From this dam a tunnel 88,8 km long with an internal diameter of 4,8 m directs water southwards to the upper valley of the Fish River. This water supplements the flow of the Fish River, irrigates its banks and then, via another tunnel 51,5 km long, flows into the Sundays River and irrigates citrus estates and other farms in the driest part of the Karoo.

A second dam, the P. K. le Roux, is named in honour of the Minister of Water Affairs under Dr Verwoerd. It has been constructed 130 km below the Hendrik Verwoerd Dam and has a storage capacity of 3 185 million cubic metres behind a wall 765 m long and 107 m high. The wall is designed to be raised to 126 m, harnessing 13 000 million cubic metres of water to irrigate 150 000 ha of land.

Near Douglas, further downriver, a third dam is to be built. This will have a 70,1-m-high wall storing 1 000 million cubic metres of water which will irrigate 25 000 ha of Karoo, reaching as far down as the town of Prieska.

A third tunnel, 103 km long, is planned to convey water from a diversionary weir at Klipfontein to irrigate land in the valley of the Skoenmakers River.

To see the H. F. Verwoerd Dam, take the tarmac main road out of Colesberg for 39 km to Norvals Pont, the site of a pont ferry over the Orange in the days before a bridge was built across the river. The name of the hotel there, the Glasgow Pont Hotel, is a reminder of the name of the actual pont, which carried many thousands of travellers across the river in the early days. Three kilometres away, across the river, is the Hendrik Verwoerd Dam Resort.

### Accommodation
★Glasgow Pont Hotel, 15 rooms, 13 with baths. R7 B/B. Phone 22.
★★ Hendrik Verwoerd Dam Hotel, 23 rooms, all with baths. R11,44 room only. Phone 60.

### Caravans and camping
★★ Hendrik Verwoerd Dam Resort, 150 sites. R2,25 D. 30 cottages, R12 rondawels, R4,25 - R5,50 D.

A road leads from Norvals Pont for 4 km to a fine viewsite overlooking the dam. During summer floods, when the river overflows the wall, the scene is awesome. From the viewsite the tarmac road continues along the southern shore of the lake, providing anglers and boat enthusiasts with access to the shores. At 36,8 km from the viewsite the road reaches the town of . . .

# VENTERSTAD

Named after Johannes Venter, who owned the farm on which the town was laid out in 1875, this is an agricultural centre and a resort catering for visitors to the Hendrik Verwoerd Dam. It became a municipality in 1895 and now has a population of 2 950.

### Accommodation
★ Union Hotel, 12 rooms, all with baths. R9,75 B/B. Phone 50.

### Caravans and camping
★ Municipal caravan park, 40 sites. R2 D.

The road continues for 34 km from Venterstad and then reaches a junction: the south branch leads to Burgersdorp and Aliwal North; a left turn north takes the road for 15 km to the town of Bethulie. On the way to Bethulie the road bridges across the eastern end of the Hendrik Verwoerd Dam. The main railway line from East London to the north also crosses the dam at this point on a 1 152-m bridge – the longest rail bridge in South Africa.

# BETHULIE

This old mission centre was founded for the Bushmen by the London Missionary Society. They transferred it in 1833 to the French Missionary Society who gave it the name of *Bethulie* (meaning 'chosen by God'). The mission buildings still stand, among them the oldest European-built house in the Orange Free State. Named after its builder, the Reverend Jean

Pellissier, the first French missionary, the house is now the Van Riebeeck Museum, housing a collection of items devoted to local history.

Though the atmosphere of Bethulie is curiously old-world, the presence of the Hendrik Verwoerd Dam has converted this almost forgotten little place into a very pleasant holiday resort which offers boating and angling. A nature reserve and a park are in the centre of the town, which has a population of 4 345. The main railway line from East London crosses the valley in which the town lies by means of a spectacular concrete viaduct.

### Accommodation
★ Royal Hotel, 20 rooms, 8 with baths. R8 – R9 B/B. Phone 154.

### Caravans and camping
★® Municipal caravan park (at municipal dam), 80 sites. R2,30 D. 12 cottages, 8 rondawels, R6,40 – R7,50 D.

# THE P. K. LE ROUX DAM

Three kilometres north of Hanover, a tarmac turnoff leads to this dam, originally known as the Van der Kloof Dam. After stretching for 73 km across flat Karoo landscape, the branch road makes a sudden descent into a valley. Here, in a relatively fertile setting, surrounded by an assembly of strangely shaped hillocks, lies the small, rather odd-looking town of . . .

# PHILIPSTOWN

Founded in 1863 as a church centre, the place remains much the same as it was when it was first built. Some interesting buildings exemplify the style of architecture popular at that period, among them the original sandstone church, whose parsonage is still in use. The town was named after Sir Philip Wodehouse, Governor of the Cape. Merino sheep farming is the principal local occupation. The population of the town is 2 200.

### Accommodation
★ Disa Hotel, 10 rooms, 3 with baths. R8,75 – R9,75 B/B. Phone 53.

### Caravans and camping
★ Municipal caravan park, 25 sites. R3 D.

The road leads north from Philipstown through interesting scenery sprinkled with a fine assembly of flat-topped and rhino-horn-shaped hillocks. After 45 km the road reaches the town of . . .

# PETRUSVILLE

Like Philipstown, this little centre lies in a fertile valley surrounded by a cluster of high hills. Named after Petrus van der Walt, owner of the farm *Renosterfontein* on which the town was laid out, *Petrusville* is an agricultural centre, with a population of 4 700.

### Accommodation
★ Petrusville Hotel, 19 rooms, 12 with baths. R7,50 – R9,50 B/B. Phone 33.

### Caravans and camping
★ Municipal caravan park, 10 sites. R1 D.

194

From Petrusville the road continues north for 7,8 km, then joins the Hopetown-Luckhoff road and 7 km further on crosses the Orange River just below the high wall of the P. K. le Roux Dam. The view of the dam and river is impressive. The road continues into the Orange Free State, to the town of Luckhoff, 38 km away.

## Chapter Eleven

# THE DIAMOND WAY

The Diamond Way to the north begins its journey at a famous landmark in the Karoo – the triple hillocks known as the Three Sisters. At this point the Diamond Way branches due north from the Great North Road which has come up from the Cape and which swings in a north-easterly direction to become the Golden Way, stretching over the maize and goldfields of the Orange Free State. Meanwhile the Diamond Way leads through Kimberley and across most of the great diamond fields of Southern Africa. Both roads link up in Johannesburg.

From Three Sisters the tarmac road twists north-westwards through a rocky pile of arid hills, following the course of the *Soutrivier* (salt river), the banks of which are shaded by green acacia trees. Farms such as *Brakfontein* (9 km) and *Jasfontein* (41 km) make effective use of the stream's erratic flow and, in the heart of the thirstland of the Karoo, reveal what can be achieved by the magic touch of water.

At intervals along the highway, a considerate roads department has planted peppercorn and other drought-resistant trees to provide shady resting places and, in addition, there is a pump supplying drinking water at a point 46 km from the start of the road. A further 14 km from this pump (60 km from the start of the road) brings the road to the town of . . .

## VICTORIA WEST

Despite the arid appearance of the countryside, Victoria West is the centre of a wealthy farming activity in the production of wool. The town seems smaller than it is when viewed from the Diamond Way which traverses it at right angles to the long main Church Street, lined with shops, garages and public buildings. The street then burrows beyond into the western hills along a watercourse.

The town originated in 1843 when the Dutch Reformed Church purchased for 23 000 rixdollars portions of the farms *Zeekoegat* and *Kapokfontein,* for the purpose of building a church and creating a centre for a then isolated but developing region. At the request of the churchwardens, the Governor of the Cape, on 25 September 1844, approved of the name *Victoria West,* in honour of the Queen. A church was built and consecrated in 1850, erven were laid out and sold, and the town began its life beneath the clear blue skies of the Karoo.

On 24 December 1855 the division of Victoria West was created by government proclamation, the specific situation in the west of the colony being emphasised in order to distinguish the place from the division of Victoria East established near Queenstown in the Eastern Cape. A municipal council was proclaimed for the town on 28 January 1859.

The discovery of diamonds at Hopetown in 1886 contributed to a surge of progress in Victoria West. The town lay on the main route to the north (the Diamond Way), followed by the flood of fortune-seekers making their way to Hopetown, and then to Kimberley, using Victoria West as a staging post.

Diamonds lured the railway from Cape Town as far as Kimberley but for obscure reasons the line bypassed Victoria West by 12 km. The town had therefore to be satisfied with a station at first named Victoria West Road, but later renamed *Hutchinson,* in honour of the Governor, Sir Walter Hely Hutchinson. In 1904 a branch line was built from Hutchinson to Victoria West and from there to Calvinia.

Years of floods (such as in 1871 when 62 people were drowned after a cloudburst sent a wall of water down the usually dry watercourse), and years of extreme aridity (in 1922 when only 26 mm of rain fell in 12 months) – as with all Karoo towns – kept the local pendulum of prosperity swinging between ruin and riches. Through it all, however, Victoria West developed, producing a surprising number of people who made a name for themselves in the outside world. With a population of 6 190, it is today a typical example of a Karoo town flourishing in the sunshine.

An interesting museum, notable for its Stone Age exhibits and some remarkable fossil fish, is housed in the library buildings. The museum is open on weekdays from 09h00 to 13h00 and from 14h30 to 18h00; on Saturdays from 10h00 to 13h00.

### Accommodation
* Halfway House Hotel, 23 rooms, 7 with baths. R7 – R9 B/B. Phone 129.

### Caravans and camping
*Municipal caravan park, 34 sites. R1,50 D per person.

From Victoria West the Diamond Way continues northwards across the railway line and over a rugged stretch of arid Karoo. The roads department has established resting places shaded by clumps of trees and boreholes to supply drinking water at points 12 km, 48 km and 49 km from Victoria West. At 55 km the road crosses the Ongers River at a place overlooked by the stool shaped hill known as Leebkop. The surface of the Karoo in this area is covered with piles of dark-coloured dolerite rock fragments, as though nature had gathered them into neat heaps in an effort to tidy up. The road leads for 32 km over an arid, flat plain with hills watching rather aloofly from the horizon. In the midst of this plain, 102 km from Victoria West, the Diamond Way reaches . . .

# BRITSTOWN

This communications centre lies half way between Cape Town and Johannesburg on the Diamond Way and is a junction point for the tarmac road which leads to Upington. The railway from De Aar to South West Africa also passes through the town.

*Britstown* was named after Hans Brits, a man who had accompanied Dr Livingstone on a venture into the interior and then settled on the farm *Gemsbokfontein*. In 1877 an association of local men, headed by T. P. Theron, purchased a portion of this farm on which they founded a community centre and built a church, giving the place to the churchwardens to manage. The town became a municipality in January 1889 and today has a population of 3 005. Of interest in the town is an historical museum.

In a region having a total rainfall of only 250 mm a year, Britstown is a centre for sheep farming. Situated 19 km from the town is an irrigated area watered by a dam in the Ongers (or Brak) River. This irrigation scheme was originally started in 1895 as the private venture of what was known as the Smartt Syndicate. This concern built two dams, planted lucerne and wheat, and grazed sheep, karakuls and Clydesdale horses. Unfortunately, the syndicate was liquidated in October 1954 and the assets of its considerable enterprise dispersed. The massive flooding of the Ongers River in March 1961 destroyed the Smartt Irrigation Board Dam, but it was reconstructed by the government in 1964 and today irrigates fertile agricultural land where crops flourish on sunshine and ample water.

### Accommodation
** Trans Karoo Hotel, 40 rooms, 20 with baths. R11 – R12 B/B. Phone 27222.

### Caravans and camping
★Municipal caravan park, 40 sites. R1,50 D.

From Britstown the Diamond Way crosses the railway line linking De Aar to South West Africa and continues northwards. After 1 km a tarmac turnoff leads east for 48 km to De Aar (see page 240). At 3 km there is a tarmac turnoff stretching to Prieska and from there to Upington. The Diamond Way proceeds across arid, harsh country, littered with dark-coloured fragments of dolerite rock. After 56 km the road reaches a resting place with shady trees and drinking water. The journey continues a further 17 km across an open, scrub-covered plain and past a low ridge of rocky hillocks, to reach (73 km from Britstown) the small town of . . .

# STRYDENBURG

Lying on the verge of a large pan filled during the rainy years with shallow, salty water, *Strydenburg* (the town of strife) received its rather lugubrious name on account of incessant squabbling over – of all things – the choice of its name! The place was laid out by the Dutch Reformed Church in 1892 on the farm *Rooipan,* originally owned by the brothers N. and B. Badenhorst. Experiencing a slow, sunbronzed growth, it became a municipality in 1914, and is today, with a population of 2 150, a neat little farming centre of the Karoo, dominated by a handsome Dutch Reformed Church built of local stone.

### Accommodation
★Excelsior Hotel, 15 rooms, 12 with baths. R9 – R10 B/B. Phone 106.

### Caravans and camping
★Municipal caravan park, 25 sites. R2 D.

The Diamond Way leads north-westwards from Strydenburg over an open, level plain covered in Karoo scrub. Several shady resting places have been made by the roads department, notably 16 km and 46 km from Strydenburg. After 59 km the road reaches the sunbaked little town of romantic memories . . .

# HOPETOWN

With a population of 4 210, Hopetown is situated on an arid slope leading down to the Orange River. In 1850 Sir Harry Smith extended the northern frontier of the Cape Colony as far as the Orange River and the few individuals in the Hopetown area – wandering Griqua and renegade Europeans – were allowed to claim ownership of land. Nineteen farms were granted to those who claimed early residence and a steady influx of new settlers occurred once the area was no longer a no-man's-land.

The need for a community centre was soon obvious and the choice for a site fell on a farm named *Duvenaarsfontein* after a nomadic cattle herder who had in former years, occasionally watered his stock there.

On 18 February 1854 the community was established by the Dutch Reformed Church and a town laid out, with the church – a rough, frontier-type building – being made of mud and manure. The origin of the name Hopetown is odd. It is said locally, that the widow of the first owner of the farm, Michiel van Niekerk, wore a necklace to which was attached a small anchor. One of her servants admired this anchor and was very impressed when told that it represented hope. The servant made an ingenious imitation from tin which was nailed above the entrance to the farmhouse. When the house was demolished, the symbol of hope was preserved and eventually fixed above the door of another local farmer's wife, Mrs Curry. The little token was considered to be the good luck emblem of Hopetown, which became a municipality in September 1858.

For the first few years, the town flourished on sheep farming. Then, in the momentous year 1866, Schalk van Niekerk, son of the first owner of *Duvenaarsfontein,* visited a neighbour, Daniel Jacobs of the farm *De Kalk.* He noticed a 15-year-old boy, Erasmus Jacobs, playing with a glittering stone. Van Niekerk was no prospector but he was so taken with the stone that Mrs Jacobs induced her son to give it to him. Van Niekerk in turn, gave the stone to John O'Reilly who took it to Colesberg and showed it to the magistrate, Lorenzo Boyes, who tested it by scratching into a windowpane of his office the two letters 'D. P.', an interesting memento which still survives. The stone was then sent to Grahamstown to a local medical man of some general scientific reputation, Dr W. G. Atherstone. He proved it to be a 21,25-carat diamond and it was bought for £500 by the Governor of the Cape, Sir Philip Wodehouse.

Nobody knew what the origin of the diamond was. It was thought to be an isolated specimen, perhaps carried into the area in the crop of a wild ostrich. But in 1868, on the farm *Zandfontein,* a Griqua witchdoctor known as Booi, picked up a magnificent white diamond weighing 83,5 carats. He took it to Hopetown where Schalk van Niekerk acquired the stone in exchange for a wagon, span of oxen, and some livestock. In due course Van Niekerk sold the stone for £11 000 to Lilienfeld Brothers, in Hopetown. It was eventually bought by the Earl of Dudley for £30 000. This stone was the Star of South Africa, the discovery of which marked the beginning of what may be called the diamond epoch in the story of Southern Africa.

Suddenly, Hopetown was living up to its name. Fortune-seekers poured into the place from all over the world. Business boomed and when the great rushes to the Kimberley area took place, Hopetown became the main source of supply, with local farmers making a fortune as transport riders.

The railway proved the evil genius in this prosperity. As with Victoria West, the line passed Hopetown 15 km to the east, leaving the town with the sole consolation of a siding known as Orange River. Hopetown sank into the doldrums.

In 1897 a disgruntled local conjured some life back into the place by claiming a rich new find of diamonds on *Rooidam* farm. Within three weeks, 10 000 diggers rushed to the place and Hopetown boomed once again. It was then discovered that *Rooidam* was a fraud; loads of diamondiferous soil disguised as bags of maize and forage had been brought to the farm. Well 'salted' with diamonds, this formed the 'bait' for a sucker-rush. Diggers abandoned Hopetown in disgust and the place fell into disrepute.

Alluvial diamonds were later found on several farms along the banks of the Orange River near the town. *Brakfontein* (or *Higgshope*) proved the richest and between 1923 and 1953, diamonds worth £1 360 666 were recovered from these fields (a total of 131 070,25 carats). Although most of the diggers rushed to Lichtenburg in 1927 and the Hopetown fields became exhausted, the occasional stone is still found in the area and no one can say for certain that another great discovery may not again bring boom times to Hopetown.

## Accommodation
★★ Radnor Hotel, 13 rooms, all with baths. R13 – R20 B/B. Phone 15.

From Hopetown the Diamond Way continues north-eastwards and after 3 km crosses the Orange River with a turnoff 2 km further on leading to Salt Lake (35 km), a prolific supplier of high grade salt, and to Douglas (73 km). The main tarmac road proceeds across the Karoo plains and after 20 km reaches a turnoff east to the mainline station of Witput. At 35 km from Hopetown the road crosses the branch railway line from Belmont to Douglas and 15 km further on there is a wayside resting place with shade and drinking water.

The Karoo now gives way to less arid thorn country and rocky hillocks. Old battlefields of the Anglo-Boer War stretch on either side of the road and at 56 km a memorial situated on a hillock

*Overleaf: A South African scene; flat-topped koppie (Coleskop), creaking windpumps and the great plains of the Karoo flooded in sunshine.*

west of the road pays tribute to British soldiers killed at Enslin and Graspan in November 1899.

In their advance to relieve Kimberley, the British, under Lord Methuen, used Orange River station as their base, fighting their way up the line of rail. The Boers first opposed them from the koppies at Belmont station, and then successively at such railway centres as Enslin and Modder River. At the Battle of Magersfontein, the versatile Boers, under General Jacobus de la Rey, introduced trench warfare for the first time. These trenches may still be seen together with graves and several memorials.

The Diamond Way continues north-eastwards along the route of the British advance, keeping in close company with the main railway line. A resting place with shade and drinking water is reached 57 km from Hopetown, while a further 7 km brings the road to a turnoff east to Jacobsdal (24 km), just before the small railway centre of Heuningneskloof. At 73 km the road passes the Riet River Agricultural Research Station where the surroundings (the site of the Battle of Modder River) become pleasantly green, irrigated by water from the Riet River. The road crosses the river at the village of the same name, 83 km from Hopetown and a further kilometre takes the road past Modder River station.

## Accommodation
* Crown and Royal Hotel (Modder River), 8 rooms, all with baths. R8,24 B/B. Phone 22.
* The Grange Hotel (Witput), 5 rooms, 2 with baths. R7 – R8 B/B. Phone Belmont 1240.

The road now leads northwards through low hillocks rising from a plain covered in grass and acacia trees. After 115 km of travel from Hopetown a long avenue of peppercorn trees provides shade and marks the approach to . . .

# KIMBERLEY

The story of the diamond city of Kimberley has made it one of the best known cities in the world and to its name is attached a considerable glamour and romance. With diamonds as the emblem of affection and Kimberley the source of the glittering stones set in many of the world's great pieces of jewellery and engagement rings, it is understandable that this sunbronzed city of the wastelands on the verge of the Kalahari Desert, has a place in the hearts of the world's lovers. For women, particularly, the place has an aura as if Eros, in conjunction with Venus and Cupid, is employed there in the design of dreams.

The saga of Kimberley and its diamonds originated during a phase of volcanic activity which occurred about 60 million years ago towards the end of the Cretaceous period. Groups of volcanic pipes (or throats) were blown up through the earth's crust from deep down. Through these pipes flowed a soft, waxy, blue-coloured volcanic rock, known as kimberlite. On the surface this kimberlite weathered to so-called 'yellow ground' and being soft, was easily eroded, along with any volcanic cones which might have piled up above the pipes. Below the surface the kimberlite in the pipes formed what is called 'blue ground', while at greater depths it became what is known as 'hardebank'.

In some inexplicable way, diamonds were accumulated by the kimberlite on its way up from the depths. A diamond is composed of carbon which has been subjected to tremendous pressure; kimberlite itself contains no carbon, but simply acts as host to the diamonds which must have been formed deep down and then carried by the material surging up the volcanic pipes. Not all the pipes contain diamonds, but of 150 found so far, 25 of them do, to degrees varying from 29 carats per 720 000 kg of kimberlite at the Premier Mine near Pretoria; 19 carats at Kimberley; and lesser quantities elsewhere.

Many other kimberlite pipes were entirely eroded away and their diamond content dispersed along the beds of rivers (as at Hopetown and Barkly West), or among the gravels of abandoned watercourses where subsequent discovery by man caused the great rushes to places such as Bloemhof and Lichtenburg in the Transvaal.

While the first diamond rush was taking place at Hopetown, a second and far greater discovery was made in 1870 in the gravels of the Vaal River at Barkly West (page 206). At the height of the rush to these river diggings, diamonds were found in the mud brick walls of the farmhouse *Bultfontein,* owned by Cornelis du Plooy. The house was rapidly dismantled and the site is now the colossal hole in the ground of Bultfontein Mine.

In December 1870 diamonds were found by the children of Adriaan van Wyk, playing next to Du Toits Pan on their father's farm *Dorstfontein.* A whole army of diggers stampeded to the place. Against such a flood of humanity a landowner could do nothing save make money from claim fees and watch his farmlands literally disappear into an appalling cloud of red dust and dumps of rubble abandoned by the diggers.

In May 1871 a new discovery was made on the farm *Vooruitzicht,* owned by the brothers Diederick and Nicolaas Johannes de Beer. Then, on Sunday night 18 July 1871, a servant named Damon, employed by Fleetwood Rawstorne, one of a party of men from Colesberg who were digging at Du Toits Pan, appeared at his master's tent with three diamonds he had found on a hillock near by. This marked the discovery of what was named Colesberg Koppie and led to the greatest of all the diamond rushes (known as the New Rush), which attracted to South Africa some of the most flamboyant characters in the world; produced a staggering fortune in precious stones; and, by the mass activity of the diggers, resulted in the sinking of the Big Hole of Kimberley Mine, the largest manmade hole in the world.

The Big Hole has a surface area of 13,38 ha and a perimeter of 1,6 km. Over 28 million tons of ground were removed from it, yielding 14 504 566 carats of diamonds (the equivalent of 3 tons) before operations ceased on 14 August 1914. As an open-cast working, it is 800 m deep. Shafts continued it to the 1 100-m level before the pipe started to pinch out. Water seepage is steadily filling up the hole and is now 133,6 m from the surface. The water is 240 m deep.

*Kimberley* (named after the Secretary of State for Colonies, the Earl of Kimberley) grew up as the centre of the new rush. A twin town, *Beaconsfield* (named after Benjamin Disraeli, the Earl of Beaconsfield) developed as the centre for the Bultfontein, Wesselton and Du Toits Pan mines. The two towns were eventually amalgamated in 1912 to become a city.

These early diamond towns were actually great tent camps which were slowly replaced by tin shanties. Life was uproarious, with rumours, rows, bad smells from non-existent sanitary arrangements, dust, heat, shortages of water, and a plethora of insects, vermin, loafers, thieves and swindlers. Political squabbles over the ownership of the diamond areas raged between Britain, the Orange Free State, the Griqua and the Tlapin tribe, emphasising the general insecurity of life.

The British, in the grand imperial manner in vogue at the time, took control of the areas which the Keate Award had declared the possession of the Griqua, whose chief promptly ceded to the British, the territory known as Griqualand West. By that time there were 50 000 people living in Kimberley and such individuals as Cecil Rhodes and Barney Barnato were amongst the throng, beginning to elbow their way from scratch to fortune.

The first rushes to diamond pipes such as Colesberg Koppie saw the entire exposure pegged out into claims. Seven hundred claims were marked off on Colesberg Koppie, many overlapping the pipe on to completely valueless ground. An area slightly less than 3 ha actually proved the most profitable. At first, each claim was separately worked and there was no indication that the pipe would extend to any depth. As the claims worked deeper, chaos resulted when separate workings became difficult and dangerous. Amalgamations of claims became the only solution and it was through this fortuitous circumstance that the organising genius of men such as Rhodes and Barnato grasped the opportunity which led to fortune.

The spectacle of these vast open-cast mines, looking like overturned ant heaps, must have been staggering. Thirty thousand men worked at one time in the Big Hole and the sounds of pounding, digging, shouting, grinding of winches, and all the hubbub of mining gave to Kimberley a strange husky sort of voice which could be heard day and night for some kilometres across the veld, as though the town was muttering to itself.

Suddenly confronted with this flood of gems from South Africa, the world price of diamonds, which until then had been extremely rare gemstones, fell very considerably. At the same time, however, diamonds were now within reach of the general public, and having such a glamorous background of rarity and mystic beauty, they became fashionable throughout the world and the accepted emblems of romance. Demand increased after the first decline and Kimberley flourished considerably, with successful diggers washing in soda water, booking all-day rides on visiting merry-go-rounds, lighting cigars with £5 notes, as well as all the other nonsense which accompanies an excess of money in such a madcap society.

Kimberley underwent a metamorphosis, with money providing the cocoon out of which a dusty caterpillar, transformed into a butterfly, emerged, complete with social graces, libraries, fine buildings, theatres, gardens and civic airs. Old Nicolaas de Beer, owner of the land on which the town was growing, took one last look at it, sold out for 6 000 guineas and moved to quieter parts in the Transvaal. The family name, in the form of De Beers, remained as a collective term for the entire activity as it was slowly amalgamated by Rhodes into the mighty concern of today, the De Beers Consolidated Mines Limited.

Kimberley became a municipality in 1877 and by 1882 a tramway connected the place to Beaconsfield, and the streets were illuminated by the first electric street lights in Southern Africa. Cecil Rhodes had begun his political career by becoming the diggers' representative for Barkly West in the Cape Legislative Assembly. In 1890 he became Prime Minister of the Cape Colony.

It was in the Kimberley market square, on 16 July 1886, that F. W. Alexander, an itinerant produce dealer, publicly crushed samples of reef which he had acquired on the newly discovered Witwatersrand, and started a rush of financiers from Kimberley to secure holdings in the world's richest goldfields. It was also in Kimberley, in 1887, that Rhodes and his cronies planned the famous concession with Lobengula and the subsequent occupation of Zimbabwe. The simple little office and boardroom in which Rhodes conceived many of his great coups still stands, in its original state in Warren Street. It is now a museum.

In 1888 the great amalgamation took place between Rhodes's De Beers Mine and Barney Barnato's Kimberley Mine. Barnato received a cheque for £5 338 650 for the Big Hole and Rhodes remained the veritable king of diamonds, the controller of the great bulk of the world's production, and the recipient of a personal daily income far beyond the earning capacity of the average man's lifetime. By means of this unparalleled income he financed his dealings on the Witwatersrand, in Zimbabwe, and elsewhere. The great holes in Kimberley provided him with an inexhaustible flow of money which, like the hair on Samson's head, was the source of his power.

Kimberley spread out around the mines. In 1889 the Kenilworth Model Village was established by the De Beers Company to house employees. At that time plans were already under way to convert the open-cast workings into underground operations, the headgear of the Kimberley Mine being erected in 1892 and all activity at the Big Hole thenceforth conducted through shafts and adits.

The year 1892 also saw the Kimberley and World Exhibition, the first of its kind to be held outside London. At that time, the diamond city was the gayest and most vivacious place in Southern Africa. Even learning and religion were flourishing in the town. A School of Mines was opened in 1896 and, strangely enough, in 1903 it was transferred to Johannesburg, where it became the University of the Witwatersrand. Among the religious groups who thrived in Kimberley were the Seventh Day Adventists. In 1885 Pieter Wessels, founder of the denomination, on reading his Bible, decided that the fourth commandment explicitly ordained the seventh day (Saturday) as the Sabbath. Arousing considerable argument over the matter in his church, he was excommunicated and promptly started the Seventh Day Adventists in Kimberley, amply financed by the sum of £451 438, paid in 1891 by the De Beers Company, in exchange for the Wesselton Mine, a Wessels family property.

The outbreak of the Anglo-Boer War in October 1899, saw Kimberley besieged by the Boers for 154 days from 14 October until 15 February 1900. Rhodes was in Kimberley for the whole of the siege and his quarters at the Sanatorium Hotel provided a favourite target for the Boer artillerists. To escape the shelling some 3 000 women and children were accommodated in underground workings at the De Beers and Kimberley mines. A famous gun named 'Long Cecil', firing a 12-kg shell, was designed and built in the De Beers workshops and used to shell the Boers. The designer, an American engineer, George Labram, was himself killed when a Boer 'Long Tom' secured a direct hit on the Grand Hotel while Labram was dressing for an appointment with Rhodes.

With the war over, Kimberley resumed its diamond mining. The Honoured Dead Memorial, designed by Sir Herbert Baker on a plan selected by Rhodes, was built in memory of the people of Kimberley who were killed in the siege. Similar in conception to the Nereid Monument of Xanthos, it was built of granite procured from the Matobo (Matopo) hills of Zimbabwe. Rudyard Kipling wrote the inscriptions and the original 'Long Cecil' stands guard on a stylobate of the memorial. The death of Cecil Rhodes in Muizenberg on 26 March 1902 saw an end to the king of diamonds but, as is the nature of life, his crown prince was already on the way, for during that year a young man named Ernest Oppenheimer arrived in Kimberley as representative of a European diamond buying concern. When Beaconsfield and Kimberley combined to become a city in 1912, Ernest Oppenheimer became its first mayor and was by then, already on his way to securing massive power in the world of finance.

In 1913 Kimberley became the home of the first flying school in Southern Africa known as the Aviation Sydicates School of Flying. An aerodrome about 2 km from Alexandersfontein and a wonderful box-kite affair of a flying machine used by an instructor named Paterson, formed the training foundation of the future South African Air Force.

The 1930s saw the collapse of the diamond industry during the world depression. Kimberley experienced a very bleak time, but its situation as the commercial, administrative and communications centre of the Northern Cape guaranteed it some importance even without the glitter of diamonds.

Today, with a population of 142 000, it is an educational centre; the seat of the Anglican Bishop of Griqualand West; and, with the restoration of diamonds to their old place of value, it remains essentially the diamond city – the headquarters of the De Beers Consolidated Mines where the gemstones of Southern Africa are sorted and despatched. It is certainly the only city in the world where – unlike the unfortunate Irishman digging for gold in a London street – men may still be seen searching for, and finding diamonds on the sites of demolished buildings and excavated pavements and roads where the 'blue ground', the kimberlite, was scattered during the first hectic days of the rush, before men quite realised the value of its content.

For the tourist, Kimberley offers an atmosphere redolent of old excitements. There is, of course, the Big Hole. From an observation platform the visitor can visualise the place and particularly the crater pipe itself, seething with a lava of human activity. A completely reconstructed street lined with the original buildings of old-time Kimberley forms a wonderful museum on the edge of the Big Hole. Here may be seen a bar, church, and Barney Barnato's Boxing Academy; tram cars; luxury private pullman railway coaches used by the millionaires and complex machinery for the recovery of diamonds; bicycles with sails for wind power, the original headgear which lowered many women and children to safety during the siege, and a replica of the original De Beers homestead. The Big Hole and the Kimberley Mine Museum are open daily from 08h00 to 18h00; closed at Christmas and on Good Friday.

In contrast are the modern workings, with their recovery processes, the glittering products of uncut diamonds and the ultra-intelligent police dogs who guard the diamond areas. Permits to visit the treatment and recovery plants of De Beers Consolidated Mines Ltd are issued (at the discretion of the company) for Mondays to Fridays, excluding Christmas Day, New Year's Day, Good Friday and the Day of the Covenant. A small charge is made in aid of local charities. No children under 12 are allowed. Permits may be obtained at the company's office, 36 Stockdale Street, from 08h30 to 16h30. Tours begin at 08h45 at the Dutoitspan Mine gate and include a display of diamonds, the mine plant and the African hostels. The tours end at about 12h30. The De Beers dogs give performances at 10h30 on the first and third Sunday of each month at the De Beers Kennels. A collection is taken in aid of the S.P.C.A.

There are several interesting museums and galleries to visit in Kimberley. The old museum in 10 Chapel Street was created as a memorial to a former mayor of the city, Alexander McGregor. This museum houses exhibits dealing with the prehistory and history of the Northern Cape, as well as geological specimens from all over the world. It is open weekdays from 09h00 to 17h00; on Saturdays from 09h00 to 13h00; on Sundays from 14h00 to 17h00 and on public holidays from 10h00 to 17h00, but not on Good Friday and Christmas Day.

Also part of the McGregor Museum is the building in 2 Egerton Road, built first as a sanatorium, then used by Cecil Rhodes as a luxury hotel and finally becoming a convent school. Displayed there now are aspects of the history of Kimberley; there is also a Hall of Religions. The hours of opening are the same as the old museum.

Also attached to the MacGregor Museum is *The Bungalow,* built for C. D. Rudd and maintained as an example of the opulence during the period of the diamond magnates. The house is situated at 7 Lock Road, but visits must be arranged by appointment with the McGregor Museum.

The William Humphreys Art Gallery was founded in 1952 when William Humphreys, the member of Parliament for Kimberley for 25 years, donated his collection of paintings to the city. Housed in the Civic Centre, this collection has been considerably expanded to include works by many South African artists, European and Cape furniture and other items. The gallery is open Mondays to Saturdays from 10h00 to 13h00 and from 14h30 to 17h30; on Sundays from 14h30 to 17h30.

The Duggan-Cronin Bantu Gallery, next to the McGregor Museum in Egerton Road, has the same opening hours and exhibits a staggering collection of over 8 000 photographs taken by Mr A. M. Duggan-Cronin who immigrated to South Africa from Ireland in 1897. Working for the De Beers Company as a manager in their labour department, he indulged in the hobby of taking these unique photographs of African tribal people before they adopted European dress. Such pictures can never be retaken and, in addition to being of historical value, they are superb photographic works of art. There is space in the building for the exhibition of only a small portion of the total collection.

On the southern outskirts of Kimberley, a portion of the battlefield of Magersfontein (428 ha) has been proclaimed a national monument. It was here, on 11 December 1899 that the Boers, 8 200-strong and commanded by General P. A. Cronje, were attacked by 12 500 British soldiers commanded by Lieutenant-General Lord P. S. Methuen. The British were attempting to relieve the siege of Kimberley but their advance was so decidedly brought to a halt at Magersfontein that it was two months before they recovered and finally relieved Kimberley. The Boers had created strong defensive positions in a single line of trenches and behind several low stone walls. The British attacked without realising the strength of the Boer positions. Altogether 239 were killed and 663 wounded, mainly men of the Highland Brigade. The Boer losses were 87 killed and 149 wounded. A field museum, viewing post, tearoom and some picnic sites are situated at the battlefield.

The Kimberley library, in Dutoitspan Road, is worth visiting; it houses one of the best collections of Africana in South Africa and is greatly used for research. It is open on weekdays from 09h00 to 20h00 and on Saturdays from 09h00 to 13h00.

Among the many memorials in Kimberley is a superb equestrian statue of Cecil Rhodes sculpted by Homo Thorneycroft. The horse was actually modelled from Rhodes's personal animal which he often rode in Kimberley. Spread across Rhodes's knees is a map of South Africa and he is dressed in the clothes he wore at the great indaba with the Ndebele in the Matobo hills.

In the gardens of the civic centre stands a fountain and statue sculpted by Herman Wald, in the form of a diamond sieve held aloft by five lifesized diggers. A bust of Sir Ernest Oppenheimer, first mayor of Kimberley City and diamond financier supreme, is also in the garden.

For recreation, the people of Kimberley frequent two pleasure resorts – Riverton and Langleg – 26 km away on the Vaal River where pastimes include boating, fishing and swimming and there are bungalows and sites for caravans, camping and picnicking.

## Accommodation
** Colinton Hotel, 10 rooms, all with baths. R13 – R20 B/B. Phone 2-4651.
* Crescent Hotel, 18 rooms, 8 with baths. R10,50 B/B. Phone 2-2413.
** Grand Hotel, 80 rooms, 45 with baths. R9,50 – R11,50 B/B. Phone 2-6251.
* Halfway Hotel, 13 rooms, all with baths. R8,50 B/B. Phone 2-5151.
** Horseshoe Motel, 56 rooms, all with baths. R10 – R14 B/B. Phone 2-5267.
**** Kimberley Hotel, 115 rooms, all with baths. R16 – R26 room only. Phone 3-1751.
* Phoenix Hotel, 13 rooms, 4 with baths. R6,50 – R7 B/B. Phone 2-7101.
* Queens Hotel, 20 rooms, 9 with baths. R7,28 B/B. Phone 2-3299.
*** Savoy Hotel, 50 rooms, 45 with baths. R15 – R20 B/B. Phone 2-6211.
* West End Hotel, 9 rooms, 3 with baths. R9 B/B. Phone 2-6661.

## Caravans and camping
* De Beers Stadium Caravan Park, 24 sites. R2 D.
** Langleg Pleasure Resort, 30 sites. R1,50 D. 20 bungalows, R2 – R3 D.
* Municipal caravan park, 40 sites. R2,50 D.
*** ®Riverton Pleasure Resort, 40 sites. R2,50 D. 6 cottages, 20 rondawels, R5 – R7 D.

# GRIQUALAND WEST AND THE NORTHERN CAPE

Kimberley is the gateway through which travellers along the Diamond Way from Cape Town to Johannesburg may turn aside off the beaten track and enter the great spaces of sunshine and bush-covered plains of Griqualand West and the Northern Cape, where spectacular developments are taking place against the background of a history involving hunters, prospectors, missionaries, and wanderers of the wastelands.

Take the tarmac road leading west from Kimberley across the bush-covered plains to the great bend of the Vaal River. After 22 km there is a turnoff to Nooitgedacht where glacial pavements and rock engravings may be seen. The engravings are of uncertain age but were probably done by Bushmen. At this point the river is a fine stretch of water which the main road crosses by means of a handsome solid-looking bridge of dolomite stonework. The original toll house still stands guard. Downriver from the bridge there is a great pool which, according to African legend, is the haunt of a giant serpent. A swimming pool and camping and recreational area has been created on the right bank of the river where the road makes its crossing.

The traveller is now in really romantic diamond country. Immediately across the bridge, on the eastern side of the road, looms Canteen Koppie, now a nature reserve preserving the site of the great rush to what was known as Klip Drift. There are signs everywhere of considerable disturbance to the landscape: mounds of gravel, pits, holes, excavations. Abandoned implements, rusty machinery, dilapidated houses abandoned at the sites of rich finds, all still remain, while the broad river flows silently by, retaining the secret of when and how the diamonds came to be mixed up in its gravel and from where they originated.

The area around Canteen Koppie almost resembles an illustrated geology textbook. Striated rocks at *Nooitgedacht* (16 km away) indicate that about 220 million years ago, the area was under ice. After the ice melted, prehistoric man moved in and Canteen Koppie is now rich in their artefacts. Iron Age people arrived, followed by Korana Hottentots, and in 1849 by missionaries of the Berlin Missionary Society who founded a station on the left bank of the Vaal and named it *Pniel* (the face of God). The most momentous occasion of all was in January 1870, with the arrival of a party of prospectors from Natal, led by Captain Loftus Rolleston. They discovered diamonds in the gravel of the river, an event which put an end to the tranquil labours of the missionaries. It was as though an earthquake had suddenly rocked the place.

Diggers rushed to Pniel, and across the Vaal River to Klip Drift where a noisy, uproarious camp established itself, notorious for gun running, strong liquor and illicit traffic in stolen diamonds. The site of this camp, just beyond Canteen Koppie (35 km from Kimberley), is now the town of . . .

# BARKLY WEST

With a population of 6 600, Barkly West, to say the least, experienced a very lively beginning. The diamond diggers had no sooner pitched their tents on the site of the town – the old fording place known as Klip Drift – than a variety of individuals appeared on the scene, claiming ownership of the ground, and the right to levy rates. First to arrive was the Korana chief, Jan Bloem. The diggers, led by Roderick Barker, armed themselves, formed a laager on the site of the English church, and offered to fight for their independence. Bloem fled. He was followed by chief Jantje of the Tlapin and then by the Griqua people, both of whom were driven away in confusion.

The Orange Free State claimed the south side of the river and a magistrate was established at Pniel. The Transvaal claimed the north side and in June 1870 President Pretorius arrived to effect control. The diggers, however, would have none of him. Led by Roderick Barker, they threatened to pull down the Transvaal flag if it was hoisted over them. Pretorius tried again three days later and introduced Hugh Owen to the diggers as their magistrate. In a yelling mob the diggers surrounded the Presidential party, tore up the flag, dumped Owen in a boat and sent him off to the south bank of the river, threatening to tar and feather him if he tried to return. Pretorius retreated to the mission station of Hebron (now Windsorton), from where he tried to negotiate with the diggers, who simply ignored him. Forming a mutual protection society, they elected Stafford Parker as President of the Klip Drift Republic and declared independence.

President Parker, with his white top hat and massive set of whiskers, was one of South Africa's classic characters. His speech, in accepting office, was simple: 'If you have confidence in me, support me loyally, and for Heaven's sake don't allow any tipsy fool to say "pitch him in the river".'

President Parker ruled with rough justice in the form of commonsense trials and punishments such as tar-and-feathering, being hauled through the river, pegging out a man on the ground, or simply running him out of camp. In December 1870 John Campbell arrived in a top hat crowned with an ostrich feather. He had been sent by the government of the Cape Colony, which also laid claim to the diamond area.

The whole unseemly squabble about ownership was eventually taken to arbitration and the Keate Award gave the area to the Griqua people. Complete chaos resulted on the diamond fields, with supporters of rival claimants threatening one another. The British eventually persuaded the Griqua to cede the area to them and at the close of the singularly stormy year of

1870, Sir Henry Barkly, the Governor of the Cape, visited the diggings to establish order, administration, and a High Court for Griqualand. As a result of this visit, the camp at Klip Drift received the name of *Barkly West* and commenced a more sober career. The majority of diggers abandoned the place when the great diamond pipes were discovered at Kimberley, but diamond recovery from the gravel beds of the Vaal River has continued and is likely to for many years to come along the 160-km stretch of the river above its confluence with the Harts.

Barkly West became a municipality on 3 January 1913. It is an atmospheric little town, especially on a Saturday morning when a row of offices is opened opposite the headquarters of the Mining Commissioner, where diamond buyers meet the local diggers and intense negotiation takes place over the sale of stones found during the week. In the offices of the Mining Commissioner there is an interesting museum containing the minerals and prehistoric artefacts found along the Vaal, as well as early photographs of the diggings. The museum is open Mondays to Fridays from 08h00 to 16h30.

The course of the Vaal River is a particularly interesting sight, characterised by breakwaters where diggers still labour during the dry season (June to November), and scars of enormous mining activity. The river has many pools, rapids, waterfalls and features with odd names such as *Gong-Gong* (a Bushman name from the sound of water falling over the rocks); *Beaumont's Folly* – the great pool below the Kimberley bridge, where George Beaumont transported piecemeal and at great expense a substantial dredger which he erected, launched and floated in 1898 in the hope of recovering diamonds from the bottom, only to be defeated by the rocks; *Bosman's Fortune,* where A. Bosman, in the same pool that had ruined Beaumont, erected breakwaters, and from the river bottom recovered a small fortune in diamonds; and many other places of forgotten hopes and stories rich enough to fill many books. St Mary's Anglican Church in Barkly West, built in 1871 and the first church building on the diamond fields, is brimming with memories of the diggers. The gravels of the Vaal River are a rich source of semi-precious stones and decorative pebbles, providing a rewarding pastime for the collector who fossicks here. Cecil Rhodes's house is now the residence of the manager of the local Standard Bank.

## Accommodation
* Grand Hotel, 10 rooms, all with baths. R8,75 B/B. Phone 38.
* Queens Hotel, 12 rooms, all with baths. R8,75 B/B. Phone 85.

## Caravans and camping
* ®Municipal caravan park, 30 sites. R1 D.

From Barkly West the tarmac road continues west, keeping a few kilometres north of the course of the Vaal River. The length of the river is lined with the signs of mining and frequent turnoffs lead to places such as Waldeck's Plant (16 km); Longlands (19 km); and Delportshoop (25 km). All these places have odd little community centres, some of them almost ghost towns, with a hotel, a few stores and government offices.

## Accommodation
* Delportshoop Hotel, 10 rooms, all with baths. R8,75 B/B. Phone 14.

Delportshoop lies close to the confluence of the Vaal and Harts rivers, at which point the Vaal swings off to the south-west. The tarmac road continues westwards. At 31 km from Barkly West the road reaches a crossroads where a turnoff leads south to Schmidts Drift, and north to various diamond mines along the course of the Harts River, including Bellsbank, where diamonds are found in strange volcanic fissures. Jasper, agate and tiger eye are common in this area. Eight kilometres beyond the crossroads lies the huge open-cast working of Ulco

(Union Lime Company) beyond which the road climbs the escarpment of what is known as the *Ghaap*, or *Kaap*, from the old Hottentot name *Ghab* (plateau). The scenery is prodigious: a featureless, open, bush-covered dolomite plain where kameeldoring trees flourish, as well as a singularly rich number of many hundreds of varieties of grass for which the northern Cape is noted.

This carboniferous landscape is of great interest to the discerning geologist for it represents the resurrected pre-Karoo surface stripped of its sedimentary cover but little changed by later erosion. To the west along the ranges of the Langeberg and Koranaberg, it merges with the Kalahari and is buried beneath the sands. Sinkholes, underground rivers and surprisingly powerful springs (all characteristic of dolomite) are a feature of this great plain.

At 65 km from Barkly West, the tarmac road reaches the railway centre of Koopmansfontein where there is a parting of the ways. One road branches north, crosses the railway line and leads through scenery of little note for 120 km across the great dolomite plateau to the historic centre of . . .

# KURUMAN

A surprisingly attractive, clean and modern little town, Kuruman was once so remote that it took eight days of hard travelling by ox wagon to reach it from Kimberley. The town lies at the foot of a range of low hills and is characterised by a remarkable feature, the famous 'eye', the source of the Kuruman River.

At a place known to the Africans as *Gaseonyane* (the small calabash), 20 million litres of crystal-clear water gush out from the dolomite every day at a rate of flow which slackens only slightly even during the worst droughts. The town draws its water supply directly from this spring, an incalculably valuable asset for any community centre in the wilderness of Africa.

The residue of water tumbles into a fine ornamental pool occupied by a parcel of fat, grossly overfed bream and barbel fish. Lilies rest on the surface of the water. Tall shady trees cluster around, beneath which are picnic sites, a tearoom and caravan park.

Water is led from the pool through two canals to irrigate a 6-km length of the valley which, as a result, is delightfully green and fertile.

The name *Kuruman* apparently derives from a Bushman chief, Kudumane, who once lived there. In 1800 a missionary, Johan M. Kok, settled near the 'eye', but he was murdered eight years later. In 1824 Robert Moffat arrived and 4 km downstream from the 'eye' built a new mission station on behalf of the London Missionary Society for the Tlapin tribe who lived in the area. This became the best known mission station in Africa, a famous frontier outpost and the base for so many historic journeys of exploration by such people as David Livingstone, that the Kuruman 'eye' was described as a fountain of Christianity in Africa.

Today the cluster of original buildings erected by the London Missionary Society still stands surrounded by a riverine forest and a garden that has run wild. Giant syringa trees (almost the trademark of missionaries in Southern Africa), huge pear trees, old figs, and pomegranates all flourish. The almond tree under which Livingstone proposed to Mary Moffat in 1845 is dead, but its trunk still stands and the wind whispers through the leaves of the tree shading it.

The original church is beautifully preserved and still in use as a mission church with clean mud floors, great wooden beams holding up a thatched roof, and wonderful acoustics. Moffat's house is restored and is in spic and span condition. The original wagon house and other outbuildings are near by. The cemetery is half overgrown and filled with the melancholy graves of the children of missionaries who found life on the frontier too much for them. About the whole station lingers an atmosphere and a character of calm confidence and complete tranquillity. All is still, as though the place is set in a dream world. Each New Year weekend sees a great gathering in Kuruman of members of the L.M.S.H. Church and impressive ceremonies are held in the mission buildings.

The town of Kuruman was laid out in 1886 by Captain Levenson and in 1916 it became a municipality. The number of inhabitants now totals 9 400. It is the centre of a substantial district particularly important for the production of cattle, butter, cheese, asbestos, manganese, lime and iron. The Kuruman hills have been mined for Cape blue asbestos since 1912. At first exploited by primitive open-cast workings, the industry developed through the enterprise of such men as O'Conner and Wiemgartner, and large-scale companies such as Dominion Blue Asbestos and Cape Blue Asbestos, which were created to exploit deposits of high grade Cape blue asbestos. High grade manganese ore at Black Rock, and high grade haematite found in 1940 at Sishen allowed for the development of enormous mining industries, with Kuruman as the central town. The creamery in Kuruman is one of the largest butter producers in Southern Africa. Visitors are welcome at the plant.

## Accommodation

★★ El Dorado Motel, 26 rooms, all with baths. R11 – R12,50 B/B. Phone 1075.
★ Grand Hotel, 15 rooms, 9 with baths. R10,50 B/B. Phone 421.
★ North Star Hotel, 10 rooms, all with baths. R7 B/B. Phone 978.
★★ Ranch Motel, 20 rooms, all with baths. R9,50 B/B. Phone 616.
★ Savoy Hotel, 27 rooms, 7 with baths. R10 – R11 B/B. Phone 139.

## Caravans and camping

★ ®Municipal caravan park, 60 sites. R4 D.

Kuruman is situated at a major crossroads in the communication network of the northern Cape. East of the town a fine, straight tarmac road leads for 139 km to Vryburg (page 215), over a seemingly boundless plain of grass, patched by shrub and low thorn trees. There are few landmarks of special note other than occasional small rural centres such as Sarsoen (72 km from Kuruman) which serves as a halfway point on the journey.

North-west of Kuruman a gravel road extends for 47 km to the manganese mining centre with the extraordinary name of Hotazel, so called, it is said, by a party of early surveyors who, planning the original Cape-to-Cairo railway, held a party there which was even warmer than the weather!

From Hotazel the road, now a gravel track, continues for 368 km and, notable only for its corrugations and potholes, eventually reaches the entrance to the Kalahari National Park at Twee Rivieren. Hotazel is the terminus of the busiest branch railway in Southern Africa. This line, 336 km long and joining the mainline system at Kamfersdam, north of Kimberley, services the great iron, manganese and lime mines. Along it the heavy ore trains find their way in an endless stream to the steel mills and ports of South Africa.

From Kuruman a road leads west for 65 km to Sishen, the great iron ore mine which lies on the railway 65 km south of Hotazel. Sishen is also the loading point for the railway to Saldanha Bay.

## Accommodation

★★ Minerva Hotel, 36 rooms, all with baths. R13,50 B/B. Phone 2451.

In company with the railway, the road continues south for a further 64 km past *Lohatlha* (place of the vaalbos or *Tarconanthus camphoratus*), and after 57 km, reaches the huge workings of the Manganese Corporation at Beeshoek. The road then enters the little town of . . . .

# POSTMASBURG

This rather unbeautiful little place is built in a hollow, with a marsh as the town centre, surrounded by a prodigious dolomitic plain covered in grass, low shrubs and stunted thorn trees. If appearance is not the strong point of this area, it is because its beauty lies beneath the surface of the earth in the form of some of the richest mineral deposits in Africa.

Postmasburg was founded when the local farming community decided that a centre was needed for a church and trade. They selected as a site the area known to the Africans as *Tsantsibane* and *Sibilung*, and to Europeans as *Blinkklip* – each name deriving from the glittering stones found there on the surface. The town was proclaimed on 6 June 1892 and named after Professor D. Postma of the Dutch Reformed Church. A village management board was created at the same time and in this state the little town remained half asleep until prospectors found rich deposits of minerals and precious stones.

First there were diamonds. In 1918, Casper Venter was prospecting in the area when an African assistant by the name of Plaatjie, found an interesting looking pebble in a mongoose burrow and took it to his employer. It was a diamond. Venter prospected the area thoroughly and with a partner named Curle, formed the West End Diamond Mine which they eventually sold for £80 000 to a company. Diamonds are still produced by this mine.

The discovery of manganese followed. A prospector, Captain T. L. H. Shone, found manganese in 1922 on the farm *Doornfontein*, 29 km north of Postmasburg. The find was examined by A. L. Hall and reported to be of excellent quality and enormous quantity. Two substantial companies commenced operation in the area: the South African Manganese Co. Ltd, and the Associated Manganese Mines Ltd. Their activities brought the railway to Postmasburg in November 1930, with an extension to Lohathla being created six years later.

As the centre for this mining activity, Postmasburg became a municipality in 1932 and since then has grown rapidly, with a present population of 11 700. It is a substantial railway marshalling yard, with the line electrified to Kimberley, doubled for most of the way and earning over R2 million a month in freight charges. Horses, sheep and cattle are the agricultural products.

### Accommodation

* Postmasburg Hotel, 20 rooms, 15 with baths. R8 – R9,50 B/B. Phone 163.

From Postmasburg, a main road leads eastwards, climbing through a low ridge of hills and after 50 km reaching the village of . . .

# DANIELSKUIL

This little place, with a population of 1 600, receives its name from a sinkhole in the dolomite known as Daniel's Den and used by the Griqua as a depository for prisoners. Asbestos, diamonds, marble and lime in the area are the source of the village's prosperity.

Danielskuil lies at the foot of a ridge of hills where several asbestos mines of various sizes are located. On a hillock overlooking the village there is a small fort built by the British during the Anglo-Boer War. Twenty-two kilometres south of the village, across what is known as The Great Pan (a dried-out lakelet), lies the railway station of Silverstreams. Eight kilometres west of this place is Lime Acres, the huge lime quarry of the Northern Lime Company.

Seven kilometres beyond the quarry, on the summit of a low ridge, is the Finsch Diamond Mine, a diamond pipe found in November 1961 by Allister Fincham while he was investigating an outcrop of asbestos on the government farm *Brits*. Backed by his partner, a local trader named W. Schwabel, he proved the richness of the pipe and in 1963, sold his discoverer's certificate for R4½ million to the De Beers Consolidated Mines Ltd who have developed the property into one of the principal diamond producers in Southern Africa. The name of the mine is a combination of Fincham and Schwabel.

**Accommodation**
* Commercial Hotel (Danielskuil), 15 rooms, 10 with baths. R6 – R7 B/B. Phone 19.
*** Finsch Hotel (Limeacres), 22 rooms, all with baths. R18 – R20 B/B. Phone 121.

**Caravans and camping**
* Municipal caravan park, 50 sites. R1,25 D.

From Danielskuil the main road continues east over a level, featureless grassy plain, covered with dense shrub and low trees. After 51 km the road reaches Koopmansfontein, situated at the junction of the road to Kuruman and from there, continues east to Kimberley (page 200).

From Postmasburg a gravel road leads south over an enormous open plain. To the west lies the long ridge of the Langeberg range. Low shrub and thornbush blanket the plain until the road reaches and crosses the low range of the Asbestos Mountains and, 52 km from Postmasburg, reaches . . .

# GRIQUATOWN

Situated in a fold of the Asbestos Mountains, amid trees and sunshine, Griquatown is small and quite nondescript to the eye but undoubtedly has a character which stems from a curious past.

When Europeans first settled in Cape Town, they encountered a small Hottentot tribe, the Xurikwa, living in the area of Piketberg. Apart from several bad habits and a considerable amount of mixed blood, these people adopted from Europeans so many corruptions of their name that the term Griqua by which they eventually became known is, in effect, a simplification.

Under the leadership of a freed slave, *Adam Kok* (Adam, the cook) who had been in charge of the kitchen of the Cape Governors, these people wandered away from their original homeland and after numerous adventures, settled in the area of what was at first known as *Klaarwater* (clear water), now Griquatown. There, in 1801, the London Missionary Society established a station for the benefit of these people and this became the centre for a very polyglot crowd of Griqua, Tswana tribal fragments, and half-breeds known, by a proud tribal name, as Bastards.

It was on 7 August 1813, that the name of Griquatown was finally adopted. The settlement had the distinction of being the first town to be founded north of the Orange River and it was here also, in 1812, that the wife of the missionary, Cornelius Kramer, had the misfortune to become the first known white woman to die north of the Orange River. In 1821, Mary Moffat, later the wife of David Livingstone, was born in the old mission house, now the Mary Moffat Museum, which houses a collection devoted to the story of missionary work in the area, especially that of Robert Moffat who worked there for many years.

During this period (the 1820s), the Griqua, under their chief Andries Waterboer, ruled over the substantial portion of country still known as Griqualand West. Griquatown became a place of some importance – a base for hunters and traders venturing into the interior – and a sanctuary for many renegades and desperadoes. The discovery of diamonds at Barkly West in 1870 terminated the dominion of the Griqua when the British, to quote President Brand of the Orange Free State, 'jumped the country' and incorporated it into the volatile British Empire. By that time the Griqua had already split up, with one section, under Adam Kok (descendant of the first chief), having moved, first to Philippolis and then, in 1862, right across the Drakensberg range to Griqualand East.

In Griquatown may still be seen the original *Raadzaal* (council chamber) of the Griqua; the execution tree where they hanged cattle thieves; the grave of the chief Andries Waterboer, guarded by two cannon, Hans and Griet (presented to the Griqua by Queen Victoria), and several other interesting mementoes of the days when this little town was the capital of an independent state, with its own flag and coinage.

The area is renowned for its semi-precious stones, notably tiger eye. The population of Griquatown is 2 830.

### Accommodation
★ Louis Hotel, 15 rooms, 4 with baths. R7,50 – R8,50 B/B. Phone 84.

### Caravans and camping
★ Municipal caravan park, 50 sites. R2 D.

From Griquatown the tarmac road stretches east over a featureless plain covered with dense, low scrub. Amongst the principal inhabitants of this wilderness are numerous kudu, a large antelope notoriously devoid of traffic sense: numerous signs warn the motorist to beware of colliding with the creatures.

After 46 km the road reaches the nondescript village of Campbell, lying in a shallow valley on the shrub-covered plain at the edge of the Ghaap Plateau. Named after the Reverend J. Campbell, this little place is situated at the head of a well-watered gorge, known to the Griqua as *Knovel Vallei* (valley of wild garlic), which provides an easy route up the escarpment of the Ghaap Plateau. The Griqua settlement was founded there in 1811, with the first mission church built in 1831 by the Reverend John Bartlett of the London Missionary Society. Bartlett's church has been restored and stands in a pleasant setting.

From Campbell the tarmac road leads for a further 39 km to Schmidtsdrif (page 213) and Kimberley (108 km). A branch road follows the gorge, revealing some handsome views over the low-lying country and after 31 km, crossing the Vaal River to reach the town of . . .

# DOUGLAS

With its inhabitants numbering 6 800, Douglas was founded in 1848 as a mission established by the Reverend Isaac Hughes on the farm *Backhouse*, close to the ford of Kokounop across the Vaal River used by early travellers making their way to the north. This strategic ford had been the site of bitter contention between the Bushmen and Hottentots, whereafter it was known to the Bushmen as *Go Koo Lume* (where we had a hard time).

In 1867 a group of Europeans from Griquatown signed an agreement with the Griqua chief, Nicholas Waterboer, giving them the right to establish a town at the ford. The place was named after Lieutenant-General Sir Percy Douglas, and flourished as an agricultural centre, with land irrigated with water from the Vaal. Attaining municipal status in 1905, its prosperity attracted a branch railway from Belmont in 1923. Lucerne, wheat, potatoes, cotton, vegetable seeds and an occasional diamond, are the products of Douglas.

Twelve kilometres from Douglas, the Vaal River joins the Orange at the irrigation area of Bucklands. A great dam on the Orange is being built south of Douglas on the farm *Torquay*. At Driekops Island in the Riet River east of Douglas may be seen hundreds of stylised engravings carved in the rock by prehistoric people, probably Bushmen. The site is reached via a turnoff on the main Douglas-Kimberley road marked Plooysburg with, after 8 km, a turnoff through a gate leading to a parking area at the site. The engravings are inundated when the river is in flood.

### Accommodation
★ Douglas Hotel, 15 rooms, all with baths. R8 B/B. Phone 20.
★ Frederick Hotel, 16 rooms, 8 with baths. R7,50 – R8 B/B. Phone 168.

**Caravans and camping**
★ Municipal caravan park, R2 D.

From Douglas the road continues south past Salt Lake to join the Diamond Way (73 km). Another road leads north-eastwards across gently rolling country, densely bushed and populated with numerous game animals such as springbok and kudu. To the east the Vaal River flows in great, lazy looking loops and coils. After 45 km the road joins the tarmac road from Campbell (32 km), the combined roads continuing eastwards for 6 km to cross the Vaal River at Schmidtsdrif. From there the tarmac road leads due east for 71 km to Kimberley over a level bush-covered plain. Situated 30 km along this road at Doornlaagte, is a prehistoric site, a Stone Age waterhole unearthed by the roadmakers. Half way between Schmidtsdrif and Kimberley, the tarmac road passes a curious, isolated hillock which has been used as a gravel quarry. This hillock, known as *Bakenkop* (beacon summit), marks the centre of South Africa at its widest point, for it stands half way between the east coast at St Lucia and the west coast at Oranjemund.

The game farm of the De Beers Consolidated Mines lies next to the road at Rooikoppies near Schmidtsdrift. Further on is a private zoo on the farm *Teneriffe*, belonging to C. P. Mathewson.

## THE DIAMOND WAY TO THE NORTH

From Kimberley the Diamond Way makes its way northwards over a level plain covered with grass and low bush. Sixteen kilometres from the city there is a turnoff west to the pleasure resort of Riverton, managed by the municipality of Kimberley. At 41 km the road reaches the small railway centre of Windsorton Road, from where a tarmac turnoff stretches eastwards for 12 km to the odd little diamond miners' village of . . .

## WINDSORTON

Built on the banks of the Vaal River, this atmospheric little place was originally the mission station of Hebron. Diamonds were discovered in the gravels of the river and a madcap crowd of diggers rushed to the place, establishing themselves in an uproarious camp. The missionaries went into retreat and the diggers' camp was named *Windsor* after P. F. Windsor, a merchant who owned the land on which it developed.

Diamonds are still found in the area but the prodigious upheaval of the past is now a memory, the scars of which are still clearly visible on the landscape. A drink in the local pub can be rewardful of yarns as well as refreshment.

**Accommodation**
★ Rand Motel, 20 rooms, 6 with baths. R9,50 B/B. Phone 9903.

From the Windsorton turnoff, the Diamond Way continues across level, shrub country. After 26 km (67 km from Kimberley), the road reaches the Vaal River and on its south bank, the town of . . .

## WARRENTON

This place originated in 1880 when a syndicate of 18 men bought the western portion of the farm *Grasbult,* on the left bank of the Vaal, with the intention of irrigating the fertile land there and producing vegetables for the Kimberley diggers. In those days and in such an area, fresh vegetables were almost as valuable as diamonds, and as a result, the enterprise of the syndicate proved highly profitable.

A town was laid out on the south bank of the river and named after Sir Charles Warren, leader of the Warren Expedition to the Tswana country and surveyor of the local frontier line with the Transvaal and Orange Free State. In 1888 diamonds were discovered on the town lands and a rush to the place ensued. Mining continued until 1926 when the last diggers wandered away. The town was then left to develop into an agricultural and railway centre with such enterprises as a cheese factory providing employment for its population, which has since reached a total of 18 325.

Warrenton became a municipality in 1948 and is today a pleasant little rural centre, producing maize, groundnuts and china clay.

### Accommodation
★ Central Hotel, 16 rooms, 7 with baths. R10 – R10,50 B/B. Phone 10.

### Caravans and camping
★ Municipal Caravan Park, 20 sites. R2,50 D.

At Warrenton the Diamond Way undergoes a major division: the main road veers north-eastwards into the Western Transvaal (page 679), while a tarmac branch crosses the Vaal and continues north. After 16 km this road reaches . . .

## THE VAAL-HARTS IRRIGATION AREA

In 1873 it was discovered that the Vaal River, in the approach to its confluence with the Harts, was 140 m higher than the latter river, with a high ridge separating the two valleys. The time was, however, inopportune for any development and the first settler in the valley of the Harts, the well-known Francis 'Matabele' Thompson, only made his home in the area on *Cornforth Hill* in 1874. Troubles with the neighbouring tribes in 1878 delayed still further any develop-ment, but in 1881, Cecil Rhodes sent surveyors into the area to devise an irrigation scheme.

Nothing came of Rhodes's plan nor of subsequent schemes, but in 1933 the government, spurred on by depression, reinvestigated the project and the Vaal-Harts Irrigation Scheme, the largest in the Southern Hemisphere and the second largest in the world, came to fruition. The Vaal-Harts storage dam was built in the Vaal River at a site above Fourteen Streams. From this dam a grand canal was dug to lead the water from the Vaal for 120 km into and up the valley of the Harts, thereby irrigating 1 200 smallholdings varying in size from 25 ha to 40 ha. From this water the valley of the Harts, originally a wilderness of vaalbos and kameeldoring trees, was transformed into a huge garden of lucerne, groundnuts, maize, watermelons and other produce. Any residual water from the canal finds its way back to the Vaal through the Harts River.

At 21 km from Warrenton the tarmac road reaches the railway station of Border, actually on the border of the Transvaal. At this point a turn east leads for 1 km to the headquarters of the water department officials who manage the irrigation scheme. This centre, originally known as Andalusia, became in January 1954 a town named *Jan Kempdorp* in honour of the Minister of Agriculture. A rural centre shaded by fine trees, it attained the status of a municipality on 1 April 1967, and has a population of 10 800.

### Accommodation
★ Border Hotel, 12 rooms, 6 with baths. R8,32 – R9,36 B/B. Phone 121.
★ Jan Kemp Hotel, 18 rooms, 8 with baths. R12,50 B/B. Phone 194.

From Border the road continues north, keeping close company with the railway and stretching in a straight line through rich, irrigated fields. After 18 km there is a turnoff east leading for 3 km to the rural centre of . . .

# HARTSWATER

Laid out in 1948 as a town for the northern section of the Vaal-Harts irrigated area, Hartswater has grown up to the sound of gurgling water in irrigation canals, and is surrounded by myriad trees and wide expanses of fertile fields. It became a municipality on 1 April 1960 and has a population of 2 602.

## Accommodation
⋆ Hartswater Hotel, 22 rooms, 14 with baths. R10 – R11 B/B. Phone 22.

From Hartswater the tarmac road continues north across the irrigated fields. The drive up the length of this great irrigation scheme is akin to crossing a vast garden 40 km long and occupying 400 000 ha. Sixteen kilometres north of Hartswater the scheme ends and the traveller feels a slight shock at the sudden transition back to the wilderness of shrub and aridity. Seven kilometres beyond this point (24 km from Hartswater) the road reaches the small rail centre of . . .

# TAUNG

From *Taung* (the place of the lion), a branch railway leads west to the Buxton quarries of the Northern Lime Co. where the celebrated prehistoric skull of Taung Man was found. The Taung Travertyn works, mining semi-precious stones, is situated in Taung itself.

West of Taung is the largest cheese factory in the Southern Hemisphere, at *Reivilo,* an odd name derived from the spelling in reverse of the name of the Reverend Mr Olivier who presented the land for the centre. Visitors to the factory are welcome.

## Accommodation
⋆ Cecil Hotel, 10 rooms, 5 with baths. R7,25 – R8 B/B. Phone 91.

The tarmac road north of Taung leads across a vast, flat savanna – park-like in places with green grass and areas of handsome trees. At 9 km a turnoff leads to Amalia (page 690). The road continues past the railway junction point of Pudimoe (12 km from Taung), leaving an area of tribal African occupation and reaching a vast, featureless, grassy plain – magnificent ranching country. Here, 60 km from Taung, sheltering in a slight hollow in the plain, lies the town of . . .

# VRYBURG

Inhabited by 23 420 people, *Vryburg* (the town of liberty) had a real swashbuckling origin. A long spell of disturbance between the Tlapin tribe of chief Mankwarane and the Korana Hottentots led by David Massouw resulted in the employment by these rivals of European mercenaries. David Massouw offered each recruit a farm as well as a share in all loot. Commanded by Sarel Cilliers, a force of over 400 Europeans was raised to support David Massouw, while Mankwarane also presided over a pocket army.

A desultory little war followed, with four of Massouw's followers being killed – two mercenaries and two of his own men. On 26 July 1882, peace was arranged and 416 farms were given to the mercenaries. The occupants of these farms decided to organise their own state and in August 1833, they formed the Stellaland Republic with Gerrit Jakobus van Niekerk elected as the first president. The name of Stellaland is said to have arisen after a comet appeared while fighting was in progress. A party of mercenaries, sitting around their camp fire in the veld, were discussing the proposed republic and its name, for which various suggestions were made. One of the group, lying on his blanket gazing at the wondrous spectacle of the sky, proposed that the republic be named *Sterland* (star land) as he considered that in no other part of the world could the stars be seen so vividly. The name was accepted, but changed to the more euphonious *Stellaland*.

As a capital for the republic, the town of Vryburg was laid out on a site known to the Africans as *Huhudi* (running stream). A postal service was organised, a flag designed, and the republic launched as a proper, if diminutive, state. Its life, however, was short. A second pocket republic, Goshen, had been established further north and disturbances there induced President Paul Kruger of the Transvaal, to annex the area. The British intervened and sent an expeditionary force under Sir Charles Warren to 'remove filibusters from Bechuanaland (Botswana) and restore order in the country'. Warren and his men occupied the area without resistance in 1885 and from then on it became part of what was called British Bechuanaland. The Stellaland flag was sent to Queen Victoria and hung in Windsor Castle until 1934 when King George V returned it to Vryburg where it is now displayed in the museum housed in the handsome town hall.

The Stellaland flag is worth seeing. In the centre, on a dark green background, is a shield surmounted by a star. On the shield is a white hand holding a *korhaan* (bustard); representative of Mankwarane are two fish (totems of the Tlapin tribe) pierced by a sword; a scale depicts justice, and there is another star. Stellaland postage stamps are rarities. The museum is open Mondays to Saturdays from 10h30 to 12h30, and from 15h00 to 17h00 on Mondays, Tuesdays, Thursdays and Fridays.

British Bechuanaland became part of the Cape Colony in 1895 and today the land of stars is a prosperous ranching area, with Vryburg a great sales yard and railage centre for livestock. Beef, butter, milk powder, buttermilk and other products are the exports of Vryburg. The days when the town was a frontier resort for renegades, freebooters, and outlaws such as the famous Scotty Smith, are gone forever although some of the atmosphere of those halcyon days still survives. On Fridays from 08h00 onwards a cattle auction is held at which about 4 000 head are sold. Heavy trucks bring in the slaughter stock and the ranchers and stockmen provide a very colourful gathering. A meat canning concern has its factory in Vryburg and 10 km away at Armoedsvlakte is situated a veterinary research and bull-testing station.

Ruins of the old gaol – a home from home for many interesting characters – may still be seen. Outside the modern civic centre plays a pretty little fountain, next to which stands a bronze of President Gerrit van Niekerk, looking very paternal in his king-sized bushy beard, and viewing with interest the rapidly changing scene around him. Six kilometres out of Vryburg, on the road to Tosca, lies the fine Swartfontein Recreational Resort, where there are facilities such as a swimming pool, café, caravan and camping sites and cottages. Next to it is a nature reserve named after Leon Taljaard, a councillor of the town. A large variety of game animals find a home in this resort which is open Mondays to Thursdays from 14h00 to 18h30 and on Fridays, Saturdays and public holidays from 08h00 to 18h30.

## Accommodation

★ Central Hotel, 31 rooms, all with baths. R13 – R17 B/B. Phone 2393.
★★ Grand Hotel, 45 rooms, 40 with baths. R13,60 – R15,75 B/B. Phone 2264.
★ International Hotel, 45 rooms, 25 with baths. R10 – R11,50 B/B. Phone 2235.

## Caravans and camping
★★★ ®Swartfontein Municipal Recreational Resort, 40 sites. R2 D. 5 cottages, R7 D.

From Vryburg the main tarmac road continues north across a seemingly boundless savanna of grass and acacia trees. After 20 km the road passes the Boereplaas Caravan Park, and 46 km from Vryburg reaches the small trading centre of Stella, laid out in the form of a star next to a salt pan known to the Africans as *Schwaing* (place of salt).

At 85 km from Vryburg lies the trading centre of Setlagoli, from where there is a turnoff to Madibogo railway station. This is a flat world of red soil, maize, groundnuts and cattle. Acacia trees are the principal natural feature.

At 114 km from Vryburg the road reaches the trading centre of Maritsane.

## Accommodation
★ Setlagoli Hotel, 5 rooms, 2 with baths. R6 – R6,50 room only. Phone 994.
★ Stella Hotel (Stella), 8 rooms, 3 with baths. R9 – R10,50 B/B. Phone 49.
★ Wayside Hotel (Maritsane), 5 rooms, 2 with baths. R7,50 – R8,50 B/B. Phone 3.

## Caravans and camping
Boereplaas Caravan Park, 20 sites. R2 D. 2 cottages, R5 D.

Beyond Maritsane (a total of 156 km from Vryburg), the road reaches . . .

# MAFEKING

The town of *Mafeking* takes its name from the Tswana *Maheking* (place of boulders), originally applied to the area by the Rolong tribe who live there.

The birth of Mafeking was similar to that of Vryburg. In 1881 the Rolong tribe was divided into two factions. Both sides recruited European mercenaries with the usual promises of farms, the consequence of which was the establishment of a pocket republic named Goshen. A 'capital' was created at Rooigrond (18 km from Mafeking) and A. Delaney was elected as president.

Goshen never amounted to much and its inhabitants squabbled aimlessly. Paul Kruger attempted to annex the republic to the Transvaal but the British Government intervened in 1885 and sent Sir Charles Warren in command of an expeditionary force to occupy the whole of what became known as British Bechuanaland. In the course of the expedition Sir Charles laid out the town of Mafeking on the banks of the Molopo River. A British administrator, Sir Sydney Shippard, was appointed and the roughneck semi-military Bechuanaland Border Police was raised to control the area. Mafeking was the administrative centre and it grew into a rough and ready frontier town inhabited by tough troopers and a rugged crowd of farmers, traders, hunters and adventurers.

In 1895 British Bechuanaland was annexed to the Cape and life in Mafeking, then the remotest town in the Colony, started to settle down into a more humdrum existence, with the Jameson Raid that same year drawing off many of the former Bechuanaland Border policemen. On 10 September 1896 Mafeking became a municipality and the population now numbers 10 800.

On 14 October 1899, a few days after the outbreak of the Anglo-Boer War, a Republican force under General Snyman besieged the town. Colonel Baden-Powell and a garrison of 800 men held the town for 217 days until 17 May 1900, when it was relieved by a combined force of Rhodesians from the north and Imperial troops from the south. The siege of Mafeking had so captivated the imagination of the British public that when news of the relief arrived, celebrations in the streets of London reached unparalleled heights of emotion. It was during the

*Overleaf: Diamonds being recovered from beneath the sea sands at Oranjemund. Their origin there, in the pipes at Kimberley and in the gravels of rivers is a mystery.*

217

siege, when Baden-Powell organised the boys of the town into a non-combatant corps to keep them out of mischief and assist in the conduct of the town, that the idea was born for the future Boy Scout movement.

There are many relics in Mafeking of the siege days. The fort on Cannon Koppie has been restored as an historical monument. The Anglican Church, designed by Sir Herbert Baker, was built of Rhodesian stone in memory of those who died in the siege. Old cannon and other bric-à-brac of battle are preserved in various parts of the town, and there is a fine museum in the old town hall, housing exhibits mainly concerned with the siege. The museum is open Mondays to Fridays from 08h00 to 17h00; on Saturdays from 09h00 to 12h00. History tours to historical sites are conducted by arrangement with the museum.

Subsequent to the war, Mafeking continued to develop slowly.Excitement erupted in 1924 when alluvial diamonds were found 5 km from the town. Some 500 diggers rushed to the area but it proved only moderately rich and eventually petered out. Prosperity in Mafeking today is based on cattle, dairy products, maize, cement and its importance as a railway junction and marshalling yard close to the border with Botswana. Until February 1965, Mafeking was the seat of the British Administration of the then Bechuanaland Protectorate, the buildings of which were situated on what was known as the Imperial Reserve, an area adjoining the town which had been preserved for the exclusive use of the British Government.

With the creation in 1977 of the Tswana homeland of *BophuthaTswana* (that which binds the Tswana), a capital was established on the outskirts of Mafeking and named *Mmabatho* (mother of the people). Situated here, apart from residences, is an administrative and council building, a large stadium and a hotel containing the usual gambling casino, nightclub and theatre presentations and varied entertainments. In 1980 Mafeking was incorporated into BophuthaTswana.

Cookes Lake provides a pleasant recreational area with fishing opportunities, picnicking, and a caravan park. Thirty kilometres from Mafeking a great sinkhole has occurred in the dolomite. Over 60 m deep, and 70 m by 50 m wide, it is filled with crystal-clear water.

### Accommodation
* Crewe's Hotel, 19 rooms, 16 with baths. R15 B/B. Phone 206.
* Fish Hoek Hotel, 23 rooms, all with baths. R11 B/B. Phone 5.
*** ® Mmabatho Sun Hotel, 110 rooms, all with baths. Sun - Thurs: single R27 B/B, double R19 B/B. Weekends: single R33 B/B, double R22,50 B/B. Phone 301.
* Protea Hotel, 20 rooms, all with baths. R13 B/B. Phone 2404.
* Surrey Hotel, 20 rooms, 10 with baths. R10,50 – R11,50 B/B. Phone 349.

### Caravans and camping
** ®Cookes Lake Municipal Caravan Park, 80 sites. R3 D.

From Mafeking the tarmac main road to the north continues, passing Mmabatho at 5 km and at 25 km reaching the customs and immigration post of the Botswana border at Ramatlabama. The post is open from 07h00 to 20h00.

# Chapter Twelve

# THE GREAT KAROO

Vast, moody, lonely, melancholy, autumnal in its moods and stillness. Remote, elusive, harsh in the midday sun, but transformed by the approach of night into a place of gorgeous sunsets, with cool shadows rising out of valleys and hollows, slowly enveloping the land in a dark blanket of sleep while the heavens gleam with so brilliant a display of stars that the Karoo seems to be washed with a soft dew of falling light.

There are several ways of seeing the Karoo. The tarmac Cape-to-Cairo road (N1) which crosses part of the area is described in Chapter Ten. For most travellers along this great north-south highway of Africa, the Karoo simply represents a hot and dreary non-scenic intrusion between the fertile Western Cape and the grasslands of the highveld. To the discerning, especially those who make the journey in the early morning or late afternoon, the Karoo is far more appealing, for at that time of day the landscape is modelled into interesting shapes by oblique light, and its crystal-clear air is cool and invigorating.

This chapter is for those who have sensed the intrinsic nature of the Karoo and who wish to know it more intimately by leaving the beaten track and journeying to distant Bushmanland, Gordonia and the verge of the Kalahari where the springbok play.

In the Hottentot language, the name *Karoo* indicates a thirstland – very dry but not actually a true desert. Geologists apply the name to a system of sediments laid down over two-thirds of the interior of Southern Africa, dry only in the south, covered in grass in the better watered highveld of the Orange Free State and Transvaal, and blanketed with trees further north in territories such as Zambia.

The sediments were laid down by water between 150 and 250 million years ago in a series of different deposits of immense thickness, in places over 7 000 m. The origin of this material, however, is a mystery. Some ancient surface comprising mountain ranges, volcanoes, hills and valleys, must have been eroded completely, the debris dispersed in solution and then redeposited as though nature, dissatisfied with some early creative work, had erased it and started again with something new.

Buried in these layers of silt are the fossils of many animals and plants which existed in the swamplands, lakes and seas during the period of the formation of the Karoo. The water subsequently dried up and vanished like a mirage in the geological history of the earth, leaving behind the high-lying surface of the central plateau of Southern Africa.

Apart from its content of fossils and coal, the layers of sediment contain a particularly notable intrusion. Some disturbance in the molten depths of the earth caused igneous matter to travel upwards through the soft layers of shale and mudstone. Forcing its way through horizontal and vertical lines of weakness in these sediments, the igneous matter cooled to form hard dolerite rock, which, when it reached the surface vertically, was exposed in the form of strange walls of stone known as dykes, stretching aimlessly across the country as though constructed by some vanished people. In places where the dolerite spread out horizontally, it solidified in layers of hard rock known as sills, which resist erosion long after the softer sediments around them have disintegrated. In the same way as a roof, the sill protects what is below it with the result that fragments of higher levels of land remain like pieces of an ancient jigsaw puzzle, the surface of which was once the face of the land but whose segments are now scattered over the floor, irregular in size but uniform in height; these are the distinctive 'koppies' of South Africa: table-tops, pouf-tops, or rhino horns, characterised by a hard dolerite top.

The sediments of the Karoo are virgin and rich but to awaken fertility, water is needed, a precious bringer of life in a region where it sometimes does not rain for years. When rain does fall, the surface, only thinly protected by vegetation, is more often damaged than aided by sudden run-offs of water from short-lived but violent storms. In addition, every watercourse is impeded by man with dams and weirs. The flow of streams is in any case erratic but even without being beset by man, the water seldom gets anywhere. It flows into hollows, lingers for a little while in shallow lakelets and then disappears leaving behind dried-out pans and ghost lakes with hard, smooth, level floors caked with mineral salts.

In 1854, in America, Daniel Hallady invented the windpump, the perfection of which in 1883 by Stuart Perry, made the Karoo habitable by significant numbers of people. Many thousands of these pumps work in the area, drawing up water through boreholes and pouring it into small reservoirs and drinking troughs. The plaintive creaking and groaning of these hardworking devices provides the Karoo with its most characteristic sound and there are few parts of this wilderness where a windpump may not be seen, either near by or on the furthest horizon.

Before the windpump was introduced, the Karoo was the home only for creatures who could tolerate drought conditions such as springbok, gemsbok, the suricate (meercat) and the tortoise. Water obtained from the windpumps made possible the introduction of sheep, about 35 million of which now flourish in Southern Africa, mainly in the Karoo.

The most prolific variety of sheep in this area is the wooled merino which originates in Spain. The black-headed Persian mutton sheep is also common, as is the Dorper (a mixture of the Dorset Horn and the Persian) and the karakul, which is bred for its handsome skin. Sheep provide the Karoo with its principal industry.

The scarcity of surface water, understandably, made the Karoo unattractive to early man. A few Bushman and Hottentot groups wandered into the area but generally departed at the earliest opportunity. Europeans entered the Karoo from the south but before the introduction of the windpump their settlement was confined to the few oases where water was available, although it was often brackish, unpalatable, with an unpleasant smell, and undependable.

The traditional southern entrance to the Karoo was from Ceres through Karoo Poort. The first track to penetrate far into the interior of Southern Africa made its way through this natural passage and it was the route followed by early explorers, hunters, missionaries and most of the extraordinary human cavalcade which, lured by the promise of diamonds and gold, poured into Southern Africa. This highway later fell into disuse and was almost forgotten when the modern road and railway were opened through the valley of the Hex River. The old road was subsequently revived and today it carries traffic to several towns such as Sutherland and Fraserburg. For the connoisseur of travel, it provides the means for a nostalgic journey off the beaten track, to places seldom visited, along a route crowded with memories of adventures and characters, and where many interesting scenes and aspects of life peculiar to the Great Karoo are revealed.

From Ceres the tarmac road stretches north-eastwards across the floor of the fertile fruit-producing area of the Warmbokkeveld. Fine farms line both sides of the road and turnoffs lead to such places as Onder-Swaarmoed (at 3 km) and Lakenvlei (at 11 km). After 12 km the road reaches the foot of the Theronsberg Pass and for the next 12 km climbs steadily to the 1 091-m-high summit. The views from this pass are superb, especially in winter when the mountains encircling the basin of the Warmbokkeveld are often covered with snow. The pass is frequently closed due to snowfalls, while the Hex River mountains to the south provide at least a minor opportunity for winter sports.

The Theron family, after whom the pass is named, settled on *Leeuwfontein* farm during the 18th century and their thatched and gabled homestead is dated 1770.

The tarmac road continues, rising and falling through a world of panoramic views and castellated mountains. The road descends the Theronsberg Pass and winds through Hotten-tots Kloof, passing a turnoff to Citrusdal and the Kouebokkeveld 30 km from Ceres. The journey is interesting and prepares the traveller for his entrance to the Great Karoo.

The road continues past a resting place with water in the midst of the kloof. *Nuwerus* farm stands beside the road 35 km from Ceres and 2 km beyond this homestead, the tarmac road veers eastwards to join N1 at Touws River. The road to the Great Karoo now becomes gravel surfaced. Ahead can be seen Karoo Poort, the cleft in the mountains which forms the gateway between the fertile, well-watered Western Cape and the arid Great Karoo.

Karoo Poort is actually the passage made through the mountains by the Doring River. For 4 km the road keeps close company with the river as it twists through the mountains. The floor of the pass is level and the journey demands no climbing or descent. Near the farmhouse at the south-western entrance to the pass a shady resting place is reached, beyond which a considerable change in vegetation and scenery occurs: the erica, proteas, renosterbos and characteristic flora of the Western Cape dwindle and disappear. Dark green karee trees *(Rhus lancea)* and the lighter green wild willows *(Salix capensis)* line the banks of the river, the bed of which is thick with reeds. As the road reaches the north-eastern side of the pass, the vegetation transforms completely, with drought-resistant succulents, mesembryan-themums, ganna, milkbush, brakbos and other shrubs taking over and a hardy acacia tree putting in an occasional appearance.

The sedimentary cliffs of the *Witteberge* (white mountains) on either side of the pass have been curved and warped by the stresses of their original deposition and drying process. The gravel road leaves the pass beneath these natural arches and the traveller sees before him the vast panorama of the Bokkeveld Karoo, a level, open, shallow valley through which the Doring River finds its way, swinging northwards and then westwards to eventually become a tributary of the Olifants just above Klawer.

The road divides beyond the end of Karoo Poort, 45 km from Ceres. One branch leads northwards up the valley of the Doring to Calvinia, 213 km away, while the other branch veers north-east across the broad valley, towards the mountain heights at its eastern end. The wheels of many wagons, the feet of many eager travellers seeking after fortunes in diamonds and gold, blazed this route into the heart of the Great Karoo.

For a while the gravel road keeps within a few kilometres of the east bank of the Doring River. Irrigation from this river and its tributaries brings life to orchards, fields and vineyards on estates such as *Inverdoorn*. Over the entire valley broods a strange, sombre pile of dark-coloured Dwyka shales, known as the Perdeberg, a remnant of a former higher level of the valley. A melancholy atmosphere surrounds it as though it remembers past years, but is now forlorn, the last of its kind awaiting an inevitable end by erosion.

The road passes the foot of this 620-m-high landmark, twice crossing the Doring River and continuing across a desert landscape painted with colour – delicate blues for the sky; olive-green hue for vegetation, splashes of vivid shades in the spring when the succulents bloom and convert the wilderness into a garden.

Ahead lies another landmark, an overhanging peak known as Klein-Hangklip (755 m high) which forms part of the mountains on the eastern side of the valley of the Doring. In former years many travellers outspanned and rested beneath Klein Hangklip, for the place marked the end of the journey across the hot and arid Bokkeveld Karoo.

Beyond this landmark, the gravel road starts to ascend the heights, reaching the summit 65 km from the exit of Karoo Poort. Behind, the traveller has his last view of the mountains of the Western Cape, the Hex River range, the Cedarberg and the Witteberge. The road continues, descending and climbing across the grain of mountains and tributary river valleys of the Doring. It is a bone dry, hot and rugged world, but nevertheless provides an interesting scenic and travel experience.

At 106 km from Karoo Poort the gravel road joins the tarmac road coming in from Matjiesfontein 71 km away on the N1, the modern great north-south trunk road of Africa. Another kilometre takes the tarmac road across the Bobbejaanskrans River, beyond which lies the entrance to the pass known as *Verlaten Kloof* (lonely or abandoned ravine). This great cleft in the face of the mountains carries the road steadily upwards. There are several pleasant resting places along the way with shade and water provided by windpumps. The summit, 1 571 m high, is reached after 21 km and the road now begins to cross the cold and often snowbound plateau of the *Roggeveld* (rocky prairie).

Five kilometres from the top of the pass, the road passes a pleasant resting place with toilets and water. After a further 10 km (188 km from Ceres and 143 km from Karoo Poort), the tarmac road reaches the isolated little town of . . .

# SUTHERLAND

Founded in 1857 and named after the Reverend Henry Sutherland, the town was created on the farm *De List* as a centre for the wool-producing district of the Roggeveld, which has the bleak reputation of consistently being the coldest area in Southern Africa. Parts of the Eastern Transvaal do, at times experience lower temperatures than Sutherland but with an average minimum temperature of −6,1°C and periodic heavy falls of snow, the town (lying 1 456 m above sea level) and its surroundings can be rather chilly.

Despite a shortage of water, Sutherland is an amiable place characterised by a few interesting buildings surviving from the Victorian period. The town became a municipality in 1884.

## Accommodation
★ Sutherland Hotel, 17 rooms, 5 with baths. R8,50 – R9,50 B/B. Phone 96.

Beyond Sutherland the gravel road continues over the Roggeveld, reaching after 13 km a turnoff to the entrance of the South African Astronomical Observatory, the buildings of which, awkwardly positioned, look down aloofly from the cold summit of a high ridge. The observatory was created in 1972 when the main instruments from the observatories in Cape Town, Johannesburg and Pretoria were moved to the site (away from the glare and pollution of cities) where the sky is brilliantly clear and unaffected by clouds. The principal instrument is the 187,96-cm (74-inch) reflecting telescope formerly housed in the Radcliffe Observatory in Pretoria. The buildings of the observatory on top of the ridge are visible from many kilometres away.

Beyond the entrance to the observatory, the gravel road continues over arid, undulating Karoo landscape, where sheep flourish on the scanty vegetation and windpumps provide the source of life. After 100 km, the road reaches the town of . . .

# FRASERBURG

Named after the Reverend Colin Fraser, this centre of wool production with a population of 2 376, is situated high on the cold plateau of the *Nuweveld* (new prairie). Fraserburg is worth exploring for in the side streets may be found several well-preserved Victorian buildings with elaborate wrought-iron decorations, verandas, doors, windows and interior furnishings of great interest to antique dealers.

One particularly extraordinary building is known as the *Peperbus* (pepper box), a six-sided building erected in 1861 and designed as an office by the Reverend Bamberger. The reason for its eccentric design is unknown. Over the years it served as an office for the municipality market master, the magistrate and for the church. A small powder magazine used by British forces during the Anglo-Boer War stands on the hills overlooking the town.

## Accommodation
* Central Hotel, 15 rooms, 5 with baths. R7,90 – R8,94 B/B. Phone 9901.

From Fraserburg, the gravel road continues across the Karoo with its sheep runs, isolated homesteads and long, clear views. After 95 km the road enters . . . .

# LOXTON

In 1899 the Dutch Reformed Church bought from Mr A. F. Loxton the farm *Phezantfontein* on which was founded a village to serve the sheep farming community. In 1905 Loxton became a municipality and today has a population of 1 305. Although it is a sleepy, hot little place, numerous trees have been planted and the town shelters in a hollow in the valley of the upper Sak River, away from the searing winds of the Karoo. There is normally a scarcity of water but occasionally the situation alters: in March 1961 a violent storm caused such flooding that the dam above the town burst and three-quarters of the buildings in Loxton were destroyed or damaged. There is no accommodation available in the town.

---

From Loxton roads diverge to several parts of the Karoo. At the town, the old road from Ceres joins the tarmac route (84 km long) leading eastwards to Victoria West, where it joins the modern 'Diamond Way' proceeding to Kimberley and the north. Along this road, 47 km from Loxton, lies the holiday resort of Melton Wold.

## Accommodation
Melton Wold Guest Farm, 30 rooms, 17 with baths. R10 – R11,50 D. Phone Victoria West 1430.

A gravel road leads south from Loxton for 111 km across an interesting stretch of Karoo, descending (as a tarmac road) the spectacular Molteno Pass to Beaufort West. Extraordinary rock formations, deep ravines, the Karoo National Park (see page 188), and some fine farms may all be seen along this road.

---

North-west of Loxton a tarmac continuation of the road from Victoria West leads for 62 km, passing a resting place with water (44 km from Loxton) and reaching . . .

# CARNARVON

The town of Carnarvon, with its population of 7 320, lies in the central Karoo in a setting of flat-topped hills. The town originated as a Rhenish mission station where, in about the year 1850, 110 African refugees from various tribal disturbances in the north were settled. In 1860 a village named Harmsfontein was established. In 1874 the name was changed to *Carnarvon* in honour of the British Colonial Secretary, Lord Carnarvon and in 1882 the village became a municipality. Trees have been planted to provide shade and water is obtained from boreholes. The town is a busy farming centre, served by the branch railway from Hutchinson to Calvinia.

## Accommodation
* Astoria Hotel, 22 rooms, 6 with baths. R8 – R9 B/B. Phone 110.
* Carnarvon Hotel, 25 rooms, 13 with baths. R7 – R9 B/B. Phone 95.

Caravans and camping
* Voortrekker Park, 20 sites. R1,50 D.

From Carnarvon, the tarmac road leads westwards, keeping company with the railway line. After 92 km a turnoff leads to an interesting national monument, the homestead of the farm *Stuurmansfontein*, an example of the corbelled style of architecture. The method of construction of the homestead on this farm in the 1850s incorporates stone and timber and effectively promotes coolness. After a further 35 km (130 km from Carnarvon), the road reaches . . .

# WILLISTON

In a setting of arid hills the town of Williston originated as a Rhenish mission station founded in 1845 on the banks of the Sak River and named *Amandelboom* after a wild almond tree under which the first missionaries, J. H. Lutz and F. W. Reinecke, pitched their tent. About 600 people of diverse origin were living in the area at the time and the purpose of the mission was to exert some order over a rather shiftless community. Sheep farmers were attracted to the area in the 1860s and a village developed around the mission. Named in honour of Colonel Hampden Willis, Colonial Secretary of the Cape Colony in the 1880s, *Williston* became a municipality in 1881 and today has a total population of 5 015.

Accommodation
* Williston Hotel, 23 rooms, 19 with baths. R9,50 – R10,50 B/B. Phone 5.

Caravans and camping
* Williston Caravan Park (at swimming bath), 10 sites. R1,50 D.

From Williston, the tarmac road continues west across the Sak River, passing a resting place with shade and water 2 km from the town and continuing across a more fertile and better watered part of the Great Karoo than has been traversed so far. The Sak River and its tributaries (when they contain water) flow sluggishly over a plain where they are easily intercepted and diverted by means of weirs, dams, polders and other constructions. By this means, farmlands are irrigated and crops such as lucerne and wheat are cultivated. The shallow valley of the Sak River is famous for the *saaidam* system of irrigated farming which takes place in the riverbed. Grain is sewn in the shallow bed of the river as soon as the seasonal flow ends. Enough water remains in the soil to allow the crop to ripen without the necessity of rain or further irrigation.

At 90 km from Williston a tarmac turnoff stretches north to Brandvlei and Upington, while the tarmac main road continues west and 111 km from Williston, reaches . . .

# CALVINIA

Founded in 1845 and named after John Calvin, the religious leader, *Calvinia* is a pleasant, if isolated little town lying at the foot of the Hantam mountain range. Sheep are bred in the area on a very considerable scale and, after Harrismith in the Orange Free State, this is the second largest wool-producing district in Southern Africa.

Calvinia (with its population of 7 530) is the terminus of the branch railway from Hutchinson which reached the town on 13 August 1917. One of the steam locomotives working this line, a class 24, built in 1949 by the North British Locomotive Company, is now preserved in the garden of the local museum. Housed in the old synagogue building, the museum was opened in 1968 and contains an interesting and well-displayed collection of items of local history. There are photographs and mounted specimens of unusual sheep, period furniture, and a delightful example of a confidence trick: a four-legged ostrich chicken skilfully contrived by a local itinerant carpenter who charged people one penny to peep at his odd little pet. The museum is open weekdays from 08h00 to 13h00 and from 14h00 to 17h00; on Saturdays from 08h00 to 11h00, Sundays from 15h00 to 17h00.

A rockery in the centre of the town contains a good collection of aloes. Four kilometres out of the town, at the foot of the mountains, lies the Akkerendam Nature Reserve, 2 568 ha in extent and conserving the flora and fauna of the area. There are picnic places in the reserve which is open daily from sunrise to sunset.

Drought is the curse of the district, with water often scarce and inclined to smell. In compensation nature delights the area with some of the most blazing sunsets and dawns imaginable. The dolerite-topped Hantam Mountains also provide a fine sight.

## Accommodation
* Calvinia Hotel, 12 rooms, 3 with baths. R7,50 – R8,50 B/B. Phone 491.
* Commercial Hotel, 17 rooms, all with baths. R8,90 B/B. Phone 20.
* Hantam Hotel, 21 rooms, 14 with baths. R8 – R9 B/B. Phone 37.

## Caravans and camping
** ®Calvinia Caravan Park, 25 sites. R2,50 D.

From Calvinia the tarmac road continues westwards. After 2 km there is a gravel turnoff leading south for 215 km to Karoo Poort and from there for 45 km to Ceres. The main tarmac road proceeds west for a further 30,5 km, reaching an interesting wayside memorial commemorating the last battle of the Anglo-Boer War which was fought at this place. The memorial contains an actual rifle used in the conflict.

The tarmac road follows the fertile valley of *Oorlogskloof* (ravine of war), reaching 35 km from Calvinia, a turnoff leading for 117 km to Clanwilliam over Pakhuis Pass. Beyond the turnoff the tarmac road continues over a high open plateau, fairly well watered and grassy, with low shrubs. At 69 km from Calvinia the road enters the village of Nieuwoudtville, consisting of a cluster of houses, windpumps and trees sheltering in a hollow in the plain. From here a road leads north to the pretty 100-m-high Nieuwoudtville Falls in the Doring River where there is a picnic and camping ground. This road continues to Loeriesfontein (63 km), while the main tarmac road to the west continues from Nieuwoudtville for 8 km across fields of wheat, heather and proteas. Reaching the edge of the escarpment, the road commences a 6-km-long descent of the Vanrhyns Pass. On the way down the road passes a picnic site with water and a tremendous view west over the coastal terrace of Namaqualand. At the bottom of the pass, the tarmac road proceeds over this terrace, famous for its wild flowers in spring. At 52 km from Nieuwoudtville the road reaches Vanrhynsdorp (page 163).

## Accommodation
* Loeriesfontein Hotel, 10 rooms, 4 with baths. R8,75 – R9,30. Phone 1.
* Nieuwoudtville Hotel, 10 rooms, 3 with baths. R8,84 – R9,50 B/B. Phone 46.

At a point 21,5 km before the tarmac road from Victoria West and Loxton reaches Calvinia, a tarmac road branches northwards for 126 km up the valley of the Sak River to . . .

# BRANDVLEI

The rather bleak little town of *Brandvlei* (burned marsh) became a municipality on 1 October 1962. The Sak River normally reaches its end at the large dried-out marsh near the town and the last trickle of water not ambushed on its journey by weirs, dams and irrigation polders, is finally evaporated by the heat. However, this despairing surrender to the Karoo does not always occur without a final show of spirit. In 1961, for example, a flash flood inundated the town to such an extent that it was cut in two. Afterwards, Brandvlei took some time to join itself together again. A scorching sun in summer and icy winds in winter pose for the townspeople certain problems with regard to personal comfort.

## Accommodation
* Brandvlei Hotel, 17 rooms, 13 with baths. R10 – R10,50 B/B. Phone 2.

From Brandvlei roads branch to places such as Loeriesfontein (121 km) and Vanwyksvlei (149 km). *Verneuk* (deception) Pan, where Sir Malcolm Campbell made an unsuccessful attempt in his car Bluebird to break the world's landspeed record in 1929, may be reached from Brandvlei but the route is complicated and involves the opening of several gates. The surface of the pan is hard, dried out and completely flat, and is notable for its mirages.

From Brandvlei, the tarmac road to the north follows the long since dried-out *Grootvloer* (great floor), the bed of the Sak River when it flows to join the Hartbees. Sheep, jackals and bat-eared foxes (whose poor traffic sense sees many of them lying dead on the road) flourish happily in a flat area devoid of any features save occasional piles of dolerite rock fragments, remnants of hills which have vanished. After 136 km there is a turnoff east to Verneuk Pan (115 km). A further 2,5 km sees the road pass through a ridge of dolerite covered with kokerbooms. Ten kilometres further on, 148 km from Brandvlei, the tarmac road reaches . . .

# KENHARDT

In the wild frontier days of the Cape Colony, this area was a lair for rustlers and outlaws. On 2 September 1868 the government promulgated a Border Protection Act calculated to bring a degree of law and order to the unruly frontiermen. A magistrate, Maximilian Jackson, together with 50 policemen, was ordered to establish an outpost on the site of Kenhardt. The police party had to fight its way to the place, driving the rustlers away and arriving on 27 December 1868, to find two ramshackle shacks on the banks of the Hartbees River and the name Kenhardt, of unknown origin, lingering over this old resort of renegades, outlaws and adventurers. The policemen made a camp under a giant kameeldoring tree.

The town developed around the tree and became a municipality in 1909. Today, 2 832 people live there. Karakul and dorper sheep provide the district with a quieter but more prosperous living than the banditry of former years.

## Accommodation
* Kenhardt Hotel, 16 rooms, 2 with baths. R10 – R11 B/B. Phone 32.

From Kenhardt, roads radiate in various directions. The main tarmac road to the north continues for 70 km, reaching the south bank of the Orange River at Neilersdrift, crossing the river by means of a bridge to reach Keimoes, 3 km away, where it joins the main Upington-Kakamas road (40 km from Upington).

---

A particularly interesting gravel road follows the course of the Hartbees River (on whose banks Kenhardt stands), leading for 90 km to Kakamas and passing on the way great dunes of red sand and many wonderful kameeldoring trees with their boughs weighed down by nests of social weaver birds. Scattered about are strange granite domes, piles of rock and, in the spring, vast areas of wild flowers bloom, an astonishing sight in a landscape basically so harsh and wild. Gemstones are numerous.

----

# UPINGTON

The island-strewn section of the Orange River between Upington and the Augrabies Falls is particularly rich in memories. For many years the densely wooded islands served as strongholds for river pirates, bandits, rustlers, renegades, and desperadoes. The renowned Captain Afrikaner had his hideout close to the site of modern Upington and his lieutenant was a Polish forger named Stephanus who had escaped from Cape Town Gaol while awaiting execution.

Stuurman was another famous river bandit who headed a crowd of vagabonds. The activities of these adventurers of the Orange eventually provoked a substantial punitive expedition whereby they were rooted out and driven away into the northern wilderness.

One of the great centres for all these people of the river, was the ford known as *Olyvenhoutsdrift* (ford of the olive wood trees). In 1870 a Hottentot chieftain, Klaas Lukas, who lived at the ford, appealed for the establishment of a mission station in order to settle the area. The Reverend Christiaan Schröder was sent up from Cape Town and from Klaas Pofadder, who claimed ownership of the area, he secured permission to establish a mission. The foundations were laid in 1873 of the Olyvenhoutsdrift Mission, as it was called. By 1875 the mission was complete and in 1883 Schröder built a parsonage next to it. These buildings are still standing today. In 1884, when the river pirates were finally driven away, a town was founded at Olyvenhoutsdrift and named after Sir Thomas Upington, Attorney-General of the Cape, and this became the administrative centre for the area north of the Orange named *Gordonia* in honour of Sir Gordon Sprigg, Prime Minister of the Cape.

Upington grew rapidly for it is the centre of a region characterised by a variety of activities and considerable natural wealth. Pioneer settlers such as Johan (Japie) Lutz and the Reverend Christiaan Schröder dug the first irrigation canal in 1890. A pontoon ferry service was started at Olyvenhoutsdrift and the town became a busy commercial centre most pleasantly situated on a river which was ideal for boating, fishing and recreation, and never likely to run dry.

The second longest railway bridge in Southern Africa (1 067 m) was built over the river to carry the railway from De Aar on its way to Namibia and a branch line was built down the north bank of the Orange as far as Kakamas. Lucerne, sultanas, raisins, peaches, apricots, cotton, wheat, maize, peas, wine, karakul pelts, cattle, wool, mutton and dates are produced in the area. Salt is obtained from several pans while scheelite (or tungsten), copper and pegmatites are mined. Wood from the wild olive trees is worked into furniture and decorations.

The celebrated Scotty Smith (George St Leger Gordon Lennox), reputedly the Robin Hood of South Africa and a highwayman, horse thief, rustler and adventurer, settled and married in Upington after he had quietened down. He died of influenza on 26 October 1919 and is buried in the local cemetery.

A fine collection of mineral specimens from the district is exhibited in the library. Spitskop, 13 km north-west of the town, is maintained as a nature reserve, open daily from dawn to dusk. Nine kilometres of roads lead through the reserve and there is a telescope at the lookout on top of the hillock. Olyvenhout Island has been beautifully developed as a park with sports fields, a caravan park, bungalows, a swimming pool, restaurant, numerous flowers and trees, and an avenue of palms 1 041 m long. In Basson Park the Upington Model Railway Club, headed by its chairman and founder, Mr Richard Henry, has created a remarkable model railway with stations, shunting yards and bridges, open to the public on Saturday afternoons.

A bright, clean and cheerful place, Upington can be excessively hot, although evenings are invariably cool. The town boasts an international airport and a population of 45 100.

## Accommodation

★Gordonia Hotel, 43 rooms, 39 with baths. R8 – R12 room only. Phone 2156.
★★ Oranje Hotel, 100 rooms, all with baths. R9,50 room only. Phone 4177.
★ Upington Hotel, 39 rooms, 35 with baths. R8 – R9 room only. Phone 3031.

## Caravans and camping

★★ ®Olyvenhout Island, 100 sites. R4,50 D. 15 cottages, 2 rondawels, 5 rooms, R6,50 – R14 D.

The mud-rich water of the Orange, like that of the Nile, is the alchemist which brings life to the arid world on both sides of the river, and to a complex of islands. Originally mudbanks formed by the river, these islands were permanently established by a dense growth of vegetation and are now intensely farmed and connected to the banks by means of bridges. Situated on Olyvenhout Island is an agricultural research station and most of the various crops cultivated along the river grow adjoining each other.

Sultana and hanepoot grapes are grown along the river in about 10 000 ha of vineyards. From the grapes wine is made in Upington by the Orange River Wine Cellars Co-operative which commenced production in 1968. Cellars at Groblershoop, Grootdrink, Keimoes, Kakamas and Upington all contribute to a total of 50 000 tons of grapes which are crushed and the juice supplied to the central winemaking co-operative, the largest in Southern Africa. Visitors are welcome at the co-operative on Tuesdays and Thursdays at 09h00 and 15h00. Wine is sold direct to the public during normal business hours.

Sultanas and muscatel raisins are dried on a vast scale and exported to many parts of the world. The cement-floored open-air drying yards may be seen on nearly every farm. The S.A. Dried Fruit Co-operative is situated south of the river at Upington and is claimed to be the most modern in the world, with 150 tons of sultanas and raisins packed each day. The product is of superb quality and is absolutely hygienic. Visitors are welcome at the factory on Mondays and Wednesdays at 09h00 and 14h00 and on Fridays at 09h00. Dried fruit can be bought at the factory during normal shop hours.

Dates grow to perfection along the Orange but have hitherto not been extensively cultivated on account of the low price of imported dates from the Middle East. This is a pity for the local date is of magnificent quality, size and flavour and the hygienic conditions under which it is handled make it an infinitely superior product. Cultivation is being expanded, however, as a result of difficulties involved with supply from the Middle East.

Dates are not easy to produce, although the palms grow without trouble in perfect local conditions. They flourish on intense heat and plenty of water from irrigation. Humidity (and especially rain) during the ripening season, has a deleterious effect on the fruit, but fortunately, this is not much of a problem locally. The difficulty lies in pollination. Although there are male and female palms, the date is not effectively fertilised by natural means, even in their home in the Middle East. A vast amount of hard work is required, with pollen being collected from the male and either sprayed over the female flowers or, less effectively, the bunch of male flowers cut off and suspended next to the female bunch for the pollen to be spread by wind and insects. Hand pollination remains the ideal, but it is a tedious job to do in the heat, and uneconomical if the palm trees grow too tall. Bunches of ripening dates must also be protectively wrapped as a defence against birds and any rain or dew.

Research is being done on the best method of date cultivation for the Orange River area and other suitable parts of Southern Africa. There are many different species of dates, such as the Deglet Noor, Thoory, and Zahidi, each with its own flavour and character. The dates ripen in March and fresh fruit bought in the area is delicious.

Cotton is another crop very largely produced along the Orange River. A ginnery in Upington is open to visitors when it is in production towards the end of summer.

Lucerne, wheat, maize, peas, lentils, citrus and numerous other products are also grown in the fertile mud of the Orange.

---

From Upington roads follow both banks of the Orange. On the south bank (the left-hand side) a tarmac road leads to the rural centre of Louisvale (15 km from Upington) and then reaches a turn to the bridge linking Kanoneiland to the banks of the river (26,5 km from Upington).

## KANONEILAND

The largest island in the Orange, Kanoneiland is intensely cultivated. A tarmac road leading across the bridge from the south bank for 3 km reaches the small commercial and administrative centre. The name of the island originates from the period of the war against the river pirates. In 1879 a force of 80 policemen under Captain Dyason was sent up from Kenhardt to deal with troublesome elements on the Orange River. The river people followed their normal tactic of hiding in the dense foliage on the island. Kanoneiland is said to have been bombarded with a small cannon for several days, and so received its name. The river people eluded capture, however, and other punitive police and military forces had to be sent to the area until, in April and July 1879, final attacks led by Commandants McTaggart and Alexander Maclean of the Cape Mounted Rifles, finally cleared the river of unruly elements.

European settlers subsequently found the valley of the Orange River to be fertile and commenced farming there, although the area was almost overpoweringly hot. Settled in 1928, Kanoneiland really consisted of a number of islets separated by narrow channels of the river. A 2 533-ha extent of rich land was available for cultivation, with unlimited water for irrigation.

The first islanders secured the aid of Johann Lutz from Olyvenhoutsdrift and dug the first irrigation canal. Crops were planted and harvests were rich. A prosperous community developed on the island and in 1939 a board of local management was created. A church was built in 1951.

Periodic floods have inundated the island but being itself an offspring of the river, it is resilient, and the retreating waters have always left behind a richer layer of soil.

---

The tarmac road crosses Kanoneiland and bridges over the Orange to the north bank. There, 4,5 km from the turnoff to the island on the south bank, the road joins the main tarmac road from Upington down the north bank of the river. From here it is 26 km to Upington.

---

From the turnoff to Kanoneiland, the road down the south bank of the Orange converts to gravel and continues to Kakamas. The road along the north bank is completely tarmac and beyond the turnoff to Kanoneiland it continues for 14 km, reaching, 40 km from Upington . . .

## KEIMOES

Klaas Lucas one of the leaders of the river people, had established a village named *Keimoes* (mouse nest) on account of the colonies of mice found living there in twig nests. The modern town, with a population of 14 390 and a municipality since 1949, is a farming centre of considerable importance. A restored waterwheel stands next to the main street. Overlooking the town is Tierberg, the highest point in the area which is preserved as a nature reserve. A road leads for 4 km from the town centre to a lookout on top of the hill from where a tremendous view of the irrigated areas of the Orange is revealed. Flowering aloes are spectacular during winter and spring sees many species of succulents in full flower.

## Accommodation
★ Keimoes Hotel, 26 rooms, 18 with baths. R9,50 – R10 B/B. Phone 29.

## Caravans and camping
★ Keimoes Caravan Park, 20 sites. R2 D.

From Keimoes, the tarmac road continues down the north bank of the Orange River, passing a range of hills composed of basement complex rocks and granite pegmatites aged well over 2 000 million years (the Kheis System). The green, irrigated fields of the river valley appear very youthful compared to these weatherbeaten ancients. Many gemstones are found in this area, notably rose quartz, amethyst, amazonite, garnet, beryl, tourmaline, felspar, river stones, agate, onyx, jasper and blue, green and brown tiger eye.

There are turnoffs north to Lutzputs and thence to the Kalahari National Park 2 km from Keimoes and again at 38 km just before the tarmac road crosses the Orange and, 40,5 km from Keimoes, reaches . . .

# KAKAMAS

Hottentot pastoralists gave *Kakamas* (poor pasturage) its name. They did not like the area very much but, in 1895, when a movement began in Cape Town for the settlement of the poor on land, the Reverend Christiaan Schröder remembered his abandoned mission station on the banks of the Orange, and his impression that the area was ideal for irrigation and intensive farming. At a conference in Worcester on 5 March 1895 he recommended the valley of the Orange River as a suitable site for the projected settlement. Under the auspices of the Dutch Reformed Church, and with the Reverend Christiaan Schröder in charge, this settlement was established in 1898.

The first irrigation canal at Kakamas was opened on 4 July 1898. By 1900 there were 95 settlers in the area each receiving £12 in capital from the church and being left on their own to clear bush, level dunes, lead irrigation water and turn the river valley into a giant garden.

The general intention was to farm fruit, with peaches growing very well. Then, in 1928, the Reverend H. P. van der Merwe sent up a few thousand sultana vines from Robertson. These took to local conditions with such enthusiasm that the sultana became the staple crop for the Orange River Valley farmers, and today the area is the principal producer of sultanas in Southern Africa. The cement-floored sultana and muscatel raisin drying yards and the overshot waterwheels used in lifting irrigation water from the canals became a characteristic sight of the Kakamas area.

As far as peaches are concerned, it is interesting to know that this area produced the mutation known as the *Kakamas Peach,* the standard canning peach of South Africa. The first peach grown in South Africa by Jan van Riebeeck was known as the *St Helena* variety for he imported the tree from St Helena island where the Portuguese had planted them. A variety known as the *Apricot Peach,* from the colour of its flesh, and a white-fleshed variety, the *Parvie,* flourished later.

The St Helena peach took to South African conditions so well (especially on the highveld) that today it grows wild in many areas such as Lesotho and is popularly known as the

Transvaal yellow peach. The Kakamas Peach is a mutation of this common yellow peach. Prior to its discovery, no satisfactory canning peach had been grown in South Africa. A great deal of experimental work was carried out to find or breed such a variety. Professor Reinecke of the Elsenburg Agricultural College in Stellenbosch, in particular busied himself in experimenting with peach varieties collected from many parts of the world.

One of Reinecke's students, Mr A. D. Collins, became a teacher of agriculture at Kakamas where he furthered the professor's interest in peach varieties. In 1933 he forwarded to Reinecke a batch of seedlings from the Kakamas area, one of which showed immediate promise. Collins forwarded propagation material from the parent tree during the same year. This was the beginning of the Kakamas Peach with its characteristics of vigorous growth, prolific cropping, large fruit of good yellow colour, perfect shape for canning, finely textured flesh, delectable flavour, and retaining its firm shape throughout the canning process. The South African canning industry developed around this peach, with 75 per cent of all canning peaches deriving from offspring of the one original tree found by chance. The first trees, sold to the public by nurserymen in 1938, came into bearing in 1943 and in their first year increased the total volume of South African canning by two and a half fold.

What had started as a settlement of economically distressed people, flourished on irrigation and grew into a prosperous community. In 1926 a branch railway was opened to Kakamas from Upington. In 1954 the town received a village management board and on 1 December 1964 it became a municipality. The number of inhabitants has now reached 4 050.

## Accommodation
★ Waterwiel Hotel, 18 rooms, all with baths. R10,50 B/B. Phone 250.

## Caravans and camping
★ Kakamas Caravan Park, 15 sites. R2 D.

From Kakamas the tarmac road continues down the south bank of the river. After 10 km a division is reached. The right-hand branch continues along the river to the Augrabies Falls while the left-hand division leads to Pofadder and Springbok.

The turn to Augrabies continues as a tarmac road passing the rural centres of Marchand (14 km from Kakamas) and Augrabies (24 km). The Augrabies Falls Hotel is reached a further 9 km along the road and the falls themselves, 39 km from Kakamas.

## Accommodation
★ Augrabies Falls Hotel, 11 rooms, 3 with baths. R9,50 – R10,50 B/B. Phone Augrabies 18.

# AUGRABIES FALLS NATIONAL PARK

Derived from the Hottentot *!oukurubes* (the noise-making place), the name *Augrabies* describes the gigantic gorge into which the Orange River falls headlong with a roaring rumble and a rising cloud of spray which can, during a flood season, be heard and seen from a considerable distance away.

The gorge of the waterfall is considered by geologists to be the finest example in the world of weathering on granite by water action. Over a passage of time, the Orange River has cut a knife-edged wound through this prodigious barrier of rock. In a succession of preliminary cascades and falls, the river drops about 100 m, shouldering its way through a narrow gap to hurtle down yet another 100 m in a combined cascade and final sheer fall of 56 m. At the bottom lies a deep pool in which there is reputed to be in residence a mighty water serpent. In addition, a fortune in diamonds is thought to have been washed down the river over the ages, and to lie trapped in this great hole. All that is certain is that the hole and the gorge provide a home for many giant mud barbel *(Clarias gariepinus),* a fish reaching a length of 2 m.

For 9 km the river boils and rushes through the granite gorge, dropping over 300 m in a series of rapids and minor falls. The average depth of the gorge is 240 m. The main gorge is joined by several tributary gorges and the entire formation presents a scene of savage power and primeval force in a setting of complete wilderness. Strange noises, echoes, and the ceaseless, darting flight of swifts who especially seem to like the gorge, add to the atmosphere.

The flow of water over Augrabies varies very considerably. In the midst of a dry winter season, the waterfall can dwindle to an insignificant stream, but at the peak of a wet summer in the main watershed of the river (Lesotho and the highveld), the spectacle can be stupendous. The river overwhelms the entire upper portion of the gorge, with 19 great waterfalls hurtling into the gorge and creating an infernal combination of spray, water and menacing sound.

Augrabies is justly regarded as one of the six great waterfalls of the world occurring in a first-class river. Each of the world's great waterfalls has its own special character: the wonderful spectacle of Victoria Falls, the queen of them all, has a feminine beauty and the intensely green surroundings soften the nature of the fall; Augrabies is essentially masculine – ruthless and brutal in a harsh and fearsomely arid landscape. During peak flood about 400 million litres of water race over Augrabies every minute. The peak flow of Victoria Falls is about 750 million litres of water a minute but Augrabies is concentrated into the head of its narrow gorge while Victoria Falls is spread out over the whole 2 000-m length of the long trough into which the Zambezi tumbles.

In former times the area of the waterfall was the resort of Bushmen and Hottentots who fed on fish and the several edible roots, wild fruits, beans and the berries of the wild raisin trees *(Rhus viminalis* and *Zizyphus mucronata)* which flourish there. Klaas Pofadder was the last of the Hottentot leaders to rule in the area, with his base on the island named after him. The first known European to see the falls was a Swedish mercenary soldier, Hendrik Wikar, who had deserted his post in Cape Town as a result of debt in 1775 and wandered north to the Orange River, reaching Augrabies in October 1778.

In 1967 the Augrabies Falls National Park, centred on Klaas Island, was opened, conserving as a wilderness area 5 403 ha of the south bank of the river. The waterfall and gorge is now accessible at all seasons of the year, whereas in former years it was impossible to reach the vicinity of the waterfall during flood times for the river spread out above and around the gorge, completely overwhelming all approaches. Bridges and causeways have now been built, as well as a series of protected outlooks on the very edge of the gorge which allow the visitor to view in safety the waterfall in full flood – one of the world's great spectacles.

The National Parks Board has its office, restaurant and shop on Klaas Island, with a museum displaying the rocks, gemstones, fauna and flora of the area. The walls of this complex of buildings contain a great variety of decorative and semi-precious stones, all found locally. Over 100 species of aloes are grown in the garden next to the central building. Trees such as the karee, wild olive, Cape willow, numerous succulents, kokerbooms, and species of acacia flourish in the area, including the beautiful *Schotia brachypetala* with its flame-red flowers.

The population of wild animals is increasing under protection. Monkeys, baboons, klipspringers, steenbok, various wild cats and other creatures may be seen. Bird life is varied and numerous and lizards are plentiful.

A road, 12 km long, has been made to reach the western portion of the park at Fountain. From this road branches lead to various outlooks over the gorge and other places of interest. A complete exploration of these roads and a return journey to the park headquarters comprises a total of 42 km. A three-day hiking trail known as the Klipspringer Trail may be followed, with overnight accommodation provided by two huts.

The north bank of the Orange, from where the best views of the waterfall may be seen, consists of 70 000 ha of wilderness area, yet to be opened. A suspension bridge above the waterfall is being built to reach this area. A visit to this first-class national park is highly recommended. Summer is the best season even though the weather can be stiflingly hot.

## Caravans and camping
★ ®50 sites, R2,60 D. 12 chalets, R12,50 D.

From the turnoff to Augrabies, 10 km west of Kakamas, the main tarmac road continues to the west over the arid plains of Bushmanland. In spring wild flowers flourish in great profusion while red sand dunes and curious piles of dolerite fragments provide variety to an otherwise flat landscape. The road passes small rural centres such as Bladgrond (67 km from Kakamas) and at 87 km a turnoff stretches north for 51 km to *Onseepkans* (the drinking place of wild animals) a village on the banks of the Orange which was laid out in 1916 as a centre for the cultivation under irrigation of citrus, lucerne, beans and other crops. With a summer temperature of about 50°C, this is a very sunbaked little place.

The main tarmac road continues for a further 48 km and, 135 km from Kakamas, reaches . . .

# POFADDER

The Hottentot chieftain, Klaas Pofadder, once had his principal centre at the springs on the site of the present town. In 1875 the Reverend Christiaan Schröder established a mission there and named the place after the chief. Pofadder himself came to grief after raiding livestock from farmers in the Springbok area. He was pursued and shot at the springs which have since borne his name.

In 1918 a town at first named Theronsville was laid out at these springs. The old name of *Pofadder* (puffadder) however, persisted and eventually became generally accepted and has given the little town the distinction of an unusual place name. In 1937 the first village management board was elected and the population now numbers 2 400.

With a rainfall seldom exceeding 50 mm a year, Pofadder is a centre for karakul and other sheep but periodic droughts in an already arid environment cause grievous damage. In 1959 the entire livestock population had to be transported by the army to better grazing until rains came to revive a remarkably resilient vegetation.

## Accommodation
★ Pofadder Hotel, 20 rooms, 7 with baths. R9,50 – R10,50 B/B. Phone 43.

## Caravans and camping
★ Municipal caravan park, 8 sites. R2 D.

From Pofadder the road leads north-westwards for 30 km to the interesting and atmospheric mission station of . . .

# PELLA

Originally founded in 1814 by the London Missionary Society as a sanctuary for Hottentots driven out of the Warmbad area of Namibia by various disturbances, the mission was named after the ancient town in Macedonia which became a refuge for persecuted Christians.

In 1872 drought induced the London Missionary Society to abandon Pella but it was reopened in 1878 and developed by the Roman Catholics into the present substantial settlement. Their pioneer missionary, Father Simon, who became the first Bishop of Namaqualand, and his associate, Father Wolf, were responsible for most of the hard work involved in establishing the station. Today they are buried side by side in the pretty little church which they built.

The situation of Pella is striking and it is particularly strange to arrive there in the evening: the date palms, the sharply serrated mountains, the dry desert air, the pervading incense-like odour (in July and August) of the wild flowers and the aromatic shrubs used for fuel by the residents, all combine to conjure up an image of Arabia. There is no other place in Southern Africa quite like this.

Pella produces dates of a very special flavour which ripen in February and March and are in considerable demand. There is also extensive activity involved in the mining of the anhydrous silicate of aluminium known as *Sillimanite,* after the American chemist, Benjamin Silliman. The mineral is exported for use in the manufacture of porcelain, enamelware and many other items used by man.

During the summer months Pella experiences temperatures of 50°C. The local inhabitants find some relief by following a track through a spectacular passage in the hills to the Orange River, where, in a grove of the salty-tasting *dubieka* trees, is situated a picnic and swimming place.

The area around Pella is a treasure house of gemstones: green malachite-stained rocks, red oxides of iron, white and rose-coloured quartz, silvery micaschists and enough other lovely things with which to build a veritable fairy city in this hot but sweet-smelling wilderness.

---

From Pofadder, the main road continues westwards, passing the Dutch Reformed Church mission of Namies after 29 km. At 68 km from Pofadder, the road reaches *Aggeneys* (place of water), where considerable mining developments concerning lead, silver, zinc and copper are taking place at Black Mountain Mine, close to what was for a long time simply a cluster of farmhouse, post office and store standing at a turnoff of a road leading for 40 km to Pella.

From Aggeneys the main road swings south-westwards, passing through a ridge of rocky hills and then crossing an immense plain covered in low scrub and broken by a few isolated and lonely-looking hills scattered around the horizon. Sheep and karakul farmers find a living in this wilderness, but drought is a curse and drinking water very precious. After 119 km the road reaches Springbok and the main highway of Namaqualand.

---

# GORDONIA

Gordonia is the area north of the Orange River which borders on the Kalahari. Hot and flat, it is nevertheless full of interesting and unusual features – great sand dunes, salt pans, lovely farms, odd little wayside trading posts, elegantly shaped kameeldoring trees, nests of the social weaver birds, and, in the north, the Kalahari National Park.

From Upington, the principal centre of Gordonia, roads radiate to all parts of the region and with their quality considerably improved through modern construction, it is possible to explore the area without the shattering experience of corrugations and potholes which made this area notorious to motorists only a few years ago.

Beyond Upington, the main tarmac road to Namibia leaves the town and stretches to the north-west over a vast plain. After 6,5 km a turnoff north to the Spitskop Nature Reserve is reached and, after 15 km, a turn north to a cluster of salt pans such as Grootwitpan and Norokel which provide visitors with the unusual spectacle of salt being gathered from the dried-out floors.

234

At 61 km from Upington there is a crossroads. The main road continues west for a further 71 km, reaching the border of Namibia at Nakop. To the south a road branches off for 11 km to the railway station of Lutzputs, from where there are roads to Keimoes (45 km) and to Kakamas (52 km). To the north, a road leads to the Kalahari National Park. This road is gravel but is now maintained in good condition after years of being famous for having some of the worst corrugations in Africa.

At 23 km from the crossroads, this road is joined by the road from Upington which serves the salt pans already mentioned. The gravel road continues northwards, ascending to a higher plateau and passing farms such as *Swartmodder* (32 km) and *Bokhare* (47 km).

A further 17 km brings the road to a turnoff to Namibia and 5 km beyond this point (69 km from the crossroads on the main tarmac road) stands a notable tree. In a landscape devoid of trees this solitary roadside specimen is worth remembering. Road engineers have considerately placed seats and a table beneath its shady boughs. People travelling with a dog should draw the attention of their pet to this tree as there is no further convenience for some distance.

The road proceeds over the seemingly boundless plains, reaching after 5 km, the Albion Pan. Thirty-five kilometres beyond the tree (104 km from the crossroads) the road passes the small centre known as *Noenieput* from a *noenie* tree which grew there at an old drinking well dug by the Bushmen. A school with a hostel provides for the education of the children from many isolated farms.

Beyond Noenieput the road passes a substantial pan at Abiquasputs. A turnoff leads to the Dutch Reformed Church mission of Rietfontein (127 km from the crossroads) and the road to the Kalahari National Park swings to the north-east. At 157 km the road passes Koopan-suid, with its store and petrol pump. A further 24 km brings the road to the turnoff to . . .

## LOCH MAREE

This salt pan lies 5 km west of the main road. The track leading to it is poor and permission must be obtained from Mr C. J. Donald whose farmhouse stands at the turnoff. The pan is an extraordinary sight and a geological marvel. It is 24 km in circumference and covered with a layer of salt 1 m thick, the equivalent of 9 million tons, with concentrated brine below the surface. The salt is particularly pure. The shimmering white surface of the pan is surrounded by red sand dunes. With deep blue skies and, around February, masses of yellow-coloured botterblommetjie flowers, the spectacle is unforgettable. When it rains, water collects in the pan but there is seldom enough to cover more than a section of the dry floor. The shallow water is blown about by the prevailing winds, sometimes covering one portion of the pan and then, within a few hours, blown over another portion by a change of wind. The pan is occasionally worked for salt but the bad road leading to it has impeded development.

---

From Loch Maree the main road continues for a further 9 km, reaching a turnoff to the Rietfontein mission station (68 km away) and Namibia. The main road continues north-eastwards. After a further 13 km (204 km from the crossroads) the road passes the turnoff to Lentlands (or Leitlands) Pan, an old retreat for Scotty Smith, the celebrated horse thief and rustler. The name of a nearby farm, *Scotty's Fort,* provides yet another reminder of the escapades of this irrepressible character. He made this area his home in the 1890s, remaining there for several years. The book *Scotty Smith* by F. C. Metrowich gives a detailed account of his life.

The countryside is now amply covered with trees, many of them acacias, laden with the cumbersome community nests of the social weaver birds *(Philetairus socius).* These little birds select a suitable tree and join forces in building a roof of twigs somewhere in the

*Overleaf: In a chaos of spray and sound, the Orange River in flood storms its way down the great gorge of Augrabies.*

branches where there is shade and security. Under this roof individual pairs build their nests in a dense 'condominium' which can remain in use for generations of birds. A few predatory snakes also take up residence, living on the eggs and chickens.

At 211 km from the crossroads, the road reaches a small garage at a division, where the east turn leads to Askham and Vanzylsrus and the main road continues north. After a further 3 km there is a turn to Molopa and Grenspan. The road now reaches the border of Botswana and follows the dry bed of the Nossob River, in the middle of which is situated the border between South Africa and Botswana.

At 270 km from the crossroads on the Upington-Namibia main tarmac road, the road enters the . . .

## KALAHARI GEMSBOK NATIONAL PARK

This is a unique national park and one of the most fascinating wilderness areas in the world. Although the park is bisected by the Botswana-South Africa border, there is no boundary fence and the wild animals have complete freedom of movement in a well-balanced ecological area. The Botswana side of the park (1 087 000 ha in extent) is a complete wilderness unserviced by roads or public access. The area consists of aeolian sand covered in shrubs and a few acacia trees. Little surface water is present. However, when it rains during summer (usually in the form of thunderstorms), water collects in shallow pans. The wild animals which frequent the area, together with a few wandering groups of Bushmen, have adapted themselves to these arid conditions and regard the area as a happy home well free of interference from the outside world, other than the activities of an occasional poacher.

The western border of the Botswana section of the reserve runs down the centre of the bed of the *Nossob* (big water) River. The floor of this shallow river valley is firm and well covered with trees and grass, with ample water below the surface. A considerable concentration of wild animals live in the valley, particularly springbok, gemsbok, hartebeest and wildebeest. Predators such as lion and cheetah prey on the game while numerous scavengers such as brown and spotted hyenas and jackals keep the area clear of any carcasses.

The border line, happily, is marked simply by a line of small concrete beacons, allowing the wild animals complete freedom of movement. The South African side of the park consists of 970 000 ha of country stretching westwards like a sea of sand to the border of Namibia. Through this area occasionally flows another river, the Auob, in a valley narrower than that of the Nossob but grassy and tree-covered. The floor of this river valley is also firm with water occurring beneath the surface and an occasional surface flow during a very wet season. Between the two rivers (which join at the southern end of the park) lies an area of dunes and scrub-covered sand scattered with several pans and watering places.

The area was originally surveyed into farms for European settlement and then used for the settlement of Coloured farmers, the ruins of whose houses may still be seen along the valley of the Auob. The heat, remoteness and unsuitability of the area for human industry became apparent and in 1931 the Kalahari Gemsbok Park was proclaimed. Today, the combined reserves are a credit to Botswana and South Africa, a delight to tourists, a field of study for scientists and a joy to conservationists.

The twin parks are managed from the South African side, with headquarters at *Twee Rivieren* (two rivers) at the southern entrance. Apart from the residences of the warden and his staff, there is also a shop and comfortable accommodation for tourists. There is no restaurant but kitchen facilities and refrigerators are available.

From Twee Rivieren a road follows the valley of the Nossob for 3,5 km to its junction with the Auob. There the road divides, one branch leading north-westwards up the valley of the Auob for 112 km to the camp, shop and ranger post of *Mata-Mata* (the very nice place). This camp lies on the border of Namibia and the road continues into that territory.

The drive up the Auob is delightful, especially for the lover of wildlife, trees and clouds (in the summer months). The trees, especially the kameeldorings, are superbly graceful and are ideally suited to a desert world of glaring, relentless sunshine, generously providing dense, cool shade pervaded by a pleasant aroma issuing from the tree. The wood provides excellent fuel for cooking fires, adding a piquant flavour to items such as meat, tea, bread, flapjacks and coffee.

A second road leads up the valley of the Nossob, adjoining and occasionally crossing the Botswana border. From the junction with the road up the Auob, this route extends for 102 km, reaching a turnoff known as the Dune Road, which traverses the sand country between the Nossob and the Auob. The 52-km journey provides travellers with the sensation of being on a ship negotiating a grassy sea of sand. Few features may be seen save occasional wind-pumps, and pans and trees are sparse. Gemsbok, hartebeest, steenbok and ostriches are particularly fond of the area. At the end of its run this road reaches the Auob Valley, joining the road at a point almost midway between Mata-Mata Camp and the junction of the Auob and Nossob valleys.

From the turnoff to the Dune Road, the road up the Nossob Valley continues for 53 km and then reaches Nossob Camp where there is a ranger post, shop and accommodation. From here the road continues for 134 km up the valley to Union End, the extreme northern tip of the park, where the road reaches a dead end. There is a resting place but no accommodation.

The Nossob Valley is not as green as the Auob but wild animals are plentiful, especially hartebeest and gemsbok. Springbok occur in very large numbers all over the park and their sprightly movements and 'pronking' (displaying) provide amusement for visitors. Wildebeest, eland and kudu are well represented. The presence of predators is unpredictable but they are always somewhere in the area. About 170 species of birds have been recorded in the park.

Late summer is the best time to visit the park, as winter is too dry. The summers are hot but the evenings cool and afternoon thunderstorms continually refresh the area. Cloud formations and sunsets are spectacular. Vegetation is at its best in summer and the wild animals concentrate in the river valley to enjoy the grass and water.

The camps are unsophisticated, clean and pleasant, and the staff courteous. There is little evidence of bureaucratic authority and the natural ecological balance of the park allows for a management devoid of culling operations, and curio and byproduct manufacture from the carcasses of its wild animal inhabitants – the usual indications whereby man considers himself a better manager of the wilderness than God.

The park is open daily from dawn to dusk, with the hours varying slightly between summer and winter.

### Accommodation

★★ ®All three camps: caravans and camping, R2,60 D. Cottages, rondawels and rooms, R5,75 – R16,15 D.

---

On the road from the south (59 km from Twee Rivieren) there is a junction with a gravel road branching east. This road, maintained in good condition, leads through rural centres such as Witdraai (where the old camel patrol of the police had their headquarters), Askham, Cramond, Ontmoeting and Vanzylsrus (159 km), which comprises a cluster of stores, houses and a hotel.

### Accommodation

★ Gemsbok Hotel, 11 rooms, 3 with baths. R8,50 – R9 B/B. Phone 9902.

From Vanzylsrus the main road veers south-eastwards and after 105 km reaches the mining centre and railway terminus of Hotazel. From there a tarmac road leads for 61 km to Kuruman, a route which is followed by travellers from the Transvaal visiting the Kalahari National Park.

From Hotazel, a gravel road stretches southwards alongside the railway for 59 km to Dibeng, and thence on a tarmac road for 30 km to Sishen with its huge iron mine. From Sishen, tarmac roads lead to Kuruman (66 km), Kimberley (263 km) and to Upington (207 km). This last road provides an interesting return journey to Upington for travellers interested in completing a grand tour from that riverside town to the Kalahari National Park and back through the rugged Kalahari sand country. Along the road, 37 km west of Sishen, is the small but enterprising town of . . .

## OLIFANTSHOEK

Founded in 1897, *Olifantshoek* is said to have taken its name from the tusk of an elephant which was used as payment for the ground on which the town stands. With a population of 3 800, the town is a ranching centre supplied with water from a nearby dam. Mining for iron is carried out in the vicinity.

### Accommodation
★ Kalahari Hotel, 15 rooms, all with baths. R10 B/B. Phone 7.

### Caravans and camping
★ ®Municipal caravan park, 25 sites. R2,50 D.

------

From Upington, the main tarmac road to the south bridges over the Orange and then follows the left bank of the river, passing many interesting scenes of agricultural activity. After 114 km the road reaches . . .

## GROBLERSHOOP

Founded in 1936 and named after Piet Grobler, the Minister of Agriculture, this is a farming and administrative centre for the Orange River Valley south of Upington. The completion in 1931 of the Buchuberg (or Boegoeberg) Dam in the Orange close to the site of the town made available a vast amount of water for the irrigation of the entire valley of the lower Orange and Groblershoop has since become a busy centre of agricultural industry. The dam is used for recreation such as fishing and camping. It is reached by a tarmac road to Brandboom followed by a short gravel road. Red sand dunes and kokerbooms decorate the surroundings.

### Accommodation
★ Grootrivier Hotel, 9 rooms, 5 with baths. R8 – R9 B/B. Phone 14.

One kilometre before the road from Upington reaches Groblershoop, a tarmac turnoff leads eastwards across the Orange for 135 km to Griquatown and thence to Kimberley. At 10,5 km along this road a gravel turnoff north to Witsand is reached. This road serves many farms, amongst them, after 66 km, the farm *Doornaar,* owned by Mr P. M. Maritz, who maintains there the Witsand Holiday Resort with bungalows and camping ground for people wishing to visit . . .

# THE ROARING SANDS

Consisting of a white dune 'island' which contrasts with a surrounding sea of red Kalahari sand, the roaring sands or *witsand* (white sands) extend in the form of a tongue about 9 km long and 2 km wide. Whereas the dry surrounding red sands are coloured by the presence of iron oxide, the white dunes are peculiar for the amount of water contained in them.

The origin of these isolated white dunes is obscure. It is probable that they originally consisted of normal windblown Kalahari red sand which accumulated over a supply of water. The water, reaching the surface under pressure, removed the iron oxide and with it the red colour. This chance freedom from a coating of foreign matter, combined with the dry atmosphere and the smoothness and uniform size of the individual sand grains as a result of ceaseless wear from wind movement, provides suitable conditions for the roaring effect.

The smooth surface of the sand grains allows for considerable contact if the sand is disturbed. Friction results and sets up vibrations which produce the strange sound. The roaring issues from completely dry sand lying on the surface. If it rains the sand is dampened and the sound vanishes until dry weather returns. Extreme cold also seems to mute the sands. It is therefore useless visiting the area in a wet season. The locals relate very conflicting stories about the sands: some say that they will only roar during months which contain an 'R' in their names. The truth is that the sands know no calendar – they roar when they are dry and conditions are suitable. The driest months are in winter, from May to October. The summer months are very hot, with frequent thunderstorms, which subdue the roaring for several days.

The southerly face of the dunes is the best place to hear the roaring, which is distinct when the sands are violently agitated and subsides to a hum when poured or gently moved. A person sliding down the dune can be heard 100 m away. Even the act of moving a finger backwards and forwards through the sand produces a roar, which will occur day or night. A strong dry wind blowing in the dunes at night produces an eerie rumbling.

The dunes are also notable for the occurrence of fulgurites caused by flashes of lightning which strike and fuse the sand. The fulgurites consist of thread- or tube-like strings of fused sand glazed and mirrored in parts, and up to 2 m long. Short, fragmented fulgurites are numerous and the local people collect and sell them as souvenirs to visitors. The white sands are very photogenic, especially towards sunset.

The road to the white sands is in reasonable condition when dry but should be negotiated in daylight. There are several signposted turns which can easily be missed at night.

### Accommodation
★ Witsand Holiday Resort, 20 caravan sites. 10 bungalows and rooms. R3 D.

---

From Groblershoop, the main tarmac road continues south, leaving the valley of the Orange and crossing arid country. After 56 km the road reaches a crossroads. To the east, 3 km away, lies the railway station of *Draghoender* (dragoons), where soldiers of that regiment were reputedly stationed during the Anglo-Boer War. To the west of the crossroads lies . . .

# MARYDALE

Established in 1902 by the Dutch Reformed Church, *Marydale* was named after the wife of Mr G. P. Snyman who owned the farm *Kalkput* on which the town was laid out. The population has now reached 2 666. Sheep and cattle are farmed in the area and considerable mining activity mainly for asbestos, is carried out in the vicinity. The Koegas Asbestos Mine, 24 km to the east, is the largest producer in the world of blue asbestos. The mine centre at Westerberg is of substantial size and a real oasis in the wilderness famous for its gardens producing oranges, fruit and vegetables.

## Accommodation
* Marydale Hotel, 10 rooms, 3 with baths. R8,50 – R9 B/B. Phone 45.

From Marydale, the tarmac road continues in a south-easterly direction through arid but asbestos-rich country, where the mining activity is extensive. After 73 km the road passes through the Doringberg range of hills and reaches . . .

# PRIESKA

Lying on the south bank of the Orange River, the town takes its name from an ancient fording place known to the Hottentots as *Prieskab* (place of the lost goat). Many early European travellers used this ford on their way to the north and it became a well-known staging post. A trading station and mission were established there and the town developed around these places. The population now numbers 9 192.

Prieska is the centre for sheep farming while irrigated farmlands in the valley of the Orange produce lucerne, vegetables, maize and fruit. Considerable mining activity is carried out. The Prieska Copper Mine situated at Copperton (64 km from Prieska) produces copper and zinc. Salt pans yield salt and Prieska is the principal centre for the production of tiger eye gemstones.

Overlooking Prieska is a hill on the summit of which stands a small fort built by the British during the Anglo-Boer War. Garrisoning the fort must have been akin to being stationed in an oven! The hill is a nature reserve where a good collection of aloes and other flowering plants flourish. Another fine collection of aloes grows in the garden named after Ria Huysamen, a local woman who collected them. Four kilometres from the town centre is a riverside resort known as Die Bos, run by the municipality. The Orange River here is fine for swimming with many trees whose deep, cool shade is a precious asset in an area extremely hot in summer.

In the municipal offices is a collection of gemstones and mineral specimens from the district.

## Accommodation
* Border Hotel, 19 rooms, 9 with baths. R8,80 – R9,60 B/B. Phone 133.
* Prieska Hotel, 22 rooms, 12 with baths. R8,80 – R9,60 B/B. Phone 94.

## Caravans and camping
* Municipal caravan park, 25 sites. R2,60 D.
* Die Bos Resort, 6 rondawels, R4 – R8 D.

From Prieska the tarmac road continues south-eastwards over arid country. After 129 km the road joins the main road, the 'Diamond Way', linking Cape Town to Kimberley (page 198). The junction point is 3 km north of Britstown. Closer to Britstown, the route continues in company with the railway for a further 52 km to the east and then reaches the important junction of De Aar where the railway from Upington and Namibia joins the rail network of South Africa.

# DE AAR

This junction, the name of which means 'the artery', is the second most important railway junction (after Germiston) in Southern Africa. When the railway was built from Cape Town to Kimberley the administration purchased a large portion of the farm *De Aar* and established there a marshalling yard and junction. Hot in summer, bleakly cold in winter, De Aar had an evil reputation among railwaymen and passengers alike. To the railwaymen it was a deadly dull place in which to live, while to passengers it was notorious for such inordinate delays that parliamentary pressure eventually had to be invoked in order to induce trains to move more quickly.

It was originally planned to name the place *Brounger Junction* after the general manager of the railways but this name did not survive. The farm name *De Aar* refers to underground water supplies, said to occur in 'arteries'. At first simply comprising a couple of gangers' cottages and a ramshackle wood and iron hotel, De Aar has now grown into a substantial, well planned modern town, with parks, gardens and amenities. The lives of the 21 384 people living there will always be dominated by the comings and goings of innumerable trains.

### Accommodation
★De Aar Hotel, 40 rooms, 24 with baths. R8,60 – R9,18 B/B. Phone 2182.
★ Walter Hotel, 30 rooms, 11 with baths. R8,30 – R8,80 B/B. Phone 2541.

### Caravans and camping
★ Van der Merwe Park, 13 sites. R2 D.

## Chapter Thirteen

# LITTLE KAROO

The Little Karoo is unique. There is nothing quite like it anywhere else on earth. It is a world all of its own; the land of ostriches and majestic sandstone mountains, cleft by spectacularly beautiful ravines, with a vast agricultural richness concealed behind a costume of apparent aridity. Wild flowers in glorious profusion and of vivid colour – especially the mesembryanthemums – must be seen to be believed.

For the tourist, the Little Karoo is a compact, accessible concentration of surprises. To the eye it consists of a plain, 100 km wide and 300 km long, lying between the Swartberg range to the north and the Langeberg and Outeniqua ranges to the south. The Hottentots called this area *Kango* (a plain between mountains). The first Europeans to explore it called it *Gannaland,* after the vast number of plants of the *Salsola* family which grow there and are known to the Hottentots as *ganna.* These plants are a favourite food of eland, also known to the Hottentots as *ganna.*

The name 'Little Karoo' has been applied to the original plain between the mountains and the more rugged area to the west, beyond the course of the Gamka River, which is also hemmed in north and south by the Swartberg and Langeberg mountains.

Geologically speaking, the Little Karoo is a minor basin contained in the folded mountain belt of the Southern Cape. Red-orange coloured sandstone and mudstone were laid down between 250 and 350 million years ago as sediments beneath water and then warped and tilted by powerful pressures as they dried in more recent times. This sand- and mudstone provide the materials for this extraordinary landscape whose colours (especially in the mountain passes) cause the traveller to think of the smouldering beauty of a dying fire.

Since the mountain tops sweep the sky clear of clouds, rainfall in the Little Karoo is slight (about 150 mm a year). But from the mountains, especially the Swartberg, flow perennial streams which provide the key to man's exploitation of the fertile soil, and which explain the appearance of vast flocks of ostriches roaming around as tamely as sheep, a sight which may be seen nowhere else on earth.

The dry climate combined with ample surface water, allows for several specialised agricultural industries. Ostriches are common to most parts of Africa but as far as they are concerned, they have found their heaven in the Little Karoo. The Arabs say that to produce perfect fruit, the date palm needs to have its roots in the coolness of a water paradise and its leaves in the sunscorched heat of hell. In the same way, the ostrich needs a dry climate for the best feather growth and running water to irrigate lucerne, the food on which they flourish most economically.

The principal rivers flowing through the Little Karoo have their sources somewhere in the Great Karoo which lies to the north beyond the great mountain wall of the Swartberg. The rivers find their way through this range by means of spectacular ravines. Fed by the perennial streams which have their source on the slopes of that great mass of mountains, the rivers gather strength, surge beneath towering precipices of rock and enter the Little Karoo.

The most important river flowing across the plain between the mountains is the *Olifants* (elephants). From its source in the Great Karoo this river meanders through the Swartberg by means of the *Toorwaterpoort* (pass of the bewitched water), so named on account of a hot spring (1 200 000 ℓ a day at 45°C) which rises there out of the Table Mountain Sandstone at the foot of the Swartberg. Subterranean gases also result in periodic surface fires in the area. Burning intermittently and unpredictably, these fires wander about like will-o'-the-wisps, causing unfounded fears among local residents of volcanic explosions.

From this strange pass through the mountains, the Olifants River meanders westwards, accumulating along its course a rich 10-m-deep alluvial deposit of Karoo soil, providing 24 000 ha of agricultural land on which fine crops of tobacco, wheat, grapes, walnuts, potatoes, beans and lucerne are produced. Twelve main tributaries originating in the mountains, feed the Olifants and each of these streams flows through a fertile valley of its own. The Olifants eventually unites with the other rivers which flow through the Little Karoo (such as the Gamka), and the combined flow is called the *Gouritz* River, after the Hottentot tribe which once lived on its lower reaches. The Gouritz drains the Little Karoo by shouldering a passage through the southern mountain barrier of the Langeberg and flowing across the coastal terrace to the sea.

In former years, the Little Karoo was inhabited by Hottentot and Bushman groups. Many of the caves in the Swartberg, Langeberg, Outeniqua and other mountain massifs, are decorated with Bushman paintings. Particularly fine galleries occur in the rock shelters on farms such as *Boesmankloof, De Hoek* and *Skildergat,* and in rocky ravines such as Caledon Kloof, through which the old road used to find its way from Calitzdorp to Ladismith.

Europeans first penetrated the Little Karoo through the beautiful cleft in the Langeberg range known as Cogmans Kloof, which nowadays carries the tarmac road from the valley of the Breë River to Montagu. A tough breed of hunters, ranchers and farmers who were trying to keep ahead of the tax gatherer in Cape Town, wandered through the mountains and explored the plain of the Kango. Hunting was good and the land appealed to the farmers. Homesteads were soon built in such delectable areas as *Op de Tradouw* (above the women's pass); *Onder de Tradouw* (below the women's pass), and northwards to the slopes of the Swartberg and the site of the modern town of Ladismith. The Bothas (grandparents of the famous General Louis Botha); Bruwers; De la Reys (grandparents of the celebrated General De la Rey); Craffords; Jouberts; Nels; Trichardts (parents of the Voortrekker leader, Louis Trichardt); Van Tonders; Van der Vywers; Van Zyls; and many others, all entered the Little Karoo during this epoch of pioneering.

# OUDTSHOORN

The largest town, principal centre and 'capital' of the land of ostriches, Oudtshoorn is congenially situated on the banks of the Olifants River and lies in a strategic, central position on the plain between the mountains. The site of the town was originally the farm *Hartenbees-rivier.* When the settler population in the Little Karoo increased, making it desirable that a community centre be established, the farm owner, C. P. Rademeyer, donated 4 ha of ground and a church to provide the nucleus for a town. The church was completed in April 1839.

In 1847 a surveyor named Ford divided the farm into 500 erven and the first sale of plots was held on 15 November of that year. The place was named *Oudtshoorn,* after the family name of the Baroness Gesina E. J. van Reede van Oudtshoorn, the wife of the Civil Commissioner of George, E. Bergh, who was the superior administrative officer for the area which included the Little Karoo. Oudtshoorn became a magistracy in 1855 and a municipality on 1 September 1863. There are at present 40 186 people living in the town.

As the principal centre of the Little Karoo, Oudtshoorn grew into a sundrenched little town. The Olifants River and its tributary, the Grobbelaars, provided water for fine gardens and the surrounding green fields of lucerne on which, in the boom days, 100 000 ostriches fed. Oudtshoorn still remains the 'feather capital', with great flocks of ostriches still providing a spectacle to be seen nowhere else in the world.

At the height of the feather boom, just prior to the First World War, many substantial buildings were erected in Oudtshoorn. The town houses of the so-called 'feather barons', the leaders of the industry, were lavish mansions, of which several survive today as fascinating architectural reminders of the years when women paid vast amounts for feathers. *Pinehurst*, built in 1911 for E. J. Edmeades, is a fine example in Oudtshoorn of an 'ostrich palace'.

Apart from feather barons, Oudtshoorn has been the home of many interesting and accomplished people. One of the most revered was Cornelis Jacob Langenhoven who, as an attorney, settled in the town in 1899. Apart from his legal work, he was a prolific writer and a great champion of the Afrikaans language. His writings are notable for their homely humour and sympathy for his fellow men. He held sway in the old coffee house in High Street, strolling there from his office, soberly dressed, with a fine walking stick and a flower in his buttonhole. He was always ready to treat his café admirers, as the French literary figures love to do, with a serial of witticisms directed at all and sundry, but especially at the English and their ways.

On his death in 1932, Langenhoven's home, *Arbeidsgenot*, was presented by his widow to the South African nation. It is open to the public and is perfectly preserved as an atmospheric example of the home lifestyle of a professional man during the period. It is filled with his personal belongings, including many odd little carvings of Herrie, the droll elephant who features in his book *Sonde met die Bure*. The carvings were sent as presents to Langenhoven by numerous admirers of Herrie.

In 1918 Langenhoven wrote *Die Stem van Suid-Afrika*, the national anthem of South Africa. His enthusiasm for his native tongue largely contributed to Afrikaans being placed on the statute book in 1925 as one of the two official languages in South Africa.

Another interesting feature of Oudtshoorn is the C. P. Nel Museum, housed in the old Boys' High School which is an elegant sandstone building with a handsome green dome. C. P. Nel was a local businessman who, in 1953, bequeathed to the town his lifelong collection of historical objects. This collection forms the nucleus of the present museum which has the ostrich as its principal theme, with a superbly presented series of exhibits displaying the evolution of this most remarkable bird.

## Accommodation
* ★ Caves Motel, 55 rooms, all with baths. R8,50 – R10 B/B. Phone 2511.
* ★ Criterion Hotel, 10 rooms, 5 with baths. R8,25 – R8,75 B/B. Phone 2981.
* ★★ Holiday Inn, 120 rooms, all with baths. R22 – R28 room only. Phone 2201.
* ★ Protea Hotel, 19 rooms, 12 with baths. R6 – R8 B/B. Phone 4772.
* ★★ ® Queens Hotel, 85 rooms, 63 with baths. R9,50 – R10,50 B/B. Phone 2101.
* ★★ Riempie Motel, 26 rooms, all with baths. R10,50 B/B. Phone 4325.

## Caravans and camping
* ★★ Municipal caravan park, 75 sites. R2 D, plus 25c D per person. 17 rondawels, R3 D.

# THE OSTRICH AND THE FEATHER INDUSTRY

The ostrich is a most peculiar bird. If it was extinct, people would gape at its relics in museums and argue that the scientists had invented the thing from disassociated fragments.

The largest among living birds, the ostrich belongs to a widely dispersed family of flightless birds of which there is no evidence that nature ever allowed or planned for them to fly. The rhea in South America; the emu and cassowary in Australia; the kiwi in New Zealand; all are relatives of this strange bird. Each has been valued by man since antique times, especially the ostrich, being killed for its tasty meat and for its leather, harnessed to carts and used as a pack bird to carry goods. Even the handsome plumage – long before it found popularity in the fickle world of fashion – was used by primitive warriors as headgear and decoration.

In Africa, the ostrich is widespread in about 12 forms. The species *Struthio australis* occurs south of the Zambezi. A big, strapping, athletic bird (the males attaining a height of 2,4 m and a weight of 226 kg), it is still numerous in many parts of Southern Africa, both in a wild and domesticated state.

The eating habits of the ostrich are as strange as the bird itself. Vegetation, insects, sand, bits of metal, glass, bullets, bones and stones; all provide good fare for the *bon vivant* bird. The stones – like iron marbles in a rock crusher – are necessary to grind up food in the gizzard of the ostrich. Items such as tin cans and bottles (full or empty), can be swallowed and, after being ground in the gizzard-mill, digested without effort.

The ostrich is admirably designed to cope with desert life. The bird can survive without water for long periods but under flood conditions, it is sufficiently versatile to be able to swim. Two-toed feet and muscular legs enable the birds to reach speeds of about 50 km an hour, making them formidable sights as they race to safety across some open space such as a dried-out pan. Their speed, however, is of short duration. They drop from exhaustion and, perhaps realising their limitations, generally hope to escape aggressive attention by hiding. The chickens scatter, melting into the grass or feigning death, while the parents lower their heads to the ground in order to reveal as little of themselves as possible.

Normally they are docile creatures, but romance can go to their heads. During the love season, the skin of the cocks turns a bright pink and with their long, naked legs, the birds look as though they are dressed in circus tights! They become aggressive and their kick can be dangerous. The cock makes his presence known by means of a booming call which is commonly confused with the distant roar of a lion. He displays his beautiful feathers to the hen in an elegant dance, bending his knees, falling to his haunches and swaying from side to side.

The hen lays a clutch of 15 to 20 eggs in a hollow scraped in the sand which is often shared with other hens. Male and female take turns in sitting on the eggs, the dark-coloured males at night and the grey-coloured females during the day. The incubating period is six weeks and the chickens take 18 months to mature. The lifespan of an ostrich is 40 years. Predators catch many ostriches on their nests and the black-backed jackal has developed a special technique for raiding nests by rolling one egg to the edge of the rim, kicking it smartly backwards against its fellows, and then dining well out of the resulting omelette! Each egg weighs just over 1 kg and provides excellent eating, especially when scrambled and sprinkled with grated ostrich biltong.

Ostrich feathers were exported from Southern Africa from the days of the first traders and hunters and were always valued as decoration and curios, as well as having a functional use in the making of dusters. A local story relates that in 1865 there was a severe drought in the Little Karoo. Only the ostriches seemed indifferent to the period of thirst, while most other creatures died or fled the place. The European settlers, who had always hunted the birds, were forced to exist entirely on the spoils obtained from ostriches. They found the meat to their liking and the handsome feathers of the cocks provided a saleable item. The idea of domesticating the birds occurred, but wire fences with which to contain them had still to be devised. Lucerne (an alfalfa grass developed in Lucerne, Switzerland) had to be introduced to the Little Karoo as a staple food, and much conservative opposition to the domestication of the bird had to be overcome. Hunters claimed that tame birds would not breed, and that their feathers were inferior and not as curly or lasting as those of wild birds. Dealers were suspicious and offered lower prices for feathers obtained from domesticated birds.

Yet the idea of domestication spread. The birds were easy to manage. Although they were accident prone (even breaking their own legs in an excess of high spirits when habitually performing a gyrating dance of welcome to the rising sun), they were free of disease and parasites in their natural home. The notion that domesticated birds did not breed, or that their feathers were inferior, soon proved to be nonsense.

A farmer in the Graaff-Reinet district, Von Maltitz by name, is said to have been the first to domesticate the bird on a large scale, while in the Oudtshoorn area, Arthur Douglas brought the idea to complete practicability. He also perfected the incubator, investing time and money into improving a primitive device he had imported in 1868, and developing the perfect control of temperature, correct humidity and automatic turning of eggs. The introduction of the wire fence and lucerne to the Little Karoo made large-scale domestication possible in perfect weather conditions. The incubator, then, was the device which allowed farmers to control hatching and, by systematic removal of eggs, to induce the hens to lay more and more eggs.

When fashion adopted the feather, there was a tremendous boom in the Little Karoo. Land values shot up to R1 200 a hectare and breeding pairs of birds fetched R2 000. By 1880, the ostrich industry was yielding profits greater than any other type of farming in Southern Africa. In fact, featherbrained mania resulted in the Little Karoo. Feather barons erected palace-like homesteads incongruously made of corrugated iron and around them, one million ostriches enjoyed a pampered existence in the lucerne fields. The cocks were clipped every nine months, each yielding about 0,9 kg of feathers. With prime plumes fetching R500 a kilogram, the profits were enormous.

During the year 1880, no less than 74 000 kg of feathers were exported, valued at R1 800 000. In 1904 the output passed 210 000 kg, valued at over R2 million and in 1913 the figures were 464 581 kg of feathers exported, worth over R6 million. In many other parts of the world – the Argentine, Australia, Algeria, America, even in Europe – attempts were made to farm ostriches but the Little Karoo remained the paradise of the big birds, the only area where, in perfect health and with a minimum upkeep of feeding them their preferred diet of lucerne and marble-sized stones, they attained complete perfection.

Then came the First World War. The feather trade collapsed and at the end of the war it did not revive. The featherbrained era was succeeded by the scatterbrained age of the 'flapper' and the Little Karoo experienced a complete depression.

The ostrich population dwindled but over the years the trade has revived. Boom times are past but today the industry is firmly established. Although quality plumes only fetch around R25 compared with over R100 per 0,4 kg in former years, duster feathers sell for R5 per 0,4 kg compared with only R1 for the same amount in previous years. Ostrich skins fetch R10 and provide fine leather for the making of shoes and handbags. In 1959, the Little Karoo Agricultural Co-operative built the first ostrich abattoir, capable of processing 2 000 birds a month, with a turnover of 90 tons of biltong a year. The intestines and blood are used in cattle feed while the bones are sent to bonemeal factories. Combining plumes, leather, flesh and bones, a mature 15-month-old bird is worth about R25. Each year, a cock will produce R8 to R10 worth of feathers, while surplus eggs are sold to bakeries. At present, good breeding pairs sell for about R100. There are approximately 60 000 birds in the Little Karoo, producing 55 000 kg of feathers a year on the 170 farms which maintain them.

One of the great tourist features of the Little Karoo is a visit to one of two ostrich show farms which cater for tourists : *Highgate* and *Safari*. From 07h30 to 17h00 daily, these two show farms conduct two-hour tours during which the visitor is shown details of one of the world's most unique industries. Each of the show farms is graced with an authentic 'feather palace' homestead, built during the boom days. There are curio shops and ostrich biltong is sold.

———————

From Oudtshoorn, a fine tarmac road leads northwards for 26 km, following the valley of the Grobbelaars River through the foothills of the Swartberg until it reaches the famous Cango Caves. The scenery is beautiful, reminiscent of the Apennines in Italy.

Three kilometres from Oudtshoorn, the road passes the Cango Crocodile Ranch, a rather novel enterprise to find in ostrich country or anywhere else. About 200 crocodiles are maintained in this ranch and tours are conducted daily every half hour.

Deep in the foothills of the Swartberg, the Divisional Council maintains two holiday resorts at De Hoek and Schoemanspoort, with bungalows and caravan and camping sites. At 22 km from Oudtshoorn a branch road stretches eastwards to the Koos Raubenheimer Dam with a fine picnic ground laid out on the farm of *Rust-en-Vreugde,* now a catchment area for the water supply of Oudtshoorn. Walks are pleasant and the scenery is superb. There is a beautifully situated 61-m-high twin waterfall on *Rust-en-Vreugde.*

## Accommodation
★★ De Hoek, chalets (6 persons), R12 – R15 D, seasonal. Dormitories, R1 – R2 per person, seasonal.
★★ Schoemanspoort, 19 rondawels (2 - 4 beds), R5 – R10 D, seasonal.

## Caravans and camping
★★ De Hoek, 100 sites. R2 – R3 D, seasonal.
★★ Schoemanspoort, 30 sites. R2,50 D, seasonal.

# THE CANGO CAVES

The foothills on the southern side of the Swartberg range contain a deposit of limestone which, occurring anywhere in the world, is an indication that systems of caves decorated with elaborate formations of dripstone may be present. Explorers of this area have not been disappointed. So far, more than 30 caves containing dripstone formations have been found in the area and there are probably many more whose entrances, perhaps because they have become blocked by landslides or matted vegetation, have yet to be discovered.

The cave system popularly known as the Cango Caves, is one of the great tourist features of Southern Africa. Its entrance lies 26 km from Oudtshoorn along the fine tarmac road leading through Schoemanspoort. Many thousands of people visit these caves each month and find every facility available; restaurant, curio shop, crèches and pet room where children and pets may be deposited for safe keeping while parents and owners explore the caves. Few visitors to this subterranean wonderland ever leave the place disappointed.

Bushmen were the first to discover the caves. The entrance was used as a dwelling by these prehistoric people and they covered the walls with paintings of the various game animals which they found in the area. These early men would have had very limited knowledge of the caves, for without portable light, it would have been impossible for them to penetrate far into the depths which, as a result, were used only by bats.

Legend has it that in 1780 a herdsman employed by a local farmer found the entrance to the caves. He told his master, Barend Oppel, who was employed as a tutor and farm manager by a local landowner, Jacobus van Zyl. Oppel visited the cave and then reported his findings to Van Zyl which led to the first attempt at exploring the cave system. With their flickering torches, Van Zyl and his men found their way to the first great chamber, 98 m long, 49 m wide and 15 m high, which they named Van Zyl's Hall. It must have been a stunning experience to be the first to see such an astonishing place, with its collection of stalactites, stalagmites and other formations glittering in the light of the torches.

Van Zyl had himself lowered to the floor of this mammoth chamber. It is pleasant to imagine the pioneer's awe as he stood looking up at tall formations such as Cleopatra's Needle, 9 m high and at least 150 000 years old.

It is not known how much further Van Zyl continued, but over the years exploration gradually took man deeper into the sequence of chambers, each one being given a fanciful name until 762 km from the entrance, a dead end appeared to have been reached. Cave experts were certain that the sequence continued, for a draught of fresh air was felt, but dripstone formations and rockfalls had blocked the passage.

This first sequence of caves was developed and opened to visitors, remaining the tourist route. It is electrically illuminated with lights of various colours, and has recorded commentary as part of the conducted tours. The floor of the caves has a rise and fall of only 15 m and is thus ideal even for the elderly tourist. There are innumerable beautiful dripstone formations to be seen in the main chambers and antechambers which branch off in different directions. The well-trodden tourist section of the cave sequence is known as Cango One. The largest chamber is Grand Hall, stretching 107 m across. The highest dripstone formation is a column 12,6 m high, which is found in Botha's Hall.

The mystery surrounding the continuation of the Cango Caves has been cleared up in modern times. In 1956 the Speleological Association did a survey of the caves and noted that when the atmospheric pressure dropped outside, there was a flow of air out of the caves. When the barometric pressure mounted outside there was a reverse flow of air into the caves. This verified the fact that there was an extensive continuation of the cave sequence.

Two of the professional guides attached to the caves, James Craig-Smith and Luther Terblanche, assisted by Dart Ruiters, devoted their spare time to exploration. In the last chamber of the recognised sequence, the Devil's Workshop, they tracked the source of a draught to a small crevice. For months they painstakingly worked on expanding this crevice. At last, on 17 September 1972, they broke through into a fairyland, a 270-m extension of the sequence never before seen by man and of overwhelming beauty in its formations.

This extension of the caves was named Cango Two, or the 'Wonder Cave'. The Speleological Association experts were then called in to thoroughly explore the discovery. At the end of the sequence they found a perennial stream flowing back towards the entrance and disappearing into a course about 20 m below the level of the cave. Two members of the Association, Dave Land and Peter Breedt, followed the stream until they reached an obstruction.

In 1975 a pump was brought into the caves to sufficiently reduce the water level of the stream to allow, on 2 August 1975, a party led by Floris Koper, to continue through the stream and find their way into what is known as Cango Three, a sequence of chambers 1 600 m long (twice the size of Cango One and Two combined) containing one chamber over 300 m long. Another cave sequence, Cango Four, is an extension of Cango Three.

The new cave sequences are closed to the public. They involve strenuous agility and Cango One is quite enough for most people. The pure, crystalline beauty of the dripstone formations in the new cave sequences is thus preserved, since human beings carry destruction into caves. Cigarette smoke is a curse, depositing a patina of nicotine over the pure white lime; humans must relieve themselves and the disposal problem in deep caves without causing bacterial complications, is impossible. Another curious local problem is that people incessantly eat biltong in the caves. Ostrich biltong is tasty and practically every visitor to the Little Karoo buys a few packets. Fragments of this and other foodstuffs thrown on to the cave floor in so humid and sheltered an atmosphere, lead to serious bacterial invasions. It is probably just as well that the inner sequences of chambers are so secluded.

The entire cave sequence originated as a fault or crack in the rock up to 91 m in width. Nature sealed up this fault with calcite. Water soaked in and after slowly eroding the huge chambers, drained away. Rain water dripping down through the roof picked up carbon dioxide from plant roots and humus in the upper soil. Passing through calcite, the carbon-rich water carried with it calcium carbonate which is only soluble in carbon dioxide.

Dripping through the ceiling of the caves, the water encountered air far less rich in carbon dioxide. With the balancing action of nature, carbon dioxide was then transferred from water to air. The calcium carbonate, unable to be transferred with the carbon dioxide, solidified, a minute amount from each drop of water, and over hundreds of thousands of years decorated the cave sequence with dripstone formations of astonishing beauty and variety of shape.

In this wonderful way, nature laboured in the dark for countless years, and finally gave man the privilege of seeing a work which is still in full progress; changing, growing and being perfected. Cango One is the introduction, the new sequences are for scientists and students to study and to guard against spoliation of any kind. Admission to the caves is R1,25 for adults, 40c for children. Visiting hours: January, February, April and December, daily every hour from 08h00 to 18h00; March, May, June, July, August, September, October and November, daily 09h00, 11h00, 13h00, 15h00. Non-European visitors are specially catered for daily at 09h30, 11h30 and 14h30.

## THE SWARTBERG

The range whose foothills contain the Cango Caves, is the *Swartberg* (black mountain), which provides a 200-km-long barrier between the Little and the Great Karoo. It is one of the most beautiful and spectacular mountain massifs in Southern Africa.

The highest point of the range is the Seven Weeks Poort Mountain, 2 326 m above sea level. The range, notwithstanding its name of *Swartberg,* is composed of red-coloured sedimentary sandstone, warped and twisted into many extraordinary shapes, and coloured still further by the presence of yellow lichens growing on the precipice faces. Visually, this magnificent range is in many parts almost overwhelmingly beautiful. It glows with a rich warmth of colour which reminds many travellers of an active volcano which is still cooling off. In fact, the only way to picture some of the great gorges and river passages – notably Seven Weeks Poort – is to sit before a dying fire, take a poker and with it, form a passage through the embers. That passage, glowing red and orange on either side, in all manner of surprising shapes and beautiful tones, would not be more colourful than Seven Weeks Poort, the chasm of Swartberg Pass, or the precipices of Meirings Poort.

The Swartberg has had a curiously romantic history. A typical tale about these mountains dates from the period of the Anglo-Boer War. A band of Boer guerillas, raiding into the Little Karoo, found themselves hotly pursued by British soldiers. They determined to cross the Swartberg and to escape into the vast spaces of the Great Karoo where they hoped to rejoin the main body of their commando, led by General Smuts.

Since the passes through the mountains were all closely guarded by the British, the raiders decided to lead their horses directly over the range. They set out to climb the great heights, the horses struggling up the cliff faces and the men sustained by the thought of reaching the summit ridge and then being able to look north into the safety of the Great Karoo.

Darkness came before they had reached the summit, and clouds swept up and enveloped the heights by the time the men finally arrived at the top. Too cold to sleep and with everything too damp to enable them to light a fire, they sat shivering until dawn. They then started to grope their way down the northern face of the mountains which was shrouded in dense mist. It was not until nearly 16h00 that they descended out of the clouds. They expected to find themselves looking down on the Great Karoo, but instead, they were astounded to find beneath them a long, narrow canyon, hemmed in by precipices. On the floor of this canyon, 305 m below, they could see a few primitive-looking mud huts scattered about amongst the aloes and the bush.

Thinking that some tribe of Hottentots must have found a retreat in this eerie place, the Boers left their horses in a ravine and, in a body, went down to investigate, reaching the bottom just after sunset. As they approached the nearest hut a shaggy giant of a white man, heavily bearded and dressed in goatskins like Robinson Crusoe, appeared and spoke to them in a strange, long drawn out, outlandish type of Dutch. He introduced himself as Cordier, who lived in the house with his wife and a brood of half-wild children. He knew all about the visitors, for one of his sons had been up in the mountains that morning. Hearing the sound of men and horses, he had stalked the party in the mist, observed their numbers and then slipped down to report to his father.

Cordier was the head of a small community living in the canyon. He offered the visitors a

249

rough but kindly hospitality, feeding them goat's meat, milk and wild honey. He had vaguely heard of the Anglo-Boer War, but none of the contestants, either British or Boer, had ever penetrated this valley of isolation in the Swartberg.

For two nights the visitors remained as guests of this 'Swiss Family Robinson'. Then their host and some of his sons guided them out along secret paths across the rugged mountains until, at last, they looked down on the northern plains, and so made their escape across the barrier of the Swartberg. This account of how the secret valley was discovered, appears in the book *Commando,* by Deneys Reitz.

The history of this hill-billy community was strange. According to them, a party of *trekboers* (nomadic farmers) had been wandering along the northern slopes of the Swartberg at the beginning of the 19th century. Smelling water and sweet grazing in the hidden valley, a number of domestic animals owned by the migrant farmers stampeded during the night and found their way through the gorge forced through the Swartberg by the Gamka River, which flows directly across the concealed valley. Following the tracks of their missing livestock, the trekboers discovered the valley and were delighted with its perennial water and the farming possibilities of its alluvial soil. It was uninhabited, although the presence of numerous paintings in caves, as well as wooden peg ladders reaching up the precipice faces to wild hives, were proof of the original existence of Bushmen.

The nomadic farmers ended their wanderings forthwith and settled in what became known as Gamkas Kloof, or *Die Hel* (the abyss). Eventually 16 small farms were occupied in the valley and the owners, shut in by the mountains and increasingly disinterested in the outside world, became self-dependent, living entirely on the produce of their farms, making their own clothes, and indulging in their one luxury – a potent alcoholic beverage made from wild honey.

In 1921 the Dutch Reformed Church established a school in the valley and since then the inhabitants have developed a cash crop of hanepoot grapes which they dry into raisins and convey out of the valley to sell to the outside world. On the proceeds they purchase clothing, sugar, coffee and a few other luxuries. In 1962 a hair-raising road which twists, rises and falls was made into the Hel, which has allowed representatives of burial societies, insurance agents, sellers of encyclopaedias and politicians at election time, to find their way into this once lost valley.

For the tourist, there are some magnificent drives through the Swartberg. One and a half kilometres before the main road terminates at the Cango Caves, there is a turnoff to the west, signposted Prince Albert. This road leads along the southern slopes of the Swartberg through 27 km of ruggedly attractive country, where the towering mountains may be viewed from many angles. After 27 km the road reaches a turnoff which leads to Kruisrivier (29 km); to a branch road to Oudtshoorn (43 km); and eventually to Calitzdorp (58 km from the original turnoff). This road provides a fascinating circular drive – Oudtshoorn-Calitzdorp-Oudtshoorn – taking the traveller through magnificent foothill scenery and past many beautiful and curious rock formations and caves.

Meanwhile, the main Prince Albert road, after the turnoff to Kruisrivier and Calitzdorp, immediately starts to climb the Swartberg by means of the Swartberg Pass, without doubt one of the most sensational road passes in Africa. The road ascends steadily for 7 km, passing magnificent mountain slopes covered in watsonias and proteas. Eventually, 1 586 m above sea level (over 1 220 m above the level of the Little Karoo), the road crosses a saddle on the summit ridge of the range. If the southern side of this pass has been scenically exciting, then the northern side can be classed as sensational.

The road immediately commences a most involved descent. Just below the summit ridge, in a stand of pine trees, lie the ruins of the old building originally erected to shelter convict labourers employed on the construction of the pass between 1881 and 1888 by Thomas Bain, son of the famous Andrew Geddes Bain, builder of Bain's Kloof Pass in the Western Cape. This ruined building is reputedly haunted by the ghosts of many unfortunate travellers caught in the snowstorms which often block the pass in winter. Just beyond the old building, 1,5 km from the summit of the pass, the road crosses a perennial stream of crystal-clear, ice-cold water around which may be seen many lovely watsonias in spring.

Directly beyond the stream is a forestry station, while 1,5 km further on, a turnoff provides a rough, wild and woolly switchback railway type drive to Gamkas Kloof (35 km to the west). This road to the secluded valley is not to be carelessly followed, but for those prepared to drive with caution, it yields many remarkable views, with a final descent into the valley of Hel that is breathtaking.

The Swartberg Pass continues to descend for 10 km with zigzags, serpentines, twists, and stiff gradients carrying it down the face of a flame-coloured precipice. The road then winds out of the mountains through a canyon full of echoes, whose rock strata is warped and arched, and daubed with splashes of vivid colour as though nature – putting on overalls and preparing to turn painter – had tested brushes and colour effects against the rocks.

Ten kilometres from the northern entrance of the Swartberg Pass, the road enters the little town of Prince Albert and then goes on to join the main Cape-to-Cairo road. From Prince Albert, however, there is a road eastwards, leading back to the Little Karoo through the Swartberg by means of another spectacular pass.

This east road from Prince Albert branches off from the Swartberg Pass road 3 km south of the town, following a settled valley, passing several handsome farms and revealing many impressive views of the mountain range. At 47 km from Prince Albert the road joins the tarmac highway stretching south from Beaufort West, at a point 59 km from Oudtshoorn and 112 km from Beaufort West. After a further 5,5 km the combined roads reach the rural centre of *Klaarstroom* (clear stream), lying in a fertile setting of lucerne fields. After 3,2 km of travel through this cultivated area, the road reaches the entrance to Meirings Poort.

*Meirings Poort* is named after Petrus Johannes Meiring who owned the farm *De Rust* which was situated at the southern (Little Karoo) entrance to the pass. In 1854 when the renowned roadmaker, Andrew Geddes Bain, was trying to find a route for a road with which to link the Great and Little Karoos, Petrus Meiring drew his attention to the great ravine penetrating the range from his farm. Bain rode through the pass and considered it to be ideal. The entire ravine had been worn through the range by escaping floodwaters which resulted from occasional downpours in the Great Karoo. The draining stream, simply known as the *Groot-stroom* (great stream), had eroded for itself a reasonably level floor littered with giant boulders, and overlooked by colossal precipices. Any road made through the ravine would have to cross and re-cross the stream 26 times, but the route was perfectly practical and just the type of pass which Bain loved; grand and majestic to behold, with brilliantly coloured sedimentary sandstone precipices, and the whole place full of odd rock shapes and echoes.

After some delay in the raising of funds, work was started on the pass in August 1856. Labour was recruited from farms on either side of the pass and under the supervision of Thomas Bain, construction proceeded quickly. On 3 March 1858, Meirings Poort was opened to traffic and was considered to be such an asset to the farmers of the Great Karoo – who could now send their produce through the mountains to be shipped from Mossel Bay – that a party of 300 horsemen and 50 carts carrying ladies, made an opening tour through the pass. The Civil Commissioner of Oudtshoorn, Lieutenant-Colonel A. B. Armstrong, opened the pass. He broke a bottle of Bass's Best Ale on a rock and named the pass after Piet Meiring, who held open house for the whole party on his farm, where feasting and dancing continued until dawn chased away the night, as well as all the merry horsemen and their ladies.

Meirings Poort remains one of the most romantically lovely of all South African road passes. It is 12,9 km long, from its northern to its southern entrance and is full of beautiful scenes and interesting features. Three kilometres from the northern entrance there is a pathway branching off from the road and leading to a waterfall. A further 3 km takes the road past a tablet commemorating the famous Senator C. J. Langenhoven and his well-beloved literary character, Herrie, the elephant. The modern tarmac road has overwhelmed several of the charming corners of the pass (well-remembered by seasoned travellers of the route), but the scenic splendour remains and there are many pleasant picnic sites and resting places where the motorist can pause a while and admire the towering cliffs with their fantastic patterns of warped and twisted rocks, numerous flowering plants and rugged piles of boulders.

It is through this splendid, natural gateway that the road makes the transition from the Great to the Little Karoo. The beauty of the pass prepares the traveller for a general transformation in the landscape. Behind is the aridity of the Great Karoo with its isolated sheep farms, scarcity of water and absence of cultivation. Ahead, the traveller is immediately confronted by the intensely cultivated and picturesque ostrich country of the Little Karoo. Three kilometres beyond the southern entrance to Meirings Poort, lies the hamlet of De Rust.

## Accommodation
★ De Rust Hotel, 10 rooms, 4 with baths. R7 – R8,50 B/B. Phone 34.

From De Rust a gravel road branches eastwards, leading for 73 km to the hot springs at Toorwaterpoort, at present having only simple facilities for visitors. The main tarmac road from De Rust continues for 34 km, following the valley of the Olifants River to Oudtshoorn. From Oudtshoorn a tarmac road stretches southwards for 33,5 km to join the road crossing the Outeniqua Pass from George (see page 308), while another tarmac road leads south-westwards, past the Safari and Highgate ostrich show farms and thence over the spectacular Robinson Pass (see page 309) to Mossel Bay, 78 km away.

# OUDTSHOORN TO CALITZDORP, LADISMITH AND MONTAGU

From Oudtshoorn, a fine tarmac road extends the full western length of the Little Karoo to the town of Calitzdorp. This is an interesting drive, passing places such as the Greylands ostrich show farm (13 km from Oudtshoorn), with its private nature reserve and beautiful 'feather palace' homestead. For the tourist interested in exploring the plain between the mountains, it is interesting to turn off this main road (10 km from Oudtshoorn) on to the old road which accompanies the branch railway line leading to Calitzdorp. Along this route lie many large ostrich farms where there is always lively activity in the handling of birds with their nests and chickens, and the growing, reaping and handling of crops. At 38 km from Oudtshoorn, along this concrete-surfaced road, a gravel turnoff leads to the hot water springs of the . . .

# CALITZDORP SPA

The mineral-rich hot springs (with a temperature of 50 °C at source) reach the surface on the banks of the Olifants River, just before it flows into a ridge of high hills and, at the bottom of the gorge, joins the Gamka to form the Gouritz River. The Divisional Council has developed a splendid resort around the springs; there are swimming pools (35 °C), private baths, saunas, a restaurant, caravan park and several chalets and huts. The chalets are built on a high viewsite with a grand panorama of the plain stretching to the Swartberg range.

## Accommodation
★★★® 22 chalets (4 - 6 beds), R13 – R15 D, in season. R7 – R8 D, out of season. 6 huts (2 beds), R10 D in season. R6 D, out of season. Day visitors 25c per car, 20c per person.

## Caravans and camping
★★★ ® 120 sites, R3 D.

Fourteen kilometres beyond the turnoff to the hot springs, lies the town of Calitzdorp, 52 km from Oudtshoorn by the old road (48 km by the new road).

## CALITZDORP

This town is situated against the western end of the valley through which the Olifants River flows before joining the Gamka. Red-coloured sandstone cliffs look down from the west upon the town lying in the acacia-shaded Cango Valley.

In former times this area was richly populated with game, especially buffalo, and many of the local farms retain the memory of these animals in their names. *Buffelsvlei,* the farm on which the town now stands, was one of these resorts of buffalo. It was granted, in September 1821, to J. J. and M. C. Calitz. In those days this area was remote, with no proper roads, and ox wagons took five weeks to journey to Cape Town and back. Hunting and ranching were the local activities, with cattle being driven to market along rough trails across the mountains.

By 1845 the local farmers had prospered sufficiently to make them think of establishing a community centre. In that year *Buffelsvlei* was selected as a church farm, with services held under a large orange tree. In 1857 a proper church was erected and around this building the town slowly grew. On 22 April 1913, Calitzdorp became a municipality and today has a population of 3 500. When the branch railway from Oudtshoorn reached the town on 14 November 1924, its development into a prosperous agricultural centre became inevitable.

The Calitzdorp Co-operative Cellars, situated on the old Oudtshoorn road, sell wines and dried fruits to the public, while several roadside kiosks sell fresh fruit in season.

### Accommodation
⋆ Queens Hotel, 10 rooms, 7 with baths. R8,50 B/B. Phone 26.

From Calitzdorp a highly attractive scenic road (gravel) leads eastwards for 48 km along the foothills of the Swartberg to the Cango Caves. The main tarmac road proceeds north-westwards and after 8 km, crosses the Gamka River situated beneath towering cliffs. Three kilometres further on, the spectacularly located Huisrivier Pass which carries the road 665 m above sea level, begins. Some splendid scenery may be viewed and the pass is a beautiful example of location and construction.

At the foot of the Huisrivier Pass, 11 km from Calitzdorp, there is a pleasant caravan and camping ground – shady, clean and picturesquely situated. The Divisional Council maintains the camp with drinking water and pit toilets. Entrance is free.

Twenty-seven kilometres from Calitzdorp, a gravel turnoff leads northwards through the Swartberg to the Great Karoo by means of what must surely be one of the loveliest and most remarkable mountain passes in the world, the famous . . .

## SEVEN WEEKS POORT

The origin of the name *Seven Weeks Poort* is elusive. It is said that it was originally named *Zerwickspoort,* after the Reverend Louis Zerwick, a missionary at the Zoar Mission Station which stands close to the turnoff to Seven Weeks Poort. This mission was established in 1816, long before the road was made and was then a real oasis in the wilderness: 'Like the Garden of the Lord, as thou comest into Zoar'. Petrus Joubert, grandfather of the famous General P. Joubert of the Transvaal, founded the station for the South African Missionary Society. After 17 years the Berlin Missionary Society took over, building a church and school next to Zoar, at Amalienstein, and growing superb fruit which, in dried form, won first prize at the Crystal Palace Exhibition in London. During the First World War, the Dutch Reformed Church took over the station. Amalienstein flourished on water from the stream which flowed out of Seven

Weeks Poort and it was during this period that, it is said, the name originated.

Another explanation of the name is that wagons smuggling Cape brandy to the interior avoided the revenue officers by travelling to the Cape through this pass, with the return journey from Beaufort West to Cape Town and back taking seven weeks. Still other stories claim that commandos flushing out rustlers took seven weeks to clear the Poort, while it is also said that the name comes from the everlasting flowers (known as Seven Weeks) which flourish there.

Even if the name is puzzling, there is not the slightest doubt about the supreme beauty of the pass. Prometheus himself must have passed this way through the Swartberg and split the range asunder with a breath of fire. Glowing coals of red, orange, and yellow seem to form the towering cliffs, while their summits, topped with dark green growth, are like blackened charred embers. What man must have thought as he first found his way through this fantastic pass, would be interesting to know. He must have had a somewhat terrifying experience.

The gravel turnoff from the main tarmac road leads through the pass for 21 km and on the northern side, joins a gravel road coming from a rural area to Laingsburg. The pass is dominated on its eastern side by the 2 328-m-high Seven Weeks Poort Mountain, the highest peak of the Swartberg range.

There are picnic sites along the pass while 13 km from the entrance, is the Aristata Caravan Park (20c per person per night), situated in very handsome surroundings. There is a swimming pool, some pit toilets and very cold water.

The main tarmac road from Calitzdorp, after passing the turnoff to Seven Weeks Poort 27 km from Calitzdorp, crosses the Zoar River 3 km further on. There is a turnoff to the mission settlement of Zoar and, 9 km from Seven Weeks Poort, a turnoff to Hoeko. This tarmac turnoff leads up a fertile valley into the foothills of the Swartberg. After 2 km the road passes the birthplace of the writer, C. J. Langenhoven, and then continues along the foothills. The tarmac ends after 7 km but a good gravel road eventually proceeds as far as Ladismith and provides an interesting drive. Beyond the turnoff to Hoeko the main tarmac road from Calitzdorp continues for 16 km and, 48 km from Calitzdorp reaches the town of . . .

# LADISMITH

Superbly set against the mountains, Ladismith is overlooked to the north by some of the finest peaks of the Swartberg, two of which are particularly notable. Directly above the town soars the 2 130-m-high *Toringberg* (towering mountain), so named because of its steep cliffs and (as seen from the east) its sharp peak.

Immediately to the west of the Toringberg stands one of the most famous mountains in Southern Africa, the *Toorkop* (bewitched peak), 2 203 m high and an extraordinary landmark from whatever direction it is viewed. A legend relates that a witch, while trying to cross the range one night, was thwarted near the summit. In her rage, she split the great rock dome before her with her wand. Today it remains divided into the eastern and western pinnacles, so oddly situated in relation to each other that the mountain takes on a different appearance in varying lights and from each point of the compass. The northern aspect, observed from the Cape-to-Cairo road between Beaufort West and Laingsburg, is particularly strange; the peak looks like a recumbent face which has a bulbous nose, protruding chin and a cigarette stump between the lips.

Climbing the bewitched mountain is an outstanding feat, for the final 122 m is a severe test. It was first attempted in 1885 by a 20-year-old local farmer, Gustaf Nefdt, while the rest of his party remained at the base of the dome. Fourteen days later he repeated the climb with two friends. The next ascent was not accomplished until 1905 and it remains one of the major climbs in Southern Africa.

The area to the south of this odd mountain was first settled by Europeans in the middle of the 18th century. As in other parts of the Little Karoo, strong men wandered across the southern mountains, hunting, grazing cattle and hoping to escape the grasping hand of the tax gatherer. Cogmans Kloof was the entrance to the Little Karoo which most of these pioneers used and, riding hard on their heels on his horse Bob, came the indefatigable Pastor Robertson, visiting the scattered pioneers, holding services in wagon houses and under trees.

Ladismith started in this way as a permanent place for worship. In 1851 a portion of the farm *Ylands Valley* was bought for £1 000 from Balthazar Kloppers. In 1852 this was laid out by William Hopley into 138 erven and named in honour of Lady Juana Smith, wife of the Governor, Sir Harry Smith. The spelling was *Ladismith* to differentiate between Ladysmith in Natal. At first administered by the Dutch Reformed Church, the town received local government in 1862 and became a municipality in 1903. The ostrich feather craze converted Ladismith into a boom town, with 50 000 birds feeding on the lucerne fields around the town and farmers paying fortunes for breeding pairs, while their wives enjoyed the profits by going on mad spending sprees.

The feather crash in 1914 brought the district to bankruptcy. Economic relief and rehabilitation only came in 1925 when the branch railway was opened connecting Ladismith to the main line at Touws River. This link provided an outlet to markets and nowadays the district produces fresh fruit, dried fruit, lucerne and dairy produce, including some notably good sweetmilk and cheddar cheese. Ostriches also flourish still but the bitter memory of the crash keeps men sober when they think of those treacherous birds. Ladismith is now a level-headed and pleasant little town of 3 161 inhabitants, with beautiful mountain scenery being its proudest asset.

### Accommodation
\* Dinnies Hotel, 18 rooms, 10 with baths. R6 – R7 B/B. Phone 56.
\* Royal Hotel, 20 rooms, 5 with baths. R6 – R7 B/B. Phone 37.

### Caravans and camping
\* Municipal caravan park, 50 sites. R2 D.

From Ladismith the tarmac road leads south-westwards for 79 km across a rugged and interesting semi-arid landscape. Rivers such as the *Groot* (great), and the *Touws* (pass), meander through this sandstone wilderness on their way to join the Gouritz, while in spring, mesembryanthemums (*vygies*) provide fantastic patches of concentrated colour. At 53 km from Ladismith a gravel turnoff stretches for 3,5 km to the hot springs of Warmwaterberg. These springs, surfacing on the farm *Uitvlugt,* have a temperature at source of 40 °C, are rich in iron and are slightly radio-active. A small resort has been created there where sufferers from skin diseases and rheumatism find relief and relaxation.

### Accommodation
Warmwaterberg Hot Springs, rooms R7 B/B. R10 D, inclusive.

### Caravans and camping
\* Sites, R2 D. Bathing in spring 50c.

From the turnoff to Warmwaterberg the tarmac road gradually approaches the southern range of mountains (which, in this part of the Little Karoo is called the Langeberg range) and directly against these heights, 79 km from Ladismith, reaches the straggling little agricultural centre of
. . .

# BARRYDALE

Barrydale lies at the northern entrance to the Tradouw Pass, which leads through the Langeberg to Swellendam. The Barry merchant family of Swellendam laid out this township in 1882 as a church and trading centre on a portion of the farm *Tradouws Hoek*. In 1921 Barrydale became a municipality and today it is the quiet little centre of a productive fruit farming area, renowned for the quality and sweetness of its crops, and the vivid colour of the mesembryanthemums (*vygies*) growing on the mountain slopes.

## Accommodation
★ Valley Inn, 14 rooms, 6 with baths. R7 – R7,50 B/B. Phone 26.

## Caravans and camping
★ Municipal caravan park, 20 sites. R1 D plus 10c D per person. Situated in the Anna Roux Wild Flower Garden and Park.

From Barrydale the tarmac road continues westwards along the foothills of the Langeberg. This is undulating, rugged country, where the valleys are full to the brim with fertility. Grapes, apples, quinces and all manner of deciduous fruit flourish here, as well as sheep and cattle. The road proceeds over the Op de Tradouw Pass (27 km from Barrydale), and past the turnoff to the Poortjies Kloof Dam (35 km from Barrydale). At 63 km from Barrydale, the road reaches the mineral baths and town of . . .

# MONTAGU

Lying at the historic entrance to the Little Karoo – the scenically splendid Cogmans Kloof – Montagu grew as a staging post for travellers coming through the kloof. An added attraction was the presence of a hot, radio-active spring (19 mach. units) which, bubbling up at a temperature of 45 °C, has been a boon to many visitors. There is another radio-active hot spring at Baden, 13 km from Montagu.

*Montagu* was founded in January 1851 when the first erven were sold in the town which had been laid out on the farm *Uitvlugt* (originally occupied in 1841 by P. Swanepoel). The town was named after the energetic and popular Colonial Secretary, Sir John Montagu who, during his ten years of office at the Cape (1843 - 1853), was originator of the first great road-building programme in Southern Africa. Montagu became a municipality in 1895 and a magistracy two years later. It now has a population of 5 927.

The town is the centre for wine and fruit-producing activities. The rugged area north of Montagu known as the *Koo*, is famous for its apples, pears, apricots and peaches. A tarmac road leads for 78 km through this region in a winding, climbing route over Burger Pass and the Roodehoogte to join the Cape-to-Cairo road at the summit of the Hex River Pass.

Montagu is graced with several Cape-Dutch style buildings, a museum and the hot springs. Fine scenery and wild flowers (particularly mesembryanthemums) have made the place a popular resort, especially during winter when the climate is mild and swimming in the hot baths and exploring the mountains provide pleasant occupations. There are several excellent walks up the various valleys.

'Lovers' Walk', between Montagu and the hot springs, leads through a magnificent ravine. It is a pleasant, easy stroll, especially at sunset when the birds are tucking themselves into bed with a last little twitter, as some hen nags her mate for coming in a trifle late. Baboons and dassies call from their retreats on the face of the cliff. The rocks are rich in colours of red, purple and orange. The warm water from the springs meanders down the floor of the ravine, gradually cooling as it goes. Trees shade the pathway and the twists and curves tempt the walker on to explore further, with new scenes and experiences around each corner. So perhaps it is with love and lovers and the path they follow; a fragment of life with new feelings, words, thoughts, dreams, hopes and disappointments occuring around each bend.

### Accommodation
★★ Avalon Hotel, 32 rooms, 15 with baths. R10 – R12 B/B. Phone 153.
★ Montagu Baths Hotel, 22 rooms, 12 with baths. R8 – R10 B/B. Phone 65.
★ Montagu Hotel, 22 rooms, 8 with baths. R7,50 – R8 B/B. Phone 83.

### Caravans and camping
★★★ ® Municipal caravan park, 68 sites. R2,75 D.

# COGMANS KLOOF

From Montagu the main tarmac road linking the Little Karoo to the valley of the Breë River continues for 6 km and then joins the main Worcester-Swellendam road on the southern side of the Langeberg range. During these 6 km, the traveller is rewarded by a wonderful concentration of scenery. *Cogmans Kloof* takes its name from a Hottentot tribe which once lived there. The road was built by the famous engineer, Thomas Bain, and opened on 28 February 1877.

In the middle of the pass is Keurkloof, a ravine which supplies drinking water to the town of Ashton. A track wanders up this gorge for 6 km while at the entrance, beneath wattle trees, there is a fine, shady camping ground with barbecue sites and pit toilets.

There is a short but picturesque tunnel, 15 m long, running under a rocky ridge known as Kalkoen Krans. Perched on the ridge above the tunnel is a small fort built by the British during the Anglo-Boer War. It served as a guard point, blocking the way to the Western Cape from the Little Karoo. The view from this fort is superb; the overlooking mountains are notable for their extraordinary, folded sandstone formations, their vivid colours, the lichen growing on the rocks, and the aloes flowering during winter.

257

## Chapter Fourteen

# CAPE TOWN TO MOSSEL BAY

From Cape Town, the main road to the east – to Mossel Bay, Port Elizabeth, East London and Natal – is one of the oldest and most romantic highways in Southern Africa. Herds of game animals wandering along the coast, Bushman hunters, Hottentot pastoralists with their herds of sheep and cattle, migrating African tribes moving down from the north into the cul-de-sac of the south; all combined to blaze this ancient route. When Europeans arrived in the Cape and explored the coastal area, they followed old trails, converting footpaths into wagon trails and wagon trails into the highways of today.

Fittingly, the highway along the east coast of Southern Africa is known as Settlers Way. It has its start on Rhodes Drive just beyond Groote Schuur Hospital, 5 km from the centre of Cape Town. It then makes its way out on to the Cape Flats passing under and over numerous traffic interchanges leading to suburbs, housing estates and satellite townships such as Pinelands (the first garden city to be established in South Africa); *Athlone* (named in honour of the Earl of Athlone, a Governor-General of South Africa); *Langa* (the sun); *Nyanga* (the moon); *Guguletu* (our hope); Epping (home of the municipal market), and, at 16 km from Cape Town, the D. F. Malan airport.

The road, a finely engineered concrete dual carriageway, has now left the built-up confines of Cape Town, with Table Mountain receding into the blue directly behind it. A forest of Port Jackson trees covers the sandy flats, laden with sweet-smelling golden blossoms each spring, while vast numbers of arum lilies flourish in the swamps and around the pools.

At 28 km from Cape Town the road passes the military training depot of the South African Coloured Corps and 3,5 km further on there is an intersection with turnoffs to Stellenbosch and to the False Bay coast at Swartklip and thence to Muizenberg. From this point the concrete highway veers eastwards, passing a turnoff to the housing estates at Macassar, to Firgrove and to the Methodist mission of Raithby, founded in 1845 as a sanctuary for freed slaves and named after Raithby Hall in Lincolnshire, home of Mrs Brackenbury who donated the land for the mission. Today the Raithby community are great producers of strawberries. Beyond this turnoff the concrete road passes the extensive grounds belonging to the explosives and fertilizer factories of African Explosives and Chemical Industries, the Cloetenberg Caravan Park and, 46 km from Cape Town, reaches a turnoff leading to Strand and the Coast of Flowers (see page 138), and to the town of . . .

## SOMERSET WEST

Lying in a superb mountain environment, the commercial centre of Somerset West – one long street – is not particularly distinguished by architecture or horticultural beauty. However, the residential area is exceedingly pleasant. Fine gardens and many beautiful homes are owned by retired people as well as business people who find the attractions of the area ample compensation for spending a significant proportion of their lives commuting to Cape Town in an electric train. The population of the town is 18 554.

The best part of Somerset West may be seen by following the road to Helderberg Nature Reserve which turns off from the main road at the top of the commercial area. This road leads for 5 km through the residential area of the town, passing the entrance to the famous

Cape-Dutch homestead of *Vergelegen* and ending at the gateway to the magnificent estate of *Lourensford,* the homestead which is of recent, but handsome, Cape-Dutch style construction.

The Helderberg Nature Reserve is reached by a turnoff to the left, 3 km from the start of this branch road. The reserve is situated on the south-eastern slopes of the 1 138-m-high Helderberg, and its 245 ha extend well up to the rock faces of this impressive mountain. The reserve, proclaimed on 23 September 1960, is intended as a permanent sanctuary for the indigenous flora of the Hottentots Holland area. Skilfully developed, it is one of the showpieces of the Western Cape. The reserve is open daily 09h30 to 18h00. Picnic places are situated in a grove of oaks.

From the Helderberg Nature Reserve a path leads up to the highest point on the mountain, the Helderberg Dome. This is a strenuous, but very worthwhile walk and, even without reaching the actual summit, the views from the lower reaches of the path magnificently reveal the whole area of the Hottentots Holland. Permission to climb the Helderberg from within the Nature Reserve must be obtained from the ranger in charge.

The *Helderberg* (clear mountain) is so named because it is seldom obscured by cloud or mist. It constitutes the northern arm of the great amphitheatre of the Hottentots Holland range and, as with all mountains which project as a spur, the view from the summit is panoramic, revealing in breathtaking detail a countryside not only handsome, but filled with the most romantic human associations.

In 1657 the first Europeans – three cattle traders from Cape Town – made their way into this area and found living there about 500 members of the small Chainoukwa Hottentot clan. The prosperity of these people and their proud claim that they were living in the choicest part of the entire world, added to which was the visual beauty of the area, induced the Europeans to improvise the rather quaint name of the Hottentots' Holland.

Fifteen years later the Chainoukwa parted with their cherished homeland. For about R1 600 worth of trade goods they sold the area to two representatives of the Dutch East India Company and the wild flowers and streams of their 'Holland' knew the Hottentots no more. The new owners only established a cattle post and outstation, but the desirable qualities of this fair countryside were too self-evident not to arouse the cupidity of every visitor to the Hottentots Holland. Among these visitors was the Governor, Wilhelm Adriaan van der Stel, and the story of how he lost his heart and reason to the fair charms of this area provides a lugubrious chapter in the records of the Cape.

It was contrary to the rules of the Dutch East India Company for its officials to own ground, but there were ways of evading such regulations. The choicest farmlands in the Hottentots Holland were soon in the possession of the Van der Stel family. *Parelvallei* (pearl valley) was granted to the Governor's brother, Frans, on 11 March 1699, while the superb stretch of country which Wilhelm van der Stel named *Vergelegen* (far away) was granted to the Governor himself by a visiting dignitary on 1 February 1700.

*Vergelegen* became an obsession with Van der Stel. He enlarged his holdings by the expedient of granting adjoining land to subordinate officials and then immediately buying it back. Along the valley of the stream known as the *Lourens* – after an individual unfortunate enough to be drowned in it – Van der Stel developed one of the most famous South African farms. A most magnificent homestead formed the centre for a whole cluster of industries: workshops, watermill, tannery, winery, granary, groves of fruit trees, cornlands, and a vineyard of over half a million vines.

Since the Governor was so preoccupied with the delights of agriculture, it was inevitable that his subordinates would follow suit. In South Africa, the most unexpected people frequently have a tendency to turn farmer at the slightest opportunity, often with unfortunate results to their farms – but that is by the way. In Van der Stel's time, senior civil servants were more engrossed in agriculture than the affairs of state. It is reputed that even the Company-

259

appointed clergyman of the Cape showed an inclination to postpone Sundays if chickens were hatching on his farm. As for the Governor, he was more often on *Vergelegen* than at his post in the Castle.

Inevitably, of course, trouble ensued. Reports started to trickle through to the Company in Holland; officials were said to be using their position to secure markets for their own produce; the Company's slaves and materials were being used on private farms, plus a whole series of detailed complaints and accusations.

Looking down on the tranquil fields of *Vergelegen* today, it is difficult to imagine the storm that raged over the question of the farm's possession. Van der Stel was not the kind of man to take accusations with a smile. Not only was his position as Governor at stake but also his ownership of these fertile acres. He tried to use force to silence his critics. The famous Adam Tas, leader of the agitation against the Governor, was imprisoned while others were summarily arrested and deported to Holland and Java.

The end was unavoidable. Van der Stel had simply allowed the charms of *Vergelegen* to run to his head. With his senior officials he was recalled to Holland in April 1707, while his brother Frans was ordered to take himself off to some territory outside the Company's possessions. *Vergelegen* was repossessed by the Company and the dwelling house, considered too ostentatious for any farmer, was ordered to be demolished. The 526 ha of ground was divided into four separate farms and sold by auction, the section on which the condemned homestead stood, alone retaining the name of *Vergelegen*.

The end of the dreams of Van der Stel lingers as a melancholy memory in the fair land of the Hottentots Holland. Down the years many other settlers came to the area and many beautiful farms were granted. None of them, however, has quite the atmosphere of Van der Stel's old farm with its intangible mood of lost human hopes and forgotten jealousies.

Upon viewing the interlinking farmlands today, it is easy to imagine the dazzling white homesteads and pleasant to think of the bustle and industry which resulted when their first owners took possession of the virgin land. Examples of these are: *Laaste Gift,* so named because it was the last grant of Governor van Assenburgh before his death in 1711; *Lourensford,* one of the divisions of *Vergelegen,* which is named after the ford leading over the Lourens River to the original watermill; *Rome,* with its seven hills which suggested the name; *Morgenster* (morning star), with its superb farmhouse; *Land-en-Zee-Zicht* (land and sea view), whose unique view inspired the name; *Brinksburg, Erinvale, Republiek* and *Weltevreden.* All these and many others providing snug livings for the people – the Munniks, Malans, Morkels, Moolmans, Hendriks, Brinks and Theunissens – who made up the community of this pleasant land during the course of the last century.

It was this community which eventually founded the village of Somerset West in a way typical of many South African centres. In 1817 the farmers of the district decided to establish a church of their own to avoid the inconvenience of having to travel to Stellenbosch. They combined to buy land which they called the Pastorie Estate and applied for permission to establish a township. By 1820 the church was ready, with building plots and wide roads radiating from it in a carefully laid-out plan calculated to place the church at the centre of the future town. On 13 February 1820, Lord Charles Somerset had the pleasure of granting permission for this centre to bear his name.

The mountains which overlook this interesting area are serenely beautiful. Attached to the Helderberg in a succession of summits are Guardian Peak (*Haelkop* or Hail Peak), *Pic Sans Nom* (peak without name), New Year Peak, the Triplets, Sneeukop (at 1 590 m the highest point), Landdrost's Kop, Klein Vallei, Vallei Berg, Langkloof Berg, Moordenaar's Kop, and the curious Sugar Loaf; after which the range loses height to the level of Sir Lowry's Pass. Attached to each of these mountains is a tale. The modern climber finds traces of many half overgrown paths wandering through the valleys and along the ridges, blazed there not only by the migrating herds of game, but by the first men – renegades, some of them, flower pickers in more recent times – or those odd souls one occasionally encounters who lead a hermit's life in the solitude of the heights.

Robbers and bandits also blazed these trails and the sinister name of *Moordenaar's Kop* (murderer's summit) serves as a reminder of a tragedy which occurred around the end of the 18th century. It was then, it is said, that travellers crossing the mountains were frequently pillaged by robber gangs hiding in the mountain valleys.

To end the misdeeds of these gangs, the government called upon a commando of Stellenbosch and Swellendam burghers. Led by four field-cornets, the commando hunted for the robbers and found them at bay in an inaccessible ravine. Thereupon a young burgher, Barend Saayman by name, together with another, volunteered to be lowered by ropes to the place where the robbers were hiding. His offer was accepted but the result of it was tragic. Barend Saayman was killed by the fugitives, while his companion barely escaped with his life. Only later were the robbers captured or shot.

Upon learning what had taken place, the directors of the Dutch East India Company ordered the Governor of the Cape to grant to the widow and children of the man who had sacrificed his life, a farm which had to be named *Barend Saayman's Eredood* (Barend Saayman's honourable death). To each of the four field-cornets, a suitably inscribed silver jug was presented. The farm, situated in the Riversdale district (its name now prosaically changed to *Surrey*), subsequently passed into hands other than those of the descendants of Barend Saayman. In recent times a gentleman in Stellenbosch, Mr Beyers, had in his possession one of the silver jugs.

Somerset West has a busy, modern commercial centre. As it leaves the shopping area, the main street crosses the Lourens River, with the original stone bridge preserved at the side of the modern structure. The road continues past many fine estates, to eventually reach the village of Sir Lowry's Pass and the foot of the great road pass over the Hottentots Holland mountains.

## Accommodation
* Alexandra Hotel, 10 rooms, 4 with baths. R7,50 – R8 B/B. Phone 2-1735.
* Cylnor Country House Hotel, 25 rooms, 12 with baths. R9 – R12 B/B. Phone 2-1641.
* Helderberg Hotel, 10 rooms, 3 with baths. R8 –R8,50 B/B. Phone 2-1536.

## Caravans and camping
** Cloetenberg Caravan Park, 100 sites. R4 D.

Beyond the turnoff to Somerset West, Settlers Way crosses the railway line leading to Strand and continues past several fine farms where grapes are grown and horses are bred. After 5 km the road passes the Happy Valley Farm Stall and at the turnoff to Gordon's Bay and Sir Lowry's Pass Village, commences the climb up . . .

## SIR LOWRY'S PASS

Migrating herds of game blazed the first way over the Hottentots Holland mountains, the range which provided so formidable a barrier between the areas of the Western and the Southern Cape. Bushmen and Hottentots followed the trail of the animals and gave the pass its original name *Gantouw* (pass of the elands).

The old pass followed a stiff route directly up the mountain wall with no twists or zigzags to ease the gradient. European pioneers used the same track and the path became a most laborious wagon route. At a point 4,3 km above the start of the modern pass the tarmac road crosses the route of the old pass. There is still a little-used gate where the old trail crosses the railway line above the modern road. This wagon trail goes directly up a small ravine, today followed by the Escom power lines, and then over the summit. It is a worthwhile scramble to follow this wagon route. The scar of the wagon wheels worn deep into the rocks may be clearly seen. It is easy to imagine the shouting, cajoling, cursing, whip-crashing, grunting, rumbling and groaning as the vehicles made their tedious way. On the summit, amid a natural garden of wild flowers, stands the ruin of a small fort with two old cannon lying at ease beside it. These weapons were mounted there in 1734 and used as signal guns, summoning farmers in the 'Overberg' east of the mountains, to Cape Town in times of trouble, or inviting them to bring provisions for sale when fleets arrived in port.

As settlement increased east of the mountains so transport pressure on this old route became a problem. A great clamour arose for the making of a new and properly graded pass. No money was allocated in those days for public roads but a benevolent Governor, Sir Lowry Cole, took a chance and authorised construction out of local resources. In 1838 the pass named in his honour was opened, to the enthusiasm of the farming community, but to the displeasure of the Governor's superiors in London who accused him of wantonly using official funds.

The new pass (substantially followed by the modern tarmac highway) reaches the summit in a setting of oddly shaped rocks. From the summit there is a superb panoramic view of the Cape Peninsula, False Bay, the Hottentots Holland and Cape Flats. Travelling up the old pass, this grand view fades away like a vignette as the rocky sides of the ravine narrow and close. The new pass has the contrary effect of opening up the view as the road reaches the summit and few travellers can resist pausing to admire the scene.

The summit is 452,6 m above the level of the great curve of False Bay and it is reached 6 km from the bottom of the pass (57 km from Cape Town). Immediately over the summit there is an entrance gate to the Steenbras reservoir (see page 140) and the first 23-km-long stage of the Hottentots Holland Hiking Trail, a magnificent walk through possibly the finest wild flower area in the world, which eventually ends in the Jonkershoek Valley above Stellenbosch.

Beyond the summit of the pass lies a new world. When the loquacious Lady Anne Barnard travelled over the pass in 1798, she described the view ahead as being that of 'the new Canaan opened to my eye, hillock upon hillock, mountain behind mountain, as far as the eye could reach'. The area actually consists of a high-lying bowl drained by the river known as the *Palmiet,* after the palm rushes which grow there. Set in a ring of mountains, the height and situation of the area combine to give it a special quality. The air is fresh and a crispness in winter is ideal for keeping fruit trees healthily dormant for months of rest. A coolness in summer and dew from the sea breezes, combined with 1 200 mm of winter rainfall each year absorbed by well-drained soil, makes the area a heaven for flowers, trees, and the agricultural industry of man.

From the summit of Sir Lowry's Pass, Settlers Way descends easily into the basin of the Palmiet with scenes on all sides of afforestation, water conservation and intense activity in the growing of fruit, particularly apples, pears, peaches and plums. After 8 km a tarmac turnoff leads for 3 km to the town of . . .

# GRABOUW

This place is the commercial centre for what is the largest export fruit-producing area in Southern Africa (26,3 per cent of the export total). With its name slightly misspelt, the town was created on the farm *Grietjesgat,* acquired on 22 November 1856 by a German, Wilhelm Langschmidt, who named the place after Grabow, the village of his birth in Germany. The farm was situated at the ford across the Palmiet River where a store had already been opened in 1832 by William Venables. Langschmidt took over the store and this was the beginning of a town which the new owner apparently resolved to populate himself, for he was the father of 23 children, including three sets of twins! The population has since risen to 5 812.

Grabouw is today a rather unbeautiful small town in a lovely setting of green trees, farms and mountains. Instead of allowing the place to remain a pleasant habitation, a forest town, the civic planners have been misguided by traffic authorities into thinking that motor vehicles are more important than people and roadside trees have been cut down. Grabouw is a town of streets, pavements, shops and garages. It became a municipality in 1956. Perhaps one day the streets will be planted with apple trees, and an annual festival held at blossom or harvest time.

## Accommodation
★ Forest Hotel, 19 rooms, 11 with baths. R8 – R11 B/B. Phone 381.

Rather to the mortification of Grabouw, the district of which it is the centre is better known by the name of Elgin. The reason for this is that in 1902, when the railway known as the Caledon Extension was built over Sir Lowry's Pass, it passed about 1,5 km from Grabouw to a station named Elgin situated on the farm *Glen Elgin*. This station was intended as the despatch point for the produce of the district, eventually becoming internationally known as the place in South Africa where the apples come from. The name *Elgin* (with the 'g' pronounced as in 'get'), originated from Scotland. The original place seems to have had nostalgic memories for several expatriates, for the name has been copied in Canada and Australia, and occurs seven times in the United States.

# THE APPLES OF ELGIN

When the railway line linking Cape Town to Elgin and thence to Caledon was opened, the principal products loaded on to the trains were wheat, oats and everlasting flowers which were exported in considerable quantities, mainly to Germany, where they were used in the making of artificial wreaths. Fruit was grown in the area but not on any substantial scale.

One of the farmers of the Palmiet River basin was a remarkable individual, Dr Antonie Viljoen of *Oak Valley*. A medical man born in Caledon in 1858, he had studied medicine at Edinburgh University, practised in the Transvaal, returned to the Cape and in 1899 purchased the portion of *Palmietrivier* farm which he named *Oak Valley*. He returned to the Transvaal to serve in the Boer forces during the Anglo-Boer War. He was captured by the British and was returned to his farm in the Cape on parole, after he had agreed to pay the salaries of the two men who guarded him, a unique way of being prisoner-of-war!

Dr Viljoen planted oaks on his farm and experimented with various crops but found nothing really remunerative. In 1902 he was elected to the Cape Legislative Council and when, in 1905, he told the Cape Minister of Agriculture, John X. Merriman, about the agricultural problems of his district, Merriman advised him to try apples; this was the beginning of a vast industry.

Dr Viljoen purchased 24 assorted apple trees from Harry Pickstone, the great nurseryman. These trees were planted close to the homestead on *Oak Valley* where followed a patient wait for them to produce a crop. In 1912 the first apples were ready and on an auspicious day, Dr Viljoen invited friends and neighbours to sample the fruit. It was excellent.

Dr Viljoen resolved to embark on the large-scale production of apples. He was aided in this industry when, in 1913, the elder of his two daughters, Hannah, married George, son of James Rawbone, a well-known forestry officer of the Cape Government. George Rawbone became a real son to his father-in-law and joined him as a partner in the apple-growing venture. From then on, the family name was Rawbone-Viljoen.

The First World War delayed the apple project. Dr Viljoen was knighted in 1916 but unfortunately died in 1918 before he could see his plans to fruition. However, he did at least see vast orchards of young trees growing on his estate and on the properties of his neighbours. On his estate he also left 20 000 oak trees, a condition of his will being that they be left undisturbed, and these lovely trees are as much his memorial as the apple industry. His second daughter, incidentally, he christened Oaklene.

The local farming community as yet had everything to learn about apples: correct varieties, cultivation, picking, packing and despatch. When Miss Kathleen Murray, a neighbour of Dr Viljoen, picked her first apple crop she sent 25 boxes to the Johannesburg market. The agent returned to her a cheque for £1 (R2) a box. At the same time he complained that the apples had reached the customers in such a state that it was hardly possible to find one good bite between the bruises.

In 1923 a number of the local farmers created the Elgin Co-operative Fruitgrowers Ltd. A library of technical books on apple cultivation was founded and a start was made to the systematic study of the problems and possibilities of apple production.

In 1931 three of the leading farmers organised the Elgin Fruit Company as a joint venture in packing and marketing. Depression followed by the Second World War impeded progress in the industry but the end of the war saw a tremendous surge of technical development in every aspect of the growing and marketing of fruit in general, and apples in particular.

The Palmiet River lent itself to water storage and irrigation. With the introduction of sprinkler irrigation the area was transformed. Instead of 100 trees to 0,4 ha, 470 trees could be planted with a consequent five-fold increase in production. Improved fertilizers and the method of sod culture (where a covering of natural grass is left between trees in order to enrich the soil with humus, retain water and impede erosion) were used. Then, in 1959, Edmond Lombardi introduced the Italian palmette system of cultivation on his farm *Applethwaite*. This idea, perfected in Italy from an ancient practice, involved the planting of fruit trees close together and training them to form continuous walls, each tree linked to its fellow for mutual support by grafting, and the main branches tied down into a horizontal position. This technique brought apple trees into bearing after four years instead of eight.

Apple production became an industry. The big farms installed computers to solve intricate problems of production and marketing. On *Applethwaite* farm the genius of its owner resulted in the creation and introduction to the market in 1966 of the pure apple juice drink known as 'Appletiser'. In creating this drink in association with Professor H. R. Lüthi of the Department of Agriculture at the Swiss Federal Institute of Technology, Edmond Lombardi solved the apple producers' problem of what to do with lower grades of fruit and gave to the world a drink absolutely pure, without any additives, adulteration or preservatives.

Picking, packing and handling techniques were transformed in a manner far removed from the traditional ways. *Glen Elgin* and *Applethwaite* farms established their own packing houses. The smaller producers banded together in 1948 to form, with the Elgin Fruit Company, the Elgin Fruit Packers' Co-operative. A second co-operative packing station, Krom-rivier Apple Co-operative Ltd, was formed in 1972 and the combined output of apples and fruit juice from all these enterprises today amounts to a significant factor in the economy of South Africa.

The main varieties of apples grown in the area of the Palmiet River are the Ohinimuri, ripening in February and originating from the Ohinimuri County of New Zealand; the White Winter Pearmain, ripening in March and originating from the Parma area of Italy; the Golden Delicious, also ripening in March and originating about 1890 from a chance seedling on a farm in West Virginia in the United States; the Granny Smith, which originated in 1867 in the garden of Mrs Maria Ann Smith, wife of the mayor of Parramatta, New South Wales, Australia; the Starking, introduced commercially in 1895 by the Stark Bros. nursery of America; the all-red bud mutation of this variety known as the Starking Delicious, found in 1921 in New Jersey; and the bud mutation known as Starkrimson Delicious, found in 1953 in Oregon. The last apple to be picked, during the month of May when the season ends, is the York Imperial, a favourite old variety which originated in the early 19th century in York, America.

There are kiosks which sell the apples and other fruits of the district. One is run by the Elgin Fruit Packers' Co-operative (Elpaco) at the entrance to their huge pack house; another is Peregrine, at the eastern turnoff to Grabouw from Settlers Way and a third situated at the Kromrivier packing station.

From the turnoff to Grabouw, Settlers Way continues eastwards, crosses the Palmiet River and, after 2,5 km, reaches a crossroads with a left turn to Grabouw, Elgin and Villiersdorp, and a right turn leading through the apple orchards to the forestry station of Highlands. The Peregrine farm stall stands at the crossroads and offers fruit, juices and other good things to eat and drink. At this point Settlers Way is 68 km from Cape Town.

Settlers Way continues past a succession of orchards, especially lovely in spring when the trees are in blossom. After 5 km the road passes the Kromrivier pack house and stall selling the fruit of the area to passing travellers. Just beyond this pack house is a tarmac turnoff, the Valley Road, which leads to the lovely farming area in the valley of the Krom River. A further 2 km takes the road past the entrance to the Lebanon Forestry Station, and ahead, on the slope of a hill, a large white 'K' forms a landmark for the farm *Korteshoven*. At 5,5 km further on (81 km from Cape Town) there is a turnoff leading to . . .

## HOUHOEK

*Houhoek* (ravine glen) lies in a narrow fertile valley known as *Poespas* (higgledy-piggledy). Down this valley where the Jakkals River flows, the old road and the railway originally found a complex twisting route out of the mountains (the railway still follows this route). The railway station of Houhoek stands at the top of the actual ravine which gives it its name and the surrounding countryside is dominated by a fine cluster of high peaks. Wild flowers and trees cover the slopes and floor of the valley.

In former years the transport wagons outspanned at this pleasant spot for a rest and refreshment. An inn was built there which became a regular staging post. Lady Anne Barnard stayed there in 1798, eating boiled chicken 'fit for an emperor'. Lady Duff Gordon was another visitor who, in 1861, recommended the place, for she found it 'all clean and no louses'. The present buildings were erected in 1834 and extended in 1861, while the gigantic eucalyptus tree which stands at the door as though hopeful of a free drink, was reputedly planted in 1875.

There are many stories about this inn. After the railway was built the inn supplied meals to passengers. It is said that the innkeeper made handsome profits by serving the soup course so hot that diners were unable to consume it in time to eat the rest of the meal before the train moved on.

The pub is notable for its collection of old school ties, stripped, cut or forcibly removed from wearers during past forgotten celebrations. There is also a collection of about 200 foreign banknotes, mostly signed by owners who nailed them to the wall of the bar for safe keeping against future need or thirst. The habit is said to have been started by a young lord who left a ten shilling note glued to the ceiling of the bar so that on his return from abroad (broke as usual) he could once again enjoy the delights of the cellar.

A story is told about the eucalyptus tree: its alcoholic tendencies are said to make it flourish on the aroma of good liquor which floats out from the bar. Its leaves rustle appreciatively when any good jokes are told inside but it drops twigs on hearing stale stories. A teller of real chestnuts is said to have been killed by a falling bough. Since then, his ghost repeatedly haunts the inn, tugging at people's sleeves in the hope of inducing them to listen to his tales. Another ghost is said to belong to a man who died of indigestion or over-indulgence; the inn is haunted by his hiccups.

The little inn has three restaurants and a dining room, with a notable variety of good food.

## Accommodation
★ Houhoek Inn, 28 rooms, all with baths. R9,50 room only. Phone Bot River 646.

Beyond the turnoff to Houhoek, the modern Settlers Way, instead of following the old route down Higgledy-Piggledy Pass, takes the mountain crossing in its stride. It rises purposefully to the 341-m-high summit, and with a glance at the view over the wheat fields of the 'Overberg', commences a sweeping descent. The summit ridge is a good place for wild flowers, especially pink everlastings. At the bottom of the pass (5 km from Houhoek) in a mass of protea bushes, there is a turnoff to Hermanus and to the small town of . . .

# BOT RIVER

This little place takes its name of *bot* (butter) from the days when the Hottentot tribes resident there supplied butter to traders from Cape Town.

## Accommodation
★ Bot River Hotel, 7 rooms, 3 with baths. R6 B/B. Phone 640.

From the turnoff to Bot River and Hermanus, Settlers Way continues on a switchback journey over hill and dale through wheat fields which are green in winter, gold in spring and drab in summer. The landscape has a spaciousness and variety of scene which adds interest to the journey. At 21,5 km from Bot River, a turnoff leads to Greyton and Genadendal (see page 268) while a further 2,5 km brings the road to the entrance (24 km from Bot River) of the town of . . .

# CALEDON

In itself a rather drab, sunbaked little town, Caledon has the saving grace of lying in a handsome environment, overlooked by the 2 607-m-high Swartberg and confronted by the 2 687-m-high Tower of Babel mountain to the south. The town also possesses two remarkable assets, one of which, in fact, stimulated the founding of Caledon.

On the slopes overlooking the town, seven springs of chalybeate (iron-rich) water bubble to the surface, one of which, curiously enough, is cold and the other six thermal. The water, in contact with rocks heated by pressure deep under the ground, is heated to a steady temperature of 50 °C, with 909 200 ℓ reaching the surface each day.

As with the 73 other known hot springs of Southern Africa, these thermal springs of Caledon are not related to volcanic activity. The principal feature of the water, besides its warmth, is that it is free of any organic matter and has a large amount of iron in solution along with a variety of other less important chemicals. Compared with the waters of the famous spas of Europe and America, the waters of Caledon rate very highly. At the Chicago World's Fair, in fact, they secured first prize against all comers.

Bushman and Hottentot tribes had discovered the springs long before Europeans came to the Cape, and it was these early people who contributed the first place names of the area. To the first Dutch explorers the name of the hot springs sounded something like *Disporekamma*, while the river into which the water flows was called the *Hacqua* or Zebra River. This is the river on whose banks Caledon, with its population of 5 661, stands today.

Whether the Hottentots made any use of the springs for medicinal purposes is not known, but Europeans have always had an irresistible urge to jump into such natural baths on sight. From the time white people settled in the Cape, the Caledon springs became increasingly famous. Actual development started in 1710, when one Ferdinand Appel secured a grant of the area on condition that he build there a house of accommodation for invalids and visitors.

Just how effective such medicinal baths are in curing human ailments has always been a matter of some debate. Taking the waters is a fetish with many, and certainly does no harm. One rather suspects that these medicinal baths were more effective in former years when people normally washed less, and then in water which was often not very pure. Relaxing in a nice hot bath of absolutely clean water would do anybody a power of good if their normal ablutions only consisted of using perfume to counter body odour!

At all events, the hot springs at Caledon became popular and were developed as the years passed, with a variety of shelters and accommodation erected there for the convenience of visitors. The town of Caledon grew almost as an adjunct of these baths, being founded in 1813 and named *Caledon* in honour of the late Governor, the Earl of Caledon.

At the beginning of the 20th century the spa reached a notable height in its development with a company, The Golden Baths Ltd, erecting quite a remarkable hotel and sanatorium, with accommodation for 200 guests, public rooms, recreational facilities and gardens of a most spacious and impressive nature. Old photographs of the place reveal it as being quite the equal of similar establishments anywhere in the world in those days of elaborate Victorian decorations and uncomfortable-looking furniture.

All this glory was, alas, destined to go up in smoke. In the early hours of 5 June 1946 the hotel was burned down, with a total loss of some £200 000. What set the blaze going is a mystery. The staff and the 29 guests just managed to get safely out of the place before the flames soared up to the heavens like a Guy Fawkes night bonfire. It was a miserable night for a fire, with a howling north-wester blowing and just enought drizzle to wet the unhappy, if fortunate, survivors. There was no fire brigade in Caledon, and at dawn a melancholy ruin was all that remained of what had once been a glittering social centre.

The place was never rebuilt. It remained a ruin until 1961 when the Caledon municipality obtained possession of the site. Now it is being rehabilitated at least as a caravansary and camping ground. The handsome gardens with a wide view over the rolling hills of the Caledon wheat country to the dominating peaks of the Tower of Babel and Shaw's Mountain, are once again open to the public. As far as swimming is concerned, the bath is certainly the easiest place in South Africa in which to jump on a cold winter's morning! Opening times are 07h30 to 21h00 weekdays; 07h30 to 18h00 Sundays. Closed on Fridays. Admission is 25c.

The second great asset of Caledon is its world-renowned wild flower garden. This garden was founded in 1927 as a result of the zealous work of a group of nature enthusiasts, J. Dunsdon, F. Guthrie, L. Langschmidt, B. Newmark and J. B. Taylor. Covering 10 ha of the slopes of the Swartberg, it was laid out in 1933 by an itinerant landscape gardener named Cecil Young, and then developed to its present standard by its curator, C. de W. Meiring.

The garden is notable for its wonderful variety of indigenous flowers, superb examples of one of the richest flora in the world. Added attractions are the pleasantly casual layout of paths and bridges, the pretty little valley, and the odd natural feature of the so-called 'Window Rock' with its spacious view of the surroundings. The garden is open daily from 07h30 to 17h00. Admission is 25c per person.

## Accommodation
* Alexandra Hotel, 11 rooms, 8 with baths. R7,50 – R8,50 B/B. Phone 2-1411.
* Baumkers Park Hotel, 16 rooms, 9 with baths. R7 – R8 B/B. Phone 2-1520.
* Overberg Hotel, 10 rooms, 4 with baths. R7,50 – R8,50 B/B. Phone 2-1128.

## Caravans and camping
* Caledon Hot Springs, 35 sites. R2 D. 10 rondawels, R3,50 D.

From Caledon a road branches south-eastwards to Bredasdorp (page 151). Caledon is also a convenient centre for a visit to Greyton and to the romantically situated mission station of Genadendal, 27 km north of Caledon up the road which branches off from Settlers Way 2,5 km before it reaches the town. This is a pleasant drive over undulating wheat fields, especially lovely in November when the colours are golden and harvesting is in progress.

# GENADENDAL

The mission station of *Genadendal* (the valley of grace) was founded by the Moravian Missionary Society in 1793 in what was called *Baviaans Kloof* (ravine of the baboons) where, in 1737, an earlier worker of the Society, Georg Schmidt, had attempted to establish a station for the conversion of the Hottentots to Christianity. This effort had failed, ending after five years in a squabble over the unordained missionary's right to administer Baptism to his converts.

The new venture, however, flourished. In 1806 it received its present name and became a model of its kind with a thriving population, converted to a Christian and Western way of life. The village, with its streets of neat black-thatched, white-walled cottages, the church and manse, the watermill (no longer working) and the magnificent groves of oak trees, all survive to this day and preserve with them the flavour of life in the Cape 150 years ago.

From Genadendal the gravel road continues eastwards for 4,5 km to the small but beautifully situated village of . . .

# GREYTON

A relaxed and pleasant little place, Greyton lies in the afternoon shadow of some of the finest peaks of the Riviersonderend range. Into one of the mountain ridges, the *Wa en Osse* (wagon and oxen), a particularly beautiful gorge known as Noupoort, finds a way close to the summit of the 1 465-m-high Kanonberg. This provides a fine walk, while a walk through the Bosmanskloof is also spectacular. On the road to Krige, 1,5 km from Greyton, a pleasant camping ground with simple facilities is situated in the wood on the banks of the Riviersonderend. There is canoeing and swimming. The fee is 50c D per person, the camp being run by the local authority.

**Accommodation**
★ Central Hotel, 12 rooms, 5 with baths. R6,50 – R7,50 B/B. Phone 682.

From Greyton the gravel road continues eastwards along the slopes of the Riviersonderend range where many fine views of mountain and rural landscape may be seen. On the farm *Nethercourt* may be viewed the little cave known as *Het Ziekenhuis* (the hospital) in which ailing travellers were sheltered in former years. After 33 km the road joins Settlers Way which has come from Caledon (48 km away) over the wheat fields, and now enters . . .

# RIVIERSONDEREND

Lying astride Settlers Way 168 km from Cape Town, *Riviersonderend* (the river without end) is a municipality with a population of 1 900. It was established in 1925 as a centre for the farming community in the fertile valley of this river with the romantic name. In itself it possesses little of tourist interest but its setting, dominated to the north by the Riviersonderend range of mountains, makes it a convenient centre for the exploration of this area.

**Accommodation**
★ Garden Route Hotel, 20 rooms, 14 with baths. R8,75 – R9,25 B/B. Phone 48.

**Caravans and camping**

★ ® Municipal caravan park, 50 sites. R2 D.

From Riviersonderend, Settlers Way continues eastwards over wheat fields where superb photographic possibilities may be found, especially when the wheat is golden ripe and being reaped. There are turnoffs to Protem after 5 km and to Napier after 10 km and then, at 20 km, a turnoff to the village of . . . .

# STORMSVLEI

A small rural centre on the banks of the Riviersonderend, Stormsvlei has a holiday resort with river swimming and camping grounds in the shade of trees on the banks of the Riviersonderend. A tarmac road crosses the river and leads through the Riviersonderend mountains for 19 km to Bonnievale in the valley of the Breë River (see page 132).

**Accommodation**

★ Stormsvlei Hotel, 5 rooms, 2 with baths. R9,65 B/B. Phone Riviersonderend 1730.

**Caravans and camping**

★ Stormsvlei Caravan Park, 20 sites. R2 D.

East of Stormsvlei, Settlers Way continues through more rugged country as the Riviersonderend mountain range peters out into hillocks covered with the red flowering *Aloe ferox*. Ahead lies the great mountain wall of the Langeberg, with the Breë River flowing down from the north-west. After 24 km there is a turnoff to Bredasdorp and 7 km further on the road reaches the bridge across the Breë River, where a tearoom and caravan park are situated on its west bank. The town of Swellendam lies 5 km beyond the river bridge (36 km from Stormsvlei).

Swellendam and the Bontebok National Park, which has its entrance 2 km further along Settlers Way from the entrance to the town, have been described in the chapter on the Breë River Valley (pages 124 to 137).

The Settlers Way proceeds over undulating wheat country. At 8 km from the entrance to the Bontebok Park the road descends into the fertile valley of the river known after some old adventure as the *Buffelsjag* (buffalo hunt). In this pleasant setting, there is a tearoom, garage and a small trading centre near the railway station. A road branches off at this point to reach the sea at the mouth of the Breë River.

Beyond Buffelsjag River the road climbs out of the shallow valley with fine views of the Langeberg range to be seen north of the road. After 1,5 km there is a turnoff leading to Barrydale and the Little Karoo through the pass known as . . .

# THE TRADOUW PASS

The branch road to the Tradouw Pass leads north-eastwards, close to the Langeberg range. At 6 km a cairn stands marking the site of *Oupos* (old post), a small military stronghold established there in 1734 by the Dutch East India Company as a defence against Hottentot and Bushman groups who were marauding and resisting settlement by Europeans in the area. Three kilometres further on, in a well-watered valley lying at the foot of the mountain range, the road reaches the station of the London Missionary Society, founded in 1809 at *Suurbraak* (sour marsh). Today it consists of a 1-km-long cluster of cottages on either side of the road.

Beyond Suurbraak, the road passes the fine *Lismore* farm of the Barry Trust and then, 6 km from the mission, reaches the turnoff north to the *Tradouw* (women's pass) which follows a most beautiful route for 17 km to Barrydale on the other side of the mountains. This pass, originally blazed by the Bushmen and named by the Hottentots, is notable for its waterfalls in winter and wild flowers in spring. Bushmen found the caves in its cliffs to their liking and their rock paintings may be seen by following a signposted path 12 km from the start of the pass. Near this path there is a magnificent swimming pool in the river, reached by a branch track. The modern pass was opened to traffic in 1873, having been built by Thomas Bain to provide a trade route between the Little Karoo and Port Beaufort at the mouth of the Breë River. It has been substantially rebuilt in modern times.

From the turnoff to the Tradouw Pass the road from Swellendam leads on for 25 km past the historic farm of the Moodie family, *Groot Vaders Bosch* with its forest of stinkwood and California redwoods, and then arrives at the town of Heidelberg.

---

From the turnoff to Tradouw Pass and Barrydale, the main coastal road, Settlers Way, finds an undulating route over wheat-covered hills. There is a turnoff to Port Beaufort 37,5 km beyond the Barrydale turnoff and after 3 km (50 km from Swellendam) the road reaches the town of . . .

## HEIDELBERG

With its population of 3 712, Heidelberg lies in an attractive setting on the banks of the *Duivenhoks* (dovecote) River. In 1689 the explorer, Izaak Schryver, first camped at this pleasant place and found so many doves there that he gave the river its rather unusual name.

Settlers found their way to the valley. As early as 1725 Andries Gous received a grant there of the farm *Doornboom*. For some years the area was considered to be a part of the Riversdale district but on 14 September 1855 the Riversdale Church Council bought (for £5 000) a portion of the farm *Doornboom*. The purpose was to lay out a town which they named *Heidelberg,* after that ancient city in Germany, the source of the Heidelberg Catechism and, like the new Heidelberg, built on the banks of a river.

A church and school became the twin centres of the new town. The first erven were sold on 21 November 1855 and in 1862 the place received its first town management board under the chairmanship of Joseph Barry (son of Thomas Barry, one of the two famous Barry 'nephews'). Wool, tobacco, corn, dairy cattle and ostrich feathers were the products which put the community on its feet. The opening of the railway in 1903 provided the essential link with the outside world.

### Accommodation
* Esperanza Hotel, 17 rooms, 5 with baths. R7 – R7,50 B/B. Phone 87.
* Heidelberg Hotel, 14 rooms, 5 with baths. R8,50 – R9 B/B. Phone 47.

### Caravans and camping
* Duivenhoks Caravan Park, 10 sites. R2 D.
* Municipal caravan park, 60 sites. R2 D.

From Heidelberg, the main coastal road continues eastwards for 29 km and then reaches . . .

## RIVERSDALE

This place was at first part of the Swellendam district. Church services were periodically held in a room set aside for the purpose on the farm *Zeekoegat* owned by Hillegert Mulder, a man renowned for his hospitality towards travellers on the road to the east. The farmhouse still stands and is known as the *Ou Pastorie.*

Watered by the Vet River, many other fine farms flourished in this area, a well-known one being *Barend Saayman's Eredood.* This farm was granted to the family of young Barend Saayman, killed while being lowered down to the cave of bandits who were hiding in the Hottentots Holland mountains. The residents of these farms decided that a community centre was desirable in an area as prosperous as theirs. Money was contributed and on 21 July 1838 the farm *Doornkraal* was purchased from Hermanus Steyn. On 16 August, the first erven were sold in a town named after Harry Rivers, the civil commissioner of the Swellendam district. Rivers, a civil servant who had found himself in hot water for autocratic behaviour while in his former post in Grahamstown, had mellowed after transfer to Swellendam, become popular, and eventually ended his career as Treasurer-General of the Cape Colony.

Riversdale today is an amiable and clean little farming centre. It has 6 638 inhabitants and is much resorted to by travellers as a staging post on the road to the east. For some reason the town has always been the home of 'characters' and there are many tales to be heard in the pubs about individuals such as Henry Meurant, a magistrate renowned for his sage decisions and the man who, in 1861 in Cradock, published the first work written in Afrikaans. A typical local story of a Riversdale character concerns one Dik Koos Saayman, a fat and happy old farmer. Dik Koos – a total illiterate who kept his farm accounts most accurately in his head – had the habit every week of visiting the town in his cart and conducting his business. At the end of the day he drove to the pub, leaving his cart in the care of a little boy. After having one for the road he would collect a couple of bottles of brandy already wrapped up for him.

The local *dominee* (parson) at this time was something of a holy terror, who strongly disapproved of Dik Koos. One evening he lay in wait. When Dik Koos went in for his drink, the parson walked up to the boy, told him to run away and stood holding the horses himself. The whole town was agog at the news of his attempt to shame Dik Koos. Dik Koos finished his drink, collected his bottles, paid his due and walked outside, watched by many. Without blinking an eye he went to his cart, paused, then fumbled heavily in his pocket for a moment. Producing sixpence, he gave it to the astounded parson, and with a 'Thank you, I usually only give a tickey but as it's the parson this evening I'll give sixpence,' he drove away.

The Riversdale district is also well known for the rather pungent and curiously antiseptic aroma produced by species of agathosma which flourish in these parts. The area is also good for wild flowers and aloes. In the Van Riebeeck Garden of the Jurisch Park there is a magnificent collection of local aloes which bloom in May and June, while mesembryan- themums are equally spectacular in spring: A skilled gardener, Werner Frehse, takes care of this collection, the spectacle of which has brought many travellers to a halt on Settlers Way.

For those travellers with the time and inclination to appreciate lovely and interesting things, there are two fascinating drives from Riversdale. To the south-west a gravel road leads down to the coast through what is almost a forgotten rural world, where may be seen some of the most primitive architecture ever devised by man. This road stretches for 41 km to the mouth of the Duivenhoks River. Projecting into the blue of St Sebastian Bay, is what is known as *Puntjie* (the little point), on which stands an extraordinary cluster of seaside buildings architecturally known as *kapsteilhuisies* (truss-style houses). This odd place started as a holiday resort for the local farmers. Shortage of modern building material stimulated somebody to erect a *kapsteilhuis* as his ancestors had once done, then others followed the style. Each building consists of a thatched roof built at ground level with no side walls at all and a floor space of about 6 m by 5 m. A window in one end and a recessed door in the other complete the primitive but extremely snug structure. Such buildings were used in Europe in ancient times.

Similar or more elaborate *kapsteilhuisies* may be seen in other parts of South Africa but nowhere quite as numerous or as lovely as these. On the way to Puntjie, where the road passes through the rural settlements of Brakfontein and *Vermaaklikheid* (jollification), elab-

*Overleaf: Protea aristata, a rare member of a flower family characterised by forms and colours of infinite variety.*

orations of *kapsteilhuisies* may be seen with low, whitewashed side walls elevating the roofs above ground level. The atmosphere of this hill-billy part of the world is rather reminiscent of Ireland – poor but pretty.

Puntjie is privately owned by Mrs Molly Lazarus (née Davids), who bought it in 1960 from a previous owner, the gentleman-politician, Major Piet van der Byl. Major Piet – the stories have it – allowed local farmers to build *kapsteilhuisies* at Puntjie for a nominal ground rental of 4/- and maybe they showed their pleasure by voting for him. However, it is a fact that in a strong Nationalist area, the locals solidly voted United Party for years and at the same time had their seaside fun. Now tenants pay R10 a year. Only *kapsteilhuisies* may be erected on Puntjie so that its charm will be preserved.

The second drive from Riversdale leads northwards to the Langeberg mountains. After 10 km the tarmac road ends at a bridge over the lovely upper reaches of the Kafferkuils River which flows through delightfully verdant country with the high peaks of the Langeberg looking down serenely. Across the river lies the Garcia Forest Station, also the start of Garcia's Pass which takes the road (now gravel) through to the Little Karoo.

In 1868 Maurice Garcia, Civil Commissioner of Riversdale, with the use of a few convicts, constructed a bridle path through the mountains, following the deep gorge of the Kafferkuils River. This pass (10 km long) provided a short link through fine scenery between Riversdale and Ladismith in the Little Karoo. Between 1874 and 1877, Thomas Bain constructed a proper road through the pass and today this route provides travellers with a most spectacular gateway into the Little Karoo. It replaces the older, now disused Platte Kloof Pass, which followed the Duivenhoks River through the mountains.

Garcia's Pass is particularly renowned for its wild flowers. For those travellers with the time, a ruggedly beautiful circular tour may be made by taking the Van Wyk's Dorp turnoff 4,5 km from the end of the pass (25 km from Riversdale). This road leads eastwards along the northern slopes of the Langeberg. High mountains, deep ravines, red-orange coloured sandstone cliffs, innumerable waterfalls in the rainy season and farmhouses against a background of serrated peaks, together form a dramatic landscape. At 72 km from Riversdale the road crosses the Gouritz River flowing in a deep gorge and 9 km further on passes an old toll house at the entrance to Bergkloof, the beginning of what is known as *Cloetespas* after the family owning ground on the southern end of the mountain passage. Cloetespas is a picturesque and little-known mountain pass, still guarded by the ruins of blockhouses built to watch over it during the Anglo-Boer War. After 23 km of twisting and turning the road reaches Herbertsdale, a former mission station founded by the Reverend Mr Herbert. Down the fertile valley of the Langtout River the road continues through masses of winter flowering aloes and eventually rejoins the main coastal road, Settlers Way, at Cooper's Siding after a 130-km drive from Riversdale. By means of the coastal road it is 59 km from Cooper's Siding to Riversdale.

## Accommodation
★ Central Hotel, 18 rooms, 5 with baths. R8 – R8,50 B/B. Phone 95.
★★ President Hotel, 31 rooms, 12 with baths. R8 – R9 B/B. Phone 192.
★ Royal Hotel, 20 rooms, 9 with baths. R7 – R8 B/B. Phone 184.

## Caravans and camping
★ ® Municipal caravan park, 50 sites. R2 D. 10 rondawels (2 beds in each), R3 – R4 D.

From Riversdale the coastal road, Settlers Way, continues eastwards for 12 km and then reaches a tarmac turnoff south to Stilbaai. This road leads over slightly undulating country for 25 km to the mouth of the Kafferkuils River where lies the fishing harbour and resort of . . .

# STILBAAI

Divided into an east (resort) side and west (harbour) side on the banks at the mouth of the Kafferkuils River, *Stilbaai* (still bay) is an almost classic example of the South African country-man's ideal of a holiday centre. There is a fine swimming beach, excellent boating on the river, and varied estuary and coastal fishing. These attractions, together with an equable climate, soon lured man to the area for his living as well as recreation. Prehistoric men made their homes on this coast. Artefacts of the middle and later Stone Age are numerous and it was on this coast that Doctor C. Heese found the evidence of what is known as the Still Bay Culture.

Interesting features of the coast dating from the period of these early men are the numerous fish traps known as *vywers* which are still in use. These are dams made of boulders built up to form low barricades between the high and low water marks. At high tide the fish enter these dams to feed among the rocks. When the tide recedes, the fish are left behind and often thousands of mullet are caught in a single trap. The traps are still maintained in their former condition and the bottoms are cleared of debris in order to make it easier to catch the fish.

When Europeans first entered the area they found several unusual natural wonders: caves, strange rock formations such as the *preekstoel* (pulpit) 3 km east of Stilbaai, and an extraordi-nary number of eels populating the streams. These eels – a local delicacy with a record weight of 7 kg – frequent all the streams and many are incredibly tame. On *Platbos* farm for instance, where the De Jager family live in the original 1814 homestead, there are springs full of these eels, so tame that they eat from the hands of visitors.

Shells and drift seeds (such as the *Entada gigas* and *Entada scandens*) washed down from the tropics to this coast by the Agulhas Current, are often found in considerable numbers, and it was here that Dr John Muir of Riversdale collected many of the shell specimens which are part of the Muir Collection in the South African Museum in Cape Town. His detailed study of the strange, wandering drift seeds is also the definitive work on the subject and is published as *Botanical Survey No. 16* by the Government Printer. It is interesting to know that some Stilbaai old-timers such as J. Dekenah (a man rich in local lore) have induced these seeds to grow. Although they have produced creepers with bean-like leaves the plants have not flourished in the temperate climate and have never developed the huge 0,9-m-long seed pods characteristic of their kind.

Until the great smallpox epidemic of 1713 wiped out most of the Hottentot tribes there was friction along this coast between settlers and the indigenous people. There is a local story that says the last of the Hottentots – a tall, light-coloured individual who had set himself up as a rustler – was eventually cornered and killed on a rock offshore where he had swum for safety. His retreat had been the rock shelter at *Jongensgat* (the cave of the young man) and his death took place at Grootjongensfontein.

Such bitter memories of the old times seem alien to this pleasant coast. Today man lives there in harmony. At *Melkhoutfontein* (fountain of the milkwood trees) there is a pleasant village of fisherfolk, with a little churchyard in which may be seen the graves – decorated with shells – of fishermen drowned in the cruel sea; for their calling, even in the waters of the still bay, is a matter of skill, risk and interminable battle with the elements.

Stilbaai itself was surveyed into plots in 1894 and early buyers such as Frans van Wyk secured choice properties for £7 10s. (R15) each. No road was made to the resort and visitors travelled by wagon to a point on the river from where boats ferried them and their belongings down to the coast. Riversdale inhabitants went there for Christmas while the farmers of the Little Karoo travelled down during March, after the grape harvest was in, with their wagons always loaded with barrels of wine, brandy and *witblitz* (white lightning). Their holiday camps were very jolly affairs, with the old folk gossiping and the young people dancing all night, every night beneath the stars on a piece of ground cleared for the occasion, which was literally danced into a smooth, rock-hard surface by the time the season was over.

With the advent of motor vehicles, a road was built. A pontoon was opened across the river in 1930 and worked (until it was replaced by a bridge in 1955) by a celebrated character named Eepie, who never seemed to forget anybody no matter how long they had been away. Wooden bungalows were erected on plots in the higgledy-piggledy fashion common to old resorts with no disciplinary local authority. Many of these shacks were built on stilts above the level of spring tides and all had freshwater wells dug into the sand underneath them. Most of these shacks were built by the Dekenah brothers, who habitually knocked up a house in ten days and nights flat. To the fury of neighbours they often worked all night by the light of the moon and even though a good many of these shacks look as though they have been built in the pitch dark, Stilbaai has always been a singularly happy and totally informal place. Concerts and church services were held in the *planksaal* (plank hall), with everybody – including the parson – barefoot and relaxed. Sports, pastimes, romances, picnics and friendships all flourished in the sunshine against the murmur of the waves on the beach.

Stilbaai became a municipality in 1965, and that same year the road was tarred. It remains a place of many happy ghosts.

## Accommodation
★ Bellevue Hotel, 11 rooms, all with baths. R9,50 – R11,50 B/B. Phone 30.

## Caravans and camping
★★ Ellensrust Caravan Park, 325 sites. R3,50 D. 8 cottages, R7,28 – R9,88 D.
★★ Jongensfontein Caravan Park, 100 sites. R3,50 D. 16 rondawels, R9 – R12 D.
★★ Riverside Caravan Park, 50 sites. R3 D.

The main coastal road continues eastwards from the Stilbaai turnoff for 24,5 km over level wheat country and then reaches the town of . . .

# ALBERTINIA

This little place was named after the Reverend J. R. Albertyn of Riversdale, who planned the establishment of a separate church community east of Riversdale. For various reasons matters were delayed and he had long left the district before the town had its birth on the old farm *Grootfontein*. It was proclaimed a town on 18 November 1904. With its population of 1 740 it has had a quiet history, but even this town, like every other, has a feature special to itself. In 1925, W. R. van As started mining yellow and red ochre from deposits first noticed by Sir John Barrow in 1797. This industry today is the principal source of ochre in South Africa which is exported all over the world as a natural earth colour used in the manufacture of paints and for imparting colour to things such as cement and linoleum.

Kaolin is also found in the area while another unusual local industry – largely practised by the Coloured people – is connected with the masses of red flowering *Aloe ferox* which flourish between Albertinia and Mossel Bay. During winter, the leaves are collected and drained of their bitter-tasting sap. This sap is concentrated by boiling and is exported from the area which is one of the world's two principal sources (the other being the West Indies) of an important ingredient in many medicines.

## Accommodation
★ Albertinia Hotel, 16 rooms, 8 with baths. R6,75 – R8,10 B/B. Phone 30.

At 8 km east of Albertinia Settlers Way reaches a gravel turnoff leading to the coast 27 km away at the mouth of the Gouritz River. The main coastal road actually crosses the deep gorge of this river 8 km further on and most travellers pause here to view the spectacular twin rail and road bridges which, 73 m long and situated over 60 m above the river, span the ravine.

274

The Gouritz River, draining the arid areas of the Little and Great Karoos, is essentially a fluctuating river with long spells of slight flow followed by short but most violent floods. The *Gouritz* is named after the Gourikwa tribe of Hottentots who once lived along its banks. At its mouth (at the end of the 27-km-long turnoff mentioned earlier) there is a good beach with the usual nondescript collection of shacks, most of them forlornly locked up for 11 months of the year. A track down the coast leads to several vantage points for fishermen, including the rocky stretch known as The Fisheries, where Mr Gulliman started an industry mining deposits of amorphous silica. Deposits of this silcrete provide the principal material for the furnace bricks used in the South African iron and steel foundries.

### Accommodation
★ Gouritz River Mouth Hotel, 14 rooms, 6 with baths. R9,75 B/B. Phone 5313.

### Caravans and camping
Gouritz Mouth Caravan Park, 22 sites. R2,50 D.

Beyond the high bridges over the Gouritz River, where a picnic area is situated at a good viewsite, the main coastal road continues eastwards for 5 km and then reaches a turnoff leading to the coast. This road follows the broad, alluvial valley of the lower Gouritz where masses of aloes grow. The local inhabitants cut off the leaves and boil the juice to produce the concentrated bitters used in the manufacture of various medicines. At 12,5 km there is a turnoff to the mouth of the Gouritz River and 2 km further on, a turnoff stretches for 7 km to Kanon, the first of three coastal resorts . . .

## KANON, VLEESBAAI AND FRANSMANSHOEK

These resorts owe their names to the visits (of varying fortune) made by three ships. On 11 September 1763 the French warship *La Fortune* was wrecked during a heavy gale near the mouth of the Gouritz at a place known as *Fonteintjies,* after a small freshwater fountain situated close to the beach. The rocky point projecting into the sea there is known as *Fransmanshoek* (Frenchman's corner) and is covered in vivid ochre-coloured lichen, making a striking picture with the waves breaking on its jagged rocks. A sandy area near by is said to be the burial site of many of the drowned sailors. Several cannon from the wreck were washed up on the beach and the Reverend M. Johnson of Riversdale, who had a bungalow near the mouth of the Gouritz, dragged three of them away and mounted them in front of his home. These cannon gave the name of *Kanon* to the huddle of seaside shacks which stands there today, forming the sort of fishermen's holiday resort which always looks windy even when it isn't.

Vleesbaai, which is reached by a 4,5-km-long turnoff 3 km beyond the turnoff to Kanon, consists of a fine (if exposed) bay, with a sandy beach and a throng of holiday shacks trying to stop themselves from sliding down the slope on which they have been built. The bay received its name on 8 July 1601 when two Dutch ships commanded by Paulus van Caerdon, sailed along this coast searching for signs of one of the Hottentot pastoral tribes who could sell them fresh meat. The local tribes were well known for their cattle trading and because of this the Portuguese had already contributed one name, *Cape Vacca* (cape of the cows). One of the two Dutch ships, the *Hop van Holland,* put into what the crew named *Visbaai* after the fish they caught there. The second ship, the *Vereenigde Lande,* found the Hottentots and their herds in what the Dutch named *Vleesbaai* after the meat they bartered there. Through some latter-day confusion, the modern resort known as Vleesbaai had been built on the shores of Visbaai.

This stretch of the Southern Cape coast is a renowned fishing area and many spectacular catches have been made. Whales frequent the coast, coming into the bays to calve. There are large kitchen middens of sea shells, artefacts, clay pots and other bric-à-brac left there by the beachcombers and fishermen of prehistoric times. Scenically the coast is dramatic: a succession of bays and cliffs, with the Langeberg range on the northern horizon.

From the turnoff to Kanon and the other resorts the main coastal road continues for 14 km, then passes a second turnoff leading to the three resorts. A further 4 km takes the road to a turnoff proceeding inland to Herbertsdale and 12 km further on, 35 km from the Gouritz River bridge, the coastal road reaches the port and holiday resort of Mossel Bay.

## Chapter Fifteen

# THE GARDEN ROUTE

## MOSSEL BAY

Mossel Bay, the fifth harbour of South Africa and a major holiday resort, has a population of 24 909 with a considerable addition in numbers during vacation periods. The town is attractively (if slightly awkwardly) situated on cliffs and a narrow terrace between them and the sea. Cape St Blaize dominates the town with an 80-m-high cliff on the summit of which stands a lighthouse winking seductively at passing ships with a 20 000 candlepower lamp. The harbour lies below this cliff with space for fishing vessels, coasters and other small craft. Heavier vessels lie out in the roadstead and are serviced by lighters.

It was on 3 February 1488 that the Portuguese explorer, Bartholomew Dias, became the first navigator to sail into Mossel Bay. After doubling the Cape of Good Hope, far out to sea in a vicious storm, this was the first landfall made by a sailor from Europe on the eastern side of Southern Africa. It is pleasant to imagine the delight and fascination of Dias and his crew as they looked over the spacious bay to the great range of mountains on the inland horizon.

Dias named the bay the *Angra dos Vaqueiros* (bay of the cowherds) after the Hottentot pastoralists and their herds who could be seen wandering along the shore. What they, in turn, thought of the miracle before them – a sailing ship appearing on the hitherto empty waters of the bay – is unfortunately unrecorded. Dias did try to communicate with them but a volley of stones rewarded his efforts and he sailed off on his voyage of discovery.

On 20 November 1497, Vasco da Gama reached the bay and his charts are marked with the name *Aguade de São Bras* (watering place of Saint Bras) for it was on the feast day of that saint that Bartholomew Dias had originally visited the place. The corrupt version of this name is still retained in Cape St Blaize.

Da Gama established friendly trading relations with the Hottentot herdsmen and thenceforth many Portuguese ships called to obtain fresh water and meat, and to leave messages, often hanging in such things as old sea boots, tied to the branches of a milkwood tree growing close to the fountain of fresh water which the sailors used to fill their casks. Messages were also left carved into rocks, and a cast of one of these may be seen in the local museum.

The old 'post office tree' and the little fountain, both now declared national monuments, may still be seen close to the beach. A letter box in the shape of a navigator's boot has been erected there and any letters posted in it receive a special post office franking. Close to the post office tree, one of the Portuguese visitors, John da Nova, in 1501 erected a small shrine and this was the first place of Christian worship in South Africa.

On 4 August 1595, Cornelis de Houtman of Holland visited the bay and he named it *Mossel* (mussel) Bay from the pile of shells of that mollusc which he found on the floor of the huge open cavern (known today as Bats Cave) just below the modern lighthouse. Mussels and oysters were collected in the tidal zone along the shore by the Dutch sailors and these shellfish are still gathered each spring tide in Mossel Bay and marketed throughout Southern Africa.

Over the years many ships called at Mossel Bay in search of refreshment or shelter from storms. With its rocky little island covered in seals, the bay became well known and was marked on all the early maps of the African coast as a sheltered and convenient anchorage. In

1734 the Governor of the Cape, Jan de la Fontaine, visited the bay by sea and erected there a stone beacon of possession, with the arms of the Dutch Republic and the monogram of the Dutch East India Company.

It was not until 1787, however, that the first permanent settlement was made on the site of the present town. In that year a granary was built there and in July of the following year the first shipment was made of wheat grown in the surrounding countryside. From that date Mossel Bay started to develop as a port for the Southern Cape and the Little Karoo. At first a ward of George, it became a separate magistracy on 18 March 1848. The name given to it was Aliwal (after the place in India where the Governor, Sir Harry Smith, had won a notable victory) but the older name of Mossel Bay proved more popular.

In the boom years of ostrich feathers, some 800 060 kg of feathers were exported annually through the port, and a breakwater and jetties – to allow small craft to dock – were built in 1912. The railway line reached Mossel Bay from Cape Town in 1905 and although ostrich feathers no longer provide a rich export cargo, ochre, wool and fruit products still attract ships to the bay. The first submarine pipeline built on the coast of Southern Africa also allows oil tankers of considerable size to discharge into a great cluster of storage tanks built in the industrial area known as the *Voorbaai* (fore bay).

With its equable climate, moderate rainfall of 375 mm a year, attractive scenery, beautiful beaches, natural swimming pool in the rocks below the lighthouse, caves (such as the Tunnel Cave) and Seal Island, Mossel Bay has always had a strong appeal to holidaymakers. Although it has developed slowly and never been 'fashionable' in the sense of smart hotels and sophisticated entertainments, the farming community of the Southern Cape and the two Karoos have a great affection for Mossel Bay and in the summer holiday season – especially over Christmas – they gather there in enormous camps. Some of the beaches (especially the ones known as *Die Bakke* (the trough) and Hartenbos are so crowded that it is said visitors have to queue there to reach the sea.

There is a museum in the town which features a collection of the seashells of the coast and exhibits related to the exploration of the area.

## Accommodation

* ★ Dias Hotel, 12 rooms, all with baths. R4 B/B. Phone 3620.
* ★★ Golden Rendezvous Motel, 68 rooms, with baths. R10 – R12 B/B, seasonal. Phone 3641.
* ★ Ocean View Hotel, 36 rooms, 22 with baths. R11,50 – R13,50 B/B. Phone 3711.
* ★ Santos Hotel, 46 rooms, 31 with baths. R10 – R15 B/B. Phone 3011.

## Caravans and camping

* ★★★® Bakke Caravan Park, 130 sites. R4,75 – R6,25 D according to position in season. 33 chalets (1 to 3 bedrooms each), R23 – R25 D, seasonal.
* ★★★® Mossel Bay Caravan Park, 76 sites. R4,50 D, seasonal. 4 cottages and 9 rondawels, R6,50 – R15 D.
* ★★★ Point Caravan Park, 230 sites. R4,75 – R6,25 D according to position in season.
* ★★★® Santos Caravan Park, 330 sites. R4,75 – R6,25 D according to position in season.

Apart from the municipal area of Mossel Bay itself, the whole stretch of the coastline of the bay is an area of recreation and holiday resorts. The main coastal road, from Mossel Bay onward, known as the Garden Route, makes a grand sweep along the verges of this bay and rewards the traveller with lovely views of blue water, an inviting beach, the islet and its seals, and the majestic Outeniqua Mountains watching serenely from the near horizon.

For the first 5 km from Mossel Bay the Garden Route is hemmed in closely between the cliffs and the shore. Past Voorbaai, with its railway marshalling yard and industrial area, the coastal belt widens slightly and 6 km from Mossel Bay the road reaches the resort of . . .

# HARTENBOS

*Hartenbos,* named after the river on whose banks grow the bushes of that name, is a resort particularly beloved by farmers. The influx into the place of recreation-seeking humanity during the holiday season is almost unbelievable and individuals employed in such enterprises as tearooms are left with a stunned expression for some weeks after the rush is over. Some 80 000 holidaymakers flock to the limited area in December and January. Most of them are farmers who habitually lead an isolated life, but enjoy a brief spell of gregarious existence; tolerating outrageous overcrowding for the sake of meeting old friends, exchanging news, lazing on a fine beach, re-opening sporting rivalries, being harangued by cultural and religious leaders, watching folk dancing in an open air amphitheatre, and allowing opportunity for the young folk to meet one another. The A. T. K. V. (Afrikaanse Taal en Kultuurvereniging) have the management of most of the area.

There is a Voortrekker museum at Hartenbos containing interesting exhibits from the pioneer days.

## Accommodation
* Riviera Hotel, 42 rooms, 27 with baths. R9 – R15 B/B. Phone 5203.
* Sea Shells Motel, 16 rooms, all with baths. R10,50 B/B. Phone 5103.

## Caravans and camping
*** A. T. K. V. Caravan Park, 1 000 sites. R3 – R6 D, seasonal. 119 cottages, 64 rondawels, 62 rooms, R3 – R16,50 D, seasonal.

The Garden Route bridges across the Hartenbos River 3,5 km from Hartenbos, and from here there is a branch tarmac road swinging northwards and leading over the mountains for 80 km to Oudtshoorn by means of the spectacular Robinson Pass. Built by the famous Thomas Bain and opened in June 1869, this pass was named after M. R. Robinson, the Commissioner of Roads. The pass carries the branch road 838 m above sea level from Mossel Bay and rewards the traveller with wonderful views. At Ruyterbos on the southern slopes of the pass is the
* Eight Bells Mountain Inn (18 rooms, all with baths. R8,50 B/B. Phone 5-8480).

Four kilometres beyond the Hartenbos River, the Garden Route crosses the Little Brak River and passes through another popular holiday resort with numerous shacks and bungalows and a pretty beach at the mouth of the river which gives the area its name.

## Accommodation
* Little Brak River Motel, 20 rooms, all with baths. R9 B/B. Phone Mossel Bay 6262.

## Caravans and camping
** Riverside Caravan Park, 100 sites. R3 D plus 75c D per person.

Ten kilometres beyond Little Brak River, the Garden Route reaches the Great Brak River, with its holiday resort, lagoon and beach. About this area there is an interesting tale.

# GREAT BRAK RIVER

Apart from being a picturesque holiday resort, with a cluster of bungalows built on a low island in the lagoon of the river (the Great Brak River), this area will always be associated with the name of one man.

When the first bridge was built across the river its construction had to be financed by means of a toll. The keeping of the toll was put out for tender in 1859 and the successful tenderer was

Charles Searle, who had emigrated to South Africa in the previous year and, with his family, was staying near George with his brother.

Searle settled next to the bridge on the farm known as *Voorbrug,* operated the toll, built a store and gradually acquired 1 713 ha of choice surrounding land. In 1875 he started a watermill and two years later a woolwashery. In 1884 he sold the growing business to his sons and two years later a beginning was made with a boot and shoe factory, employing only two men. The following year a tannery was opened and soon a village of 2 500 inhabitants, nearly all dependents of the Searle enterprise, grew up at Great Brak River. Searles Limited is today one of the best known shoe and boot manufacturers in Southern Africa.

From the Great Brak River village there is a gravel road (the original road) leading to George and from this road there is a most beautiful drive leading to the forestry station of Jonkersberg and the Ernest Robertson Dam which supplies water to Mossel Bay. A permit to visit the dam is necessary and is obtainable from the Mossel Bay municipality. It is worth the trouble.

## Caravans and camping
*Municipal caravan park, 186 sites. R4 D.
** Pine Creek Caravan Park, 140 sites. R4 D.

From the Great Brak River bridge the Garden Route climbs above the coastal strip. With a lingering view behind of Mossel Bay and Cape St Blaize and an exciting glimpse up the coast of beaches, bays and cliffs, the road twists inland and for the loss of the seascape the traveller is compensated by handsome panoramic views of the whole length of the Outeniqua Mountains.

The traveller is now in a different world – a higher terrace about 250 m above the sea. The change in scene is so remarkable that few can disagree with the description given of it in the 1780s by the French traveller, Le Vaillant:

'We had to climb a difficult and very steep mountain. The scenery which now appeared richly rewarded all our trouble. The land bears the name of *Outeniqua,* which in the Hottentot tongue means 'a man laden with honey'. The flowers grow there in millions, the mixture of pleasant scents which arises from them, their colour, their variety, the pure and fresh air which one breathes there, all these make one stop and think nature has made an enchanted abode of this beautiful place.'

The Garden Route leads across this amiable landscape, crossing such torrents as the Gwayang and the *Maalgat* (whirlpool) rivers. Several branch roads tempt the traveller to turn off and explore the surrounding countryside. Eight kilometres from Great Brak River a gravel road branches off south (right) and leads down to the developing coastal resort of Glentana. This is a fine 7-km-long drive descending steeply to the coast and yielding impressive views of Mossel Bay. There is a nice beach at Glentana, the usual collection of bungalows and, about 1 km up the coast, the wreck (visible at low tide) of a 120-m-long floating dock which came to grief there in a howling gale while being towed to Durban in October 1902. The crew escaped but the brand new R150 000 worth of dock was a total loss.

## Caravans and camping
* Glentana Caravan Park, 55 sites. R5 D.

Seventeen kilometres from Great Brak River there is another turnoff south (right). This leads 7,5 km along a tarmac road to the singularly pretty little bay known as . . .

## HEROLD'S BAY

*Herold's Bay,* named after the Reverend Tobias Herold of George, is set in the steep cliffs with a collection of bungalows looking down on a safe swimming beach. Paths lead along the coast to such fishermen's vantage points as Voëlklip and Skotsebank and it is altogether a pleasant and intimate little resort.

## Accommodation
★ Searle's Inn, 13 rooms, 6 with baths. R8 – R8,50 B/B. Phone 4528.

## Caravans and camping
★★ Dutton's Cove Holiday Resort, 36 sites. R5 D plus 25c D per person.
★ Herold's Bay Caravan Park, 53 sites. R5 D.

From the turnoff to Herold's Bay, the Garden Route continues its pleasant way past the P. W. Botha airport and then, 27,5 km from Great Brak River, it reaches the town of . . .

# GEORGE

George, with its population of 45 190, is one of the great junctions on the Garden Route, for it not only lies astride this wonderful coastal trunk road, but is the terminal for an important road leading over the Outeniqua Pass to the Little Karoo and the Long Kloof (see page 310).

In a setting of great natural beauty, 226 m above sea level on the plateau terrace between the Outeniqua Mountains and the sea, George has always been the admiration of visitors, for it can hardly help being beautiful, even though many of its lovely trees have vanished beneath the axe of a modern age which shows little inclination to replace them.

The town of George had its birth shortly after the second British occupation of the Cape. The earlier Dutch administration had already felt the need to establish an administrative centre further east than Swellendam in order to provide more effective control over this part of the Cape; and the new British Governor, the Earl of Caledon, was in agreement with this need. He sent Lieutenant Collins to investigate the matter and, as a result, on 12 October 1809, the Governor recommended to the Colonial Secretary that a new magistracy be established in the area of Outeniqualand.

The new district was proclaimed on 23 April 1811, and Adrianus van Kervel appointed as the first landdros. To Van Kervel fell the interesting task of laying out the new town known as George Town, named after the reigning king of England, George III. The first erven were presented free to six woodcutters whose labours would provide materials for the construction of the new town.

York, Meade and Courtenay streets were the first to be laid out. The landdros decreed their width to be 91 m and trees had to be planted on both pavements 'not only for ornament but for defending passengers from the scorching rays of an almost vertical sun'.

With plentiful supplies of amber-coloured water, good soil, and an amiable climate, gardens flourished in the town and it became a place of flowers, with the beautiful Outeniqua Mountains providing a background to a middle distance of green forest and a foreground of every flower colour imaginable.

In 1837 George Town became a municipality. The growth of the town was leisurely. It was simply an administrative outpost, a staging post for travellers proceeding east, and a centre for the timber cutting industry in the surrounding forests. Mine props, railway sleepers, hardwood for furniture and softwood for boxes all came from the George area. The industry was at first parasitic, simply cutting down existing trees, but in 1896 a nursery was established at Witfontein for the purpose of reafforestation, and from then on considerable planting of trees began around George, mainly exotic softwoods such as pines.

The railway line from Cape Town reached George on 25 September 1907, and was carried on over the mountains to Oudtshoorn by means of seven tunnels, involved cuttings and steep gradients. The picturesque branch line through the coastal lake country to Knysna was opened in 1928.

Dairy farming, the growing of hops for beer making (first started by a man named Stietz in 1829) and vegetables are the principal agricultural products of the George district.

Close to George the London Missionary Society, in 1813, established a station named *Pacaltsdorp* after the Reverend Charles Pacalt, the German missionary who founded it.

At Saasveld, 8 km east of George, is South Africa's training centre for foresters. It was established in 1932 and is housed in a handsome building with furnishings and woodwork made of a large variety of indigenous timber.

George is famous for its wild flowers. The scarlet lily is unique to the area while proteas, erica, watsonia and the *Gladioli splendor* cover the mountain slopes with carpets of colour.

The George Museum, which owes its creation to a public-spirited resident, Mr E. O. Sayers, is housed in the old town hall where its large collections are well displayed. One of its many interesting exhibits is a collection of old phonographs, many still in working order. It is open on Mondays, Tuesdays, Thursdays and Fridays from 09h00 to 13h00 and 15h00 to 17h00; Wednesdays 09h00 to 13h00 and Saturdays 09h00 to 12h30. Admission is free.

## Accommodation

* ★ Criterion Hotel, 18 rooms, 7 with baths. R8 – R9,50 B/B. Phone 2403.
* ★ Garden Route Hotel, 30 rooms, 16 with baths. R8,50 – R9,50 B/B. Phone 3600.
* ★ Gelderland Hotel, 15 rooms, 6 with baths. R9 – R10,50 B/B. Phone 2303.
* ★ George Hotel, 37 rooms, 16 with baths. R8,50 – R9,50 B/B. Phone 2003.
* ★★ Hawthorndene Hotel, 32 rooms, 28 with baths. R10,50 B/B. Phone 3391.
* ★ Outeniqua Hotel, 16 rooms, all with baths. R12 B/B. Phone 2920.

## Caravans and camping

* ★★★® George Tourist Camp, 400 sites. R3,50 D. 44 rondawels and bungalows. R4 – R6 D.
* ★★★★® Caravan Park International, 200 sites. R5 – R7,50 D, seasonal.

## THE PASSES ROAD

The prodigious difficulties encountered by road engineers in the building of the great coastal trunk road between Cape Town and Durban are perfectly illustrated by the complex stretch of country encountered between George and Knysna. Here, between the mountains and the sea, there is a narrow belt of country averaging 24 km in width. It consists of a plateau terrace at the foot of the mountains, falling sharply to a narrow coastal belt of lakes and lagoons. The terrace is deeply bisected by the gorges and ravines of successive streams and rivers and to add to these formidable barriers the well-watered landscape – with a rainfall of up to 2 540 mm a year on the mountains – is densely wooded with luxuriant primeval forests, tangles of shrubbery and such masses of wild flowers, heath and creepers as to fully justify its description as the garden of Southern Africa.

To fully appreciate the difficulties of the road engineers, and the way they surmounted them, take (before following the great highway of today) the earlier alternative route, known as the Passes Road, which was the first link between George and Knysna. This gravel road is maintained in excellent condition as it feeds several important forestry stations as well as providing tourists with a fascinating and leisurely scenic drive.

The Passes Road branches off from the modern Garden Route 3 km outside George. It immediately leads into difficult roadmakers' country with a 3-km-long descent into the valley of the *Swart* (black) River. In former times this descent was a nightmare. The first wagon track simply slithered almost straight into the valley and, with their wheels *remmed* (braked with blocks), the wagons wore the road into a deep channel, more than 2 m deep and so narrow that a man could not pass between the banks and the sides of the vehicles. Down this chute the wagons went, with a loud cracking of whips by the drivers to warn any travellers not to start coming up in the opposite direction, for a first-class disaster would occur if two wagons encountered each other on the pass.

This hazardous pass, and the rest of the pioneer trunk road to the east, became so notorious that eventually, in 1861, a select committee was set up to investigate the matter. As a result work eventually began on the first properly made road between George and Knysna in 1867. The famous Thomas Bain had the task of locating and constructing the new road, and the Passes Road followed today is substantially his work. He must have had a fascinating and energetic time sorting out the difficulties of the route, and a great deal of satisfaction in seeing it completed.

Across the Swart River there is a shady picnic site. The road rises for 3 km through the forest to the level of the plateau where, against a magnificent background of the Outeniqua Mountains, stand the gates of Saasveld, the college for the Department of Forestry. There, in a delightful environment, the young foresters of South Africa receive their training.

*Saasveld* takes its name from the ancient castle in Holland, the original seat of the ancestors of the Van Reede van Oudtshoorn family. Baroness Gesina E. J. van Reede van Oudtshoorn became the wife of E. Bergh, civil commissioner of George, and owned a portion of the ground on which Saasveld now stands.

This ridge was originally occupied by a farm with the rather lowly name of *Pampoenkraal* (pumpkin corral), the property of Barend Stander, a man fortunately renowned for his hospitality. He was often called upon to extend this courtesy for, 1,5 km east of his farm, the road descends to the crossing of the *Kaaimans* (alligators) River. It is now an easy descent but before the engineering of Thomas Bain, it required the labours of 32 oxen to effect a wagon crossing of the murderous gradient and torrent which often ran so wild that travellers were delayed for days on end. The notorious *Kaaimans Gat* (alligator's hole) near which the old road found its passage was reputedly a merman's pool, haunted by water spirits.

No sooner is the road across the Kaaimans River than it has to cross the Silver River in a pretty pass and then climb 1,5 km up to a crossroads at a little rural post office and store known as Ginnesville, 14 km from George. From here a road known as White's Road branches down to the coast at the Wilderness.

Beautiful farms such as *Woodfield* and *Pieter-Koen* (Jan Pieter Koen, grandson of a famous director of the Dutch East India Company, settled here in the 1750s), may be seen on either side of the road. *Barbierskraal* (barber's place) is another old name in this area, where a foreman labouring to improve the original track swore that he would not shave until the task was achieved. It is on record that he grew an uncommonly long beard!

Six kilometres east of Ginnesville the road traverses another thickly wooded river valley, this time the valley of the river nowadays known as the *Touw,* said to be a corruption of the original Hottentot name, *Krakede Kau* (maiden's ford). A picturesque river pass today, it was a fearsome toil for the oxen before Bain relocated the road. Right on its eastern summit there is a tarmac road branching off to the Wilderness while the gravel road veers left and continues across another of the plateau segments of this terraced country.

Six kilometres further on (26 km from George) the road reaches the turnoff to the forest stations of Woodville, Bergplaas and Kleinplaat. If one has the time it is worth turning aside here. For 16 km the road burrows through the forest right up close to the mountains where the forestry settlements of Bergplaas and Kleinplaat lie. From here the energetic can follow the original road, now quite disused, which gave up the struggle with the river crossings and made its way over the mountains by the pass known as *Duiwelskop* (devil's peak) and descended on the northern side of the range into the Long Kloof. This was the route all the early travellers took including Sir Harry Smith on his 950-km six-day ride to reach Grahamstown when news spread to Cape Town that the Xhosa had invaded the Eastern Cape.

One and a half kilometres before Woodville there is a turnoff north leading to an enormous yellowwood tree, 600 years old, 31 m high with a girth of 9 m.

Bain pushed his own new road due east over all obstacles: across the valley of the Diep or Swart River, past Lancewood (34 km from George) across to Hoogekraal valley, over the plateau where the Karatara Forestry Station and rehabilitation settlement of the Department of Social Welfare lie; down and up the sides of the shady valley of the Karatara River; past the forestry centres of Barrington (where Henry Barrington had his farm) and Farleigh. Then, winding, twisting, climbing and falling through forests, plantations, wild flowers and fields of erica, with cottages peeping from the wayside, contentedly smoking their chimneys, the road (42 km from George) comes to the deep and beautifully wooded valley of the *Homtini* (the place of the passage).

Bain completed the Homtini Pass in 1882. It is a classic piece of old-time roadmaking with dramatic views and the indefinable elegance of its curves. The river itself is a gorgeous torrent of amber-coloured water, tumbling down from the deep forests of the mountain slopes to the north.

All travellers along this road should turn aside at some stage in their journey and drive into the primeval forest. An excellent opportunity occurs 1,5 km beyond the east summit of the Homtini Pass. Here, just where the tarmac starts, there is a road branching off to the *Goudveld* (goldfield) Forestry Station. The intriguing name is itself an invitation. Take this side road.

The entrance to the forestry station lies 1,5 km from the start of the turnoff. Drive in through the arch and secure a permit from the forester (during normal working hours only). Continue past the forestry offices, across the grid and into the forest: a most entrancing drive runs along a good gravel track which tunnels through the tall indigenous trees. After 3 km there is a junction. Take the Jubilee Track to the left. A thick carpet of ferns covers the verges of the road and the trees meet overhead. Another 3 km further on a sign directs the traveller to the left for 1,5 km down a track to a picnic site on the banks of an exquisite little stream known as Forest Creek. Here gold was prospected in former times, and one can still find a 'tail' of yellow dust in a pan today, if one tries one's luck.

The track continues across the creek for 1,5 km to Natbos where there is a picnic site in the shade of a gigantic 400-year-old yellowwood tree, and then ends at another picnic site at Droërug.

Back on the main track, continue out of the indigenous forest, through a plantation and after 3 km, the road reaches the forestry settlement of Millwood. Here in the late 1880s, there was a bustling town of prospectors and gold diggers. One thousand men rushed into this sylvan area in 1886 when alluvial gold was found in several of the streams by an inspector of roads named C. F. Osborne. On 6 August 1886, John Courtney found reef gold in the overlooking hills and excitement reached a fine pitch. By the end of 1887 the town of Millwood had seven hotels, 25 shops, three banks, seven butcher's, four baker's, a police station, post office, three newspapers, and 40 mining syndicates. Machinery was brought in; adits, shafts and trenches dug and the sound of dynamite explosions rumbled incessantly through the trees. Now nothing remains. One has to search and scramble to find the foundations of the houses, the rusty machinery, the caved-in excavations. The gold was there, but only enough to tantalise. The prospectors went broke. The heath, the trees, the wild flowers and mountains reclaimed their own, and all that is left today is the ghost of a vanished town.

The Oudtshoorn Mine was the most promising venture on the Millwood field. When it proved a failure the spirit went out of the rush. Millwood was so named after an overshot sawmill waterwheel originally run there by a Mr Franzen.

Back on the main Passes Road, (now tarmac), pass the forestry centre of Rheenendal and for 6 km continue over a fertile plateau with many fine views of the mountains and the long belt of forest. Then the road reaches a turnoff. The tarmac road sweeps on to Keytersnek and Knysna, 13 km away. The Passes Road proper reverts to a gravel surface and turns sharply left. For 3 km it descends steeply down the Phantom Pass (so named after the phantom moths common there), rewarding the traveller with charming views of the delightfully green and completely rural valley of the Knysna River lying below. From the bottom of the pass the road runs for a further 5 km along the banks of the river and then joins the modern coastal road just before it bridges across the upper end of the Knysna Lagoon (82 km from George by the Passes Road).

By modern standards this old road is quite inadequate except for sightseeing. When the modern road came to be built, P. A. de Villiers – that prince of location engineers – abandoned the plateau terrace entirely and boldly took the road from George straight down to the sea, blasting and cutting a spectacular route through country totally impossible to the old-time engineers. In the process of this construction a classic example was presented of the changes which can be brought to an area by a new road. The whole coastal stretch from George to Knysna was completely transformed by this road. From a remote wilderness of bush and lake it developed within a few years of the coming of the road into a lotus land of pleasure and recreation with a considerable industry in hotels, motels and caravan parks.

---

From George the modern coastal road (the Garden Route) descends steadily to the coast. Passing after 3 km the turnoff to the Passes Road and, 5 km further on, the turn to Victoria Bay, the road crosses the Swart River and sweeps downwards, revealing some of the finest roadmaking in Southern Africa. The view here has given delight to countless travellers. In all the world there can be few more serenely beautiful scenes of river and coast. Here the dark amber-black waters of the Kaaimans and the Swart rivers merge and, with a great tidal ebb and flow, make their way down a deep valley to the sea.

## VICTORIA BAY

Victoria Bay, 3 km from the turnoff by a tarred road, is worth seeing. It consists of a small bathing beach set in a tiny bay from which there is clearly no exit by land at either end. A row of seaside houses, a small concrete pier, a tearoom and caravan park make up the amenities. In the 1840s there was a project to turn this little bay into a landing harbour. There are several places of accommodation in the vicinity, mostly higher up at the main road. It is considered to be one of the best surfing areas of Southern Africa. During the winter months some very big waves work this part of the coast.

All land masses with shores exposed to deep water have surf but the waves are not always entirely suitable for the sport of surfing. Southern Africa possesses several beaches where conditions are ideal or almost ideal for surfing. Surfers regard as perfect, a wave which breaks sufficiently early and far from the shore to give them a long run and provide the chance of trying out manoeuvres and skills. A big wave breaking too near the shore is spectacular to see but useless fur surfing. The waves must be powerful, with all the muscle and weight of a heavy swell, having a wall at least 3 m to 5 m high and the ability to summarily 'wipe out' or 'dump' a surfer, thereby making the ride high and wild, taxing his stamina, skill and experience. The surfer does not compete with the wave; he wishes to harmonise with its movement, stealing some of its power to carry him along. He cannot fight such a wave; he can only ride it to the point of its tolerance. If its power exceeds his capacity, he will be wiped out, his board broken and he will possibly have the nasty experience of being unceremoniously dumped on the rocks or beach.

The isolated volcanic islands of Hawaii (the home of surfing) rise abruptly from the tremendous depths of the Pacific Ocean and are exposed to waves originating from a vast variety of disturbances. Huge seismic waves originate from earthquakes; so-called tsunami waves are caused by earth movement on the bed of the sea, while the complex play of wind on water over the huge expanse of the Pacific Ocean produces waves of prodigious power.

Waves emanating from such disturbances can travel for immense distances without losing much energy. As they finally approach a land mass they come under the influence of the shallowing sea bed. Wildly undisciplined in the outer ocean, the waves travel at speeds varying from 25 km to 32 km an hour. As the water shallows they are braked from below by the rising sea bed. The crest eventually falls forward over its own base, the power of the wave is broken and it expires on the beach.

The principal surfing beaches of Southern Africa are at Elands Bay on the south-west coast of the Cape Province, where the south-east winds of summer produce a heavy swell; Chapmans Bay on the Cape Peninsula, where the summer south-easter produces some giant waves at Long Beach and De Hoek; Muizenberg and Kalk Bay, where the north-westerly wind of winter produces small but lively waves; Victoria Bay; the celebrated St Frances Bay (see page 305); and Nahoon at East London where a very consistent reef wave of great power breaks.

## Accommodation
* Seabreeze Tearoom, 8 furnished chalets. R25 D.

## Caravans and camping
** Sea Glimpse Caravan Park, 8 sites. R5 D.
* Victoria Bay Caravan Park, 58 sites. R5 D.

Just beyond the Kaaimans River bridge (a handsome curved concrete structure), a somewhat inconspicuous gravel turnoff on the right leads down to a place ideal for riverside picnics, and provides access to a handful of houses on the opposite bank. The Kaaimans River is a pleasure for canoeists, and the waterfall up the course of the Swart River can only be seen from such a craft.

The road then follows the east bank of the river, rising steadily as it nears the sea. The branch railway from George to Knysna crosses the mouth of the river by means of a bridge, after making its own spectacular descent to the coast through tunnels and cuttings. Countless photographers must have paused at this point in the hope of seeing a train crossing the bridge. (The railway service follows an erratic schedule: about 07h00 and 13h15 from George daily except Sundays, with an occasional special. About 12h00 and 15h30 back to George).

This branch railway, built in 1928, has a 68-km route which the puffers take about 3 hours to complete. It is a highly diverting journey and a most enjoyable alternative way of seeing the lake country.

The coastal road now swings sharply around a shoulder of the cliff and ahead and below stretches one of the loveliest views imaginable of seascape and forest-covered downland. The road descends to sea level and 13 km from George reaches . . .

# WILDERNESS

Wilderness had its start on 16 January 1877 when George Bennet purchased for £500 what was known as Lot 497 (H) originally surveyed in 1850 by M. J. Adams. Bennet decided that his purchase should have a name and called it what it was, a wilderness of dense forest and bush falling from the interior right down to the edge of the lagoon of the Touw River.

With no road access of any kind, Bennet constructed a rough track down from the Passes Road and built a homestead on the site of the famous modern luxury hotel. There he lived until his death, the property (in 1886) passing into the hands of his widow's second husband. In May 1905 the property was acquired by The Wilderness Estate Company (Montagu White and Associates) who divided it into plots, built a new road (White's Road) tò provide access, and converted the farmhouse into a boarding house run by Hannie and Alida van Niekerk.

The venture did not prosper. In 1921 the estate was auctioned. A new company, The Wilderness (1921) (Pty) Ltd, took over, with one of the directors, Owen Grant, later acquiring sole ownership. With some genius he converted the farmhouse-cum-boarding house into the beginnings of the renowned Wilderness Hotel. Plots were sold and the modern resort came into being. With its beautiful (but dangerous) beach, spacious lagoon, superb boating river and magnificent scenery, Wilderness is today one of the finest of all South African resorts.

There is a small nature reserve entered from the road at the right hand side of the Wilderness Hotel, in which a footpath leads up one side of a thickly wooded valley and back to the starting point, with three signposted alternatives each a little longer than the preceding one. This is the haunt of many of the area's birds and a recommended excursion.

### Accommodation
*® Fairy Knowe Hotel, 48 rooms, 29 with baths. R10,50 – R14 B/B. Phone George 9100.
** Holiday Inn, 106 rooms, all with baths. R23 – R30 room only. Phone George 9014.
**® Wilderness Hotel, 107 rooms, all with baths. R17,50 – R30 B/B. Phone George 9110.

### Caravans and camping
* Ebb and Flow Caravan Park, 78 sites. R5 D. 15 rondawels, R6,24 D.
** Island Lake Caravan Park, 40 sites. R3,50 D. 4 rondawels, R6 – R11 D.
** Kleinkrans Holiday Resort, 60 sites. R2 D. 6 bungalows, R4,16 D.
** ® Lakes Holiday Resort, 72 sites. R2,50 – R5,50 D. 7 cottages, 2 rooms.
** ® Siesta Caravan Park, 80 sites. R2 – R3,50 D.

From Wilderness the coastal road continues in a fine drive running along the narrow strip between the sea and the chain of lakes: the Langvlei, Rondevlei, Swartvlei and Groenvlei. Oddly enough, each of these beautiful little lakes has the reputation of being haunted. Groenvlei, with its green-coloured waters, is reputedly a particular haunt of water spirits who can be heard singing as they float on the surface in the light of the moon. Bushman paintings in several caves in the Outeniqua Mountains and Little Karoo, strangely enough, depict women with fish tails, so the legends date from a long time ago. Ghostly carts with horses are also said to have been seen galloping across the waters of this still and peaceful little lake. All these lakes have resorts on their banks and any ghosts present certainly do not interfere with the pleasures of boating, yachting, swimming and fishing!

The main lake is Rondevlei which forms part of a Nature Conservation research station whose buildings stand on the eastern shore. All the lakes are saline to varying degrees, Rondevlei being 15 parts per 1 000 saline content. Swartvlei is the deepest of the lakes, the average depth being around 6 m. The water of all the lakes is rich in food and fish flourish, especially the smaller species which have found a sanctuary for themselves where there are no predatory fish and only a few otters with the numerous birds which feed in the calm waters.

Swartvlei is best for fishing with steenbras, grunter and harder in its waters. Groenvlei is good for bass. About 160 species of birds frequent the lakes, exploring the surrounding coastal terrace for food by day and returning to the trees around the lakes at night when a rich symphony of calls and songs provides an accompaniment to the kaleidoscopic changes of dawn and sunset. The chorister robins of the area seem to act as the prima donnas.

Eilandsvlei, Langvlei and Rondevlei are connected to the sea by a natural channel known as the Serpentine which joins the rivers at Ebb and Flow to feed the lagoon at Wilderness. Canoeing through the Serpentine or up the Touw and Ebb and Flow is a delightful experience, for the river valleys are natural wildlife sanctuaries, with glorious trees and such singing of birds as makes the verdant valleys resemble the entrance to paradise.

Thirteen and a half kilometres from Wilderness, the Garden Route reaches a turnoff leading to the Nature Conservation office at Rondevlei, and to several holiday resorts on the shores of the lakes.

## Caravans and camping
★★★® Jooris Caravan Park, 90 sites. R2 – R4 D plus 60c D per person, seasonal.

★★★® Pine Lake Marina, 150 sites. R3 – R6 D, seasonal. 8 flats and 25 cottages, R7 D, seasonal.

★★★® Trails End Caravan Park, 150 sites. R3 – R6 D plus 50c D per person, seasonal.

From this turnoff to Rondevlei, the coastal road continues eastwards for 1 km and then bridges across Swartvlei. A further 2 km of pleasant driving along the coastal terrace brings the road (16,5 km from Wilderness) to the village of . . .

# SEDGEFIELD

Sedgefield has inactivity as its most considerable industry. It is the centre for several holiday resorts situated on the lakes and sea coast. The coast is reached by a tarmac turnoff from the Garden Route as it passes through the village. The turnoff follows the verge of Swartvlei and leads to a pleasant assembly of seaside houses overlooking a sandy beach. Just before crossing the bridge to the coastal resort, there is a gravel turnoff signposted Swartvlei. This passes the caravan park and camping ground and then climbs the dunes to end at a sort of belvedere overlooking a wide bay with its right arm ending in a barren crag, Gerickespunt, accessible only on foot at low tide. Notwithstanding this inconvenience, the point is a fishing harbour, with several boats generally resting on the beach. In an easterly direction, the beach extends smooth and level, past the estuary of Swartvlei to Buffels Bay.

## Caravans and camping
★★ Cloverdale Caravan Park, 100 sites. R4,50 D.

★★★ Landfall Caravan Park, 48 sites. R4,50 D.

★★★ Sedgefield Caravan Park, 20 sites. R3,50 D plus 25c D per person.

★★ Swartvlei Caravan Park, 157 sites. R3,50 D.

Four kilometres east of Sedgefield, the main coastal road reaches the lake known as Groen-vlei or Lake Pleasant. This beautiful lake is in a delightful setting and its charms are well appreciated by a discerning flock of swans who live there permanently, breeding in the beds of reeds and providing a pretty spectacle as they cruise over the calm waters. Black bass and blue gill fish abound in the lake. For the bird watcher there are many interesting scenes and studies in this area. A canoe allows for exploration of the lake, with opportunities for photographing the nests of birds who live in the reeds. Sunset on the lake is often very lovely.

## Accommodation
★★ ® Lake Pleasant Hotel, 21 rooms, 11 with baths. R17 – R19 D/B/B. Phone Sedgefield 10.

## Caravans and camping
★★★ ® Lake Pleasant Caravan Park, 120 sites. R2 – R6 D plus 50c D per person, seasonal.

Beyond Lake Pleasant, the coastal road continues for 2 km, then passes a turnoff to Karatara (see the section on the Passes Road). A further 9 km of driving through a natural garden brings the road to the Goukamma River and a tarmac turnoff leading for 6 km to the resort of Buffels Bay and to the . . .

# GOUKAMMA NATURE RESERVE

This reserve was created by the Cape Provincial Administration to protect a characteristic area of the coastal dunes and the natural bird sanctuary of the Goukamma River.

The public are admitted to a spacious and shady picnic site by the riverside during daylight hours, but the reserve proper is only accessible by permit obtainable from the ranger's office, Mondays to Fridays, between 07h30 and 16h30. To reach the ranger's office, drive through the gate (marked 'no admittance') and continue up the hill and round the bend past two houses, to the end of the road, where a double-storeyed house contains the office on the ground floor. At other times, permits may be obtained by post from the Senior Nature Conservation Officer, Groenvlei, P. O. Sedgefield, 6573. Phone Sedgefield 50.

Once in possession of a permit, a member of the public has access to several attractive nature trails; the adventurous visitor may continue through the whole reserve, to emerge at Groenvlei by the Lake Pleasant Hotel.

The entire area is a good place to see water birds, the commoner ones, and those most likely to be seen by the casual walker are the Egyptian goose, yellowbill duck, blacksmith plover, both the Cape and water dikkops, crowned plover and black-backed gull. There are three species of kingfisher, the pied, giant and brown hooded, and the black Cape raven is a common sight. In the bush there are many greater double-collared sunbirds, red-winged starlings and Cape canaries. The total number of species so far recorded is 174.

Beyond the turnoff to the nature reserve, the tarmac road continues for 3,5 km to the small resort of Buffels Bay (Buffalo Bay), where there is no hotel, but a large beach café and a caravan park.

### Caravans and camping
★ Buffels Bay Caravan Park, 80 sites. R2 D plus 25c D per person out of season. R4 D plus 50c D per person in season.

Beyond the turnoff to the Goukamma Nature Reserve and Buffalo Bay, the main coastal road continues for a further 6 km, climbs a rise and then makes a grand descent to the great lagoon of Knysna. At the bridge, the Passes Road comes in to join the coastal road. At this point there is a branch road turning off to Brenton and the pretty little church of Belvidere. This road is worth taking. The church lies 2 km from the turnoff and is surrounded by trees, the Belvidere homestead, and a few creeper-covered cottages.

Belvidere Church might well be regarded as a lesson in Norman (12th century) architecture to anyone who has not seen it in its native Europe, for it has many of the features of that style, including interlaced arcading, a massive entrance arch in two orders, a round-headed chancel arch, rounded apse, and capitals based on Norman originals. The stained-glass windows are interesting, especially those in the apse, which came from the bombed ruins of Coventry Cathedral in Britain.

Belvidere was acquired from George Rex by Lieutenant Thomas Duthie when he married Rex's daughter Caroline. Belvidere House was their homestead and they built the church in the 1850s. One and a half kilometres before the church, the main branch road turns sharply to the right and climbs steeply through plantations of pine and gum trees. Wild flowers and erica are in profusion, while the views are spectacular of the great lagoon of Knysna on the one side and Buffalo Bay on the other. The erica in many varieties bloom around April. After 7 km the road reaches the resort of Brenton-on-Sea. Brenton, originally part of the famous *Melkhout-kraal* estate, was named after Sir Jahleel Brenton, the British Admiral who opened Knysna harbour.

### Accommodation
★ Brenton Hotel, 28 rooms, all with baths. R14 – R18 D/B/B. Phone Knysna 4140.

289

*Overleaf: Deep in the high forest on the road from Knysna to Avontuur; the dale of ferns, a legendary retreat for supernatural creatures.*

**Caravans and camping**

★★ Lake Brenton Holiday Resort, 80 sites. R4 D plus 50c D per person. 14 cottages, 28 rondawels, R15 – R22 D.

From the bridge across the upper end of the Knysna lagoon, the Garden Route makes a handsome 6-km-long drive down the northern shores to the town and holiday resort of . . .

# KNYSNA

Knysna is one of those places to which most people who see it say they would like to retire. Its 17 805 inhabitants live in the mildest of climates, with 762 mm of rain considerably falling mainly at night and distributed over the four seasons in order to keep the area perennially green. Its situation between the great inland forests and the shores of the tranquil lagoon, the wonderful sunsets reflecting over the waters, the Outeniqua Mountains watching from the horizon, the spectacular gateway to the sea through the Heads, are all additional attractions.

The Knysna lagoon is a rich field of study for the scientists. Its bottom varies from a deep mouth to the sea, through deep to shallow channels and mudbanks further inland. Over 200 different species of fish flourish in it, including a rare species of seahorse unique to the lagoon.

At the lagoon end of Long Street, just past Thesen's factory, are found the premises of the Knysna Oyster Company. Here the gastronome may buy those delectable dainties fresh from the sea at a most reasonable price — provided he buys a hundred or more at a time. Those who like their shellfish in smaller quantities, should go to Melville's department store, at the top of the same street, where they are sold in multiples of ten.

Adjoining the oyster company's office, a division of the Fisheries Development Corporation maintains an oyster hatchery, Knysna Lagoon being one of the few places on this coast whose water is (so far) sufficiently unpolluted to allow for such an undertaking.

For anglers the Knysna estuary is one of the world's great sporting areas. The variety and number of fish, the pleasant climate, varied conditions and beauty of seascape, all combine to make an exciting experience. There is an ample supply of bait.

The concreted road leading from Knysna around the east shores of the lagoon to The Heads yields many handsome views. Near the end of this road, a tarmac turnoff climbs to the top of the eastern Head and terminates at Coney Glen. The views from this road (especially towards sunset) are superb. Wonderful as these views are, however, the aspect of the shore at the foot of the steep, concrete road, presents one of the most magnificent seascapes in South Africa. A more splendid confusion of red rocks and blue ocean can scarcely be imagined.

A puzzling thing about Knysna is the meaning of its name. It apparently originated as the Hottentot name of the river flowing into the lagoon. The original form of the name is uncertain, but it is said to have been *Xthuys Xna* (place of wood).

The first settlers of the Knysna area were all attracted to the place by its beauty, although once there they were inclined to think that perhaps they had been lured to ruin by a siren. Almost impossible lines of communications made the area seem more difficult to get out of than it was to get in, and only a South African bullock wagon made of the hard timber of the Knysna forests could have survived the first dreadful track that was blazed to connect Knysna to George.

The first settlers – Van Huysteen, Van Rooyen, Jerling, Read, Meeding, Weyer, Barnard, Vosloo, Terblans and others of the days of Dutch rule – all selected superb farms for themselves. Of these farms the finest was without doubt *Melkhoutkraal* (milkwood corral) first granted in 1770 to Stephanus Terblans. It was this farm which included the whole basin containing the Knysna lagoon.

On the death of Terblans the farm was sold by his widow in 1798 to her second husband,

Johan van Lindenbaum. He resold the property to a trader, Richard Holiday, who died in 1802, and two years later the ownership of *Melkhoutkraal* was taken over by the man who will always be identified with Knysna as the real founder of the town, George Rex.

So much romance has been attached to the person of George Rex that it is interesting to learn a little about this extraordinary character whose enigmatic and forceful personality has become part of the folklore of Southern Africa. He arrived in the Cape in 1797, at the time of the first British occupation. A man of distinguished bearing, he was well educated, accomplished, intelligent, obviously well connected, but extremely taciturn.

In Cape Town, George Rex was appointed marshal of the Vice-Admiralty court, notary public to the Governor, and advocate to the Crown. He met Johanna, the young widow of a well-to-do merchant, and settled down with her and her children.

When the British occupation ended he remained in the Cape and in 1804, at the age of 39, he purchased the farm *Melkhoutkraal,* on the shores of Knysna lagoon, from the estate of the late owner, Richard Holiday. To reach this farm, George Rex made a coach journey on a grand scale. His lady and four children rode with him in a coach bearing a coat of arms and drawn by six fine horses. Riding alongside the coach was a retinue of friends and retainers. To the awed locals the journey resembled a royal procession – even the name of the man, George Rex, conjured up images of royalty travelling incognito.

Stories spread that George Rex was the son of George III of England and the fair Quakeress, Hannah Lightfoot. Modern research does not confirm this belief and there is no record of George Rex ever having made any such claim. But his lifestyle and grand manner convinced the residents of the Cape, and especially those of Knysna, that the man in their midst was indeed of royal descent and his company was sought by many distinguished visitors.

At Knysna, Rex found a fellow Briton, James Callander, a retired shipwright, already in residence in a home he had built near the Heads. Rex rebuilt the farmhouse of *Melkhoutkraal,* as the place had been burned down during a Xhosa raid along the coast. Rex turned it into a magnificent home known as the 'old place'. When his common law wife Johanna died, Rex married her daughter from her original marriage, and with the amiable aid of this pretty young woman his family increased to a total of six sons and seven daughters. Edward, the eldest son, was deaf and never married. John, the second son, was his father's right-hand man and considered by those who met him to be an individual of 'princely manners and conspicuous ability'.

The daughters, mainly educated in Cape Town, were comely, made good marriages, and attracted to Knysna sundry gallants such as Lieutenant Thomas Duthie who married Caroline Rex, and made his home at *Belvidere* on the west side of the lagoon, Captain John Fisher Sewell, who married Maria Rex, and Mr Atkinson of Arnagh, who married Sarah Rex.

*Melkhoutkraal* blossomed into one of the show estates of the Cape. Gardens, watermill, blacksmith's shop, orchards, vineyards, oak trees, all flourished under the care of George Rex. The farm was expanded to cover an area of 10 125 ha including the whole lagoon area and The Heads. On this estate, Rex engaged in a great variety of enterprises. He kept ostriches; his daughters spun silk from the silkworms fed on groves of mulberry trees; Rex men hunted elephants in the forests, sealed at Plettenberg Bay, cut timber, and influenced the government to develop Knysna into a port.

Knysna as a harbour seemed to be the answer to the problems of transport. It was surveyed by James Callander, the scheme was considered practical and on 11 February 1817 the naval transport brig, *Emu,* made an attempt to enter the lagoon. Unfortunately the vessel struck a sunken rock as she entered The Heads and was damaged so badly that it became necessary to run her ashore within the entrance. Nobody was drowned. A second naval vessel, the *Podargus,* was hastily sent up from the Cape in May 1817 to rescue the stranded crew and retrieve the stores of the *Emu.* Captain Wallis, of the *Podargus,* accomplished his mission, sailing in and out of the lagoon, and reported so favourably on the harbour and the vast forests, that the Admiralty decided to commence shipbuilding there. Rex promptly presented them with 16 ha of lagoonside land, and this site, named *Melville* – after Viscount Melville, the First Sea Lord at the time of the British occupation of the Cape – became the scene of a great deal of labour as the hull of a large brig slowly took shape from local timber. Unfortunately a fire seriously damaged the hull on its stocks and the project was abandoned. The site of the George Rex Slipway, situated by the lagoon side, is marked by a pillar and is most easily visited by river. The nearest land access would be from the point where the old Passes Road takes a sharp left-hand bend, by a side road to the right, barred by a gate and 'private' notices. Doubtless the farmer would allow any serious enquirer to cross his land.

The wood from which the ship had been constructed was salvaged and part of it now forms the handsome triangular table in the council chamber of the Knysna Divisional Council, whose offices are in Market Street. The wide stinkwood planks have acquired a beautiful lustre through continual polishing, and the table may be inspected by permission. Ask on the first floor, at the 'Enquiries' counter.

Knysna, however, was established as a port. Up to the time of his death, on 3 April, 1839, Rex had the satisfaction of seeing 162 ships call at Knysna with only four wrecked in the course of their visits. In 1831 Rex even launched his 127-ton vessel, the *Knysna*. In this ship, built at Westford on the Knysna River, just below Phantom Pass, John Rex explored the coast, becoming the first to sail into the Buffalo River (at East London). Fifty years after she was launched, the stout little *Knysna* was still in service carrying coal along the coast of England.

George Rex's grave may be seen close to the site of his original homestead on *Melkhout-kraal*. The turnoff from the Garden Route is marked. It can also be reached by taking the Assegaaiweg, about 600 m from The Heads road, but on the left-hand side. Opposite this road by two large shady trees, a gravel road turns right. Take it, and then turn almost immediately left to cross a deep stream, beyond which is a stone-walled enclosure sighed over by two tall pine trees. Rex's son, George junior, and his wife Jessie are also buried there. The younger Rex family lived at *Hunter's Home,* adjoining *Melkhoutkraal.* Their house has vanished but the beautiful little wood known as Ashmead, once part of their estate, survives as a holiday camp.

No descendants of the male line of the Rex family remain in Knysna. One of the best known of George Rex's descendants is the celebrated clown Stompie, really Wentworth Fitzwilliam Edward Dupreez, sometimes known as King Stompie from the romantic stories of his ancestor's origin.

In 1825 the Governor, Lord Charles Somerset, decided to found a village at Knysna. Fortunately for once he did not also name the place after himself or any of his relatives. George Rex granted 121 ha for the proposed town, while the old Admiralty dockyard area of Melville was added to it in 1844. This was the beginning of the present town.

The beauty of the situation and, perhaps, the social standing of the Rex family, made it fashionable to settle in Knysna. The Honourable Henry Barrington, younger son of Viscount Barrington, came in the 1840s and founded an estate at Portland, on land bought (like Belvidere) from the Rex family. William Newdigate, another younger son of a British aristocrat, settled in the Piesang River Valley. Colonel John Sutherland also came soon after the death of George Rex and, when Rex's heirs fragmented the *Melkhoutkraal* estate, purchased the old homestead. The Rex family moved to Rexford, known to them as the 'new place', closer to The Heads, and thereafter they gradually faded from the local scene. The Sutherland family laid out the township of Newhaven, now part of Knysna town, and the process of fragmenting the old Rex lands was well under way. They were divided into erfs, plots, smallholdings and otherwise 'improved' in estate agents' jargon.

Apart from the Rex family, another family particularly associated with Knysna is that of the Thesens. This family of 12 sailed from Norway in 1869 intending to settle in New Zealand. A storm off Cape Agulhas blew their schooner *Albatross* back to Cape Town. While there, one of the sons, Hans, sailed to Knysna on contract and reported so enthusiastically about the place that the family settled there, purchased an island in the lagoon and on it commenced boat building and furniture manufacture. In 1974 the business was acquired by a Johannesburg finance house bringing to an end the long association of the family and the firm.

In its heyday, Knysna as a port exported wool, timber and railway sleepers. An average year, such as 1886, saw 89 vessels trading with the place. The Thesens, with their Knysna Steamship Service, had two coasters, the 635-ton *Ingerid* and the 23-ton *Agnar*, permanently on the service and trade was flourishing.

The village became a magistracy on 29 April 1858, and a municipality in 1881. The first railway was planned as a narrow-gauge half-metre-wide line by the South Western Railway Company, who hoped to connect with the Port Elizabeth-Avontuur line. The present standard gauge line was opened on 17 October 1928. The railway killed local shipping. The harbour was deproclaimed in December 1954 and a picturesque activity ended, with the last pilot, Reuben Benn, fourth generation of Benns to hold that post, transferred to Port Elizabeth.

There is a small museum at the end of Queens Street, on the left-hand side, close to the municipal buildings. Although still young, it contains a wealth of material concerning the history of the town, with hundreds of old photographs of absorbing interest. A collection of George Rex items has been started, and, as the years pass, this will become a museum of truly national rank.

Today Knysna is a favourite holiday resort, residential area and scene of considerable activity in the making of furniture and boats. Speculation in property and improving the natural beauty of the area by means of townships, suburbs, and so on are standard preoccupations of the population.

Across the lagoon is a glaring example of local insensitivity to the natural beauties of the site. The Heads have been ruined for all time through the building of houses over the heights on the left-hand side. This acquiescence by the authorities to the claims of profitmaking has irreparably spoilt one of South Africa's most famous views by covering a noble bastion with a scattering of nondescript houses that could just as easily have been built anywhere else.

Leisure Island is another example of local development. Originally a sandy island known as Steenbok Island, it was purchased from the Duthie family in 1929 by George Cearn, a wealthy visitor to Knysna. Considered to be a crank by the locals, he built a causeway to the island, spent £500 000 and ten years in draining and laying out his treasure island, and then another ten years in selling at substantial prices, building plots with fabulous views and a romantic atmosphere.

## Accommodation
* Imperial Hotel, 24 rooms, 7 with baths. R9,50 – R10,50 B/B. Phone 110.
* Knysna Hotel, 18 rooms, 11 with baths. R9 – R9,50 B/B. Phone 97.
** Leisure Isle Hotel, 40 rooms, all with baths. R13 – R18 D/B/B. Phone 136.
* Newhaven Hotel, 19 rooms, 9 with baths. R9,90 – R10,40 D/B/B. Phone 100.
* Royal Hotel, 23 rooms, 8 with baths. R7 – R8 B/B. Phone 26.

## Caravans and camping
**® Ashmead Park, 50 sites. R6 D plus 50c D per person. 4 flats, 6 cottages, 4 rondawels, R4 – R35 D.
** Knysna Caravan Park, 80 sites. R5 D plus 50c D per person.
** Lagoonside Caravan Park, 20 sites. R4,50 D plus 40c D per person. 10 rondawels, R17,50 D.
** Monks Caravan Park, 32 sites. R3,50 D plus 25c D per person. 2 flats and 6 rooms, R6 – R12 D.

293

** Waterways Caravan Park, 45 sites. R3 – R5 D plus 50c D per person. 10 cottages, R19 – R24.
** Woodbourne Caravan Park, 70 sites. R2 – R5,50 D plus 50c D per person. 20 rondawels, R3 – R4,75 D per person.

# THE KNYSNA FOREST COUNTRY

Southern Africa is notable more for its wide open spaces and savanna country than for great forests of timber trees. Such forests require for one thing, at least 750 mm of rain a year, and only limited humid areas in the country attain or exceed this annual figure. In South Africa there are 255 150 ha of indigenous forest, mainly controlled by the state, and 972 000 ha of exotic forests or plantations owned by the state and private enterprise. Altogether, therefore, only one per cent of South Africa is covered in trees, compared to 25 per cent of the United States.

Of all the indigenous forests in South Africa, the coastal forest stretching from George to near Humansdorp is the largest, covering some 40 500 ha with a further 68 860 ha planted with exotics (pines, eucalyptus and wattle). Known as the Midland Conservancy, this forest area is 177 km long and 16 km broad, lying along the coastal terrace between the sea and the inland mountains. The indigenous areas are covered with a luxuriant mixture of tall and ancient trees, wonderful ferns, creepers and wild flowers. Animal life, as in most great forests, is limited to a few varieties of forest-dwelling antelope, numerous birds, and a lingering remnant (seven animals) of the herds of elephant which once frequented the area.

From the time Europeans discovered this forestry area it was ruthlessly exploited. The finest hardwood trees, 600 years old and more, were cut down to provide railway sleepers and timber for ships. It was not only the mature trees which were cut, but wagon tracks were blazed to reach them, crushing down literally hundreds of young trees in the course of dragging out logs and sawn timber.

An entire parasitic community of professional woodcutters derived their livelihood from the Knysna forests. Like fishermen who incessantly take and never replenish, they were all firmly persuaded that the forest was inexhaustible, and they cut at will. Government control came very late. In 1874 Captain Christopher Harison was appointed conservator, but he had limited control over the tree cutters.

In 1886 a French forester, Comte de Vasselot de Regne, was appointed by the Cape Government to investigate the state of the forests. He was apalled to find that fully three-quarters of the indigenous forest had been seriously damaged by wanton cutting. He prohibited further indiscriminate cutting and divided the forest into sections. The felling was thenceforth permitted only in specific sections of the forest, while other sections rested. Those portions of the forest which had been completely destroyed, as well as other suitable areas, were reafforested with exotics.

Notwithstanding these measures, the demand for timber continued to bring destruction to the forest. In 1913 the Forestry Department introduced fresh control measures by marking trees for destruction and these were allocated to registered woodcutters by means of the drawing of lots. The woodcutters had to pay a nominal charge for the trees, and were then free to sell the timber for what they could get. It was an absurd arrangement. The woodcutters on the whole were not a particularly intelligent crowd and, left to the hazards of chance on one side and the hard bargaining of timber merchants on the other, their situation became increasingly miserable.

The number of woodcutters dwindled. In 1932 there were 500 of them registered. In 1939 this number had decreased to 258, and their average annual income was little more than R40 a year per man. The government then realised the absurdity of a situation where some of the most beautiful and majestic trees in Africa were being destroyed with no significant gain to the state: the ultimate prospect was a community of poor whites – no matter how picturesque their way of life – and no profit to anybody save a crowd of timber dealers and speculators.

In March 1939 the Woodcutters Annuities Bill passed its final stage in Parliament. The 258 remaining woodcutters were banned from further private work in the forests, and compensated with a pension of R50 a year. Settlements were established for them, and employment found in public works and in the Forestry Department. Considerable public agitation and resentment arose over this abolition of the ancient Knysna profession of woodcutting, but it was obvious to all save romanticists that the primeval forests were simply being destroyed by a group of men whose hard work was completely misplaced in a mass destruction which rewarded them, if they were lucky and healthy, with a pittance of about R2 a week.

From 1939 onwards trees for cutting were carefully selected by the Forestry Department and auctioned as they stood to the dealers. The ancient forests of Knysna are now solely under the control of the state, and it would be a tragic day indeed if any caprice of politics once again allowed wanton destruction of one of the most beautiful and tranquil areas on earth.

From Knysna there are several very fine drives through the forest country, while the walker will find that the finest scenes are reserved for him alone as a reward for his exertions.

A short but exceptionally interesting drive from Knysna starts with the gravel turnoff leading up the left bank of the Salt River, just as the coastal road enters the built-up area of Knysna town. This Salt River road makes its way up the river valley and then climbs north into the overlooking hills, revealing many handsome views.

At the summit there is a junction. The left-hand branch continues north over rugged country to an open plateau on which stands the Gouna Forest Station, whence there is a magnificent forest drive to Diepwalle on the Avontuur road. The right-hand branch swings eastwards and after 3 km of varied views reaches the Concordia Forest Reserve. At this point there is a branch to the right leading down the slopes to Grey Street in the town of Knysna. The views are memorable.

The longest route through the Knysna forest country is the road leading to Avontuur across the Outeniqua Mountains by means of Prince Alfred's Pass. This road starts as a tarmac turnoff from the main coastal road 3 km east of Knysna on the way to Plettenberg Bay. After 1,5 km there is a gravel turnoff west leading to the Concordia Forest Station and linking up with the Salt River Road already described.

The main road (tarmac) leads on northwards through pine and eucalyptus plantations. After a further 3 km the tarmac ends and the gravel road enters the indigenous forest. Fourteen kilometres from the start of the road it reaches the Ysterhoutrug picnic site, considerably laid out there by the Forestry Department. One and a half kilometres beyond this site, there is a turnoff to the west leading for 183 m to what is known as King Edward's Tree, one of the big trees of the forest. This one is a yellowwood 700 years old and 46 m high from the ground to the start of its branches.

The traveller is now in the main forest of Knysna and the feeding ground of the elephants. One and a half kilometres beyond the turnoff to King Edward's Tree, there is a turnoff east to the Diepwalle Forest Station.

## ELEPHANT WALK

The forestry station of *Diepwalle* (deep walls) is in the heart of the main Knysna forest. The road from Knysna to Avontuur over Prince Alfred's Pass takes the traveller past this forestry station, and it is from there that hikers commence what is known as the Elephant Walk, a circular trail of 18,2 km leading through some of the most beautifully luxuriant high forest imaginable. The walk takes about six and a half hours, with two shorter alternatives. The path is well marked, many of the trees are numbered, there are eight giant yellowwoods to be seen on the way, together with a host of interesting smaller trees, plants, and wildlife. Elephants are often in the area. Each spring they migrate through the area changing from their winter feeding grounds in the Harkerville forest to those in the Gouna forest for the summer season. In autumn, they move back again and it is on these wanderings that they are most frequently seen. A permit to do the Elephant Walk must be obtained from the forestry station at Diepwalle.

A second and even more spectacular hiking trail, known as the Outeniqua Hiking Trail starts from Diepwalle. It runs for 150 km along the full length of the Outeniqua range, ending at the Witfontein forestry station near George. There are seven huts along the way. The trail can be divided into sections and joined or left at various points. It is an outstanding wilderness trail and a delight for all lovers of nature.

---

One and a half kilometres beyond the turnoff to Diepwalle there is a turnoff to the Kransbos Forest Station. Another 6 km (26 km from the start of the road) leads to the beautiful *Dal van Varings* (dale of ferns) where there are picnic sites and a fine walk through an enchanting forest world of giant ferns. On the left-hand side of the road a short distance away from the Dal van Varings, a signposted track will take one to the top of Spitskop (933 m), a fine viewpoint.

One and a half kilometres beyond the Dal van Varings, the road reaches the Buffelsnek Forest Station perched on a hilltop looking out on majestic views of the inland mountains. The road now makes a steady 5-km-long descent until it reaches the valley of the Kruis River, 32 km from the start of the road. Here there is a tearoom and store, and a turnoff to the east leading to Plettenberg Bay 39 km away. Seven kilometres along this turnoff there is the famous viewsite of Perdekop, and the continuation of the road makes a pleasant return route to Knysna via Plettenberg Bay.

The main road to Avontuur continues for 6 km and then reaches a picnic site in a pleasant river valley. Another 11 km of rugged travelling leads to the tiny rural centre of De Vlugt where there is a store, petrol, and a causeway across the clear waters of the Keurboom River. The road is now 50 km from its beginning, and at the start of the spectacular Prince Alfred's Pass. For 13 km the gravel road makes a convoluted ascent up this pass before reaching the summit, 1 046 m above sea level. The descent on the northern side of the mountains is much easier, and only 5 km long before the road reaches Avontuur and joins the tarmac road leading down the Long Kloof. Avontuur, 872 m above sea level, is the terminus of the narrow-gauge railway up the Long Kloof from Port Elizabeth. For 68 km we have travelled along this beautiful road, from its start at the turnoff on the Garden Route 5 km east of Knysna.

## PRINCE ALFRED'S PASS

This fine pass, still in much the same condition as when it was originally built, is one of the most spectacular mountain crossings in Southern Africa. Andrew Geddes Bain located the route of this pass in 1856 and his son Thomas had the actual task of constructing it, using for labour a force of about 270 convicts who were housed in a station erected for them at De Vlugt. Construction work was exceedingly heavy. A complex passageway had to be blasted up what was known as Reeds Poort, with bridges crossing the Fuchs River which at this spot tumbles down through a canyon in a series of lovely cascades and rapids. The road had to continue, skirting the slopes of a valley known as Fuchs Kraal, climbing over a saddle (known as Voor die Poort) at the head of this valley, and then twisting and steadily rising to the place where the mountains touch the clouds.

The pass was completed in May 1867. It was named after Prince Alfred, the Duke of Edinburgh, who, in company with the Rex family, had hunted elephants in the Knysna forests in 1864. It is a fine example of the work of Andrew Bain and his son Thomas, two of the greatest road builders who ever worked in Southern Africa. It is a pass full of charm, of majestic views, of lovely forest vistas, and in the latter part, of gentle rural scenes. There is no way of traversing this pass quickly. By modern standards it is narrow and twisting but, aesthetically, throughout its length it is a complete scenic delight.

---

From Knysna, the coastal road leads eastwards. One and a half kilometres from the town centre there is a concrete turnoff to The Heads. The main tarmac road climbs steadily out of the basin containing the Knysna lagoon. After 5 km there is a crossroads. A tarmac turnoff to the north leads to Prince Alfred's Pass and Avontuur (as already described). A gravel turnoff south leads for 5,5 km to the beach at the mouth of the *Noetzie* (black) River, a pretty little place hemmed in by seaside houses, several of which, through some whim of their owners, are designed like castles. There are camping sites on the left bank of the Noetzie River. Permits must be obtained from the Kransfontein Forestry Station.

The coastal road continues eastwards through the eucalyptus and pine plantations of the Kruisfontein Forest Station. Ten kilometres from Knysna there is a gravel track branching off south into the plantation, and leading to the Brackenhill Falls, a series of cascades in the Noetzie River, 1,5 km away. Six kilometres beyond this turnoff, 16 km from Knysna, the coastal road enters the indigenous forest known as the Garden of Eden. Here there is a picnic site and a very beautiful walk through a portion of the forest where the Forestry Department has identified many of the trees.

One and a half kilometres beyond the Garden of Eden, 18 km from Knysna, there is a gravel turnoff to the Harkerville Forest Reserve. A permit from the forester will allow one to drive for 11 km through the reserve, ending at a clearing, with a path leading for 91 m to a fine viewsite over the rocky coast.

The coastal road is now traversing a beautifully forested landscape, but one which also possesses some unhappy memories. It was in this area, in October 1802, that a Xhosa raiding army swept through the forest. At *Moordleegte* (the dale of murder), the warriors surprised five wagons carrying to safety families of the local farmers. The women and children were seized as hostages and four men killed. One of them, Wolfaardt by name, was brutally ill-used and his body tied to a tree in a copse known as Wilke's Kraaibos. *Benekraal* (corral of bones) is another place name marking the site where the raiders slaughtered a large number of cattle. Retribution came on the elevation known as *Kaffirs Kop* (peak of the Kaffirs), where a commando attacked the raiders, rescued the captive women and children and killed most of the Xhosa.

### Accommodation

★ Stromboli's Continental Inn, 16 rooms, all with baths. R8,50 B/B. Phone Plettenberg Bay 1922.

One and a half kilometres beyond Harkerville, 19 km from Knysna, there is a turnoff to the south leading to the Kranshoek Forest Station 11 km away and the local airport, 13 km away. Six kilometres further on there is a turnoff on the left leading to Wittedrif, 8 km away, and then over Prince Alfred's Pass to Avontuur, 79 km away. Five kilometres further along the coastal road there is another turnoff to the south, this one leading to Robbeberg, 10 km away, and to Beacon Island, 3 km away. One kilometre beyond this junction, there is the main turnoff to the south leading for 1 km to the amiable little coastal resort, 32 km from Knysna, of Plettenberg Bay. The road leads first to the village, the street of which is lined with an assortment of commercial buildings. The village lies well above the sea and from it roads stretch down to the shore. Views from the village are panoramic, embracing a vast sweep of ocean, shore, coastal terrace and mountain range. The variety of scenery is exciting to every taste.

# PLETTENBERG BAY

With a permanent population of 4 769, Plettenberg Bay has a vast influx of visitors during the Christmas holiday season. Fortunately, its three spacious beaches, and the grass-covered slopes of the hills looking down on them, have ample room to contain the holidaymakers.

Plettenberg Bay, sheltered by the great natural breakwater of Cape Seal (Robbeberg) offered sailors a degree of protection from storms. The early Portuguese explorers named the bay *Formosa* (beautiful), for its situation, backed by the handsome Outeniqua and Tsitsikama ranges, was very satisfying to the eye. The present name resulted from a visit to the bay of the Governor, Joachim van Plettenberg who, after a rough journey from Cape Town, reached the place on 6 November 1778 and erected there a stone pillar as a mark of possession by the Dutch East India Company. Van Plettenberg's Pillar still stands on the site of its original placement.

Ten years later, the government erected a shed at the bay and attempted to establish the place as a port for the forest area, the ship *Meermin* loading the first cargo of timber there in August 1788. The harbour never flourished, for the bay was only a tricky roadstead. The warehouse fell into ruin and the relics remain today as a memento of wasted effort.

Attached to the shore of Plettenberg Bay is a rocky islet known as Beacon Island after a navigational beacon erected there in 1772 as an aid to the checking of chronometers. This islet, in 1912, became the site of a Norwegian-run whaling industry. A collection of corrugated-iron buildings grew up on the islet. When the Norwegians abandoned the place in 1920, the buildings were converted into a rather rough and ready boarding house. In 1940 the Beacon Island Hotel was erected on the unique site, with the islet tied to the mainland by a tarmac road. A new hotel was built on the islet in 1972. The beacon of Beacon Island, several times renewed, still stands on the islet.

Safe swimming, excellent fishing, a most equable climate and a beautiful situation, are the assets of Plettenberg Bay. A gravel road, 10 km long, leads from the little town (a municipality since 24 October 1960) south down the coast to Cape Seal and the prominent, red sandstone peninsula known as the *Robbeberg* (mountain of seals). This famous fishermen's resort is a nature reserve 243 ha in extent. Scenically spectacular, with pathways providing many interesting walks, the peninsula has a rich intertidal life, a considerable variety of birds and a remarkably varied environment. There is a huge cave (once the home of prehistoric beach-combers), and there are many dramatic viewsites showing towering cliffs and white waves breaking on rocks. The Greek ship *Athena* was run aground in the north lee of Robbeberg in 1967 and still lies there just below the spectacularly situated Robbeberg Caravan Resort.

## Accommodation
★★ Archerwood Hacienda Hotel, 12 rooms, all with baths. R13,50 – R17,50 B/B. Phone 184.
★★★ Beacon Island Hotel, 190 rooms, all with baths. R33 – R47 B/B. Phone 411.
★★ Formosa Inn, 38 rooms, all with baths. R13 – R17,50 B/B. Phone 51.
★ Look-Out Hotel, 24 rooms, 20 with baths. R12 – R14 B/B. Phone 10.

## Caravans and camping
★★ Archerwood Hacienda Caravan Park, 20 sites. R2 D plus R1 D per person.
★★★ ® Piesang River Caravan Resort, 100 sites. R4 D plus 50c D per person, out of season. R8 D plus 50c D per person, in season.
★★ Plettenberg Bay Caravan Park, 280 sites. R6,50 D plus 50c D per person.
★★ Robbeberg Caravan Resort, 115 sites. R4 D plus 50c D per person. 3 cottages, 8 rondawels, R10,50 – R15 D.

From Plettenberg Bay, the main coastal road continues north-eastwards. After 8 km the road bridges over the Bitou River, and 1,5 km further on crosses the handsome river known as the

*Keurboom,* after the trees of that species (*Sophors capensis*) which grow on its banks. This is a superb boating river and the Provincial Administration maintain a fine holiday resort on the west bank.

## Accommodation
★ Frederick Hotel, 10 rooms, all with baths. R9 B/B. Phone Keurboom River 2.

## Caravans and camping
★★® Keurbooms River Public Resort, 86 sites. R2 – R4 D. 21 cottages, R5 – R15 D.
★★★® Lagoon Holiday Resort, 50 sites. R5,50 D plus 50c D per person. 2 cottages, 10 rondawels, 2 rooms, R14 – R15 D.
★★★® San Marino Caravan Park, 200 sites. R2,50 – R5 D plus 25c – 50c D per person. 2 rondawels, R10 – R12 D.

The Keurboom and the Bitou unite at their mouths to form a broad lagoon. Just across the river there is a 5-km turnoff to the south-east, leading to the holiday resort much beloved by fishermen, of . . .

# KEURBOOMSTRAND

This small resort lies at the end of a tarred by-road where the hills slope steeply down to a sandy shore broken by many outcrops of rocks. Once a collection of ramshackle huts, Keurboomstrand has become respectable in recent years, though many of the houses remain tightly bolted for most of the year.

From the road's end, through Arch Rock Caravan Park, a narrow path (signposted) leads through lush coastal bush to Matjies River Cave (20 minutes' walk). Where the path forks, towards its end, take the left-hand path. The cave is really a characteristic overhanging shelter, occupied for many thousands of years in the Late Stone Age, that has yielded much valuable information about the men who lived there to excavators in 1928 and in the fifties. Much of what the archaeologists found may be seen in the National Museum in Bloemfontein. All that the visitor now sees is a narrow path between the rock face and a pile of sea shells. What he may not realise is that the pile is a gigantic midden, slowly accumulated over countless generations by a shellfish eating people who, not unlike those of our own day, carelessly chucked their rubbish over the edge. When one thinks about it, and studies the size of their dump, it can be a sobering thought!

## Accommodation
★ Keurboomstrand Hotel, 28 rooms, 21 with baths. R15 B/B. Phone Keurboom River 3.

## Caravans and camping
★★® Arch Rock Caravan Park, 84 sites. R3,50 – R5,50 D plus 25c D per person.
★★ Cons Caravan Park, 106 sites. R4,50 – R5,50 D plus 50c D per person.

The Keurboom River is usually considered the boundary between the two forest worlds overlooked by the Outeniqua and the *Tsitsikama* (clear water) mountain ranges From the bridges across the Keurboom River, the Garden Route climbs steeply and diagonally up the face of the cliffs until it reaches the level of the coastal terrace, twisting, rising and falling through attractive wild flower and forest country. For the roadmakers this Tsitsikama country has always provided considerable difficulties for it is split by the deep ravines of several rivers, and covered in dense primeval forest. For many years, in fact, this stretch of country was considered to be impassable.

Only in 1868 did Thomas Bain (the great roadmaker) and Captain Harison (the forester) cut an arduous path through the forest and discover that a practicable route could be found for a road linking Plettenberg Bay to Humansdorp. Work on this road started in 1879, with the indefatigable Thomas Bain in charge. Convict labour provided muscle for the work while the engineering skill and aesthetic taste of Bain located and controlled a complex route including three superb crossings of the great chasms of the Groot, Bloukrans and Storms rivers. The completed road was opened to Humansdorp in 1885. The route located by Bain is still followed substantially by the road today. It is a stunningly beautiful drive, a real garden route, and a lasting reminder of the genius of Thomas Bain.

Eleven kilometres from Keurboom River, the road passes the Keurbooms River Forest Station and after 10 km of varied plantation, forest and open country where watsonias are spectacular in spring, commences the steep descent in to the gorge of the *Groot* (great) River. For 3 km the road descends steep slopes covered in forest and ferns. After losing 223 m in altitude the road reaches the floor of the gorge, near the lagoon and mouth of the Groot River, in what is known as Nature's Valley. Here, on a small alluvial plain more than half buried beneath the forest, stands a cluster of attractive seaside cottages. There are picnic sites on a pretty little beach and on both sides of the bridge across the Groot River. This is a cool and beautiful place for a roadside luncheon. At the first of these picnic sites a signposted path leads through the forest to Kalender Kloof, a fine walk with the air filled with the calling of the sombre bulbul birds.

### Caravans and camping
★ Groot River camping site, 45 sites. R2 D.

The Groot River marks the western boundary of the Tsitsikama Coastal National Park, which is described further on. From the bridge over the river, 34 km from Plettenberg Bay, the road begins to climb out of the gorge. After 3 km of twists, rises and handsome views, the road regains the altitude of the coastal terrace and continues eastwards through dense plantation country and, 3 km from the top of the pass, through the Platbos indigenous forest. On the roadside in the Platbos forest there are several pleasant picnic sites and a gravel turnoff leading to Covie.

Six kilometres from the top of the Groot River Pass, the road passes the Bloukrans Forestry Station and then commences the descent of the Bloukrans Pass. As with the Groot River Pass, the road has to lose 183 m in altitude in 3 km of winding down the sides of the river gorge and then bridging across the Bloukrans River. This is a particularly charming pass and the 5 km the road takes to climb the height on the left bank of the river provides travellers with many lovely views.

The top of the Bloukrans Pass is 50 km from Plettenberg Bay. The road now leads over the coastal terrace through great plantations. After 3 km the road passes the Coldstream Saw Mill. A further 3 km takes the road through the Lottering Plantation, and 5 km east of this settlement, 64 km from Plettenberg Bay, there is a turnoff to the south leading for 11 km through plantations and forest, and then descending the coastal cliffs to the narrow and spectacularly rocky stretch of coastline at the mouth of the Storms River. The traveller is now in the . . . .

# TSITSIKAMA FOREST AND COASTAL NATIONAL PARK

The Coastal National Park consists of a narrow strip of coast, about 76 km long, lying between the mouth of the Groot River in the west and, in the east, the mouth of another river also known as the *Groot* (great). Between these two namesake rivers, the cliffs press close to the sea, making a bold, rocky coastline, wild, unspoilt and beautiful to the eye.

On the seaward side, the great rollers pound incessantly on the dark-coloured rocks. On the landward side the forest tumbles over the cliffs like a green waterfall, with arum lilies and other flowers providing splashes of colour like spray. Through these high cliffs, the Storms River has washed a narrow cleft through which its amber-coloured waters flow to the sea.

Boating, swimming, skindiving, walking, and (strangely, for one would expect all marine life to be protected in a national park) angling, are the pastimes in this pleasant coastal wilderness.

At the end of the road are beach cottages (some of a remarkable unloveliness for such a spot) the restaurant and office, to which intending visitors must repair immediately, to make or to confirm their bookings. The restaurant stands on the site of another of the many strandloper middens of the coast, and a showcase there contains specimens of the objects found when the restaurant was constructed.

From here a rough path makes eastwards to the mouth of the Storms River, passing, a short distance from the start, a small field museum. The river is spanned by a suspension bridge but walkers are reminded that this path eventually comes to a dead end. Here is a cave once used by strandlopers, with an interesting museum showing some of the things they used, and bones of the animals and fish they fed on. From a small jetty canoes go up the Storms River for 3 km through primeval forest scenery of great beauty and interest.

In the opposite direction, from the restaurant, a coastal path known as the Otter Trail, follows the length of the entire national park to Nature's Valley, and provides a fairly strenuous three-day walk. Shelter is provided in bungalows at two staging points, but all food and bedding must be carried.

There is a first-rate book on sale in the shop, *Tsitsikama Shore* by R. M. Tietz and Dr G. A. Robinson, packed with information and illustrated with colour photographs. It is compulsory reading for anyone staying more than a few hours and who wishes to learn more about the fascinating life of the shore.

## Caravans and camping
** ® Caravan park, 100 sites. R2,90 D. 23 cottages, R5,80 – R20,80 D.

From the turnoff to the Storms River mouth, the coastal road continues westwards. After 5 km there is a gravel turnoff to the south leading for 366 m to Storms River village (a small centre serving the Tsitsikama forest area), and then continuing down the original pass made by Bain across the Storms river, rejoining the modern road at Pineview. This is a very beautiful drive 16 km long and well worth doing. The Blue Lily Forest Station lies east of the river crossing.

## Accommodation
* Tsitsikama Forest Inn, 25 rooms, 20 with baths. R10 B/B. Phone Tsitsikama 4.

The modern coastal road, after passing the turnoff to Storms River village, traverses the Tsitsikama Forestry Reserve and 1 km beyond the turnoff to the Storms River village there is the entrance (on the northern side of the road) to what is known as De Plaat (admission 10c), the magnificent indigenous forest section of the Tsitsikama Forest and Coastal National Park. At a turning place for vehicles there are a few showcases with drawings of plants, and wood sections. A path to the right leads to a truly magnificent yellowwood tree, of a majesty and nobility that transcends anything that the human race has, so far, produced. There are several others in the vicinity of impressive size, whilst the forest itself is usually loud with the unfamiliar calls of the birds of the canopy, whose audibility is greater than their visibility.

Three kilometres east of this forest turnoff, the road reaches the gorge of the Storms River and the spectacular Paul Sauer Bridge which carries the road across the deep gash washed by the river through the sandstone. The bridge is 191 m long in a single span 130 m above the river. It was designed by Ricardo Morandi of Rome, and built like two giant drawbridges made of concrete. A platform was first constructed on either side of the gorge. The two halves of the bridge, in vertical form, were then erected on hinges. On completion the two halves were lowered, meeting perfectly in the centre. The bridge cost R200 000 to build. It was opened to traffic in 1956 after two and a half years' construction work. It replaced the entire original Storms River Pass. Purely functional, but cleanly beautiful in appearance, it is one of the very few bridges of its kind in the world.

There is a restaurant overlooking the Storms River Bridge. There is also a picnic and camping ground on the south side of the road just before it reaches the bridge and a small caravan park.

## Caravans and camping
★ Caravan park, 50 sites. R2,90 D.

The Storms River marks the end of the Garden Route, and the road, after crossing the river, leads on towards the Eastern Cape.

## Chapter Sixteen

# THREE ROADS TO ALGOA BAY

After crossing the Storms River by means of the spectacular 130-m-high bridge, the main coastal road continues eastwards along the coastal terrace, with the Tsitsikama Mountains looking serenely down from the north, and the Indian Ocean a few kilometres to the south. Between ocean and mountain there lies a natural garden of trees and flowering plants and through this lovely wilderness the road finds a pleasant entry into the Eastern Cape.

The Blue Lilies Bush Forest Reserve is situated 4 km from the bridge, and the Witelsbos Forest Reserve is 14,5 km further on, dominated by the handsome 1 251-m *Witelskop* (peak of the white alders), the great landmark of this eastern end of the Tsitsikama range.

Thirty-two kilometres from the Storms River bridge the road passes the eastern end of the Tsitsikama range where there is a turnoff leading over a saddle in the mountains to join the tarmac road running up the Long Kloof (see page 310) 6 km away. This turnoff, known as the *Kareedouw* (pass of the karee trees) provides a handsome drive with many lovely wild flowers along the roadside.

Forty kilometres from the Storms River, the coastal road passes the mission station of *Clarkson,* established in 1839 by the Moravian mission and named after the co-worker of Sir William Wilberforce, the great campaigner for the abolition of slavery. The mission was created for the benefit of the Fingo, Hottentot and other people who had found a refuge there from various tribal disturbances.

Clarkson is overlooked by the last substantial peaks of the Kareedouw Mountains, a short range which is a continuation of the Tsitsikama chain, running from the Kareedouw Pass eastwards. Eight kilometres further east, the road passes close to a prominent, 359-m-high peak and the range then peters out, literally passing under the road and continuing only as a ridge which eventually sinks beneath the sea at Cape St Francis.

Beyond the ridge, the road traverses the open mouth of the famous fruit-producing valley of the Long Kloof and, 68 km from the Storms River, reaches the junction of the main tarmac road into the Long Kloof (see page 310). As the mountains have dwindled, so rainfall, no longer precipitated by the heights, has diminished, and the country is drier and more spacious; it has become undulating scrub-covered terrace. After a further 18 km of travelling (86 km from Storms River) the road reaches the town of . . .

## HUMANSDORP

This town is an agricultural and railway centre on the narrow-gauge line from Port Elizabeth to Avontuur in the Long Kloof.

The area of Humansdorp was originally known as the Parish of Alexander, after the Reverend Alexander Smith, the Dutch Reformed minister of Uitenhage who periodically visited the community and held services in a building on the farm *Geelhoutboom,* 11 km from the present town.

In the 1840s the local community began agitating for a church and district centre. The administration was not keen on the idea, but in 1849 Matthys Human of the farm *Zeekoe,* offered a gift of 606 ha for a township and commonage. The government accepted it and in 1853 a town was laid out with 300 erven, half being sold to endow a church.

The Humansdorp district produces forage, oats and sheep, but it was always a difficult area for agriculture, with extremes of drought and flood. Numerous stories have resulted from the colossal fire which swept the whole coastal terrace in 1869. Entire spans of oxen were caught in yoke and roasted alive. Many people died and homesteads were destroyed.

The fire broke out on 9 February, 1869 when the thermometer registered 59°C in the sun, and a fierce north-westerly wind was blowing. The Civil Commissioner of Humansdorp, Mr J. J. le Sueur, has left an interesting account of this disaster:

'A very wet season about the middle of 1868 had been succeeded by drought and great heat which prevailed for some months before the fire occurred. The heat had prepared for instant ignition the grass, shrubs, and brushwood, then unusually plentiful in consequence of the heavy rains that had preceded the dry weather. Veld burning (that barbarous system or "want of system" of agriculture) had been going on for some time, and on a calm night, bright dots and streaks and reflections in the sky marked the localities where it was being practised. The heat was most intense on 9 February; a scorching hot wind from the north, blowing like a sirocco, withered and dried up all that came within its influence. Everything, therefore, combined to make ready for combustion the plentiful grass and bushes so that where there fell cinders or sparks (from the fires kindled to burn the veld), which a strong gale of wind bore along to an almost incredible distance, a new centre of flame instantly burst into destructive activity, and then in turn gave origin to many others.

'The loss of life in this district amounted to 20. Of these, four were Europeans and the rest Natives. Of the Europeans three consisted of a mother with an infant in her arms and a child by her side, who fled before the fiery blast until they were overpowered, and then sank victims to the flames.'

This fire covered the coastal area from near Port Elizabeth to the vicinity of George. Many of the wonderful forest areas it destroyed have never recovered and are today little more than open expanses of scrub.

Humansdorp became a municipality in 1906 and its population has now reached 6 000. It is a busy centre for the area of St Francis Bay.

Humansdorp Park, laid out originally on the plan of the crosses of a Union Jack, with an ornamental fountain in the centre, shelters several rare and interesting trees and also contains the municipal caravan park.

## Accommodation
* Grand Hotel, 14 rooms, 6 with baths. R8 – R8,50 B/B. Phone 302.
* Humansdorp Motel, 30 rooms, all with baths. R8,50 B/B. Phone 17.
* New Star Hotel, 12 rooms, 5 with baths. R8 – R8,50 B/B. Phone 42.
* Royal Hotel, 13 rooms, 9 with baths. R7 – R7,50 B/B. Phone 169.

## Caravans and camping
** Tourist Park, 100 sites. R2 – R3 D. 4 rondawels, R3 – R4 D.

From Humansdorp a gravel road leads southwards over the undulating coastal plains which are notable for brilliant displays of erica in May and many other flowering plants throughout the year. After 16 km there is a turnoff leading for 10 km to Oyster Bay, a coastal resort especially favoured by fishermen. After a further 13 km the road reaches the seaside resort of Sea Vista and a further 10 km (36 km from Humansdorp) brings the road to its end at the Cape St Francis lighthouse.

## Caravans and camping
** Oyster Bay Caravan Park, 36 sites. R5 D. 10 cottages, 5 rondawels, R20 D.

# ST FRANCIS BAY

This handsome and spacious bay is one of the great recreational areas in Southern Africa. It was first named in 1575 by the Portuguese navigator, Manuel Perestrello, who described the landfall well, naming the cape *serras* (mountains) for it was there, in his own words, that 'all the mountain ranges, which are continuously tacked on to one another from the Cape of Good Hope along the coast, give out here and come to an end'. This is the cape now known as Cape St Francis. The 2 750 000 candlepower lighthouse built in 1876 actually stands on Seal Point, at the western end of Seal Bay, which has Cape St Francis for its eastern end. This lighthouse is a massive cylindrical tower, 28 m high, with the original keeper's quarters at its base.

In his description of the bay, Perestrello does not say whether he actually landed there. But if he did walk upon that wonderful beach of shimmering sands, it is certain that he would have stooped immediately to collect a shell, for in all the world there are few beaches more richly supplied with these beautiful jewels of the sea.

Scenically, the environment of Cape St Francis is a rather drab, flat, scrub-covered wasteland and the air is saturated with the pungent, almost antiseptic odour of the *agathosma* species of plants which flourish there. The Cape itself is not dramatic, just a flat, sandy promontory petering out into the sea. But the bay on the south-western side, sheltered between the arms of Cape St Francis and Seal Point, is handsome with a spacious beach and excellent swimming and surfing. The white tower of the lighthouse dominates the bay with, unfortunately, the usual nondescript collection of seaside shacks and cottages boarded up forlornly for most of the year.

For many years, Cape St Francis was very difficult to reach, its only access a sandy track. Seaside resort developers gradually discovered the possibilities of the area and its real fame began in 1961 when Bruce Brown produced his surfing film *Endless Summer*. He visited the area and found the 'perfect' wave washing along the eastern side of Cape St Francis. These waves, called Bruce's Beauties after their discoverer, work with a north-westerly wind coupled to a ground swell at low tide. This combination occurs mainly in the winter months (May to September) and provides a ride of at least half a kilometre. The waves are immensely powerful – relentless surges of water sweeping in from the outer ocean with a crashing, rumbling rush – and riding them is a wild experience in which the surfer is called upon to use every skill and reflex he possesses as he is carried forward at such speed that there is just no time to think.

Smaller waves known as 'Bruce's', are fairly common, but they too, require a westerly wind, a low tide, and a light swell. These waves also work on the east side of Cape St Francis. Generally superb waves occur on the west side (Seal Bay), especially with the westerly winds in winter. They do not reach the size of Bruce's Beauties, but are always exciting and very lovely to watch, with their long, white plumes trailing behind them as though each wave were a line of knights in armour, charging down upon a trembling shore, with pennants and banners flying.

Apart from surfing, the swimming is good and the fishing exciting on this western side of St Francis Bay. Sea Vista, situated on this part of the coastline, is a holiday house area of the more superior kind with some very attractive homes, white-walled and black-thatched, but as usual boarded up for most of the year.

The Sea Vista resort looks out over a spacious beach, across the surfing waters of what is known as *Krombaai,* from the *Krom* (crooked) River which reaches the sea there. The lower reaches of this river have been developed into a marina and the banks are lined with the holiday houses of boating enthusiasts. The Krom River, apart from its boating, is notable for the wild flowers growing along its banks. In winter, the aloes flower, and erica and arum lilies bloom to perfection. Countless birds make their homes in the area. The Churchill Dam, which supplies Port Elizabeth with much of its water, lies across the middle reaches of the Krom River.

### Accommodation
★★ Cape St Francis Hotel (Sea Vista), 26 rooms, all with baths. R8,50 – R12,50, seasonal. Phone Sea Vista 28.

### Caravans and camping
★★ Cape St Francis Caravan Park, 150 sites. R4,50 D plus 40c D per person.

From Humansdorp, the old coastal road continues eastwards for just over 6,5 km and then reaches a turnoff leading to the resort known as Paradise Beach 11 km away. Paradise Beach lies on the right bank of the lagoon formed by the Zeekoe and the Swart rivers. This is a famous sanctuary, resorted to by at least 57 varieties of birds including flamingos and swans. It is said that when the ship *Cape Recife* was wrecked on Cape St Francis on 20 February, 1929, two swans escaped from a crate on the deck. They settled in the Krom River and as a result of their breeding, the number of swans has increased enormously. At times 150 of these lovely birds may be seen together in such sanctuaries as the one at Paradise Beach.

There is good swimming and fishing at Paradise Beach and a considerable seaside resort housing development.

### Caravans and camping
★★ Paradise Beach Caravan Park, 80 sites. R2 D plus 50c D per person.

Back on the old coastal road, 5 km east of the turnoff to Paradise Beach, there is a turnoff to Aston Bay, a coastal resort being developed on the left bank of the same lagoon of swans as Paradise Beach (which is on the right bank). Fishing, swimming and the birds are the attractions.

### Caravans and camping
★★ Aston Bay Caravan Park, 100 sites. R5 D.

On the main coastal road, 10 km east of the turnoff to Humansdorp, there is a turnoff leading for 4 km to the coastal resort of . . .

# JEFFREY'S BAY

Jeffrey's Bay had its beginning as a trading store built in 1849 on the shores of St Francis Bay. In those days, before the opening of the narrow-gauge railway from Port Elizabeth to Humansdorp and on to Avontuur (the Apple Express), the beach in front of the store was used for landing and offloading cargo. It was named *Jeffrey's Bay* after the senior of the two partners in the venture, Messrs J. A. Jeffrey and Glendinning.

The coasters vanished after the railway was opened but the beach of Jeffrey's Bay was soon discovered by holidaymakers. The swimming is excellent and this part of St Francis Bay is especially rich in shells. The children living in the area spend most of their time collecting shells for sale to visitors, or for making into ornaments and novelties. Known as *skelpie* (shell) hunters, the children have provided apt common names for several of the shell varieties found on their familiar beaches. Violets, tops, rosebuds, angel wings, dollies, butterflies, jam tarts, plates, tear drops, and many others may be found lying on those spacious beaches. The book *Marine Shells of Southern Africa* by D. H. Kenelly, describes these shells in detail. In Jeffrey's Bay the Charlotte Kritzinger Shell Museum houses a wonderful exhibition of shells originally collected by the late Miss C. Kritzinger.

In modern times, surfers have discovered the great rollers of St Francis Bay and Super Tubes Point at Jeffrey's Bay is one of the finest surfing areas in the world. Winter is the best season, with westerly winds bringing in the big rollers. The surfing community, dominated mainly by visitors from Australia, provides Jeffrey's Bay with its most picturesque inhabitants. To watch them riding the wild waves is a spectacle not easily forgotten.

Jeffrey's Bay became a municipality on 3 January, 1968. It is growing rapidly as the usual real estate developers cover the landscape with seaside homes. The population is now 3 197.

### Accommodation

★ Beach Hotel, 15 rooms, 7 with baths. R8 – R9 B/B. Phone 14.
★★ Savoy Hotel, 40 rooms, 28 with baths. R8 – R10 B/B. Phone 27.

### Caravans and camping

★★ Municipal caravan park, 137 sites. R2,50 D plus 20c D per person.
★★ Jeffrey's Bay Holiday Resort, 60 sites. R2,50 D.
★★ Kabeljous-on-sea Holiday Resort, 60 sites. R3 D.

From the turnoff to Jeffrey's Bay 10 km from Humansdorp, the main coastal road continues eastwards, descending into the shallow valley of the Kabeljous River. After traversing a stretch of open sandveld country (well covered with wild flowers in a good rainy season), the road, now 25,5 km from Humansdorp, reaches the bridge over the Gamtoos River.

The *Gamtoos* takes its name from a Hottentot tribe which once lived in these parts. It is a river of major importance in the economy of South Africa for its broad, alluvial valley has lent itself to irrigation. At the mouth of the river there is a fishermen's resort, with a camping site. A hotel is situated just upstream from the bridge, at the site of the original ferry service across the river. A tarmac road runs along the left bank of the river for 7 km and then joins the tarmac road leading from Loerie to the picturesque little railway junction of Gamtoos. This is an interesting drive (see under the section on the Baviaans Kloof).

### Accommodation

★Gamtoos Ferry Hotel, 6 rooms, all with baths. R7 B/B. Phone 9901.

### Caravans and camping

★Divisional Council caravan park, 300 sites. 20c – 50c D per person.

The main coastal road continues eastwards from the Gamtoos River, climbing steadily to a higher coastal terrace. After 11 km the road reaches a tarmac turnoff leading to Hankey and the Baviaans Kloof (see page 318).

Beyond this turnoff, the main coastal road continues for 4,5 km to a turnoff leading to the rural centres of Thornhill and Sunnyside and after a further 3 km, reaches the spectacular bridge over the . . .

## VAN STADENS GORGE

The *Van Stadens River* is named after Martinus van Staden, a pioneer farmer in those parts. With its precipitous sides, the gorge was a major road obstacle for years. The first proper road across it was completed in 1867, but floods repeatedly destroyed the river crossing however often it was remade, and traversing the gorge was always hazardous. Eventually a better road and bridge was constructed in the early 1880s but the descent on both sides of the river remained dangerously steep.

*Overleaf: Baviaans Kloof, a wilderness of red-orange coloured sandstone mountains, wild flowers, trees and crystal streams teeming with fish.*

Finally, on 12 October, 1971, after four years of construction and the expenditure of R1 275 000, the spectacular modern bridge was opened. It eliminates completely all descents and ascents, and spans the deep gorge so smoothly that many travellers speed over it without even realising that they have just crossed one of the greatest bridges of the world.

The four-lane bridge is the longest concrete arch bridge in Southern Africa and the sixth longest in the world. Its main span is 198 m long, or twice the length of a rugby field. There are also several approach spans. The bridge deck rises 125 m above the bottom of the gorge. The overall length is 366 m and the overall width 26 m. It was built by the Italian engineering firm of Impresa Ing, A & P di Penta.

The earlier road may still be followed to the bottom of the gorge, where there is a picnic and camping site (20c per vehicle). It is a beautifully forested gorge and there are pleasant walks up and down the banks of the river.

The eastern side of the gorge has been preserved as the Van Stadens Gorge Wild Flower Reserve and Bird Sanctuary. It conserves 373 ha of fine wild flower and forest country. There are many attractive walks in this reserve and a pleasant picnic ground. The reserve is open daily from sunrise to sunset. The book *Wild Flowers of the Eastern Cape* by Batten & Bokelman is the standard guide to the flora, which is amazingly varied.

**Accommodation**
★ Thornhill Hotel, 14 rooms, 10 with baths. R7 – R7,50 B/B. Phone 653.

The turnoff to the Van Stadens Gorge Wild Flower Reserve (and down to the bottom of the gorge) is 1 km east of the bridge. At this point there is also a turnoff leading to Uitenhage 22,5 km away. The main coastal road continues eastwards across a level, well-wooded plain. There are several turnoffs to such places as Van Stadens Mouth, Sea View and Kragga Kama and after 42 km the coastal road reaches the city of Port Elizabeth (see page 322).

## GEORGE TO PORT ELIZABETH THROUGH THE LONG KLOOF

This all-tarmac road from George climbs over the Outeniqua Mountains, giving access to routes on the northern side into the Little Karoo, the Great Karoo, and a route through the Long Kloof which links up with the coastal road near Humansdorp. It is a magnificent alternative to the coastal road.

From its start in the pleasant little town of George, the road confronts the massive mountain barrier of the Outeniqua range. For 3,5 km the road leads westwards below the face of the range, searching for a gap through which to pass. Deciding that the only course to choose is the bold one of climbing directly over the barrier, the road sweeps northwards, passing the Witfontein Forestry Station, the gravel turnoff signposted Montagu and a turnoff to the small village of Blanco, originally the construction camp of Henry Fawcourt White (after whom it is named), the engineer who built Montagu Pass. The road then ascends still further by means of the magnificent Outeniqua Pass, one of the most majestic road passes on the whole continent of Africa.

Six kilometres up this pass there is a viewsite with a parking bay and a toposcope built on a vantage point and identifying various interesting parts of the countryside. This is a fitting place to pause awhile and to learn something of the Outeniqua range and its remarkable road and rail passes.

## THE OUTENIQUA PASSES

The *Outeniqua* Mountains were named after the Hottentot tribe who formerly lived there. This pleasant name actually means 'the men laden with honey' as the Hottentots used to remove rich stores of honey from the swarms of bees flourishing on the nectar of the wild flowers growing on the mountain slopes.

The range, rising to 1 579 m on George Peak, acts as the barrier between the coastal terrace and the unique world of the Little Karoo, the *Kango* (plain between the mountains) which acts as an intermediate step up to the central South African plateau. The problem of crossing the barrier of the Outeniqua has provided travellers and road builders with no little exertion.

The first Europeans to cross this range consisted of a party led by Izaak Schryver. Hykon, then chief of the Inkwa tribe of Hottentots living near the modern town of Aberdeen, had sent messengers to Cape Town in 1687 offering to trade, and the result of this was Schryver's expedition. In January 1689, he led his men over the mountains, following an ancient elephant path through what was known as Attaqua's Kloof, where the Hottentot tribe of that name once lived.

Attaqua's Kloof remained for years the regular pass through the Outeniqua. It lay just to the west of the modern Robinson Pass in the area of the Ruiterbos Forestry Station, but it has now reverted to an overgrown and forgotten track.

A second pass over the Outeniqua lay east of George. This climbed the slopes of the 1 113-m-high *Duiwelsberg* (mountain of the devil) and descended the northern slopes of the Outeniqua into the Long Kloof. This old pass, known as the Duiwelskop Pass, with its splendid scenery (like Attaqua's Kloof) is no longer used, but provides a fascinating walk for those energetic enough to follow its route from the modern forestry settlement of Bergplaats.

The third pass over the Outeniqua was built in 1812 after the establishment of George. This pass, known as *Cradock Kloof* in honour of the Governor, Sir John Cradock, was built by the first magistrate of George, Adrianus van Kervel. It was an appalling 8-km-long climb. From the viewsite at the toposcope on the Outeniqua Pass it is easy to see the route that the Cradock Kloof Pass follows. Its course is clearly marked by whitewashed cairns erected during the time of the Voortrekker Centenary. The pass climbs steeply up a shoulder of the mountain on the right, crosses the railway line in a clump of trees, and then rises in a fierce gradient to the summit. This was a dreadful pass and from the time it was built, travellers' complaints about it were incessant.

The fourth pass over the Outeniqua Mountains was the *Montagu Pass,* opened in 1847 as a replacement for Cradock Kloof. This pass is still in use and may also be seen from the toposcope on the Outeniqua Pass. Its gravel surface seems to curve like a yellow-brown cobra up the valley immediately east of the viewsite. The pass was named after John Montagu, Colonial Secretary of the Cape in the 1840s, whose enthusiasm for good roads resulted in the first ambitious programme of construction in Southern Africa. The old toll house still stands at the foot of this pass, while the ruins of a blacksmith's shop may be seen half way up the pass, where it was built to repair vehicles damaged in the difficult mountain passage. The original toll fees for users of Montagu Pass were ¾d a wheel if using a patent brake; 3d a wheel if not using a brake; 1d for each animal drawing a vehicle; ½d for sheep, goats and swine, and 2d for any other animal.

The modern Outeniqua Pass, which carries the tarmac road over the mountains, was located by Mr P. A. de Villiers, the National Road Board's location engineer, who will always rank as one of the great road builders of South Africa. Its whole conception and execution – bold and majestic – ensures its status as one of the world's grand road passes and makes it a pleasure to use.

The summit (799 m above sea level) is reached 14 km from George, 10 km from the foot of the pass. The altitude of George is 226 m above sea level.

From the summit of the Outeniqua Pass, the road descends into a fertile valley, so full of fruit farms that it resembles the bounteous harvest basket of Ceres. Having descended 10,5 km from the summit (24,5 km from George), the road reaches the northern foot of the pass and at this point there is a turnoff north-westwards to Oudtshoorn and the Cango Caves (see page 247).

From this junction, the road leads eastwards through the northern foothills of the Outeniqua Mountains, down the long, fertile valley between this range and the mountains known as the *Kammanasie* from the Hottentot *T'Kami 'Nasi* (the place of perennial water). The scenery is impressive, the tarmac road excellent, and the valley becomes increasingly fertile as the road travels further eastwards. Seven and a half kilometres from the turnoff to Oudtshoorn, the original gravel road turns off to George over Montagu Pass; while 72 km from the Oudtshoorn turnoff the road reaches an important division where one branch veers north-eastwards to Uniondale (see page 313) and the other branch continues eastwards for 12 km to Avontuur. This is a rural centre and terminus of the narrow-gauge railway running down the Long Kloof and popularly known as the Apple Express.

## THE LONG KLOOF

After the Western Cape Province, the Long Kloof is the second largest deciduous fruit producing area in Southern Africa. Its fertility is very evident to the eye, for practically the entire length of the valley is one huge export fruit orchard, backed by handsome mountains and watered by perennial streams.

The fine tarmac road running down the Long Kloof passes through a succession of rural fruit growing and despatch centres such as Avontuur, Haarlem, Misgund, Louterwater, Joubertina, Assegaaibos, and so on, each a cluster of houses and commercial buildings scattered around a railway station, church and school. Spring in the Long Kloof (September and October) is a period of blossoms and wild flowers. During the summer months wayside stalls sell the fruit of the valley to passing travellers.

Towering mountains crowd in on the valley from north and south, now advancing, now receding and leaving some new vale filled with farms and homesteads. The tarmac road and the narrow-gauge railway run down the centre of the valley, criss-crossing each other like two strings holding together a necklace made of farms, towns, villages and packing stations.

In former times the valley was the home of Bushmen. Their paintings may still be seen on the walls of many of the rock shelters. Hottentot pastoralists who supplanted the Bushman hunters have contributed many of the place names which are still in use in the valley: *Gwarina* or *Querina* (the ravine of the eland); *Kouga* (place of the blue wildebeest); *Traka* (place of the women); *Humtata* (plain where the Hottentot figs grow). These, and many other names, survive as reminders of a vanished people whose disappearance was largely due to epidemics of smallpox.

Izaak Schryver's expedition of 1689 was the first European venture into the area. Hunters, botanists and explorers followed after him. The first European settlers appeared in 1740. These people always the despair of the authorities in Cape Town, were of the breed of pioneers who, on their own initiative and quite contrary to the wishes of government, constantly expanded the frontiers in attempting to keep one step ahead of the tax gatherer. He, however, inevitably followed after them.

By 1773, about eight homesteads had been built in the Long Kloof. Men such as R. Kamfer (at *Kamfer*); M. Zondagh, on the farm *Avontuur* (adventure); John Kritzinger on *Onzer;* Tjaart van der Walt on *Warmbad;* and Jan de Buys on *De Ezeljacht,* were some of the pioneers of the area. Jan de Buys was the father of one of the most notorious and toughest of all South African frontiersmen, Coenraad de Buys. He was born on the farm *Wagenboomrivier,* but had his own farm *De Opkomst* near Kareedouw. His wild lifestyle and his practice of polygamy on a large scale, sent him wandering off as an outlaw into the northern wilderness where, at Mara on the southern slopes of the Soutpansberg in the Northern Transvaal, he founded a tribe of his own descendants, the Buys people.

During the early Kaffir wars, the Long Kloof was invaded by marauding Xhosa warriors, and many memories survive of wild fights, escapes and adventures. In those days the valley was remote and tediously difficult to reach by wagon or horse. Even now there are minor valleys – such as the Hoeree Valley – attached to the main Long Kloof, which are as difficult to enter as the famous valley of Hel in the Swartberg.

Avontuur is a small village at the head of the narrow-gauge railway running down the valley to Port Elizabeth. This line is of considerable interest to the railway enthusiast. The train service, popularly known as the Apple Express, is busy during the fruit picking season when thousands of trucks of fruit are conveyed to the harbour at Port Elizabeth for shipment. Passengers are not much catered for on the Apple Express – a bus service provides a faster alternative – but enthusiasts can always find a seat in 2nd- and 3rd-class accommodation in the caboose. During holiday periods a special passenger train runs from Port Elizabeth to Loerie.

From Avontuur there is a magnificent drive over Prince Alfred's Pass to Knysna (see page 289). Avontuur is situated in the Long Kloof, 12 km from the point where the road to Uniondale and the Great Karoo branches off. Just 0,5 km from the turnoff to the village on the main road, there is another turnoff leading 9 km to Uniondale. This road runs through a beautiful ravine filled with the rich colours and extraordinary formations of the local sandstone. Resembling a miniature Seven Weeks Poort, Uniondale Poort is resplendent with flowering aloes, flaming red- and orange-coloured cliffs, yellow lichens, and caves containing galleries of Bushman paintings.

Twenty-three kilometres down the Long Kloof from Avontuur there is a turnoff to the farming area of the Bo-Kouga. The village of *Misgund* (envied) lies 8,5 km further on, and the village of Louterwater a further 16 km down the valley. Fruit orchards which line both sides of the road provide a magnificent spectacle in spring when the trees are in blossom.

Seventeen kilometres from Louterwater there is a turnoff to the farming area of the Onder-Gouga, and after another kilometre (65,5 km from Avontuur) the road reaches the principal town of the Long Kloof . . .

# JOUBERTINA

Named after the Reverend W. A. Joubert, pastor of Uniondale from 1879 to 1892, *Joubertina* was founded in 1907 as a church centre. It became a municipality in July 1971, and now has a population of 2 101. With its position in a handsome setting of mountains, it is a busy farming centre and station for the Apple Express.

**Accommodation**
★Kloof Hotel, 26 rooms, 11 with baths. R8 – R8,50 B/B. Phone 34.

Keeping company with the puffing billies of the narrow-gauge railway, the road continues down the valley for a further 43 km and then reaches the village of . . .

# KAREEDOUW

*Kareedouw* (pass of karee trees), is a timber and farming centre. From it a tarmac road branches off to cross the mountains and join the coastal road, traversing the pass which has given the village its name. Wild flowers on the mountain slopes are prolific. Three kilometres down the Long Kloof from the village is the narrow-gauge railway centre of Assegaaibos. Here a gravel road branches off on a spectacular route to Zuuranys, the lower Kouga valley and the strange area of the Moordenaars River.

**Accommodation**
★ Assegaaibos Hotel, 15 rooms, 9 with baths. R7 – R8 B/B. Phone 33

# GHOSTS, AND THE MOORDENAARS RIVER

The gravel road from Assegaaibos railway station climbs steeply for 7 km to the summit of the *Zuuranys* (sour anys shrubs) and then descends into a broad farming valley where (9 km from Assegaaibos) it joins a gravel road which has come 18,5 km from Essenbos in the Long Kloof. From this junction the road leads past several farms and then makes a sudden steep descent into the ravine of the Kouga River. The causeway across this river is 17 km from Assegaaibos and is situated in a spectacular setting of cliffs. A fine series of pools lies up- and downstream. The whole area, however, is private property and the very tempting camping grounds can only be used with the permission of the farmers.

The road climbs steeply out of the ravine and after 2 km reaches a turnoff leading to farms such as *Joubertkraal* and *Sewefontein*. This left-hand turnoff rewards the venturesome traveller with spectacular scenery. The right-hand road continues for a further 2 km and then passes through the farmyard of *Brandekraal*. For the next 5 km there is some rugged travelling to be done as the road yet again descends steeply, this time into the ravine of the *Moordenaars* (murderers) River. The floor of the ravine lies 24,5 km from Assegaaibos. At the bottom of the pass there is a sharp turn downstream just before the road crosses the river and climbs the further slope to reach farms on the northern side of the valley.

The road downstream is rough and leads through a wild and eerie landscape, terminating after 4 km on the farm *Boskloof* owned by Mr J. H. ('Bang Jan') Ferreira. Half way to this farm lies the abandoned farm of *Jammerfontein* (fountain of sorrow) which is reputedly the most haunted place in South Africa. The story behind this reputation has been related in detail in books such as *Myths and Legends of Southern Africa* by Penny Miller.

The farm was originally the possession of Jan Prinsloo, an individual renowned for his breeding of horses and notorious for the harsh manner in which he treated his servants. Eventually, a number of his servants decided to kill him after he had flogged two of their women to death. Prinsloo heard of the plan and tried to escape on one of his horses. He was chased back into his horse corral and among the terrified animals, Jan Prinsloo was skinned alive and parts of his body were eaten.

This event took place on the stormy night of 15 January at the beginning of the 19th century. Since then the farm has had several owners, all of whom have abandoned the place. Unpleasant manifestations are said to take place on the same night each year, invariably accompanied by a thunderstorm and always in the presence of horses.

The original farmhouse of Jan Prinsloo is a total ruin overgrown with dense bush. It lies close to the Moordenaars River 1 km from the start of the road. A second farmhouse was built 0,5 km further down the road by an owner hoping to avoid any unpleasant occurrences. This farmhouse is also in ruins. A further 0,5 km down the road among the trees, are some graves said to be those of British soldiers killed in the area during the Anglo-Boer War. *Boskloof* farm is 1,5 km further on.

*Jammerfontein* farm lies in a setting of high, red-coloured sandstone mountains. In former times this area was the lair of renegades and men who preferred the solitude of the wilderness and wanted nothing to do with government, law or any other restraints of society. By all accounts, Jan Prinsloo was a brooding, erratic, violent character. He found his way into this forbidding and remote gorge and there defied the efforts of the tax gatherer, police and parson to reach him. He built the homestead himself, dug a water furrow to irrigate his lands, and built stables and a corral to house the horses he bred, the only living things for which he had any affection.

Perhaps it was inevitable that something violent would take place in so wild and remote a setting with such a strangely hostile atmosphere. To visit the place is an experience. In January the air is hot, and thunderstorms charge the atmosphere with electricity as the dark shadows of the clouds drift over the hills. For those who wait through the night for something to happen, the day dawns with the visitor only realising long afterwards that perhaps something did occur and what was thought to be natural at the time – a sound, or a horse in the thicket – cannot now be reasonably explained.

Giant tortoises move ponderously through the undergrowth which is also inhabited by snakes. There is a tangible silence in the night and even the stream seems muted. Some birds do sing, and horses, wild or tame, conceal themselves from man in the thickets. There is no need for signs saying 'Keep out' or 'No Trespassing'. Many little things conspire to make the place repellent.

From the turnoff at Assegaaibos to Zuuranys and Jan Prinsloo's ill-starred kloof, the main road down the Long Kloof continues for 18 km and then joins the main coastal road at a point 18 km from Humansdorp. The coastal road then proceeds to Port Elizabeth and Algoa Bay (see page 303).

## UNIONDALE, WILLOWMORE AND BAVIAANS KLOOF

At the head of the Long Kloof, 96,5 km from George, the road divides. One branch leads to Avontuur. The left-hand tarmac road veers towards the north-east, climbing and twisting over a high ridge of hills, and after 12,5 km it reaches a sunburned-looking cluster of houses gathered attentively around a tall church, like a rural congregation attending an open-air revival campaign. The town lies in a dale overlooked by an assemblage of odd-shaped hills, flat-tops and pointed peaks. This is the town of . . .

## UNIONDALE

Uniondale had a rather odd beginning. In 1856 the owners of each of the two portions of the farm *Rietvallei* laid out two rural townships named Hopedale and Lyon. The townships adjoined one another but the owners disagreed until the Dutch Reformed Church settled the rivalry by building a church there in 1865 and marking the union of the townships by naming the place *Uniondale*.

For some years Uniondale was a very quiet backwater, hindered by lack of communications. It acquired municipal status on 12 February 1884. The ostrich feather boom gave it an injection of prosperity, for feathers not only fetched high prices but could be relatively easily transported through the Swartberg range to what was then the nearest railway station, Prince Albert Road in the Great Karoo.

Wagon and cart building, the manufacture of furniture and the rearing of cattle, horses, sheep and Cape goats, also flourished in and around the little town. With a rainfall of 250 mm a year, and the surrounding hills looking pretty arid, the dale of Uniondale is fortunately still well watered by a perennial stream. A disused watermill with a fine, big wheel, is a reminder of another local industry of former times. The town is now inhabited by 3 780 people. The drive from Uniondale through Uniondale Poort to Avontuur is magnificent.

### Accommodation
★ Royal Hotel, 24 rooms, 6 with baths. R7 – R7,50 B/B. Phone 9904.

313

**Caravans and camping**
Municipal caravan park, free.

Beyond Uniondale, the road rises steeply for 4,5 km. At the summit of the rise there is a left turn to Oudtshoorn (132 km away), while ahead, along the edge of the dry, arid north-eastern corner of the Little Karoo, lies the Swartberg range. The Swartberg has lost much of its height by the time it reaches its eastern extremity here, but it still presents a formidable barrier to the road seeking a way of escape from the Little Karoo. The road leads north-eastwards towards the mountains. Forty kilometres from Uniondale there is a turnoff to Oudtshoorn and immediately beyond this point the road enters what is known as Ghwariespoort, a dry, shallow valley full of flowering aloes, which provides a natural passage around the eastern end of the Swartberg, out of the Little Karoo and on to the higher plateau of the Great Karoo. After 17 km of steady climbing the road emerges from the pass on to an arid plateau encircled by mountains. On the far side of this plateau, 63 km from Uniondale, against a backing of the *Witberg* (white mountain), lies the town of . . .

# WILLOWMORE

This is a curiously old-world Karoo town with several interesting buildings dating from the Victorian and Edwardian periods. It is the administrative centre of a large district lying on the border of the summer and winter rainfall areas and it would be pleasant to imagine that it enjoys the best of both worlds, but this is uncertain. The weather never seems to have made up its mind about the Willowmore district, resulting in an interesting effect on the vegetation. Drought-resistant plants such as *Obesa euphorbia* and *Horrida euphorbia* grow in the area and find conditions congenial if only because most normal plants have long since given up in despair and left space for others.

The town had its beginning in 1864 when J. P. Aughanbough purchased from William Moore a portion of the farm *Willow*. A tennis court was built on part of the ground which became the focal point of local sporting activities; this thereafter led to the establishment of trade. The name Willow-Moore was first applied to the place and later simplified to *Willowmore*. Ten years after the tennis court had been built, a church and a magistracy were established and after a further ten years, on 28 February 1884, Willowmore became a municipality. The railway connecting Cape Town to Port Elizabeth reached the town in 1900.

Today, Willowmore has a population of 4 720 and remains the centre for a considerable farming industry which produces ostriches, sheep, goats, lucerne and in the fertile Baviaans Kloof, citrus and tobacco.

**Accommodation**
⋆ Royal Hotel, 25 rooms, 9 with baths, R8,55 – R9,05 B/B. Phone 225.

**Caravans and camping**
⋆Willowmore Caravan Park, 20 sites. R3 D.

From Willowmore, the main tarmac road to the north climbs steadily through stony hills covered with stunted bush. Three kilometres from the town there is a turnoff to Steytlerville (89 km away) and 20 km from the town a turnoff to Beaufort West, 136 km away.

Thirty-two kilometres from Willowmore, the road reaches the bridge over the Groot River, where there is a picnic site at the Beervlei Dam of the Department of Water Affairs. At this point the road to the north penetrates the final barrier of hills and emerges on to the high plains of the Great Karoo, reaching, 116 km from Willowmore, the town of . . .

314

# ABERDEEN

Another curiously old-world type of Karoo town is Aberdeen (with a population of 5 064), situated on the plains and backed by the Sneeuberg range. The town was laid out as a community centre in 1856 by the Dutch Reformed Church and named after the birthplace in Scotland of the Reverend Andrew Murray, then the Dutch Reformed Church minister of Graaff-Reinet, of which district Aberdeen was an offshoot. The Aberdeen Dutch Reformed Church claims to have the highest steeple in South Africa. The principal farming activity of the area is the production of wool.

A pleasant picnic site is situated at Fonteinbos, on the banks of the Kraai River, 100 m from which may be seen some odd fossilised footprints.

### Accommodation
★ Aberdeen Hotel, 19 rooms, 8 with baths. R8 – R8,50 B/B. Phone 62.

### Caravans and camping
★★ Municipal caravan park, 20 sites. R2 D.

Beyond Aberdeen, the tarmac road leads north-eastwards over an arid plain. Eleven kilometres from the town the road bridges over the river known as the *Kamdeboo* (green elevations) from the relative fertility of its surroundings. Fifty-eight kilometres from Aberdeen, the road reaches the town of . . .

# GRAAFF-REINET

One of the historic towns of the old Cape Colony, Graaff-Reinet still retains some of the atmosphere and presence of the days when it was a frontier town, and its streets were peopled by a picturesque crowd of wanderers, hunters, explorers and pioneers. The district gave birth to a hardy, independent and rugged assembly of human beings, some of whom were to become great Voortrekker leaders, such as Andries Pretorius and Sarel Cilliers.

The town had its beginning on 19 July 1786, when the Governor of the Cape, Jacob van de Graaff, in an effort to settle a troubled frontier, proclaimed the establishment of a new district embracing the sprawling, sunburned area which extended from the Gamtoos River to the Great Fish River, and from the sea to the Zeekoe River. A new town was planned to administer this district, and the site chosen was in a most spectacular concentration of scenery near the source of the Sundays River. At this place the river burrows into a complex cluster of flat-topped mountains which form part of the Sneeuberg massif. In the course of finding a way through this range the river has formed into a huge horseshoe bend and deposited a rich layer of alluvial silt which, with the perennial flow of water, the crisp, sunny climate and 250 mm of rain a year, combines to make the area particularly fertile. Overlooking the site is a guardian peak, *Spandau Kop*, named by a Prussian settler, Werner, after the fortress in Spandau near Berlin.

The site of the town (originally the farm of Dirk Coetzee) was well chosen by Herman Woeke, the first landdros appointed to the new district. The name of *Graaff-Reinet* was given to the town in honour of the Governor and his lady. A *drostdy* (residency) was built in 1786 on a site between Seamans Garage and the Gem Garage, but was replaced in 1804 by a more imposing official residence erected on the site of the present Drostdy Hotel. Both of these early homes have long since vanished; in its early years Graaff-Reinet was a rough and ready little town in which most of the early buildings met their end by simply collapsing as a result of their primitive construction.

After the first drostdy came a church and school and 11 years after its founding the town could boast one street lined with clay buildings. Progress was slow, however, impeded by frontier uncertainties and political disturbances. In 1795 the local inhabitants assembled in the town, whereupon they expelled the resident landdros and declared a republic with Adriaan van Jaarsveld as president. In addition, the Great Trek lured away many of the best local farmers, and economic conditions remained in a state of depression for many years with inadequate communications isolating the district from any worthwhile market for its produce.

The passage of years did not, however, prevent Graaff-Reinet from developing its special character and some most interesting buildings were erected: Reinet House, built about 1805 as the parsonage of the first minister of the local Dutch Reformed Church, is a supreme example of Cape-Dutch architecture. In the garden may be seen growing the largest grapevine in the world. Planted in 1870 by the Reverend Charles Murray, the son of the famous Dr Andrew Murray, this vine is of the Black Acorn variety, the stem of which is 1,5 m in circumference. At present the vine covers 125 square metres and still bears excellent grapes. Reinet House is now a museum containing many interesting period pieces. Included among the exhibits is a gloriously Heath-Robinson-type invention – a hand-held machine for pipping raisins – and a machine for peeling peaches. In the yard of the museum is a working waterwheel and mill. Reinet House is open in winter, Mondays to Fridays from 09h00 to 12h00 and from 15h00 to 17h00; in summer, Mondays to Fridays, from 15h30 to 17h30 and on Saturdays from 09h00 to 12h00.

A tragedy occurred on 1 April 1980 when the building was partially destroyed by fire. However, the museum is in the process of being rebuilt.

Parsonage Street, leading from the museum to what was originally the drostdy (now a hotel) is lined with some fascinating examples of South African architecture, perfectly restored by the Simon van der Stel Foundation. Number 1 Parsonage Street is now the Jan Felix Lategan Museum of Historical Firearms, open Mondays to Fridays from 09h00 to 12h00 and from 15h00 to 17h00; on Saturdays from 09h00 to 12h00. Also in Parsonage Street is the restored church building of the London Missionary Society, which now houses the John Rupert Art Gallery.

A powder magazine built in 1831 still keeps a rather sinister watch over the town from an overlooking hill. The present Dutch Reformed Church, surely the most graceful in Southern Africa, was built in 1886 and designed by the architect J. Bisset on similar lines to Salisbury Cathedral in England. The town hall, constructed in Renaissance style, was opened on 1 May 1911. The charming little Dutch Reformed Mission Church, consecrated in 1821, now the Hester Rupert Art Museum, is another unique asset, preserved and restored for the town by the Rembrandt group of companies and named after the mother of Dr Anton Rupert, the guiding spirit of the company, who was born in Graaff-Reinet. The Hester Rupert Art Museum exhibits an admirable and provocative collection of the work of many leading South African artists, which is constantly being expanded. The museum is open on weekdays from 10h00 to 12h00 and from 15h00 to 18h00; in winter from 15h30 to 17h30 and on Saturdays from 10h00 to 12h30.

The main building of the Drostdy Hotel has been restored to its original charm, while behind it is the superb *Stretch's Court,* named after Captain Charles Stretch, government surveyor of Graaff-Reinet, who bought the area in 1855 and sub-divided it. Cottages were built there, mainly for labourers. These later fell into disrepair, but in 1966, the Historical Homes of South Africa acquired the properties and perfectly restored the entire court. The cottages now form part of the Drostdy Hotel, splendidly managed by Mr David Rawdon.

On the banks of the Sundays River has been laid out a beautiful little park, named after Herbert Urquhart, a popular mayor of the town. This park is particularly pretty at night when the trees are illuminated by lights and the atmosphere is almost tropical. It contains a caravan park and some bungalows.

Graaff-Reinet (with a population of 17 728) is the centre for many sheep, cattle, horse and dairy farms. Wool and mohair are the principal products and the town is an important educational centre with a large Teachers' Training College for men and women. The cultural history of Graaff-Reinet is outlined in detail in the book *Graaff-Reinet* by Dr C.G. Henning.

## Accommodation
★★® Drostdy Hotel, 41 rooms, all with baths. R10,35 – R16,35 B/B. Phone 2161.
★ Graaff-Reinet Hotel, 27 rooms, 9 with baths. R9,50 – R10,50 B/B. Phone 3655.
★★ Panorama Hotel, 40 rooms, all with baths. R11 – R11,50 B/B. Phone 2233.

## Caravans and camping
★★® Urquhart Park, 120 sites. R1,50 – R2 D. 7 rondawels, R3 D.

# THE VALLEY OF DESOLATION

From Graaff-Reinet an interesting 14-km-long drive leads to the summit of the overlooking mountain massif west of the town, ending at what is known as the Valley of Desolation.

The tarmac road leaves Graaff-Reinet on its way to Murraysburg. Passing the Urquhart Park (1,5 km from the town centre) the road skirts the verge of the Vanryneveldspas Dam in the Sundays River. The dam, covering 1 000 ha, has a wall 353 m long and 32 m high. The South African Nature Foundation is developing a Karoo Park in the 2 600-ha area adjoining the dam.

The road continues past the memorial to Gideon Scheepers, designed by E. Hough. Commandant Scheepers was executed near there during the Anglo-Boer War. Six kilometres from Graaff-Reinet a gravel turnoff leads south to *Winterhoek* farm. At 1,5 km along this turnoff there is another gravel branch which takes the traveller in a steady, steep climb of 8 km up to the summit (1 500 m above sea level) of the mountain massif. The views of the surrounding country and Graaff-Reinet, make the diversion well worth while.

The road terminates at a picnic site, from where a footpath marked with whitewashed boulders leads to the various viewsites along the edge of the Valley of Desolation. The valley is actually a cleft in the rock-strewn plateau summit of the massif and is an example of bizarre natural erosion. Littered with rocks and boulders, and with the crumbling edges of the precipice worn into all manner of jagged shapes, the valley falls sharply away from the plateau summit, yielding fine views over the plains of the Great Karoo.

_____

From Graaff-Reinet the main tarmac road continues in a northerly direction, passing at 1,5 km, the memorial to Andries Pretorius, the dominant leader of the Great Trek. Sculpted by Coert Steynberg, the memorial faces Pretorius Kloof where Andries Pretorius had his farm *Letskraal.* After crossing the Sundays River just above the point where it flows into the Vanryneveldspas Dam, the road proceeds to climb into the hills.

At 28 km from Graaff-Reinet a turnoff is reached leading eastwards for 19 km to New Bethesda, founded in 1875 and lying at the foot of the 2 500-m-high Kompasberg, the highest point of the Sneeuberg massif. This small town with a total of 2 925 inhabitants, had its start as a mission station.

The main road leads on through fine sheep country, rising to successive levels of plateau country interspersed with hills and mountains. Naudesberg Pass, 39 km from Graaff-Reinet, provides a steady 3-km-long climb which carries the road up to a bowl in the mountains, situated at 1 440 m, in which the Sundays River has its source. From here (48 km from Graaff-Reinet) another turnoff leads over Witnek Pass to New Bethesda.

**Accommodation**

★ Good's Motel (close to the turnoff to New Bethesda), 10 rooms, 6 with baths. R7 – R16 room only. Phone Bethesda Road 718.

The tarmac road crosses the infant Sundays River and continues north-eastwards across the floor of this bowl in the mountains. At 47 km from Graaff-Reinet there is a turnoff east to Cradock (89 km), just beyond which point the road begins an ascent of the Lootsberg Pass, reaching the summit (1 785 m above sea level) after 5 km. From here the road keeps company with the railway along the eastern verges of the Renosterberg, until, 106 km from Graaff-Reinet, it reaches the important junction with the tarmac road coming from Port Elizabeth. The combined roads enter the town of Middelburg (see page 346).

# BAVIAANS KLOOF

From Willowmore a gravel road leads eastwards through Baviaans Kloof to join the coastal road and to reach Port Elizabeth. For the traveller exploring Southern Africa, this road, rough in places with steep gradients and incessant curves, provides an exciting drive through 171 km of rugged, brilliantly coloured sandstone mountains and ravines.

At a junction 30,5 km from Willowmore, the road is joined by a gravel road coming from Uniondale, 50 km away. The combined roads now leave the Karoo area and enter the great *Baviaans Kloof* (ravine of baboons). For 43,5 km the road runs through a narrow cleft in the mountains, filled with plants such as geraniums and arum lilies, and many lovely acacia trees.

Seventy-four kilometres from Willowmore, the road reaches the principal centre of the Baviaans Kloof, a cluster of stores with a police post, named *Studtis* after a German who once traded there. Fine wild fig trees shade the area and a branch road leads 24 km into the Baviaans Kloof Forest Reserve where in places such as Doringkloof in the Kouga mountains the rare and unique Baviaans Kloof cedar trees *(Widdringtonia schwarzii)* may be seen growing.

The road continues beneath red-coloured cliffs with many strange rock formations. After 25 km of travelling the road reaches a small farming centre known as Colesplaas where there is a store and petrol supply. Beyond this place the road begins climbing a high ridge and for 8 km the journey is graced with magnificent scenes of rocks, ravines, a richly varied flora and majestic views.

At the far side of the pass, after a steep descent, the road winds through a valley shaded by fine peppercorn, acacia and wild fig trees. Thirty-two kilometres from Colesplaas, the road reaches a gate at what was originally an agricultural settlement, now taken over by the Forestry Department. From this gate the road commences a steep ascent and the summit is reached after 10 km of climbing. The views are superb and the mountain slopes are richly covered with proteas, erica and other flowering plants.

On the summit there is a solitary farm, *Berg Plaatz*, owned by Mr F. F. Botha, and the road passes the signpost demarcating the boundary between the Willowmore and Humansdorp districts. The road traverses a high plateau where the traveller can admire the wheat fields, proteas, pincushions and panoramic views of the towering mountains. The road then descends steeply down a narrow pass occasionally edged by hair-raising precipices.

Forty-five and a half kilometres from Colesplaas the road reaches the bottom of the pass in a valley quite choked up with vegetation. A beautiful, clear stream, the Wit River, flows down this valley and the road crosses it by means of 12 successive causeways. It is a delightful drive with several fine, shady places in which to rest and picnic.

The valley suddenly opens into a basin in the hills containing the Cambria Forestry Station and the Goedehoop Nedersetting, a church settlement. Flowering aloes, orange groves, cacti, succulents, geraniums and acacia trees with their sweet-smelling blossoms grow on the alluvial floor. There are several fine farms.

Fifty-six kilometres from Colesplaas the road reaches a turnoff at a small store. This turnoff leads to Armmansvriend and to a memorial to Tjaart Johannes van der Walt. He was killed on 8 August 1802 about 8 km away on a site marked by a small, white commemorative stone in the centre of a field in the farming area of the Cambria agricultural settlement. His death occurred during one of the wars of the period. His remains were exhumed and removed to the present site where a memorial hall has been erected to serve the local community, and a plinth stands over his grave.

From the turnoff to this memorial site, the road twists through a most magnificent cleft in the mountains. The colours and folded formations of the cliffs reflect in the river pools and the journey is extremely winding and varied for 13 km. Then the road emerges from what is known as the Groot River Pass, and enters the alluvial valley of the Gamtoos River with its beautiful, irrigated farmlands. After 2 km the road reaches the small centre of Heroncliff 71 km from Colesplaas. From here the road, now tarmac, continues down the Gamtoos valley for 24,5 km to the village of Patensie.

Any traveller venturing through Baviaans Kloof, the 171 km from Heroncliff to Willowmore, will have lasting memories of the journey. In summer the air is sweet with the smell of acacia blossom. Plumbago is in flower, as well as agapanthus, red-hot pokers, oleanders and some proteas, although their season is really winter. Wild fig trees, pelargoniums and a mass of greenery grow in vividly red soil.

Birds chatter, talk, squabble and call. The air is warm. Crystal-clear streams tumble down the slopes in cascades and waterfalls. Rivers such as the Kouga work their way through complicated scenery. Odd farms linger in isolated places, with men, some of them hill-billy types, dressed in blue overalls and women bare-footed, gazing in curiosity. A visitor is usually suspected of being a revenue, forestry or water department official come to expropriate their property.

Guineafowl call, baboons bark, an occasional fat puffadder slithers across the road, sluggish and sinuous – doing no harm to anyone if no one harms it. Tortoises large and small abound; this is their primeval sort of country. Echoes sound in the hills – a distant shot – fish glide silently in the pools, there is stillness and solitude.

The wind whispers and tells of old adventures. The streams gossip interminably as they bustle along. *Mtunzini* (the place of shadows) the Fingo people called this area. It is a good place for ghosts: it is their scene. One can understand their reluctance to leave it.

## THE GAMTOOS VALLEY

When the road through Baviaans Kloof emerges from the Groot River Pass, the traveller is confronted with an altogether different scene. The mountains are still there, crowding in on either side, but the valley is densely settled, highly developed, and has an atmosphere far removed in years of progress from the wildness of Baviaans Kloof.

The Gamtoos Valley lends itself splendidly to irrigation and it has water supplies which at times have proved more than ample when heavy rains bring the rivers down in flood. Five and a half kilometres from Heroncliff, on the main tarmac road to Patensie, there is a turnoff leading to the Paul Sauer Dam 8 km away, in a deep gorge of the Kouga River. This fine dam contains 130 million cubic metres of water. It was completed in 1967, with a wall 365 m long and 94 m high. It feeds irrigation water to many farms in the valley. Its scenic setting is pleasant and there is a picnic ground situated below the dam wall.

Beyond the turnoff to the dam, the main tarmac road continues down the valley, with irrigated farmlands on either side and many lovely gardens of flowers cultivated around the homesteads. Aloes flowering in May and June turn the hillsides red. Twenty and a half kilometres from Heroncliff there is a gravel turnoff to the north leading to the valley of the Elands River and thence to Port Elizabeth. The main tarmac road, 24,5 km away from Heroncliff, reaches the town of . . .

# PATENSIE

A busy little agricultural centre and the terminus for a branch of the narrow-gauge railway from Port Elizabeth, this town has a population of 1 108. The name of *Patensie* is said to have originated from the Hottentot place name indicating a resting spot for cattle. Citrus, tobacco and vegetables for the Port Elizabeth market are the principal products.

## Accommodation
★ Ripple Hill Hotel, 14 rooms, 3 with baths. R7,80 – R8,80 B/B. Phone 12.

## Caravans and camping
★ Municipal caravan park, 20 sites. 50c D per person.

From Patensie, the tarmac road leads down the valley through a landscape covered in flowering aloes. The narrow-gauge railway follows the road closely. After 14,5 km the road reaches the town of . . .

# HANKEY

With a present population of 1 100, *Hankey* had its beginning in 1822 when the London Missionary Society purchased ground on both sides of the Gamtoos River. To this area they transferred some of the surplus population from their overcrowded mission station at Bethelsdorp. The Reverend J.G. Messer was appointed first missionary and the station was named in honour of William Hankey, the treasurer of the society in London.

The irrigation possibilities of the flat, alluvial valley floor were only too apparent. William Philip, a son of Dr Philip, one of the leading missionaries of the society, cut a tunnel to divert water from the river to the fields. The young man was sadly rewarded for his enterprise as he was drowned with John Philip Fairbairn, on 1 July 1845 in the Gamtoos during a flood. Sudden floods, in fact, have always been a menace in such a wide, flat valley. The years 1847, 1905, 1916 and 1932 all saw prodigious floods which did great damage and caused considerable loss of life. Emma Hughes and Alice Hullock, 17 years old and 13 years old respectively, were drowned in the Klein River on 27 February 1875.

In 1876 the London Missionary Society sold their property. Hankey was proclaimed a public village in 1881 and a municipality in 1905. This first municipality was abolished in 1951 but, after a spell under local area management, Hankey was once again given village management board status on 1 March 1963. Today it is the centre for a superb stretch of irrigated farmland producing citrus, tobacco, fruit, vegetables and general agricultural produce.

Camping is allowed in the pleasant park known as Yellowwoods, situated 1 km from the town on the road to Klein River.

## Accommodation
★ Hankey Hotel, 11 rooms, 5 with baths. R7 – R8,50 B/B. Phone 61.

From Hankey, the main tarmac road climbs a ridge with a turnoff 1 km away leading to a fine viewsite looking out over the whole valley. After a further 17 km the road reaches the railway centre of . . .

320

# LOERIE

Named after the bird *Turacus corythair*, *Loerie* is simply a railway station with a few shops and houses but several things contribute to give it an importance beyond its size. It is the site of one of the main water storage dams of the Port Elizabeth municipality.

The station is one of the busiest on the narrow-gauge railway from Port Elizabeth. The limestone quarries of the Eastern Province Cement Company are connected to the station by an aerial ropeway 9 km long. There are two separate parallel ropeways. One, a bi-cableway built in 1932, consists of two steel ropes, a stationary track rope and a haulage rope. The second ropeway, built in 1954, is a mono-cableway and consists of one endless rope which carries as well as hauls.

The speeds and carrying capacities of the two ropeways are very similar. They run simultaneously or individually and take an hour to carry a bucket container from the quarry to Loerie where the narrow-gauge railway takes over the load, hauling about 120 trucks of limestone a day to the junction of Chelsea, from where the cement company has its own narrow-gauge railway to take the trucks to their factory in Port Elizabeth.

The ropeway is completely straight. It climbs for about a third of its route and then descends to Loerie. The descending weight of the evenly-spaced buckets helps to raise the ascending buckets and consequently makes the ropeway very economical to operate. The driving engines are at the Limebank quarry which was first worked in 1932 when the ropeway was opened.

From Loerie a tarmac road branches off and leads to Gamtoos, 9 km away, where the narrow-gauge railway has a junction, with a branch going up the valley to Patensie and the main line continuing to Humansdorp and the Long Kloof. The situation of Loerie is handsome. Each year, from 1 June to 31 January, the railway authorities run a special Apple Express excursion, departing from Port Elizabeth each Saturday at 09h00 to Loerie and returning at 17h30. For railway enthusiasts this is a delightful trip. There is a pleasant picnic area just outside Loerie on the road to Patensie.

From Loerie, the tarmac road climbs steeply out of the valley of the Gamtoos, winding through hills covered in aloes, cacti and dark-green bush. After 7 km of climbing, the road reaches the summit where there is a viewsite and resting place offering a grand view of the valley and the ranges of the Elandsberg and the Groot Winterhoek. The scene is dominated by the 1 759-m-high peak known to Europeans as the Cockscomb but named by the Hottentots the *T'Numkwa* (mountain of the clouds). To some the outlook is so vast that it is known as the Valley of a Thousand and One Hills.

The tarmac road continues for a further 3 km, and then 10 km from Loerie, joins the main coastal road at a point 38 km from Port Elizabeth (see page 322).

## Chapter Seventeen

# PORT ELIZABETH AND THE SETTLER COUNTRY

## PORT ELIZABETH

With a population of 526 381, Port Elizabeth is the third port and fifth largest city in South Africa. Originally founded on a narrow coastal shelf compressed between the sea and a steep rise to a high plateau, it was most awkwardly situated. The city has escaped its early constriction by spreading up the rise and then projecting its new suburbs in all directions over the high plateau, where gardens and mankind flourish in a more spacious environment generously endowed with water, sunshine and good soil. All things grow well and places such as Walmer enjoy the shade of many magnificent trees planted there in previous years by considerate people.

Originally, a Hottentot tribe grazed livestock in the area, and watered them in the stream they named *Kragga Kama* (stony water), now changed to Baakens, at whose mouth there was a small lagoon and the best landing beach on the shores of Algoa Bay. The first Europeans to visit the bay were the early Portuguese navigators who named it the *Bahia de Lagoa* (bay of the lagoon). Bartholomew Dias, on his pioneer voyage of discovery in 1488, sailed along the east coast as far as a headland now known as *Kwaaihoek* (angry corner), 14,5 km west of Cape Padrone, the sandy *Pòntas do Padrão* (point of the pedestal) which marks the eastern end of Algoa Bay. On Kwaaihoek, called by the Portuguese the *Penedo das Fontes* (rock of the fountains), Dias erected a pillar in honour of St Gregory, hence the modern corrupted name of Cape Padrone. Another Portuguese name lingers over the western cape of Algoa Bay, *Cape Recife* (cape of the reef). A replica of the pillar of St Gregory, hewn from the same quarry in Portugal, stands in the mayor's garden of Port Elizabeth.

The Portuguese made no use of the Bahia de Lagoa (Algoa Bay) since it offered scant shelter and the few Hottentot residents on the shore had little to trade. Not until January 1690 was any interest shown by Europeans in taking possession of the area. A galiot from the Cape, the *Noord,* visited the bay at that time for the purpose of securing possession but the skipper, viewing the bay lashed by a howling gale, considered it worthless and sailed away again.

In 1752 Ensign August Beutler visited the shores of Algoa Bay during an overland journey from the Cape. He camped on the shores of the bay and erected at the mouth of the *Baakens* (beacon) River, a beacon of possession, bearing the arms of the Dutch East India Company. Nothing further was done, for the exposure of the bay to the south-east gales of summer made the place a death trap for shipping. A harbour to serve the Eastern Cape, however, became increasingly essential and, for want of anything better, Algoa Bay slowly came into use as a landing place for men and goods.

In August 1799, the authorities of the first British occupation of the Cape built a stone redoubt, 24 metres square, overlooking the mouth of the Baakens River and dominating the landing place of Algoa Bay. It was named *Fort Frederick,* after the Duke of York. A garrison was stationed there and this was the beginning of the present city which, with the landing of the 1820 Settlers, was visited by the acting Governor, Sir Rufane Shawe Donkin, on 6 June and named by him *Port Elizabeth* in memory of his beloved wife who at the age of 28, had died of fever in India two years earlier. The old fort was the first stone building to be erected in the Eastern Cape and is well preserved on a handsome viewsite overlooking the harbour. Sir

Rufane Shawe Donkin built a stone pyramid to the memory of his wife on the hill above the landing place of Algoa Bay. The monument with its touching inscription still stands on the Donkin Reserve, with the old 15 000 candlepower lighthouse beside it watching the shipping in the busy harbour of today.

Port Elizabeth became a seat of magistracy in February 1825. Notwithstanding many dreadful shipwrecks in the bay when entire fleets were sometimes blown on to the beach by sudden gales, Port Elizabeth developed as a major port with a secure artificial harbour eventually being built in 1928. The worst shipping disaster occurred on 31 August 1902 when 19 out of 38 ships in the anchorage were wrecked.

Industry flourished in the growing town with Frederick Korsten founding the first manufactory (a tannery and smithy) in 1811. The city today is the principal centre in Southern Africa for the automobile industry (notably the Ford and General Motors plants), while over 700 diverse factories are engaged in the production of a great variety of commodities.

As a holiday resort, Port Elizabeth has much to offer in the way of fun and the enjoyment of life in the sunshine. Summer sea temperatures are pleasantly warm (21°C to 25°C) without becoming sticky and the beaches of Algoa Bay offer splendid swimming. Humewood and King's Beach (where the British Royal Family swam during their 1947 visit) are imaginatively developed with change rooms, tearooms, a miniature railway, promenades, tidal baths and children's paddling pools. A particularly pleasant adjunct to this ocean front is Happy Valley, once the boggy course of a stream but now most skilfully converted by the municipal gardeners into something of a playground of fairies from *A Midsummer Night's Dream,* with reflecting pools, lights, masses of flowers and the greenest of lawns.

The famous Port Elizabeth snake park, tropical house, museum and oceanarium is also on the Humewood beachfront. The museum has many beautifully displayed exhibits of natural history (especially marine life), settler history, early transport vehicles, sailing ships, and so on. Of considerable literary interest are some of the original illustrations and text pages from *Jock of the Bushveld* by Percy Fitzpatrick, the classic work of South Africa's gold rush and hunting days. *Jock of the Bushveld,* with nearly 100 editions to its credit, has never been out of print since its publication in 1907 and has given pleasure to countless people. Its author, James Percy Fitzpatrick, died in his home *Amanzi,* some kilometres from Port Elizabeth, on 24 January 1931.

The snake park next to the museum is one of the best known of its kind in the world and the display of assorted reptiles is fascinating. The tropical house contains an especially well-presented collection of reptiles, birds and plants.

The oceanarium contains a varied, animated and colourful collection of fish and marine life. The stars of this assembly, occupying a large central tank, are a number of delightful dolphins whose antics, acrobatics, histrionics and pure show-off are a joy to see. The bottle-nosed dolphins were all caught in Algoa Bay or bred in the aquarium. The first two 'stars' of the dolphin show were the females, Haig (caught off King's Beach on 16 October 1962) and Lady Dimple (caught in November 1963).

The museum is open daily, 09h00 to 12h45 and 14h00 to 17h00. Sundays 10h00 to 12h30 and 14h00 to 17h00. Admission is free. The snake park has the same hours as the museum. Demonstration times are 10h00, 10h30, 11h45, 12h15, 14h15, 15h00, 16h30. Admission is 45c adults and 15c children. The oceanarium is open daily. The dolphins perform at 11h00 and 15h30 daily. Admission is 45c adults and 15c children.

Another considerable asset to Port Elizabeth is the Settler's Park Nature Reserve, a 54-ha wild flower reserve situated on the banks of the Baakens River. Proclaimed a reserve in 1938, this interesting piece of riverine scenery preserves something of the landscape, flora and fauna of the area as it was in past years. Indigenous flora; water lilies on the pools of the river; trees such as yellowwood, milkwood and keurboom in the deep gorges; coral aloes on the cliff faces, the orange-scarlet-coloured *Aloe pluridens* flowering in June and July; the Namaqualand daisies and other spring flowers; and a variety of fauna – springbok, blue wildebeest and waterfowl – animate an attractive scene.

Yachting and boating on the lower reaches of the *Swartkops* (black hills) River, at Redhouse and the North End Lake, and a great variety of organised sports on excellent playing fields, all contribute to the enjoyment of life in Port Elizabeth.

Port Elizabeth is the home of the dual medium (Afrikaans and English) University of Port Elizabeth, which began its first academic year on 1 March 1965. Several fine schools such as Grey High School are also established in the city. The King George VI Art Gallery, opened in June 1956, is accumulating an interesting collection of works of art and frequently exhibits loan collections. Admission to the art gallery is free, Mondays 14h00 to 18h00. Tuesdays to Saturdays from 10h00 to 12h45 and 14h00 to 18h00. Sundays 14h30 to 17h30. There is an interesting historical museum in the restored parsonage of the Reverend Francis McCleland in Castle Street. He was the colonial chaplain and lived there until his death in 1853. The parsonage is open Tuesdays to Saturdays from 10h00 to 12h45 and 14h00 to 18h00. Sundays and Mondays from 14h00 to 17h00.

A campanile, 52 m tall, stands on the harbour landing as a memorial to the 1820 Settlers. Built in 1923, it has a 204-step spiral staircase leading to the top. It is open, weekdays from 09h00 to 13h00 and 14h00 to 16h00. Wednesdays and Saturdays from 08h30 to 12h30. Closed on Sundays. A carillon of 21 bells rings changes from the campanile every day at 08h32 and 18h02. Another notable memorial in Port Elizabeth is the Horse Memorial standing at the junction of Cape and Russel roads. The work of Joseph Whitehead, it was erected by public subscription in recognition of innumerable horses which perished during the Anglo-Boer War.

## Accommodation

★★★ Beach Hotel, 63 rooms, all with baths. R14,50 – R17 B/B. Phone 53-2161.

★★ Campanile Hotel, 66 rooms, 57 with baths. R14 – R22 B/B. Phone 2-7766.

★ Clarendon Hotel, 17 rooms, 6 with baths. R6 – R7 B/B. Phone 2-1558.

★ Criterion Hotel, 10 rooms, 3 with baths. R4,50 – R5 B/B. Phone 2-7533.

★★ Edward Hotel, 124 rooms, 118 with baths. R10 – R19 B/B. Phone 2-2111.

★★★★★ Elizabeth Hotel, 204 rooms, all with baths. R29 – R46,50 room only. Phone 52-3720.

★ Farmers Home Hotel, 12 rooms, 3 with baths. R5,75 – R6,80 B/B. Phone 2-1991.

★Grand Hotel, 42 rooms, 26 with baths. R8,50 – R9,50 B/B. Phone 2-7341.

★ Green Bushes Motel, 20 rooms, all with baths. R9 B/B. Phone 72-1311.

★ Griffin Hotel, 22 rooms, 13 with baths. R7,50 – R8,50 B/B. Phone 52-1218.

★★ Holiday Inn, 180 rooms, all with baths. R28,50 – R31,50 room only. Phone 53-3131.

★ Hollywood Hotel, 20 rooms, 16 with baths. R8,50 B/B. Phone 53-2154.

★★ Humewood Mansions Hotel, 58 rooms, all with baths. R9,85 – 11,85 B/B. Phone 2-8961.

★★ Hunters Retreat Hotel, 20 rooms, all with baths. R11,40 B/B. Phone 30-1244.

★ Hynch's Algoa Hotel, 22 rooms, 6 with baths. R6,50 – R8 B/B. Phone 2-6788.

★★★ Marine Hotel, 113 rooms, 98 with baths. R20 – R42 B/B. Phone 53-2101.

★★ Markham Hotel, 20 rooms, 10 with baths. R6,50 – R8,75 B/B. Phone 2-2301.

★★ Park Towers Hotel, 119 rooms, all with baths. R11,50 – R16 B/B. Phone 2-9583.

★ Phoenix Hotel, 14 rooms, 5 with baths. R6,50 – R7,50 B/B. Phone 2-3622.

★ Red Lion Hotel, 22 rooms, 15 with baths. R6 – R7 B/B. Phone 41-3749.

★ Springbok Hotel, 30 rooms, 8 with baths. R6,25 – R7,25 B/B. Phone 41-4871.

★ Summerstrand Hotel, 56 rooms, 48 with baths. R7,50 B/B. Phone 53-2144.

★ Sydenham Hotel, 19 rooms, 5 with baths. R8 – R9 B/B. Phone 41-3835.

★ Victoria Hotel, 12 rooms, 3 with baths. R4,75 – R5,75 B/B. Phone 2-4318.

★ Zwartkops Hotel, 14 rooms, 5 with baths. R5,50 – R6,50 B/B. Phone 6-2663.

**Caravans and camping**

★★★ ® Brook's Hill Caravan Park, 127 sites. R3 D.

★★ Humewood Caravan Park, 500 sites. R2,50 D. 30 huts, 7 rondawels, R3,50 – R8 D.

# PORT ELIZABETH DISTRICT

There are several roads from Port Elizabeth leading to beautiful places. The Marine Drive from the city around Cape Recife and along the western coast is one of the most interesting.

From the city hall drive south along North Union Street, leading first into Humewood Road, then Beach Road, and eventually becoming Marine Drive. On the way the harbour is passed on the east side, and then the terminus and depot of the narrow-gauge (61 cm) railway (the so-called Apple Express) which connects Port Elizabeth with Avontuur in the great fruit-growing valley of the Long Kloof, and also with Patensie in the Gamtoos Valley. A journey in the Apple Express is a fascinating experience, not only for lovers of trains, for the scenery along the route is superlative. The line does not normally carry passengers but each Saturday from 1 June to 31 January, special excursions are arranged which offer an unusual day-long outing as far as Loerie and back, departing at 09h00 and returning at 17h30.

The road develops into a fine double carriageway running along the ocean front with a long line of hotels, apartments and residences situated on the landward side, all with fine views over the playgrounds of King's Beach, Humewood, and the blue haze of Algoa Bay.

Three kilometres from the city hall, the road passes the oceanarium, museum, snake park and the hill named after Alfred Brooks, mayor in 1928, with the fine modern caravan park on the summit overlooking the bay and, on the south side, Happy Valley.

The road leads onwards past sunny beaches and green lawns. Six kilometres from the city hall there is the bus terminus of Summerstrand and from there the road becomes Marine Drive proper. Past the Humewood golf links the road cuts across the base of *Cape Recife* (cape of the reef), with its black and white banded lighthouse with a 4 067 000 candlepower lamp. The cape is covered in dense thickets of Port Jackson willows planted there in 1873 to settle drift sands. Fourteen kilometres from the city hall, the road reaches the south-western shores of the cape and leads along a rocky coast liked by fishermen for its vantage points and the variety of catches to be made there. Numerous camping sites lie sheltered among the trees and permits to camp may be obtained at the Divisional Council resort known as The Willows, which the road reaches 18 km from the city hall.

The Willows is a first-class and justly popular resort, with a tidal swimming pool, restaurant, some fine walks along the rocky shore, interesting fishing and a grassy, clean camping and caravan area.

**Caravans and camping**

★ The Willows Caravan Park, 65 sites. R4,20 – R6,30 D, seasonal. 27 rondawels, 8 cottages, R3,70 – R10,50 D, seasonal.

Beyond The Willows, the Marine Drive continues along a rocky, fishermen's and walker's coastline, with numerous parking areas, benches and barbecue sites. Six kilometres from The Willows, the road reaches *Skoenmakerskop* (shoemakers' hillock), a small coastal residential area with a line of houses watching the sea and a tearoom for refreshment.

From Skoenmakerskop, the road turns inland through thickets of Port Jackson willows and tall gum trees. After 3 km there is a turnoff westwards leading for 8 km past many pleasant little country estates and ending at the fine, sandy beach of Sardinia Bay. The main tarmac road continues northwards inland for 4 km beyond this turnoff and then, 30,4 km from the city hall, joins the Port Elizabeth-Sea View Drive. A turn right (east) into this road would lead directly back to Port Elizabeth (6 km), passing on the way the pleasant residential municipality of . . .

*Overleaf: The classic horseshoe bend in the Kowie River as it flows through forest country where crane flowers grow and antelope lurk in the shadows.*

# WALMER

Notable for its fine flowering and evergreen trees, the present site of Walmer was originally the farm *Welbedacht* belonging to Anthony Muller. This forested area was laid out as a town in 1853 and named after the seat of the Duke of Wellington in Kent. Walmer has been a municipality since 22 April 1899.

## Accommodation
★★ Walmer Gardens Hotel, 26 rooms, all with baths. R14 – R15,50 B/B. Phone 51-4322.

If the left turn (west) is taken at the intersection of the Port Elizabeth-Sea View Road, the road continues over a green, undulating and well-bushed countryside, past such residential areas as Charlo, Greenshields Park and Mount Pleasant township and eventually reaches the coast again at Sea View, 24 km from the junction (30,5 km from Port Elizabeth via Walmer, or 27 km by an alternative inland road branching off at Sea View).

# SEA VIEW

A coastal resort popular with anglers, Sea View is the start of a particularly handsome stretch of the coastal drive leading to many fine beaches and fishermen's vantage points. The road rises and falls along the slopes of the coastal hills, providing the traveller with panoramic views of sea, beach and stretches of rocky coast. Picnic and camping sites are numerous.

## Accommodation
★★ Minhetti Hotel, 32 rooms, 20 with baths. R10 B/B. Phone 7-4611.

Six kilometres from Sea View the road reaches the Maitland River Mouth, where a fine beach is dominated by enormous sand dunes. The road swings sharply inland at this point, passing a nice, grassy camping site (Divisional Council) towered over by a gigantic sand dune. Three kilometres from Maitland River Mouth, the road reaches a left turn (west) to Van Stadens River Mouth, a pleasant 19-km-long drive ending at the mouth of the river, with a magnificent beach lying below a cluster of huge sand dunes. At the mouth of the river (a lagoon for most of the year) the Divisional Council has created another fine recreational area with bungalows, caravan and camping sites and a restaurant. Boating, swimming, walking, fishing and sliding down the steep sides of the dunes, are the pastimes here. From Van Stadens Mouth, there is a road running inland for 16 km to the main coastal road and thence for a further 16 km back to the Port Elizabeth city hall.

## Caravans and camping
★★ Beach View Caravan Park, 90 sites. R4,20 – R5,20 D.
★★ Van Stadens River Mouth Holiday Resort, 150 sites. R2,10 – R3,20 D. 13 rondawels, R4,20 – R7,30 D.

# ADDO AND THE ELEPHANTS

A most interesting and varied circular drive from Port Elizabeth leads to the Addo Elephant National Park, the famous Sundays River Valley, and back to Port Elizabeth through the town of Uitenhage.

From the city hall of Port Elizabeth, the route leads up the long Main Street of the city, then branches right along the old Grahamstown road through the industrial areas and continues slightly inland to the small centre of *Swartkops* (black hills) on the river of that name, one of the greatest yachting waters in Southern Africa. Swartkops is situated 13 km from the city hall on the original Grahamstown road, and 6,5 km further on across the river, there is a tarmac turnoff left (north-west) leading to Addo and the Sundays River Valley.

This road leads through level scrub country for 34 km (53 km from Port Elizabeth) and then reaches the small railway centre of Addo, originally called *Kadouw* (river passage) by the Hottentots, from the fording place there across the Sundays River. Addo (the European corruption of the name) is the junction of the branch railway up the Sundays River Valley from the main Port Elizabeth-Johannesburg line. One and a half kilometres north of Addo, there is a tarmac turnoff leading north-westwards up the Sundays River Valley.

## Accommodation
★ Commando Kraal Hotel, 15 rooms, 11 with baths. R6,50 – R7 B/B. Phone 34.
★★ Zuurberg Inn, 28 rooms, 24 with baths. R8,50 – R13 B/B. Phone 1612.

The road to the Addo Elephant Park continues northwards for 9,5 km to the railway station of *Coerney* (the small bush). Here the tarmac ends and there is a division, the left-hand road continuing northwards to the *Suurberg* (sour mountains), the right-hand branch crossing the railway and, 67,5 km from Port Elizabeth, entering the . . .

# ADDO ELEPHANT NATIONAL PARK

The 9 712-ha Addo Elephant National Park is an area of singular interest to botanists, zoologists and lovers of big game. An extraordinary assembly of tough, drought-resistant plants, shrubs and stunted trees combine to produce the famous, and in the old days notorious Addo bush, blanketing the slopes and heights of a cluster of foothills of the Suurberg range. Spekboom (particularly palatable to elephants), boerboom, with its lichen and long strands of moss, ghwarrie, acacia species, aloes, creepers, mesembryanthemums, and a great variety of other hardy evergreen plants find conditions to their liking in this rugged wilderness and combine to produce a thicket which requires the full power of modern bulldozers and tools to penetrate it. In former years it was quite impenetrable.

The Addo bush (of which the elephant park is a part) covers a total of about 26 300 ha. As the Eastern Cape became settled, game animals – elephant, buffalo and numbers of antelope – retreated into this bush, trampling erratic pathways through the thicket, and developing so evil a temper against mankind that hunters who persisted in harrying them in this last retreat, did so at considerable hazard. Even donkeys, fleeing from hard work, found sanctuary in the Addo bush and reverted to a state of wildness and cunning.

A crisis in relations between settlers and the game animals of the Addo bush took place when the adjoining Sundays River Valley was being developed under irrigation as a great citrus and farming area. There was an increasing demand that all wild animals, and especially elephants, be exterminated from the area. A professional hunter, Major Pretorius, was accordingly employed in 1919 by the Provincial Administration for the purpose of eradicating the elephants from the Addo.

Pretorius spent 12 months in what he described as a 'hunter's hell, a 250 square kilometres or so of all you would think bad in Central Africa, lifted up by some Titan and plonked down in the Cape Province.'

In a systematic hunt in these difficult conditions, and with numerous narrow escapes, Pretorius shot 120 elephants in the Addo bush. Only 15 elephants were known to survive but it was at this stage that the vast publicity given to Pretorius' hunting adventures produced a reaction from the public sympathetic to the unfortunate animals fighting so resolutely for life in an erstwhile sanctuary which had now been turned into a slaughterhouse.

The hunt was called off and the surviving elephants – some wounded, all completely terrified of man – were left alone in a retreat in what was known as the Harvey Bush, where they fed on spekboom, prickly pears, and the results of occasional nocturnal raids on adjoining farmlands. There was much uncertainty about their future, and farmers once again started to vociferate their complaints about damage to crops.

On 3 July 1931, however, a far-sighted Minister of Lands, P.G.W. Grobler, proclaimed the Addo Elephant Park, and Ranger Harold Trollope was sent there from the Kruger National Park, with instructions to concentrate all elephants in the area proclaimed a national park, and to find a means of retaining them there. This was no easy task.

Trollope reached the Addo area in August 1931 and, supported by Mr R.A. Hockley, a member of the National Parks Board, and the Harvey brothers (local farmers who were sympathetic to the elephants and had left them undisturbed in the bush on their property), he studied the new national park and its problems. His decisions were practical and sensible. Firstly the park had to be prepared to receive its population of elephants, with water supplies assured. Secondly, the elephants would have to be driven into the area by making the greatest possible noise behind them and lighting fires. Once in the confines of the new park they would have to be retained there by log fires kept alight at 457-m intervals all night every night, until they became used to their permanent homes, or a better way was found of containing them.

The big elephant drive took place in the first week of October 1931, and was a success. By 8 October, 12 elephants were in the park, with only a few stragglers remaining outside – a cow and a small calf who had been left behind in the stampede and a lone bull. The drive had been quite an epic of hard work, in most difficult and dangerous conditions. The cow and calf followed the herd into the park while the lone bull, an outcast and full of old bullet wounds, charged Trollope and his men and had to be shot, making him the only casualty of the operation.

The next few years in the history of Addo Park saw a prolonged struggle to contain the elephants in their area. It proved an impossible task despite the most painstaking efforts of Ranger Trollope and his successor, Graham Armstrong (who took over in 1944). Under protection the number of elephants increased to 25 and they made, from their point of view, most intelligent use of their sanctuary, raiding the neighbouring farms and retreating back to the park when the farmers' tempers made outside conditions hazardous.

Stories became commonplace of the raids, of narrow escapes by human beings and of brushes with trains and railwaymen at sidings such as Lendlovu (place of elephants), where guards switching points for a crossing in the dark hours, occasionally mistook an elephant for a pile of maize sacks. Coerney railway station was also the scene of periodic visitations by the elephants, with trains being held up and the operating staff fleeing for safety. Two elephants were killed in collisions with trains.

Once again the clamour mounted for the elephants to be totally destroyed. They were said to be purely a destructive nuisance and in the dense bush, not even visible to tourists, therefore why maintain them? Hundreds of letters of complaint and claims for compensation for damaged fences and crops reached the National Parks Board, while in 1949, a petition was sent to Parliament by the farmers praying for a definite end to the matter.

The elephants, however, cantankerous as they were, also had their supporters and wildlife enthusiasts did their best to defend them. An Addo Park Advisory Committee was formed under the chairmanship of the mayor of Port Elizabeth; individuals such as James and Eileen Orpen donated boreholes to provide the elephants with dependable water supplies; and the Citrus Co-operative dumped low-grade oranges into the park as supplementary food.

Then, in 1951, the real turning point came in the history of the park. Mr L.D. Summerley, local manager of the Waygood-Otis Lift Company, offered to donate old lift cables for the building of an elephant-proof fence to enclose the park. Old tram lines from Port Elizabeth and

Johannesburg were also presented for use as posts and in this way the famous Armstrong Fence evolved.

The idea of some form of fence around the park had always been considered. In 1934 Ranger Trollope had suggested that an electrified fence be used and 16 km of this was actually completed in 1940 before the work was abandoned. The elephants, at first frightened by the electric shock, had discovered that the standards could be pushed down with impunity and the fence no longer presented a barrier to them.

The Armstrong Fence, made of steel wire lift ropes, however, proved to be the answer. Ranger Armstrong, with prodigious exertion, built the fence. A post office hole-digging machine made the post holes; 64 km of lift cable and the old tram lines provided the material. In September 1954, the fence was completed whereby the elephants were most successfully contained.

Today the Addo Elephant Park is so magnificent an asset to the Eastern Cape, that it is difficult to imagine the place as ever having been endangered. The elephants (67 at present), secure in their fenced reserve, have recovered confidence and are easily seen. Buffalo, rhino, and numerous antelope also flourish, along with a great and most fascinating diversity of flora. Water supplies have been further assured by incorporating into the park what is known as Caesar's Dam, an old elephant wallow scooped out into a dam by an ostrich shepherd named Caesar. The present dam was built by the Cape Sundays River Settlement Company.

The park is open 1 March to 31 August from 07h00 to 17h30 and 1 September to 28 February from 06h00 to 19h00. Entrance fee is R1 per car containing up to five persons and 10c for each additional person. There is a good restaurant and curio shop.

### Caravans and camping
★★ Caravan park, 50 sites. R2,60 D plus 25c D per person. 6 rondawels, R9,35 D.

# THE SUNDAYS RIVER VALLEY

One kilometre north of the village of Addo (53 km from Port Elizabeth) on the way to the Addo National Park, there is a tarmac turnoff leading in a north-westerly direction up the magnificently fertile valley of the Sundays River.

The Sundays River has its source in the Sneeuberg range in the Great Karoo. Dependent on the periodic Karoo thunderstorms, the river flows erratically in its upper reaches but its original Hottentot name, *Nukakama* (grassy water), emphasises that, relative to the drought-subject landscape across which it flows, the river verges have always been attractive to man. The origin of the European name of the river is obscure, but possibly it is derived from a family, the Sontags, who originally settled on its upper reaches.

European settlers first appeared in the valley between 1818 and 1820. Farms were granted but life was fraught with hazards such as wild animals – especially elephants who regarded the valley as being their own – while the whole area was dangerously near the strongholds of the African tribes, then pressing down from the north.

The first settlers, nevertheless, pioneered irrigation from the river, leading water over the rich alluvial soil which covered the 48-km length of the valley, and experimenting with a variety of crops. One of these farms, owned by Jacobus Scheepers, was purchased on 3 April 1818 by the Moravian Mission and converted into the mission station of Enon.

The year 1819 saw fighting with the Xhosa people and the entire valley was plundered by raiding bands with 31 people killed. Everything had to be rebuilt and a particularly attractive little church was opened at Enon in 1821. With its solid walls and cool white interior, this church survives as a reminder of the frontier passions and hardships of the past.

Successive raids into the valley during the various frontier upheavals seriously disrupted farming. Nevertheless the natural fertility of the valley made it inevitable that prosperity would follow as soon as tranquillity came to the old frontier areas. Meanwhile, men lived with one hand on a plough and the other hand on a gun. The name Commando Kraal, applied to the area round the village of Addo, comes from the rallying point on the site of the area's present primary school which the local men used as a strongpoint commanding the historic fording place across the Sundays River. Something of the atmosphere of the days of alarms and the constant coming and going of the early travellers still lingers about the place with its relics of old-time inn, wagon works and forges.

The late 1870s saw significant changes coming to the Sundays River Valley. In 1878 the Trappist monks established a mission named *Dunbrody* after the ancient abbey in the county of Wexford. This mission was a failure, largely on account of drought, but in 1882 the Jesuit order took it over and they still run the place.

Far more momentous was the arrival of James Somers Kirkwood, a well-known auctioneer from Port Elizabeth, who travelled up the valley in 1877 to attend a sale. He climbed to the Lookout at Hillside where the spectacle of the alluvial valley floor covered in lush vegetation fired his imagination. He visualised a tremendous development in irrigation, including barge transport on the river, with a port at its mouth.

After settling at Hillside and proving his irrigation theories in practice, Kirkwood started to buy farms in the valley and by 1883 he owned 21 of them. He then formed the Sundays River Land and Irrigation Company Limited and shares were offered to the public for a major enterprise in irrigation. The flotation proved a total failure and most bitter disappointment to Kirkwood and his colleagues. The public were just not interested. In a time of depression there was no capital for such a long-term project, no matter how worthy. The quick returns of ostrich farming were at the time, far more interesting to those with money.

Kirkwood's dreams simply collapsed. He was declared insolvent in 1887 and died two years later. It is fitting that the memory of this worthy man will always remain in the valley he loved so much. The principal modern centre and terminus of the branch railway up the valley, the town of *Kirkwood,* bears his name and was founded in 1913.

Kirkwood's assets were taken over by the Guardian Assurance and Trust Company. A manager, a renowned character named Arthur Goldhawk, was appointed to manage the estate and farming continued on an individual basis. Then, in 1893, a syndicate of valley farmers and Port Elizabeth businessmen bought the Sundays River Estate. They formed the Strathsomers Estate Company (so named after one of Kirkwood's christian names, and the Scots word *strath,* meaning a broad valley), and commenced a substantial farming activity in lucerne and ostriches.

The first large-scale irrigation work in the valley (and indeed in South Africa) was the Korhaans Drift weir completed at the end of 1913. This weir irrigated 4 856 ha of land which the company offered for sale at £20 (R40) per hectare in order to attract settlers.

A comprehensive new Irrigation Act introduced in 1912 by Colonel H. Mentz, the Minister of Lands, really exposed to the discerning the full potential of the Sundays River Valley. A consolidated effort was needed and the stimulant for this came largely from the lower end of the valley where, in 1906, the Addo Land and Irrigation Company had been formed with one of its directors, J.W. Babcock, planting the first large-scale citrus orchards on his farm *Carlton.* A second company operating in this lower area was the Cleveland Estate Syndicate, formed in 1912, with its highly ambitious projects of irrigating vast stretches of land towards the mouth of the river.

The man destined to weld into a whole the various enterprises in the lower part of the valley was Sir Percy Fitzpatrick, the mining financier and politician always remembered best by the public as the author of *Jock of the Bushveld.* On a visit to the valley in 1913 he saw the fine orchards on Babcock's farms, and immediately appreciated the potential of the area. He purchased a block of farms near Addo and formed the Sundays River Settlements Limited with the intention of attracting an influx of new settlers to the valley.

In 1914 Sir Percy's company absorbed the Cleveland Syndicate with its assets of irrigation development. With great vigour he set out to raise capital and to prepare ground for an influx of settlers expected at the end of the war but he experienced many setbacks. The war years saw the collapse of the ostrich feather industry, while the Eastern Cape was in the grip of a ruinous drought. Substantial water storage during good years would have to be effected to tide the valley over such periods of crisis. A prodigious flood in 1916 gave the government the embarassment of having to grant drought and flood aid to the same valley farmers. The Sundays River would definitely have to be disciplined. The result, after considerable discussion, planning, argument and inevitable court litigation, was Lake Mentz, completed in 1922.

While the government built Lake Mentz, the land-owning companies continued their programmes of development. Many settlers were attracted, but unfortunately, few of them had much capital. The years of waiting for the waters of Lake Mentz ruined several of them and caused considerable recrimination that the companies had stimulated sales of land by over-sanguinary propaganda. The usual glowing real estate brochures had been published and many British settlers had purchased land simply by selecting smallholdings from a map. On arrival in South Africa they had found their property still under bush with no prospect of any financial return for several years and, to make the situation worse, a drought so serious that drinking water had to be brought in by the railways. Life in the sunshine so rosily advertised in the brochures, became a matter of sweat and dust.

Sir Percy Fitzpatrick and his company were the most severely criticised as it was his enthusiasm which had attracted most of the immigrants, who now felt aggrieved at their hardships. A great argument also developed in the valley towards the end of 1921 when, with Lake Mentz nearly completed, it began to appear that there would be a shortfall in the long-awaited water supply and irrigation plans would have to be curtailed. Management squabbles and a major lawsuit over the dismissal of its managing director, General Byron, added to the difficulties of the Cape Sundays River Settlements Company. In 1923 it went into voluntary liquidation and the unfortunate Sir Percy Fitzpatrick, like Kirkwood, must have regarded the valley as something of a beloved mistress turned traitor. The assets of the Company were taken over by the government.

Through all the squabbles and disappointments, the shattering of over-rosy dreams and the heartbreak of facing the reality of water limitation even with Lake Mentz, the valley progressed. Lucerne provided a cash crop; citrus groves were being planted and in 1924 the Sundays River Citrus Co-operative Company was formed to control marketing. At its start it had 60 members owning 60 000 trees.

March 1928 saw Lake Mentz overflowing for the first time. The railway from Addo to Kirkwood had been opened in January 1927, and now with water, transport and organised marketing, the valley changed from a duckling into a swan. Sir Percy Fitzpatrick at least had the satisfaction of seeing many of his predictions become reality before he died in 1931 and was buried beside his wife on the top of Outlook Hill which dominates the valley.

Droughts, floods, the siltation of Lake Mentz and many other problems have plagued the valley, but in 1936, 220 000 cases of oranges were exported under the Outspan trademark, introduced in that year for South African citrus. In 1947, after the setback of the war years, 1 000 000 cases were exported. In 1979 the Sundays River Valley produced 58 746 tons of the total South African citrus crop of 665 844 tons.

A drive up the Sundays River Valley leads the traveller through a superbly fertile and most charming world. From the tarmac turnoff north of Addo, the road leads north-westwards and after 3 km reaches the packing station at Hermitage of the Sundays River Citrus Co-operative. On all sides stretch the citrus groves, particularly beautiful in October when the trees are in blossom and the air is sweet with perfume. The fruit is picked in early winter.

Five kilometres from Hermitage lies Sunland, where there is a turnoff leading to the fine viewsite known as The Lookout. One and a half kilometres further on, the tarmac road crosses the Sundays River, and for the next 18 km continues through beautifully tilled citrus groves and farmlands with the dark-green trees as neat and disciplined as an army on parade. The road then crosses the Sundays River for a second time and after a further 3 km (32 km from Addo) reaches the principal centre of the valley, the town of . . .

# KIRKWOOD

Named after the unfortunate James Kirkwood, whose story has already been told, Kirkwood was founded in 1913 as a centre for the valley. It became a muncipality in March 1950 and today has a population of 6 500. It is the terminus of the branch railway from Addo, and the site of a pack house of the Sundays River Citrus Co-operative. The town is particularly notable for the beautiful roses which grow there.

### Accommodation
* Kirkwood Hotel, 15 rooms, 7 with baths. R6,55 B/B. Phone 294.

Eight kilometres beyond Kirkwood, the tarmac road ends, but the gravel stretches only 11 km before the road joins the main tarmac road linking Uitenhage to Jansenville. Immediately ahead, dominating the landscape, looms the 1 799-m-high bulk of the Cockscomb Mountain, the highest peak of the Groot Winterhoek range. The road has found its way through a valley any visitor will long remember. In summer (the best time to see it), it can be oven hot but the late afternoons are cool and have something of the atmosphere of a man who has worked hard all day in the heat but now relaxes with a sundowner.

The road now traverses a level, alluvial, arid valley covered in low scrub, aloes, cacti and euphorbia. Botanically this area is the home of the elegantly angular crane flower (*Strelitzia reginae*) which blooms from January to May. Ostriches, angora goats and sheep are the principal products of the area. The tarmac road, turning left (south-east), leads over the foothills of the Groot Winterhoek range, past (after 27 km), a turnoff stretching eastwards to Steytlerville, after 32 km a turn to Addo, after 37 km a turn to the Springs recreation resort, and then, 6,5 km further on (43,5 km from the junction with this tarmac road), reaches the town of . . .

# UITENHAGE

With a population of 87 760, Uitenhage is a clean, modern and bustling industrial town, notable for its fine trees and pretty gardens.

The town had its start when Jacob Abraham Uitenhage De Mist – Commisary General sent by the Batavian Government in 1802 to take over the Cape from the British – toured the colony, inspecting even its remoter frontier regions.

De Mist found four families settled in the valley of the Swartkops River. These people had found their way to the area in 1790 when a party of hunters roamed into the valley, found it to their liking and petitioned for permission to settle there. De Mist considered their choice of home so handsome that he decided to establish a town there as a seat of a frontier *drostdy* or magistracy. (The word *drostdy* actually comes from *drossardschaap,* meaning a bailiwick).

De Mist selected the farm of Gert Scheepers as the site of the town, for it was well watered by a cluster of powerful perennial springs. In November 1804 the government purchased this farm for £400, with the widow Scheepers retaining until death, the right of residence in the farmhouse. She lived in the loop-holed two-roomed mud-walled house on the site of the later locomotive works, until the fine old age of 90, spending some of her time with her son-in-law, the well-known Van Staden of *Winterhoek* (winter glen).

*Uitenhage* was given its name in honour of Jacob Abraham Uitenhage De Mist, on 25 April

1804, by the first landdrost, Captain Alberti, formerly commander of Fort Frederick at Algoa Bay. Notwithstanding numerous alarms of Xhosa raids, the town grew fairly rapidly as a centre for the frontier area. The residency of the landdrost remains as a fine piece of construction from this period. A municipality was created on 11 June 1841. Apart from being a centre for mixed farming, Uitenhage began its industrial life in the considerable activity of wool-washing, and in the 1870s, 11 businesses were in operation on the Swartkops River.

At one time Uitenhage was world renowned as being the home of a working baboon. The signalman at Uitenhage railway station, James Wide, had lost both legs in an accident. He trained a large baboon to work the points and to harness a collie dog to a trolley on the line and see that his master was conveyed to and from his cottage.

The baboon's method of working the signals was a famous spectacle: he pulled the levers, looked around to ensure that the correct signal had been moved, and then turned to watch the approaching train, catching the various offerings thrown to him by passengers. For nine years he carried out his work without a mistake until his death in 1890.

The principal modern industries in Uitenhage are concerned with transport. The South African Railways workshop repairs rolling stock and manufactures spares in 18 workshops. Goodyear Tyres, Volkswagen, and several component manufacturers have their plants close to the town. Visitors are welcome on conducted tours.

The municipality maintains a fine recreational area at The Springs, 12 km north of the town on the tarmac road to Jansenville. At this resort there is a swimming pool, picnic area, caravan park and some rondawels. Uitenhage draws part of its water supply from this source and visitors are shown the springs at 15h00 on weekdays and on weekends and holidays at 14h00 and 16h00.

There is an historical museum situated 5 km from the town on the Port Elizabeth road while in the town, the old railway station has been converted into a railway museum, a delight for many visitors, who can roam through a completely authentic station of the Victorian period, complete with all furnishings, equipment, and with locomotives and carriages on the permanent way.

In the town, the Court House, built in 1911, with its fine clock tower, is worth seeing. The Municipal Botanical Garden in Magennis Park has a fine collection of plants and trees, with a caravan park and a nearby Olympic-size swimming pool.

## Accommodation

* Crown Hotel, 14 rooms, 4 with baths. R7 – R7,50 B/B. Phone 2-4417.
* Jubilee Hotel, 10 rooms, 5 with baths. R5 – R6 B/B. Phone 2-4830.
* Phoenix Hotel, 10 rooms, 3 with baths. R6 – R7 B/B. Phone 2-6646.
* Rose and Shamrock Hotel, 20 rooms, 9 with baths. R9,50 B/B. Phone 2-1351.
* Solly Kramer's Hotel, 14 rooms, 4 with baths. R8 – R8,50 B/B. Phone 2-4034.
* Waterford Hotel, 14 rooms, 8 with baths. R6,50 – R8 B/B. Phone 2-3433.

## Caravans and camping

** ® Magennis Caravan Park, 10 sites. R1,50 D.
** ® Springs Caravan Park, 20 sites. R2 D. 11 rondawels, R3 – R7 D.

A tarmac road leads south-eastwards over the aloe-covered foothills of the Groot Winterhoek, Elands River and Van Staden ranges of mountains. After 14 km of travel along this tarmac road there is a crossroads, with a left turn to Port Elizabeth (34 km) and a right turn up the Elands River Valley, a fine drive leading to the Gamtoos Valley. A further 8 km (22,5 km from Uitenhage) sees the road join the main coastal road linking Port Elizabeth to Cape Town.

The main direct road from Uitenhage to Port Elizabeth leads eastwards, past the Historical Museum (5,5 km) and, at 10 km, reaches a turnoff to the town of . . .

## DESPATCH

The rather odd name of Despatch seems to have stemmed from the days when the town was originally a railway centre. It became a municipality in 1945 and with its population of 19 800, is now a residential centre for many people working in Uitenhage and Port Elizabeth.

Accommodation
* Despatch Hotel, 10 rooms, 4 with baths. R7 – R8 B/B. Phone 3-1411.

Beyond the turn to Despatch, the tarmac road continues past outlying residential areas of Port Elizabeth such as Redhouse, Perseverance and (21,5 km from Uitenhage) a turn to Bethelsdorp. This place was founded in 1862 by Dr Vanderkemp of the London Missionary Society as a settlement area for remnants of the original Hottentot tribes. The community developed around a huge salt pan, 3 km by 1,5 km in extent. Each holder of a residential plot in the settlement was entitled to a *baan* or polder in the salt pan. In this polder the owner could evaporate brine and secure the salt. Nowadays a company leases the whole area, pays a rental each year and works all the 'baans' as one unit. In summer the salt pan resembles a frozen lake with piles of snow-like salt gathered ready for packing.

Beyond the turn to Bethelsdorp the road continues for 13,5 km and then reaches Port Elizabeth.

## PORT ELIZABETH TO GRAHAMSTOWN AND THE SETTLER'S COUNTRY

From Port Elizabeth, Settlers Way leads northwards out of the city by means of a magnificent double carriageway, complete with a spectacular series of traffic interchanges and flyover bridges. Hugging the shores of Algoa Bay, the road reveals to travellers many fine views over the sparkling beaches and the spacious reaches of the great bay. Offshore, to the north, may be seen the two rocky islets of *Jahleel* and *Brenton,* named after Admiral Sir Jahleel Brenton, while further out to sea lies the islet of *St Croix* (the islet of the Holy Cross), so named because it was once thought that the pioneer explorer, Bartholomew Dias, had erected a cross there in 1488 to mark the furthest point of his voyage of exploration. The actual remnants of this cross, dedicated to St Gregory, were later found 14 km west of Cape Padrone (originally known as the *Pontas do Padrão,* point of the pedestal). A replica stands there today on the headland now known as *Kwaaihoek* (stormy corner) as originally named by the Dutch, but which the Portuguese called the *Penedo das Fontes* (rock of the fountains) and the British, False Islet.

At 7,5 km from the centre of the city, the road crosses the mouth of the Swartkops River by means of the Settler's Bridge. This is a great river for yachtsmen and the left bank is lined with a free and easy looking collection of water-edge bungalows and unconventional houses.

Beyond the river, the road continues north-eastwards, leading over level country covered in low, stunted scrub. The coast veers off in a more easterly direction, with the road gradually finding its way inland.

At 12 km from the city there is a turnoff north-westwards leading to Addo and the Sundays River Valley. A further 4,5 km (16,5 km from Port Elizabeth) brings the road to the mouth of the river known as the *Coega* (place of acacia trees) where the Salnova Salt Company recovers salt from a pattern of geometrically shaped evaporation polders built in the shallow water of the lagoon.

A further 14 km (30,5 km from Port Elizabeth), brings the road to the Sundays River, with a holiday resort known as Colchester situated on its banks. This lower reach of the Sundays River offers fine boating and a track leads down to the beach at the mouth where there is a massive barrier of sand dunes.

## Accommodation
★ Coega Hotel, 12 rooms, 6 with baths. R7,50 B/B. Phone P.E. 6-9975.

## Caravans and camping
★★ Sundays River Caravan Park, 50 sites. R4 D plus 25c D per person..

From the valley of the Sundays River, the road climbs over low, scrub-covered hills. At 45,5 km from Port Elizabeth there is a traffic interchange, where the main tarmac road branches off on the start of its journey inland to join the Cape-to-Cairo road at Colesberg and to carry traffic on to the great north-south trunk road of Africa (page 191).

Settlers Way continues north-eastwards. One kilometre from the interchange there is a turnoff stretching eastwards to Alexandria and Port Alfred (page 340). The road now traverses an area of low, undulating hills, with pineapple, dairy and sheep farms worked in difficult conditions of unreliable and moderate rainfall. Spineless varieties of prickly pears are cultivated to provide stock feed in times of drought.

The road curves downwards into the shallow valley of the Bushman's River, where it crosses the river 78 km from Port Elizabeth. The road then climbs steadily out of the valley, over undulating hills covered in shrub and numerous aloes which flower in May and June. This is the country where descendants of the 1820 Settlers occupy most of the farms. The area is enriched by memories of these settlers and the contentions they experienced in the form of a difficult, erratic climate; periodic and seemingly interminable droughts; raids and wars with the frontier tribespeople, and all the uncertainty of existence in a primeval land.

Frequent turnoffs from the main road lead to 1820 Settler villages such as Seven Fountains, Salem, Sidbury and Alicedale. For those who are able to explore these byways at leisure, there are many interesting scenes of beautiful rural landscapes and frontier-type farmhouses of the period to be seen. Salem is particularly worth visiting. The turnoff leading southwards to this village (situated 16 km from the main road), is 101 km from Port Elizabeth. *Salem* (peace) was founded in 1820 by Hezekiah Sephton and his party of 344 settlers. Several of the houses they built are still standing; compact, double-storied (for economy in roofing material), and stoutly built. The church with its thick, strong walls served as a fortress in times of danger.

In the records of this church there is an account of the last time it was used as a stronghold. The people of Salem retreated to the church when a band of Xhosa warriors raided the area and there was a great bustle of calling on the Lord, cleaning of guns and drying of powder. In the midst of this excitement there walked a man of peace, Richard Gush. Wearying of all the talk of approaching bloodshed, he took off his coat and went out unarmed to the warrior chieftain.

The Xhosa received him in silent surprise and he fell to lecturing them severely on the impropriety of their conduct. Abashed, the chief excused the behaviour of his people. 'We are hungry,' he said, 'that is why we attack you.' Gush eyed the settler's livestock in the hands of the raiders, but decided to take the chief at his word. Returning to the church, Gush collected 6 kg of bread, 4 kg of tobacco and 12 pocket knives. These he carried back as a gift to the warriors. As the records have it, he once more 'expostulated with them on their great wickedness. The parties then shook hands and the Caffres went away and were seen no more in the vicinity of Salem'.

The original fortress-church of Salem is now a school for the descendants of the Xhosa warriors. It is an atmospheric old building filled with contrasting memories of old alarms, of happy little weddings, of baptisms and long sermons, sombre funerals, of simple rustic schoolteachers and pupils such as Theophilus Shepstone (who became so famous in Natal) and Mary Moffat who grew up to marry Livingstone. The village green outside the church (especially on a summer afternoon with a game of cricket in progress) could have been transported with the settlers all the way from England.

At 4,5 km north-east of the turnoff to Salem, Settlers Way reaches a turnoff to Alicedale (30 km) and Highlands (16 km). Another kilometre takes the road across the upper reaches of the river known as the *Kariga* (place of steenbok). Patches of typically stunted Eastern Cape bush alternate with cultivated lands. A further 6 km (113 km from Port Elizabeth) brings Settlers Way to a turnoff leading south to Kenton-on-Sea (48 km) and to Alexandria (48 km). Settlers Way now reaches the picturesque Howison's Poort, where a reservoir is situated immediately downstream in one of the tributaries of the Kariga River. There is a pleasant picnic site at the foot of Howison's Poort. The reservoir has been stocked with trout and black bass, and is used for boating. The first road up the valley was built in the 1830s by Alexander Howison, working on a public subscription from the inhabitants of Grahamstown who wanted a dependable link with Port Elizabeth. The modern road, following the same route, climbs steadily up the fertile valley of the stream. It is a pleasant drive, with the Stone Crescent Hotel providing refreshment halfway up the valley. After 6 km the road reaches the top of the valley and descends for 6 km down a well-wooded hill slope, past the caravan park and turnoff to the mountain drive, and, 120 km from Port Elizabeth, enters the miniature city of . . .

# GRAHAMSTOWN

The capital of the Eastern Cape Province, *Grahamstown* was founded in 1812 by Colonel John Graham. The intention was to establish a military outpost on the troubled frontiers in order to effect pacification after the Fourth Kaffir War. A line of blockhouses was built to guard from the heights the prodigious valley of the Fish River which formed the frontier line – the line of collision – between European settlers expanding from the south and African tribal groups migrating from the north.

The choice of the site of Grahamstown was admirable. It was made by Colonel Graham while he was resting in the shade of an acacia tree which grew on a position marked by a memorial on an island in High Street opposite Fishers Building. The river known to the Xhosa as the *Qoyi* (rushing) had its headwaters near by in a number of streams bubbling to life on the slopes of the overlooking heights. In the valley below, close to the tree under which Graham rested, they united to form the river whose name was corrupted by Europeans into the familiar *Kowie* of today.

A struggling little town grew up around the military camp. In its early years it was reputed to be a slovenly place, simply a camp following of traders and canteen keepers leading a precarious life at the whim of the soldiers and very much dependent on the ability of the military to defend it from the onslaught of primitive tribes. The site of the town was actually the abandoned farm of *Rietfontein,* and the original farmhouse of Lucas Meyer was restored from its burnt-out and looted condition, and converted into the officer's mess of the garrison.

Grahamstown became the administrative capital of the district named *Albany* (after the city of Albany in America where the father of the first magistrate, Colonel Cuyler, had once been mayor). An interesting and most varied population was attracted to the town. The famed (and ill-fated) Voortrekker leader, Piet Retief, was one of the leading businessmen in the place, owning (among numerous other ventures) a windmill for the grinding of wheat.

In April 1819 Grahamstown was attacked by 10 000 warriors led by the renowned witch-doctor Makhanda and only a most resolute defence saved the town from total destruction.

The following year saw the advent of the 1820 Settlers to the Eastern Cape and Grahamstown became their particular centre. A great bustle came to the place with 174 registered ivory traders dealing in tusks, and many more engaged in the traffic of skins. In those days great herds of game animals wandered through the frontier areas. Regular fairs were held and 50 000 skins and many tons of ivory passed through Grahamstown each year.

By 1830 the town of Grahamstown had grown considerably with an imposing High Street and many fine buildings, including the drostdy house (official residence) completed in 1826, which subsequently became part of Rhodes University. The erection of this building by Piet Retief had been commenced in July 1822, but during the four years it took to complete, several other contractors had a hand in the work. The house was demolished in 1935 to make way for the modern administrative centre of Rhodes University and only the arched gateway remains.

The present St George's Cathedral also had its beginning in this period; firstly as a rather ill-constructed church completed in 1828 as the first Anglican church in Southern Africa, and secondly, after Grahamstown became a bishopric in 1853, converted piecemeal (as funds became available) into the imposing structure of today with its numerous memorials, tablets, regimental colours and other items.

In the 1830s Grahamstown ranked as the second largest town in Southern Africa. It had a horticultural society; a weekly newspaper, the *Grahamstown Journal* (December 1831); a substantial commercial hall where social occasions could be held (today the Eastern Districts Court of Justice); a municipality promulgated in April 1837, and the Albany Library, founded in 1842. All this progress was made in the teeth of periodic alarms, frontier disturbances and wars with the wild tribes who were still trying to migrate southwards.

Frontiermen, ivory traders, farmers, hunters and soldiers thronged the streets of the town, but with them mingled an increasing number of men of culture and learning: Robert Godlonton and L.H. Meurant, journalists and authors of note; Thomas Pringle the poet; John Centlivres Chase; the famous road builder, Andrew Geddes Bain; and Dr William Atherstone whose versatile genius saw him perform the first successful operation in the Cape using an anaesthetic; he was also the originator of the Botanic Gardens, a scientific and literary society, and the identifier of the first diamond found in Southern Africa in 1867.

The first school in Grahamstown was opened in 1849 and the building is still in use as the Good Shepherd School for Coloured Children. The second, opened in January 1850, was the Assumption Convent school for girls. In August 1855, St Andrew's College was founded by Bishop John Armstrong and this was the first of the prestigious public schools of Grahamstown. The purpose of its founding was to provide the type of church-controlled training in Christian citizenship which was the pride of the illustrious English public schools.

The second prestigious school to be established in Grahamstown was Graeme College (1873). In the following year Bishop Merriman established the Diocesan School for Girls as a sister school to St Andrews. In 1876 the first Catholic Bishop of the Eastern Cape, the Right Reverend Bishop Rickards, founded St Aidan's College under the management of the Society of Jesus (Jesuits). In 1894 the Methodist Church founded Kingswood College for boys, and in 1896 the government rebuilt a small private school founded in 1892 by Miss Bertha Mingay, and converted it into the Victoria Girls High School. In 1894 the Grahamstown Training College was founded by the Anglican Sisterhood of the Community of the Resurrection, responsible for the training of many female student teachers. The principal educational institution in Grahamstown is Rhodes University, founded in 1904. The main building of the university was designed in 1911 by Sir Herbert Baker. At first a university college, Rhodes attained full status in 1951 and today accommodates about 3 000 students.

Among the other schools in Grahamstown are St Pauls Theological College; the P.J. Olivier High School; a School of Art; and a School of Music. The buildings in which these schools and colleges are housed, are notably handsome while the grounds in which they stand are spacious and exceedingly beautiful. The Students' Union of Rhodes University occupies a particularly interesting old building known as *Selwyn's Castle,* a castellated house built in 1835 as a home for Major C.J. Selwyn.

337

Grahamstown is truly a city of schools. Its original commercial importance as a frontier town largely vanished in modern times with the building of railways. Grahamstown was left well off the main routes from the coastal ports to the interior. With little significant industry (save ceramics and electric lamps) to motivate its way of life, it has, instead of the overall of the workman, accepted the cap and gown of the student as its characteristic dress. Social and commercial life is very much influenced by the school and university calendar and activities are very relaxed during vacation periods. The population today is 43 240.

Apart from its public library, Grahamstown is the home of the South African Library for the Blind. It also possesses a first-class museum, the Albany Museum, which contains many interesting relics of the 1820 Settlers and some fine paintings by Thomas Baines. Among the architectural relics of past days is the Provost building with its round tower and loop-holed walls, built in 1836 as a military prison. Another interesting building is *Fort Selwyn,* a redoubt on Gun Fire Hill built in 1836 and named after Major Selwyn who was the commanding officer of the Royal Engineers in the Eastern Cape. It still contains a battery of guns.

Behind Fort Selwyn stands the imposing 1820 Settlers National Monument. This building was the result of a campaign started by Thomas Bowker to revive pride in the heritage of the English-speaking people of South Africa. In 1960 the South African Parliament voted R100 000 towards the cost of the monument. Mr Bowker died in 1964 but his enthusiasm lingered on to carry the project forward with numerous supporters and contributors. The result was the construction of a complex of two conference halls, one seating 500 people and the other 200 people, a theatre with a seating capacity of 914, a restaurant, shop and a magnificent commemorative interior containing an eternally bubbling fountain rising from a millstone, depicting man's dependence on bread and the skill and labour which produce it.

The abstract sculpture of the interior created out of indigenous yellowwood, is a three-dimensional integration with the concrete wall and represents the merging of the cultures of Britain and South Africa. The rectangles and diagonals symbolise the Union Jack with the Cross of Christ dominating the whole. The yellowwood radiates towards the lantern roof which is open to the sky in good weather.

The theme of the monument is taken from St John, Chapter 10, verse 10: *That all might have life and have it more abundantly.* The design was by Richard Wade and Kevin Alkinson. The building was opened on 13 July 1974.

Outside the complex there is a bronze of a settler family by Ivan Mitford-Barberton. The building stands in a floral reserve where the flora of the Eastern Cape is cultivated and there is a nature reserve on the slopes of Gun Fire Hill. The view from the monument presents a superb panorama over Grahamstown in its setting of hills and valleys.

The Botanic Gardens were founded in the 1850s and contain a variety of interesting trees and cycads. There is a small military cemetery in the gardens and by repute, a ghost. The beautiful Lady Juana Smith, wife of the Governor Sir Harry Smith, is said to have liked the gardens so much that she lingers there as an occasional intangible (and inexplicable) whiff of Spanish perfume in the evening air. Another reserve, the Thomas Bains Reserve, has been established in Howison's Poort with a variety of game animals originally indigenous to the area being reintroduced.

A particularly fine feature of the Grahamstown environment is the Mountain Drive which turns off from Settlers Way at the caravan park. This road leads for 17 km through handsome stands of trees and there are many panoramic views. The drive passes such interesting places as the first reservoir of Grahamstown, built in 1860 and named after Sir George Grey, Governor of the Cape. The road climbs to the summit of the ridge, Dassie Krans, where the view provides a fitting climax to any visit to this amiable, atmospheric and serene little city, sometimes known as the City of the Saints on account of the 40 churches situated there.

## Accommodation

★★ Cathcart Arms Hotel, 12 rooms, 6 with baths. R10,50 – R11,50 B/B. Phone 3024.
★ Goodwood Hotel, 27 rooms, 8 with baths. R7,50 – R9 B/B. Phone 2921.
★★ Graham Hotel, 38 rooms, 19 with baths. R8,50 – R10 B/B. Phone 2324.
★★ Grand Hotel, 45 rooms, 22 with baths. R12,70 B/B. Phone 2621.
★★ Settler's Inn Motel, 36 rooms, all with baths. R12,25 – R14,25 B/B. Phone 5013.
★ Stone Crescent Hotel, 23 rooms, all with baths. R7,50 – R8 B/B. Phone 2622.
★ Victoria Hotel, 12 rooms, all with baths. R8 B/B. Phone 3811.

## Caravans and camping

★★® Municipal caravan park, 125 sites. R3,12 D. 4 rondawels, R5,20 D.

# GRAHAMSTOWN TO PORT ALFRED AND PORT ELIZABETH

The route from Grahamstown through Port Alfred, and thereafter west along the coastal road to Port Elizabeth, provides the traveller with an interesting and scenically most pleasantly varied journey. The exit from Grahamstown is especially spectacular. The tarmac road rises out of the city, climbing a hill slope covered in plantations of fir and gum trees. Reaching the summit line, the road follows the top of a high ridge with fine views on either side of the downlands of the coastal terrace, and many well-cultivated farms of citrus and pineapple.

After 15 km the tarmac road starts to descend, passing farmstalls selling the seasonal products of the area such as oranges and pineapples. At 20 km from Grahamstown the road reaches the Bloukrans Pass, a 5-km-long traverse across a valley whose slopes are thickly grown with flowering aloes and bush. It was here, on 22 April 1911, that there occurred the so-called Blaauwkrantz Bridge Disaster. A mixed train was derailed while crossing the high railway bridge, and 28 people were killed when their coaches tumbled into the gorge.

Beyond the pass, the tarmac road continues south-eastwards across an undulating grass-covered plain, patched with light acacia bush and huge pineapple fields. At 38 km from Grahamstown there is a turn eastwards leading to Trappes Valley and 3 km further on (41 km from Grahamstown) the road reaches the picturesque little town of . . .

# BATHURST

One of the tiniest municipalities in Southern Africa, *Bathurst* has a population of 1 142. It was named after Earl Bathurst who was the British Colonial Secretary at the time of the 1820 Settlers. The town was originally planned as the principal centre of the Settlers' area and in May 1820, Captain Charles Trappes of the Seaforth Highlanders was appointed its first magistrate. The tent he pitched as a combined residence and office, heralded the beginning of the town, but unfortunately, the seat of magistracy was transferred to Grahamstown and Bathurst was left as a quiet little rural centre. In this rustic state it still remains with its buildings dominated by some magnificent trees, notably flowering kaffirbooms which grow in the streets and many gigantic wild figs, one near the hotel with a spread of 120 m. The atmosphere of Bathurst is enriched by memories of early Settler alarms, achievements and disappointments.

The Anglican and Wesleyan churches are both national monuments and each contains a Settler Bible. In their stormy day, both acted as retreats and strongpoints for the Settlers during times of attack by Xhosa warriors. Christmas Day 1834 saw Bathurst abandoned entirely as a result of one of these attacks, with the district overrun by raiders for several days.

Bathurst is generally considered to be the pineapple capital of Southern Africa. Back in 1865 a local farmer, Charles Purdon, went into the shop of a Grahamstown barber, Lindsay

Green, for a haircut. In his shop the barber had some pineapples from Natal. Purdon secured about 40 of the crowns and planted them on his farm *Thorndoh* in the Bathurst district where they grew to perfection. Everything suited pineapples in that area. The novelty of the fruit rewarded growers with high prices and pineapples became the rage. Cultivation spread from Bathurst to the southern sector of the Albany district, and up the coastal belt to East London. Overproduction has caused sharp variations in prices but about 145 000 tons of pineapples are now produced in this area each year.

### Accommodation
★ Pig and Whistle Hotel, 10 rooms, 4 with baths. R10 B/B. Phone 26.

### Caravans and camping
★ Newman Walker Tim Park, 24 sites. R1,50 D plus 50c D per person.

From Bathurst a gravel road leads westwards to the Horseshoe Nature Reserve, 6 km from the town. Near the entrance to the reserve there is a viewsite overlooking the horseshoe bend in the Kowie River, a classic example of a river meander. The road descends steeply, ending at a fine picnic site on the banks of the Kowie River, 9 km from Bathurst. This is a very worthwhile drive. Several species of antelope and numerous birds find sanctuary there. Among the flowering plants is *Strelitzia reginae* (the crane flower) which flourishes to perfection.

From Bathurst there is a turnoff leading eastwards for 2 km to Bailies Beacon where, on a fine vantage point, there is a toposcope identifying the various interesting points in the surrounding countryside, including the different places where parties of the 1820 Settlers were allocated land.

The main tarmac road continues southwards across a richly grassed coastal plain, where there are sheep and cattle farms. After 15 km the road makes a fine scenic entrance to the quaint little old-time Settler town and port of . . .

# PORT ALFRED

One of the most attractively informal and picturesque of all the holiday resorts of Southern Africa, where the Kowie or *Qoyi* (rushing) River reaches the sea with a spacious beach situated at its mouth. It is a fine river flowing through a well-wooded valley with innumerable twists, and the horseshoe meander which is often described by geologists as a classic of its kind.

When the 1820 Settlers came to the Eastern Cape they viewed the mouth of the Kowie with interest. At that time the estuary consisted of a swampy mixture of islets, canals and reeds confined east and west by the low hills known as the East and West banks. The area was entirely unpopulated, and a great resort of birds and fish.

Several individuals conceived the idea of a port at the mouth of the river. In 1821, the government at their suggestion, sent a small brig, the *Locust,* to sound the entrance to the river and this was the first vessel ever known to sail the waters of the Kowie. The bar across the entrance to the river varied from 1 m to over 3 m in depth, with reasonably deep water further inland. A rich fishing ground lay in the roadstead east of the river mouth, close to the Fountain Rocks, so named on account of the swell which at high tide, spouted up there in a jet of water.

As a result of this investigation, Mr J. Dyason was appointed pilot and harbour master of the Kowie, a flagstaff was erected on the East Bank and a boat's crew appointed. This was the beginning of Port Kowie. A special light-draft schooner, the *Elizabeth,* was built to serve the port and on 9 November 1821, this little vessel successfully entered the river. Unfortunately, on her next voyage from Port Elizabeth, the schooner was totally wrecked on Cape Recife.

Other coasters soon replaced the wreck, for there was a genuine need for a port to serve the Settler country. Unfortunately, like all shallow river mouths, the Kowie was a death trap for sailing vessels. A sudden drop in wind or an unexpected rush of tidal water could defeat the genius of any sailing master and land his vessel unceremoniously on the beach.

For the next ten years the government struggled to develop Port Kowie into a harbour. The little town which grew up on the banks of the river was at first called *Port Frances* in honour of the wife of Colonel Somerset (son of the Governor) but in 1860 the name was finally changed to *Port Alfred* in honour of Prince Alfred who was on a visit to South Africa at the time.

The efforts to develop a harbour failed. In 1831 the office of harbour master was abolished and the port was left to a few fishermen and the enterprise of private individuals. Among these was William Cock who, in 1836, settled there, building on the west bank what became known as *Cock's Castle*. His daughter, Mary, has left her name on *Mary's Cove*. For years these private individuals laboured, trying a series of schemes to open the river mouth. Cock was the motivating force for most of these efforts, and it was he who changed the flow of the river to a new channel below the west bank.

A vast amount of energy and money was expended on the Kowie by Cock and other people. Ships came and went, but the number that were wrecked was considerable and professional shipmasters detested the place because of its dangers and uncertainties. The only saving grace was that Port Elizabeth, the nearest harbour, was also a great hazard to shipping.

In 1857 the government once again launched a scheme to develop the port. Piers were built, a steam tug was stationed there in 1863, and a dredger employed in deepening the channel. A company, the Kowie Harbour Improvement Company, had the running of the port. This was the golden age of the harbour, with ships such as the 350-ton *Icon* trading there. Larger ships anchored in the roadstead and were serviced by lighters. In this way the mailships of the Union Steamship Navigation Company paid regular visits from 1875 onwards, with 101 ships landing 12 750 tons of cargo in Port Alfred in 1876.

The year 1881 saw great activity with a railway being built to Grahamstown and the constructional materials and rolling stock all being shipped to the harbour. Included with this material was the steelwork for the 61-m-high bridge over the Bloukrans, where the railway disaster took place in 1911, killing 28 people. The railway was built by a private company, the Kowie Railway Company, which went into liquidation in 1886 and was taken over by another concern. It is interesting to know that two of the locomotives used on this railway are still preserved, one on a pedestal in the Cape Town railway station and the other in the Port Elizabeth Museum.

Port Alfred harbour fell into disuse in the 1890s. There has been periodic talk of re-opening it, but today the river is confined to pleasure only, with yachts, power boats and canoes being used in a paradise of fine scenery. The climate is pleasant and there is excellent swimming, fishing and recreation. The beaches of Port Alfred too, provide superb swimming and surfing and are renowned for their variety of shells. The river is navigable by small boats for 24 km. The population of the town is 8 954.

## Accommodation
* Fullers Inn, 23 rooms, all with baths. R9,50 B/B. Phone 36.
* Grand Hotel, 24 rooms, all with baths. R8,85 – R9,85 B/B. Phone 39.
* ® Langdon Hotel, 43 rooms, 12 with baths. R8,50 – R9,50 B/B. Phone 25.

## Caravans and camping
* Lagoon Caravan Park, 95 sites. R2 – R3,50 D plus 25c D per person, seasonal.
** ® Medolino Caravan Park, 90 sites. R2,50 – R3,50 D, seasonal.
* Rainbow Caravan Park, 35 sites. R3 D plus 25c D per person. 10 rondawels, R6 D.

From Port Alfred the tarmac coastal road leads westwards through exceedingly pleasant downland country, with grass-covered hill slopes rolling towards the sea. An interesting feature is the number of dew ponds, each with a collection of wild ducks and geese. Patches of trees and fine herds of cattle ornament the landscape.

At 13 km there is a gravel turnoff to the small hamlet of Southwell (19 km) while at 23 km from Port Alfred the road crosses the *Kariga* (steenbok) River, a spacious and most attractive expanse of water with an informal huddle of cottages on its banks. A further 0,5 km brings the road to a turnoff leading to the seaside township of Kenton-on-Sea, which lies on the east side of the broad mouth of the Bushman's River. Superb boating on the river, a spacious beach, and handsome sand dunes all contribute towards a pleasant recreational area. Besides a hotel, there are cottages available for rent.

## Accommodation
★ Kenton Hotel, 14 rooms, 7 with baths. R9 – R10 B/B. Phone 3.

One kilometre beyond the turn to Kenton-on-Sea, the road crosses the Bushman's River with its water-edge bungalows and boat houses.

## Caravans and camping
★ Bushman's River Mouth, 60 sites. R4 D plus 25c D per person.

Five kilometres from Bushman's River there is a tarmac turnoff to Bokness and Cannon Rocks. The main road continues for 20 km over pineapple and chicory fields and fine dairy country, then reaches the town of Alexandria. The turnoff to Bokness and Cannon Rocks provides an alternative scenic route to the same town. It is along this turnoff, after 1,5 km that a gate on the eastern side takes the traveller on to a track (1,5 km long, with three gates) ending at a path which stretches over bush-covered dunes and across a miniature 'Sahara'. Beyond this 1-km-wide stretch of windswept sand there looms the curious island-like, isolated rock known to the Portuguese as the *Penedo das Fontes* (rock of the fountains). It was here that Bartholomew Dias, the first navigator from Europe to double the Cape of Good Hope, reached the furthest point of his great exploration and erected on this rock a stone cross dedicated to St Gregory. The fragments of this cross were found in modern times and a replica today stands on the point where the original was erected by Dias. It is a moderately stiff walk to the rock (apparently once an islet), but the experience is worth the trouble.

At 4,5 km beyond the turnoff to the Dias cross there is a crossroads. A left turn (tarmac) leads for 1,5 km to the beach and lagoon of the small holiday resort of Bokness where there is a camping ground. A right turn (gravel) leads to a turnoff after 6 km to the fishing resort and sandy beach of Cannon Rocks. Two old cannon and an anchor are mounted at the beach.

## Caravans and camping
★ Cannon Rocks, 100 sites. R2,50 D plus 20c D per person.

Beyond the turnoff to Cannon Rocks, the gravel road continues along the coast, past Rustfontein store and Cape Padrone. After 13 km the road reaches a turnoff to Midfor. The coastal scenery is spectacular with a sandy mass of high dunes and a view seawards of the cluster of Bird islands.

The road now veers inland and leads through the beautiful Alexandria State Forests. This is an indigenous high forest with many superb trees, well populated with vervet monkeys, bushbuck and wild pigs. There is a picnic site at Langebos, 4 km from the Midfor turnoff while a further 1,5 km takes the road past the Alexandria Forest Station.

For a further 8 km the road leads across open pasturage country, patched with forest. Then,

27,5 km from the turnoff to Cannon Rocks, the gravel road, after a most enjoyable journey, joins the main tarmac Port Elizabeth road, 0,5 km from the town of . . .

# ALEXANDRIA

Named after the Reverend Alexander Smit who ministered to the population in the district in pioneer days. *Alexandria* is a small rural town with a population of 4 381. It is the centre of a considerable industry in the growing of chicory and pineapples, and the railhead of a branch line from Port Elizabeth.

### Accommodation
★ Alexandria Hotel, 12 rooms, 5 with baths. R6,50 – R7 B/B. Phone 24.

### Caravans and camping
★ Municipal caravan park, 12 sites. R3 D.

From Alexandria, the tarmac road continues westwards across a pleasant agricultural countryside of chicory, pineapple, wheat and mixed livestock farms. Passing through a small, bushy valley (Soutkloof), the road (20 km from Alexandria), climbs into a pile of hills. At 30 km from Alexandria, the tarmac road reaches the summit of an attractive pass and descends easily through the shallow Thorn Kloof, with wheat and maize land set among low, undulating hills. At 49 km from Alexandria, the road joins the main Port Elizabeth-Grahamstown road at a point 54 km from Port Elizabeth. The circular drive Port Elizabeth-Grahamstown-Alexandria; Alexandria-Port Elizabeth, provides a diverting and varied tour of a total of 338 km through the best parts of the 1820 Settler country.

# PORT ELIZABETH TO THE NORTH

The tarmac route from Port Elizabeth to the north, for the first 45,5 km of its journey, is part of Settlers Way leading to Grahamstown (page 336). A major traffic interchange marks the parting of the ways and the road to the north has its own start in life by leading over a slightly undulating plain. After 21,5 km it reaches the small twin rural and rail centres of Paterson and Sandflats where there is a gravel turnoff leading for 27 km to the Addo National Park. The main road crosses the railway line and is immediately confronted by a steady climb up the densely bushed slopes of the Suurberg range. After 19 km of interesting journey up this Olifantskop Pass, the road reaches the summit of the range, 720 m high, where there is a comprehensive view over a countryside covered in the blue-green coloured bush typical of the Eastern Cape.

The inland side of the range is far more arid than the coastal belt. The road descends into this drought-ridden wilderness, crosses after 12 km from the summit the erratically flowing upper reaches of the Bushman's River, then, 36,5 km from Paterson, passes through the small rural centre of Middleton. The traveller is now in the valley of the Great Fish River and for many kilometres the effects of irrigation can be seen as the road leads northwards.

At 14 km from Middleton, the road passes a memorial to the Slagtersnek rebellion and a further 2,5 km sees the road pass the small rural centre of Golden Valley. After 7 km the road reaches the important railway and road junction of Cookhouse, in itself an insignificant place, notable for little other than its oven-like heat in summer.

### Accommodation (Paterson to Cookhouse)
★ Cookhouse Hotel, 15 rooms, 4 with baths. R7,50 – R8,50 B/B. Phone 20.
★ Golden Valley Hotel, 13 rooms, 6 with baths. R7 – R8 B/B. Phone 9916.

*Overleaf: Lithe, alert and as full of energy as a coiled spring, a herd of springbok caught in the rays of a setting sun.*

* Middleton Oase Hotel, 9 rooms, all with baths. R8,65 B/B. Phone 20.
* Sandflats Hotel, 7 rooms, 2 with baths. R8 – R14 B/B. Phone 12.

From Cookhouse, there is a turnoff leading for 24 km westwards to the town of . . .

# SOMERSET EAST

Lying firmly against the well-bushed 823-m-high cliffs of the Bosberg range, Somerset East is rather a nondescript town with a long main street devoid of trees. The mountain background, however, is impressive, with patches of forest, numerous waterfalls (16 of them visible from the town), good walks, and a 33-km scenic Auret Drive leading to the summit of the range from where many impressive views may be seen. The district is famous for its sheep stud farms. Somerset East, in fact, originated as a farm (known as the *Somerset Farm*), which was founded there in 1815 by the Governor, Lord Charles Somerset. This farm was developed to supply meal and oat hay to the frontier garrisons, and also to experiment with crops such as tobacco. Although the farm served a useful purpose, its production was ended in 1825 and a village (later to be named *Somerset East,* after the Governor), was laid out on its grounds. On 13 April 1825, the first erven were sold. In February 1837 it became a municipality and today has a population of 10 231.

The original Georgian-style farmhouse built in 1818 for the superintendent of the *Somerset Farm,* and subsequently the *drostdy* (seat of magistracy), then the Methodist manse and then the Dutch Reformed Parsonage, is now the Somerset East Museum. Somerset East is notable for its flowers, both cultivated and wild. Roses flourish to perfection, producing some wonderful displays in summer.

### Accommodation
* Royal Hotel, 25 rooms, 6 with baths. R7,50 – R8 B/B. Phone 205.
* Somerset Hotel, 18 rooms, 7 with baths. R7,80 – R8,85 B/B. Phone 214.

### Caravans and camping
* Max Clarke Caravan Park, 20 sites. R2 D. Selley camping area, 20 sites. 25c D.

From Cookhouse, the tarmac road continues northwards up the valley of the Great Fish River which is now closely hemmed in by high cliffs covered in thornbush. The alluvial valley floor, wherever suitable, is intensely irrigated and very productive. Several turnoffs mark the way. At 13 km there is a tarmac turnoff to East London, another one to the same place after 6 km and, at 24 km from Cookhouse there is a turnoff stretching westwards to that place of lugubrious memories, Slagtersnek.

After 80 km of travel up the valley from Cookhouse, the tarmac road reaches the pleasant, busy town of . . .

# CRADOCK

A major road and rail centre on the route to the north from Port Elizabeth, Cradock is an exceedingly pleasant, spacious and clean country town built on the banks of the Great Fish River and dominated by a handsome Dutch Reformed Church erected in 1868 as a replica of St Martins-in-the-Field in London.

The story of Southern Africa consists of a series of leapfrogs: government draws boundaries; pioneers leap over them; government is forced to re-draw boundaries. In such a manner Cradock had its beginning. Families such as the Van Heerdens, Lombards and Van

Rensburgs settled in this area when it stretched well beyond the recognised frontier.

After the 1812 Kaffir War, the soldier-Governor of the Cape, Sir John Cradock, decided to strengthen the frontier by creating the two sub-districts of Uitenhage and Graaff-Reinet. On 10 June 1812, Andries Stockenstroom became deputy magistrate at Van Staden's Dam in the valley of the Great Fish River. He soon changed his seat to the farm *Buffelskloof* owned by Pieter van Heerden, which lay in a particularly pleasant and strategic position, close to a spring of sulphur water.

Sir John Cradock visited the place and approved it as the site for a town. The farm was bought for 3 500 rixdollars, the homestead converted into a gaol, official buildings erected and from Stockenstroom came a suggestion that the place be named Cradock. On 21 January 1814, this was officially approved and from then on the town grew, becoming a municipality in 1873 and developing a considerable charm and character over the years. The town now has 23 382 people living there.

With rich soil irrigated from three government irrigation dams (Grassridge, Lake Arthur and Kommandodrift), Cradock is the centre for considerable farming activity in lucerne, fruit, dairy and poultry produce. Lake Arthur is a favourite recreational place for boating of all kinds.

There is a good viewsite overlooking the town from Oukop, a hillock next to the road just as it leaves Cradock for the north. At the Karoo Sulphur Springs, the municipality has developed a pleasant resort with swimming, caravan and picnic facilities. The Van Riebeeck Karoo Garden, with its succulents, shrubs and wild pomegranates, is also a place to visit.

## Accommodation
* ★ Masonic Hotel, 27 rooms, 19 with baths. R6,50 – R8 B/B. Phone 79.
* ★ Victoria Hotel, 30 rooms, 9 with baths. R8 – R8,50 B/B. Phone 196.

## Caravans and camping
* ★★ Karoo Sulphur Springs, 100 sites. R2 D. 4 cottages, 7 rondawels, R4 – R10 D.
* ★★ Municipal caravan park, 60 sites. R2 D.

# THE MOUNTAIN ZEBRA NATIONAL PARK

Situated 24 km from Cradock, this is one of the most scenically beautiful and interesting of all the national parks in Southern Africa. It may be reached by following the main road running northwards from Cradock. After 3 km there is a tarmac turn leading westwards to Graaff-Reinet. At 5 km along this tarmac road there is a gravel turnoff leading southwards into the foothills of the Bankberg range. Eleven kilometres of travel brings the road to the entrance of the park, where the ranger's house and office lie tucked away in a valley 3 km further on.

The park was started in 1937 when the National Parks Board bought the farm *Babylons Toren* to use as a sanctuary for one of the rarest animals, the Cape mountain zebra (*Equus zebra zebra*). The smallest of the zebras, the mountain zebra stands a mere 1,2 m high. Beautifully striped, with a distinct dewlap beneath the throat, it is a lively, sure-footed creature which once inhabited many of the mountain ranges of the Cape, especially the Outeniquas. European hunters largely shot them out, but today there are 140 mountain zebra in the park while a further 42 are known to exist elsewhere. These are the only survivors of a breed once quite numerous.

The Mountain Zebra National Park covers an area of 6 633 ha on the slopes of the Bankberg. Apart from the zebras, there are mountain rietbok, grey rhebok, klipspringers, steenbok, duikers, eland, black wildebeest, red hartebeest, springbok and 150 species of birds, including ostriches.

Vegetation is particularly interesting and typically Karoo, with many fine karee, acacia, wild olive, white stinkwood and kiepersol trees, and a great variety of flowering plants, shrubs and aloes growing there. Mesembryanthemums make a handsome display and after good rains in April, the entire landscape is covered with flowers such as the purple-mauve *Moraea poly-stacha* (blue tulp).

From the ranger's house, tracks lead to several parts of the park and those climbing to the heights of the range (especially to Kranskop) reveal magnificent panoramas of a landscape covered with oddly shaped hillocks. Walking is permitted in the park along the many paths. Horses may be hired at 50c an hour. This is classic commando country where armies could manoeuvre like fleets on the surface of a seemingly boundless ocean. With the herds of antelope grazing on the heights, the wild flowers and the Bushman paintings on the rocks, the scene is superb and a living museum piece of the romantic days of old. The park is open daily from 07h00 to 18h00 (1 October to 30 April), and 08h00 to 18h00 (1 May to 30 September).

Meals are available in the original farmhouse of *Berghof*. There is a museum in the original homestead of *Doornhoek*.

### Accommodation
2 cottages, 10 rooms, R6,50 – R8,20 D.
Youth Hostel, 60 beds.

### Caravans and camping
Caravan park, 25 sites. 50c D per person.

From Cradock, the main road crosses the Great Fish River by means of the Gilfillan Bridge and then climbs steeply northwards out of the river valley, taking a last look at the little town resting on the banks. At 3 km north of Cradock there is a tarmac turnoff stretching westwards to the Mountain Zebra Park (17 km) and to Graaff-Reinet (140 km).

The road continues northwards over the great plains of the Karoo. Scattered over the high-lying landscape is an assemblage of rocky hillocks (the genuine, unique breed of South African *koppie*). Among their assorted shapes may be seen table tops, pointed tops, round tops and pouf-seat tops. Their presence gives this scene a peculiarly and very distinctive South African touch to be viewed nowhere else on earth. In such a setting it is easy to understand the hardiness and independence of the pioneers. The landscape is on a prodigious scale, seemingly infinite, always with more distant hills lurking over an endless horizon. Such a scene is an insidious temptation to trek on, to escape from authority and the irksome taxman, and to lose oneself 'in the blue'.

After 35 km the road crosses the upper reaches of the Great Fish River. Twenty-four kilometres further on there is a turnoff stretching eastwards to Hofmeyr (50 km) and then 97 km from Cradock, the road merges with the tarmac road coming from George and Graaff-Reinet. Together, the combined roads lead past the town of . . .

## MIDDELBURG

Founded in 1852 as the middle point (hence the name) between the older towns of Cradock, Colesberg, Richmond and Hofmeyr, *Middelburg* lies on the banks of the Little Brak River in the great basin which forms the watershed of that river. The town attained municipal status in 1913 and today has a population of 12 400. Middelburg is the centre for a substantial farming activity concerned mainly with sheep. The Grootfontein College of Agriculture is situated 3 km from the town.

### Accommodation
★ Commercial Hotel, 32 rooms, 16 with baths. R7,75 – R8,50 B/B. Phone 22.
★ Grand Hotel, 33 rooms, 19 with baths. R7,75 – R8,50 B/B. Phone 236.

### Caravans and camping
★ Municipal caravan park, 30 sites. R3 D.

From Middelburg, the tarmac route to the north stretches on past the Grootfontein College of Agriculture and in company with the railway, begins climbing up the Carlton Hills, reaching the summit 1 804 m above sea level, 10 km from Middelburg. Three kilometres further on, the road passes through the *Noupoort* (narrow pass), with the railway now running below it in a tunnel, and descends to the level of another high plain on which, 39 km from Middelburg, lies the coldly situated, bleak railway junction and marshalling yard of . . .

# NOUPOORT

When the railway being constructed from Port Elizabeth cut its way through the 'narrow pass' and reached the site of the town in 1884, *Noupoort* had its beginning. The town was actually laid out on the farm *Hartebeesthoek,* but because the narrow pass was the principal feature of the area, the name of Noupoort came into use. As a coaling depot, junction (to De Aar), staging post and marshalling yard, Noupoort became one of the most important railway centres in South Africa. Its existence is dominated entirely by the continuous passage of trains.

### Accommodation
★ Imperial Hotel, 16 rooms, 6 with baths. R6,75 – R7,75 B/B. Phone 71.
★ Noupoort Hotel, 18 rooms, 5 with baths. R5,75 – R6,75 B/B. Phone 69.

### Caravans and camping
Drikkie du Toit Caravan Park, 15 sites. R1 D.

From Noupoort, the tarmac road continues northwards across a high, open and windswept plain, bitterly cold in winter. Rocky hillocks are scattered around in general disorder. At 16 km north of Noupoort the traveller sees for the first time one of the best known of all these hillocks, and one of the principal landmarks of Southern Africa, the famous Colesberg Koppie. A further 34 km of travel brings the road to the slopes of this distinctive beacon on the way northwards. At this point, 50 km from Noupoort, the Cape-to-Cairo road coming from the south, joins the road from Port Elizabeth and the united roads lead to the crossing at the Orange River and the long journey northwards.

## Chapter Eighteen

# CISKEI AND EAST LONDON

From Grahamstown, Settlers Way stretches eastwards, climbing out of the valley of the Kowie up the slopes of the hill named after Makhanda, the leader of the Xhosa attack on Grahamstown, and along the summit of a high ridge. At 4,5 km from Grahamstown a tarmac turnoff leads northwards to Fort Beaufort, while a further 12 km brings the road to one of the most impressive and romantic viewsites in Southern Africa.

The end of the ridge is marked by a pair of radio and telecommunication towers erected on the 847-m-high Governor's Kop. From the summit may be seen a superb view across the valley of the Great Fish River, the old frontier of Kaffraria, the meeting place of two great migratory waves of humanity – black from the north, white from the south – and the scene of innumerable clashes, brawls, fights, wars, heroics and outrages.

The line of watchtowers built by the British army to guard this troubled frontier still looks out from the heights. The scene stirs the imagination and is beautiful at all seasons with the range known as the *Amatole* (place of weaned calves) across the valley, often topped with snow in winter.

The road steadily descends into the valley. Wayside stalls offer pineapples, oranges and iced fresh fruit juices for sale. At 23 km from the summit (39 km from Grahamstown) the road passes *Frasers Camp,* named after Colonel G. S. Fraser who led several commandoes during the frontier wars. At this place a stall sells ice-cold pineapple juice and a variety of snacks. Accommodation is available.

For a further 12 km the road continues its tortuous descent which is enhanced by many interesting views. At 49 km from Grahamstown, the road reaches the bridge across the Great Fish River, the old frontier line of so much disturbance, and for 4,5 km climbs the steep, euphorbia-covered eastern side of the great valley. At the top of the rise the road emerges on to an open grassy plain. After 3 km there is a gravel turnoff leading to the mouth of the Great Fish River, while a further 6 km takes the road to a gravel turnoff leading through Ebb and Flow (41 km), and Kidd's Beach (72 km), and on to East London.

The tarmac road continues eastwards for a further 2 km and then (73 km from Grahamstown), reaches the small town of Peddie, lying in a bowl in a cluster of hills covered with stunted acacia trees.


## PEDDIE

Beginning its existence as an earth-stockaded fort, shaped like an eight-pointed star, which was built in 1835 to protect the Fingo (amaMfengu) tribe who took refuge there from troubles in the Transkei, *Peddie* was named after Colonel John Peddie of the 72nd Highlanders.

On 28 May 1846 in this fort, the Europeans and Fingo residents of the district were besieged by 9 000 Xhosa warriors until a relief force eventually reached them from military posts situated at the Great Fish River.

Fort Peddie became a magistracy in 1848 and the town developed around the old fort and government buildings. The earth fort has long since vanished but the line of watchtowers built in 1841 to protect communications with Grahamstown may still be seen at the original sites: Fort Peddie, Piet Appel, Fraser's Camp, Governor's Kop, and Fort Selwyn (Grahamstown). A few relics of the old military buildings (hospitals, church, and quarters) from the troubled period of the successive frontier wars, still stand in the town.

Peddie became a municipality in 1905 and with a population of 1 074, is an agricultural and trading centre.

### Accommodation
★ Peddie Hotel, 10 rooms, all with baths. R6 B/B. Phone 9902.

From Peddie, the tarmac road continues northwards across undulating country lightly covered in low acacia trees. At 6 km from Peddie a gravel turnoff stretches to Hamburg (46 km) where men of the old German Legion settled. At 15 km from Peddie, the road begins a descent into the valley of the river known as the *Keiskamma* (shining water). Thick acacia and euphorbia bush cover the slopes of the valley. On the right bank of the river stands the old Line Drift Hotel. The road bridges over the river at this point (18 km from Peddie) and then climbs up the left-hand side of the valley to the level of the semi-arid plain thinly covered in grass and acacia trees.

After proceeding 31 km from the Keiskamma River there is a tarmac turnoff which leads to Alice (59 km) and Keiskammahoek (41 km). One kilometre further on (50 km from Peddie) the road crosses the Buffalo River and enters the town of . . . .

# KING WILLIAM'S TOWN

Originally established by the London Missionary Society in 1826, King William's Town has had a somewhat chequered career. In 1835 the Xhosa destroyed the mission and drove the missionaries away. In due course the Xhosa in their turn were chased away by Sir Benjamin D'Urban, the formidable Governor of the Cape, who, on 24 May 1835, in the hope of bringing peace to the troubled area, proclaimed a new district which was named Queen Adelaide. Here a new town was to be created at the site of the old Buffalo River Mission Station. The town was named after the reigning British monarch, William IV.

Plans for the first King William's Town proved abortive because the British Government was reluctant to expand territorial ownership over the area. The mission continued, however, and the name of King William's Town remained attached to this part of the warm valley of the Buffalo River. A few traders were attracted to the place and a local industry developed in the spinning of coarse silk from cocoons gathered from the acacia trees. Gum arabic was also prepared.

In 1846 King William's Town and the mission were destroyed by the Xhosa. At the end of the war, Sir Harry Smith, Governor of the Cape, revived the idea of a town and the old site became the administrative centre of the newly proclaimed province of British Kaffraria. As a military centre, the new town soon outgrew the ruins of the old. It became the principal base for operations in the subsequent Kaffir wars and was a very colourful, bustling type of frontier town, abounding with the rumours, ceremony, and comings and goings of a garrison stronghold. Many bizarre and exciting scenes must have taken place in the town: Red-coats drilling; prisoners in chains; transport riders bringing in the impedimenta of war; hordes of human skeletons fleeing in 1856 from the mystical cattle killings which ruined the Xhosa people.

In approximately the year 1857, the German Legion was disbanded and 2 500 men settled in the area. The empty countryside became populated with stolid farmers. After Prince Alfred's visit in 1861, King William's Town became a royal borough and later, after the annexation of British Kaffraria to the Cape and the final pacification of the frontier areas in 1878, King William's Town became a prosperous centre of trade for the tribal areas. The town remained a garrison station for imperial regiments until 1914 and it is easy to imagine the place at the time when social life was dominated by the doings, scandals and gossip of the officers' mess. Legacies of those days include a town hall which contains an excellent little theatre for concerts and stage shows, and the Kaffrarian Museum, housed in a graceful building. This museum, founded in 1884 by the King William's Town Naturalists' Society, contains among its treasures one of the world's finest and most complete collections of African mammals. This unique assembly of 25 000 specimens was largely the work of the late Captain Guy Shortridge, a former curator of the museum, an author, and a world authority on his subject. To the mammalians of the world this is the most comprehensive of all African study collections. To the layman it is staggering, with a variety of rarities such as a black lechwe from Zimbabwe (only one other is known); web-footed hares from Calvinia; silver moles from Namaqualand; a 5,5-m-high giraffe from the Kaokaveld (the world record specimen); and, dear to the hearts of all animal lovers, that most famous of all hippos, Huberta, who, after ambling a full 800 km down the coast of South Africa, endearing herself as the country's national pet, eventually came to an unhappy end in the Keiskamma River in 1930. The Kaffrarian Museum is open weekdays from 09h00 to 12h45 and 14h00 to 17h00; Saturdays from 09h00 to 12h45; Sundays from 15h30 to 17h00.

The public library, founded in 1861, contains a fine collection of books on Africa, while King William's Town also possesses a botanical garden where five conservatories are laid out in a most pleasant environment on the left bank of the Buffalo River, opposite the caravan park.

The well-known Dale College for boys, founded in 1861 as the Diocesan Grammar School but renamed in 1877 after Sir Langham Dale, the Superintendent of Education, is an important part of the life of King William's Town, along with the Kaffrarian High School for girls (founded in 1875), the school of the Convent of the Sacred Heart, and the De Vos Malan School for Afrikaans-speaking children (founded in 1933).

Industrially, King William's Town is the centre for tanning, footwear, soaps, candles, clothing, sweets, cartons, light engineering, grain milling and toy soldiers. On the outskirts of the town lies *Zwelitsha* (new era), the site of the huge mill of the Good Hope Textile Corporation and its housing estate for workers. There are now 22 680 people living in the town.

## Accommodation
★★ Barkly Hotel, 12 rooms, 6 with baths. R7,50 – R8,50 D. Phone 2-2963.
★★ Central Hotel, 32 rooms, 22 with baths. R9,35 – R13 B/B. Phone 2-1440.
★ Commercial Hotel, 21 rooms, 8 with baths. R10 B/B. Phone 2-2361.
★ Crown Hotel, 17 rooms, 10 with baths. R6,50 B/B. Phone 2-3025.
★ Grosvenor Hotel, 20 rooms, 7 with baths. R8,50 – R9 B/B. Phone 2-2301.
★ Masonic Hotel, 10 rooms, 5 with baths. R8 – R8,50 B/B. Phone 2-2611.
★ Oddfellows Hotel, 12 rooms, 4 with baths. R7,50 – R8 B/B. Phone 2-1011.

## Caravans and camping
★★ ® Municipal caravan park, 100 sites. R1,50 D plus 30c D per person.

King William's Town is the junction for many major roads; a road to the north; the important link road through Fort Beaufort to Port Elizabeth and the north; a short link through Komga rejoining the main coastal road (63 km) north of East London; and, of course, the continuation of the main coastal road to East London. All these roads reveal many interesting and beautiful scenes.

## KING WILLIAM'S TOWN TO COOKHOUSE
This important all-tarmac road links the main coastal road and the road from Port Elizabeth to the north. It also allows the traveller access to the beautiful mountain country of the Amatole range, the Hogsback and the Katberg.

The road branches off from the main coastal road just before this route crosses the Buffalo River from Grahamstown into King William's Town. From this point (1 km from King William's Town), the tarmac road climbs out of the valley of the Buffalo River and continues over an undulating plateau covered in stunted acacia trees. To the north loom the forest-covered slopes of the *Pirie* (named after the Reverend A. Pirie of the Glasgow Missionary Society) and the Amatole mountains. The huts, lands and herds may be seen of the Ngqika (Gaika) section of the Xhosa people who inhabit this part of what is known as the Ciskei.

At 19,5 km from King William's Town there is a turnoff to the industrial township of Dimaza. Two kilometres further on a turnoff leads to the village of Keiskammahoek, 19 km away. The road travels a further 3 km over the saddle of land known as Debe Nek, where the Debe stream has its source. The forest-covered mountain slopes crowd in from the north. Passing the railway station, store and hotel of Debe Nek, the road continues westwards, traversing an arid plain whose thin grass contrasts with the green of the indigenous forest on the overlooking mountain slopes.

After a further 12 km (39 km from King William's Town) there is another turnoff north to Keiskammahoek (94 km) and Fort Cox. Yet another kilometre takes the road across the *Keiskamma* (shining water) River and into the nondescript village of Middeldrift which lies in the shallow valley of the river. For a further 19 km the tarmac road continues westwards over an open undulating plain (notable for its flowering aloes in winter), and then, 57 km from King William's Town, enters the picturesque town of . . .

# ALICE

Named after Princess Alice, daughter of Queen Victoria, *Alice* is pleasantly laid out around a central park. It was the magisterial and administrative centre of the district of Victoria East and is now the capital of the Ciskei.

Alice had its start as a mission station founded in November 1824 and named *Lovedale* after Dr John Love of the Glasgow Missionary Society. After being abandoned during the 1834 Kaffir War, this station was re-established in 1836 on its present site on the west bank of the Tyumi River, and it was there, in 1841, that a school was opened. Although the mission had to be abandoned during the 1846 war, with the buildings converted by the military into a fort, the importance of the place as an educational centre began to increase.

The military later built a fort for themselves on the east bank of the Tyumi River, named *Fort Hare* (after Major-General Hare, the Governor of the Cape) and from 1847 the missionaries returned to Lovedale, developing schools and a hospital. In the same year the town of Alice was founded and named.

Today Alice has a population of 11 010 and is the centre for the University College of Fort Hare, founded in 1916 and now developed to accommodate over 2 900 students. Also situated in the town is the Lovedale High School (457 pupils), and the Lovedale Hospital (with 260 beds) which provides training for 150 student nurses and midwives. The Federal Theological Seminary of Southern Africa, consisting of four colleges representing the Anglican, Congregational, Methodist and Presbyterian denominations, stands in a fine parkland and annually trains 100 theological students. The Lovedale Mission of the Church of Scotland operates the Lovedale Press, which has a considerable output of educational books, as well as the Lovedale Farm which supports a superb herd of dairy cows.

Citrus, beef, milk, wool, mohair and tobacco are the agricultural products of the district.

## Accommodation
★ Amatola Hotel, 11 rooms, 5 with baths. R10 – R11 B/B. Phone 106.

# THE ALICE COUNTRYSIDE

Alice and the district of Victoria East provided the setting for many battles during the frontier wars. The scenery becomes dramatic nearer the mountains of the north, or down the colossal valley of the Great Fish River, where relics of the old military forts make an exploration of the area an interesting experience.

The road to the south descends into the Great Fish River Valley through Victoria Post and Breakfast Vlei. The river is crossed at Committee's Drift (57 km from Alice). A steady climb of 2 km brings the road to a junction with the tarmac road stretching from Fort Beaufort (64 km) to Grahamstown (15 km). An interesting circular drive through Fort Beaufort, back to Alice is provided.

The road to the north branches off from the main tarmac road just as it enters Alice from King William's Town. Passing the Fort Hare University College, the gravel road makes its way up the valley of the Tyumi River, enhanced with aloes (flowering in June) and fine citrus estates. In previous years this valley was the stronghold of the Xhosa chief, Ngqika, and the road passes the site of the old British settlements of Woburn, Juanasburg and Auckland, which were destroyed on Christmas Day during the frontier war of 1850.

After 16 km a turnoff leads for 20 km to the pretty little village of Seymour. This is a beautiful drive which passes the shores of the Kat River Dam on the way. The road to the north continues past this turnoff and after 5 km (21 km from Alice) starts to climb the Amatole mountains by means of a spectacular pass. At 31 km from Alice the road reaches the summit, and enters the popular resort area known as . . .

# THE HOGSBACK

The Xhosa call the Hogsback area *Qabimbola* (red clay on the face). The Xhosa obtained the type of clay they traditionally used to cover their faces from numerous clay pits in the area. The valley of the Tyumi River was a stronghold of the tribe, and the mountain known as Gaika's Kop is said to have been the particular centre of the great Xhosa leader, Ngqika.

The first Europeans in the area were soldiers stationed at Fort Mitchell, built on the slopes of the height known as Tor Doone, where a watch was kept on the stronghold of the Xhosa chief. The outline of Fort Mitchell is still visible, as well as traces of the first road built from Fort Hare to this outpost. The graves of several soldiers, killed during the frontier wars, lie next to this old military trail at places such as Komkhulu. Colonel Mitchell built the fort, and the road pass was also named after him.

After the frontier wars ended, European farmers settled on the high plateau overlooked by the three mountains whose summit ridges give rise to the name of *Hogsback*. The gorgeous indigenous forest growing along the escarpment of the Amatole range became a forestry area, while a hotel, the Hogsback Hydro, was built to convenience travellers. Farmers such as Colonel Bowker, owner of the farm *Arminel*, and Mr Summerton, a professional gardener who introduced apples, hazelnuts and berry fruits to the area, were among the first to build homes in the vicinity of the village of Hogsback.

There are several beautiful forest walks at Hogsback, with drives for vehicles, viewsites, big trees, and a waterfall known as the Kettlespout which, when the wind is strong, is actually blown upwards for about 10 m curling back to fall behind the ridge of the escarpment. There is interesting trout fishing in the area and superb wild flowers abound.

From Hogsback village the main road continues over high grassland, set among hills and mountains. Well watered and richly grassed, this is excellent cattle country. With turnoffs after 11 km to Happy Valley and, after 18 km to Whittlesea, the road, 47 km from Hogsback, reaches Cathcart.

A beautiful and most interesting road also leads back to the main King William's Town-Alice road. This route is known as the Wolf Ridge road. It descends the western slopes of the Amatole escarpment, through the forest reserve where there are fine views of the Amatole range and the basin of the Wolf River. The gravel road descends on the right bank of the Wolf River past numerous tribal villages until it joins the Middeldrift-Fort Cox-Keiskammahoek road after a total of 28 km. Middeldrift, on the main King William's Town-Alice road, is 17 km away along the right-hand turnoff. Turning left to Keiskammahoek 7 km away, the traveller is taken through the notorious Boma Pass where 700 men of the British army were ambushed by Xhosa warriors on 24 December 1850. Twenty-three of the soldiers were killed before the rest fought their way through to Keiskammahoek. This was the bloody beginning of the Eighth Kaffir War. On the following day, Christmas Day, the Xhosa attacked the settlements of Woburn, Juanasburg and Auckland in the Tyumi Valley and totally destroyed them, killing 84 European settlers during the course of a hectic series of fights.

From Keiskammahoek an interesting scenic road passes the Devil's Staircase on its way to Stutterheim, or branches south to Pirie and the Alice-King William's Town road.

## Accommodation
★ Grosvenor Hotel (Keiskammahoek), 9 rooms, 6 with baths. R6,50 – R7 B/B. Phone 9906.
★★ Hogsback Inn, 37 rooms, 27 with baths. R13,25 – R18 D/B/B. Phone 6.
★ Kings Lodge Hotel (Hogsback), 24 rooms, 18 with baths. R8,50 – R9,35 B/B. Phone 24.

## Caravans and camping
Forestry Department camping ground.
★ Waterfall Caravan Park (Hogsback), 20 sites. R2 D.

## ALICE TO FORT BEAUFORT

From Alice, the main tarmac road continues westwards across the foothills of the northern escarpment. It is semi-arid cattle country, covered in acacia bush. After 21 km the road reaches . . .

## FORT BEAUFORT

This town was started during the interminable disturbances of the successive Kaffir Wars. The *Kat* (wild cat) River – on whose banks the town stands – flows through a warm, fertile valley which is ideal for citrus. This valley was the scene of many contentions as it was too fruitful to escape the competitive and envious attentions of man. For some years after the Fifth Kaffir War of 1819, government forces, having driven the Xhosa across the Keiskamma River, attempted to maintain the whole area between the Great Fish and the Keiskamma rivers as a neutral buffer zone. Forts were built to preserve the peace and in this way, *Fort Beaufort* was founded in 1823 as a military stronghold named after the ducal title of the father of Lord Charles Somerset, the Governor of the Cape.

The position of the fort was extremely strong, built on a level tongue of land between the Kat and Brak rivers, whose steep banks enclosed the place almost like a moat. This natural strength served the place well, for it was often used as a place of safety during the disturbances of the time and, on 7 January 1851, withstood a full-scale assault from a Xhosa army.

Fort Beaufort was surveyed as a town in 1837 and a strategic military highway known as the Queen's Road' was constructed from Grahamstown across the valley of the Great Fish River, through Fort Beaufort and onwards to the mountain strongholds of the Xhosa, ending at the foot of the Katberg. The road was built by that indefatigable roadmaker, Andrew Geddes Bain, using military labour. Completed in 1842, it was named in honour of Queen Victoria who was crowned in the year the building of this road commenced. It was the first major South African highway to be properly constructed. Its route is still followed by the modern tarmac road to Grahamstown, and the original fine stone bridges still span the Kat and Great Fish rivers.

Fort Beaufort became a municipality in September 1883. Today it is a pleasant and modern little town with a population of 13 200. It is the centre for considerable farming activity, especially citrus, with the Kat River Packing Sheds despatching many thousands of cases of oranges every June to October.

The original fort, a Martello Tower, may still be seen. A permit and key to visit the fort must be obtained from the town clerk. There is an interesting little museum which contains many a relic from the years of frontier incident and uproar. The museum is housed in the original military mess house and is open on Wednesdays from 10h00 to 12h00, and Mondays and Wednesdays from 19h30 to 21h00. Ten kilometres from Fort Beaufort, on a most picturesque site, stands the Methodist Healdtown Institute, established in 1855, where African students receive technical education.

## Accommodation
* Commercial Hotel, 17 rooms, 5 with baths. R9,50 – R10,50 B/B. Phone 63.
* Royal Hotel, 21 rooms, 5 with baths. R9,50 – R10,50 B/B. Phone 139.
** Savoy Hotel, 10 rooms, all with baths. R9,50 – R10,50 B/B. Phone 62.

## Caravans and camping
* Municipal caravan park, 12 sites. R1,20 D plus 20c D per person.

## THE FORT BEAUFORT COUNTRYSIDE

From Fort Beaufort there are several interesting drives. To the south, the original 'Queen's Road' now provides an all-tarmac route directly across the valley of the Great Fish River to Grahamstown. At 9 km from Fort Beaufort, this road passes a turnoff to a sulphur spring, frequented by many local people. Climbing and winding, the tarmac road reveals many grand views of the valley of the Great Fish River, and eventually bridges the river at Fort Brown (49 km from Fort Beaufort). This fort is now a police post, its tower still watching over the vast valley and its flowering aloes, cattle and sheep farms, thick stunted bush, and sunbronzed farmhouses. Fort Brown was built in 1813 and was first known as Hermanus' Kraal. During the 1834 war it was held against several attacks. After the war it was strengthened with a tower containing a powder magazine, a swivel gun, and an underground tunnel which led to a water supply. From then on it was named after Lieutenant Robert Brown of the 75th Regiment and was completed in 1838. During the 1846 and 1851 wars it survived several attacks and finally, in 1873, it became a police post.

Six kilometres from Fort Brown the road, by means of the Ecca Pass, descends to the lowest level of the valley, thereafter commencing a steep climb up the southern cliffs of the valley through thick bush, where many euphorbias and aloes grow. Superb views of a prodigious and most atmospheric valley are revealed. At 64 km from Fort Beaufort a turnoff leads to Peddie (69 km) via Committee's Drift. The bush begins to thin out with the rise in altitude and prickly pears and aloes cover the slopes. At 69 km from Fort Beaufort the road reaches the summit of the climb, a grassy undulating plateau covered in wattle, fir and eucalyptus trees. At 73 km from Fort Beaufort, the road joins Settlers Way and leads to Grahamstown, 6 km away.

From Fort Beaufort a magnificent modern tarmac road follows the valley of the Kat River through an amiable, rural landscape of citrus groves and fine irrigated farms such as *Millbank* and *Olive Cliff*. Today the area is peaceful, but during the frontier wars this valley was the scene of violent fighting.

There are small wayside villages such as Lower Blinkwater (13 km) and Tidbury's Toll (22 km), with a turnoff to the east at *Lorraine* (23 km) which provides a pleasant drive along a tree-lined road past Bonkazana to Alice. At 53,3 km a turnoff leads to the village of Balfour and thence to several interesting places such as Maasdorp, Retiefs Post, Jurieshoek, McKomens-hoek and other rural hamlets snuggling in the valleys below the towering Kat Mountains. A road also ascends the Katberg Pass from Balfour (see page 356).

## Accommodation
★ Kat Tavern (Balfour), 8 rooms, all with baths. R11,50 B/B. Phone Balfour 16.
★ Tidbury's Toll Hotel, 6 rooms, all with baths. R7 B/B. Phone Fort Beaufort 1520.

Beyond the turnoff to Balfour, the main tarmac road continues up the valley of the Kat River, passing close to the shores of the irrigation dam. There is a turnoff to a recreational area 39 km from Fort Beaufort and, after a further 3,5 km, a turnoff to the town of . . .

# SEYMOUR

With a population of 2 636, Seymour is a small rural village and the terminus of the branch railway from Fort Beaufort. It originated in 1862 as a military stronghold called Elands Post. It was subsequently named after Colonel Seymour, private secretary to Sir George Cathcart, Governor of the Cape. It is an atmospheric little place, although a trifle decayed through the closing down of various enterprises. It is handsomely situated and the Kat River Dam, built in 1869, provides a fine recreational area.

## Accommodation
★ Seymour Hotel, 10 rooms, 3 with baths. R10 – R10,50 B/B. Phone 36.

Beyond the turnoff to Seymour (from where a road skirts the verges of the dam to join the Alice-Hogsback road), the main tarmac road proceeds directly towards the face of the overlooking mountains and steadily climbs the magnificent Nico Malan Pass. At 61,5 km from Fort Beaufort the road reaches the summit, 1 438 m above sea level, after climbing 650 m from the level of Seymour in the valley below. The journey is delightful, passing fine scenery on the way.

From the summit of the pass, the road crosses a high grassland watered by many clear streams where trout play in the rapids and pools. At 24,5 km from the summit there is a turnoff to Hogsback and Cathcart. The tarmac road continues on its easy, sweeping way, past the Waterdown Dam and, 38,5 km from the summit of the pass, reaches the village of Whittlesea, a small rural centre for a prosperous sheep and cattle area. A road branches off beyond the village to the Katberg Pass.

## Accommodation
★ Masonic Hotel, 5 rooms, all with baths. R6,50 B/B. Phone 24.

Beyond Whittlesea, the tarmac road proceeds for 34,5 km and 132 km from the start at Fort Beaufort, reaches Queenstown (see page 359).

# WHITTLESEA DOWN THE KATBERG PASS

A road (mainly gravel) from Whittlesea provides a spectacular scenic journey down the Katberg Pass to the valley of the Kat River. For the first 25 km this road winds sinuously over high grassland. It then climbs the northern slopes of the Winterberg range, by means of what is known as Devil's Bellows Nek, reaching the summit after 14 km. Passing a turnoff 2,5 km further on which leads through Doringkloof to Post Retief and Adelaide, the road starts to descend the Katberg Pass.

The road winds and zigzags through a deep indigenous forest where trees, ferns and flowering plants cascade down the cliff faces like a green waterfall. The Katberg Forestry Station lies 12 km from the summit and from this place there are drives and walks into the Branderskop area and the Katberg Forest area, where picnic spots are situated and lovely scenery may be viewed. The Highlands Caravan Park lies near the forestry station while another kilometre brings the road to a turnoff leading to the Katberg Hotel (51,5 km from Whittlesea).

A further 5,5 km of descent brings the road to a turnoff to the village of Balfour. Six kilometres further on (63 km from Whittlesea) the road joins the main tarmac road which stretches up the valley of the Kat River from Fort Beaufort (see page 353). The drive is unforgettable and has splendid photographic possibilities. It should be done in good weather.

## Accommodation
* Katberg Hotel, 70 rooms, all with baths. R11,50 – R13,50 D. Phone Katberg 3.

## Caravans and camping
** Highlands Holiday Resort and Caravan Park, 50 sites. R3 D. 9 rondawels and 9 rooms, R6– R10 D.

---

From Fort Beaufort the main tarmac road continues westwards along the foothills of the mountains. After 15 km there is a turnoff which descends into the valley of the Great Fish River, to Gardiner's Drift and Riebeek East. A further 21 km (35 km from Fort Beaufort) brings the road into the small town of . . .

# ADELAIDE

Named after the Queen of England, *Adelaide* has a population of 10 270 and became a municipality in October 1896. Built on the banks of the Koonap River, it is a pleasant little town with a central square faced by an array of shops and business premises. A museum with an interesting collection of glassware may be visited.

## Accommodation
* Commercial Hotel, 20 rooms, 8 with baths. R7,60 – R8,60 B/B. Phone 155.
* Midgleys Hotel, 19 rooms, 9 with baths. R8 – R8,50 B/B. Phone 119.

## Caravans and camping
* Dunvegan Caravan Park, 25 sites. R2 D plus 30c D per person.

From Adelaide, the main tarmac road continues westwards, through the foothills of the Baviaansrivier range, with the great Winterberg range lying to the north. At 2 km from the town a turnoff south leads to Tarkastad (98 km). After a further 13 km (24 km from Adelaide) the main tarmac road reaches the town of . . .

## BEDFORD

Lying at the foot of the Kaga Mountains, Bedford was laid out in 1854 on the farm *Maastrom*, belonging to Sir A. J. Stockenstrom. The town was named after the Duke of Bedford and is today the centre for considerable industry in the rearing of cattle and sheep with several stud farms situated in the area. The population is 5 385.

### Accommodation
★ Bedford Hotel, 14 rooms, 6 with baths. R9 – R10 B/B. Phone 110.

From Bedford, the main tarmac road proceeds in a westerly direction beneath the heights of the Kaga Mountains. After 15 km there is a turnoff to the north which leads to Cradock, while a further 8 km brings the road to a junction with the main tarmac road travelling from Port Elizabeth to the north at a point 13 km north of the railway junction of Cookhouse (see page 343).

## KING WILLIAM'S TOWN TO THE NORTH

King William's Town is the starting place for the main tarmac road to the north which, after leaving the town, steadily climbs through foothill country covered in dense medium-high acacia trees. Ahead lies the high mountain ridge which marks the end of the coastal shelf, and the steady rise of the country towards the central plateau of Southern Africa. During winter the high peaks of the *Amatole* (place of weaned calves) are covered in snow, looking down aloofly from the north-west on a landscape of brown grass and acacia trees.

At 11 km the tarmac road crosses the Izeleni Stream and 1 km further on a turnoff west leads to the Pirie Trout Hatcheries and the Rooikrans and Maden dams, all lying in handsome mountain and forest country. The trout hatcheries at Pirie are open to the public daily except on Sundays, from September to April. The road now traverses a densely inhabited tribal area, climbing steeply up a well-bushed ridge, decorated with aloes which flower in June. It is a picturesque drive with interesting views of the downland country.

At 27 km from King William's Town the road reaches the summit of the ridge. Here, in a clump of wattle trees, a turnoff to the west provides a magnificent scenic drive to the Evelyn Valley, Mount Kemp and to a memorial built over the grave of the great Xhosa chief, Sandili, situated behind the Mount Kemp store (11,5 km). The road continues northwards across a grassy, open plateau, covered in cattle, maize fields and wattle plantations. The peaks of the Amatole are well revealed to the west. At 35 km from King William's Town a turnoff to the west leads to the Kubose and Kologha forests and to the Forest Sanctuary. Sandili's grave may also be reached along this road (21 km). Three kilometres further on (40 km from King William's Town), the road enters the town of . . .

## STUTTERHEIM

Lying on the southern slopes of the Kologha mountains which form an eastern spur of the Amatole range, Stutterheim is pleasantly situated with forest-covered mountain slopes providing many recreational possibilities such as good walks, fishing, boating, swimming in the rivers and numerous picnic spots and scenic features such as waterfalls and viewsites. Ferns and wild flowers are numerous.

The first Europeans to settle in this well-watered area were missionaries of the Berlin Missionary Society who established the Bethal Mission Station in 1837. Twenty years later men of the disbanded British German Legion were settled in the area and in the same year the town was founded and named after their commander, Baron Von Stutterheim.

On 20 May 1879, Stutterheim became a municipality and at present 14 150 people live there. Today it is the centre for a considerable timber industry, with sawmills producing things such as transmission poles, mosaic floor blocks and building materials. The town is also the centre of the Eastern Cape Grassveld Region. The Dohne Agricultural Research Institute conducts extensive experiments (especially with sheep and cattle) on its research farm 8 km north of the town. Merino sheep, Jersey cows and Bonsmara beef animals are bred in the district. Citrus fruits and timber are produced.

## Accommodation
* Bolo Hotel, 5 rooms, 1 with bath. R3 – R4,50 B/B. Phone Bolo 7.
* Scoonie Hotel, 13 rooms, 5 with baths. R6 – R9 B/B. Phone 42.
* Stutterheim Hotel, 15 rooms, 9 with baths. R8 B/B. Phone 45.

## Caravans and camping
* Municipal caravan park, 30 sites. R1 D.

From Stutterheim, the main road continues northwards climbing the steep slopes at the eastern end of the Kologha range. Alongside the road, the main railway line also proceeds in an involved, serpentine climb up the same ridge. After 5 km the tarmac road passes the small rail centre of Dohne, with its turnoff to the east which leads to Komga 48 km away. A further 5 km of steady climbing through plantations of pine and wattle trees takes the road past Fort Cunynghame. The old fort was built during the Ninth Kaffir War (1878), and named after General Cunynghame. Eight kilometres further on the road reaches the top of the ridge and continues its journey over rugged, grassy, stony country, patched with wattle tree plantations. After 9 km the road crosses the Thomas River and then proceeds over an undulating plateau for a further 21 km until (48 km from Stutterheim) it reaches the town of . . .

# CATHCART

In the early 1850s Cathcart was originally a military post built on the overlooking Windvoël-berg. In 1876 the first erven were sold to create a town named after Lieutenant-General the Honourable George Cathcart, Governor of the Cape from 1852 until 1854. In 1881 the town became a municipality and today has a population of 4 220. It is a quiet little rural centre surrounded by extensive sheep farms.

## Accommodation
* Royal Hotel, 10 rooms, all with baths. R7,50 B/B. Phone 145.

## Caravans and camping
* Municipal caravan park, 10 sites. R1 D.

From Cathcart, the road carries on climbing over a rugged countryside with the main railway line tunnelling and twisting in close company. After 19 km both the road and the railway reach a fine viewsite which has an expansive outlook across the valley of the Swart Kei River into a great bowl, dominated to the north by the high, stool-shaped mountains of the Stormberg range and its numerous spurs and outliers. This is a majestic scene peculiar to South Africa –

rocky, arid, enormous, romantic in atmosphere and strangely comforting in its harshness.

The road and railway descend into this bowl and continue northwards across its floor, through stunted acacia bush past numerous sheep farms. Stony hillocks (many flat-topped), look down on a rugged landscape.

At 40 km from Cathcart there is a turnoff east to Engcobo (130 km). After a further 17 km the road (57 km from Cathcart) reaches the town of . . .

# QUEENSTOWN

The principal town of the Cape Midlands, Queenstown is also the commercial, administrative and educational centre of a prosperous farming area. As well as being a communications, road and railway centre, it is a staging post of considerable importance.

*Queenstown,* named after Queen Victoria, was founded in 1853 by the Governor, Sir George Cathcart. It was intended to be one of a chain of border outposts and had a most unusual layout. In accordance with the instructions of the Governor that the town be a stronghold for the defence of the frontier area, the surveyor, Thomas Holden Bowker, designed the town around a hexagonal open piece of ground from where cannon or rifle fire could be directed down the six thoroughfares which radiated from it. This hexagonal town centre is now a handsome garden with a pleasant fountain as its dominant feature.

Lying on the banks of the Komani River, with a refreshing climate and plentiful water obtained from the surrounding heights, Queenstown grew rapidly. In 1879 it became a municipality and is today one of the most important smaller towns in Southern Africa.

Queenstown possesses an impressively modern commercial centre and its cultural, sporting and recreational assets are numerous. The Frontier Museum and Municipal Art Gallery both contain many worthwhile exhibits, and at the beginning of June each year, the Queenstown Art Society holds an exhibition of paintings and sculptures by artists from many parts of Southern Africa. There is a well-stocked library, while the collection of shell work of Miss R. Lock, exhibited in a gallery in 1 Lamont Street, has a unique charm.

Queenstown is pleasantly situated and from the overlooking heights many handsome views are provided. The slopes of the Madeira Mountain were proclaimed as a nature reserve in May 1964. A 7-km-long gravel road leads through this reserve to the summit of the mountain from where a sweeping panoramic view may be seen. Blesbok, springbok and ostriches roam the reserve, while the flora is varied and interesting. In winter (July/August) the *Aloe ferrox* is in full bloom, while in spring and early summer (October/November) the numerous species of acacia tree are covered in yellow and red flowers. The tambookie thorn *(Erythrina acanthocarpa)* is especially notable at this time. Cycads may also be seen and fine specimens may be found 6 km south of the town at Fincham's Nek. The reserve is open daily all the year round except in wet weather.

Five kilometres from Queenstown on the road to Lady Frere, lies the Bongolo Dam, the town's main source of water. In a fine setting of hills, the dam has been developed as a recreational area where there are picnic sites. The Queenstown Power and Yacht Club is based at the dam and has a summer weekend tearoom in its clubhouse. The dam is stocked with black bass and bluegill fish. Another substantial dam is the Waterdown Dam, 50 km from Queenstown on the road to Fort Beaufort. With an earth wall 55 m high and 260 m long, this dam supplies water for irrigation and is well stocked with trout. The Walter Everitt Sunken Gardens has been developed where the road enters Queenstown from the south. The garden has a succession of ponds frequented by swans and aquatic birds, and a great variety of ornamental shrubs, trees and flowers. A municipal caravan park has been laid out here next to a drive-in tearoom.

Queenstown is altogether a pleasant and modern country town with an amiable and relaxed atmosphere. At present there are 49 048 people living there.

## Accommodation

★ Central Hotel, 26 rooms, 17 with baths. R8,50 – R10 B/B. Phone 3868.
★ Gardens Hotel, 40 rooms, 20 with baths. R8 – R9 B/B. Phone 2244.
★ Grand Hotel, 49 rooms, 30 with baths. R9 – R10 B/B. Phone 2266.
★★ Hexagon Hotel, 41 rooms, 26 with baths. R11 – R13,50 B/B. Phone 2262.
★ Queens Hotel, 16 rooms, all with baths. R10,50 B/B. Phone 2953.
★ Royal Hotel, 22 rooms, 8 with baths. R9 – R10 B/B. Phone 2415.
★ Windsor Hotel, 27 rooms, 8 with baths. R9,50 – R10,50 B/B. Phone 2393.

## Caravans and camping

★★ Municipal caravan park, 50 sites. R2 D plus 25c D per person.

From Queenstown, the main tarmac road climbs northwards through the mountains, with Hangklip dominating the landscape from the east. Angora goats and aloes flourish in its rugged setting and laybys created by a considerate roads department allow travellers to rest awhile and view the surroundings. Numerous flat-topped mountains crowd the horizon. The landscape is wild and the air has the clarity of the verges of the Great Karoo.

At 49 km from Queenstown there are turnoffs west to Sterkstroom (12 km) and Dordrecht (48 km – see page 501). The road continues northwards and after a further 5 km crosses the branch railway line from Sterkstroom to Maclear. Ahead looms the high continuous ridge of the *Stormberg* (stormy mountain) running east to west, and 57 km from Queenstown the road starts to climb the range by means of the Penhoek Pass. For 7 km the road climbs steadily up the grassy, rock-strewn slopes. The summit of the pass is 1 844 m high (65 km from Queenstown), from where the road traverses a grassy and windswept mountain plateau, with no trees or bush to be seen. Cattle and sheep farms cover the heights. At 7 km from the summit there are turnoffs, east to Dordrecht (34 km) and west to Molteno (35 km).

The road continues through rugged rock and hill country, where fine farms abound and after a further 33 km (106 km from Queenstown), reaches the town of . . .

# JAMESTOWN

A rural centre for a substantial farming activity in sheep and grain, Jamestown lies huddled in a hollow on the northern slopes of the Stormberg. It is the terminus of the branch railway from Molteno and has always been a staging post on the route to the north, the early transport men using it as a place of rest and repair after or before crossing the Stormberg.

The farm on which the town stands, *Plessies Kraal,* was owned by Johannes Jacobus Wagenaar, known to his English-speaking friends as 'James'. With a syndicate of his friends he laid out a village on a portion of his farm and the first 405 lots were auctioned on 22 December 1874. Eight years later what had become known as *Jamestown* after the farm owner, received its first village management board and on 4 December 1943 eventually became a municipality. Its growth has not been very spectacular, but Jamestown has no pretensions of being anything other than a friendly little rural centre and the terminus of the branch railway built as far as the town in 1930.

## Accommodation

★ Central Hotel, 18 rooms, 4 with baths. R8,50 – B/B. Phone 20.

## Caravans and camping

★ Municipal caravan park, 20 sites. R1 D.

From Jamestown, the road continues northwards through rugged, rocky sheep country, where the cliff faces of numerous high hills provide ideal resting ledges for a large population of vultures. After 6 km there is a turnoff leading eastwards to Lady Grey (58 km). After a further 6 km the road finally emerges from the Stormberg range and makes its way on to a superb agricultural plateau where wheat, barley, dairy cows and sheep are farmed. On the far eastern horizon looms the great pile of the *Witberge* (white mountains), covered in snow in winter, and the complex massifs which build up to the Drakensberg.

At 24 km from Jamestown the tarmac road passes the Vineyard Cheese Factory. For a further 16 km the road traverses fertile farming country, dominated to the west by the bulk of Stormberg Peak. At 40 km from Jamestown the road travels through a spur of hills dominated by the Plaatkop. A further 5 km takes the road across the branch railway line linking Aliwal North to Barkly East. There is a turnoff to the east 6 km further on leading to the hot springs at Aliwal North. Fifty-six kilometres from Jamestown, the road enters the town of . . .

# ALIWAL NORTH

With its population of 22 055, Aliwal North was founded as a centre for the territory north of the Stormberg which had been newly annexed by that volatile Governor, Sir Harry Smith. On 19 September 1848, Sir Harry had visited the site and at a meeting of local settlers had been requested to establish a town. The following year, on 12 May 1849, John Centlivres Chase, newly-appointed magistrate for the area, laid the foundation stone for an administrative building and held an auction sale of erven in the town named after Sir Harry Smith's great victory in 1846 over the Sikhs at Aliwal in India.

The site of the new town was at the strategic ford across the Orange River known as Flotfontein, where a frontiersman, Pieter Jacobus de Wet, had settled on a farm named *Buffelsvlei* in 1828. On this farm two powerful thermal springs at a temperature of 94°C reached the surface. The larger, 2 182 000ℓ a day, and the smaller, 1 227 000ℓ, were both highly mineralised, principally with sodium chloride, calcium chloride, calcium carbonate and aluminium sulphate. They contained so high a content of methane, nitrogen and carbon dioxide, that a funnel placed over the eyes of the springs could trap enough gas to maintain a cooking fire in the first restaurant built there. These springs originate at a depth of about 1 280 m where the water is heated and through artesian pressure, rises to the surface so rapidly that much of the heat from the depths is carried upwards as well. From early times these springs were highly regarded for their properties for curing rheumatism, arthritis, lumbago, neuralgia, etc., and people became accustomed to visiting them to enjoy their special qualities.

Aliwal North grew as a frontier town of the Cape, a transport centre and health resort. A pontoon was floated in 1872 to convey travellers across the Orange River. Just below the pont, D. C. Greathead erected a giant watermill which was driven by the river water, while pleasant homes were built on vantage points along the banks.

In 1882 Aliwal North became a municipality and in 1885 became the railhead of the line from East London competing for trade with the booming diamond fields of the north. Hotels and warehouses were built and many colourful gardens were cultivated. The streets were shaded by handsome trees, and a park was developed and named after the romantic and beautiful Lady Juana Smith, bride of the Governor.

The continuation of the railway across the Orange destroyed the old importance of Aliwal North as a railhead but it remained an important staging post and railway junction, the centre of rich farming activity and gifted with boundless water from the Orange River and the hot springs.

The hot springs have been lavishly developed. In a setting of green lawns, a warm Olympic-sized swimming pool holding 2 273 000ℓ of water (27,7°C) has been constructed.

*Overleaf: The Katberg; mountains and forests where memories linger of frontier wars with their bitter-sweet episodes of heroism, tragedy, despair and hope.*

There is a second outdoor pool built over the eye of a hot spring containing water at a temperature of 31,1°C. Built directly in the eye of the main spring is a completely enclosed 'wonder' pool where the water is 34,4°C. Since the water is heavily impregnated with natural gases, the effect is like bathing in warm champagne.

There are two warm children's pools (27,7°C), turkish baths, saunas, private baths, playgrounds, picnic areas, caravan and camping parks, and numerous other worthwhile amenities which today attract over 150 000 visitors each year. The Hot Springs Resort is open from 06h00 to 22h00 (October to March); from 07h00 to 18h00 (April to May); from 08h00 to 17h00 (June to August); and from 07h00 to 18h00 (September). Entrance fee is 50c for adults, 25c for children.

## Accommodation
★ Aliwal Hotel, 18 rooms, 5 with baths. R6,50 – R7,50 B/B. Phone 2341.
★★ Balmoral Hotel, 15 rooms, 12 with baths. R9,50 – R10,50 B/B. Phone 2453.
★ Criterion Hotel, 43 rooms, 21 with baths. R10 – R12 B/B. Phone 2471.
★★ Juana Maria Hotel, 21 rooms, all with baths. R9,50 B/B. Phone 2475.
★ Somerset Hotel, 14 rooms, 6 with baths. R7 – R8 B/B. Phone 2861.
★ Spa Hotel, 18 rooms, all with baths. R12,60 B/B. Phone 2772.
★ Radio Hotel, 23 rooms, 6 with baths. R7,50 B/B. Phone 3311.
★★ Umtali Motel, 33 rooms, all with baths. R10 – R11 B/B. Phone 2408.

## Caravans and camping
★★ Municipal Holiday Resort, 450 sites. R1,50– R2 D. 20 cottages and 5 rooms, R4,60– R6 D.

Beyond Aliwal North, the main tarmac road crosses the Orange River by means of the General Hertzog Bridge. There is a turnoff to the west immediately after the bridge which leads to the town of Bethulie. The road continues northwards through picturesque hill country – stony and lightly bushed – which flattens out into the great central plains of the Orange Free State. At 33 km from Aliwal North, the road enters the town of . . .

# ROUXVILLE

Founded in 1863 when the town was laid out as a church centre on the farm *Zuurbult,* owned by Petrus Weppenaar, *Rouxville* was named after the Reverend Pieter Roux who ministered to the district from the older town of Smithfield.

It is a quiet, rural town, with a population of 3 298, and is the centre for prosperous farming with merino sheep and Afrikander cattle. Its situation, in a hollow overlooked by some handsome hills to the north-east, is pleasant.

## Accommodation
★ Criterion Hotel, 12 rooms, 5 with baths. R7 – R7,50 B/B. Phone 55.

From Rouxville the road swings north-westwards through low hillocks and makes its way over grassy cattle and sheep country. After 24 km the road bridges over the handsome Caledon River and then, 15 km further on (40 km from Rouxville), reaches the drowsy, neat little town sheltering in the lee of a ridge of hills called . . .

# SMITHFIELD

With a population of 3 601, Smithfield had its start in September 1848 when the hard-riding and popular Governor, Sir Harry Smith, laid the foundation stone for a church to be the centre for a town named in his honour and laid out on the farm *Waterval,* belonging to C. S. Halse. The site was soon found to be unsuitable through lack of water. In November of the following year, erven in a new Smithfield were sold on the present site of the town, the well-watered farm *Rietpoort.* It became a municipality in 1860 and has always been an important church and farming centre for the southern Free State and Lesotho border areas.

Accommodation
★ Smithfield Hotel, 12 rooms, 3 with baths. R6 – R6,50 B/B. Phone 46.

Beyond Smithfield the road travels through the ridge of overlooking hills by means of a natural passage known as Wilcocks Poort, where a dense thicket of acacia trees covers the banks of the stream and the Kinderman Park is situated on the far side, with picnic sites, a golf course, and the substantial Smithfield Dam.

The road continues north-westwards over the high, grassy plains, dotted with low, bush-covered hillocks and numerous ant heaps. There are endless vistas of the type of highveld scene (especially attractive towards sunset), peculiar to South Africa. The roads department has considerably created several laybys (notably on the banks of a stream 56 km from Smithfield) and a fine road makes the way pleasant. At 72 km from Smithfield, the road reaches the end of its journey when it merges with the great north-south Cape-to-Cairo trunk route on the outskirts of Reddersburg (see page 506).

## KING WILLIAM'S TOWN TO KOMGA

From King William's Town a tarmac road leads directly towards Transkei through Komga, thereby saving 52 km compared with the main road which goes to East London before continuing to Transkei. This road stretches over open grassland, crosses the main railway line to the north at Kei Road station and, 64 km from King William's Town, reaches the town of . . .

## KOMGA

The name of *Komga* is a European corruption of the Hottentot *Gama* (red clay). The town is an agricultural and railway centre. On the road between it and Kei Road there is an interesting little memorial marking the spot where Major H. G. Moore won the first Victoria Cross to be awarded in South Africa on 24 December 1877. This occurred at the beginning of the Ninth Kaffir War.

Accommodation
★ Hangmans Inn (Kei Road), 5 rooms, 2 with baths. R7 – R8 B/B. Phone 14.
★ Royal Hotel (Komga), 14 rooms, 5 with baths. R7,25 – R7,75 B/B. Phone 29.

Caravans and camping
★ Municipal caravan park (Komga), 10 sites. R3 D.

Six kilometres beyond Komga (74 km from King William's Town) the road rejoins the main coastal road and descends into the valley of the Kei River (see page 372).

## KING WILLIAM'S TOWN TO EAST LONDON

From King William's Town the main coastal road climbs out of the acacia-covered valley of the Buffalo River. Passing the industrial area of *Zwelitsha* (new era), the road reaches the level of a grassy, acacia-dotted plain where, 19 km from King William's Town, stands the town of . . .

# BERLIN

Founded in 1857 by men of the disbanded German Legion who settled in the area, Berlin was for years simply a small, rural centre. Now it is changing into an industrial area, a part of the general development of the Ciskei.

## Accommodation
★ Berlin Hotel, 14 rooms, 6 with baths. R6,30 – R8,40 B/B. Phone 1.

Beyond Berlin the main road gradually descends to the coast, passing a vast housing area created for African industrial workers and then, 60 km from King William's Town, reaching . . .

# EAST LONDON

The fourth largest harbour in South Africa, East London is the only river port in the country of any significance. Developed at the mouth of the Buffalo River, the harbour has a working depth of 12 m at low water, and its six quays on the east bank and seven wharfs and quays on the west bank can accommodate substantial ocean-going ships. Among other facilities is the Princess Elizabeth Graving Dock.

The harbour possibilities at the mouth of the river originally named by the Hottentots *Ingaad! ab* (river of buffaloes), were apparent to the first European explorers, but the need for development there only arose in 1835. After the Sixth Kaffir War, when British control was extended to the area between the Keiskamma and the Kei rivers, Colonel Harry Smith, then Chief of Staff to the Governor, rode to the river mouth to examine its potential as a port where supplies could be landed. As a result of the visit, the brig *Knysna,* owned by the famous George Rex, was sent to the Buffalo River to trade, arriving on 19 November 1836. A Union Jack was nailed to a tree on Signal Hill, overlooking the left bank of the river, and a mixed cargo was landed by means of the ship's boats.

The success of this experiment was marked by giving the river mouth the name of Port Rex. For ten years nothing more was done to the harbour since the British Government had relinquished control over the area. Then in 1847, the Seventh Kaffir War broke out and the mouth of the Buffalo River immediately became of major importance. Fort Glamorgan was built to defend the place and on 28 April 1847, the barque *Frederick Huth* arrived to unload military stores. After this, the harbour began to be used regularly. A village soon grew up and on 28 December 1847 was officially (if rather stupidly) named East London. The following month it was annexed to the Cape Colony. From 1851, organised parties of settlers, many of them German, made their homes on both banks of the river. Since most of these ex-legionaries were bachelors, the *Lady Kennaway* was sent out from Britain in 1857 with a cargo of 157 Irish lassies. These beauties arrived in East London on 20 November, probably the most welcome cargo ever landed in the Buffalo River harbour!

In 1856 work commenced on the first training walls at the mouth of the river and from then on the harbour was steadily developed into its present state. Today East London has a population of 113 245 and is a centre for the export of wool, for numerous industries and for extensive trade with Transkei and Ciskei. As a holiday resort, it has tremendous potential, being richly endowed with a congenial climate and a string of superlative beaches and river mouths where boating, fishing, swimming and recreational delights are available for those who like to enjoy themselves in the sunshine and fresh air.

The commercial centre of East London, built along the principal thoroughfare of Oxford Street, is not particularly notable and inclined to be dull but the suburbs are attractive. The coastline is superb, combining most of the best features of the Cape and Natal beaches: the clear water of the Cape and the warm sea temperatures of Natal; the spacious, sandy beaches of the Cape and the shady, evergreen shoreline trees of Natal; the absence of excessive summer heat and humidity experienced in Natal combined with the safe swimming conditions of the Cape, where there are few sharks or dangerous back or side washes. All these characteristics unite to make a most enjoyable playground for man.

Among the principal suburbs and places of interest in East London are *Panmure* (named after Lord Panmure, Secretary of War at the time when members of the German Legion settled); *Vincent* (after Mr Vincent, a leading figure on the town council in the 1870s); *Quanza Terrace* (named after the wreck of the *Quanza* in 1872); and *Cambridge* (after the Duke of Cambridge, British Commander-in-Chief when the German Legion was disbanded).

The three main beaches are *Orient* (named after the Russian sailing ship *Orient,* wrecked there on 29 July 1907), Eastern Beach and Nahoon Beach, situated at the mouth of the Nahoon (Nxaruni) River. These are only a few among the delectable necklace of bays, lagoons, inlets, promontories and beaches strung along the length and breadth of coast where the Indian Ocean meets the shores of Africa north and south of the mouth of the Buffalo River.

East London possesses one of the best museums in Southern Africa. Among its fine natural history exhibits is the first coelacanth to be discovered in modern times. This strange fish, long thought to be extinct, was caught in 1938 near East London. The museum also exhibits the only dodo's egg in the world, as well as a magnificent collection of marine shells and a finely presented series of exhibits depicting man through the ages. The museum is open weekdays from 09h30 to 17h00; Saturdays from 09h30 to 12h00; Sundays from 09h30 to 12h30 and 14h30 to 16h30.

There is a zoo containing about 1 200 animals in Queen's Park. It is open daily from 08h30 to 17h00. On the beachfront an aquarium is open daily except Tuesdays from 09h00 to 18h00. Feeding times are: small fish, 10h30 and 15h00; large fish and sharks, 16h00; penguins, 12h00 and 16h00; seal shows, 11h30 and 15h30.

The Ann Bryant Art Gallery is open on weekdays from 09h30 to 17h00; Saturdays and Sundays from 14h30 to 17h00.

Gately House, situated at the bottom of Caxton Street, is another interesting place to visit. This was the home of John Gately, the first mayor of East London in 1875. In 1966 the house with its Victorian period furnishings was bequeathed to the municipality and is preserved as a national monument, a delightful example of the lifestyle during the last century. It is open daily except Mondays from 09h30 to 12h30 and 15h00 to 17h00; Sundays from 13h00 to 17h00.

There are several buildings in the city which are historically interesting: the railway station, built in 1877; the Drill Hall, built in 1906; St Peter's Church, constructed in 1857, and the city hall situated in Oxford Street where stands the equestrian memorial to the men of the Colonial Division who fell during the Anglo-Boer War.

An interesting feature in East London is the auction sales held in the Wool Exchange, from September to May on Tuesdays at 09h30. Visitors are welcome.

Surfing is spectacular off Nahoon beach, a favourite area where a reef wave of considerable power occurs sufficiently reliably to allow competitions on an international level to take place.

## Accommodation

★ Belgrave Hotel, 16 rooms, 5 with baths. R7,50 B/B. Phone 2-3486.
★★ Carlton Hotel, 54 rooms, all with baths. R9,75 – R13,75 B/B. Phone 2-3174.
★ Continental Hotel, 42 rooms, 17 with baths. R6,88 – R8,88 B/B. Phone 2-2229.
★ Deals Hotel, 76 rooms, all with baths. R9,03 B/B. Phone 2-3771.
★★ Dolphin Hotel, 40 rooms, all with baths. R7,25 – R11,06 room only. Phone 8-7515.
★★ Dorchester International Hotel, 52 rooms, 40 with baths. R11,50 B/B. Phone 2-4253.
★★ Esplanade Hotel, 88 rooms, 45 with baths. R7 – R11,50 B/B. Phone 2-2518.

★ Grand Hotel, 30 rooms, 12 with baths. R7,75 – R9,25 B/B. Phone 2-3106.
★ Highgate Hotel, 11 rooms, 8 with baths. R6,78 B/B. Phone 8-7085.
★★ Holiday Inn, 116 rooms, all with baths. R18 – R28 room only. Phone 2-7260.
★★★ Kennaway Hotel, 89 rooms, all with baths. R20 room only. B/B. Phone 2-5531.
★★★ Kings Hotel, 57 rooms, all with baths. R18 – R45 B/B. Phone 2-2561.
★ Majestic Hotel, 34 rooms, 8 with baths. R6,65 – R14,35 B/B. Phone 2-6228.
★ Oceanic Hotel, 10 rooms, 3 with baths. R6 B/B. Phone 2-4767.
★ Orange Grove Hotel, 10 rooms, 4 with baths. R6,25 B/B. Phone 46-1330.
★★ Osner Hotel, 126 rooms, all with baths. R15,50 B/B. Phone 2-0654.
★ Protea Hotel, 10 rooms, 4 with baths. R9,50 B/B. Phone 2-2667.
★★ Queens Hotel, 70 rooms, 36 with baths. R13 – R15 B/B. Phone 2-3631.
★ Royal Hotel, 15 rooms, 5 with baths. R8,50 – R16 B/B. Phone 2-4248.
★★ Weavers Hotel, 53 rooms, all with baths. R11,20 – R13,60 B/B. Phone 2-3186.
★ Windsor Hotel, 42 rooms, 16 with baths. R6,75 – R7,45 B/B. Phone 2-6081.

### Caravans and camping
★★★★ Eastern Beach Caravan and Camping Ground, 232 sites. R3,64 D plus 25c D per person.
★ Nahoon Beach Caravan Park, 113 sites. R3,64 D plus 25c D per person.

# THE EAST LONDON COASTLINE

Exploring the coastline of East London, the traveller is rewarded by the discovery of many pleasant and amiable resorts where rivers become calm lagoons before reaching the sea, and waves play lazily upon the beach.

As already mentioned, many of these resorts combine some of the best features of the Natal and Cape beaches. They have the intimacy and tropicality of the Natal beaches, without shelving steeply and having tricky back and side washes. Water and air temperatures are warm, without the stickiness of Natal summers. The climate is equable and the water, although not quite as clear as the Cape seas further south, is seldom as turgid as the ocean off the Natal coast where it is muddied during summer by the floodwaters of numerous rivers. Fishing is interesting and richly varied, as are shells (especially on the beaches north of the Kei), which combine species from the tropical seas of the north with those from the temperate waters of the south.

The roads following the coast north and south from East London pass through green and attractive countryside where picnic and camping sites can be found. African tribal life is in many parts picturesque, and it is interesting to know that it was here that the Xhosa people migrating down from the north encountered and mingled with the Hottentot tribes who first inhabited the area. The Hottentots have now vanished from the region, but many traces of their original presence are retained in the culture and dress of the local tribespeople. The language of the local Xhosa tribespeople (especially with its strange-sounding clicks) has been influenced, as have most of the place names (particularly river names), which have been hopelessly corrupted into Xhosa, English or Afrikaans forms.

# THE COASTAL RESORTS SOUTH-WEST OF EAST LONDON TO PORT ALFRED

The tarmac road travelling down the coast south-west of East London leaves the city at the seaward end of Oxford Street. It descends into the valley of the Buffalo River, passing Queen's Park and its zoo set among trees and gardens. The road then crosses the river by means of a handsome bridge built immediately upstream from the curious old double-decker steel bridge which the road originally shared with the railway. The view of the river from the bridge is impressive. Downstream may be seen the bustle of the harbour; upstream, where the river flows down from the interior, magnificent opportunities for boating are provided.

Immediately beyond the bridge a turnoff descends the west bank to the mouth of the river and continues from there as a marine drive along the coast, rejoining the main road after 15 km.

The main road proceeds from the bridge in a south-easterly direction, passing the Ben Schoeman airport at 9 km and rewarding travellers with a delightful journey along a level, green, lightly bushed coastal terrace. At 12 km the road is joined by the marine drive and at 17 km there is a crossroads, with a turnoff to the west leading to Mount Coke and east to the coast and the mouth of the Igoda River where there are camping sites and holiday cottages.

Another kilometre takes the road across the *Igoda* River, whose name (meaning a shallow) valley) accurately describes the course it follows through hills, well covered with a considerable variety of bush, euphorbia species and trees. The area is pleasantly park-like. At 24 km the road descends into another attractively wooded, shallow valley, through which flows the river known as the *Gxulu* (agitated). On the right bank of this river is Rayners Caravan Park, and the Aqualea Caravan Park is 1 km further on.

### Caravans and camping
★★ Aqualea Caravan Park, 80 sites. R2,50 D plus 50c D per person.
★★ Rayners Caravan Park, 30 sites. R5 D plus 50c D per person.

At 6,5 km from the Gxulu River (30,5 km from East London), the road reaches a turnoff which leads for 3 km to the coastal resort of . . .

## KIDD'S BEACH

Named after Charles Kidd, a mayor of King William's Town in the 1860s, *Kidd's Beach* originated as a coastal resort particularly popular with the people of King William's Town. Today it is an amiable (if untidy) huddle of seaside cottages which look out on to a rocky shoreline. There is a tidal pool for swimming and a sandy beach at the mouth of the river.

### Accommodation
★ Kidd's Beach Hotel, 12 rooms, all with baths. R10 – R11 B/B. Phone 715.

### Caravans and camping
★ Kidd's Beach Holidays, 25 sites. R4 D.
★★ Palm Springs Caravan Park, 50 sites. R5 – R6 D plus 50c D per person.
★★ Seavale Caravan Park, 70 sites. R2 – R5 D plus 50c D per person.

From the turnoff to Kidd's Beach, the tarmac road continues south-westwards along the park-like coastal terrace. After 1,5 km (33 km from East London) a turnoff west leads to Mount Coke and King William's Town. The coastal road swings left, passes substantial fields of pineapples and then descends into the well-wooded valley of the river known as the *Ncera* after the species of grass used for thatching which grows there. At 1,5 km beyond this river (39 km from East London) a turnoff stretches for 4,5 km to Christmas Rock and for 9 km to . . .

## KAYSER'S BEACH

Named after John Kayser, who owned the land during the 1880s, *Kayser's Beach* is a popular resort for fishermen. Their wives, however, seem to spend most of their time sitting around watching, presumably to see that their husbands catch only fish!

### Caravans and camping
★★ Christmas Rock Caravan Park, 100 sites. R4 D plus 50c D per person.

Beyond the turnoff to Kayser's Beach, the winding tarmac coastal road continues, passing fields of pineapples and swinging more inland across a gentle succession of green, lightly-bushed hills. At 49 km from East London the road descends steeply to the river known to Europeans as the *Chalumna* and to the Xhosa as the *Tyalomnga*.

Three kilometres beyond the river crossing there is a turnoff leading southwards for 9 km to the mouth of the Chalumna. The main tarmac road continues through a tribal area, lightly bushed with low acacia species and covered with green grass, sisal plantations and maize fields. After 11 km (67 km from East London) the road descends into the ruggedly handsome, thickly bushed valley of the river which still bears the pleasant original Hottentot name of *Keiskamma* (shining water). The scenery of rolling hills and an interesting collection of succulents and euphorbias growing along the riverbanks, is dramatic.

Eight kilometres beyond the river (80 km from East London), an important junction is reached. One branch veers westwards and makes its way inland for 25 km over gentle hills covered in thick bush. The Crossroads Supply Store is passed on the way after which the tarmac road reaches Peddie and joins the main Cape Town-Durban road.

The left-hand branch at the junction continues for 4,5 km and then reaches a turnoff to the east which descends to the alluvial floor of the valley of the Keiskamma and then follows the bank of the river for 16 km before reaching its mouth where lies the holiday resort of . . .

# HAMBURG

An informal little fishermen's resort with a spacious beach, excellent swimming and boating on the river, Hamburg has a population of 1 215. A huddle of cottages and stores stands on the bush-covered hill slopes which overlook the estuary of the river.

### Accommodation
★ Hamburg Hotel, 22 rooms, 16 with baths. R6 – R6,50 B/B. Phone 4.

### Caravans and camping
★ Hamburg Board Camping Ground, 40 sites. R2 D.

Beyond the turnoff to Hamburg, the main tarmac road proceeds, passing a turnoff to the mission station of Wesley and then approaching the coast. This is a delightful coast which is, as yet, unspoilt by developers or other 'vepers' (venal persons) who assault nature by looting it for their own profit. The road crosses a succession of rivers – the Gqutywa, Bira, Mgwalana and Mtati – each with a pretty lagoon at its mouth. The Mpetweni River, 25 km from the turnoff to Hamburg, has a camping ground on its left bank, with an entrance charge of R1 per car and R1 D per person.

The Old Woman's River is 10 km further on, where a turnoff north leads to Peddie. A further 2,5 km brings the tarmac road to the bridge across the Great Fish River. On the southern side of the bridge there is a turnoff of 1,5 km to the mouth of the river where there is a fine, sandy beach and a scattering of rather ramshackle fishermen's cottages.

The ruins of Fort D'Acre, built during the days of the frontier wars, lies 1 km further down the main tarmac road. A turnoff to the Great Fish Point lighthouse lies a further 4,5 km down the road. The lighthouse is in a prohibited area reached by a 5-km-long gravel road.

The main tarmac road continues for 4,5 km and then reaches the twin rivers known as Kleinemonde West and East, both of which have fine lagoons at their mouths and small resorts consisting of private bungalows and shacks.

At 4 km from West-Kleinemonde, the road crosses the Riet River, where there is a gravel turnoff to its mouth. A further 7,5 km takes the road to the Rufane River and a turnoff to the beach at its mouth. Four kilometres further south-west, this beautiful coastal drive on an all-tarmac road ends 178 km from East London at Port Alfred (page 340).

# THE COASTAL RESORTS NORTH-EAST OF EAST LONDON

The coastline stretching from East London as far as the mouth of the Great Kei River, shelters a succession of popular holiday resorts all of which are endowed with fine beaches, lagoons and river mouths, rocky vantage points for fishermen, and patches of coastal forest where campers and picnickers can find shady retreats.

Immediately north-east of East London proper, lies the mouth of the river known to Europeans as the *Nahoon,* a corruption of the Xhosa *Nxaruni* (said to have been a chief who once resided there). The Nahoon area is nowadays a suburb of East London, lying 3 km from the centre of the city. The river provides a fine stretch of boating water and there is a spacious beach pleasantly situated at the mouth of the river, where the swimming is safe and there is exciting surfing.

The second coastal resort north-east of East London is Bonza Bay, reached by a turnoff from the main road to Transkei, 9 km from the city centre. This is a 4,5-km turnoff to the sea at the mouth of the river known to Europeans as the *Quenera,* a name which has, through the years, undergone a succession of involved corruptions from the original Hottentot *!Kani !ab* (river of elands). At the mouth of the river lies Bonza Bay, an attractive little bay which has a pleasant beach and good sea and lagoon swimming and boating. The township area is known as *Beacon Bay,* combining the names of the original farm, *Beaconhurst,* and *Bonza Bay* (whose name is said to have been given to it by an admiring Australian). The Quenera and Nahoon rivers border the area and provide kilometres of interesting possibilities for boating, canoeing, aquaplaning, swimming and fishing.

## Accommodation
★ Bonza Bay Hotel, 28 rooms, 23 with baths. R5 – R10 B/B. Phone East London 47-2401.

## Caravans and camping
★★★ ® Blue Bend Holiday Resort, 32 sites. R2 D plus 50c D per person. 22 cottages, R3,50 D per person.
★★ ® Pirates Creek Caravan Park, 120 sites. R2 D plus 25c D per person. 4 cottages, R10 – R17 D.

The third coastal resort north of East London lies 12 km from the city along the main Transkei road and is reached by a 7,5 km turnoff to the coast.

# GONUBIE

With its population of 5 100, the pleasant little seaside town of Gonubie lies at the mouth of the river known to the Xhosa as *Qunube* after the wild bramble berries which grow along its banks. Apart from giving the town its name, this river, and the lagoon and beach at its mouth, provides a delectable recreational facility for visitors to this sunny and relaxed part of the world. Apart from these natural assets, the local municipality has with commendable energy, created several amenities such as a tidal paddling pool for children and, in a shady setting along the banks of the river, one of the loveliest caravan parks in Southern Africa.

## Accommodation
★ Gonubie Hotel, 32 rooms, 8 with baths. R8,70 – R11,70 B/B. Phone 94-1010.

## Caravans and camping
★★★ ® Gonubie Mouth Caravan Park, 104 sites. R4,75 D plus 60c D per person.

The coast north-east of Gonubie supports a necklace of pretty little bays, river mouths and recreational resorts casually strung out along the shoreline and reached by a tarmac loop road which branches off from the main Transkei road at a point north of the turnoff to Gonubie (17 km from East London): This loop road, leading to the East Coast Resorts area, provides a very pleasant 23-km-long drive, traversing a green and very gentle rural landscape.

Crossing the old East London-Transkei road, the loop road travels eastwards for 3 km before reaching a turnoff of 7,5 km to the coast at the mouth of the Kwelera River where a cluster of seaside shacks and cottages looks out over a rocky, fishermen's shoreline, and a lagoon and beach are situated at the river mouth. From this branch road to Kwelera Mouth, there is a turnoff stretching for 3 km to Sunrise-on-Sea.

From the turnoff to Kwelera Mouth, the main tarmac loop road continues across fields of pineapples. After 4,5 km a turnoff leads eastwards for 3 km to the Yellow Sands Caravan Park and the Glengariff Hotel. A splendid beach at the mouth of the Bulugha River, where swimming is safe and the fishing is interesting, makes this area (known as Fisherman's Cove) a fine holiday resort throughout the year.

From the turnoff to the Glengariff Hotel, the tarmac loop road continues past the Glen Eden Caravan Park (3 km), the turnoff to Cintsa Mouth West (4,5 km) and at 7,5 km from the Glengariff turnoff, a turnoff 6 km long, leading to the mouth of the Kefani River and thereafter travelling 7,5 km to Cintsa Mouth East. At both these river mouths there are fine beaches, lagoons, good swimming and fishing, holiday camps and caravan parks. At Cintsa Mouth East there is also a Divisional Council parking and camping ground. The *Kebani* (or *Cebane*) River is said to take its name from a man who once resided there. The *Cintsa* is said to be named after the 'crumbling' of its banks by floodwaters.

From the turnoff to the mouths of the Kebani and Cintsa rivers, the tarmac loop road proceeds. After 1,5 km a turnoff stretches for 12 km through pretty scenery and tribal country past the Tainton School, joining the main Transkei road at a point 40 km from East London. The tarmac loop road meanwhile continues for 4,5 km and then rejoins the main Transkei road at a point 32 km from East London.

## Caravans and camping (on the East Coast Resorts loop road)
★ Cefani Mouth Caravan Park, 25 sites. R2 D. 2 cottages, 9 rondawels, R1 D per person.
★★★ ® Cintsa Bay Holiday Resort, 85 sites. R3 D plus 50c D per person. 32 cottages, 14 rondawels, R5,50 – R15 D.
★★ ®Cintsa Mouth East Caravan Park, 40 sites. R4 D plus 50c D per person.
★★★ ® Cintsa West Holiday Resort, 50 sites. R5 D plus 25c D per person. 10 cottages, 40 rondawels, R5 – R15 D.
★ Four Seasons Holiday Resort, 50 sites. R2,50 – R3,50 D. 24 cottages, R4 – R15 D.
★★ Glen Eden Caravan Park, 100 sites. R3,50 – R6 D. 18 cottages, R9,50 – R16 D.
★ Glen Muir Caravan Park, 50 sites. R4 D plus 50c D per person. 26 cottages, R4 – R21.
★★ Glen Navar Holiday Resort, 80 sites. R3 D plus 50c D per person. 13 cottages, R16 D.
★★ Quinera Lagoon Holiday Resort, 15 sites. R5 D plus 50c D per person. 7 cottages, R6– R10 D.

★ Rondalia Holiday Resort, 20 sites. R3 D. 5 cottages, R7 – R9,50 D.
★★★ ® Yellow Sands Caravan Park, 120 sites. R3 D plus 50c D per person.

At a point on the main Transkei road, 41 km from East London, there is yet another turnoff, which leads to the coast at Haga-Haga. This road travels eastwards over gentle hills with euphorbia-covered slopes, and passes well cultivated farmlands. After 12 km a crossroads is reached where stands St Anthony's Store. The road leads for a further 12 km in an easterly direction directly to the coast, past pineapple and maize farms and numerous tribal settlements nestling in lightly bushed country. Once at the coast, the road descends suddenly and steeply to a line of cottages, stores and places of accommodation built along a rocky coastline at a resort with the odd-sounding name of . . .

## HAGA-HAGA

A small coastal village, *Haga-Haga* looks out at the sea from the foot of a pair of hills. It is said to take its name from the ceaseless murmur and movement of the waves upon the shore. It is the centre of an interesting stretch of coast, where a spacious beach at the river mouth provides lively fishing and a good area for collecting sea shells. There are several beautiful walks.

### Accommodation
★ Haga-Haga Hotel, 36 rooms, all with baths. R7 – R11,50 D/B/B. Phone 2412.

### Caravans and camping
★ Bosbokstrand Caravan Park, 50 sites. R2 – R2,50 D plus 50c D per person. 10 cottages, R8 – R14 D.

From the junction at St Anthony's Store, a road marked Kei Mouth turns to the north. For 9 km this road crosses gently rolling downland country, lightly bushed and very green, where occasional trees, fine farms (pineapples and sheep) and tribal settlements can be seen. This road then joins the road connecting with the main Transkei road which travels to Morgan Bay and Kei Mouth.

The road to Morgan Bay and Kei Mouth branches off from the main Transkei road at a point 57 km north-east of East London. This road leads eastwards over gently rolling hills for 29 km before reaching the turnoff south to Haga-Haga, described above. From this junction the road continues for a further 15 km and then reaches a turnoff of 8 km to the delightful little resort of . . .

## MORGAN BAY

*Morgan Bay* takes its name from A. F. Morgan, master of the royal naval ship *Barracouta* which was used in the survey of the coast of south-east Africa in 1822, made by Captain W. F. Owen. The master's name was applied to Cape Morgan (on which there stands today an automatic lighthouse) and the little bay sheltered in its southern lee.

The holiday resort lies on the right bank of the *Ntshala* (or *Nchara*) River, so called from the crabs found there. The river forms a pretty lagoon which is the centrepiece for a singularly romantic and quite charming stretch of coastline. South-west of the village, with its atmospheric hotel and water's edge caravan park, the coastline develops into a handsome line of cliffs, over the top of which leads a track to one of the most beautiful and unspoilt areas in Southern Africa. This area is known as Double Mouth and consists of the lagoon formed by two small rivers, the *Quko* (or *Khukho*), meaning something spread out, and the *Gondwane*

371

(river of wild figs). The traveller is confronted with an almost dreamlike scene of calm water, green hills, and an exquisite coastline of rocks alternating with dark-yellow coloured beaches. Fine shells litter these stretches of sand, and amongst the natural gems of the sea may be found cornelian beads and fragments of Ming china, washed up on the shore from the forgotten wrecks of early sailing vessels.

North-east of the village a pleasant 5-km-long walk takes one to Kei River Mouth over the base of Cape Morgan, past a drowsy indigenous forest where bushbuck and duiker lurk. In this forest may be seen the workings of the Cape Morgan Titanium Mine. In 1954 an asbestos miner, Trevor Miller, on holiday in Morgan Bay, noticed a black deposit on the beach. Samples showed this deposit to be rich in ilmenite, rutile and zircon. He followed the traces, pegged claims, and exported the first 150 tons in 1958.

## Accommodation
∗ Morgan Bay Hotel, 30 rooms, 12 with baths. R8 – R9 B/B. Phone Kei Mouth 130.

## Caravans and camping
∗∗ Double Mouth Camping Site, 50 sites. R2 D plus 20c D per person.
∗∗ ® Morgan Bay Caravan Park, 40 sites. R2,50 D plus 50c D per person.

Once again on the main road to Morgan Bay, a turnoff (after 8 km) passes pineapple fields and travels over the hills for a pleasant 9 km to the village and holiday resort of . . .

# KEI MOUTH

This little place takes its name from the *Kei* (great) River which flows sedately through a jumble of low hills, depositing upon the beach a peace offering to the ocean of flotsam, jetsam and tree trunks carried down from the inner parts of South Africa.

The village consists of an informal collection of cottages, stores and places of accommodation built on the slopes of a pile of hills which tumble down to the sea. There is a spacious beach and good rocky vantage points for fishermen. Sea shells can be collected, and a walk of 1 km through a coastal forest (a haunt of blue duikers) takes the visitor to the mouth of the river. The climate is cool and the sea water warm. With the addition of plenty of sunshine but no humidity, all these factors contribute to make an attractive holiday resort.

Beyond the Kei River of course, lies Transkei. Kei Mouth is the last of the holiday resorts on the East London and Border coastline.

## Accommodation
∗ Beach Hotel, 28 rooms, 12 with baths. R7 B/B. Phone 17.
∗∗ Florence Hotel, 26 rooms, 17 with baths. R7,75 – R8,25 B/B. Phone 47.

## Caravans and camping
∗∗ Kei Mouth Camping Site, 100 sites. R2,10 – R2,60 D plus 30c – 60c D per person.

## Chapter Nineteen

# TRANSKEI AND THE WILD COAST

From East London, the main road to Transkei proceeds in a north-easterly direction, leaving the city via the suburb of Nahoon. A turnoff to Beacon Bay is reached after 4,5 km and a further 2 km sees the road join the main coastal road, Settlers Way, which has its beginning in Cape Town. This great highway extends across the undulating and perennially green expanse of the coastal terrace, where deep valleys have been eroded by a multitude of streams and rivers during the course of their journey to the sea. Banana and pineapple farms, clumps of acacia bush bedecked with gold-coloured, sweet-smelling flowers in spring, and numerous tall evergreen trees cover the attractive park-like landscape.

There is a turnoff to Gonubie after 10,5 km (page 369) and at 16,5 km the turnoff to the East Coast Resorts loop road (page 369). This loop road returns to rejoin the main road 30,5 km from East London. At 40 km there is the turnoff to Haga-Haga (page 371) and at 56 km the turnoff to Morgan Bay and Kei Mouth (page 372).

The main road swings inland and at 60,5 km is joined by the direct road from King William's Town through Komga. After 2,5 km the road begins to descend into the valley of the river known to the Hottentots as *Kei* (great). This river truly deserves its name, not only for the enormity of its valley, but for the fact that it has long been a divider in the affairs of man, providing a natural frontier between tribes and a memorable landmark for all travellers.

The road sweeps down the southern side of the valley through a hot wilderness of euphorbias, aloes and acacia bush. The railway line follows a more circuitous descent with the Great Kei Cuttings being famous among railway enthusiasts. The road completes its route after 7,5 km but the train takes 24 km to descend the 330 m to the bridge across the river.

The valley is spectacular in all seasons. During winter the aloes are in flower; in spring the blossoms of the acacia trees perfume the warm air with a sweet fragrance. Dominating the valley on the southern side are the cliffs of the 576-m-high *Moordenaars Kop* (murderers' peak) where, in September 1847, during the War of the Axe, five British officers were surprised and killed. To the Africans the height is known as *Sihota* (place of seclusion).

The Kei River, 70,5 km from East London, marks the frontier of . . .

## TRANSKEI

The self-governing state of Transkei consists of 41 620 square kilometres of agricultural and pastoral land extending along the coast from the Kei River to the border with Natal on the Mthamvuna River. Prior to receiving its independence on 26 October 1976, the area consisted of three distinct tribal territories divided into 26 magisterial districts, all of which formed part of the Cape Province.

The first tribal territory consisted of Transkei proper, the area between the Kei and Mbashe (Bashee) rivers; the second was known as Tembuland which lay between the Mbashe and Mthatha rivers; and the third was Pondoland, extending from the Mthatha to the Natal border.

These territories covered 480 km from north to south, while east to west, they extended about 160 km from the coast to the Drakensberg range. As a whole these areas are graced with extremely beautiful scenery such as the magnificently rugged Wild Coast and a grassy midland, emerald green in summer, drab brown in winter, traversed by several fine rivers flowing through deep valleys. The entire landscape is given an extraordinarily picturesque appearance by the spontaneous distribution, as well as sheer number of rondawel-type homes in which the resident population live.

Inhabiting Transkei are about two million people who belong to the various tribal groups. They are pastoralists and agriculturalists by occupation, their land supporting 1 386 000 head of cattle, 2 226 000 sheep, 1 400 000 goats, 101 000 horses, and 415 000 pigs. Fully 70 per cent of the land is for common grazing; 24 per cent is arable; 3 per cent is planted with forest; and 3 per cent is residential. Apart from wool and mohair, the area each year produces substantial crops of maize and corn which, together with milk, form the staple diet of the people. About 1 000 tons of tea are produced each year on two estates at Magwa and Majola in Pondoland and fibre is produced from *Phormium tenax* plants. Forestry is being extended, with 73 505 ha of indigenous forest and 60 000 ha of plantations being cultivated.

Tradition says that the first inhabitants of Transkei were Bushmen and Hottentots. In approximately the year 1600, a section of the Hlubi tribe of Natal wandered southwards, hunting and seeking new lands in which to settle. The Hlubi people were part of the great migratory wave of humanity which was steadily moving down the coastal belt of south-east Africa. All speaking a similar language (the Zulu-Xhosa of today) this group claimed a common origin in a place called eMbo in the far north. One section of these migrants, under a leader named Nguni, developed into the great tribe of the Zulu. Another migratory wave under a leader named Dlamini entered the area of Natal.

The Hlubi section of these people sent still further south an advance party who in some way rebelled against its parent group and (it is said) killed their leader. Led by a woman known as Xhosa they encountered the Hottentots, found sanctuary with them, and blended to form the great tribe which the Hottentots apparently named after the woman who was its first leader. The language of the newcomers was retained by the combined group but was much influenced by Hottentot speech, especially the use of 'click' sounds. The use of these strange clicks was apparently regarded as fashionable and became widespread. It is notable that the migrants who remained in the north employed fewer words containing such clicks. The Zulu language, for example, has the same variety of clicks as Xhosa, but a much smaller number of words which contain them.

Other related people followed behind the Xhosa vanguard, and the pressure shifted the pioneers forward as far as the Great Fish River where they encountered Europeans advancing from the south in a similar but counter-migratory movement.

The inevitable clash resulted in the nine successive 'Kaffir Wars' and the ultimate annexation of the Transkeian territories by the Cape Government in 1879.

The territories were then divided into magisterial districts for the imposition of law and order, but the tribal chiefs always had a considerable measure of local authority. District Councils were established in the 1880s and in 1895 these councils combined to form two General Councils, one meeting at Butterworth in the south, and the other in Pondoland. These two councils, which exercised local control over tribal life, were amalgamated in 1931 to form the United General Council of the Transkeian Territories, popularly known as the *Bunga* (meeting and discussion). In May 1963 this became the Legislative Assembly of Transkei when the territories received their independence and Paramount Chief K. D. Matanzima became Prime Minister of the new government.

Beyond the bridge over the Kei River, the main tarmac road commences a steady and scenically spectacular climb out of the valley. The road ascends for 16 km before reaching the 765-m-high level of the grassy, undulating midland plateau. The road continues for a further 18 km across this spacious world of summer thunderclouds, grassy slopes, cattle herds and white-coloured rondawels scattered over the landscape like grains of starch dropped on an emerald green carpet.

At 34 km from the Kei River bridge, the road reaches the valley of the Gcuwa River on whose acacia-covered slopes lies the town of . . .

# BUTTERWORTH

Known to the Africans as *Gcuwa,* Butterworth is the oldest town in Transkei. It was originally a Wesleyan mission station built in 1827 on the banks of the Gcuwa River near the seat of Hintsa, chief of the Gcaleka section of the Xhosa tribe. The first missionary, the Reverend W. S. Shrewsbury, named the station after Joseph Butterworth, the treasurer of the Wesleyan Missionary Society. Although burnt down three times during the Kaffir Wars, the mission was always rebuilt. In December 1877, a magistrate was stationed there and upon the establishment of law and order, a collection of traders and commercial persons created by their joint activity a town which became a municipality in 1904. The population now numbers 28 514.

Butterworth is at present developing as a substantial industrial centre. In the vicinity of the town are two handsome waterfalls, the Bawa Falls in the Qolora River with a drop of nearly 100 m, and the cascades on the Gcuwa River tumbling down 90 m.

**Accommodation**
★ Bungalow Hotel, 40 rooms, 10 with baths. R12,75 – R13,75 D.

# GCALEKALAND

From Butterworth several drives traverse the charming countryside inhabited by the section of the Xhosa tribe known as the *Gcaleka* after a witchdoctor chief who ruled over them around 1750. These drives lead by devious scenic ways down to the coast, here truly 'wild' and quite magnificently beautiful. The most important of these side roads stretches south-east from Butterworth and after 31 km of winding, reaches the village of . . .

# CENTANE

With its tiny population of 276, *Centane* takes its name from a nearby hill named *kwaCentane* after a local headman who once had his home there. It is a picturesque and typical little Transkeian village: one street of shops, a post office and magistracy; a few horsemen, and womenfolk in their tribal costume. The regal gait of these women results from their practice, handed down from generation to generation, of balancing loads on their heads.

Centane, notwithstanding its diminutive size, features largely in the history of South Africa for the area around it was the scene of many clashes between elements of the Xhosa tribe and British forces. The village was established as a military post where, on the misty morning of 7 February 1878, the last battle of the Ninth (and final) Kaffir War took place.

Captain R. Upcher was in command of the post at the time, having under him 436 European and 560 Fingo soldiers. A combined, 5 000-strong army of Xhosa consisting of warriors from the Gcaleka and the Ngqika (Gaika) sections of the tribe, attacked the government force which was entrenched in a rough quadrangular earthen fort built near Moldenhauer's Hill Store. The Xhosa had been well doctored by Xito, a renowned witchdoctor, who had so thoroughly assured them that they were invulnerable to bullets that they attacked *en masse*. The two great chiefs, Kreli and Sandili, were present to witness the promised total defeat of the government troops. Instead, a sad debacle followed.

The advancing warriors were simply mown down by heavy fire. With their faith shattered they broke and fled, pursued by cavalry. Three hundred of them were killed while the government force lost only two men. Sandili and his Ngqika fled south of the Kei River while Kreli and his Gcaleka became refugees, hiding in the forests and endless hills of their homeland until the chief eventually surrendered and spent the rest of his life in retirement near Elliotdale. His followers were resettled in the Willowvale district while their former homeland, largely depopulated, was united with Fingoland and Idutywa to become the nucleus of the present Transkei. Centane grew into an administrative and communications centre with a village management board proclaimed on 21 June 1932.

## Accommodation
Royal Hotel, 9 rooms, R3,50 B/B. Phone Centane 17.

From Centane, roads lead down to several coastal resorts whose scenic beauty and angling, swimming and recreational possibilities make them superb holiday resorts. The most southerly resorts are reached by a gravel road which turns off just before the road from Butterworth enters the village.

The road descends steadily for 6 km through a handsome jumble of bush-covered hills where the tilled fields and rondawel huts of the Xhosa tribespeople occupy all suitable ground. The road then reaches a turnoff stretching for 20 km to the mouth of the Khobonqaba River where a cluster of seaside shacks stands watching the wreck of the *Jacaranda* (see further on). The main road continues its winding descent. At 20 km it passes the Kei Mouth Forestry Station with a turnoff just ahead leading down to the left bank of the Kei.

The main road now traverses a green coastal terrace, where clumps of palm and indigenous forest grow. At 26 km it reaches the coastline at the pleasant resort of . . .

# QOLORA MOUTH

The *Qolora* (steep place) River is named after the gorge through which it reaches the sea. This stretch of coastline is very typical of the Wild Coast. The river emerges from its gorge and, as though weary after its tortuous journey through the hills, rests in a pretty lagoon until at last it finds its way to the sea. A spacious beach extends between the lagoon and the sea and a series of rocky promontories provide fishermen with ideal vantage points. Green grass, sundu palm trees, wild banana palms and a variety of indigenous trees crowd on the verges of the sand. The general effect created is pleasing and relaxing to the eye and mind.

Holidaymakers come here to fish, swim and play golf on a scenic course. There are walks or rides to several interesting places such as the Boiling Pot, a rough inlet from the sea; the Gates, where the river flows through a narrow crevice; and the Blow Hole, where high tide forces a spurt of water high into the air. A 7-km walk along the beach leads to the mouth of the Kei River, while a similar walk in the opposite direction ends at Khobonqaba Point and the wreck of the *Jacaranda*.

The *Jacaranda* was a 2 000-ton Greek coaster. On the windy night of 18 September 1971, while riding high with empty holds, her engines are said to have failed. The little vessel ended up so securely wedged in a narrow crevice in the rocks that it looked as though she had been snugly berthed. Captain Kokkios Paulos phoned his owners in Greece by means of his ship's radio informing them of his predicament. Nothing much could be done about the situation at that distance but the conversation between them would have made interesting listening. The captain, his wife and 14 crew members then abandoned ship by means of a rope ladder strung from the prow to the rocks, leaving the good ship *Jacaranda* to her fate. There she remains with no intention of ever leaving.

Another interesting walk or drive over a rough track can be followed inland for 4 km, to that pool of poignant memories where the young medium Nongqawuse (sometimes known to

Europeans as Nongqause) claimed to have held communion with the ancestral spirits. The pool lies in the river known as the *Gxara* (the precipice) after the deep gorge through which it flows. At this pool Nongqawuse used to sit and look into its waters where she saw the faces of the ancestral spirits. Their voices came to her promising that they would help the Xhosa drive the Europeans away providing that, as a sign of faith, the tribespeople would destroy all their cattle and crops.

A great commotion arose amongst the Xhosa at news of this revelation. Men travelled from far to speak with the medium and her witchdoctor uncle, Mhlakaza. Crowds gathered to gaze into the pool where many claimed to see the faces of their own ancestors and hear them demanding total faith as the price of support from the supernatural world. Some witnesses told in bated breath of how they had seen whole armies of ghost warriors waiting to emerge, eager for war and jeering at the timidity of the Xhosa.

There commenced a dreadful fever of cattle killing and crop destruction, the great majority of the Gcaleka section of the Xhosa implicitly obeying the dream voices heard by Nong-qawuse. Fortunately, the Ngqika section of the tribe kept their reason and remained aloof.

For those who believed, the climax was destined for 18 February 1857: the sun would rise blood-red and the land would be filled with fat cattle, new crops and vast armies of reincarnated spirits ready to restore the Xhosa tribe to its past glory and greatness.

It was truly a terrible dawn for many thousands of deluded people when the sun climbed out of the Indian Ocean as usual and the Gcaleka saw before them ruination and the prospect of starvation; they had nothing left. It is estimated that 25 000 people died of hunger and the remainder only survived through the compassion of neighbouring tribes and Europeans who fed them. The discredited medium fled for safety but was arrested by European police, ending her days in obscurity on a farm near King William's Town. The pool of spirits in the Gxara, with its troubled surface and wild surroundings, remains as a memorial to folly. In winter flowering aloes provide a particularly handsome setting, although the area is always beautiful. The river meanders through the hills until it comes to rest in the lagoon at its mouth before finally rushing through the barrier of sand to the waiting sea.

## Accommodation
* Seagulls, 40 rooms, 8 with baths. R11 – R14 D, seasonal. Phone Seagulls 9901.
* Trennerys (named after the original housekeeper, Mrs Trennery), 57 rooms, 11 with baths. R12 D, February to November. R15 D, December to January. Phone Butterworth X3011.

## Caravans and camping
Forestry Department sites at Qolora Mouth and Khobonqaba Point. Simple facilities, R1 D.

# EXPLORING THE WILD COAST
The best way to explore the Wild Coast is to follow the gravel road which twists, rises and falls parallel to the coast from Centane to Port St Johns and Lusikisiki. From this road, branches lead off to the various coastal resorts. The scenery is entrancing throughout the journey; for the photographer and artist there are innumerable views and scenes which are charming and often overwhelming. The road crosses the homelands of the principal section of the Xhosa, Tembu and other tribes where is displayed to the traveller in splendid variety, one of the most unique landscapes on earth: green hills, deep valleys and gorges; grassy pastures ornamented by clumps of indigenous forest and palm trees; herds of grazing cattle, goats and sheep; neat rondawel dwellings, with doorways invariably facing east, and roofs decorated with odd charms against lightning; friendly little pigs who act as mobile garbage disposal units; beautifully poised and almost statuesque women in their tribal dress; and the absence of fences or any other sign of private property (land ownership is communal). These

are merely a few of the ingredients comprising the atmospheric, elegant and curiously old-world land of Kaffraria.

In the same way as the other administrative and trading centres in Transkei, Centane lies on top of a ridge, with its avenue of tall trees providing a landmark which is visible from many kilometres away. The road follows a north-easterly direction and commences a winding descent into the valley of the river whose name *Khobonqaba* is said to indicate a deserted precipice. After 8 km the road crosses this river and 1,5 km further on reaches the first of the turnoffs leading to coastal resorts. This turnoff stretches for 24 km over pleasant downland country and ends at a fine lagoon formed at the mouths of two rivers, the *Nxaxo* and the *Nqwasi*, both said to be named after former tribal headmen.

The lagoon provides a fine stretch of water for boating and aquaplaning while the islets and swamps further up the two rivers are good nesting places for crested cranes. These beautiful birds are numerous along the Wild Coast and very conveniently for themselves, are regarded as taboo by the tribespeople. It is believed that if one of these birds is killed, death will come to the killer's family.

A fine beach lies between the lagoon and the sea. Swimming is safe, there are oysters in season and fish all through the year. Birds, monkeys and shells are numerous while the local tribespeople are expert bead workers.

### Accommodation
* Wavecrest Hotel, 45 rooms, 7 with baths. R11 D, out of season. R14 D, in season. Phone call office, Wavecrest via Butterworth.

### Caravans and camping
Forestry Department sites, simple facilities. R1 D.

At the turnoff to the Nxaxo mouth, the main road from Centane continues its undulating way north-eastwards. After 8 km (17 km from Centane) there is a junction with a road branching westwards which eventually leads to the main inland road traversing Transkei. The road being followed veers eastwards and proceeds along what is known as the Cats Pass, the summit of a narrow ridge from where tremendous views, especially northwards into the valley of the river known as the *Qora* (place of clay), may be seen.

At the end of the Cats Pass there is a junction. One road (which shall be followed eventually) descends the river valley while the other continues eastwards, passing the cluster of buildings of the Dutch Reformed Church mission hospital at *Tafalofeffe* (the plain of help), 24 km from Centane.

A further 15 km takes the road to the forestry station of Manubi. This forest, comprising 1 361 ha of indigenous trees and shrubs, provides a very fine drive for those who turn aside and, with the permission of the forester, explore some of the tracks. The forest has always been a stronghold for game animals and its name is said to have been derived from a local chief, Manyobi, who hunted in the area.

The road continues its descent. After travelling a further 7 km from the forest station it eventually terminates 46,5 km from Centane at the coastal resort of . . .

## MAZEPPA BAY

Without doubt one of the most beautiful coastal areas in Southern Africa, this bay was named after a coastal trading ship, the *Mazeppa*, which, captained by a man named Allen, used the place in the 1930s in order to land goods.

Swimming and fishing are good at Mazeppa Bay. A little island connected to the mainland by a suspension footbridge provides vantage points for fishermen as well as some handsome views up and down the rugged coastline. Between the island and the Clan Lindsay rocks, where the ship of that name was wrecked in 1898, there is a sheltered beach fringed by sundu palms. Known as First Beach, this is a splendid swimming area while further south lies the spacious Second Beach, with Shelly Beach still further south but both within pleasant walking distance.

The attraction of shells, numerous middens left behind by prehistoric beachcombers (*strandlopers*), fine walks, kite fishing and the clear air of the Wild Coast, make Mazeppa Bay an outstanding holiday resort.

### Accommodation
★ Mazeppa Bay Hotel, 46 rooms, 16 with baths. R11 D, out of season. R14 D, in season. Phone Mazeppa Bay.

### Caravans and camping
Forestry Department sites, simple facilities. R1 D.

The main road from Centane continues past the turnoff to Mazeppa Bay and immediately descends to the bottom of the Qora Valley. This is a magnificent scenic drive. The river is crossed after 6 km and the road then makes an involved climb up the northern slopes. After 11 km a branch leads westwards to Butterworth and a further 10 km brings the road to a junction with the main gravel road running from Willowvale (west) to Qora Mouth (east). This junction is 51 km from Centane.

## QORA MOUTH

From the junction point of the Centane road, 33 km of very pleasant driving is provided to the mouth of the Qora River. The landscape is typical of the lovely Transkeian downland countryside: rich grass, deep gorges, patches of indigenous forest, the innumerable huts of the Gcaleka, and the buildings of several wayside trading stations. It is worth stopping at some of these trading stations where the bustle of a group of tribespeople doing their shopping provides an animated scene and the costumes seen are fascinating. Some of the stores, such as the one at *Ncizele* (the grassy place) sell beadwork, carvings and curios – prices are not exactly cheap but there are many interesting items to examine.

At the mouth of the Qora River lies a fine beach and an oyster bed. The swimming and fishing possibilities are excellent. It was at this place on 14 November 1887, at about 23h45 that the 1 390-ton fully rigged iron ship *Idomene,* bound for London from Rangoon and carrying a full cargo of rice, ran straight into the rocks. The ship was totally wrecked. The captain and 12 of the crew were drowned while 11 men safely reached the beach.

From a botanical point of view it is interesting to note that the Qora River marks the northern limit of the sundu palms. Beyond the river palm trees are absent for some distance before the lala palm appears, being the characteristic plant of the lower Natal coast.

Fishing has yielded some great sport at the mouth of the Qora and the resort situated there takes its name of Kob Inn from the good catches there of that species of fish.

### Accommodation
★ Kob Inn, 40 rooms, 25 with baths. R11 D, out of season. R14 D, in season. Phone Qora Mouth 01.

Resuming the journey from the junction point where the road turns off to Qora Mouth, the main gravel road continues westwards for 1 km and then enters the village of . . .

---

*Overleaf: Rolling green hills, the murmur of voices, the lowing of cattle and the distant thudding of drums in the land of Kaffraria.*

# WILLOWVALE (GATYANA)

With a population of 510, Willowvale receives its name from a number of willow trees which originally grew in the valley behind the old Residency. The local tribespeople know the place as *Gatyana* after a former headman who had his kraal there. The Paramount Chief of the Gcaleka section of the Xhosa tribe has his seat (great place) at Nqadu close to Willowvale.

The tribal history of the Willowvale district is particularly interesting. Bushmen and Hottentots originally inhabited the area, but towards the end of the 17th century they were displaced by the Xhosa who absorbed many characteristics of the Hottentots, including the use of 'clicks' in speech and the amputation of the top joint of the little finger.

In about the year 1750 the Xhosa split into two great sections. The senior section remained in the Willowvale area and became known as the *Gcaleka* after their chief. The second section moved south of the Kei River and were known as the *Rarabe*, also after their own chief.

The first half of the 19th century saw great troubles in the land of the Xhosa. Disturbances in far-off Zululand sent waves of refugees southwards in search of new homes. The Xhosa were themselves restless and inclined to push southwards where they clashed with European settlers, the result of which were the successive Kaffir Wars. Eventually the British were obliged to invade the land of the Gcaleka in 1837 and William Flynn was established as a political agent at the then Xhosa capital of Holela in the Centane district. A long series of brawls took place, forcing the British to apply ever firmer control over the Xhosa people.

In 1856 the disaster concerning the medium Nongqawuse and the cattle killing occurred. Further disturbances caused the British to drive the Gcaleka northwards across the Mbashe River, and to leave their old homeland almost denuded of population. In 1864 their chief, Sarili, was allowed to return to the area with some of his followers. A British officer was stationed with him as consul and 40 000 Fingo tribespeople (Mfengu) were also settled in the area.

Fighting inevitably broke out between the Xhosa and the Fingo. This was the start of the Ninth (and last) Kaffir War in 1877. After several minor clashes, the Xhosa were defeated at the Battle of Centane and the bulk of the Gcaleka were once again driven north of the Mbashe River. In 1878 a police camp was erected on the site of Willowvale and on 2 January 1879 a magistrate, Mr F. N. Streatfield, was appointed. He surveyed the district and was the actual founder of Willowvale which became a village management on 17 July 1933. Since the Gcaleka were allowed to return to their old homeland, the district has been at peace.

Europeans had first arrived in the Willowvale area in about 1839 when the Wesleyan Missionary Society founded a station named *Beecham Wood* after the Reverend John Beecham, the general secretary of the society. This station was abandoned in 1858 when the population was depleted as a result of the cattle killing episode of Nongqawuse. Nothing remains of the station today except the place name.

The Malan Mission was founded in 1876 by Major C. H. Malan, officer commanding the 75th Regiment. He intended it to be an interdenominational mission but it was later taken over by the United Free Church of Scotland. *Fort Malan*, built in 1877, was named after the mission and *Fort Bowker*, built in 1860, was named after Colonel J. H. Bowker. Apart from these places, Europeans made no attempt to settle and the whole Willowvale district remained a tribal reserve.

## Accommodation
Willowvale Hotel, 15 rooms, R4,80 D. Phone Willowvale 31.

Beyond Willowvale the gravel road continues north-eastwards parallel to the Wild Coast, following a meandering, up-and-down route through superb scenery. Initially the road descends to the bottom of the pretty valley of the river known as the *Nqabara* (place of the steep descent). On its banks, under the Mbongo hill, lies the grave of the great chief Hintsa, who was shot in the valley in 1835 when he tried to escape from a British force. A road leads down to the mouth of the Nqabara River and the Dwesa Forestry Station and Nature Reserve, the first reserve to be established in Transkei. It comprises a fine stretch of indigenous forest where various species of antelope have been reintroduced. The walking is excellent and a camp provides accommodation in five log cabins at R6 D, as well as sites for caravans and tents.

The Nqabara River is crossed at a point 28 km from Willowvale. A further 12 km of travelling brings the road to the Mpozolo trading station on the verge of the prodigious valley of the Mbashe River. This is one of the great viewsites of Southern Africa. The Mbashe (also known to Europeans as the Bashee) finds so tortuous a way through the seemingly interminable hills that a portion of its middle course bears the amusing name of Colley Wobbles. Few travellers at this point in their journey fail to pause and admire an outlook that is airy and most serenely beautiful.

The name *Colley Wobbles* originated in 1859. Lieutenant George Pomeroy Colley, a Transkeian Special Magistrate, surveyed the area and upon looking down at the extraordinary meander in the river, remarked to his staff, 'How that river wobbles!'

'Yes, Sir,' said one of his staff. 'In fact, it Colley wobbles!'

Lieutenant Colley eventually attained the rank of General Sir George Colley, and was killed in the Battle of Majuba.

At 45 km from Willowvale, the road bridges the Mbashe River and ascends the northern slopes in a stiff climb. On the summit, 54 km from Willowvale, the road joins the main gravel road stretching from Elliotdale (Xhora) and the main inland road to the mouth of the Mbashe River. The drive down to the coast, 35 km from this junction, crosses fine hill country yielding handsome views of the great river valley and dense coastal forest. Where the road ends, the Mbashe relaxes after its journey in a fine, lazy lagoon bordered by another good beach and a series of rock outcrops which oblige fishermen with vantage points. This assembly is watched over by a 225 000 candlepower lighthouse which stands on a tall steel trestle like a lonely being from another world looking for its fellows who are lost somewhere in space.

**Accommodation**

The Haven, 42 rooms, 4 with baths. R10,50 D, out of season. R13 D, in season. Phone The Haven 01.

The coastal road from the mouth of the Mbashe (35 km long) rejoins the original route from Willowvale which now continues inland. After 4 km a turnoff leads to the mouth of the Qora River and a further 1,2 km brings the road to a turnoff to Mpame and Mqanduli. The road now descends to the floor of the beautiful valley of the Qora River where many fine views may be seen before the ascent to the other side.

At 12,5 km from the junction of the Willowvale road, there is a pleasant camping spot next to the Qora River at the bridge. The surroundings are completely wild and well wooded.

A further 6,4 km brings the road to a turnoff to Mpame. Continuing left (west), after a further 13 km the road reaches the Lutubeni Mission and a junction with the main gravel road leading from Mqanduli and the interior to the coast. It is 30,8 km from the Willowvale junction to this point.

Once the main gravel road is joined (turning right or eastwards), the traveller is conveyed towards the coast through green and pleasant hill country. After 7 km there is a turnoff to the Wilo Forestry Station and a further 11,6 km brings the road to the trading station of Ncwangu-ba, standing in a tall cluster of eucalyptus trees. At this point there is a junction with a turnoff to the right (south-east) stretching over the hills for 19 km to one of the most remarkable coastal scenes in Africa.

# THE HOLE IN THE WALL

This natural feature consists of a huge detached cliff rising up from the sea in the form of a precipitous island at the mouth of a small river known as the Mpako. Through the centre of the cliff the pounding waves have worn a substantial tunnel.

The Hole in the Wall is known to the local Africans as *esiKhaleni* (the place of the sound). The great rollers shoulder their way through the cavern with a rumbling, sullen roar which, in stormy weather, can be heard for a considerable distance. The cavern is regarded with suspicion among the Bomvana tribespeople who inhabit this part of the coast. They are great eaters of shellfish and many a food gatherer, tempted to explore the cavern at low water, has been caught by an unexpected roller and chafed to death on the barnacles.

A local tale tells of a rough and over-intrepid trooper of the old Cape Mounted Rifles who, for a wager of a bottle of whisky, attempted to swim through the cavern. He vanished inside and was never seen again. Numerous people have attempted to climb the 'wall' containing the hole. It is possible but proves no easy exercise. A Bomvana tribesman who watched a party of experienced European mountaineers reach the summit, tried his hand the next day. He climbed to the top, but when he had to get down again, he lost his nerve and sat plaintively hollering for help for the next three days until news of his plight reached a camping party whose members, fortunately for him, could climb.

The name of the *Hole in the Wall* was applied to it in 1823 by Captain Vidal of the *Barracouta* which was one of the ships on an expedition (under Captain W. F. W. Owen R.N.) sent out by the British Admiralty to survey the coast from the mouth of the Keiskamma River to Lourenço Marques. Vidal reported to Owen that 'twice they approached the beautiful but harbourless Kaffir Coast, the first time, within half a mile, at a most interesting spot, where two ponderous black rocks arose from the water's edge, upwards of eighty feet above its surface, exhibiting through one of them the phenomenon of a natural archway, called by us the Hole in the Wall'.

The coast on either side of the Hole in the Wall is precipitous and notorious for the number of ships wrecked there. Divers constantly find odd fragments of many unfortunate vessels, while beads and coins are often discovered in the pools. Among the tribes living along the coast are many descendants of people shipwrecked whose ancestors, of European and Asian descent, mingled with the African population who gave them shelter. One small tribe resident in the vicinity is known as the *abeLungu* (European people) who claim that they originate from these shipwreck survivors.

There is no accommodation available at the Hole in the Wall, although there is a cluster of privately owned seaside shacks. Camping is delightful but there are no facilities.

At the Ncwanguba trading station, where the road branches off to the Hole in the Wall, the main gravel road continues to the coast and after 16,5 km reaches the resort known as . . .

# COFFEE BAY

The origin of the name Coffee Bay is obscure. A local story tells of a ship which was wrecked in 1863, depositing its entire cargo of coffee beans on the beach. Some of the beans are said to have taken root and for several years coffee shrubs tried to grow but eventually gave up the struggle and died, unable to flourish so far from their natural home.

Three small rivers, the *Nenga* (river of the whale), *Bomvu* (red) and *Maphuzi* (place of pumpkins) reach the sea in the area of Coffee Bay and the local tribespeople usually refer to the place as *Tshontini,* the name applied to a dense wood there. Today Coffee Bay is one of the most popular holiday resorts on the Wild Coast. An informal little village is fronted by a superb beach, snugly contained in a setting of green hills. Swimming, fishing, riding, walking and having a thoroughly enjoyable and lazy time are the major occupations. There is a spectacularly situated golf course.

## Accommodation

★ Lagoon Hotel, 40 rooms, 34 with baths. R11 – R14 D, seasonal. Phone Coffee Bay X03.
★ Ocean View Hotel, 38 rooms, 16 with baths. R11 D, out of season. R14 D, in season. Phone Coffee Bay X02.

## Caravans and camping

★ Coffee Bay Caravan Park, 20 sites. R2,25 – R3,50 D, seasonal.

After 3,5 km of travelling on the road from Coffee Bay to the interior, just before the trading station of C. R. Ilott, there is a turnoff north which will take the more venturesome traveller on to the scenic route running parallel to the Wild Coast. This road (rough but passable for the first few kilometres) descends into the valley of the river known as the Umtata or *Mthatha* (the taker) after its destructive and dangerous floods. At 3 km from the turnoff the road reaches a low-level causeway which is impassable when the river is in flood.

Beyond the causeway the road improves and climbs steeply out of the valley. At the summit (5 km from the causeway) a turnoff leads westwards to the Cancibe Hospital. A further 1,5 km brings the road to a junction with the gravel road which stretches to the mouth of the Umtata River from Nqwelini and the interior. This junction is 10 km from the turnoff on the Coffee Bay road. A turnoff eastwards down this road reaches the coast at the mouth of the Umtata River after 7 km where there is a spacious beach, fishing, a cluster of seaside shacks and one hotel.

## Accommodation

★ Anchorage Hotel, 24 rooms. R10,50 room only, seasonal.

Seven kilometres after leaving Umtata Mouth the gravel road passes the junction of the road leading from Coffee Bay. The gravel road continues westwards and soon begins to descend into the well-wooded and most beautiful valley of the river known as the Mdumbi. This is one of the most verdant valleys in Transkei. At 4 km from the junction of the Coffee Bay road, the bridge over the river is reached where the climb back to the summit begins. At the top, the road reaches a junction. The main road continues ahead to Ngqeleni and the interior. The scenic route, signposted 'Presley Bay' and 'Old Bunting', swings off to the right (northwards) providing a fine drive through rugged hill and forest country. After 4,8 km there is a turnoff eastwards to Presley Bay and Lwandile. A further 2 km brings the road to a turnoff leading to the coast at the mouth of the Mtakatye River. The road crosses the Mtakatye River in the midst of a fine valley and after a further 5 km, joins the main gravel road (which is in good condition) stretching from Libode and the interior down to the coast at Hluleka. At the coastal terminus of this road lies the Hluleka Nature Reserve which comprises some delightful beaches, a rich flora and excellent walking while accommodation is provided in fully furnished log cabins at R6 D. Turning westwards (to the left), this road ascends smoothly for a further 22 km (46 km from the junction of the Coffee Bay-Umtata Mouth road), until it reaches the site of the long abandoned mission station of *Buntingville,* founded in 1830 by the Wesleyans and named after the Reverend Dr Jabez Bunting. The mission was removed to New Bunting in 1864 and the site is now known as Old Bunting.

At this point there is a turnoff to the right (eastwards) leading to Tombo and the coast, which passes through some fine scenery. After 6 km of travel along this road, the road divides with the left fork veering off to Tombo. Take the right-hand fork which leads close to the coast and then veers northwards past the turnoff to the pretty Mpande Beach. After 26 km the road reaches the Dutch Reformed Church Mission hospital of *Tsilemele* (the place where help is given), built on a slope in the green valley of the Singangwana River. After a further 16 km the road joins the main gravel Umtata-Port St Johns road. This junction is 42 km from Old Bunting and 88 km from the junction of the Coffee Bay and Umtata Mouth roads.

Turning eastwards down this road, a turnoff is reached after 7 km which follows a very beautiful route for 11 km down the left bank of the river known as the *Mngazi* (place of blood) after tribal battles which took place in its valley in former times. At the mouth of this river lies a spacious lagoon and a fine beach, with a rugged coastline stretching south to the great cliff face known to Europeans as the Brazen Head and to Africans as *Ndluzulu* after the thundering sound of the surf. Bird life is especially rich, abounding with about 130 recorded species. The entire valley of this river is a supreme example of the genius of nature in devising a perfectly balanced landscape of hills, river, forest and seascape. A project for the development of a harbour for Transkei is under way on the southern side of this area at the mouth of the Mngazana River.

## Accommodation

★★ ® Umngazi Bungalows Hotel, 43 rooms and family cottages, 27 with baths. R12 D, out of season. R15 D, in season. Phone Umngazi Mouth 01.

From the turnoff to the mouth of the Mngazi River, the main Umtata-Port St Johns road continues eastwards through superb scenery for 12 km and on reaching the banks of the great river known as the *Mzimvubu* (home of the hippos), comes to a major junction. The left branch veers sharply to the north and crosses the Mzimvubu River by means of the Pondoland Bridge. The right branch (now tarmac) continues straight down the right bank of the river, past wayside kiosks selling fruit, curios, basketwork and carvings, and after 3 km reaches that most delightful little place at the mouth of the river . . .

# PORT ST JOHNS

Known to the Africans as *Mzimvubu,* Port St Johns with its population of 2 600, has one of the most beautiful and scenically spectacular situations imaginable. The Mzimvubu River reaches the sea after cutting its way through a high ridge. This passage, known as the Gates of St Johns, is dominated by two great cliffs of sandstone. On the right (western) bank stands the 378-m Mount Thesiger; on the left (eastern) bank looms Mount Sullivan. Both are thickly covered in indigenous forest and provide the giant 'posts' for the gateway which heralds the river's approach from the interior to the sea.

Port St Johns takes its name from the saint, but the reason for this is obscure. The name does not appear on any of the early Portuguese maps although in 1552 one of their galleons, the *Saint John,* was wrecked 89 km north of Port St Johns at the mouth of the Mthamvuna River. The popular theory is that the site of the disaster was in later years mistakenly thought to have been the mouth of the Mzimvubu and the name applied accordingly. Another theory is that the buttress of Mount Sullivan (on the left bank) resembles a full-length figure of a man, robed and hooded in the same way as the apostles are depicted in biblical paintings. This likeness may be viewed from the right bank on the site of the original harbour works of Port St Johns.

The Portuguese named the Mzimvubu River after Saint Christovão while the first English name of the place was Rosebud Bay. In October 1846 the schooner *Rosebud* became the first vessel known to attempt a passage across the sand bar at the mouth of the river and to open the harbour to trade. Other ships followed and in spite of many of them being wrecked, the river mouth became the accepted port of call for coasters conveying goods for trade with the Pondo and other local tribes.

Notwithstanding the considerable difficulties of transporting goods inland from the mouth of the river, an increasing number of ships visited the harbour. The name of Port St Johns became established and the British Government decided that it was essential to exert control over the area, especially in view of the possibilities of foreign powers landing there and the place being used by gun runners. In July 1878, an agreement by means of which the harbour of Port St Johns was ceded to the British, was made with the chief Nqwiliso, who ruled over the independent Pondo tribe living on the western side of the Mzimvubu River. In August 1878 General Thesiger and Commodore Sullivan arrived at Port St Johns in the *Active* and on 31 August hoisted the British flag at what was known as White's landing place, downstream from the lower ford across the river known as Davis Drift. *Fort Harrison,* a stronghold named after the captain commanding the garrison, was built on the right bank close to the ford and was held by troops until 1882 whereafter the garrison was stationed at the mouth of the river. The site of the fort is about 6 km above the Pondoland Bridge.

The area along the riverbanks was at first administrated as an enclave, known as the St Johns River Territory, with a resident magistrate and harbour master. On 15 September 1884 the territory was annexed to the Cape Colony. The population at the time comprised 110 officers and men of the garrison, 92 European officials and traders with their families, and 106 African servants. A small wooden wharf was built on the right bank of the river where a succession of small craft landed cargoes such as whisky, beads, blankets and trade goods, and carried away maize, ivory, hides and other products of the Pondo.

In the warm, drowsy atmosphere of Port St Johns, the garrison and traders led lives of extreme isolation. Drinking and gambling were the principal pastimes. Some renowned dice games were held beneath a drooping wild fig tree growing near by the wharf. During one of these games a visiting Norwegian ship's captain was obliged to wager parts of his vessel. The bell of his ship, the *Clan Gordon,* is still in use outside the town hall.

The days of the river trade are over. The last coaster, the *Border,* called at the harbour in December 1944, and today the bar across the mouth allows only very light craft to enter the river. The garrison has also long since vanished, but the atmosphere from the picturesque early days remains. Now there are very few visitors to Port St Johns who are not receptive to the relaxed easy-going feeling inherited by the little town from its past.

Port St Johns became a municipality in 1935. The first councillors had the management of an almost dreamlike little place inhabited by a picturesque crowd of individualists, beach-combers and escapers from society. Memories of many of these individuals form part of the amiable story of the town. There was a ragamuffin known as Captain Kettle with his dog Billy Bones. Together, these two roamed the countryside, making a dashing entrance into the town on the odd occasion. On one such occasion, when Port St Johns was *en fête* to receive the Prime Minister, Captain Kettle made his appearance and dressed in his usual rags strolled down the centre of the main street bowing to the crowd, while his mongrel dog trotted proudly at his heels.

The famous wandering hippopotamus, Huberta, arrived in the village in March 1930, and for six months took up residence in the river where, notwithstanding its name of *Mzimvubu* (home of the hippos), none of her kind had been seen for years. She grazed on the gardens in the village, overturned a few boats, caused several upsets and quite a few laughs, and then wandered off southwards to her untimely death.

Relics of old shipwrecks, such as cannon retrieved from the celebrated wreck of the *Grosvenor,* salvaged silver coins and sea-washed beads, may be seen in the town. Gardens and vegetation are luxurious and handsome beaches stretch on either side of Cape Hermes, on which promontory there stands a 5 000 candlepower lighthouse and a radio beacon.

There are many magnificent walks to be taken through the forests, over the hills, and along the coastline. Pathways meander to most of the places and viewsites and picnic spots are scattered along the way. Many of these trails were blazed and also described by one of Port St Johns' characters of former years, the author C. R. Prance, who wrote an interesting little booklet, *Rambling Routes for Hikers,* giving details of the paths. Fishing, swimming, walking, boating and sleeping in the sun, are the activities and inactivities in Port St Johns. The booklet *Highways and By-Ways* by Mrs S. Taylor contains many interesting facts about Port St Johns.

## Accommodation

★★ ® Cape Hermes Hotel, 64 rooms, all with baths. R10,25 – R11,25 D, seasonal. Phone 35.
★ Needles Hotel, 33 rooms, 8 with baths. R8,90 – R9,25 B/B. Phone 11.
★ Winston Hotel, 35 rooms, 4 with baths. R9,50 – R11,50 D, seasonal. Phone 12.

## Caravans and camping

★ ® First Beach (municipal): 1 cottage (6 beds), R1,50 – R2 D per person, seasonal. 1 rondawel (2 beds), R1,50 – R2 D per person, seasonal. 4 bungalows (4 beds), R1,50 – R2 per person, seasonal.
22 caravan sites, minimum of 2 people. 30c – 40c D per person, seasonal.
★★★ ® Second Beach (municipal): 13 rondawels (2 beds), 60c – 80c D per person, seasonal. Minimum of 2 people. 23 bungalows (5 beds), 60c – 80c D per person, seasonal. Minimum of 5 people.
46 caravan and 65 camping sites, 30c – 40c D per person, seasonal.
★★★ ® Second Beach Holiday Resort, 30 Caravan sites, 42 bungalows, rondawels and cottages. R1 – R1,50 D plus 50c D per person, seasonal.
★★ ® Sikiligindi Caravan Park (at Pondoland Bridge), 100 sites. R1 – R1,50 D, plus 25c D per person, seasonal.

From Port St Johns, the main road (3 km upriver) crosses the Mzimvubu by means of the Pondoland Bridge, which, in May 1953, replaced the picturesque but unhurried Camerondale Pontoon. On the left bank of the river the road enters Eastern Pondoland and begins a steep, winding and most beautiful climb out of the valley of the Mzimvubu, where many fine views of the towering Gates of St Johns may be seen.

At the Gemvale Trading Station, 11 km from the bridge, stands a small roadside memorial to the indefatigable Bishop Bransby Keys who was fatally injured there in an accident. At this point a turnoff leads for 10 km to the coast at Seaview and the mouth of the Mntafufu River where there is a cluster of cottages. Gold was once found here and efforts were made by two successive companies to extract the metal. The latter company, floated in 1932 by Eli Tom Ball, a famous Pondolander who ran the store at Gemvale, proved that although gold was present, it occurred in unpayable traces.

Beyond Gemvale, the main road twists and climbs for 13 km in a most picturesque journey through the hills of Eastern Pondoland. It then reaches a turnoff to the coast which ends at Manteku and Bucele. After a further 1,5 km the road arrives at the summit of its climb where it traverses a lovely green rural plateau sprinkled with the white-walled rondawel huts of the tribespeople and patched with dense indigenous forest in the valleys.

A further 16 km (42 km from the Mzimvubu bridge) brings the road to the village and magisterial centre of . . .

# LUSIKISIKI

This pleasant name is derived from the sound of the reeds which rustle in a nearby marsh. Proclaimed a village in 1932, Lusikisiki is now a bustling trading and road transport centre.

A long central street provides an animated spectacle of tribespeople in their national costume doing their shopping or gossiping in the shade of the stores' verandas. The men (often riding into the village on horseback) attend to business at the offices of the government or at the various labour recruiting offices, particularly those of the Witwatersrand mines which are invariably identified by the sign *Kwa Teba* (place of Mr Taberer). The late Mr Taberer was a pioneer of labour recruiting in the territory whose name is immortalised by the organisation which took over his personal activity.

Thirteen kilometres north of the village lies the seat of the Paramount Chief of East Pondoland. This centre, named *Ohwakeni* (the elevated place), is also a scene of considerable activity.

**Accommodation**
★ Royal Hotel, 20 rooms, 7 with baths. R7,50 – R8 D. Phone 29.

## THE LUSIKISIKI DISTRICT

One and a half kilometres south of Lusikisiki, on the main road to Port St Johns, a gravel road branches off eastwards, leading through fascinating and varied scenery to one of the wildest stretches of the famous Wild Coast where features such as the site of the *Grosvenor* wreck and the superb Magwa waterfall can be seen. Fishing on this coast is among the finest in Southern Africa.

Six kilometres along this road a turnoff stretches southwards for 27 km to the coastal resort of Embotyi and to the Magwa Falls. Following this turnoff for 8 km, a second turnoff is reached which leads to the waterfall. This road traverses grassy downland country where large plantations of tea are grown and after 3 km there is another turnoff which leads through these plantations. The traveller is advised always to bear right at any division not signposted as there are several branch roads through the plantation. After 5 km (22,5 km from Lusikisiki) the road ends at the beautiful and dramatic Magwa Falls where the river leaps a sheer 142 m into a narrow gorge below.

The Embotyi road, meanwhile, continues to the coast past the three-step cascade known as Fraser Falls, through a fine primeval forest and terminates on the Wild Coast at the delightful little fishermen's and campers' resort of Embotyi (31 km from Lusikisiki).

The main gravel road continues eastwards from the point where the Embotyi-Magwa road turns off (6 km from Lusikisiki). After 1,5 km a track branches off north-eastwards to the Mateku Mission Station and the 142-m-high Mateku Falls where a stream tumbles headlong into the densely forested valley of the Msikaba River. The Mateku Falls are worth seeing only after rain. The track is poor but a good view is yielded from the Msikaba road.

The main gravel road continues for a further 36 km and ends at South Sand Bluff at the mouth of the Msikaba River where an automatic 2 000 candlepower lighthouse stands. On the left bank of the Msikaba River lie the grounds of the Mkambati Leper Hospital established in 1922 as a sanatorium for those suffering from what is today considered a perfectly curable disease. The area is also worked as an immense cattle ranch. A pathway extends along the coast to groves of carefully protected palm trees belonging to the species *Jubaeopsis caffra* (known to the Pondo as Mkambati), and to several magnificent scenic attractions such as the Waterfall Bluff where a river plunges straight into the sea over a high cliff. The entire coastal area between the Msikaba and Mtentu rivers is being developed as the Mkambati Nature Reserve, the largest nature reserve in Transkei, with accommodation to be provided in log cabins and hiking trails which lead to many lovely places, including Waterfall Bluff.

On its way to the Msikaba River, the main road sends tracks down the coast to several interesting coastal points such as the mouth of the Mkweni River and Kilroe Beach. One of these places is known as Port Grosvenor where, in 1885, an abortive attempt was made to develop a harbour for Eastern Pondoland which would rival Port St Johns, then considered to be the harbour for West Pondoland. The attempt proved disastrous. The East Pondoland chief, Mqikela, gave two identical monopoly concessions to two rival traders, a Captain Turner and a man named Rethman, neither of whom would allow the other to function. Only one ship, the *Sir Evelyn Wood*, called there with a cargo for Captain Turner whereupon Rethman disputed landing rights so effectively that it was forced to sail away.

# THE WRECK OF THE GROSVENOR

The name of *Port Grosvenor* was taken from one of the most celebrated of all shipwrecks. A few kilometres down the coast from Port Grosvenor (the turnoff is 26 km from the turnoff to the Mateku Mission) lies a rocky little bay known as Lwambazi where, on 4 August 1782, the English ship, *Grosvenor,* sailing in from India on a dark night, literally collided head on with Africa. The consequences were dismal. Although only 14 of the 150 people on board were drowned, the survivors experienced severe hardships on land. Having no strong character to bind them together, they split up into groups, each one making its own way in search of shelter and distant Cape Town.

After four months, six sailors managed to reach a frontier farm near the site of modern Port Elizabeth. The news they brought of the disaster prompted the government to send a relief expedition. The party found 12 more survivors but the fate of the rest remains undiscovered. For years rumours persisted that some of them, including several white women, were living with the tribespeople.

In 1790 an expedition set out from the Cape to investigate these rumours. On a tributary of the Mngazi River the expedition found a mixed community comprising about 400 descendants of people of various non-African origin who had been shipwrecked along the coast. Among them were three old white women, apparently English, whose origin was obscure.

The expedition arrived at the site of the wreck of the *Grosvenor* but saw nothing of the ship and no survivors.

Over the years, other travellers journeying along the coast visited the site of the wreck, finding several ship's cannon, ballast and other fragments. Included among these fragments, however, were reported to be gold and silver coins, the result of which was an increasingly eager search for a fortune in bullion (£1 314 710) which was reputed to have been listed on the bill of lading. Rumours persisted that even the fabulous peacock throne of Persia (looted at about this time) was part of the ship's cargo.

A succession of syndicates and companies went bankrupt in their search for the treasure of the *Grosvenor*. These days, on visiting the site of the old disaster, more interest is likely to be found in viewing the wreckage left behind by the various companies than in expecting to see something of the ship itself. The amount of debris is impressive as is the variety and ingenuity of the techniques which have been employed.

The first *Grosvenor* treasure recovery syndicate known was formed in 1883 when a group of spiritualist-hypnotists, guided by a ghost, made an idiotic effort at searching for buried treasure!

Several individuals followed in the hunt including a local trader, Alexander Lindsay, who, in 1896, systematically blasted away rubble and sifted sand to recover a substantial number of coins. Lindsay showed his findings to others and in 1905 he formed the Grosvenor Recovery Syndicate. A steam-driven crane was dragged to the site where it scraped the sea bottom with a heavy chain. Many coins and fragments of the wreck were dragged to the surface by this means, but the company's finance was exhausted without any worthwhile return.

In 1907 Lindsay organised a second venture, the Grosvenor Treasure Recovery Company, and with £10 000 as capital, planned to use a suction dredger and divers to reach the wreck. The dangerous situation of the wreck (close inshore in a rocky little bay, combined with rough seas and the lack of shelter of the Wild Coast) totally defeated the venture which ended in disaster after a diver was drowned when his air hose was severed by a sharp rock.

In 1921 Martin Webster, a Johannesburg mining engineer, floated the Grosvenor Bullion Syndicate Ltd with a capital of £35 000 and a plan of tunnelling under the sea bed, solidifying the sand with liquid cement and boring directly into the hull of the wreck. This involved a substantial mining operation. A diver was employed to examine the sea bottom and he claimed to have located a mound in the floor of the bay large enough to be the wreck buried under the sand. By November 1922 the tunnel had bored 122 m through sandstone, which was easy to work but allowed a dangerous amount of seepage from the sea. At one stage a black mamba took up occupation in the tunnel and refused to budge which delayed work by several days until the reptile could be located and despatched. Then the money ran out, work became desultory and in 1925 the tunnel collapsed. A new tunnel was started and in 1927 a wealthy individual, Theodore Pitcairn, bought out the venture. He allocated £27 000 to a continuance of work, but when the funds were exhausted in 1929, the venture was abandoned.

In 1938 the Grosvenor Salvage Co. Ltd was formed by Gerhardus van Delden. His project was to build a horseshoe shaped breakwater, 396 m in length, around the site of the wreck. The water inside would then be pumped out and the treasure recovered from dry land. £35 000 was needed as capital and work started in January 1939. Rock was blasted from a quarry and carried by a tramway to the two arms of the breakwater which groped out to embrace the bay. The trouble was that the bay had no intention of being embraced. As fast as the breakwater arms were extended, storms simply lashed them to smithereens. By the end of the year the whole venture had collapsed in chaos to the recriminations of shareholders and putting disgruntled employees out of a job.

Next to appear on the scene was F. W. Duckham, whose project was to use a Michigan mobile grab crane to fish up the wreck piecemeal in a steel bucket. The Second World War delayed this venture but in 1946 the Grosvenor Salvage Co. (Duckham) Ltd was floated, a road was built and the crane ordered. When it arrived in South Africa there was insufficient money to pay for it and the venture collapsed.

Duckham then organised the Duckham Marine Salvage Co. (Pty) Ltd. Another crane was ordered but again there was no money to pay for it on its arrival. Investors were now becoming very chary of risking money in the recovery of *Grosvenor* treasure. A few private enthusiasts were left to carry on the search. The idea of the grab crane was abandoned (unfortunately, perhaps for the little steam crane used by Lindsay in his pioneer effort had at least produced some results). Instead, water jets worked at high pressure from a raft were used in an effort to remove the overburden of sand. Frogmen were employed and the Grosvenor Treasure Co. (Pty) Ltd was floated in 1951 to work on the project.

It appeared that three major fragments of the wreck lay beneath water less than 10 m deep but were also buried under about 2 m of sand as well as rubble from the ill-fated breakwaters of Van Delden. A professional diver was employed to work from a small ship, the *Steenbok*. Several cannon and other bric-à-brac were located on the bed of the bay (which is actually a gully). Explosives were used in an attempt to reveal more of the wreck but work was made difficult and dangerous by heavy weather, treacherous currents, turgid water and sharp rocks. In June 1952 the venture was abandoned.

The only items so far recovered from the *Grosvenor* have been cannons (one placed at the Old Fort, Durban; two in the Umtata Museum; one in the park at Port St Johns; one in the grounds of the Royal Hotel, Lusikisiki) and the various gold and silver coins recovered by individual searchers. Sidney Turner, the trader, found enough of these in 1880 to make a bracelet for his daughter, to melt down for a silver cup, and to sell about 3 000 coins to a bank. Alexander Lindsay's steam crane also collected several hundred coins. The remaining cargo still lies at the bottom of that dangerous little gully in the Wild Coast. How much is there, and how best to reach it, no man knows.

## LUSIKISIKI TO NATAL AND KOKSTAD

The main gravel road leads north-westwards out of Lusikisiki and over the seemingly endless hills of Pondoland. After 1,5 km a turnoff stretches eastwards to Ohwakeni (11 km) and the important mission station of Holy Cross (40 km) founded in 1911 by an Anglican missionary, Robert Callaway, and famous for its hospital and the handsome church built in 1925.

Providing a contrast, the extraordinary residence of the renowned herbalist, Mr Khotso, is passed by the main gravel road 3 km beyond the turnoff to the mission. Painted entirely a pale-blue colour, this mansion is known as *Mount Nelson* and reflects the scale on which the late Pondo healer practised.

The main gravel road continues for a further 27 km over the green grassy hills. Thirty-three kilometres from Lusikisiki there is a turnoff on to an interesting 49-km-long scenic drive to the small village of *Tabankulu* (the great mountain). On the way may be seen a spectacular example of a river meander, a great horseshoe bend in the course of the Mzimhlava River. Tabankulu originated in 1894 when two traders, Blenkinsop and Meth, opened a store there. Other traders joined them and in 1909 a village was laid out. Beyond Tabankulu the road joins the main Transkei road.

The main gravel road continues for 11 km beyond the turnoff to Tabankulu along a high ridge sprinkled with myriad huts on either side. After 46 km of travel from Lusikisiki, the road reaches the trading centre and village of . . .

## FLAGSTAFF

This little place had its origin in 1875 when two traders, Z. G. Bowles and G. Owen, secured rights to the area from the Paramount Chief of Eastern Pondoland. They erected a store and did a roaring business, but found it difficult to keep customers away when they closed on Sundays or holidays. Accordingly, the traders erected a flagstaff next to their store on which a white flag was flown on the days when the store was closed. This not only kept customers away, but gave the future village its European name. Today it is a busy trading and road transport centre surrounded by substantial plantations of black wattle trees which grow on the village commonage. Flàgstaff is known to the Africans as *Siphageni*.

At 1,5 km out of Flagstaff, a turnoff leads eastwards to Holy Cross Mission and the Mkambati Leper Hospital (72 km away). Five kilometres beyond the wattle plantation, in a handsome avenue of tall eucalyptus trees, there is a turnoff to *Emfundeswani* (the place of learning), the training school for young men destined for the high office of administration.

The main gravel road continues through fine, rolling, high hill country, with deep wooded ravines. Incessantly rising and falling through this lovely country – one of the most romantically beautiful expanses in Africa – the road (31 km from Flagstaff) reaches an important junction close to the trading station of *Magusheni* (place of sheep), where a large flock of these animals is once said to have perished after being caught in a storm.

From this junction, a tarmac road turns north-westwards and leads for 49 km over high hill country, joining the main Transkei road at the foot of Brooks Hill (see page 396). The second branch turns eastwards and after passing a turnoff (at 19 km) to Harding and Durban, makes its way over a beautiful green pastoral landscape, covered in innumerable rondawel huts, maize fields and herds of cattle. A further 8 km sees a turnoff south to Mtentu and Holy Cross Mission, while another kilometre down a hill slope takes the road into the magisterial village (27 km from the junction at Magusheni) known as *Bizana* (the little pot), after the stream of that name which meanders near by.

From this trading centre, the gravel road continues eastwards over a high undulating plateau covered in green grass, huts, maize and cattle. To the north there are views across the great valley of the Mthamvuna River which marks the boundary of Transkei and Natal. At 16 km from Bizana there is a turnoff which descends steeply into the valley of the Mthamvuna, amid spectacular views. This road crosses the river after 27 km and after climbing out of the valley, traverses some superb hill country and eventually (41 km from Bizana) joins the main Port Shepstone-Harding road at Izingolweni, from where the surface is tarmac to Durban. This route provides a very beautiful alternative to continuing from Bizana directly to the coast. The latter road descends steadily across green hills. The blue sea emerges from the distant haze and, 37 km from the turnoff to Izingolweni (53 km from Bizana) the road crosses the Mthamvuna River by means of a handsome bridge, entering Natal 3 km south of Port Edward (see page 404).

---

## BUTTERWORTH TO IDUTYWA

From Butterworth, the main inland road of Transkei continues north-eastwards over the undulating grassy plateau, surrounded by the rondawel homes of the tribal people, all conservatively the same, with their doorways invariably facing east towards the rising sun. On many of the thatched roofs may be seen small patches of soil supporting a species of succulent plant used as a charm against lightning.

The costumes of the people are particularly striking, especially those of the women. Braided skirts and orange-ochred shoulder cloths are the convention, and although rigid conservatism demands that everybody dress exactly the same, the cumulative effect is extraordinarily charming. The women smoke long-stemmed pipes and wear innumerable metal armlets and turban head cloths. Custom dictates that all items of costume and every colour, bead or decoration have a particular meaning.

Periodically the traveller may see boys dressed in the weird costume of the *Khwetha,* the circumcision lodge of puberty. With their faces and bodies daubed with white clay and strange reed dancing skirts wound around their waists, they provide a touch of ancient magic to a unique landscape.

At 33 km from Butterworth, the road crosses a stream with the singular name of Nqxakaxa and after travelling north-eastwards for a further 2 km, reaches the town on the acacia-covered slopes of the Mputi River called . . .

## IDUTYWA

The name *Idutywa* (place of disorder) originated from a tribal disturbance which occurred in that area during an invasion by raiders from Natal.

The town was laid out in 1884 on the site of a military and police post established in 1858 at what was known as the Idutywa Reserve. It is today a magisterial, railway and trading centre with a population of 2 688. It became a municipality in 1913, with its first mayor, W. E. Warner, holding office for 20 years.

**Accommodation**
★ Idutywa Hotel, 50 rooms, 20 with baths. R6 – R7 B/B. Phone 114.

**Caravans and camping**
Municipal caravan park, free. Simple facilities.

---

From Idutywa a branch road leads south-eastwards for 32 km to the magisterial centre of Willowvale. This little village, with its cluster of stores and hotel, is the point of departure for the popular fishermen's resort at the mouth of the Qora River (see page 379).

---

# IDUTYWA TO VIEDGESVILLE

The main Transkei road continues north-eastwards from Idutywa, steadily climbing out of the acacia-covered valley. At 16 km there is a turnoff west stretching to the pretty little town of *Engcobo* (place of long grass) founded in 1875 by Sir Walter Strandford, Resident Commissioner, as the administrative centre for the Tembu tribe. A further 8 km of travelling along the main Transkei road over the grassy plateau takes the road to the brink of the acacia- and aloe-covered valley of the Mbashe (Bashee) River. The tarmac road winds down for 5 km to the valley floor where the river makes its sultry way towards the sea.

At 28 km from Idutywa the road crosses the river and rises out of the valley for 13 km, passing through the Mtentu Cuttings. Returning to the level of the plain, the road continues across this quaint world of rondavels, ox-drawn sledges, horsemen, and statuesque women in their elegant orange-ochre costumes. After 5 km there is a 31-km turnoff south-east to Elliotdale, known to the Africans as *Xhora*. After a further 17 km (64 km from Idutywa), the road reaches the trading post, railway and road centre of *Viedgesville,* named after a German trader who established his headquarters there.

# VIEDGESVILLE TO THE WILD COAST

From Viedgesville, a road branches eastwards to some of the most popular resorts on the Wild Coast. At 13 km from Viedgesville, this road reaches the small magisterial centre of *Mqanduli* (the dresser of grindstones) where a man once lived who was famous for this skill. The centre comprises a cluster of stores, administrative buildings, garages and a hotel.

At 23 km from Mqanduli lies another small magisterial village originally named *Elliotdale* after Sir Henry Elliot, chief magistrate of the Transkeian territories from 1891 to 1902 and now known as Xhora. It is the administrative centre for the Bomvana tribal area. The village was founded in 1878 and is situated in handsome, rugged hill country. The Bomvana people who live in these parts are a picturesque and amiable crowd: notable tobacco growers and smokers, and inclined to be conservatively primitive. Their tribal name derives from a chief, Bomvu, who ruled over them in about the year 1600. A younger son of this ruler created a tribe of his own and these became known as the *Bomvana* (little Bomvu tribe). The tribe is closely related to the Pondo living further north.

Beyond Elliotdale, a good road leads for 40 km through delightful scenery to the mouth of the Mbashe River where there is a great resort of fishermen at what is known as The Haven, with a superb setting for this sport and fine beaches and forest-clad hills rolling down to the sea (see page 381). A couple of kilometres from Elliotdale along the road to the Mbashe mouth, it is worth turning aside to view the famous Colley Wobbles, the series of involved curves in the Mbashe River, one of the world's most remarkable examples of a river meander (see page 381).

Just outside Mqanduli, on the road to Elliotdale, a turnoff proceeds eastwards for 67 km through delectable downland scenery, and to several interesting spots on the Wild Coast. One of the best known of these is the Hole in the Wall (see page 382).

# VIEDGESVILLE TO UMTATA

From Viedgesville the main Transkei road continues north-eastwards over the undulating coastal plain, where the hill slopes are scattered with rondavel huts almost as numerous as the stars in the milky way. Also prominent are cattle herds and herdboys, sheep and their shepherds; groups of women who balance their water containers so skilfully on their heads that, even if the container happens to be an unglamorous paraffin tin, they still contrive to look graceful and dignified, a feat unmatched by any other race or nation on earth.

At 17 km from Viedgesville the tarmac road commences an easy descent down the southern slopes of the valley of the Mthatha River, approaching (3 km ahead) the town of . . .

# UMTATA

The capital of Transkei, Umtata has a population of 40 000. It is a pleasant hill slope town, the terminus of the railway from the south, and a road junction and communications centre of considerable importance.

The nearby Mthatha River is said to have received its name from the number of *thathe* or sneezewood trees (*Pteroxylon utile*) which flourish along its banks. It supplies the town with a generous amount of water and contains several beauty spots, including a pretty cascade a couple of kilometres downstream. A notably treacherous river when it floods, another theory suggests that the name is derived from the word *thatha* (the taker), owing to the damage and the fatalities through drowning caused by the flooding river.

From early times the Mthatha was regarded as the boundary between the lands of the Tembu and the Pondo tribes. The *Tembu,* who take their name from a chief who ruled over them about the middle of the 16th century, were amongst the earliest people to settle in the Transkeian area. Their origin is rather obscure, but they are generally considered to be part of the Lala offshoot of the great Karanga tribe of Zimbabwe.

Incessant border brawls with the Pondo north of the Mthatha River gave the chiefs of both tribes the idea of creating a buffer strip between them. To this end both the Tembu and Pondo tribes granted farms along the river to Europeans in the 1860s. In 1875 Tembuland was ceded to Great Britain and divided into four magisterial districts. A site about 8 km west of the present Umtata was selected as the seat of one of these magistracies, with Major J. F. Boyes pitching his tent there in 1876.

In 1877 Bishop H. Callaway arrived as the first bishop of the new Anglican Diocese of St Johns, which serviced the Transkeian territory. He acquired one of the Mthatha River farms where he erected his headquarters, including a church, school and hospital, the forerunner of the present substantial Sir Henry Elliott Hospital.

The township of Umtata was laid out in 1879 and grew rapidly. In 1882 the first village management board was elected and on 10 November of the same year it became a municipality.

There is a handsome building in Umtata which seats the *Bunga* or Parliament, and an impressive town hall, built in 1907, stands overlooking a superb garden. Other features are a substantial Anglican cathedral, numerous official buildings, and many pleasant homes in the residential areas. The University of Transkei, founded in 1977, is situated on the southern side of the town.

### Accommodation
★ Grosvenor Hotel, 50 rooms, 13 with baths. R8 – R9 B/B. Phone 4418.
★★ Holiday Inn, 60 rooms, all with baths. R19,50 room only. Phone 2181.
★★ Imperial Hotel, 50 rooms, 11 with baths. R8,65 – R9,50 B/B. Phone 2205.
★★ Royal Hotel, 33 rooms, 2 with baths. R9 – R9,75 B/B. Phone 2231.
★ Savoy Hotel, 59 rooms, 21 with baths. R9,10 – R10,15 B/B. Phone 4403.
★★ Transkei Hotel, 40 rooms, 20 with baths. R7,25 – R14,55 B/B. Phone 4445.

### Caravans and camping
★ Municipal caravan park, 35 sites. R2 D.

---

# PONDOLAND

North of the Mthatha River lies the land of the Pondo, an area of immense scenic variety: precipitous river valleys; the greenest of downland country; lovely patches of indigenous forest; and as rugged a piece of coastline as any fisherman could desire.

Two closely related tribes inhabit this area, the Pondo and the Pondomise. Both had a common origin and were involved in the great migration of people down the east coast from a legendary home in the far north known as eMbo. Tradition has it that Mpondo and Mpondomise were brothers who divided the original tribe in about the year 1500. They formed part of the vanguard of the main migration and their language belongs to the modern Zulu-Xhosa group.

The people of Pondoland dress in a manner similar to their Xhosa and Tembu neighbours, but incorporate a different colour scheme. Pale blue is the dominant colour instead of red-orange. Apparently, white – originally the colour of mourning – was worn after the death of a revered chief, when the mourning period was so protracted that this colour became permanently established. Subsequently, the habit of using blue in washing was adopted from the Europeans and this new shade of clothing became popular as opposed to the less practical white. Nowadays, all gala dress is a pretty shade of pale blue while red-orange is still worn by young boys and girls.

Residences are of the same rondawel type as those built by the Xhosa, and in Pondoland the doorways also face the east, towards the rising sun.

The principal road through Pondoland branches off eastwards at Umtata and leads through some of the most spectacular and fascinating scenery in Africa.

Crossing the Mthatha River (1,5 km from the town) the road proceeds eastwards over hills densely settled by tribal people. At 6 km from Umtata a turnoff to the south-east leads to the village and magistracy with the bleak name of *Ngqeleni* (the cold place). From this point the road continues down to the Wild Coast and fishing and camping resorts such as the mouth of the Mthatha River. Fishing along this coast is particularly good and the mouths of the several small rivers which reach the sea there provide suitable vantage points and pleasant camping sites.

The main road continues past the turnoff to Ngqeleni and (26 km from Umtata) reaches the small magisterial village named after the Pondo chief, *Libode*. From now on the road finds an involved way through spectacular scenery. Steadily losing altitude, the road descends into the valley of the river bearing the sombre name of *Mngazi* (place of blood), where vicious tribal fights of former years took place.

Dominating this great valley (51 km from Umtata) is a gigantic pile of rock, a veritable fortress known as *Mlengani* (the hanging one). Its huge cliffs seem to lean out over the valley, and the atmosphere is one of brooding savagery. This is one of the most memorable of all landmarks about which there are many legends. Europeans like to call it Execution Rock and fancy that some early chief had his victims dragged to the summit from where they were thrown to their deaths. However, on the northern side of the river there is a precipice (also known as Mlengani) which was actually used as a place of execution. The great rock itself can be climbed from its eastern face. Among the legends surrounding it is one in which a circumcision lodge of tribal youths attended their mystic training in seclusion on the summit. A fire swept the grassy top and all of them perished, either by being burned to death or in their attempt to jump to safety.

The road curves around the great rock, yielding superb panoramic views of the valley. The best time to do this journey is in the cooler hours of the late afternoon, when the cliff faces are modelled by the deep shadows of oblique light. The atmosphere of this rugged area is then both wild and romantic, and the colours are varied and deep.

At 81 km from Umtata, at the Tombo trading station, a turnoff stretches for 16 km to the mouths of the Mngazi and other rivers, where fishermen find sport and holidaymakers relax in fine camping grounds. For a further 12 km the main road climbs and twists, with handsome indigenous forest covering the slopes. Running along the right bank of the great river known as the *Mzimvubu* (home of the hippos), the road (95 km from Umtata) reaches a junction. The left branch crosses the river while straight ahead, the road continues along the riverbank for 3 km and then (97 km from Umtata) reaches the small and most picturesquely situated town of Port St Johns (see page 384).

---

## UMTATA TO KOKSTAD

The tarmac main Transkei road leaves Umtata, lying on the banks of the Mthatha River in a great bowl in the hills and climbs over slopes green in summer but sleepily brown in winter. Sheep, cattle, maize and the rondawel huts of the Pondomise tribespeople may be seen on all sides. After 35 km a turnoff west is reached, leading for 4,5 km to the village of *Tsolo* (sharply pointed), so named after a pointed mountain which provides a landmark 23 km away. The village was originally established in 1879 under this mountain, whereafter the first 30 European inhabitants were besieged in the stone prison building for eight days during the Pondomise uprising in 1880. Close to the modern village is the Mbuto School of Agriculture established in 1903.

The main road continues past the turnoff to Tsolo. After 11 km it descends into the densely inhabited valley of the fine, often flooded river known as the *Tsitsa* (the one that spouts out). A magnificent 125-m-high waterfall occurs in this river downstream from the bridge and is reached from the road which branches off down the left bank to the *Shawbury Mission* (15 km) founded by the Wesleyans in 1839 and named after the mission benefactor, William Shaw. The waterfall is especially worth seeing during the flood time. A guide should be obtained from the mission station, if only to control numerous urchins who volunteer their services and can be a nuisance. The track continues for a rough 2 km and then there is a walk of another kilometre to a handsome viewsite. Afternoon light is best for photography.

From the bridge across the Tsitsa, the main road climbs out of the valley over undulating grassy slopes. Traversing a densely populated area, the road (57 km from Umtata) descends a slope after 10 km and passes through the small village of *Qumbu* (place of budding or bursting), with its avenue of jacarandas.

Continuing over undulating, grassy hills, the main road proceeds from Qumbu for 11 km and then descends into the badly eroded valley of the river known as the *Tina* (said to be named because of the otters there). With its complex meanders, this river provides some interesting scenery as the road climbs its left bank. At 27 km from the river (39 km from Qumbu) the road descends steeply and passes through the village of *Mount Frere* and its long street of commercial buildings, situated on the hill slope. Founded in 1876 as a magisterial centre for the Bhaca tribe, the village was named after Sir Bartle Frere, the Governor of the Cape. The Africans know it as *kwaBhaca* (the place of the Bhaca).

The main road continues through the village and descends steadily over 10 km of attractive countryside into the valley of the river known as the *Mzimvubu* (home of the hippos) which has its spectacular mouth at Port St Johns. There is a pleasant picnic site at the bridge across the river.

The main road climbs out of the valley over 11 km of rugged country, then leads along a high ridge from where fine views may be seen to the north of deep valleys, mountains and a regular milky way of the white-painted rondawels of the Bhaca tribespeople.

The impressive Insiswa Mountains, with their periodically worked copper deposits and patches of forest, dominate the road to the north. Many streams tumble down the slopes in waterfalls and cascades during the summer rainy season. Passing (at 33 km from Mount

Frere) the turnoff to Tabankulu (see page 390), and the Insiswa Forest Reserve (1,5 km further on), the road descends to the crossing of the river known as the *Mzimhlava* (home of the *mhlava*, the mealie grub parasite of maize) at the foot of the mountain range. At 6 km beyond the river (41 km from Mount Frere), the road passes *Mount Ayliff*, a cluster of houses, trees and stores sheltering at the foot of a high ridge. The place was named after William Ayliff, Secretary for Native Affairs in the Cape Government who visited the area in 1878 and accepted the local Xesibe tribe as subjects of the Cape. The diminutive village grew as the administrative centre for this tribe and is known to the Africans as *Maxesibeni*.

Beyond Mount Ayliff, the road continues up the valley of the Emvalwini stream, densely populated by the Xesibe tribespeople, with high hills towering on either side of the road. At 19 km from Mount Ayliff there is a gravel turnoff to Bizana (39 km) and Port Edward (119 km).

The main road now commences a steady climb up the slopes of Nolangeni, the 2 013-m-high mountain which dominates the area. After 6 km of climbing, the road reaches a point 1 610 m high at *Brooks Nek* where L. M. Brooks once had a trading station. From this point the road starts to descend, passing (after 6 km) the turnoff to Pietermaritzburg and the south coast of Natal and then, after a further 3 km (35 km from Mount Ayliff), entering the town of Kokstad (page 460).

Chapter Twenty

# THE SOUTH COAST OF NATAL

The great eastern coastal highway of Southern Africa, Settlers Way from Cape Town and the main highway of Transkei, descends the northern side of Brooks Nek over the often snow-covered heights of Nolangeni Mountain and reaches a turnoff leading for 4 km to the town of Kokstad (page 460). Beyond this turnoff the main tarmac road stretches north-eastwards across an undulating grassland dominated to the north by the bulk of Mount Currie.

After 21 km the road reaches the mountains known as *Ingeli* on account of their fragmented, precipitous nature. Amid slopes and ravines blanketed with fine patches of indigenous trees, the road passes through the Langerwacht and Ingeli forests, crossing and recrossing the Natal border which lies along the summit ridge of the range. At 29,5 km the road reaches the Ingeli Motel and a turnoff to the government forestry settlement of . . .

## WEZA

This centre, whose name means a fording place, is one of the largest forestry plantations in Natal. The plantation was started in 1923 as a labour settlement, mainly for people who had been involved in the Rand riots of the previous year.

Additional people were settled there during the period of the depression of the 1930s. With the return of better economic times, the majority of settlers rehabilitated themselves and wandered off to more rewarding fields of employment. The original corrugated iron buildings erected to house the first settlers remained and during the Second World War, Weza became a prisoner-of-war camp for Italians captured in North Africa.

A timber sawmill had been built in 1939 and when the main plantations began to reach maturity, this small mill was replaced in 1953 by what was then the largest mill in South Africa.

**Accommodation**
★★ Ingeli Forest Motel, 34 rooms, all with baths. R11 B/B. Phone Ingeli 2.

At 8 km beyond the turnoff to Weza (37,5 km from the Kokstad turnoff) the road reaches a major division. One branch leads on to Umzimkulu and Pietermaritzburg (see page 450), while the second branch swings south-eastwards through superb forest country and, descending gently, passes a second turnoff to Weza (after 13 km), and at 52,5 km from the Kokstad turnoff, reaches the town of . . .

## HARDING

This little place was established in 1813 as a magisterial and police post on the rather unruly frontier between Natal and Griqualand East. Named after Walter Harding, the Natal Supreme Court Judge, it became the capital of the district of Alfred, replacing the earlier centre of Murchison. The area is inhabited by a number of tribes of diverse origin such as the Mau and the Jali who derive from the Pondo; the Cele, Nhlangwini and Nyuswa who are of Zulu origin; and one mixed tribe, the Nkumbini, founded by the British ivory trader Frank Fynn and still ruled by one of his descendants, Wilson Fynn.

*Overleaf: Overlooked by the hanging rock, the Mzimkhulu River forces its way through the rocks and rapids of a mighty gorge.*

For a lengthy period, the border area was a no-man's-land of gun runners, smugglers and a retreat for a number of shady characters. In this setting Harding grew into an atmospheric little town, becoming a municipality in 1911. The population has now reached 3 380. At first very remote, Harding was eventually connected to the outside world by means of a modern road and subsequently a narrow-gauge railway from Port Shepstone, opened in 1917. The considerable timber exports of the district are transported by this railway.

The complex nature of the countryside around Harding is aptly demonstrated by the narrow-gauge railway. The road from Harding to Port Shepstone is 77 km long. To complete the same journey, the narrow-gauge railway follows a circuitous 95-km-long route which winds, climbs, and descends, giving the little puffers a very hard time. What with stops, starts, hesitations, reversals, shuntings, heavings and squealing of brakes, the procedure resembles the lovelife of a nervous spinster.

The trains take 14 hours to make the journey. Railways enthusiasts would find a travel experience such as this fascinating, if only to discover what happens to the train during its lengthy trip. An outing at night, particularly, seems like a venture into complete darkness. The puffer is completely masculine: a bundle of pipes exuding hot air (amid various grunts, steams, pants, gasps, blowoffs, swear words when one of the crew puts his hand on a hot pipe), and peculiar smells, all of which comprise the body odour of a living, mechanical creature working very hard for its living of coal, water and a spot of grease. It moans and complains incessantly, sizzling at other engines when it meets them at crossing points; it rattles merrily downhill, groans at the gradients and zips along the straights, squealing around curves like a small boy pretending to go fast. In the darkness, the headlight illuminates only two fragile-looking rails which stretch ahead into a void so inky that it seems as though the puffer has taken a wrong turning and has abandoned the world around the previous bend.

**Accommodation**
★ Southern Cross Hotel, 10 rooms, 7 with baths. R9 – R10 B/B. Phone 70.

**Caravans and camping**
Municipal caravan park (in town hall garden), 6 sites. Free water and toilets.

From Harding the main tarmac road continues, descending towards the coast through a seemingly interminable jumble of hills. At 35 km there is a turnoff to Gundrift and after a further 5 km, a turnoff to the farming area of the Oribi Flats. Passing the trading centre of *Izingolweni* (place of wild cats), founded in 1870 as a halfway point and police post between Harding and Port Shepstone, the road continues its winding descent. There is a turnoff to Port Edward 1 km beyond Izingolweni (39 km from Harding) and at 53 km the road passes the trading centre of Paddock. At 4,5 km beyond this little place there is a loop road turnoff to the Oribi Gorge Nature Reserve, with the second leg of the loop to the gorge being reached after a further 4,5 km. Beyond this point the road descends rapidly for 12 km past many smallholdings and shacks before reaching Port Shepstone, 77 km from Harding.

## THE ORIBI GORGE AND NATURE RESERVE

The loop road to this reserve provides a magnificent scenic spectacle. From the turnoff on the Harding road 12 km from Port Shepstone, the tarmac road leads through a densely settled tribal area. Hugging the edge of the escarpment, the road reveals fine views of the valleys of the Mzimkhulu River and its tributary, the *Mzimkhulwana* (little Mzimkhulu).

At 16 km from Port Shepstone the road commences a steep descent into the valley of the Mzimkhulwana River which forms the lower end of the Oribi Gorge. Scenically splendid, the slopes of this ravine are covered in a dense indigenous forest.

At the end of the descent, 21 km from Port Shepstone, the road crosses the river near the ruins of the buildings formerly occupied by the Umzimkhulu Lime Company, now removed to another quarry site. The road climbs steeply to the heights dominating the left (north) side of the river. The summit is a plateau known as the Oribi Flats, consisting of a tongue of high land between the deep valleys of the converging Mzimkhulu and Mzimkhulwana rivers. On the edges of this tongue of land are a series of wonderful sites from which to view the two valleys.

Once on the summit (24 km from Port Shepstone), the road reaches a turnoff to the Oribi Gorge Hotel, in whose grounds lie most of the viewsites for the Oribi Gorge. The hotel stands 1,5 km from the turnoff and for an entrance fee of R1, visitors are allowed to follow a private road leading to oft-photographed scenes such as Baboon's Castle, Lehr Falls, Horseshoe Bend and The Heads, all of which are worth seeing. The Fairacres Estate, in which the hotel stands, is a green and pleasant natural parkland where there are many fine trees, wild flowers, and exotics such as flamboyants, bougainvillaea and the 'yesterday, today and tomorrow' flowers which are at their best in spring. There are many picnic spots.

## Accommodation
★ Oribi Gorge Hotel, 13 rooms, 8 with baths. R6 – R7 B/B. Phone Paddock 753.

Beyond the turnoff to the hotel, the main road, now gravel, continues westwards over the grassy Oribi Flats, with fields of sugar cane and plantations of trees stretching on both sides. After 3,5 km there is an unmarked turnoff to the right leading for 0,5 km to one of the most impressive views of Southern Africa. The track is rough but at its end lies the Hanging Rock, projecting over the edge of the precipice of the Mzimkhulu River. The gorge is immense and the great river provides a fine spectacle as it rushes through rocky rapids far below.

From the turnoff to the Hanging Rock, the main gravel road continues westwards over the Oribi Flats. After 3 km there is a junction: straight ahead, the road continues over the Oribi Flats to rejoin the main Harding road at Izingolweni (29 km); turning left (south) the scenic road commences a descent through an exquisite indigenous forest into the gorge of the Mzimkhulwana River where the road enters the Oribi Gorge Nature Reserve. At a point 37 km from Port Shepstone the road crosses the river and then starts to climb the southern side of the gorge. After 3 km of climbing, the road passes the entrance to the tourist camp and rangers' quarters, all built on a handsome viewsite.

The Oribi Gorge Nature Reserve, 4 461 ha in extent, was proclaimed in 1950 and to the delight of botanists, ornithologists and walkers, conserves a large portion of the great gorge of the Mzimkhulwana River. Towering sandstone cliffs – red-orange in colour – dominate a gorge choked with a tangle of trees, flowering plants and ferns. Baboons and leopards find a home on the faces of the precipice. Duikers, bushbuck, oribi, monkeys and a variety of wild cats roam through the forest while many beautiful birds rest in the branches of trees.

## Accommodation
6 squaredawels with central kitchen, ablution block and lounge. R4 D per person.

Immediately beyond the entrance to the camp, 40 km from Port Shepstone via the scenic drive, the road joins the main tarmac Harding road at a point 24 km from Port Shepstone. The entire 64 km provides a superb circular drive.

# PORT SHEPSTONE

The terminus of the South Coast Railway from Durban and the narrow-gauge railway to Harding, Port Shepstone is also the principal administrative, commercial, educational and transport centre on this portion of the Natal coast.

The town has experienced a romantic history. The presence of marble on the north bank of the broad Mzimkhulu River a few kilometres from its mouth, attracted attention in the 1860s and a sprinkling of settlers made their homes in the area. Among them were several men of enterprise; it was the Aiken family and William Bazley who endeavoured to open the river mouth for shipping. Bazley was an engineer whose labours made it practical for the first coaster to enter the river on 8 May 1880, and to anchor at what had been named *Port Shepstone,* in honour of the famed native administrator of Natal, Sir Theophilus Shepstone.

From then on, a regular shipping service linked Port Shepstone to Durban: sugar, lime and marble blocks were shipped out and a great variety of goods were brought in for local trade. Harbour facilities were built and a town was laid out in 1882. In that year a party of 246 Norwegian immigrants landed at the place which has since then, benefited from a substantial community of these hardworking people. A charming little church on the outskirts of Port Shepstone continues to serve as a centre for those of Norwegian descent.

With the opening of the railway from Durban in 1901, Port Shepstone harbour fell into disuse but the importance of the town as a distributing centre continued and it became a municipality in 1934. The population has now reached 3 500. The river remains one of the handsomest rivers in Southern Africa, although sadly it has silted up in modern times. A 27 000 candlepower lighthouse keeps watch over the entrance and serves as a beacon to passing ships.

The attractions of Port Shepstone as a holiday resort, apart from the river, are: a beautifully situated 18-hole golf course; varied coastal and river mouth fishing; a tidal swimming pool and sandy beach; and superb scenery inland. Industrially, substantial amounts of sugar are produced through the mill of the Umzimkhulu Sugar Company as well as timber and lime. Subtropical fruits such as litchis, bananas, pawpaws and avocado pears are grown.

## Accommodation
★★ Bedford Inn, 11 rooms, all with baths. R12 B/B. Phone 2-1085.
★ Marine Hotel, 12 rooms, 8 with baths. R6,44 – R6,94 B/B. Phone 2-0281.
★ Milton Hotel, 27 rooms, 12 with baths. R7,50 – R8,50 B/B. Phone 2-1396.
★ Port Shepstone Hotel, 21 rooms, all with baths. R8,50 B/B. Phone 2-1378.

## Caravans and camping
★ Municipal caravan park, 24 sites. R2 D.

# THE LOWER SOUTH COAST OF NATAL

The Mzimkhulu River, reaching the sea at Port Shepstone, marks the division between the South Coast and the Lower South Coast of Natal. From this point a subtle change occurs; the climate south of the river is more temperate, the humidity far less in summer, there is less coastal forest and green, grassy plains predominate. A succession of sandy bays, rocky promontories and river lagoons provide the setting where a great deal of enjoyment may be had from living and holidaying in the sunshine.

From Port Shepstone, the tarmac road leads south-westwards down the coast past a succession of cottages and resorts, and crosses a number of rivers, the first of which is reached 1,5 km from Port Shepstone. This is the *Mbango* (disputed) River, a boundary line of past squabbles between rival tribes. At 5 km from Port Shepstone, the road crosses the *Boboyi* River, named after a type of grass growing on its banks. After 1,5 km the road reaches the *Izotsha* River, where the Zotsha clan once lived.

The perky little narrow-gauge railway from Port Shepstone to Harding has so far kept the road company, but at a point known as Shelly Beach, it now turns inland, crosses the road and vanishes into the hills.

## Accommodation

★ Dawn View Hotel (Shelly Beach), 16 rooms, all with baths. R8,50 B/B. Phone Port Shepstone 4841.

## Caravans and camping

★★★★® Karapark (Shelly Beach), 235 sites. R4,75 – R6 D plus 50c D per person.

The road continues close to the coast from Shelly Beach, over a green terrace of grass and lala palms. At 11 km from Port Shepstone, the road crosses the *Mhlangeni* (place of reeds) River, and enters the municipal area of the resort of . . .

# UVONGO

This little town takes its name from the river known as *iVungu,* itself named on account of the onomatopoeic sound of the wind and the waterfall murmuring through the gorge. The river reaches the sea after tumbling 23 m over a pretty waterfall into a lagoon, where a compact little beach is situated on the seaward side. Features such as wild bananas and trees clinging to the overlooking precipice face combine with the whole to form a delectable miniature resort.

The municipal area consists of three coastal resorts: St Michaels-on-Sea, on the right bank of the Mhlangeni River; Uvongo Beach 3 km further south, the commercial centre and resort at the mount of the Vungu River; and Manaba Beach, 1,5 km further south, aptly named after a Zulu word indicating a place of much ease and relaxation. The three resorts combined in October 1954 to form a pleasant holiday town which possesses a considerable variety of attractions: boating and swimming in the rivers; bathing beaches at St Michaels-on-Sea and Uvongo Beach protected from sharks; three tidal swimming pools; and interesting fishing from vantage points such as Shad Bay at Manaba Beach, Beacon Rocks and Orange Rocks at Uvongo Beach, and the Point at St Michaels-on-Sea. The scenic setting is a green coastal terrace covered in a lala palm parkland. *Uvongo Beach,* originally the farm of the great fisherman, T.G. Lilliecrona, was fortunate in being thoughtfully laid out by an owner who was also a professional surveyor. Consequently it is one of the prettiest coastal resorts. The Thure Lilliecrona Park on the banks of the Vungu River commemorates this owner.

## Accommodation

★★ Golf Course Hotel (St Michaels-on-Sea), 48 rooms, 40 with baths. R11,50 D/B/B. Phone Margate 5-1230.
★★ La Crete Hotel (Uvongo Beach), 103 rooms, all with baths. R12,50 – R19,50 B/B. Phone 5-1301.

## Caravans and camping

★★ Blue Seas Caravan Park, 58 sites. R2,50 – R4,50 D plus 50c D per person.
★★★★ Kingfisher Caravan Park (St Michaels-on-Sea), 44 sites. R5 D plus 50c D per person.
★★ Oasis Caravan Park (Uvongo Beach), 30 sites. R7,50 D plus R1 D per person.
★★ Surf Bay Caravan Park (St Michaels-on-Sea), 44 sites. R2,50 – R5 D plus 50c D per person.
★★ Uvongo Beach Caravan Park, 42 sites. R5 D plus 75c D per person.
★★ Uvongo River Caravan Park, 32 sites. R5 D plus 50c D per person.

Beyond Uvongo (19 km from Port Shepstone), the tarmac main road immediately crosses into the municipal area of . . .

# MARGATE

The popularity of Margate as a holiday resort among Transvaal and Zimbabwean visitors is so immense, that it has occasionally been described as the seaside suburb of Johannesburg. It is a bright and cheerful place, particularly favoured by young people who like plenty of organised entertainment.

Margate is built around a fine, sandy beach where there is a pretty swimming pool for children and shark-protected sea swimming, as well as a tidal swimming pool, a fishing pier and numerous other vantage points for anglers, pleasant walks up and down the coast, and a small lagoon for canoeing at the mouth of the river known as *iNkhongweni* (the place of entreatment). This name stems from an old legend that the tribal people living there were so mean that travellers had to entreat them for hospitality. Things have changed in Margate since those churlish times!

*Margate* was originally a coastal farm owned by Hugh Balance. In 1919 he began to develop the farm as a resort and after a slow start, the place received international publicity in 1922 when a so-called sea monster was washed up on the beach. The controversy surrounding the nature of this creature created considerable attention which resulted in the charms of Margate being publicised at the same time. In 1948 Margate became a municipality and today 12 126 people live there. In April 1973 a modern airport was opened in the town.

## Accommodation
* Faerie Glen Hotel, 31 rooms, all with baths. R8,50 D/B/B. Phone 2-1280.
* Lucien Hotel, 50 rooms, all with baths. R8,50 – R12 D/B/B. Phone 2-1423.
** Margate Hotel, 60 rooms, 42 with baths. R10 – R13 B/B. Phone 2-1410.
** Marina Hotel, 42 rooms, 37 with baths. R11,50 – R13 D/B/B. Phone 2-0990.
* Palm Beach Hotel, 55 rooms, 15 with baths. R7,50 – R10 B/B. Phone 2-1512.
* Regent Hotel, 32 rooms, 17 with baths. R5 – R7,50 B/B. Phone 2-1320.
* Sunlawns Hotel, 33 rooms, 13 with baths. R6,50 – R8 B/B. Phone 2-0091.

## Caravans and camping
* Constantia Caravan Park, 50 sites. R2 – R6 D plus 30c – 60c D per person, seasonal.
** De Wets Caravan Park, 60 sites. R4,50 D plus 75c D per person.
** Margate Caravan Park, 75 sites. R2,50 D plus 30c D per person and R6,50 D plus 75c D per person, seasonal.

From Margate, the main tarmac coast road continues south, following its scenic marine route. After 5 km (24 km from Port Shepstone) it reaches the holiday town of . . .

# RAMSGATE

This resort was originally a coastal farm situated at the mouth of the river known as the *Bilanhlola* (marvellous boiler) because some of its pools appear to bubble and boil as if by magic.

In 1922 a wandering painter and violin maker named Paul Buck discovered the beauty of the area and settled on the right bank of what he called 'Blue Lagoon'. The romantic home of the amiable Paul Buck was soon unearthed by journalists and writers whose accounts of his carefree way of life and the delightful setting of his self-built home, attracted the attention of many others. A holiday resort grew up around the lagoon and despite its rather stodgy name of Ramsgate, it remains a colourful and sunny little place on the coast of lala palms.

The art gallery attached to the Teahouse of the Blue Lagoon is worth a visit. There is boating on the lagoon and river, and protected sea bathing; fishermen's vantage points such as Little

Billy and Blue Bay are numerous. Together with a fine sandy beach, these are the assets of a resort town whose sole industry is the enjoyment of living.

## Accommodation
★ Bilton Hotel, 30 rooms, 27 with baths. R7,50 – R10 B/B. Phone 4305.
★★ Crayfish Inn, 19 rooms, all with baths. R10,50 – R14,50 D/B/B. Phone Margate 4410.

From Ramsgate, the main coastal tarmac road continues southwards, crossing the Little Bilanhlola River, closely following the shoreline for 3 km and then sweeping more inland. After 5 km the road crosses the river with the name (of which there are various corruptions) of *Mbizana* (the place of little pots), so called on account of the small potholes in its rocky bed. At 1,5 km beyond the river there is a turnoff to the resort of . . .

# SOUTHBROOM

Established by Alfred Eyles on a farm which he named after his family home in Wiltshire, *Southbroom* has a pleasant beach with a shark-protected bathing area, several fishing vantage points and a sheltered lagoon at the mouth of the Mkobi River. There is also a spacious area for aquaplaning, two tidal pools and an 18-hole golf course.

## Accommodation
★ Golf Course Hotel, 35 rooms, 11 with baths. R9,50 – R10,50 B/B. Phone 6004.

## Caravans and camping
★★ Belle Vista Caravan Park, 140 sites. R2,50 – R4 D plus 50c D per person, seasonal.
★★ Ooteekalia Caravan Park, 27 sites. R5 D plus 60c D per person.
★★★ Paradise Caravan Park, 150 sites. R1,95 D plus 50c D per person.

Beyond the turnoff to Southbroom, the main South Coast road proceeds southwards over an undulating mass of hills, well covered in trees and lala palms. After 2 km (34 km from Port Shepstone) there is a turnoff to the resort of . . . .

# MARINA BEACH

This is one of the most spacious beaches in Natal where there is shark-protected bathing, a tidal swimming pool and a lagoon in the mouth of the river known as the *Mhlangakhulu* (place of big reeds).

## Accommodation
★Marina Beach Hotel, 32 rooms, 16 with baths. R6,50 B/B. Phone 3795.

## Caravans and camping
★ Sherwood Forest Caravan Park, 100 sites. R6,50 – R7,50 D plus 50c D per person, seasonal.

The main road continues beyond the turnoff to Marina Beach over undulating coastal hills covered in sugar cane, banana plantations, pawpaws, lala palms and patches of bush. During the next 20 km, the road passes a number of turnoffs to coastal resorts. At 1,5 km there is a turnoff to the private township of San Lameer; at 3 km a turnoff to Trafalgar; and at 5,5 km, to Palm Beach, lying just south of the river known as the *Mpenjati* after the reedy species of grass growing on its banks.

The coastal resorts of Munster and Portobello lie 10 km from Marina Beach with Glenmore and Ivy Beach immediately to the south. *Munster* was named by an Irish surveyor after his home town and lies in a particularly verdant setting with safe bathing and interesting fishing possibilities. The Von Baumbachs and the Stoppels, two German missionary families, were the earliest European settlers in the area.

On 24 January 1933, Glenmore Beach was the scene of the wreck of the 150-ton fishing trawler *Nightingale*. The vessel was totally lost but the crew were all saved. The anchor, rudder and propeller are displayed on the lawn in front of the Kinderstrand Building at Glenmore Beach.

A more celebrated wreck was that of the *Ivy* which occurred at Ivy Beach on 22 March 1878. The ship was a barque of 287 tons carrying a full cargo of liquor from London to Durban. The ship became securely wedged on a tongue of rock about 60 m from land and was left high and dry at low tide. The lower south coast of Natal, in those days, was not very populated but every individual (and there were some wild ones) in the area, rushed to the scene. A lengthy party commenced which still rates as the most hectic ever held on the coast, with several individuals developing delirium tremens. The anchor of the *Ivy* may be seen at the holiday resort run by the Transvaal Teachers' Association (the T.O. Strand) which fronts on to Ivy Beach.

## Accommodation
★ Glenmore Beach Hotel, 23 rooms, 16 with baths. R7,50 – R9 B/B. Phone V. Strand 612.

## Caravans and camping
★★★ Greenheart Caravan Park (Palm Beach), 43 sites. R5 – R7 D.
★★ Leisure View Caravan Park (Glenmore Beach), 100 sites. R3,50 D plus 50c D per person.
★★ Mittenwald Caravan Park (Munster), 70 sites. R4 D plus 50c D per person.
★★ Port o' Call Caravan Park (Trafalgar), 90 sites. R4,50 – R8,50 D plus 50c D per person.
★★ T.O. Strand Caravan Park (Ivy Beach), 130 sites. R2,50 D plus 50c D per person.

After the turnoffs to these various coastal resorts, the main road continues across a green parkland. At 21 km from Marina Beach there is a turnoff to . . . .

# PORT EDWARD

This little place (with a population of 800), had its start when T.K. Pringle acquired the area and named it Banner Rest, for it was there that he intended to 'strike the banner' and retire. He laid out a township on the coast and named it *Port Edward* in honour of the then Prince of Wales.

Port Edward has a pleasant beach overlooked by what is known to Europeans as Tragedy Hill, and to the tribespeople as *isaNdlundlu* (that which is shaped like a hut). The 'tragedy' occurred in 1831 when a Zulu raiding band cornered on the hill a refugee party of Langeni tribespeople and some of the followers of Frank Fynn. They were all killed and up until recent times, their bones still covered the hill.

## Accommodation
★ Port Edward Hotel, 16 rooms, all with baths. R7,50 B/B. Phone 828.

## Caravans and camping
★★® S.A. Police Holiday Resort, 41 sites. R4 D. 143 cottages, R2,50 – R10 D.

The road to Port Edward turns off at a crossroads, with the right-hand (west) turnoff leading to the Banner Rest store and then inland for 35 km to Izingolweni, or branching off for 3 km down to the banks of the Mthamvuna River, the frontier with Transkei. The road ends at the site of the original pont which for years was the only means of crossing the river and which provided a most picturesque scene on the coastal road to the Cape.

The ferry service started in 1935 when the storekeeper of Banner Rest launched a boat on the river in order to attract customers from the areas south of the river. The name *Mthamvuna* (the reaper of mouthfuls) was given to this river on account of the damage done to crops by its floodwaters. It is a beautiful river, flowing through fine scenery and its water is to a large extent, still unpolluted and unsilted. Many legends have been attached to it: its pools are said to be inhabited by water spirits, mermen and mermaids; evil people are said to be swept out to sea if they do not confess their sins before attempting to cross the river.

In 1943 a proper vehicular ferry service was commenced about 1 km above the mouth of the river. This position was found to be unsuitable and the ferry was moved to its final position at the site of the present caravan park where it worked until 1959 when it was swept out to sea during a violent flood. A new pont was introduced and this continued in service until 1967 when the handsome Mitchell Bridge was opened nearer to the mouth of the river.

At the peak of its activity, the pont carried an average of 4 720 vehicles and 60 000 passengers across the river each month. Many travellers still remember with pleasure when their journey was broken by the picturesque pont being hauled across the river on a thick rope pulled by a crew of singing men.

**Caravans and camping**
★® Pont Caravan Park, 50 sites. R3 D.

Beyond the crossroads leading to Port Edward and the pont site, the main road continues down the coast, passing through an extraordinary deposit of deep-red coloured sands. After 3,5 km (55 km from Port Shepstone) the road reaches the end of Natal on the banks of the Mthamvuna River. Crossing the C.H. Mitchell Bridge, the road continues into Transkei, degenerating from tarmac to a gravel surface, reaching Bizana after 53 km and eventually, after 116, km, joining the main Cape Town-Transkei-Natal road.

# PORT SHEPSTONE TO DURBAN

From Port Shepstone, the main tarmac road crosses the Mzimkhulu River by means of a bridge spanning the mouth. Now badly silted, the river still ranks as the largest to reach the sea on the South Coast of Natal and fully justifies its name which means 'the great home of all rivers'. It marks the boundary between the Lower South Coast of Natal and the South Coast, sometimes known as the Strelitzia Coast, on account of the number of wild banana plants of that family which grow there.

Two kilometres after crossing the bridge the road reaches a turnoff to the coastal resort of . .

# UMTENTWENI

A relaxed little resort town, *Umtentweni* receives its name from the river which, in turn, is named after the spiky mtentweni grass which grows on its banks.

As its assets, this town of 2 389 people has the handsome river, a lagoon and a pretty, sandy beach with fishermen's vantage points such as Shaka's Rock, Splash Rock and Shad Alley. For swimming, there is a tidal pool and bathing area protected from sharks, while a balmy climate and an agreeable environment complete the list of attractions for retired people as well as those in search of a peaceful and easygoing holiday.

## Accommodation

★ Umtentweni Hotel, 24 rooms, 11 with baths. R5,75 – R6,75 B/B. Phone Port Shepstone 5-1138.

★ Venture Inn, 23 rooms, all with baths. R7,75 B/B. Phone Port Shepstone 5-0110.

## Caravans and camping

★★ Umtentweni Caravan Park, 34 sites. R5 D plus 50c D per person.

North of Umtentweni the main road twists through green hills, descending and climbing a succession of valleys of rivers such as the *Mhlangakhulu* (river of big reeds); the *Dombe* (a species of sweet wild cane growing there); the *Kotswana* (little dried-up one); and the *Njambili* (the two dogs). This river receives its name, the tribespeople say, because it consists of two streams flowing side by side, like two dogs coursing after an antelope; where the streams meet at the mouth, the dogs have pounced on the antelope (represented by the sea). In between these rivers are turnoffs to four small coastal resorts which combine to form the municipality of . . .

# BENDIGO

Four seaside resorts were created on the coastal farm of *Bendigo* : Sea Park, South Port, Anerley and Sunwich Port. In 1967 these resorts amalgamated and adopted the original farm name for the new municipality. Each resort retains its individuality and has special features such as bays, beaches, tidal pools, surfing, shark-protected swimming, fishing and recreational facilities.

## Accommodation

★ Southport Hotel, 18 rooms, all with baths. R9,50 – R11,50 B/B. Phone 3319.

## Caravans and camping

★★ Banana Beach Holiday Resort, 100 sites. R3 – R8 D.

Three kilometres north of the Njambili River, the road reaches a turnoff to the coastal resort of . . .

# UMZUMBE

It is said that in former years a band of cannibals and renegades created a stronghold for themselves on the banks of the river known today as the *Mzumbe* (the bad kraal). In 1828, when Shaka himself led the Zulu army on a great raid down the coast, the local Hlongwa tribe suffered severe loss of life and massive destruction of their villages and farmlands.

One very interesting relic survives in the area from this great Zulu raid. Following a path which stretched towards the coast, the Zulus climbed a ridge overlooking the valley of the Malkake, a tributary of the Mzumbe. On this high ridge, Shaka followed the custom of propitiating the spirits; he picked up a pebble in the toes of his left foot, placed it in his right hand, spat on it and deposited the pebble by the side of the path. His followers observed this procedure and one by one, as they passed the site, every member of the Zulu army duplicated Shaka's action and a large mound of pebbles was accumulated next to the path.

A pile of pebbles such as this is known as *isivivane* (a luck heap). They are regarded with great reverence by Africans, particularly this one, on account of its connections with the memory of the great Shaka. It is a classic specimen of its kind, impressively situated on a strategic height in the midst of a rolling sea of hills. The pathway beside which it stands seems to be as old as the hills themselves and the feet of countless travellers have tramped it deep into the ground. Surrounded by the superb panorama of scenery, the pile of pebbles stands next to the pathway which climbs, descends and twists incessantly through this prodigious landscape, conjuring up a picture that is completely African. The luck heap lies 10 km from Umzumbe up District Road D453. A guide should be obtained from Govender's Store, beyond which the road is rough for 3 km, degenerating into a track and involving a final walk of 0,5 km along the path.

The coastal resort of Umzumbe is a pleasant place half lost in trees and palms. Fishing from the rocks is good.

### Accommodation
★ Pumula Hotel, 35 rooms, all with baths. R10 – R20 D/B/B. Phone 6717.

### Caravans and camping
★★ Hideaway Caravan Park, 26 sites. R4 – R7 D plus 70c D per person.

Beyond the Mzumbe River, the main South Coast road traverses a 3-km-wide expanse of bush, crosses the *Mzimayi* (place of cattle) and, 21 km from Port Shepstone, reaches the coastal resort of . . .

## HIBBERDENE

Named after C. Maxwell-Hibberd, a former Postmaster-General of Natal who was the first to retire to this pleasant place, *Hibberdene* possesses a tree-fringed beach and fishing vantage points such as the flat rocks known as Reef End. It is a good place in which to have a thoroughly lazy time.

### Accommodation
★ Alexander Hotel, 20 rooms, all with baths. R10 – R12 D/B/B. Phone 723.

### Caravans and camping
★★ Happy Days Holiday Resort, 10 sites. R2,50 – R7 D, seasonal. 20 cottages, R7 – R17 D.
★★★ Hibberdene Caravan Park, 134 sites. R2,50 – R6,50 D, plus 50c D per person, seasonal.
★★★ Rondalia Holiday Resort, 85 sites. R3,60 – R6,30 D, seasonal. 181 rondawels, R8,25 – R17,70 D.
★ Umzumbi Caravan Park, 28 sites. R7,50 D plus 50c D per person.

From Hibberdene the coastal road continues northwards. After 4,5 km the road bridges across the river known as the *Mhlungwa* (the division) for it was there that Shaka, on his great raid down the coast, is said to have divided his army into two sections to form a great pincer attack against the Pondo.

At 10,5 km from Hibberdene (32 km from Port Shepstone) the road reaches the resort of . . .

## MTWALUME

The river which gives the area its name, is itself named after the mtwalume trees growing on its banks. The bark of these trees is used as a specific against dysentery and the name means 'what it carries must stand upright', an odd reference, presumably, to the effect it has on loose stomachs. The beach is pretty and there is a tidal pool and shark-protected swimming area.

## Accommodation
★ Mtwalume Hotel, 6 rooms, 2 with baths. R5 – R6,50 B/B. Phone 751.

## Caravans and camping
★ Mtwalume Caravan Park, 105 sites. R2 – R3,50 D plus 50c – 75c D per person, seasonal.
★★ Long Beach Caravan Park, 225 sites. R7,50 D.

The road crosses the Mtwalume River whose valley is thickly bushed and after 4,5 km reaches a turnoff to the resort of . . .

## IFAFA BEACH

The *Ifafa* (sparkling) River reaches the sea through a lagoon at Ifafa Beach. Swimming is good, there is a plentiful supply of karanteen bait for fishermen, and the area has a reputation for shad, rock fish, salmon and sharks. The lagoon and lower reaches of the river offer fine boating and canoeing possibilities.

## Accommodation
★ Ifafa Beach Hotel, 22 rooms, all with baths. R6,75 B/B. Phone 670.

## Caravans and camping
★★★★® Ifafa Marina, 190 sites. R3 – R15,60 D plus 35c – 60c D per person, seasonal. Chalets R8,50 – R30 D, seasonal.

After crossing the Ifafa River, the main coastal road continues through a hilly landscape covered in sugar cane. After 8 km (44 km from Port Shepstone) the road reaches a turnoff to the sugar-producing centre of . . .

## SEZELA

Legend has it that the Sezela River was named after a notorious crocodile, responsible for the deaths of many people. This reptile was known as *Sezela* (the one who smells out) for it persistently hunted its prey like a dog, or a witchdoctor 'smelling out' victims. Shaka, when he led his army down the coast, was told about the monster and he decided to procure its skin. A great hunt was organised and the crocodile was found and killed, but its name lingers about the river which was originally known as the *Malangeni* after the tribe living on its banks.

In 1914 the Reynolds Brothers Ltd, one of the largest sugar-producing concerns of Southern Africa, erected a mill at Sezela. The mill is fed with cane brought in on an extensive narrow-gauge railway system and the company produces over 120 000 tons of sugar each year.

The Reynolds brothers were Frank and Charles, sons of Thomas Reynolds, who with his brother Lewis, acquired vast landholdings on the Natal South Coast. Before that they had developed a considerable sugar industry on the North Coast on Oaklands Estate near Shaka's Kraal, where, among other things, they produced a rum known as Umhlali Water.

Their first sugarmill, named Esperanza, was built in 1882 at Umzinto on the South Coast. This mill was served by a narrow-gauge railway system whose route included one tunnel over 230 m long through solid rock, and a suspension bridge over the Mzinto River spanning 80 m at a height of 10 m. The old Esperanza mill was replaced in 1899 by the new Esperanza mill which was eventually (in 1952) removed to the Phongolo River in Northern Zululand to crush the cane grown on the Pongola Irrigation Settlement. The mill at Sezela now handles all cane grown by the company on the South Coast.

## Accommodation
* Sezela Hotel, 14 rooms, 4 with baths. R4,50 – R5 B/B. Phone 5330.

Beyond the Sezela River, the main coastal road continues northwards over a fine rolling mass of hills, well covered in sugar cane and patches of indigenous forest. This area was originally owned by the Pennington family and their name remains over the coastal resort of . . .

# PENNINGTON

The original Pennington was killed by a leopard in the bush on his estate but his two sons continued to farm in the area and to run a transport business. The estate was a superb piece of natural parkland, well watered, with two rivers flowing through it, the *Nkhomba* and the *Nkhombana*, both named after the palm trees *Jubaeopsis caffra* which flourish there.

The Penningtons sold part of their estate to the sugar producer, Sir Frank Reynolds, who built a home there on what he named *Umdoni Park* after the *mdoni* (water myrtle) trees growing there. On this beautifully wooded estate, Sir Frank built a seaside mansion for General Louis Botha, the first Prime Minister of the Union of South Africa, whom he admired. This lovely home, *Botha House,* eventually became a holiday residence for the Prime Ministers of South Africa. A public holiday area has developed close to the beach.

## Caravans and camping
*** Pennington Caravan Park, 50 sites. R2 – R4 D plus 50c – R1 D per person.
** Umdoni Caravan Park, 60 sites. R7 D.

Pennington lies 1,5 km south of the river known as the result of its destructive floods as the *Mzinto* (doer of things), 51 km from Port Shepstone. On the north bank of this river lies the railway junction and resort of . . .

# KELSO

Named by the original owners of the estate after their family home in Scotland, *Kelso* is graced by a small lagoon and a pleasant beach.

## Caravans and camping
***® Happy Wanderers Caravan Park, 100 sites. R7 D. 18 flats, 8 cottages, R9 – R17 D.
** Kelso Valley Caravan Park, 40 sites. R2 – R6 D plus 50c D per person.

The main coastal road leads north from Kelso through a green parkland of trees, palms and grass. It crosses the river known as the *Mzimayi* (place of cattle) and after 5 km reaches . . .

# PARK RYNIE

In 1857 the land on which Park Rynie has been developed was acquired by the firm of Norsworthy & Co. A partner in this firm was a Mr Hoffman whose wife, Catherine Renetta, was nicknamed 'Rynie'. Consequently, *Park Rynie* is named after her. During the First World War a whaling station was created at Park Rynie by a company known as Park Rynie Whales Ltd. A breakwater and landing ramp was built which is now used by fishing craft.

## Accommodation
* Oceanic Hotel, 10 rooms, all with baths. R6 – R7 B/B. Phone 2-0080.
* Park Rynie Hotel, 12 rooms, 2 with baths. R5 – R5,50 B/B. Phone 2-0191.

### Caravans and camping
*** Caravan Cove, 165 sites. R2 – R6 D plus 60c D per person, seasonal. 16 chalets, R4 – R10 D, seasonal.
** Park Rynie Camping, Parking and Picnic Ground, 200 sites. R3 D.
** Rocky Bay Caravan Park, 90 sites. R3 – R4 D plus 60c D per person, seasonal.

From Park Rynie, a turnoff from the main coastal road leads for 7,5 km to the town of . . .

# UMZINTO

The centre for one of the principal sugar-producing areas of Natal, Umzinto is a busy railway terminus of a branch of the main South Coast line, and also for the narrow-gauge line inland through Highflats to Ixopo and Umzimkulu. The road from Umzinto to Highflats (59,5 km) leads through superb hill scenery, passing on its way the small trading centre of Braemar.

*Umzinto* is named after the river known to the Africans as *umezi wezinto* (the doer of things) on account of its destructive floods. It was in the Umzinto area that the first public sugar company in Natal commenced production in 1858, using as labourers the first Asians to be imported for the purpose, a group of men from Java. By 1865 Umzinto had grown to be the magisterial and principal centre for the Alexandra District of Natal. It remains a major industrial town on the South Coast of Natal; a busy, rather ramshackle-looking place with one long main street and a population of 6 180.

### Accommodation
★ Alexandra Hotel, 11 rooms, 3 with baths. R7 – R8 B/B. Phone 4101.
★ Archibalds Hotel, 18 rooms, 5 with baths. R6 – R7 B/B. Phone 4204.
★ Plough Hotel, 10 rooms, 2 with baths. R5,50 – R8 B/B. Phone 4490.
★ Royal Hotel, 11 rooms, 4 with baths. R5,50 – R8 B/B. Phone 4205.

From the turnoff to Umzinto, the main South Coast road continues through a green parkland for 4,5 km and then, 52 km from Port Shepstone, reaches a turnoff to the town and resort of . . .

# SCOTTBURGH

This resort was named after John Scott, Governor of Natal when the place was originally surveyed in 1860 as the first township in Natal south of Durban. Before the railway was built, an attempt was made to use the bay for the export of sugar and although several coasters traded there, the bay offered scant shelter from rough seas. A number of fishing vessels also used the place as a base at the beginning of the 20th century. The nearby Aliwal Shoal provided a rich fishing ground and the industry flourished for several years.

Scottburgh became a municipality in 1964 and the population now numbers 6 100. Today it is a popular seaside resort with a fine beach fringed by a coastal forest. Attractions include shark-protected bathing, tidal pools, a miniature railway and an 18-hole golf course.

### Accommodation
** Blue Marlin Hotel, 104 rooms, 68 with baths. R7,50 – R10,50 B/B. Phone 2-1214.
** Cutty Sark Hotel, 56 rooms, all with baths. R9 B/B. Phone 2-1230.
★ Golf Inn, 37 rooms, all with baths. R9 – R11 B/B. Phone 2-1308.
★ Southern Cross Hotel, 11 rooms, all with baths. R8,50 B/B. Phone 2-0770.

### Caravans and camping
**® Municipal holiday resort, 306 sites. R2 – R4 D plus 50c D per person, seasonal.

From Scottburgh, the main South Coast road descends into the valley of the river which the Africans rather ingeniously name the *Mphambinyoni* (confuser of the birds) for its course meanders to such an extent that (it is said) even the birds fail to find their own nesting places. Across the river the road finds a way through dense coastal forest where so many palms of the *Strelitzia* family grow, that this part of the coast truly deserves its name of the *Strelitzia Coast*.

Crossing the river known as the *Hlongwa* (the resident tribe bears that name), the road, after 6 km, reaches the resort of . . .

# CLANSTHAL

The site on which *Clansthal* developed was originally a farm named by its German owner after a place in Hanover, Germany. On the hill overlooking the resort stands the 240 000 candlepower lighthouse of Greenpoint which beams its warning light over the offshore shipping hazard of the Aliwal Shoal.

The Aliwal Shoal is a 1,5-km-long, 1-km-wide ridge of rock lying in the sea 4 km off the coast. It is so near the surface that in rough weather, the ocean swells break on it in a line of white foam. The shoal was first reported in 1849 by the captain of the barque *Aliwal* which narrowly avoided colliding with it. The first ship known to be wrecked on the shoal was the *Nebo*, a 2 600-ton steamer on her maiden voyage in 1884. The crew were all saved but the ship was totally lost as well as 4 500 tons of railway material destined for Natal. Several other ships, such as the *H.C. Richards* in 1893 and the *Amy Lykes* in 1970, have come to grief on this shoal. The *Amy Lykes* was on a record-breaking run to Durban when she hit the shoal at 11h00 on a calm morning. Over 3 000 tons of cargo had to be dumped before she could be pulled off by two tugs. The shoal at least provides the South Coast of Natal with its finest deep-sea fishing ground.

## Caravans and camping
★★★ Clansthal Caravan Park, 58 sites. R6 D plus R1 D per person, seasonal.

From Clansthal, the main coastal road follows its scenic route through a forest of palms, casuarina trees and indigenous bush interspersed with fields of sugar cane. The road crosses the Hlongwana River and veers slightly inland to pass through the residential area of Widenham, returning to the coast to reach, 74 km from Port Shepstone, the river and resort of . . .

# UMKOMAAS

The European name of *Umkomaas* is a corruption of the African name for the river, the *Mkhomazi* (place of cow whales). The shallow waters of the river mouth have always provided a favourite place where cow whales can give birth to their calves and Shaka, the Zulu chief, is said to have witnessed this spectacle and then named the river.

The town of Umkomaas with its present population of 2 113, originated with an attempt in 1861 to develop a harbour in the mouth of the river. Several coasters called there to load sugar but the river entrance was made hazardous by a sand bar and difficult currents. As a result, the shipping venture failed. The opening of the South Coast Railway in 1897, however, finally solved the transport difficulties of the planters.

Umkomaas was established as a town in 1902 and is today the centre for the factory of the South African Industrial Cellulose Corporation (SAICCOR). There is a fine 18-hole golf course. The beach is rather restricted and the sea generally muddied in summer by the floodwaters of the river. There is however, an enclosed tidal pool for swimming, boating on the river and angling for fish such as salmon, garrick, grunter and shad. A notably excellent Italian restaurant in the town is worth visiting.

## Accommodation

★ Golf Course Hotel, 31 rooms, 14 with baths. R7 – R9 B/B. Phone 3-1230.
★★ Lido Hotel, 33 rooms, all with baths. R8 – R9 B/B. Phone 3-1002.
★ Ocean Park Hotel, 23 rooms, 6 with baths. R4,50 – R5,50 B/B. Phone 3-0181.
★ Umkomaas Hotel, 12 rooms, 5 with baths. R5,50 – R6,50 B/B. Phone 3-1004.

## Caravans and camping

★★★ Widenham Caravan Park, 60 sites. R2 – R4 D plus 50c – 75c D per person, seasonal.

The main coastal road bridges across the mouth of the Mkhomazi River and continues northwards, passing a wayside market place where fruit and handicrafts may be bought. This is the area where the Luthuli tribe live. After 6,5 km the road crosses the river known as the *Mngababa* (place of jealousy) on account of an old tribal feud. On the north bank stands another wayside market place where a line of stalls offer for sale a great variety of beadwork, baskets, carvings, curios, handicrafts and fruit. Litchis, sold in January, are notably sweet while bananas of several different varieties are sold.

## Caravans and camping

★★★ Umngababa Holiday Resort (for Africans), 50 sites. R1,50 – R2 D, seasonal. Chalets, R12,50 D. Rooms, R6,25 – R7,50 D. Dormitory beds at various prices.

The coast on either side of the Mngababa River is rich in titanium and a considerable industry developed here in the years after the Second World War. Recovery of titanium, unfortunately, caused the sea to become badly polluted and the industry was ended.

The coastal road passes through the area of titanium-rich sands, crosses the Msimbazi River and enters the area known as . . .

# KINGSBURGH

This borough receives its name from Dick King who passed along this coast on 26 May 1842 at the start of his great ride to Grahamstown to secure reinforcements for the British garrison besieged in Durban.

Kingsburgh has a population of 9 780 and consists of several separate coastal resorts each with its own individuality. The combined urban area became a borough on 1 August 1952. The most southerly of the resorts is Karridene, 9 km from Umkomaas. The man after whom the resort is named, W. Karri-Davis, was a Rand mining magnate who built there a recuperative home for people suffering from mining phthisis. It has a pleasant beach, there is boating on the river and a fine golf course.

Adjoining Karridene is the resort of *Illovo Beach* situated on the south side of the river named after the *mlovo* trees growing there. The road bridges across the broad river and reaches a turnoff leading inland for 87 km to Pietermaritzburg. On the coast opposite this turnoff lies the resort of *Winklespruit,* the name of which, with a slight misspelling, is derived from the Afrikaans *winkel* (trading store). On 10 May 1875 the schooner *Tonga,* carrying a mixed cargo of groceries, was wrecked there. The salvors erected on the beach a small store from which the salvaged goods were sold.

Further up the coast lies the residential area and resort of *Warner Beach,* founded in 1910 as a settlement for pensioners and named after the Government Surveyor, T. A. Warner. Over the years this settlement changed into a commuter residential area for people working in Durban. There is a fine, sandy beach, with fishing and shark-protected swimming.

Warner Beach ends on the south banks of the Little Amanzimtoti River. On the north side stands the residential area and resort known as *Doonside,* originally a railway station of that name, built close to a house called *Lorna Doone,* after the heroine of R.D. Blackmore's famous novel. Doonside is the most northerly of the resorts included in Kingsburgh.

## Accommodation
★ Illovo Hotel, 14 rooms, 4 with baths. R5,50 – R6,50 B/B. Phone 95-1900.
★ Karridene Hotel, 33 rooms, 14 with baths. R5 – R6 B/B. Phone 95-1515.
★ Kingsburgh Hotel (Winklespruit), 31 rooms, 12 with baths. R6,50 – R7,50 B/B. Phone 93-3790.
★ Park Beach Hotel (Winklespruit), 32 rooms, 14 with baths. R6 – R8 B/B. Phone 95-1644.
★ Seaward Hotel (Warner Beach), 28 rooms, 8 with baths. R6,50 – R7 B/B. Phone 93-2351.
★ Strand Hotel (Warner Beach), 28 rooms, 7 with baths. R7 – R8 B/B. Phone 93-2678.

## Caravans and camping
★★ Illovo Beach Caravan Park, 26 sites. R4,30 D plus 60c D per person. 13 cottages, R7 – R10 D.
★★★® Karavana Caravan Park (Winklespruit), 240 sites. R3 – R7 D, seasonal.
★★ Karridene Holiday Camp, 120 sites. R3 – R8,50 D, seasonal.
★★★ Mount Carmel Caravan Park (Winklespruit), 40 sites. R5 D plus 50c D per person, seasonal.
★★★ Natalia Holiday Resort, 110 sites. R5 D plus 50c D per person. 75 flats and 50 rooms, R5,50 – R15,50 D.
★★★★ Ocean Call Caravan Park (Winklespruit), 48 sites with private bathrooms. R4,40 – R6,60 D plus 80c D per person, seasonal. 20 sites with communal bathroom, R3 – R4 D plus 60c D per person, seasonal.
★★® Oom Dicks Caravan Park, 70 sites. R2 – R3,50 D plus 50c D per person, seasonal.
★★★® Patlyn (Illovo Beach), 75 sites. R5 – R6 D plus R1 D per person, seasonal.
★ Pot Luck (Doonside), 45 sites. R3 – R6 D, seasonal.
★★★ Uitspan Caravan Park (Winklespruit, on PMB road), 120 sites. R6 D.

The south bank of another river named by Shaka forms the northern limit of Kingsburgh. It is said that in the year 1828 when he was returning to Zululand with his army after raiding the tribes of the south, he camped on the banks of this river. Shaka's attendant filled a calabash of water to drink; upon sipping it, Shaka murmured with pleasure, *'Kanti amanza mtoti'* ('So, the water is sweet'). As always, his followers acclaimed his every saying and from this event arose the name of both river and the modern town situated on its north bank . . .

# AMANZIMTOTI

Acquiring municipal status on 1 January 1962, Amanzimtoti has a population of 16 020. It combines the residential assets of a beautifully wooded coastal ridge within easy commuter reach of Durban, 27 km away; the industrial area of the Isipingo Flats; and the Inyoni Rocks Beach. This seaside resort consists of a long stretch of coast with a sandy beach, several rocky vantage points for fishermen, swimming pools and shark-protected sea swimming areas.

There is boating on the river, an interesting 4,5-ha bird sanctuary on Umdoni Road, and a nature reserve, Ilanda Wilds (20 ha in extent) with walks along nature trails where 126 species of indigenous trees and shrubs flourish.

## Accommodation
★ Beach Hotel, 53 rooms, 24 with baths. R9 – R10 B/B. Phone 93-2680.
★ Lagoon Hotel, 46 rooms, 42 with baths. R8 – R11 B/B. Phone 93-2346.
★ River Gardens Hotel, 16 rooms, 7 with baths. R6,50 – R7,50 B/B. Phone 93-3355.

From the business centre of Amanzimtoti, the main South Coast road continues northwards, passing through the residential and industrial area of Umbogintwini and then descending to cross the river called *emBokodweni,* meaning 'a place of round stones', after which the industrial area is named. Durban is now only 19 km away and its buildings are clearly visible over a flat expanse of ground, once covered in sugar cane but now being developed as the industrial area of *Isipingo,* so called after the river of that name, derived from the siphingo shrubs *(Sentia indica)* which grow on its banks.

## ISIPINGO

Today, Isipingo is an Indian township and holiday resort with a pleasant beach. The population has reached 17 700. The industrial and commercial areas are centred on what is known as Isipingo Rail.

Dick King, celebrated for his great ride from Durban to Grahamstown in 1842, owned a farm on the site of Isipingo Rail. The homestead is now the headquarters of the local traffic department. If this had been the case in his day he might possibly have been caught for speeding!

### Accommodation
* Island Hotel, 37 rooms, 10 with baths. R7 – R11 B/B, seasonal. Phone 92-3400.
* Railway Hotel, 12 rooms, 8 with baths. R5 – R6 B/B. Phone 92-1310.
* Royal Hotel, 12 rooms, 3 with baths. R5 – R6 B/B. Phone 92-2729.

The main South Coast road continues from Isipingo directly across the coastal plain, past the Louis Botha airport, across the river known on account of its colour as the *Mlazi* (river like whey), through the industrial area of *Mobeni* (place of sugar cane), and the congested business area of Clairmont and then into Durban, 118 km from Port Shepstone.

## Chapter Twenty-one

# DURBAN

With a population of 751 265, not only is Durban one of the loveliest and cleanest great harbours of the world (and South Africa's principal harbour), it is also an industrial centre of considerable importance, and a major holiday resort which enjoys a non-stop, all-year-round season.

In the beginning it would appear that the present harbour of Durban consisted of a great lagoon which was fed by streams such as the Mhlatuzana and the Mbilo. About 100 million years ago the entire coastline subsided beneath the sea. The land eventually rose again, but to a lower level than before its submergence. The former lagoon had now become a bay almost landlocked by two elevated spits of sand formed from the silt brought down by the rivers. Sandspits such as these are a common feature of the Natal coast where the powerful inshore current carries the silt north of the river mouths. The two sandspits of Durban comprise: in the north, what is known as the Point, composed of silt brought down to the former lagoon by its rivers; and in the south, what is known as the Bluff, probably composed of silt washed down by the river known as Isiphingo.

It is interesting to imagine this drowned lagoon at the time of the advent of man: a spacious and grand expanse of water with nothing to break its solitude save the play of the wind, the sea birds flying incessantly over the surface, and the splashing and grunting of hippos lazing in the shallows. Around the verges of the lagoon, where the city of Durban stands today, grew a forest, dense and secret; a place where the silence was broken only by the isolated sounds – plaintive or menacing – of wild animals.

A few African people, consisting initially of the Lala tribe and later mainly of the Luthuli clan, refugees from tribal disturbance in the north, found sanctuary in the forest around what they called *Thekwini* (the lagoon), and in the almost impenetrable bush of the high ridge of the Bluff, known to them as *siBubulungu* (the long, bulky thing). In constant fear of raids from their neighbours, these people eked out a living by planting crops in burned-out patches of bush, hunting game, and catching fish in the lagoon, using complex traps consisting of long fences made of reeds and poles which encircled the shallows.

The first Europeans to visit the area were mostly survivors of shipwrecks who tramped up and down the coast in search of rescue. One of these individuals was Rodrigo Tristão, who, surviving the wreck in 1552 of the Portuguese galleon *Saint John,* became the first European known to make his home in the area. He settled among the local Africans and found a living by hunting and fishing. Little did he realise that the simple hut in which he lived was standing on the site of a future city, and that the tranquil lagoon would one day be lined with wharves and sheds.

Over the years, other odd characters found their way to the shores of the bay. It is noted in old shipping chronicles, that even a penitent pirate who turned honest sequestered himself from his former companions in that lonely place. A few traders occasionally visited the area but there was little of commercial value since the resident Africans were poverty stricken and possessed neither ivory nor slaves for export. To this stretch of coast the Portuguese navigator, Vasco da Gama, had applied the name *Natal* (Nativity) because he had first seen it on Christmas Day 1497. The entrance to the bay became known as the *Rio de Natal* (river of the nativity).

*Overleaf: A balancing skill that comes naturally in Africa; a Bhaca woman dances to a record playing on her head, the needle staying perfectly in place.*

415

Fate took a hand in shaping the future of the Rio de Natal. In the north, 250 km away, the Zulu nation was born at the beginning of the 19th century. Their wealth provided a market for trade and in 1823 merchants from the Cape sent up two separate parties of men to find a practical harbour from which the Zulu could be reached.

It was one of these parties, led by Lieutenant James King and Lieutenant George Farewell, which examined the coast of Natal without finding any suitable harbour, and which eventually anchored in front of the entrance to the Rio de Natal in November 1823. The explorers hesitated thinking that the entrance would prove too shallow for a ship to pass. Fate once again took a hand in the game. A squall blew up. The ships were anchored dangerously close to the shore and if their anchors dragged the consequences would be disastrous. The traders found their minds made up for them; with a few rolls and an alarming bump they sailed straight across the bar and to their delight found themselves safely on the waters of the great harbour, completely secure and protected from the weather.

This was the real beginning of Durban. The traders were jubilant at what they had found. They returned to the Cape to organise a substantial trading venture, hopeful of government support in the establishment of a settlement. The government proved hesitant, but private means and men were found. In May 1824 the 25-ton *Julia,* under the command of a young man, Henry Francis Fynn, was sent to the area with a party on board who were to commence the settlement. It was these men who cut the first clearing in the bush 'opposite the present church of St Paul's in Durban, where the present railway station stands', and built there a house, 4 metres square, made of wattle and daub.

Thus Durban was created by a population of 26 hard-living, picturesque traders and ivory hunters. Life for these men was solitary and precarious; the Zulu tolerated the settlement as being convenient for trade, but kept a sharp watch on the activities of the settlers by means of a garrison established in a stronghold suggestively named *uKangel' amankengane* (watch the vagabonds). From this fortress has been derived the modern corruption of *Congella,* nowadays a suburb of Durban.

The name of Durban was itself bestowed on 23 June 1835 when the settlers held a meeting for the laying out of a town. They named the place after the Governor of the Cape, Sir Benjamin D'Urban, the apostrophe being later conveniently forgotten.

The advent of the Voortrekkers in 1838 and the dismal events surrounding the killing of Piet Retief and many of his followers, left the settlers of Durban in a state of alarm. They joined forces with the Voortrekkers and Durban became a part of the short-lived Natal Republic. In May 1842, Durban reverted to British control with the arrival of a garrison under Captain Smith. The soldiers made their stronghold in what is now known as the Old Fort and in this defensive work they withstood a siege of 34 days (relieved on 26 June 1842). It was during this siege that Dick King made his celebrated 950-km ride in ten days to carry news to Grahamstown of the predicament of the garrison.

## DICK KING AND HIS RIDE

Richard (Dick) Philip King was born in England in 1811 and was nine years old when his family came to South Africa in a group of 1820 Settlers. He grew up in the hard environment that was the frontier and consequently became resolute, tough, and taciturn, prepared to try his hand at anything.

He first arrived in Natal in 1828 as the servant of two explorers, Dr A. Cowie and B. Green. King liked what he saw of Port Natal and remained there while the two explorers went on to eventually die of fever in Moçambique.

Dick King worked for several of the ivory traders and accompanied Captain Allen Gardiner, the missionary, on his exploration of the inland areas and the Drakensberg in 1835. He was in Durban when news of the murder of Piet Retief and his men at uMgungundlovu reached the ivory traders. Dick King set out immediately to warn the Voortrekker encampments below the Drakensberg, reaching them a day after the Zulu army had wiped out their advance camps. He remained with the trekkers, defending the rear camps, and then returned to Durban when the Zulu withdrew.

Together with Robert Biggar, several other ivory traders and their African followers, Dick King fought the Zulu and narrowly escaped when most of their little army was wiped out at Ndondakusuka. A few surviving traders and Dick King hid on Salisbury Island. He remained in Durban when the Voortrekkers arrived and the area became part of the Natal Republic.

When the British arrived and the Voortrekkers besieged them in the little fort, Dick King was on board the trading vessel *Mazeppa,* which was anchored in the bay. The British garrison was in a hopeless position: short of food and ammunition, and completely isolated. Their only hope was relief from the Cape.

On the night of 25 May 1842 one of the senior traders, G. C. Cato, went aboard the *Mazeppa* and woke Dick King. The commander of the garrison, Captain Smith, had sent a message asking King to ride to Grahamstown and to warn the authorities there of the danger in Port Natal.

King asked no questions. He dressed hurriedly, went ashore, woke his 16-year-old servant Ndongeni and selected two good horses, a saddle and stirrups. At midnight a boat ferried them across the bay, with the horses swimming behind. They landed on Salisbury Island and there Ndongeni decided to ride with his master, although he had no saddle. They whispered a farewell to the boatmen and set out across the shallow mangrove swamps, following a secret path to avoid Voortrekker piquet posts.

On the far side of the bay dwelt a friendly chief named Mnini, who agreed to obliterate their trail. Then began a journey of nearly 1 000 km: there were 122 rivers and streams to ford and no road or continuous path to follow; there were wild animals and unknown dangers to face as well as the prospect of descending and climbing one deep valley after another.

For Ndongeni the journey became unbearable. Without saddle or stirrups he still managed about half the distance and was then forced to stop. Dick King reached Grahamstown after ten days, despite a delay owing to sickness. Reinforcements were hastily shipped from Port Elizabeth to relieve the siege in Port Natal. The first of these arrived in the bay on 24 June, followed shortly afterwards by others. On 26 June the siege was broken.

Dick King and Ndongeni were rewarded for their ride. Ndongeni settled on a grant of land he was given on the northern bank of the Mzimkhulu River, where his grave lies today. Dick King also received a grant of land at Isipingo, south of Durban. He opened a butcher's shop in Kings Street, Durban and later, in 1859, moved to Isipingo where he ran a sugarmill. He died in Isipingo in 1871 and his house is now the headquarters of the Isipingo Traffic Department.

The impressive equestrian monument to Dick King was erected on the Durban embankment in 1915. It was designed by Wallace Paton and sculpted by H. H. Grellier. The monument was financed by public subscription organised by Miss Ethel Campbell, who knew Ndongeni and wrote a book about the great ride.

When Natal was at last proclaimed a British colony and annexed to the Cape on 31 May 1844, Durban commenced its growth as a port and gateway to the interior of Southern Africa. Settlers came from Europe; explorers, hunters and prospectors passed through the place with their eager eyes fixed on distant horizons; merchants established stores and warehouses.

An early problem concerned the depth of the bar (the shallow entrance to the harbour). This bar was formed by the debris eroded from the interior by the rivers and deposited along the coast, forming sand barriers across the entrance of all river mouths or inlets. Deepening this bar, which in 1855 had a low water depth of little over 3 m, was an exceedingly difficult problem. Years of hard work by the primitive dredgers of the period eventually improved the position by removing 10 million tons of spoil from the entrance and increasing the depth to 6 m by 1898. Today it is over 15 m deep at low water, and the harbour is by far the principal cargo port of Southern Africa, with 18 million tons of cargo handled each year compared to the 6 million tons handled in Cape Town, South Africa's second largest port. Among the facilities of Durban harbour is a graving dock and a grain elevator storing 42 000 tons; specialised ore-loading facilities, coaling and oil fuelling facilities, and bulk oil storage.

The city of Durban originated with a scattering of wattle and daub shacks, half hidden in the dense coastal forest. As it grew, streets were hacked through the trees, with *West Street* (named after the Governor, Martin West) becoming the principal thoroughfare and *Smith Street* as the second most important street, named after Major Smith, commander of the British garrison during the siege. Other important streets are: *Aliwal,* named after the victory in India of the Governor of the Cape, Sir Harry Smith; *Gardiner* named after Captain Allen Gardiner, the pioneer missionary of Natal; *Field* named after William Field, first magistrate; *Grey* was named after Earl Grey, Secretary of State for Colonies; and *Russell* named after Lord John Russell, the British Premier. To lend a touch of sanctity to the proceedings, *George* and *Andrew* streets were named after the saints. The rest of the city and its suburbs steadily expanded around this commercial nucleus. These residential areas, with their freely growing gardens, handsome flowering trees, brilliant sunshine, almost tropical warmth, and long views over the blue of the Indian Ocean, are amongst the fairest on earth.

The famed Botanical Gardens had its beginning in 1848 when the Natal Agricultural and Horticultural Society was formed and acquired the ground for a garden.

The Durban Philharmonic Society, organised in 1853, brought music to the town with a 12-piece band which was the ancestor of the later Durban Symphony Orchestra.

Horse racing started in 1852. The July Handicap (one of the richest horse races in Africa) is run in Durban which today remains a major venue for this sport, where the Greyville Race Course is the scene of spectacular social gatherings.

Rickshaws, as a picturesque form of transport, were introduced to the town in 1893 by Sir Marshall Campbell, a sugar magnate who imported the idea from Japan and trained stalwart Zulu to pull the rickshaws by himself demonstrating the techniques of drawing them. The rickshaws he imported were single-seaters but these were adapted locally into the present two-seaters. Notwithstanding the hostility of modern traffic authorities (who consider them a hindrance on the streets) they remain a feature of the Durban scene, enjoyed by visitors and the pride of the lavishly costumed Zulu who draw them. There is an annual parade and award of a silver plaque to the best dressed rickshaw puller. The costumes are fantastic and the presence of these curious vehicles is a unique aspect of Durban life. The oddly decorated vehicles and gaudily outfitted drawers provide a colourful sight along the beachfront. So bizarre are these man-drawn vehicles, in fact, that it is surprising to learn that they were invented by an American missionary, the Reverend Jonathan Goble, who went to Japan in 1853 with Commander Perry. As his wife was an invalid, the missionary needed some form of transport for her. As a result, the idea became fashionable in Japan, especially with high-class Geishas while tourists also thought the vehicles novel and amusing.

Durban became a municipality in 1854 and a city in 1935. In many ways it is unique. Although it is the busiest port on the continent of Africa, it is spruce, clean and well ordered. Within easy reach of the great inland mining and industrial complexes of the Transvaal and Orange Free State, it is almost a seaside suburb or playground for those areas. The climate is hot during the months of January to March and warm to temperate throughout the year. The beaches are highly developed as recreational areas, having amusement parks, games, rides, gardens, entertainments and varied facilities for fishing, surfing and swimming. Although bathing is complicated by shelving slopes and a notorious back and side wash, the water has a temperature of around 25° C and swimmers are protected by effective anti-shark netting.

The city hall, a close replica of the city hall in Belfast, Northern Island, was opened in 1910.

Apart from municipal offices, the building houses an art gallery exhibiting a substantial collection of paintings, statuary, ceramics and other art.

The museum (also contained in the city hall) displays a notable collection of mammals and birds, including the most complete dodo (the long-vanished bird king of the old pigeon empire of Mauritius) to be seen anywhere in the world. Attached to the main museum but housed in the Old Court House behind the city hall, is a local history museum exhibiting many interesting items concerned with past years in Durban. The art gallery, museum and library, all housed in the city hall, are open from 09h30 to 17h00 on weekdays; 09h30 to 14h00 on Wednesdays; 14h30 to 17h00 on Sundays.

Another interesting museum is the Old House Museum featuring a replica of an original Durban house in a garden setting, built in 1849 by John Goodricke. The story of Natal is revealed here in a collection of pictures, maps, guns, and other items of interest. The Old House Museum is open weekdays from 09h30 to 17h00; 09h30 to 14h00 on Wednesdays; 14h30 to 17h00 on Sundays.

The Old Fort in which the British garrison withstood the siege, is perfectly preserved and in it seems to linger the atmosphere of the pioneer days of Port Natal. The warriors' gate, shrine and headquarters of the Memorable Order of Tin Hats (M.O.T.H.s) are situated in the Old Fort where numerous military relics and trophies are contained. There are conducted tours from 10h00 to 12h00 daily except Saturdays and public holidays.

On the ocean front may be found the famous Fitzsimons Snake Park where a remarkable collection of reptiles is exhibited and anti-venom serum sold. The snake park is open daily from 09h00 to 16h30.

Durban's Marineland (comprising aquarium and dolphinarium) at the foot of West Street, exhibits in huge tanks many of the fish fauna of the Indian Ocean, including a group of sharks, on which considerable research is being done with a view to a better understanding of their habits and reactions to man and his attempts to devise effective protective measures against their attacks. The Marineland is open daily from 09h00 to 21h00. The fish are fed at 11h00 and 15h00.

Some of the attractions of Durban's beachfront include: miniature golf courses and putting games; a model yacht pond, a children's centre with safe swimming, motor boating and other delights; numerous novelty rides and amusement park entertainments, a miniature railway and a lovers' rendezvous at the Blue Lagoon (the mouth of the Mgeni River); a mini-town with its own drive-in cinema and replicas of buildings in 1-in-24 scale; a sunken garden and a large ice-skating rink close to the beach. Of considerable interest to visitors is the Indian market in Warwick Avenue, just off the top end of West Street. African and Eastern curios, as well as many different varieties of curry may be obtained here, blended to order from volcanic eruption strength to newly-wed mild.

Most of the Indian population of Durban follows the Hindu religion and the Sri Vaithianatha Easvarar Alayam temple in Umgeni Road is the oldest and largest in South Africa. The Moslem section of the population makes use of a large mosque at the corner of Grey and Queen streets. Both of these groups stage annual festivals in Durban. The Hindu fire-walking rituals, held at Easter, and the Kavady festivals in February and July, when penitents pierce various parts of their bodies with daggers, fish hooks and needles, are fascinating spectacles.

The beautiful gardens of Durban have already been mentioned. Apart from the Botanic Gardens and its renowned orchid house exhibiting over 3 000 plants, there is Albert Park with its sporting facilities; the Amphitheatre and sunken garden on North Beach, which has an open-air auditorium; Mitchell Park and its superb lawns, trees, monkeys, aviaries and penguin pool. Medwood Gardens in West Street opposite the city hall provides a pleasant little retreat in the centre city, with a graceful illuminated fountain; the Robert Jameson Park has a magnificent rose garden and a Japanese water garden on the north side of the Umgeni River.

Private gardens, especially in the residential areas of the Berea, are lovely, and the views of the city and harbour from this elevation are worth seeing. Also in the Berea area (for those interested in Africana) is the Killie Campbell library and museum, bequeathed to and now managed by the University of Natal. This museum is open to the public daily except on Sundays and holidays from 08h30 to 13h00 and from 14h00 to 16h45. Apart from one of the world's most important collections of Africana, visitors may see the unique series of paintings by Barbara Tyrrell depicting the costumes worn by the tribal peoples of Southern Africa. On this assembly of several hundred exquisitely detailed paintings was based Barbara Tyrrell's great book *Tribal Peoples of Southern Africa*. Included in the Africana are many unpublished manuscripts. The material for several important books has been researched from the wealth of information contained in this elegant home.

The late Miss Killie Campbell was also a renowned gardener. In the grounds of the house her professional gardener, William Poulton, bred several new varieties of bougainvillaea including one named after Killie Campbell. On the death of Miss Campbell, the house and its collection was presented by her brother William to the University of Natal as a study centre.

Burman Drive, a short, very attractive route from Durban (Umgeni Road) to North Ridge, winds for 3 km along forest country where birds and monkeys abound.

Another drive leads along the Esplanade and Maydon Road around the head of the bay. Branching east into Edwin Swales V. C. Drive, off the main South Coast road, the route climbs the Bluff where fine views are revealed of the panorama of shipping in the great harbour, the fair city of Durban, and the blue waters of the Indian Ocean sweeping in to a golden shore.

## Accommodation

* Alexandra Hotel, Point Road, 13 rooms, 4 with baths. R8 – R10 room only. Phone 37-1664.
* Argyle Hotel, Umbilo Road, 19 rooms, 5 with baths. R7,40 – R9,50 B/B. Phone 35-2241.
* Astra Hotel, Russell Street, 114 rooms, all with baths. R7,78 – R9,78 B/B. Phone 6-0571.
** Athlone Hotel, Northway, 160 rooms, all with baths. R12 – R18 B/B. Phone 84-1251.
* Baldwin Hotel, West Street, 22 rooms, 9 with baths. R5,50 – R7,50 B/B. Phone 37-3987.
** Balmoral Hotel, Marine Parade, 97 rooms, 49 with baths. R5,45 – R9,60 B/B. Phone 37-4392.
** Beach Hotel, Marine Parade, 106 rooms, all with baths. R15,50 B/B. Phone 37-5511.
** Belgica Hotel, St Georges Street, 33 rooms, all with baths. R8,50 – R14,50 B/B. Phone 31-1064.
* Bell Inn, Northway, 21 rooms, 8 with baths. R7 – R8,50 B/B. Phone 84-1341.
* Berea Hotel, Berea Road, 21 rooms, 11 with baths. R7,50 – R8,50 D/B/B. Phone 21-8782.
* Berkeley Hotel, Old Fort Road, 83 rooms, 10 with baths. R7 B/B. Phone 37-8365.
*** Blue Waters Hotel, Snell Parade, 264 rooms, all with baths. R13 – R23 B/B. Phone 33-3781.
* Brighton Strand Hotel, Brighton, 22 rooms, 16 with baths. R10,50 – R11,50 B/B. Phone 47-7991.
** Caister Hotel, Musgrave Road, 45 rooms, all with baths. R11,50 – R23 B/B. Phone 21-1291.
** Claridges Hotel, Marine Parade, 162 rooms, all with baths. R15 B/B. Phone 37-6261.
* Congella Hotel, Sydney Road, 11 rooms, 6 with baths. R10 B/B. Phone 35-7282.
* Coogee Beach Hotel, Tyzak Street, 133 rooms, 41 with baths. R6 – R9 B/B. Phone 37-2444.
* Crown Hotel, North Coast Road, 20 rooms, 4 with baths. R8 – R20 room only. Phone 83-5761.
* Cumberland Hotel, Snell Parade, 69 rooms, 40 with baths. R5,15 – R9,25 B/B. Phone 37-3501.
*** Edenroc Hotel, Snell Parade, 120 rooms, all with baths. R15 – R19 B/B. Phone 37-4321.
**** Edward Hotel, Marine Parade, 101 rooms, all with baths. R27,50 – R76 room only. Phone 37-3681.

★★★★ Elangeni Hotel, Marine Parade, 453 rooms, all with baths. R17,50 – R30 B/B. Phone 37-1321.

★★ Empress Hotel, Marine Parade, 46 rooms, 29 with baths. R6 – R9 B/B. Phone 37-2783.

★★ Fairhaven Hotel, Marine Parade, 90 rooms, all with baths. R6 – R9,50 room only. Phone 37-2515.

★★★ Four Seasons Hotel, Gillespie Street, 195 rooms, all with baths. R10,50 – R15 B/B. Phone 37-3381.

★ Grosvenor Hotel, Soldiers Way, 40 rooms, 18 with baths. R7,50 – R8,50 B/B. Phone 32-4912.

★★ Himalaya Hotel, Grey Street, 26 rooms, 9 with baths. R5 – R6 B/B. Phone 6-5522.

★★★ Holiday Inn, Sol Harris Crescent, 268 rooms, all with baths. R21 – R32 room only. Phone 37-1211.

★ Imperial Hotel, Umgeni Road, 50 rooms. R5 – R6 B/B. Phone 2-6424.

★ Killarney Hotel, Brickhill Road, 224 rooms, all with baths. R5,15 – R8,85 B/B. Phone 37-4281.

★★ Lonsdale Hotel, West Street, 330 rooms, all with baths. R14,50 B/B. Phone 37-3361.

★ Los Angeles Hotel, Musgrave Road, 50 rooms, all with baths. R5,03 – R7,03 room only. Phone 21-1351.

★★★★★ Maharani Hotel, Marine Parade, 270 rooms, all with baths. R32 room only. Phone 32-7361.

★★★ Malibu Hotel, Marine Parade, 400 rooms, all with baths. R13 – R22 B/B. Phone 37-2231.

★ Mayfair Hotel, Smith Street, 74 rooms, 58 with baths. R11,75 – R21,50 D/B/B. Phone 32-6232.

★ Mayville Hotel, Jan Smuts Highway, 20 rooms, 5 with baths. R7,50 – R8,50 B/B. Phone 88-5111.

★ Metropole Hotel, Smith Street, 30 rooms, 7 with baths. R10 – R11 B/B. Phone 37-1711.

★ Milner Gardens Hotel, Mariott Road, 130 rooms, 50 with baths. R6,90 – R11,90 B/B. Phone 33-5561.

★★ Moon Hotel, South Coast Road, 16 rooms, 7 with baths. R4,25 – R4,50 B/B. Phone 81-7681.

★ Natalia Hotel, Gillespie Street, 58 rooms, 21 with baths. R5,50 – R6 B/B. Phone 37-3631.

★ New European Hotel, Umgeni Road, 14 rooms, 4 with baths. R4 – R6 B/B. Phone 33-7776.

★ New Rand Hotel, West Street, 29 rooms, 8 with baths. R7,20 – R8,50 B/B. Phone 37-6655.

★ New Savoy Hotel, Berea Road, 40 rooms, 35 with baths. R6 B/B. Phone 21-1381.

★ Normandie Hotel, Lancers Road, 21 rooms, all with baths. R6,50 B/B. Phone 6-5821.

★ Oceanic Hotel, Sol Harris Crescent, 286 rooms, all with baths. R5 B/B. Phone 37-5381.

★★ Osborne Hotel, Musgrave Road, 85 rooms, 79 with baths. R11,50 – R12,25 B/B. Phone 21-5101.

★★ Outspan Hotel, Umbilo Road, 63 rooms, all with baths. R6,50 B/B. Phone 35-1561.

★★ Palm Beach Hotel, Gillespie Street, 88 rooms, 75 with baths. R12,95 B/B. Phone 37-3451.

★★ Palmerston Hotel, Palmer Street, 172 rooms, 47 with baths. R7 – R9,50 B/B. Phone 37-6363.

★ Parade Hotel, Marine Parade, 78 rooms, 43 with baths. R6,50 – R9,75 B/B. Phone 37-4565.

★★ Park View Hotel, Sea View Street, 182 rooms, all with baths. R11,45 – R16,25 B/B. Phone 37-4311.

★ Pavilion Hotel, North Beach, 75 rooms, 48 with baths. R6,50 – R7,25 B/B. Phone 37-7366.

★ Plaza Hotel, Broad Street, 41 rooms, all with baths. R5 – R9 room only. Phone 6-2591.

★ President Hotel, Chamberlain Street, 60 rooms, 15 with baths. R7 – R12 B/B. Phone 48-2471.

★ Raj Mahaal Hotel, Bombay Square, 16 rooms, 6 with baths. R3,50 – R4 B/B. Phone 82-3926.

★ Riviera Hotel, Esplanade, 41 rooms, 16 with baths. R8,95 – R14,95 B/B. Phone 32-3681.

★★★★★ Royal Hotel, Smith Street, 280 rooms, all with baths. R28 – R34 B/B. Phone 32-0331.

★ Rydal Mount Hotel, Gillespie Street, 240 rooms, 148 with baths. R4,20 – R6,25 B/B. Phone 37-6371.

* St Georges Hotel, St Georges Street, 22 rooms, 16 with baths. R8,75 – R9,75 B/B. Phone 6-4137.
* St James Hotel, Point Road, 22 rooms, 6 with baths. R4,50 room only. Phone 37-6960.
* Stamford Hill Hotel, Umgeni Road, 25 rooms, 5 with baths. R6– R6,50 B/B. Phone 33-9879.
* Tudor House Hotel, West Street, 28 rooms, 8 with baths. R8 – R9,25 B/B. Phone 37-4782.
* Wagonwheels Hotel, Florida Road, 34 rooms, 32 with baths. R5,50 B/B. Phone 33-3602.
** Wentworth Hotel, Brighton Road, 19 rooms, 9 with baths. R10,50 B/B. Phone 47-3839.
* West End Hotel, Pine Street, 14 rooms, 4 with baths. R6 – R7 B/B. Phone 32-2814.
* Westville Hotel, Jan Hofmeyr Road, 20 rooms, 8 with baths. R8,80 – R9,90 B/B. Phone 85-4141.
* White House Hotel, Marine Parade, 57 rooms, 50 with baths. R4,75 – R6,75 B/B. Phone 37-8231.
* Willowvale Hotel, Umbilo Road, 31 rooms, all with baths. R7,50 B/B. Phone 35-7859.

## Caravans and camping
** Ansteys Caravan Park (Brighton Beach), 60 sites. R4 D plus 50c D per person.
*** ® Durban Caravan Park (Greys Inn Road, Bluff), 400 sites. R3,50 D plus 50c - R1 D per person, seasonal.

---

# ANGLING FISH AND SHARKS

The angling calendar of the Natal coast is varied and exciting. The commonest fish is barracuda, taken from the shore or by line during two seasons: December to April and June to August. Bream and musselcrackers are caught from October to January; salmon from May to September; shad from April to January; skate from September to March; and sharks principally between November and March.

The main event in the angler's calendar takes place during the first half of June when enormous shoals of sardines appear with such regularity that opinionated anglers lay bets and endeavour to prophesy the exact day when the first shoals will be sighted. The sardines perform this annual migration along the coast as far north as Durban. Their proximity to the shore depends on winds and other local influences; sometimes they keep well out to sea and frustrate the shore anglers; in other years the little fish are driven into the waves and hundreds of them are actually washed up on the beaches.

Throughout their migration the sardine shoals are accompanied by predators such as game fish, sharks and masses of birds, especially gannets. A prodigious number of the fish (really pilchards) are eaten, but their breeding rate is so high – each female lays about 100 000 eggs – that an enormous casualty rate is essential to prevent the sea from being swamped with fish. Anglers follow the shoals to catch the predators, while the little fish are sought by everybody interested in tasty eating. Near Durban (where water temperatures are presumably too warm) the shoals turn tail and, keeping further out to sea, return to the southern end of Africa to complete their breeding life cycle.

Sharks, who practically feed themselves to death on the sardines and the larger fish which eat them, are unpleasant creatures, little more than stomachs with fins. There are many of them in the warm waters of the South African east coast and the visitor to these areas should bear their presence in mind and know something about their habits and the precautions which have been adopted against them.

Eighty of the 400 known species of sharks and their close relations, dogfishes, inhabit the sea around Southern Africa. The reason for this concentration is that the fish, seals, penguins and other creatures to which sharks are partial, are in plentiful supply. Although man is more of a novelty on the shark's menu, he nevertheless provides very acceptable provender for eight species of shark and if, through accident or carelessness, he appears within easy reach in water conditions suitable to sharks, he will be attacked.

Little is known about the habits of sharks, but for some reason records show that very few attacks take place in water below 20° C, while in water above 25° C attacks are common. Most of the eight species of man-eating sharks are concentrated in the warm Moçambique Current and, off the Natal coast, conditions throughout the year make them extremely dangerous. The sharks are at the height of their activity during summer owing to the high water temperature and the fact that flooding rivers discharge so much silt into the sea on the Natal coast, that the water becomes turgid the result of which is a 3-km-wide brown ribbon running the length of the coast. It is in this strip that death lurks.

Natal beaches tend to shelve steeply into deep water, a condition which attracts sharks, while further down the Moçambique Current off the Cape coast, the beaches shelve more gradually. The shallow water deters the sharks from venturing in too close, the water temperature dwindles below the danger level, and the rivers do not pollute the sea with mud to anywhere near the same extent as in Natal. Sharks are still present – they are found in all oceans – but they cause little trouble unless provoked. In False Bay where the Moçambique Current ends, many great white sharks (the most fearsome of all) live on the rich concentration of fish and seals, but almost never attack people swimming and surfing off the gently shelving Muizenberg beach. Occasionally there is a clash between shark and fishing boat. Sharks apparently resent competition and in the deeper waters off Macassar Beach they have been known to rub tentatively against the sides of boats, an ominous action they employ to 'taste' a potential victim. They generally disregard the boats once the tasting proves them unpalatable, and swim off. One gigantic specimen, known locally as 'the submarine', is a great white shark of such formidable proportions that it would be perfectly capable of stoving in the sides of a fishing vessel. It is renowned for its exploratory rubbing against the sides of boats but it has never attacked. Giant great white sharks have been caught in False Bay and exhibited in America and Europe.

Many vicious attacks have been made on human beings along the Natal coast. To prevent this from occurring and to study the sharks, the Provincial Council maintains the Natal Anti-Shark Measures Board which has its headquarters at Umhlanga Rocks.

Under the control of the board, bathing beaches at various resorts are protected by large nets suspended in the water but not necessarily forming continuous barriers. In order to survive, sharks have to keep moving constantly and can never sleep, therefore they are highly nervous of either a reef or net standing between them and the open sea where they might be trapped at low tide or prevented from making a quick getaway. Every year off Durban, about 400 sharks are caught in these nets and die as a result. Their struggles, in turn, serve to drive other sharks away.

Where the use of nets is impractical owing to powerful currents at certain resorts along the coast, continuous metal fences are erected around bathing areas. Persistent fishing and hunting for sharks also helps to reduce the menace. Fortunately, several species have some commercial value; their flesh, livers and fins are exported to the East where they are regarded as delicacies.

One of the most notorious sharks, the great white, is also known as the white death, blue pointer or simply as the man-eater shark. The film *Blue Water, White Death* depicts these and other species of sharks in all their power and ruthlessness. Many of the remarkable underwater sequences in the film were taken in the deep sea off Durban. Great whites grow to about 12 m in length and are capable of swallowing a human being whole. Even larger specimens are sometimes sighted, such as 'the submarine' in False Bay, reputed to be at least 15 m long. Teeth 127 mm in length have been found and it is estimated that the fish from which they come must have been about 30 m long! One shark of 5 m caught off the South African coast contained in its stomach the foot of a man, half a goat, two pumpkins, a wicker-covered scent bottle, two large fish, another shark and various other oddments!

Also a very dangerous shark is the Zambezi. Similar in nature to the great white, it is an aggressive, mobile, ever-hungry stomach that swims. It favours shallow, muddy water and frequents estuaries, lagoons and even ventures up rivers for some distance. A nasty, formidably audacious creature, it reaches a length of 3 m.

The ragged-toothed or brown shark is the third of the man-eaters. It reaches 5 m in length and is a menace along much of the coast, but becomes subdued in the cooler waters of the Cape. Its fins are valued in the East for soup and its liver oil is excellent for lamps, poor compensation for the fact that most shallow water attacks on the South African coast are made by this species!

The blue shark, attaining a length of 6 m, is a deep water shark, which seldom approaches near enough to shore to be a nuisance to man.

The mako shark is also a deep water shark. Speedy and dangerous, up to 5 m in length, it generally keeps out to sea, but does not hesitate to charge boats which disturb its hunting. It leaps clear of the water, sometimes landing in the boats, creating havoc and huge splashes.

Hammerhead sharks have weirdly shaped double-hammer heads with eyes on the extremities and grow to more than 7 m. They are aggressive but for some reason are not as dangerous in South African waters as in some tropical parts of the world. They provide anglers with great sport on the Wild Coast, where kite fishermen catch them in deep water at places such as Mazeppa Bay.

Whale sharks, a whopping 15 m in length, usually do not attack unless provoked.

Long-fin and bulldog sharks are also killers but fortunately avoid shallow water close to the coast.

The grey shark grows to 3 m but remains out to sea. It provides good eating and is considered a fine sporting fish by fishermen. The dusky or ridgeback grey shark is the commonest species to be found off the Natal coast.

The tiger shark reaches a length of 5 m and is a great menace along the coast, endlessly scavenging close to shore. A 5-m specimen taken at Durban had in its stomach the head and forequarters of a crocodile, the hind leg of a sheep, three seagulls, two intact 1-kg tins of green peas and a cigarette tin!

---

## THE OLD NORTH COAST ROAD

Along this road (essentially the Sugar Way), the traveller journeys as though on a ship, across an undulating sea of green sugar cane where occasional inhabited islands, consisting of towns and mills, emerge from the plantations. An interesting circular drive leads from Durban up this Sugar Way to Stanger, and back via the main road (Shaka's Way) which, coming down from Zululand, joins the old North Coast route at this point and then sweeps on southwards to Durban hugging the coastline.

From Durban, the old North Coast road leads out of the city past the beautiful fairways and trees of the Windsor Park golf course and, at 4,5 km crosses the river known as *Mngeni* (place of acacia trees). On the left bank of the river, the road meanders through the handsome northern suburbs of Durban, with their sunny looking houses, gardens and trees.

At 10 km from Durban the road passes through the Indian residential area of Avoca and at 11 km reaches a junction. Straight ahead (north-westwards) a road continues through the Indian residential area of Duffs Road, past the great African township of *kwaMashu* (the place of Mashu, the name given to Sir Marshall Campbell, the sugar magnate and introducer of the rickshaw to Durban). From here a fine scenic drive stretches up into the green hills, reaching the magisterial centre of *Inanda* (the pleasant place) 24 km from Durban. The tarmac road ends at this point, but two gravel branches (especially the left-hand branch) lead to some stunningly beautiful viewsites overlooking the great Valley of a Thousand Hills through which flows the Mngeni River. This is a superlative piece of hill country, a special feature of interest being the dense population of Africans.

The Inanda Game Park may be reached from Inanda or from Verulam, further up the Sugar Way. This park, 550 ha in extent, contains a variety of wild animals and there are five camps accommodating guests at R6 to R8 daily for adults and R3 to R4 daily for children. It is open daily from 07h00 to 18h00.

The old North Coast road meanwhile continues northwards from the point where the Inanda road branches off (12 km from Durban), crossing fields of sugar cane, with tall gum trees providing a shady avenue. Five kilometres from the junction the road passes the White House Hotel in a superb garden setting. Another kilometre takes the road past the spacious Mount Edgecombe Estate of Messrs Huletts, with the sugarmill of Natal Estates Ltd forming the centre of the township, 18 km from Durban, known as . . .

# MOUNT EDGECOMBE

Named after Mount Edgecumb in Cornwall (and with its name slightly misspelt), the Natal Mount Edgecombe is a sugar township in a garden setting of hibiscus in many shades, cannas, bougainvillaea and fine trees. A picturesque Hindu temple graces the exit of the town on its northern side.

———

Five kilometres further on, the road passes through the village of Ottawa and a further 3 km (27 km from Durban) brings the traveller into the atmospheric village of . . .

# VERULAM

Lying on the slopes of the valley of the river known as the *Mdloti* after the wild tobacco plants found on its bank, Verulam was established in 1850 with the influx of British immigrants to Natal. A party of these people, under the patronage of the Earl of Verulam, made their home around the future village which later became the magisterial seat for the county of Victoria. Today, Verulam is an Indian township where intriguing glimpses may still be seen of the elegant homesteads, gardens and cemeteries dating back to the genteel but antique days of 'sugar barons'.

**Accommodation**
★★ Railway Hotel, 10 rooms, 3 with baths. R5 – R7 B/B. Phone 37.
★ Starlite Hotel, 29 rooms, 9 with baths. R7 – R12,50 B/B. Phone 66.

Crossing the Mdloti River (28 km from Durban), with a turnoff north-west to Canelands (1 km) and Ndwedwe (32 km), the old North Coast road continues northwards across the cane fields, passing the Shortlands Hotel and, 34 km from Durban, reaches the straggling village of . . .

# TONGAAT

A long main street of untidy shops and a cricket pitch on an English looking village green, comprise the village of *Tongaat* which receives its name from the river known as the *Thongathi* after the *Strychnos mackenii* trees growing on its banks. Jacarandas, casuarina trees and bamboos flourish and fruit stalls sell subtropical fruits (including exceptionally sweet litchis). North of the village, the old North Coast road bridges the Thongathi River (41 km from Durban), passing the handsome, white-coloured head office and its pretty fountains, of Messrs Moreland Molasses. Just beyond this complex stands the equally imposing entrance to the Tongaat Sugar Estate mill and office. A beautifully laid out golf course in a setting of palms and trees, surrounded by a green sea of sugar cane, make this one of the pleasantest parts of the North Coast.

## Accommodation
* Chelmsford Hotel, 10 rooms, 5 with baths. R4,50 – R5,50 B/B. Phone 15.
* Fairbreeze Hotel, 14 rooms, 4 with baths. R5,50 – R6,50 B/B. Phone 98.

This area is the historic home of the sugar industry of Natal. Past the wayside Fairbreeze Hotel, the road (48 km from Durban) reaches *Compensation,* the farm on which the pioneer, Edmund Morewood, produced the first commercial sugar in Natal in 1851. There is an interesting memorial to this endeavour; from *Compensation* a gravel road branches west-wards for 1 km where a turnoff south leads for another kilometre to the site of Morewood's first sugarmill. In a pleasant garden surrounded by undulating hills of sugar cane stands a replica of this little mill. Its capacity was only 54ℓ of juice an hour but the product was excellent and Morewood's success was the beginning of a major industry which today produces about 2 million tons of sugar a year from 20 large mills fed by cane grown on over 232 680 ha of farmland.

From the turnoff to Morewood's mill, the old North Coast road continues northwards over the fields of cane. After 4 km (55 km from Durban) the road passes the small rail centre of Umhlali, dominated by the white building of the Victoria County Farmers' Association, overlooking the surrounding ocean of sugar cane from a hilltop.

Another kilometre takes the road across the river known as the *Mhlali* after the monkey-orange trees growing on its banks. On the left bank of the river stands the great Shaka's Kraal sugarmill, with a ramshackle township attached to it. Each spring a few jacaranda trees near by shed their blossoms like purple tears at the sight of such dilapidation.

## Accommodation
* Shaka's Kraal Hotel, 5 rooms, 1 with bath. R6 B/B. Phone Umhlali 106.

Passing a turnoff to Glendale (28 km), the old North Coast road continues northwards through a tribal area covered with grass and lala palms. At 63 km from Durban, the road passes the site of the *Groutville Mission Station,* established in 1844 by the Reverend Aldin Grout of the American Board of Missions.

Three kilometres beyond Groutville, the old North Coast road twists down into the valley of the river known as the *Mvoti* after a man who once resided on its banks. Immediately ahead, clustered on a hilltop which emerges island-like from the ocean of sugar cane, may be seen the town of Stanger. Passing the mill and workers' houses of the Melville Sugar Estates, the old North Coast road (72 km from Durban) enters the busy centre of . . .

# STANGER

Originally laid out as a European town in 1873 and named after William Stanger, the Surveyor-General of Natal, *Stanger* was built on the site of Shaka's last great capital, *kwaDukuza* (the place of he who was lost). It was here, towards sunset on 22 September 1828, that the great Zulu king was assassinated by two of his half-brothers, Mhlangana and

Dingane. In the centre of what is now largely an Indian commercial town, a memorial stands in a small garden marking the site where the founder of the Zulu nation died.

Stanger became a municipality in 1949 and has a population of 16 890. It is the commercial, magisterial and railway centre for one of the most important sugar-producing districts.

## Accommodation
★ New Gelderland Hotel, 5 rooms, all with baths. R7 B/B. Phone 667.
★★ Stanger Hotel, 26 rooms, 18 with baths. R9 – R9,50 B/B. Phone 291.
★ Victoria Hotel, 35 rooms, 15 with baths. R7 – R10,50 B/B. Phone 303.

From Stanger the old North Coast road continues northwards for 6 km past the small centre of New Gelderland, then joins the main road, Shaka's Way, which links Durban with Zululand.

---

## SHAKA'S WAY

The main road from Durban to Zululand leads north from Durban along the Snell Parade. It provides a handsome exit from the city and keeping close to the shore is lined with tall hotels and apartments on one side, and on the other the Indian Ocean, sweeping on to a dark golden-coloured beach. Along this route Shaka and his army tramped the first paths. The great tarmac highway of today follows these old trails blazed by warriors, hunters and ivory traders.

Five kilometres from the centre of Durban, the road crosses the Mngeni River at what is perhaps ironically known as Blue Lagoon, a muddy expanse of water in an untidy setting of concrete blocks. Across the river the road continues through the well-to-do suburbs of Durban North, where the roadside is beautified by flowering plants, especially a great variety of cannas which provide a gorgeous spectacle in November.

At 9,5 km from Durban the road passes the Virginia airport, used by light aircraft. The farm on which the airport stands was originally owned by a Mauritian sugar planter, Melidor Cheron who named the place after his daughter Virginia, a singer once known as the 'nightingale of Natal'. She and her Irish husband, Ancrum McCausland, built the first hotel, the Victoria, in 1920, 6 km further up the coast near the mouth of the river known as the *Mhlanga* (place of reeds). This was the start of the holiday resort of . . .

## UMHLANGA ROCKS

The site of this fashionable resort was originally part of the sugar estate of Sir Marshall Campbell, Natal Estates Ltd, which had its headquarters at Mount Edgecombe. A track was made from Mount Edgecombe to Umhlanga Rocks and the area became popular with local farmers who leased small plots on the ocean front where they built vacation cottages. William Alfred Campbell, son of Sir Marshall, built his family home *Nganalana* there in 1925 and in the coastal forest of Hawaan (an Indian name) he staged annual hunts. This lovely coastal forest has been preserved as part of the green belt of Umhlanga and is notable for its trees, including the rare *Cava coa aurea*.

In 1931 Umhlanga Rocks became a village under its own health committee. Additional cottages, places of accommodation and stores were built and the first hotel, the Victoria, was rebuilt and named the Umhlanga Rocks Hotel. The first beach cottage, *The Oyster Box,* became the Oyster Box Hotel of today. The cottage had been built in 1869 and for years was used as a navigational point by passing shipmasters who found its corrugated-iron roof easy to spot amid the green setting of coastal forest. The automatic lighthouse was built in 1953.

In December 1957, the entire Natal coast suffered a severe setback as a holiday area when several shark attacks on bathers took place. Sharks, of course, were always present in the Indian Ocean but had never been a major problem. With the tremendous increase in holidaymakers along the coast and the pollution of the sea by the spoil of rivers, drainage and sewage systems, sharks seemed suddenly to have become aware that human beings were tasty.

As a solution to the predicament, Umhlanga Rocks erected shark nets in 1962 and two years later the Natal Anti-Shark Measures Board was established to study and to deal with the problem of sharks. The headquarters of this board was built on a hill overlooking Umhlanga Rocks and from here, the field staff service 256 nets which protect 39 recreational beaches in the 250-km stretch of coast from Port Edward in the south to Zinkwazi in the north. There is also a base station at Uvongo on the South Coast. Visitors are welcome at the Umhlanga headquarters at 14h30 on Wednesdays. There is a lecture on sharks, a film and a conducted tour of the laboratories.

In 1970 Umhlanga Rocks became a municipality and two years later it amalgamated with the adjoining residential township of La Lucia to become the borough of Umhlanga. The population is now 12 515.

## Accommodation

★★★★★ Beverly Hills Hotel, 83 rooms, all with baths. R31 – R43 B/B. Phone 51-2211.
★★★ Cabana Beach Hotel, 214 rooms, all with baths. R15 – R21 room only. Phone 51-2371.
★ Durban View Hotel, 42 rooms, all with baths. R8 – R10 B/B. Phone 51-1301.
★★ Edge-of-the-Sea Hotel, 33 rooms, 29 with baths. R13,50 – R15 B/B. Phone 51-1341.
★★★ Oyster Box Hotel, 98 rooms, all with baths. R19,80 – R33 B/B. Phone 51-2233.
★★ Umhlanga Rocks Hotel, 98 rooms, all with baths. R11 – R12 B/B. Phone 51-1321.
★★★ Umhlanga Sands Hotel, 237 rooms, all with baths. R14 – R47 room only. Phone 51-2300.

## Caravans and camping

★★ Bennetts Caravan Park, 36 sites. R5 D plus 60c D per person.
★★ Umhlanga Rocks Caravan Park, 36 sites. R5 D plus 60c D per person.

Crossing the Mhlanga River, the coastal road continues north and after 7,5 km joins the main highway which runs the full length of the Natal coast. Three kilometres north along this road there is a turnoff to La Mercy Beach and the resort at the mouth of the Mdloti River known as . . .

# MDLOTI

This river receives its name from a species of wild tobacco plant growing on its banks. A spacious lagoon, a pleasant beach with a rock-enclosed tidal pool and a cluster of hotels and bungalows comprise this resort, amongst trees and flowers.

## Accommodation

★ Selection Hotel, 32 rooms, 18 with baths. R7 – R8 B/B. Phone 20.
★★ Umdloti Strand Hotel, 62 rooms, all with baths. R7,50 – R9 B/B. Phone 1.

The coastal road, Shaka's Way, continues up the coast where many pleasant glimpses of the sea and beach are provided. Casuarina trees growing along the shoreline are an indication of the many Mauritians who have settled on the North Coast, producing sugar and remembering their island home by introducing to Natal their favourite trees (originating from Madagascar, where it is known as the *filaos* tree).

After 8 km of pleasant travel from the Mdloti River, the road reaches a turnoff to . . . .

# TONGAAT BEACH

The *Thongathi* River takes its name from a species of tree which grows on its banks. The resort is a relaxed, informal little place with bungalows shaded by whispering casuarina trees. The beach is pleasant and there is good fishing.

### Accommodation
** Tongaat Beach Hotel, 29 rooms, all with baths. R14,75 – R16,75 B/B. Phone 200.

Beyond Tongaat Beach the road continues north for 2 km, crosses the Thongathi River and then veers slightly inland, leaving the sea out of sight behind bush-covered coastal dunes. After 7 km a turnoff is reached, leading to the coast at Compensation Beach, Ballito Bay and 2 km further on, a turnoff to the resort of Shaka's Rock.

# BALLITOVILLE AND SHAKA'S ROCK

Shaka's Rock is said to have been a seaside resort favoured by Shaka during the last years of his life when his capital was established on the site of modern Stanger. Together with the adjoining resort of Ballitoville, Shaka's Rock forms a fine recreational stretch of coast with shark-protected swimming, a large tidal pool and a pleasant coastal pathway.

### Accommodation
* Shaka's Rock Hotel, 39 rooms, all with baths. R8 – R10 B/B. Phone 99.

### Caravans and camping
**® Dolphin Caravan Park, 79 sites. R4,50 D plus 90c D per person.

At a point 2,5 km beyond the turnoff to Shaka's Rock, there is another turnoff to the coastal resort of . . .

# SALT ROCK

A pleasant little resort, popular with fishermen and those people who prefer a quiet holiday beside the sea.

### Accommodation
** Salt Rock Hotel, 79 rooms, all with baths. R11 – R12,50 B/B. Phone Umhlali 25.

### Caravans and camping
** Salt Rock Caravan Park, 85 sites. R5,50 D plus 70c D per person.

North of the turnoff to Salt Rock (46 km from Durban), the road continues for 6 km reaching a turnoff to Tinley Manor Beach. Sugar cane covers the coastal terrace and there are turnoffs to small coastal resorts such as Blythedale Beach and Zinkwazi. At 73 km from Durban, the main coastal road, Shaka's Way, is joined by the old North Coast road, the Sugar Way. The combined roads continue through vast plantations of cane, passing the sugarmill at Darnall, crossing the river known as the *Zinkwazi* after the white-headed fish eagles and then, 85 km from Durban, reaching a gravel turnoff which stretches for 11 km to the mouth of the Tugela River.

### Caravans and camping
** Zinkwazi Beach Caravan Park, 125 sites. R6,50 – R9 D plus 50c D per person.

The gravel turnoff to the mouth of the Tugela River takes the traveller to several interesting places. One kilometre from the start of the turnoff stands Fort Pearson, looking out from a hilltop over the Tugela River, far north into Zululand. This fort was built by the British army in 1878 when they were preparing to invade Zululand. The fort dominates what was known as the lower Tugela drift. A great military camp was pitched beneath it, close to the river where the British army prepared their attack.

Little more than 1 km beyond the fort, the road passes the so-called 'Ultimatum Tree'. Under this wild fig tree which grows on the banks of the river, the Zulu headmen sent to meet the British commander on 11 December 1878, were given the ultimatum to take back to their king, Cetshwayo. The demanding terms of this ultimatum resulted in the Anglo-Zulu War.

The gravel road continues down the right bank of the Tugela River, and leaving the canelands behind, penetrates an attractive belt of coastal forest and then ends at the shallow bay at the mouth of the river. Some attractive camping sites are situated under the trees but this is a generally wild and unspoilt piece of coast where the waves tumble ashore like invaders on a solitary beach.

Beyond the gravel turnoff to the mouth of the river, the main tarmac road continues northwards for 4,5 km and then (89,5 km from Durban) reaches the traditional boundary between Natal and Zululand, the great river known to the Zulu as the *Thukela* (startling) on account of its size, the power of its floods, and the colossal valley which it has eroded in its middle reaches. Across this river, known to Europeans as the *Tugela,* lies Zululand.

# Chapter Twenty-two

# ZULULAND

The main coastal road, Shaka's Way, which links Durban to Zululand, Swaziland and the Eastern Transvaal, crosses the traditional southern frontier of Zululand, the Thukela (Tugela) River, by means of the John Ross Bridge. John Ross was a 15-year-old boy who, in 1827, under the instructions of his master walked from the ivory trading settlement of Durban, all the way to the Portuguese fort at Lourenço Marques (Maputo) to obtain urgently needed medicines. The courtesy of the Zulu saw him safely through his journey and he duly returned to his sick comrades with medicines and assorted comforts.

The road is at this stage 88 km from Durban and once across the river, climbs out of the valley of the Thukela. After 1 km there are turnoffs – west to the Mandini mill of S.A. Pulp and Paper Industries Ltd, and east to a recreational area on the northern side of the mouth of the Thukela River where a cluster of vacation cottages and a caravan park have been built.

### Caravans and camping
** Tugela Mouth North Bank Caravan Park, 10 sites. R3 D plus 30c D per person.

Beyond these turnoffs, the main coastal road continues northwards over an undulating terrace covered in sugar cane. At 16 km from the Thukela River the road bridges across the Matikulu River (*matigulu* – 'water that scrapes away') with the Huletts sugarmill standing on its banks. A further 4 km across the cane fields takes the road past the railway junction of . . .

## GINGINDLOVU

This place was named 'the swallower of the elephant' after a kraal established there in 1856 by the young Zulu prince, Cetshwayo, after he had defeated his brother Mbulazi in a struggle for succession to the Zulu throne. It is now a village and railway junction from where a branch line leads to Eshowe. In April 1879 a British force, on its way to relieve Eshowe (besieged by the Zulu), defeated a Zulu army at a site marked by a monument 3 km from Gingindlovu. The Battle of 'Gin gin I love you', as the British soldiers called it, opened the way for an advance on Eshowe.

### Accommodation
* Imperial Hotel, 16 rooms, 5 with baths. R8 – R10 B/B. Phone 20.

One kilometre north of Gingindlovu, a tarmac turnoff stretches for 21 km to Eshowe (see page 443). The main coastal road continues through the green sea of sugar cane, and 21 km from Gingindlovu, reaches a turnoff to the coastal resort of . . .

## MTUNZINI AND THE UMLALAZI NATURE RESERVE

The pleasant name of *Mtunzini* (the place in the shade) applies to an attractive little resort on the shores of the Indian Ocean. This was a favourite holiday place for John Dunn, the white chief of a section of the Zulu people living along the coast between the Thukela and the

Mhlathuze rivers. By the time he died in 1895, at the age of 61, Dunn had married 49 wives! His offspring numbered 117 and these, together with numerous followers and dependants, formed a small group of their own to add yet another patch to the complex ethnic 'quilt' of South Africa.

The Umlalazi Nature Reserve, established in 1948, receives its name from the *Mlalazi* (the place of whetstones) River. The reserve lies 1,5 km east of Mtunzini and covers 908 ha of coastal dune country, inhabited by numerous bushbuck, reedbuck, blue and grey duiker and many birds. The river is amply populated with crocodiles and the vegetation is interesting; a mangrove-covered lagoon in the river and several small lakelets and marshes.

## Accommodation
★ Mtunzini Hotel, 22 rooms, all with baths. R12 – R14 B/B. Phone 1.

## Caravans and camping
★ Casa Benri Camping Resort, 100 sites. R3 D plus 50c D per person.
★★ Forest Caravan Park, 24 sites. R3,50 D plus 35c D per person.
★ Umlalazi Nature Reserve, 65 sites. R1,20 D per person. 8 cottages, R5 D.
★★★ Xaxaza Caravan Park, 100 sites. R5,50 D plus 50c D per person.

Beyond the turnoff to Mtunzini the main coastal road crosses the Mlalazi River, passing the Forest Inn Motel and Caravan Park (after 11 km) and entering the area of the Port Durnford State Forest. Port Durnford simply consists of an exposed roadstead which was occasionally used by the British for landing supplies during the Anglo-Zulu War. A 6 000 candlepower lighthouse watches over the place today.

## Accommodation
★ Forest Inn, 47 rooms, R9 B/B. Phone Mtunzini 95.

## Caravans and camping
★ Caravan park (at above motel), 20 sites. R3 D.

The main coastal road proceeds in a northerly direction passing, after 5 km, the entrance to the University College of Zululand, opened in 1960. A further 3 km sees the road crossing the river known on account of its floods as the *Mhlathuze* (forceful). After 9 km of travel through the cane fields, the road, 29 km from Mtunzini, reaches the busy town and sugar centre of . . .

# EMPANGENI

In 1851 a mission was established by the Norwegians near by a stream on whose banks grew a number of *mpange* trees (*Treema guineensis*). It is from these trees that the name of *Empangeni* is derived. The mission was later moved to Eshowe but the original site was still regarded as a pleasant situation and in 1899 a magistracy was established there. The opening of the Zululand railway in 1903 made Empangeni a major staging post, and later, the junction of the branch line to Nkwalini and the sugar estates in the productive valley of the Mhlathuze River.

By 1906 Empangeni had become a village. In 1913 George Armstrong built a large sugarmill there, now run by Zululand Sugar Millers and Planters Ltd. As a result, the place progressed into a town which achieved full municipal status in 1960. Today, Empangeni is inhabited by 17 500 people.

Sugar, cotton, cattle and timber are the products of the district. In 1905 the first experimental timber plantations in Zululand were established by the government near Empangeni.

Some of the eucalyptus trees planted at that time are still flourishing, having reached heights of over 60 m.

## Accommodation
★ Imperial Hotel, 62 rooms, 19 with baths. R12 – R15 B/B. Phone 2-1522.
★ Royal Hotel, 14 rooms, 6 with baths. R10 – R13 B/B. Phone 2-1601.

From Empangeni, the main coastal road continues northwards, past the mill of Zululand Sugar Millers and Planters Ltd, through the cane fields and timber plantations. After 14 km the road crosses the Enseleni River, where there is a turnoff to the . . .

# ENSELENI NATURE RESERVE

Established in 1948 at a bend in the Enseleni River, this 293-ha reserve incorporates a picnic ground and nature trail. Amongst the wildlife are antelope species such as nyala, impala, zebra and blue wildebeest, while a very rich plant life comprises mangroves, papyrus, and some grand old wild fig trees lining the banks of the river.

One kilometre beyond the Enseleni River, a turnoff of 15 km leads across a level, grassy plain to . . .

# RICHARDS BAY

Admiral Sir F. W. Richards, after whom this great natural harbour is named, was commander of naval units during the Anglo-Zulu War. The bay lies at the mouth of the spacious lagoon in the Mhlathuze River. In its original state this lagoon provided a home for a vast population of aquatic birds, attracted to the area by a rich supply of fish. Crocodiles and sharks also frequented the lagoon, occasionally eating each other as well as the fish. Hippos were numerous and the celebrated wandering hippo, Huberta, is thought to have started her strange travels from this lagoon in 1928. She eventually walked as far down the coast as the Keiskamma River, south of King William's Town, where she was killed by hunters. Huberta is now the star exhibit in the Kaffrarian Museum.

Hunters and fishermen frequented the lagoon and it was there that John Dunn shot a giant crocodile just over 7 m long, the South African record. The potential of the lagoon as a harbour was apparent to all the early visitors and in 1826 two ivory traders, King and Isaacs, planned to develop the area. In 1897 a detailed survey of the lagoon was carried out, the results of which proved its suitability as a harbour. The area of the sheltered expanse of water was twice that of Durban; the mouth was open to the sea and although only 3 m deep, could be dredged to allow the passage of very large vessels. A second survey in 1902 again confirmed the harbour possibilities of the lagoon.

In 1935 the 1 200-ha lagoon was proclaimed a game reserve while the adjacent land on its northern side was, in 1945, declared the Richards Bay Park. The township of Richards Bay was laid out alongside this park, on the elevated northern shore of the lagoon, overlooking a fine stretch of water. Established as a health committee in 1954 and a municipality in 1959, the town has a population of 22 209.

From being a quiet little holiday resort, Richards Bay has developed into a major port, connected by railway to the coal and other mines of the Transvaal and accepting for loading, bulk carriers of very deep draught. The new harbour was opened in 1976.

## Accommodation
★ Bay Shore Inn, 60 rooms, 22 with baths. R15,50 B/B. Phone 3-2451.
★★★ Richards Hotel, 68 rooms, all with baths. R17 – R35 B/B. Phone 3-1301.

*Overleaf: Strange but true that the presence of tsetse fly in Zululand kept hunters at bay and gave the white rhino its last but enduring sanctuary.*

**Caravans and camping**
★★ Richards Bay Caravan Park, 200 sites. R3 D.

The main coastal road continues northwards from the turnoff to Richards Bay, through vast plantations of gum trees and sugar cane. Magnificent casuarina trees grow at railway centres such as Nseleni. After 13,5 km the road passes the state forests at *kwaMbonambi* (place of the Mbonambi tribe), and a sawmill at Denecuik siding 3 km further north. A turnoff to the east leads for 40 km to the coast at Mapelane where the Natal Parks Board maintains a camping ground and nine furnished log cabins.

Kilometres of gum plantations stretch off to the north. Twelve kilometres from kwaMbonambi, the road crosses the river known as the *Msunduze* (the pusher) on account of its destructive power during floods. A further 5,5 km takes the road to the bridge across one of the most important rivers in Zululand, the *Mfolozi* (zigzag) River, notorious for its violent floods and famous for the big game area, the Umfolozi Game Reserve, contained between the two upper divisions known as the White and Black Mfolozi rivers.

There is a turnoff, 5 km north of the bridge over the Mfolozi, to . . .

## MTUBATUBA

The railway centre of *Mtubatuba* receives its odd-sounding name – in corrupted form – from the chief of the local section of the Zulu people, Mthubuthubu. It is a small but busy trading centre bustling with labourers from the timber and cane plantations, trains loaded with timber, cane and other products of the area, constantly coming and going.

Mtubatuba was originally a siding when the North Coast railway was built in 1903. In 1911 the alluvial flats of the lower Mfolozi River were opened to sugar planting and a mill was built in 1916 at Riverview, close to Mtubatuba. This was the actual beginning of Mtubatuba as a commercial centre which, in 1950, achieved village status under the control of a health committee.

**Accommodation**
★★ Safari Motel, 51 rooms, all with baths. R12,50 – R14,55 B/B. Phone 107.
★ Sisalana Hotel, 9 rooms, 4 with baths. R8,32 B/B. Phone 202.
★ Sundowner Hotel, 16 rooms, 6 with baths. R8 – R13 room only. Phone 153.

Twenty-eight kilometres east of Mtubatuba, across a grassy, bush-covered coastal plain, lies the estuary, game reserve and resort of . . .

## ST LUCIA

During the Cretaceous period, about 100 million years ago, the flat coastal area of Zululand, Tongaland and Moçambique lay beneath the sea. The Indian Ocean washed against the slopes of the Lubombo mountains and laid down a rich deposit of coral and shells for man to unearth whenever he excavated the former sea bed.

This ancient sea bed eventually became the coastal plains of today when the waters, for some unknown reason, receded. Rivers which had originally reached the sea along the line formed by the Lubombo range, were now confronted by a barrier of sand in Zululand about 100 km wide. This flat coastal terrace proved a complex obstacle to the rivers whose flow was impeded by the flat nature of the plain, and by chance depressions which trapped the water, forming shallow lakelets. A final ridge of sand dunes piled up by wind action along the shore, held the rivers back, creating shallow lagoons and lakes.

Lake St Lucia originated in this way, forming a vast estuary system, roughly in the shape of the letter 'H'. The left limb of the 'H' consists of what is known as False Bay, 25 km long, 3 km wide and about 2 m deep. The crossbar of the 'H' is the so-called Hell's Gates, a windswept, treacherous stretch of water lying between two cliffs. The southernmost gate is formed by what is known as Goose Point, frequently used in former years as a base camp for hippo hunters.

The right-hand limb of the 'H' is Lake St Lucia proper, a vast and beautifully wild stretch of water, 40 km long, 10 km across and an average of 2 m deep. Three reed-covered islands lie on its surface; the largest is Bird Island, and the other two are *Lane Island,* named after William Lane of the Natal Parks Board who used to fish there, and *Fanie's Island,* named after a Zulu headman who lived on the opposite mainland.

Fanie's Island separates the lake from its southern reach, which empties into the estuary channel. A shallow finger of the lake beset with mudbanks, this channel gropes towards the sea where it unites with the mouth of the Mfolozi River.

The whole lake system has always been fed as much by the sea as by the various rivers flowing into it. Immense evaporation of water in the hot climate has caused the residue to become increasingly saline, with False Bay having a salinity of 52,6 parts per 1 000, compared to the 35 parts per 1 000 of the sea.

Large shoals of fish – salmon, grunter, mullet, mud bream and others – have always frequented the lakes. At the estuary they are prey to numerous big game fish and sharks, while crocodiles haunt the entire lake, particularly at the mouths of the tributary rivers. About 400 hippos comprise a resident population of mammals. Over 25 species of aquatic birds find rich feeding in the area, with flamingos, pelicans, sea eagles, duck, geese, goliath herons, kingfishers and cormorants being particularly prolific and providing many wonderful spectacles.

Since as far back as 1897, the 36 826 ha covered by the waters of Lake St Lucia have been an official game reserve. The land surrounding the lake, 1 km wide and comprising a total of 12 545 ha, was proclaimed the St Lucia Park in 1939, while an area of 2 247 ha at False Bay was also declared a park in 1944. In these reserves live reedbuck, bushbuck, nyala, impala, grey and red duiker, suni, steenbok and bushpigs. The whole expanse has an exceedingly varied and interesting vegetation consisting of grasslands, patches of forest, mangroves and ferns. For walkers there are wilderness trails which follow the verges of the lake. These outings are conducted between April and October by professional rangers and usually last three or four days. Launch trips in the lake are also organised by the Parks Board.

Fishing, boating and the enjoyment of nature are popular pastimes at Lake St Lucia. The best time to visit the area is in winter, when it is cooler. Apart from the hotels at the estuary, the Natal Parks Board maintains four open-air camping areas and two hutted camps.

## Accommodation
★ Estuary Hotel, 20 rooms, all with baths. R9,50 – R10,50 B/B. Phone 9.
★★ Lake View Hotel, 30 rooms, all with baths. R12 – R13 B/B. Phone 6.
Charters Creek, 15 rondawels (2 beds each), with cooking facilities. R3 D per person.
Fanie's Island, 12 rondawels (2 beds each), with cooking facilities. R3 D per person.

## Caravans and camping
★ Cape Vidal, 50 sites. R1,20 D per person.
★ Fanie's Island, 50 sites. R1,50 D per site.
★ False Bay Park, 45 sites. R1,20 D per person.
★ St Lucia Resort, 239 sites. R1,80 D per person.
★★ St Lucia Travel Lodge and Caravan Park, 40 sites. R2 D plus R1 D per person.

# MTUBATUBA TO THE GAME RESERVES

Three kilometres north of the turnoff to Mtubatuba and Lake St Lucia, the main coastal road reaches a second turnoff of considerable importance to tourists. This is the road leading to the game reserves of Hluhluwe and Umfolozi, and thence to Nongoma, Melmoth and Eshowe. The very heart of Zululand is penetrated by this route which passes the sites of many historic kraals and battlefields, and reveals some of the most majestic scenery of a romantic little country.

After 21 km this turnoff reaches yet another turnoff (15 km) which leads northwards through an open area of tribal settlement to the entrance gate (and thence for 17 km to the camp) of the . . .

## HLUHLUWE GAME RESERVE

Without doubt one of the best known and most popular game reserves in the world, Hluhluwe is 23 067 ha in extent. The reserve covers a superb piece of Zululand hill country, cut by the deep valley of the Hluhluwe River which has given the place its name. The river, in turn, receives its Zulu name from the thorny monkey ropes (*Dalbergia armata*) which grow on its banks. Hluhluwe was proclaimed a game reserve in 1897 and its varied landscape, ranging from densely forested lowlands to open hill summits, provides a sanctuary for a considerable diversity of flora and fauna. Rhino, both black (about 250) and white (about 100) are easily seen. There are also buffalo, nyala, kudu, waterbuck, impala, giraffe, zebra, blue wildebeest, bushbuck, steenbok, reedbuck and red and grey duikers, warthog, bushpig, leopards, cheetahs, monkeys and baboons, hyenas, an occasional lion, crocodiles, and vast numbers of birds.

Hluhluwe has an atmosphere entirely its own and remains imprinted in the memories of innumerable tourists on account of the variety of sights, experiences, impressions, and most satisfying tranquillity experienced there. The reserve is open throughout the year.

### Accommodation
Hutted camp: 4 self-contained cottages (4 beds each), R6 D per person. 25 rondawels (2 beds each), R4 D per person. Communal kitchen and ablution block. Bedding and utensils provided but only petrol, curios and film sold in camp.

From the turnoff to Hluhluwe Game Reserve, the main gravel Mtubatuba-Nongoma road continues north-westwards for 7 km over low hills covered in acacia bush and fairly densely inhabited by tribal people.

At 27 km from Mtubatuba, the road reaches a turnoff south leading for 23 km to the . . .

## UMFOLOZI GAME RESERVE

A 47 753-ha expanse of wilderness, Umfolozi is one of the most important game sanctuaries in the world. At the time of its proclamation in 1897 the last significant numbers of white (square-lipped) rhino in Africa lived in this lovely wilderness. This species, once on the verge of extinction, has been carefully safeguarded at Umfolozi and today flourish to such extent that each year a surplus population is immobilised by tranquillising darts and shipped off to zoos and other game reserves. Over 500 surplus white rhinos have been removed in this way leaving a balance of about 750 white rhinos, the number estimated as being safe for the carrying capacity of the reserve.

Umfolozi is an undulating, bush-covered wilderness area contained between the two great branches of the *Mfolozi* (zigzag) River, the *Mfolozi emnyama* (black Mfolozi) and the *Mfolozi emhlophe* (white Mfolozi). Hills overlook the reserve from the north and the atmosphere is particularly romantic. As with Hluhluwe, Umfolozi may truly be said to preserve not only the wildlife of Zululand, but also something of the indefinable charm and tradition surrounding one of the most storied and fascinating parts of Africa.

Apart from rhino, the reserve also carries a substantial population of bushbuck, zebra, blue wildebeest, waterbuck, duiker, steenbok, reedbuck, klipspringer, kudu and nyala. There are numerous buffalo, giraffe, baboons, hyenas, cheetahs, leopards and a very remarkable group of lions whose story provides one of the most incredible episodes of conservation in Africa.

Lions in Zululand had long since been shot out. But in 1958, motivated by some totally unknown factor, a male lion found his way from Moçambique across 300 km of inhabited country and established himself in Umfolozi. Throughout his travels he had been tracked, hunted and pursued by the usual trigger-itchy goon squad but had given them all the slip. In his book *Bushlife of a Game Warden* Nick Steele has described very well the feelings of the rangers and conservationists regarding the adventures and perils of this lion, and their delight when he safely reached the reserve. The arrival of this lone animal was in itself remarkable but even more curious was the fact that, after a few years of celibate existence, he was joined by several females. The result of this is a healthy and happy lion population in Umfolozi, who occasionally visit Hluhluwe to feed on the plump antelope there.

The reserve is open throughout the year. About half of the area has been set aside as a wilderness through which parties of up to six people are escorted on three-day walking tours.

### Accommodation

Hutted camp: 12 squaredawels (3 beds each) and 6 rest huts, all with bedding and utensils. R4 D per person. Communal kitchen and ablution block. Only petrol, curios and limited photographic material is sold in the reserve.

From the turnoff to the Umfolozi Game Reserve, the main Mtubatuba-Nongoma road continues north-westwards, climbing steadily through taller and denser bush. Numerous game animals, including rhino, may be seen for the road is now traversing what is known as the Corridor, a belt of unsettled virgin land which provides a natural link between the Hluhluwe and Umfolozi game reserves. The future of this lovely piece of wilderness is as yet undecided, but it will be a great loss to mankind if people are ever allowed to settle there. The demand is high for accessible recreational and wilderness areas in the world today and with Africans now taking as much interest in the natural splendours of this continent as European tourists, the pressure on existing conservation areas will become overwhelming. It is the hope of all conservationists that this region, rather than be spoilt, should be retained for future game reserve development.

The road continues for 23 km beyond the turnoff to Umfolozi, climbing through lovely hill country and yielding many pleasant views of a green and almost classic expanse of Zululand scenery. With a final panoramic view over game areas, the road tops the escarpment and leads over a grassy, undulating plateau to enter, after 4 km (53 km from Mtubatuba), the magisterial seat and small village of *Hlabisa,* named after the Zulu clan of that name.

The gravel road proceeds across grassy hills, densely settled with tribal people whose cattle and maize lands are spread out on either side. The road finds a way through a narrow valley, well wooded with trees and wild banana palms. Climbing steadily, the road reaches another plateau; an open grassveld, with low hill slopes. At 87 km from Mtubatuba there is a turnoff north to Mkuze (47 km). The road climbs a ridge of hills on a summit of which, 99,5 km from Mtubatuba, stands the village and administrative centre of . . .

# NONGOMA

*KwaNongoma* (the place of the diviner) comprises one street lined with stores, houses and administrative buildings which overlook a vast stretch of surrounding country. Founded in 1887, the high perch on which the village is built was selected as a good strategic situation in what was then a very troubled part of Zululand. In fact, Nongoma was destroyed in June 1888 by supporters of the chief Dinuzulu and was only re-occupied two months later by government forces.

## Accommodation
* Nongoma Hotel, 20 rooms, 7 with baths. R11 – R12 D. Phone 37.

# MTUBATUBA TO THE NORTH

From the turnoff to Nongoma, 3 km north of Mtubatuba, the main coastal road continues north-eastwards through plantations of eucalyptus, pine trees and sugar cane. At 17 km from Mtubatuba, at Nyalazi railway siding, a turnoff east leads for 12 km to Charters Creek on Lake St Lucia (see page 434).

After 3 km the road crosses the Nyalazi River, and after a further 8 km crosses the Hluhluwe River. Occasional patches of light bush and lala palms appear amongst the sugar cane and eucalyptus trees.

At 49 km from Mtubatuba, the road reaches the small railway centre of Hluhluwe, from where turnoffs lead to False Bay (17 km east) and to the Hluhluwe Game Reserve (17 km west to the entrance, plus 12 km to the rest camp). For those sections, see pages 435 and 436.

## Accommodation
** White Rhino Holiday Inn, 65 rooms, all with baths. R19 – R32 room only. Phone 46.
*** Zululand Safari Lodge, 42 rooms, all with baths. R23 – R29 B/B. Phone 64.

The main tarmac road continues north-westwards across gently rolling country covered in huge plantations of sisal. Elegantly shaped fever trees grow along the watercourses. Nine kilometres from the village of Hluhluwe, the road passes the small railway centre of *Ngweni* (place of the leopard), situated in the midst of the sisal estate. Beyond, the road continues and in the distance on the eastern side, emerges the southern beginning of the *Lubombo* (ridge), a continuous mountain wall of dark basalt rock which stretches far to the north.

At 33 km from Hluhluwe, the road crosses the Msunduze River on whose banks lie the plantations of the Msunduze Sisal Estates where piles of white sisal may be seen at the drying sheds. The road continues across fields of sisal alternating with patches of savanna, covered in grass and acacia trees of various species. Fever trees growing in the watercourses are especially handsome with their deep green leaves and greenish-white bark.

At 47 km from Hluhluwe, the main tarmac road reaches a turnoff leading eastwards for 8 km to the entrance of the . . .

# MKUZI GAME RESERVE

The approach to the Mkuzi Game Reserve is picturesque; the road finds a natural passage through the Lubombo mountains, forested with many tall trees and clustered with tribal huts. At the entrance to the reserve is a caravan park, with the office and hutted camp 3 km further on. The reserve, quite apart from its game population, is a botanist's delight, consisting of 25 091 ha of beautiful natural parkland. The variety and elegance of the trees must be seen to be appreciated.

Mkuzi contains a dense population of impala, blue wildebeest, nyala, kudu, zebra, bushbuck, reedbuck, red duiker, steenbok, and black and white rhino. Bird life is extremely diverse and their songs very lovely. Excellent roads, three well-designed hides (ideal for photography) and a comfortable hutted camp, make this a delightful piece of wilderness.

The reserve is named after the *Mkhuze* River which forms its northern and eastern boundary. The river receives its name from the aromatic trees *(Heteropyxis natalensis)* which grow along its banks and is also notable for handsome trees such as the giant wild figs. The river is one of the principal feeders of Lake St Lucia and its mouth has always been a notorious lurking place for crocodiles. Most of the water, however, is nowadays used for irrigation and the flow is therefore erratic.

Mkuzi (a misspelling of Mkhuze) was proclaimed a game reserve in 1912. For some reason it has always existed under the threat of deproclamation and conversion into farmland. Such an event would be tragic; in future years the need for such wilderness areas of recreation and refreshment will be so pressing that governments will be buying back farmland and re-establishing trees and game animals. For any modern government to abandon an established reserve would be folly indeed.

There are one-day walks and three-day wilderness trails through the reserve which is open throughout the year. Summer months, however, are very hot.

## Accommodation
6 squaredawels, R3 D per person. 3 rustic huts, R2 D per person. Communal ablution and kitchen facilities. Bedding and utensils but no food.

## Caravans and camping
★ 24 sites, R1,80 D plus R1,20 D per person.

From the turnoff to the Mkuzi Game Reserve, the road continues north-westwards along the bush-covered slopes of the Lubombo range. After 9 km the road reaches the small rural and rail centre of Mkuze, baking in a warm summer sun, in the midst of sugar cane fields near where the Mkhuze River passes through the Lubombo. Overlooking Mkuze is the 520-m-high peak which Europeans call Ghost Mountain. Known more prosaically to the Zulus as *iTshaneni* (the place of the small stone) this mountain is considered taboo. A secret cave somewhere near the summit is used as a burial site for the chiefs of the Gasa clan (the ruling family of the Shangane tribe of Moçambique). Tales are told of strange lights and weird sounds which issue from this mountain and the superstitious will not approach its slopes.

At the foot of this enchanted mountain in the valley of the Mkhuze, lies the battlefield where, on 5 June 1884, the bold Zibebu and his Mandlakazi section of the Zulu were defeated by the Suthu of Dinuzulu, supported by 115 European mercenaries. Until recently, the battlefield was still littered with bones from this fight.

## Accommodation
★★ Ghost Mountain Inn, 30 rooms, 26 with baths. R13 B/B. Phone 18.

From Mkuze, the road continues north-westwards, crossing the Mkhuze River. Three kilometres from the village is a turnoff which leads eastwards for 12 km, in a steep and spectacular climb to the magisterial village of Ubombo, on the plateau summit of the Lubombo range. This is a most interesting drive and the variety of flora is especially fascinating. The display of flowering aloes in late summer is superb.

Ubombo is the administrative centre for a part of the forest-covered coastal belt known as Tongaland. Beyond the village, a road descends steeply into this wilderness of trees for 89 km, reaching the coast at the . . . .

# SODWANA BAY NATIONAL PARK

This park comprises a narrow coastal strip of forest-covered sand dunes, 413 ha in extent. Proclaimed in 1950, its camping ground is particularly popular with fishermen, especially during the winter holiday season. However, in summer it is hot and humid. A few antelope such as suni, duiker, steenbok and reedbuck as well as bushpig, frequent the area along with a wealth of bird life. The name is derived from an isolated streamlet known to the tribespeople as *Sodwana* (little one on its own).

## Caravans and camping
★ 600 sites, R1,20 D per person.

From the turnoff to Ubombo, the main tarmac road continues north-westwards for a further 7,5 km reaching a turnoff to the east. From here the turnoff stretches for 23 km, climbing a well-located route 600 m up the Lubombo to Jozini, the site of the J. G. Strydom Dam in Pongola Poort. *Jozini* (named after a tribal headman) overlooks the wall of what is one of the largest irrigation dams in Southern Africa. The village was created to house the constructional workers on this project, which was completed in 1969. The dam impounds the waters of the river named by the tribespeople the *Phongolo* (like a trough) because, being long and deep, there were few crossing places. The dam is intended to irrigate a vast area for the cultivation of sugar, rice, coffee, fibre crops and subtropical fruits.

## Accommodation
★ Jozini Ho-Motel, 11 rooms, 6 with baths. R7 – R8 B/B. Phone 20.

# TONGALAND, NDUMU AND KOSI BAY

The sweltering hot, feverous and bilharzia-ridden but otherwise happy wilderness of Tongaland, seems destined to be considerably altered from its present primeval state. For some reason its totally undeveloped condition has always been an irritant to certain people. Many schemes for the development of this flat, sandy, forest-covered area have been promoted. Few bother to think that Tongaland might conceivably be best left in its present state – a giant wilderness where game animals could be ranched for the world venison market and edible fish farmed in the shallow lakelets; where wild fruits can be propagated to provide mankind with new flavours; and where magnificent winter recreational areas might be developed, including controlled safari hunting areas as well as game-viewing resorts.

A visit to Tongaland as it is now, is a unique experience for the botanist, the bird and game enthusiast, and for the person who simply wants to relieve his mind of the tensions of city life by returning to nature.

Tongaland occupies an area of 7 000 square kilometres. In Cretaceous times (100 million years ago) this flat, sandy tract of country was the sea bed and waves washed against the cliffs of the Lubombo. The sea receded, leaving a stretch of sand amply covered with shells. Shallow depressions, gathering fresh water spilled into them by rivers such as the Phongolo and Mkhuze meandering their way to the sea, formed the numerous shallow lakelets which are such a feature of Tongaland today.

A prodigious number of trees flourish in the area, among them some of the most majestic wild fig trees in Africa. Several acacia species, including the elegant fever trees, also grow to perfection.

The trees form a belt about 40 km wide stretching from the Lubombo eastwards. They then peter out into a strip of lala palms which in turn, give way to open grassy coastal flats, followed by a thin line of coastal forest and a wall of tall sand dunes, resembling a dyke built by nature to keep the sea from flooding these lowlands. These topographical features terminate in a stretch of glistening beach where rocky fishermen's promontories jut out into the languid blue of the Indian Ocean.

This wilderness was always a great resort for game animals and over 200 species of birds are to be found here. Fish, crocodiles and hippos teem in the lakelets and rivers.

Several tribal fragments also inhabit the area, the largest of these being the Tembe people, who are, curiously enough, related to the Karanga tribe of Zimbabwe. The name of *Tonga* was indiscriminately applied to all the people in this part of the world by the Zulu who were aware of the existence much further to the north of a tribe of this name.

---

Jozini acts as a gateway to Tongaland. From the village, one road leads south along the Lubombo to the magistracy of Ubombo, and to Sodwana Bay. Another road proceeds north, crosses the Phongolo at the foot of the dam wall and, after 3 km, reaches a junction. Both branches from this junction stretch north to Ndumu Game Reserve, but one road keeps to the high country, while the other makes its way through the trees of the lowlands. The latter road is the shorter, but enquiries should always be made in Jozini as to which road is the more suitable; their condition varies from fair to execrable.

The lowland road travels eastwards down the left bank of the Phongolo to the old fording place and store at Otobotini (6 km from Jozini). From here it swings northwards, finding a picturesque way through the trees for 41 km before rejoining the upland road.

The upland road, meanwhile, makes its way northwards high up on the slopes of the Lubombo, yielding interesting views over the low country. After 48 km the road reaches a junction from where a turn left leads for 8 km to the magisterial and trading village of *Ingwavuma* (named after the river, itself named after the species of tree, *Pseudocassine transvaalensis*). From this isolated little centre and its tremendous views, a road (not always open) descends for 23 km down the Cecil Mack Pass to Swaziland where it joins the main Golela-Manzini road. A turn right at the junction before Ingwavuma, takes the road down the eastern slopes of the Lubombo through a dense forest, to join the lowland road after 24 km (72 km from Jozini).

The united roads continue northwards through the forest, where many interesting succulents (including the carrion flower) grow by the wayside. After 19 km the road crosses the Ngwavuma River, with tall fever trees thriving on its banks. One kilometre further on the road passes the Ndumu trading station and after a further kilometre (72 km from Jozini via the lowland road) reaches the entrance with the camp 6 km away of the . . .

## NDUMU GAME RESERVE

This reserve, 10 117 ha in extent, was named after a Tembe chieftain who once lived on the slopes of the overlooking hill. Proclaimed in 1924, it conserves one of the most gorgeous arboral and riverine landscapes on earth. Here the tree has found a perfect home; exquisitely beautiful and of infinite variety, they form a primeval forest through which the roads literally tunnel.

Game animals roam this forest: shy nyala (about 2 000 of them), impala, suni, bushbuck, duiker, bushpig, black and white rhino. The density of the forest makes it difficult for the game to be seen, nevertheless the animals haunt the forest like elusive ghosts, lending a subtle piquancy to the place.

The trees, however, are the stars of the reserve and of the estimated 200 different species, there are no examples more beautiful to be seen anywhere else. The riverine forests of fever trees and wild figs are superlatively lovely, and the powerful, majestic uSuthu River which forms the northern boundary of the reserve (and the frontier between South Africa and Moçambique), is made more so by the handsome trees growing on its banks.

Some 390 species of birds may be seen in the reserve, while the series of shallow lakelets fed by floodwater overflow from the Phongolo and uSuthu rivers, contain an astonishingly rich population of fish, crocodiles (feeding on the fish), and about 400 hippos living well on the luxuriant grazing around the verges. With fish eagles sending their eerie cry over the calm waters, hippos 'gallumphing', fish splashing, spur wing geese honking and hissing, and the crocodiles moving with such sinister silence and stealth that scarcely a ripple reaches the surface, these lakelets almost belong to a dream world.

There is a crocodile breeding station at Ndumu, where eggs are hatched and the young protected for the first three years of life. They are then released in waters where their kind has been depleted by hunters, the result of whose activities has seriously affected the balance of fish life.

Ndumu is open throughout the year, but November to March is excessively hot and humid. From April the weather becomes cooler and vast numbers of birds flock to the area. May, June and July are the coolest months when bird life is at its most prolific. But at all seasons, even in sweltering heat, Ndumu is worth visiting.

### Accommodation
7 squaredawels (3 beds each), R5 D per person. Central kitchen and ablution block. Bedding and utensils but no food.

For those adventurers who wish to see still more of the Tongaland wilderness and who possess a four-wheel-drive vehicle, a sandy track stretches eastwards from the road to Ndumu at the point where the road from Ingwavuma joins the lowland road from Jozini (31 km from Ingwavuma). This track tunnels through the forest for a further 23 km and then crosses the Phongolo at the fording place, *Makhane's Drift,* named after a chieftain who once lived there.

The track then continues through the forest and across the belt of lala palms whose fermented sap provides the local tribespeople with the unique facility of being able to acquire unlimited quantities of intoxicating liquor. The result is that many alcoholic mothers give birth to inebriated babies who, when they eventually die of old age, are still in that presumably happy state, never having known sobriety!

At 57 km from Makhane's Drift the track reaches the remote trading post of *Maputo* (named after the chief Mabudu). From this little centre, the track proceeds north-eastwards over an open grassy landscape of flats and sandy hillocks. Branch tracks lead eastwards to the chain of lakes known to Europeans as Kosi. These magnificent lakes – *Hlangwe* (the reedy lake), 8 km long, 5 km wide and 50 m deep; *oKhunwini* (place of firewood); *uKhalwe* (the distant one); and their estuary *enKovukeni* (ebb and flow) – received their European name as the result of a mistake made by the pioneer marine surveyor who marked them on his chart as being the mouth of the 'omKosi' (Mkhuze) River. The lakes contain numerous fish which are caught in complex reed traps constructed by the local tribespeople.

The Kosi Bay Nature Reserve of 20 ha was proclaimed in 1950, on the shores of Lake Hlangwe. The ranger in charge has the additional task of patrolling the beaches where the leatherback and loggerhead turtles nest in one of the few sanctuaries provided for these interesting creatures.

The track from Maputo, meanwhile, continues north-eastwards for 24 km past the Kosi Bay store, crossing the frontier line between South Africa and Moçambique. Eight kilometres beyond the Kosi Bay store, a turnoff to the coast leads through an exquisite parkland, ending at a lazy little bay with a high, sandy headland jutting protectively into the sea to form Oro Point. Originally the Portuguese called the mouth of the Kosi lakes the *Rio de la Medãos do*

*Oro* (river of the sands of gold), of which name Oro Point is the sole remnant. A small lighthouse watches over the point, a lonely little outpost marking the frontier between South Africa and Moçambique and the most easterly point of South Africa. Good fishing, and the beautiful phosphorescent sands at night, make this an interesting place for the adventurous to visit.

**Caravans and camping**
★ Kosi Bay Nature Reserve, 12 sites. R1,50 D.

From the turnoff to Jozini and Tongaland, 10,5 km from Mkuze, the main tarmac road travels north-westwards across a bush and aloe-covered plain dominated to the east by the massive wall of the Lubombo. At 19,5 km from Mkuze the road crosses the railway line at Candover station, passes a turnoff west to Magudu (40 km) and continues over a rolling plain, covered with acacias and sisal estates.

At 30 km from Mkuze, the road climbs a ridge and in a finely located route, descends into the valley of the Phongolo River where fields of sugar cane are irrigated. At 33,5 km from Mkuze, the road crosses the Phongolo into the Transvaal and leads westwards up the valley of this important river. After 3 km there is a turnoff north-eastwards to the border of Swaziland at the Golela railway terminus (9 km).

From the turnoff to Swaziland, the left-hand branch of the road continues westwards to the township of Pongola and the Eastern Transvaal (see page 617).

---

# ESHOWE AND THE ZULU COUNTRY

One kilometre north of Gingindlovu, on the main coastal road of Zululand, a tarmac turnoff stretches westwards to Eshowe and from there to several interesting places in the heart of traditional Zulu country. One kilometre after this turnoff commences, a monument is passed, marking the site of the Battle of Gingindlovu, fought in April 1879 when a British force on its way to relieve Eshowe from a Zulu siege, defeated a Zulu attack. Beyond this battle site the road climbs 500 m up the sugar cane-covered hill slopes, from where the lovely countryside may be viewed. After 21 km the road reaches the summit, entering the municipal area of . . .

# ESHOWE

The pretty town of Eshowe is built on the site of a gorgeous hilltop forest known on account of its silence and dark recesses as the *Dlinza* (a grave-like place of meditation). Since 1952, 187 ha of this forest have been protected as a nature reserve, with the town surrounding it. Within its confines live bushbuck, blue and red duiker, wild pigs, vervet monkeys and numerous birds. Fine drives and walks yield many delightful scenes of tall trees, fern-grown glades, streams and waterfalls. In a central glade, known as the Bishop's Seat, church services are occasionally held and every three years a nativity play specially written in 1953 by Selwyn Moberley, is performed in this natural 'amphitheatre'.

Eshowe overlooks a fine view from its hilltop and the altitude contributes to a refreshing climate. The sounds of the cool breezes of Eshowe sighing through the trees are, in fact, said to have given the place its attractive name. This may be so, although the Zulu say the name is derived from the xysmalobium shrubs growing there, which they call *ishowe* or *ishongwe*.

Eshowe originated in 1860 when Cetshwayo built his *eSighwagini* (abode of robbers) kraal in the area and granted the Norwegian missionary, Ommund Oftebro, permission to establish what became known as the *kwaMondi* Mission, from the Zulu version of Oftebro's first name. It

443

was here, after the disaster of iSandlwana, that a British force was besieged by the Zulu for ten weeks until 3 April 1879, after the battle of Gingindlovu (known to the soldiers as 'Gin, gin I love you').

After the Anglo-Zulu War, Eshowe became the administrative centre for the British Resident Commissioner, Melmoth Osborn. To support him, a force of Zulu, the Reserve Territorial Carbineers, popularly known as the *Nongqayo* (restrainers) was created. A Beau Geste-type fort, built for them at Eshowe, is now a picturesque museum housing an interesting collection of Zululand relics. It is open daily from 10h00 to 17h00.

In 1887 Eshowe became the capital of the whole of Zululand and in 1892 the first sale of erven established its future as a town. Tall trees and colourful gardens, a magnificent swimming pool in the forest, Rutledge Park with its lake full of waterfowl and Ocean View Game Park just off the road to Gingindlovu, contribute towards making Eshowe one of the most pleasant small towns in Southern Africa. The population is 7 030.

### Accommodation
* Provincial Hotel, 25 rooms, 16 with baths. R11 – R11,50 B/B. Phone 4.
* Royal Hotel, 25 rooms, 16 with baths. R10,50 B/B. Phone 2.

### Caravans and camping
** Municipal caravan park, 20 sites. R2,60 D.

From Eshowe a very interesting scenic route to Empangeni may be followed. This gravel road branches off from the Eshowe-Melmoth tarmac road 8 km from Eshowe, and runs along the verge of the tremendous valley of the Mhlathuze River, once one of the great game areas of Zululand but now extensively planted with sugar cane. Impressive views, the numerous Zulu huts and tribal villages, the acacia trees and euphorbias; all make the journey picturesque.

At 27 km from Eshowe, a monument on the left (north) side of the road marks the site of Shaka's great capital of *kwaBulawayo* (place of the man who was killed) which was situated on the summit of a rounded hill, now overgrown with thick grass and a few euphorbia and other trees. It is fascinating to imagine the day in 1824 when Henry Fynn, the ivory trader, was the first European to visit the place from the new settlement at Port Natal (Durban). There the rugged adventurer found an African city of several thousand huts. He was ceremoniously welcomed by the great Zulu king in the presence of 12 000 warriors in full war dress, while 10 000 girls in exquisite bead costumes danced in his honour. It must have been a spectacle of barbaric splendour unsurpassed on the whole continent of Africa.

One kilometre beyond the site of kwaBulawayo, a memorial draws attention to a kei apple tree growing at the roadside, known as Coward's Bush, where Shaka reputedly tested, by means of some ordeal, those of his men accused of cowardice.

The gravel road descends to cross the *Mhlathuze* (forceful) River and, 45 km from Eshowe, joins the tarmac Nkwalini-Empangeni road 12 km from the latter town.

## ESHOWE TO ULUNDI AND NONGOMA

This road takes the traveller through fine scenery to several of the most interesting historical sites of Zululand. From Eshowe the tarmac road leads for 6 km, passes a turnoff to the site of kwaBulawayo (see above) and then makes a grand descent into the valley of the Mhlathuze River. This huge valley, overlooked by a jumble of high hills, was once a haunt of big game and a favourite hunting ground of the Zulu kings. This is a supreme piece of Zulu country, with the huts of the tribespeople perched on the hill slopes and the river twisting lazily down the valley like a sinuous python.

The road bridges across the Mhlathuze River 17 km from Eshowe, passing the trading centre and railhead of Nkwalini 3 km further on, with a tarmac turnoff leading down the valley to Empangeni. The road then starts to ascend the steep northern side of the valley, a magnificent drive which reveals many exciting views. After 6 km the road reaches the summit and continues through the high hills until, 48,4 km from Eshowe, it reaches the village of . . .

# MELMOTH

When the British Government annexed Zululand in 1887, several magistracies were established, one of which was named *Melmoth* after Melmoth Osborn, the Resident Commissioner and chief magistrate of the country. The high hill country surrounding the village was ideal for the growing of trees, particularly wattle. In 1926 a factory was established in Melmoth to process the bark of the wattle trees to make tanning extract. The village is now a trading centre for considerable industry in the growing of trees to obtain timber, wattle extract and paper-making material.

### Accommodation
★ Melmoth Inn, 12 rooms, 3 with baths. R10 – R10,50 B/B. Phone 44.

From Melmoth the main tarmac road climbs steadily through fields of sugar cane and plantations of trees. After 4,5 km a turnoff leads to Babanango and Dundee while 14 km further on there is a turnoff to Katazo (*Ntaba Khathazo,* the hill of khathazo plants) and from there to Nkandla. The road is now on the summit of the escarpment, in what is known as the mist belt, where the plantations of trees are particularly dense and green as a result of the water which condenses from the winds as they rise from the coast and top the summit ridge of the hills.

On the summit the road passes a monument marking the *Mthonjaneni* (place of the little fountain) which gives this ridge its name. From this spring the Zulu kings drew their own drinking water which was reserved for their personal use. A grand view reveals to the west, the valley of the Mkhumbane, the traditional birthplace of the Zulu nation and the residence of all their early kings.

The road descends the western slopes of the Mthonjaneni ridge and at 24 km from Melmoth reaches a turnoff leading westwards to Vryheid. Five kilometres along this turnoff there is a turnoff signposted Dingane's Kraal, an important historical site 4,5 km away in the valley of the Mkhumbane.

# DINGANE'S KRAAL

About 300 years ago, according to tradition, the man named *Zulu* (heaven) who founded the Zulu nation, found his way into the warm, bush-covered valley of the stream known as the *Mkhumbane* (stream of the hollow). He settled in the valley with a handful of dependants, eventually dying there. His grave is marked with a euphorbia tree planted at what is known as *kwaNkosinkhulu* (place of the great chief).

When Shaka became king of the Zulu he built a capital on the right bank of the Mhodi tributary of the Mkhumbane. This capital he named *kwaBulawayo* (place of the man who was killed) in memory of the persecutions of his youth. When he expanded his territorial control over what is now Zululand, he moved this capital south to a site overlooking the Mhlathuze Valley (page 444).

In 1828 Shaka was assassinated by two of his half-brothers, Mhlangana and Dingane. Dingane became king and built a new capital in the valley of the Mkhumbane. This capital he named *uMgungundlovu* (the secret plot of the elephant), a name which referred to the intrigue surrounding the assassination of Shaka.

It is worth visiting the site of uMgungundlovu, where the hard floors of many of the huts and other interesting relics may be seen. In its heyday, uMgungundlovu was an enormous hut city and the centre for endless ceremonial activities, military parades, dances and affairs of state of the Zulu nation. The scenic setting of the valley is impressive: to the north looms the principal landmark of this part of the world, the flat-topped 1 448-m-high *Nhlazatshe* (green stone) Mountain; immediately west of this mass of rock stands the stool-shaped mountain known as *isiHlalo sikaManyosi* (the seat of Manyosi).

Manyosi was a famous fat man and favourite of Dingane who found it amusing to display his gluttony to visitors by letting Manyosi eat, at one sitting, his fill of an entire goat and then look for more. Manyosi's pampered life ended when he said something out of place and Dingane had him starved to death. The stool-shaped mountain is his memorial.

It was at uMgungundlovu on 5 February 1838 that Dingane massacred Piet Retief and 70 of his men. The scene of the murder was the Zulu place of execution, known as *kwaMatiwane* after a chief named Matiwane who had been killed there. A memorial marks the site. This massacre resulted in war between the Zulu and the Voortrekkers. After the Battle of Blood River a Voortrekker force advanced on Dingane's capital, reaching uMgungundlovu on 20 December 1838. They found the entire place, with its 2 000 huts, abandoned and set on fire by the Zulu.

A large mission of the Dutch Reformed Church was later built on the ridge overlooking the site of uMgungundlovu. The mission occupies the position where the Reverend Francis Owen made his camp in 1837 and endeavoured to persuade Dingane to allow the establishment of a permanent mission. From this height, the pioneer missionary watched with horror as the Zulu killed Retief and his men, and then marshalled their army for a great raid against the camps of the Voortrekkers, situated below the Drakensberg. A tangible atmosphere still lingers about the scene where these events took place. The valley remains in its original state, covered with a parkland of flowering aloes, euphorbias and flat-topped acacia trees.

---

From the turnoff to Vryheid and Dingane's Kraal, the main road continues for 11 km and then bridges over the White Mfolozi River, flowing through an acacia-covered bowl in the hills. In the centre of this bowl, 4 km beyond the bridge, the road reaches a turnoff leading to the memorial on the site of . . .

## ULUNDI

In 1873, when Cetshwayo became king of the Zulu, he founded a new capital which he named *uluNdi* or *oNdi* (the heights) and which Europeans know as Ulundi. On 4 July 1879 the British army under Lord Chelmsford, advanced on the capital and the last battle of the Anglo-Zulu War took place there. About 17 000 Zulu made a rather dispirited advance on the British who, 5 000-strong, were drawn up in square formation about 2 km from the capital. The Zulu lost about 1 500 men in the attack, while British fatalities amounted to 12 – the spear was simply no match for the rifle. The battlefield is still sprinkled with numerous bullets and other bric-à-brac of war. Visitors to the site (marked by a memorial building), are usually received by urchins who offer for sale various items presumably recovered by them from the scene of battle. Ulundi was burned down by the British, and by this act, the independence of the Zulu nation was ended.

The modern administrative centre of Ulundi has been built 3 km from the memorial.

### Accommodation
★★ Holiday Inn, 50 rooms, all with baths. R16 – R24 room only. Phone 03572-96.

The main road continues northwards, climbs the hill slopes overlooking the Ulundi basin and, after 10 km, reaches the small centre of *Mahlabathini* (the place of white sands), founded in 1896 as a seat of magistracy. From this rather dilapidated place, a commanding situation being its principal asset, the road descends into the bush-covered valley of the Bekamuzi River, 13,5 km from Mahlabathini. This valley was once a hunting area renowned for its elephants but wildlife has long since been replaced by man. The road climbs another bush-covered ridge and after 9,5 km, descends to cross the Black Mfolozi River. Rising, falling, twisting and turning, the road continues for a further 23,5 km and after a long climb, reaches Nongoma (page 438) and a choice of roads stretching to the coast or inland.

## ESHOWE TO NKANDLA, ISANDLWANA AND RORKE'S DRIFT

From Eshowe a spectacular scenic drive follows the edge of the valley of the Thukela (Tugela) River to Nkandla and thence to Kranskop or Babanango, Nqutu, iSandlwana and Dundee. The first part of the road to Nkandla is mainly gravel and should be avoided in wet weather. Careful driving in dry weather rewards the traveller with superb scenery.

The road leads westwards from Eshowe through extensive plantations of sugar cane. After 13 km there is a turnoff to the Entumeni Nature Reserve, a 393-ha area of evergreen mist belt indigenous forest. Proclaimed a reserve in 1970 but as yet not developed for the public, the name is derived from the wild bitter apple trees growing in the vicinity. Dabulamanzi, a renowned officer of the Zulu army during the Anglo-Zulu War, had his stronghold there. The British garrison of Eshowe attacked it on 1 March 1879 but without notable success.

At 22 km from Eshowe a turnoff stretches for 4 km to the sugarmill and village of Entumeni. The road (now gravel) continues for a further 24 km through the cane plantations and then reaches the first of a number of superb viewsites looking out over the huge valley of the Thukela to the distant landmark of Kranskop on the Natal side of the river.

For the next 31 km the road follows the edge of the prodigious valley which justifiably gives the river its Zulu name of *Thukela* (startling one). Patches of indigenous forest cover the hills which are also clustered with numerous tribal huts.

The name *Nkandla* (place of exhaustion) is applied to the rugged forest-clad edge of the Thukela Valley. This wildly beautiful piece of country was the scene of the Bambatha Revolt in 1906. A number of tribesmen led by the petty chief Bambatha, made an armed protest against the imposition of taxes. The Mhome Gorge in the heart of the Nkandla forest where Cetshwayo is buried, was their stronghold and some bitter fighting took place in the area before the revolt was suppressed and Bambatha killed.

The village of Nkandla, 77 km from Eshowe, was established as a seat of magistracy in 1887. It is a straggling little place, shaded by wattle and eucalyptus trees.

### Accommodation

★ Nkandla Hotel, 7 rooms, 3 with baths. R7,60 – R8,10 B/B. Phone 16.

Two kilometres outside Nkandla a road branches off for 32 km to join a road from Dundee and Nqutu. The combined roads make a spectacular descent into the valley of the Thukela, crossing the river after 18 km at Jameson Drift. The road then climbs the cliffs on the Natal side of the valley, reaching Kranskop after a further 34 km of scenic splendour.

From the junction outside Nkandla, the west road continues for 2,5 km reaching a turnoff to Melmoth 48 km away. A further 13 km takes the road to a turnoff of 3,5 km which joins the tarmac Melmoth-Babanango road at a point 12 km from the small rural centre known as *Babanango* (father, there it is). The name is derived from a high hill which serves as a landmark for the area and is a convenient place from which to explore the grassy middleveld and the battlefields of iSandlwana and Rorke's Drift.

### Accommodation
★ ® Babanango Hotel, 6 rooms, 2 with baths. R10,50 B/B. Phone 36.

From Babanango the tarmac road leads westwards over the grassy hills. There are turnoffs after 16 km to Nkandla; after 18 km to Vryheid (75 km); after 30,5 km to Kranskop (100 km); and 40,5 km from Babanango a turnoff leading for 9,5 km to the site of the battle of . . .

## ISANDLWANA

The scene of this renowned battle of the Anglo-Zulu War is the foot of the isolated, sinister-looking hillock which the Zulu called *iSandlwana* (something like a small house). This is the name given to the second stomach of a cow, the shape of which the hill is considered to resemble.

On 20 January 1879 the British army, about to commence an invasion of Zululand, set up camp on this site which consisted of open, high ground and which seemingly dominated the surrounding country. Deep dongas, however, invisible from ground level, lay scattered at the approach to the site, providing magnificent cover for any attacker with the wit to exploit them.

On 22 January, while the British commander Lord Chelmsford was out on reconnaissance, a Zulu army of about 17 000 men, led by Ntshingwayo, overwhelmed the camp and killed 864 British soldiers and 470 of their African allies. The Zulu suffered about 1 000 casualties.

The battlefield is clearly marked with whitewashed boulders which indicate the position of the various units engaged in the action. A small field museum is situated on a hill overlooking the battlefield, where maps and a relief model of the scene on the day of the battle are displayed. There is also a collection of shields from the different Zulu regiments and uniforms and badges of the British units.

To reach Rorke's Drift, where a small British garrison was attacked immediately after the main Battle of iSandlwana, the main tarmac road must be rejoined and then followed through the trading centre of Nqutu (23 km). From here the main road to Dundee must be taken, across the Buffalo River to a turnoff 19 km from Nqutu (32 km from Dundee), which leads for 18 km to the Swedish mission station at . . .

## RORKE'S DRIFT

James Rorke farmed and traded on the site of the mission until his death on 24 October 1875. In 1878 the Swedish Missionary Society acquired the property and founded the *Oscarberg Mission,* named after the Swedish king. The mission, under the Evangelical Lutheran Church of Southern Africa, is still very active.

At the outbreak of the Anglo-Zulu War, the main British force was marshalled near the mission and on 11 January 1879 invaded Zululand by crossing the Buffalo River at the drift named after James Rorke. It was this force which made its camp at iSandlwana and suffered such grievous defeat. A small garrison under Lieutenant Bromhead, with Lieutenant Chard of the Royal Engineers in overall command, had remained at the mission station. When news of the disaster at iSandlwana reached them at 15h15, the 139 men at the mission hurriedly braced themselves for a Zulu attack.

Two Zulu regiments commanded by Dabulamanzi were sent to pursue refugees from iSandlwana and at 16h30 they approach the mission. They had received no orders to attack the place but were heady with the victory of iSandlwana. About 600 Zulu charged the sandstone buildings of the mission but were driven back, trying a second time without success. The main body then lined up on the overlooking hill and peppered the buildings with bullets, meanwhile launching a series of onslaughts, during which the parsonage, which was being used as a hospital, was set on fire. The attack went on until about 04h00 of the next day,

23 January. Dabulamanzi then realised that he was badly exceeding his orders in conducting an attack on entrenched soldiers. He had so far lost about 400 men while 15 British soldiers had been killed and most of the others wounded.

The two Zulu regiments withdrew, leaving the members of the little garrison to bandage wounds and put out the fires. They ultimately received high praise for stubborn courage and heroism shown in the face of heavy odds.

## Chapter Twenty-three

# PIETERMARITZBURG AND THE NATAL MIDLANDS

The capital of Natal, Pietermaritzburg, is situated in green, park-like surroundings and is a city of flowers and bright colours. The hollow (sometimes known on account of its warmth as 'sleepy hollow') in which the city has developed, is actually the valley of the river called the *Msunduze* (the pusher) from its habit of 'pushing' masses of driftwood down its course during flood time. With good rainfall (1 000 mm a year), deep soil and a climate inducive to the growth of vegetation, the site of the city also happened to be directly on the pioneer wagon road from Port Natal (Durban) to the interior.

The Voortrekkers, who appreciated fertile and pleasant situations for their towns, chose the site for the capital of their Republic of Natal. After the defeat of the Zulu in the Battle of Blood River they laid out a town on the banks of the Msunduze in the traditional Dutch manner: wide streets with water furrows for irrigation of gardens on either side, and plots so large that they seemed more like small farms.

The town was founded in 1839 and named in honour of the two leaders of the Voortrekkers in Natal, Pieter Retief and Gerrit Maritz. The former was killed by the Zulu and the latter died of natural causes just prior to the establishment of Pietermaritzburg. Statues of the two men stand in the garden outside the Voortrekker Memorial Church. Next to this church (a modern building in Voortrekker style) is the Voortrekker Museum which displays an interesting collection of relics of the period. The museum is open daily except Sundays and religious holidays from 09h00 to 13h00 and from 14h00 to 16h30. It is closed on Saturdays after noon.

In the halcyon days after it was first established, Pietermaritzburg must have perfectly resembled the capital of a rural republic of extreme simplicity: white-walled, black-thatched cottages built in Cape-Dutch style, each surrounded by an irrigated garden of fruit trees, vegetables and flowers; the streets filled with an unhurried traffic of wagons, horsemen and pedestrians; picturesque and rugged-looking hunters, traders and visiting farmers conducting business, coming and going to and from the far interior of Southern Africa.

Simple government buildings were erected, including a small hall in which, on the first Monday of January, April, July and October, assembled the august members of the *Volksraad* (people's council), the ruling body of the Republic of Natal.

Unfortunately, only one of these early buildings survives, a double-storeyed residence built in 1846 by Petrus Pretorius at 333 Boom Street. Originally black-thatched, this interesting house still retains its original yellowwood ceilings and tiled floor and now contains a small private museum and an antique and herb shop.

The collapse of the Natal Republic in 1843 brought British administration and a garrison to Pietermaritzburg. A small military stronghold, Fort Napier, was built on an elevation overlooking the town. In December 1845 the first British Governor, Martin West, was established in the town, which from then on became the capital of the British colony of Natal.

Fort Napier is well preserved and contains several artillery pieces and other interesting military relics. St Georges Garrison Church was built in 1897 and also contains relics of the British military units. It is open to the public on Wednesdays from 14h30 to 16h00 and on Saturdays from 08h00 to 09h15.

The market square of Pietermaritzburg was a meeting place for traders, hunters, travellers and explorers. Transport vehicles outspanned there, resting or repairing, or offering for sale a great variety of skins, tusks, horns, agricultural produce and goods imported from foreign countries. Shops, hotels and small industries were founded. The first newspaper of Natal, the *Natal Witness,* made its appearance on 27 February 1846. Its editor, David Buchanan, used the local gaol as his editorial office while he was imprisoned there for contempt of court. The address 'Pietermaritzburg gaol' appears on several issues of the paper!

In 1848 Pietermaritzburg received a village management committee and in 1854 it became a full municipality. The Legislative Council of Natal sat in Pietermaritzburg and in 1893 when Natal received responsible government, the town became the seat of Parliament with two Houses, a Legislative Council and a Legislative Assembly. The Assembly building is now used by the Natal Provincial Council, and the Legislative Council building contains the offices of the Natal Provincial Administration. Both buildings may be visited by appointment: phone 4-1666 for the Assembly and 2-6721 for the Council.

The imposing city hall, said to be the largest all-brick construction in the Southern Hemisphere, was completed in 1900 on the site of the original Volksraad hall of the Natal Republic. The hall contains some fine stained glass windows, a clock tower 47 m high with a Westminster chiming clock and a carillon of 12 bells. The second floor of the city hall houses the Tatham Art Gallery which exhibits a number of French and English paintings, china, glassware and an elaborately gilded ormolu clock. This fine piece with moving figures was built in London in the last century, reputedly for an Indian rajah. The gallery is open weekdays only from 10h00 to 17h00.

The Natal Museum, founded in 1905, is one of the five national museums of South Africa. A large collection of African animals is displayed and there is a notable exhibition of marine molluscs, fish, geological specimens and a first-class ethnological gallery. The Hall of Natal History contains a reconstructed street from Victorian Pietermaritzburg. The museum is open daily from 09h00 to 16h30 and on Sundays from 14h00 to 16h30 only.

Another interesting museum is Macrorie House, maintained by the Simon van der Stel Foundation. The house, built about 1862, was the residence from 1869 to 1891 of William Macrorie, Bishop of Pietermaritzburg, who arrived at a time of great dissent in the Anglican Church. The renowned Bishop John William Colenso challenged various dogmas and established the Church of England in Natal, with its own cathedral of St Peters. Bishop Macrorie became head of the Episcopal Church of the Province of South Africa, with St Saviours as his cathedral. Bishop Colenso is buried in front of the altar of his church.

In Macrorie House are displayed many items from Victorian times. It is open Tuesdays to Thursdays from 09h00 to 13h00 and on Sundays from 09h00 to 12h30 and from 14h00 to 16h00.

Other notable buildings in Pietermaritzburg include the Supreme Court, completed in 1871 and built of the bright red brick characteristic of several other local structures. The old Government House is another reminder of the past. Originally the official home of Lieutenant Governor Benjamin Pine during the 1800s, it is now part of the Teachers Training College.

Gardens, trees and parks are the city's chief glory. *Alexandra Park,* 65,6 ha in extent, was founded in 1863 and named after Queen Alexandra of England. This park comprises the Jan Smuts Stadium, the cricket oval, a cycle track, swimming bath, the superb Rock Gardens, created during the great depression by unemployed men and the Mayor's Garden with its roses and avenue of palms. In May each year, an open-air art festival, 'Art in the Park' is held in the shade of an avenue of plane trees along the banks of the Msunduze River. The Diamond Jubilee Pavilion and Bandstand are interesting reminders of Victorian elegance in the park.

Next to Alexandra Park is Kershaw Park with its public tennis courts. *Wylie Park,* 8 ha in extent, was presented to the city by Mrs. G. H. Wylie, together with a legacy to finance its development, particularly as a garden for indigenous plants and the lovely azaleas which are the floral emblem of Pietermaritzburg. The park was opened in 1958.

The Botanic Gardens (44,5 ha) were founded in 1870 by the Botanic Society of Natal and in

*Overleaf: Who named it the Valley of a Thousand Hills? To each hill cling many stories of fights, adventures, cannibals and rustlers.*

1969 was taken over by the National Botanic Gardens of South Africa. This garden contains a superb collection of trees gathered from many parts of the world, some of them the largest of their kind growing in South Africa. There is an avenue of plane trees, spectacularly beautiful when their leaves change colour. Plants indigenous to Natal are cultivated in a special section of the garden.

The Queen Elizabeth Park was established in 1960, 8 km from the city centre on the main road to the north. This 93-ha park contains the headquarters of the Natal Parks, Game and Fish Preservation Board as well as indigenous trees, shrubs and flowering plants, many birds (including blue and crested cranes) and numerous antelope of different species. There are walks and picnic sites.

The Bird Sanctuary, situated next to the main road to the north, is a popular roosting place in the evenings for hundred of egrets. A number of beauty spots on the outskirts of the city provide pleasant drives and recreational areas for residents and visitors. Eight kilometres from the city centre (on the old Howick road which branches off from the main road to the north) is the viewsite known as Worlds View, 1 083 m above the city. Traces of the original wagon road to the interior may still be seen climbing the escarpment at this point and a map set into the paving stones identifies landmarks of interest. There are picnic sites under the trees.

Henley Dam, 22 km from the city on the Bulwer road, is another recreational area worth visiting. The Natal Canoe Club uses the lake and pleasant picnic spots are provided. The area is open daily from dawn to dusk. Permits for parties of over six people must be obtained from the city engineer.

Pietermaritzburg has a population of 151 131 and is a considerable centre for industry. It retains its administrative and judicial importance and is the home of many fine schools and also of the University of Natal. The principal thoroughfare, Church Street, has a variety of shops and several attractive buildings, including one of the best-known bookshops in Southern Africa, the strangely named partnership of Shuter and Shooter. Between Church and Longmarket streets is an interesting pedestrian shopping area, free of traffic. Lawyers have their offices here and there was once a stock exchange when Pietermaritzburg was the capital of the colony of Natal.

## Accommodation

★★ Ansonia Hotel, 45 rooms, all with baths. R9 B/B. Phone 2-2251.
★★★ Camden Hotel, 80 rooms, 38 with baths. R15,50 – R26,50 B/B. Phone 2-8921.
★★★ Capital Towers Hotel, 78 rooms, all with baths. R14,50 – R22 B/B. Phone 5-3333.
★ Cosy Hotel, 11 rooms, 3 with baths. R6,50 – R7,50 B/B. Phone 2-3279.
★ Crown Hotel, 12 rooms, 6 with baths. R6,95 – R7,50 B/B. Phone 4-1601.
★ Cumberland Hotel, 12 rooms, 2 with baths. R6 – R7 B/B. Phone 2-4150.
★ Foresters Arms Hotel, 17 rooms, 7 with baths. R7,50 – R9,50 B/B. Phone 5-1401.
★★ Imperial Hotel, 65 rooms, all with baths. R9,25 – R13,25 B/B. Phone 2-6551.
★ Kismet Hotel, 24 rooms, 9 with baths. R7,50 – R9 B/B. Phone 5-1141.
★ Norfolk Hotel, 34 rooms, 14 with baths. R7 – R9 B/B. Phone 2-8981.
★★ Plough Hotel, 30 rooms, 19 with baths. R10,50 – R11 B/B. Phone 2-8981.
★★ Royal Hotel, 32 rooms, 16 with baths. R10 – R12 B/B. Phone 2-8555.
★ Taj Mahal Hotel, 17 rooms, 4 with baths. R8 – R9 B/B. Phone 7-2241.
★ Thistle Hotel, 14 rooms, 4 with baths. R6,50 – R7,50 B/B. Phone 2-4204.
★ Watson Hotel, 32 rooms, 17 with baths. R7,45 – R8,60 B/B. Phone 2-1604.
★ Windsor Hotel, 10 rooms, 7 with baths. R6 – R7 B/B. Phone 2-3819.

## Caravans and camping

★★ ® Pietermaritzburg Corporation Caravan Park, 100 sites. R2 D.

# PIETERMARITZBURG TO DURBAN

There are several ways of travelling to Durban from Pietermaritzburg: one of the more strenuous routes is by canoe! In January of each year a race begins in the centre of Pietermaritzburg on the Msunduze River, as far as its confluence with the Mngeni and from there to the sea at Durban. This race is spread over three days.

Another testing route (by road) is the Comrades Marathon, held on 31 May each year. Reputedly one of the world's most demanding athletic events, this race was started in 1921 by Victor Clapham, an ex-soldier member of the Comrades of the Great War, hence the name of *Comrades Marathon*. The course is over 90 km long, and alternates each year with either the uphill or downhill route. The first race was won by 39-year-old Arthur Newton, who, at 72 years of age, was still running competitively and had by then covered over 160 000 km.

The race is now organised each year by the Collegians Harriers and is a gruelling test of endurance, ranging in altitude from 30 m at the Durban post to 610 m in Pietermaritzburg. In the first race, 34 men took part; now over 3 000 men and women of different races and nationalities compete. All hope to at least complete the course within 11 hours in order to secure a medal proving that they are Comrades of the Road. A silver medal is awarded to those who finish within seven and a half hours. The record for the downhill race was set in 1978 by Alan Robb at 5 hours, 29 minutes and 14 seconds. The uphill record, also set by Alan Robb, is 5 hours, 47 minutes and 9 seconds.

For the more conventional road user, the superbly located dual carriageway from Pietermaritzburg to Durban, provides a delightful drive through kaleidoscopic views. From Pietermaritzburg the road stretches south-eastwards past the borough caravan park and commences a winding, steady descent through the green hills of Natal. The outlying suburbs of the city are reached via turnoffs and near the turnoff to Mkondeni stands the little church built by Italian prisoners-of-war during the Second World War. About 5 000 Italians detained in a camp at this spot, transported stone on foot from a quarry 2 km away, in order to build the church. Consecrated on 19 March 1944, it is the only remaining feature of the camp. The stone lion in front of the building, sculpted by the Italians, once stood in the middle of the camp.

The road, 11 km from Pietermaritzburg, passes the residential area of *Ashburton*, originally the farm of William Ellis who, having made money in the Australian gold rush, settled in Natal and named the property after his home town in Dorset.

Four kilometres beyond Ashburton a turnoff leads to the Natal Lion and Game Park, the Zoological Gardens and the Ibhubesi Motel and Caravan Park. Entrance to the lion park is R3 per car. It is open from 07h30 to dusk and contains a considerable variety of wild animals, apart from lions. This was the first lion park to be established in Southern Africa by Dick Chipperfield of Chipperfield Circus fame, and is scenically handsome on the verge of the Valley of a Thousand Hills and very well maintained.

## Accommodation

★ Ibhubesi Motel, 20 rooms, all with baths. R12 – R18 room only. Phone Cato Ridge 274.

Three kilometres beyond the turnoff to the lion park, a tarmac turnoff (18 km from Pietermaritzburg) provides a direct route to the South Coast resorts of Natal. A further 5 km takes the traveller past the village of Camperdown, where the South African wattle industry had its beginning. The original owner of the land on which Camperdown stands was John Vanderplank, an Englishman of Dutch descent who settled in Tasmania as a shipbuilder. An unhappy love affair sent him off on his travels. Visiting Natal to trade, he liked the place and decided to settle there. He acquired the farm which he named *Camperdown* and to it he removed from Tasmania all his portable belongings, and also the seeds of the wild black wattle shrub, used in Australasia to cultivate windbreaks and hedges.

Vanderplank planted the wattle seeds around his homestead, hoping that when the hedge grew, it would protect the place from wind and wild animals. Protection was essential for the first homestead merely consisted of a large packing case!

To Vanderplank's surprise, the wattle seeds developed into trees instead of shrubs; the soil and climate had obviously affected the growth of the seeds. It was not until 1887 that the value of wattle bark as a derivative of tannic acid became known. By that time, seeds from Vanderplank's pioneer trees had been carried to many parts of Southern Africa and mass cultivation was commenced.

### Accommodation
* ★ Camperdown Hotel, 8 rooms, 1 with bath. R6,30 B/B. Phone Cato Ridge 261.
* ★ Mandalay Hotel, 41 rooms, 30 with baths. R6,30 D/B/B. Phone Cato Ridge 92.

Four kilometres beyond Camperdown (27 km from Pietermaritzburg) the road reaches the railway junction of *Cato Ridge* originally the estate of G. C. Cato, one of the pioneers of Durban. Cato Ridge has developed as a railway centre and is the parting place of both rail and road, the original route to Durban providing a scenic way along the edge of the Valley of a Thousand Hills while the new routes swing off more to the west.

### Accommodation
* ★ Cato Ridge Hotel, 14 rooms, 6 with baths. R5,50 – R6,50 B/B. Phone 151.

## THE VALLEY OF A THOUSAND HILLS

The Valley of a Thousand Hills is the deeply eroded and most majestic valley of the river known as the *Mngeni* (the place of acacia trees). The course of the river is not very long but from its source in the well-watered hills near the height known as Spioenkop in the Natal Midlands, and fed by numerous tributaries, the Mngeni has been a vigorous influence on the landscape and economy of Natal: it feeds the Midmar Dam; provides the spectacle of the Howick and Albert falls; and in its final 65-km journey to the sea, finds an involved way through the beautiful Valley of a Thousand Hills.

At the head of the valley looms a dominant, flat-topped height, monarch of all the 'thousand hills'. To the Africans this mass of sandstone is known as *emKhambathini* (place of giraffe acacia trees). Europeans know it as the Natal Table Mountain. A climb to the top (960 m) is very rewarding. The plateau summit should be a nature reserve for it is the home of many magnificent wild flowers and the views are breathtaking. The mountain is best climbed from the Pietermaritzburg side by taking the road past Bishopstowe.

At the foot of emKhambathini the Mngeni River flows into the lake formed by the Nagle Dam, one of Durban's principal sources of water. This dam is reached by a tarmac turnoff from the old Pietermaritzburg-Durban road, 3 km from Cato Ridge. This superb 16-km drive descends to the floor of the valley, where the Debe tribe have their homeland. These people, whose residences and farmlands may be seen on every suitable site in the valley, were formerly much harried by Zulu raids and also by gangs of cannibals who once haunted the area like evil figures in a nightmare. The mountain tops, especially emKhambathini, provided sanctuaries for the tribespeople, who stubbornly clung to the valley. Today they may be seen often wearing traditional dress, and are renowned for their beerdrinks, weddings, dances and faction fights (mainly over women and cattle rustling).

The road ends at the dam where there is a tearoom and picnic area situated in a handsome parkland of trees. Many lovely flowers flourish in the valley: the ink flower, *Cynium adoensis*, with its snow-white petals which turn ink-black on being crushed; the orange-coloured snake lily, *Haemanthus natalensis*, which blooms in spring from buds resembling the heads of snakes; arum lilies, *Richardia africana*, abounding in marshy places; red-hot pokers (*Kniphofia* sp.) and magenta-coloured watsonias, blooming in February; exotic Mexican sunflowers which have run wild; coral-coloured fire lilies (*Cyanthus* sp.) which spring up in winter, especially in areas where grass has been burned; *Aloe ferox* and other flowering aloes ornamenting the rock faces.

---

From the turnoff to the Nagle Dam, the old Pietermaritzburg-Durban road continues along the southern verge of the Valley of a Thousand Hills, revealing many panoramic views, especially along the top and around the cliffs of what the Africans know as the *Ntshangwe* (sharp ridge). Bird life is worth watching with kestrels and white necked rovers soaring past the cliff faces and ground hornbills foraging along the slopes.

The road passes the Inchanga Caravan Park 5,5 km from Cato Ridge, and the small centre of Inchanga (a European misspelling of Ntshangwe) 3 km further on. At 12,5 km there is a viewsite which generally seems to be infested with people persistently offering bazaar curios for sale. This area is known as *Drummond*, apparently in honour of Sir F. C. Drummond, an immigration commissioner during the 1870s. The road passes the railway station of the same name 14 km from Cato Ridge and the two hotels in the area, Rob Roy and the Thousand Hills Hotel, both of which have grand outlooks over the valley.

A further 6 km takes the road to *Bothas Hill*, a small trading centre named after Philip Botha, grandfather of the famous General Louis Botha who once lived there. From here a gravel road descends very steeply into the Valley of a Thousand Hills and eventually joins the road to Nagle Dam at the base of the valley. A permit, obtainable from a magistrate, is necessary for use of this road.

For 6,5 km the road continues from Bothas Hill along the verges of the valley, then reaches the residential area of Hillcrest and, 27,5 km from Cato Ridge, rejoins the main Pietermaritzburg-Durban road. The old scenic road cannot be driven at any speed; it is essentially for those who have the time to sightsee and is thoroughly worth taking. On a clear day the views into the great valley are breathtaking.

## Accommodation
* ★ Bothas Hill Hotel, 8 rooms, 6 with baths. R6,50 – R7,50 B/B. Phone Durban 75-2508.
* ★ Chantecler Hotel, 17 rooms, 4 with baths. R6,50 – R9,50 B/B. Phone Durban 75-2613.
* ★★★ Rob Roy Hotel, 37 rooms, all with baths. R18,50 – R31 B/B. Phone Durban 75-1320.
* ★ Thousand Hills Hotel, 27 rooms, 8 with baths. R8,50 – R9,25 B/B. Phone Cato Ridge 16.

## Caravans and camping
* ★★★ Inchanga Caravan Park, 60 sites. R4 D plus 25c D per person.

From Cato Ridge the main freeway linking Pietermaritzburg to Durban sweeps eastwards, losing altitude steadily but rising and falling over lovely downland country. There are turnoffs to places such as Shongweni and Assagay (47 km from Pietermaritzburg). The Polo Pony Hotel and the Durban municipal Shongweni Dam are situated near the road. At 22 km from Cato Ridge (49 km from Pietermaritzburg) the road reaches the residential area of Hillcrest and is rejoined by the old road which follows the verge of the Valley of a Thousand Hills.

## Accommodation
* ★ Hillcrest Hotel, 12 rooms, all with baths. R8 B/B. Phone Durban 75-2616.
* ★★ Polo Pony Hotel, 20 rooms, all with baths. R13 – R20 B/B. Phone Durban 7-9729.

The road descends from Hillcrest, through a green parkland where trees and flowers flourish. There are many delightful residential areas on the cool heights where man finds relief from the humidity and summer heat of the Durban coast. The first of these garden towns is reached 56 km from Pietermaritzburg.

## KLOOF

In 1851 William Swan Field, first collector of customs for Natal, and first magistrate of Durban, was rewarded for his services by the British Government who granted him a farm named *Richmond* (after the Duke of Richmond), on the hill slopes high above Durban. The following year, William Field brought his brother, John, from the Cape and settled him on the farm, eventually transferring ownership of the 2 268-ha estate to him in 1867.

John Field became a well-known man in the area. *Field's Hill* is named after him while his son-in-law, William Gillitt, acquired a neighbouring farm which he named *Emberton* after the family home in England. Another piece of this farm was named *Hill Crest,* both portions being the sites of modern residential townships. *Richmond* farm remained in the possession of the Field family until 1901 when, on the death of John Field's widow, it was subdivided into residential areas. The attractiveness of the area at once made it popular, with several well-known businessmen from Durban building homes in what was at first known as Krantzkloof (later abbreviated to Kloof).

Kloof became a municipality in 1961 and has at present, 14 239 inhabitants. The name is derived from a deep 10-km-long cleft through the hills. The stream known as *eMolweni* (the place of high cliffs) flows into this cleft over a fine waterfall. The Krantzkloof Nature Reserve was established in 1950 over a 500-ha area and is 5 km from the centre of Kloof along a tarmac road. There is a picnic site immediately above the waterfall and the forested cleft is a sanctuary for bushbuck, bushpigs, blue, red and grey duiker and numerous birds.

### Accommodation
★ Field's Hotel, 37 rooms, 13 with baths. R10 – R10,50 B/B. Phone Durban 74-1313.
★ Tina's Hotel, 12 rooms, 6 with baths. R7,50 – R10 B/B. Phone Durban 74-1325.

From Kloof the main road descends the steep Field's Hill and it is from this point that travellers first see Durban in the distance, half lost in the blue haze of the Indian Ocean. At the bottom of the hill, 60 km from Pietermaritzburg, the road reaches . . .

## PINETOWN

In 1849 the Wayside Hotel was built as a staging post on the coach road from Durban to Pietermaritzburg. The following year a town was surveyed around this hotel and named after the Governor, Sir Benjamin Pine. The situation was pleasant – a park-like setting of flowering trees. The place must also have been very atmospheric, what with lions and elephants roaming about; travellers along the road simply did not know what to expect around the corner!

Pinetown became a municipality in 1948 and has a population of 78 500. It is a popular residential area for people working in Durban as the altitude of 343 m is sufficient to elevate it above the heat and humidity of the coast. Numerous industries have also been established in the area.

### Accommodation
★ Fairydene Hotel, 34 rooms, 10 with baths. R9 – R12,50 B/B. Phone Durban 72-2015.

★ Imperial Hotel, 10 rooms, 6 with baths. R9,50 B/B. Phone Durban 72-3541.
★ Rugby Hotel, 25 rooms, 7 with baths. R7 – R16,50 B/B. Phone Durban 72-7622.

From Pinetown a road branches southwards for 5 km to the Mariannhill Monastery, founded in 1882 by the order of Trappists. Another road branches off to Sarnia, an industrial and residential area named by its first owner, Captain Drake, after his birthplace in England. From here a road leads to Durban through . . .

# QUEENSBURGH

In 1924 the townships of Malvern, Escombe, Northdene, Moseley and Cavendish were united under one local authority which, in 1954, became a municipality. With a population of 18 885, the town is a residential area on the outskirts of Durban. The North Park Nature Reserve, 52 ha in extent, was established in 1968 in the municipal area and preserves a stretch of coastal lowland forest rich in bird life. There are paths and a picnic site.

Near Queensburgh is the Kenneth Stainbank Nature Reserve, a 214-ha area established in 1963 on a piece of land granted by Mr Kenneth Stainbank. A Zulu military outpost Ndaba nKhulu (the great discussion) once stood in this area which later became part of a farm named Bellair, granted to Robert Dunn in 1847. The Stainbank family acquired it in 1857. A delightful wilderness area to find on the outskirts of a big city, it provides nature trails and picnic spots. Bushbuck, grey, blue and red duiker, impala, zebra and nyala inhabit the reserve, as do many birds and small mammals.

## Accommodation
★ Malvern Hotel, 14 rooms, 5 with baths. R10,50 room only. Phone Durban 44-7931.

The main Pietermaritzburg-Durban road continues eastwards from Pinetown. After 1,5 km it enters the municipal area of . . .

# NEW GERMANY

In 1847 two enterprising men, H. Jaraal and P. Jung bought 6 272 ha of virgin ground on the outskirts of Durban where they planned to grow cotton. Naming the estate Westville after the Governor of Natal, Martin West, they set out to attract settlers. A group of 183 Germans immigrated to the place in 1848, making their homes on small farms, each 85 ha in extent.

Cotton proved unsuccessful but the settlers cultivated vegetables and New Germany, as the area came to be called, flourished. Today it is an industrial and residential area with a population of 2 632.

The main road continues through a parkland of flowering trees: scarlet-flowered kaffir-booms (Erythrina sp.) blooming in July and August; the blood-red kaffir honeysuckle, Tecomaria capensis, flowering in April; cassia species producing golden blossoms in May and June; wild bananas (Strelitzia sp.) with their orange and purple 'bird of paradise' flowers; and in autumn, the orange flowers of the Lion's Tail (Leonutis leonuris), blooming by the roadside. Many other indigenous plants flourish on these green slopes, while man has introduced many shades of bougainvillaea and so many other ornamental trees, shrubs and creepers, that no season is without some plant in full bloom.

The road steadily descends Cowie's Hill, named after William Cowie who came to Natal with the Voortrekkers. Close to the road on the hill slopes lies the Paradise Valley Nature Reserve (28 ha) established in 1963, with walks and picnic sites on the banks of the river known as the Mbilo (bubbling). At the foot of the hill, 64 km from Pietermaritzburg, lies . . .

# WESTVILLE

The town of Westville is a pleasant residential area on the outskirts of Durban, sufficiently elevated (about 300 m) so as to enjoy a cool climate and a fine outlook. With a population of 26 000 it has grown on the old farm named after Martin West, the first Governor of Natal. The 200-ha campus of the Durban-Westville University for Indians is situated in the municipal area.

## Accommodation

★ Westville Hotel, 20 rooms, 8 with baths. R8,80 – R9,90 B/B. Phone Durban 85-4141.

Beyond Westville, the main road continues eastwards to Durban. Crossing the north-south coastal highway, the road passes through the suburb of Mayville, climbs over a rise where in former years there was a tollgate and on the summit of what is known as Berea, enters Durban, terminating in the centre of the city, 80 km from Pietermaritzburg.

# PIETERMARITZBURG TO KOKSTAD

The main tarmac road to the south from Pietermaritzburg climbs through the suburbs and out of the valley of the Msunduze River. The road leaves the built-up areas through an avenue of palm trees lined with pleasant homes and lovely gardens. After 16 km the road passes through the trading centre of Thornville from where a turnoff leads eastwards to join the main Pietermaritzburg-Durban road.

## Accommodation

★ Thornville Hotel, 11 rooms, 8 with baths. R7,50 – R8,50 B/B. Phone 290.

Beyond Thornville the road proceeds across a succession of green valleys and hills, superlative dairy, poultry and general farming country. The first creamery in Natal was, in fact, established in this area, at Nelsrust, in 1899. Sugar cane, wattle, pine and gum trees flourish in the region which forms part of the mist belt of high rainfall lying along the edge of the middle-veld escarpment of Natal. In October and November the wattle trees are in blossom and the air is rich with their perfume. Farm stalls sell citrus fruits in November and a delicious tangy blackberry jam is made from local wild brambles.

Thirty-six kilometres from Pietermaritzburg the road reaches . . .

# RICHMOND

During the influx of British settlers in 1850 several villages and towns were founded in the midlands of Natal. The first settlers in the area of modern Richmond were all from Beaullieu, the seat of the Duke of Buccleuch in England. The settlers established a trading centre they at first named Beaullieu, but the difficult pronunciation, especially for Africans (who cannot pronounce two vowels together), caused them to change the name to *Richmond* after another estate of the Duke of Buccleuch. Today the population is 3 200.

Lying on the banks of the Lovu River, Richmond lacks any special features as a town and is cursed with a main street lined with tin shanty stores. However, it is at least notable for the beauty of its gardens. The Bhaca tribespeople who live in the area are also renowned for their costumes and beadwork. On Tuesdays, in particular, Bhaca brides have a habit of coming into the town in order to register their marriages and are always superbly dressed for the occasion.

The luxuriance of the surrounding countryside is delightful. Branch roads leading to rural centres such as Eastwolds take the traveller through some stunning scenery. The road to Eastwolds descends into the valley of the Mkhomazi River, crossing the river below the huge red-coloured sandstone cliffs known as Hela Hela. Across the river, half way up the southern slopes, there is a resting place with a fine view. Slightly higher, where the road crosses a small stream, a pathway leads to the summit of Hela Hela where a tremendous viewsite overlooks a world of hills and river valleys. Below the cliffs in the river valley, lies the 498-ha Soada Forest Nature Reserve, established in 1967 to preserve a lovely expanse of indigenous forest.

## Accommodation
* Central Hotel, 16 rooms, 4 with baths. R8 – R9 B/B. Phone 78.
* Richmond Hotel, 10 rooms, all with baths. R8,50 B/B. Phone 84.
* The Oaks Hotel, 34 rooms, all with baths. R7 – R8 B/B. Phone Oaksbyrne 9901.

From Richmond the tarmac road to the south crosses undulating plantations of sugar cane. After 6 km there is a turnoff stretching to Mid Illovo and just beyond this point the road starts a descent into the spectacularly beautiful valley of the Mkhomazi River. For 9 km the road finds a way down the slopes of the valley, revealing many impressive views of the landscape and homes of the Bhaca tribespeople. The floor of the valley is warm and a picnic site is situated on the far side of the bridge across the river.

The road climbs the southern side of the valley and if possible, the views are even better than those seen from the northern heights. After 3 km a turnoff leads eastwards for 33 km to Highflats. The main road tops the heights of the river valley and continues for a further 24 km before reaching a turnoff to . . .

# IXOPO

The village of *Ixopo* is situated in the gentle rural valley of the stream from which it receives its odd-sounding name (correctly spelt *exobo*), an onomatopoeic word representing the sound of a person squelching through a bog. Established in 1878, it is an amiable little rural centre in a green setting of trees and luxuriant grazing. A narrow-gauge railway carries the agricultural produce of the area down to the coast at Umzinto.

## Accommodation
* Off Saddle Hotel, 20 rooms, 14 with baths. R9,50 – R10 B/B. Phone 27.
* Plough Hotel, 18 rooms, 11 with baths. R9,50 – R10 B/B. Phone 80.

The pleasant drive to the south continues over grassy hilltops covered in wattle trees and patches of indigenous bush. The narrow-gauge railway closely follows the road and although trains are not very numerous, it provides a picturesque touch to a charming landscape.

After 1,5 km of travel from Ixopo there is a turnoff to Highflats (24 km) and from there to Umzinto on the coast, providing a beautiful drive through a veritable sea of hills. Eighteen kilometres from Ixopo the road reaches the Mzimkhulu River, the border between Natal and Transkei. Across the river stands a huddle of stores, a hotel and the terminus of the narrow-gauge railway, together comprising the hamlet known as Umzimkulu. An immigration post is maintained here by the Transkeian Government.

The road proceeds through a densely settled area, especially in the valley of the Bisi River where a vast assembly of huts may be seen. At 39 km from Umzimkulu the road joins the main Cape Town to Durban coastal road (N2) and continues for 40 km to Kokstad. From there, the road leads southwards across Transkei to the Cape (page 396).

# KOKSTAD

The town of Kokstad (with a population of 18 650) had its beginning in 1862. In that year the Griqua – an assorted group of Hottentots and people of mixed blood – migrated from Philippolis in the Orange Free State across the Drakensberg to what was originally a no-man's-land but which from then on was called Griqualand East. The Griqua leader was Adam Kok III. After an adventurous journey he and his followers formed a *laer* (camp) on the slopes of the mountain which they named after Sir Walter Currie whose support had allowed them to settle in these new lands.

Kok allotted a 1 214-ha farm to every male Griqua over the age of 18. It was superlative farming country, but winter was bitterly cold with regular snowfalls on the mountains. The Nguni tribes had for this reason avoided the area, and the Griqua, inclined to be improvident and indolent, soon began to sell their fine farms to Europeans and to live merrily on the proceeds.

In September 1869 Adam Kok founded *Kokstad* as the capital of Griqualand East. Surrounded by high hills and mountains, it lies on the banks of the bustling upper reaches of the *Mzimhlava* (home of the mealie grub) River.

In 1874 Griqualand East was annexed to the Cape Colony, the district of Mount Currie defined, and Kokstad converted from the seat of a rough and ready Griqua republic, into a magisterial centre. On 5 April 1892 Kokstad became a municipality and developed into an important agricultural centre and railhead from which is despatched a considerable proportion of the cheese and other dairy products of South Africa. Horsebreeding, stock raising and general agriculture flourish in a notably crisp, healthy climate.

Many magnificent farms surround the town. Trout in the streams, finely bred horses for polo, and numerous sporting facilities make Kokstad a social centre of some importance. The town is graced with a rather elegant little civic hall, with a bandstand and a memorial to the men of the Cape Mounted Rifles who played an important part in the frontier disturbances of former years.

## Accommodation
* ★ Balmoral Hotel, 54 rooms, 18 with baths. R8,50 – R9 B/B. Phone 406.
* ★ Mount Currie Motel, 20 rooms, all with baths. R8 – R14 room only. Phone 279.
* ★ Royal Hotel, 54 rooms, 32 with baths. R8 – R9 B/B. Phone 212.

## Caravans and camping
* ★★ Mount Currie Caravan Park (at motel), 6 sites. R3 D.
* ★ Oval Caravan Park, 20 sites. R2 D.

---

# PIETERMARITZBURG TO KRANSKOP

The road to the north-east climbs out of the 'sleepy hollow' in which Pietermaritzburg shelters and for 9 km curves up the slopes, revealing fine views of the city and its well-wooded surroundings. Once on the summit of the rise, the road continues over a plateau covered in acacia trees. At 13,5 from Pietermaritzburg there is a turnoff to Wartburg and 3 km further on the road starts to descend into the valley of the Mngeni River. At 17 km from Pietermaritzburg a turnoff leads for 3 km to the oft-photographed . . . .

# ALBERT FALLS

The Mngeni tumbles over the Albert Falls in a very attractive setting of trees and plants.

Unfortunately the waterfall, only 7 m high, has been considerably disfigured by pipes. The path from the parking area provides a pleasant walk and there are picnic sites and fishing is interesting. Immediately above the waterfall a lake has been created in lovely surroundings. On its shores, the Natal Provincial Council has established the Albert Falls Public Resort, where boating and fishing are favourite pastimes. The 3 012-ha area around the lake contains a nature reserve, proclaimed in 1975. Swimming in the lake is not advisable as there is a slight risk of bilharzia infection.

## Accommodation
** Public Resort, 16 rondawels and 2 chalets, R4 D – R5 D per person. 40 sites, R1,20 D per person.

A little over 1 km from the turnoff to the Albert Falls, the main tarmac road bridges across the Mngeni River, climbing the northern slopes of the valley. Passing another turnoff to the Albert Falls, the road after 15 km, reaches the village of . . .

# NEW HANOVER
Pleasantly situated in the timber country of the mist belt, New Hanover consists of a simple cluster of stores, post office and police buildings, a railway station and hotel.

## Accommodation
* New Hanover Hotel, 6 rooms, 5 with baths. R7 – R8 B/B. Phone 72.

From New Hanover the road climbs steeply out of the valley up *Garbutts Hill,* named after a man who had an inn to succour those stuck on what was once a very muddy road. The summit is reached 7,5 km from New Hanover and yields a grand view of a mass of hills and green valleys.

The road traverses an undulating plateau covered in plantations of wattle, gum and pine trees, sugar cane and sisal. At 52 km from Pietermaritzburg there is a turnoff of 15 km to the village of Dalton. For a further 16 km the main tarmac road crosses a landscape of maize, wattle and dairy farms and reaches a turnoff of half a kilometre leading to the birthplace of the famed General Louis Botha, now an historical monument. Five kilometres further on (73 km from Pietermaritzburg), the road enters . . .

# GREYTOWN
In 1850 a town was surveyed on the banks of the Mvoti River and named after Earl Grey, the British Colonial Secretary. Since its founding the town has experienced a lively and, at times, amusing history. Close to the frontier of Zululand, it was subject to periodic alarms of invasions and occasionally resembled an armed camp.

Claims concerning the discovery of gold, silver and coal in the vicinity also caused local excitement. But the introduction, around 1890, of the cultivation of wattle for the tannic acid in its bark, actually gave the area its principal industry. Today the whole countryside surrounding Greytown is covered in trees and timber is the economic king of what is known as the Umvoti District.

Greytown became a municipality in July 1915 and has a population of 13 280. Situated in the mist belt of Natal, it has a congenial climate and a green and refreshing environment.

## Accommodation
* Umvoti Hotel, 42 rooms, 15 with baths. R8,25 – R9,25 B/B. Phone 728.

461

**Caravans and camping**

★ Lake Merthley Caravan Park, 25 sites. R2 D.

From Greytown the main tarmac road continues north-eastwards through plantations of trees and across fertile farmlands. After 21 km there is a turnoff to the Natal Tanning Extract factory, and to Hermansburg, the headquarters in Natal of the Hanoverian Missionary Society, founded there in 1854.

At 33 km from Greytown, the road reaches an important junction. A turn right (east) stretches for 69 km to Stanger and the north coast of Natal, an interesting drive through a spectacular jumble of hills and deep valleys. Tea estates and timber and banana plantations line the way and there are tremendous views of the valleys of the Mvoti and Thukela rivers.

At the junction of this road to the coast, the main road from Greytown continues northwards and after 1,5 km enters the village of . . .

# KRANSKOP

Founded in 1894, *Kranskop* (precipice peak) receives its name from one of the great scenic landmarks of Natal, the 1 230-m-high peak which stands 12 km away like a sentry keeping eternal watch over the prodigious valley of the Thukela (Tugela) River. Known to the Zulu as *iTshe lika Ntunjambili* (the rock with two openings), this mass of sandstone has several legends attached to it. A cavern may be seen near the summit and it is said that there is a second entrance to the mountain which opens magically. Maidens weary of carrying water from the river below the cliffs need only say *'iTshe lika Ntunjambili,* let me come in to your house,' and the secret doorway would roll open. The sound of revelry would lure them in to what at first seemed to be a wonderland but which always became a prison. No maiden ever returns and the sound of sobbing is said to be heard when the nights are quiet, lingering about the precipice face like a sigh.

The village of Kranskop is the terminus of the railway from Pietermaritzburg and is a centre for timber plantations.

**Accommodation**

★ Kranskop Hotel, 16 rooms, 8 with baths. R7,50 – R8,50 B/B. Phone 39.

From the village, a road descends into the valley of the Thukela River, providing travellers with one of the most spectacular road journeys in Africa. From Kranskop village, the road leads for 4 km through plantations of trees, then reaches the edge of the gigantic valley which fully deserves its name of *Thukela* (startling). An involved descent along the edge of this great gash in the landscape, begins. At 23 km from Kranskop there is a viewsite from where is revealed an almost overwhelming panorama of the valley, the river below doing a great 'U' turn, and the lovely hills of Zululand to the north.

At this viewsite stands a simple memorial to H. B. Jameson, the Engineer Superintendent of Roads of Natal who pioneered the construction of this road, known fittingly as the Jameson Road. From the memorial the road continues its descent down slopes overgrown with a rich variety of trees, shrubs, euphorbias and flowering plants. The valley is densely inhabited by a number of Zulu-speaking clans whose thatched huts provide a completely African touch to the landscape. After 12 km (35 km from Kranskop) the road reaches the river and crosses into Zululand by means of the Jameson Bridge. The northern side of the valley is as spectacular as the southern side. For 19 km the road finds a difficult and steep way until it finally reaches the summit where it joins the road to Nkandla (see page 447).

# PIETERMARITZBURG TO THE NORTH

From Pietermaritzburg the main road to the north makes a handsome exit from the city, rising steadily through suburban areas where the homes are notable for their flowers and trees. At 6 km from the city lies the Natal Parks, Game and Fish Preservation Board headquarters in the Queen Elizabeth Park, a pleasant setting of trees, picnic spots and drives on the right-hand side of the road. There are panoramic views of the city and the surrounding hills.

At 11 km from Pietermaritzburg the road reaches the summit of the climb and passes through the residential area of . . .

## HILTON

In 1857 Joseph Henderson bought a farm named *Ongegund* on the cool green heights above Pietermaritzburg. He renamed his farm after Hilton Park in Staffordshire where his wife had enjoyed walking as a girl. In 1860 Gould Lucas, magistrate of Ladysmith, purchased a portion of this farm, intending to retire there one day. In 1868, a friend of his, the Reverend W. V. Newnham, organised a school in Ladysmith but the venture did not flourish and in 1872 was transferred to the original farmhouse on *Hilton*. From this small beginning, the Hilton College of today has developed as one of the most prestigious schools in South Africa. The area of Hilton is made pleasant by trees and gardens.

### Accommodation
★ Crossways Hotel, 22 rooms, 12 with baths. R9 – R13,50 B/B. Phone 3-1143.
★★ Hilton Hotel, 46 rooms, all with baths. R27,50 – R30 B/B. Phone 3-1611.

From Hilton the finely graded double carriageway road to the north continues through the midlands of Natal. To the left of the road, 2,5 km from Hilton, lie the immaculate farmlands of the Cedara Agricultural College. There are turnoffs to Bulwer and Merrivale 3 km further on and 4 km further on (30,5 km from Pietermaritzburg), turnoffs to . . .

## HOWICK AND MIDMAR DAM

The town of *Howick*, named after the Northumberland home of Earl Grey, British Colonial Secretary, was founded in 1850 on the site of the staging post where the road to the north crossed the Mngeni River. Its luxuriant setting makes this one of the most amiable regions in the midlands of Natal: 1 048 m above sea level, well-watered and having a temperate climate. The Mngeni River was originally crossed at a shelf of rock just above a 93-m-high waterfall. Generally a dangerous crossing and especially during flood time, a number of travellers and their vehicles were carried over the falls. In later years it became quite a fashionable place in which to commit suicide; about 20 people are known to have lost their lives there.

Howick was first established with only one inhabitant, a ferryman and hotel keeper named Lodge, whose son had recently been carried over the falls during a flood. His grave, a pile of stones next to the pool at the bottom of the falls, provided a melancholy object of interest for travellers. The town now has a fair-sized population of 14 377.

Howick became popular as a holiday resort for people seeking to escape the humidity of the Natal lowlands. The beauty of the waterfall always proved an attraction while in the vicinity were three other waterfalls, all in tributaries of the Mngeni River: Cascade Falls, 25 m high; Shelter Falls 37 m; and the highest, Karkloof Falls, 105 m. On the banks of the Karkloof River just above the waterfall, 15 km from Howick, a superb picnic area has been created through the generosity of the SAPPI Company, who own the surrounding timber plantations. There are toilets and the river is fine for swimming. It is a pleasant place in which to spend a lazy summer day. There is no charge, so the least visitors can do is to keep the area clean. If everybody removed not only their own litter but at least one thing discarded by somebody else, the world would be a cleaner place.

Howick Falls is probably the most photographed waterfall in South Africa. There is a tearoom and viewsite at the summit and a pathway which descends steeply to the bottom.

Just upriver from Howick the Mngeni River has been contained to form a lake known as *Midmar,* from a castle in Scotland. In 1968 the Natal Parks Board created a public resort and nature reserve encompassing 2 831 ha of the lake and its verges. Fishing for carp or bass, yachting, swimming and various sports on water and land are popular pastimes. Riding and hiking trails may be followed and launch trips are organised. There is a restaurant and camping ground while chalets and bungalows provide accommodation. The game park is a home for white rhino, zebra, eland, impala, blesbok, springbok, wildebeest, gnus, reedbuck and red hartebeest. Waterfowl flock to the area in large numbers. It is altogether, a first-class, splendidly managed development which harmonises with its surroundings.

## Accommodation
★ Howick Falls Hotel, 34 rooms, 10 with baths. R9 – R12 B/B. Phone 9.

## Caravans and camping
★★ Howick Municipal Caravan Park, 26 sites. R2 D plus 50c D per person.
★★★ ® Midmar Public Resort, 260 sites in 3 camps. R1 – R1,20 D per person. 17 rustic cabins and 31 chalets, R3 D – R5 D per person.

From the turnoff to Midmar and Howick, the main tarmac double carriageway continues, winding and climbing through the grassy hills of Natal. This is a delightful journey along a finely located and expertly constructed road. Turnoffs lead to villages such as Tweedie, Lions River, Currys Post, Balgowan and Nottingham Road, all of which are worth exploring if the traveller has the time. Without exaggeration, this may be described as one of the loveliest pieces of downland country in Africa. The valleys are filled with the murmur of streams, cascades and waterfalls; fat herds of dairy cows grazing; horses, patches of indigenous forest and many handsome farms contribute to a delightful landscape. At *Balgowan,* named after a village in Scotland, stands a famous school, and nearby, on the *Tetworth* farm of John Parker, the first trout were introduced to Natal in 1882.

## Accommodation
★ Hebron Haven Hotel (Lions River), 10 rooms, all with baths. R9 B/B. Phone Howick 4031.
★ Nottingham Road Hotel, 12 rooms, 6 with baths. R7 – R8, B/B. Phone 51.
★★★ Rawdens Hotel (Nottingham Road), 20 rooms, all with baths. R22,50 – R26,50 B/B. Phone 44.
★★ 3J Motel (Nottingham Road), 30 rooms, all with baths. R12,50 – R18 B/B. Phone 96.

After 39 km of travel from Howick, the road sweeps down over the hills to the valley of the willow-lined Mooi River on whose banks stands the town of . . .

# MOOI RIVER

Named after the river which flows through this green and fertile valley, *Mooi River* (beautiful river) originated in 1921 on the farm of *Mooirivier* owned by J. N. Boshoff, the man who became the much-esteemed President of the Orange Free State. The town became a municipality in 1959 and at present has 7 803 inhabitants.

Stockbreeding is a major activity in the area and the stock sales held on the first Wednesday of each month provide an animated spectacle. The National Co-operative Dairies, the Mooi River bacon factory, Midlands Hides and Skins and Mooi River Textiles all carry out substantial industries in the town.

Trout fishing in the rivers of the district is good while the Giants Castle Game Reserve is reached 63 km west of the town. The Mooi River Waterfall is about 24 km from the town on the Middle Rest road.

## Accommodation
* Argyll Hotel, 12 rooms, all with baths. R9 B/B. Phone 116.
* Sierra Ranch Hotel, 70 rooms, 60 with baths. R10 – R13 B/B. Phone Glengrove 2.

Beyond Mooi River the road to the north passes a turnoff after 25 km, to the rural centre of Willowgrange and 31 km from Mooi River, the road reaches . . .

# ESTCOURT

In the pioneer days, when the road to the north was simply a rough wagon track, a fort was erected on a hill dominating the fording place over the Bushmans River. This fort, first occupied in 1847, is still standing and is reputedly haunted by numerous ghosts who, for various reasons, have become attached to the place. The fort was designed as a substantial stronghold, with watertanks in the basement, a drawbridge, moat and, reputedly, two secret tunnels. A trading station, blacksmith's and inn were established under the protection of the garrison and by 1863 it was decided that a name be given to what had become a village. *Estcourt* was the name selected by the inhabitants, in honour of Thomas Estcourt, an English parliamentarian who had sponsored the immigration of settlers to the area. Estcourt became a municipality in 1914 and there are at present, 11 500 people living in the town.

Lying at the edge of the thorn country of the Natal Midlands, Estcourt is the centre for considerable industry in livestock. The Estcourt Co-operative bacon factory produces great quantities of sausage, ham and other foodstuffs. Nestlés have a large factory there while other products include hard and soft board, nylon goods, plastics, animal feeds and textiles.

The Bushmans River provides trout fishing possibilities while 4 km upstream from the town lies the Wagendrift Dam, greatly used for fishing and water sports. In 1973 the Natal Parks Board converted 745 ha of the lake and surrounding area into a public resort and nature reserve with campsites and picnic places. The waters of the lake cover the site of Veglaager where the Voortrekkers withstood an attack by the Zulu on 10 August 1828.

At the head of the lake is the 264-ha Moor Park Nature Reserve, established in 1967 as a sanctuary in the acacia thorn country for blesbok, zebra, wildebeest, impala, kudu and other game animals. There is a picnic site for visitors.

## Accommodation
* Andrew Motel, 20 rooms, all with baths. R12,35 – R13,20 room only. Phone 4720.
* Estcourt Hotel, 29 rooms, 11 with baths. R9 – R10,20 B/B. Phone 3044.
** Plough Hotel, 25 rooms, 17 with baths. R13 B/B. Phone 3040.
* Willow Grange Hotel, 11 rooms, all with baths. R9 B/B. Phone 4622.

## Caravans and camping
** Municipal caravan park, 50 sites. R2,40 D.
* Wagendrift Public Resort, R1,20 D per person.

Estcourt is connected to the historic Voortrekker centre of Weenen by means of a road and narrow-gauge railway which is a delight to enthusiasts from many parts of the world.

# WEENEN

The railway to Weenen is 0,5 m (2 ft) gauge and 46,5 km long. It was opened in 1907 and is a perfect specimen of its kind. The train depot is at Weenen from where, each weekday, it leaves at 08h15, reaching Estcourt at noon. The return journey is commenced at 13h15, ending in Weenen at about 16h20. On Saturdays the train leaves Weenen at 07h15. Two locomotives (Hanomag Garretts) work the line, relieving each other every three weeks. Built in Germany in 1928, these locomotives can haul 185 tons on 52 axels on a ruling gradient of 1-in-33.

Weenen is an interesting place to visit in its own right. Situated 35 km from Estcourt in acacia thornbush country, it was founded in 1838. The name means 'weeping' a reminder of the massacres inflicted on the Voortrekker camps in the area after the assassination of Piet Retief and his men by the Zulu. The Bushmans River provides water for irrigation and crops produced are vegetables, lucerne, citrus and groundnuts. The town is also a trading centre for the Cunu and Thembu tribes who live in the vicinity.

Weenen became a municipality in 1910 and has a population of 2 989. A small museum housed in a building erected in 1838 by Andries Pretorius, is open from 08h00 to 16h00 Mondays to Fridays and from 08h00 to noon on Saturdays. A nature reserve, 2 929 ha in extent, was established in 1975 in the thorn country outside the town. Picnic sites have been laid out in the reserve.

## Accommodation
Weenen Lodge, 14 rooms, 12 with baths. R9 D. Phone 838.

From Estcourt, the main tarmac road continues north-westwards over grassy hill country, patched with herds of cattle and numerous acacia trees. After 2,5 km there is a turnoff to Weenen and at 18 km a turnoff to Winterton and the Drakensberg. Shortly after this turnoff the road passes a wayside plaque marking the site where a British armoured train was wrecked by the Boers on 15 November 1899. During this event, Winston Churchill was taken prisoner. Those killed are buried in a cemetery nearby.

A further 1,5 km brings the road to a turnoff leading for 8 km to a monument marking the site of the Blaauwkranz massacre on 16 February 1838. The Zulu army, fresh from the killing of Piet Retief and his men at uMgungundlovu, surprised a number of Voortrekker camps. During a wild night they killed 41 men and 56 women, 185 children and 250 African retainers. About 500 Zulu died in the fighting.

Battlefields and military graves may be seen on either side of the main road as it continues for a further 14,5 km from the Blaauwkranz turnoff. Thirty-five kilometres from Estcourt, the road reaches the town of ....

# COLENSO

Colenso is another of the wayside towns on the road to the north which originated as a simple collection of business establishments and hotel at the crossing place of a river. The river in this case was the Thukela, the largest in Natal. The Zulu still refer to Colenso as *eSkipeni* (the place of the boat). Bishop Colenso, after whom the town is named, was a renowned religious leader in those days. Founded in 1855, Colenso has a population of 3 620, and became a municipality in 1958.

The British army made attempts to relieve the siege of Ladysmith, using Colenso as a base. One of the major battles of the Anglo-Boer War was fought on 15 December 1899 when the British tried to drive the Boers off the heights north of the town and instead were themselves driven down to the south bank of the river with 165 men being killed and 1 002 wounded.

The Thukela River provides the water for a large Escom generating station and is also used for boating and fishing. The Tugela Drift Nature Reserve, 98 ha in extent, was created in 1973, from where the Colenso battlefields may be viewed.

### Accommodation
* Colenso Hotel, 14 rooms, 6 with baths. R9 – R10 B/B. Phone 2242.

### Caravans and camping
** Colenso Caravan Park, 30 sites. R2 D.

From Colenso, the main road bridges across the Thukela River and climbs easily up the same Colenso Heights which gave the British army so much trouble. Once on the summit of the ridge the road continues through a tribal area of grass and acacia trees. This is cattle country, with views of the Drakensberg to the west. At 23 km from Colenso the road reaches a turnoff leading into the town of . . .

# LADYSMITH

The Klip River, on whose banks the town lies, is, to say the least, very erratic – sometimes hardly moving, at other times almost washing away the town. This is good cattle country and the ranchers who first settled in this region were a rugged crowd who, in 1847, proclaimed the independent Klip River Republic, with Andries Spies as commandant. This pocket republic only survived for a few months before British authority over the area was declared.

The British planned a town as an administrative centre for the Klip River District proclaiming it on 20 June 1850. It was named *Ladysmith* in honour of the wife of the Governor, Sir Harry Smith, providing a suitable partner for the town of Harrismith, just across the border, founded at the same time by the Orange Free State Republic.

Ladysmith became world famous during the Anglo-Boer War when it was besieged by the Boers from 2 November 1899 until 28 February 1900. Several of the most celebrated battles of the war were fought around the town, the sites of which are easy to reach: Wagon Hill and Caesar's Camp are within walking distance while Lombards Kop and Umbulwana Hill are located after a short drive. A museum, housed in the municipal buildings in the town, displays many interesting relics of the siege days.

Ladysmith became a municipality in 1899 and today has a population of 38 200. It is an important road and rail junction where the main routes from Durban to the interior diverge to the Orange Free State and Transvaal. Ranching and horse breeding is a considerable activity as is the cultivation of corn, soya beans, oats, fruit and vegetables. The climate is warm to hot and with ample water from the river and the Windsor Dam (8 km away), gardens flourish and there are facilities for water sports. Aloes thrive in great numbers on the surrounding hills and a visit to the various battlefields is recommended.

### Accommodation
** Andrew Motel, 26 rooms, 16 with baths. R9,75 – R15,65 room only. Phone 6909.
** Crown Hotel, 34 rooms, 10 with baths. R11 – R11,50 B/B. Phone 2267.
** Royal Hotel, 63 rooms, 32 with baths. R11 – R15 B/B. Phone 2176.

### Caravans and camping
** Ladysmith Caravan Park, 66 sites. R3 D.

# SPIOENKOP PUBLIC RESORT

This resort and nature reserve (4 562 ha in extent) was created in 1975 at the dam in the Thukela River, 40 km west of Ladysmith. Also included is a game park, and there are facilities for water sports, swimming and accommodation.

## Caravans and camping
★★ ® 22 sites, 50c D per vehicle. 38 chalets (6 beds), R6 D.

The main road to the north reaches a parting of the ways at Ladysmith: one branch veers north-westwards to the Orange Free State (page 526); the other branch continues to the Transvaal. Passing the railway marshalling yard of Danskraal, the road proceeds over open, grassy, undulating country. The Platberg Colliery stands next to the road 23 km from Ladysmith. The road crosses the barrier of the range known to the Africans as *uNdi* (the heights). Europeans know it as the *Biggarsberg* after Alexander Biggar, one of the pioneers of Port Natal who had a slight accident in his cart there when accompanying the Voortrekkers on their way to the Battle of Blood River.

In the midst of the Biggarsberg, 49 km from Ladysmith, is a motel pleasantly situated in an area known as Fort Mistake. This name refers to the ruin of a small fort, known as Fort Selby, built on a high summit overlooking the area. By whom was this fort built, for what reason and when was it built, are questions that have intrigued many historians. The fort consists of two structures built of stone without mortar or foundations. One of the structures is conical in shape and the only one of its kind in South Africa. The buildings were never roofed and since there was no supply of water near by, the military value would have been very doubtful.

Various persons have considered the buildings to be of either British or Boer origin, built during one or other of the wars during the last century. Neither Boer or Briton, however, was in the habit of designing such fortifications and erecting them in situations quite so awkward. The fort was certainly a folly. Oddly enough, there is a resemblance to the roofless stone buildings of Zimbabwe, although in this case, the embrasures in the walls were created for firearms.

Whatever its origin, the little fort makes every passerby aware of its presence. Perched on the heights of the Biggarsberg, it looks out into the great power heart of South Africa – the area of coal and electricity – and seems to brood over memories as it watches the changes of today. Perhaps it should be called 'Fort Mystery' rather than Fort Mistake?

## Accommodation
★ Andrew Motel, 38 rooms, all with baths. R10 room only. Phone Dannhauser 2052.

Beyond the motel the main tarmac road continues for 6 km and at the Sunset Rest Hotel, reaches an important junction: the main road continues north to Newcastle (see page 472) and a turnoff east leads for 26 km to Dundee and the coalfields of Natal.

## Accommodation
★ Sunset Rest Hotel, 21 rooms, 10 with baths. R8,50 – R9 B/B. Phone Dannhauser 2100.

# DUNDEE

The presence of coal in Natal was observed by many early travellers. The Voortrekkers, during their battles with the Zulu, found coal in the beds of streams such as the *Steenkoolspruit* (coal stream) and in 1839 the British garrison commander in Durban, Captain Jervis, sent samples of coal to the Governor of the Cape.

In their kitchens farmers burned coal obtained from surface outcrops on their lands and it was one of them, Peter Smith of *Talana* farm, who started sending wagonloads of coal to be marketed in Pietermaritzburg. This action, in 1862, actually started the coal industry. In 1880 the first proper geological survey was made of the Natal coalfields by which it was proved that workable deposits existed in an area of nearly 3 000 square kilometres. Exceptionally rich deposits were found on the farms *Dundee* and *Coalfields*.

By that time, Peter Smith had already marketed over 7 000 tons of coal. With Dugald MacPhail and Charles Wilson as partners, he developed mining substantially, forming the Dundee Coal and Estate Company. In 1882 he laid out a town on the farm *Dundee* to create a centre for the coalfields. In 1902 this township became a municipality and today has 20 420 inhabitants.

The town has an interesting museum which is largely devoted to coal, displaying a collection of geological specimens and the surprising variety of lamps used by coal miners during the early years. The museum is housed in the government administrative building and is open by request during normal working hours.

Coal mines are not the most beautiful examples of man's impact on the environment but in this part of the world, they at least occur in a green, pleasant and healthy area. There are estimated to be reserves of 2 700 million tons of high quality coal in northern Natal, lying close to the surface.

### Accommodation
★ El Mpati Hotel, 48 rooms, 28 with baths. R10 – R11 B/B. Phone 2-1155.
★ Royal Hotel, 42 rooms, 15 with baths. R10,50 – R12 B/B. Phone 2-2147.

### Caravans and camping
★ Municipal Park, 30 sites. R2,50 D.

Tarmac roads lead from Dundee to nearby coal mining centres such as Glencoe (population 10 206) and Dannhauser (population 3 280), both of which are on the main railway line from Durban to the Transvaal.

### Accommodation
★ Dannhauser N. C. Hotel, 9 rooms, all with baths. R6 B/B. Phone 2210.
★ Glencoe Hotel, 20 rooms, 12 with baths. R6,50 – R7,50 B/B. Phone 198.
★ Regent Hotel (Glencoe), 10 rooms, 8 with baths. R7 – R8 B/B. Phone 3-1175.

Beyond Dundee the main tarmac road continues north-eastwards. After 6 km there is a turnoff past the Dundee Agricultural Research Station leading to Nqutu and the battlefields of Rorke's Drift (46 km) and iSandlwana (see page 448). The main tarmac road proceeds, reaching 27 km from Dundee, a turnoff stretching for 20 km to the battlefield of . . .

# BLOOD RIVER

The site of this clash is marked by a laager of 63 full-sized wagons cast in bronze and erected around a pile of rocks placed in the centre of the site by survivors of the battle. A strangely deceptive position for a decisive conflict, it is situated in the midst of a wide, grassy, treeless plain which is today peacefully covered with farmhouses and grazing cattle. A few isolated hills look down aloofly on the scene.

The Blood River (known to the Zulu as the *Ncome* or 'praiseworthy' River from its plentiful water and green banks) meanders tranquilly across the plain. Deeply eroded dongas, causing unexpected hindrances, hold the secret to the military character of the area.

*Overleaf: The Mngeni River tumbles over a sheer 95-m precipice at Howick, creating one of the loveliest waterfalls in Southern Africa.*

It was here, on 15 December 1838, that Andries Pretorius and 464 men, riding towards Dingane's capital uMgungundlovu to obtain vengeance for the murder of Piet Retief and his followers, found a campsite which either Providence or the perspicacity of their leader had selected for its invulnerability. A sharply edged donga, 4 m deep and invisible from the level of the plain, leads down to a junction with the Blood River. The camp was situated on the tongue of land where the donga joined the river, thus being securely protected on three sides. With their wagons drawn up in a tight defensive laager, the men inside were secure from all save cannon fire.

Only foolhardiness could have caused the Zulu to attack such a camp. At dawn on 16 December 1838, a force of about 10 000 Zulu, commanded by Ndlela, found the camp. Charles Celliers, who was present, described the battle:

'They came down on the camp with great courage and, if I am not mistaken, endeavoured four times to take it by storm. Each time they were driven back. We could both hear and see their commander, who wished to repeat the attack, but the men refused to do so.'

About 3 000 died in the course of that clamorous morning. By the time they had been driven off the donga was choked with corpses and the river so stained with blood that it will for ever more, be known as Blood River. Only four Europeans had been wounded.

The details of this battle and the events surrounding it, may be found in *Natal and the Zulu Country*.

---

From the turnoff to Blood River, the main tarmac road continues north-eastwards over open, grassy country. After 41 km the road passes the Stilwater Motel and a further 6 km (74 km from Dundee) brings the road to the town of . . .

## VRYHEID

After the Anglo-Zulu War of 1879 the British fragmented Zululand into 13 petty states. In this way they hoped to control the area by reducing the Zulu people to minor tribal elements. However, considerable rivalry and fighting resulted between the 13 appointed chieftains. Cetshwayo, the Zulu king, was given only a small portion of his original state and on his death in 1884, his heir, Dinuzulu, became involved in heavy competition with Zibebu, chief of the Mandlakazi section of the Zulu.

In order to obtain support, Dinuzulu offered rewards of land to any mercenaries who would fight for him. In 1884 a group of Europeans formed the Committee of Dinuzulu's Volunteers and after several clashes, defeated Zibebu in the Battle of Ghost Mountain. Details of this complicated chapter in South African history are recorded in *Natal and the Zulu Country*. The mercenaries then expected their payment and Dinuzulu found himself confronted with demands from 800 applicants who claimed to have supported him. Zululand was not big enough to allocate to all these land-hungry individuals, farms the size of which they wanted.

After some unpleasantness and intervention from Britain, the mercenaries had to be content with a grant of land in the northern part of the country. On 5 August 1884 this area was declared the 'New Republic' with the town of *Vryheid* (liberty) founded as its capital. This independent state only survived until 1887 when it was absorbed into the South African Republic and after the Anglo-Boer War, Vryheid became part of Natal.

The town became a municipality in 1912 and at present the population is 17 556. It is a centre for coal mining and ranching and is particularly important for communications. A museum has been created in the original *Raadsaal* (council hall) of the New Republic and at the back of this building there is a small fort. The museum is open on Mondays, Wednesdays,

Thursdays and public holidays from 10h00 to 12h00 and from 15h00 to 16h00; on Saturdays from 10h00 to 12h00.

## Accommodation
* President Hotel, 32 rooms, 13 with baths. R11 – R12 B/B. Phone 5201.
** Stilwater Motel, 61 rooms, all with baths. R13,50 B/B. Phone 3802.

## Caravans and camping
** Vryheid Caravan Park, 20 sites. R2,25 D.

Beyond Vryheid a road stretches southwards for 96 km to Babanango (see page 447). At 48 km along this road stands the Mhlungwane trading store from where a turnoff leads to the monument erected on the site where the Prince Imperial of France was killed on 1 June 1879 during the Anglo-Zulu War.

The main tarmac road continues northwards from Vryheid, climbing gently through grassy country, with the Skurweberg lying to the west and the Zungwini mountain to the east. At 12 km the road passes the site of the Battle of Nkambule where, on 29 March 1879, a Zulu army of 17 000 men attacked a British fort held by 2 000 men. The Zulu were driven off, losing about 2 000 men, an event which marked the turning point of the Anglo-Zulu War.

The road continues through pleasant, hilly country scarred by numerous coal mines and forested by dense plantations of trees. At 50 km from Vryheid the road reaches . . .

# PAULPIETERSBURG

Situated beneath a high ridge and dominated by the bulky mass of rock known as *Dumbe* from the edible tubers of that name which grow there, *Paulpietersburg* was named after President Paul Kruger and Commandant-General Pieter Joubert of the South African Republic. The town became a municipality in 1958 and has a population of 29 751. It is a centre for coal mining, timber cultivation and for the hot springs of the Natal Spa which, 16 km away, have been considerably developed into a pleasant resort offering swimming, recreation and accommodation. The Pongola Bush Nature Reserve, 850 ha in extent, was created in 1972 to conserve an evergreen forest in the vicinity of Paulpietersburg.

## Accommodation
* Dumbe Hotel, 10 rooms, 6 with baths. R8,50 – R9,40 B/B. Phone 131.
** Lurula Natal Spa Hotel, 74 rooms, 41 with baths. R8 – R14,50 B/B. Phone Natal Spa 4.

From Paulpietersburg, the main tarmac road continues northwards for 56 km to Piet Retief (see page 616).

---

From the turnoff at the Sunset Rest Hotel which leads to Dundee, the main tarmac road from Pietermaritzburg to the Transvaal continues northwards across grassy country. Herds of dairy cows, maize fields and several coal mines provide visual evidence of the richness of the area. To the west are fine views of the highveld escarpment while the Chelmsford Dam in the middle distance further enchances the scene. The Chelmsford Public Resort covering 6 014 ha was created at this lake in 1975. There are facilities for boating, fishing and swimming, as well as a game park and sites for camping, caravanning and picnicking.

The road crosses the Ingagane River, passing the Ballengeich and Kilbarchon collieries, the Ingagane Power Station (the largest in Natal) and a turnoff to the Normandien Pass, an interesting but precipitous route into the Orange Free State – not to be attempted in wet weather. At 41 km from the Sunset Rest Hotel, the road reaches . . .

# NEWCASTLE

Founded in 1864 and named after the British Colonial Secretary, the Duke of Newcastle, the town is today a major centre for the production of steel. The Iron and Steel Corporation has substantial works there and the glare of blast furnaces at night is a characteristic sight.

Coal and water are in plentiful supply, and form the basis of local industry. A major portion of South Africa's pig-iron requirements originate from Newcastle as well as high carbon ferro-manganese, red oxide and calcium carbide. The factory of the Durban Falkirk Iron Company manufactures Defy stoves, enamel baths and other items in the town.

Newcastle is inhabited by 32 150 people. The Chelmsford Dam provides recreation, there is good fishing in the rivers and there are beauty spots such as the waterfall in the Ncandu River 16 km from the town on the road to Mullers Pass.

## Accommodation
★ Castle Arms, 33 rooms, all with baths. R10,40 – R13,50 B/B. Phone 2-7064.
★★ Holiday Inn, 169 rooms, all with baths. R20,50 – R31 room only. Phone 2-8151.
★ Kings Hotel, 18 rooms, 7 with baths. R8 – R9 B/B. Phone 2-6101.

## Caravans and camping
★ Newcastle Caravan Park, 50 sites. R2 D.
★ Incandu Caravan Park, 16 sites. R3 D.

From Newcastle a fine tarmac drive leads to the town of Memel in the Orange Free State. After 16 km this road passes a turnoff to the Schuinshoogte Battlefield, where, on 8 February 1881, a British force of 311 men clashed with a Transvaal patrol. In the skirmish 65 of the British and eight of the Transvaal patrol were killed. Also on this road, 3 km away, stands *Fort Amiel* named after Colonel Amiel who built it during the Anglo-Zulu War. The escarpment is climbed by means of *Botha's Pass*, a finely graded ascent up grassy hill slopes yielding pleasant views. Numerous sheep, cattle, storks and sakabula birds live on these slopes. The pass was named after a farmer, Rudolf Botha, who lived on a farm at the foot of the pass. At 47 km from Newcastle the road reaches the town of . . .

# MEMEL

Situated in a bowl in the hills, the site of Memel has always been renowned for the richness of its grass. In 1890 it was reported by a traveller that the basin was so overgrown, his wagon was invisible from 15 m away! The first farm, *Allenvale,* was acquired by a Mr Green and the opening of the pass attracted to the site of the town a blacksmith, a toll keeper and a trader. During the Anglo-Boer War the British built a line of forts along the top of the escarpment from Botha's Pass to Klip River. The town, laid out in 1911, became a municipality in 1913 and has a population of 1 478. The 1914 Rebellion was largely planned on *Allenvale* farm by General C. R. de Wet, the then owner. The name *Memel* (surrounded by water) is of Prussian origin.

## Accommodation
★ Memel Hotel, 10 rooms, 7 with baths. R7,50 - R8 B/B. Phone 9909.

From Memel the main tarmac road continues north-westwards to Vrede, 56 km away. An interesting return drive to Newcastle is possible via a gravel road (64 km long) down *Mullers Pass,* named after Joel Muller who lived on *Eikenhof* farm at the foot of the pass. Below Mullers Pass a gravel branch road leads southwards, serving farms on the lower slopes of the escarpment. This is an interesting route to take in good weather conditions. Several passes lead from it up the escarpment into the Orange Free State.

Under no circumstances should these roads be attempted in wet weather. The author, who has covered over a million kilometres of African roads of all kinds, once found himself in a pickle near the summit of Normandien Pass, in pouring rain, and the car had to slide down part of the way in reverse.

This road running along the face of the escarpment eventually joins the main Ladysmith-Newcastle road at a point 41 km from Ladysmith, or 58 km from Newcastle at a turnoff marked Collings Pass. This drive is recommended, being enhanced by pretty cascades and many lovely trees and scenes – but, please, only in dry weather!

From Newcastle a tarmac road stretches eastwards for 37 km to the town of . . .

## UTRECHT

In 1854, six stock farmers secured permission to graze their cattle in the area, promptly declaring the creation of an independent republic named after Utrecht in Holland. In 1860 this cattlemen's republic joined the South African Republic (Transvaal) and after the Anglo-Boer War, Utrecht became part of Natal. With a population of 5 993, it is a centre for agriculture, beef production and coal mining.

### Accommodation
★ Grand Hotel, 26 rooms, 14 with baths. R9 – R9,50 B/B. Phone 661.

### Caravans and camping
★ Utrecht Caravan Park, 14 sites. R2,50 D.

The main tarmac road from Newcastle to the Transvaal proceeds northwards from the town. Immediately outside Newcastle, there is a turnoff to Memel (page 472) and at 6,5 km a turnoff to Utrecht and the Iscor Steelworks. The road begins climbing steadily up the slopes of the escarpment.

At 35 km the road reaches the foot of the pass of Laings Nek with the Inkwelo Motel and a turnoff to O'Neill's Cottage. Majuba Mountain dominates the scene, surrounded by memories of the Anglo-Transvaal War.

## MAJUBA AND LAINGS NEK

*Laings Nek Pass,* 1 676 m high, is named after Henry Laing who farmed on the Natal side of the escarpment. At the outbreak of the Anglo-Transvaal War, the Transvaal forces occupied the summit of the pass, a very strong natural position. On 28 January 1881 the British tried to force a way up the pass, but from this excellent shelter, the Transvaal men held them at bay and then drove them back with 82 men killed and 112 wounded. Only 14 Transvaal men were killed and 29 wounded. It was a sobering setback for the British and in an effort to outflank the defence of Laings Nek they were lured into a sad folly.

The flat-topped height of *Majuba* (the place of rock pigeons) is 2 146 m high and overlooks

Laings Nek. On the moonless night of 20 February 1881, a British force of 554 men led by Sir George Colley, quietly climbed to the summit of the mountain. The intention was to entrench themselves on the top during the night and by dawn to have the Transvaal force blocking Laings Nek Pass at a considerable disadvantage.

When it grew light on 21 February, the 3 500 Transvaal men holding Laings Nek discovered the British presence on Majuba. Expertly using every scrap of natural cover, they worked their way up the slopes. The British soon found themselves in sad trouble; the Transvaal men were magnificent shots and completely outnumbered the British. Any soldier revealing himself on the skyline of the mountain was immediately shot. The fight became a rout and ended at 18h00, when nature mercifully intervened, bringing mist, rain and darkness. By then the summit of Majuba was littered with the dead bodies of 92 British soldiers and a further 134 wounded. Among the dead was General Colley. The Transvaal force had lost only one man and a mere five had been wounded.

As a result of this and other setbacks, the British were prepared to negotiate. Under the mediation of the kindly President Brand of the Orange Free State, a British representative met Paul Kruger and other Transvaal representatives in the homestead of the *Mount Prospect* farm owned by John O'Neill. A treaty of peace was signed on 23 March 1881, thus terminating the Anglo-Transvaal War. O'Neill's Cottage is now a national monument.

The summit of Majuba is best reached from the northern side. At 6 km from the turnoff to O'Neills Cottage the main road reaches the summit of Laings Nek Pass and a further 2,5 km takes the road to a turnoff to Kwaggasnek and Majuba. The turnoff runs for 4 km to a gate bearing a sign marked Majuba. Through this gate the tracks lead for 0,75 km to a parking place very agreeably situated in the shade of an old wattle plantation. Here visitors may leave their cars and walk up a path to the summit. Some scrambling is required in steep places, but the path is otherwise quite practical. The views are superb and there are many lovely wild flowers. On the summit stands a stone memorial cairn erected on 7 October 1935 by veterans of the battle and by public subscription. Graves may be seen as well as a memorial marking the place where General Colley fell. A trigonometrical beacon has been placed on the highest point. There is a windwept airiness about the place, with waving grass and the clouds very near overhead. A sudden thunderstorm in summer will send visitors down the slopes with a strong impression that the battle is still being fought!

### Accommodation
★ Inkwelo Motel, 15 rooms, 12 with baths. R9,50 – R10 B/B. Phone Ingogo 737.
★ Valley Inn, 20 rooms, all with baths. R10,40 B/B. Phone Ingogo 737.

---

From the turnoff to Majuba the main tarmac road continues for 5 km and then, 46,5 km from Newcastle, reaches . . .

## CHARLESTOWN

When the railway from Durban to the Transvaal was opened on 7 April 1891, it terminated at a customs and immigration point named *Charlestown* in honour of Sir Charles Mitchell, the Governor of Natal. Charlestown remained the terminus of the line until 1895 when it was eventually opened all the way to Johannesburg. Today, the town is a small trading centre.

At 3 km north of Charlestown the tarmac road crosses the Coldstream which acts as the border between Natal and the Transvaal. A further 1,5 km (51,5 from Newcastle) takes the road into the town of Volksrust (see page 618).

# Chapter Twenty-four

# THE DRAKENSBERG

The extraordinary scenic and botanical diversity of Southern Africa has, by the genius of nature, been created over a prodigious period of time. A succession of distinct zones ranges from pure aolian desert (the Namib) to the arid sedimentary areas of the Karoo; the Kalahari thornveld of windblown sand; the grassveld continuation of the Karoo; the coastal terrace of high forest; the Cape mountain area of folded sedimentary rock; the windblown and spectacularly beautiful cave sandstone formation in the central part of the country. Providing the ultimate climax was an outpouring on the very top of a mass of basaltic lava which originated about 200 million years ago.

The geological disturbance associated with this eruption must have been truly colossal. The crust of the earth split open allowing a mass of molten matter to surge up from the depths and to spread out over the surface. This matter congealed to form a 1 500-m thick layer of dark-coloured volcanic basalt which cooled without any pressure. Exposed to wind and rain, the basalt was soft and porous, containing numerous pockets and bubbles of gas which formed cavities known as amygdales, filled with mineral matter such as agate and quartz crystals.

This 'roof' of basalt once covered a substantial part of Southern Africa, and being exposed to the weather, was continually drenched with rain by clouds which swept in from the Indian Ocean. The crumbly basalt summit was thus eroded into deep ravines and the sides were washed away to form sheer cliffs. The whole island-like mass of rock eventually dwindled in size and today remains as the highland of Lesotho, the principal watershed and rainy 'roof' of Southern Africa.

On the eastern side, this island of basalt appears as a continuous wall of dark-coloured rock, known to the Zulu of Natal as *uKhahlamba* (the barrier) or simply as *uluNdi* (the heights). For the Sotho living on the heights, the edge of their world is an abrupt 1 500-m precipice which they call the *Dilomo tsa Natala* (cliffs of Natal). A party of European hunters or travellers in the last century heard the story of a legendary dragon which had its lair somewhere in the southern part of the basalt mass. Out of this legend came the name of the *Drakensberg* (dragon mountain), at first applied to one height (Draken's Rock, 2 727-m high) 50 km west of Matatiele, but then covering the full length of the eastern wall of the basalt mass as named by the pioneers of Natal and the Voortrekkers.

From the east, the summit line of the basalt island is as level as the top of a badly decayed, crumbling wall. Few isolated sharp points emerge above the general level. The Drakensberg creates an overpowering impression of tremendous rock faces, deeply eroded into crevices and gorges; crumbling buttresses and isolated ridges left behind by the retreat of the main wall; the ceaseless wear and tear of rain, ice, snow and wind; and the sound of innumerable streams combining to produce a veritable symphony of erosion on a gigantic scale.

The summit maintains an average height of about 3 200 m above sea level. The highest point, 3 482 m, is incongruously named *Tabana Ntlenyana* (nice little mountain). On its heights the Mkhomazi River has its source.

The wall of basalt is 250 km long, stretching from the Sentinel in the north to the southern end. Along this entire length, the basalt, from the 1 800-m level, rests on top of a series of sedimentary deposits. Laid down over this is a 300-m-thick layer of cave sandstone vivid with colours – orange, yellow and red – which contrast brilliantly with the dark basalt. Below this cave sandstone lies a succession of sediments known to geologists as the Red Beds, the Molteno Beds and the Beaufort Beds. Each rock system provides variation of scenery, form and colour, and each tends to erode into shapes peculiar to it. A cross-section of these different formations, as revealed in a deep gorge, is a fascinating visual display of the ceaseless power of creation at work with the tools of fire, water and wind: eroding, erupting, washing, blowing away and piling up.

The tremendous variation in altitude of the Drakensberg cliffs makes the area a home for diverse forms of life. The summit is an Alpine belt, where life is adapted to conditions of snow, hail, ice and vicious thunderstorms. Species of erica thrive in these harsh conditions as well as tough grasses and everlastings (Helichrysum sp.). On the rocks grow algae, lichens and mosses. Apart from a few birds, animal life is scarce.

Below the 2 800-m level of the Alpine belt is the sub-Alpine belt extending down to 1 800 m. This is a zone of tussock grass and scrub, where ferns, cycads and trees shelter in the gullies. The lower and more protected the gullies the denser the trees and the richer their variety. Below this belt, at the 1 200-m level, is the Montone belt where proteas such as the sugarbush (Protea multibracteata) flourish and also many grasses. In areas sheltered from the weather and protected by rock from grass fires, grow podocarpus forests of yellowwood and other timber trees. About 1 000 species of plants thrive in the three belts of altitude.

Most of the wild animals of the Drakensberg live in the Montone belt. The rich grazing and ample drinking water attract many antelope, gnus, blesbok, eland, red hartebeest, zebra, reedbuck, mountain reedbuck, grey rhebuck, grey duiker, klipspringer and oribi. Some are permanent residents, others migrating with the seasons.

Man was attracted to the Drakensberg from prehistoric times. The antelope provided food, the pure water of the streams was good to drink. The forests yielded firewood and the cave sandstone was eroded into numerous overhangs, shelters and caves which accommodated people such as the Bushmen. In fact, it was in the Drakensberg that the Bushmen reached the heights of their Latter Stone Age culture. Unfortunately, it was also in the Drakensberg that their kind was brutally wiped out when later African and European immigrants seized their ancient hunting grounds, regarding them as mere cattle rustlers when they resisted encroachment.

There were never many Bushmen in Southern Africa. They lived in small groups, hunting in specific territories and claiming as their possessions the caves in these areas, decorating many of them with galleries of paintings. About 2 100 caves and rock shelters containing 150 000 paintings, have been found so far. The caves situated around the basalt 'island' contain perhaps the most splendid of these galleries. The sandstone surface leant itself to rock painting and a considerable range of natural colours was available, mainly drawn from earth colours mixed with alluminoid binders made out of animal blood. The colours were applied with brush-like instruments in so expert a manner that mistakes or signs of accident are very rare. The artists must have learned their skills on less permanent surfaces and only applied themselves to rock faces when they were proficient.

Most of the paintings in the Drakensberg were completed between 200 and 800 years ago. They are fading rapidly, their deterioration inevitable because the rough rock surfaces are exposed to air, dripping water, damp and smoke from fires. Some of the colours, more fugitive than others, have already vanished.

Nothing is known of the artists and very little about the history of their people. The paintings give the impression that they lived well and enjoyed life. The men hunted and feuded; the women collected wild fruits and roots. At night they made merry, with feasts and festivals, mimes, rituals and dances. All these activities were depicted by the rock artists, whose paintings serve as the only record. Even the names of the clans and their leaders are only sketchily remembered by their supplanters, and then only in connection with conflict.

It was in the early 18th century that the Bushmen first confronted intruders to their hunting grounds. Iron Age people migrating from the north entered Natal and a section of these newcomers, the Zizi tribe, reached the Drakensberg. The Zizi were not a martial people but they were decidedly stronger and far greater in number than the Bushmen. They were pastoralists, attracted to the lower slopes of the Drakensberg where their livestock could graze. They steadily pushed the Bushmen back against the wall of rock, fighting with them, capturing their women and at the same time, adopting some of their customs and peculiar manner of speech, notably the clicking sounds which were a novelty to the newcomers.

The Zizi largely eliminated the Drakensberg Bushmen, but soon experienced trouble themselves. Other migrating groups of Iron Age people started crowding them from the north-east. In the same way as the Bushmen, the Zizi found themselves pressed against the Drakensberg. They retreated up the passes and eventually found sanctuary in the deep gorges of Lesotho where the Bushmen had also found their last retreat.

Along the grassy foothills of the Drakensberg, the Zizi were replaced by the people known as the Ngwaneni. A period of chaos in the area ensued. A few Bushmen remnants clung to the most inaccessible areas and resorted to cattle raiding in order to compensate for the loss of their former hunting grounds. Surviving groups of the Zizi hid in caves and were reduced to such destitution that they turned cannibal. Their hideouts are still remembered as the scene of many horrible feasts.

Raiding Zulu bands periodically looted their way through the foothills of the Drakensberg. The Ngwaneni were driven off, to seek sanctuary far in the south, only to return after the death of the Zulu king, Shaka. Under a chief named Zikhali, the remnants of the tribe once again built snug beehive-shaped huts along the lower slopes of the Drakensberg. Here they still reside, especially in the area dominated by the mountain once known after their chief as *Zikhali's Horn* but now called Cathedral Peak.

The first known Europeans to see the Drakensberg were, strangely enough, the survivors of a shipwreck. In 1593 the Portuguese ship, *Saint Albert* was wrecked on the Wild Coast. The survivors, 125 Portuguese and 160 slaves, set out to walk to the old trading station of Lourenço Marques (Maputo). They decided to march inland hoping to find more food and to have less trouble fording rivers. It was May when they reported sighting on the horizon, the Drakensberg covered in snow.

Hunters from the Cape reached the southern portion of the basalt mass during the first quarter of the 19th century. In October 1835 the missionary, Allen Gardiner, with two wagons driven by Dick King and Henry Ogle, arrived at the area near the modern town of Underberg. In his diary Gardiner described how he saw a rugged mountain which he named *Giants' Castle,* for he fancied that it resembled Edinburgh Castle. This mountain was renamed in 1865 by the surveyor Dr Sutherland. He called it *Garden Castle* in honour of the maiden name of his mother. The name Giants Castle was then applied to another height of the basalt wall, the 3 314-m-high mass of rock which provides a great landmark and cornerstone of the main basalt mass 50 km north of Garden Castle.

The Voortrekkers descended the escarpment from the central plains to the midlands of Natal by means of several passes north of the main wall of the Drakensberg. However, the mountain wall was still clearly in view and many of them hunted and selected farms for themselves in the foothills. These were men such as Adriaan Olivier, who settled on *Tugela Hoek* at the foot of the pass known as *Sungubala* (where you overcome a difficulty). This was one of the traditional routes up the escarpment to the central plains. The modern road is named Oliviershoek Pass.

Missionaries such as the Reverends K. W. Posselt, W. Gulden-Pfenning and C. Zunckel commenced work at Emmaus, Emangweni and Hoffenthal, stations run by the Berlin Mission Society. Woodcutters also arrived, attracted by the forests of timber trees, to commence a destructive industry.

# MONT-AUX-SOURCES

In 1836 two French Protestant missionaries, the Reverends T. Arbousset and F. Daumas, explored the summit of the basalt mass, travelling from the Caledon River Valley in the west. They reached the edge of the Drakensberg cliffs at the plateau summit known to the Sotho as *Phofung* (place of the eland). The missionaries soon realised that they had found one of the natural wonders of Southern Africa – the continental divide and the source of many important rivers. They therefore named the 3 282-m-high summit *Mont-aux-Sources* (mountain of springs). On the slopes of this crest, overlooking the high Mont-aux-Sources plateau, the Thukela (Tugela), Elands and Western Khubedu rivers have their source. The Thukela flows eastwards, reaches the edge of the plateau and leaps into space, falling 614 m at a horizontal distance of 284 m. The fall is not sheer, being broken, but the main fall is 183 m high. Near its source, the Thukela flows alongside the Elands River before tumbling over the edge of the cliffs. The Elands river veers away northwards, plunges over the edge of the basalt in a spectacular fall of its own and, while the Thukela flows eastwards across Natal to reach the Indian Ocean, the Elands joins the Vaal, its waters eventually reaching the Atlantic Ocean on the west side of Africa.

At the foot of the Mont-aux-Sources plateau, where the main mass of basalt forms a prodigious amphitheatre, a woodcutter named Dooley commenced work cutting trees on land named after him. Near by, a farm named *Goodoo* was purchased in 1903 by Walter Coventry who, in a casual way, started to accommodate the occasional visitor who wanted to explore the Drakensberg. The spectacular beauty of the Mont-aux-Sources area became renowned and in 1906, the Natal Government minister for agriculture and lands, W. F. Clayton, proclaimed as a national park the unoccupied area below the amphitheatre. The Natal Government railways publicity department sent a photographic team to the area, as a result of which practically every guidebook to Natal and passenger coach on the railways was from then on decorated with photographs of the Drakensberg.

Lack of funds badly hindered any development and at one stage just prior to Union in 1910, the government actually decided to abandon the whole scheme. Fortunately, one of the members of the management committee of the park, Colonel J. S. Wylie, bought the area containing the park and after the formation of the Union of South Africa, sold it back to the government on condition that it be retained for all time as a recreational area and national park. The park was initially 3 300 ha in extent. More land was added, including the 762-ha Rugged Glen Nature Reserve. The park attained its present size of 8 094 ha, administered at first by an advisory committee, and then, from 1942, by the Provincial Council of Natal. Since 1947, the park has been run by the Natal Parks, Game and Fish Preservation Board.

The first hostel accommodating visitors had been opened when Mr and Mrs F.C. Williams leased *Goodoo* farm from its owner, Walter Coventry, and converted the original farmhouse into quarters for 12 visitors. Mr Coventry became lessee of the whole park in 1919 and was appointed park superintendent in 1924, earning a salary of £5 (about R10) per month. He busied himself in building a road from the outside world to the hostel, as well as blazing a series of bridle paths to various interesting places in the park.

Climbers steadily began to explore the precipices. The 3 165-m-high peak known as the Sentinel, which looms up as a jagged mass of isolated rock marking the northern end of the basalt wall of the Drakensberg, was first climbed on 17 October 1910 by W. J. Wybergh and N. M. McLeod. The Inner Tower was first scaled on 13 June 1913 by Father A. D. Kelly and J. E. Miller, the same two climbers conquering the 3 047-m-high Eastern Buttress on 10 July 1914.

The mountaineer, Tom Casement, ran the climbers' hostel of Rydal Mount in the Orange Free State. Accompanied by his renowned Sotho guide, Mlatu, he brought parties into the Mont-aux-Sources area from as early as 1908.

In 1926, when Walter Coventry resigned as superintendent of what was called the Natal National Park, he was succeeded in turn by Otto and Walter Zunckel, of the early missionary family. The hostel in the park was enlarged and became an atmospheric place, filled with talk of climbing, hiking and adventure in this superb rock wilderness.

In 1910 a Drakensberg Club had been formed with Judge Broome as first president. During the First World War this pioneer association became defunct but on 15 April 1919 the Natal Mountain Club was established and in July 1920 held its first regular camp in the Mont-aux-Sources area. As a result, the national park received vast publicity from the photographs and glowing descriptions taken back home by those who had participated in the outing.

The first guidebook to the Drakensberg was published in 1927 by a member of the Natal Mountain Club which, during this period, built a stone hut on the summit of the Mont-aux-Sources Amphitheatre. This shelter gave many people the pleasure of spending at least one night on the heights, and of watching the dawn break over the lowlands of Natal.

Walter Coventry had built the bridle path from the hostel to the summit of the Mont-aux-Sources Amphitheatre – a distance of 22,5 km. With two chain ladders spanning the final rock face, this path has allowed several thousand people to experience the thrill of walking or riding to the summit of Mont-aux-Sources at all seasons of the year. Other paths stretching to most parts of the national park were made, including a superb 11-km-long path leading up the Thukela River, to its spectacular gorge near the foot of the waterfall. Without any climbing necessary, this is one of the finest walks in Southern Africa.

The popularity of the Mont-aux-Sources area increased very rapidly. The national park contained such a variety of scenes, climbs, walks, swimming and fishing facilities, flora, picnic spots and riding trails that few visitors failed to return home with pleasant memories. Otto Zunckel, the lessee of the hostel, ran his establishment in a relaxed manner which made it a natural resort for outdoor lovers. Climbers came from all over the world and the Zulu guide, Charlie Sentinel, escorted so many people to the top of the Sentinel that overseas newspapers carried reports when he fell and suffered serious injuries while climbing. The Amphitheatre Wall was first climbed during this period. On 19 April 1935 Doyle Liebenberg, Amlee Metter, Mary Lear and Mark Frank found a route up the precipice.

The atmospheric old hostel, unfortunately, was burned down on 10 December 1941. The larger establishment was built in far more luxurious style and in March 1947, when the British Royal Family stayed there, the title of 'Royal' was added to the name of Natal National Park. Carefully conserved by the Natal Parks Board, the Royal Natal National Park has become one of the tourist showpieces of Southern Africa and a delightfully exciting place to visit.

There are 31 different walks in the area of the park and climbing possibilities are innumerable, ranging from easy to extremely severe. The famous Devil's Tooth, an isolated spire of rock, was first climbed on 6 August 1950 by David Bell, Peter Campbell and Ted Scholes. It remains one of the most complex climbs in the Drakensberg where many exposed parts of the rock wall provide mountaineers with sensational challenges.

### Accommodation
★® Little Switzerland Hotel, 20 rooms, 14 with baths. R16 D/B/B. Phone Robbers Roost 2.
★® Mont-aux-Sources Hotel, 49 rooms, 35 with baths. R13 – R16,50 D/B/B. Phone Mont-aux-Sources 7.
★★® Royal Natal National Park Hotel, 56 rooms, all with baths. R16 – R17 D/B/B. Phone Mont-aux-Sources 1.

### Caravans and camping
★★★® Royal Natal National Park, 100 sites. R1,50 D. 13 rondawels and 2 cottages, R5 – R6 D.

The main access road to the Royal Natal National Park is through the town of Bergville, 46 km away. The approach road yields some grand views of the Drakensberg, with many of the best known heights clearly visible.

# BERGVILLE

In 1897 a cluster of trading stations and houses was built close to the banks of the Thukela River on the farm *Kleine Waterval*, owned by a retired sea captain named Wales. In 1903 this village received the name of Bergville, progressing slowly as the natural trade, administrative and communications centre for the tribal area of the Ngwaneni, a European farming area and the overlooking stretch of the Drakensberg. Bergville became a municipality in 1962 and is the terminus of a branch railway from Estcourt. During the Anglo-Boer War the British built a blockhouse near the town and this is now a museum and national monument. Scenery and climate are both superb and the municipality maintains a tourist resort. The population is 835.

## Accommodation
★ Walter Hotel, 15 rooms, 7 with baths. R10 – R11 B/B. Phone 12.

## Caravans and camping
★★® Municipal caravan park, 30 sites. R2 D. 12 cottages, R3,50 D.

South of the Royal Natal National Park is a ruggedly beautiful stretch of the Drakensberg which overlooks the tribal area of the Ngwaneni people. The foothill country is wild and not easily accessible. Valleys lead up to the basalt wall and dominating the rocky landscape is a height considered by many to be the most beautiful of all Drakensberg peaks, *Mnweni* (place of fingers), so named from the spires of rock which provide a severe test for climbers. Sometimes known as The Rockeries, this peak is 3 116 m high. Behind it, the Orange River has its source on the high moorlands of Lesotho. There is a magnificent cave next to a waterfall at the foot of Mnweni which is generally used by climbers for accommodation.

Immediately south of the Mnweni area a ridge of mountains projects eastwards from the main wall of the Drakensberg. This ridge is known as *abaMponjwana* (the place of little horns), on account of its sharply pointed assembly of peaks. On this ridge are grouped some of the best known heights of the Drakensberg: the 3 004-m-high Cathedral Peak; the 2 918-m-high Bell; the 3 009-m-high Outer Horn; the 3 017-m-high Inner Horn; and an oddly shaped collection of lesser peaks known by names such as the Mitre and the Chessmen.

## THE MPONJWANA RIDGE

The spectacular Mponjwana ridge overlooks on its southern side, one of the most beautiful gorges eroded into the basalt wall of the Drakensberg. Here the river known as the *Mlambonja* (river of the dog) draws its water from at least a hundred separate springs. Tumbling down in waterfalls and rapids and broadening into many deep pools where trout dodge from sun-beams to shadows, this river finds a tortuous way through the sandstone foothills, flowing off to join the Thukela, as one of its most important tributaries.

The valley of the Mlambonja attracted human beings from as far back as Stone Age times and the sandstone formations are filled with caves and rock shelters. The valley was sheltered, there was plentiful water and game animals were attracted to the area by the excellent grazing; thus the Bushmen pioneers lived well. In the valley of the Mlambonja there are about 150 rock shelters formerly used by the Bushmen which contain some of their finest galleries of rock art.

The largest gallery is found in what is known as the Elands Cave in the sheltered and verdant valley of a tributary stream of the Mlambonja. This stream is called the *Mhlwazini* from the Bushmen's tea trees *(Catha edulis)* growing there. In the Elands Cave are painted 1 639 separate figures, including some of the most beautiful polychrome artwork done on rock faces in the world.

Close to the Elands Cave, the river known as the *Ndidima* (place of reverberations) flows down to join the Mhlwazini as a tributary. The Ndidima originates on the summit of the Drakensberg. Tumbling over the cliff face in a tremendous fall and with a ceaseless rushing and roaring, the river flows through a deep, narrow valley half choked with gigantic boulders, while the other half is covered in one of the most dense and unspoilt indigenous forests to be found in the whole area of the Drakensberg.

Bushmen found the valley of the Ndidima particularly idyllic: protected by its situation and depth from the worst of the Drakensberg weather, there were spacious rock shelters, permanent water, firewood in the forest, fat antelope grazing on the grassy foothills. Even modern visitors are tempted to take up residence in so favourable a retreat.

There are 17 main rock shelters in the Ndidima Valley which contain nearly 4 000 separate rock paintings, most of them polychrome and many attaining a high standard of art. Notable among these rock shelters is the one known as *Sebayeni* (the corral) from its use by later pastoralists as a shelter for livestock. In this shelter are 1 146 paintings and although they have regrettably faded, they still reveal the art of the Bushmen at its highest level.

It would be interesting to know when the last Bushmen vanished from this area. In 1925 two European sheep farmers, grazing their animals in the foothills, took shelter from a storm in the Elands Cave. On a ledge they found carefully hidden away, a Bushman's complete hunting outfit – bow, leather case, bark quiver, 22 poisoned arrows, poison and iron knives. All the items were in such excellent condition that they hardly looked as though they had been there for six months. The bundle was carefully wrapped in fresh-looking skins and was concealed beneath some grass which looked as though it was not more than four months old. The find was sent intact to the Natal Museum in Pietermaritzburg. Of the owner there was no trace. Perhaps this was the only remaining Bushman in the Drakensberg who was the last of his kind to view the high peaks and fading paintings left by forgotten artists on the rock walls of the caves.

During the period of this discovery in the Elands Cave, the foothills between Cathedral Peak and Champagne Castle were being used as seasonal grazing grounds. Each winter farmers from the Orange Free State sent flocks of sheep and herds of cattle to the area, grazing them on land leased or bought from the government. A farmer from Kransfontein in the Orange Free State, I. J. M. Buys (Ryk Isak Buys), was the principal user of the area for grazing. In the watershed of the Mlambonja River he had, by 1918, acquired eight farms: *Solar Cliffs, Brotherton, Gewaagd, Tryme, Inhoek, Schaapkraal, Hopeton* and *Leafmore*. The names of these farms still feature on modern maps although they are no longer used for producing sheep.

*Tryme* farm, said to have been named by its surveyor in honour of his horse, was sold by Buys to one of his foremen, Sybrand Vermeulen, who made his home there. Visitors to the mountains today are familiar with the name from the massive hill overlooking the Cathedral Peak Hotel and from the little shop, the Tryme Store, attached to the hotel.

Another of Buys's foremen, Willem Oosthuizen, bought *Leafmore* and *Hopeton* from his employer. *Solar Cliffs* was sold to Anton Lombard, *Brotherton* to Stoffel van Rooyen, *Gewaagd* to Jan Roux, and in 1937 the farms *Inhoek* and *Schaapkraal* were sold to Philip van der Riet, then farming on *Olivia*. Van der Riet bought these farms for the specific purpose of creating a mountain holiday resort. His son Albert, who had hunted, fished and climbed in the area, told his father of the immense possibilities. The two farms lay close to the Drakensberg in a superb setting dominated by Cathedral Peak and the Ridge of Little Horns. The Van der Riets wasted no time. They carefully selected the site for their hotel and started to build. The bad access road was improved to a rough road and during Christmas 1939 the first guests arrived at the Cathedral Peak Hotel, today one of the outstanding resort hotels in Southern Africa.

Another interesting development in the Cathedral Peak area started in 1935 at the Empire Forest Conference. A problem was raised at this meeting concerning farmers who complained that streams were running dry on account of trees being planted at their headwaters.

It was decided to commence intensive research on this controversial matter and, after much study, the watershed of the Mlambonja River was selected as the site of what became the Cathedral Peak Forest Influences Research Station and Cathedral Peak Mountain Catchment Research Station.

In 1938 H. M. (Mike) de Villiers was appointed officer in charge of this research station and a start was made in erecting headquarters on what was originally the farm known as *Gewaagd* (vigilance). The Second World War halted research plans. When Mike de Villiers returned to his post in 1945, he really began work. An entire complex of access roads and paths were made. The main access road had to climb steeply up a route which De Villiers most skilfully located. This is fittingly named Mikes Pass, in his memory. The contract to blast the cuttings was given to G. R. Monzali, an Italian engineer who had built, amongst other things, the railway bridge over the Gouritz River in the Cape. Unfortunately, Monzali broke his back in a truck accident just after he started work on the cuttings. He persevered with the job, however, and the summit of what is known as the Little Berg was reached in May 1949. A drive up Mikes Pass is quite a scenic experience during which the traveller cannot fail to admire the ingenuity of the road's location and construction.

On completion of Mikes Pass, the top of the Little Berg could be reached and research commenced. The initial programme was to select ten catchment sites. Each of these streams was gauged. A central meteorological station was established with a network of raingauges over each catchment. One catchment was subjected to light intensive grazing while the rest were planted with trees. Research proceeded until 1972 with results proving that pines consumed far more water than natural grassland; the farmers' original complaints were therefore justified.

This research having been carried out, a new programme of work was commenced. The Mountain Catchment Act had stipulated that the principal function of the Drakensberg was to provide optimum water and to allow environmental management and human recreation – the basic concept of wilderness areas. Afforestation was therefore terminated and now no farming or other development is allowed in the area. Pure water and human pleasure are the two products of the Drakensberg. The wilderness is to be maintained in its present state with (strange as it may seem) fire being the principal tool of the conservationists.

Totally protected grasslands create enormous fire hazards. Complete protection is therefore impractical, since fires – accidental or deliberate – are inevitable. Total preservation would in any case, allow the encroachment of secondary, woody vegetation over the grassland. Different burning techniques are being studied and this experience will influence future management of the whole Drakensberg catchment area.

The paths made by the Forestry Department have opened up the entire area from Cathedral Peak to Champagne Castle. Permits to enter the catchment areas are readily available from the forestry offices, since nature lovers, walkers and climbers are welcome in wilderness areas especially during summer when the grass is green and fire hazards are low. It must be remembered, however, that they are carefully controlled areas. An unplanned fire can cause immense damage and for years retard an entire complex programme of experiment.

## THE CATHEDRAL PEAK AREA

This portion of the Drakensberg is essentially the catchment area of the Mlambonja River. The main access route is via the gravel road which branches westwards from the Bergville-Loskop road at a point 10 km from Bergville and 20 km from Loskop. The gravel road stretches directly towards the Drakensberg up the valley of the Mlambonja. After 4 km the road passes the Emmaus Mission with its large hospital. For the next 14 km the road leads through the homeland of the Ngwaneni people, many handsome views of the mountain wall providing a background to the huts and fields of the tribal farmers. At 18 km from the junction, the road first passes the turnoff to Mikes Pass, and then, near by, the turnoff to the Cathedral Peak Forestry Station. Opposite lies the turnoff to the caravan park and camping ground maintained by the Forestry Department. A further 4 km brings the road to its terminus at the Cathedral Peak Hotel, 22 km from the junction with the Bergville-Loskop road.

A closer approach to the main wall of the Drakensberg can only be achieved on foot, horseback or (accompanied by foresters) in a four-wheel-drive vehicle. A network of paths spreads from the hotel towards the mountains. The upper valley of the Mlambonja provides a particularly beautiful walk. In its upper reaches, the river is joined by tributaries such as the *Qalweni* (place of bamboos); the *Tseketseke* (place of red ants); and the *Xheni* (place of the bundle). In these deep valleys are innumerable waterfalls, deep swimming pools, towering cliffs and cool forests of trees and ferns.

Another tributary of the Mlambonja, joining it just below the hotel, is the *Mhlonhlo*, which receives its name from the elbow-shaped precipice of sandstone projecting into the valley like a cape. The path finds a way up the Mhlonhlo to beauty spots such as the Doreen, Albert and Ribbon falls, and to a magnificent forest of ferns. These paths up the river valleys are pure delight for walkers, with crystal-clear water to drink, many delightful picnic spots and a constant change of scenery as the valleys twist and rise.

Yet another tributary of the Mlambonja which reaches that river below the hotel is the *Ndumeni* (the place of thunder), named after the dome-like summit in the Drakensberg where the noise of summer storms always seem to reach a climax and where the river has its source. The path following the valley of this river provides the walker with a joyful experience of majestic scenery: a constantly changing panoramic view; a dream-like indigenous forest; the Rainbow Gorge; and branch paths climbing steeply up to the bulky sandstone massif of Tryme.

A different path leads from the hotel up the Mhlonhlo Valley. Branching north to climb the steep sandstone cliffs, the path passes the landmark known as Mushroom Rock and from there ascends to the top of the Little Berg, the intermediate stepping stone between lowland and the actual escarpment. From this high, grassy plateau, the entire length of the Drakensberg from Cathedral Peak to Champagne Castle may be viewed. The path leads to a little tarn, a real enchanted pool where lovely reflections are captured on its surface. It is, however, a strangely elusive pool; one day it may contain water but the next day there is no sign of such a pool. Photographers and artists are left wondering whether they had, in fact, ever seen in it the glorious reflections of the mountain massif.

Beyond the tarn, the path continues until, as do most of the other paths, it joins the contour path which runs along the foot of the escarpment all the way from Cathedral Peak to Champagne Castle. This path provides enthusiastic walkers with a full two- to three-day walk if the whole journey is completed. Otherwise, part of the way may be done, which takes less time. Whichever length is chosen, there are few walks in Southern Africa to equal it.

Above the contour path is climbing territory. The great heights loom like a battle phalanx of heavily armoured giants. They have their occasional weakness, where steep passes lead to the summit but most of them present a formidable challenge.

Cathedral Peak (3 004 m) at the end of the Mponjwana ridge, is actually one of the easier climbs with a choice of 'C' category routes. It was first climbed in July 1917 by D. W. Bassett-Smith and R. G. Kingdon. At that time it was already called Cathedral Peak but the person who gave it that name remains unknown. Only by a long stretch of the imagination can any similarity between the mountain and a cathedral be found, but the name was probably suggested by the adjoining presence of the extraordinary, and unmistakably shaped peak known as the Bell.

The Bell (2 918 m) provides one of the most interesting climbs of the Drakensberg and was conquered for the first time on 17 January 1944 by Hans and Else Wongtschowski. The easiest ascent is in the 'E' category, but it has attracted so many climbers in recent times –

many of them sadly lacking in experience – that it is a wonder that more people have not been killed climbing it. Fatalities include Ian Dawson and Charles Barber, killed in September 1970.

Next to the Bell looms the Outer Horn (3 009 m). A 'D' climb, the Outer Horn was first conquered in July 1934 by a party comprising some of the best known climbers of the Drakensberg: Doyle P. Liebenberg, T. Wood, H. G. Botha-Reid, 'Doc' Ripley and F. S. Brown. Although easier to climb than the Bell, the Outer Horn is exposed and on 13 October 1959, Miss Fielette van Rooyen was killed there.

Next to the Outer Horn is its twin, the Inner Horn (3 017 m). A 'C' climb, it was conquered in 1925 by a group headed by H. G. Botha-Reid. On 13 July 1942, Auguste Hellemans, from what was then the Belgian Congo, was killed on this mountain. He is buried in the forest of wattle trees close to the hotel. Next to him lies Hans Marcus who, on 21 October 1947, was killed in a fall from Baboon Rock.

On the main face of the Drakensberg, south of the junction with the Mponjwana ridge, are several remarkable mountains. Projecting out on their own are two jagged-looking peaks, the Pyramid (2 914 m) and the Column (2 926 m). The Pyramid, an 'E' climb, was first ascended in 1936 by H. F. Howes-Howell, O. B. Godbold, Naomi Bokenham, H. C. Hoets, C. Axilson and S. Rose. On 29 December 1950, Michael Stephens was killed while climbing this mountain.

The Column, an 'F' climb, was first scaled on 9 December 1945 by one of the most legendary of all Drakensberg climbers, the New Zealander, George Thomson. Thomson, a builder by profession who deliberately sought contracts in the Drakensberg area so that he would be able to climb, was responsible for many sensational first climbs. Climbing alone, and watched with bated breath from below, he managed to reach the summit of the Column using no mechanical aids whatsoever. On his way down he fell about 15 m, badly gashing his leg, yet managing to reach the bottom safely.

Just south of the Column and the Pyramid, the summit line of the Drakensberg reaches one of its highest points by means of the 3 281-m Cleft Peak, so named from the deep vertical gash on its face. There is an easy 'A' category climb with a first recorded ascent in 1935 by Doyle P. Liebenberg, 'Doc' Ripley and party. There are harder ways of reaching the top of the Cleft Peak but the path, followed by many groups in modern times, is a magnificent experience for walkers, yielding particularly sensational views.

Just to the south of Cleft Peak looms the 3 285-m dome of Ndumeni with, just below the summit, the strange assembly of spires and buttresses known to the Africans as Qolo la maSoja (ridge of the soldiers) and to Europeans as the Organ Pipes. Easy paths lead to the Organ Pipes and through a gap in the Organ Pipe wall, to the summit of Ndumeni.

Still further southwards rear the buttresses of the 3 065-m Windsor Castle, the 3 076-m Little Saddle, lesser heights such as the Sugar Loaf and the Sphinx, and finally, the 3 078-m Ndidima (the place of reverberations) Dome where the magnificent waterfall of the Ndidima River leaps down from the summit plateau.

Next may be seen the Witch, the Vulture's Retreat, and in the foreground, the lower 2 596-m Eastman's Peak, a climb of 'C' category first conquered in 1935 by H. A. Eastman and party. This peak marks the end of the Drakensberg area usually climbed or walked by people based in the Cathedral Peak Hotel and caravan park. Beyond this point is the Cathkin Peak-Champagne Castle area.

## Accommodation
★★⑩ Cathedral Peak Hotel, 86 rooms, all with baths. R12,50 – R18 D/B/B. Phone Peak 1.

## Caravans and camping
★⑩ Forestry Department Caravan Park, 25 sites. R1,50 D.

# THE CATHKIN PEAK-CHAMPAGNE CASTLE AREA

From the point 16 km from Bergville where the access road branches off to the Cathedral Peak area, the main gravel road continues south-eastwards. Keeping parallel to the Drakensberg, the road crosses undulating foothill country, particularly beautiful around Easter when cosmos flowers are in bloom. After 8 km, the road passes a short turnoff to the Kelvin Grove Caravan Park, pleasantly situated and from where fine views of the Drakensberg may be seen.

## Caravans and camping

** Kelvin Grove Caravan Park, 20 sites. R2,50 D plus 25c D per person. Rooms, R2,50 D per person. Camping hostel, R1,50 per person.

The main gravel road continues south-eastwards. After a further 5 km it reaches a crossroads: to the north, a road branches off for 13 km to the agricultural centre of *Winterton,* founded in 1905 and named after H. D. Winter, Secretary for Agriculture; ahead the road proceeds for 11 km to Loskop; to the south the access road stretches to the Cathkin Peak-Champagne Castle area. This road leads up the valley of the *Sterkspruit* (strong stream), taking the traveller through some superlatively beautiful foothill country.

The valley of the Sterkspruit, like the valley of the Mlambonja, was always attractive to human beings. For some reason, a very odd assortment of Europeans made their homes there at different times: hermits, woodcutters, nameless men who lived and died in solitude, cattle rustlers such as Pat McCormick, remittance men, and also a more respectable breed of farmers who settled in the valley and worked hard to establish farms and build homesteads. It was to this valley in 1858 that David Gray, who ran a hotel at Weston, moved. He settled first on a farm named *The Nest* and then in 1863 transferred to an adjoining site which he named *Cathkin* after Cathkin Braes near Paisley, his home town in Scotland.

The imported name of Cathkin was rather unfortunately applied to one of the most handsome of all the Drakensberg peaks, the 3 194-m Cathkin Peak. This fine mountain, one of the cornerstones of the whole escarpment, stands at the point where the basalt wall veers to the south. Cathkin Peak stands on its own, dominating the whole escarpment in so definite a manner that the Africans have called it *Mdedelele* (make way for him), the name applied to a bully!

David Gray and Captain Grantham, a surveyor of the Royal Engineers, were jointly responsible for naming another of the Drakensberg peaks, this time with a bit more originality. Grantham was busy on a survey of the Drakensberg when he and Gray decided to try and climb Cathkin Peak, a formidable prospect. After climbing two-thirds of the way, they felt that they had gone far enough. They settled down to rest and to drink a bottle of champagne they had carried with them, destined for enjoyment on the summit.

On removing the bottle from the haversack, they found it to be half empty. After some argument as to who had snatched a surreptitious drink (they had taken it in turns to carry the haversack) they resolved to blame the mountain. They renamed Cathkin Peak, Champagne Castle, and for years the mountain was inflicted with the unwieldy name of Cathkin Peak or Champagne Castle. Only in comparatively recent times did the confusion end when mapmakers transferred the later name to the hitherto unnamed 3 351-m summit on the main wall of the escarpment. The Champagne Castle of today is one of the highest points on the summit of the escarpment.

Another interesting settler in the Sterkspruit Valley was Carter Robinson. In July 1910, when he was only 21 years old, he bought the farm *Benjamin* which nestled in the afternoon shadow of Cathkin Peak and he erected the first buildings on the site of the present Monks Cowl Forest Station. He was a lover of trees and pleaded so strongly to the government for conservation that in April of 1922 the Cathkin Peak Forest Reserve was proclaimed covering some 40 400 ha between the Njesuthi and Mlambonja rivers.

In January 1924 Carter Robinson was appointed honorary forester and the following year was placed on a salary basis of £5 (R10) per month. He resigned in 1934 and in that year the government bought his farm *Benjamin,* developing it into the Monks Cowl Forestry Station with J. van Heyningen appointed as the first full-time forester.

Apart from agriculture, recreation and forestry, the area beneath Cathkin Peak has seen diverse excitements such as claims of gold discoveries. The first occurred in November 1891 when J. T. Howe reported finding gold on a spur of Cathkin Peak. In February 1892 there was a rush to the Phutini Valley where J. M. Sayman claimed a find. Nothing worthwhile resulted. In 1916 it was claimed that cinnabar had been discovered in the valley of the Nkosasana where the earth is notably red in colour. There was a short-lived rush by fortune-seekers.

In the field of recreation, however, no disappointment has been experienced in the Cathkin Peak area. A string of recreational resorts has been built along the access road. Eight kilometres from the junction with the main Bergville-Loskop road stands the hotel known as The Nest, built in 1943 by David Gray, grandson of the original David Gray who settled on the farm of that name. A further 3 km takes the road past the El Mirador Hotel built in 1940 by Captain H. G. Whelan on part of *Heartsease* farm. Just beyond the hotel is the M.O.T.H. sanctuary of Mount Memory, dedicated in 1948 as a place of reflection and memorial to those killed in the two world wars.

One and a half kilometres further on a turnoff leads to the Cathkin Park Hotel started in 1929 by Carter Robinson. After 3 km the road passes the turnoff to the Dragon Peaks Park attached to the Drakensberg Boys Choir School. This was founded in 1954 when R. W. Tungay, a Durban journalist, bought the farm *Dragon Peaks* and on 23 January 1967, his son John opened the school. Today it houses 120 boys whose touring choir groups are known throughout Southern Africa and in many overseas countries.

Five kilometres beyond the turnoff to the Dragon Peaks Caravan Park the road reaches a turnoff to the Monks Cowl Forestry Station, and then ends in the grounds of the Champagne Castle Hotel, founded in about 1930 by H. Martens on the farm *Woestyn.* From the forestry station and the hotel, foot- and bridle paths stretch into the mountains and to beauty spots such as the Sterkspruit Falls. This is magnificent walking country and the assembly of great peaks provides a challenge to mountaineers.

## Accommodation
★® Cathkin Park Hotel, 48 rooms, 40 with baths. R12 – R15 D. Phone Cathkin 1.
★® Champagne Castle Hotel, 54 rooms, all with baths. R13,50 D/B/B. Phone Champagne Castle 1.
★® El Mirador Hotel, 41 rooms, all with baths. R14 – R15,40 D/B/B. Phone El Mirador 1.
★® The Nest Hotel, 43 rooms, all with baths. R8 B/B. Phone Nest 2, via Bergville.

## Caravans and camping
★★★® Dragon Peaks Park, 80 sites. R6 D plus R1 D per person. Chalets R6 D per person.

Cathkin Peak is a stiff 'E' climb. After resisting many early attempts it was first conquered on 12 September 1912 by a party consisting of G. T. Amphlett, Tom Casement, W. C. West, Father A. D. Kelly and two guides, Tobias and Melatu. A relentless mountain to climb, Cathkin Peak demands great stamina and perseverence. It is always dangerous; on 20 September 1955 Keith Bush was killed in a fall on this mountain. The Mountain Club hut in the Mhlwazini Valley is named in his memory.

Champagne Castle is an easy 'B' category climb up Grays Pass, first explored in 1860 by David Gray and Captain Grantham.

Immediately behind Cathkin Peak is the sinister-looking Monks Cowl, 3 261 m high. This is an 'F' climb first completed in May 1942 by H. Wongtschowski, A. S. Hooper, E. Rhule and J. Botha. On 28 January 1938, Richard Barry had been killed trying to scale this mountain which demands great respect from all climbers.

Just to the north of Champagne Castle is the strangely shaped ridge known as the Dragon's Back, culminating in one of the oddest of all Drakensberg peaks, the 2 408-m-high *Ntunja* (the eye). Also known as *Gatberg,* this mountain contains a great natural hole gouged out immediately beneath its summit, which stares out over the countryside like a one-eyed giant. It was first climbed in 1888 by A. H. and F. R. Stocker, and the more difficult south peak, an 'F' climb, by the same two mountaineers on 19 August 1888.

--------

From the turnoff to the Cathkin Peak area, the main Bergville-Estcourt gravel road continues south-eastwards through a park-like area of tribal huts, cattle and trees. Crossing the Little Thukela River (7 km from the turnoff) the road leads for 3 km past the railway station of Loskop (34 km from Bergville). For a further 9 km the road continues through the tribal area and 48 km from Bergville, reaches a junction. Ahead lies Estcourt 19 km away; to the right (south-west), lies Ntabamhlope (25 km) and Giants Castle (57 km).

The south-western turnoff leads past the little rustic railway station of Draycot, with a turnoff to the agricultural research station of *Die Hoek.* The gravel road now climbs steeply up a sandstone height from whose slopes may be seen a panoramic view of the acacia-covered, badly eroded tribal area of timber plantations. Wild cosmos flowering in late summer provide a magnificent display.

Passing many fine farms with richly grassed hill slopes, the road skirts the western slopes of the massive sandstone pile of the 1 983-m-high *Ntabamhlope* (white mountain) which is a landmark in this area. At 25 km from the turnoff the road reaches a junction with a gravel road coming from Estcourt. At this junction point stands the White Mountain Resort.

### Accommodation
★⑧ White Mountain Resort, 25 rooms, 11 with baths. R9,50 D. Phone Estcourt 4437.

The combined roads continue past the resort in a southerly direction, rising and falling, with many lovely views of the Drakensberg to the west and Ntambamhlope, like a giant table, to the east.

The road proceeds through a tribal area and descends into the valley of the Bushmans River, a great trout stream which bustles in a rush of crystal water. Massive displays of cosmos flower on its banks in late summer. At 11 km from the junction at White Mountain the road joins the main gravel road leading directly from Mooi River (46 km) and following the valley of the Bushmans River for 9 km to the entrance, and then for a further 9 km to the tourist camp of the . . . .

## GIANTS CASTLE GAME RESERVE

This park and game reserve consists of 34 284 ha of beautiful, unspoilt country – a wilderness of grassy hills and deep river valleys lying at the foot of the great wall of the Drakensberg.

The Drakensberg is at its most majestic where it overlooks this game reserve. For a distance of 35 km the great mountain wall maintains a height of around 3 000 m with many prominent peaks rearing their heads to the clouds. North of the reserve may be seen the distinctive landmark of Cathkin Peak beyond which the Drakensberg swings out of sight to the west. South of Cathkin and its companion, Champagne Castle, the Drakensberg stretches in a

*Overleaf: The snow, clouds and mists of a winter storm envelop the Drakensberg ridge known as* Mponjwana *(the place of little horns).*

southerly direction, where may be seen peaks such as the 2 986-m *kwaMfazo Gaya Mabele* (the old woman grinding corn), and the 3 212-m *Njesuthi* twins, at the source of that quaintly named river, the *Njesuthi* (well-fed dog). Following these is the unmistakably shaped Thumb; Bannerman (resembling the profile of Campbell Bannerman, seen very clearly from the warden's house at Giants Castle); several other high peaks and finally, the majestic 3 314-m mass of basalt known as Giants Castle.

This is one of the great landmarks of the Drakensberg. Like Cathkin Peak, it acts as a cornerstone behind which the main wall swings to the south-west. The rock mass of Giants Castle remains so prominently exposed that the Africans have their own name and legend for it: *iNtabayikonjwa* (the mountain at which one must not point). They say that the mountain resents being pointed at, creating bad weather as a result.

In former years, the rich grazing and perennial water in the area of the present game reserve attracted a substantial population of game animals. Eland, red hartebeest, gnu, blesbok, and a considerable variety of smaller antelope such as oribi, klipspringer, grey rhebuck, reedbuck, and mountain reedbuck especially, flourished in the area. Now under conservation, they may be observed in a superb scenic setting.

Drawn by the antelope and the congenial environment, Bushman hunters of the Latter Stone Age made their homes in the sandstone caves of the Giants Castle area where some of their finest rock art may be seen in numerous galleries of polychrome paintings. There are more than 50 rock shelters in the area, containing about 5 000 paintings. Main Cave and Battle Cave are the two most important where there are 546 and 750 paintings respectively. A site museum at Main Cave displays an excavated hearth, models of Bushman figures and a collection of tools.

The area of Giants Castle was proclaimed a game reserve in 1903. A most beautiful camp, situated in a garden of wild flowers, has been built to accommodate visitors. Mountain huts have also been erected at various points. Hikers and riders may use the paths, the streams are well stocked with trout and climbers and walkers find endless fascination in what is one of the scenic showpieces of Southern Africa. Of special interest is the Lammergeyer Hide where, every Saturday morning from May to September, meat and bones are put out on which the huge Lammergeyer vultures feed. The path from the main camp to the summit of Giants Castle is 34 km long, yielding 13 hours of unforgettable walking and easy climbing.

Of historic interest is the monument on the top of Bushmans Pass. On this site three men from Major Durnsford's force were killed in 1873 when in pursuit of Langalibalele and his Hlubi tribe, who were fleeing into Lesotho after refusing to surrender their guns to the government of Natal.

**Accommodation**
4 cottages and 13 squaredawels, R5 – R6 D.

South-west of Giants Castle, the great rock mass of the Drakensberg not only maintains its imposing height, but actually culminates in the 3 482-m *Ntabana Ntlenyana,* the highest point in Southern Africa. The river valleys and foothills below this stretch of the Drakensberg are particularly beautiful and a drive through the area is a memorable scenic experience. The principal route of access to this region is from Pietermaritzburg to Underberg. From Underberg a road leads northwards, traversing the Drakensberg foothills and providing a fine circular return route through Nottingham Road and Mooi River back to Pietermaritzburg.

# PIETERMARITZBURG TO UNDERBERG

The tarmac road leaves Pietermaritzburg, passing the Fort Napier Hospital and the non-European residential area of Edendale with its hospital. Twelve kilometres from the city, at what is known as Plessislier, the road starts to climb out of this thickly populated valley of the Msunduze River. A turnoff leads to the Henley Dam at 15 km. With fine views of the river valley, the road continues climbing steadily. At 40 km from the city, the road reaches the head of the valley, where flowering aloes on the heights provide a magnificent display.

The road traverses high, rolling hill country, covered with plantations and rich, grassy farmlands. At 44 km from Pietermaritzburg the road passes the Boston rural centre. Six kilometres further on a turnoff to the north-west leads to Impendle (10 km). The road climbs Lundy's Hill, reaching the verge of the spectacular valley of the Mkhomazi River. An involved descent commences to the alluvial floor, a densely inhabited tribal area. At 65 km from Pietermaritzburg the road crosses the Mkhomazi River and climbs the slopes of the right bank, revealing many panoramic views of the great valley, where both its beauty and severe erosion (resulting from abuse of the soil by primitive farmers) may be seen.

After 10 km of curves and gradients, the road reaches the level of the midland plateau traversing an area of plantations and tribal settlement. At 82 km from Pietermaritzburg the road enters the village of *Bulwer,* named after the Governor, Sir Henry Bulwer. Founded in 1889 as the seat of the magistrate of the Ipolela Division, it is a quiet little trading and administrative centre.

## Accommodation

★ Bulwer Hotel, 12 rooms, 3 with baths. R6,50 – R10 B/B. Phone 9.
★ Mountain Park Hotel, 19 rooms, 18 with baths. R10,75 – R14 D/B/B. Phone 26.

From Bulwer the road continues over plantation-covered hills. This rural landscape is extremely pleasant and 11 km from Bulwer there is a particularly superb panoramic view of hills, mountains and grassy slopes. The road proceeds across farming country, with the Drakensberg ahead and the isolated peak now known as Garden Castle looming in the foreground of the range. At 37 km from Bulwer the road curves around the 1 905-m-high *Hlogoma* (place of echoes) making an impressive descent into the beautifully situated village and railhead of . . .

# UNDERBERG

The position of *Underberg* (below the mountain) yields a handsome view of the Drakensberg, as well as the bustling, crystal-clear trout waters of the Mzimkhulu River which meanders across the town lands. Grass – velvet-green in summer and golden-brown in winter – completely carpets the spacious landscape.

Underberg originated as a store at the railhead and although still a quiet little place, it is a great centre for trout fishermen and a junction point from where roads lead to several mountain resorts.

## Accommodation

★ Underberg Hotel, 14 rooms, 7 with baths. R9 – R9,50 D/B/B. Phone 22.

From Underberg, a tarmac road leads northwards for 5 km to the village and magisterial seat of *Himeville,* founded in 1902 and named after Sir Albert Hime, the Governor. It is a small rural centre set in an environment of green fields and hills. A nearby nature reserve comprises two trout fishing lakes situated in a grassy valley. Boats are available for hire and trout fishing permits may be obtained from the Fisheries Inspector in the reserve.

## Accommodation

★ Himeville Hotel, 10 rooms, all with baths. R8,50. B/B. Phone 5.

Caravans and camping
* Himeville Nature Reserve, 10 sites. R1,50 per person.

Beyond Himeville the main road continues northwards for 3 km, crossing the fine, rushing trout stream of the *Polela* (cold) River. A turnoff is reached which involves a most spectacular and fascinating drive westwards over the green foothills into the valley of the *Mkomazana* (little Mkomaas) River. The road then passes the Sani Pass Hotel (10 km) and from there carries on to the police border post (25 km) situated at an altitude of 1 950 m at the foot of the *Sani* (Bushman) Pass over the Drakensberg to Mokhotlong, 55 km from the border post. The last 10 km of this road up the river valley to the border post is only accessible to four-wheel-drive vehicles. Even then, the 7-km-long drive to the summit of the pass takes an hour. Passports and means of identification are needed if the traveller intends proceeding beyond the border post. The post is open 08h00 to 16h00 daily.

The valley of the Mkomazana is romantically beautiful, scattered with a jumble of giant boulders and traced by innumerable streams, waterfalls and cascades. Sandstone cliffs tower over an area of rich vegetation, where an interesting wildlife of baboons, birds and other animals flourish. There are many delightful camping sites for fishermen, walkers, climbers and nature lovers who find a paradise in this lovely valley.

The Sani Pass climbs the wall of the Drakensberg between two notable peaks: to the north of the pass looms the highest point in Southern Africa, the 3 482-m Ntabana Ntlenyana; to the south stands the twin *Hodgson's Peaks,* named after Thomas Hodgson who, in 1862, was most tragically killed there while pursuing a band of Bushman rustlers. The twin Hodgson's Peaks were named the Giants Cup by the missionary, Allen Gardiner.

Accommodation
** Sani Pass Hotel, 97 rooms, 92 with baths. R15,75 – R21,50 D/B/B. Phone Himeville 30.

From the turnoff to the Sani Pass (3 km north of Himeville), the main gravel road continues through magnificent foothill scenery, with the main wall of the Drakensberg looming in the west. At 12 km from Himeville there is a turnoff east to Impendle while at 32 km from Himeville the road reaches the rural centre of Lower Loteni and the 15-km-long turnoff to the . . .

# LOTENI NATURE RESERVE

This reserve, 3 984 ha in extent, was created in 1953. Reminiscent of Giants Castle Game Reserve, it is an attractive, open foothill area, with excellent walks, brown trout fishing on a 12-km length of the Loteni River, and an interesting population of birds and antelope such as reedbuck, eland, oribi, duiker and bushbuck. The scenery is superb.

Accommodation
Loteni Nature Reserve Camp: 2 cottages, 12 squaredawels, R5 – R6 D.

The main gravel road continues north-eastwards from the Lower Loteni rural centre, crossing handsome foothill country revealing many superb views. After 16 km there is a turnoff south-eastwards to Impendle. A further 10 km brings the road to a turnoff leading north-westwards for 12 km to the rural centre of Kamberg and the . . .

# KAMBERG NATURE RESERVE

Established in 1951, this 2 232-ha reserve offers pleasant walks and good brown and rainbow trout fishing along a 12-km length of the Mooi River which flows through a delectable landscape of grass slopes and sandstone heights, backed by the Drakensberg. The reserve is the home for the white herd of Zulu royal cattle, the *Nyonikayipumuli* (birds that have no rest), which have been carefully bred over the years by successive Zulu kings.

## Accommodation
Kamberg Nature Reserve Camp, 5 squaredawels, R4 – R6 D.

From the turnoff to the Kamberg area, the main gravel road continues north-eastwards across superb dairy country. After 30 km (92 km from Himeville) the road reaches Nottingham Road on the main Durban-Johannesburg railway and the old tarmac main road, now a loop road to the modern dual carriageway.

---

Beyond Underberg a tarmac road stretches westwards towards the Drakensberg. After 4 km the tarmac ends at a division of the road; the right-hand division continues for 2 km to the Drakensberg Gardens Hotel. Dominating this area is the remarkably shaped mass of sandstone which, in 1835, Captain Allen Gardiner named *Giants Castle*, on account of its close resemblance to the castle of Edinburgh. In later years the surveyor, Dr Sutherland, renamed this interesting mountain *Garden Castle*, after the maiden name of his mother. The name of Giants Castle was then applied to the mountain further north, on the main wall of the Drakensberg.

The road continues beyond the hotel as far as the Garden Castle Forestry Station from where a bridle path climbs the valley of the Mlambonja River, passing Pillar Cave to eventually reach the summit of the Drakensberg at Mashai Pass. The upper valley is dominated by the sharp peak of *Ntabangcobo* or Rhino Horn, 2 997 m high. The main wall of the Drakensberg averages about 3 100 m in height in this part of the basalt mass.

## Accommodation
★® Drakensberg Garden Hotel, 70 rooms, all with baths. R19,50 D/B/B. Phone 6-3148.
  10 caravan sites, R9 D.

At the division of the road, 4 km from Underberg, the left-hand fork continues in a south-westerly direction past a turnoff to Swartberg 5 km from Underberg and, at 29 km, reaching a junction. The left-hand turnoff is a beautiful drive on a fair gravel road stretching for 38 km and then joining the main Underberg-Swartberg road (see page 492). The views of the Drakensberg along this road are superb. The right-hand turnoff at the junction leads for 5 km to the Bushmans Nek Hotel, situated in the valley of the Ngwangwe River.

The road ends 3 km further up the valley at the Bushmans Nek Police Post border point. Beyond this post (open from 08h00 to 16h00 daily) there is a bridle path which ascends the Drakensberg to Jonathans Gate on Bushmans Nek. A five-hour walk along this path takes hikers to Jonathans Lodge in the Sehlabathebe National Park, a place notable for its rock formations and scenic beauty. The Bushmans Nek Pass is dominated by the 3 028-m-high Devils Knuckles, known to the Sotho as *Barowa Babararo* or *Tabantsu* (the mountain of eagles).

The Bushmans Nek Hotel is built on *Silverstreams* farm, the original farmhouse of which is the starting or terminal place for hikers undertaking the Drakensberg Hiking Trail – a five-day walk between this place and the Sani Pass. The old farmhouse and four huts provide overnight accommodation at staging posts along this trail. This is a fine walk which tempts many holidaymakers to linger over the journey, swimming or fishing in the mountain streams, taking photographs or simply revelling in a world of mountains and hills.

**Accommodation**

★★® Bushmans Nek Hotel, 70 rooms, all with baths. R12,60 – R18 D/B/B. Phone Bushmans Nek 3.

# THE SOUTHERN DRAKENSBERG

The Drakensberg lying south of the Cape/Natal border yields some spectacular scenery and the road following its length passes through an attractive landscape of hills and farmlands. However, there have as yet, been few recreational developments in this area comparable to the Natal Drakensberg resorts. But for the motorist, the climber, the walker, the trout fisherman, the photographer, and the skier (for the southern Drakensberg experiences the heaviest falls of snow), this stretch of massive rock precipices provides many exciting possibilities.

To explore this area it is best to start from Underberg. Three kilometres back on the road to Bulwer a gravel turnoff leads to Coleford, traversing some of the most superlatively beautiful farming country on earth, especially so in late summer when the grass is velvety and masses of cosmos flower in patches of vivid colour.

Three kilometres from the turnoff, the road crosses the Mzimkhulu River, a bustling, rushing flow of clear trout water. Twisting, rising and falling over endless grassy hills, the road continues southwards. At 20 km from Underberg there is a turnoff east to Bulwer and 3 km further on the road descends into the green, immaculate farming valley of the Ngwangwe River. In this fertile valley lies . . .

# THE COLEFORD NATURE RESERVE

Created in 1959 as a public resort for walkers, riders and trout fishermen, this reserve is 1 272 ha in extent. Immediately across the river (20 km from Underberg) lies the hutted camp of the Natal Parks Board. The reserve is good for rainbow trout. Bird life is interesting and gnus and blesbok graze on the hill slopes. Eland are bred here.

**Accommodation**

Coleford Nature Reserve Camp: 6 squaredawels and 5 bungalows, R4 – R5 D.

One kilometre beyond the camp a turnoff to the west stretches to Bushmans Nek (43 km). The main road now leaves the Coleford Nature Reserve and after 3 km (32 km from Underberg) reaches the crystal-clear Ndwana River, cascading through a shallow valley carpeted with luxuriant green grass and cosmos flowering during Easter.

The Ndwana River marks the border line of Griqualand East. Leaving behind the fair land of Natal, the road climbs the southern heights of the valley, revealing fine views of mountains and river. At the summit (46 km from Underberg) lies the small rural centre of Kingscote. Continuing southwards, after a further 17 km, the road reaches Middel Valley with a turnoff west to St Bernards Peak. A further 9 km of pleasant travel (72 km from Underberg) brings the road to the rural livestock sales yard, and rail centre of *Swartberg* (black mountain), lying in a spacious, grassy bowl in the hills, and flanked by a dark-coloured range in the south.

From Swartberg the gravel road leads westwards, traversing superb cattle country; a rich, grassy upland graced with many charming rural scenes. At 23 km from Swartberg the road crosses the Mzimvubu River, where a turnoff on its right bank stretches to Cedarville. A further 23 km of rural travel brings the road to another turnoff (12 km) to Cedarville, a little dairy farming centre founded in 1912 which shelters at the foot of the Cedarberg on a richly grassed plain.

A further 12 km brings the gravel road to a junction with the tarmac road coming in from Kokstad 52 km away to the east. After joining this road and turning west, after 5 km (63 km from

Swartberg) a pleasant valley is reached, set against a background of the Drakensberg. In this valley lies the town of . . .

# MATATIELE

The name *Matatiele* is apparently derived from the Sotho *Madi-i-Yila* (the ducks have flown), which is applied to the wild fowl who used to frequent the marshes in the area. However, it could well also refer to some of the rough customers and tough 'birds' – the pioneer inhabitants of this town on the frontiers of Lesotho, Natal and the Cape; an ideal area for the livestock rustlers of old.

The town originated with the arrival of Adam Kok and his Griqua in 1864. Near a broad, reed-grown lakelet frequented by innumerable aquatic birds, Adam Kok established a so-called magistrate: a grimy, half-drunken character by the name of Peter O'Reilly. With a mud hut serving as a courthouse built on top of a hillock known as Materies Kop, this representative of civilization attempted to effect law and order over a turbulent countryside. It was said that any rustler wishing to run stock through the area need only send O'Reilly a bottle of whisky the day before and a bleary eye would be closed on proceedings. The isolated state in which the man lived was described by the missionary, William Dower, who, approaching the magisterial seat on a visit, received an urgent message from the incumbent: 'Hold hard. Send me some soap and in an hour I'll be presentable enough to see you.'

The general turmoil in Griqualand East (as the area was called) induced the Cape Government to intervene in 1874. A respectable magistrate, G. P. Stafford, replaced the pioneer, but times remained unsettled. The outbreak of the Basuto Gun War in 1880 saw the area in so uproarious a state that the four Europeans stationed on Materies Kop were forced to slip away on 4 October of that year and to abandon the magisterial post. The place was overrun and 11 Hlubi tribesmen who were part of a force attempting to guard the place, were killed.

For 12 months the area remained chaotic, but the rule of law was eventually reasserted. Troublesome elements were driven away and the district was opened to European settlement. A new magistracy was built on the site of the present Matatiele town hall, with a detachment of the Cape Mounted Rifles to garrison the place.

Gun running, smuggling and cattle rustling continued in the area for years. Some rather picturesque individuals made their homes in old Matatiele. The local hotels – the Royal and the Masonic – were notorious places for brawls and gambling (especially the Royal, whose owner, Alec Payne, was a great card player). Many tales, both lurid and amusing, date from this period. A typical example concerns a memorable game which took place in the Royal Hotel one night. A visiting commercial traveller cleaned out the local gamblers. At 05h00, everyone retired to sleep with the game due to be resumed at 11h00 to allow losers a chance to recover their losses. However, the commercial traveller sneaked out with his winnings, left enough to pay his bill, and fled for Natal.

When Alec Payne woke up and heard the news he ordered a fleet horse to be saddled. Stuffing cards and money into the saddlebags, he jumped on and rode in pursuit of the traveller. He returned triumphantly the next day, bringing with him the traveller's trousers, and all his money!

Men such as Bill Wollenschlaiger habitually rode their horses right inside the hotels and into the bars, standing their horses as well as themselves to a drink. Charles Castle staked his farm *Compensation* in a game and lost it to Alec Payne. Payne left in the postcart next day to transfer the farm to his name in Kokstad. Castle clambered into the cart with him. The two gambled all the way to Kokstad, with Castle winning not only his farm back, but half the hotel as well!

A regular character in the area was the trader James Cole. Known as 'King Cole', he arrived penniless in the area and on his death in 1943, was reputedly a millionaire. Another successful early trader was J. A. E. Taylor. Apparently he had family troubles; on his death he bequeathed R140 000 towards the founding of hospitals in Matatiele and Mount Fletcher, on condition that nobody with the name of Taylor would ever be admitted to them, alive or dead!

From the beginning of the 20th century, Matatiele started to reform. More women and policemen arrived and the hitherto predominantly masculine society was subdued. On 1 January 1904, Matatiele became a municipality and the arrival of the railway in April 1924 finally ended the town's isolation. Today it is a prosperous agricultural centre, the railhead of the line from Pietermaritzburg and a great place for trade with the Sotho people who ride in from the Drakensberg. Horses (especially polo ponies) are bred here and the town is also a centre for the dairy industry in the fertile *Mabele* (kaffircorn) Valley. The Wilfred Bauer Nature Reserve has been established on the road to Qacha's Nek. The population is 4 300.

## Accommodation
* Imperial Hotel, 20 rooms, 10 with baths. R10 B/B. Phone 5.
* Royal Hotel, 17 rooms, 6 with baths. R9 – R10 B/B. Phone 100.

## Caravans and camping
*® Municipal caravan park, Haigh Park. Free.

From Matatiele a scenic drive (gravel) leads for 34 km to Qacha's Nek in Lesotho. The border posts are open daily from 08h45 to 16h00.

The main road to the south ascends from Matatiele over a ridge, yielding fine views of the Drakensberg. The road passes through a tribal area largely settled by Sotho people. After 8 km a turnoff stretches to *Ongeluks Nek,* the pass over the Drakensberg used by the Griqua on their migration. The name of the pass refers to an unfortunate incident when one of the Griqua was killed there during an eland hunt. Immediately north of Ongeluks Nek, dominating Pack Ox Nek, is the 2 726-m-high Draken's Rock, said to have been the origin of the name *Drakensberg.*

The main road continues southwards, following the course of the Kenega River which flows through a jumble of rocky hills. At 38 km from Matatiele, the road crosses the river at Kenega Drift, close to the site of some sulphur springs. Proceeding southwards through the eroded, arid, rocky tribal area, the road, after a further 24 km, crosses the Tina River. There is a pleasant picnic and camping site on the right bank of the Tina River where the road bridges across it. After a further 9 km (71 km from Matatiele) the road reaches the village and magisterial centre of Mount Fletcher, built on a ledge on the slopes of the 2 142-m-high Castle Rocks. *Mount Fletcher* was named after the Reverend John Fletcher, one of the leading British Methodists. Founded in 1882 as an administrative centre for the surrounding district, it is largely inhabited by members of the Hlubi tribe. Although only a small one-horse type of place, Mount Fletcher is at least notable for the castle-shaped mass of rock towering above it.

From Mount Fletcher, the road climbs southwards over a stony ridge, revealing panoramic views of the Drakensberg and the rugged landscape of the tribal area. Descending into the valley of the Lusi River, the road crosses the river by means of a bridge 12 km from Mount Fletcher. A turnoff on the right bank leads westwards to Naudes Nek Pass and Rhodes.

The main gravel road continues southwards, climbing a rocky slope and passing over what is lugubriously known as *Moordenaars* (murderers) Nek. Traversing a grassy, less stony and level plateau for 9 km, the road then descends into a wide valley littered with picturesque huts and dominated to the west by the Drakensberg. In the centre of this valley (44 km from Mount Fletcher) the road crosses the willow-lined Tsitsa River at Halcyon Drift whereafter the countryside improves rapidly.

South of the river the road traverses the Maclear District, a farming area of red earth and fine alluvial river valleys watered by streams stocked with trout. The traveller is rewarded with many pleasant views of the Drakensberg and its foothills, handsome and blue in the clear air.

The road leads through the hills and 64 km from Mount Fletcher, makes an impressive descent into the valley of the Mooi River, on whose pleasant banks lies the town of . . .

## MACLEAR

Named after Sir Thomas Maclear, the celebrated and popular Astronomer Royal at the Cape from 1834 to 1879, *Maclear* was established in 1875 as the magisterial centre for the district originally (and rather hideously) known as the *Gatberg* (hole mountain) from a weirdly shaped mountain in the vicinity.

The little town experienced trouble during its early existence. During the rebellion of 1880, Maclear was besieged for over a month and the pioneer magistrate, J. R. Thomson, supported by loyal Fingo tribesmen, had a bad time. It was at this stage that Hamilton Hope, the magistrate of Qumbu, with three other Europeans, attempted to reach Maclear but were foully murdered on the road.

At the end of the insurrection in 1881, the Maclear district received its present name, becoming an area of European settlement. Mount Fletcher was simultaneously detached from it as a district inhabited by African people. From then on Maclear became a prosperous farming area, notable for its cheese and dairy products. The railway from Sterkstroom was opened in 1902. The population of Maclear numbers 3 310.

### Accommodation
★ Central Hotel, 11 rooms, 5 with baths. R8,50 – R9 B/B. Phone 5.
★ Royal Hotel, 13 rooms, 7 with baths. R8,50 – R9,50 B/B. Phone 9907.

## NAUDES NEK TO STERKSTROOM

From Maclear a road branches westwards on a most spectacular journey. For the traveller exploring the southern Drakensberg this is an exciting experience in both driving and scenic beauty.

From Maclear the gravel road leads up the beautiful green valley of the Pot River, a clear, fast-flowing stream whose banks are shaded by many graceful trees. Handsome farms shelter below towering cliffs of sandstone. After 24 km the road crosses the Pot River and commences a steady climb up the slopes of the Drakensberg. Scenery is on a large scale and many examples of soil erosion are interesting. At 73 km from Maclear, the road reaches the summit – 2 920 m high – of Naudes Nek Pass.

For 19 km the road makes a steep and involved descent. Snows in winter are often heavy and red-hot pokers flower in March staining the slopes with colour. Immediately to the north-west looms the 3 300-m bulk of *Makhollo* (great mother), known to Europeans as Ben Macdhui, one of the principal peaks of this part of the Drakensberg.

At the foot of the pass is a picnic site and memorial to Stefanus Naude and his brother Gabriel who first blazed this route over the Drakensberg. The road was located by the engineer George Mandy and constructed, finance allowing, between 1890 and 1911. It was intended as a military road linking Maclear with Lundeans Nek and built to facilitate the pursuit of rustlers and the movement of troops around the southern border of Lesotho.

Beyond the memorial the road finds a way down the valley of the Bel River, passing a succession of farms and after 12 km (105 km from Maclear), reaching the village of . . .

## RHODES

Now gradually fading away, the village of *Rhodes* was established in 1893 as a church centre on the farm *Tintern*. It was named after the famous Cecil Rhodes, who sent the village a gift of stone pine trees which today provide the place with so handsome a feature. The village comprises a couple of dozen earth-walled shacks and corrugated iron cottages, most of them used only occasionally by the mountain farmers when they come to the village to attend *Nagmaal* (Communion) or to escape from the winter snows.

In its day, however, Rhodes experienced hectic times. Race meetings were held regularly with bookies travelling from Durban and wagonloads of liquor being dragged over the mountains from East London. The polished horns of Wydeman, doyen of the oxen who drew the liquor wagons, were mounted in the bar of the Horseshoe Hotel when he died, and toasts were regularly proposed in his honour.

Dice, billiards, and some celebrated fights provided the nightly entertainment at the hotel. Visiting wool buyers such as Maurice Rosenberg presided over big card games. Bill Hocking, the host, and Joey van der Walt, the barman, saw piles of coins changing hands. So many cowboy types habitually rode their horses directly into the hotel that a Bushman, Thys Volstruis, was employed on a piecework basis to sweep up droppings. Costs were debited to the rider's bill! When business was slack, the Bushman, keen to make a fast buck, would anxiously slap the horse's hindquarters. His plaintive plea *'Kom, toe jong'* ('Come, please fellow') is still remembered, although the hotel has long since been closed.

From Rhodes the road continues amid fine scenery down the valley of the Bel River. Red-orange coloured sandstone cliffs and high, black basalt peaks crowd the side of the fertile valley. After 8 km there is a turnoff to Maartens Hoek where a giant cavern contains a gallery of Bushman paintings. At 17 km there is a turnoff to Bokspruit and after a further 12 km the road reaches Moshesh's Ford, where memories of the splashing hooves of rustler bands and the passing of raiding warriors, linger beneath the willow trees.

At Moshesh's Ford the road divides: one branch leads down the valley; the other branch crosses the river, climbing the steep northern slopes of the valley, an area littered with great blocks of sandstone and a lovely place in which to rob a stage coach! There are turnoffs to Barkly East and to Funnystone. The road seems to ascend to the skies and the atmosphere is wildly beautiful. Past the trading station of War Trail and the police post, the road, 30 km from Moshesh's Ford, reaches the summit of what is known as *Lundeans Nek* from a Swede who owned a lonely trading station there in the 1880s.

From Lundeans Nek on the summit of the Witteberge is revealed a tremendous view over the mountains of the southern part of Lesotho. The summit is a place of winds, snow and airy solitude. The police post at the summit (now rebuilt in a more protected situation 1 km lower down the south slope) was the base for a ceaseless war against rustlers. In the records are many accounts of raids, pursuits, escapes and captures among the valleys and heights of this mountainous world.

In former years a police outpost stood even higher in the Witteberge on the mountain named Snowdon. For 14 years a celebrated individual, Constable Erasmus, was stationed there. His only connection with the outside world was a bridal path to Lundeans Nek. When winter came, the bleak weather forced him to retreat to the main police station but in spring he returned to the heights. While he was there, rustlers lay low or followed more distant trails, for his administration of justice was swift, rough and ready.

The road descends the steep northern slopes of the Witteberge and after 8 km passes the Upper Telle trading station. Three kilometres below this station is a turnoff leading up the valley of the Telle River to what is known as *Dangers Hoek,* after Richard Dangers who owned a trading station there. The road comes to a dead end after 12 km. The valley is stunningly beautiful, burrowing into the private underwear of the great basalt Drakensberg, revealing the frilly, delicate coloured cave sandstone undergarments. The road ends at the village of Nomlengana, dominated by the great heights of Nduzikontaba and Makhollo.

Beyond the turnoff to Dangers Hoek, the main road continues down the rocky slopes of the

Witteberge, following the valley of the Telle River, the boundary of Lesotho. After 17 km there is a turnoff of 15 km leading to the border post of Telle Bridge. The post is open 08h00 to 16h00. The main road swings westwards into the valley of the Famine River. Climbing through this valley and overlooked by brilliantly coloured sandstone cliffs, the road makes its way over a ridge, passing the hospital of Mlojinini, built on a picturesque site. Sixty-four kilometres from Lundeans Nek, the road reaches the dusty village of Sterkspruit, built on the left-hand side of the rocky valley of the *Sterkspruit* (strong stream).

The road described, from Maclear to Sterkspruit, can be classed as one of the most spectacular scenic routes in Southern Africa. Gravel throughout, it has tremendous gradients. There is no pleasure in doing the journey in wet weather, but in fair weather, and when the mountains are covered in snow (not thawing), it is a dramatic experience.

From Sterkspruit a road leads for 49 km to the town of Zastron in the Orange Free State (see page 537).

## STERKSPRUIT-BARKLY EAST-ELLIOT

The road from Sterkspruit through Barkly East and back over the Drakensberg to Elliot is almost as spectacular as the road from Maclear, just described. From Sterkspruit this road swings westwards, climbs out of the valley and continues across a rugged, rocky and densely settled tribal area. Prickly pears grow amongst the rocks and everywhere erosion and abuse of the soil by poor farming techniques is apparent. After 25 km the road passes through the small rural centre of Herschel.

The road climbs and twists over the ridge which forms the western end of the Witteberge range. At 11 km from Herschel a turnoff leads westwards to Aliwal North. A further 4 km takes the road past Lady Grey station and 3 km away, in a cul-de-sac in the Witteberge range, lies the picturesquely situated town of . . . .

## LADY GREY

With its population of 2 383, Lady Grey is completely dominated by the high, rocky and often snow-covered range of the *Witteberge* (white mountains). The town originated in 1858 when the Dutch Reformed community purchased the farm *Waaihoek* from the Botha brothers and laid it out as a church centre. The first handsome church was built, establishing the site as a town, named after the wife of the Governor, Sir George Grey.

Lady Grey, a trading and administrative centre for the rugged area at the foot of the Witteberge, is beautifully situated. Its valley is well wooded and a journey up to the reservoir at the head of the gorge rewards the traveller with some fine scenery. The reservoir is the centre for a nature reserve and was built in 1925. A steep road climbs out of the valley over Joubert's Pass, crossing some pretty rugged country until it eventually joins the main Lady Grey-Barkly East road near a railway station with the rather damp name of Drizzly! The drive is rough but worthwhile, and the snow-covered mountains are very lovely in winter.

### Accommodation
★ Mountain View Hotel, 15 rooms, 6 with baths. R8,50 – R9 B/B. Phone 12.

### Caravans and camping
★ Lady Grey Caravan Park, 50 sites. R1,50 D.

The main road and railway both follow difficult routes between Lady Grey and Barkly East. The railway route is particularly involved, involving eight successive reversing sections where the train zigzags its way up and down steep slopes.

From Lady Grey, the main road skirts the southern slopes of the Witteberge range yielding many tremendous views, especially at 9 km from Lady Grey station, where the road climbs steadily towards the fourth reversing station on the railway, and 15 km further on where the road crosses a high ridge.

The gravel road continues eastwards along the southern slopes of the Witteberge which are grassy and ideal for sheep. At 53 km from Lady Grey station, the road passes the station of New England, a centre for many handsome farms. Five kilometres further on is a turnoff north-eastwards to Lundeans Nek and a further 4 km takes the road across the willow tree-lined Kraai River, swiftly flowing through a precipitous gorge which provides several zigzags and other engineering problems for the railway to surmount.

Climbing out of this gorge, the road reveals fine views of the whole length of the Witteberge range, a fairyland when covered in snow. At 73 km from Lady Grey station there is a turnoff to Dordrecht, and 3 km further on the road enters the town of . . .

# BARKLY EAST

Lying 1 820 m above sea level, Barkly East has the chilly distinction of experiencing some of the coldest weather in Southern Africa, with an average of 93 nights a year where the temperature drops below freezing point. Snow is usual in winter.

Notwithstanding the coldness of winter the district has always been desirable to man. Bushmen hunted the game animals grazing on the rich pasturage in the area and found shelter in sandstone caves. European settlers wandered in during the first half of the 19th century. To provide a religious, educational and trading centre for this community, Sir Henry Barkly, the Governor of the Cape, proclaimed the establishment of a town in December 1874 which received his name in the form of *Barkly East*. A portion of the farm *Rockypark* was purchased as the site of the town and on it the Dutch Reformed community built a church. Captain Nesbitt, a survivor of the wreck of the *Birkenhead*, established a watermill in the Lang Kloof River, having apparently resolved to move as far away from the sea as possible. By 1881 the town had reached the status of a municipality (the population is now 4 568). In 1886 a newspaper, the lively little *Barkly East Reporter*, was published and the town became the busy centre of considerable agricultural activity in the production of wool, maize, wheat and potatoes. Eventually, by means of a 1-in-36 gradient and eight reversing stations, the railway managed to reach the town in December 1930.

Today 600 000 sheep and many thousands of other livestock graze in the surrounding mountains, often in areas so remote that a farmer has to be a pretty agile mountaineer in order to visit his pasturage. The cold winters kill livestock parasites, thus sheep and cattle flourish. Rustlers also flourish, however, and this jumble of mountains still sees a never-ending war between farmers and the men who cut their fences at night and spirit away a rich loot of prime cattle and sheep into secret valleys and hideaways in Lesotho and elsewhere.

## Accommodation
* Drakensberg Hotel, 16 rooms, 10 with baths. R9,50 B/B. Phone 277.
* Barkly Hotel, 17 rooms, 5 with baths. R5 – R5,50 B/B. Phone 176.

## Caravans and camping
* Municipal caravan park, 20 sites. R1 D.

From Barkly East, a particularly beautiful drive leads up the valley of the Lang Kloof and over Barkly Pass to Elliot. Leaving Barkly East lying in the midst of a great bowl in the mountains, the gravel road stretches southwards, commencing a long, steady climb up the river valley, overlooked on both sides by high sandstone buttresses, containing many caves and weirdly shaped rock formations. Magnificent sheep and cattle farms are scattered along the floor of the valley.

At 43 km from Barkly East, there is a turnoff east to Rhodes, through the Tembu Pass. At this point, the main road reaches the summit of Barkly Pass, built in 1885. Spectacularly beautiful, it reveals many majestic views of crumbling sandstone cliffs. The view from the summit, especially to the west along the great wall of the Drakensberg, is magnificent, with a superb crumbling 'castle of the giants' (Van Zyl's Berg) dominating the road. The Tafelberg lies further west, and the range ends 35 km away at the towering sandstone cliffs of *Xalanga* (the vulture).

From this summit point the road starts to descend and after 9 km, reaches the foot of the mountains. After a further 9 km of travel across undulating grass country at the foot of the massive wall of the Drakensberg, the road reaches the town of Elliot, 63 km from Barkly East. It is a memorable drive.

## MACLEAR TO DORDRECHT

The main road leads south-westwards from Maclear, traversing the foothills of the Drakensberg – beautifully grassed slopes, sandstone cliffs, and willow-lined river courses. After 19 km the road crosses the Nxu River, passing through, on the south bank, the small village of *Ugie*, founded in 1863 by the missionary, William Murray, and named after the Ugie River in his Aberdeenshire home. The pleasant Nxu River flowing through the green fields, with cattle grazing on the slopes, reminded the missionary of his Scottish homeland, hence the odd name.

### Accommodation
★ Central Hotel, 10 rooms, 3 with baths. R7,50 – R8 B/B. Phone 9906.

From Ugie, the road continues south-westwards in a beautiful scenic route through the foothills of the Drakensberg. Fine farms, richly grassed dairy country, stands of wattle trees and handsome views of the Drakensberg make the journey continually interesting. At 30 km from Ugie there is a turn west to Noahs Ark, from where may be seen the curious looking mountain which gave the district the original name of *Gatberg* (hole mountain). Known to the Africans as *uNtunjenkala* (the crab's opening), it provides a memorable landmark. A further 20 km (50 km from Ugie) takes the road into the neat little town of . . .

## ELLIOT

Named after Sir Henry Elliot, Chief Magistrate of Tembuland, *Elliot* lies in a grassy, spacious valley at the foot of the Drakensberg, towered over by curtain-like buttresses. A farming and railway centre, the town has 6 080 inhabitants.

### Accommodation
★ Merino Hotel, 16 rooms, 5 with baths. R7,50 – R9,50 B/B. Phone 45.
★ Stanford Hotel, 13 rooms, 5 with baths. R7,50 – R9 B/B. Phone 90.

Leaving Elliot, the tarmac road crosses the railway line and continues south-westwards, steadily climbing a spacious, grassy slope – treeless save for clumps of wattle – and providing handsome views of the Drakensberg range. After 15 km the road reaches the summit of the slope and descends the steep Cala Pass, a natural passage through rocky, aloe-covered hills. At the bottom of the pass, nestling into the hill slopes 30 km from Elliot, lies the town of . . .

# CALA

With a total of 3 550 inhabitants, Cala is the administrative centre for the district known as *Xalanga* (the vulture) from the high cliffs which mark the southern end of the Drakensberg range. Cala was laid out as a town in 1884, the magisterial seat for part of Tembuland where the tribe of that name had settled. It has grown into a rather wild west type of town, notable for its sandstone buildings and the aloes flowering on the heights above it. The Drakensberg range, including the Xalanga cliffs, lies 30 km northwards. The name *Cala* (or *Caba*) originates from the stream regarded as an old boundary which flows across a 'flat plain'.

Beyond Cala, the road crosses the Tsomo River by means of a sandstone bridge and reaches a crossroads. The left-hand branch continues south-eastwards across the flat floor of the Cala Valley. This road climbs and then traverses a high ridge of grassland dotted with tribal huts. Descending to cross the Ndwe River (32 km from Cala), the road, in a rather dehydrated landscape of rocks and stunted acacias, passes through the tiny town of Lady Frere, and 3 km beyond it, the large Catholic mission hospital of Glen Grey. *Lady Frere,* with a population of 2 383, was named after the wife of the Governor, Sir Bartle Frere. Founded in 1884, it is a quiet rural centre.

The road now ascends from the densely populated, eroded tribal area. Traversing a high ridge, the road, 15 km from Lady Frere, descends Mackays Nek Pass into the rocky, eroded valley of the Wit Kei River. After a further 5 km there is a turnoff north to Dordrecht via the Glen Grey Falls. The road climbs out of the valley with its numerous huts and winds its way to *Nonesi's Nek,* named after a renowned chieftainess. With a sweeping view of the wide, hut-covered river valley set amongst fortress-like mountains, the road descends, passing the Bongola Dam and recreational area and 6 km further on (31 km from Lady Frere) reaching Queenstown (see page 357).

From the turnoff to Queenstown (5 km out of Cala) the main road continues up the valley of the Cala stream, climbing easily through a jumble of flat-topped stoney hills settled by Tembu tribespeople. At 17 km from Cala, the road reaches the summit of a rolling, grassy plateau which stretches westwards to the foot of the Drakensberg. After a further 15 km the road descends through a steep stony pass leading to the course of the Ndwe River, where there is a pleasant picnic site. Five kilometres further on (41 km from Cala) the road enters . . .

# INDWE

This place receives its name from the blue cranes which have always frequented the pleasant valley of the Ndwe stream flowing past the town. Founded in 1896, the town (with a population of 3 117) is situated at the southern end of the Drakensberg, with the high cliffs of Xalanga looming 15 km to the north-east. From here the Drakensberg dwindles into a pile of outlying hills – many of them table-topped – which guards its south-western end.

Indwe lies in the centre of an extensive deposit of low-grade coal which has been worked periodically.

## Accommodation
* Blue Crane Hotel, 11 rooms, 3 with baths. R8 – R9,50 B/B. Phone 116.
* Indwe Hotel, 13 rooms, 6 with baths. R8,50 – R9 B/B. Phone 66.

From Indwe, the road continues westwards across farming country overlooked by fine outlying sandstone cliffs at the end of the Drakensberg. As the Drakensberg diminishes into hills, so the rainfall lessens and the country becomes increasingly arid. At 23 km from Indwe the road climbs a ridge, traversing a high plateau covered with sheep and cattle farms. Passing turnoffs north to Mackays Kop and Barkly East (37 km from Indwe), the road reaches the town of . . .

# DORDRECHT

With a population of 5 474, Dordrecht lies in a shallow valley on the banks of a lake-like dam in the Holspruit. Tall sandstone cliffs overlook the town whose long main street is dominated by the tower of the Dutch Reformed Church.

Dordrecht was laid out in 1856 on the farm *Boschrand*. Named after the ancient city in Holland, it became a municipality in 1867. Bleakly cold in winter, Dordrecht is a sunny little town in summer and the centre for a considerable industry in sheep and cattle raising.

## Accommodation
★ Highveld Hotel, 14 rooms, 4 with baths. R7,50 – R8 B/B. Phone 9903.

## Caravans and camping
Municipal caravan park, 10 sites. 60c D.

The road leaves Dordrecht, climbing out of the river valley. After 5 km, it reaches a high, scrub-covered, arid plateau, surrounded by a jumble of hills which mark the beginning of the Stormberg range. At 38 km from Dordrecht, the road reaches the main tarmac road linking East London to the north.

## Chapter Twenty-Five

# THE GOLDEN WAY

### ORANGE RIVER TO THE VAAL RIVER

From the various points at which they cross the Orange River, the three branches of the Cape-to-Cairo road find separate ways into the Orange Free State and then converge to form a 'Golden Way' as far as the Vaal River border with the Transvaal, crossing a golden-coloured land of wheat, maize and sunflowers, and the rich subterranean treasure chest of the gold and uranium fields.

The western road, which branched off from the main Cape-to-Cairo-road, 3 km north of Hanover, crosses the Orange River just below the wall of the P. K. le Roux Dam. From there it traverses a grass-covered prairieland for 38 km and then reaches the town of . . .

## LUCKHOFF

Established in 1892 and named after the Reverend H. J. Luckhoff, it is a quiet little sheep farming and agricultural centre, with a population of 1 011.

### Accommodation
★ Luckhoff Hotel, 10 rooms, 5 with baths. R7,35 – R8,35 B/B. Phone 12.

From Luckhoff, the road continues northwards across a grass-covered plain – sheep and maize country – until, after 45 km, it reaches the town of . . .

## KOFFIEFONTEIN

The habitual making of coffee by transport riders at the fountain there, is said to be the reason for the sociable name of *Koffiefontein*. The town recognises this pleasant tradition by means of an ornamental fountain (situated at its eastern entrance), designed to resemble a huge coffee pot pouring out a drink.

In June 1870 one of the transport riders picked up a diamond near the fountain. This started a rush to the area and by 1882 Koffiefontein was quite a boom town with four mining companies working there. Several buildings in the town remain from this period, notably the Central Hotel with its corner tower.

In 1892 Koffiefontein became a municipality and today has a population of 8 778. Diamonds obtained from a volcanic pipe, are still being mined there by the De Beers company. The mine is in a security area but visitors are occasionally permitted to tour the workings if they apply to the manager. A game farm in the vicinity of the town, also owned by the mine, is open to visitors on Sundays.

During the Second World War Koffiefontein was a prisoner-of-war camp for about 2 000 Italians and a few memorials of their presence remain, including two wall paintings of Mussolini and the Italian king. These are protected to mark the former site of the camp. Eight hundred pro-Nazi South Africans were also interned there, including John Vorster, who, many years later, became Prime Minister and then State President of South Africa.

Bushman paintings may be seen in the area. A local factory produces cheese.

## Accommodation
* Central Hotel, 12 rooms, 5 with baths. R12 B/B. Phone 69.
* Koffiefontein Hotel, 11 rooms, 5 with baths. R9,25 B/B. Phone 64.

## Caravans and camping
* Municipal caravan park, 35 sites. R2 D.

From Koffiefontein the traveller has several roads to choose from. To the west, a road leads for 43 km to the town of . . .

# JACOBSDAL

Named after Christoffel Jacobs, owner of the farm on which the town was laid out, *Jacobsdal* has a population of 3 000. It became a municipality in 1860 and is an attractive little place, its streets shaded by trees. Ample water is available from the Riet River on whose banks the town stands. An Anglo-Boer War blockhouse is situated on the outskirts of the town and numerous salt pans may be seen in the vicinity.

## Accommodation
* Jacobsdal Hotel, 10 rooms, 8 with baths. R7 – R8 B/B. Phone 38.

North of Koffiefontein, a road leads for 55 km to the town of . . .

# PETRUSBURG

Named after Petrus Venter who provided money for the purchase of the farm *Diepfontein* on which the town was laid out, *Petrusburg* was founded in 1896 and has a present population of 2 500. The town is a farming centre and railage point on the line from Kimberley to Bloemfontein which is 80 km to the east. Numerous salt pans are found in the area.

## Accommodation
* Petrusburg Hotel, 10 rooms, 5 with baths. R9 – R9,50 B/B. Phone 4.

South-east of Koffiefontein a road leads along the southern side of the Kalkfontein Dam. After 53,5 km of pleasant travel through fine sheep and maize country, with the poplar trees a superb golden colour in early winter, the road reaches the town of . . .

# FAURESMITH

Named after two individuals, the Reverend Philip Faure and Sir Harry Smith, the popular British governor, *Fauresmith* was founded in 1849, making it the second oldest town in the Orange Free State. It became a municipality in 1859 and now has a population of 2 673.

Fauresmith is set among high ridges which have squeezed the growing town into a horseshoe shape. An extraordinary feature of the town is the railway line which runs up the centre of the main street. The spectacle of a steam locomotive happily puffing its way through traffic is almost unique. At Inhambane in Moçambique there is a similar line running down the main street and Berlington in the state of Iowa, U. S. A., has the same feature. The local flyer hits the main 'drag' of Fauresmith at 06h00 and at 11h00 return on weekdays. Train enthusiasts and nervous motorists should check these times beforehand in case of changes!

A retired puffer is permanently mounted in the middle of the main street in the centre of town. As if it was one of the town's oldest inhabitants confined to his rocking chair, this elderly locomotive now spends its time watching the traffic go by and wishing there was still enough steam in its boiler to allow it at least a few more whistles at the girls. A fitting companion for this retired puffer is the quaint little town hall which also stands on the main street. A piece of genuine Victoriana, it definitely disapproves of both the puffer and modern goings-on.

In 1926 a veld reserve and laboratory was established on ground situated just outside the town. Dr M. Henrici, a Swiss expert, was in charge of a research project for 30 years, which involves studying the effects of weather and grazing on the vegetation of this part of the grass-covered veld.

**Accommodation**
★ Phoenix Hotel, 14 rooms, 5 with baths. R7,50 – R8,50 B/B. Phone 19.

The road continues eastwards from Fauresmith across the grassy plains where blue cranes (the bird emblem of South Africa), gather in many groups. Each group generally consists of three birds but whether all are male or female or an agreeable mixture, is known only to the birds. After 12,5 km the road reaches the diamond mining centre of . . .

# JAGERSFONTEIN

The town had its start in 1870 when Mr J. J. de Klerk found a diamond on the farm of *Jagersfontein* which was originally owned by a Griqua, Jacobus Jagers. A great rush to the area resulted. The diamonds were found in a volcanic pipe and many stones of superb quality and great beauty have since been recovered, ranging from blue-whites to sapphires. In 1893 the Excelsior Stone (971 carats) was found, the largest diamond to be discovered until the Cullinan diamond was located near Pretoria in 1905.

At the start of the rush, the government proclaimed the farm a public diggings on 29 August 1870 and bought the farmhouse to serve as an administrative office. A large eucalyptus tree provided a 'gaol', where prisoners were tied to its trunk. The diamond workings were subsequently consolidated to form one big mine run by the De Beers company. The town, which became a municipality in 1904 has a population of 4 629. Pleasantly situated, it is an interesting example of a mining boom town of former years. Original mine staff quarters have been converted into the Charlesville Old Age Home.

---

From Jagersfontein a road leads north-eastwards for 113 km to Bloemfontein, while three other roads lead to various points on the Golden Way, such as Trompsburg, 50 km away.

The original route of the Cape-to-Cairo road north of Colesberg, crossed the Orange River by means of a bridge built at Bothasdrif 30 km from Colesberg. In the Orange Free State the road continues for 24 km through a mass of hillocks, passes the small rural settlement of Waterkloof and 4,5 km further on, reaches the town of . . .

# PHILIPPOLIS

Founded in 1823 when a mission school was established for the benefit of the local Hottentot and Bushman clans, *Philippolis* was named after the Reverend Dr John Philip, superintendent of the London Missionary Society's operations in South Africa.

In 1826 a section of the Griqua Hottentot tribe, led by Adam Kok, settled there. A straggling village of shacks and huts grew up around the church while a few trading posts, the residence of Adam Kok, his council chamber, gaol (including gallows), and the homes of the missionaries, gave the place some importance.

The Griqua eventually decided to move away. On 10 February 1862 the Orange Free State Government bought the area for £400 from the Griqua, who then wandered off to Griqualand East. A magistrate, Jean Francis van Iddekinge, was appointed to Philippolis and it developed as a European village, although the narrow streets survive as reminders of the original Griqua owners. Today the place consists of one long main street and a few tortuous sideways. Its inhabitants now number 2 425.

### Accommodation
★ Oranjehof Hotel, 16 rooms, 10 with baths. R15 – R18 B/B. Phone 8.

### Caravans and camping
★ Dew Drop Caravan Park, 20 sites. R2 D plus 20c D per person.

From Philippolis the Golden Way to the north swings north-eastwards. After 3 km there are branches to Springfontein and Jagersfontein, while 23 km from the town the road crosses the branch railway from Springfontein to Koffiefontein. At 56 km from Philippolis the road reaches the town of . . .

# TROMPSBURG

Named after Bastian Tromp, owner of the farm *Middelfontein* on which the town was laid out in 1892, *Trompsburg* has a population of 3 088. The railway – then being constructed to Bloemfontein – reached the site in the same year and the village grew as a centre for a productive cattle and sheep district – 200 merino sheep farms carrying 200 000 sheep. Plentiful underground water and a brisk climate are the principal assets of this little town, a municipality since 1902.

### Accommodation
★ Beau Vista Motel, 12 rooms, all with baths. R6,50 room only. Phone 111.
★ Commercial Hotel, 10 rooms, 4 with baths. R8,25 – R9,95 B/B. Phone 93.

### Caravans and camping
Municipal caravan park, 40 sites. Free. Toilets and water available.

At Trompsburg the old Cape-to-Cairo-road joins the new road which leads from Colesberg for 35 km, crosses the Orange River, passes a turnoff to Springfontein at 85 km and then reaches Trompsburg at 108 km. The combined roads lead northwards and, keeping close company with the railway line, continue for 38 km across the Free State plains before reaching . . .

# EDENBURG

The town was founded on 15 January 1862 when the farm *Rietfontein* was bought for 60 000 rixdollars as the site for a church centre. With good water available and situated on the main transport road from the south, the little town had an optimistic beginning when the first erven were sold on 24 February 1862 and the name of Edenburg was given to it by the church elders. It became a municipality in 1890 and today, 2 838 people live there. Originally a great area for plains game, it is now a prosperous cattle and sheep farming centre. The old Berlin Mission Society station of Bethany lies on the Riet River, 22 km away.

### Accommodation
★ Edenburg Hotel, 17 rooms, 9 with baths. R9,50 – R10,50 B/B. Phone 147.

*Overleaf: Near Oranjemund the ruins of Hohenfels, a German camel police post, silently watch the moody Orange as it approaches the sea.*

Veering sharply eastwards, the Golden Way crosses the plains for 14 km to reach another church settlement called . . .

## REDDERSBURG

On 20 August 1859 the farm *Vlakfontein* was purchased for £1 500 by the Dutch Reformed Church, who laid out a town and named it *Reddersburg* (town of the saviour). With a population of 3 063, it is an agricultural centre and the junction for the main road coming from King William's Town and East London.

### Accommodation
★ Sarie Marais Hotel, 12 rooms, 3 with baths. R8,50 – R9,50 B/B. Phone 138.

The Golden Way now leads directly northwards over the Free State plains, past the cluster of masts of the South African Broadcasting Corporation's transmitters at Paradys (46 km from Reddersburg) and then, 62 km from Reddersburg reaches the city of . . .

## BLOEMFONTEIN

With its population of 234 900, Bloemfontein is the capital of the province of the Orange Free State and also the judicial capital of South Africa, the seat of the Court of Appeal. Centrally situated on the highveld plains, at an altitude of 1 392 m above sea level, it experiences a warm summer and a dry, cold winter. With an average rainfall of 500 mm, the countryside is intensely green in summer, gardens flourish and the soil is fertile. The city is attractively situated at the foot of a cluster of flat-topped hillocks, with spacious views from the summits of heights such as Naval Hill.

*Bloemfontein* (the fountain of flowers), originated as an outspan at a spring where water could always be found, and game animals and wild flowers abounded. The site of this fountain marked by a column and a mosaic of the city emblem, is now rather unromantically confined in a large concrete drainage canal. Behind it, in Victoria Park, there is a fine municipal caravan park situated where many travellers of old must have camped as they rested and watered their draught animals at the fountain.

To the African tribes the fountain was known as *Mangaung* (place of the leopards). In 1840, the first European known to settle there was Johannes Brits, who built a simple homestead and started to farm. Six years later, in March 1846, the farmer was startled to see a group of horsemen and wagons approaching across the veld. In the van of this party rode an officer of the Cape Mounted Rifles, Major H. D. Warden, seconded to the responsibility of being official British Resident on the central plains of South Africa.

Major Warden was something of a romantic figure: the son of an illegitimate offspring produced by one of the lusty Stuart princes and an Edinburgh beauty, Warden had, early in life, become a professional soldier. Now here he was, far from the elegance of Princes Street, Edinburgh, riding across the veld in search of a suitable site for his official residence, and where a strongpoint for a small garrison could be erected.

Warden liked Bloemfontein. Its central situation and the dependable supply of water from the fountain made him choose the place as his official residence. After some hard bargaining with Johannes Brits, Warden bought the farm for £37 10s. Brits (who later complained about the sale price and received another £50) and his somewhat bemused family, moved to a new farm in the vicinity of the present town of Harrismith. Warden and his men built a tiny fort of mud and stones which they named Fort Drury, of which nothing remains today. Only the ghost of the name lingers above a residential hotel erected on the site of the fort that watched over the original fountain of flowers.

Warden had been sent to his post simply as official British Resident on the central plains. At first he had little power other than the influence of his personality on the sunbronzed farmers, hunters and traders who either settled or wandered over the face of the veld. To Warden's little fort, however, on 14 January 1848, came the glamorous Governor of the Cape, Sir Harry Smith, and a meeting of plainsmen voted for the establishment of British rule over what was to be called the Orange River Sovereignty.

There was violent disagreement over this development. Many plainsmen had trekked away from snug homesteads in the Cape to escape from British rule and they had no intention of meekly allowing it to overtake them yet again. Six months after the meeting these hardy dissidents mustered their strength and received reinforcements from the Transvaal. Led by Commandant-General Pretorius, they appeared before Fort Drury on 17 July, giving Warden summary notice to quit.

Warden was helpless. His supporters at the fountain of flowers consisted of a mere 45 Hottentot soldiers, 42 loyal civilian males and 200 of their dependants. After a short parley Warden received three days to abandon his fort and within that time he led his men away. Back on the double came the doughty Sir Harry Smith. Pretorius rode south to meet him and on 29 August 1848 at Boomplaats, a tough, day-long skirmish occurred which resulted in the flight of Pretorius and the return of Warden to the fountain of flowers.

For the next six years the sovereignty prevailed and Bloemfontein grew as an administrative centre. With a garrison of 450 men, Warden built a new stronghold (Queen's Fort) on one of the dominant hillocks and this became the key British military base on the central plains of South Africa. Lion hunting was the principal diversion for the officers of this garrison. The surrounding plains at that time still teemed with such enormous numbers of game that the antics of the herds provided standard amusement for the residents of the village who watched from the shade of their verandas.

The Sovereignty did not flourish. Many of its inhabitants were resentful towards British control and the British Government in turn, was not enthusiastic about this addition to their empire calling it 'a valueless territory not worth retaining, always causing trouble, and moreover an endless expense to the Home Government'.

To the consternation of the loyalists, Sir George Clark arrived in Bloemfontein in February 1854, with the news that he had been sent to liquidate the Sovereignty. For a few days there was an uproar in Bloemfontein, with celebrations on the one side and blank despair on the other. On 11 March 1854, the British flag was lowered over Queen's Fort and replaced with the flag of the new republic. Sir George rode out of the town at the head of the garrison and the republicans were left to elect for themselves a *Volksraad* (people's council), and as first president, an amiable, intelligent trader by the name of Josias Hoffman. The old *Raadsaal* (council chamber) built in 1849 by Major Warden is now preserved as a national monument and may be seen in St George's Street.

The diffident little village of Bloemfontein then found itself to be one of the world's capitals, albeit of a diminutive rural state whose total population numbered only 12 000 souls scattered over a vast plain with hardly any communications or assets and a threat of trouble from the Sotho people who lived in the east.

President Hoffman tried his best, drawing up a liberal constitution and, by personal friendship with Moshesh, ruler of the Sotho, maintaining a precarious peace. But he had many enemies. After nine months he was ousted from office, accused of high treason for presenting to Moshesh a keg of gunpowder. He was replaced as president in 1855 by Jacobus Boshoff, a magistrate from the Cape and Natal.

President Boshoff found that it was required of him to be a combination of superman, lawyer, diplomat, administrator and soldier. Under the circumstances he managed extremely well. His pocket republic and its village capital were placed on a business footing and as a result of basic administrative order and the stirrings of prosperity in a fertile and healthy land,

507

immigrants started to trickle into the place. Bloemfontein grew and in spite of troubles and petty wars with the Sotho and the people of the Transvaal, the old fountain of flowers soon found itself at the centre of a town.

President Boshoff resigned in 1859 and was somewhat ineffectively replaced by M. W. Pretorius, the President of the South African Republic in the Transvaal. He soon went and on 5 November 1863, Johannes Brand – a lawyer from the Cape – was elected President of the Orange Free State. Under this wise and amiable man the little rural republic entered its golden age of independence and some spectacular changes were made during Brand's 25-year term of office.

President Brand's daughter, Kitty, told the author that when her father arrived with his family in Bloemfontein, the members of the Volksraad gathered to greet them, all sombrely dressed in black, correctly mannered, grave of demeanour and densely bearded. Suddenly, in the midst of formalities, they all hurriedly left the room in some agitation. The Brands asked what was happening, half expecting to be told that some emergency had occurred. They were informed that no calamity, rumour or war ever disturbed the Volksraad members half as much as the fact that coming up the garden path was Mr Drinkwater, the local debt collector!

Through wars with the Sotho, quarrels with Britain over ownership of the diamond fields, and nagging economic problems, Brand steered the republic along the stony road of independence. The simple little phrase he used when things looked bleak, *Alles sal reg kom mits elkeen sy plig doen* (everything will come right providing everybody does his duty) was sometimes the only hope of a gloomy Volksraad.

There was a lengthy struggle to secure finance to build a railway, and to persuade the more rural republicans that its advent would not drive the state to ruin. Eventually, in the midst of great public celebration, the railway to Bloemfontein from the Cape was opened on 7 May 1888. Unfortunately, President Brand had not lived to see the culmination of one of his fine projects. He had died two months after finally persuading his Volksraad to approve its construction. His successor, Frederik Reitz – also a lawyer – found himself at the head of a republic which, through Brand's good work, was in a far healthier financial state than it had ever been in the past.

President Reitz could relax in a handsome presidency (built in 1884) and be saluted by the cannon and band of a smartly dressed state artillery – 100 men led by a finely whiskered German officer, Captain F. W. Albrecht. The population of Bloemfontein had by then reached 2 000 (Europeans), and the original frontier character of the place had changed. More substantial buildings had been erected and the days when wild animals wandered through the streets had gone forever. The vast herds of plains game had been hunted almost to the point of extinction. In this massive slaughter a local farmer, Andrew Bain of *Bainsvlei*, had particularly excelled. Among his hunting achievements was the organisation of entertainment for the visiting Prince Alfred in August 1860. Prodigious herds of antelope were stampeded through a narrow pass on Bain's farm where numerous hunters were concentrated. Five thousand head of game were slaughtered during the course of this particular hunt.

President Reitz was an intelligent man in the same kindly mould as Johannes Brand. He lived, however, in far more complex political times than his predecessor had. The graceful *Raadsaal* (council chamber), built in 1893 and now the seat of the provincial council, housed many acrimonious debates on issues such as unity with the South African Republic in the Transvaal. Reitz, like Brand, was against unity but when he resigned in 1896 – the difficult year of the Jameson Raid into the Transvaal – he was replaced by M. T. Steyn, a farmer and lawyer, who was an ardent supporter of union. The Orange Free State was drawn into the quarrels which culminated in the Anglo-Boer War.

Bloemfontein was declared an open city and five months after the war had started, it became the unhappy duty of Dr B. Kellner, who was then mayor, to surrender the capital to Lord Roberts, whose footsore but cheerful 'Tommies' marched in without opposition on 15

March 1900. The occupation marked the end of an epoch in the history of Bloemfontein. For the remainder of the war, the town was a major communications and remount centre for the British army.

With Lord Roberts had marched a naval brigade with a small battery of 4.7 guns. In the general search for suitable campsites, the sailors were allocated the flat top of what was known as the mountain of Bloemfontein, from then on known as Naval Hill. Other units occupied this elevated site after the sailors had left and a remount camp for the Wiltshire Regiment was established below the slopes, where some of the troopers – inspired by the famous white horse of their home country – laid out a similar figure with the words *For Remounts* worked underneath in whitewashed boulders.

At the end of the war, Bloemfontein became the capital of the Orange River Colony and developed considerably. As the centre of a communications complex and a rich agricultural area, it was destined to grow. With the Union of South Africa proclaimed in 1910 Bloemfontein became the judicial capital – the seat of the Supreme Court of Appeal – and an important educational centre with the establishment there of the University of the Orange Free State, and many fine schools such as Grey College, founded in 1856 on a financial grant from Sir George Grey, Governor of the Cape Colony. Glen Agricultural College, opened in 1919, is situated just outside the modern city and (among many other achievements), is famous for its experiments in proving the fertility of the Kalahari aeolian sands, the basic research which started the great Vaal-Harts irrigation scheme.

With its central position and crisp climate Bloemfontein is a suitable place for conventions and sports gatherings. Its sports facilities are excellent – the Free State Stadium for rugby and athletics (68 000 seats); the fine rifle range belonging to the headquarters of the South African Bisley Association; and the largest freshwater swimming bath in the Southern Hemisphere (135 m long) at Mazelspoort.

The clear highveld air has also made the city attractive to astronomers. The great Boyden Observatory was built at Mazelspoort in 1927 by the Harvard University of America and is today an international research station equipped with a fine 152,40– cm reflecting telescope.

On the summit of Naval Hill stands the original building of the Lamont-Hussey Observatory, built in 1928 for the purpose of observing binary stars, of which it discovered over 7 000. Its principal instrument was a 68,5-cm refracting telescope. The observatory was originally under the control of the University of Michigan in America but astronomical work was completed there in 1972. The building now houses a unique theatre and cultural centre.

Today Naval Hill is a pocket-sized game reserve known as the Franklin Game Reserve, established in 1928 and named after J. S. Franklin who was then mayor. Its 198-ha area is maintained in its original wild state and serves as a home for herds of springbok, eland, zebra and blesbok. The road which encircles the summit of the hill yields fine photographic views of the city, its suburbs and surroundings. Couples will find it a pleasant place in the moonlight!

There are many interesting and unique things to see in Bloemfontein apart from stars. There is a fine zoo and a magnificent rose garden in Kings Park; *Mazelspoort* (oddly named 'Measles Pass'), has river boating, swimming and holiday facilities; the National Museum with its outstanding anthropological exhibition is open daily 09h00 to 13h00 and 14h00 to 17h00. Sundays 14h00 to 17h00 only; the War Museum, with its relics of the Anglo-Boer War is open daily 08h30 to 17h00 but 14h00 to 17h00 only on Sundays and holidays. Many historic buildings and impressive memorials may be seen, such as the General J. B. M. Hertzog statue with its 33 fountains, the 34-m-high obelisk of the National Women's War Memorial (underneath which lie the ashes of the famed Emily Hobhouse who did so much to alleviate the plight of Boer women and children in the concentration camps during the Anglo-Boer War) and the garden of remembrance column and city emblem where the original 'fountain of flowers' came to life in Bloemspruit (next to Victoria Park with its caravan park).

Bloemfontein became a city on 17 March 1945. It is a neat, amiable and bustling city of the sunny veld and a pleasant stopover for those travelling north or south along the great trunk road of South Africa.

## Accommodation
★★★★ Bloemfontein Hotel, 115 rooms, all with baths. R19 – R35 room only. Phone 7-0595.
★ Capitol Hotel, 35 rooms, 13 with baths. R8,50 – R11,50 B/B. Phone 7-7711.
★★ Cecil Hotel, 52 rooms, 38 with baths. R12,50 – R15 B/B. Phone 8-1155.
★★ Fontein Hotel, 30 rooms, 15 with baths. R14 – R26 B/B. Phone 7-6197.
★★ Maitland Hotel, 82 rooms, all with baths. R10 – R12 D/B/B. Phone 8-3121.
★ Oranje Hotel, 31 rooms, 9 with baths. R8 – R9 B/B. Phone 7-9849.
★★★ President Hotel, 100 rooms, all with baths. R23 – R50 B/B. Phone 7-0666.
★ Roadhouse Motel, 12 rooms, 6 with baths. R8,25 – R9 B/B. Phone 33-2023.
★ Roberta Hotel, 53 rooms, 7 with baths. R9 – R10 B/B. Phone 7-6126.
★ Victoria Hotel, 19 rooms, 4 with baths. R7,50 – R8,50 B/B. Phone 7-9869.

## Caravans and camping
★ Caravan and General (212 Andries Pretorius Str), 10 sites. R3 D plus 50c per person.
★ ® Mazelspoort Holiday Resort, 60 sites. R1 – R2,50 D. 12 cottages and 32 rondawels, R2,50 – R9 D.
★★ ® Rayton Caravan Park, 60 sites. R3,50 D plus 30c per person.
★★ ® Victoria Park, 60 sites. R5 D.

# BLOEMFONTEIN TO KIMBERLEY

From the central position of Bloemfontein, roads stretch to most parts of the Orange Free State. West of the city, a tarmac road crosses the level plains to Kimberley, passing numerous salt pans – shallow depressions in the veld where rainwater collects during summer, washing in mineral salts from the surface of the plains and over vast periods of time, concentrating deposits which are now recovered by various salt-producing companies.

It is interesting to see the vast number of smallholdings on the outskirts of Bloemfontein. Each one is owned by some individual who generally works in the city but devotes his spare time to the growing of vegetables or other cash crops to be sold at the local markets. Each smallholding usually has at least one windpump on a borehole raising water which is used for irrigation. After 69 km of travel, the road reaches the town of . . .

# DEALESVILLE

Laid out on the farm *Klipfontein,* owned by John Deale, the town became a municipality in 1914 and has a present population of 1 705. Dealesville is a centre for general farming (sheep and maize), for the recovery of salt, and for a number of thermal mineral springs frequented by sufferers of a variety of ailments. One of these springs reaches the surface on the town lands. Fifteen kilometres from the town lies the spring known as Baden-Baden, while 37 km away is the spring of Florisbad, famous for its fossil deposits. In 1930, Professor Thomas Dreyer discovered there a skull of Florisbad Man, which dates back more than 41 000 years.

## Accommodation
★ Olien Hotel, 10 rooms, 3 with baths. R7 – R7,50 B/B. Phone 20.

The road continues westwards past several salt pans which lie on a prairieland so flat that there is little opportunity for rainwater to drain away so it collects in hollows, forming temporary shallow pans or lakelets and then evaporates to leave a glistening deposit of mineral salts on the floor of the depression. After 54 km, the road reaches the town of . . .

## BOSHOFF

Named after President Jacobus Boshoff, the town was founded in 1858 as an administrative centre for the western part of the Orange Free State. Today, 3 150 people live there. Of interest is a municipal nature reserve situated on the outskirts of the town.

**Accommodation**
★★ Boshoff Hotel, 16 rooms, 10 with baths. R9 – R10,50 B/B. Phone 91.

West of Boshoff, the road crosses a more arid landscape dotted with a few acacia trees to break the monotony. After 45 km the road crosses the provincial boundary with the Cape Province and after 53 km reaches the city of Kimberley (see page 200).

## BLOEMFONTEIN TO THE NORTH

The road leaves the centre of Bloemfontein and after 12 km joins the Golden Way, which has bypassed the built-up areas. The road leads northwards for 6 km then reaches a turnoff where the original road branches off north-westwards to Brandfort and the goldfields (see page 514). and the new road continues straight across the central plains, past maize and sunflower lands, sheep and cattle pasturage and acacia thorn trees. The road crosses the Great and Little Vet rivers, and eventually, after 96 km, reaches the town of . . .

## WINBURG

This place has the distinction of being the oldest town in the Orange Free State. Built around a central square and overlooked by low hills, Winburg possesses an atmosphere of the rural tranquillity of former times. Without possessing any notable architectural features, it is nevertheless a typical agricultural town of the central plains. Cattle, sheep, horses, wheat and maize flourish in a brisk highveld climate (1 441 m above sea level) with a rainfall of 550 mm a year.

The town originated with the advent of the Voortrekkers. In 1835, the famous Andries Hendrik Potgieter led a party of trekkers into the area and for 42 head of cattle purchased from the local African chief, rights to the vast stretch of country between the *Vet* (fertile) and the *Vaal* (tawny coloured) rivers. An administrative, church, educational and commercial centre for the area was essential and a search for a suitable site began. After some argument the farm *Waayvontein* was selected and the owner, Jacobus de Beer, named the place *Wenburg* (victory town) because he had defeated rival offers of alternative sites. The name was later spelt Winburg.

For several years the little town was the only administrative centre on the central plains. At first it was an outpost of the Natal Republic, and from 1841 the seat of a landdros who was appointed by the Volksraad in Pietermaritzburg. The British annexation of Natal left Winburg independent as the capital of the central plains. With the advent of the British in 1846, Bloemfontein was founded as the centre of their administration and in 1848, Winburg became the seat of a British-appointed magistrate. Although Bloemfontein developed as the main centre of the Orange Free State and the capital of the republic which replaced British government, Winburg always remained the administrative centre of its own district.

The population has now reached 7 064. A monument to the Voortrekkers stands on the southern outskirts of the town.

**Accommodation**
* Fords Hotel, 20 rooms, 5 with baths. R9,50 – R10,50 B/B. Phone 183.
* Winburg Hotel, 19 rooms, 7 with baths. R7,30 – R8,35 B/B. Phone 160.

**Caravans and camping**
* Municipal caravan park, 40 sites. R1,50 D.

From Winburg, the road to the north stretches through extensive fields of maize and sunflowers. Six kilometres from the town, a main road branches eastwards towards Ladysmith and Natal (see page 523). At 32 km north of Winburg the Golden Way suddenly descends into the bush-covered valley of the Sand River and at this point a most interesting diversion is made possible by taking the tarmac branch road leading eastwards for 9 km to the irrigation dam at . . . .

# ALLEMANSKRAAL AND THE WILLEM PRETORIUS GAME RESERVE

In 1960, at Allemanskraal on the Sand River, the Department of Lands completed the construction of an irrigation dam designed to supply water for the cultivation of produce for the nearby Free State goldfields. The great dam and its shores have been developed into a major recreational area with black bass, yellowfish and carp in the dam providing interest for anglers. Boating, yachting, aquaplaning and swimming (in a beautifully situated swimming bath built on a site overlooking the dam), are other activities to be enjoyed.

The well-bushed heights surrounding the dam were a favourite resort for prehistoric man. The summit of Doringberg contains the ruins of an extensive settlement (about 7 000 huts) of early Iron Age people, presumed to be the long-vanished Leghoya tribe, who built huts and cattle kraals out of stone. The huts were so tiny that only one person (they were normal-sized individuals), at a time could occupy them in any comfort.

This interesting area, and much of the dam's surroundings have been converted into a 10 520-ha game reserve named in honour of Senator Willem Pretorius, a former member of the Orange Free State Executive Committee, whose enthusiasm for the project materially furthered its successful development.

A game reserve was urgently needed to provide a sanctuary for the fast vanishing species of highveld game – springbok, black wildebeest, blesbok, red hartebeest, eland, zebra, impala and white rhino – which had once flourished there in prodigious numbers. An earlier attempt to establish a game reserve on the 10 278-ha farm *Somerville* near Bultfontein was unsuccessful as it was too removed from tourists routes, situated in drought-stricken country, and had, in any case, degenerated rather dismally into something of a private shooting area reserved for a favoured few.

The new reserve however, was beautifully grassed, well watered and accessible to the public. Its wooded ravines and heights provided a most attractive scenic setting for the game animals. The more fortunate amongst the surviving game population of *Somerville* were translocated to the new area, and white rhino were reintroduced from Zululand. Today the Willem Pretorius Game Reserve is well established, an asset to the Orange Free State, and a delight to all lovers of the wilderness and the rich wildlife of birds and game animals. It is thoroughly worth visiting and the accommodation provided, together with a restaurant and store, is excellent. The entrance fee to the Allemanskraal area is R2 per car.

**Accommodation**
* Allemanskraal Dam, 72 rondawels (2 beds), R5,50 – R14 D. Additional beds and bedding R1,50 – R2 D.

**Caravans and camping**
★★ ® 150 sites. R2,75 D.

From the turnoff to Allemanskraal, the Golden Way continues northwards across the Sand River. On the northern bank of the river on an elevation just off the road, stands a small monument marking the site of the signing of the Sand River Convention on 17 January 1852 by which the independence of the Transvaal was recognised by the British.

Seventeen kilometres north of the Sand River (49 km from Winburg), the Golden Way reaches the small town of . . . .

# VENTERSBURG

The centre for an agricultural district producing maize, wheat and livestock, Ventersburg lies on the farm *Kromfontein,* which was originally owned by P. A. Venter, the chief field cornet of the area and a great friend of the renowned Sotho chief, Moshesh. Venter died in 1857 and his son, B. G. Venter, inherited the farm, allowing his farmhouse to be used for church services when a community was created in the area in 1864. The town grew up around this farm-church, with the first erven being sold in 1871. There are now 3 645 people living there.

Ventersburg is connected by a short road to the main railway line at a station formerly known as Ventersburg Road but, since 1927, called *Henneman* after P. F. Henneman, a local farmer.

**Accommodation**
★ Ventersburg Hotel, 14 rooms, 5 with baths. R8,50 – R14 B/B. Phone 76.

The Golden Way continues due north from Ventersburg across rich agricultural lands. One kilometre from the town it crosses the tarmac road linking the goldfields to Senekal, on the main road to Natal, while 46 km from Ventersburg the road is rejoined by the division which left it just before Brandfort to travel north over the goldfields. Three kilometres from this junction lies the substantial town of Kroonstad but before this town is described, let us examine the branch of the Golden Way which has travelled up from Bloemfontein through Brandfort and the Free State goldfields.

--------

From the division of the Golden Way, 18 km north of Bloemfontein, the north-western branch leads through a wood of acacia trees with several shady resting places at the roadside. After 5 km the road crosses the Modder River, where there is a turnoff leading for 1,5 km to the Glen Agricultural College and to Mazelspoort (16 km away). After a further 30 km of travel the road, now 53 km from Bloemfontein, reaches the outskirts of the town of Brandfort, with a turnoff bypassing the built-up area and leading on to the goldfields.

# BRANDFORT

An agricultural and communications centre, Brandfort was established on the farm *Keerom,* first occupied in about 1838 by Jacobus Van Zijl. Van Zijl became an elder in the community of the Bloemfontein Dutch Reformed Church and in 1866 planned a church centre on his farm as a convenience for the local inhabitants. He named the place *Brandfort* (burned fort) after a small fortification on *Keerom* farm which had been burned down during one of the frequent brawls with the Sotho tribespeople. The first erven were sold on 30 October 1866, houses were built and in 1874 Brandfort was proclaimed a town. It has grown into a centre for wool, maize and general farming activity and has 7 201 inhabitants.

## Accommodation
* Elgro Hotel, 30 rooms, 12 with baths. R10 – R10,75 B/B. Phone 73.
* Walmay Hotel, 13 rooms, 2 with baths. R9,40 – R10,20 B/B. Phone 412.

## Caravans and camping
* Municipal caravan park, 20 sites. R2 D.

From Brandfort a road leads north-eastwards for 59 km to join the Golden Way at Winburg. The main road to the goldfields bypasses the outskirts of Brandfort, curves past the hillock overlooking the town and stretches northwards across a gently undulating plain covered in maize, sunflowers and (in winter) long, golden-coloured grass. Maize is the important product here, and the road enters the outskirts of both the Free State goldfields and what is known as the 'maize triangle' of South Africa, the principal agricultural pantry of the country. The first town to be reached, 42 km from Brandfort, is landmarked and dominated by a huge silo holding 350 000 bags of maize. This is the town of . . .

# THEUNISSEN

Named after Colonel Helgard Theunissen, commandant of the local commando during the Anglo-Boer War, *Theunissen* was proclaimed a town in August 1907. The Colonel was the founder of the town and also its first mayor. Amply watered from the Erfenis irrigation dam, the town is the centre for a rich farming district and has a population of 7 157. There is fishing, boating and swimming in the dam and camping space on its banks. Many fine farms may be seen in the area.

## Accommodation
** Elgro Hotel, 10 rooms, all with baths. R12 B/B. Phone 338.

Beyond Theunissen the road continues northwards, passing the Star diamond mine and then, after 24 km, reaching a major parting of the ways. To the north-west, a branch leads to the goldfields (see page 516). To the north-east the road proceeds to the mining centre of Virginia, 16 km away.

# THE GOLDFIELDS OF THE ORANGE FREE STATE

There is a bitter-sweet element about the discovery of most of the renowned goldfields in the world. The Orange Free State goldfields are no exception. To the eye this goldfield consists of a plain so flat and featureless that the pioneers considered the one small hillock in the area remarkable enough to be named *Koppiealleen* (lonely hillock). Particularly subject to droughts, the area was regarded as a wasteland, and the few farmers resident there made a precarious living.

During the great gold discoveries on the Witwatersrand, an occasional prospector wandered south into this area. It so happened that 13 km north of the modern town of Odendaalsrus, a trader named Gustav Furst owned a tin shanty store on a farm named *Zoeteninval*. Near this store there appeared a definite reef on the sandy surface of the veld. Furst pointed this out to one of the prospectors, Archibald Megson, and a syndicate was formed consisting of Furst, Megson, Alick Donaldson and George Haines.

The syndicate sank an adit into the reef and found traces of gold of which samples were taken to Johannesburg in 1894 but the mining houses there were not interested; the samples were unimpressive and the area was considered unlikely to possess any major gold deposits.

As a last resort, the syndicate (it was rumoured), after salting their samples to make them more spectacular, scraped up enough money to send two of their members, Donaldson and Haines, to London. The two men sailed from Cape Town on the *Drummond Castle* which struck a rock off Ushant at midnight on 16 June 1896. Donaldson and Haines were among the 250 people who drowned in the disaster.

The remaining two partners gave up in despair. For 35 years the prospect shaft in the Zoeteninval reef lay abandoned. Gustav Furst vanished from the scene but Megson still wandered around the area, doing odd jobs and periodically trying to induce some visitor to take an interest in the reef. He was considered to be a local 'crank', but he nevertheless persisted.

In 1930 Megson happened to meet Allan Roberts, a Johannesburg mining engineer. Megson told him about the reef whereupon Roberts inspected it and collected samples from the adit. Megson's faith was infectious and Roberts decided on a gamble. In Johannesburg he floated a £50 000 company called Wit Extensions Ltd. Megson received £400 for his remaining interests in the reef and the company secured options on the surrounding farms. This was the first worthwhile sum of money invested in the area.

A few hundred metres away from the original prospecting adit, the company sank a drill on the farm *Aandenk*. The drill bored down 1 263 m and found nothing payable. At this stage, the company had exhausted its funds. The borehole was abandoned and the company withdrew, ceding its rights to the Transvaal Mining and Finance Co. Ltd. The new company searched around for a while and then ceded its rights to the African German Investment Company run by the well-known mining man, Hans Merensky. Merensky's reputation as a prospector was such that others became interested in the area simply because he was active there. A second company, Western Holdings, took options south of Odendaalsrus.

The geologist of Western Holdings, a Hungarian named Oscar Weiss, examined the area with brilliant perception. He noticed that all the geological evidence indicated that any extension of the Witwatersrand into the Orange Free State was not likely to be part of the Main Reef series, but of the associated Elsburg series. Unfortunately, this series was not related to magnetic shales which could be detected at deep levels by the type of magnetometer used in the spectacular discovery of the Western Rand gold area. Weiss knew, however, that the Ventersdorp System of basic lavas lay immediately above the Witwatersrand System and was a fairly reliable indicator of the latter's presence. By means of a gravitational torsion balance he could delineate the areas of the Ventersdorp System, since its masses of thick lava produced local anomalies in gravitation which could be measured with his instrument. The thickness of the lava could also be reasonably gauged, and drilling could be directed to areas where the lava was at its thinnest and most fragile.

The gravitational torsion balance of Oscar Weiss proved to be the key which fitted the locked door, previously tapped upon so feebly by the first syndicate of prospectors. Using this delicate instrument, Weiss directed his clients to a spot where the lava was thin and the Witwatersrand System (if, indeed, it lay below) was reasonably accessible.

The place selected by Weiss was on the farm *St Helena* and it was there, in April 1938, that the diamond drill first broke through into the subterranean treasure-vault of the Orange Free State. At a depth of 737 m, a reef was intersected which yielded on assay, 11,8 dwt to the ton. This find shook the mining world. The reef (like the Zoeteninval reef) was a freak bearing no relationship to the Witwatersrand System, but its discovery and gold content were enough to spur on the search.

The Second World War hindered work, but the discovery on *St Helena* and the development there of a payable mine, largely occupied the thoughts of all prospectors. At the end of the war the whole area bustled with prodigious activity. About 500 boreholes were sunk at a cost of well over £3 000 000. The result certainly justified the effort; 100 boreholes produced samples yielding gold in excess of what was then the payable minimum of 150 inch-dwt; 15

boreholes produced values of over 500 inch-dwt; nine boreholes produced values over 1 000 inch-dwt. The champion of them all was sunk on the farm *Geduld* – on 16 April 1946, the entire mining world was thrown into a dither by the announcement that this drill at a depth of 1 195 m, had intersected the Basal Reef and returned an assay amounting to the staggering figure of 23 037 inch-dwt.

The Orange Free State was now proved to be the new El Dorado with an estimated R7 000 million worth of gold waiting to be mined from a field roughly 50 km long by 20 km wide. Amid the general excitement, it is interesting to know that one of the prospecting companies remembered the borehole which had been sunk by Allan Roberts at *Aandenk*. They cleared out this borehole, resumed drilling and, after going down 135 m further, reached the great gold-bearing Basal Reef.

The effect of all these discoveries on the area can best be appreciated by a visit to the modern towns which have sprung up with extraordinary rapidity in order to house the mine workers.

From the division of the road 24 km of Theunissen, the north-eastern branch continues for a further 10 km, then reaches the mining town of . . .

# VIRGINIA

The place grew up around the original railway station of that name and today has a population of 58 150. Virginia became a town in 1954 and within three years had become the second largest town on the goldfields and the fourth largest in the Orange Free State. With the development of the goldfields, the Harmony Gold Mining Co., the Merriespruit O. F. S. Gold Mining Co. and the Virginia O. F. S. Gold Mine were established in the vicinity.

The town lies in attractive surroundings on the south bank of the Sand River where the municipality has developed a recreational resort in Virginia Park, with a 9-km-long boating stretch, swimming, fishing and a variety of holiday accommodation and sportsfields.

## Accommodation
* Doringboom Hotel, 27 rooms, 15 with baths. R13 – R14 B/B. Phone 3-4124.
* Harmony Hotel, 28 rooms, all with baths. R13,50 B/B. Phone 3-2191.
* Virginia Park Hotel 26 rooms, all with baths. R14 B/B. Phone 3-2306.

## Caravans and camping
** ® Municipal caravan park, 150 sites. R3 D. 20 rondawels, R8 D. 10 cottages, R14 D.

From Virginia a tarmac road continues in a north-westerly direction and after 16 km, reaches the town of . . .

# HENNEMAN

The town had its beginning as a railway station called Ventersburg Road, which served the town of Ventersburg 17 km to the east. The discovery of limestone in the area resulted in two cement factories, Anglo Alpha and Whites Portland, being constructed and a town grew up around the railway station. On 25 May 1927 at a public meeting held on the railway station, it was decided to rename the place in honour of P. F. Henneman, a local farmer of Dutch descent who had settled in 1860 on the farm *Swartpan* on which the town was now being built.

The discovery of gold on 16 April 1946 on the farm *Geduld* which lay to the west of Henneman, stimulated the growth of the town considerably. Today there are 8 820 people living there.

**Accommodation**
* Henneman Hotel, 21 rooms, 17 with baths. R11,50 B/B. Phone 50.

Welkom, the largest town of the goldfields, lies 32 km east of the road division between Theunissen and Virginia. The road passes several pans much frequented by aquatic birds such as flamingos. These days the pans are fed by additional saline water pumped from the mines, whose deep-level workings encounter great quantities of it.

# WELKOM

This city was laid out in 1947 on the farm with the pleasant name of *Welkom* (welcome) by the Welkom Township Company. From the beginning it was planned as a garden city with a commercial centre built around a handsome central square. It became a municipality in 1961 and a city on its 21st birthday, 14 February 1968. The population has reached 84 000.

Understandably, it has no historic monuments, being entirely dominated by the headgears of the gold and uranium mines of the St Helena Gold Mining Co., The Welkom Gold Mining Co., Western Holdings, Free State Geduld Mines, President Brand Gold Mining Co., and President Steyn Gold Mining Co.

**Accommodation**
* Dagbreek Hotel, 23 rooms, 8 with baths. R13,50 – R14,50 B/B. Phone 2-4269.
** Golden Orange Hotel, 50 rooms, 28 with baths. R16,25 – R16,75 B/B. Phone 2-5281.
* Los Angeles Hotel, 23 rooms, 10 with baths. R15,60 B/B. Phone 7-2291.
** 147 Hotel, 42 rooms, all with baths. R16,75 B/B. Phone 2-5381.

**Caravans and camping**
** Municipal caravan park, 40 sites. R2 D.

The oldest town on the goldfields of the Orange Free State lies 5 km from Welkom . . .

# ODENDAALSRUS

When the Dutch Reformed Church established a village on the *Kalkkuil* farm belonging to Jesaja Odendaal, the name *Odendaalsrus* (Odendaal's rest) was given to the little place. A few traders established themselves there but the village was short of water and extremely isolated, being connected to the outside world only by a sandy track leading for 33 km to the railway whistlestop which later became the town of Henneman.

Memories still remain in Odendaalsrus of the original postal contractor, Weber, who used to stagger into the village late at night, carrying mail bags on his shoulders and using his horses as pack animals, having abandoned the cart which had stuck fast in the sand.

One ramshackle little hotel run by Harry Woodburg provided an ever-open door (it was broken and couldn't be closed); water was sold from a well owned by I. J. van Vyver; there was a mill worked by MacMaster; four stores were owned by J. Bridger, H. Levy, J. Cohen and a curmudgeon of an Irish bachelor, J. Stewart, who periodically went on a spree and provided business for a solitary lawyer, Andries Hauptfleisch. Altogether, Odendaalsrus lived up to its name of 'rest'. It was a quiet but curiously cheerful little place, with Archibald Megson, the prospector being one of two reigning characters. The other was Piet Nelson, who claimed by devious connections, to be a descendant of Admiral Lord Nelson.

The secretary of the village management board, W. Furst, received a salary of £2 a month. He couldn't live on such a sum and so he eked out a living by playing for hand-outs an old horned gramophone in the local pub. He received a slight increase in his salary in 1912 when Odendaalsrus became a municipality, but things still remained very quiet!

Thirty-four years later, when the golden bombshell burst with the sensational results of the borehole on *Geduld* farm only 4,5 km away, there were still only 40 dwellings in the place, but Odendaalsrus is now a bustling mining town of 21 249 people. There is little to remind it of the past save a memorial marking the site of the first abortive borehole sunk by Allan Roberts, and the original prospect adit on the Zoeteninval reef.

### Accommodation
★ Outspan Hotel, 25 rooms, 7 with baths. R12 – R13 B/B. Phone 4-2876.
★ President Hotel, 20 rooms, 7 with baths. R13 B/B. Phone 4-1256.

### Caravans and camping
★★ Mimosa Park, 50 sites. R1,50 D.

From Odendaalsrus a tarmac road runs north for 9 km and reaches the newest town of the goldfields . . .

## ALLANRIDGE

Named in honour of Allan Roberts, the man who sank the pioneer borehole at *Aandenk,* the town of *Allanridge* was founded in 1950 and designed by William Backhouse, who also planned Welkom. It became a municipality on 21 December 1956 and is a fine example of a modern mining boom town with a population of 10 700. The place is hygienic, well ordered and a far cry indeed from the rip-roaring towns of former days.

Allanridge is the centre for the Lorraine Gold Mining Co. Huge fields of maize surround the town like an ocean. A large pan is situated on the outskirts of the town and is a favourite resort for flamingos.

From Allanridge, the road to the north continues for a further 50 km through the maizelands and then reaches the agricultural centre of . . .

## BOTHAVILLE

This place was laid out in 1891 on the farm *Gladdedrift* owned by Theunis Botha who planned to call it Bothania. It was proclaimed a town in 1893 under the name of Bothaville and became a municipality in 1914. At present, 12 500 people live there. The town is pleasantly situated on the banks of the Vals River where there are recreational facilities with swimming, boating and angling. The vast maizelands of the 'maize triangle' stretch interminably around the town.

### Accommodation
★ Bothaville Hotel, 17 rooms, 7 with baths. R8,75 – R10,50 B/B. Phone 304.
★ Elgro Hotel, 30 rooms, 12 with baths. R9,50 – R12,50 B/B. Phone 450.

### Caravans and camping
★★ Doring Park, 40 sites. R2 D plus 20c D per person.

From Bothaville the road leads northwards over highly productive agricultural country with pasturage for sheep and cattle and fields of groundnuts, maize, wheat and sunflower seeds. The road descends into the shallow valley of the Vaal River, crossing the river after 41 km. A further 6 km brings the road to the mining town of Orkney in the Western Transvaal (see page 695).

From Odendaalsrus a tarmac road stretches eastwards for 61 km to join the main Golden Way at the entrance to the town of . . .

# KROONSTAD

It is said that *Kroonstad* (the city of Kroon), was named after a horse. This interesting animal appears to have been rather a loser. Owned by one of the Voortrekkers, the horse reputedly came to grief in a pothole in a stream which flowed over the site of the town. The stream became known as *Kroonspruit* after the horse's misfortune and in August 1854 when Joseph Orpen, the landdros of Winburg, selected the site of a new town on the banks of the Vals, he simply applied to it the established place name. The first erven were sold on 20 April 1855.

Lying on the main route to the north, Kroonstad became a major staging post. The railway reached it on 20 February 1892 and over the years it became a strategic junction and marshalling yard on the north-south line and the line to Natal.

Today Kroonstad is a bustling agricultural, educational, and administrative centre, with a population of 75 000. A fine recreational area known as Kroonpark, has been developed along the banks of the Vals River.

## Accommodation
* Emilio Hotel, 31 rooms, 26 with baths. R12,50 B/B. Phone 3271.
* Selborne Hotel, 29 rooms, 27 with baths. R10,50 B/B. Phone 4269.
** Toristo Hotel, 48 rooms, all with baths. R13,50 B/B. Phone 5111.
* Zeederberg Hotel, 15 rooms, all with baths. R12,50 B/B. Phone 2138.

## Caravans and camping
*** ® Kroonpark, 150 sites. R2,50 D. 16 rondawels (2 beds), R2,25 D. 28 luxury huts (4 beds), R8,50 D.

From Kroonstad, the Golden Way continues northwards over flat maize and sunflower farmlands. At 76 km from Kroonstad the road reaches the small town of . . .

# VREDEFORT

The area in which *Vredefort* (the fort of peace) lies, is devoid of any great scenic beauty, but is extremely fertile, and was once the home of prodigious herds of game – blesbok, springbok and black wildebeest. Bushman hunting clans also roamed the area and their paintings may still be seen in numerous rock shelters, especially along the banks of the Vaal River. With the arrival of the Voortrekkers, and their defeat of the Ndebele at the battle of Vegkop (19 km south-west of Heilbron), the Vredefort area was settled by cattle farmers such as the Van Rensburgs, Schoemans and Bothas.

Hunting was the principal industry in the old Vredefort area, and at first it was popularly called *Riemland* (thongland), after the quantity of skins and thongs produced there. The name Vredefort originated during the period when there was dispute in the Transvaal over the question of the presidency. A Transvaal commando under Marthinus Pretorius invaded the Orange Free State. At *Laerplaas* on 19 May 1857 this commando was halted by men of the Orange Free State. After the usual wild threats being made, good sense prevailed and everybody returned home without there being any casualties.

The area was left to develop in peace. More settlers arrived and a community centre became necessary. A commission from the Kroonstad Dutch Reformed Church visited the area and selected as the site of the proposed town the farm *Vredefort* whose owner, Jacobus

Scheepers, had named it in memory of the peaceful conclusion to the threatened war between the Transvaal and Orange Free State. The town was laid out in 1876 and the first erven were sold on 20 April of that year. As a staging post on the north-south road, and the centre of a prosperous agricultural industry, Vredefort soon grew into a small town, the present population of which is 3 490. It received an added boost in 1886 when a discovery of gold was claimed by C. J. Bornman, on the farm *Weltevreden*. Other claims of gold finds were made on the farm *Lindequesfontein* and for a few years the so-called Vredefort Goldfields attracted some attention, with one moderately-sized mine, the Great Western, producing gold for a few years before the field fell into disuse.

The Vredefort area is well known to geologists on account of the so-called Vredefort Dome which is exposed there (see page 521). Maize, sunflowers, kaffircorn, corn, groundnuts and cattle provide the riches of the Vredefort area today.

## Accommodation

★ Vryst-a-a-a-t Hotel, 14 rooms, 5 with baths. R6 B/B. Phone 142.

Lying only 15 km across the farmlands north of Vredefort, is the town of . . .

# PARYS

The man who surveyed the place, Schilbach, a German who had participated in the siege of Paris, found that the site of the proposed town, lying on the banks of the Vaal River, reminded him of the French capital on the Seine and so he named it *Parys* (Paris).

Parys became a town in 1887 and today has a population of 24 400. Its attractive situation makes it one of the most popular of all the highveld holiday resorts. The broad river (about 1 km wide in places) is studded with tree-covered islands and several of these, such as Woody and Long islands, have been developed as resorts by the town council. Boating, fishing and swimming provide relaxation on the river and the left-hand bank has been turned into a first-class resort for caravanners, campers and picknickers, with holiday bungalows available for hire. This is a very pleasant place for a stopover on the Great North Road of Africa. The willow trees of the Vaal are curiously old world in their character and fireflies dart like fairies through their graceful leaves at night. Fish rise to feed where the willow leaves touch the water and trap insects carried down by the stream.

A wonderful variety of birds rest and call in this green paradise of trees and water. At night it is pleasant to walk beneath the willows. Cross to one of the islands. All is quiet and it is nice to be alone for a little while. Listen to the silence – only the gentle gurgling of the water; the sound of frogs; the twittering of a bird comforting its chickens in some tiny nest; the sighing of the willows as the night breeze whispers stories of seeing a river nymph hiding in the shadows.

The town is a centre for the growing of tobacco as well as the production of maize, groundnuts, sunflower seeds and corn.

## Accommodation

★ Bridge Motel, 16 rooms, all with baths. R5 room only. Phone 2791.
★ Echoes Hotel, 23 rooms, 8 with baths. R8,50 B/B. Phone 2752.
★ Polana Hotel 14 rooms, 7 with baths. R7 – R8 B/B. Phone 3555.
★★ Riviera Hotel, 40 rooms, all with baths. R12 – R14 B/B. Phone 2143.

## Caravans and camping

★★ Festival Park, 500 sites. R2,50 D plus 50c D per person.
★★ Mimosa Gardens, 200 sites. R4 D. 36 bungalows (2-5 beds), R10 - R15 D.

Parys, as we have seen, lies on the willow-shaded banks of the Vaal River. However, the Golden Way does not cross the river into the Transvaal at this point. It swings north-eastwards and takes the traveller across a landscape which is of interest to the discerning who know that the ridges of low hills over which the road crosses, form part of what is known to the geologists as the Vredefort Dome, a fascinating exposure of ancient granites emerging from the thick cover of the later-Karoo sediments. The form of the dome consists of a central cone of granite surrounded by concentric ridges of quartzites belonging to the Witwatersrand System. The exact nature and origin of this exposure is still a controversial issue.

At 17 km from Parys, the Golden Way reaches a junction. The left hand road continues straight to the Vaal and crosses into the Transvaal. The right-hand division is signposted Sasolburg and Vereeniging. This road swings almost due west for 22 km, then turns north-wards again where it joins the tarmac road which leads south for 3 km to the great chemical industrial complex of . . .

## SASOLBURG

As its name indicates, *Sasolburg* is the township established on 8 September 1954 to house the workers of S. A. S. O. L. (South African Coal, Oil and Gas Corporation). A modern town with a population of 42 703, Sasolburg is completely dominated by the chemical works which, night and day, reveal proof of enormous activity by belching out flames, fumes, smoke and an all-pervading, not altogether unpleasant (but certainly king-sized) 'body odour' which can be smelt from a considerable distance.

The siting in 1954 of the Sasol plant in this part of the Orange Free State was determined by the presence of vast deposits of low-grade coal (an estimated 600 million tons), and the Vaal River situated in the immediate vicinity, from which Sasol satisfies its thirst for 36 million litres a day. In exchange for its diet of water and low-grade coal, Sasol produces about 279 million litres of petrol and liquid chemicals of a considerable variety each year. A gas pipeline feeds gas to industrial users on the Witwatersrand, while a number of major chemical manufacturers of fertilizers, super phosphates, synthetic rubber, plastics, soft detergents, etc, have their plants in the immediate vicinity of Sasol and draw on it for essential materials. Sasol exports considerable quantities of hard, high-melting point Fischer-Tropsch waxes, and also koga-sins, both essential materials in a great variety of manufactured products. A full list of the chemicals produced by Sasol makes bewildering reading.

### Accommodation
★ Indaba Hotel, 58 rooms, all with baths. R9,75 B/B. Phone 6-1881.

Four kilometres north of the turnoff to Sasolburg, the Golden Way bridges over the *Vaal* (tawny-coloured) River, the borderline between the Orange Free State and the Transvaal. This great river, the principal tributary of the Orange, supplies nearly three million people with water and supports the most important industrial complex in Africa.

## THE VAAL RIVER

Known to the Bushmen as the *Gij 'Gariep* (tawny-coloured), and to the Zulu and Sotho as the *iliGwa* (erratic) river, the Vaal has its source near Breyten in the Eastern Transvaal. It has been thoroughly harnessed at many points along its course.

In 1923 the Rand Water Board built a barrage across the river creating a reservoir some 65 km in length and 7 m deep, with a storage capacity of 62 million cubic metres. From this rather hideously named *Loch Vaal*, the Rand Water Board extracts 1 045 million litres of water a day and supplies an area of 12 000 square kilometres including the whole Witwatersrand, Pretoria, Southern Transvaal and Sasolburg.

In 1936, the Vaal Dam was built upstream from Vereeniging. This dam, storing 2 500 million cubic metres is nearly 10 km wide in places and stretches back for 100 km. It has a circumference of 700 km and is up to 52 m deep. It controls the flow of the Vaal and feeds the barrage of the Rand Water Board, and also water users lower down the river, such as the Free State goldfields, which draw 218 million litres a day through a pumping station near Bothaville; the Western Transvaal Regional Water Company which abstracts 68 million litres a day for use in the Klerksdorp mining area; and numerous riparian and other users all the way downriver.

Famous for its yellowfish and barbel, the Vaal also provides great recreational possibilities. Angling, boating, swimming, and aquaplaning – all are enjoyed on the waters of this majestic river which meanders its way across the sunny veld, its banks lined with handsome willow trees.

Chapter Twenty-Six

# THE EASTERN ORANGE FREE STATE

The eastern area of the Orange Free State is composed of one of the most beautiful sandstone landscapes to be seen anywhere on earth. Its ingredients are: isolated flat-topped mountains; strangely shaped or balancing rocks; meandering rivers whose banks are lined with willow trees; deep soil, richly rewarding to the producer of maize, fruit (notably cherries and yellow peaches), dairy products, wheat and vegetables; spectacular cloud formations and summer thunderstorms on a vast scale; a romantic history and an untapped literary treasure trove of legends, fairy tales and traditions about long-vanished Bushmen, early Sotho tribes, cannibals, and the first European settlers such as that droll character, Renier du Wennaar, whose tall tales are still told, with many a chuckle, in the homesteads of today.

Three kilometres north of Winburg, on the Great North Road of Africa, the road to the Eastern Free State and Natal begins, branching off eastwards across the open, gently undulating highveld. At first there are few features of note. The landscape is sundrenched, spacious and airy, green in summer, brown in winter. At 7 km a turnoff stretches to Marquard and Clocolan; at 60 km there is a crossroads with a turn south to Marquard and north to Ventersburg and Welkom; after a further 3 km (63 km from the start of the road) the hollow of the Klipspruit stream is reached, on whose banks stands the town of . . .

## SENEKAL

The centre for an important food-producing district, *Senekal* is a busy and modern little rural centre named in honour of the unfortunate Commandant Frederick Senekal, who was killed in the Basuto Gun War of 1856. The town was laid out in 1874 on the farm *De Put,* owned by F. Malan, and it grew slowly as the church, school and trading centre for the farming community. The population now numbers 10 881.

### Accommodation
★ Senekal Hotel, 20 rooms, 6 with baths. R7,50 – R9,50 B/B. Phone 5.

The road to the east climbs easily out of the shallow valley sheltering Senekal and continues eastwards. After 5 km there is a turnoff to Arlington and Lindley, and 1,5 km further on brings the road to a turnoff to Rosendal and Ficksburg. The road is now making its way through rugged country dominated by isolated flat-topped hills. In this setting it is interesting to see the homes of the local Sotho tribespeople, decorated by the womenfolk in gay colours and designs, providing many striking examples of folk architecture in the rural landscape.

At 34 km from Senekal, the road reaches a turnoff to the small town of . . .

## PAUL ROUX

A rural centre lying among sandstone cliffs in the valley of the upper Sand River, its site was once an early resting place of the Voortrekkers and a staging post of the old postcarts. The modern town, which has a population of 2 640, is notable for its characteristic sandstone

*Overleaf: Sunset on Golden Gate in the cave sandstone area of the Eastern Free State, a landscape of subtle charm and elegance.*

buildings. It was founded in 1911 on the farm *Wassou* as a centre for an area of mixed farming, including the growing of poplar trees for making of safety matches from the poplar wood. The name of the village comes from the Reverend Paul Roux of the Dutch Reformed Church.

---

From the turnoff to Paul Roux the road to the east continues its way, traversing a pleasant rural landscape of farmlands and isolated hillocks. After 36,5 km the road reaches the busy, progressive town of . . .

# BETHLEHEM

This is a major farming, communications, administrative and tourist centre in the Eastern Orange Free State. It was founded in March 1860 on the farm *Pretorius Kloof*. The church and administrative centre for a very fertile and productive area, its site was well selected: the Jordaan River, flowing through Pretorius Kloof, provided a dependable supply of water and the climate was healthy. The town was proclaimed on 27 February 1864 and became a municipality in 1902.

A brisk climate and an attractive situation, enabled Bethlehem to grow rapidly, especially after February 1905, when the railway reached it along the important route from Bloemfontein to Harrismith and on to Natal.

Today Bethlehem has a population of 42 000 and is the centre for the regional offices of several government departments and commercial concerns operating in the Eastern Free State. There is an agricultural research station near the town. An interesting museum is housed in the old Nazareth Mission Church which, built in 1906, was the second mission church in the Orange Free State. The town has always been an important church and educational centre – its name (and that of the Jordaan River) was given by F.P. Naude, a great churchman and one of the original owners of the site. In Hebrew, *Bethlehem* means a house of bread, and the original Jordan River flows through some of the most fertile areas in the Holy Land.

In addition to being a centre for tourism in the Eastern Free State, Bethlehem is a pleasant holiday resort in its own right. The Jordaan River has been dammed to form what is known as Loch Athlone and on its shores a magnificent municipal pleasure resort has been created, with a complex of bungalows, club buildings, slipways, a caravan park, swimming pool and tearoom. The centrepiece, however, is a most unusual feature in an inland resort: a restaurant in the form of the favourite old Union Castle mail steamer, *Athlone Castle*. Painted in the same colours as the ship, the building houses many items retrieved from the *Athlone Castle* when it was scrapped. Mr C.M. van Heerden, manager and creator of the pleasure resort, collected these items – steering wheel, lamps, compass etc – and designed the restaurant, which was opened on 6 December 1957. Boating, fishing and swimming are recreations in this resort. Pretorius Kloof, below the dam wall, is a nature reserve with a rich bird life.

## Accommodation
★ Greens Hotel, 43 rooms, 23 with baths. R9 – R10 B/B. Phone 5140.
★ Park Hotel, 45 rooms, 25 with baths. R9,50 – R19 B/B. Phone 3117.
★ Royal Hotel, 84 rooms, 38 with baths. R10 – R11 B/B. Phone 5119.

## Caravans and camping
★★★® Loch Athlone Holiday Resort, 100 sites. R2 D plus 50c D per person. 15 bungalows (2 beds in 1 room), R5 – R7 D, bedding extra. 29 bungalows (4 beds in 2 rooms), R10 – R15 D, bedding extra. 6 bungalows (6 beds in 3 rooms), R15 D, bedding extra.

From Bethlehem, the road to the east continues through beautiful hill country. This part of the route makes a very pleasant drive: the landscape is fertile and varied, with rocky ridges and lovely farms in the valleys. In July wattle trees bloom and perfume the air, while masses of cosmos adorn the roadsides over Easter; there are many fine views of the Maluti mountains of Lesotho in the south – always beautiful, particularly when covered in winter snow.

At 7,5 km from Bethlehem a turnoff stretches to Clarens and the Golden Gate (see page 531), and at 45,5 km from Bethlehem, the road reaches the small town of . . .

# KESTELL

Taking its name from the Reverend J.D. Kestell of the Dutch Reformed Church, this little rural centre is inhabited by 1 499 people and is dominated by its rather odd-looking church. The village was founded in 1905 on the farm *Mooi Fontein* and has slowly grown into a trade, church, school and administrative centre for the farming area.

**Accommodation**
* Mont-Aux-Sources Hotel, 13 rooms, 6 with baths. R6,25 – R7,25 B/B. Phone 50.

The road to the east continues from Kestell across the rolling highveld. All around are spacious well-kept farmlands, sheep runs, maize lands, wheat fields, herds of blesbok and cattle, and to the south are views of the Maluti and Drakensberg ranges. At 19 km there is a turnoff to Witsieshoek, and another turnoff to the same place 19 km further on (for a description of Witsieshoek see page 529). At 43 km from Kestell, the road reaches the important Eastern Free State town of . . .

# HARRISMITH

The centre for one of the five principal wool-producing districts in Southern Africa, the town has a population of 19 630. Lying 1 615 m above sea level, Harrismith has a fine, crisp climate and a handsome situation in a valley where the *Wilge* (willow tree) River flows beneath the slopes of a 9-km-long, 2 377-m-high table-topped sandstone pile known as the *Platberg* (flat mountain).

Founded in 1849, *Harrismith* was named after the glamorous, hard-riding British Governor, Sir Harry Smith, whose beautiful Spanish wife is commemorated in the name of the neighbouring town of Ladysmith in Natal.

The first Harrismith was laid out by Robert Moffat (son of the famous missionary) on a site near Mayors Drift, about 25 km from the present town. Erven were sold in May 1849. The site was found to be deficient in water, however, so the present situation of the town, on the farm of Jan Snyman, was selected. Jan's house stood in a little valley, still known as the Old Homestead, along which courses the clear water of the Halle Stream, and this supply has quenched the thirst of the town since it was relocated in January 1850.

Afrikaans and English settlers were attracted to the area, the latter mainly people who had been brought to Natal under the Byrne Scheme and found the climate of Harrismith more congenial.

During the diamond rush to Kimberley, Harrismith boomed, becoming a busy staging post on the Natal transport route. At least 50 wagons toiled up the escarpment from Natal each day and Harrismith became a customary place of rest and refreshment. Hotels, public buildings and stores sprang up. The discovery of gold on the Witwatersrand attracted still more transport vehicles and in 1892 the railway from Natal to Harrismith was opened. Political problems, however, kept the railhead in Harrismith until 1905; then the link to Kroonstad through Bethlehem was opened.

A major base of the British army during the Anglo-Boer War, Harrismith has since then progressed steadily to become what it is today – a pleasant, spaciously laid out town with several handsome churches and public buildings. The beautiful President Brand Park, along the banks of the Wilge River, boasts fine trees, a prolific bird life, a caravan park and a zoo. The environment of the town offers enjoyable riding, walking and climbing; canoeing and angling are popular on the Wilge River.

The annual Harrismith Mountain Race is one of the foremost cross-country athletic events in Southern Africa. The course comprises a stiff 609-m climb in 5 km up *One Man's Pass* (named from a solitary rock figure there) to the top of the Platberg, then a run along the summit and down to the town by means of an old zigzag bridle path used by pack animals of the British army during the Anglo-Boer War.

The slopes of the Platberg are forested, and among the trees are many fine oaks. A mountain drive branches off the road (which goes to Johannesburg) 2 km from Harrismith and leads for 6,5 km to the plantation gate. There are fine views, picnic spots and easy routes to the summit of this very majestic mountain. Permits to enter the municipal forests are available at the town hall, or at the entrance to the forest.

The municipal waterworks, 4 km from the town, along the slopes of the Platberg, are also worth seeing, and from there a blockhouse, built by the British garrison, and now a national monument, is easily reached.

Next to the town hall is a remarkable petrified tree, 33 m long and estimated to be 150 million years old. A small museum is housed in the town hall.

## Accommodation

* Central Hotel, 40 rooms, 15 with baths. R11,50 B/B. Phone 31.
* Grand National Hotel, 34 rooms, 11 with baths. R11 – R12 B/B. Phone 33.
** Holiday Inn, 120 rooms, all with baths. R18,50 – R28 room only. Phone 550.
* Sir Harry Motel, 48 rooms, 28 with baths. R6 – R7 room only. Phone 813.
* Royal Hotel, 40 rooms, 21 with baths. R8 B/B. Phone 191.

## Caravans and camping

** President Brand Park, 100 sites. R3 D.

Continuing eastwards from Harrismith, the main road penetrates an impressive mass of sandstone mountains which tower on both sides of the road like sentinels guarding the verges of the highveld plains. This makes a fine drive, and an impressive gateway between the Orange Free State and Natal. After 19,3 km, the road reaches the small centre of Swinburne. At 31 km from Harrismith, the road enters the village of Van Reenen.

At this point the road is on the 1 680-m-high summit of the Van Reenen Pass and with the beginning of the descent, it enters Natal. At 2,5 km from Van Reenen, a turnoff down the old road leads to a fine viewsite known as Windy Corner. This is a worthwhile detour to follow, and while looking at the view of Natal and the long line of the Drakensberg, it is interesting to learn something of the history of this great strategic pass.

## Accommodation

* Montrose Hotel (Swinburne), 18 rooms, all with baths or showers. R8,50 B/B. Phone 19.
* Green Lantern Inn (Van Reenen), 28 rooms, 9 with baths. R7 – R8,50 B/B. Phone 13.

# THE VAN REENEN PASS

Built in 1856 and named after Frans van Reenen, who farmed at its foot and pointed out to the road surveyors the feasibility of the route, this finely located, sweeping pass is one of the major road and railway passes in Southern Africa. Over bridges, through tunnels and by means of great curves along the contours, the electrified railway climbs 681 m on the 61-km journey from Ladysmith to the summit. From the Windy Corner summit, the road loses 580 m in the 15 km to the bottom of the pass.

These great passes down the South African escarpment all have an atmosphere of romance. Most of them were originally blazed by herds of game animals – notably zebra, hartebeest, blesbok, wildebeest – migrating up and down between winter grazing in the warm midlands of Natal, and the sweet young grass which sprouts each spring after the bleak winter on the highveld plains.

The hooves of countless antelope unerringly found the line of least resistance up the escarpment. Man followed after, firstly in the form of nomadic hunters living on the game animals and then (especially during the Zulu disturbances at the beginning of the 19th century) as migrating or refugee groups in search of the safety of new homes.

Europeans arrived; at first only isolated adventurers, hunters, renegades and deserters from army garrisons on the coast. Then, on 7 October 1837, the Voortrekkers, led by Pieter Retief, reached the edge of the escarpment and, at a point 30 km south-west of Van Reenen Pass, looked down for the first time on the fair land of Natal. The scene so overwhelmed them after their long journey from the Cape, that Retief named the viewsite *Blijde Vooruitzicht* (the joyful prospect). From this viewsite a gentle pass known as the *Oudeberg* (old mountain) Pass provided a convenient route which Retief followed on his ill-fated journey to see Dingane, the Zulu king. The rest of Retief's followers descended into Natal by means of historic passes such as De Beers, Bezuidenhouts and Middledale, all of which are near the modern Van Reenen Pass.

Van Reenen village was originally founded as the border post between Natal and the Orange Free State. From the village the main road (passing after 2,5 km the turnoff to Windy Corner) makes its way down the pass. At 8,5 km from Van Reenen the road passes the Andrew Motel. At 16,5 km the road reaches the foot of the pass and at 49,5 km from Van Reenen, enters the town of Ladysmith where the road ends at its point of junction with the road from Johannesburg to Durban.

**Accommodation**

★ Andrew Motel, 16 rooms, all with baths. R9 room only. Phone Van Reenen 22.

## THE ROAD FROM HARRISMITH TO HEIDELBERG

This road provides an attractive alternative to the conventional road linking Natal with the Transvaal. The road leads northwards from Harrismith, curving around the western end of the massive landmark of the Platberg. After 3 km there is a turnoff to the mountain drive and just beyond that, a turnoff to Memel.

The tarmac road continues north-westwards over a landscape which is beautifully verdant in summer; streams are willow-lined; there are fine farmlands and maize fields. Handsome isolated sandstone hillocks, resembling feudal castles, tower over the countryside and the great pile of basalt mountains of Lesotho may be seen on the southern horizon.

After 50,3 km the road reaches a turnoff to the town of . . .

## WARDEN

This little place with its 4 800 inhabitants, was named after Major Henry Warden, a well-liked British administrative official during the years of the Sovereignty. The tall grain storage silo and the towering church steeple denote the town's importance as a church, school and agricultural centre.

**Accommodation**
★ Warden Hotel, 14 rooms, 8 with baths. R9 – R10 B/B. Phone 133.

From Warden, the road continues north-westwards. At Easter, the countryside is covered with huge patches of cosmos flowers – pink, plum and white – making a lovely sight as they wave in the wind. The mountains of Lesotho are gradually lost in the haze of the southern horizon. Gently undulating maize and sunflower fields stretch all around, where few prominent landmarks are seen. The colourful, tastefully decorated homes of the Sotho farm workers are worth noting.

At 45 km from Warden there is a turnoff to Memel and Vrede, and at 60 km a turnoff to Heilbron and Frankfort. At 75 km the road passes the small village of Cornelia, which, in summer, is beautifully set among emerald-green pasturage and fat herds of sheep and cattle. *Cornelia* was founded in 1918 and named in honour of Cornelia Reitz, wife of the last President of the Orange Free State. On the banks of the Skoonspruit, 10 km north of the village, lies an important fossil site. At 108,6 km from Warden, the road reaches the town of . . .

# VILLIERS

Situated in the great maize-producing triangle of the Orange Free State, *Villiers* was founded in 1891 and was laid out on the two farms *Pearsons Valley* and *Grootdraai,* owned by Lourens de Villiers, after whom the town was named. The town lies on the left bank of the Vaal River where a pleasant recreational area with fine willow trees shading a good stretch of water has been created.

**Accommodation**
★ Toeriste Hotel, 15 rooms, all with baths. R8,50 B/B. Phone 284.

**Caravans and camping**
★★ Villiersdorp Pleasure Resort, 37 rondawels, R5,20 – R10,40 D (depending on number of beds). 50 caravan sites, R2 D. 50 camping sites, R2 D. Admission is 10c per adult, 5c per child.

From Villiers, a tarmac road branches westwards for 34,5 km to . . .

# THE JIM FOUCHÉ HOLIDAY RESORT

Run by the Provincial Council of the Orange Free State, this resort is situated on the shores of the great Vaal Dam, near where the Wilge River joins the Vaal. The resort is named after Mr J. J. Fouché, a former president of South Africa. It is a spacious and handsomely laid out resort and appeals particularly to anglers who catch yellowfish, carp and barbel there.

Bird life is very rich in the area. Horse riding is pleasant and boating superb.

**Accommodation**
26 rondawels (3 beds), with kitchenettes and showers, R6 D. 6 rondawels (3 beds), nó kitchenette, R5,50 D. Family rondawels (6 beds), R10,50 D.

**Caravans and camping**
★★® 75 caravan sites, R2,75 D. 24 tents, R4 D. Entrance fee is R1.

From Villiers the road continues northwards, crossing the Vaal River. Maize, sorghum and wheat fields cover the landscape, while sheep and cattle graze on rich pasturage. After 26 km there is a turnoff to Grootvlei Power Station. At 31 km a crossroads is reached with turnoffs to Vereeniging and Balfour and at 53,7 km from Villiers, the original Durban-Johannesburg road joins the Harrismith road at a point 9 km south-east of Heidelberg.

## HARRISMITH TO KERKENBERG AND OLIVIERSHOEK

The gravel road running from Harrismith to Bergville in Natal by means of the Oliviershoek Pass, provides the traveller with some dramatic changes of scenery. The road commences at a turnoff to the south from the tarmac main road, 1,5 km from Harrismith on the way to Bethlehem.

The gravel road crosses a pleasant agricultural landscape where colourful patches of cosmos flower during Easter, and the grassy countryside is dominated by several high, isolated flat-topped hills. These flat-topped hills or mountains have great character; resembling islands in a sea, they tend to be atmospheric, each having some legend or history attached to it. Early tribes used many of them as strongholds similar to the feudal castles of Europe, for the summits were easy to defend and generally accessible by only one or two routes. It was also sufficiently easy to support (at least for short sieges) quite a number of people and their livestock on the summits.

At 32,5 km from Harrismith, a turnoff leads for 3,5 km to Retiefs Klip situated at the foot of a particularly stately example of these flat-topped massifs, the impressive 2 083-m-high sandstone pile known as *Kerkenberg* (church mountain).

It was here, on 7 October 1837, that Pieter Retief and his Voortrekkers arrived in 54 wagons and made camp. From the edge of the escarpment, close to Kerkenberg, Retief first viewed Natal. This was the viewsite which he named *Blijde Vooruitzicht* (the joyful prospect). Close to this viewsite, an easy pass led downwards. Known today as *Oudeberg* or *Step Pass,* it was used by Retief and 14 of his men, when he set off on his first visit to Port Natal and to Dingane in Zululand.

From Port Natal (Durban), Retief sent two of his men back to the camp at Kerkenberg with samples of fruits from Natal, and with the good news that the trekkers would be welcomed by the ivory traders already resident there. There was jubilation at the Kerkenberg camp. The day after the arrival of this good news was a Sunday, and also the 57th birthday of Pieter Retief. His 22-year-old daughter, Deborah, marked the occasion by painting her father's name on the side of a very strange rock formation at the foot of the Kerkenberg. This little memorial (carefully protected) may still be seen on what is known as *Retief's Klip.* Each year, on 16 December (the Day of the Covenant), a church service is held at Kerkenberg.

Beyond the turnoff to Retief's Klip, the main gravel road continues southwards. The road crosses the canal bringing water pumped from the Thukela River in Natal to feed the Vaal River. At 44,2 km from Harrismith the road reaches the Natal border at the summit of Oliviershoek Pass, 1 737 m above sea level. From this point the road makes a curving descent and eventually reaches the town of Bergville, 80 km from Harrismith.

## WITSIESHOEK AND ITS MOUNTAIN RESORT

The river known to Europeans as the Elands and to the Sotho people as the *Namahadi* (place of plenty), has its source on the summit of Mont-aux-Sources. It tumbles down in a spectacular waterfall and then flows northwards through an extremely rugged glen, in itself magnificent and made doubly impressive because it is backed by the high Maluti range of Lesotho.

Dominating the glen to the north is a magnificent specimen of a flat-topped sandstone mountain, named by the Bushmen *Qwa-Qwa* (whiter than white) either because of its winter snows, or because it is coloured by the droppings of vultures who, from time immemorial, have used it as a nesting area.

In approximately the year 1839, a group of Kgolokwe tribespeople led by a chief named Whêtse, made their way to this glen where they found a precarious sanctuary during the Zulu disturbances. Made destitute by incessant raids, they turned rustlers themselves and set out to recoup their losses by stealing the cattle belonging to European farmers who settled in the Free State. This enterprise provoked a punitive reaction. In 1856 a commando was sent out against Whêtse's rustlers. The chief and his followers retreated to a great cave, still known as Whêtse's Cave, near Monontsha. Besieged there, Whêtse made his escape through a tunnel, but his power was broken and only his name, in the corrupted form of *Witsie,* remains in the area.

The government of the Orange Free State retained possession of Witsieshoek but in August 1867 allocated a portion of the area to the friendly chief, Paulus Mopeli, a brother of the famous Moshesh, chief of the ruling Kwena tribe of Lesotho. With 200 of his followers, chief Paulus made his home in the area and in 1874 at his earnest request, the Dutch Reformed Church opened, on ground given to them by the Orange Free State, a mission station in Witsieshoek to serve the inhabitants. The Reverend G. Maeder was the first missionary. From this mission originated the Elizabeth Ross Hospital (named after the wife of one of the missionaries), and a theological school.

In 1873 Chief Koos Mota of the Tlokwa tribe was also allocated a portion of Witsieshoek and it is the descendants of the Kwena and the Tlokwa people who live in the area today. On 19 June 1953 these people became the first tribe in South Africa to be granted tribal authority of their homeland being the first step towards self-government. Since 1969 the Witsieshoek area has become the official homeland of the *baSotho ba Borwa* (Sotho people of the south) where territorial authority is exercised and a developing capital known as *Puthaditjhaba* (meeting-place of the nations) has been established. To its inhabitants the Witsieshoek area is known as *Qwa-Qwa,* after the flat-topped hill which dominates the region. The tribal area is 47 385 ha in extent and more than 40 000 people are settled there.

On 27 October 1972, a holiday resort was opened by the Bantu Development Corporation in a superb setting near the terminus of a spectacular road leading up the slopes of the Drakensberg to the Sentinel Peak and Mont-aux-Sources. This road provides one of the most stunning scenic experiences in Southern Africa.

Witsieshoek can be easily reached: four kilometres from Kestell, on the road to Golden Gate, a well-maintained gravel road branches off for 29 km to the Witsieshoek post office; another road branches off from the main road 7 km from Harrismith on the way to Bethlehem; this gravel road leads for 31 km to join the Kestell-Witsieshoek road at a point 15 km from the Witsieshoek post office; from the post office the road continues past Whêtse's Cave to Monontsha and the Lesotho border; one kilometre before the post office, a road branches eastwards to the mountain resort.

It is a drive enhanced by superlative scenes. After 20 km the road reaches a tollgate where a permit costing R1 must be obtained before proceeding. The road continues climbing past some remarkable rock shelters, caves and overhangs. After a further 4 km there is a junction, the left turn leading for 1 km to the rest camp, the right turn continuing for 6,5 km to a terminus confronting the Sentinel. At this point, 30,5 km from the start in Witsieshoek, the road is 2 680 m above sea level. From the road terminus, the original bridle path carries on to the chains which provide access to the summit of Mont-aux-Sources. This is a superb one and a half hour walk which should not be missed by any lover of beautiful scenery, fresh air, high mountains, summer flowers and winter snows.

Accommodation at the resort (which is 2 100 m above sea level) is comfortable. Winter snows are usual and violent summer thunderstorms are always spectacular. To experience one at this altitude is to be part of it, not beneath it. In fact, it is almost the same as being in a box of fireworks into which a lighted match is dropped. Everything literally seems to blow up in a strangely abrupt sequence of bangs, rumbles, flashes, patterings, downpours, hailings, floods, clatterings, rattles and finally a dead silence. One gets the feeling that the thunderheads (the *donderkoppen* of legend) are really alive – rough, noisy fellows, barging around the sky, pushing one another, brawling, shouting, cursing, roaring and swearing like a gang of toughs on the rampage, who suddenly vanish down an alley when the police arrive. Sometimes they return just as suddenly after the police have left and have another turn at tearing up the sky and flushing it down the drain. It can be quite an experience!

**Accommodation**
Double rooms: R9 one person, R16 for two people. Family units, R6 per person B/B, minimum tariff of R24 per night, R6 for each extra person. No preparation of food is allowed in above-mentioned accommodation. Meals are served in restaurant.
Chalets, R5 per person, minimum tariff of R20 per night, R5 for each extra person. Fully equipped for 6 people.
The restaurant is fully licensed. Horses, haversacks etc are available for hire.

# THE GOLDEN GATE

At a point 7,5 km before the main road reaches Bethlehem from Harrismith, a tarmac turnoff leads southwards in a pleasant drive through elegant sandstone country past fields of wheat and maize, and orchards of yellow peaches. Then, by means of the *Noupoort* (narrow passage), the road passes through the Rooiberg range and, at 28 km, reaches the straggling and curiously old-world little town of . . .

# CLARENS

Laid out in 1912, *Clarens* was named after the place in Switzerland where President Paul Kruger died. It is a quaint little place, spread over a slope where some odd public buildings are looked down upon by a collection of high, very superior sandstone mountains. Three kilometres from the town lies a pleasant picnic and recreational area known as Leibbrandt Kloof.

**Accommodation**
★ Maluti Lodge, 14 rooms, all with baths. R10,50 B/B. Phone 35.

From Clarens, the tarmac road swings up the valley of the Little Caledon River which is one of the world's most beautiful examples of a sandstone valley, deeply eroded and modelled by the bustling river. The road leads beneath a series of towering cliffs, one of which is known as Gladstone's Nose, a prominent appendage situated in the middle of an unmistakable face. In this lovely area, 21 km from Clarens, lies the . . .

# GOLDEN GATE HIGHLANDS NATIONAL PARK

This unique national park was established in 1963 to conserve 4 792 ha of sandstone highlands unsurpassed in their variety of rock shapes and colour. A great number of wild flowers – notably arum lilies, watsonias, fire lilies and red-hot pokers – flourish in the area. Bird life includes the magnificent lammergeyer, with a wingspan of nearly 3 m, the black eagle, jackal buzzard, blue crane, secretary bird, rock pigeon, guineafowl and numerous waterfowl. Game animals include eland, red hartebeest, springbok, gnu, and smaller mammals.

The whole area provides superlative riding, walking and climbing opportunities, which yield innumerable interesting scenes. Great caverns and rock shelters are set in a landscape where the colours are spectacular, the rock shapes surprising and where an undeniable elegance is conjured up by the old-world farmhouses and graceful trees (especially willows and poplars) which line the banks of the streams.

There is crisp mountain air to breathe, crystal-clear water to drink; the atmosphere is serene and quiet. Amid the many lovely scenes which charm the eye, the National Parks Board has developed a magnificent recreational area, complete with a variety of accommodation ranging from luxury in the Brandwag camp to chalets, huts, rooms and a fine caravan park and campsite. There are restaurants, snack bars, curio shops, and a museum. Tours are conducted, there is a stable of riding horses and a network of paths for walkers to follow.

The road through the park is always open and admission is free. One kilometre beyond the headquarters camp of *Glen Reenen* (named after the Van Reenen family, the original owners of the area, who are buried in the little cemetery near Gladstone's Nose), there is an entrance gate leading to the game park where a number of antelope live in their natural state. Admission is 50c per vehicle. Overnight guests in the camp are admitted free. There are many fine picnic spots along the roadside which are open from one hour before sunrise to half an hour after sunset. Trout fishing is popular in summer.

Beyond the turnoff to the game park, the tarmac through road deteriorates into a gravel road which traverses fine scenery for 37 km as far as Kestell, where it joins the main road to Harrismith.

## Accommodation

Glen Reenen Rest Camp: 13 huts (2 beds), R7,50 – R9 D. 7 rooms (2 beds), R7,50 D.
★ ® 100 caravan and camping sites, R2,50 D.
Brandwag Rest Camp: 34 double rooms, all with private baths, R8,50 – R12,50 D. 34 chalets (with 4 beds, bathroom and refrigerator), R15 D for 2 people. R2 each extra adult, R1 each extra child.

# THE ROAD ALONG THE LESOTHO BORDER

This road provides an all-tarmac drive through some of the finest scenery in Southern Africa. Starting in Bethlehem, it stretches southwards past the Loch Athlone pleasure resort and across a fertile, green, agricultural landscape. After 50 km this road reaches the town of Fouriesburg. This first section of the road actually yields the dullest scenery, but an alternate route starts from Clarens and joins the road which skirts the Lesotho border at Fouriesburg. This is the recommended scenic route which rewards the venturesome traveller with some stunningly beautiful scenery during any season of the year.

From its beginning at Clarens where it turns off from the tarmac road to the Golden Gate, this road leads through the little town itself and, after 1 km, beyond the turnoff to Leibbrandt Kloof with its picnic spots (2 km away).

The tarmac road continues south-eastwards down the valley of the Little Caledon River, an undulating rural landscape adorned with willow- and poplar-lined streams, sandstone cliffs, weird rock formations and neat farmlands. After 13 km, the road starts climbing to the summit of a long ridge. On the summit, 14,5 km from Clarens, the traveller is treated to a view almost overwhelming in all directions, but particularly to the south and east into the massive mountain pile of Lesotho, and the great range of the *Maluti* (mountains).

At 19 km from Clarens there is a turnoff to Hendriksdrift and the Lesotho border. At 26 km from Clarens, the road joins the main road leading from the Lesotho border post of Joels Drift to Fouriesburg and at 36,5 km from Clarens the road reaches the town of . . .

# FOURIESBURG

This little place, with its population of 4 367, was laid out as a township in 1892 on the farm *Groenfontein* owned by Stoffel Fourie, after whom the town was named. Although a somewhat nondescript little town, it is handsomely situated with the mountains of Lesotho only a few kilometres away, a picturesque assembly of sandstone flat-topped hillocks in the surrounding area, and the pretty picnic area of Meiringkloof (also a nature reserve) near by. The town has considerable trade and traffic relations with Lesotho through the Caledon Bridge border post 8,8 km away.

**Accommodation**
* Fouriesburg Hotel, 10 rooms, 5 with baths. R8 – R9 B/B. Phone 30.

From Fouriesburg, the border road continues south-westwards across well-cultivated farmlands dominated by high, flat-topped sandstone hills with vividly-coloured cliff faces. At 32 km from Fouriesburg, the road passes through a lovely, park-like valley, where fine orchards of peach trees are laid out, and the heights of the Witteberge look down from the west.

Continuing south-westwards across a landscape of grass and maize lands, beneath skies notable for their summer blueness and gigantic afternoon thundercloud formations, the road passes numerous flat-topped hillocks; especially remarkable is the one 43 km from Fouriesburg at the Sekonyela railway siding. Three kilometres beyond this hill, the road is joined by the road coming south from Rosendal. A further 3 km sees a turnoff north to Senekal (66 km). One and a half kilometres beyond this turnoff (46,5 km from Fouriesburg), the road enters the pleasantly situated town of . . .

# FICKSBURG

Sheltered by the tree-covered heights of the 1 854-m-high Mpharane mountain to the west with the Caledon River boundary with Lesotho immediately to the east, Ficksburg has a fine, crisp, highveld climate (the town is situated 1 629 m above sea level), a good rainfall and an attractive environment. Consequently, the area has always provided a pleasant home for human beings.

Numerous paintings in caves and rock shelters indicate that Bushmen found the area around Ficksburg to their liking. Various Sotho tribes settled in the area where many memories still linger of raids and invasions, especially those which occurred during the troubled early years of the 19th century when the whole interior of Southern Africa underwent a period of war and ferment.

Europeans wandered into the area in the middle 1830s and made their homes along the fertile banks of the Caledon River, even though life on the frontier was precarious and subject to the endless depredations of expert rustlers and stock thieves. Among the pioneers, however, was Commandant-General Johan Fick, after whom the future town was destined to be named and who was a renowned figure during the frontier wars with the Sotho. He and his wife are buried in front of the town hall which was built in 1895.

The frontier area remained in a state of turmoil for over 30 years and the history of this prolonged period reads with greater excitement than the most romantic fiction.

During these troubled years, Johan Fick rose to the rank of Commandant-General and upon the founding of a town on the frontier in June 1867, *Ficksburg* was the name given to it, in his honour. The town of Wepener, further south, was founded simultaneously with the similar purpose of pacifying the newly conquered territory along the Lesotho border.

Ficksburg rapidly developed into a pretty, busy little town, always having considerable trade relations with Lesotho. Today it remains an amiable and attractive place with 13 183 inhabitants and is notable for its fine gardens, parks and recreational areas, such as Morgen-zon Spruit and Meul Spruit. Grain, maize, fruit and livestock are the products of the district.

Ficksburg is also the principal cherry-producing centre in South Africa. Blossoms in springtime are exquisite and at the height of the season each year in November, a cherry festival is held in the town.

Summer thunderstorms and violent hailstorms are a problem to farmers and Ficksburg is the home of the Farmers' Hail Insurance Co-operative which provides compensatory protection for more than 10 000 members.

### Accommodation
★ Commercial Hotel, 14 rooms, 6 with baths. R8,50 – R9 B/B. Phone 22.
★ Ficksburg Hotel, 47 rooms, 38 with baths. R12,50 B/B. Phone 5.

### Caravans and camping
★ Municipal caravan park, 30 sites. R1 D. In Thom Park.

From Ficksburg, the road continues south-westwards close to the Caledon River border of Lesotho. The countryside, neat and park-like in appearance, with tall gum, pine and willow trees flourishing, is well grassed and there are numerous fine farms. Handsome and curiously elegant sandstone hills dominate the scene.

At 34 km from Ficksburg a turnoff leads for 3 km into the centre of the town of . . .

# CLOCOLAN

Lying in the centre of a rich agricultural area, where maize, potatoes, wheat and cattle are produced, Clocolan has a fine, crisp, well-watered climate, and, set among green grass, is dominated to the north by the 1 820-m-high *Hlohlowane* (ridge of the battle) mountain.

The Kwena people under the renowned chief Mohlomi, made their homes in this area but were often raided by other tribes who envied them their prosperity. Memories of many fights linger about the area. Matiwane and his footloose Ngwaneni people raided the area; the Zulu came, and also the Ndebele. Endless disturbances drove away most of the early inhabitants.

Europeans arrived and a trader built a store beneath Hlohlowane mountain, corrupting its name into the *Clocolan* of today. In 1906 the town was laid out in a hollow close to the store on the two farms *Rienzi* and *Harold* (named by their surveyor after the Italian hero and the last Anglo-Saxon king of England). The town adopted the name of the store. Built around a central square, it has grown to its present modern state, with a population of 7 052. There is a large grain silo and industries include maize, corn, fruit, and trade with Lesotho.

### Accommodation
★ Clocolan Hotel, 20 rooms, 6 with baths. R6,76 – R8,32 B/B. Phone 19.

### Caravans and camping
★ Municipal caravan park, 20 sites. R1,20 D.

From Clocolan, the road continues southwards across a landscape of grass, maize and low, flat-topped sandstone hillocks, many of which display on their slopes queer, balancing and oddly shaped rocks. The countryside is neat and immaculate especially in summer when the grass is green and the sky a rich blue filled with wonderful cloud 'castles'. After 32 km the road reaches (in a fine setting of hills and trees) the pleasant little town of . . .

# LADYBRAND

With a population of 11 048, Ladybrand is sheltered in the rocky sandstone arms of the high ridge known as the *Platberg* (flat mountain). This area has long been an attraction to man, for in the caves of the Ladybrand district may be seen many interesting and beautiful Bushman paintings. Especially notable are the caves at Rose Cottage (3 km from the town); in two caves at Modderpoort (11 km from the town) and on the farm *Tandjiesberg* (22 km from the town). Unfortunately, most of these paintings have been badly disfigured by vandals who have scrawled graffiti over them. Fossils and prehistoric artefacts are also found in the district. In 1934 the fossilised remains of *Diarthrognatus* was found close to the Leliehoek Pleasure Resort. Scientists consider this prehistoric animal to be the link between mammals and reptiles. The fossil (the only one in the world), is now exhibited in the museum in Bloemfontein.

There was tribal chaos in the first half of the 19th century, as was the case in the whole Lesotho border area. Cannibalism in the mountains and raiding and renegade bands from Natal (mainly Zulu and Ndebele), combined to make life unpleasant in the region.

The first Europeans arrived in the Free State plains towards the end of this period which was then succeeded by an interval of frontier disturbance and war between the Sotho people, the British and then the Orange Free State governments. Eleven kilometres north from Ladybrand is the flat-topped hill of Viervoet where, on 20 June 1851, a British-led force suffered defeat at the hands of the Sotho. The hill was the stronghold of the Taung people under chief Molitsane. It was stormed by the British force. Sotho reinforcements counter-attacked, retook the stronghold and drove the British force off to Bloemfontein.

Battles and quarrels continued along the frontier until, in the 1860s, Europeans finally secured the area as far as the Caledon River. To pacify and hold this so-called 'Conquered Territory', towns such as Ficksburg, Wepener and Ladybrand were created.

*Ladybrand* was founded in 1867 and named after Lady Catharina Brand, mother of the President of the Orange Free State. The site was originally known as *Mauwershoek,* after a famous half-breed who once lived there. With plentiful supplies of water, the town rapidly grew into an important trade, administrative and agricultural centre, in an environment made pleasant by the presence of several pretty ravines in the surrounding heights. Places such as Leliehoek have been developed into beautiful parks and the sheltered situation of the town stimulates fine gardens and the growth of handsome trees. There are pleasant walks and riding trails leading from Leliehoek to interesting places such as The Stables, a cleft in the rock where the Boers concealed their horses during the war with the Sotho in 1858.

Connected in 1905 by means of a branch line to Modderpoort, on the main Bloemfontein-Bethlehem railway, Ladybrand is a trade centre on the Lesotho border. Maize, grain, cheese, dairy products and livestock are the agricultural industries.

At Modderpoort a unique cave church was created in 1869 by the Anglican Society of St Augustine, a small monastic group who used the cave as a chapel and also as living quarters for more than a year until they managed to build a house. In 1902 the Anglican Society of the Sacred Mission took over the area and they continue to work with Modderpoort serving as their headquarters. On the fourth Sunday of each August, a special service is held in the cave church.

## Accommodation
★ Central Hotel, 28 rooms, 15 with baths. R7,50 – R9 B/B. Phone 2.

## Caravans and camping
★★ ® Leliehoek Municipal Resort, 50 sites. R2,50 D. 4 bungalows (6 people), R11,23 D from 1 October to 15 April. R7,42 D from 15 April to end September. 4 rondawels (2 people), R5,62 D throughout the year.

From Ladybrand the tarmac border road continues south-westwards, climbing up the ridge which overlooks the town. After 3,5 km, a tarmac turnoff leads for 18 km to Caledon Bridge, the main border post of Lesotho, with the capital of Maseru lying just across the Caledon River which forms the frontier at this point. The customs and immigration office is open from 06h00 to 22h00. The Riverside Lodge Hotel is immediately upstream from the border post, on the South African side.

## Accommodation
** Riverside Lodge Hotel, 38 rooms, all with baths, R12 B/B. Phone Ladybrand 345.

The main tarmac road proceeds from the turnoff to the Lesotho border post, reaching a fork after 12 km. The right-hand branch stretches to Thaba Nchu and Bloemfontein. The left-hand branch continues over green and pleasant border country, where the Maluti range of Lesotho lies to the east and isolated hillocks loom like precipitous islands in an undulating sea of grass. Lying at the foot of one of these hillocks (which rather resembles a Stone Age mound), 54,5 km from Ladybrand, is the small town of . . .

# HOBHOUSE

This little place, with its population of 1 398, was named after Emily Hobhouse, who laboured during the Anglo-Boer War to alleviate conditions in the British concentration camps. It was founded in 1912 and is the centre for an agricultural area producing cheese, maize, wheat and livestock.

From Hobhouse, the road continues south-westwards across fertile country bordering on the Caledon River. This is a spacious, well-grassed and open area where occasional sandstone hills look down serenely on well-kept farmlands.

After 31 km the road crosses the Caledon River and, 36,3 km from Hobhouse, enters the town of . . .

# WEPENER

With a population of 5 665, Wepener was one of the towns established in the newly conquered territory along the Lesotho border. It was laid out in 1867 and named in honour of Lourens Wepener who was killed on 15 August 1865 while leading an attack on Thaba Bosiho in the war against the Sotho. It is an agricultural and trading centre, sheltered by a high ridge and pleasantly situated on the banks of the Jammersberg stream.

## Accommodation
* Wepener Hotel, 19 rooms, 10 with baths. R8,50 B/B. Phone 87.

## Caravans and camping
* Municipal caravan park, 30 sites. R2,50 D.

From Wepener, the border road continues southwards, crossing open grasslands, maize fields, herds of cattle, and passing flat-topped hills which dominate an amiable rural landscape. One and a half kilometres from the town there is a turnoff to Bloemfontein (117 km), while a further 26 km takes the road past a turnoff to the fine Egmont Dam at Boesmanskop, and a turnoff east to Sephapo's Gate on the Lesotho border.

At 62 km from Wepener the border road reaches a turnoff to the south-east leading for 4,5 km to the town of Zastron. The main road continues south-westwards for 30 km, ending its route at Rouxville.

# ZASTRON

The town of Zastron grew up as a commercial centre on the farm *Verliesfontein* owned by J.H. du Wennaar, who had made his home on the site in 1838. Driven away by frontier disturbances, he later returned and brought with him a brother named Renier, an individual who has a peculiar renown in the folklore of the Orange Free State.

The two Du Wennaars led a Rip van Winkle type of life. Renier, particularly, with a huge flowing beard, and dressed in *velskoen*, ragged trousers, and a peaked hat, roamed around the countryside, hunting and telling a type of story which became a byword and treasured anecdote throughout Southern Africa. Renier's inseparable companion was a wizened old Bushman (known simply as Boesman), who followed him faithfully, squatting at his heels when Renier spun his stories and, if he saw doubt on the faces of the listeners, would eagerly add *'Dis reg, baas'* ('quite correct, sir'), after even the most outrageous claim made by his master.

A typical Renier du Wennaar story relates how the Aasvoëlberg behind Zastron received the hole through its rocky crag which watches over the countryside like an eye. With vultures nesting on its ledges, it provides a singular landmark.

It appears that Renier and Boesman were hunting on this height one afternoon when they encountered an individual who, although he had long hair and curling finger nails, and was dressed in filth and rags, was polite enough.

'Morning,' said this individual, surveying the equally ragged Renier with appreciation. 'You look like my father-in-law. What have you there?' He pointed at Renier's *pangeweer* (an old type of gun requiring liberal doses of gunpowder and a steady nerve to fire it off). Renier realised that this was the devil. He thought rapidly.

'It's my pipe,' he replied. 'I like to smoke, but my wife won't let me, so I come up here for a puff.'

'Good,' said the devil. 'Let's have a draw.'

Renier loaded his gun with a triple charge of gunpowder and a pile of lead and nails. 'Here,' he said kindly. 'Hold it to your mouth and draw while I strike a light.'

The devil put the muzzle in his mouth. Gleefully, Renier lit the fuse. There was a huge explosion. Through the smoke, Renier saw the devil's head hurtling through the air. It hit the mountain with a thud, boring a hole through the rocks. As it flew off through the other side, Renier could faintly hear the devil's startled voice exclaiming, *'Wraggies, jong! Daardie twak was darem sterk!'* (Hell, man! That tobacco was a bit strong!). The devil's body sped off in search of its head!

The Zastron area was always favoured by Bushmen and the caves in the surrounding sandstone hillocks provided some of their most celebrated strongholds. Visiting these caves today is a fascinating and (if their history is known) at times, poignant experience. On the farm *Lichtenstein*, for example, is the Cave of the Hippopotamus, so named because the hippo is the dominant figure in that gallery of rock paintings. Some of the last surviving Bushmen lived in this cave, the floor of which is still littered with the fragments of their pots. It is said that they were all treacherously murdered by a vicious half-breed freebooter named Danster whose stronghold was nearby, at Danster's Nek. Jealous of the Bushmen, he invited them to a carousel, let them get drunk and then had their throats cut.

Close to *Lichtenstein* is another farm, *Glen Roza*, whose owner, hunting dassies in 1946, was caught by a sudden storm. Seeking shelter he stumbled into what is now known in his honour as the Hoffman Cave. This cave contains one of the finest galleries of polychrome rock paintings to be discovered. Farmer Hoffman found a frieze 4,5 m long and 1,5 m wide, which, in a splash of vivid, almost unfaded colour, gracefully preserves the memory of a vanished people and the game animals they hunted. This is a veritable gallery of Bushman masterworks, where eland, especially, are magnificently depicted. The cave is situated in a deep and broken ravine which leads down to the Orange River.

The fate of the inhabitants of the Hoffman Cave is not known. But in the 2 026-m-high rock massif known as Genadeberg (19 km south-east of Zastron) there are a number of Bushman caves about which there are particularly poignant memories. It was here, in the year 1830 that a punitive commando cornered a band of Bushmen accused of rustling cattle. The commando found the Bushmen on the western side of the heights, living in rock shelters beneath a series of waterfalls.

A succession of fights and sieges followed. The Bushmen withdrew cave by cave towards the innermost valleys of the massif. Finally, they fled to the great cave of their chief in the eroded corner of the heights known as Poshudi's Hoek. This cave (big enough to house a thousand people), is made of a colossal arch of rock thrown across a scooped-out shelter in the sandstone. During the rainy season a fall of water thunders noisily across the entrance and a tangle of thorn trees and loose boulders makes the approach most difficult.

The name of the Bushman chief was Korel. He was a wizened, one-eyed little man whose daring and skill as a bowman gave him a formidable reputation. One of the commando, 14-year-old Jacobus du Plessis, who could speak the Bushmen's language, made his way to the cave. Waving the Bushman sign of truce (a jackal's tail tied to the end of a stick), he nervously entered the rock fortress.

The Bushmen received him courteously. He was conducted to the innermost recesses of the cave where he found the wild little chieftain seated in the centre of a circle of his followers. It must have been a barbaric sight; this great cave full of echoes, shouts and dark shadows, in whose depths sat a savage circle of near-naked hunters, with bows in hand, their heads bedecked with poisoned arrows filleted into thongs fastened around their foreheads.

In the centre of the circle, Du Plessis faced the chief and nervously stuttered out his message; futile to resist, safe conduct if the chief surrendered, with Du Plessis himself to take the chief by the hand and walk beside him to the commandant's presence. The wrinkled little face peered at the boy from the shadows. 'Go! My eyes cannot bear the sight of you. Begone. Tell your commandant that our hearts are strong, and we will claim a price today before the score between us is settled.'

Twice again Du Plessis returned to parley with the Bushmen. Each time the number of warriors who received him was less, but their resolution remained. Seven Europeans fell to the whizzing arrows until at last a storming party, protected by shields formed by their duffel coats, rushed the cave. The silence was final. No Bushman survived, and today the cave remains a place of memories, scarred by the marks of innumerable bullets.

The *Genadeberg* (mountain of grace) was named much later when a surveyor, M.C. Vos, scrambling up to erect a beacon, unsettled a rock which so narrowly missed the head of one of his assistants that it was considered an act of grace that the man escaped. The 2 209-m-high peak immediately east of the town is *Vegkop* (battle summit), originally known to the Sotho people as *Bloke* (stony). This was the stronghold of the chief Poshudi which, in 1849, was stormed by Lourens Wepener and his men in a bitter and bloody battle.

*Zastron* itself was named after the maiden name of the wife of President Brand (Miss Johanna Sibilla Zastron). The town was proclaimed in 1876 and today has a population of 4 337. The famous Renier du Wennaar died on 10 December 1883 at the ripe old age of 102. Some say, however, that he is still to be seen roaming the mountains and smokers are warned to beware of his pipe. His grave is shaded by a copse of trees on the outskirts of the town.

Cattle, maize, wheat and trade with Lesotho are the activities of the district.

## Accommodation
★ Maluti Hotel, 23 rooms, 11 with baths. R11,75 B/B. Phone 107.

## Caravans and camping
★★ ® Municipal caravan park, 30 sites. R1,50 D.

## Chapter Twenty-Seven

# VAAL TO THE LIMPOPO RIVER

The Vaal River, fully harnessed to the industries of man, is also a great recreational asset. Its water is naturally muddy but unpolluted by industry and, happily, completely free of the curse of bilharzia which makes the more tropical rivers of Africa dangerous to man. Anglers and boatmen frequent the river and its banks are lined with willow trees, waterside residences and pleasure resorts.

Where the Cape-to-Cairo road crosses the Vaal, yellowfish and barbel of large size can be caught, and travellers are rewarded with glimpses of canoeists, boatmen and aquaplaners. The Vesco Caravan Park, shaded by willows, lies just above the bridge.

**Accommodation**
★ Loch Vaal Hotel, 8 rooms, all with baths. R13 D/B/B. Phone 2471.

**Caravans and camping**
★ ® Vesco Caravan Park, 100 sites. R2,50 D.

Across the river, in the Transvaal, the road reaches a crossroads. Straight ahead the main road leads on to Johannesburg, passing the steelworks of the Iron and Steel Corporation. To the right the road continues up the banks of the river for a further 1,5 km, and then reaches a turnoff to . . .

## VANDERBIJLPARK

This town was born on the flat and treeless plains of the highveld in 1951, when the South African Iron and Steel Industrial Corporation (Iscor) erected a new steel foundry in the area. The township, which was to house the employees of this enterprise, was named after Dr H. J. van der Bijl, the chairman of the corporation. The place became a municipality on 29 October 1952, and today 101 440 people live there. Laid out on spacious modern lines and equipped with all the amenities – half a million trees have been planted to beautify its streets – Vanderbijlpark is a classic example of an industrial township of the 20th century.

**Accommodation**
★★★ Holiday Inn, 170 rooms, all with baths. R20 – R24 room only. Phone 31-1810.
★★ Killarney Hotel, 45 rooms, 25 with baths. R9 – R16 B/B. Phone 33-4021.
★ Park Hotel, 73 rooms, 22 with baths. R8,50 B/B. Phone 33-4821.
★ Van Riebeeck Hotel, 47 rooms, 18 with baths. R8 – R8,50 B/B. Phone 33-4461.

The tarmac road continues eastwards for 10 km from the turnoff to Vanderbijlpark, and then enters the industrial town of . . .

## VEREENIGING

In 1878 the geologist and author, George Stow, discovered coal on the farm *Leeuwkuil*, on which Vereeniging stands today. These so-called Vaal Valley Coalfields were rapidly exploited by a company floated by Isaac Lewis and Samuel Marks, which was given the imposing name of *De Zuid Afrikaansche en Orange Vry Staatsche Kolen en Mineralen Myn Vereeniging* (The South African and Orange Free State Coal and Mineral Association).

At the same time, the railway line from the south was under construction and had reached what was known as Viljoen's Drift, directly opposite the site of the future town. The latter was already starting to grow as a centre for coal miners and as a railhead, for there was a delay before the Transvaal republican government completed the link from the Vaal to the Witwatersrand. The first train completed this journey from the south through Vereeniging to the Rand on 15 September 1892.

The town at the bridge across the Vaal was named *Vereeniging* (association or union) because it was there that the Cape, Orange Free State and Transvaal joined hands through the medium of the railway.

Vereeniging was richly endowed for an industrial town, and record prices were paid at the sale of the first erven on 29 April 1892. Not only were coal and water in plentiful supply in the vicinity, but there was also glacial conglomerate to provide fire clay, dolomite for calcium and lime, black reef to supply silica, and excellent quarry stone for building purposes. The railway provided transport and it was even proposed at one time that steel barges be used to carry coal down the Vaal to the point nearest to Kimberley.

Vereeniging today has a population of 122 325, and is the centre of considerable industry. With an estimated reserve of 4 000 million tons of high-grade coal in the area, coal mining is a major activity; mines, such as the Cornelia Colliery produce over four million tons each year. An entire battery of giant thermal power stations – Highveld, Klip, Taaibos, Vereeniging and Vaal – cluster around the coal mines and the landscape is festooned in every direction with high-tension grids carrying power to the Witwatersrand and to busy industries.

The town of Vereeniging is itself the venue for diverse industrial activity. The Vereeniging Brick and Tile Company, the Union Steel Corporation (which produced South Africa's first steel ingot in 1913), the McKinnon Chain Company, African Cables Ltd, Stewarts and Lloyds, Massey-Ferguson, and the South African Farm Implement Manufacturers Ltd, are among the substantial industrial concerns, which produce a wide variety of heavy and light industrial items in Vereeniging.

Situated on the Vaal, midway between the Barrage and Vaal Dam, the town is also a popular resort. The river is broad and deep, lined with fine willow trees on its banks, which offer many pleasant sites for campers and picnickers. Boating, swimming, aquaplaning and fishing are all pastimes to be enjoyed along the tranquil course of the great Vaal River. An interesting little museum can be visited in the town.

### Accommodation
* Central Hotel, 42 rooms, all with baths. R7,50 B/B. Phone 22-1471.
* Hilton Hotel, 28 rooms, 9 with baths. R7 – R8 B/B. Phone 22-1904.
* Maxime Hotel, 28 rooms, 9 with baths. R7,50 – R8,50 B/B. Phone 4-2041.
* National Hotel, 52 rooms, 14 with baths. R7 – R8 B/B. Phone 22-4401.
** Riviera Hotel, 54 rooms, 22 with baths. R8,50 – R16,50 B/B. Phone 22-0033.
* Royal Hotel, 25 rooms, 8 with baths. R6 – R7 B/B. Phone 22-0521.

### Caravans and camping
**® Dickinson Park, 150 sites. R2 D.

Continuing due north from Vereeniging, 3 km on, the main tarmac road reaches a large traffic circle from which branch roads radiate to industrial areas such as Duncanville and Unitas Park, and to the town of . . . .

# MEYERTON

With a population of 18 574 Meyerton lies 8 km east of the Vereeniging road. First proclaimed in November 1841, the town was named after Jan Meyer, then the Witwatersrand member of the Volksraad. The place is now a busy maize and industrial centre.

## Accommodation
* ★ Meyerton Hotel, 17 rooms, 6 with baths. R7 – R9 B/B. Phone 2-1448.

After the turnoff to Meyerton, the main tarmac road leads on northwards into the hills of the *Gatsrand* (ridge of caves). Smallholdings – vegetable, dairy and poultry farms – line the roadside and the subtle change in atmosphere – it might be described as the 'body odour' – makes one sense the approach to a great city. At 18 km from Vereeniging the road passes through the small centre of *De Deur* (the door), then climbs easily over the heights of the Gatsrand and descends into the valley of the *Klip* (stony) River, crossing the river at Jackson's Drift, 39,5 km from Vereeniging. The shallow valley is grassy and fertile. In former years it was a great area for transport men who brought loads of everything imaginable to the booming Witwatersrand, and grazed their draught animals in the valley. More than 1 000 wagons reached Johannesburg each week and the demand for grass and water was insatiable. At Jackson's Drift itself a man named Jackson opened a small store and hostelry; today there is still a hotel and resort there. Near by a miller named Wienand once had a watermill with a great lumbering wheel. The watermill has long since vanished. The area is now known as Eikenhof.

## Accommodation
* ★ Lido Travel Lodge, 15 rooms, 14 with baths. R6,50 – R7,50 B/B. Phone 943-4413.

Across the Klip River, the main road confronts the long rise of the *Witwatersrand* (the ridge of white waters), the lid of one of the world's richest geological and mineral treasure chests. The main tarmac road makes its way up the heights of the Witwatersrand, following the course of a tributary stream of the Klip River. After 4 km the road passes the Safari Caravan Park and at 6,5 km the Meredale Caravan Park.

## Caravans and camping
* ★★★ Safari Caravan Park, 75 sites. R2,50 D plus 50c D per person.
* ★★★ Meredale Pleasure Resort, 60 sites. R2,50 D.

Eight kilometres from the Klip River crossing (46,5 km from Vereeniging), the road reaches a junction with the Diamond Way, from the Cape to Johannesburg which has made its way north through Kimberley and the Western Transvaal.

The road is now on the heights of the Witwatersrand, on the outskirts of Johannesburg at Baragwanath, an area named after John Baragwanath who, in the early days of Johannesburg, owned a small but celebrated hostelry (the Concordia Hotel), which stood at the junction of the roads. Baragwanath's son, Orlando, was one of a greathearted company of prospectors in Southern Africa, and, together with Fred Lewis, he was the first to peg the Copper Belt of modern Zambia. The Baragwanath Hospital for Non-Europeans is one of the largest and most modern hospitals in the Southern Hemisphere.

From its entrance into Johannesburg at Uncle Charlie's Roadhouse until it leaves the built-up area of the city at the Johannesburg Drive-In the Cape-to-Cairo road becomes a spectacular 26-km-long freeway which passes at some places over the roof of the city and at others cuts deep into the ground. There are many spectacular views of Johannesburg; but the story of this great mining city and that of the Witwatersrand are told in separate chapters (see chapters 28 and 29).

*Overleaf: North of the Soutpansberg stretches a mighty parkland where the brachystegia tree is queen, adorned with spring leaves of every shade – brown, plum, scarlet, green.*

The Cape-to-Cairo road leaves Johannesburg and, as the magnificent dual carriageway known as the Ben Schoeman Highway, leads northwards, gradually losing altitude as it crosses undulating, grassy country with pleasant views of the Magaliesberg range of mountains to the north-west. Several streams make their way beneath the road and among them is the *Jukskei* (yoke key) along whose course the first tantalising traces of gold on the Witwatersrand were found by Pieter Marais in 1853. The fine Ben Schoeman Highway, named after a former minister of transport, is beautifully located and built, but shamefully ill-used by some of the most irresponsible, idiotic and abusive drivers to be found anywhere on earth. Youths use this highway as a missile track and, for some reason, before the fuel crisis the authorities allowed a speed limit of 130 km an hour on parts of the road. As a result there were 18,4 deaths for every 100 accidents – the worst record for any highway on the continent of Africa. Recent speed restrictions imposed as a result of the fuel crisis have improved matters.

Thirty kilometres from Johannesburg there is a turnoff to the small centre known as Halfway House, where a cluster of shops, garages and a hotel stands on the site of an old staging post of the original coach service. In summer the countryside here is extremely pleasant; the roadside farms produce fine crops of peaches, plums and other deciduous fruit and, along with eggs, honey, cream and homemade jams, these edibles are sold to passing travellers from stands and kiosks.

### Accommodation

★ Halfway House Hotel, 18 rooms, 6 with baths. R7,50 – R8,50 B/B. Phone 805-2319.

At 8,5 km north of the turnoff to Halfway House, there is a parting of the ways: the Ben Schoeman Highway continues for a further 20 km, culminating in a grand approach to Pretoria, 58 km from Johannesburg (the story of Pretoria is told in chapter 29); and the Cape-to-Cairo road swings off to bypass Pretoria. After 6,5 km it reaches a turnoff to . . .

## VERWOERDBURG, LYTTELTON, IRENE AND DOORNKLOOF

Verwoerdburg was created in 1964 as a municipality by merging the townships and municipalities of Doornkloof, Irene and Lyttelton. The combined municipality has a population of 48 642. The 20 000-ha area received the name of Verwoerdburg in honour of the then Prime Minister of South Africa, Dr Hendrik Verwoerd, who was assassinated in 1966. Lyttelton, established in 1904, was named after General Lyttelton. It soon became a popular residential area for people working in Pretoria, who found its rural atmosphere relaxing. Two large country clubs, Zwartkop and Irene, provide recreation. The Waterkloof Air Force Station is in the immediate vicinity of Lyttelton.

Irene was named after the daughter of a well-known figure in the days of the South African Republic, a Hungarian named Alois Nellmapius, who promoted various industrial and property developments, including a block of nine model farms at Irene. In addition to being a residential area, Irene is also the centre of the South African film production industry.

*Doornkloof* was the farm of Field Marshal Jan Christian Smuts until his death in 1950. His ashes, and those of his wife Isie, are scattered on the nearby Smuts Koppie. The house is now a museum containing the original furniture and many personal belongings of a politician and soldier of world stature. The museum is open to visitors daily from 09h00 to 12h00 and, from 14h00 to 16h30, except on Christmas Day and Good Friday.

Four kilometres beyond the turnoff to Verwoerdburg there is a turnoff to Kempton Park and Pretoria; two kilometres further on a turnoff leads to the Pretoria suburb of Waterkloof; and after 8,5 km the road reaches a traffic interchange with the eastern highway to Komatipoort and Moçambique. This crossing is 53 km from the centre of Johannesburg.

The Cape-to-Cairo road continues on its sweeping way north. After 3 km a turnoff branches to the Pretoria suburbs of Waverley and East Lynn, after 7 km to Wonderboom and Cullinan and at 18 km to Pyramid and Walmansthal.

To the north, the road now traverses a most interesting geological area. With a far mountain rim still out of sight, fully 100 km away, this acacia-covered plain seems boundless. To the untrained eye it is merely an immense and completely flat plain, but to the discerning scientist this landscape is a lopolith on a colossal scale, known as the Bushveld Igneous Complex. Its formation was spectacular . . .

## THE BUSHVELD IGNEOUS COMPLEX

About 600 million years ago a considerable disturbance occurred beneath the surface of this part of the world. In between the sedimentary layers of the Transvaal System a molten mass of magmatic material intruded, consisting of a mixture of dark-coloured basic rocks (which carry platinum, chromite, nickel and iron), and later a reddish acid granite which carries tin and tungsten.

As this material forced its way into the subterranean layers of the Transvaal System it was fluid and soft. The centre of the overlying landscape subsided into this undermining fluid, much as the lead in a pot subsides when heated from below. A gigantic flat-bottomed basin formed (a lopolith) whose rim consisted of remnants of the original high-lying Transvaal System, now in the form of an encircling chain of mountains known in its various parts as the Magaliesberg, Strydpoort, etc. This mountain rim dips inward towards the basin, whose floor is extraordinarily flat; below it the lopolith, shaped by the weight and pressure of the intrusive magma, takes the form of the bulging curve of a convex lens pointing down into the depths. This is the Bushveld Igneous Complex, famous for its succession of rock types and associated ore deposits. It also has a small, beautifully preserved volcanic crater (the Pretoria Salt Pan) which was blown into the lopolith by minor volcanic activity; the pan is filled with a commercially valuable mud impregnated with chloride and carbonate of soda.

At 37 km there is a turnoff to the small centre of *Hammanskraal,* where a road branches off west to the Pretoria Salt Pan. Hammanskraal was named after an individual who built a corral there in the old days to protect his cattle against lions. This area was always frequented by lions and right up until the 1930s an occasional lion still hunted the thornbush. There are numerous stories of desperate adventures with these lions and quite a number of early travellers vanished without trace in the course of traversing what was known as the Springbok Flats. Today groundnuts and maize replace much of the thornbush and a tall grain elevator at Pienaars River (57 km) is one of the principal landmarks in the flat landscape.

The Springbok Flats is the home of the interesting and colourfully dressed Ndebele tribe and on the old road to Pretoria from Pienaars River there is a *papatso* (market place) where curios and arts and crafts made by the Ndebele can be purchased.

### Accommodation
★ Pienaars River Hotel, 16 rooms, 5 with baths. R8,50 – R10 B/B. Phone 1.

At 93 km from Pretoria, the Cape-to-Cairo road reaches a group of boarding houses, hotels, cafés and shops at . . .

## WARMBATHS

Jan Grobler and Carl van Heerden were hunting in this area one winter when they noticed a cloud of vapour rising in the cold air. They rode to the spot, and found a powerful hot spring (22 730 ℓ an hour, at a temperature of 62° C) bubbling to the surface amid a morass of soggy vegetation. The spring was later found to have been a death trap for numerous wild animals, for when it was cut open, a vast accumulation of skeletons – including those of elephants – were recovered from the mud.

The Sotho tribespeople knew the area as *Bela Bela* (the boiling place). The two European discoverers of the hot spring settled in the vicinity of what first became known as Het Bad. Carl van Heerden established a farm around the hot spring, draining the swamp with a furrow and cleaning out the morass. People with ailments began to arrive to take the waters, camping and digging their own baths in the mud, which they encircled with screening shelters of reeds and blankets.

The baths soon attained considerable renown, and became as popular in the Transvaal as the Caledon baths in the Cape. In 1873 President Burgers visited the place and considered it so great a national asset that he persuaded his Volksraad to purchase the area of the baths which from then on came under state control. Little development took place in the area for another ten years. Then it was surveyed by the government and the hot springs were proclaimed as 'public baths'. They were enclosed and roofed, and a township was laid out on an adjacent farm. But the township site proved unpopular; hotels and boarding houses were built closer to the baths, and eventually the present town of Warmbaths was laid out, receiving its first health committee in 1921. Today 9 080 people live in the town.

The hot baths have been fully developed and over 260 000 people visit them each year, not only for health reasons but also for the pleasure (especially in winter) of swimming in the fine hot water – 32° C – swimming bath. Medicinally, the springs are rich in sodium chloride, calcium carbonate and other chemicals. They are also slightly radio-active. Anything immersed in the water is subjected to a degree of irradiation and visitors are confident that the baths have a definite effect on them, especially after a course of the waters lasting at least two weeks, when what the Germans describe as 'bath reaction' is very marked. Devotees believe that taking the water is beneficial in cases of rheumatism and other arthritic ailments. The Warmbaths hospital has a special institute for rheumatic research, developed by the Transvaal Provincial Council in conjunction with the baths.

Wheat, groundnuts, maize and citrus are the products of the district. Commerce in the town itself is principally orientated towards catering for visitors to the hot springs.

The Warmbaths swimming bath is open from 07h00 to 12h45 and from 14h00 to 16h45 daily. Admission for adults is 40c and for children 20c; private baths 40c; de luxe baths 90c; mud baths R2,50.

### Accommodation
★ Browns Hotel, 39 rooms, 20 with baths. R9,50 B/B. Phone 9.
★ Grand Hotel, 28 rooms, all with baths. R11 B/B. Phone 352.
★ Warmbaths Hotel, 66 rooms, 34 with baths. R11 – R12 B/B. Phone 427.
★ White House Hotel, 23 rooms, 12 with baths. R10,50 B/B. Phone 15.

### Caravans and camping
★ ® Mineral Baths Caravan Park, 400 sites. R2,10 D. 52 flats and 35 chalets, R8,50 – R17,20 D.

Veering in a north-easterly direction from Warmbaths, the Cape-to-Cairo road finds a scenically striking way through the tree-covered foothills of the *Waterberg* (water mountain). Several shady resting places are located along this stretch of the road. An arresting landmark 8 km from Warmbaths is the 1 308-m-high Buyskop. A story is told of this height. A group of followers of the notorious outlaw, Coenraad de Buys, was once attacked in the region and retreated to the hilltop, where they withstood a stubborn siege. Days passed and their food and water supplies approached exhaustion. Suspecting, however, that the besiegers were also suffering privations in the summer heat, the leader of the Buys party, in sheer bravado, scaled a vantage point atop the cliffs and from there taunted the besiegers by offering them his last skin bag of water. When the besiegers sent a man up the slopes to collect the bag, the leader insolently threw it at his head. This apparent proof of plentiful water supplies on the summit dispirited the besiegers so much that they withdrew, leaving the Buys party to continue their journey in peace.

Immediately beyond Buyskop is a turnoff east to the railway station of *Eersbewoond* (first habitation) and the Loskop Dam. The road then continues through the foothills, past the Klein Kariba holiday resort (11,5 km from Warmbaths) and the Valhalla Motel, 19,5 km from Warmbaths.

### Accommodation
★ Klein Kariba Hotel, 24 rooms, all with baths. R7,50 – R9 B/B. Phone Warmbaths 571.
★ Floyd's Valhalla Motel, 19 rooms, all with baths. R9,85 B/B. Phone Warmbaths 44.

### Caravans and camping
★® Floyd's Valhalla Motel, 90 sites. R3 D.
★ Ronwil Caravan Park, 50 sites. R3 D.

The Cape-to-Cairo road crosses the upper reaches of the Nylstroom, which the Voortrekkers mistook for the headwaters of the Nile (hence the name), and 31 km from Warmbaths, reaches the town on the banks of that river . . .

# NYLSTROOM

The principal centre of the fertile Waterberg area, this town was proclaimed on 15 February 1866 and founded in 1867, when it was laid out on the farm *Rietvallei,* purchased from Ernest Collins. It slowly grew to be an agricultural centre and railway junction for the line to Vaalwater. The headquarters of the largest agricultural co-operative in the Transvaal, the N.T.K., is in Nylstroom, and the manufacture of peanut butter from the enormous local groundnut crop is an important industry. The town has a population of 8 952.

### Accommodation
★ Nylstroom Hotel, 18 rooms, all with baths. R9,50 B/B. Phone 36.

### Caravans and camping
★★® J. G. Strydom Park, 50 sites, R3,50 D plus 40c D per person.

The Cape-to-Cairo road continues from Nylstroom in a north-easterly direction along the foothills of the Waterberg. Fine trees provide shade along the undulating road, the scenery is pleasant and there are many wayside resting places. After 8 km the road passes the Stokkiesdraai Motel and, at 21 km, the Stork's Rest.

### Accommodation
★ Stokkiesdraai Motel, 50 chalets, all with bath or shower. R10 – R16 room only. Phone Nylstroom 792.

### Caravans and camping
★® Stokkiesdraai Motel, 100 sites. R3,50 D.

The road twists around the foothills. To the east, there is a good view of a famous landmark of the Springbok Flats, the 1 337-m Kranskop, which the Voortrekkers are reputed to have regarded as the remnant of a pyramid. Known to the local tribespeople as *Modimolle* (place of spirits) the mountain is thought to be a resort of ghosts and the taboo site of graves of ancient chiefs.

At 41,5 km from Nylstroom, the main road reaches the town of . . .

# NABOOMSPRUIT

This town, whose name means 'stream of euphorbia trees', is all red and green in colour. The rich, deep-red colour of the soil is perpetuated in the locally made building bricks, and the trees are vividly green. Fine jacarandas line the streets.

Naboomspruit has often been the butt of big-city newspaper jokes: for years it was considered the epitome of a South African dorp, and certainly in the 1920s it was an odd little town, complete with a private, patent narrow-gauge railway which ran for 34 km to Singlewood on the Springbok Flats. This railway, the creation of Major Frank Dutton, boasted a locomotive known as *Tshongololo* (the centipede) which could jack itself off the line, undergo a change of wheels, and take to the road to cope with an unscheduled service!

The Waterberg, behind the town, is a richly mineralised area. A discovery of tin made there in 1910 by a renowned local prospector, Adolph Erasmus, led to the founding of the town. The discoveries, made on the farms *Doornhoek* and *Welgevonden* attracted a rugged crowd of miners to the area. A collection of bars, stores and a gaol was erected to serve them at the nearest railway point. This centre grew until, in 1919, it became a village.

In 1925 Adolph Erasmus found platinum on the farm *Rietfontein* and the fresh influx of miners gave Naboomspruit the impetus to become a town. This was achieved in 1938, and today Naboomspruit has a population of 8 500.

In addition to mining, Naboomspruit is the centre for considerable farming activity. Maize, groundnuts and citrus flourish in the area. The original narrow-gauge railway was later converted to standard-gauge and extended to reach the enormous privately run citrus estate of Zebediela, 84 km away. Named after an Ndebele chief, Zebediela, the estate is today claimed to be one of the largest citrus producers in the world, with more than half a million trees bearing 60 000 tons of fruit each year.

The Waterberg has many beauty spots, streams, gorges, valleys and hot springs. The larger hot springs have been developed by various private enterprises; temperatures are about 39° C.

## Accommodation
★ Naboom Hotel, 16 rooms, 8 with baths. R7,50 – R8,50 B/B. Phone 126.

## Caravans and camping
★ Municipal caravan park, 20 sites. R2 D.

## MINERAL BATH RESORTS IN THE VICINITY OF NABOOMSPRUIT

★★ Constantia Mineral Spa, 110 rondawels, R9,50 – R19 D. 50 caravan sites, R4 D plus 50c D per person.

★★ Lekkerrus Mineral Baths, 97 rondawels, R5 – R10 D. 250 caravan sites, R2,50 D plus 35c D per person.

★★ Libertas Mineral Spa, 10 cottages and 69 rondawels, R7 – R16 D. 50 caravan sites, R3 D plus 25c D per person.

★★ Maroela Camp, 11 cottages, R9,50 D. 10 caravan sites, R3 D.

★★ Rondalia Spa, 200 rondawels, R7,50 – R17 D. 150 caravan sites, R4,50 D.

From Naboomspruit, the Cape-to-Cairo road continues north-eastwards along the foothills of the Waterberg. Trees shade many wayside resting places and travelling is pleasant. At 22 km from Naboomspruit there is the Fiesta Park Motel, which also has a caravan park. Eighteen kilometres further on the road reaches a picnic and resting place at a site of poignant memories, *Moorddrif* (the ford of murder), where the road bridges across the Nylstroom.

Moorddrif was the scene of a gory event which took place in September 1854. Two Voortrekker parties, totalling 33 people, were travelling in the area with Hermanus Potgieter, when they were attacked at Moorddrif and slaughtered by the local Tlou tribespeople. What started the massacre will never be known, but once it began, the murderers made a particularly brutal job of things. Then, realising the inevitability of retribution, the 2 000 Tlou tribespeople fled for safety into the depths of a prodigious cave known today as *Makapans-gat*, after their chief Makapane. What befell them there is told on page 548.

## Accommodation
* Fiesta Park Motel, 20 rooms, 12 with baths. R7,25 – R9,25 B/B. Phone 5641.

## Caravans and camping
* Fiesta Park Motel, 18 sites. R2 D plus 50c D per person.

Immediately across the Nylstroom which is known to the tribespeople as the *Mohalakwena*, meaning 'place of fierce crocodiles', the Cape-to-Cairo road reaches a branch leading eastwards to Groblersdal (124 km), the Loskop Dam, Middelburg and down to Natal. This all-tarmac route is much favoured by travellers from Zimbabwe as it avoids the congestion of Pretoria and the Witwatersrand.

Eleven kilometres beyond this turnoff (51 km from Naboomspruit), the Cape-to-Cairo road enters the town of . . .

# POTGIETERSRUS

*Pieter Potgietersrus,* to give this place its original name, was named in memory of Commandant-General Pieter Potgieter who was killed at Makapansgat while directing a punitive attack on the tribespeople responsible for the massacre at Moorddrif. The town was founded on 25 September 1858 and today it is a busy and modern little place, with a population of 9 830. Its residential streets are shaded by handsome trees and its gardens overflow with bougainvillaea, poinsettia and jacarandas, all of which thrive in the warm and well-watered climate.

The town lies on the floor of a wooded pass which provides the national road and the branch road into the north-western Transvaal bushveld with an easy natural route through the Waterberg. The centre for a considerable industry in tobacco production, Potgietersrus has huge sheds for sorting, grading and packing the leaves. Groundnuts, sunflowers, castor oil plants, cotton, rice, citrus, maize, kaffircorn and wheat also flourish in the region, while the north-western bushveld is a major cattle ranching area.

Thirty-seven kilometres from Potgietersrus is the Zaaiplaats tin mine and its refinery.

The Arend Dieperink Museum, named after its founder, is one of the finest small town museums in Southern Africa and is well worth a visit. Its aloe garden contains more than 4 000 plants of 212 different species. They flower in about June and July.

## Accommodation
** Jones Hotel, 21 rooms, 14 with baths. R10 – R13,50 B/B. Phone 1281.
* Orinoca Hotel, 46 rooms, 14 with baths. R9 – R10,50 B/B. Phone 901.

**Caravans and camping**

★★ Municipal caravan park, 25 sites. R2 D.

Beyond Potgietersrus, the Cape-to-Cairo road makes its way up the long valley which provides a route through the mountains. At 3 km from the town there is a turnoff to the Percy Fyfe Nature Reserve. Fourteen kilometres from the town a gravel turnoff stretches for 11,5 km to the celebrated caves of . . .

# MAKAPANSGAT

These extraordinary limestone caverns lie on the private farm of Mr G. R. Peppercorn, whose homestead is passed on the way to the caves; his permission must be obtained in order to visit them. The gravel road terminates at a gate. Beyond this point a rough track leads for about 2 km to the entrance of the caves, which lie in a wild and beautiful ravine whose slopes are covered in aloes, euphorbias, and forest trees. To the right the valley is bordered by a high cliff of red sandstone. This rugged and primeval setting was the scene of sanguinary events which were climactic in the history of the caves.

The caves themselves are colossal and only when one enters them can one fully appreciate their size. The two main entrances, one below the other, slope into each other and huge chambers branch off from them into the depths. Stone barricades, ashes of long-dead fires and sinister memories are all that remain in the caves from the days of the siege.

Much excavated by archaeologists, the caves have yielded many important discoveries, dating as far back as the Upper Chelles Acheul period, well below the level of the Early Stone Age. Man continued to discover and make use of these strange caverns after those distant days and, exploring them today, it is fascinating to visualise the long succession of primitive people who made their homes there.

After the Moorddrif massacre in 1854, the caverns became a stronghold for the Tlou tribe. With their leader (whose proper name was Makapane) these people retreated into the great caves, believing that the natural cave water and their stores of grain would see them through any siege.

A punitive commando led by Commandant-General Piet Potgieter, made its way to the cave and a grotesque struggle followed. The tribespeople fired from the impenetrable dark in the depths of the caves at anybody who appeared in the bright light at the 600-m by 150-m entrance. This fire was formidable: on 6 November 1854, Potgieter himself was shot dead by a sniper lurking in the shadows of the cave. The 29-year-old Paul Kruger (then a field cornet), was nearby and he dragged Potgieter's body away.

For 30 days the commando besieged the cave. Then a party of Europeans, observing that the defence had become notably weaker, stormed the cave. They found it to be a place of death, permeated by an overwhelming stench of putrefaction: some 1 500 tribespeople lay dead of starvation and thirst; only a handful had managed to slip away.

Once more the great cave was left to itself, and now only rock pigeons bill, coo and flutter through the shadows and the silence of Makapansgat . . .

From the gravel turnoff to Makapansgat, the Cape-to-Cairo road continues its easy climb to the plateau summit above the pass. Twenty-two kilometres from Potgietersrus the road reaches the summit of the rise and finds itself 1 279 m above sea level, on an open, grassy plateau with the high ridge of the Strydpoort mountains stretching off to the east.

Five kilometres further on (27 km from Potgietersrus) the road reaches a junction east, and the sign, Eersteling, is a reminder that travellers are passing through an interesting mining field; it was at Eersteling that the first gold rush in the Transvaal occurred. In 1871 Edward Button, a pioneer prospector from Natal, claimed a find of payable gold. The discovery did not prove to be significant but it attracted a flood of fortune-seekers to the Transvaal.

The old goldfield at Eersteling is worth visiting. It lies 4,5 km from the Cape-to-Cairo road in a superb setting backed by a range of mountains. It is a small field around a central hillock and the surrounding area is scarred with old adits, rubble dumps, rusting machinery, stamp bases, and the famous chimney. This chimney, built of imported Aberdeen granite, was the smoke stack of the Eersteling Mine. Once the tallest building in the Transvaal, it is a fine example of industrial architecture. A legend spread at the time that the chimney represented the strength of the British Empire and if the former could be pulled down the latter would collapse. During the Transvaal War of 1881 several local inhabitants tried to destroy the chimney using spans of oxen, but it survived and still stands today, a curiously elegant ruin.

As befits an old field, tales are told of hauntings. It is said that at certain times on particular days and nights, sounds of digging may be heard, although there is never any sign of work done; the clamour of nocturnal jollification is also sometimes heard. The old diggers were a happy breed even in their poverty, and one who enjoyed some luck would give a party. The sounds of merriment are said still to echo over the field, to the accompaniment of midnight sharings of bottles of Hollands Square-face Gin.

Five kilometres beyond the turnoff to Eersteling, the Great North Road of Africa (the Cape-to-Cairo road) passes the handsome grounds of the Ranch Motel.

### Accommodation
★★★® Ranch Motel, 61 rooms, all with baths. R8,50 – R18 room only. Phone Pietersburg 7-5377.

At 11 km beyond the Ranch Motel the road passes the turnoff south-east to Zebediela (40 km). Thirteen kilometres further on (a total of 64 km from Potgietersrus), the Cape-to-Cairo road enters the principal town of the Northern Transvaal . . .


# PIETERSBURG

Lying 1 280 m above sea level in a slight hollow (known to the Africans as *Pholokwane,* the protected place) amid an open, grass-covered plateau, the town originated on 11 November 1884 when the Volksraad approved the farm *Sterkloop* selected by Commandant-General Pieter Joubert, as the site of a new town. The farm was bought for £1 500 and on 31 July 1886 a magistracy was established there. The town, named after Pieter Joubert, gew rapidly, for the site was a natural centre for communications and agriculture in the Northern Transvaal.

A bright and modern town, decorated with flowering trees and pretty fountains, Pietersburg has a population of 79 000 and enjoys a considerable amount of commercial bustle. It is a major staging post on the road to the north, and along the scenic branch road which leads east over Magoebaskloof to Tzaneen and the Kruger National Park. Garages, hotels and shops line the Great North Road as it passes through the town, offering travellers the goods, fuel, repairs and refreshment they need to continue on their journey. The town has a nature reserve which shelters more than 1 000 head of game. There is an air force station west of the town. At the northern entrance to Pietersburg the verges of the Cape-to-Cairo road have been converted into a gallery of industrial sculptures similar in concept to Frogner Park in Oslo. Various artists have created some very unusual looking pieces, using improbable material such as steel pipes, old railway sleepers and diverse pieces of scrap metal. The results are diverting. A collection of about 250 paintings is housed in the civic centre, including work by many of South Africa's leading artists. Silica quartz is mined at Witkop, on the outskirts of the town, and silicon metal is produced in large quantities.

Accommodation
** Great North Road Hotel, 50 rooms, 25 with baths. R15 D/B/B. Phone 7-1031.
** Holiday Inn, 132 rooms, all with baths. R18 – R24 room only. Phone 6585.

Caravans and camping
** Union Park, 50 sites. R3 D.

The Cape-to-Cairo road continues northwards from Pietersburg, descending gently off the plateau and entering an area which becomes increasingly heavily bushed with stunted acacia trees. The road passes through a cluster of hillocks and, 40 km after leaving Pietersburg, the traveller sees ahead of him, in the haze of the northern horizon 72 km away, the long line of the Soutpansberg range.

Fifty-one kilometres from Pietersburg the road passes through an assembly of small granite domes, a foretaste for the traveller to the north of the enormous granite domes the road must pass in Zimbabwe. These granite domes are disfigured by idiots daubing their initials on them and a gentleman from the public works has to be frequently employed there with ladder and paint remover.

An important milestone is passed 61 km from Pietersburg: the Tropic of Capricorn, indicated by a sign at the point where it crosses the road. Immediately ahead a forest of magnificent euphorbia trees serves to emphasise the great changes in the vegetation as the road leads on into warmer and lower-lying regions.

Seventy-two kilometres from Pietersburg a tarmac turnoff stretches east to Soekmekaar (22 km) and Tzaneen (97 km). Five kilometres further on, the road crosses the railway near by the small centre of Bandelierkop.

The 1 171-m-high hillock of that name is immediately to the east of the road. Six kilometres beyond Bandelierkop lies the Lalapanzi Motel and 11 km further on (95 km from Pietersburg) is the Adams Apple Motel with caravan park.

Accommodation
* Bandelierkop Hotel, 12 rooms, 3 with baths. R8,50 – R9,50 B/B. Phone 10.
** Lalapanzi Motel, 18 rooms, all with baths. R5,50 – R9 room only. Phone Wilharsin 9901.
* Adams Apple Motel, 27 rooms, all with baths. R7,50 room only. Phone Louis Trichardt 4117.

Caravans and camping
* Adams Apple Caravan Park, 20 sites. R1 D.

The Cape-to-Cairo road reaches the southern slopes of the Soutpansberg range 113 km from Pietersburg, and then enters the pleasant little town of . . .

# LOUIS TRICHARDT

Set in an extremely beautiful situation, backed by the Soutpansberg range, this town has a warm climate, 940 mm of rain a year and rich soil all of which combine to produce a green and congenial environment, inhabited by 14 115 people.

The history of this area is singularly romantic. In the year 1836, two advance parties of Voortrekkers reached the Soutpansberg. The first party, under Johannes van Rensburg, pushed on eastwards, hoping to reach a Portuguese trading port. Somewhere in the bush, they were massacred.

The second party, under Louis Trichardt, camped somewhere near by the site of the modern town. They planted crops and made exploratory journeys into what is now Zimbabwe and also to the east in search of the lost Van Rensburg party. In a valley in the Soutpansberg, at Mara, Louis Trichardt and his followers discovered a community of Coloured offspring of the renowned frontier adventurer named Coenraad de Buys, who had made his home there in about 1820.

Trichardt and his followers left the Soutpansberg in September 1837 in an attempt to reach Lourenço Marques (now Maputo). This venture cost most of them their lives. Later, other pioneers followed Trichardt's trail to the Soutpansberg and in 1847 a renowned leader, Hendrik Potgieter, explored the area and selected the site of a town which became known as Zoutpansbergdorp.

At that time, the area of the Northern Transvaal was teeming with game animals. Zoutpansbergdorp, the northernmost town of the Transvaal, became a base for the ivory trade and an unruly crowd of hunters and traders made the place their home. After the death of Hendrik Potgieter in 1852, the town fell under the control of Stephanus Schoeman, who married the widow of Potgieter's son (who was killed at Makapansgat). The town was renamed Schoemansdal and conditions there became chaotic. The incessant brawling, and the quarrels between ivory hunters and local African tribes culminated on 15 July 1867, when the town was abandoned by the Europeans and totally destroyed by the Venda tribespeople. Today nothing remains of the place other than piles of rubble and a few fruit trees growing wild in the bush.

For some years the surrounding area remained under the control of the Venda people of the Soutpansberg. Few Europeans ventured into the area and those who did, such as the famous safari trader, João Albasini, made their homes in private forts. It was only at the end of 1898, after a petty war with the Venda, that the Transvaal Republic regained control of the area. The modern town of Louis Trichardt was proclaimed as an administrative centre for the Soutpansberg on 15 February 1899. Today it serves as a centre for communication, administration, afforestation and large-scale vegetable farming.

Angling and boating can be enjoyed on the Albasini Dam, 20 km east of the town.

### Accommodation
★★ Clouds End Hotel, 40 rooms, all with baths. R9,50 B/B. Phone 9621.
★ Louis Hotel, 33 rooms, 10 with baths. R8,50 – R9,50 B/B. Phone 2715.

### Caravans and camping
★★® Municipal caravan park, 50 sites. R1,20 – R1,70 D plus 10c D per person.

Beyond Louis Trichardt, the Cape-to-Cairo road begins to climb the Soutpansberg range. The road finds a way up the southern slopes of the range over a winding and attractive scenic pass. The summit is reached 10 km from Louis Trichardt, and at this stage it is fitting to know something of . . .

## THE SOUTPANSBERG

This range takes its name, which means 'salt pan mountains', from a large salt pan lying at its western end. The pan has a powerful brine spring, and has been a source of salt for different tribes from prehistoric times.

The mountain range is slightly longer than 130 km and its highest point is the 1 753-m Lejume. Its composition is sedimentary – rather coarse, reddish-coloured sandstones, grits and conglomerates, part of the Waterberg System laid down about 400 million years ago.

The summit of the range is a fertile, well watered and healthily cool plateau which has proved attractive to human beings since very early times. Bushmen made their homes there and, about the beginning of the 18th century, a fragment of the Rozvi people of Zimbabwe wandered south and discovered the delights of this delectable range of mountains. They named them *Venda* (said to describe a pleasant area), ejected the Bushmen and settled there themselves to become the Venda people of today.

The Venda still live on their pleasant plateau atop the mountains. Their huts, the picturesque costumes of their women, their traditional way of life, may still be observed; at night their drums thud as young girls are put through the elaborate and prolonged rituals of puberty, including the famous *domba* (fertility) dance of the python.

In the Nzhelele valley are ruins of the Zimbabwe-style stone walls the Venda erected around their first settlement, Dzata. In the valley of the Mutale River lies the curiously sinister lake of Fundudzi, an old venue for tribal sacrifice, enveloped in superstition and reputedly the retreat of the python god of fertility. There are enchanted waterfalls such as Phipidi, named after a chieftainess and haunted forests, the latter said to be so full of ghosts that few men dare to venture through them. Magnificent walks can be taken through the forests and plantations as well as interesting climbs to the summits of peaks such as Hangklip (1 718 m), where lies the taboo burial ground of the early chiefs of the Venda tribe: the famed Maghato, the Lion of the North, and his son Mphephu. From the heights there are striking views of the flat bushland of the Northern Transvaal.

A worthwhile drive leads west from Louis Trichardt, past the site of Schoemansdal, now just a cemetery (15 km), as far as the western end of the range (73 km), where it joins the tarmac road from Pietersburg to Dendron. From here it is possible to drive on a gravel road for 71 km eastwards along the northern slopes of the range, past the salt pan and Waterpoort, to rejoin the Cape-to-Cairo road 33 km north of Louis Trichardt.

Sibasa, reached from the Louis Trichardt-Punda Malia road, is the administrative centre for the Venda tribal area. Permits must be obtained there for visits to the tribal area proper.

As has already been described after leaving Louis Trichardt (948 m above sea level), the Cape-to-Cairo road immediately commences its ascent of the southern slopes of the Soutpansberg, through the beautifully forested country of the Hangklip Forestry Reserve. Five kilometres from Louis Trichardt the road passes the well-wooded ground of the Clouds End Hotel. Eight kilometres from the town the road passes the Mountain Caravan Park, and 10 km from Louis Trichardt lies the Mountain Inn, right at the top of the pass.

At the top of the pass, 1 524 m above sea level, a gravel turnoff west is marked Bluegumspoort, 16 km. This is a beautiful drive along the summit ridge of the western Soutpansberg revealing a succession of charming rural scenes – only to be seen in Africa – of European farms and African tribal huts. Here are fine trees including one remarkable avenue-like stretch of tall bluegums, serene indigenous forests, and arresting views across the lowveld. The gravel road ends at a farm gate.

After the turnoff to Bluegumspoort, the Cape-to-Cairo road curves in to the heart of the Soutpansberg, passing the grounds of the Punch Bowl Hotel and Caravan Park (11 km from Louis Trichardt). The road then begins a circuitous and scenic descent into the central valley of the range. At 16 km from Louis Trichardt, the Ingwe Motel regards the view from a vantage point on the slopes; from here the road enters a final descent to the fertile valley floor, where citrus groves and farmlands flourish on the red soil. At 22 km from Louis Trichardt the Cape-to-Cairo road reaches the famed scenic pass known as Wylie's Poort. The old gravel road through the pass is still open, and the modern road burrows straight through the cliffs by means of the two Hendrik Verwoerd tunnels, opened on 18 November 1961. These two, the north 274 m long and the south 457 m long, were built after serious washaways destroyed the original pass in 1958.

## Accommodation

★ Ingwe Motel, 19 rooms, 15 with baths. R8,50 B/B. Phone 9687.
★★ Mountain Inn Hotel, 35 rooms, 27 with baths. R11,70 B/B. Phone 9631.
★ Punch Bowl Hotel, 18 rooms, all with baths. R8 B/B. Phone 9688.

Caravans and camping
* Mountain Inn Caravan Park, 16 sites. R1 D plus 10c D per person.
* Punch Bowl, 10 sites. R1 D.

# WYLIE'S POORT AND TSHIPISE

*Wylie's Poort* was named after Lieutenant C. H. Wylie, who located the original road to the north through it in 1904. To the Venda, the passage is known as *Manaledzi* (place of the stars). Before the deep gorge was blasted open to allow construction of the first road, its facing cliffs almost touched at the top. Baboons could jump across and it was said that from its depths the stars could be seen shining in the middle of the day. The yellow-coloured lichen high on the dark red sedimentary cliffs of Wylie's Poort gives a spectacular touch to an impressive and atmospheric mountain passage.

Immediately north of Wylie's Poort a gravel turnoff stretches east towards the Venda tribal lands. At 29 km from Louis Trichardt another turnoff leads west to Waterpoort (27 km) and a little place with the odd name of Alldays (97 km). The Cape-to-Cairo road now makes its way through a charmingly sylvan passage which leads out of the Soutpansberg and, 31 km from Louis Trichardt, into the northern bushveld. Children stand by the roadside selling seedpods of baobab trees, and the first baobab trees appear just after the road leaves Wylie's Poort.

The landscape is a gently undulating, densely bushed plain. Evergreen mopane trees replace thorny acacia as the predominant species and the botanical world is dominated by the wonderful baobab trees, which are carefully protected here. The Cape-to-Cairo road continues northwards through this parkland. At 39 km from Louis Trichardt there is a turnoff to the Njelele Dam (22 km). This dam, completed in 1948, has a storage capacity of 31 million cubic metres and irrigates 1 867 ha of farmland. Nineteen kilometres further on is the tarmac turnoff to the well-known Tshipise Mineral Bath (31 km). The name *Tshipise* is a Venda word meaning hot spring. A popular resort, under the same administration (the Transvaal Board of Public Resorts) as Warmbaths, Tshipise makes an agreeable stopover for the travellers who have the time. The spring which yields 227 306 l a day at a temperature of 65° C, has been attractively developed in a fine natural parkland of acacias and baobab trees. Poincianas (flamboyants), jacarandas, frangipani and bougainvillaea flourish in the area. The spring is open daily from 07h00 to 12h45 and from 14h00 to 17h45. Adults 50c, children 30c; private baths 30c. Near by, on the farm *Nonsiang,* there is a particularly huge baobab – 25,9 m tall and 19,2 m in circumference. It is estimated to be about 4 500 years old and contains about 181 840 l of water.

At Tshipise are shops, a restaurant, butchery, post office and bank.

Accommodation
* Tshipise Hotel, 36 rooms, 9 with baths. R7,70 B/B. Phone 15.

Caravans and camping
** ® 400 sites. R3,60 D plus 40c D per person. 150 rondawels, R4,60 – R16,50 D.

From the turnoff to the Tshipise springs, 60 km from Louis Trichardt, the Cape-to-Cairo road continues for a further 34 km through a fine parkland of mopane and baobab trees. Then, 90 km from Louis Trichardt, the road enters the mining centre of . . .

# MESSINA

This town takes its name in corrupted form from *Musina* (the spoiler), the word used by early

African miners to describe copper, which they found intruding into the iron ore they were smelting. From prehistoric times the area of Messina has been the scene of mining activity and today, in addition to being the largest copper producer in South Africa, the Messina district also produces substantial amounts of iron ore, magnesite and asbestos. The town itself has a population of 10 507.

The Messina area is rich with relics of prehistoric people. In the valley of the Limpopo River stand several flat-topped segments of an ancient eroded plain. To early man, these isolated, steep-sided hillocks made natural strongholds and his paintings, on the walls of caves, old barricades, fortifications and piles of rubble, provide archaeologists with a valuable field of study. One of these hillocks, *Mapungubwe* (place of the jackal), was a stronghold of the long-vanished Leya tribe and now it remains a taboo place of many strange legends and superstitions. To archaeologists it has proved to be a veritable mountain of treasure, having yielded beads, bangles, ornaments and plate – all of gold. Mapungubwe is 72 km west of Messina, near the junction of the Shashi and Limpopo rivers. It is an interesting drive through well-wooded ranching country. Near Mapungubwe is another notable hill, *Matshete,* and the hot springs at Evangelina.

By the time Europeans appeared on the scene, the area of modern Messina was covered with bric-à-brac from primitive mining activities – adits, shafts and rubble dumps were numerous. The early miners, known as the Musina people, used their women as labourers; utilising iron tools fastened on to wooden handles, ladders made of thongs, and haulage systems consisting of baskets attached to leather thongs, they could work as far down as the water level, after which they were forced to dig new shafts as they had no pumps or pipes with which to drain their mines.

The ore from the mines was broken by hammers, winnowed in baskets and then placed in furnaces fanned by bellows made of skins. The molten metal – iron or copper – was poured into moulds scooped out of the ground and generally shaped somewhat like a cooking pot, with a cluster of small legs at the bottom. These strangely-shaped ingots were standard trade items, accepted all over South Africa and hammered by smiths into a variety of tools and ornaments.

In the 1880s a prospector in Zimbabwe, John Pasco Grenfell, met a renowned hermit known as Wild Lotrie, who told him of the group of disused primitive mines at Messina. The Anglo-Boer War delayed explorations but in 1901 Grenfell visited the site, guided by Magushi, last known survivor of the Musina tribe. A quick inspection of the workings made Grenfell certain that he was on the surface of a great copper deposit long since abandoned by the primitive miners.

At the end of the Anglo-Boer War, Grenfell organised a company and sent a prospecting expedition led by Everard Digby to examine the Messina area thoroughly. Their findings staggered the expedition members: the farm *Bergenrode,* on the Sand River, was, as they described it in a report, 'a veritable mountain of copper . . . there must be millions of tons of copper'.

On 11 March 1904 Grenfell secured a 'discoverer's certificate' for the first claims pegged in the Messina area and in January 1905 the Messina (Transvaal) Development Company Limited was established to mine the area. The road from Louis Trichardt through Wylie's Poort to Messina was opened in 1907 and from then on the Messina area developed. At first the copper ore was carried south in ox wagons, but when the railway reached Messina from the south on 4 May 1914 the improved transportation enabled production at the copper mines to be increased to a high level.

The village of Messina, the residential and trading centre for the workers, grew with the mines. In 1915 a health committee was formed and on 1 December 1968 Messina became a municipality. The town is notable for its beautiful poinciana (flamboyant) trees, which flower in spring. Just outside the town, on the road to Malala Drift, a wonderful old baobab tree grows, known from the shape of one of its branches as the Elephant's Trunk baobab. It is preserved in a special little park named after Eric Mayer, a well-known painter of baobabs.

## Accommodation
* Impala Motel, 32 rooms, all with baths. R8,75 B/B. Phone 542.
* Limpopo Inn, 23 rooms, 15 with baths. R8,25 – R10,25 B/B. Phone 128.
* Messina Hotel, 23 rooms, 15 with baths. R5 – R5,50 B/B. Phone 425.

## Caravans and camping
** Municipal caravan park, 200 sites. R2 D plus 10c D per person.

The Cape-to-Cairo road continues northwards from Messina through densely wooded mopane country. A gentle incline leads for 16 km to the banks of the Limpopo River. Here the Beit Bridge, opened in 1929, and the customs posts of South Africa and Zimbabwe, mark the end of the South African section of the Great North Road, which has led all the way from Cape Town through 1 996 km of remarkably diverse scenery.

The customs post is open from 06h00 to 20h00 daily. Beyond it, across the 'great, grey-green, greasy Limpopo River' where, if Kipling is to be believed in his *Just So* story, the curious elephant received its trunk, there lies Zimbabwe and a long, long journey through the heart of Africa for those travellers with an urge to explore far places, to cross savanna and desert, to behold great rivers, mighty waterfalls, the snows of Kilimanjaro, vast herds of game, secret lakes full of flamingos – and at long last the shores of the Mediterranean.

## Chapter Twenty-eight

# JOHANNESBURG

Johannesburg, the golden metropolis of the Witwatersrand, and the largest city in Southern Africa, has a population of 1 416 700. Its history has been singular and romantic . . .

Before the discovery of gold, the site on which Johannesburg now stands was solitary and inhabited by a few farmers who barely managed to eke out a living, let alone entertain hopes of becoming wealthy. Agriculturally, the area was limited to the production of food crops such as maize and pumpkins. In summer the grazing was good, but winter (being frosty, windy and bleak), caused the grass to become brown and dormant. There was no town, market, post office or trading centre in the vicinity.

In the 1880s news concerning the discovery of gold in the Eastern Transvaal stirred up hope in every farmhouse in the Transvaal. Traces of gold had been found as early as 1853, in streams flowing off the watershed of the Witwatersrand and in 1884 a small mine was worked without much success on a farm named *Wilgespruit,* close to the site of Johannesburg. It was this little mine, however, which attracted two men, George Walker and George Harrison, who had journeyed from the Cape in search of fortune in the Eastern Transvaal.

Walker was given temporary work in the mine, while Harrison was employed in building a new homestead on the farm *Langlaagte.* Harrison spent his spare time prospecting and in March 1886, found an outcrop of the gold-bearing reef of the Witwatersrand.

The effect of his discovery on South Africa, was staggering. A mass of people converged on the area: prospectors, speculators, adventurers. The greatest gold rush ever known took place; all along the Witwatersrand tents and shelters were erected at such speed that parked vehicles would frequently be hemmed in by newly built shacks and owners, on their return, would be compelled to dismantle the wagons in order to extricate them!

Harrison travelled to Pretoria to report his find and to obtain the usual prospector's reward, the privileged tax-free 'Discoverer's Claim'. The government hardly had time to assess the situation before the flood of fortune-seekers arrived. Two commissioners, Johannes Rissik and Christian Johannes Joubert, were hastily appointed and dispatched to inspect the discovery and its implications. After all, the discovery could have been deceptive or superficial. A town could not be laid out simply on the basis of a report by an enthusiastic prospector.

Strangely enough, from the beginning, nobody expressed any real doubts about the permanence of the Witwatersrand. The two commissioners declared the farms along the line of reef as public diggings and F.C. Eloff, private secretary to the State President, Paul Kruger, was sent to find a central site suitable for a town.

Eloff rode over the area, gazing in wonder at the hodgepodge of humanity. Every day more people arrived on the scene. Off the actual reef Eloff found a vacant piece of ground, a government-owned farm named *Randjeslaagte* (dale of little ridges). It had never been considered important, but it was situated well away from the gold reef and, unwanted by the prospectors, would never be undermined by any workings. *Randjeslaagte* was chosen as the site of the town, surveyed as quickly as possible and the first 980 stands were auctioned on 8 December 1886. The site was named *Johannesburg* after the christian names of the two commissioners who had confirmed the substance of Harrison's discovery.

The first official building in Johannesburg was a shack erected to accommodate the patriarchal, white-bearded Carl von Brandis, sent there as a one-man government, magistrate, mining commissioner, tax gatherer, law enforcer and general administrative factotum of the goldfields.

In those days, life in Johannesburg was about as comfortable, private and quiet as being in the midst of a major construction site. Holes were being dug on every side, buildings were being erected or demolished. An appalling cloud of dust covered everything. Wagons rumbled in day and night bringing foodstuffs, mining tools, people and still more people.

The diamond diggings of Kimberley provided men during the first rush. As soon as the Witwatersrand discovery was confirmed, the diamond magnates raced to the area for concessions. Johannesburg automatically became the centre of their activities. Shacks fetched premium prices and offices and rough hotels charged small fortunes for accommodation.

The first hotel was the Central, consisting only of a bar, dining room and three bedrooms, but whose holding capacity was in some mysterious way, elastic. The Central Hotel was already in business when the two commissioners arrived from Pretoria to assess the gold discovery. They were welcomed at the hotel by a gathering of 250 financiers and the agents of several of the greatest financial houses in the world: Cecil Rhodes, J.B. Robinson (representing the Wernher Beit Company who in turn represented the Rothschilds) – all were there. A full list of those present even before the birth of Johannesburg reads like a who's who of the great speculators of the world.

In several unusual ways, Johannesburg quickly developed into a ready-made town. It was the age of corrugated iron, and traders moving to Johannesburg from other areas brought with them their stock and premises, the latter being dismantled and carried in pieces on wagons. In other South African towns, spaces began to appear along the commercial streets; buildings simply accompanied their owners in the rush to the golden city.

Even newspapers such as the *Star* transplanted, removing staff, press and accommodation from other centres (in this case from Grahamstown) to commence publishing in Johannesburg. Grog shops, canteens and bars sprang up like weeds and in an effort to counter the influence of these establishments, the government offered free stands for churches in the new town. Anglicans, Roman Catholics, Baptists, Presbyterians and the Salvation Army all hastened to the scene. Despite the fact that many Jews took part in the gold rush (Johannesburg was nicknamed 'New Jerusalem'), a rabbi only arrived to claim a stand long after the Christians did. It is said that President Paul Kruger at first granted the rabbi only half a stand because of his belief in only half the Bible!

Within 12 months, Johannesburg was the second largest town in the Transvaal, rapidly overtaking Barberton, then the biggest, with Pretoria the third largest. The delivery service of the first post office in the town consisted of a clerk who announced the names of addressees to an expectant crowd milling around the building. Joubert Park had been laid out as a recreational area and there was a morning market and hospital. Clubs – the Johannesburg Club and the Rand Club – appeared, as did a steady stream of entertainers, prize fighters, cardsharps and confidence tricksters to distract the public. There were 68 mining companies working in the vicinity of the town and the gold they produced attracted an astonishing assortment of people.

By 1889, Johannesburg was the largest town in Southern Africa. Each day, nearly a thousand ox wagons carried supplies to the goldfields. Stage coach services connected Johannesburg to the outside world, and one company, Hays & Co, used 38 coaches and 1 000 horses to maintain a daily express service to Kimberley.

By the end of 1889, 630 499 ounces of gold had been recovered from the Witwatersrand reef. Businesses were booming; a stock exchange had been founded; the Chamber of Mines was organised in April 1889 as the representative body for the mining industry; and workers were forming unions. The first strike, on 7 September 1889, aimed at achieving a 48-hour week as well as pay increases. Citizens began agitating for a municipality and direct representation in the government of the South African Republic.

To supply a rapidly growing city such as Johannesburg with services would have taxed any government. In 1890, drinking water was still supplied by a public company and the demand on the limited supplies was so great that taps yielded little more than a trickle of liquid mud. The transportation of goods was chaotic. Vast numbers of draught animals consumed all the grazing and the environment of Johannesburg, littered with the skeletons of numerous unfortunate oxen and horses which had died of starvation or overwork, began to resemble a desert. The projected railway to Johannesburg met with considerable opposition: transport riding had become a major industry, and the men working this service would be ruined by the railway. They had a powerful anti-train lobby in the Transvaal *Volksraad* (parliament) and every effort was made to stop the construction of a railway line.

The first railway service was surreptitiously introduced into the town under the guise of being a 'tram'. This line ran from Johannesburg to Springs, where coal was being mined. The rolling stock and rails were brought up by wagon from the coast to Johannesburg and the service was opened on 17 March before the opposition realised what was happening. However, as soon as the transport men learnt of events, they took action: on 8 May 1890 the puffing billy hauling the train collided violently with an ox wagon loaded with coal which had been deliberately outspanned across the line in order to wreck the service.

Despite opposition, however, the railway from the Cape reached Johannesburg on 15 September 1892, and there was great excitement when the first train arrived. The last stage coach to carry mail departed the next day, after which the trains took over.

For the first six years, an entire town and a considerable mining industry had been built and maintained by the carrying power of wagons and coaches. Bricks, timber, water, food, clothing, cumbersome machinery – all were brought to the town by thousands of stoic oxen, mules and horses. The story of these draught animals and the transport men who ran the service provides a romantic chapter in the history of South Africa.

The opening of the railway heralded a new epoch in Johannesburg. The tempo of its growth accelerated as a result of the greater carrying capacity of the trains. Amid the glitter of opulence now appearing, black and white miners laboured in primitive conditions and lived in bleak, company-provided accommodation, while the self-styled upper social strata – financiers, company promoters, businessmen, gamblers, swindlers, illicit gold buyers, thieves and prostitutes – lived in style and gave the town its ostentatious façade.

Gambling became a mania in Johannesburg. Pritchard Street was the main trading thoroughfare in those days, but the hub of the town was a portion of Simmonds Street in front of the stock exchange. This area, known as 'The Chains' (since all vehicles were kept out by means of chains) contained rows of offices which housed various brokers. The street was always filled with people of all nationalities, and it was here that the cosmopolitan nature of Johannesburg could really be appreciated. In a number of diverse languages and accents, trade was conducted and deals were made, shares were sold, and rumours, gossip and tips abounded. Horse races, prize fights, claim jumping, swindles, chorus girls, organised coups against rivals or the great gambles of the previous night when £80 000 and more changed hands at cards – all were subjects for excited discussion, debate and dissension.

By the middle of the 1890s there were 200 separate mining companies working from head offices in Johannesburg. A gold mine was cynically described as consisting of 'a hole in the ground with a fool at the bottom, a liar on top, and a crook in the office in Johannesburg'. There were then 75 000 men working in the mines whose excavations had resulted in colossal profits for the financiers and considerable grief for the many women left widowed. For every 11 858 tons of ore mined (worth, at the time, £23 702 in recovered gold), one man had been killed and the number injured or totally disabled in accidents was high. Those who survived the perils of the mines, fell prey to the dangers of Johannesburg – strong drink, footpads, confidence tricksters, the high cost of living, incessant gambling. From the time a miner collected his pay, he was fair game to a host of parasites. On paydays, lines of cabs waited at the mines to take the men to town where the bars, girls and cardsharps were waiting expectantly.

Dominating Johannesburg at this time were the so-called 'rand lords' – the heads of the principal mining houses, men whose profits were astronomical. Chiefs among these mining financiers were Julius Wernher and Alfred Beit, who ran Wernher, Beit & Co. and many of the most profitable mines, including the fabulously rich Crown Mines and the Rand Mines.

The second largest company was the Consolidated Gold Fields of South Africa, run by Cecil Rhodes and Charles Rudd. From this company Rhodes drew a personal income of £300 000 a year. Next in line was the Johannesburg Consolidated Investment Company, run by the flamboyant Barney Barnato, who revelled in the moneymaking scramble of Johannesburg. He built himself a huge mansion in the town, complete with imported English butlers, chambermaids and footmen, and spent most of his spare time playing poker for high stakes with a crowd of big-time gamblers.

Sigusmund Neumann, J.B. Robinson, George Albu, George Farrar, Carl Hanau, Sam Marks and his cousin Isaac Lewis (who, conducting their business in Hebrew, acquired control of more than 300 farms in the Transvaal), and Abe Bailey (also a large-scale speculator), were all men whose audacious achievements and ruthless coups were regarded by themselves and the envious lower levels of the population as worthy of knighthood (received by several of them from King Edward VII) or the Nobel Prize.

Early in the second half of the 1890s, the rand lords conflicted with the Transvaal Government. The financiers considered the government to be inept and standing in the way of still bigger profits; the government had its policy and members had their own vested interests. The clash resulted in the Jameson Raid, a futile effort on the part of Cecil Rhodes and his financial allies to dislodge the Transvaal Government by means of a paramilitary invasion of armed men from Zimbabwe and Botswana, led by Dr Leander Jameson, Rhodes's principal assistant.

The population of Johannesburg kept aloof from the squabble since they had nothing to gain from it. The government rewarded them for their neutrality by granting Johannesburg municipal status. The first *burgemeester,* Johannes de Villiers, was appointed in September 1897 to preside over an elected council.

The town continued to grow. A family of suburbs was steadily spawned from the original parent: Hillbrow, Mayfair, Rosebank and others. Johannes de Villiers found himself mayor of a town with more than 100 000 inhabitants. Half these people were European – mainly British, and Russian Jews. European males outnumbered females by three to one, while African males outnumbered females by 24 to one. As a result of this disparity, there were 591 hotels and bars within the municipal limits, and almost the same number of houses of ill repute.

The first motor car was brought to Johannesburg in January 1897 by J.P. Hess and within two years, traffic was complicated by an assortment of animal-drawn and motorised vehicles. Streets and shops were electrically lit, entertainments were diverse – flashy music halls, circuses, open-air prize fights, lotteries, horse racing at Turffontein, waxworks and a great variety of dingy dives.

Over the heads of this boisterous community the political storm continued and, on 11 October 1899, the Anglo-Boer War broke out. Johannesburg became almost deserted as trainloads of refugees fled. The rumbling noise of ore being ground day and night was stilled as mill after mill closed down. For the people of Johannesburg the quiet seemed like the end of the world, so accustomed were they to this 'voice' of the town.

For two years, Johannesburg remained silent. Finally, under the new dispensation of British control, work resumed and former citizens rushed back, together with demobilised soldiers and a mass of newcomers. The mills began operating and, once again, their roar became a

559

*Overleaf: Johannesburg, a bitter-sweet city built of gold from the reef and the blood of the men who mined it.*

familiar sound night and day, continuing without a pause for the next 70 years until the mines of the central Rand began closing down owing to technical complications at deep levels and as the mining industry began to spread east and west of the city. The 'voice' of the mills, now much quieter, can still be heard in Johannesburg.

Johannesburg became a city in 1928 and by 1960 it had more than one million inhabitants. Today it is the centre of the most densely concentrated population in Southern Africa, all of whom live along the Witwatersrand in various municipalities which, with little vacant ground separating them, form one golden metropolis nearly 100 km long.

The city of Johannesburg, then, developed from a gauche, untidy and quite unbeautiful mining camp. From the beginning it was purely mercenary, a regular painted lady with all the characteristics of her kind. Few of its citizens regarded it as being anything other than a convenience. It was knocked around, subjected to a great deal of ill-usage, exploitation and harsh treatment, and regarded by many people as a purely temporary affair which grew against all expectations. This growth often astonished its inhabitants who, having made their fortunes, left Johannesburg with a smirk, and on returning for a nostalgic visit in later years, found the place transformed like Cinderella.

In the space of the lifetime of a single human being, Johannesburg has grown through every stage: bouncing babyhood; brawling, tarty girlhood; mindless teenager; wanton; and finally, reaching a degree of maturity preoccupied with money and having the self-consciousness of a respectably married one-time dancing girl now primly hugging a fur coat around the bosom she once displayed with brazen abandon.

It is not possible to see much of the 'old' Johannesburg since it has always been a place in the process of being pulled down and rebuilt. Local architecture tends to be admired for little more than its height. In slum suburbs such as Jeppestown, Fordsburg and Vrededorp, odd glimpses may be seen of the original mining camp – bleak and sordid – where some rather sleazy-looking characters wander around the tougher areas. An extreme contrast is provided by the northern suburbs, residential areas as handsomely and beautifully developed as in any city on earth. By means of these suburbs – Houghton, Rosebank, Saxonwold, Killarney, and others – man has turned a former, treeless grassveld into a parkland of shady trees, lawns, gardens and pleasant homes.

The best way to begin an exploration of Johannesburg, is by viewing the city from some high observation point. The highest natural point in the area of the city is at Northcliff, the 1 808-m-high *Aasvoëlkop* (peak of vultures). A fine panorama of the northern and north-eastern suburbs may be seen after an easy climb to the top of this peak. For the less energetic there are three manmade viewsites, each of which yield comprehensive vistas of the city.

The highest of these manmade observation points is the J.G. Strijdom Tower situated on Hospital Hill. This unbeautiful tower, resembling a large ramrod used by old-time artillery men, was completed in 1971. It was erected as a microwave transmitting centre for the South African Post Office. Its construction in the midst of a congested residential area was controversial and at times, local residents pelted rubbish at the monster growing in their midst. Telecommunications engineers, however, are a breed not notable for their aesthetic considerations. The site of the tower suited them and up it went with no concession being made to appearance. The tallest building in Africa, the tower (named after a former Prime Minister of South Africa) is 269 m high, and has an observation room, revolving restaurant and souvenir shop near the top. The view of the city area as seen from the top is dramatic, especially at sunset. The tower is open daily from 10h00 to 22h00 and admission is 20c per person.

The suburb of Hillbrow in which the tower stands has some pretensions of being a cosmopolitan hang-out of vagrants, layabouts, drug addicts and drop-outs. Several of the shops in the area remain open until a late hour, however, providing the nights with a little more liveliness than the funereal state of some other areas, but unfortunately, the few local residents trying desperately to live up to the pseudo-Bohemian reputation of Hillbrow are as drab and boring as similar mindless people the world over. Scenically, there is a fine artifical waterfall on Pullinger Kop, on the approach to Hillbrow.

The second highest building in Johannesburg is the tower erected in the suburb of Brixton for the South African Broadcasting Corporation. This tower is 235 m high, and has a steel transmitting antenna on top, adding a further 52 m in height. Used for television and audio high frequency radio transmissions, the tower (otherwise known as the Brixton Tower) was named in honour of Albert Hertzog, a former Cabinet Minister. This is a notably graceful construction, especially at night when skilful lighting causes it to resemble a giant red-hot poker.

The tower is open to the public on Mondays from 14h00 to 22h00, Tuesdays to Saturdays from 09h00 to 22h00, and Sundays from 11h30 to 22h00. Admission is 25c adults, 10c children. The view from the observation platform is superb and reveals the whole of the Witwatersrand stretching out from east to west, where so many lights twinkle at night that the area seems to be a continuation of the Milky Way. The scene is not only impressive but also instructive and should be an essential item on the agenda of all visitors to the city for it effectively dispels the popular misconception that Johannesburg is built on top of underground mine workings.

From this elevated viewpoint it is easy to see that the gold-bearing reef, running from east to west, approaches the surface in a narrow belt, plunging diagonally downwards to tremendous, as yet unplumbed depths. Mining operations are concentrated along this belt of reef, known as the Main Reef of the Witwatersrand. No mining takes place on either side of the reef as all workings are vertical or lateral. Work in the central part of the reef has now ceased for levels have been reached below which it is unprofitable to mine and to haul ore to the surface. The deepest mine in the central area, adjoining Johannesburg, was the Crown Mines, in its day one of the richest mines in the world. The workings of this mine reached a depth of over 3 000 m before operations were discontinued.

As seen from the Brixton Tower, the mine workings – headgears, slag dumps, mills, dams storing water pumped from the mines as well as storm water – stretch in a long line, dividing the city into two halves with the southern suburbs on the south side, and the city area, Hospital Hill and northern suburbs to the north.

In both used and disused mine workings, constant movements of rock occur as the earth adjusts to the stresses and strains which result from the removal of vast quantities of material. These subterranean adjustments cause dreadful accidents in mining and it has been calculated that one man has died for every R22 000 worth of gold recovered from the Witwatersrand. However, their only physical effect on Johannesburg is to send tremors through the ground beneath the city. Buildings shudder but the vibrations are not strong enough to do significant damage. The periodic rumbles and shakes are part of the life of Johannesburg and while visitors find them mildly alarming, the true 'Joburger' (as the residents of Johannesburg or 'Joeys' are called) regards them with indifference.

Another instructive aspect of the towers is their play with lightning, especially during summer when electrical storms involve them in high drama. Both towers have been struck on countless occasions by the full force of lightning on a grand scale common to the South African highveld. The towers simply shrug off bolts of lightning which could illuminate a fair-sized town. The steel antennae on top of the towers are connected to the steel reinforcement of the concrete structures and this in turn is connected to copper strips buried in the earth. Nobody in either tower even realises that the structure has been hit.

Apart from revealing the lie of the gold reef and the spectacle of thunderstorms, the two towers of Johannesburg show visitors a 320-degree view from their windows, of most of the main buildings, streets, suburbs and parks of the city, which are identified by means of accurately positioned indicators.

The building most notable (at least for its bulk) in the centre city, is the Carlton Centre,

561

claimed to be the tallest all-concrete office block in the world. On the top (50th floor) of this building, an observation area is open to the public from 10h00 to 24h00 daily. Admission is 30c. There is a restaurant on the top open to all races and the view, especially of the built-up areas, is very impressive.

As seen from above, it is particularly obvious that the original surveyors of Johannesburg laid out the town in straight streets and square blocks – a completely functional plan without any adornment of boulevards, ornamental approaches or open squares.

The principal streets of the city are: *Commissioner*, named in honour of the government commissioners involved in the proclamation of the goldfields and the establishment of the city; *Eloff*, named after F.C. Eloff, private secretary to President Kruger when Johannesburg was laid out; *Harrison*, named after George Harrison who found the first payable gold of the Witwatersrand; *Hollard*, with its fountain of dolerite boulders and reflecting pools, named after Emil Hollard, lawyer and financier; *Jeppe*, named after Carl Jeppe, pioneer miner and property developer; *Joubert*, named after one of the first mining commissioners; *Loveday*, named after R.K. Loveday, first representative of the diggers in the *Volksraad; Pritchard*, named after W.A. Pritchard who surveyed much of early Johannesburg; *Rissik*, named after Johann Rissik, one of the government commissioners after whom the city itself is named; and *Von Brandis*, named after Carl von Brandis, the first mining commissioner.

The buildings in the city centre are contrived mainly of concrete and glass and simply designed to occupy the maximum space permissable. One of the few buildings linking Johannesburg with its past is the Rissik Street Post Office, designed by Sytse Wierda, head of the Public Works Department in the Transvaal. The laying of the foundation stone of this building in 1897 was a great occasion for the people of Johannesburg. The erection by the government of so substantial a building was visual reassurance that authority considered the town to be permanent, and that it would not become a dilapidated, abandoned place of ghosts, exhausted mines and long-departed dancing girls.

The post office had a ground floor and two upper floors, and was attractively designed and faced with red bricks. With two cupolas and a central bell tower, the building was the pride of Johannesburg.

After the Anglo-Boer War, the British added a top storey and a clock tower. In the process they removed the cupolas and the central bell tower, but in exchange, to commemorate the coronation of King Edward VII in 1902, they installed a clock which had been made in England by the same firm which had manufactured Big Ben, and its chimes were identical. Ever since it was first set in motion, this clock has, despite a few technical interruptions, told Johannesburg the time in a loud, clear, authoritative voice.

A new main Johannesburg post office of the usual concrete type was opened in Jeppe Street in 1935, but the Rissik Street Post Office is still in use. There has been talk of demolishing it and planting a garden in its place, but this would be a pity. Though now quite dwarfed by the towering modern glass and concrete skyscrapers, this building has a subtle charm, a mellowness of design and colour which makes it architecturally superior to the buildings around it.

Immediately behind the Rissik Street Post Office, on a site once occupied by the Standard Theatre, there is a garden in which a fountain plays with 18 bronze impala antelope jumping through the jets of water and a rainbow which is formed at various times of the day. The fountain was given to Johannesburg by Harry Oppenheimer, in memory of his father, Sir Ernest, the renowned mining magnate. The bronze impalas are the work of the sculptor Hermann Wald.

On the opposite side of the post office in Rissik Street, stands the Johannesburg City Hall, with its solid stone facings. It was designed in the Italian Renaissance style by a Cape Town firm of architects, Hawke & McKinley. Constructed between 1910 and 1915, it is still in use, but the new Civic Centre and the Civic Theatre on Hospital Hill have taken over most of its functions. The old building, although solid and imposing, and containing a sumptuous mayoral parlour, resembles a mausoleum, with high ceilings and cold, echoing corridors and stairwells.

One and a half kilometres west of the Johannesburg City Hall, off Bree Street, stands the Oriental Plaza, a lively and interesting modern shopping centre containing about 300 shops in an area of 9 ha. Opened in 1974, this shopping centre replaces the hotchpotch of shops under Indian management which lined Fourteenth Street, Pageview. Though picturesque, these shops were hopelessly cramped, unhygienic and dilapidated, and the street considerably congested.

The new centre is a joint project in urban renewal of the State Department of Community Development and the Johannesburg City Council. The architecture is imaginative and it consolidates the separate businesses in one attractive, harmonious building complex. The oriental atmosphere is stimulating and, as in the original Fourteenth Street, there are many unusual novelties and bargains to be found.

A major feature of the central city area is the railway station, the largest on the continent of Africa and very nearly the size of Grand Central in New York. The entrance to the original concourse building is at the northern end of Eloff Street. Erected in the 1930s and decorated with murals by the South African artist J.H. Pierneef, this concourse contains the first locomotive to serve the Witwatersrand. The little 'puffing billy' was carted in pieces up to Johannesburg by ox wagon in 1890.

Behind this building is the modern station, completed in 1966 and covering 22 ha with platforms and tracks. Over 250 000 passengers use this station every day, the main concourse of which is 168 m long, 43 m wide and 18 m high and contains a variety of shops, restaurants and snack bars. Escalators convey passengers down to the various platforms. Adjoining the station is the airways terminal and railways head office buildings in a garden setting. A railway museum is housed in a part of the station building.

The churches of the city area also add some architectural interest to the mass of buildings. Among them is an impressive mosque, the Madressa Himayatil Islam. This building, standing at the corner of Market and Nugget streets, has a minaret 30 m high which is equipped with a powerful public address system in order to save the muezzin from climbing for the five daily obligatory calls to prayer. The floor is electrically heated for the comfort of the devout at prayer. The mosque was founded in 1916 and has been enlarged in recent years.

The Roman Catholic cathedral of Christ the King, built in 1960 in End Street, is of unusual design: a variety of materials were used to produce a finish of mellow brick, red granite and stained glass which floods the interior with crimson, viridian and golden light.

The Anglican St Mary's Cathedral was built in 1926 and designed by Sir Herbert Baker, an architect whose creative genius gave South Africa many of her finest buildings. The cathedral, with its imposing appearance, was constructed from hammer-dressed sandstone.

The Great Synagogue in Wolmarans Street was built in 1913 and designed with a magnificent dome by Theophile Scheerer in the style of Santa Sophia in Istanbul.

Overlooking the city area of Johannesburg from the north is the Hospital Hill ridge, densely covered with flats and other buildings. Part of this ridge is named after the old Johannesburg General Hospital which is situated on it. On the summit of the ridge stands the Johannesburg Fort, a grim old stronghold built in the 1980s and designed by Colonel A.H. Schiel, a professional German soldier in the employ of the South African Republic. The purpose of the fort was to keep the boisterous digger community in order, and a garrison of the state artillery was maintained there together with armaments of cannon and machine guns.

Happily, the fort was never used for aggressive purposes. After the Anglo-Boer War it was converted into a prison, in which form it is still in use. Above its main entrance is the carved coat of arms of the former South African Republic (Zuid Afrikaansche Republiek), reputedly the work of the famous sculptor Anton von Wouw.

Close to the fort, built on the original parade ground of the garrison, is the Medical Research Institute. To the west is the Civic Centre, the vast administrative office block of the city council, and near it the Civic Theatre, the home of ballet, opera, drama and music, staged mainly by PACT (Performing Arts Council of the Transvaal). In front of the theatre is a fountain consisting of three bronze figures dancing with water playing at their feet. The sculptor Ernest Ullman created the bronzes.

Still further to the west along the same ridge lie the two universities of Johannesburg. The oldest, the University of the Witwatersrand, originated, strangely enough, in Kimberley in 1896, as a training institute for the mining industry. An offshoot of the institute was established in Johannesburg after the Anglo-Boer War. In 1906 it became the Transvaal University College, with a branch opened in Pretoria in 1907, which later became the University of Pretoria.

For some years the Johannesburg College only taught mining and technology but various other departments were gradually added and in 1922 it became the University of the Witwatersrand. The Johannesburg City Council had already presented a 32-ha site to the college at Milner Park, and from the handful of buildings erected there in 1932, the present massive complex has arisen, housing over 10 000 students. Opposite the entrance to the university there is a delightful little fountain with two bronze antelopes drinking. The bronzes were sculpted by Ernest Ullman. The University of the Witwatersrand uses English as the medium of tuition. To its west, close to the Brixton Tower and the audio visual studios of the South African Broadcasting Corporation, lies the campus of the Rand Afrikaans University. Established in 1966 this Afrikaans-medium university is housed in a magnificent complex of modern buildings.

Johannesburg is fortunate in that it possesses many open areas in the suburbs around the central city. There are approximately 500 parks and gardens within the city limits, providing over 4 000 ha of open space, recreational areas, picnic grounds and walks.

The best known is *Joubert Park,* the oldest in Johannesburg, laid out in 1887 on 6,43 ha of vacant ground close to the city centre. Named after Christian Johannes Joubert, first chief of the Mining Department, this park is a green oasis set among asphalt streets and concrete buildings where office workers eat their lunch under the trees; mothers, children and old people emerge from the shadows of their flats and enjoy the sunshine and fresh air. Situated in the park is a floral clock, giant open-air chess board, conservatory of tropical plants, restaurant and fountain. Carols are sung at Christmas and the park is illuminated. There is an art gallery and an open-air art mart where any artist can exhibit his work and sell directly to the public.

The art gallery is housed in a building designed by Sir Edwin Luytens as a fine example of British classical architecture. The gallery started as the private collection of Lady Phillips, wife of one of the mining magnates. Between 1904 and 1909 she collected from her wealthy friends a considerable amount of money for the purpose of creating an art gallery for Johannesburg. The first part of the building was opened in 1915 and another portion in 1940. The rest of the gallery remains unfinished, awaiting a donor.

The gallery is open daily except Mondays (or Tuesdays if the previous day was a public holiday), from 10h00 to 17h00.

Bezuidenhout Park lies in the eastern suburbs, at Dewetshof, and is of considerable historical interest. It was originally the heart of the farm *Doornfontein,* owned by F.J. Bezuidenhout when the rush to the Witwatersrand took place. The farm lay well away from the gold-bearing reef and although it was prospected, nothing was found on it. The Bezuidenhouts, however, made a fortune by selling land for townships; suburbs such as Bezuidenhout Valley, Doornfontein and Judith's Paarl were laid out on their property. The nucleus of the farm, with the homestead and a graveyard, remained intact. Old Bezuidenhout died in 1900 and his son, Barend, in the 1920s. The Johannesburg City Council subsequently bought what remained of the farm. The deed of sale contained the condition that 40 ha, encompassing the homestead, garden, dam, cemetery and the original trees (mainly *Acacia karoo*), be preserved intact.

Bezuidenhout Park is therefore a unique combination of historical monument and recreational area, where facilities such as a miniature railway, children's playground and swimming pool, restaurant, some sports grounds, picnic spots, a superb caravan park and excellent walking area are provided in a refreshingly unspoilt parkland.

In the suburb of Houghton Estate, a 17,45-ha expanse of ground covering part of the foothills of the Witwatersrand was presented to the city in 1937 by one of the major mining houses, the Consolidated Investment Company. This area was to become a permanent home for the spectacular collection of South African wild flowers exhibited at the 1936 Empire Exhibition which was held in Johannesburg. Since then the rocky hillocks have been converted into a garden of indigenous flora dedicated to the memory of Field-Marshal Smuts, a great naturalist as well as politician. The garden originally formed part of the grounds of *Hohenheim*, the home of Sir Percy Fitzpatrick, author of *Jock of the Bushveld*, and also a director of the mining company which presented the property. The garden is known as The Wilds.

Another notable park donated to Johannesburg by a mining house is the Hermann Eckstein Park just over 100 ha in size in Saxonwold. In 1903 Wernher Beit & Co. offered the area to Johannesburg, asking that it be named after a late senior partner in the firm who had started a private zoo on the estate before his death. These animals formed the nucleus for the Johannesburg Zoological Garden which today covers 55 ha of the area and exhibits 600 mammals, 1 300 birds and numerous reptiles. Also in the Hermann Eckstein Park is the South African National War Museum, where a collection of military hardware, paintings, uniforms and medals is displayed. The artillery park, one-man submarine and aircraft exhibits are fascinating. In another portion of the park (45,32 ha in extent) is a lake, very popular with boating enthusiasts, while other attractions include extensive picnic grounds, an illuminated fountain, and a restaurant.

The western suburbs are provided with a 45-ha reserve known as Mellville Koppies. Left entirely in its natural state, with the original flora and remains of an Iron Age furnace, it is a national monument and a sanctuary for birds and other wildlife.

Brixton has the Kingston Frost Park – 3,39 ha devoted to the cultivation of numerous aloes collected from various parts of Southern Africa. Emmarentia, in the northern suburbs, has the attraction of a fine 79,41-ha area under development known as the Johannesburg Botanic Garden, where a garden of herbs flourishes in one part and in another section more than 12 000 rose trees are under cultivation.

Other parks include Rhodes Park in Kensington (24,90 ha), containing a small lake and a restaurant, and Pioneers' Park in La Rochelle, on the shores of Wemmer Pan (88,87 ha). In this park stands the James Hall Museum of Transport, housing a collection of ancient automobiles, trams, buses, steam rollers and tractors, and many other vehicles of former years. A restaurant provides refreshment and there are picnic grounds for relaxation. Boat trips are taken on the lake and on the northern shores stands a miniature town known as Santarama. Inspired by the famous Madurodam miniature city in Holland, Santarama has a scale of 1:25 and is run for charity by the South African National Tuberculosis Association. A magnificent musical fountain plays on the southern verge of the lake. Built in 1970 ('Water Year'), it has 225 jets, 642 underwater lights in five colours and is driven by 22 pumps. A computer synchronises the play of water and light to music. The fountain operates from September to March 19h30 to 21h00, and from April to June 18h30 to 20h00. It is closed during July and August.

In the suburb of Doornfontein, 3 km east of the city hall, lies *Ellis Park*, named after a former mayor, J. Dowell Ellis. It is the principal venue in the city for rugby, tennis and swimming.

The headquarters of the Transvaal Rugby Football Union are situated at Ellis Park where many great matches have taken place on its playing fields. With a seating capacity of nearly 100 000 people, the Ellis Park rugby ground is an international test match venue for all visiting teams.

The Southern Transvaal Lawn Tennis Association also has its headquarters and 23 courts at Ellis Park. All major tennis tournaments in Johannesburg are played there and it is a standard venue on the international circuit.

The largest swimming bath in Johannesburg is also to be found at Ellis Park. Built to full Olympic standards, this bath, too, is the scene of international competitive swimming.

Open-air boxing matches are also staged at Ellis Park.

In 1888, a group of sportsmen banded together and formed a sports club called the Wanderers. They rented from the government a substantial piece of ground which became known as Kruger's Park. The main railway station of Johannesburg was eventually built near by and named Park Station. An English cricket team, captained by Aubrey Smith, was the first international side to visit Kruger's Park, where they played against the local team in January and February 1889. From that time onwards, the Wanderers became internationally known as a centre of sport in Southern Africa and where many great sporting events subsequently took place.

In later years, the sportsfields were encroached upon by the growing city and the club moved to Kent Park in 1945. On the old site of the club, where Aubrey Smith (later a famous actor) had once led his white-flannelled men into combat, the gigantic modern railway station was built. The headquarters of the South African Railways and Harbours, as well as the airways, are also housed here in an imposing array of outlying buildings. The Wanderers Club in Kent Park is today the setting for many important sporting events.

Milner Park, next to the Witwatersrand University, is the home of the Rand Show (the largest of its kind in Africa), staged each Easter by the Witwatersrand Agricultural Society. Smaller agricultural, livestock and industrial shows are also held during the year in the 40,5-ha showground.

Other recreational areas, such as the 44-ha Gillooly's Farm in Bedfordview, are used for staging events such as dog shows as well as being used for picnicking. James Gillooly ran a dairy on this farm until the City Council bought it in August 1943 and opened it in 1944 as a picnic resort.

While possessing many parks, Johannesburg is also richly endowed with libraries, museums and galleries, several of which contain unique collections. One of the proudest possessions of the city is the Public Library and the group of specialised museums contained in the same building.

The library originated as a privately run subscription service housed in the boardroom of the City Chambers. By 1891 this infant library had grown to such an extent that a librarian was appointed and a series of moves to a succession of ever larger accommodation commenced. In 1905 the Reference Library was founded by the addition of the technical books owned by Major Seymour, an American mining engineer.

The present home of the library in Market Square, facing the city hall on the west side, is one of the handsomest buildings in Johannesburg and was built in 1935 from a design by John Perry. In this building the library occupies the ground floor while above it is the famed Africana Museum which started as the private collection of John Gubbins. It has become a splendid museum in which the history of Southern Africa is presented in three divisions. The first division exhibits some magnificent Cape-made furniture of the solid kind which alone could survive the long ox wagon journeys into the interior during the pioneer days. Cape silver, glass, china and other domestic items of former years are displayed, including a charming little 'peep' show.

The second division is devoted to Johannesburg and local history and it includes a real

Zeederberg mail coach which was used on the run from Pretoria to Bulawayo, a trail fraught with lions, highwaymen and warring tribes. In an effort to neutralise the presence of tsetse fly, the coach was at one time hauled by a team of zebra. Unfortunately the experiment failed as they lacked the stamina of oxen.

The third division covers tribal life encompassing Bushman paintings, musical instruments, trade beads, costumes, carvings and ceremonial masks.

Throughout the museum, displayed on the walls, are the paintings of artists such as Thomas Baines, T.W. Bowler, W.S. Burchell, Samuel Daniell and Barbara Tyrrell whose work is accepted as being the classic representation of the life and scenery of Southern Africa.

Also housed in the library building is the Geological Museum, in which the Draper Gemstone Collection of ore specimens containing visible gold, and collections depicting the geological history of the earth are exhibited. Adjoining the Geological Museum is the Harger Archaeological Museum containing a collection of the prehistoric artefacts of Southern Africa. The museums in the library building are open Mondays to Saturdays from 09h00 to 18h00 and on Sundays and public holidays from 14h00 to 18h00.

A branch of the Africana Museum is the James Hall Museum of Transport which has now outgrown its parent building and has moved to Pioneer's Park on the shores of Wemmer Pan where it displays a remarkable assembly of ancient automobiles, steam tractors, tramcars, fire engines and other interesting vehicles dating from the past. The museum is open Mondays to Saturdays from 09h00 to 18h00 and on Sundays and holidays from 14h00 to 18h00.

Among the specialised museums in Johannesburg are the following:

The Bensusan Museum of Photography is housed in a building in 17 Hillside Road, Parktown. It displays the history of photography by means of many interesting examples of early photographs and equipment. There are magic lanterns, cinematographic cameras and equipment, and a perfect reproduction of an amateur's dark room and a photographer's studio at the turn of the century. There are hundreds of photographs from classics by pioneers such as Fox-Talbot, daguerreotypes, calotypes, early specimens of colour and a comprehensive library covering all aspects of photography. Dr and Mrs Bensusan started this collection and presented it to the City Council.

The Bernard Price Museum of Palaeontology is the premier museum in South Africa wholly devoted to palaeontological research. It forms part of the University of the Witwatersrand, but is housed in a separate building off Showground Road in Brixton.

The museum depicts the geological periods of the earth and contains a vast collection of fossils, including a treasure trove of ancient bones recovered from the huge cave of Makapansgat in the Northern Transvaal. The deposits in this cave are so enormous and of such scientific value that teams of excavators will be kept busy for years to come. Detailed collections feature the bone, tooth and horn artefacts of early men such as Australopithecus, the discovery of which revealed that man was present very much earlier than was previously thought.

The Bernard Price Institute of Geophysical Research is separate from the museum although named after the same man. Bernard Price was an electrical engineer and a considerable benefactor of the University of the Witwatersrand. The Institute of Geophysical Research is famous for its study of complex subjects such as thunderstorms.

Summer weather in Johannesburg is pleasantly mild – days are warm to hot, and nights are cool and refreshing. Most of the rainfall occurs in summer, usually in the form of spectacular afternoon thunderstorms which occur suddenly and are of short duration.

In the early morning the sky is generally clear. At about 11h00, white cumulus clouds appear which build up steadily until they form gigantic cloud 'castles' resembling great dollops of whipped cream floating lazily through the warm air.

At lunchtime, the clouds convert into an ominous black mass and tremendous electrical charges (both positive and negative) separate within them. Drops of water turn to ice and fall as hailstones, sometimes as large as pigeons' eggs, which cause immense destruction to crops, motor car windscreens, insect and bird life. The contact in the clouds between hail and water seems to generate still greater electrical imbalances – flashes of 100 million volts are not uncommon in such huge clouds.

Lightning flashes as the clouds disgorge their electrical burden. Most of the lightning is hidden within the clouds but about one in every six bolts strikes the earth releasing energy for a mere one thousandth of a second. Currents of approximately 100 000 amps are possible but about 58 per cent of them are less than 30 000 amps. Electrical storms such as these provide an awesome spectacle, but should be viewed from a safe place. About 60 people are killed by lightning in South Africa each year, but they have generally been struck in exposed situations. Modern buildings are fairly indifferent to lightning and the two high telecommunications towers in Johannesburg are sometimes struck several times in the course of a single storm. Conductors take the discharge safely to earth without anyone in the buildings even being aware that anything untoward has taken place. Motor vehicles are unaffected, aircraft are occasionally struck but survive with minor damage. Electrical power lines and telecommunication networks suffer the greatest inconvenience.

A considerable amount of research on lighting has been carried out in South Africa. Dr (later Sir) Basil Schonland started studying the subject at Somerset East in the 1920s. When the Institute of Geophysical Research, named after Bernard Price, was founded in Johannesburg, Dr Schonland became the first director. Between 1933 and 1935 particularly, much information on lightning was accumulated by this institute, as well as information on radar and earth tremors. Working with an improved version of a camera invented in England by G.V. Boys, Dr Schonland and co-workers such as Dr E.C. Halliday and Professor D.J. Malan, all renowned authorities on lightning, managed to secure many high-speed photographs of lightning and to time the flashes to a few millionths of a second.

Other aids were developed, such as cathode ray oscilloscopes and counters which could check the number of strikes on power lines and exposed points. It is an intensely interesting but very difficult and dangerous subject to study. Many problems remain unsolved, including weird phenomena such as ball lightning, often seen in Zimbabwe and occasionally in the Transvaal. Since the Second World War, however, several protective systems against lightning have been devised and much more is now known about these spectacular disturbances.

Experimental work has been carried out extensively by the universities and by organisations such as the Electricity Supply Commission and the Post Office, because of the effect of lightning on electrical transmission and communications services. The Council for Scientific and Industrial Research (CSIR) is conducting research on lightning and the improvement of protective measures. When protection systems are contrived, instruments known as lightning flash counters are used to establish the number of flashes which occur during a storm. Ground flashes are ones that cause damage to life and property and the CSIR's National Electrical Engineering Research Institute has developed, to a degree not possible before, a counter which differentiates between intercloud flashes and flashes to ground.

The high-lying areas of the Transvaal, Lesotho, Zimbabwe, Zambia, Madagascar and parts of Australia experience some of the most violent electrical storms on earth. As with Johannesburg, these are areas of summer rainfall which occurs in very localised thunderstorms. In the tropics of Africa, Malaysia and South America, thunderstorms take place on more than 100 days a year.

The Bernberg Museum of Costume is contained in a suburban house on the corner of Jan Smuts Avenue. The house has been reconstructed to include a complete circuit covering two different displays: the first comprises costumes of various periods worn by models standing in beautifully designed period interiors; the second involves collections of various accessories displayed in wall cases. A fascinating range of fashion plates is exhibited on the walls.

Also included are complete wedding groups, a reconstructed dress salon of the 1920s, an art gallery from 1810, a kitchen, various children's costumes and all the bric-à-brac of high fashion – underclothing, smoking hats, buttons, gloves, shoes, shawls, bags, purses, cigarette holders and jewellery. The collection is superbly mounted and should not be missed as there are no other museums like it in Southern Africa.

The Jewish Museum is housed in the offices of the South African Jewish Board of Deputies at the corner of Main and Kruis streets. It is devoted to Jewish religious art and the history of the Jewish people of Johannesburg.

Because of their unsettled past, the Jews have no great world monuments of antiquity, no medieval buildings, palaces or castles. Their past was portable, and most of the surviving works of art are associated with religion. Superb examples of cases holding the Torah (holy scrolls), are displayed. There are many ritualistic items such as pointers used for reading the Torah (which is not to be touched by hand), elaborate boxes for holding spices, seven- and eight-branched candlesticks, silver cases set with precious stones, six seals and the 12 signs of the zodiac. The museum is open on Mondays to Thursdays from 09h30 to 15h00. It is closed at lunchtime.

The Museum of Man and Sciences is housed in a suburban residence at 111 Central Street, Houghton. It contains some splendid exhibitions of the history and way of life of the Bushmen and other peoples of Southern Africa. Artefacts, costumes and photographs are used in an exposition of primitive lifestyles and the endless ingenuity of man in fashioning, out of minimal resources, his basic necessities.

The Pharmacy Museum, maintained by the Pharmaceutical Society of South Africa, displays a collection of medicinal plants and antique laboratory equipment. The museum is accommodated in Pharmacy House, 80 Jorissen Street, Braamfontein.

The Planetarium is situated in the grounds of the University of the Witwatersrand. It was brought to Johannesburg at the time of the town's 70th birthday celebrations and later sold to the University by the Festival Committee. Since its opening to the public in 1960 this wonderful place of optical magic has introduced nearly one million spectators to the beauty and mystery of the universe. The images of about 9 000 heavenly objects can be presented in any period from 2 000 years ago to 5 000 years ahead. There are demonstrations from Tuesdays to Fridays at 20h30 and on Saturdays at 15h00 and 20h30. Sundays at 16h00. School holidays (Tuesdays to Fridays) and extra sessions take place at 15h00.

The Railway Museum is housed in the railway station at the top of Eloff Street. One entire wall of the museum is devoted to scale models of locomotives and rolling stock dating from early days to modern times. Cases are devoted to various local systems of former years as well as tickets, signalling systems, uniforms, badges, lamps, equipment, dining car menus, a working lighthouse, road motor transport, harbour equipment and air services. A number of models actually work.

The Museum of Reza the Great, 41 Young Avenue, Mountain View, is a memorial to the Shah of Iran who died in South Africa while in exile. The museum exhibits superb examples of Iranian metalwork, ceramics, carpets and other works of art. The museum is open Tuesdays to Fridays from 09h00 to 13h00 and on Sundays from 09h30 to 13h00.

The South African National War Museum contains a lavish display of lethal equipment and the uniforms (equally lavish) of the military men of past years. The exhibition is mounted in the Hermanus Ekstein Park, off Erlswood Way, Saxonwold. More people visit the museum than any other in Johannesburg. Tanks, armoured cars and military aircraft are displayed, including a Hawker Hurricane, a De Haviland Mosquito, and a Spitfire, together with planes of the First World War. There are battle flags, medals, decorations uniforms, insignia, war photographs, steel helmets, rifles, hand guns, swords, daggers, knives and bayonets. Also included is a German one-man submarine, and many fine paintings of battle scenes and portraits adorn the walls.

On a 10-ha site surrounding the No 14 shaft at Crown Mines, a great mine museum is in the process of creation. There are replicas of a mine village, a railway, milling area, study facilities and opportunities for visitors to go underground.

Many of the suburbs and satellite townships around Johannesburg contain places of interest which are worth visiting and some of the original suburbs have grown into towns in their own right, especially in the northern areas.

## RANDBURG

With a population of 106 760, Randburg is one of these young municipalities mothered by Johannesburg. It was created in 1959 when 13 of the original northern suburbs combined to form one municipality, complete with a shopping centre, civic centre, light industrial area and built-in seeds of future civic indigestion in the form of traffic congestion and pollution.

Randburg has 37 parks, an art gallery exhibiting contemporary South African art housed in the municipal building, and a privately owned vintage car museum situated at a picnic site on the banks of the Kleinjukskei River which is open to the public during weekends. An open-air fresh produce market is held all day on Saturdays when farmers bring their produce to the town and sell directly to housewives in an animated scene of bargaining in the sunshine.

## SANDTON

Another child of Johannesburg situated in its northern areas is the municipality of Sandton, whose population numbers 71 370. The name *Sandton* is a combination of the names of the original suburbs of Sandown and Bryanston which combined with north-eastern Johannesburg in 1966 and formed a new town in a spacious park-like setting. There is a spectacular modern shopping centre, plenty of room for recreation and an African market in Atrium Centre where curios and handicrafts are made by some very talented workers and artists.

In the Sandton area lies the original 1 000-ha farm named *Kyalami,* after the Zulu *kaya lami* (my home). This old farm is now the site of the Kyalami Country Club and the Kyalami motor racing track, built in 1961. On 1 January 1968 this track became the venue for the annual Grand Prix of South Africa, one of the races included in the World Championship circuit.

The South African National Equestrian Centre also has its home in Sandton, next to the Kyalami Country Club. At 11h00 every Sunday displays of dressage in the unique riding disciplines of the Spanish Riding School in Vienna, are given. White Lipizzaner stallions perform under the direction of Major George Iwanowski, a former Polish cavalry officer, in the only riding school outside Vienna to display this precision training.

A breed which originated from a mixture of Kladruber horses from Bohemia, small Italian horses, and Arabian horses, produced these magnificent stallions. They were a species bred at Lipizza stud farm, founded in 1580 by the Austrian archduke Charles. From the beginning, this breed was trained in dressage in the celebrated Spanish Riding School founded in Vienna by the English Duke of Newcastle and Antonius de Pluvinal, riding master to Louis XIII of France, who developed extraordinary training methods for the techniques riders call 'high school', 'carriage work', 'hunting' and 'hack'.

Several noblemen in the Austro-Hungarian empire obtained some of these horses and at the time of the Second World War, Count Jankovich Besan had a number in his stables at Oregelak, in Hungary. With the collapse of the Nazis, he fled while about 12 of the horses were removed from the war zone by the stud manager and accountant. These horses reached Bavaria where the count reclaimed them. In 1946 they were transferred to the estate of Lord Digby in England and in 1948 the count brought them to South Africa where they were placed on a farm in the Mooi River district of Natal. In 1964 six of the horses were sold to National Chemical Products, a manufacturer of horse feed, who transferred them to Waterkloof in Natal and used them to establish a South African lipizzaner breed, the offspring of which perform at Kyalami.

The southern suburbs of Johannesburg are less glamorous than those in the north but they contain some of the principal sporting venues, such as the horse racing course at Turffontein and the Rand Stadium in La Rochelle, scene of soccer and open-air boxing matches. In the extreme south of the city limits lies *Soweto* (south-western township), the principal residential area of the African population and a substantial town with its own administration.

To the east of Johannesburg lie associate towns such as Bedfordview (16 800 inhabitants) and Kempton Park (84 016 inhabitants). Situated in this area, 12 km from the centre of the city, is the international airport named in honour of Field-Marshal Jan Smuts. This is South Africa's .principal airport, opened in 1953 and enlarged over the years to cope with bigger aircraft and ever-increasing numbers of passengers. The main runway is 4 411 m long and can accept all modern aircraft at maximum loads. The airport is the home base of South African Airways, the largest airline in Africa. The road from the airport to the centre of Johannesburg makes an impressive entrance to the city through Settlers Park and its three gold-lit fountains.

Five kilometres west of the centre of Johannesburg, in an unbeautiful industrial setting, lies the small George Harrison Park which preserves the actual site of the first discovery by George Harrison, of payable gold from the main reef of the Witwatersrand. Old mine workings may also be seen there as well as an interesting 10-stamp battery of the type used to crush ore in the early days of gold mining.

From the site of this memorial park, the spirit of the original prospector might well look out at the city, the mines and the factories which have developed all around the original exposure of reef. He would see a vast, sprawling, burgeoning, energetic city where everybody always seems to be in a rush, preoccupied with getting to work to make money, getting home again, and then rushing back to the city at night in order to spend some of their gains.

At night Johannesburg is a glittering place to see from the air, or from the two towers. Cinemas and theatres attract the crowds while restaurants feature the foods of many nationalities, particularly German, Greek and Portuguese, large communities of whom live in the city. Their characteristic music – from oompah bands to the soulful singing of *fado* – is part of the song of the city of gold, a sound it hums and murmurs to itself by day and night, as it works and plays. It is the song of a bass drum beat of industry, a baritone of men at work that is hard and dangerous; a song of the falsetto of moneymen safe on the surface, counting profits, losses, and loot; and of the lonely sighs of families who have lost somebody in the utter darkness and profound silence of what seems to be the bowels of the earth.

## Accommodation

★★★ Airport Hotel, Jan Smuts Airport, 250 rooms, all with baths. R15 – R25 room only. Phone 36-2687 or 36-6911.

★ Alba Hotel, 90 De Korte Street (Braamfontein), 76 rooms, 12 with baths. R7 – R9,50 B/B. Phone 724-2131.

★★ Ambassador Hotel, 52 Pretoria Street (Hillbrow), 54 rooms, all with baths. R7,50 – R13 B/B. Phone 642-5051.

★ Ascot Hotel, Grant Avenue (Norwood), 14 rooms, 5 with baths. R7 – R8 B/B. Phone 45-6253.

★★ Astor Hotel, 264 Smit Street (Hospital Hill), 72 rooms, all with baths. R11 – R22 B/B. Phone 724-1771.

★ Astra Hotel, 88 Corlett Drive (Birnam), 28 rooms, all with baths. R8 – R12,50 B/B. Phone 40-6811.

★ Bellevue Hotel, 314 Main Road (Fordsburg), 14 rooms, 4 with baths. R6,50 B/B. Phone 834-8557.

★★ Belmont Hotel, Banket Street (Hillbrow), 76 rooms, 44 with baths. R7,50 B/B. Phone 642-4985.

* Booysens Hotel, 33 Booysens Road, 14 rooms, 5 with baths. R7 B/B. Phone 838-7986.
*** Capri Hotel, 27 Aintree Avenue, Savoy Estate (Bramley), 50 rooms, all with baths. R19,75 – R21,25 B/B. Phone 786-2250.
***** Carlton Hotel, Main Street, 600 rooms, all with baths. R40 – R310 room only. Phone 21-8911.
*** Casa Mia Hotel, 37 Soper Road (Berea), 150 rooms, all with baths. R10,95 – R14,95 B/B. Phone 642-7231.
* Chelsea Hotel, Catherine Avenue (Berea), 72 rooms, 42 with baths. R5,50 – R7,75 B/B. Phone 642-451.
* Commissioner Hotel, 297 Commissioner Street, 13 rooms, 4 with baths. R5 – R6 B/B. Phone 24-1564 or 24-5971.
* Constantia Hotel, 35 Quartz Street (Joubert Park), 24 rooms, all with baths. R7,50 B/B. Phone 725-1046.
** Coronia Hotel, 45 O'Reilly Road (Berea), 380 rooms, all with baths. R12,50 B/B. Phone 642-7334.
* Cosmopolitan Hotel, 285 Commissioner Street, 11 rooms, 4 with baths. R8 – R9,50 room only. Phone 24-2650.
* Courtleigh Hotel, 38 Harrow Road (Berea), 108 rooms, all with baths. R11,50 – R17,50 B/B. Phone 648-1140/7.
** Connoisseur Kosher Hotel, Leyds Street, 100 rooms, all with baths. R10 – R30 B/B. Phone 724-5211.
*** Crest Hotel, 7 Abel Road (Berea), 195 rooms, all with baths. R13 B/B. Phone 642-7641/9.
*** Devonshire Hotel, Melle Street (Braamfontein), 64 rooms, all with baths. R19 – R22 room only. Phone 28-7926.
* Diggers Inn, 157 Bree Street, 19 rooms, 4 with baths. R7 – R8,50 B/B. Phone 834-5932.
** Diplomat Hotel, Klein and Bree Streets, 81 rooms, all with baths. R13,50 – R17,50 B/B. Phone 21-9171.
* Doornfontein Hotel, 32 Beit Street, 14 rooms, 4 with baths. R7,50 D/B/B. Phone 725-4716.
* East London Hotel, 54 Loveday Street, 32 rooms, 9 with baths. R8 B/B. Phone 838-6291.
* Elizabeth Hotel, 16 Pritchard Street, 42 rooms, 14 with baths. R7,50 – R8,50 D/B/B. Phone 838-7897/8.
* Ellis Park Hotel, 19 Derby Road (Bertrams), 27 rooms, 13 with baths. R7 B/B. Phone 24-1453.
* Europa Hotel, 63 Claim Street (Joubert Park), 65 rooms, 40 with baths. R5 – R6 room only. Phone 724-5321.
* Federal Hotel, 181 Commissioner Street, 28 rooms, 8 with baths. R5,25 – R10,50 B/B. Phone 22-8848.
* Flamingo Hotel, Caroline Street (Hillbrow), 98 rooms, all with baths. R8 – R13 B/B. Phone 642-7571.
* Fontana Inn, cor. Twist and Smit streets, 166 rooms, all with baths. R6,95 – R8,95 room only. Phone 725-3980.
* Forest Hill Hotel, Forest Street (Forest Hill), 30 rooms, 11 with baths. R6,50 B/B. Phone 683-6400.
* Fountain Hotel, Kruger Street (Langlaagte), 10 rooms, 4 with baths. R6,50 – R10 B/B. Phone 35-3785.
* Franklyn Hotel, 52 Esselen Street (Hillbrow), 150 rooms, all with baths. R6 – R10 B/B. Phone 724-9221.
** Gardens Hotel, cor. O'Reilly Road and Tudhope Avenue (Berea), 358 rooms, 195 with baths. R12 – R24 B/B. Phone 642-5071.
* Golden Crest Hotel, 57 Abel Road (Berea), 129 rooms, all with baths. R9 D/B/B. Phone 642-4371.

* Grand Hotel, 93 Kerk Street, 39 rooms, all with baths. R5,50 room only. Phone 22-9557.
* Grand Station Hotel, 302 Main Street (Jeppe), 14 rooms, all with baths. R9 B/B. Phone 618-1320/1.
* Gresham Hotel, 13 Loveday Street, 30 rooms, 18 with baths. R6,50 B/B. Phone 834-5641.
*** Holiday Inn Jan Smuts, Jan Smuts Airport, 276 rooms, all with baths. R28 — R36 room only. Phone 975-1121.
*** Holiday Inn Milpark, cor. Owl Street and Empire Road (Braamfontein), 249 rooms, all with baths. R25 – R35 room only. Phone 31-4760/9.
*** Holiday Inn President, Eloff and Plein streets, 230 rooms, all with baths. R36 – R46 room only. Phone 28-1414.
** Hyde Park Hotel, 52 Jan Smuts Avenue (Craighall), 40 rooms, all with baths. R11,50 – R30 B/B. Phone 42-7451.
** Jacaranda Hotel, Banket Street (Hillbrow), 300 rooms, all with baths. R7,50 – R8,50 D/B/B. Phone 642-7625.
*** Johannesburger Hotel, cor. Smit, Twist and Wolmarans streets, 400 rooms, all with baths. R11,50 – R13,50 room only. Phone 725-3753.
* Kontinental Hotel, 75 De Villiers Street, 66 rooms, all with baths. R7,50 – R13 B/B. Phone 23-7301.
*** Kyalami Ranch, Kyalami (Bergvlei), 121 rooms, all with baths. R15 – R21 room only. Phone 702-1600.
***** Landdrost Hotel, Plein Street, 265 rooms, all with baths. R27 – R42 room only. Phone 28-1770.
** La Rosa Hotel, 50 Abel Road (Berea), 111 rooms, all with baths. R9,75 – R15,75 B/B. Phone 642-7438.
* Libertas Hotel, 40 Central Avenue (Mayfair), 22 rooms, 6 with baths. R9,50 – R16 B/B. Phone 839-1012.
** New Library Hotel, 67 Commissioner Street, 33 rooms, all with baths. R8 – R12 B/B. Phone 834-1441.
* Lido Travelodge, Johannesburg/Vereeniging road, 15 rooms, 4 with baths. R6 – R10 B/B. Phone 943-2800 or 943-4413.
* Linden Hotel, 4th Avenue (Linden), 23 rooms, 6 with baths. R9,80 – R19 B/B. Phone 46-9477.
** Little Roseneath Hotel, Smit/Quarta Street (Joubert Park), 72 rooms, all with baths. R10,50 B/B. Phone 724-3322.
** Lloyd Hotel, Paul Nel Street (Hillbrow), 192 rooms, all with baths. R10 B/B. Phone 642-7665.
** Mariston Hotel, Koch Street, 107 rooms, all with baths. R10,50 – R15,50 room only. Phone 725-4130.
** Mark Hotel, 24 O'Reilly Road (Berea), 167 rooms, all with baths. R8,85 D/B/B. Phone 642-4931.
*Mellville Hotel, 20 Main Road (Melville), 16 rooms, 4 with baths. R7,50 B/B. Phone 31-1892.
* Milner Park Hotel, 71 Juta Street (Braamfontein), 14 rooms, 6 with baths. R5,50 B/B. Phone 724-4815.
* Mimosa Hotel, 26 Claredon Place, 320 rooms, all with baths. R8,50 D/B/B. Phone 642-7471.
* Monte Carlo Hotel, Bree/Von Wielligh Streets, 39 rooms, 19 with baths. R7 – R8 B/B. Phone 22-2367.
*** Moulin Rouge Hotel, Claim Street (Hillbrow), 146 rooms, all with baths. R14,90 – R23,60 B/B. Phone 725-4840.
* Newlands Hotel, 183 Main Road, 10 rooms, 3 with baths. R8,50 – R15 room only. Phone 27-1524.
* New Nugget Hotel, 25 Nugget Street, 18 rooms, 5 with baths. R6 B/B. Phone 23-0779.

★ Ophirton Hotel, 29 Garland Street, 14 rooms, 4 with baths. R5 B/B. Phone 834-4035.

★ Oxford Hotel, Oxford Road (Rosebank), 40 rooms, 22 with baths. R10 – R15 room only. Phone 42-9216.

★★ Park Lane Hotel, 54 Van der Merwe Street, 150 rooms, all with baths. R7,50 – R9,50 B/B. Phone 642-7425.

★★ Quirinale Hotel, 27 Kotze Street (Hillbrow), 117 rooms, all with baths. R13,50 – R19,95 B/B. Phone 724-1725.

★ Radium Hotel, 308 Marshall Street, 16 rooms, 8 with baths. R6 – R9,50 B/B. Phone 24-3562.

★★★★ Rand International Hotel, 290 Bree Street, 143 rooms, all with baths. R26 – R36 room only. Phone 836-7911.

★ Rebel Inn (Belgravia), 139 Jules Street, 11 rooms, 2 with baths. R7 – R14 B/B. Phone 24-1922.

★ Rebel Inn (Braamfontein), 159 Smit Street, 15 rooms, 4 with baths. R7,50 – R8,50 B/B. Phone 725-4380.

★ Rebel Inn (Malvern), 452 Jules Street, 26 rooms, 7 with baths. R7,50 – R8,50 B/B. Phone 25-1651.

★ Rebel Inn (Mayfair), 106 Central Avenue, 24 rooms, 6 with baths. R7,50 – R8,50 D/B/B. Phone 35-2200.

★★ Rebel Hotel, Mynpacht, 224 Main Road (Fordsburg), 9 rooms, 6 with baths. R7,50 – R8,50 B/B. Phone 838-7054.

★ Rebel Inn (Rosettenville), 200 Main Street, 20 rooms, 5 with baths. R7,50 – R8,50 B/B. Phone 26-4175.

★ Regent Park Hotel, 31 Augusta Road, 21 rooms, all with baths. R8 B/B. Phone 26-6414.

★ Ridge Hotel, 56 High Street (Mayfair W.), 19 rooms, 12 with baths. R7 B/B. Phone 35-1319.

★ Robertsham Hotel, Harry Street (Robertsham), 29 rooms, 15 with baths. R9,10 – R9,60 B/B. Phone 680-3606.

★ Rondebosch Hotel, 24 Edith Cavell Street (Hillbrow), 68 rooms, 26 with baths. R6 – R7 B/B. Phone 724-4151.

★★★★ Rosebank Hotel, 13 Tyrwhitt Avenue (Rosebank), 147 rooms, all with baths. R23,50 – R32 room only. Phone 788-1820.

★ Rosettenville Hotel, Verona Street (Rosettenville), 22 rooms, 11 with baths. R7,50 – R14,50 room only. Phone 26-5582.

★ Sacks Hotel, 89 Main Street (Fordsburg), 24 rooms, 6 with baths. R6,50 B/B. Phone 838-3717.

★ Salisbury Hotel, 118 Anderson Street, 12 rooms, 3 with baths. Phone 21-7749.

★★ Sands Hotel, Fife Avenue (Berea), 197 rooms, all with baths. R8 – R10 B/B. Phone 642-7211.

★ Sans Souci Hotel, 10 Guild Road (Parktown W.), 42 rooms, 26 with baths. R6,50 – R15 B/B. Phone 31-2578.

★★ Skyline Hotel, 27 Pretoria Street, 84 rooms, all with baths. R9,50 – R15,70 B/B. Phone 643-4941.

★ Solly Kramer's Hotel, 184 Main Road (Fordsburg), 14 rooms, 5 with baths. Phone 834-6664.

★ Springbok Hotel, 73 Joubert Street, 52 rooms, 29 with baths. R8 – R9,50 B/B. Phone 22-4177.

★ Station Hotel, 39 Berlein Street (Denver), 14 rooms, 4 with baths. R5 B/B. Phone 25-4198.

★★★® Sunnyside Park Hotel, 2 York Road (Parktown), 85 rooms, all with baths. R20 – R80 room only. Phone 43-7193.

★★★ Taylor's Travelodge, 400 Heidelberg Road, 60 rooms, all with baths. R16,62 – R23,92 B/B. Phone 869-5381/9.

★★★★ Towers Hotel, Kerk Street, 150 rooms, all with baths. R20 – R150 room only. Phone 37-2200.

* Troyville Hotel, 25 Bezuidenhout Street, 24 rooms, 7 with baths. R5,75 B/B. Phone 24-2319.
* Tudor (Rebel Inn), 116 Harrison Street (Braamfontein), 12 rooms, 3 with baths. R7,50 – R8,50 B/B. Phone 724-6995.
** Turffontein Hotel, Turf Club Street (Turffontein), 16 rooms, 7 with baths. R8,50 – R9,50 B/B. Phone 683-8343.
* Van Riebeeck Hotel, High Street (Brixton), 14 rooms, 4 with baths. R9,20 B/B. Phone 35-6791.
** Victoria Hotel, 25 Plein Street, 300 rooms, all with baths. R11,50 – R16 room only. Phone 28-3000.
* Village Main Hotel, 39 Gold Street, 21 rooms, 7 with baths. R5,50 – R6,50 B/B. Phone 22-5715.
* Waverley Hotel, 79 President Street, 24 rooms, 6 with baths. R8,50 B/B. Phone 834-3428.
* Wayside Hotel, 3 Stanhope Road (Cleveland), 40 rooms, 20 with baths. R6,50 B/B. Phone 25-2155.
* Whitehall Hotel, 8 Abel Road (Berea), 195 rooms, all with baths. R7,50 B/B. Phone 643-4911.
** White Horse Inn, Ford Avenue (Bushhill), 40 rooms, all with baths. R14 B/B. Phone 675-2091.
* Whitehouse Hotel, 152 Marshall Street, 31 rooms, 9 with baths. R8 – R17,50 B/B. Phone 21-9815.
* Wyntonjoy Kosher Hotel, Catherine Avenue (Berea), 57 rooms, 19 with baths. R16 – R28 B/B. Phone 642-4881.
* York Hotel, 6 Sauer Street, 21 rooms, 7 with baths. R7,50 B/B. Phone 834-2770.

## Caravans and Camping
***® Bezuidenhout Park, 55 sites. R2 – R4 D. Phone 43-3399.
Blossom Valley Caravan Park, 41 sites. R2 D plus 25c D per person. Phone 443-1508/4400.
** Essexwold Caravan Park (Bedfordview), 43 sites. R2,50 D plus 25c D per person. Phone 53-4631.
Ferreira's Caravan Park (10 km from Johannesburg on road to Vereeniging), 51 sites. R3,70 D for five persons. Phone 942-2600.
** Honeydew Caravan Park (Bramley), 45 sites, R3 D. Phone 675-2605.
** Johannesburg Caravan Park (Bramley), 26 sites, R3 D. Phone 802-2100.
Meredale Pleasure Resort (10 km from Johannesburg on road to Vereeniging), 60 sites. R2,50 D. Phone 942-1008.
Panorama Caravan Park (14 km from Johannesburg on Little Falls road), 60 sites. R1,50 D plus 25c D per person. Phone 679-1225.
** Rivonia Caravan Park (Rivonia), 40 sites. R2 D per person. Phone 802-1108.
Safari Caravan Park (12 km from Johannesburg on road to Vereeniging), 75 sites. R2,50 D per person. Phone 942-1404.
** Willow Grove Caravan Park (Lyndhurst), 70 sites. R2,50 D plus 50c D per person. Phone 608-2491.

# Chapter Twenty-nine
# THE WITWATERSRAND

The *Witwatersrand* (ridge of white waters) has long been the world's principal source of gold and one of its great natural wonders. To the eye it consists of a narrow rocky ridge about 80 km long, stretching east to west, with its centre point or hub, the city of Johannesburg, lying 1 748 m above sea level. Bleak, dry, hazy and swept by frost-laden winds in winter (May to August), the Witwatersrand is green, warm, and pleasantly well washed during the summer months (November to March) by a rainfall of 813 mm which generally falls in the form of spectacular afternoon and evening thunderstorms.

Geologists find the mystery of the Witwatersrand and its treasure house of gold most intriguing. Many theories have attempted to explain the origin of the complicated exposure of rock known as the Witwatersrand System. This system is sedimentary and is composed of rocks such as quartzite (hardened sandstone), shale and slate (hardened shale). The actual outcrop on the Witwatersrand is about 8 km wide and consists of a succession of upward sloping layers or series of beds, known from north to south as the Hospital Hill Series, the Government Reef Series, and the Jeppestown Series, all grouped together to form the Lower Witwatersrand Beds. Two other layers, the Main-Bird Series and the Kimberley-Elsburg Series, are together classed as the Upper Witwatersrand Beds.

The nature of the lower beds is largely shale while the upper beds consist mainly of quartzites impregnated with bands of conglomerate which are composed of quartz pebbles bound together in a fine matrix of siliceous cement containing iron pyrites. The conglomerate is similar in appearance to the favourite old Dutch sweetmeat of almonds in burnt sugar known as *banket,* and it is by this name that it is popularly known.

On the Witwatersrand itself there are three important bands containing this conglomerate: the Main Reef, the Main Reef Leader, and the South Reef. They occur close together and are collectively called the Main Reef Group of Conglomerates. On the Far West Rand, a less important member of this group, the Carbon Leader, is present. At Klerksdorp and in the Orange Free State, the Vaal Reef and the Basal Reef, both belonging to the Bird Reef Group, are the principal gold carriers. For the past 70 years these reef groups have together yielded the great bulk of the world's gold.

The origin of this remarkable rock system is cause for much controversy. That it was deposited by water action about 1 000 million years ago has been confirmed, but whether by means of marine, river, or even glacial action remains a mystery. It seems most probable that the site was once an inland sea or lake. Rivers flowed into this ancient sea depositing a rich spoil eroded from the higher lying landscape of the Primitive System. Included in this deposit, apart from pebbles, sand and silt, were green diamonds, gold and other minerals such as carbon, uranium, iron pyrites and chromite. The distinct layers at the bottom of the sea resulted from variations in the nature of the sediments carried in from time to time, the effects of currents, and the changing level of the inland sea.

Eventually this basin (a dream sea of gold) silted up and vanished. Its ancient bed was left to dry and solidify. During the course of time it was twisted, tilted, faulted, and subjected to extreme fluctuations of heat and cold. Lava intruded into it from subterranean depths. Its richly varied mineral content was partly dissolved and re-precipitated. The ghost of the old dream sea of gold was metamorphosed and the only verification of its existence today is that the gold is there and that water played some part in its establishment; all else is conjecture.

Little more is known about the prehistory of the Witwatersrand other than its geological origin. Relics of the primitive people who lived on the Witwatersrand before the dawn of history may easily be seen. On many of the heights of the Rand (especially in the south in the hills of the Kliprivviersberg, around the suburb of Mondeor) still stand whole complexes of low stone walls surrounding the ruins of huts erected there by primitive Iron Age people who apparently spoke the Tswana language.

The situation of these ruins (always on the tops of hills) made them easily defensible. What battles, sieges and sackings took place in these old settlements there is no way of knowing. The inhabitants were eventually totally wiped out – killed, captured or driven away – by the invasion of the Ndebele in 1822. When the first Europeans appeared on the scene, only ruins remained and now even these are vanishing rapidly, overwhelmed by modern housing estates, or being half buried beneath long grass. Their stone walls serve only as wild rockeries for aloes and succulents whose crimson flowers contain, perhaps, a little of the blood of a vanished people.

With the advent of the Voortrekkers, the Witwatersrand, by then completely devoid of human occupants, was settled by a number of farmers (about 75 families in all) who made a rather drab living growing maize and pumpkins in what was an isolated situation.

There is no indication that any of the prehistoric inhabitants or the early farmers found any mineral deposits other than iron, but somehow a rumour that gold was present in the Witwatersrand spread abroad as early as 1806, when John Barrow published a map of the Transvaal on which the high-lying ridge was indicated and marked as supposedly rich in gold.

The first discovery of gold on the Witwatersrand was in 1853 when Pieter Marais, a man with experience of the Australian and Californian goldfields, searched the verges of the ridge in the hope of finding alluvial gold. On 8 October he found a few tantalising specks of gold in the *Jukskei* (yoke key) River which has its source on the summit of the Witwatersrand. The specks had almost certainly been washed down from those heights, but Marais found no positive lead and abandoned the search. The detailed story of the Witwatersrand and the discovery of its gold is told in the book *Lost Trails of the Transvaal.*

The next discovery in the area of the Witwatersrand was made in 1874 when an Australian, Henry Lewis, found gold on a farm named *Bloubank* in the Magaliesberg, about 29 km north-west of Krugersdorp. Quite a rush to the scene of this discovery resulted, but little gold was ever found there and the excitement petered out.

*Bloubank* had simply been on the outskirts of the Witwatersrand proper; the next exciting gold find was much nearer the real pay lode. In 1881 Stephanus Minnaar found gold on the farm *Kromdraai* 16 km north of Krugersdorp. A small-scale rush to this area took place and gold was actually produced, but only in disappointingly small amounts. Three years later, in 1884, Fred Struben found another gold reef on the slopes of the Witwatersrand, on a farm named *Wilgespruit* near the burgeoning modern township of Florida. This find also proved disappointing but it played a major role in the chain of events which culminated in the discovery of the Main Reef of the Witwatersrand.

Among the individuals attracted to the Witwatersrand by the rumours of gold at *Wilgespruit* were two rough-looking men tramping up from the south to try their luck at Barberton. Struben employed one of these men, George Walker, while the other, George Harrison – the man of destiny – trudged on up to the summit of the Witwatersrand and made his way to the *Langlaagte* (long dale) farm of Jan Oosthuizen, where he had heard that a workman was needed to build a new farmhouse. While he was employed on this task, George Harrison indulged in spare-time prospecting. Some time in March 1886, on a day which he never even bothered to record, this silent man found an outcrop of the Main Reef on a portion of *Langlaagte* farm owned by Gerhardus Oosthuizen.

*Overleaf: Like a range of mountains on another planet; the manmade rubble, rock and tailing dumps of the Witwatersrand gold mines.*

For his discovery, Harrison was awarded the usual tax-free privileged claim (Claim 19) known as the Discoverer's Claim, but this he soon sold for £10 and vanished from the scene entirely. His fate is not known, but his discovery lives on in the vital, pulsating mining and industrial complex of the Witwatersrand which has developed around the site (almost poignantly left abandoned) of the actual reef outcrop on which George Harrison, in his shabby, itinerant labourer's clothes, must have sat as he looked down in wonder and disbelief, at the signs of gold in his battered old prospecting pan.

The site of the discovery of the Main Reef is preserved as the George Harrison Park, 5 km west along the Main Reef Road from the centre of Johannesburg. Old mine workings may also be seen there, as well as an interesting 10-stamp battery of the type used to crush the ore in the early days.

The reason for George Harrison's abrupt disappearance from the scene was probably due to his own disappointment at the nature rather than the value of his discovery. Gold is found in two main types of deposit: alluvial and lode or reef. The prospector, generally an individualist, always dreamed of finding a rich alluvial deposit in a stream. With minimum requirements of capital, the prospector could set up a simple recovery plant and extract gold with little investment other than hard work.

The gold-bearing reefs of the Witwatersrand were lode deposits, however, which required the investment of enormous amounts of capital. Individual prospectors could not cope with such discoveries for they were immediately at the mercy of financiers. Of these gentlemen it was said that the only time one of them ever seemed at least to have a glint of kindliness in his eyes was an individual whose one glass eye happened to reflect the light!

A simple prospector such as George Harrison fled the scene when the financiers moved in. If one such as he was lucky he took something away with him; if unlucky, he left in rags. Out of the spoils these prospectors left behind them, the financiers created a colossal industry. A lode such as the Witwatersrand Main Reef might be difficult to work, involving complex chemical problems of how to release the gold from the rock; but from a business point of view, while an alluvial deposit was patchy and unpredictable, a reef could be measured, tested, assayed and evaluated as a long-term industrial prospect worthy of vast investment and the employment of an enormous concentration of money, labour, and technical expertise.

When the gold-bearing reef of the Witwatersrand was first discovered, it was exposed by open trenches which were dug along its length. The reef was narrow – only 1 m wide for most of its length – and dipped steeply below the surface at an angle of about 20 degrees. The trenches were made as deep as possible, but there were limits to such surface workings. The average proportion of gold in the Witwatersrand reef was 15 g per metric ton (8,75 pennyweights per short ton). For payability or maximum profit a very minimum of non-gold carrying ore would have to be extracted, and with the reef being so narrow this meant that highly specialised mining techniques were called for. When it became evident that the reef would reach a very deep level, it was even more essential that as little non-productive waste matter as possible be mined, for every rock would have to be hoisted to the surface. The deeper the mine the more costly the hoisting would be; the more non-productive matter fed into the mill, the more expensive the whole process of gold recovery would become.

In practice, a shaft is sunk to the lowest level planned for current working. On the Rand the deepest level reached so far is 3 500 m. From the shaft, drives are sent out at various levels to intersect the sloping reef. From these drives stopes are worked up the reef with the excavated ore gravitating down to the drives where it is trammed by electric haulage to the hoisting shaft. The stopes are kept as narrow as possible, excavating the width of gold-bearing reef with just enough space on either side to allow the miners to work. Ventilation and refrigeration on a massive scale have to be provided to make conditions tolerable for human beings since the deeper the mine, the greater the heat and humidity.

The ore hoisted to the surface is crushed in mills to a fine powder. Mercury is then introduced and this amalgamates with about 70 per cent of the gold. This amalgam is separated from the rest of the material and heated to vaporise the mercury; the gold which remains is bullion. The mercury vapour is condensed for re-use. The balance of the gold has a recalcitrant nature and its recovery demands a more complex chemical process. A solution of sodium or calcium cyanide is introduced which dissolves the gold, producing gold cyanide. Extremely fine zinc powder is then added which displaces the gold in the cyanide solution. The mixture is filtered and the gold is precipitated in the form of a black powder. This powder is mixed with fluxes and subjected to heat. Most of the impurities separate to form waste slag and what is known as bullion or unrefined gold is produced.

Bullion contains an average of 88 per cent gold, 10 per cent silver and 2 per cent base metals. Bullion is sent to a central refinery, the Rand Refinery in Germiston, for the elimination of all undesirable matter by means of the standard treatment, the Miller Chlorination Process, invented in Australia.

This process introduces chlorine gas to the molten gold. Impurities form metallic chlorides with the gas and, being lighter than gold, rise to the surface where they are skimmed off. The remaining matter is known as monetary gold, 99,5 per cent pure while 0,5 per cent is silver. This refined gold is cast into bars weighing about 12,5 kg each. On these bars the exact purity as determined by assay is stamped: a bar stamped 9960 would mean that it is 99,60 per cent pure gold, and is acceptable for monetary and most industrial purposes, as well as for the making of jewellery.

The space age and modern electronics demand gold of ultimate purity. To achieve this purity, refined gold is subjected to additional treatment such as electrolytic refining, during which an electric current is passed through the gold. This current deposits absolutely pure gold on to a cathode. Pure gold is used in electronics to plate vital contacts, and also in printed circuits where high conductive reliability and corrosion resistance are essential. Space apparatus, too, demands this gold. Thin layers are used to provide an outer casing for satellites since the metal reflects 98 per cent of infra-red radiation and acts as a barrier against solar radiation of high intensity. Astronauts' visors are plated with pure gold to protect them from both ultra-violet and infra-red radiation.

Since gold was discovered in the Transvaal, more than 35 million kilograms (1 100 million ounces) have been recovered, realising more than R25 000 million. Large mines such as the Vaal Reefs and the Harmony Mine mill more than five million metric tons of ore each year. The world's richest mine, West Driefontein, produces 74 000 kg (2,4 million ounces) of gold every year. Apart from gold, also recovered are uranium, silver, platinum and various base minerals of considerable value to industry. Over 400 000 men are employed in the gold mining industry in the Transvaal.

The deepest gold mine in the world is the East Rand Proprietary Mine near Boksburg, the main shaft of which goes down 3 428 m. The second deepest gold mine is the City Deep Mine on the south-eastern outskirts of Johannesburg, with a shaft of 3 245 m. To maintain a reasonable working temperature for the miners, the East Rand Proprietary Mine uses 36 284 tons of ice each day.

On the Witwatersrand, the temperature rises 12,2°C for every 61 m under the ground. The deep mines are working in temperatures of 46,1°C. Although ore is known to extend beyond the 15 244-m level, the technical difficulties of operating at such depths would be staggering and the costs of hauling ore to the surface immense.

Visits to the gold mines are arranged by the Chamber of Mines, corner of Main and Hollard streets in Johannesburg (phone 838-8211). Advance booking is essential and no children under 16 years of age are allowed.

The Simmer and Jack Mine at Germiston has been restored as a fascinating living museum of gold mining. Visitors can descend in the mine hoist to underground workings, or walk down an incline shaft to the number nine level where gold mining can be seen. A horse-drawn tram takes passengers through a perfect facsimile of a miner's residential area of the 1890s. There are working stamp mills, sluice boxes, winches, and demonstrations of how to pan gold. In the reduction mills, extraction plant and smelt house, visitors can watch gold being extracted from the rock and poured into bars. A museum, curio shop and an Ndebele village are housed in one of the historical buildings. Admission is R6,50 per person. The mine is open Mondays to Fridays at 08h30. Phone 51-8571 for details of daily tours.

A fine, entertaining spectacle on the Witwatersrand is the competitive tribal dancing that takes place every second and fourth Sunday of each month on one or other of the gold mines. Tickets and information about these dances may be obtained from the Chamber of Mines, corner Main and Hollard streets, Johannesburg. Phone 838-8211. Admission is free.

The African loves to dance. He regards it as recreation, an exercise, an opportunity for display; the supreme expression of his zest for life. A miner's work is arduous and dangerous, his society exclusively male. He lives in barracks for the duration of his contract period (usually about one year), and his women are far away back home. For him the journey to *eGoli* (the place of gold) is the greatest experience of his life; a completely new environment, lifestyle, type of labour and society.

Men from about 50 different African tribes work on the Witwatersrand. To converse with one another, and the European mine workers, they quickly learn a simple language common to all, known as *Fanakalo* (like this). Fanakalo consists mainly of Zulu vocabulary interspersed with odd words from several other African languages while English and Afrikaans provide the technical terms.

In his leisure time, the African mine worker takes part in sport, watches films, attends self-improvement classes in subjects such as reading, writing and various handicrafts. There is singing, tribal music, African jazz – and also dancing; in this manner he can revert to his tribal way of life, can change his clothing from European overalls to the skins and adornments of his own people, can look and feel his best when dancing in groups of his own kind, displaying to others his physical prowess and competitive spirit.

The dancers organise themselves into teams, each having a manager as well as a music and dance director. Costumes are designed, rehearsals are held in preparation for Sunday mornings – the big day for tribal dancing.

The music is powerful, the rhythms explicit and demanding. Variations are imposed on a basic rhythmic theme which is established at the beginning of the piece. Most of the melodies are pentatonic (consisting of five notes) but some of the tribes, particularly those from the Northern Transvaal and Zimbabwe, use hexatonic (six-note) and even heptatonic (seven-note) scales. The principal dances are as follows:

The various tribes of the Nguni-speaking group – Zulu, Hlubi, Bhaca, Nhlangwini, Pondomise, Pondo, Zingili and Swazi – who live along the south-east coast, specialise in what is known as the *Ndlamu* dance, performed by young men in single or double lines who stamp their feet in different ways to diverse tempos. Each tribe has their own complex variation of this dance. Music is provided by clappers, bells and various kinds of drums. From all the groups, individuals spring forward at different times and perform a *giya* or war dance; jumping, brandishing sticks, throwing their bodies about and shouting vainglorious self-praise.

In the same Nguni-speaking group, the Xhosa perform an *amaKhwenkwe umteyo* (young men's shaking dance): with a rapid backward and forward movement of the knee, the dancers make their chests and spines ripple, tinkling small bells strapped across their upper bodies.

The Bhaca tribe have an amusing dance of their own, known as the *isiCathulo* (boot dance). Of this dance it is said that a missionary once forbade his community from performing their traditional dances as he considered them to be pagan. They were taught a more 'genteel' Austrian folk dance. It happened that some of the tribesmen working in the docks in Durban were issued with wellington boots. The 'new' dance, performed in these cumbersome boots, became popular and there was nothing the missionary could do, since the idea was originally his!

The Sotho-Tswana-speaking tribes have a completely different series of dances from the Nguni-speaking tribes. The Sotho perform a *Mohobelo* (striding dance), making a unique entrance to the dancing area by sliding, striding, slithering and hissing. They favour high kicks and stamping, leaping and twisting into the air. Another of their dances is the *Stapu* (walking dance), in which they move rhythmically backwards and forwards.

The Pedi tribe of the central Transvaal are the performers of a *Kubina dithlaka* (pipe dance). Each dancer plays a pipe of a different tone. As they dance, they blow their pipes in succession, producing a series of unique melodies, like the chords on a concertina. Leg rattles and drums provide the rhythm.

The Tswana or Lete people from Botswana also have a *Kubina dithlaka* (pipe dance) which is similar to that of the Pedi, but varies slightly in sound, melody and performance.

The Shangane-Tsonga people from Moçambique perform a modern dance known as the *Makwaya*. A source of great amusement, the participants poke fun at the modern world and the ways of the white man, their bosses on the mines, the missionaries back home, the tax collectors and government officials.

The Tswa from Moçambique perform a complex *Nzumba* or *Ngalanga* (step dance), using small wooden xylophones for music.

The Tshopi tribe from Moçambique have the *Ngodo* (orchestral dance) and, musically, this is the most fascinating sound in Africa. Wooden xylophones are used and the standard of playing is excellent. An outstanding player is highly regarded and honoured by his people. Orchestral performances in the homelands are superb – a full *Ngodo* has up to 16 movements.

The Ndawu tribe, also from Moçambique, performs a *Mutshongolo* (tumbling dance), which involves skilled acrobatics. The men burst into the dancing area, somersaulting, throwing themselves on to the ground and bouncing along on their hands and toes, clowning in many ingenious and amusing ways. Their drummers are masters of rhythm and a good performance always brings the house down.

## EXPLORING THE WITWATERSRAND

The Witwatersrand is not notable for its scenic beauty and few people regard it as a holiday resort. Any traveller condemned to negotiate the full 96-km length from Springs to Randfontein during a rush-hour period (from 16h30 onwards on a Friday), would consider himself to be in purgatory.

The towns and cities are all linked together by kilometres of similar-looking streets congested with demoniac drivers and heedless pedestrians. Look-alike shops – commercial clones – line the streets and there are few exceptional features.

Towns such as these may be seen in most of the industrial and mining areas of the world but at least the inhabitants of the Witwatersrand have the consolation of being able to breathe reasonably upolluted air. They can bask in generous sunshine and, leaving their high ridge, can escape to the vast, rolling kilometres of open veld where claustrophobia is unimaginable.

Winter is a bleak season; dry, hazy and swept by frost-laden winds. Grass-burning is common, blackening the landscape which as a result, seems to be in mourning. Spring transforms the place into a beautiful Cinderella – green, warm, well-washed by thunderstorms, she is sparkling, vivacious, stimulating and competitive. But in autumn, she reluctantly sneaks back as late as possible before the stroke of midnight into the drab colours, smog, smut, cold and toil of winter.

Exploring the East Rand, the first town is reached 14,5 km from the centre of Johannesburg . . .

# GERMISTON

This town was established at the height of the rush to the Witwatersrand. A trader from Lake Chrissie, John Jack, happened to pass over a farm named *Elandsfontein* where, amidst the general mania for gold, he tried his hand at prospecting, with such interesting results that, with his partner, August Simmer, he floated the Simmer & Jack Gold Mining Company. In May 1887 a town to house the workers on this mine was laid out on *Elandsfontein* farm and named *Germiston* by John Jack in memory of the farm near Glasgow on which he had been born.

Germiston became a municipality in 1903 and a city in 1950. It is today the largest railway junction in Africa as well as being a major industrial area. It is the site of the world's largest gold refinery, the Rand Refinery, which has an annual output of 73 per cent of the world total of gold produced outside Russia. There are over 600 industries in Germiston and it is the sixth largest city in South Africa, having a population of 216 123. Among its recreational facilities is the Germiston Lake (a manmade dam), the largest on the Witwatersrand, which is a favourite place for boating, swimming and picnicking.

At the western entrance to Germiston stands a remarkable illuminated fountain which resembles the working headgear of a gold mine. The Simmer and Jack mine is now a museum (see page 579). The various tailings dumps around Germiston include some of the largest and most colourful of their kind. Photographers and those interested in mining history find the area rich in fascinating scenes and relics. On the old Balmoral mine a huge tailings wheel, 16 m in diameter, still stands on its original supports.

## Accommodation

* Caledonian Hotel, 24 rooms, 6 with baths. R8 B/B. Phone 58-1516.
* Clarendon Hotel, 29 rooms, 9 with baths. R6 – R7 B/B. Phone 825-1610.
* Constantia Hotel, 10 rooms, 4 with baths, R7 – R16 B/B. Phone 58-1020.
* Court Hotel, 32 rooms, 8 with baths. R8,50 B/B. Phone 51-2845.
* Edward Hotel, 13 rooms, 3 with baths. R6,75 B/B. Phone 51-2270.
* Germiston Hotel, 60 rooms, 23 with baths. R10 – R12 D/B/B. Phone 51-8371.
* Grand Station Hotel, 16 rooms, 4 with baths. R4,50 – R6 B/B. Phone 51-2698.
* King's Hotel, 14 rooms, 4 with baths. R8 B/B. Phone 51-5834.
* Masonic Hotel, 13 rooms, 3 with baths. R8 – R16 B/B. Phone 51-1457.
* Primrose Hotel, 23 rooms, 11 with baths. R8 B/B. Phone 58-5762.
* Railway Hotel, 12 rooms, 4 with baths. R7,50 – R8,50 B/B. Phone 51-1724.
* Witwatersrand Hotel, 12 rooms, 4 with baths. R7 – R8 B/B. Phone 58-3958.

## Caravans and camping

* Cresta Caravan Park (Elandsfontein), 200 sites. R1 D. Phone 36-5060.

From the centre of Germiston, the centre of the next East Rand town is reached after 11 km.

# BOKSBURG

Founded in August 1887 as an administrative centre for the surrounding mining areas, *Boksburg* was laid out on a portion of the farm *Leeuwpoort* and was named after Eduard Bok, the Attorney-General of the Republic. Apart from gold (a notable producer being the great East Rand Proprietary Mines), coal was also mined in the area and the place soon attained considerable importance, becoming one of the pleasantest towns on the East Rand. Its first mining commissioner, Montague White, set out to beautify the place by planting numerous trees. He also built a dam across the Vogelfontein stream, planning a lake on so magnificent a scale that at first it was known as White's Folly. Now called Boksburg Lake, this handsome stretch of water provides a fine recreational area for the town. President Kruger was particularly fond of the place. He owned a farm nearby named *Geduld* (patience) which he sold at a profit when gold was found there.

Boksburg became a municipality in 1903 and has a population of 151 650. It is an industrial centre with a considerable variety of factories producing items such as electric motors, transformers, nuts, bolts, bitumen, veneered and laminated board, concrete piping, detergents, domestic appliances and many other things.

## Accommodation

* Angelo Hotel, 13 rooms, 7 with baths. R7,50 – R8,50 D/B/B. Phone 826-2213.
* Boksburg North Hotel, 13 rooms, 4 with baths. R7,50 – R8,50 B/B. Phone 52-5206.
* Central Hotel, 23 rooms, 7 with baths. R7 – R8 B/B. Phone 52-7479.
* East Rand Hotel, 14 rooms, 4 with baths. R7 B/B. Phone 52-1361.
* Kings Hotel, 16 rooms, 6 with baths. R8,50 room only. Phone 52-3572.
* Masonic Hotel, 20 rooms, 6 with baths. R12 – R15 D/B/B. Phone 52-4389.
* Rebel Inn, 14 rooms, 5 with baths. R7,50 – R8,50 B/B. Phone 826-2424.
* Transvaal Hotel, 11 rooms, 3 with baths. R7 – R9 D/B/B. Phone 52-3072.

From the centre of Boksburg it is 8 km to the centre of the town of . . .

# BENONI

The irregular shape of the farm on which the modern town stands gave its original surveyor so much trouble that he borrowed from the Bible the name Rachel had given Benjamin – *Benoni* (son of my sorrow). Gold was discovered on this farm in September 1887 and in due course a mine by the name of The Chimes commenced production there. For some reason this mine was a great centre for Cornishmen who comprised the total work force. The book *Lost Trails of the Transvaal* relates that the collection of shanties which served as the mine's housing estate was a favourite place for gambling and dog fights. Paydays also provided a unique spectacle; a long line of cabs would arrive from Boksburg, then the nearest town, and as soon as the men knocked off, they would choose their cabs and for high stakes race one another to the nearest pub, causing an appalling cloud of dust to rise from an execrable road.

The town of Benoni only came into existence in March 1904 when the first sale of stands took place. On 1 October 1907 it became a municipality and today 186 823 people live there. The foundation and early development of the town was largely due to the work of Sir George Farrar, chairman of the mining syndicate which owned the ground. On his instructions thousands of trees were planted, the lake was stocked with rainbow trout, and the town laid out on spacious grounds.

Benoni is one of the most pleasant towns on the Rand. A 61-ha nature reserve, the Korsman Bird Sanctuary, has been established and there are first-class sporting facilities at Willowmore Park. Rynfield Children's Park, commonly known as Bunny Park, provides a delightful playground with hundreds of rabbits, tame sheep and birds. A considerable variety of industries are centred in the town, producing batteries, jute, asbestos products, light castings, valves, brake-linings and wheel rims, railway trucks, hose-piping and teapots.

## Accommodation

* Rebel Inn, 24 rooms, 9 with baths. R7,50 – R8,50 B/B. Phone 54-6745.
* Regent Hotel, 25 rooms, 6 with baths. R6,50 – R7 B/B. Phone 54-3425.
* Rex Hotel, 23 rooms, 10 with baths. R8,32 B/B. Phone 54-2299.
** Van Riebeeck Hotel, 19 rooms, all with baths. R11,50 B/B. Phone 54-9591.

Caravans and camping
** Cairngorm Tea Gardens, 100 sites. R1 D plus 50c D per person.
** Fairwinds Caravan Park, 52 sites. R7 D.
** Sonop Caravan Park, 59 sites. R4,50 D. Phone 973-1489 or 973-3089.

Eight kilometres from the centre of Benoni lies the next East Rand town of . . .

# BRAKPAN

With its population of 89 480, *Brakpan* was originally a farm named on account of a small lakelet of brackish water which was found in the vicinity. The area came into prominence when coal was discovered and the first railway in the Transvaal, the old 'Rand Tram', was built to carry coal from this and other East Rand coal mines, to Johannesburg.

The town of Brakpan had a slow beginning and only became a municipality in August 1919. Besides mining, it has developed into a modern industrial centre. Recreational facilities include Hosking Park and Jan Smuts Park created on the shores of the V.F.P. Dam.

## Accommodation
* Brakpan Hotel, 37 rooms, 7 with baths. R7 B/B. Phone 55-1285.
* Masonic Hotel, 12 rooms, 3 with baths. R7,50 – R8 B/B. Phone 55-2328.
* Park Hotel, 33 rooms, 10 with baths. R8 – R19 B/B. Phone 55-1871.
* Savoy Hotel, 22 rooms, 6 with baths. R7 B/B. Phone 55-1226.
* Station Hotel, 16 rooms, 4 with baths. R8 – R9 B/B. Phone 55-1211.

## Caravans and camping
* Jan Smuts Park, 25 sites. R2 D.

The last East Rand town is reached 6 km from the centre of Brakpan.

# SPRINGS

The town was established on the farm of *Springs* which was named on account of the number of fountains there. The importance of the area increased when coal was discovered in 1888 and in 1890 the first railway in the Transvaal, the so-called 'Rand Tram', was built to carry coal from the East Rand coal mines to Johannesburg. The line terminated on the *Springs* farm and six collieries commenced operations in the area.

The railway terminus formed the nucleus of a town whose first inhabitants were principally Welshmen employed as coal miners. Inevitably, the Springs Male Voice Choir was established and became well known in the Transvaal. The coal mines, however, underwent several unfortunate experiences. The Z.A.S.M. Colliery, situated between the present railway station and the town hall, caught fire early in 1899 and had to be closed; on 21 March 1907 a major subsidence occurred in the Great Eastern Colliery, causing the houses of the mine captain and the engineer to collapse into the hole, with one of the mine captain's children being killed.

Coal mining in the area was gradually abandoned, but was replaced by gold and industry. Springs became a municipality in November 1904 and has a population of 173 553. It is now a substantial industrial centre where factories produce paper (S.A.P.P.I.), cosmetics (Watkins), glass (Pilkington), foodstuffs (Maconochie) and many other items.

Recreational facilities include the Murray Park pleasure resort, the Martiens Kotze Park with its novel layout, a game park and the spacious P.A.M. Brink stadium, home of the Eastern Transvaal Rugby Union. In the library is a fine frieze painted by the wandering artist, Conrad Genal.

## Accommodation
* Casseldale Hotel, 20 rooms, 11 with baths. R10 – R20 B/B. Phone 56-2735.
* National Hotel, 16 rooms, 4 with baths. R9 B/B. Phone 53-6301.
* Park Hotel, 22 rooms, 5 with baths. R10 – R12 B/B. Phone 818-5115.
* Protea Hotel, 31 rooms, 9 with baths. R11,50 B/B. Phone 56-0708.
* Riebeeck Hotel, 25 rooms, 6 with baths. R8,50 B/B. Phone 56-5734.
* Springs Hotel, 41 rooms, 10 with baths. R12,50 B/B. Phone 56-2613.
* Township Hotel, 12 rooms, 3 with baths. R6 – R7 B/B. Phone 56-1678.
* Veld and Vlei Hotel, 20 rooms, 9 with baths. R9 B/B. Phone 56-6849.
* Vossies Royal Hotel, 22 rooms, 8 with baths. R5,50 – R7 B/B. Phone 56-2076.

## Caravans and camping
*® Murray Park, 200 sites. R3 D.

From Springs, the main road eastwards leaves the Witwatersrand, crossing typical highveld maize country. After 29 km the road passes through a rural centre with the French name of *Delmas* (the little farm) which, with a population of 9 700, is the rail and commercial centre for the surrounding farmers.

A further 42 km brings the road to the rural coal mining centre of Ogies, built on the farm *Ogiesfontein* (fountain of little eyes) belonging to Jan Visagie.

Another rail centre in this flat world of coal, maize, beans and potatoes is *Kendal,* named after the town in north-western England which lies at the gateway to the Lake District.

Twenty-seven kilometres beyond Ogies (98 km from Springs) the road joins the main road from Pretoria to Moçambique at Witbank, the coal metropolis of Southern Africa.

## Accommodation
* Delmas Hotel (Delmas), 10 rooms, 4 with baths. R7,50 B/B. Phone 441.
* Ogies Hotel (Ogies), 27 rooms, 7 with baths. R7,50 – R8,50 B/B. Phone 93.

# THE WEST RAND TOWNS

From Johannesburg, the Main Reef Road to the west passes the old workings of the Crown Mines, in its day one of the richest gold mines ever worked, but now no longer in production. Part of it has been converted by the Chamber of Mines into the Gold Mine Museum with an old time restaurant, smelter, underground workings and rides on steam trains. The museum is open daily except Mondays.

The Main Reef Road continues through a confused complex of mines, dumps and industries. At 6 km the road passes the George Harrison Memorial Park where the first payable gold was found on the Witwatersrand. At 13 km from Johannesburg there is a turnoff to Florida with its lake and recreational area.

## Accommodation
* Killarney Hotel (Florida), 19 rooms, 6 with baths. R6,50 B/B. Phone 672-4742.
* Lake Hotel, 34 rooms, 9 with baths. R8 – R18 B/B. Phone 672-0540.
* Retreat Hotel, 15 rooms, 6 with baths. R6,50 – R10,50 D/B/B. Phone 672-2895.
* Richmond Hotel, 16 rooms, 4 with baths. R7 B/B. Phone 672-5129.
* Uniflor Hotel, 15 rooms, 4 with baths. R7,50 – R8,50 B/B. Phone 672-4311.

At 19 km from Johannesburg the road reaches the town of . . .

# ROODEPOORT

Many of the pioneer miners of the Witwatersrand worked in this area where Roodepoort was first established as a mine camp. On the farm *Wilgespruit* just north of Roodepoort, Fred and Harry Struben worked their Confidence Reef, and others such as J. G. Bantjies, G. Lys, H. G. van der Hoven on *Florida* and A. P. Marais on *Maraisburg,* were all pioneers of this area.

A town to serve these various mining enterprises was laid out on the farm *Roodepoort* (the red pass) and the first stands sold in February 1887. With its 'family' of suburbs and associate townships such as Maraisburg, Florida, Hamburg, Discovery and Ontdekkers Park, Roodepoort now occupies a 140-square kilometre extent of the Witwatersrand and apart from its mines, is a rapidly developing industrial area. It became a city on 1 October 1977 and the population now numbers 165 618. The area around Florida Lake facilitates activities such as swimming, boating and picnicking. A monument commemorating the discovery of gold in the area stands on its shores. The bronzes were sculpted by Dale Lace. A museum in the town exhibits interesting relics of early mining and the pioneer days.

### Accommodation
* Delarey Hotel, 19 rooms, all with baths. R9,50 – R10,50 B/B. Phone 27-3610.
* Golden West Hotel, 13 rooms, 4 with baths. R7,50 – R9 B/B. Phone 763-1396.
* Karina Hotel, 25 rooms, 9 with baths. Phone 763-1226.
* Savoy Hotel, 22 rooms, 4 with baths. R7 – R8,50 B/B. Phone 763-1815.
* Solly Kramer's Hotel, 12 rooms, 3 with baths. R7 B/B. Phone 763-3293.
* Station Hotel, 12 rooms, 9 with baths. R8,50 B/B. Phone 763-6064.

### Caravans and camping
** Florida Lake, 65 sites. R1 D. Phone 672-2711.
** Pondorosa Caravan Park, 20 sites. R2 D plus 50c D per person. Phone 765-0635.

From Roodepoort, the Main Reef Road continues westwards through *Witpoortjie* (the small white pass), a popular picnic resort. From the Witpoortjie railway station a path leads for 8 km down the pretty ravine to the fine 76-m-high waterfall and pleasure resort accessible only by road a long way round through Krugersdorp. Facing the Witpoortjie railway station is a small wayside hotel which for many years has offered refreshment to passers-by.

In 1889 a famous gunfight took place near the bar of this hotel. Two bank robbers, John McKeone and Joseph Terpend, had held up the Standard Bank in Krugersdorp, absconding with £4 500. A posse set off in pursuit of the thieves who were making good their escape. While passing Witpoortjie, one of their pursuers remembered that a well-known racehorse named Atlas was quartered in a stable behind the hotel. He flung himself on to the horse and raced after the robbers, who, to their dismay, found themselves being overtaken by what seemed to be a whirlwind.

On passing the wagon of an impoverished woodcutter, they tried to lighten their load of £1 503 worth of gold nuggets by tossing their saddlebags on to the wood piled on the wagon in the hope of retrieving the gold later. This strategy was to no avail, for nemesis in the form of the racehorse overtook them and a blazing gunfight ensued. The two men surrendered and were imprisoned. It is said that when the woodcutter unloaded his wagon and found the bags of gold, he gave thanks to the Lord for gifts received, retired to the Bushveld and bought a farm on the proceeds!

### Accommodation
* Witpoortjie Hotel, 16 rooms, all with baths. R7,50 – R15 B/B. Phone 664-6009.
* Lewisham Hotel, 26 rooms, 9 with baths. R7,50 B/B. Phone 664-6112.

Passing through Lewisham and the Luipaardsvlei Estate mining area, the road, 11 km from Roodepoort, reaches the town of . . .

# KRUGERSDORP

For a variety of reasons, Krugersdorp is the most atmospheric town on the Witwatersrand. During the period between 8 and 18 December 1880, a great gathering of Transvalers was held on the farm *Paardekraal* just outside modern Krugersdorp. The stalwarts of the old Transvaal Republic had assembled to stage a massive protest against the annexation of their country by the British. A triumvirate was appointed – Paul Kruger, Piet Joubert and M. W. Pretorius – with full powers to act, and the 6 000 men at the gathering all solemnly swore to stand united until independence had been restored. As proof of their oath, each man placed a stone on a cairn. After the short but salutary Anglo-Transvaal War when independence had been won, it was resolved that once every five years on 16 December, a celebration would be held at the cairn combining the giving of thanks for independence and remembrance of the victory over Dingane. A permanent monument to mark the site was erected at *Paardekraal*, but unfortunately the original cairn of stones has vanished.

On 26 April 1887 the Republican Government resolved to purchase a portion of *Paardekraal* and on this was founded the town of *Krugersdorp*, named in honour of the State President. This town became the administrative centre of the West Rand goldfields and its importance was soon established with substantial government buildings, the handsome 37-ha Coronation Park, first-class sports amenities and a bustling commercial centre. Enhanced by flourishing vegetation, it became one of the most pleasant towns on the Rand and its council has systematically set out to beautify the place with gardens and trees.

At Doringkop, 13 km south of Krugersdorp, the Jameson Raid came to a sudden end and the renowned Dr 'Jim' and his band – now a forlorn collection of prisoners – were marched into Krugersdorp, which he regarded as his special 'Krugerloo'. The five burghers who fell in the fight were buried in Krugersdorp, while the graves of Jameson's men lie alongside the railway line to Randfontein.

Krugersdorp lies a brisk, 1 740 m above sea level on the summit of the Witwatersrand and its population has reached 116 000. Its situation is near the western end of the ridge, where there is within walking distance of the centre of the town, some very fine rugged scenery, with the heights falling away sharply to the bush-covered lowlands. Several attractive picnic, camping and swimming places are situated in the ravines along the edge of the escarpment where the Crocodile River has its headwaters in a number of tributary streams which flow off the watershed of the Witwatersrand.

The road from Krugersdorp to Pretoria passes through some particularly dramatic scenery. The Muldersdrift Hill is the scene of many famous hill-climbing races for automobiles, cyclists and athletes and the sweeping panorama seen from the top of the hill is known as 'World's View'. Immediately west of the town on the Rustenburg road is the Krugersdorp Game Reserve which preserves the indigenous fauna and flora of the Witwatersrand prior to the discovery of gold. A fine example of conservation has been set by the Krugersdorp Municipality. The reserve is grassy and supports a dense population of eland, zebra, springbok, blesbok, oryx and other antelope, as well as lion and white rhino which are contained in separate enclosures. An attractive camp with bungalows (3 beds, R9 D) has been built in a sheltered valley. A tearoom offers refreshment and a circular road 16 km long provides a very pleasant drive. Entrance is R3 per car. Below the Muldersdrift Hill, on the road to Pretoria, is the South African Lion Park, a 354-ha, privately run game reserve where visitors can drive along 16 km of trails viewing a variety of game animals, especially lions. The game reserve and the Lion Park are open daily from 8h30 to 18h00. Admission for the Lion Park is also R3 per car.

587

Apart from gold, a considerable variety of economic minerals is mined in the Krugersdorp district, including high-grade manganese, iron, asbestos, dyes, lime and dolomite. There are three uranium plants within the municipal area, one of which was the first recovery plant in Southern Africa, opened on 8 October 1952 on the first mine in the world (the West Rand Consolidated) to produce uranium as a byproduct of gold.

## Accommodation
* Bacchus Inn, 10 rooms, 3 with baths. R10,50 B/B. Phone 660-6027.
* Luipaard Hotel, 39 rooms, 11 with baths. R10,19 – R11,34 B/B. Phone 660-1161.
* Majestic Hotel, 16 rooms, 4 with baths. R7,50 – R9,50 B/B. Phone 660-3247.
* Victoria Hotel, 18 rooms, 5 with baths. R7,50 – R9,50 B/B. Phone 660-2965.
* West Krugersdorp Hotel, 10 rooms, 7 with baths. R8,50 B/B. Phone 660-1632.

## Caravans and camping
** The Pines Resort, 88 sites. R3,50 D per site.
Pretorius Park (overnight only), 15 sites. Free.

From Krugersdorp, the Main Reef Road veers sharply south-westwards past the vast mining property of the West Rand Consolidated Mines (5 km) and the Randfontein Gold Mining Company at Robinson (11 km). At 14,5 km from Krugersdorp the road reaches the town of . . .

# RANDFONTEIN
The last of the West Rand towns, Randfontein was originally attached to Krugersdorp but became a municipality of its own in January 1929. *Randfontein* (fountain of the ridge) was originally a farm owned by Louis le Grange. During the first wild scramble for mining areas after the discovery of the Main Reef, J. B. Robinson, acting on little more than rumours of gold and his own instinct, secured options over the area.

Robinson's instinct proved wonderfully rewarding. In 1889 the Randfontein Estates Gold Mining Company was floated, then the largest mining enterprise on the Rand, which was destined to produce a fortune in gold. A town to serve the mine was proclaimed on *Randfontein* farm in May 1890 and with its 50 070 inhabitants, is today a major mining and developing industrial centre. There are two pleasant recreational areas at Riebeeck and Robinson lakes.

## Accommodation
* Central Hotel, 18 rooms, 5 with baths. R7 – R8 B/B. Phone 663-3068.
* Rand Hotel, 16 rooms, 4 with baths. R7,50 – R8 B/B. Phone 663-2086.
* Station Hotel, 12 rooms, 3 with baths. R8 B/B. Phone 663-2106.
* West Rand Hotel, 16 rooms, 5 with baths. Phone 663-1134.

## Caravans and camping
* Riebeeck Lake, 55 sites. R1,50 D.

From Krugersdorp, two main roads continue westwards, taking the traveller through interesting scenery to Rustenburg and the Cape border at Mafeking. One road leaves Krugersdorp from the suburb once known as *Blikkiesdorp* (shanty town) but which has now become the respectable Dan Pienaarville. Immediately beyond this suburb, the road reaches the edge of the Witwatersrand where fine views to the north are displayed with the well-bushed escarpment falling away sharply to the low country.

A turnoff leads to the African Fauna and Bird Park, a picnic and swimming resort run by Mr Nicholaas Boshoff whose collection of birds provides an interesting exhibit for visitors.

Past the Saronde Valley pleasure resort (caravans and camping, R2 D), the road begins to descend. The scenery is now ruggedly hilly and the vegetation changes rapidly. At 8 km from Krugersdorp the road passes the Proranda Pleasure Resort, and after turnoffs at 10 km to Muldersdrift (13 km) and Pretoria (64 km), reaches the 8-km turnoff (12 km from Krugersdorp) leading to the world famous . . .

# STERKFONTEIN CAVES

One of the world's most important archaeological sites, these caves have their entrance in a low, rounded hillock of dolomite forming part of the Isaac Edwin Stegmann Nature Reserve. His children donated the area to the University of the Witwatersrand who manage the caves.

The caves were discovered in 1896 on the farm *Sterkfontein* by an Italian prospector, Guigimo Martinaglia. The caves were rich in bat guano. Extracting the guano unfortunately led to considerable destruction of the spectacular dripstone formations in the cave, many of which were broken up and used for the making of lime.

The caves consist of six large chambers connected by means of passages. The largest is the Hall of Elephants, 23 m high and 91 m long. The other chambers are: Milner Hall, Fairy Chamber, Bridal Arch, Lumbago Alley, Fossil Chamber and the Graveyard. At a depth of 40 m lies an underground lake which is completely still and has about it an atmosphere of such enchantment that local African tribes regard it with considerable awe. Its waters are reputed to have healing properties, and to be effective against blindness. Ceremonies are performed on the verges of the subterranean lake and water is carried away for the sick.

Prehistoric creatures once inhabited the caves where many interesting traces discovered have placed the caves among the world's major archaeological sites. Between 1936 and 1951, Dr Robert Broom carried out considerable excavations in the caves, and among his discoveries is the exceptionally well-preserved skull of *Plesianthropus transvaalis,* now known as *Australopithecus africanus,* a species of early man who lived about two million years ago. The skull, that of a female, is nicknamed 'Mrs Ples'.

The *Sterkfontein* farm was acquired in 1921 by Mr Stegmann whose heirs presented the site of the caves to the university in 1958. The Robert Broom Museum at the caves exhibits many fossils found in the area. There is a restaurant and picnic area. Guided tours are held at frequent intervals from 09h00 to 17h00 Thursdays to Sundays. A bust of Dr Broom examining the skull of 'Mrs Ples' stands at the exit of the caves.

## Chapter Thirty

# PRETORIA

With a total of 650 600 inhabitants, Pretoria is the administrative capital of South Africa and also the provincial capital of the Transvaal. Lying 1 363 m above sea level (382 m lower than Johannesburg), the city enjoys a warm well-watered climate very conducive to gardens (beautiful throughout the year) and the production of subtropical fruit. Summer is hot, winter dry and cool; spring, however, is the best time to visit Pretoria for the colours of the flowers can then only be described as brilliant.

The city is attractively situated where the highveld falls away to the lowveld in a succession of parallel valleys separated by rocky ridges. In this sheltered setting Pretoria has spread out in a colourful complex of green gardens, shady streets, red roofs and reddish-coloured ridges of rock. There are some notably imposing and beautiful buildings in the central area, such as the Union Buildings, containing the principal government offices and standing in a magnificent formal garden; the city hall in Paul Kruger Street, surrounded by superb jacarandas; the headquarters of the Transvaal Provincial Council; several elegant old buildings surviving from the days of the South African Republic; many handsome modern commercial centres; the vast municipal offices *(Munitoria);* and the almost overpoweringly dominant building belonging to the University of South Africa situated on the hills at the southern entrance to the city.

Pretoria has experienced a lively and romantic past. The first known settlers in the area were sections of the Nguni people migrating down the east coast into modern Natal, where they fragmented into tribes such as the Zulu. Some disturbance sent a small group of these people westwards where they made their homes on the future site of Pretoria, on the banks of a river which became known as the *Tshwane* (little ape) or in Afrikaans, *Apies,* from one of their early chiefs.

This first settlement was established about 350 years ago. The people involved were dubbed *maTebele* (refugees) by the earlier Sotho-speaking groups living on the highveld. The title, in the Nguni language, became the tribal name of *Ndebele* by which these pioneers are still known and their descendants may be seen in and around Pretoria. Ndebele residences are usually elaborately decorated with bizarre patterns painted by the women, who also affect a complex, colourful but rather unwieldy ornamentation of heavy bead anklets and necklaces.

In about the year 1825 a second group of refugees from the Zulu country arrived in the valley site of the future Pretoria. These newcomers – also dubbed maTebele by the Sotho people – were a formidable crowd of bandits led by a renowned chief, Mzilikazi. They built villages along the valley of the Apies River and it was there that the first known Europeans to reach the area (traders and missionaries) visited Mzilikazi.

In 1832 a Zulu army drove Mzilikazi westwards, out of the sheltered valley of the Apies. He and his followers eventually settled north of the Limpopo River. The site of Pretoria was abandoned with only a few of the original Ndebele people remaining, scattered in hiding places in the vicinity. In this state the Voortrekkers found the Apies Valley when they entered the Transvaal in 1837.

Several farms were established along the banks of the Apies and farmers irrigated their fields from the river, finding profitable relaxation in hunting the herds of antelope which abounded in the area. The famed trek leader, Andries Pretorius, owned a fine farm *Grootplaats* near the junction of the Apies and Crocodile rivers. Shortly after his death in 1853 it was suggested that a central capital be founded for the Transvaal and named in honour of the dead leader.

Pretorius's son, Marthinus, selected as a site for the new capital, portions of the farm *Elandspoort* which he purchased for £825. On 11 August 1854 work was started on the erection of a church in the centre of the present Church Square. After initial uncertainty about the exact form of the name of the new town, the Volksraad of the Republic, on 16 December 1855, accepted the pleasant-sounding version, *Pretoria,* based on the distinguished family name of Andries Pretorius.

The town was laid out by a self-trained surveyor, Andries du Toit, and by 1860 incorporated large gardens and snug little houses. The first suburb, Arcadia, was already being developed by Stephanus Meintjes, whose name has been commemorated by *Meintjes Kop,* the hillock site of the Union Buildings. Traders had built the first stores and overlooking the central square, the government erected a simple *Raadsaal* (council chamber) where the *Volksraad* (people's council) held its meetings.

The peaceful, rustic atmosphere of early Pretoria did not prevent the place from experiencing exciting events. At the time Marthinus Pretorius was the President of the South African Republic and had many political rivals. Quite a small-scale civil war raged over Pretoria in the early 1860s when Pretorius attempted to unite the Orange Free State with the Transvaal. Bullets flew and the squabbles culminated in a minor battle fought on 5 January 1864 in the bush near Silkaatsnek, a passage through the Magaliesberg.

Pretorius resigned in 1870 and was replaced as President by the kindly and cultured Reverend Thomas Burgers who had to steer the little republic through some troubled times of near bankruptcy, incessant disturbances with primitive tribes, the excitement of the first discoveries of payable gold in the Eastern Transvaal, and the political crisis culminating in the British annexation of the Transvaal on 12 April 1877.

By this time, Pretoria had grown into a far more imposing town, for Burgers had stimulated the building of schools and the creation of amenities such as public parks. The British established a garrison in the place and attracted an influx of immigrants and money. New buildings were erected and the future generally looked golden. However, trouble was soon to come.

Between December 1880 and March 1881, Pretoria was besieged during the Anglo-Transvaal War and several skirmishes took place on the outskirts of the town. When the British withdrew, Paul Kruger was established in Pretoria as the President of the restored Republic and for the next 19 years his forceful personality dominated life in the developing town, as it did throughout the Transvaal.

Pretoria grew rapidly as the capital of what had now become a real golden republic, after the dramatic discoveries of gold at Barberton (1884), the Witwatersrand (1886), and the subsequent massive influx of diggers and *uitlanders* (foreigners) attracted by the prospect of fortune.

The handsome new Raadsaal, built on the site of the original council hall, saw many tense and momentous debates. The Palace of Justice also overlooks the square. The great trial of the Jameson raiders in 1896 was held in Pretoria, and the town experienced the mounting tensions which culminated on 11 October 1899 in the outbreak of the Anglo-Boer War. The Raadsaal is open to the public on weekdays from 09h00 to 21h00. It is an interesting place to visit, especially if one has some knowledge of the events and intrigues which centred on this building. The book *Lost Trails of the Transvaal* contains an account of these times.

Pretoria survived the war unscathed as an open city. Occupied by the British under Lord Roberts on 5 June 1900, it was there that the peace of Vereeniging was finally signed late at night on 31 May 1902. Having achieved its new status as the capital of a British colony,

Pretoria continued to grow and on creation of the Union of South Africa in 1910 it became the administrative capital. The handsome Union Buildings, designed by Sir Herbert Baker, were built at this time out of orange-red coloured sandstone.

An ever-growing community of civil servants expanded the population of Pretoria while in 1928 the Union Government decided on the establishment there of the South African Iron and Steel Industrial Corporation (Iscor). This great venture into steel production commenced operation in 1934 and since then, the glow of blast furnaces has become a feature of the night sky of Pretoria. Many other industries have been developed around the steel foundry. The steelworks of Iscor allow visitors on Wednesdays and Saturdays at 14h00. No children under 12 allowed. Strong shoes are essential.

Pretoria became a municipality in 1877 during the first British annexation and on 14 October 1931 was proclaimed a city, which today covers an area of 570 square kilometres. The two principal streets are Church and Paul Kruger streets which cross each other at the original Church Square, still the centre of the city. The square is graced with a superb statue of Paul Kruger guarded by four burghers and sculpted by Anton von Wouw.

At the southern end of Paul Kruger Street stands the railway station, founded in 1910 and designed by Sir Herbert Baker. A fine old steam locomotive, Z.A.S.M. No. 1283, is preserved in the station as a national monument.

Also in Paul Kruger Street is the city hall whose massive clock tower contains a carillon of 32 bells. A tympanum by Coert Steynberg symbolises the growth of the city. There is a colonnade of fountains as well as murals and statues of Andries Pretorius and his son Marthinus, the founder of the city. Superb jacarandas grow in the garden.

In Church Street, west of the square, is the imposing opera house and theatre complex built on Republic Square. Next to it plays an impressive fountain erected in memory of Johannes Strijdom, Prime Minister from 1941 to 1958. The fountain comprises a sculpted group of charging horses and a giant bronze bust, the work of the sculptor Coert Steynberg.

In spring (September-November) the whole city is transformed into a magnificent floral picture and it is at this time that the marvellous spectacle of flowering jacarandas may be seen – a feature that is world famous.

About 60 000 of these trees grow in Pretoria, introduced purely by chance. A few trees had been grown in private gardens, notably a pair imported from South America and planted by Mr J. D. Celliers in 1888 in his home *Myrtle Lodge* in Sunnyside. Then James Clark, a local horticulturist, ordered some mixed seed from Australia. Included in the selection were seeds of *Jacaranda mimosifolia* from Brazil. The seeds developed into healthy seedlings and in 1906 Mr Clark presented some trees to the Pretoria Municipality. The trees were planted in Bosman Street and from these ancestors originated the beautiful avenues of today.

In 1962 Mr H. Bruinslich, the Director of Parks, saw the white jacaranda in South America and introduced this variety to Pretoria where it may be seen today growing in several streets.

The handsome formal gardens of the Union Buildings (open all the time) are ablaze with colour in spring. The amount of photographic film exposed there by visitors must add significantly to the profits of the photographic industry! The clock in the right-hand tower is known as 'Oom Paul'. In front of the building stands a fine equestrian statue of General Louis Botha, South Africa's first Prime Minister, and there are statues of two later Prime Ministers, General J. C. Smuts and General J. B. M. Hertzog.

East of the Union Buildings lies the residential area of Bryntirion where, set amongst magnificent gardens, the State President, the Prime Minister and the Administrator of the Transvaal have their official residences. The State President's home was designed by Sir Herbert Baker in Cape-Dutch style and built in 1906. The home of the Prime Minister was designed by Gerhard Moerdyk and built in 1940.

The National Zoological Gardens contains 3 500 species of animals and is one of the best in the world. Mammals and birds are displayed in beautiful park-like surroundings. A reptile house includes 260 reptiles while an aquarium houses 500 species of fish. An overhead aerial ropeway provides a spectacular way in which to view the whole zoo, open from September to April from 08h00 to 18h00; May to August from 08h00 to 17h00.

The Transvaal Museum in Paul Kruger Street is renowned for its exhibits of prehistory and natural history. Included is the Austin Roberts Bird Hall, a model on which to base all collections of birds. This exhibition is definitive and will one day show all examples of South African avifauna, arranged according to 'Roberts' order. Dr Austin Roberts compiled the standard work *Birds of South Africa* in which every bird, in addition to being arranged in natural order, was given a number, now the standard reference in all books on South African birds.

The lower part of this hall is devoted to bird life in general, showing by means of excellent mounted specimens, features such as the 27 orders of living birds, feeding methods, flight, nests and nesting, falconry, and the usefulness of predatory birds. There is also a collection of eggs.

A 'quiz' case contains a number of the commoner birds. Visitors may guess the name of a particular bird, then press a button which illuminates the correct bird. A more ambitious display stands at the far end under the staircase. Operating on 5c pieces, it contains about 20 of the songbirds. When fed with a coin, the song is first heard and afterwards the name of the bird is announced and the bird itself illuminated. Both these exhibits are splendid ideas having interest and educational value.

Two other things are notable: a Dodo skeleton and an accurate reconstruction of the first known bird, the Archaeopteryx.

The museum is open Mondays to Saturdays from 09h00 to 17h00 (August to April); from 09h00 to 16h00 (May to July); on Sundays from 14h00 to 17h00. Closed on Christmas Day, Good Friday and New Year's Day.

Also for bird lovers is the Austin Roberts Bird Sanctuary, established in 1955 by the city council and situated in Boshoff Street off Queen Wilhelmina Avenue. The hide is open on weekends and public holidays from 09h00 to 18h00. A small museum displays some of the birds frequenting the sanctuary.

Adjoining the Transvaal Museum is the Museum of Geological Survey, of particular interest to those with some knowledge of geology and mineralogy. Beautifully housed and displayed in a new building, it is one of the most attractive museums in the country. The exhibits are splendid and the labelling equally so.

The collection commences with the basics of the solar system, the planets, the earth and its interior. Passing on to a study of geological processes at work, the origins of different rocks are shown, with a comprehensive section devoted to the chemical construction of minerals. Chemical analyses of a large number of these minerals are carefully indicated by means of coloured symbols.

Precious and semi-precious stones are included in a section, where there is a case containing reproductions of the world's largest diamonds.

There is a fossil collection and a special display dealing with the Karoo; its history, rocks and remains of ancient life. Here may be found one of South Africa's best fossil skeletons, that of a Jonkeria, which flourished about 250 million years ago.

Some of the geological systems are explained by means of rocks and fossils arranged on a time scale, and there are useful relief models of the Pilanesberg and Bushveld complexes.

The room devoted to economic minerals is packed with information and the maps showing where they occur in the world together with production statistics are interesting even to the non-geologist.

A large oval stone, used as a simple crusher, is an interesting relic in the museum, dating back to the early days of gold mining in South Africa when, in 1871, rumours of payable gold sent hundreds of prospectors rushing to Eersteling (beyond Potgietersrus). All that remains of the site today is one of the crushing sheds and a solitary smokestack standing in the veld. For a further account of this event, see page 549.

A notable exhibit is an exquisite Italian mosaic table inlaid with semi-precious stones. It is a masterpiece.

The National Cultural History and Open-Air Museum (adjoining the zoo) is a crowded museum containing many interesting exhibits. In the courtyard there are several old horse-drawn vehicles and two highly dangerous-looking cannon – dangerous for their operators rather than for the enemy – made from wagon wheel rims during the first Transvaal War of Independence in 1881. The British coat of arms from the old government building in Church Square is preserved here.

Also displayed in the courtyard is a fine collection of about 100 rock engravings, most of them from the South-Western Transvaal, South-Western Free State and Northern Cape. It is estimated that these date from the Middle Stone Age, between 12 000 and 8 000 years ago. The collection was carefully reorganised in 1967 and a useful guidebook, available at the museum, is a mine of information on what is the largest assembly of rock art in South Africa.

The archaeological room contains a small collection of objects from a number of scattered ancient cultures. The cast of the famous 'Venus' of Willendorf, one of the earliest nude female figures, is worth attention as it shows that the attraction of women, as far as the maker was concerned, lay purely in the bearing of children. Also of interest are some Inca objects, a mummy, a few Egyptian figures and some pots.

In two adjoining galleries is a superb collection of old furniture, furnishings and objets d'art, which ranks among the finest in the country. Particularly notable is a large armoire with Cape silver escutcheons and attractive inlay and a gilt clock with an enamel face, operated by weights, and mounted on an elaborately decorated wall bracket. There is a grandfather clock that could rank as the tallest in the Republic.

The Sydney Muller collection of Cape silver has been presented to the museum and is quite superb. Beautifully displayed, this silverware is worth a special journey to Pretoria. Not only is there a vast amount of tableware, but some of the sugar basins, bowls and teapots, etc, are of a workmanship and design that can compare with similar work anywhere in the world.

Each of these galleries is most attractively set out and every large case contains a variety of objects, concisely described and dated. Among the smaller objects is an inlaid backgammon table, probably of Batavian origin and a green glass goblet with a lid of Dutch make, dating from the 16th century.

In other rooms may be seen some Woodstock glass and a stinkwood and yellowwood panelled cabinet inlaid with ebony and ivory in a star pattern, a very rare exhibit in museums.

The rooms surrounding the courtyard are more historical in their intention and there are sections devoted to Generals Botha and Smuts and other of the country's leaders. There is a replica of the room in which General Smuts died in 1950 and another of General Botha's study.

There are collections of coins, comprising beautiful examples of the exquisite taste of the ancient world and an interesting set of foreign money used at the Cape, exhibits of medals, orders and decorations may also be seen.

Other parts of the museum display pottery, domestic utensils and arts and crafts of the Transvaal tribes. There is also a fine collection of Chinese porcelain and a small, but extremely well-executed costume section.

The museum is open Mondays to Saturdays from 08h00 to 17h00; Sundays from 10h30 to 17h00. Closed on Christmas Day, Good Friday and Ascension Day.

Of great historical interest is Paul Kruger's house in Church Street. A great deal may be learnt about the character of one of South Africa's most famous Presidents by a visit to this house in which he lived from 1883 to 1900, before he went into exile in Switzerland. The impression is gained of a man who had little regard for elegance, even less for comfort and none at all for pomp and show.

The surroundings are simple and modest, and even the official reception room holds little to impress those whom he met there. One exception to the general austerity of the house is the tasteful curtaining, handsomely draped in the fashion of the time.

The museum contains many relics of Paul Kruger – small things such as his pipes and personal belongings. One of the first telephones installed in Pretoria may be seen; also the *Vierkleur* (flag) that flew for the last time in 1900 when he left for Clarens, little realising that he was leaving his home for ever. There is the desk before which he must have spent many an anxious hour, and the chair bearing the arms of the Transvaal Republic, in which he was often photographed. The official dinner service bears the same arms and two porcelain cups are ornamented with his portrait.

At the back of the house stands the President's state coach in which he was installed as President for the fourth and last time in 1898, and his private railway coach. This railway coach should be compared with that exhibited at the Kimberley Mine Museum for the contrast between Cecil Rhodes and the austere President is another pointer to character! This coach, built for the Z.A.R. in the Netherlands, was originally two coaches which were joined together in South Africa on arrival. A painted board with the arms of the Republic is said to have been attached to the coach when the President travelled in it and is thought to have been removed by British soldiers. It was subsequently found in London and returned to the museum.

In addition, the museum is a repository for documents and other material concerning the life of President Kruger. An illustrated brochure is available for sale which gives detailed information about the exhibits. It is open Mondays to Saturdays from 08h00 to 17h00; on Sundays from 11h00 to 17h00. Closed on Christmas Day, Good Friday and Ascension Day.

Also of considerable historic interest is Melrose House, in Jacob Maré Street near Burgers Park. This magnificent example of a Victorian home was built in 1886 by George Heys who, born in 1852 in Durban, had settled in Pretoria during the first British annexation. He established a coach service which extended to many parts of the old Republic. His Pretoria home contains some superb period furniture, stained glass, porcelain, silver and works of art. On 31 May 1902 the Treaty of the Peace of Vereeniging was signed in this house, finally bringing to an end the tragedy of the Anglo-Boer War. Melrose House is open to the public Tuesdays to Saturdays from 10h00 to 17h00; on Sundays from 13h00 to 18h00. Closed on Mondays and religious holidays.

The Pioneer open-air museum in Silverton preserves a restored house and farmyard of the pioneer period. It is open daily from 09h00 to 17h00.

The Pretoria Art Museum in Arcadia Park is open Tuesdays to Saturdays from 10h00 to 17h00; on Sundays from 13h00 to 18h00; on Wednesday nights from 19h30 to 22h00. Closed on Mondays and religious holidays. Contained here are several hundred paintings by South African artists, as well as the Michaelis Collection.

The Museum of Science and Technology in Skinner Street is open Mondays to Fridays from 10h00 to 16h00. Closed on Saturdays, Sundays and all holidays. It is the only one of its kind in Africa, where the exploration of space is depicted.

The Police Museum is open Mondays to Fridays from 07h30 to 16h00; on Saturdays from 08h00 to 12h00. The museum exhibits several relics – some of them gruesome – of past crimes including gambling, smuggling and narcotics.

The Pretoria National Botanic Gardens (on the road to Witbank) are open daily from 07h00 to 16h30. The gardens, 60 ha in extent, contain several thousand species of indigenous plants grouped according to the various climatic regions of South Africa.

Protea Park in Groenkloof is the home of a collection of proteas, aloes and Namaqualand flowering plants while in Springbok Park in Pretorius Street grow numerous indigenous trees.

The beautiful Johann Rissik Scenic Drive which is reached from the Fountains traffic circle and along Maria van Riebeeck Avenue, provides fine views of Pretoria. On the summit ridge of the drive stands the perfectly maintained Fort Klapperkop.

*Overleaf: The artistry of the Ndebele people reflected in the superb costumes of the women and their finger paintings on the walls.*

As a sequel to the Jameson Raid the government of the South African Republic erected this fort and three others in 1897, in order to protect the capital. Formerly occupied by the military in 1898, it has now been lovingly restored in landscaped grounds and equipped with a series of dioramas and other exhibits to illustrate the military history of the South African Republic from 1852 to the end of the Anglo-Boer War.

The building is worth studying and would have been a difficult place to storm before aircraft rendered all such positions almost indefensible. On the lawns around the fort are arrayed a collection of ironmongery from the 1939-45 war, as well as some aircraft: a Ventura a Harvard trainer and a Vampire bomber.

The fortress itself, entered by means of a drawbridge and gate, is built around a small courtyard. Here stands one of South Africa's most remarkable curiosities in the shape of a nine-seater cycle, apparently constructed by the British from parts of other bicycles and equipped with wheels enabling it to travel on railway lines. A seat in the centre was presumably intended for the officer in charge. Eight men (four each side), seated on bicycle saddles, would then pedal for dear life. It seems that it was used for locating boobytraps, for despatch riding and conveying wounded. A less mobile and manoeuvrable conveyance can scarcely be imagined!

Various small rooms should be examined from left to right. The doors of these rooms are named in High Dutch and the first, *Stal,* is dedicated to horses throughout the ages including military horses, equipment, blacksmith's tools, those horrible anti-horse *voetangels,* and a very sympathetic diorama of a characteristic Boer trooper with his horse.

*Officieren* contains many documents and a photographic survey of the origin, erection, subsequent neglect and dilapidation and final rehabilitation of the fort.

*Proviand* displays uniforms of the volunteers from various districts, and badges, buttons, medals and decorations from both the South African Republic and Orange Free State armies during the Anglo-Boer War.

*Manschappel* leads into a series of rooms, starting with a diorama of a general's office (the desk having been used by several South African Prime Ministers). Following this is a collection of weapons from Bushman arrows to recent rifles, including a rifle dating from 1740. A general transport wagon (horse-drawn) may be seen. Next on display are various forms of military signalling, from heliographs – effective up to a distance of 112 km – tappers, buzzers and field telephones. Here also is the 'red duster' flag flown at Mafeking during the siege. On exhibition are coins made at the Field Mint, set up at Pilgrims Rest for safety – the actual coinmaking machine is outside the fort at the flagpole, some distance away. It was installed in the buildings of Transvaal Gold Mining Estates but seems to have produced little coinage. This series of rooms ends with a gruesome diorama of a field hospital where an amputation is in progress; a reminder, if ever such things are heeded, that war is a nasty business for its victims. Emily Hobhouse is justifiably honoured and her photograph may be seen in this section.

At the higher level outside, in the room marked *Ammunitie,* is a large collection of projectiles. This level yields a superb view of Pretoria, nestling under the shadow of the Magaliesberg and to some extent, the smokestacks of Iscor. The museum is open Mondays to Fridays from 10h00 to 16h00; on Saturdays, Sundays and holidays from 10h00 to 18h00. Closed on Christmas Day and Good Friday.

Pretoria is the home of the State Library, the University of South Africa, which teaches by correspondence, and the Afrikaans-medium University of Pretoria, the largest residential university in Southern Africa. It has 11 faculties and 141 departments. There are also many fine schools. The South African Mint and the Government Printer have their plants in the city. The Mint may be visited by arrangement through the Visitors' Bureau. Phone 44-1121. The laboratories of the South African Bureau of Standards maintain a nation-wide vigilance over the standards of manufacture throughout the country.

At 8 km on the road to Witbank stands the headquarters of the South African Council for Scientific and Industrial Research (CSIR), home of 16 national research institutes and a staff of 3 500. Visits by appointment only.

Fifteen kilometres north lies the famous Onderstepoort Veterinary Research Laboratory. Founded in 1908, this is the first facility of its kind on the continent of Africa and is one of the best in the world. The laboratory was responsible for finding vaccines for the control of veterinary illnesses such as distemper, blue tongue, horse sickness and botulism. It was at Onderstepoort that mineral deficiencies were proved to be the cause of livestock diseases, a discovery which prompted research on similar problems throughout the world.

The first director of Onderstepoort, Dr Arnold Theiler, was knighted for his work. Today the institute covers 200 ha, with a farm of an additional 7 000 ha. It provides the only faculty of veterinary science in South Africa where students from many parts of Africa train as veterinary surgeons.

The Premier Diamond Mine allows visits on Tuesdays, Wednesdays, Thursdays and Fridays at 19h30 and 11h00. Bookings can be made through the Public Relations Office, Cullinan. Phone Cullinan 368.

An Ndebele village may be visited from Pretoria on any day except Sundays and religious holidays. A permit must be obtained from Room 6, corner Von Wielligh and Struben streets, between 08h00 and 15h00, Mondays to Fridays. A map is supplied to show the way (40 km from Pretoria).

On the northern outskirts of the city is the Wonderboom Nature Reserve, containing a huge wild fig tree and the remains of one of the forts built to defend Pretoria (see page 596).

Pretoria is an attractive, sunny, colourful city, with many areas of recreation and sport, such as the 85 000-seat rugby stadium named after Robert Loftus Versveld, a former administrator of the game. Another pleasant recreational area may be found at Fountains at the source of the Apies River, where there are gardens, picnicking grounds, a swimming pool and caravan park. Shady trees, green lawns, flowers, swans, water birds and a delightful miniature railway with a real 'puffer' following an attractive route are features of this resort.

## Accommodation

★★ Arcadia Hotel, 515 Proes Street, 143 rooms, all with baths. R14 B/B. Phone 2-9311.

★★ Assembly Hotel, Van der Walt/Visagie streets, 84 rooms, 38 with baths. R10 B/B. Phone 3-3075.

★ Bachelors Hotel, 585 Pretorius Street (Arcadia), 120 rooms, all with baths. R10 B/B. Phone 44-8148.

★ Bel Hotel, 705 Church Street, 41 rooms, 14 with baths. R7 – R8 B/B. Phone 74-5581.

★ Belgrave Hotel, 22 Railway Street, 13 rooms, 8 with baths. R6,75 – R7,30 B/B. Phone 3-5578.

★ Bergsig Hotel, 505 Karel Trichardt Avenue, 13 rooms, 5 with baths. R7,50 room only. Phone 77-3614.

★★★ Boulevard Hotel, 186 Struben Street, 75 rooms, all with baths. R18 B/B. Phone 2-4806.

★★★★ Burgers Park Hotel, Van der Walt/Minnaar streets, 252 rooms, all with baths. R25 – R36 room only. Phone 48-6570.

★ Caledonian Hotel, 424 Pretorius Street, 28 rooms, 7 with baths. R8,50 B/B. Phone 2-6475.

★★ Continental Hotel, Visagie Street, 70 rooms, all with baths. R12,50 – R13,50 B/B. Phone 3-2241.

★★ Culemborg Hotel, 295 Pretorius Street, 120 rooms, 70 with baths. R12 B/B. Phone 48-6900.

★ Eaton Hall Hotel, 266 Visagie Street, 202 rooms, 101 with baths. R6 – R7 B/B. Phone 48-7232.

★ Edward Hotel, Paul Kruger Street, 34 rooms, 10 with baths. R8,50 – R9,50 B/B. Phone 2-3275/6.

★ Eureka Hotel, 579 Church Street, 135 rooms, 93 with baths. R8 – R16 B/B. Phone 44-6064.

★★ Hamsin Hotel, 675 Pretorius Street, 211 rooms, all with baths. R11 B/B. Phone 42-5154.

★ Hellenic Hotel, 517 Church Street (East), 95 rooms, 60 with baths. R10 – R18 B/B. Phone 44-2361.

★ Hercules Hotel, 512 Van der Hoff Road, 21 rooms, 5 with baths. R10 B/B. Phone 77-3314.

★ Hi-Way Hotel (Bon Accord), 25 rooms, all with baths. R9 B/B. Phone 57-1138.

★ Hotel 224, cor. Leyds and Schoeman streets, 224 rooms, all with baths. R9,50 B/B. Phone 44-5366.

★ Indwe Hotel, 90 Relly Street, 80 rooms, all with baths. R8 B/B. Phone 44-5245.

★ Louis Hotel, 599 Schoeman Street, 95 rooms, all with baths. R5 – R13 B/B. Phone 44-4238.

★ Lynnhof Hotel, 19 Baviaanspoort Road, 15 rooms, 8 with baths. R7 – R8 B/B. Phone 86-4580.

★ Madeline Hotel, 562 Pretorius Street, 112 rooms, all with baths. R8 B/B. Phone 44-4281.

★ Mader Hotel, 723 Paul Kruger Street (Mayville), 25 rooms, 15 with baths. R10 B/B. Phone 75-2099.

★★ Mahem Hotel (Sandfontein), 30 rooms, all with baths. R10 B/B. Phone 7-2201.

★ Majella Hotel, 564 Pretorius Street, 150 rooms, 65 with baths. R7,50 B/B. Phone 44-6370.

★★ Manhattan Hotel, 247 Scheiding Street, 294 rooms, all with baths. R12,50 – R25 B/B. Phone 48-6061.

★ Maroela Hotel, 485 Rachel de Beer Street (Pretoria North), 20 rooms, 10 with baths. R8,50 B/B. Phone 55-3885.

★★ Monria Hotel, 151 Skinner Street, 95 rooms, all with baths. R8,50 – R9 B/B. Phone 48-7174.

★ National Hotel, 386 Voortrekker Street, 17 rooms, 5 with baths. R10 – R10,50 B/B. Phone 70-3774.

★★ Nido Hotel, 230 Hamilton Street, 136 rooms, all with baths. R10,40 B/B. Phone 42-3006.

★★ Oklahoman Motel, Pretoria Road (Silverton), 59 rooms, all with baths. R15 – R22 B/B. Phone 86-4941.

★ Palmos Hotel, 340 Church Street (West), 32 rooms, 12 with baths. R6 – R7 B/B. Phone 2-3888.

★★★ Palms Hotel (Silverton), 89 rooms, all with baths. R13 – R26 B/B. Phone 86-1014.

★ Polaris Hotel (Erasmia), 8 rooms, all with baths. R7 B/B. Phone 40-3361.

★ President Hotel, 397 Potgieter Street, 32 rooms, 8 with baths. R9,50 B/B. Phone 3-6301.

★ Pretoria Hotel, 611 Schoeman Street, 134 rooms, 46 with baths. R7,50 – R10 B/B. Phone 42-5062.

★ Pretoria Gardens Hotel, 482 Van der Hoff Road, 26 rooms, 19 with baths. R7,50 – R8 B/B. Phone 7-4247.

★ Republique Hotel, 47 Schoeman Street, 32 rooms, 12 with baths. R7,25 – R8,25 B/B. Phone 48-1037.

★★ Residensie Hotel, 185 Schoeman Street, 62 rooms, all with baths. R14,50 B/B. Phone 3-4956.

★ Sharbel Hotel, 1061 Michael Brink Street, 28 rooms, 7 with baths. R6 – R8 B/B. Phone 49-6721.

★ Summerhill Hotel (Bon Accord), 22 rooms, all with baths. R7 B/B. Phone 5-9215.

★ Van Riebeeck Hotel, 388 Andries Street, 68 rooms, 22 with baths. R8,30 – R9,40 B/B. Phone 48-3640.

★ Victoria Hotel, 200 Scheiding Street, 28 rooms, 15 with baths. R7,50 – R8,50 B/B. Phone 3-1910.

★ Wagon Wheel Inn, 397 Church Street, 42 rooms, 15 with baths. R7 – R8 B/B. Phone 3-7406.

★ Western Hotel, 53 Mitchell Street, 18 rooms, 4 with baths. R4,50 – R5 B/B. Phone 2-1271.

★★ Xanadu Hotel, 573 Church Street (Arcadia), 93 rooms, all with baths. R15 – R25 B/B. Phone 42-5001.

### Caravans and camping

★★® Fountains Valley Caravan Park, 80 sites. R1,25 D plus 50c D per person.

★★★® Joos Becker Caravan Park, 60 sites. R1,25 – R2 D plus 50c D per person.

On the high ridge dominating Pretoria from the south stands the military centre of Voortrek-kerhoogte; the Zwartkop airforce station; the army and airforce residential area of Valhalla; the head office building of the Iron and Steel Corporation, constructed out of stainless steel; the South African Airforce memorial commemorating members of the South African Airforce who sacrificed their lives in war and peace-time service; and ...

# THE VOORTREKKER MONUMENT

This monument is the most imposing in South Africa, and originated in 1936 when the Sentrale Volks Monumente Komitee invited international architects to submit designs for the work. The fundamental idea of the monument, whatever form it took, was that it should commemorate the fortitude, courage and intransigence of the Voortrekkers. At the same time the monument had to harmonise with Africa's vastness, solitude, mystery and the underlying drama of a savage and often brutal past.

Gerhard Moerdyk, a South African architect specialising in churches and public buildings, produced the design which resulted in the Voortrekker Monument of today. His conception of the great structure was bold; searching for a design homogeneous to Africa, he accepted the fact that, apart from the Cape-Dutch style, the European on this continent had still to produce something which had not been copied from Europe or America.

The Cape-Dutch style would have been gauche in the severe setting of the Transvaal highveld and its relaxed tranquillity did not, in any case, reflect the stormy dynamism of the Voortrekker period. The Voortrekkers themselves had not built any great structures; wagons and simple *hartbeeshuisies* and *kapsteilhuisies* suited their needs. Since the Bible was their greatest cultural influence, the Voortrekkers, had they set out to build anything imposing, would doubtless have followed precedent and erected an altar of thanksgiving. Accepting this postulate, Gerhard Moerdyk set out to design an altar in African style, using pure African motifs for decoration and theme.

The great medieval ruin of Zimbabwe gave Moerdyk his solution to the problem of an architecture which was truly homogeneous to Southern Africa. In the erection of Zimbabwe and other stone-walled buildings of similar type in Zimbabwe and the Northern Transvaal, the Karanga-Rozvi builders devised a unique structural form which harmonised with the vastness of Africa without being overwhelmed by it.

In designing the Voortrekker Monument, Moerdyk adopted the Zimbabwe technique of piling small stone units one on top of the other to give the effect of massive scale. He also incorporated the leading decorative motif of Zimbabwe – the zigzag chevron line representative of water and associate fertility, the dominant influence in African life controlling so much human migration and activity. With its small stone unit construction and the chevron decorations, the façade of the monument is essentially African in its patterns and forms.

Grafted on to the four corners of this mighty altar are four busts depicting four leaders of the Great Trek: Piet Retief, Andries Pretorius, Hendrik Potgieter, and a symbolical, nameless leader. In the front stands a bronze by Anton von Wouw of a Voortrekker woman with two children huddled at her skirts.

Above the figure of the woman loom the heads of wildebeest, representing the dangers confronting civilisation. This symbolism was suggested by the episode during which Piet Retief was seated chatting amiably to the Zulu king, Dingane, and their conversation was disturbed by a thunderous singing and stamping outside the royal enclosure.

'What is that?' asked Retief.

'My regiment of wildebeest dancing,' answered Dingane with a smile.

Over the main entrance is mounted the head of a solitary buffalo, the most dangerous and determined of all animals when wounded. Inside is a spacious crypt, designed with the idea that it might be used as a repository for the remains of great South Africans. In the centre of the crypt lies the sarcophagus, planned to contain relics of some of the pioneers. On it are the words *Ons vir jou, Suid-Afrika* (we are for you, South Africa). The surrounding shadows and quietness are tomb-like, but in the roof a circular well has been left, which drenches the entire 30-metre square hall with light.

The great hall is dominated by African patterns and designs. Light filtering into the lower portion is tinted with the peculiar brown-yellow of the African landscape, while the heights are the colour of the deep blue sky.

Radiating in the floor from the centre wall are symbolic wave patterns representing the expanding influence of the pioneers, while all around on the wall where these waves break, is a bas-relief frieze made of Italian marble. It is 92 m long and 2,3 m high, reputedly the second largest in the world, the larger being the frieze at the altar of Zeus at Pergamum.

The frieze depicts in tableau form scenes and episodes from the history of the Great Trek: Louis Trichardt with the kindly Portuguese Governor of Lourenço Marques; the descent of the Drakensberg; Piet Retief and Dingane signing the ill-fated treaty, surrounded by their men. Well in evidence is the Zulu king's mobile human spittoon (a kneeling youth with outstretched cupped hands).

One by one the scenes are presented to the promenading visitor. Each depiction has been created with careful attention to authentic detail. Direct descendants of the Voortrekkers posed for the human figures. Original items of furniture and dress were carefully copied. When it became desirable to include a Voortrekker's dog, for lack of any positive guidance in the records, a special dog was deliberately bred and then modelled from life. Two casual references in Voortrekker records suggested a breed. In Louis Trichardt's diary he noted, 'The bitch caught a rietbok this morning.' This suggested a female greyhound, for reedbuck are very quick. In Voortrekker records of the Bloukrans Massacre, a passage relates, 'The people awoke to the barking of the dogs.' As the watchdog the Dobermann pinscher was selected. The pup produced by the greyhound-Dobermann pinscher match was featured in the frieze.

The frieze was modelled in clay in South Africa and translated in Italy into marble from the Apennines, the same as that used by Michelangelo.

Thirty metres above the floor of the great hall is the domed ceiling which forms the roof. Two hundred and sixty steps lead to the roof and from it may be obtained a sweeping view of the surrounding countryside. The domed roof adds a final touch of drama; the dome is a segment of a globe on which South Africa is marked in bas-relief. Marking the position of Blood River is an aperture, so situated that once a year, at precisely 11h00 on 16 December (the date of the Battle of Blood River), a ray of sunlight shines directly through this opening, illuminating that portion of the frieze showing the Voortrekkers making their vow to God to build a church if He granted them victory over the Zulu. At noon exactly, this ray of sunshine floods over the words *Ons vir jou, Suid-Afrika*.

Construction of the monument began late in 1937. Granite was quarried from an outcrop in the North-Western Transvaal which had yielded material for the building of a prehistoric walled settlement. The monument cost £350 000 to erect and was opened on 16 December 1949. The monument is surrounded by a wall carved to represent a laager of 64 full-sized wagons standing in a garden of indigenous flowers. Close by is a large amphitheatre where open-air religious services, meetings and exhibitions of folk dancing are staged. A great national gathering takes place there every year on 16 December.

The monument is open to the public Mondays to Saturdays from 09h00 to 17h00; on Sundays and Good Fridays from 14h00 to 17h00. Closed on Christmas Day. Adjoining the tearoom is a museum which displays many interesting relics and contains a series of dioramas showing well-reconstructed interiors of Voortrekker homes. The three rooms, together comprising a Voortrekker cottage, house many interesting objects of the time.

Among other exhibits are weapons, bullet moulds, African artefacts, leatherwork and clothing. One case contains 22 types of women's bonnets.

There are some photographs of considerable interest, including one of Louis Trichardt and another of his surviving children taken in Lourenço Marques. Two trek wagons in good condition stand outside the museum.

A curiosity in the form of a lampshade made from a tin, with perforations allowing light to shine through, is parallelled in Morocco, where similar shades are still used and also sold to tourists in large quantities.

The series of 15 tapestries stitched by nine ladies of the Railways Cultural Society, to designs by Mr W. H. Coetzer, are notable. Depicted are scenes of Voortrekker history, a task which took eight years to complete, with 3 353 600 stitches and 130 different colours of wool being used. The museum has the same opening times as the monument.

## THE HARTEBEESPOORT DAM

Thirty-two kilometres west of Pretoria lies the great irrigation dam of Hartebeespoort, completed in 1923 and overflowing for the first time in March 1925. With a wall 149,5 m long and 59,4 m high, the dam is fed by the waters of the Crocodile and Magalies rivers and covers 1 883 ha at a maximum depth of 45,1 m.

The dam supplies irrigation water through 544 km of canals to 15 976 ha of land on which is produced tobacco, wheat, lucerne, fruit and flowers.

Also a great recreational area, Hartebeespoort Dam is used by several boating and fishing clubs as well as by innumerable private people. On its shores lie residential areas such as the picturesque assembly of weekend cottages and hideaways known as Cosmos, and the township of Schoemansville. A tarmac road skirts the dam, passes through a tunnel 56,6 m long and crosses the dam wall, yielding many fine views. Cosmos, 9 km beyond the dam wall, is a particularly colourful little place enhanced by bougainvillaea, poinsettias, jacarandas, flamboyants *(Poinciana regia)*, hibiscus and other flowering plants.

Numerous places of recreation such as tearooms, wayside kiosks, camping grounds, amusement parks, a hotel, snake park, menagerie, etc, have been created around the lake. Especially notable is the aerial ropeway run by the Hartebeespoort Dam Cableway Company. This ropeway, 1,2 km long and rising 400 m from the lower station to the highest point of the Magaliesberg range, provides a dramatic 6-minute ride ending with a superb view from the summit. It is open daily from 08h00 to 18h00 and on Saturday nights until 22h00.

The Hartebeespoort Aquarium, said to be the largest freshwater aquarium in Africa, is another interesting feature of the area. Displayed here is a vast collection of exotic and indigenous fish, seals, crocodiles and marine birds. It is open daily from 08h00 to 19h00. Performing times for the seals are 11h00 and 15h00 (and, in addition, at 17h00 on Sundays).

### Accommodation
★ Lake Hotel (Schoemansville), 10 rooms, all with baths. R7,50 B/B. Phone 3001.

### Caravans and camping
★★ Hotaki Caravan Park, 500 sites. R3 D.
★★ Iscor Angling Resort, 100 sites. R1,50 D. 12 rondawels (3 beds), R3 D. 6 chalets (4 beds), R7 D.

Close to the Hartebeespoort Dam is the atomic research centre built at *Pelindaba* (end of the discussion), the former home of the author Gustav Preller who gave the place that name when the waters impounded by the Hartebeespoort Dam enveloped his farmlands. Around July, flowering aloes are very beautiful in the vicinity, especially where the road to Johannesburg passes through the hills alongside the Hennops River. A picnic place is situated on the river.

# Chapter Thirty-one

# THE EASTERN TRANSVAAL

The grassy plains of the Eastern Transvaal highveld are deceptive. To the eye they are open areas – green in summer, drab brown in winter. Rural by nature, they provide farmlands where crops such as maize, sorghum and sunflowers are cultivated and are also the adopted homeland of prodigious numbers of cosmos; white, pink and maroon flowers originating from Mexico, brought to Southern Africa as cultivated plants which have since escaped over garden walls and run riot on these wide plains.

This calm rustic simplicity is little more than skin deep. Immediately beneath the surface is hidden a gigantic powerhouse, a source of energy so vast that it will keep the heart of South Africa beating for perhaps a thousand years or more. How did this powerhouse originate?

Between 125 and 250 million years ago, nature, using water as a creative tool, laid down a thick series of sediments known to geologists as the Karoo System. In rainy, humid and swampy conditions, a huge forest grew, providing a home for many strange primeval creatures. As the trees flourished, died and were replaced by others, their trunks, together with the carcasses of dinosaurs and other animals, were interred in a cemetery of mud.

As the mood of nature changed, water was replaced by fire and wind in the creation of a new landscape; the cemetery dried up, grass covered its surface and perhaps, as a kind gesture before the creative spirit departed, the cosmos flowers were sprinkled over the area in fond memory of trees long since gone and deep forests that have vanished. It is this burial ground beneath the grass and flowers that contains an estimated 60 billion tons of coal, at least half of which is bituminous and lies within 300 m of the surface. It is this deposit – the eighth largest in the world – which provides South Africa with its energy heart; coal that can be burnt, converted into electric power, gas, liquid fuels, chemicals and raw materials for innumerable complex industrial processes.

Complementing these deposits of coal is water, of which there is ample in the Eastern Transvaal. The west-flowing Vaal River and the east-flowing Nkhomati and Usuthu rivers originate on the watershed running north-south through the Eastern Transvaal. A feature of the highveld plains is the number of shallow lakelets or pans – hollows in which water collects – which provide happy homes for a considerable population of waterfowl. After a good rainy season, the view from an aircraft reveals many hundreds of these lakelets scattered over the plains like blobs of blue paint dropped by accident on a beautiful green tablecloth.

Endowed with energy and water, the area is, understandably, bustling with human activity in the harnessing, conversion, packaging, export and marketing of its assets. As far as holidaymakers are concerned, the region would not exactly be regarded as a paradise. However, the area possesses a certain drama and impressiveness and there are recreational features worth exploring. Roads are excellent and to journey past some of the huge thermal power stations, coal mines and liquid fuel plants of Sasol II and III at Secunda, is an awesome experience.

The electric grid system of South Africa run by Escom (Electricity Supply Commission) is based in this region. The grid system begins at the 1 600 000-kw generating plant built in 1962 at Camden, near Ermelo. Eighteen other large generating stations have been constructed to contribute energy to this grid which strides across the face of South Africa by means of 80 000 km of transmission line feeding electric power at 400 000 volts from one end of the country to the other. The largest of these power stations in the South-Eastern Transvaal are Kriel, generating 3 000 000 kw, and the new stations at Matla and Duvha, each with an output of 3 600 000 kw. Two more giants, Ilanga and Tutuka, are to be built in the area and each will have a capacity of 6 000 000 kw. They will be the largest thermal power stations in the world.

The two Sasol plants, producing liquid fuel from coal, are far and away the largest of their kind in the world and at the time of construction, comprised the largest single engineering project in the world. These plants gulp one third of the coal produced in South Africa. In order to feed Sasol II, the largest coal mine in the world, Bosjesspruit Mine, is designed to yield up to 25 million tons of hard black coal a year. Mines in Germany produce 45 million tons each year, but of the type known as lignite, a soft brown coal with a high water content.

The two Sasol plants, together with the original Sasol I in the Orange Free State, are designed to produce about 50 per cent of South Africa's oil requirements. Various coal mines – some open-cast, others underground – provide all domestic requirements and are calculated to eventually export from Richards Bay, 40 million tons of bituminous coal and 4 million tons of anthracite each year. On the open-cast mines such as Rietspruit, Kleinkopje and Ermelo, massive machines remove overburden, gulping 80 tons of earth at a time. Huge mechanical shovels load the coal into 136-ton haulers which convey the coal to a crusher. It is then stockpiled, blended and loaded on to trains over 1 km long, destined for Richards Bay.

The first main road and rail communication to penetrate this natural powerhouse of South Africa, was the route from Pretoria to the east. Originally created to connect the then South African Republic with the sea, this route unwittingly found its way across the surface of the powerhouse of South Africa, opening the area for discovery and development.

The road to the east starts from the centre of Pretoria, in Church Square, where Anton von Wouw's fine statue of President Paul Kruger stands surveying the bustle and noise of the modern world.

The route leads for 6,5 km along Church Street, through the densely built-up city. After 1,5 km Church Street crosses the Apies River by means of a bridge guarded by a set of stone lions presented to Paul Kruger by Barney Barnato, one of the Rand mining 'lords' of the last century. Another kilometre takes the street past the Union Buildings, looking down aloofly from the splendour of their garden setting. Shops and flats give way to suburban houses and gardens. Then, quite abruptly, Church Street reaches the open countryside and becomes the Eastern Highway, a smoothly graded, gracefully curving dual carriageway, which snakes across the gently rolling highveld.

Immediately outside the built-up area 8 km from Church Square, the road crosses the main road to the north, the Cape-to-Cairo road.

Across the road a turnoff to the left stretches to the suburb of Silverton, originally laid out as a recreational area for the citizens of Pretoria on 1 January 1890 on Mundt's farm. Today it is a small town, but it still possesses some rural charm, with greenery interspersed amongst the concrete and some open space preserved as the Pretoria National Botanic Garden and Botanical Research Institute (open to the public daily from 08h00 to 17h30).

Passing the entrance to this lovely garden, the road continues eastwards. The vast complex of buildings occupied by the Council for Scientific and Industrial Research (CSIR) stand on the right-hand side of the road. There are turnoffs to suburbs such as Val de Grace, Menlo Park, Willows, Eerste Fabrieke, the site of the first manufactory (a distillery) in the old Transvaal, Rayton, and Cullinan, the site of the Premier Mine discovered in 1902 by Thomas Cullinan. It was here, in 1905, that the largest of all diamonds was found; a 3 024,75-carat stone from which was cut the 530-carat Star of South Africa, the smaller Cullinan ii, iii, and iv stones, and several brilliants all of which are set in the British Crown Jewels. Visits to this diamond mine are allowed by appointment on Wednesday mornings only. Phone Cullinan 368.

**Accommodation**
* Premier Hotel, 36 rooms, 6 with baths. R5 – R6 B/B. Phone 8.

The road now follows the shallow valley of the Pienaars River, well wooded with acacia trees and sheltering many fields of maize and lucerne. At 18,5 km from Church Square, the road crosses the Pienaars River, commencing a gentle climb through a low range of hills. There are turnoffs to places such as Avondzon, Cullinan and Bapsfontein, a recreational resort renowned for its 'pop' music concerts.

**Accommodation**
* Bapsfontein Hotel, 17 rooms, all with baths. R6,50 – R8,50 B/B. Phone Petit 92.

**Caravans and camping**
* Bapsfontein Pleasure Resort, 250 sites. R2 D.

Leaving the valley of the Pienaars River, the road continues eastwards over a spacious, sundrenched expanse of highveld, richly green in summer and at Easter, brilliant with the colours of countless cosmos flowers. Clumps of eucalyptus, pine and wattle trees provide shade from the brightness. At 45 km there is a turnoff to Witfontein and Forfar and 7 km further on a turnoff to the town of . . .

# BRONKHORSTSPRUIT

Named after the Bronkhorst family, *Bronkhorstspruit* is a farming centre with a population of 1 400. Originally a station opened when the Eastern Line reached the site in 1894, it was laid out as a town in 1905. The town is famous chiefly for being near the site of the ignominious defeat suffered by the British 94th Regiment on 20 December 1880 at the commencement of the Anglo-Transvaal War.

**Accommodation**
* Park Hotel, 11 rooms, all with baths. R7,50 – R8,50 B/B. Phone 135.

The road proceeds eastwards, crossing the actual Bronkhorstspruit 56 km from Pretoria, and traversing the airy, spacious highveld plain. There are few landmarks save turnoffs to places such as Delmas and the town of Bronkhorstspruit (58 km); Wilgerivier and Nooitgedacht (70 km); Balmoral and Kendal (82 km); Verena and the Highveld Steel and Vanadium Corporation (92,5 km) usually disgorging a horrible pollutant into the highveld atmosphere. There are also turnoffs to Clewer and Verena (98 km); Lynville and Ferrobank (101 km); and 104 km from Pretoria, a turnoff to Springs and to the town of . . .

# WITBANK

Named after a large outcrop of white stones, *Witbank* (white ridge) was formally used by transport drivers as an outspan place for wagons.
  The presence of coal in the area was perceived in the early years, for it was visible on the surface and in the beds of streams. Sporadic attempts were made to exploit the deposit but wagon transport was too impractical. The building of the Eastern Railway made mining possible and in 1896 Samuel Stanford started to work a mine at Zeraatsfontein. This was the beginning of the original Witbank Colliery Company. Today, the Witbank district is the largest coal producer in Africa, having 22 mines, a carbide plant and a cyanide factory. An estimated 75 000 million tons of coal lie close to the surface in this part of the Transvaal. In seams 2 m to

5 m thick, it is ideal for mechanical mining, thus securing the future of Witbank as a coal producing centre for centuries to come.

Witbank was proclaimed a town in 1903. Becoming a municipality on 13 May 1910, it has 83 550 inhabitants. It is a typical modern mining centre, with no pretensions to beauty, but at least the atmosphere is reasonably unpolluted for such an industrial centre and the climate is brisk and healthy. The Witbank Dam in the Olifants River provides a recreational area with boating, fishing and swimming facilities as well as a nature reserve.

A particularly fascinating fragment of history linked with Witbank, concerns Winston Churchill. On the night of 13 December 1899 this bedraggled-looking but quite irrepressible character appeared out of the dark and knocked on the door of the house owned by the manager of the Transvaal and Delagoa Bay Colliery. During the previous night, he had escaped from a prisoner-of-war camp in Pretoria and travelled to Clewer siding near Witbank concealed in an empty coal truck. Now he was in need of food and shelter and fortunately for him, the occupant of the house was an Englishman, John Howard. Churchill was hidden, first in the underground stables of the mine and then behind some packing cases in the mine office. Meanwhile, a hue and cry for him raged all over the Transvaal, with a reward of £25 being offered to bring him in 'dead or alive'.

Early on the morning of 19 December Churchill stowed away in a railway truck loaded with wool consigned to Lourenço Marques (Maputo). It was a tedious journey; that night the train stopped at Waterval Boven; the next night it stopped at Komatipoort. At last, late in the afternoon of 21 December, the train reached Lourenço Marques. After some argument with the British Consul, the grimy escapee was identified as Winston Churchill and a telegram sent to mine manager Howard with the terse news 'Goods arrived safely'.

As a token of his thanks, Churchill presented inscribed gold watches to the six men at Witbank who aided his escape. The mine shaft where he was hidden (now disused), was named the Churchill Shaft. A plaque was erected there to mark the event but vandalism resulted in its removal to a safer place in the grounds of the local MOTH organisation.

## Accommodation
★ Athlone Hotel, 47 rooms, 12 with baths. R8,50 – R9,50 B/B. Phone 3831.
★★★ Boulevard Hotel, 68 rooms, all with baths. R17 B/B. Phone 2424.
★ Carlton Hotel, 49 rooms, 12 with baths. R8 B/B. Phone 2805.

## Caravans and camping
★ Witbank Recreation Resort (11 km from town), 200 sites. R2,50 D plus 50c D per person.

The road continues from Witbank for 30 km in an easterly direction across the highveld, reaching the town of . . .

# MIDDELBURG

In 1859 the Republican Government decided to found a town half way between Pretoria and Lydenburg (hence the name of *Middelburg*). Nothing resulted from the plan, but in 1864 the Dutch Reformed Church bought the farm *Sterkfontein* from L. de Jager and in 1866 a town was laid out which the Church named Nazareth. A few houses and stores were built around the new church, but for years the settlement remained so lifeless that a popular jibe developed about nothing good ever coming out of Nazareth. This joke stung the residents (altogether only seven houses in the town), who petitioned that the name revert to the original Middelburg.

The town has since grown into a modern agricultural and communications centre with a population of 35 650. Situated near the coalfields, there is plenty of water and power is supplied by the giant Komati Power Station and two others in the district. A ferrochrome mill produces stainless steel and other industries have been established in the vicinity.

The Little Olifants River flows past the town and the Kruger Dam (3 km from the town) is a well-developed recreational facility, offering swimming, fishing, a restaurant and accommodation. The town is, in fact, a convenient staging post along the road to the east and also for north-south travellers who, on their way to and from the coast, bypass the traffic congestion of the Witwatersrand-Pretoria complex by taking the all-tarmac shortcut from Potgietersrus, past the Loskop Dam to Middelburg and then on to join the Durban road at Standerton.

There are several interesting structures in the town which date from the days of the Transvaal Republic. These include the railway station (built in 1890); Meyers Bridge (built in 1890); and the Memorial Church which now serves as a museum. Fort Merensky lies 13 km from the town and is described in the next section.

## Accommodation
★ Middelburg Hotel, 37 rooms, 33 with baths. R12,50 B/B. Phone 2116.
★ Olifants Hotel, 16 rooms, 10 with baths. R13,50 B/B. Phone 3003.
★★ Towers Motel, 48 rooms, all with baths. R13 B/B. Phone 5285.

## Caravans and camping
★★® Kruger Dam Park, 100 sites. R1,50 D plus 25c D per person. 24 bungalows (4 beds, furnished), R5 – R8 D.

## LOSKOP DAM AND FORT MERENSKY

From Middelburg a fine tarmac road branches north from the road to the east and descends from the highveld through varied scenery to Loskop Dam (48 km) and from there to Groblersdal and Potgietersrus (198 km).

After 8 km of travel along this road there is a turnoff left (west) leading for 5 km to Fort Merensky. In 1865 the Berlin Mission Society bought a farm in the valley of the Olifants River where the Reverend Alexander Merensky established a mission named *Bothsabelo* (place of refuge). Out of local stone he built a flat-roofed residence, church and protective fort. Local Sotho tribesmen were employed as builders and the construction of the little fort is an interesting example of combined African and European ideas. It is perfectly preserved and open to the public daily from 09h00 to 17h00.

From the turnoff to the fort, the tarmac road continues northwards across the highveld plain, traversing an area densely settled by African people. The road then drops into a bushy, shallow valley and 38 km from Middelburg, descends a spectacular pass, flanked by impressive cliffs and lovely trees. Beyond this pass the road reaches a handsome alluvial valley, covered in bush, and dotted with several farms. In the valley, at 44 km, lies the Rietbok Caravan Park and Kloof Motel. At 48 km the road reaches the Loskop Dam in its setting of bush-covered hills.

Completed in 1938, the 40-m-high, 475-m-long wall of the Loskop Dam stretches across the Olifants River, impounding 182 million cubic metres of water which irrigate 28 168 ha of land. The area round the dam has been developed by the Transvaal Council for Public Resorts as a recreational area offering boating, fishing, a swimming bath, restaurant and varied accommodation. A 12 755-ha nature reserve surrounding the dam is well stocked with game animals such as white rhino, giraffe, blue wildebeest, zebra, sable antelope, kudu, waterbuck, impala, nyala, bushbuck, blesbok, reedbuck, mountain reedbuck, klipspringer, grey duiker, oribi, steenbok and bird life, which is particularly rich. Bus tours are conducted into the reserve and nature trails lead from the camp. Water from the dam is used for irrigation on many farms in the lower reaches of the river valley.

## Accommodation
* Kloof Motel, 22 rooms, all with baths. R10 B/B. Phone c.o. Florabeau.

## Caravans and camping
* Kloof Motel Caravan Park, 20 sites. R1,50 D.
*** ® Loskop Dam Public Resort, 400 sites. R3,50 D plus 50c D per person. 22 bungalows, R8,10 – R17,20 D.

From Middelburg the main road to the east continues a gentle climb out of the valley of the Little Olifants River. Traversing typical highveld country, the road passes plantations of wattle trees and numerous shallow pans (lakelets) which are a feature of this part of the Transvaal. The decorated huts of Ndebele people may also be seen, adding touches of bright colour to a landscape already painted by nature with green grass and a deep blue sky. From January to April the cosmos flowers provide a brilliant spectacle.

There are turnoffs to Hendrina (4 km); Arnot Power Station (26 km); Carolina (45 km and 65 km); and then, at 65 km, a turnoff left (north) leading for 3 km to the town of . . .

# BELFAST

With a population of 8 032, Belfast is the highest railway station (2 025 m above sea level) on the Eastern Line. The farm *Tweefontein* was proclaimed a town on 30 June 1890 in anticipation of the opening of the railway fours years later. The owner, Richard O'Neill, had come from a family living in Belfast, Northern Ireland and so the new town was named after his ancestral abode. He opened the first store and was for a long time the principal figure in the community.

The Belfast district is high lying, well watered and has a crisp, healthy climate, ideal for sheep and dairy farming. Numerous mist belt plantations of wattle and gum trees flourish. The rivers provide good fishing with trout and bass being found in several dams.

A branch railway meanders northwards from Belfast over the principal watershed of the Transvaal. The railway serves rural centres such as Dullstroom, 35 km away, which, at 2 076 m above sea level, is the highest railway station in Southern Africa. The name of *Dullstroom* does not refer to a lack of social life but is derived from Wolterus Dull, who directed an immigration scheme there in 1883.

The area around Dullstroom is a windswept grassland of numerous streams, merino sheep and wild flowers. Dominating the landscape is the 2 332-m-high *Die Berg* of the Steenkampsberg range, the highest point in the Transvaal.

## Accommodation
* Belfast Hotel, 17 rooms, all with baths. R12 B/B. Phone 60.
* Excelsior Hotel (Dullstroom), 12 rooms, 4 with baths. R9 – R10,50 B/B. Phone 11.

## Caravans and camping
* ® Belfast municipal caravan parks (two), 20 and 84 sites respectively. R1,50 D.

The road to the east continues from the turnoff to Belfast, losing altitude as it traverses increasingly broken country. After 6 km the road passes a monument to the Battle of Berg-en-Dal, fought there on 27 August 1900. This was one of the most vicious small battles of the Anglo-Boer War.

The Boers, commanded by General Louis Botha, held exceptionally strong positions on the ridge at Berg-en-Dal. They were determined to delay any further British advance along the Eastern Line and at the same time, the British mustered over 20 000 men in order to take the position by storm.

608

At 11h00 the British artillery opened fire on the homestead buildings of *Berg-en-Dal* farm and the surrounding hillocks. The Johannesburg Police (some of Botha's best men) who were holding these positions experienced a barrage of fire. Nevertheless, they held their positions and when the British infantry tried to advance, they were received with a murderous hail of bullets which killed 12 men and wounded 103. However, the British resolutely saw the attack through and by evening, the Boers were forced to abandon the position and retreat to Machadodorp.

Beyond the monument to this battle, the road makes its way for a further 16 km across the highveld before reaching a turnoff to the town of . . . .

## MACHADODORP

This place was named in honour of Joachim Machado, the Portuguese surveyor and Governor of Moçambique who located the route of the railway from Lourenço Marques to Pretoria. The town started as a railway station, built when the line was opened on 10 July 1894. There are now 3 240 people living there. Machadodorp is the junction of the line to Natal through Breyten and 1,5 km from the town are radio-active thermal sulphur baths resorted to by sufferers from gout and rheumatism. The springs reach the surface at a temperature of 27°C and radio-activity is 12,3 mache units. Cattle, horses and sheep flourish on the surrounding farmlands. Trout fishing in the streams is good and the climate is brisk and cool.

### Accommodation
★ Hydro Baths Hotel, 36 rooms, all with baths. R9,50 B/B. Phone 114.

From the turnoff to Machadodorp, the main road continues eastwards through more rugged country. After 1,5 km there is a turnoff to Dullstroom and 6 km further on a division to the right of the road leads to Waterval Boven and on to the lowveld down the valley of the Elands River (see page 622). To the left, the road continues eastwards for a further 15 km with the landscape gradually building up to a most dramatic change. Passing the Bambi Motel and a turnoff to Lydenburg, it is there, 248 km from its start in Pretoria, that the road reaches the edge of the highveld and commences a steady descent down Schoemanskloof to reach the lowveld. The change in climate, scenery, vegetation and atmosphere is striking (see page 623).

### Accommodation
★★★ Bambi Motel, 40 rooms, 31 with baths. R12,50 – R13,50 B/B. Phone Bambi 1.

---

The road from Pretoria to the east traverses the northern side of the South African powerhouse, while other roads penetrate the heart of the area. The tarmac road leading eastwards from Springs on the Witwatersrand leads directly to some of the largest centres and thence to the borders of Swaziland. From a sightseeing point of view the journey is not recommended in winter for the area is most unattractive – a hideosity of smog so foul that it stifles the breathing, chokes the throat and stings the eyes. Understandably, the grass is dead during this season, much of it burned black and the atmosphere still further polluted by fires. It takes the summer rains to wash the manmade dirt from the face of the land and the sky. The grass then turns emerald green and the clouds pile up like huge masses of snow-white whipped cream.

Beyond Springs the road stretches across a vast plain covered with maize and sunflowers, and with cosmos plants flowering by the million at Easter time. After 37 km the road passes the village of Devon, a cluster of buildings gathered in a hollow around a bulky grain silo. A further 12 km takes the road through Leandra, a small centre whose name incorporates the names of the neighbouring townships of *Evander* (after Evelyn Anderson, wife of the managing director of the Union Corporation Ltd which developed the Far East gold mines) and Leslie.

These townships provide commercial facilities for a cluster of mines, power stations and the prodigious conglomeration of pipes, towers, smokestacks and chemical-mechanical processing bric-à-brac known as Sasol II and III built at Secunda. The headgears of the Far Eastern mining area mines such as Winkelhaak, add to the complexity of an industrial scene. The giant power stations of Matla and Kriel are worth visiting, especially Kriel with its curiously Aztec-shaped pyramid buildings, curved cooling towers, tall straight chimneys and mirror-surfaced lake, providing artists with extraordinary opportunities in composition. Incongruously interspersed among this futuristic array of structures are the cottages of Ndebele and Sotho farm labourers, most of which are decorated with elaborate patterns and colours by proud housewives.

### Accommodation
★★ Holiday Inn (Secunda), 120 rooms, all with baths. R22,50 – R26 room only. Phone 5649.
★ Leslie Hotel, 20 rooms, 12 with baths. R9,50 – R11,50 B/B. Phone Leslie 37.
★ Werda Hotel (Kinross), 18 rooms, 4 with baths. R10 B/B. Phone Kinross 124.

Passing, at 87 km from Springs, the rural centre of Trichardt, the main road continues past turnoffs to power stations and mines and 113 km from Springs, reaches the town of . . .

# BETHAL

Potatoes, maize and sunflowers are the principal products of this town, named after the first and last parts of the christian names of Elizabeth du Plooy and Alida Naudé, owners of the farm on which the town was laid out. In 1921 Bethal became a municipality and has since grown into a substantial commercial, educational, communications and administrative centre with a population of 22 330. The Eastern Transvaal Agricultural Co-operative and the Transvaal Potato Co-operative have their headquarters in the town while there are 20 coal mines and three gold mines in the vicinity. A recreational area and caravan park have been established on the verge of the Bethal Dam.

### Accommodation
★★ Christo Motel, 32 rooms, all with baths. R20 B/B. Phone 3931.
★ Douglas Hotel, 12 rooms, 5 with baths. R7,50 B/B. Phone 2469.
★ Selborne Hotel, 23 rooms, 7 with baths. R10 – R11 B/B. Phone 2501.

### Caravans and camping
★★ Municipal caravan park, 60 sites. R2,86 D.

From Bethal the main tarmac road continues over the plains for a further 55 km and then reaches the town of . . .

# ERMELO

In 1871 the Reverend F. L. Cachet founded a parish which he named *Ermelo* after a town in Holland where he had once lived. A town was laid out for the parish and its situation soon made it the largest centre in the Eastern Transvaal. The area is rich in coal and anthracite, worked by three large coal mines – Ermelo, Spitzkop and Usutu. The Camden Power Station, opened by Escom in 1967 and fed with coal from the Usutu Mine, forms the beginning of the South African grid system.

Maize, potatoes, beans, lucerne, sunflowers, sorghum, wool, cattle, pigs and timber are the products of the district. The Nooitgedacht Research Station, 4 km from the town, conducts research on the agriculture of the Eastern Transvaal highveld. The station has been responsible for the breeding (from Basuto stock) of the Nooitgedacht Indigenous Pony.

The population of Ermelo is 26 960. The civic centre, completed in 1977, is one of the most impressive to be found in the smaller towns of South Africa. Housed in the centre is a spacious administrative office block and two halls. The attractive garden surrounding it is enhanced by a magnificent fountain designed by a local resident, Mrs Heila Brink.

Several large dams in the vicinity of Ermelo, such as the Jericho and the Westoe, provide recreational areas with fishing and boating possibilities. A nature reserve and municipal tourist resort is situated on the shores of the Douglas Dam, 6 km from the town, and there is a bird reserve at the Det Dam.

## Accommodation
∗∗ Holiday Inn, 119 rooms, all with baths. R19 – R28 room only. Phone 2315.
∗∗ Libertas Hotel, 33 rooms, all with baths. R13,50 B/B. Phone 2234.
∗ Merino Hotel, 28 rooms, 8 with baths. R10 – R10,50 B/B. Phone 2321.

## Caravans and camping
∗∗® Republic Park (Douglas Dam), 50 sites. R2 D. 8 rondawels, R5 D.

Roads diverge from Ermelo to several towns in the Eastern Transvaal, to Swaziland, and southwards to Natal. To the north-east, a tarmac road leads for 8 km, reaching a branch with a left turn continuing for 22 km to Breyten and the north (see page 613) and a right turn proceeding north-eastwards for 29 km to reach . . .

# LAKE CHRISSIE

The village of Chrissiesmeer has developed on the western side of Lake Chrissie, a natural lake 24 km in circumference and up to 3 m in depth. Numerous aquatic birds, including flamingos, congregate there. The lake lies in a hollow surrounded by grasslands and has always attracted vast herds of plains game which have, unfortunately, been destroyed. However, to meet the demand for venison, local farmers breed blesbok, substantial herds of which may be seen. *Lake Chrissie* was named after Christiana, the daughter of President M. W. Pretorius. Good views of the lake may be had from a gravel road leading to Rooibank, via the northern shore of the lake.

## Accommodation
∗ Chrissie Hotel, 10 rooms, all with baths. R8,25 B/B. Phone 15.

From Lake Chrissie there are turnoffs to Breyten and Carolina. The main tarmac road continues eastwards into the timber country of the Eastern Transvaal mist belt where high precipitation along the edge of the highveld makes conditions ideal for the cultivation of trees, particularly wattle, fir and eucalyptus. At 27,5 km from Lake Chrissie (3,5 km beyond a turnoff to Carolina) the road passes the Jessievale Sawmills, with a turnoff to Lothair after a further 25 km. There is a pleasant wayside resting place 2 km beyond this turnoff.

The tarmac road continues east through plantations of trees. There are turnoffs to Amsterdam (33,5 km) and Badplaas (59,5 km). At 61 km from Lake Chrissie the road passes Lochiel with its store, garage and the Lochiel Estate Hotel. At 78,5 km from Lake Chrissie a turnoff provides a very steep and rough descent for 10 km to the Mhlondosi Valley, the site of the New Paarl Goldfield and the ghost mining town of . . .

# STEYNSDORP

Today, little more than a store bearing the name of Steynsdorp remains. The mounds of several hundred buildings lie buried under bush and long grass as though in a graveyard, unmarked by memorial or tombstone. The story of this place, and its rise and fall, is strange.

In July 1885 two prospectors, Austin and Painter, worked their way through the valley. They found traces of gold down the entire course of the stream and somewhere in its middle reaches they thought that they had discovered payable deposits. They pegged claims and a rush of prospectors ensued after the news had leaked out. By April 1886, what was at first known as Painters Camp, was the centre for a considerable gathering of prospectors who were all busy seeking a share in this new find.

Gold was certainly present in the area; a prospector's pan will today reveal traces of gold from many parts of the stream and the overlooking heights. Unfortunately, the gold occurred only in patches and finding a payable deposit defied the most energetic prospectors. Traces simply tempted them to search on and on.

Painters Camp was renamed in honour of Commandant J. P. Steyn who visited the place as a government representative in 1886. The field was declared a public diggings on 21 February 1887 and Steynsdorp was laid out as a town. It grew at a phenomenal rate with about 3 000 diggers using it in a secondary capacity as a hub for commerce and administration and in a primary capacity as a drinking centre. Canteens, grog shops, so-called hotels and other places of accommodation, were more numerous than anything else. Upon viewing the mounds in the grass today, it is difficult to imagine Duprats Royal Hotel, Bremers Store, Fullertons Store, Sheriffs Store, the government offices, banks, or the office of the local newspaper *The Observer*.

All that remains of the several hundred hopeful little mines and the thousands of claims, are the half-healed scars of adits, shafts and cross-cuts. The reefs which proved so hard to find, and so deceptive to those who did discover them, but which were famous in their day – the Ingwenya, Bank of England, Mint, Southern Cross, Unity and Comstock – have been forgotten.

The stone walls of the gaol were the last of man's structures to withstand the wind and rain. The gaol was the scene of one of the few lynchings to occur in the course of uproarious events during South African gold rushes. One of the local constables, G. Milhorat and his wife Lizzie (formerly a well-known Barberton barmaid), were murdered by their servant, Jim Zulu, on the night of 19 January 1889. He was arrested and locked in gaol. The next night a crowd of diggers – some with their faces blackened, others masked – broke into the gaol, seized the murderer and hanged him from the slaughter poles of one of the local butchers.

The Steynsdorp rush was an excitable affair. The very uncertainty of the finds allowed speculators and swindlers to run rife. Salting was practised to a fine art. The pubs harboured whispers of rumours. Just how much genuine gold was mined remains uncertain. What is definite, though, is that through the years men met with more disappointment in this valley than anything else.

The prospectors, miners, businessmen, gamblers, boozers and crooks, began to drift away. The town already lay in ruins at the outbreak of the Anglo-Boer War and it was then abandoned entirely to looters and the odd vagrant. Eventually, the bush and grass silently reclaimed the New Paarl Gold Field. Only memories and the ghosts of the excitable company of gold-mad men and women linger in that dark valley. Silence blankets the hills and valleys; the rumours, arguments, quarrels and shouts have been blown away by the winds into the vastness of eternity.

The gravel road continues down the valley of the Mhlondosi for 10 km and 20 km from the turnoff on the main tarmac road near Lochiel, joins the gravel road leading from Badplaas to the asbestos mine at Diepgeziet (see page 615).

The main tarmac road proceeds from Lochiel past the turnoff to Steynsdorp and after a further 7 km (85,5 km from Lake Chrissie), reaches the Oshoek police, customs and immigration post on the border of Swaziland (see page 794). The post is open from 08h00 to 22h00.

## ERMELO TO MACHADODORP

Eight kilometres from Ermelo, the tarmac road to the north-east (after the road to Lake Chrissie and Swaziland has veered off) continues for a further 22 km, reaching the town of . . .

## BREYTEN

Named after Nicolaas Breytenbach who owned part of the farm *Bothasrust* on which the town stands, *Breyten* lies on the watershed between the Vaal River system which flows westwards to the Atlantic Ocean and the Khomati and Olifants rivers, which flow eastwards to the Indian Ocean. The source of the Vaal River is a spring situated 2 km from the town from where it courses through a mass of cosmos flowers. The spring is easily accessible along a road branching off from the main tarmac road to Carolina at the end of the railway yards where 'puffer' enthusiasts may observe a whole collection of retired steam locomotives gently rusting away in well-earned leisure.

Breyten was founded in 1906 when the railway line from Springs reached the site of the town and today has 11 073 inhabitants. Sheep, maize and coal are the principal products of the district, supplemented by high rainfall which provides plentiful water and rich grazing. Klipstapel, the highest point on the watershed, is close to the town and ruins of early Sotho stone settlements are scattered in the vicinity, especially on Tafelkop, where the Leghoya tribe inhabited a substantial village on the summit of a flat-topped hill. As a tribe they have disappeared and the settlement is in ruins.

#### Accommodation
★ Breyten Hotel, 12 rooms, 6 with baths. R9,50 – R11 B/B. Phone 5.

From Breyten the main tarmac road continues northwards over grassy sheep and maize country. After 2 km there is a turnoff to Lake Chrissie and at 22 km, the road reaches the town of . . .

## CAROLINA

In 1882 the farmers of the present Carolina district decided that it was time to found a town as a centre for their area. The wagon trail to the newly discovered goldfields in the Kaap Valley passed through the area and the stream of traffic induced the need for a trading and staging post. Mr C. J. Coetzee offered a section of his farm *Steynsdraai* as a site, providing that the town was named after his wife, Carolina. Other land was added to this nucleus and on 22 June 1885 the town was proclaimed. Apart from being an important communications and trading centre with a population of 6 592, Carolina produces wool, timber, cattle and milk.

Carolina can be very cold in winter. The lowest temperature ever recorded in South Africa (—14,7°C) was recorded there on 23 July 1926.

#### Accommodation
★ Carolina Hotel, 12 rooms, 6 with baths. R10 B/B. Phone 356.

*Overleaf: Water and power; the great thermal generating station of Kriel reflected in the mirrored surface of a highveld pan.*

**Caravans and camping**

★★ Joubert Park, 40 sites. R3 D.

From Carolina the tarmac road to the north continues for 48 km to Machadodorp (see page 609), crossing on the way (at 23 km) the Khomati River, with the original elegant stone bridge still standing next to the modern structure. Another tarmac road leads westwards from Carolina for 44 km to the town of . . .

# HENDRINA

Named after Hendrina Beukes, wife of the owner of the farm on which it was established, *Hendrina* became a village in 1923. It is a centre for maize production, coal mining and two Escom power stations – Arnot and Hendrina. There is a museum of local history which includes among its exhibits a spinning wheel brought to the country by Emily Hobhouse. The museum is open Mondays and Fridays, 10h00 to 13h00 and 15h00 to 17h30; on Tuesdays, Wednesdays and Thursdays 15h00 to 17h30; Saturdays 10h00 to 13h00.

**Accommodation**

★ Hendrina Hotel, 16 rooms, all with baths. R9,50 – R11 B/B. Phone 39.

**Caravans and camping**

★★ Van Riebeeck Square Caravan Park, 50 sites. R1,50 D.

From Carolina a tarmac road stretches eastwards passing through patches of tree plantations and making a winding, easy descent into the valley of the Khomati River. After 50 km the road reaches the resort of . . .

# BADPLAAS

During the period 1860 to 1870, Jacob de Klerk traded with the Swazi people living in the valley of the Khomati River. They showed him a natural feature in the area in the form of a thermal spring, reaching the surface at 50° C at a rate of 25 000l an hour. The Swazi found the waters beneficial for a variety of complaints and De Klerk spread its fame amongst Europeans. From then on the spring was resorted to by people suffering from rheumatism and during the cool months from May to August, a tent town was erected in the vicinity of the healing water.

As the years passed, a few shacks were erected at the site, a tent boarding house flourished for a while and then the Transvaal Government erected a few brick rondawels, followed by a hotel. The spring was led into a reservoir and the water piped to a series of baths. Thus the place was launched as an established health resort.

There is today on the site of the old *Badplaas* (bath farm), a considerable variety of accommodation, several shops, restaurants, and other facilities. The medicinal water is fed into several private baths for use by invalids and into four magnificent recreational swimming baths (two warm and two tepid). The Transvaal Board of Public Resorts manages the place, set in spacious surroundings, with the great valley backed by the handsome range of high hills known to the Swazi as *Ndlumudlumu* (place of thunder).

**Accommodation**

★★ Badplaas Hotel, 63 rooms, 37 with baths. R11,40 – R15,30 B/B. Phone 42.

★ Lebombo Motel, 22 rooms, all with baths. R9,50 – R10 B/B. Phone 26.

**Caravans and camping**

★★★® Badplaas Mineral Baths Caravan Park, 300 sites. R3,50 D plus 40c D per person. 100 bungalows, from R4,50 D.

★ Moreson Caravan Park, 30 sites. R2,50 D. 15 bungalows and cottages, R8,50 – R16,50 D.

★ Therons Rest Camp, 25 bungalows, from R5,50 D.

From Badplaas, the tarmac road continues across the valley of the Khomati River. After 1 km there is a turnoff to Lochiel and Diepgeziet (see page 611). The road passes Therons Rest Camp and drive-in cinema and a turnoff to Machadodorp 8 km from Badplaas. A further 3 km takes the road across the river known as the *Khomati* (river of cows). Immediately upstream stands the wall of the Kafferskraal Dam. The road climbs the northern slopes of the river valley where the country is grassy and open and many pleasant views are revealed. Near the top of the climb the road leads through the plantations of the Nelshoogte Forestry Station. The summit is 40 km from Badplaas and from it may be seen the prodigious Kaap Valley – the Valley of Death of the prospectors – lying to the north amidst seemingly endless hills.

There is a viewsite and resting place on the summit. The road makes a bold descent down a finely located pass, reaches the valley floor and, in a forest of gracefully canopied *Acacia siebeviana* trees, 63 km from Badplaas, joins the main Nelspruit-Barberton road 10 km from Barberton (see page 631).

# BADPLAAS–MTSAULI–BARBERTON

From Badplaas a dramatic scenic road leads to Barberton through the valley of the river known to the Swazi as Mtsoli. This gravel road is very steep in places, and sometimes rough, but quite usable in dry weather if carefully negotiated. It is 116 km to Barberton via this route for which a full day's journey should be allocated.

The drive commences with the turnoff to Lochiel, 1 km out of Badplaas on the direct tarmac road to Barberton. The gravel road leads down the valley of the Khomati River. After 12 km a junction is reached from where a turnoff leads southwards for 22 km to Lochiel to join the main Lake Chrissie-Swaziland road. The scenic road to Barberton, marked Diepgeziet, continues down the river valley. At 13 km there is a turnoff to Tjakastad and at 49 km a turnoff up the Mhlondosi Valley to Steynsdorp which, after 20 km, joins the main Swaziland-Lake Chrissie road (see page 611).

The main gravel road leads on through a mountainous, bushy landscape. At 57 km the road crosses the Khomati River and 2 km further on passes the open-cast workings of the Msauli Asbestos Mine owned by African Crysotile Asbestos Ltd. The deposit was discovered in 1942 by two prospectors, Eyssel and Cronje.

Beyond the mine, the road crosses the Mtsoli River, the corrupted name of which (Msauli) is applied to the mine. This fine torrent of water comes down in violent flood periodically, hence the name, meaning 'unpredictable'. The road commences an involved climb through impressive mountain country along the border of Swaziland. The road reaches the summit 13 km from the mine, to join the Barberton-Havelock Mine road at a point 2 km from the Swazi border. The view from here is majestic.

Turning towards Barberton, the road follows the contours of the high country, a scenic wonderland with mountains stretching as far as the eye can see. Above the road runs the spectacular 20-km-long aerial ropeway connecting the Havelock Mine to Barberton (see page 801).

The gravel road penetrates dense plantations of trees as it twists around the mountain contours. At 27 km from the junction with the Havelock road, the road reaches the verge of the Kaap Valley. The views are tremendous with endless variations in lighting, clouds and atmosphere. For 12 km the road makes a steep descent which demands very careful driving.

An unforgettable experience, there are endless possibilities for the photographer along the whole 116-km-long route from Badplaas. Barberton lies at the foot of the descent (see page 631).

From Ermelo a road leads eastwards for 79 km to the town of . . .

## AMSTERDAM

Originally known as Roburnia, the town was founded in 1866 by a Scot, Alexander McCorkindale, who organised the settlement of a number of his compatriots in this portion of the Eastern Transvaal. McCorkindale divided the area into three, with Lake Chrissie as the centre for what he called Industria; Derby as the centre for Londina; and Roburnia as the capital of New Scotland.

Fifty Scottish settlers arrived and began farming sheep on estates such as *Lochiel, Waverley* and *Bonni Brae.* Unfortunately, the rest of McCorkindale's schemes never matured, for he died of fever while planning the construction of a harbour in the bay of Lourenço Marques. Roburnia was renamed Amsterdam in 1882 and is today a quiet little town with only McCorkindale Square to commemorate its founder.

### Accommodation
★ Amsterdam Hotel, 12 rooms, 6 with baths. R8 B/B. Phone 10.

From Amsterdam the road continues for 16 km to the customs and immigration post on the Swazi border at Nerston (see page 803). The border post is open from 08h00 to 16h00 daily.

## ERMELO TO NATAL

Beyond Ermelo the main tarmac road leads southwards over the grassy plain, passing after 13 km, the Camden Power Station whose thermal generating plant is fed coal on an endless conveyer belt by the Usutu Colliery. The road passes rural centres such as Sheepmoor, crosses the Vaal River 12 km from Camden and the Ngwempisi River after a further 8 km and continues through dense plantations of trees. Sawmills are situated at Iswepe and Panbult and the Ngoye Papermill is passed at 96,5 km from Ermelo. At 104 km the road reaches the town of . . .

## PIET RETIEF

In 1883 the surveyor Anton von Wielligh laid out a town in the mist belt of the Eastern Transvaal, named *Piet Retief,* after the ill-fated leader of the Voortrekkers. With an annual rainfall of 1 000 mm, trees flourish in the area and the town is a centre for timber, paper and wattle bark production. Mica, kaolin and iron are also found in the district. Piet Retief became a municipality in 1932 and today has a population of 15 850. The district includes the 100-square kilometre area of the 'Little Free State', surely one of the smallest independent states ever known. Between 1886 and 1891 this pocket state of 72 inhabitants was ruled by its own president. On 2 May 1891 the republic was incorporated into the district of Piet Retief as Ward I.

Living in Piet Retief are a number of German families, descendants of settlers of the last century. Their brass bands are a feature of the social life of a pleasant, modern town, notable for its gardens and the jacarandas enhancing its streets.

**Accommodation**
★★ Imperial Hotel, 30 rooms, 14 with baths. R14 – R16 B/B. Phone 7.
★ Central Hotel, 34 rooms, 8 with baths. R8,50 – R9 B/B. Phone 71.

**Caravans and camping**
★★ Municipal caravan park, 25 sites. R2 D.

From Piet Retief the tarmac road to Natal continues southwards for 4,5 km through dense plantations of saligna trees. The road reaches a junction from where the tarmac road continues to the south, descending into the valley of the river known on account of its tortuous course as the *Mkondo* (zigzag), but through a faulty translation, called by Europeans the *Assegai*. The road continues through plantations of trees until, 18 km from Piet Retief, it passes through the rural timber centre of Moolman.

**Accommodation**
★ Moolman Hotel, 11 rooms, 5 with baths. R9 – R18 B/B. Phone 22.

After a further 4,5 km of travel through plantation country, the road steadily descends into the great shallow valley of the Phongolo River. At 31 km from Piet Retief a turnoff leads for 12 km to the Piet Retief Mineral Baths. The main tarmac road continues to descend, traversing open, grassy downland where cattle are farmed. At 41 km from Piet Retief the road bridges over the Phongolo River which forms the boundary between the Transvaal and Natal. For a further 15 km the road continues southwards over a grassy plain, covered with plantations of saligna and wattle trees. Fifty-six kilometres from Piet Retief the road reaches the town of Paulpietersburg (see page 471).

---

Back at the junction 4,5 km from Piet Retief, the main tarmac road swings south-eastwards, soon commencing an easy descent into the valley of the Mkondo River, which it crosses 16 km from Piet Retief. At 38 km there is a turnoff north leading for 23 km to the Swazi border post of Mahamba. The post is open from 07h00 to 22h00 daily. The road descends through bush-covered hills with fine canopied acacia trees and plantations of sisal growing by the wayside. At 66 km the road passes the mission hospital known *Itshele Juba* (rock of the dove). At 98,5 km from Piet Retief, the road reaches the sugar producing centre of . . .

# PONGOLA

The Pongola Government Water Scheme was started in 1932 with an extension being completed in 1956. There are 154 irrigated plots and a sugarmill is situated near the village. Subtropical fruits are grown in the area and farm stalls sell produce to passing travellers.

**Accommodation**
★ Pongola Hotel, 36 rooms, all with baths. R8 – R9 B/B. Phone 22.

**Caravans and camping**
★★ Pongola Caravan Park, 35 sites. R3 D.

The tarmac road down the valley provides an interesting and varied drive, rising and falling over riverside hills, with fertile farmlands and forests of acacias and euphorbias lining the way. At 27 km there is a turnoff leading for 6 km to the Swazi border post at Golela. The post is open from 07h00 to 22h00 daily. After 3 km the road bridges across the Phongolo River which forms the border with Natal. The village of Mkhuze lies 34,5 km further on (see page 439).

---

To complete a tour through the South-Eastern Transvaal, a tarmac road should be followed which leads westwards from Piet Retief past the village of Dirkiesdorp (51 km) and from there for a further 43 km across the grassy plains to the town of . . .

# WAKKERSTROOM

Originally known as Martinus-Wesselstroom, this quiet little rural centre became a village in 1904 and has a population of 2 174. It lies on the banks of the river known to the Africans as the *Taga* or *Taka* (angry; wakeful). Europeans eventually adopted this name, calling the town *Wakkerstroom.* Sheep and cattle are bred in the district, which is amply supplied with water. Fish frequent the rivers and dams and since the town lies close to the edge of the highveld escarpment, the climate is crisp and healthy.

### Accommodation
★ Utaga Inn, 10 rooms, 4 with baths. R6,78 – R7,30 B/B. Phone 48.

From Wakkerstroom, the tarmac road proceeds westwards for 29 km through an assembly of grassy hillocks, reaching the town of . . .

# VOLKSRUST

In 1888 the Transvaal Government decided to create a town on the border with Natal where the road from the coast reached the top of the escarpment at Laings Nek Pass. The town was named *Volksrust* (peoples' rest) for it was there that the Republican army had concentrated and rested during the battles of the Anglo-Transvaal War.

Volksrust has a population of 14 045 and is the communications centre of a district which produces maize, sunflowers, sheep and cattle. The main railway and road linking Durban with the Transvaal passes through the town, hence there is a constant coming and going of trains from the marshalling yards. The mountain of Majuba overlooking the town from the south, may be easily climbed (see page 473).

### Accommodation
★ Transvaal Hotel, 22 rooms, 11 with baths. R9,50 B/B. Phone 129.

### Caravans and camping
★ Municipal caravan park, 30 sites. R2 D.

The main tarmac road from Natal to the north continues across the highveld plains which turn emerald green in summer, elegant willow trees lining the banks of the streams. High hills add variety to a rural landscape of maize and dairy farms. After 6 km the road passes the Andrew Motel.

### Accommodation
★★ Andrew Motel, 16 rooms, all with baths. R9,75 – R15,65 room only. Phone Volksrust 296.

618

Beyond the motel, 29 km to the north, looms the landmark of *Perdekop* (horse peak), 1 920 m high. In former years when horse sickness was endemic on the highveld, the area surrounding this miniature mountain was inexplicably free of the disease, with the result that the village of Perdekop became a centre for the breeding of horses.

## Accommodation
★ Perdekop Hotel, 8 rooms, all with baths. R8,60 – R9,60 B/B. Phone 95.

At 45 km from Perdekop the tarmac road reaches the town of . . .

# STANDERTON

Pleasantly situated on the banks of the Vaal River, *Standerton,* with a population of 28 970, was founded in 1876 and named after Adriaan Stander, the owner of the farm *Grootverlangen* on which the town was created. The 1 641-m-high Standers Kop overlooks both the town and the site of the original fording place across the Vaal River.

In former years great herds of antelope frequented this area, attracted by the ample water and rich grazing. Nowadays the district produces wool, meat and dairy products. During the Anglo-Transvaal War 350 British soldiers were besieged in Standerton while the Republican force occupied Standers Kop from where they peppered the town with bullets. A newspaper, *The Standerton News,* was published in the town throughout the siege. A pleasant park is situated on the banks of the Vaal River.

## Accommodation
★ Masonic Hotel, 20 rooms, all with baths. R10 B/B. Phone 2031.
★ Standerton Hotel, 39 rooms, 13 with baths. R9,50 – R11 B/B. Phone 2220.
★ Toristo Hotel, 45 rooms, 11 with baths. R7,50 – R9,50 B/B. Phone 2380.

## Caravans and camping
★★ Municipal caravan park, 100 sites. R2,50 D.

Leaving behind the landmark of Standers Kop, the main tarmac road continues across maize and dairy country, delightful in summer but hideously drab in winter when the grass is dead and generally burned to induce early grazing. After 56 km the road reaches . . .

# GREYLINGSTAD

The Dutch Reformed Church established *Greylingstad* in 1909 and named it after one of the pioneers of the district, Mr P. J. Greyling. A maize, dairy and railway centre, it has a population of 3 175. During the Anglo-Boer War a fort was built on an overlooking hill by the Scottish Rifles, who also painted the initials of the regiment, 'S.R.', on the rock.

## Accommodation
★ Grand Hotel, 10 rooms, 3 with baths. R8,50 – R9,50 B/B. Phone 45.

Crossing a landscape of grassy plains, rocky hillocks, maize and sunflower fields, the tarmac road, after 24 km, reaches . . .

# BALFOUR

Originally proclaimed a town in 1896 with the rather un-euphonious name of McHattiesburg,

*Balfour* was renamed in 1906 in honour of Arthur Balfour, the British Prime Minister who made a speech on the local railway station and was highly regarded during those difficult years. A municipality since 1920, Balfour has 7 800 inhabitants. The Springfield Collieries are situated a few kilometres away while maize is the principal local product.

## Accommodation
★ Balfour Hotel, 13 rooms, 3 with baths. R8,50 B/B. Phone 99.

The tarmac road continues across grassy, farming country with ridges of rocky hills protruding to the north and south. At 33 km the road joins the main route from the Witwatersrand to Natal through the Orange Free State. A further 6 km brings the road to . . .

# HEIDELBERG

The town of Heidelberg is pleasantly situated at the foot of the 1 903-m-high ridge of the *Suikerbosrand* which receives its name from the number of sugar bushes *(Protea caffra)* which grow there, along with numerous other species of highveld flora.

The town was founded in 1862 when a German, H. J. Uekermann, established a trading station at the crossroads of the original wagon trails linking Pretoria, Potchefstroom, Durban and Bloemfontein. Being an important communications centre, Uekermann purchased for £7.10s (R15) a portion of the farm *Langlaagte,* laying out a town which he named after his old university and the town of Heidelberg in Germany.

During the Anglo-Transvaal War, Heidelberg was temporarily the seat of the triumvirate government of the South African Republic, bustling with excitement of commandos and politicians coming and going. After the war, the discovery of gold on the Witwatersrand resulted in a flood of traffic along the roads and the town flourished, also becoming something of a pleasure resort with two hotels built beside the willow-lined banks of the Blesbok stream.

Today, Heidelberg retains its importance as a communications centre the population of which numbers 19 000. Agriculture is carried out together with numerous industries. A pleasant recreational area may be found in the *Kloof* (cleft) where visitors may swim, picnic and camp in a setting of trees, flowers and lawns. Attractive walks lead from this resort into the Suikerbosrand where great numbers of wild flowers have their home.

## Accommodation
★ Grand Hotel, 20 rooms, 7 with baths. R8,50 – R9,50 B/B. Phone 2782.

## Caravans and camping
★® Kloof Resort, 100 sites. R1,50 D. Huts R3 D.

From Heidelberg the tarmac road sweeps over the highveld past maize, dairy and vegetable farms and many nondescript modern housing developments. After 35 km the road reaches . . .

# ALBERTON

After the Anglo-Boer War, a syndicate of developers bought the farm Elandsfontein from Johann Meyer who had trekked there in 1844 from Prince Albert in the Cape. A town was laid out and named after one of the members of the syndicate, General Hendrik Alberts.

Possessing little scenic beauty the town at least has the asset of being situated on the outskirts of the Witwatersrand where the air is cleaner away from the pollution of dusty mine dumps. It was for this reason that it became popular as a residential area and with a population of 102 297, it is now an industrial and dormitory town. The Newmarket horse racing track is in the town area.

## Accommodation
** Alberton Hotel, 36 rooms, all with baths. R12 B/B. Phone 869-4618.
* Newmarket Hotel, 34 rooms, 9 with baths. R6,50 – R8 B/B. Phone 869-6251.

From Alberton the great modern dual carriageway sweeps onwards. Climbing the ridge of the Witwatersrand, the last open spaces left behind, the road passes the workings of the City Deep Mine whose shaft probes 3 245 m into the earth to reefs of gold whose riches penetrate depths well beyond the reach of man. The built-up areas of Johannesburg envelop the road and 11 km from Alberton it reaches the centre of the city of gold.

## Chapter Thirty-two

# THE LOWVELD

The transition from the Transvaal highveld to the lowveld is achieved within a few kilometres, involving a complete transformation of landscape. From the cool, open, grassy plains, the escarpment falls away to a veritable ocean of greenery – trees and bush – surging in from the east. Plants and soil have their own distinctive perfume and the atmosphere is laden with memories of the adventures of hunters and prospectors. Winds and weather are so warm and sultry that they seem to have been carried by the Indian Ocean all the way from the mysterious East.

The main road and the Eastern Line railway, linking Pretoria and the Witwatersrand to Moçambique, run side by side, reaching the edge of the escarpment to make a dramatic descent down the pass of the Elands River, the historic gateway between the highveld and the lowveld of the Transvaal. At the summit of the pass, 13 km from Machadodorp, the main road divides into a loop, with one division descending Schoemanskloof (see page 623), the other passing the railway centre of . . .

## WATERVAL BOVEN

The building of the Eastern Railway (as it was then called) between Pretoria and Lourenço Marques (now Maputo) constitutes a very lively chapter in the history of railroad construction. Building commenced from Lourenço Marques in 1887 and reached the site of Waterval Boven in 1894. It is said that by that stage, as many men as there were sleepers on the permanent way had died in the construction of the line. Fever, heat, lions, alcohol, fights and accidents had resulted in the deaths of many good men. On the station platform of Waterval Boven stands a poignent little memorial to all those forgotten workers. It consists simply of one of the countless boulders moved to make way for the line and a short section of the rack railway which enabled locomotives to haul the trains up the steep face of the escarpment. Once the line reached Waterval Boven, the remainder of the construction over the highveld to Pretoria was a simple matter.

*Waterval Boven* (above the waterfall) receives its name from the waterfall at the head of the valley of the Elands River. To reach this point on the highveld, the railway had to climb 208 m between the stations of *Waterval Onder* (below the waterfall) and Waterval Boven, 14 km away. From Waterval Onder the railway and road ran steadily down to the sea at Lourenço Marques (Maputo) 290 km away. Pretoria, the terminus of the Eastern Line is 1 400 m above sea level and 566 km from Lourenço Marques.

When the line reached Waterval Boven, a marshalling yard and railway depot were created there and in 1898 the place became a village, the population of which is now 6 870.

Accommodation
* Boven Hotel, 14 rooms, 7 with baths. R8,50 – R9,50 B/B. Phone 39.

Caravans and camping
* Elandskrans Holiday Resort, 80 sites. R2,50 D.

From Waterval Boven the tarmac road makes its way to the edge of the escarpment and then descends through a tunnel. At 4 km there is a viewsite and a turnoff leading to the original railway tunnel – 213 m long – through which the rack railway made a 1-in-20 gradient climb. The rack railway was 4 km long and was worked by three special locomotives each capable of hauling a 140-ton load. Puffing and grinding along at about 8 km an hour, these little locomotives pushed the trains up from the rear, while the normal locomotive pulled at the head of the trains. In this way, passengers had ample opportunity to view the beauty of the rushing waterfall tumbling down right next to the line. The modern railway pass, relocated to the other side of the valley, may be seen from the viewpoint. A walk through the old tunnel is interesting and the waterfall is always worth seeing, especially during summer when the Elands River is in flood.

At the bottom of the pass, 8 km from Waterval Boven, the road and railway reaches Waterval Onder, a small railway centre drowsing in a warm, sylvan setting. It was here that President Paul Kruger and his government enjoyed a brief sanctuary from 30 June to 28 August 1900 during the last stages of the Anglo-Boer War. The corrugated iron building used by President Kruger as a temporary state residence and office has been preserved. Known as Krugerhof, it stands in the grounds of the Wayside Inn, built in 1879 as a staging post for coaches.

## Accommodation

★★★ Malaga Hotel, 50 rooms, all with baths. R22,50 D/B/B. Phone Waterval Boven 431.
★★ Wayside Inn, 23 rooms, all with baths. R15 B/B. Phone Waterval Boven 425.

Trout, tropical fruits, nuts and other good things are offered for sale at wayside stalls. The journey down the valley is delightful as the road traverses a parkland of trees and flowers where the busy Elands River flows through a succession of pools and rapids well stocked with trout.

At 10 km from Waterval Onder the road passes the Malaga Hotel and at 31,5 km reaches the small centre of *Ngodwana* (the place of little stumps), sometimes known in corrupted form as Godwan River. Here the South African Pulp and Paper Industries (SAPPI) have a papermill, accompanied by the odours apparently unavoidable in this type of activity. At 3 km beyond the trading centre, a turnoff climbs the eastern heights of the valley, through the Berlyn forestry conservancy and after 14,5 km reaches the old gold rush centre of Kaapsehoop, from where the road makes a scenic descent for 29 km to Nelspruit. (see page 626).

Beyond this turnoff to Kaapsehoop the main tarmac road continues down the valley of the Elands River, past the small centre of Elands Hoek half buried beneath tall trees. Twenty kilometres from Ngodwana the road reaches Montrose Falls, rejoining the loop road which has descended . . .

# SCHOEMANS KLOOF

In 1848, P. A. Schoeman settled on *Mooiplaas* farm in the valley named after him. The left-hand loop of the main road to the east reaches the top of this valley at a point 248 km from Pretoria. The Bambi Motel (see page 609) stands on the summit of the descent to the lowveld.

The drive down Schoemans Kloof is a memorable experience for, apart from being a natural gateway between the high- and lowvelds, it is extremely beautiful in its own right. With handsome trees, high cliffs, and fine farms where the road reaches the valley of the Crocodile River, the greenness and fertility of the area becomes more apparent, metre by metre, as the road loses 800 m in altitude during the course of its journey.

Tobacco and maize fields, groves of citrus trees, lines of silver oaks, elegantly canopied acacia trees, flowering plants and trees splash the scene with colour. Farm stalls sell local produce. There are shady resting places, spectacular views and a new scene around every bend, contributing towards an atmosphere of exhiliration and excitement.

After 47 km the road down Schoemans Kloof rejoins the loop which has come from Waterval Boven down the valley of the Elands River. The roads together cross the Crocodile River just above the Montrose Falls, where the river tumbles 12 m into a deep pool.

## Accommodation

* Montrose Falls Motel, 14 rooms, all with baths. R9,50 B/B. Phone Montrose Falls 3.

## Caravans and camping

* Montrose Falls Caravan Park, 30 sites. R2,50 D plus 50c D per person.
* Schoemans Kloof Rest Camp, 25 sites. R2,50 D. 15 rondawels, R5 D.

From Montrose Falls the road climbs over the shoulder of a high ridge. Descending the eastern side, the road reveals fine views of the valley of the Crocodile River and after 5 km, reaches a tarmac turnoff leading for 8 km up the valley of the Houtbosloop to the Sudwala Caves and from there to Sabie.

## THE SUDWALA CAVES

One of the principal tourist attractions of Southern Africa, these caves are of special interest to geologists and speleologists. Beautifully situated, the entrance is hidden in a green forest which cloaks the precipitous side of the hill known as *Mankelekele* (crag on crag).

The caves are surrounded by a natural botanical garden. Aloes, blooming around August, are particularly prolific with the yellow blooms of *Aloe recurrifolio* daubing the rocky slopes with gold. Wild pear trees blossom in white, while the scarlet-flowered kaffirbooms and many other creepers, trees and plants provide colour throughout the year.

In this superb setting, Mr P. R. Owen, the late owner of the area and his two sons, Theo and Philip, have created a unique dinosaur park where there are displayed, life-sized replicas of these creatures of the past modelled by Jan Theron van Zijl, under the supervision of paleontologist, Dr Andre Keyser. A tour through the park takes the visitor back between 100 and 250 million years, providing a stimulating experience not to be forgotten.

Prehistoric man discovered the Sudwala Caves and at the beginning of the 19th century they were used as refuges by sections of the Swazi people, one of whose kings, Sobhuza I, is said to have hidden in the caves to escape Zulu raiders. On Sobhuza's death, his heir, Mswazi, was still a minor, hence an elder brother, Malambule and one of Sobhuza's brothers, Somcuba, acted as joint regents. When Mswazi came of age, both regents decamped with substantial portions of the royal cattle.

Somcuba built a *stad* (town) for himself close to the caves at what is still known as *Stadspruit* (town stream), using this place as a retreat whenever Mswazi attempted to recover the stolen cattle. He even created a defensive alliance with the Lydenburg Republic about which there is an old legend that the caves (whose end had not yet been reached) led all the way under the mountains to the town of Lydenburg.

In approximately the year 1854, Somcuba was taken by surprise and killed by a Swazi punitive regiment. Those of his followers who were not wiped out, continued to live in the area under one of Somcuba's headmen – Sudwala by name – with the caves becoming his sanctuary and subsequently being named after him.

The area later became a farm, *Sudwala's Kraal,* and in the early years of the 20th century the caves were exploited for their deposits of bat guano. A few visitors explored the caves but it was only when Mr P. R. Owen acquired the farm that a road was built to the entrance and a resort developed to accommodate visitors on the floor of the valley of the Houtbosloop.

This stream has its origin in a superb amphitheatre of forest-covered mountains. It tumbles over in a high waterfall, notable for its rainbow during the summer rainy season and then flows down to join the Crocodile River through one of the loveliest valleys in South Africa.

Serious exploration and mapping of the caves was largely the work of Harold Jackson, a master speleologist who devoted much of his leisure time to a systematic probing of the secrets of Sudwala. It was difficult work; the tourist sections of the caves comprise a minute proportion of the full length which simply vanishes into the dolomite mass. Local legend decrees the end to be many kilometres away.

A pleasant characteristic of these caves is a steady current of fresh air which provides some comfort to explorers. Unfortunately, falls of rock, underground streams and mud make exploration difficult. The rewards have been the discovery of many superb speleothems and entire chambers magnificently decorated by nature with all manner of dripstone and flow-stone formations.

In the 500-m length of the caves open to tourists may be seen dripstone formations such as the oft-photographed Screaming Monster, so dominant and powerful that those who first discovered it could be pardoned for regarding it with superstitious awe. It is highly likely that this formation was worshipped by prehistoric man.

The ceiling of these caves is tremendously interesting providing a perfect complement to the dinosaur park outside. On the ceilings, especially on the domed ceiling above the Screaming Monster, are colonies of fossilised algae known as *collenia*. These primitive algae were alive when the earth's atmosphere consisted mainly of nitrogen and carbon dioxide. Floating on the surface of warm shallow water, this algae converted the carbon dioxide into oxygen by means of photosynthesis and was largely responsible for creating an atmosphere suitable for the higher forms of life we know today.

The algae, having done its job, eventually vanished as did the dinosaurs. At Sudwala, fortunately, some colonies floating on water – which then filled the caves – were transmuted by silica into fossils. Such *stromatolites,* the earliest identifiable form of life in Southern Africa, flourished about 800 million years ago.

The largest cavern in the sequence of the Sudwala Caves has been named the P. R. Owen Hall, the high ceiling of which is decorated with stromatolite fossils. Having excellent acous-tics, fresh air, a natural stage and seating on the tiered sides, this hall of the mountain kings is often used for concerts by visiting choirs and orchestras.

The caves are open daily from 08h00 to 17h00. On the first Saturday of every month, special tours are conducted lasting six hours and penetrating as far as the Crystal Rooms, well beyond the normal tourist route. This tour is strenuous but very rewarding. Booking is essential.

### Accommodation
Family rondawels (5 beds), R10,40 D. Luxury double rooms, with baths. R9,90 D/B/B.
★ 100 caravan sites, R1 D plus 50c D per person.

From the turnoff to the Sudwala Caves the main road continues down the fertile valley of the Crocodile River. Handsome scenery comprises granite domes dominating a rugged valley where every portion of arable land is planted with groves of citrus trees, litchis, mangoes and avocado pears. Pecan trees shed their ripe nuts in July and August and roadside stalls offer them and many other tasty things for sale to passers-by.

Plants flower continuously throughout the year: aloes in June; bougainvillaea, poinsettia and golden shower creepers during winter; jacaranda and poinciana (flamboyant) trees in spring and early summer.

After 5 km the road crosses the Crocodile River, passing a turnoff to the rural centre of Schagen and the Crocodile Motel.

**Accommodation**

★★ Crocodile Motel, 32 rooms, all with baths. R12 – R15 B/B. Phone Nelspruit 4421.

**Caravans and camping**

★★ Allamanda Caravan Park, 45 sites. R3,25 D.

★★ Eureka Park Caravan Park, 10 sites. R5,05 D.

At 3 km beyond the Crocodile River bridge there is a turnoff to *Alkmaar* railway station, named after the small town in Holland, and which serves a rich agricultural area. Magnificent subtropical fruit estates adjoin one another, among the most beautiful of these being *Riverside*. This famous farm was created by Hugh Hall, a pioneer of the valley who settled there in 1890. He commenced a tremendous agricultural industry, producing so many tomatoes and mangoes that the railway authorities granted him a special siding, which combined the names of the two crops in the form of *Tomango*. When this title achieved fame as a trade name, the siding was renamed *Mataffin*, in honour of Matafini, a Swazi chief who had, in 1887, eloped from his native land with a girl intended as bride for the Swazi king. In the as yet uninhabited valley of the Crocodile River, Matafini had found a love nest for himself, where he lived until changing times and tax collectors made life unbearable.

Beyond the Crocodile River bridge the road finds a pleasant way for 22 km through this great garden of cultivated and indigenous plants, reaching the principal centre of the valley . . .

# NELSPRUIT

Half buried beneath flowering jacaranda and poinciana trees, Nelspruit is one of the most attractive towns in Southern Africa. Situated in the middle of the valley of the Crocodile River, the town is well laid out in a park-like setting. Warm to hot in summer, the climate is pleasantly cool in winter. The town has developed into the most important commercial, communications and administrative centre of the valley and has 15 940 inhabitants.

*Nelspruit* is named after the Nel brothers – Andries, Gert and Louis – who, in 1890, at an auction of farms in the valley, purchased the farm on which the town now stands. Two years later the Eastern Line was opened to the place and the town was born as a tin shanty railway station around which were built a couple of stores, hotel and police station. Nelspruit was proclaimed a town in 1905.

The conquest of malaria in the 1930s freed the entire valley of the Crocodile River from the domination of the mosquito. Nelspruit became a municipality in 1940 and since then has grown steadily. One third of South Africa's export oranges are produced in the district, while tobacco, nuts, litchis, mangoes, avocado pears, vegetables, cattle and timber are also produced on a large scale.

The Research Institute for Citrus and Subtropical Fruit has its headquarters outside Nelspruit and the Lowveld Botanical Garden is situated in the town itself.

Nelspruit is a major tourist centre, from where roads radiate to many of the most beautiful and interesting parts of the lowveld. Hotel and caravan parks in the town are convenient for stopovers and in addition, several days can be profitably spent exploring the surrounding countryside.

**Accommodation**

★ Fig Tree Hotel, 27 rooms, all with baths. R13 – R23 B/B. Phone 2264.

★ Paragon Hotel, 34 rooms, 17 with baths. R7,50 – R10,50 B/B. Phone 2283.

★★ Shonalanga Hotel, 40 rooms, 21 with baths. R11 – R15 B/B. Phone 3223.

**Caravans and camping**
- ★ Municipal caravan park, 20 sites. R3 D plus 75c D per person.
- ★ Shonalanga Caravan Park, 30 sites. R2,50 D plus 50c D per person. 25 bungalows, R8 B/B.

From Nelspruit, the main road and railway to the east continue down the valley of the Crocodile River. Immediately outside the town the road passes through the immaculate citrus groves, orchards and fields of Crocodile Valley Estates (Pty) Ltd. At 6 km from Nelspruit the road passes the head office, packing station and wayside kiosk of this company. It is interesting to learn something of its history . . .

# CROCODILE VALLEY ESTATES

In 1925, Ivan Solomon, a young Pretoria lawyer, was engaged to liquidate a company formed to sell plots in the Eastern Transvaal. This company had sold about 600 plots, mainly to soldiers returning from the world war and to would-be immigrants from Britain. The intention had been to develop a community citrus estate with large-scale irrigation and a central packhouse.

Unfortunately, the company went bankrupt although many plots had been sold, mainly in Britain. Ivan Solomon visited the plots in the Crocodile Valley and became convinced that the scheme, in fact, had considerable potential but simply needed more capital. He set out to persuade the plot holders to provide more money and not merely to liquidate the venture. He visited Britain and consulted the Plot Holders Association, formed by owners to look after their interests. They declined to 'throw good money after bad' so Ivan Solomon returned to South Africa where he prompted a small group of people to support him. In this way the interests of the Plot Holders Association were acquired. The remaining plot holders, scattered in many parts of the world, were all traced and persuaded to sell their interests.

During the depression years of the 1930s, Ivan Solomon struggled to establish the fortunes of the company. He ran his legal practice, served as mayor of Pretoria for a record term, and in addition, possessed the enthusiasm to turn farmer on a vast scale. In the face of pessimism and criticism, he struggled to finance the venture and to gather the help of a staff whose zest kept them working even when there was no ready cash to pay their salaries. In the company's archives may be found an old school slate on one side of which is written 'cheques have arrived' and on the other side 'no cheques yet'.

Faith triumphed. In the citrus groves of the estate today, 100 000 trees bear fruit, yielding 5 per cent of the total South African export crop of oranges. From mid-April until early September the packhouse is the scene of tremendous activity in the packing each day, of about 250 tons of fruit, or one and a half million oranges.

Ivan's son, Dennis, joined his father in management in 1955. Dennis's son, Mark, was born on the estate and by the African workers made an honorary chief, *Nkosi Mabale Ingwe* (chief of the spots of the leopard).

The original 20-km-long irrigation canal built by the old Plot Holders Association, still serves as the main artery of the irrigation system, using water from the Crocodile River. This water also drives the turbines which generate power for pumping and light.

Irrigation is by sprinkler system and the estate is highly mechanised. A system of bulk handling designed by Dennis Solomon, who has a Master of Science Degree in engineering, is used today by many other estates.

The estate is also the home of one of the the finest pedigreed herd of Jersey animals in Southern Africa, the Croc Valley Jerseys. Three of the bulls produced by this herd have received the highest award possible, that of Preferent Sire. Beef cattle are farmed by the estate on a separate ranch in the Bushveld near Phalaborwa, and a new breed of cattle, known as Huguenots, are bred on the estate itself from Charolais and Âfricander parent stock. These animals combine the hardiness and ability of the Africanders to calve easily with the large frame and beefiness of the European Charolais.

In 1956 the estate acquired a forestry area in the Pilgrims Rest district – Goedgeloof Plantations and Sawmill – in order to manufacture wooden boxes for the packhouse. Another acquisition has been the *Kloof* farm in Schoemanskloof. This estate, almost derelict when purchased in 1967, is now a large producer of wheat, avocado pears and pecan nuts.

--------

The main tarmac road continues eastwards past a roadside garden of red *Bauhinia galpini* (the pride of the Kaap), yellow acacia and elegant palm trees. At 7,5 km from Nelspruit the road passes through a gateway of granite domes. On the eastern side of this ridge lies a resting place and picnic spot in the shade of some wild fig trees. This pleasant place is unfortunately ill-used by certain individuals who will carry a *full* can of beer a thousand kilometres but who decline to place the *empty* can in the nearest rubbish bin, a mere metre away.

The road continues through beautifully wooded country down the valley of the Crocodile River. Oleander and frangipani trees line the verges of the road. At 13 km a turnoff leads to White River, providing tourists with an interesting alternative scenic route back to Nelspruit.

Three kilometres beyond the White River turnoff is a turn off south to Uitkyk. This gravel road supplies the connoisseur of scenery with an exciting off-route drive with a choice of two ends. The road climbs steeply into the granite mountain complex. After 5,5 km there is a turnoff to Mara. By following this turnoff the traveller will, after 23 km of scenic switchback journey, rejoin the main tarmac road near Boulders station. The other branch of the gravel road, after a great deal of winding and climbing, eventually joins the Claremont-Nelspruit road and, after 30 km, finds its way back to Nelspruit down Henshall Road.

The main tarmac road, after the turnoff to Uitkyk, travels through the spectacular Crocodile River Poort where the river forces its way through a narrow boulder-strewn pass in the ridge of granite mountains. Some of the heaviest work in the construction of the Eastern Line was undertaken in this passage. Earth and rock moving machinery was unknown in those days and all labour was done by humans. The tough cosmopolitan crowd of navvies recruited for the work were housed in a construction camp known as Poort City, built at the east end of the passage. This was a notorious place for riotous living, rough customers, and a daily lottery run by the doctor, based on the highest temperature reached by any of the numerous malaria sufferers.

Another memory of those days is the name Gould's Salvation Valley, applied to a valley leading into the Crocodile River Poort. This valley was reputed to be free of tsetse fly and during the Barberton gold rush, it was located by a transport man, Tom Gould, and used as a route for wagons carrying goods from the railway at Krokodilspoort station.

The tarmac main road passes the Salvation Valley 22 km from Nelspruit. After a further 15,5 km the road leaves Crocodile Poort, bridges over the Crocodile River and 40 km from Nelspruit, reaches turnoffs leading to Barberton (page 631) and to the railway junction of Kaapmuiden.

## Caravans and camping
★ Lowveld Rest Camp, 30 sites. R2,70 D. 19 rooms, R6 D.

From Kaapmuiden the main road continues eastwards, past the Lowveld Rest Camp and through a warm world of sugar cane, citrus and pawpaws. Intensive cultivation under irrigation may be observed. At 13 km there is a turnoff to Magnesite, Kaalrug and the Senekal

Mine. At 18 km the road reaches *Malalane* (place of small lala palms) set in an ocean of sugar cane dominated by a sugarmill.

## Accommodation
** Lelane Hotel, 19 rooms, all with baths. R11 – R19 B/B. Phone 13.

At 4,5 km beyond Malalane, the main road reaches turnoffs to Piggs Peak in Swaziland and to the Malalane gate of the Kruger National Park. Sugar cane now prevails over the landscape like a green flood of vegetation which has drowned the original bush.

At 18 km from Malelane there is another turnoff to Piggs Peak and 1 km further on the road passes the small centre of Hectorspruit which had its start in 1891 when the surveyor of the Eastern Line, Servaas de Kock, named a station after – of all things – his pet pointer dog!

## Accommodation
* Buffalo Hotel, 20 rooms, all with baths. R10,25 B/B. Phone 34.

A further 10 km takes the road past the railway centre named *Tenbosch* after the Dutch royal palace, *Het Huis ten Bosch*. Here a turnoff leads to the Crocodile River Holiday Township. The road to the east passes a turnoff to the Strydom block of agricultural farms 25,5 km from Hectorspruit, and after a further 2 km (64 km from Kaapmuiden) reaches a division where the left-hand turn leads for 3 km to the frontier town of . . .

# KOMATIPOORT

The Crocodile River reaches the end of its course when it becomes a tributary of the *Nkhomati* (river of cows). The confluence occurs immediately west of the *Lubombo* (the ridge) which, like a wall dividing two properties, forms the frontier between South Africa and Moçambique. The combined rivers, together with the road and railway, have forced a passage through this high ridge to reach the coastlands of Moçambique.

When the railway was built from Lourenço Marques (Maputo) it reached this natural passage through the Lubombo mountain and the first construction contract ended on the border. In 1890 a Dutch company took over construction from the border to Pretoria and this concern established the town of Komatipoort as a base depot.

The situation of Komatipoort was hot and feverous. Malaria was then endemic in the area and numerous men died. Strong drink and riotous living also took their toll, making the Komatipoort of those days an uproarious construction camp.

During the Anglo-Boer War the town was used as a base by the celebrated character, Colonel Ludwig Steinacker and his Forty Thieves, a group later enlarged to become Steinacker's Horse. This force of adventurers, rough-riders, mercenaries and bush whackers, were recruited into an irregular troop for the purpose of fighting Boer guerillas in the bushveld. The escapades of these men, and the variety of characters, would comfortably fill a big book.

Today, Komatipoort is a sedate place which still retains its memories. Fever has been eradicated and only summer heat remains. The streets are well shaded by jacaranda and poinciana trees and the town is still a railway centre, marshalling yard and road junction. The Crocodile Bridge entrance gate to the Kruger National Park lies 13 km to the north.

## Accommodation
* Komati Hotel, 20 rooms, 8 with baths. R6,50 – R7,50 B/B. Phone 166.

## Caravans and camping
** Komatipoort Caravan Park, 40 sites. R2 D plus 50c D per person.

From the turnoff to Komatipoort, the main road continues eastwards. Bridging across the Nkhomati River, with a turnoff south to Swaziland after 1 km, the road passes the Douane Motel, and, at 4 km from the turnoff to Komatipoort, reaches the South African customs and immigration post on the Moçambique border.

## Accommodation
★ Douane Motel, 15 rooms, all with baths. R8,50 room only. Phone Komatipoort 176.

# NELSPRUIT TO BARBERTON

From Nelspruit a tarmac road branches southwards from the main road to the east, just before it enters the town. This road climbs steadily past numerous fruit-growing smallholdings with wayside kiosks offering a variety of agricultural products for sale. At 14 km from Nelspruit the road tops the rise whereupon the traveller is confronted by one of the great views of Southern Africa, a most majestic panorama of the famous Valley of Death of the old-time prospectors.

This great valley received its sinister name on account of the malaria fever once endemic there. Innumerable prospectors died during the search for gold in this, the valley of the river known to the Africans as the *Ngwenyana* (little crocodile) but to Europeans as the *Kaap* (Cape) from the high cliffs which project into the valley like a cape projecting into a sea. The effect is particularly suggestive of this idea when the valley is shrouded in mist.

The verges of the valley are covered in vegetation, including flowering plants such as *Bauhinia galpini,* the Pride of the Kaap, indigenous to this area and producing masses of blood-red coloured flowers in summer. On the floor of the valley grow many of the graceful paperbark thorn trees *(Acacia siebeviana)* with their canopied branches.

At 29 km from Nelspruit, a turnoff leads for 32 km to . . .

# KAAPSEHOOP

The old mining village and former boom town of *Kaapsehoop* (hope of the Cape) is situated on top of the cliffs overlooking the valley from the west. The scene is atmospheric and beautiful. Near the village is a cluster of more than a thousand sandstone rocks, many of them weathered into such strange shapes that they seem to have been sculpted by an artistic demon. A stream runs down the valley in the midst of this assembly of rocks and in the upper portion lies one cluster of rock shapes which so resembles a group of petrified demons on convention that the area is known as the *Duiwelskantoor* (reception office of the devil). Old fortifications made by early tribespeople may also be seen among the rocks.

Gold was discovered in the streams in 1882. A rush to the area ensued and Kaapsehoop was created as a centre for the prospectors. Traces of gold and asbestos were found, together with many signs of prehistoric mining, but no really payable deposits were located. Kaapsehoop, however, became the base for prospecting in the Kaap Valley and it was there that one of the most persistent prospectors, 'French Bob' (Auguste Robert) discovered the Pioneer Reef on 3 June 1883. This was the greatest discovery of gold yet made in South Africa resulting in a great rush to the Kaap Valley and the eventual founding of Barberton.

Kaapsehoop was largely abandoned but in later years asbestos mining and afforestation commenced in the area. Odd prospectors still search the streams, finding an occasional nugget or enough alluvial gold to tempt them into continuing long after all hope should have vanished. In 1976 the author met an irrepressible character named Ernest George Sparg, 74 years old and with 32 years of prospecting in the area behind him. He was sitting panning gold in a furrow, removing pebbles from the pan with his fingers and throwing them over his shoulder to add to an accumulation of several hundred thousand piled up in a long ridge behind him as he periodically changed his operating position.

Accommodation
* Kaapsehoop Hotel, 10 rooms, all with baths. R8,25 D/B/B. Phone 15.

Roads lead from Kaapsehoop down to Ngodwana in the Elands Valley (14,5 km) and back to Nelspruit (29 km) along the verge of the cliff. The latter road is very spectacular and numerous interesting stones may be seen such as asbestos, serpentine, stitchtite and others.

From the turnoff to Kaapsehoop on the floor of the Kaap Valley, the main tarmac road continues for a further 8 km, reaching a turnoff to Badplaas (see page 614). Just beyond this turnoff the road crosses the Queens River, named after a Swazi queen who once ruled over a military kraal established there. Passing through a fine forest of paperbark acacias, the road, at 45 km from Nelspruit, leads into the romantic gold mining town of . . .

# BARBERTON

In the midst of all the excitement surrounding the discovery by French Bob of the Pioneer Reef at what was known as Moodies, a party of prospectors comprising Graham Barber, his two cousins, Fred and Harry Barber, and two other men, found their way into the narrow gorge just to the east of the modern town of Barberton. They noticed a white thread of quartz high up on a cliff. Graham Barber scrambled up and took some samples. With his companions he panned the samples in the stream which ran through the gorge. The result sent a wave of excitement throughout the world and resulted in one of the greatest gold rushes ever known.

On 24 June, three days after Graham Barber had reported his find, the mining commissioner of the area arrived to inspect the discovery. Already local prospectors were stirring and it was inevitable that a great rush would follow and that a town would come into being almost overnight. The mining commissioner broke a bottle of Holland's Squareface Gin over a sample of Barber's Reef and named the site of the prospector's camp, *Barberton*.

The speed with which the town grew was astonishing. Shacks and shanties sprang up like weeds, and in almost similar disarray. At first, town planning was influenced by the whereabouts of 200 canteens, dozens of gin palaces, two stock exchanges and numerous bars! These were the social pivots of the boom town and streets were directed towards them, around them, into them – but never past them. Nor was there a shortage of hitching posts for horses or pack donkeys outside them.

For the first few years Barberton's population was predominantly masculine, some very remarkable characters emerging among the thousands who used the town as their base. The few reigning beauties in the town (such as 'Cockney Liz') did a roaring trade with some of them auctioning themselves off in the evenings, and using top-hatted auctioneers such as the famous Stafford Parker, one-time president of the 'diamond diggers republic'. Cockney Liz arrived in Barberton in June 1887, leaving in September 1889. Where she came from and where she went, including details of her life, would make good reading.

Rumours and excitement were the order of the day. Many impudent frauds were perpetrated, but many real finds were made, among them the richest and most famous gold mine in the world at that time. This was Bray's Golden Quarry on the Sheba Reef, found in May 1885 by Edwin Bray. In this mine it was said, the gold was not imbedded in rock but rather the rock was set in solid gold. It was the greatest producer in the world for some years. A separate town, known as Eureka City, grew up to serve this mine. When the gold was exhausted the town was abandoned and its ruins today provide an interesting sight for visitors.

The riches of Bray's Golden Quarry, were, curiously, among the factors contributing towards the ruin of Barberton. The world began to expect too much of the place. Fraudulent company promoters easily sold shares in useless properties simply by describing them as being close to the Golden Quarry. The entire Kaap Valley was covered in claims and hopelessly over-capitalised. The vast numbers of loafers, layabouts and deadbeats attracted

631

*Overleaf: The awesome Screaming Monster in the Sudwala Caves holds court beneath a ceiling encrusted with fossils of the earliest forms of life.*

to the place were a curse, while the profits from the payable mines hardly equalled the amount of capital being poured into the valley by overseas investors.

The crash was inevitable. The Valley of Death lived up to its reputation, for dozens of companies collapsed and the hopes of innumerable overseas (particularly British) investors were ruined. Many a titled board chairman found himself dodging missiles in the form of ornate but worthless share certificates in Barberton properties. The name of the town is said to be indelibly printed in the memories of investors. By 1888 the great boom was over and investors were turning their attention to the newly discovered Witwatersrand.

Barberton and the Kaap Valley were left to settle down to a more humdrum, hardworking but quite prosperous life. The valley, richly if erratically mineralised with gold, nickel, chrome, titanium, copper, asbestos and gemstones such as jasper, onyx, budstone and verdite, will be a centre of mining for an indefinite period. Chert from Daylight Mine, containing the earliest known form of life – fossil algae – was used by the American National Aeronautics and Space Administration to compare with moon rock samples. The rich soil of the valley floor and the warm climate allows for the production of crops such as cotton, tea, coffee, subtropical fruits, pecan nuts and sisal. Eucalyptus and fir trees flourish on the mountain slopes.

Barberton has a total of 12 901 inhabitants and is the terminus for the 20-km aerial ropeway which carries to the railhead the entire output of the Havelock Swaziland Asbestos Mine.

From a tourist point of view, Barberton is not only an atmospheric and interesting little place, with its flamboyant and jacaranda trees, but it is also a convenient base from which several fine scenic drives diverge to places such as Kaapsehoop, the Havelock Mine in Swaziland, the Agnes Gold Mine and Eureka City. Many mining sites, such as the Pioneer Reef at Moodies, either working or disused, are also linked by usable gravel roads leading through breathtaking scenery.

Barberton was for some years the home of Percy Fitzpatrick, the author of the classic tale of the low country, *Jock of the Bushveld.* In the Fitzpatrick Park stands a bronze of the famous dog, Jock, modelled by Ivan Mitford-Barberton. The lounge of the Impala Hotel is adorned with a *Jock of the Bushveld* frieze painted by Conrad Genal, an itinerant artist who, born in Germany in 1875, joined the Foreign Legion, deserted, and then made his way from Cairo to South Africa, earning a living by decorating the walls of many hotels in his distinctive and talented style.

The flora of the Kaap Valley is magnificent and includes the much-cultivated Barberton Daisy *(Gerbera jameoni)* named after R. Jameson, a member of the Durban Botanic Garden who found the flower growing at Moodies when he visited it in 1885. He took the flower back to Durban. The nature reserve above Moodies is named after Miss Cynthia Letty, the renowned botanical artist.

### Accommodation
★★ Impala Hotel, 39 rooms, 23 with baths. R11,70 – R13 B/B. Phone 8-4371.
★ Phoenix Hotel, 17 rooms, all with baths. R11 B/B. Phone 12.

### Caravans and camping
★★ Municipal caravan park (Fitzpatrick Park), R2,40 D.

From Barberton the main tarmac road runs down the valley of the Kaap River to Kaapmuiden on the eastern road from Nelspruit to Komatipoort.

Three kilometres along this road is a gravel turnoff climbing up the steep heights to the Havelock Mine (39 km), in one of the most spectacular drives in Southern Africa. At 8 km from Barberton a gravel turnoff leads to Fairview Mine (11 km) and to the ghost town of Eureka City. One kilometre beyond this turnoff there stands what is known as Jock's Tree, a shady acacia tree whose canopy provided shelter for many of Jock's and his master's camps.

Five kilometres further on (14 km from Barberton) the road reaches the small centre of Noordkaap, where the Bougainvillaea Roadhouse is the proud possessor of a superb group of acacia trees whose canopies are perfect. Inside the hotel the wandering artist, Conrad Genal, painted (in 1936) a lively series of monochrome friezes depicting a tribal hunt, a Zeederberg coaching episode, and other scenes of the African bush.

## Accommodation
★ Bougainvillaea Roadhouse, 11 rooms and 8 bungalows, all with baths. R6,50 B/B.

The tarmac road continues northwards down the river valley. Turnoffs lead to the Consort Mine (3 km) and the Sheba Mines (8 km), the latter a very fine drive. At 39 km from Barberton the road passes Louws Creek, an old mining area now concerned with the production of sugar cane and mangoes. A further 5 km of travel brings the road to *Revolver Creek,* named after the murder there of a prospector, James Mayne, in July 1887. When a search was made in the little creek for his belongings, his revolver was found lying on a rock which he had chipped for gold. The rock did contain gold and the name of Revolver Creek was attached to the discovery. Ten kilometres on (53 km from Barberton) the tarmac road joins the main eastern road at Kaapmuiden and from here the traveller has the choice of turning west to Nelspruit (39 km) or east (68 km) to the frontier of Moçambique at Komatipoort.

## NELSPRUIT TO THE NORTH-EASTERN TRANSVAAL

The tarmac road to the North-Eastern Transvaal leaves Nelspruit, crossing the Crocodile River after 1,5 km. Immediately, a parting of the ways is reached; the right-hand fork leads to White River and northwards across the lowveld; the left-hand fork travels north-westwards along the edge of the escarpment, eventually rejoining the lowveld road far north, at Tzaneen. A pleasant journey is provided by taking the left-hand fork northwards along the edge of the escarpment, returning along the lowveld road.

The road commences a long and steady climb out of the valley of the Crocodile River, on the verge of which grows a lovely avenue of African flame trees flowering around January. Stretching over the hill slopes into the distance are sweetly scented orchards of oranges, mangoes, avocado pears, litchis, pawpaws, pecan nuts, and other tropical fruits, creating a scene of warmness and fertility.

Turnoffs lead to places such as the Houtbosloop Valley ( 33 km), the Sudwala Caves (17 km away) and, 21 km further on, to White River. As the road gains altitude, the air cools and freshens, the road entering a zone of the most extensive plantations of pine and eucalyptus found anywhere on earth. This area is not only of considerable beauty, but also retains many memories of some of the earliest Transvaal alluvial goldfields.

It was here, on 6 February 1873, that one of the most renowned of the old-time prospectors, Tom McLachlan, found alluvial gold. A public diggings around the slopes of the dominating peak known as Spitskop was proclaimed by the government and a lively crowd of diggers rushed to the place in the hope of finding fortune.

Stories about the adventures of these diggers make fascinating reading. Some of them made fortunes, some were ruined by delusions. One of the diggers, John Swan, found gold, but in an awkward situation where there was no water to allow for alluvial working. Carefully keeping the site of his discovery a secret, Swan started to dig a 'race' (artificial watercourse) to lead water from a stream several kilometres away. Swan's Race, as it came to be known, was one of the diggers' marvels during the age of gold. Swan had begun digging his race in 1878 and for five years he laboured intermittently, financing operations with gold nuggets removed from his secret find. Then a company secured a concession over land which neatly blocked his contour line. The company made him an offer: if he would reveal the situation of his mine, they would form a company to work it and he would receive 20 per cent interest. He refused, abandoned his race and went off to the Barberton area where he died of fever while prospecting in the Valley of Death. His mine has never been found, but portions of his race may still be traced, following the contours for several kilometres and then ending abruptly.

The main tarmac road continues to climb steadily passing Hendriksdal station, and revealing many views of tree-covered hills and distant valleys. At 54 km the road passes over a high saddle, reaching a junction with a tarmac road which has crossed the famous Long Tom Pass over the Drakensberg from Lydenburg. This is a grand viewsite.

# LONG TOM PASS

The majestic Long Tom Pass, with its smooth tarmac surface and carefully planned gradients and curves, closely follows the route blazed by the pioneer wagon drivers transporting goods from Lourenço Marques to Lydenburg. The section from Lydenburg over the Drakensberg was notorious for its gradients and hair-raising drops. The old route may still be seen twisting precariously up the western heights to what was known as Sabiesnek. Rising and falling across the four so-called Devils Knuckles (a graveyard of many wagons), the road dropped down to Spitskop and from there crossed the lowveld in a dangerous journey through bush haunted by big game, mosquitoes and tsetse flies. The wagons took an average of ten days to reach the coast at Lourenço Marques (Maputo) via this road.

This old transport road was blazed in 1871 by a commission appointed to that task by the people of Lydenburg. The discovery of gold brought heavy traffic to the route and it became one of the most romantic of roads, with a host of picturesque characters tramping along it in search of fortune.

The modern all-tarmac road provides fine panoramic views of the valley of the Sabi River. Densely planted with pine and eucalyptus trees, this green valley is dominated by the peaks of the *Mauchberg* (2 210 m) – named after Carl Mauch, the German geologist who predicted the discovery of gold in the Transvaal – and Mount Anderson (2 287 m).

At the junction with the road from Nelspruit there is a pleasant picnic and camping ground with a spectacular outlook. From here the road climbs through the plantations of *Olifantsgeraamte* (elephant's skeleton) and *Renosterhoek* (rhinoceros glen). After 3 km the road passes the Olifantsgeraamte Forest Station. The journey is altogether pleasant and diverting, enhanced by views and rich vegetation.

At 11 km from the junction the road passes a sign marking the last position held by the Boer forces during the Anglo-Boer War covering one of their famous Long Tom cannons, after which the pass is named. A fine picnic site with a superb view is situated 400 m further on where it is interesting to pause awhile and to imagine the Long Toms in action.

'Long Tom' was the nickname applied by the British soldiers to the Creusot artillery pieces used by the Boer forces. With a calibre of 15 cm and firing a 38 kg shell for 10 000 m, these ponderous guns were laboriously trundled by the Boers into a few situations both awkward and surprising for the British.

On 7 September 1900 General Buller and his Natal army captured Lydenburg after marching, against slight resistance, from the valley of the Crocodile River. The defending Boer forces withdrew to the heights of the Drakensberg up the road now known as the Long Tom Pass. With them they dragged a Long Tom and some smaller artillery pieces. The British had no sooner made themselves comfortable in Lydenburg than Long Tom opened fire on them from the mountain top.

On 8 September the British advanced up the pass in order to dislodge the Boers. A series of clashes took place, with the Boer rearguard withdrawing to a succession of strong positions along the road. Memories of the tumult, drama and echoes of that day, still linger about this road pass. A cold mist eventually enveloped the mountain and fighting died away. The next morning (9 September) Buller resumed the attack, his men reaching the summit of the pass from where, to the east, the stupendous view of the lowveld was revealed to them.

Below the summit the road fell away abruptly and the British could observe the Boer wagon convoy slowly retiring over the Devils Knuckles, a particularly tortuous portion of the old road. The British sent their cavalry in pursuit as fast as the steep slopes would allow, but soon found themselves under heavy fire, with the deep voice of Long Tom rumbling through the valley and his shells causing considerable damage to the attackers.

All day the action continued with the Boers stubbornly keeping the British at bay. Night saw the British bringing up artillery to dislodge the Boers. At dawn on 10 September the British opened fire, with the Gordon Highlanders being given the task of clearing the road over the Devils Knuckles. Battle raged for most of the day and only at 16h00 did the Boers withdraw from the Knuckles, sending 13 of their wagons tumbling down a precipice to prevent them from being captured by the British. The main Boer force had meanwhile escaped with Long Tom, bag and baggage, to new and secret positions in the far off hills.

The Devils Knuckles lie 13 km up the pass from the junction with the Sabie-Nelspruit road. The position where the Long Tom was last in action is marked by a sign, and if men had to die in battle, it was at least in a setting of overwhelming beauty.

Three kilometres further up the pass lies the Long Tom Forest Station and after a further 5 km, the Blyfstaanhoogte Forest Station. The summit of the pass – 2 149 m above sea level – is reached after a further 6,5 km from the junction with the Nelspruit road. The entire length of the road is dotted with interesting things to see; just beyond the Blyfstaanhoogte Forest Station is a sign marking the portion of the old road known as The Staircase. Near by is preserved one of the Long Tom shell craters. There is a fine viewsite and, just before the summit, a camping place at what is known as Whisky Spruit.

The summit acts as the division between the headwaters of the Sabi River, flowing east, and the Spekboom River, flowing west. The area of the division was, in the 1920s, the scene of a minor gold rush to what was known as the Mount Anderson Gold Field. The signs of mining activity may still be seen in the form of rubble dumps, trenches, shafts and adits. Here the Jackpot, Little Joker, Formosa, and several other little mines, flourished for a short while.

West of the summit, the road descends steadily through a rocky, undulating moorland, with flocks of sheep and troops of baboons wandering through the grass. After 19 km of easy descent, the road reaches the town of Lydenburg, 46,5 km from the junction with the Nelspruit-Sabie road (see page 634).

---

Back at the junction point on the Nelspruit road, the road sweeps downwards, curving easily for 10,5 km through gum and pine plantations, to the town of . . .

# SABIE

The beautifully situated little town of Sabie is named after the river originating on the divide at the summit of the Long Tom Pass and which then flows down through a handsome tree-grown valley to a waterfall where the town has been built. The name of the river – Sabi – derives from the Shangane word meaning 'fearful' and refers to the crocodiles and sudden floods which formerly made this river dangerous.

Sabie was originally a farm named Grootfontein, pioneered by D. J. Badenhorst and then sold to P. de Villiers in 1864 for £7.10s (R15). In 1880, H. T. Glynn bought it for £600 (R1 200), and he and his son (also H. T. Glynn) farmed and became celebrated as big game hunters.

The Glynns were renowned for their hospitality. Early in 1895 they were entertaining a party of friends at a picnic at the Klein Sabi Falls. The bottles remaining from lunch were placed on a ledge of rock and used as targets in a shooting match. The bullets chipped the rock and exposed what seemed to be a gold-bearing reef. From then on, the picnic was forgotten with the guests turning prospectors. Samples were crushed and panned, the results of which revealed good gold. The Glynns and their friends pegged a long stretch of what they named the Sandstone Reef. One of the picnickers, Captain J. C. Ingle, prospected the reef in detail to prove its extent and mining operations were commenced.

Thus the town of Sabie had its start. The Glynns-Lydenburg Gold Mining Company was floated to exploit the discovery. Mining operations were subject to immense technical difficulties: the rock was dolomite and subject to flooding, while chemically the ore was very refractory. Nevertheless the miners persisted, and by the time the mine closed down in July 1950, 1 240 646 oz of gold had been extracted.

The town of Sabie grew up as the child of the mine, with the branch railway from Nelspruit reaching it in 1913. On 24 September 1915, it attained the status of a village with a health committee under the chairmanship of the popular Mr H. T. Glynn, known as the Squire of Sabie. On 1 January 1924, Sabie became a town. Today, with a population of 8 917, it is a bustling trading and communications centre, whose principal industry is the considerable production of timber.

The timber industry developed from the mines. The slopes of the mountains, acting as catchment areas for the Sabi River, had always been well covered with trees. With the opening of mines arose a demand for pit-props. A number of private woodcutters started work causing enormous destruction to the natural forests, cutting down innumerable beautiful hardwood trees to make props or poles. The names of several of the old parasitic woodcutters still linger over the areas where they worked: Vosloo's Forest, Gabriel's Forest, Bokwa's Forest (named after Jan Stolz, brother of Gabriel), Maritz's Forest and others. Several sawmills were started, most of them worked by water power.

The demand for timber soon reached such a peak that the exhaustion of the natural resources was inevitable. The first man to start planting trees was W. Patrick, of Elandsdrift mine. Other mines followed his example. The first government plantations were established in the Transvaal in 1903 at places such as Lichtenburg, Machavie, Woodbush, Pan and Ermelo. In 1920 the Department of Forestry opened an office in Sabie. In 1922 the first white labour forestry settlement was started at Berlyn (Kaapsehoop) and several others followed. As a result of these settlements, millions of trees were planted and the area around Sabie today contains one of the largest manmade forests in the world. In Sabie itself, is a museum devoted to forestry.

Sixteen kilometres from Sabie on the road to the east, lies the D. R. de Wet Tree Breeding Station where experimental breeding and cross pollination of trees takes place with a view to improved timber quality and yields.

Trees dominate the entire landscape. The main tarmac road to the north makes its way through green wooded country, where ferns line every stream and watsonias, proteas, red-hot pokers, nerinas, ericas and a rich profusion of other wild flowers flourish. The road leads along a narrow shelf of land with the Drakensberg towering to the west and, to the east, the dramatic cliff face of the escarpment rears up with the lowveld nearly 1 000 m below.

Driving or walking through these vast plantations is a delight. There are many lovely views, and waterfalls are spectacular, the Sabi Falls being within the confines of the town. The Bridal Veil Falls are 7,5 km from the town and the Lone Creek Waterfall 12 km, while the Horseshoe Falls may be seen 1 km further along the same road which wanders through the trees up the left bank of the Sabi River, past the beautifully situated municipal caravan park.

## Accommodation
** Floreat Motel, 40 rooms, all with baths. R12,50 B/B. Phone 391.
* Sabie Falls Hotel, 35 rooms, 21 with baths. R8,50 – R9,25 B/B. Phone 77.

### Caravan and camping

★★ Castle Rock Caravan Park, 120 sites. R2,50 D plus 50c D per person.
★★ Merry Pebbles Rest Camp, 150 sites. R2,50 D plus 50c D per person.

Several minor roads branch off east and west to various forestry stations, down the lowveld or to pleasant places such as the Mac-Mac pools (11 km from Sabie) where there are changing rooms and picnic and barbecue sites next to some fine swimming pools. In this pretty river, alluvial gold was discovered in 1873 by Johannes Muller whereafter an excited crowd of diggers pegged claims all along its course. The odd name of Mac-Mac was given to the field by President Burgers who encountered so many Scotsmen there when he visited the area. Most of the gold was recovered from the portion of the stream above the 100-m-high twin waterfall which tumbles down into a spectacular ravine. A fine roadside view may be had of the Mac-Mac Falls (sometimes known as the Two Scotsmen), 13 km from Sabie along the tarmac road to the north.

After a further 3 km of travel along this road, a fine picnic site created by the Forestry Department is reached. A further 6,5 km (22,5 km from Sabie) brings the road to a junction. The east turn (right) leads for 5 km to the town of Graskop; the west turn (left) climbs up the mountains, crosses over a saddle known to the prospectors as the Divide, and then, amidst many beautiful views, descends into a lovely, misty valley, surely one of the most romantic in the world. Through this valley flows the Pilgrims Creek and 9,5 km from the junction of the road to Graskop (32 km from Sabie), the tarmac road enters that most delightful little mining centre of many memories . . .

## PILGRIM'S REST

With a population of only 625, Pilgrims Rest has thoroughly enjoyed a past which has been naughty, uproarious, gay, tragic, adventurous and, at times, outrageous. To connoisseurs of mining history the story of the Pilgrims Rest rush is a classic, and the little town – now merely a wistful ghost of itself – thoroughly deserves preservation as one of the most perfect specimens to be seen anywhere in the world of a mining town born during the excitement of an alluvial gold rush.

In 1873 a prospector known as 'Wheelbarrow' Alec Patterson (on account of his habit of pushing his belongings ahead of him in a wheelbarrow) found alluvial gold in the middle reaches of the stream running through the valley. He settled down to work his find and was soon joined by a second prospector, William Trafford, who, since it seemed to him that his weary pilgrimage in search of fortune was at last over, named the valley Pilgrims Rest.

A tremendous rush took place to the valley as soon as news of the discovery spread. The middle reaches of the stream proved the richest and some very fine nuggets of alluvial gold were found there, especially during 1875. By the end of that year Pilgrims Rest comprised 21 stores, 18 canteens, three bakeries and a variety of other establishments.

Disturbances between the Transvaal Government and the Pedi tribe, who lived close to Pilgrims Rest, caused a setback in 1876, by which time there was a tendency for syndicates and companies to take over from the more happy-go-lucky diggers. The Anglo-Transvaal War of 1880-81 also affected the field and it was taken over in 1881 by a financier, David Benjamin, who offered the government a monthly payment of £1 000 (R2 000) in exchange for a concession.

Benjamin formed the Transvaal Gold Exploration and Land Company to exploit the field. For some years the company was poorly rewarded for its efforts. Then in the 1890s, a prospector, C. Robinson, was employed to explore the area where he unearthed a complete Pandora's Box of mineral treasures. One of his discoveries, the Theta Reef, alone yielded over 5 000 000 oz of gold in 50 years of continuous working.

In an environment healthier, more beautiful and romantic than any other goldfield in the world, Pilgrims Rest was a persistent producer of gold right up to 1972 when mining ceased. Towards the end of its mining life, the holding company diversified and developed into the largest forestry enterprise in Southern Africa. A detailed history of Pilgrims Rest may be found in the book, *Lost Trails of the Transvaal*. An interesting museum is housed in the old post office of the town, and is open Mondays to Saturdays from 19h00 to 13h00; from 14h00 to 17h00. On Sundays and holidays from 08h00 to 10h00.

## Accommodation
★® Royal Hotel, 24 rooms, 16 with baths. R5 – R6 B/B. Phone 4.

## Caravans and camping
★® Ponies Caravan Park, 55 sites. R2,25 D plus 50c D per person.

# THE PANORAMA ROUTE

From Pilgrims Rest, the road finds an amiable way down the left bank of the stream. Immediately outside the town across a bridge over one of the tributaries of the stream, there is a division. The west branch (left) leads over the mountains to Lydenburg (58 km), climbing steeply through the Morgenson Forestry Reserve. At 10 km the road reaches the summit where there is a plaque commemorating Jock of the Bushveld and the transport riders who used this route in former years. After a further 3 km there is a turnoff leading for 10 km to the Mount Sheba Hotel, set in a beautiful natural forest. From the turnoff to the hotel, the main road descends the western side of the Drakensberg and after 15 km joins the tarmac Ohrigstad-Lydenburg road (see page 641).

## Accommodation
★★★® Mount Sheba Hotel, 25 rooms, all with baths. R20 – R40 room only. Phone 17.

The northern branch (right) of the road outside Pilgrims Rest continues down the left bank of the Pilgrims stream, meandering through a green and delightful stretch of country, with tall hills crowding the valley and innumerable signs, relics and bric-à-brac of mining visible on the slopes.

Past the Vaalhoek Mine, the gravel road, 21 km from Pilgrims Rest, reaches a turnoff (west) to Ohrigstad (30,5 km). The gravel road at present being followed bears east (right) and after 1,5 km reaches another turnoff, the right-hand branch continuing east to Graskop (34 km) on the scenic Panorama Route. The left-hand branch continues past a little tearoom (the Manx Café) and then makes its way to the Blyde River Gorge.

The Panorama Route provides the traveller with a superb circular tarmac drive back to the junction where the road from Sabie divided east to Graskop or west to Pilgrims Rest.

From the junction near the Manx Café at Vaalhoek, the Panorama Route leads through an area settled by African people and rises steadily to cross over a divide after 5 km, entering the Goedgeloof Plantation. The road winds through extensive plantations, passes at 13 km the London Plantation and at 16 km the Blyde Forest Reserve.

At 19 km the road reaches Waterval Spruit where there is a fine picnic site just downstream from the bridge, with a superb natural swimming pool set among tree ferns and green grass. A further 5 km (24 km from the start) brings the road to a turnoff leading for 3 km to the Blyde Forest Station and State Sawmill and the Berlyn Falls. This lovely waterfall should not be missed with a sheer, 80-m fall and excellent vantage points revealing the entire drop and the deep pool at its foot. Afternoon light is the best for photography. Wild flowers are spectacular, especially watsonias in late summer.

Continuing from the turnoff to this waterfall, the main road, after 1 km, reaches a turn to some fine swimming pools in the Blyde River. Little more than 500 m brings the road (25,5 km from the start) to a turnoff left leading for 8 km to what is known as Gods Window, a cleft in the edge of the escarpment which provides a grand view down into the lowveld. From the parking site at Gods Window, a path and motoring track lead along the verge of the escarpment to the Lowveld Panorama and Nature Reserve, a lovely patch of indigenous forest with a stunning view. In this reserve flourish many flowering and aromatic plants. The air is delightfully cool and some of the subtle fragrance of the low country rises up to merge with the crisp winds of the highveld.

From the turn to Gods Window, the main road continues to meander and after 1,5 km crosses a river, reaching a turnoff to the right stretching for 1,5 km to the Lisbon Falls, a fine double waterfall set among superb scenery. There is a picnic site at the falls. Afternoon light is the best for photography.

From the turnoff to the Lisbon Falls (27,5 km from the start of the road), the Panorama Route continues for 5 km and then reaches a turnoff left leading to the much-photographed Pinnacle and Driekop Gorge. Proceeding for a further 1,5 km, the road (34 km from its start) reaches the village of . . .

# GRASKOP

A pleasant little centre from which to explore the escarpment falling away to the east, *Graskop* (grassy peak) was originally the farm of Abel Erasmus, a renowned character during the 1850s who played a considerable role in the adventurous days of hunting, prospecting and the imposition of law and order over a turbulent area. The village is now a timber centre and the terminus of the branch railway from Nelspruit.

## Accommodation
** Kowyn Hotel, 28 rooms, 21 with baths. R12,50 B/B. Phone 44.

## Caravans and camping
* Municipal caravan park, 36 sites. R2,50 D. 25 rondavels, R3 – R5 D.
  Panorama Rest Camp, 30 sites. R2 D plus 30c D per person. 24 rooms, R3,50 D.

From Graskop, the circular drive is completed with an easy 5-km run to the junction with the Sabie-Pilgrims Rest road. The circular drive, stretching from this point, through Pilgrims Rest, down to the junction at Vaalhoek, and then returning via the Panorama Route through Graskop, is 48 km.

A very interesting and beautiful 37-km drive leads from Graskop down Kowyn Pass to the lowveld. From Graskop this tarmac road skirts the edge of the escarpment, revealing magnificent views of the low country. After 3 km the road passes the Panorama Caravan Park and a further 1,5 km brings it to the top of the pass known as *Kowyn* after the Sotho tribal chief who once lived there. Near the top of the pass is a picnic spot and a plaque marking the opening of the modern pass on 3 October 1959.

The road continues to descend the escarpment, passing through dense plantations of gum and pine trees and altogether providing a fine drive. At the bottom of the pass, 14,5 km from Graskop, Rand Mining Timber have their depot. One more kilometre brings the road to a branch leading to Bushbuck Ridge. The road continues eastwards, rising and falling incessantly through plantations and luxuriant, green, rural countryside settled by people of the Shangane tribe. There are many impressive views. At 37 km from Graskop, the road joins the main tarmac road leading from Tzaneen and Phalaborwa in the north down to White River and Nelspruit.

# THE BLYDE RIVER GORGE

Back at Vaalhoek, where the Panorama Route branched off, the left-hand road continues northwards along the edge of the escarpment. Passing the little Manx Café, post office and garage, the road proceeds for 7 km and crosses the *Blyde* (joyful) River just above its confluence with the *Treur* (sorrowful) River, close to a turnoff leading to the remarkable potholes of Bourkes Luck.

The origin of the various names is interesting. In 1840 the renowned Voortrekker leader, Hendrik Potgieter, led a party on an exploratory journey to Lourenço Marques. The womenfolk remained on the cool and healthy heights near Graskop while most of the men rode down across the lowveld searching for a route to the coast.

The time for their return came and passed. After the disasters which had befallen other trekkers on the route to the coast, the waiting party became despondent. They named the pleasant stream on whose banks they were then camped, the *Treur* (sorrowful) and set out for home. Potgieter, however, after an adventurous journey, returned safely, overtaking the women as they were fording the river, from then on known as the *Blyde* (joyful) on account of the happy reunion.

Near the confluence of the two rivers there was, in recent times, a profitable little gold mine known as Bourkes Luck, where a hydro-electric power station supplied electricity to Pilgrims Rest. The course of the rivers, especially at their junction, is notable for strange rock formations and potholes. A parking place and a series of footbridges allow visitors clear views of the gorge.

Below its confluence with the Treur, the Blyde River tumbles down into one of the most spectacular gorges in Africa. The two best viewsites are easily reached by means of tarmac turnoffs from the main road following the edge of the escarpment. Thick, green grass covers the heights, and the verges of the gorge are fringed with stamvrug shrubs *(Bequaertioden-dron megalismontanum).* In January these shrubs are covered with bright red fruit, which is sold in baskets by children. The fruit has a distinctive flavour and is delicious to eat, either fresh or as jam.

Tremendous panoramas of the lowveld are revealed in the distance and the prodigious flat-topped bulk of Marieps Kop may be seen in the middle distance. The river, 800 m below, forces a tortuous passage beneath towering red-coloured sandstone cliffs, daubed with yellow lichen and modelled with shadows and a lovely haze of blue. Dominating the gorge are the triplet peaks known on account of their shape as the Three Rondawels.

The viewsite turnoffs are at 9,5 km, 16 km and 19,5 km from Vaalhoek. The last turnoff leads to the sumptuous Blydepoort Holiday Resort run by the Transvaal Provincial Council (Board of Public Resorts). This is a real luxury establishment complete with restaurant, supermarket, sporting facilities, piped music, heated swimming baths etc. Nature trails for walkers and riders lead to many interesting places. Paths meander into the gorge below where, in a magnificent setting of towering red-coloured sandstone cliffs, lies the Blyderiverspoort Dam with its 72-m-high wall. All this development and the roar of motors on roads and lake, contrasts sharply with the erstwhile remote and tranquil gorge. However, portions still remain where the sweet sound of silence may be heard by those with the energy to walk or ride away from the throng.

Caravans and camping
★★★® 21 sites, R2,50 D. 150 chalets, R10 – R21 D.


# THE ECHO CAVES, LYDENBURG AND OHRIGSTAD

From the entrance to the Blyde Gorge Resort, the tarmac road winds onwards for 28 km up a fertile valley and then joins the tarmac road coming from Lydenburg.

Turning left (southwards) from the Blyde River Gorge road junction, the tarmac road leads through farmlands and after 1,5 km reaches a gravel turnoff to the right stretching for 3 km to the Echo Caves.

The Echo Caves are situated in a hill spur at the head of the Molapong Valley, and occur in dolomite, a rock notable for water-worn caves and sinkholes. There are two entrances to the caves, one of which, on the eastern side of the spur, is open to the public from 08h00 to 17h00. There is a tearoom and curio shop at the entrance. The second entrance (popularly known as the Cannibal Cave) is on the south-western side of the spur and consists of a vertical shaft leading down to a complex sequence of passages which eventually joins the series of caverns linked to the first entrance. The caverns connected to the public entrance contain some fine stalactites and stalagmites and the name of the caves derives from the echoes made when some of these formations are gently tapped. The caverns from the vertical shaft are home to a vast colony of bats and hopefully, their dark retreats will not be disturbed, for they are invaluable and interesting little creatures, fully entitled to being conserved.

One section of the cave is 400 m long, the second section is 307 m, and the largest chamber is 100 m long by 49 m high.

The area of the Echo Caves was occupied by man during the Middle and Late Stone Ages (51 000 B.C. to 10 000 B.C.) and many interesting artefacts have been found. Bushman paintings may be seen in several rock shelters and the various caverns served as sanctuaries for the local African tribes in times of war. In 1923 Mr J. A. Claasen bought the farm containing the area and the tribespeople showed him the caves. He opened the Echo Caves to visitors and created the interesting Museum of Man in one of the Bushman rock shelters next to the main approach road. Here may be seen skeletons and artefacts recovered from the caves. There is also a picturesque little art gallery exhibiting the paintings and sculptures done by a local missionary, the Reverend Paul van Zyl. Mr Claasen died in July 1978 and is buried below his museum.

### Accommodation
* Echo Caves Motel, 11 rooms, all with baths. R11 B/B. Phone Ohrigstad 1221.

### Caravans and camping
* Echo Caves, 25 sites. R2,50 D.

From the turnoff to the Echo Caves, the main tarmac road continues southwards down a rugged valley where many flowering aloes and euphorbia trees grow. Fruit, tobacco and vegetables are farmed in deep, red soil. At 21 km from the Blyde River junction there are turnoffs, left to Kaspersnek (18 km) and right to Burgers Fort (32 km). A further 3 km brings the road to the village of Ohrigstad with its memories of past days and troubled times.

# OHRIGSTAD

The village was founded in 1845 by the Voortrekker leader, Andries Hendrik Potgieter, who had heard that the British claimed all land south of the 25 degree of south latitude. Accordingly, he abandoned the early Voortrekker settlement at Potchefstroom and moved to the new town, which he named *Andries-Ohrigstad* in joint honour of himself and a Dutch merchant in Holland, George Ohrig, who had sent aid and encouragement to the trekkers.

The site of Ohrigstad was safely above the 25 degree of south latitude, but unfortunately was soon found to be plagued by mosquitoes and excessively hot in summer. As a result of malaria being endemic in those days, Potgieter abandoned the town in 1848 and removed with his followers to the Soutpansberg where he established a new settlement. The remaining inhabitants of Ohrigstad stayed in the place for another year and then were also forced to move by the voracious mosquitoes. They established the town of Lydenburg, leaving Ohrigstad to the ghosts. Only in recent years, with the conquest of malaria, has the fertile valley of Ohrigstad been resettled. Ruins and graves of the original settlement may still be seen.

From Ohrigstad, the tarmac road continues southwards down an intensely cultivated valley. The landscape is fertile and pleasant, with the sandstone cliffs of the valley at times crowding in and then receding. Roadside kiosks offer for sale cold milk, vegetables and fruit. Tobacco, peaches, sunflowers, maize and other crops flourish on almost every part of the valley floor.

At 42 km from the Blyde Gorge turnoff, a turnoff left leads over the mountains for 29 km to Pilgrims Rest. The stage coaches used this road during the gold rush, and memories linger on of highwaymen and ambuscades. After a further 5 km the road climbs over *Verraaiers Nek* (traitor's pass) where a handsome view is revealed from the summit. The road descends the other side through the fertile alluvial valley.

At 60 km the road crosses the Spekboom River in whose upper valley several small gold mines were once worked. A further 11 km brings the road to a turnoff right leading to Burgers Fort (56 km) and Pietersburg (209 km). Immediately ahead, 72,5 km from the turn to the Blyde River Gorge, lies the town of . . .

## LYDENBURG

The lugubrious name of *Lydenburg* (the town of suffering) was applied to the town when it was founded in 1849 by those disgruntled inhabitants of Ohrigstad who did not choose to move further north when Hendrik Potgieter abandoned the fever-stricken settlement.

During the Anglo-Transvaal War a small British garrison was besieged in the town. The powder magazine they used is still in existence and is a national monument. Lydenburg is today a pleasant and healthy little town of 10 680 people, situated in a warm valley. It is a centre for farming, administration and communications. The Transvaal Provincial Fisheries Institute has a large hatchery and aquarium there where trout are bred in great numbers. Fishing in local rivers is good and the Gustav Klingbiel Nature Reserve on the road to Long Tom Pass is a sanctuary for birds and mammals. A fine 244-m-high waterfall may be seen 16 km from the town.

### Accommodation
★★ Morgans Hotel, 29 rooms, 15 with baths. R12 – R16 B/B. Phone 226.

### Caravans and camping
★ Lydenburg Tourist Park, 25 sites. R2 D. 5 rondawels, R4 – R6 D.

## ABEL ERASMUS PASS

Beyond the turnoff to the Blyde River Gorge, the tarmac road continues northwards and immediately begins to climb the bush-covered slopes of the Drakensberg by means of the Abel Erasmus Pass. The ascent is 6,5 km during which fine views of the mountains are revealed. Once the summit is reached, the road commences a long and involved descent down the northern side into a grassy, bush-covered valley settled by African people. The route followed by the original road may still be seen and is marked by signs as the Old Coach Road.

At 18 km from the Blyde River Gorge turnoff, there is a track branching left and leading for 2,5 km to a viewsite known as the Devils Pulpit. The road now enters a spectacular gorge dominated by high, red-coloured cliffs, daubed with yellow lichen. There are picnic sites by the wayside, cleaned somewhat erratically, and a plaque commemorating the opening of the pass on 8 May 1959 which was named after Abel Erasmus, the well-known early inhabitant of the Graskop and Ohrigstad areas. The pass took three years to build and rises 365 m over the Drakensberg from Ohrigstad, and then descends 800 m to the lowveld.

At 21 km from the Blyde River Gorge turnoff, the road reaches the tunnel named after a former Prime Minister of South Africa, Mr. J. G. Strijdom. The tunnel, 133,5 m long, provides a dramatic gateway to the low country. The views are spectacular, especially of the Olifants River emerging from the mountain range and flowing off across the mighty bushveld.

Beyond the tunnel, the tarmac road continues its sweeping descent. At 24 km from the Blyde River Gorge turnoff, the road reaches the bottom of the pass where, in a pleasant setting, lies the Manoutsa Caravan Park with a restaurant and inviting swimming pool.

Six kilometres further on is a turn left leading for 96,5 km to Tzaneen, while 3 km beyond this turnoff, on the banks of the Olifants River, under the shade of some huge wild fig trees, lies the Strijdom Tunnel Motel.

## Accommodation
★ Strijdom Tunnel Motel, 32 rooms, all with baths. R8 – R8,50 B/B. Phone Hoedspruit 1913.

## Caravans and camping
★ Manoutsa Caravan Park, 40 sites. R2 D.
★ Strijdom Tunnel Caravan Park, 30 sites. R1 D plus 50c D per person.

The tarmac road proceeds eastwards. After 13 km the Blyde Park shopping centre, close to the bridge over the Blyde River, is passed. Across the bridge 2,5 km further on, is a turnoff south leading for 27 km to the Blyde Poort Dam and also to places such as Kampersrus and White River.

A further 3 km takes the road past the Blyde Trading Store, with a turn right (south) to Bedford and Klaserie. The Rietspruit Jam and Canning Factory stands beside the road 2,5 km further on. A further 9 km brings the road to the railway centre of Hoedspruit where it joins the main north-south road of the lowveld (Tzaneen to Nelspruit).

## ABEL ERASMUS PASS TO TZANEEN

At the foot of the Abel Erasmus Pass, between the Manoutsa Caravan Park and the Strijdom Tunnel Motel, the tarmac road leading to Hoedspruit branches northwards, crossing the Olifants River at a point overlooked by a handsome baobab tree. The bridge lies at a point 26 km from the summit of the Abel Erasmus Pass (101 km from Lydenburg and 100 km from Pilgrims Rest). Here the Olifants River flows powerfully and many pools occur in which lurk crocodiles, hippos, barbel and yellowfish. Handsome trees line the riverbanks.

After crossing the bridge, the tarmac road stretches northwards through a wild garden of trees, flowering shrubs and plants which blanket the gently rolling plains of the lowveld. Immediately to the west lies the long line of cliffs of the Drakensberg, a romantic sight, both visually beautiful and filled with memories of tribal wars and the bitter-sweet story of Louis Trichardt's trek.

As the road proceeds northwards, roads branch off, several of them to extremely interesting parts of the lowveld. Nine and a half kilometres from the Olifants River bridge there is a turnoff east to Leydsdorp, a gold rush centre of the 1890s. After 26 km of travel through thick bush country a turnoff leads westwards for 6,5 km to the rural centre of Trichardtsdal, while 8 km further on (43,5 km from the Olifants River bridge) there is a crossroads where turnoffs lead east to Gravelotte and west to Ofcolaco (Officers Colonial Land Company), formed co-operatively by a number of British army officers as a settlement scheme after the First

World War. The gravel road through Ofcolaco is worth taking for those who have the time and a rugged vehicle. The road passes through citrus groves and over fertile fields, heading for the Drakensberg. Climbing the escarpment by means of a spectacular pass, it reaches the plateau summit known as The Downs (from its resemblance to the Surrey Downs) where the family of the renowned prospector, Orlando Baragwanath, used to farm potatoes amidst the clouds. The road then drops by means of the Jan Smuts Pass into the wild valley of the aptly named *Mohlapitse* (clear, deep water) stream whose upper reaches are a paradise for walkers and climbers. Finally, the road stretches off to the west across the lunar-like scenery of the Bushveld Igneous Complex with its asbestos and chrome mines.

---

The main tarmac road, meanwhile, continues northwards. Eight kilometres from the Ofcolaco turnoff (51,5 km from the Olifants River bridge) another turnoff leads for 18 km to Leydsdorp.

## THE MURCHISON RANGE

The Murchison Range which rises abruptly from the bush-covered lowveld was, during the last century, considered remote and sinister and cursed with malaria fever, relentless heat and wild animals. In 1870 Edward Button and James Sutherland prospected the area and found gold traces in several streams in the range they named after the famed geologist, Sir Roderick Murchison. The finds were not payable, but in 1888 new discoveries attracted a considerable rush of prospectors and the entire range was pegged out into claims, with dozens of little mines being started by a pretty wild crowd of men.

Among these men was a famous character known as French Bob, whose camp became a veritable epicentre of activity and disturbance in the Murchison Range. In 1890 the site of this camp was laid out as a town and named *Leydsdorp* in honour of the State Secretary, Dr Leyds. The little mining town was notorious for the size of its cemetery, strong liquor and even stronger mosquitoes being the principal culprits.

The Murchison Range soon proved a richly mineralised area although the deposits of gold and other precious minerals and stones (such as emeralds) were patchy and erratic and contained in refractory ore. Very few of the mines showed a worthwhile profit and in London it was said that a new grade had been added to the list of liars: a liar, a damn liar, and a prospector of the Murchison Range!

Despite these difficulties, mining still persists in the Murchison Range. It was while the first rush was still booming that the notorious Selati Railway Concession fraud was perpetrated. A pair of Continental company promoters secured a concession to build a railway from Komatipoort to a terminus in the Murchison Range, at a point somewhere on the stream known as the *Selati,* from a local tribal chieftainess of that name. The swindling, intrigue and double-crossing surrounding this so-called Selati railway contributes to a very involved story indeed; contractors even put additional curves into the line in order to make it longer.

The country around the Murchison Range is beautifully wooded and the main tarmac road continues north through very attractive lowveld country. Nine and a half kilometres beyond the turn to Leydsdorp, the road passes the Shiluvane Mission Station of the Swiss Presbyterians, founded in 1886 in the territory of the Shangane chief Xiluvana.

The road now crosses a fertile and densely settled portion of the lowveld, with tribal areas and European farms lying on either side. From this lovely parkland, fine views of the mountains may be had to the west and east. Nine and a half kilometres from the Shiluvane Mission there is a turnoff west up the valley of the *Letsitele* (river of the wide crossing place) where fine subtropical fruit estates flourish on the water of the mountain streams.

Roadside kiosks offer fruit to passing travellers (especially during summer) and the road finds an attractive way through well-wooded foothills until, 13 km from the Letsitele turnoff (83,5 km from the Olifants River bridge), it enters the attractive, modern town of . . .

# TZANEEN

This place lies in a hollow on the banks of the Letaba River, a bustling mountain torrent along whose length are situated some of the most productive farms in the low country. Tea, all kinds of subtropical fruits, nuts, flowers (especially carnations), winter vegetables, potatoes, and enormous quantities of timber, are produced in this area. As the rail, commercial and administrative centre for so prosperous an activity, Tzaneen is the principal town of the northern Transvaal low country, and has a population of 11 000.

The origin of the name *Tzaneen* derives from a section of the Bokgaga tribe who broke away from the parent group and settled in the area, calling themselves the *Batsaneng* (people of the small village). In 1905 Lord Milner established an experimental tobacco farm in the area of the present Merensky High School and as a result, Tzaneen cigars and Letaba cigarettes became well known.

The development of farming stimulated the extension of the famous Selati railway line as far as the farm *Pusela* in 1912 and it was there, around the sheds of the railway, that the town of Tzaneen was laid out, eventually receiving its first public body (a health committee) on 24 May 1924. The conquest of malaria fever, largely (as in Zululand) the result of a visit by the famed Professor Swellengrebel of the League of Nations, as well as the tireless work of Dr Siegfried Annecke, vanquished the old mosquito phantom of the low country and today life is as pleasantly healthy there as in any other part of Southern Africa. The Dr Siegfried Annecke Research Institute is a stimulating place to visit and is open on weekdays from 08h30 to 16h30.

## Accommodation

★★ Tzaneen Hotel, 89 rooms, all with baths. R16 – R25 B/B. Phone 2-1056.

## Caravans and camping

★ Fairview Caravan Park, 25 sites. R2 D plus 35c D per person.

# MAGOEBASKLOOF

The circular drive up Magoebaskloof returning to Tzaneen through Georges Valley and the Letaba Valley, or straight on to Pietersburg, is a scenic delight for any traveller. The magnificent road leads under the slopes of the 2 127-m *Wolkberg* (cloudy mountain), passing the lovely cascades of the upper Letaba, the waters of the Ebenezer Dam, the trout streams of the Haenertsburg district, and the forest-covered gorges of Magoebaskloof containing the handsome waterfall of Debegeni. The tour is a superlative botanic experience, for the valleys are veritable gardens of fruit, flowering plants and forest trees of great variety and the escarpment edge is green, cool and delightful.

Travellers should take the tarmac road up Magoebaskloof which branches off west 4 km from Tzaneen on the road to Duiwelskloof. Plantations of trees, tea and subtropical fruit cover the valley. The roadside is lined with Pride of India trees (flowering in December and January in shades of bright pink and mauve); bauhinia or Pride of De Kaap, in pink and red; cassias and acacias in yellow. Eleven kilometres from the turnoff the road passes the sawmill of De Hoek where a gravel turnoff to the north is worth taking. The main tarmac road continues in a steep spiral, reaching the summit after 10 km from where the branch road will eventually rejoin it after 19,5 km of complex travelling.

This gravel branch road is steep and sometimes slightly rough, but it passes through a vast primeval forest containing waterfalls, cascades, ferns, majestic trees, fine views and other delights. Five kilometres from the start an 800-m-long branch leads down to the spectacular waterfall known as *Debegeni* (place of the big pot) on account of the deep pool shaped like a pot at the foot of the waterfall. The Ramadipa River which feeds the waterfall, is a powerful flow of clear water. In former times, the tribespeople believed that this waterfall was the home of several spirits, and left presents of food and beer beside the pool to be consumed overnight by supernatural diners.

Swimming and picnicking at the foot of the Debegeni waterfall is allowed but no camping. The rocks are very slippery and several people have been killed trying to climb the waterfall or attempting too much of the big slide.

It was in 1894 in this sylvan setting that a vicious petty war was fought between the Transvaal Government and the Tlou tribe of chief Makgoba whose name, corrupted to *Magoeba*, is applied to the valley today. Times were generally restless and there was resistance against paying taxes. Makgoba's followers (about 500 warriors) made so skilful a use of the deep forests of the gorge that the European punitive force found it exceedingly difficult to dislodge them. Only in 1895 was Makgoba finally cornered in his forest retreat. A party of Swazi warriors, fighting on the government side, tracked him down. In single combat he was defeated, his head cut off, and today only his name lingers on in memory of a long-forgotten quarrel.

Beyond the turnoff to the Debegeni waterfall, the gravel road follows a steep and very lovely route through patches of dense indigenous forest and plantations. After 3 km the road passes De Hoek Forestry Station. A further 2 km brings the road to a camping ground with simple facilities, in a woodland setting.

At 11 km from the Debegeni waterfall, the road reaches the summit and joins the main gravel road leading from the Tzaneen-Pietersburg road to Woodbush. A turn left along the road brings the traveller, after 5 km, to the main tarmac road at the top of the Magoebaskloof Pass, 25,5 km from Tzaneen, thus ending a very fascinating drive. Just before joining the tarmac road, the forestry road passes a memorial to Alexander James O'Connor (1884 to 1957), a one-time Director of Forestry who was responsible for much of the afforestation of this area and was the first forester of the Woodbush district.

The Woodbush Forestry Station is reached on turning right at the junction of the road coming up from the Debegeni waterfall and De Hoek. This is another magnificent drive along the edge of the escarpment. A particularly fine view may be had from a site 600 m from the junction. At 6,5 km from the junction, the road reaches the Woodbush Forestry Station which has always been renowned for its trees. Heavy rainfall and deep, rich granite soil are ideal for trees such as yellowwoods, red stinkwoods, ironwoods, cabbage trees, and many others, including the lovely *Ochna o'connorii* (redwood) named after the pioneer forestry officer in the district. The spring leaves of this tree are at first a deep red, changing to green while its masses of flowers are a brilliant yellow in late spring and its seeds are red. The resulting colour combinations are superb.

Beyond the Woodbush Forestry Station, the gravel road continues through beautiful avenues of oak trees, plantations and indigenous forests, where moss drapes the trees. At 5 km from the Forestry Station the road reaches the wall of the D.A.P. Naude Dam, built in 1958 to supply Pietersburg with water. There is a fine camping ground beneath the trees and the area is popular with anglers, for the Broderstroom River is amply stocked with trout. Permits for camping and fishing must be obtained from the forestry office.

After a further 2 km the gravel road leaves the area of the Woodbush Forestry Station. Continuing down the verdant valley of the Broderstroom, it passes beautiful farms such as *Greymists* and *Cloudlands* and then, 13 km from the Woodbush Forestry Station, joins the Magoebaskloof-Haenertsburg gravel road which, after 9,5 km, joins the main tarmac Tzaneen-Pietersburg road. Many interesting side roads in this area lead through fine scenery and, although they meander considerably, eventually take the traveller to some identifiable junction with a main road. Particularly lovely is the drive to Houtbosdorp (actually a trading station), and thence to Duiwelskloof, a route described further on.

## GEORGES VALLEY AND THE LETABA VALLEY

This circular route (the first part being the main Tzaneen-Pietersburg road) provides one of the loveliest drives in Southern Africa. The 15-km section from Tzaneen to the turnoff to the De Hoek forestry area and the Debegeni waterfall has already been described. Beyond this gravel turnoff, the main tarmac road winds and climbs steadily for 10,5 km, reaching the summit of Magoebaskloof. The scenery is superb, grand views being revealed of tree-covered mountain slopes and the lowveld stretching off to the east like a mysterious green sea.

The two great tea estates – *Grenshoek* and *Middelkop* – of *Sapekoe* (South African Tea, from the Chinese word for tea) cover vast areas of the hill slopes with a dense green blanket constantly moistened by sprinkler irrigation. In 1963 tea cultivation was started in South Africa on these estates when Douglas Penhill, former managing director of the Kenya Tea Development Association, was persuaded to immigrate to South Africa. With the Industrial Development Corporation providing finance, and experts recruited from several tea-growing areas of the world, the venture proved enormously successful. Tea of a quality considered superlative on the international market is now being produced to a significant extent.

The estates are continually humming with activity: plucking from September to May, pruning in June and July and tidying up in August.

Half way up the valley (22,5 km from Tzaneen) lies the Magoebaskloof Rest Camp and above it a fine viewsite. At 25,5 km from Tzaneen, the road reaches the summit and the gravel turnoff to the Woodbush area already described including the circular route back to Tzaneen past the Debegeni waterfall. The main tarmac road continues towards Pietersburg, 69 km away. After a further 3 km it passes the Magoebaskloof Hotel spectacularly situated at the head of the spacious valley after which it is named.

### Accommodation
★★ Magoebaskloof Hotel, 50 rooms, all with baths. R14 – R15 B/B. Phone 3.

### Caravans and camping
★★ Lakeside Chalets, 25 sites. R6 D. 16 flats, 6 cottages, R10 – R32 D.
★★ Magoebaskloof Rest Camp, 28 rondawels, R18 D.

Just beyond the hotel (1,5 km) is a gravel turnoff which leads southwards through fine scenery for 9 km to the Ebenezer Dam and, at 12 km, joins the tarmac road running down Georges Valley to Tzaneen (see further on). The tarmac road to Pietersburg passes this turnoff and the Lakeside Holiday Resort after a further 1,5 km.

A further 5 km brings the road to a junction just outside the old mining and forestry village of Haenertsburg. The main road proceeds westwards for 61 km to Pietersburg. A magnificent return route to Tzaneen is provided by taking the tarmac turnoff branching southwards, an opportunity which should not be missed.

Passing the Ebenezer Dam, completed in 1958 and designed to stabilise the flow of the Letaba River, the tarmac road is joined by the gravel road which branched off from the top of Magoebaskloof. A series of lovely cascades in the Letaba River is passed and the road leads on down the valley known as Georges Valley, 11 km from the turnoff. Overlooked by the towering *Wolkberg* (cloudy mountain), this valley received its name from George Deneys, a road ganger who lived there. He was an amiable soul who liked his work so much that he often included detours in his roads to allow travellers a better chance of viewing the scenery. Aloes and flowering shrubs were also planted to beautify the verges and seats and picnic tables made of rock are scattered along the wayside for the relaxation of passers-by.

The road descends the escarpment through Georges Valley in a sweeping pass, with massive mountains overlooking the Bergplaas Plantation and the lush farmlands of the Letaba Valley with their crops of subtropical fruits and nuts. The road terminates at Tzaneen, 50 km from the top of Magoebaskloof. It is altogether a magnificent 75,5-km circular route.

---

From Tzaneen, the main lowveld tarmac road continues northwards past the great dam in the Letaba River and thence up a densely wooded valley, passing the turnoff to Magoebaskloof (4 km); the fine Westfalia Estate of the late eminent geologist, Dr Hans Merensky, its romantic-looking manmade lake in a setting reminiscent of Tchaikowski's *Swan Lake;* the turnoff to Politsi; the tree-breeding station of the Forestry Department at Zomerkumst, and the tea plantation of Messrs Sapekoe at Grenshoek. At 18 km from Tzaneen, the road reaches the picturesque little town of . . .

## DUIWELSKLOOF

The name *Duiwelskloof* (cleft of the devil) originally belonged to a farm there and is said to have arisen on account of the sticky mud which impeded the passage of transport wagons in the old days. Rainfall is normally high in the area, but modern tarmac roads have defeated the mud and travellers may therefore admire the forest-covered, intensely green hills which crowd the valley. Gardens are magnificent. Especially notable are bougainvillaea, poinsettia and frangipani in many different colours; jacaranda trees which flower in October and November; potato trees, flowering in December and January; bauhinia creepers, cassias and acacias, flowering in January. Duiwelskloof is a rail centre for the timber and subtropical fruit-growing industry. The population is 1 530.

### Accommodation
★ Imp Inn, 26 rooms, 15 with baths. R9 – R9,50 B/B. Phone 3254.

### Caravans and camping
★★® Duiwelskloof Caravan Park and Rest Camp, 50 sites. R2D. 18 rondawels, R3– R10,10 D.

## DRIVES FROM DUIWELSKLOOF

The plantation and forest-covered hills around Duiwelskloof are threaded with roads which take the venturesome traveller to many interesting places. A short but very beautiful drive leaves the town centre via Mabel Street, climbing the hill slopes west of Duiwelskloof. After 2,5 km there is a branch left leading to a private estate. Continuing right, the road, at 5,5 km, enters the famous Westfalia Estate of the late Dr Hans Merensky, always to be remembered for his work in the discovery of platinum and diamond deposits in South Africa. For 8 km the road winds through the trees of this fine estate, then crosses the railway line and joins the main Tzaneen-Duiwelskloof road at point 5,5 km from Duiwelskloof. The round trip is 19 km long.

---

A very spectacular drive through the tree-covered hills begins opposite the old railway station of Duiwelskloof. Turn left up the road marked Modderspruit, which climbs the slopes of the 1 368-m Dickiesberg. After 2,5 km there is a fork, the right turn of which, marked Weltevreden, should be taken. After 3 km of climbing, the road tops the summit at a magnificent viewsite known as World's View, from where may be seen a breathtaking panorama over the Letaba Valley, with Tzaneen in the middle distance and, in the background, the great range of the Drakensberg, dominated by peaks such as the Wolkberg and Krugers Nose.

From this viewsite, the road descends steadily through plantations of tall gum trees. At 9,5 km it passes through the indigenous forest known as the Donald Grant Nature Reserve, preserved by his family in memory of a local farmer who was killed during the war. At 11 km the road joins the main gravel road linking Tzaneen with the realm of Modjadji and her Lovedu tribe. A right turn leads for 14 km to join the main tarmac Tzaneen-Duiwelskloof road at a point 10,5 km from Duiwelskloof. The total distance for the round trip is 35,5 km.

If the traveller turns left at the junction with the Tzaneen-Modjadji road he will enjoy an equally fine drive stretching 21 km from the junction and returning to Duiwelskloof, a total of 32 km. This road passes the turnoff leading to *Narina,* the home and private nature reserve of the late naturalist, artist, author and great character of the lowveld, Charles Thomas Astley Maberly. Named after the gorgeous *Narina trogon* birds which live there, this little sanctuary of nature was used by 'Mabs' (as he was known) as his own retreat where he studied and painted birds and game. Wild boars, monkeys and many other animals made the place their home and lived on such amiable terms with the beloved Mabs, that it would have been easy to believe stories that even he, like Dr Dolittle, could talk to them. He was brutally murdered by some vagrant in his home in 1972, but his memory will continue to linger over an area he knew and loved so well.

## THE REALM OF THE RAIN QUEEN

Duiwelskloof is the principal centre for the tribal area of the Lovedu people the ruler of whom, with the dynastic title of *Modjadji,* is the famed Rain Queen whose mystic reputation and claim to enternal life provided Rider Haggard with the idea for his novel *She.*

The Lovedu (pronounced Lo-*veh*-du) tribe is an offshoot of the Karanga people of Zimbabwe whose unique culture of building stone walls around their settlements has enriched the country with so many interesting ruins. During the 16th century a princess of this great tribe fled south with a few followers, finding a sanctuary in the valley of the Molotutse. The princess had carried with her the rainmaking magic of her ruling family. She and her successors used this magic to considerable effect, instilling in tribes as far away as Swaziland, a fear that if they offended the Lovedu queen, she would withhold the rain.

The successive queens of the Lovedu found it politic to remain invisible. Legend spread that *Modjadji* (the ruler of the day), as the Lovedu queens were titled, was immortal and terror caused by the magic powers of this strange being not only prevented the tribe from being attacked, but brought them prosperity from the propitiatory gifts sent to the queen.

The inner secrets of Modjadji remain a mystery. The ritual of rainmaking was highly complex, involving strange sacrifices and many magic ingredients – some gruesome, such as the skins of previous Modjadjis who, when they had become too old to rule, were obliged to sip poison from a cup and were thus replaced by a young person.

Modjadi is now far more accessible but is not likely to be seen on a casual visit.

From Duiwelskloof, the main tarmac road leading northwards up the valley towards Muketsi and Munnik should be taken. After 5,5 km there is a turnoff right leading to Modjadji's capital. At 9,5 km there is a turnoff left to Leeudraai, and at 11 km another turnoff left stretching to Gakgapane, the offices of the Balobedu Regional Authority. It is essential to secure a permit from the administrative officer here. Gakgapane was named after a chief of that area.

*Overleaf: The bush of the lowveld surges up against the cliffs of the highveld escarpment like a green sea.*

Beyond the turnoff the road continues for a further 2,5 km to a turnoff left leading to the Medingen Mission Station. Shortly afterwards (14,5 km from Duiwelskloof) there is a junction. Straight ahead the road stretches on towards Tzaneen in the drive already described, passing the old home of Mr C. A. Maberly and after 6,5 km the turn to Duiwelskloof via World's View.

Turn sharp left to reach Modjadji's capital. The road leads eastwards down the densely settled valley of the Molututse, well wooded, warm and overlooked by high hills. After 10 km there is a turn right running for 4 km up to the slightly cooler heights where Modjadji's capital lies 27,5 km from Duiwelskloof.

Modjadji's capital is a rather dusty and hot place, shaded by a few wild fig trees. It is necessary to pay a fee for sightseeing at the tribal office. The queen's courtyard is worth a glimpse but visits to the whole place are complicated by hordes of urchins who need to be very resolutely handled. One guide should be obtained from the tribal office and all visitors should take the short drive (3 km) to the summit of the ridge where there are fine views and a remarkable forest of cycads may be seen. December to February sees many of these strange plants in seed and there are also scarlet bauhinia creepers, yellow and white acacias and other flowering plants. The hill ridge is possessed by a wild, primeval loveliness, like some lost island rising steeply above the surrounding ocean of bush.

A careful watch must be kept for urchins who damage motor vehicles by climbing on them or by pilfering from them. The cycads are protected plants and urchins offering to sell seedlings should be discouraged.

––––––––––

From Duiwelskloof the main tarmac road continues northwards, passing the turnoff to Modjadji (5,5 km) and the vegetable farming centre of Muketsi (16 km). In a spectacular climb, the road ascends the escarpment to Munnik (21 km) and from there crosses the highveld plateau to join the national road or to reach Pietersburg (58 km). From Muketsi a gravel turnoff left provides another spectacular route up to the highveld, past the trading centre of Houtbosdorp (36 km from the turnoff) and thence over the 2 000-m-high summit ridge into the lovely Woodbush forestry area already described, and to places such as Magoebaskloof (53 km) where the main Tzaneen-Pietersburg road is joined.

## TZANEEN TO NELSPRUIT

From Tzaneen a fine tarmac road stretches south-eastwards through a veritable garden of subtropical fruitlands, with wayside stalls offering produce to passers-by. Rich, deep soil, rain, mountain streams and near-tropical warmth together combine with industrious man to transform this entire area into a farmland of immense productivity. On the western side stretches the Drakensberg; to the east the mighty bushveld extends seemingly to the other side of the earth.

In August the citrus groves are laden with both fruit and sweet-smelling blossoms. Bougainvillaea in many shades grows to perfection and the wild flowers of spring are profuse.

After 27,5 km the road crosses the Letaba River and 1 km beyond it a tarmac turnoff leads eastwards to Eiland and Letaba Ranch. This turnoff passes vast citrus groves and a succession of homesteads notable for their gardens and flowering trees such as poincianas and silver oaks. After 35 km the road enters the . . .

## HANS MERENSKY NATURE RESERVE

In October 1950 the Transvaal Provincial Administration purchased the farm *Eiland* (island), named after an island in the Letaba River which flows through the property. In a small marsh on this farm, a thermal spring bubbled to the surface with an occasional surge of gas. The flow of water – about 18 184 l an hour – remained at a constant temperature of 104°C and from early times had been used by the local Africans as a source of salt and as a medicinal treatment for rheumatism.

Other farms were added to *Eiland* and the whole was proclaimed a nature reserve. The area around the spring was transferred to the Mineral Baths Board of Trustees (now the Transvaal Board of Public Resorts), who set out to transform the area into a magnificent holiday resort, possessing a fine restaurant, garden and a variety of accommodation built in a park-like setting of indigenous trees. The thermal spring is fed into a large open-air swimming bath, surrounded by lawns.

The rest of the nature reserve – a parkland of mopane and combretum trees – was conserved as a sanctuary for game animals and a very rich bird life. Dr Hans Merensky, the famous mining magnate, provided a fully equipped borehole and the administration named the place in his honour as he had played a large part in mining developments in nearby Phalaborwa. The reserve shelters a growing population of impala, zebra, blue wildebeest, sable, kudu, waterbuck, warthog, duiker, steenbok, klipspringer, bushbuck, reedbuck, eland, giraffe, tsessebe and Sharpe's grysbok.

### Caravans and camping
★★★★® 500 caravan sites, R2,50 D. 81 rondawels: luxury (A type), 5 persons, R10,25 D; self-contained (B type) 4 persons, R7 D; ordinary (C type), 4 persons, R6 D.

The tarmac road traverses the Hans Merensky Nature Reserve and 3 km from the entrance, passes the impressive cluster of buildings of the Eiland Mineral Bath. A further 5 km takes the road out of the reserve on the eastern side. The road now has a well-maintained gravel surface and it continues past several fine subtropical fruit and cotton estates. There are turnoffs to Rubbervale (10 km), Gravelotte (19 km) and to Phalaborwa (32 km). At 37 km from the Hans Merensky Reserve, the road ends at the old . . .

## LETABA RANCH GAME RESERVE

This reserve was an expanse of wilderness which was converted by several previous owners into a game reserve. Adjoining the Kruger National Park, it contains a lively wild animal population: 4 000 impala, 400 wildebeest, 300 zebra, 200 buffalo, 100 kudu, 50 sable and a mixed batch of giraffe, duiker, klipspringer, steenbok, waterbuck, warthog, hippos, crocodiles, lions, leopards, cheetahs, hyenas, wild dogs and baboons. Previous owners developed the place as a resort with a hotel and 18 camps, each having five to nine rondawels where visitors could look after themselves and view the game at will. The South African Bantu Trust now owns the property.

---

From the turnoff to Eiland the main tarmac road continues southwards past Rubbervale, the rail centre where a forgotten attempt was made to produce rubber from wild vines. Twenty-five kilometres from the turnoff (53,5 km from Tzaneen) the road reaches a crossroads at the small mining and commercial centre of Gravelotte.

## GRAVELOTTE AND THE MURCHISON RANGE
Named after the battle fought on 18 August 1870 in the Franco-German War, *Gravelotte* is a

railway and trading centre for mining activity in the Murchison Range which is richly mineralised. Gold, cinnabar, mica, felspar, silica and emeralds are produced in the vicinity, while the Alpha shaft of the Consolidated Murchison Mine – the largest and richest antimony mine in the world – is the deepest sunk by man in the recovery of any base metal.

Overlooking the little centre is the 874-m-high Spitskop, the highest point in the Murchison Range. The entire area is rugged and bush-covered, profusely scarred by the continuous mining acitivty of the past as well as the present and is enriched by a human story abounding with lost hopes, weird characters, deadbeats, hardups and never-say-diers.

From Gravelotte a gravel road leads westwards to Leydsdorp, the former centre of the Murchison Range. At 4 km along this road there is a short turnoff to an enormous baobab tree whose hollow trunk was once used as a bar by an enterprising liquor seller. This individual, catering for some very thirsty men in a very hot climate, found that the hollow trunk kept the bottles cool and used it accordingly.

Leydsdorp is a further 7 km along the gravel road beyond the baobab tree. Nothing much is left of the once roaring mining camp. It has been said that the substantial cemetery is the liveliest part of the remaining town. This is rather unfair; the cemetery may be full – drink, the devil and the mosquitoes conquered the prospectors of the Murchison Range – but at least some of the houses along the main street are still occupied. The canteens, hotels and stores have all closed down and the local newspaper, *The Leydsdorp Leader,* first published as a neatly printed little eight-page tabloid on 24 October 1891, is now a rare collector's piece. Its pages, filled with the excitement of gold rush days, read like a piece of elaborate fiction. Could such things have happened in this quiet little place?

The boom days of this part of the Murchison Range began in 1888 when about 600 prospectors, lured by rumours of gold, rushed to the area, pegging many hundreds of claims. Old maps still record the names of their hopeful claims: French Bob, Homeward Bound, Horseshoe, Dirty Dick, Great Bonanza and many more.

French Bob (Auguste Robert) was the leading prospector in this rush. Around his camp, which was pitched on the site of Leydsdorp, mushroomed a centre comprising shacks, stores and bars. In 1890, this place received the unromantic name of the State Secretary, Doctor Leyds, when the government laid out a town as the seat for a mining commissioner for what was called the Selati Gold Fields, after Shalati, chieftainess of the Tebula tribe who lived in those parts.

The first rush soon petered out, but others followed and since then there has always been some mining (and quite a bit of salting) in the Murchison Range. Leydsdorp went into a long decline, with waves of men coming and going but always leaving behind a few hopefuls to keep at least a fragment of the town alive.

It was to serve this erratic mining area that the notorious Selati Railway Company was floated in Brussels on 23 February 1892. From its inception this organisation was a fraud. By the time construction started in 1893 there was almost nothing for the railway to serve. The line never penetrated the bush further than the Sabi River bridge in the present Kruger National Park, but a vast amount of money was mulcted from investors in Europe and from the government of the South African Republic. The promoters eventually landed in gaol but the money was never recovered. The line was only completed in 1922 to serve the farming and forestry industries around Tzaneen and to carry copper to the coast from Messina.

On the 33-km journey through the Murchison Range from Gravelotte, the railway and the gravel road together find a way past many small emerald, mica and other mines. Claim beacons are scattered all over and the treasures still hidden in the ground remain a challenge to prospectors. The gravel road eventually links up with a tarmac road and the railway with a heavy mineral line from Phalaborwa. The Murchison Range area still shelters a fair number of wild animals. Kudu and giraffe are frequently seen from the road. A drive through the range at night can be rewarding.

**Accommodation**

★★ Casa Creda Hotel, 20 rooms, all with baths. R11,50 B/B. Phone 35.

**Caravans and camping**

★ Kudu Caravan Park, 8 sites. R6 D.

From Gravelotte the main tarmac road turns eastwards and, passing the mine workings of the Consolidated Murchison Ltd and the huge Croc Ranch, proceeds across a level, tree-covered plain. After 45 km there is a turnoff to the Kudu Rest Camp and a further 6 km takes the road to a junction with the tarmac road coming up from Mica and the south. Ahead looms a line of oddly shaped hillocks, and immediately beyond them, 61 km from Gravelotte, lies the mining town of Phalaborwa, with the Lion Inn Caravan Park and the entrance gate to the Kruger National Park 4 km further on. This entrance gate is open throughout the year from dawn to dusk.

# PHALABORWA

A town with a romantic past, geologists say that about 2 000 million years ago a gigantic volcanic eruption took place in the area. A volcanic pipe resulted, richly loaded with minerals and metals such as phosphate, copper, circonium, vermiculite, iron, mica and gold. On the surface the mouth of the pipe is 10 square kilometres in extent. It was first discovered by a party of skilled metal workers from the great Karanga tribe of Zimbabwe who wandered into this area many generations ago. Finding themselves in a fever area, they retraced their steps northwards to a wild parkland contained by rocky hillocks rising sharply from the plain, an area they found to be more salubrious. They named the region and themselves *Phalaborwa* (better than the south) and settled there, mining iron and copper at the base of the rocky outcrop known as the *Lule* (steep hillocks).

At the beginning of this century, European miners rediscovered the prehistoric workings and men such as William Valentine, Tucker, Cleveland and Scannell defied the curse of fever to work copper in the area. Their industry attracted the attention of the famous geologist, Dr Hans Merensky, who investigated, prospected and proved the colossal and varied mineral wealth of the area. In 1938 his Transvaal Ore Company commenced mining vermiculite in the area from the world's largest known deposit and in 1953 the Merensky Trust amalgamated Vermiculite (Pty) Ltd and the Phalaborwa Phosphate Co.

Phosphate production by the Phosphate Development Corporation Ltd (established in 1952) resulted in the birth of the town of Phalaborwa which was laid out and in 1957 proclaimed a business, recreational and administrative centre for the area.

Foskor (the Phosphate Development Corporation), a R15 million concern, was financed by the government through the Industrial Development Corporation, the purpose of which is to make the country self-sufficient in the vital phosphate concentrate used in agricultural fertilizers and hitherto largely imported from Morocco. At Phalaborwa there are sufficient reserves of apatite to provide Southern Africa with all phosphatic requirements for many hundreds of years.

Close to the apatite deposit is a huge outcrop of copper ore. The Phalaborwa Mining Company Ltd, a R74 million project financed by a consortium of international companies, is delving into a deposit estimated at 300 million tons. In place of the once-solid Lule Kop, a colossal open-cast working, 1,5 km long and 2,4 km wide, is being excavated by bulldozers at a rate which, per day, fills 2 000 vehicles each containing 40 tons. The intention is to mine 12 million tons of ore a year, producing 80 000 tons of copper and not only supplying South African requirements of blister and anode copper, but leaving two-thirds of the outcrop for export. Of this output, 45 per cent is destined for West Germany. Magnetite (iron ore) is also produced in the area and 8 800 000 tons of concentrate are sent each year to Japan.

With a total of 13 515 inhabitants, the town of Phalaborwa is spaciously laid out in a natural parkland setting. Watered by 457 mm of rain a year and basking in a summer temperature of around 37,8°C, it is a garden town enhanced by flowering trees (flamboyants, jacarandas, frangipani), bright flowers and intensely green grass.

## Accommodation
★★ Andrew Motel, 28 rooms, all with baths. R9,75 – R15,65 room only. Phone 2381.
★★★ Impala Inn, 47 rooms, all with baths. R12 – R24 B/B. Phone 2181.

## Caravans and camping
★ Lion Inn Caravan Park, 130 sites. R2,50 D.

Five kilometres before the tarmac road enters Phalaborwa from Gravelotte, a tarmac turnoff south leads through woodland so dense and level that it seems like a green ocean in the midst of which odd islets of rocky hillocks provide occasional landfalls. After 8 km the road passes the Andrew Motel. At 38 km the road reaches a junction with the gravel road coming directly from Gravelotte (33 km). Five kilometres from this junction (43 km from Phalaborwa) the tarmac road passes the small mining and rail centre of Mica comprising a store, station and some storage sheds shimmering in the heat. Mica may be seen glittering in nearly every rock.

Four kilometres south of Mica, the road crosses the Olifants River, a fine, typically African river full of hippos, crocodiles and fish. The flat bushveld scenery is interrupted by a line of weirdly shaped hillocks. A further 2 km sees a turnoff to the Hippo Pool Holiday Resort.

## Caravans and camping
★ Hippo Pool Holiday Resort, 300 sites. R3 D plus 80c D per person.

The tarmac road continues southwards, with the Drakensberg looming to the west over the sea of bush. Several private game reserves are maintained in the area and game animals such as giraffe are often seen. At 22 km from the Hippo Pool turnoff the road reaches the communications, road and rail centre of *Hoedspruit* (hat stream) consisting of a cluster of stores and a motel standing at a crossroads where a tarmac road branches off westwards to the Abel Erasmus Pass and to Lydenburg.

## Accommodation
★ Fort Coepieba Motel, 22 rooms, all with baths. R10 B/B. Phone 35.

Seven kilometres south of Hoedspruit there is a gravel turnoff to Shlaralumi; at 9 km to the Mariepskop Game Reserve and at 23 km a tarmac turnoff to Caskets (a trading station) and the Thorny Bush Game Lodge. The game lodge is 22 km along this road and is one of several private game reserves in the area such as Shlaralumi and Sohebele. Most of them are open to guests and offer game viewing from hides, motor vehicles or on foot. Each has a varied population of wild animals comprising most of the species found in the Eastern Transvaal.

## Accommodation
★ Cheetah Inn, 19 rooms, 13 with baths. R8 – R12 room only. Phone Klaserie 6.
Klaserie Nature Reserve (Ingwe Lodge), 8 beds, R75 D.
Motswari Game Lodge, 10 beds, R75 – R90 D.
Shlaralumi Game Lodge, 12 beds, R8 – R24 D.
Sohebele Game Lodge, 12 beds, R80 D.

Thorny Bush Game Lodge, 24 beds, R60 D.
Tunda Tula Game Lodge, 8 beds, R65 – R85 D.

Beyond the turnoff to the Thorny Bush Game Lodge, the main tarmac road continues south for 1 km (24 km from Hoedspruit), passing the small railway centre of Klaserie, where a tarmac road branches off west to Kampersrus, Mariepskop and the Abel Erasmus Pass. Seven kilometres further south, the main tarmac road reaches a turnoff leading eastwards for 3 km to the railway station of Acornhoek and from there for 38 km through the private game reserve of Timbavati to the Orpen Gate of the Kruger National Park. This is one of the most interesting routes of entry to the park, passing through excellent game country. The Orpen Gate is open throughout the year from dawn to dusk.

*Acornhoek,* which seems to have received its curious name as a result of a mispronounciation of the Afrikaans *eekhorinkie* (squirrel), is the centre for a large area settled by African people. From it a tarmac road leads south-eastwards for 10 km to a turnoff to the railway station of Rolle. From this turnoff the road, now gravel, continues for a further 33 km, reaching the entrance to the . . .

# MANYELETI GAME RESERVE

This reserve was opened on 27 June 1967 for particular use by the African tourist and lover of wildlife. At 3 km from the entrance there is a fine camp from where a network of game viewing roads explore an area of bush adjoining the Kruger National Park.

The name *Manyeleti* (place of the stars) comes from a stream and marsh in which the reflections of the stars is notable. Originally the reserve consisted of five privately owned farms whose owners used them principally for shooting. In the 1960s these farms were bought by the Department of Bantu Affairs for the purpose of converting this handsome piece of wilderness into a game reserve and resort for Africans. Its popularity is such that over 30 000 people visit it each year.

The Manyeleti Game Reserve contains a population of 7 000 impala, 1 400 wildebeest, 500 zebra, 375, giraffe, 140 waterbuck, 16 white rhino and a number of buffalo, sable, nyala, steenbok, reedbuck, bushbuck, duiker and elephant. Amongst the predators are usually about 100 lions, 25 cheetahs and numerous leopards, hyenas, jackals, and wild dogs. Bird life is rich and there are many fine trees, notably mahogany.

The reserve is open daily from sunrise to sunset between 1 March and 15 January.

**Accommodation**
Ordinary huts, R2 D per adult, 50c per child. Minimum R3 D.
Luxury huts, R2,80 D per adult, 50c per child. Minimum R4,60 D.
Dormitories (sleeping mats) for parties of school children, 20c per pupil.

**Caravans and camping**
50c per caravan, 20c per adult, 10c per child.

From the turnoff to Acornhoek, Orpen Gate and Manyeleti, the main tarmac road continues south through a green, fertile area densely settled by peasant farmers. There are fine views to the west of the Drakensberg and patches of plantations in between areas of cultivation and natural parkland.

After 30 km the tarmac road starts to climb the Bushbuck Ridge, reaching the trading and administrative centre of Bosbokrand on its summit (34 km from the Acornhoek turnoff). Magnificent views are revealed of the surrounding country from the heights and a turnoff leads for 35 km to Graskop.

The Bushbuck Ridge is a densely settled area occupied mainly by Shangane people. The main tarmac road continues over cultivated fields, with yellow flowering acacias growing on the verges and many fine views to be had over the lowveld and the Drakensberg escarpment. The F. C. Erasmus Forestry and Nature Reserve of the Department of Forestry lies on the eastern side of the ridge and there is an entrance 6 km from the summit. After 9 km of travelling from the summit, the tarmac road descends the southern side of Bushbuck Ridge, passing a turnoff to Graskop (35 km). Ten kilometres from the administrative centre on the summit, the road reaches a turnoff leading through the F.C. Erasmus Forestry and Nature Reserve and then eastwards across the lowveld for 30 km to the small trading centre of Newington and the entrance to the . . .

## SABIE-SAND GAME RESERVE

This reserve, named after the two principal rivers (the Sabi and the Sand) which flow through the area, is a private game reserve consisting of a block of 20 farms situated on the western boundary of the Kruger National Park and occupying 62 308 ha. The area was originally surveyed by W. H. Gilfillian, who, although the farms were buried in the African wilderness, gave them rather incongruous names such as *Nantes, Toulon* and *Alicecot*. The area passed into the hands of various farmers and prospectors who tried, without notable success, to work the farms for profit. Eventually, 39 owners combined their holdings into what is today the largest private nature reserve in South Africa and appointed a full-time professional warden to watch over it. Each owner cares for his own residence but there are no fences dividing the properties.

The Sabie-Sand Game Reserve was declared a game reserve and flora area on 27 January 1965. It is separated from the Kruger National Park by a veterinary fence, and a similar fence on the western border where it adjoins areas of tribal settlement. The wildlife population of the area is varied and the approximate figures for the main species are as follows: 25 000 impala, 3 000 wildebeest, 2 000 zebra, 1 000 giraffe, 500 kudu, 200 warthog and 100 waterbuck.

Predators – lion, leopard, cheetah, hyena, jackal and wild dog – are scattered over the whole area. Elephants wander at will. Bird life is rich and the flora is varied and beautiful, with many magnificent trees growing and trails tunnelling through a lovely wilderness.

In their lodges – several of which are picturesque and luxurious – the fortunate owners find relaxation from the stresses of big business. Visitors are allowed into the Sabie-Sand Game Reserve only by invitation, but three of the farms have been opened to guests, Londolozi, *Mala Mala* (sable antelope) and Toulon.

Newington was once a station on the Selati Line and was always renowned for its lions. African passengers waiting for trains, generally spent the nights perched in thorn trees. The attention of the authorities having been directed to this discomfort, they obligingly sent ladders to what was then a siding in order to facilitate emergency tree-climbing! The railway has now been relocated and Newington is a ghost station.

### Accommodation
Londolozi Game Reserve, 16 beds, R57 D. Phone Skukuza 166.
Mala Mala Game Reserve, 30 beds, R135 D. Phone Johannesburg 21-96711.
Toulon Game Reserve, 8 beds, R50 D. Phone Skukuza 211.

From the turnoff to Newington and the Sabie-Sand Game Reserve the main tarmac road continues south over undulating foothill country. After 4 km the road passes the Jock Caravan Park. A further 8 km takes the road past the Meriti Huts and Nursery, notable for spectacular bougainvillaea and bauhinias, as well as many other flowering plants.

A further 4 km takes the road to a turnoff leading westwards to Graskop. Immediately beyond this turnoff, the road crosses the Sabie River to reach a turnoff west to the town of Sabie. Along this road, 1,5 km away, lies the magnificent Sabie River Bungalows Hotel and, further along the road turning to White River, the Don Carlos and the Casa Do Sol hotels, each in a setting of trees and gardens.

## Accommodation
** Casa Do Sol Hotel, 32 rooms, all with baths. R13,50 – R29,50 B/B. Phone Hazyview 22.
** Don Carlos Hotel, 32 rooms, all with baths. R11 B/B. Phone Hazyview 51.
** Numbi Hotel, 20 rooms, all with baths. R13,50 B/B. Phone Hazyview 6.
*** Sabie River Bungalows Hotel, 66 rooms, all with baths. R20 – R23 B/B. Phone Hazyview 12.

## Caravans and camping
**® Jock Caravan Park, 20 sites. 50c D per site plus 50c D per person.
** Meriti Huts, 20 chalets. R4 D.
** Numbi Garden Bungalows and Caravan Park, 10 sites. R2 D plus 25c D per person. 25 bungalows, R12,50 D.
** Sabie River Mineral Bath, 20 sites. R5 D. 40 flats and rondawels, R8 – R16 D.
** Sabie Villa Caravan Park, 30 sites. R5 D. 30 cottages and rooms R3,50 D.
**® Safari Caravan Park, 50 sites. R1,50 D plus 50c D per person. Flats and rondawels, R4,50 – R8 D.

One kilometre beyond the turnoff to Sabie, the main tarmac road reaches a turnoff stretching east for 54 km to Skukuza in the Kruger National Park via the Paul Kruger Gate. Less than 1 km beyond this point (35 km from Bushbuck Ridge) the road reaches the small commercial centre known as Hazyview.

A further 2 km south takes the main tarmac road to a turnoff leading to *Kiepersol* (cabbage tree) and 1 km beyond this lies the Safari Caravan Park. At 9 km from Hazyview there is a tarmac turnoff leading eastwards for 8 km to Numbi Gate, the most popular entrance to the Kruger National Park. The gate is open daily from dawn to sunset throughout the year. The landscape is rolling, fertile and profusely settled by peasant farmers. At 1 km beyond the Numbi turnoff, the main road passes a roadside market place known as *eDayizenza* (the place where things are made and sold). A variety of locally made curios and handicrafts are sold here.

Ahead looms one of the great landmarks of the Eastern Transvaal, the rocky height known as *Lugogodo* or *Legogote* (place of the klipspringer). The road passes to the west of this distinctively leaning mountain. The road climbs steeply up an attractive pass and at the summit reaches an area of plantations and farms, where the magnificent Winkler Hotel is situated in the midst of a spacious garden and lawn. Two kilometres beyond this hotel is a turnoff leading to the farming centre and railways terminus named *Plaston* after an old-time ganger, Dirk van den Plas.

## Accommodation
* Bushman Rock Hotel, 30 rooms, all with baths. R10 B/B. Phone White River 15.
***® The Winkler Hotel, 44 rooms, all with baths. R22,50 D/B/B. Phone White River 293.
*** Pine Lake Inn, 71 rooms, all with baths. R15,50 – R18,50 B/B. Phone White River 468.

Another kilometre sees a tarmac turnoff leading north-westwards and providing an alternative parallel route to the main road from Hazyview. A short turnoff branches off this road to the Pine Lake Inn. After a further 3 km (37 km from Hazyview) the main road reaches the pleasant town of . . .

# WHITE RIVER

The situation of this town is a well-watered and intensely green plateau elevated slightly above the level of the surrounding lowveld. Flowering trees shade its streets while the area is irrigated and tilled into beautifully productive farmland where vegetables, timber and subtropical fruit flourish in great variety and profusion.

*White River* receives its name from the stream which waters the area. Known to the tribespeople as *Manzemhlope* (white waters) this fertile area attracted European settlers in the 1890s when families such as the De Beers, Swarts, Stoltz's and Wolhuters made their homes there.

After the Anglo-Boer War the so-called White River Settlement was launched for the settlement of demobilised soldiers. A 26-km-long canal was dug which led water to the farm *Witrivier*. A town was laid out and a school and government buildings erected as a nucleus.

Irrigated smallholdings were provided on easy terms, but the project was a failure as it was nearly impossible to farm economically on such small units in that area. Many of the settlers went bankrupt but others, planting crops such as tobacco, managed to pull through. The White River Farmers Association was formed but had a chequered career. By 1911 the area was practically ruined and in 1914 the *Witrivier* farm was sold to a syndicate for £10 000 on easy terms. This syndicate, mainly comprising local men, brought new life to the place. Sixty thousand citrus trees were planted. The enterprise flourished, with a branch railway being built from Nelspruit in 1926 and in 1928, the White River Estate being formed to manage the area. The Danie Joubert and the Longmere dams were built to irrigate the area and today more than one million cases of citrus are exported each year, along with pine and gum wood, vegetables, subtropical fruit and flowers. More than 2 500 Europeans, living on smallholdings and farms within an 8-km radius of the town, make this the most densely populated farming area in Southern Africa.

The town received its first public body, a health committee, on 29 October 1932 and became a municipality on 1 January 1974. The population now numbers 3 515.

## Accommmodation
★ White River Hotel, 40 rooms, all with baths. R10,50 B/B. Phone 40.

## Caravans and camping
★★ Municipal caravan park, 35 sites. R1,50 D per person.

From White River the main tarmac road continues southwards passing through a fertile landscape of fruit farms, beautiful trees and flowering plants. After 4 km there is a turnoff west to Sabie and a further 3 km sees a turnoff east to Plaston. Just beyond this turnoff is a roadside market place (known as Kraal Kraft) which sells locally made curios and agricultural produce. A further 5 km (13 km from White River) takes the road past the Drum Rock Hotel. The road descends into the great citrus and subtropical fruit-growing valley of the Crocodile River. At 18 km from White River there is a tarmac turnoff to Sabie. The road then crosses the Crocodile River and at 21 km from White River, reaches the busy town of Nelspruit (see page 626).

## Accommodation
★★★ Drum Rock Hotel, 48 rooms, all with baths. R19 D/B/B. Phone Nelspruit 2154.

# Chapter Thirty-three

# THE KRUGER NATIONAL PARK

The story of conservation is dramatised by many climaxes, disappointments and achievements. It was not so long ago that a wild animal was merely considered a God-given target for hunters. It was thought that the number of bison in America and antelope in South Africa was such that they could survive a continuous bloodbath.

Man had to surmount quite an emotional and intellectual watershed before conservation was accepted as being anything other than the emotion of fools. At first, the idea of preserving wilderness for recreation was simply received with hilarity and scorn by the 'vepers' (venal persons) who consider any open space as an opportunity to secure options, raise bonds, carve up, play the game of jiggery-pokery and re-sell at a profit (for themselves but not for their fellows).

The Swiss are credited with the establishment in 1592 of the first known prohibited hunting area. The United States of America in 1872 proclaimed the first national park, at Yellowstone. In South Africa the Hluhluwe and Mfolozi game reserves were declared in 1897 and on 26 March 1898 President Paul Kruger signed a proclamation for the founding of a government game park in the Eastern Transvaal, between the Crocodile and the Sabi rivers. In this way, the Kruger National Park was born.

The area placed under protection was a small portion of the present national park but contained a variety of natural forms in three main vegetative areas: a grassy, rather sour thornless parkland in the west; a strip of bush willow parkland with sweet grazing in the centre; and on the eastern side, a dry acacia parkland with sweet grazing. These three areas provided habitats of considerable difference for all forms of animal life. The palatability of grazing largely influenced the distribution of antelope and the associate presence of predators. The eastern part of the newly proclaimed government game park was therefore a resort for the greatest numbers of wild animals.

Adversely, the area had attracted the most intensive hunting by man. So drastically had the wild animal population been reduced, that it had become apparent that without protection, none of them would survive. As an area of human settlement the new game sanctuary was limited. Malaria fever was endemic, bilharzia was present in all the rivers. Tsetse fly had, until 1896, killed off any domestic livestock and it had yet to be proved that the pestilential fly had disappeared during the rinderpest epidemic of that year. Their absence was noted, but they could just as suddenly reappear.

The mosquito and the tsetse had therefore prevented the settlement of Europeans in the area, allowing them to play the role of temporary predators during the winter hunting season when fever was not so prevalent. A few African people, mainly refugee elements from neighbouring tribes, found an uneasy sanctuary in the bush, but fever and bilharzia debilitated them and the tsetse destroyed their livestock.

The area had at least been well explored. Pathways blazed by safari traders, led directly from the coast inland across the lowveld of the Eastern Transvaal. In addition to the safari traders, the paths were tramped by ivory hunters and slave raiders. Voortrekkers such as Louis Trichardt, Johannes van Rensburg and Hendrik Potgieter also crossed the area trying to open communications with the Portuguese coastal ports.

The advent of the Voortrekkers to the Transvaal stimulated increased trading traffic along the paths. Traders such as the Italian, João Albasini (the famous *Juwawa,* as the Africans called him), sent so many parties of porters carrying goods along the paths that he created a depot and staging post near Pretorius Kop and planned to turn the entire lowveld into a new Portuguese colony named the Colonoa Da Santa Luz.

The demand for trade goods in the Transvaal soon far exceeded the carrying capacity of porters. Albasini claimed that the path his porters followed was free of tsetse and this gave rise to the hope of a wagon route. The Voortrekker settlers in the Ohrigstad area blazed the route which became known as the 'Old Wagon Road' and although found to be not entirely free of tsetse, it came into use as the first negotiable route with no physical difficulties such as mountains or rivers to surmount. The name *Pretorius Kop* dates from this period, either as a result of the death there of a hunter by that name or the visit in 1865 of President M. W. Pretorius, who travelled down the road as far as that point (a landmark on the road), to inspect the route and to indulge in a little hunting.

The discovery of gold in the Eastern Transvaal at Spitskop in 1873 opened a romantic chapter in the story of South Africa. The transport of goods along the Old Wagon Road became a way of life for a singular breed of men known as transport riders – rough, resourceful, and courageous. These men and the patient spans of oxen, took the lumbering ox wagons into the most improbable and difficult places. They paid a price for their audacity, however, by leaving the wrecks of vehicles, graves, and skeletons of their oxen scattered along the Old Wagon Road.

In 1875 Alois Nellmapius formed a transport company and experimented with exotic draught animals such as camels, mules and donkeys, hoping to find them resistent to tsetse fly, but they died as easily as the oxen. The only real solution to the problem of transport was provided by the building of the railway from the coast to Pretoria in 1895. Thus the era of the transport riders ended and the Old Wagon Road was left to its ghosts, of whom, it is reputed, there are many!

After it was proclamed a game park, the area saw no further hunting except for the activities of poachers. The police sergeant at Komatipoort was allocated the task of looking after the 4 000-square kilometre area, but there was no further development before the outbreak of the Anglo-Boer War in October 1899. Komatipoort was at the time occupied by a rather irregular British force of cavalry known as Steinacker's Horse, after its commanding officer, a German, Colonel Ludwig Steinacker. This force indulged in a good bit of hunting for the pot but their presence at least kept out the professional game slaughterers (known as 'biltong hunters') who have been responsible for the heaviest onslaughts on game animals in Southern Africa.

At the end of the war, the new British administration accepted the idea of the game sanctuary and appointed a warden for what was called the Sabi Game Reserve. The person selected for the post was Major J. Stevenson-Hamilton, a short, peppery man of considerable intelligence, resolution, and sympathy as far as wildlife was concerned. For his headquarters, the new warden selected a point on the Sabi River where the railway known as the Selati Line, a branch from the main line at Komatipoort, reached the river. Originally known as Sabi Bridge, the place soon adopted the name which the Africans gave to Stevenson-Hamilton – *siKhukhuza* (he who scrapes clear). The modified form of *Skukuza* is today the name of the principal camp and administrative centre of the park.

The facilities at Skukuza were at first rather primitive. The railway had been constructed in 1893 as part of a fraud perpetrated largely on overseas investors. It had never been completed and consisted of a pair of light-weight rusty rails vanishing rather unevenly into the bush, a blockhouse at the railhead and a gangers' trolley. Nevertheless, the line provided a link with the outside world, and the trolley could carry in stores.

Stevenson-Hamilton appointed to his staff two rangers, both former members of Steinacker's Horse: Gaza Gray who was stationed at Lower Sabi, and Harry Wolhuter who was stationed at Pretorius Kop. The three men had to look after the entire area, patrolling on horseback or on foot. To add to their responsibilities, they had also taken charge of a block of ranches lying north of the Sabi River. These ranches were in private hands but were undeveloped, with no communications or occupants.

It was in August 1903 during the investigation of a report of poaching in the area of the ranches that Harry Wolhuter had his incredible encounter with a lion. Caught after sunset in desolate country, Wolhuter came upon a lion in search of dinner. The lion was probably more interested in the horse than the rider, but the horse bolted and Wolhuter fell on top of the lion who then turned his attention to the man. Seizing Wolhuter by the right shoulder, the lion dragged him 55m, purring with gruesome satisfaction at the thought of a meal and snarling viciously each time Wolhuter's spurs caught in a root or stone.

Wolhuter lay on his back, his face pressed into the lion's mane. The stench was foul and the thought of being eaten infuriated him. He suddenly remembered his small sheath knife attached to his belt. It had always been loose however, and he was afraid that it might have fallen off. He groped for it cautiously, the lion growling as he moved. To his delight the knife was still there. Wolhuter drew it out. Feeling for the lion's heart beating above him, he stabbed upwards twice. With a great howl of agony the lion dropped him. Before it could bite again, Wolhuter stabbed it in the throat. Drenching the prostrate ranger with blood, the lion stumbled off to die.

In fearful pain, Wolhuter staggered up and managed to climb a small tree. Using his belt, he strapped himself to the trunk in case he fainted. It was just as well he did. A second lion arrived to investigate the commotion. Rearing up against the fragile tree it gave Wolhuter a lengthy, soul-chilling stare. At this critical stage, one of Wolhuter's dogs, all of whom had bolted when the lion attacked, returned to find its master. It began to bark at the lion and so goaded it that the animal left the tree and tried to catch the dog.

After about an hour, some of Wolhuter's African game guards who had ridden ahead to prepare a camp, came to find out what was delaying him. They fired shots to drive the lion away and helped Wolhuter to camp where they dressed his wounds.

At daylight they found the first lion dead with two knifewounds in the heart. The second lion had vanished. The skin of the lion and the knife are exhibited in the library at Skukuza. Also on display is a remarkable composite knife, presented to Wolhuter by T. Williams of London, the manufacturer of the knife which had saved his life. The site of Wolhuter's adventure is marked by a memorial stone and the preserved stump of the long-dead tree.

In the same year as Wolhuter's misadventure the area of the park was considerably enlarged. Between the Letaba and the Luvuvhu rivers stretched a 5 000-square kilometre extent of wilderness – hot, inclined to be arid and dominated by mopane trees. The area was proclaimed the Shingwidzi Game Reserve and placed under the control of Stevenson-Hamilton. With his small staff, however, there was nothing much he could do with the new reserve. He travelled up to inspect the area which seemed to be almost devoid of any kind of animal life.

The Shingwidzi (place of ironstone) River, after which the area was named was lined with tall trees and contained deep pools of water, even in times of drought. At a place called Malunzane, Stevenson-Hamilton found a hut deserted by a labour recruiter for the mines. He selected this lonely place for a ranger post and in 1904 stationed there a curious character by the name of Major Fraser, who became one of the legends of the lowveld. He was a man whose principal diet seemed to consist of pipe tobacco and whisky, his friends a very mixed pack of dogs, and his recreation the reading and re-reading of a vast collection of back numbers of Field magazine. He was not much interested in anything else. The area under his authority was so huge that it was not really possible to control the poachers, blackbirders (illegal labour recruiters) and renegades who frequented it, especially at the junction of the Limpopo and Pafuri rivers, known on account of their presence as Crooks Corner.

The area at least partially protected now included most of the present Kruger National Park, but as it consisted of three parts – the Sabi Game Reserve, the Shingwidzi Game Reserve, and the block of ranches between the Sabi and Letaba rivers – there was no guarantee of permanency to this protection. Also, Stevenson-Hamilton was disturbed at loose talk of the whole area being 'thrown open' for shooting. He countered with the idea that the area should rather be consolidated into one national park and 'thrown open' to the public as a magnificent spectacle of wildlife. He realised that as long as the area remained closed to the public they could hardly be expected to support its preservation, especially as their tax money was its only means of finance.

In 1912 the Selati Railway was at last completed. Only one return train a week travelled the line but the existence of the railway generally attracted more attention to the lowveld, with much talk of future development.

The First World War broke out and Stevenson-Hamilton went off to rejoin the army. Major Fraser, with his pack of 25 dogs, took charge of the three areas for most of the time. He was not a great man for paper work; a story relates how he dumped a bag of coins on the desk of a surprised magistrate and told him that it was the tax gathered from staff in the reserve. The magistrate asked for copies of vouchers and receipts at which Fraser simply snorted and walked out, asking over his shoulder whether the magistrate had no memory!

One very important event occurred during the war years. In 1916 a commission was appointed by the government to inquire into the matter of game conservation. When Stevenson-Hamilton returned at the end of the war, with the rank of Lieutenant-Colonel, he was delighted to learn that this commission had recommended that the area under protection be converted into a great national park 'where the natural and prehistoric conditions of our country can be preserved for all time'.

The end of the war unfortunately also saw a clamour for land for the resettlement of returned soldiers. African squatters were generally pressing; prospectors were fossicking around in search of coal, gold, copper and other precious minerals. All that was needed was a big discovery to send conservation ideals to their doom on a mining tailings dump. The principal landowner north of the Sabi River, the Transvaal Consolidated Land Company, was also very restive. In 1922 they commenced ranching on the farm *Toulon,* just across the Sabi River from Stevenson-Hamilton's headquarters and provoked a test case (which they lost) by shooting a wildebeest on the grounds that it was destroying plants or crops by eating grass.

In the midst of this renewed controversy, the South African Railways had a real brainwave. During the winter months of 1923 they introduced a novel tourist service, a 'round in nine' tour by train which would take holidaymakers through the best scenery of the Eastern Transvaal, including a gay night at Lourenço Marques. At first the tourist train was scheduled to pass through the game reserve at night without stopping, an arrangement so stupid as to be unbelievable. It was soon changed, however. The train stopped for the night at Sabi Bridge where the tourists were treated to a campfire and a round of yarns about big game. The next day the train continued slowly through the reserve, stopping at places such as Newington (then part of the reserve) where a ranger escorted the tourists on short walks into the bush. The public adored it. At last the hitherto forbidden areas of the wilderness were open to them and a visit to the game reserve became the most exciting prospect for any holiday.

In August 1923 Colonel Deneys Reitz, the Minister of Lands, accompanied by members of the Transvaal Provincial Council, made an inspection tour of the reserve and left it, enthusing about the concept of a national park. The Wild Life Protection Society was also agitating for a national park and the South African Railways had started featuring the game reserve in its publicity. The biggest problem in fact, was private ownership of the country between the Sabi and the Olifants rivers. Great controversy raged over these ranches.

As a compromise, a western boundary line was devised, leaving in the area of the future park, 70 privately owned ranches which had to be expropriated. The remaining ranches, forming the big block between the Sabi and its tributary, the *Moyetlamogale* (river that is fierce when in flood), known to Europeans as the Sand River, were excluded and deproclaimed. This unfortunately included some of the best sable and roan country and all of the mountain reedbuck and red duiker country in the south-west. However, the park would at least remain a self-contained block and most of these ranches now form part of the privately owned Sabi-Sand Game Reserve (see page 656).

Before the National Parks Bill could be considered by Parliament there was a change of government. Fortunately, the new government (Nationalist) was also sympathetic to the concept of conservation but a delay ensued while they settled down to office. The new Minister of Lands, Piet Grobler, a grand-nephew of President Kruger, was enthusiastic about the idea of a national park.

During the final period of waiting there were several events. Brown locusts were plaguing the entire country in 1925 and had to be resolutely battled. Farmers along the southern border complained vociferously about the acitivities of lions. To deal with this, a new post was established at *Malalane* (place of the small lala palms) and a new ranger, Harold Trollope, appointed to it. An experienced hunter, he tackled the lion problem to such effect that most of the predators in the southern area were totally destroyed. Trollope, who was somewhat over-daring, took his elderly father-in-law, Glen Leary, on a leopard hunt. The leopard surprised the inexperienced Leary in long grass and killed him.

Many enthusiasts rallied to the support of the national park concept during a final period of anxiety when it was thought that perhaps something might yet cause it to be stillborn. Keen photographers such as Colonel F. R. Hoare and the American, Paul Selby, distributed excellent pioneer game pictures throughout the world. Charles Astley Maberly, the artist-naturalist, wrote letters to the press and to individuals, his exquisite drawings of mammals and birds winning considerable support. The publicity department of the Railways appointed Stratford Caldecott, an artist, to promote the park as a tourist attraction. In creating posters, articles and pictures, he also, in close consultation with Stevenson-Hamilton, conceived the name of the Kruger National Park. It was the ultimate inspiration and an apt choice, serving as both a memorial to a remarkable man and a sentimental touch to win the support of many additional people.

Enemies of conservation also tried to rally. Sheep farmers sent a deputation to their members of Parliament condemning the idea. Would-be landowners tried to pull individual strings. Veterinarians, whose reputation in the history of conservation in Africa is particularly notorious, also raised their voices in support of slaughter, talking hysterically about a possible return to the reserve of tsetse fly or the uncontrollable spread from there of some dire livestock disease.

Considerable negotiation took place in the acquisition of the privately owned ranches north of the Sabi. Alternate land was exchanged outside the reserve; direct purchases were made; the government-owned mining ground between the Olifants and Letaba rivers was transferred and then, at last, on 31 May 1926, Mr Piet Grobler moved in Parliament the second reading of the National Parks Act. There were no dissentients.

Under the administration of a board of control comprising ten members – eight appointed by government, one by the Transvaal Administration and one by the Wild Life Protection Society – the park was launched. It was Mr Grobler's intention that each province would eventually appoint a member, the government four and the Wild Life Protection Society, one. None were to receive payment save for expenses. Politics would not influence appointments or preferments.

Stevenson-Hamilton hurried to Pretoria to congratulate and to be congratulated. Piet Grobler immediately insisted that there be no more shooting of lions. The park was to be a sanctuary for all living things except man, who would alone be controlled.

It was a year of great change and activity in the newly created national park. It was the

663

desire of the Board of Trustees that roads should be made as quickly as possible and the park opened to visitors forthwith. The economics of the park were that the state would pay for management and maintainance, but the public would pay for development. They could hardly be expected to do that unless they could visit the park and learn to regard it as something peculiarly theirs.

The first road was laid down from Sabi Bridge to Olifants River; the second from Sabi Bridge to Pretorius Kop; and the third from Sabi Bridge to Crocodile Bridge. The first three tourist cars entered the park in 1927, using the entrance at Pretorius Kop. Among the passengers was a seven-year-old boy, Douglas Jackaman who was so impressed by what he saw that he later became a camp manager in the park.

No accommodation was provided for visitors; they made their own camps in thornbush enclosures, the only facility the park could provide. Nobody knew how the estimated 100 000 wild animals living in the park would react to motor cars of the 'tin lizzie' type, so visitors carried weapons for their protection. There was never any need to use them; from the beginning the wild animals seemed completely indifferent to motor cars and tourists as long as they remained in their vehicles.

Some of the old hands in the game reserve were glad to retire before the expected flood of tourists came. Both new and experienced rangers found themselves heavily involved with rapidly increasing tourist traffic and until rondawels could be built, had to accommodate many visitors in their own restricted little homes. Pulling motor vehicles out of the mud; repairing broken cars; advising and entertaining visitors; all demanded considerable time until separate tourist officers could be appointed as the flow of visitors increased to justify the expense. Proper camps were built and placed in the hands of private contractors who negotiated rights of catering and trading from the Board of Trustees. These contractors varied as much as the celebrated parson's egg.

Everything was casual. Tourists could come and go at any time, day or night. Speeding was no problem – the roads were too bad, but night driving soon had to be stopped, as too many wild animals were being dazzled by headlights and killed as a result.

The opening of the park to visitors throughout the year also had to be summarily ended. The effects of rain on the primitive roads were chaotic. In March 1929 a large party of round-the-world American tourists arrived by luxury train at Crocodile Bridge. With the train serving as a base, groups set out in two big trucks to visit the park. A tremendous rainstorm completely bogged them down and one truck overturned on crossing a stream. People in summer dress were drenched and had to perch in thorn trees to avoid lions. Hector Macdonald, the local ranger, and his African staff, eventually reached them with blankets and food. They spent the night crammed into two small picket huts at a place named after the old headman, Gomond-wane. The tourists regarded it as an adventure, but trouble followed when several of them contracted malarial fever. The resultant publicity was bad. From the following year (1930) only the Pretorius Kop area, with its better roads and freedom from mosquitoes, was left open throughout the year. The rest of the park was closed from the end of October until the end of May. Fortunately the Pretorius Kop area experienced its best game concentration during the summer months when several species (notably zebra and wildebeest) moved into it from the east. A large permanent camp for tourists was created there, and in 1931 a full-time camp manager, Captain M. Rowland-Jones, was appointed to its control.

The popularity of the park increased at a tremendous rate. More roads and accommodation were built, but every year the number of visitors reached a new record. In 1931 it was decided to open to the public the area north of the Letaba River. For this purpose, a low-level concrete bridge was constructed across the Letaba and a road built as far as the ranger camp of Punda Malia, where it joined the original Ivory Trail, now a proper road leading to Pafuri and laid down by the Witwatersrand Native Labour Association. The road was opened in 1933 and a new ranger, H. R. Kirkman, a Natal farmer and former manager of the Sabi Ranch, was appointed to the staff so that three ranger posts could be maintained in the northern area. *Punda Maliya* (as it is correctly spelt) had originally been established by a celebrated ranger, Captain Coetser, who, in Swahili, jocularly named the place *Punda Maria* (striped Maria) after his wife who liked striped dresses.

Apart from roads and tourist accommodation, the park was confronted with the problem of water supply. Tourists needed pure water and the existing surface water supplies in many parts of the park, notably the northern areas, were so insignificant and subject to erratic drought conditions that it would never be possible for wild animals to concentrate in any appreciable numbers even though the grazing was sweet and plentiful. The establishment of artificial waterholes seemed to be the answer, but for this finance was needed.

It was the subject of boreholes that first brought the public to the aid of the park. A Mr J. H. Cloete of Clocolan bequeathed money for the erection of a windpump; Bertram Jeary, a wildlife enthusiast from Cape Town, launched a nationwide movement to raise money for boreholes. The park authorities were quite overwhelmed at the response. Towns subscribed money; individuals such as Mrs Armour Hall and Mrs Eileen Orpen each donated money for one borehole; Mrs Orpen and her surveyor husband (J. H. Orpen) surveyed the western boundary and cleared bush at their own expense; Mrs Orpen presented the park with land and considerable amounts of money for water boring and windpumps. Many other benefactors followed suit. By the end of 1933 two drills were at work and within the next two years, 20 productive boreholes were sunk, with windpumps erected to raise the water to the surface. Most of the water was rather saline, unpleasant to human taste, but highly palatable to wild animals.

A new problem presented itself. Game animals prefer muddy water to clean water in such things as troughs. The most successful boreholes were those that augmented existing supplies. Lion would drink anywhere, preferring clean water; antelope and elephant liked their drinks dirty; while elephant and buffalo enjoyed a wallow. Such was their habit and they wanted nothing else. To encourage them to accept clean water or to remain in arid areas dependent on artificial supplies when instinct warned them to migrate because of prevailing drought, would be a time-consuming, if not impossible task.

In 1938 foot-and-mouth disease spread amongst domestic livestock throughout Moçambique and the Eastern Transvaal. Veterinarians immediately resorted to large-scale extermination of all infected cloven-hoofed animals, generally making themselves unpopular amongst the local inhabitants. A great deal of panic and confusion resulted. On the one hand, movements were being restricted (motor vehicles were even being made to drive through troughs of disinfectant to prevent the tyres from transmitting the disease) and on the other, cattle were being gathered in vast herds for periodic dipping or inspection. To the lay public, the position was tragically ludicrous.

To add to the local problem, the summer of 1938-39 was excessively wet. All the rivers were in flood and vast numbers of carcasses of cattle slaughtered by the veterinarians were washed out of mass graves into which they had been bulldozed, and swept away downriver. The stench of carcasses simply left to rot in the veld was insufferable and there was a feeling of total disgust at the mishandling of a disease whose pathology still remained a mystery. Fortunately, the antelope population was highly resistant to foot-and-mouth disease and no outbreak occurred in the park. However, all domestic cloven-footed animals in the park, whether infected or not, were destroyed. The loss of several thousand head of cattle, including those which had recovered from the disease, was incomprehensible and, to the African population especially, unforgivable.

At the peak of this tragedy, the Second World War broke out in September 1939. No little panic resulted over the long, unguarded border with Moçambique, with tales spreading of German spies slipping backwards and forwards across the park, and of planned invasion by mythical forces. The Portuguese however, exercised reasonable control over Moçambique and apart from alarums and excursions on the South African side,nothing occurred. In fact, the wild animals benefited from the war. Poaching ceased almost entirely with ammunition being used elsewhere and until petrol was rationed during the final years of the war, more tourists – particularly soldiers on leave – visited the park than ever before, carrying its fame to many far countries. During the last three years of hostilities, only the Pretorius Kop section of the park remained open to tourists at any time during the year. It seemed like old times in the rest of the park; the rangers were left in solitude and a car on the roads was considered an event.

At this time a few hermits and outcasts found their way into the wilderness, for such a place has always been the resort of the lost and lonely. In the early 1940s one particular wild man made his home along the banks of the Olifants River and for about five years roamed around what was then a very remote stretch of country.

The man was usually quite naked and had a number of lairs secreted in the bush. He made particular use of antbear holes which he enlarged and improved into reasonably snug retreats. He had apparently originated from the Acornhoek area where some domestic upheaval had deranged him.

He lived reasonably well on roots, fruit and venison. The park tolerated his presence, if only because he seemed harmless, happy and, since the war had depleted the staff, very difficult to catch. He was an expert at hiding; if discovered, he bolted with the speed of a tsessebe, leaping over bushes as if pursued by a lion and apparently impervious to such things as thorns or fatigue.

Unfortunately he developed a habit of raiding rangers' picket posts and pilfering items such as knives, pots and clothing. A patrol of five African rangers were so irritated by one of his raids that they tracked him down to a hollowed out anthole. At 02h00 they stormed the place. The wild man was asleep behind a fire, into which the rangers threw a blazing stick so that they would have more light. The wild man shot up and charging through the cordon of rangers, simply vanished into the night.

Ranger Ledeboer then sent an anti-poaching patrol down the right bank of the Olifants River. They surprised the wild man drinking at a pool. He bolted, but this time was out of luck; he tripped over a rock, injuring his leg so badly that his flight was reduced to a hobble. The rangers pounced on him. He lay on the ground, trussed up, his eyes filled with the terror of a captured beast. The rangers followed the trail back to his lair which consisted of a cave filled with the spoils of many hunts and not a few raids on picket posts. He was taken away to be tried for killing game and ended his days in a lunatic asylum.

Another outbreak of foot-and-mouth disease occurred in the Eastern Transvaal in 1944. On the double, the veterinarians again arrived with their rifles, but this time they encountered resistance. Farmers saw them off their property. At meetings with veterinarians, fat cows and calves which had completely recovered from the disease were produced. There was no further killing. A cordon system was introduced to isolate infected areas and the disease died out by itself without the slightest contamination of the park.

The end of the war in 1946 saw great changes of staff. Most momentous and sad of all was the departure of the revered warden. Lieutenant-Colonel J. Stevenson-Hamilton had been born on 2 October 1867 and at the end of the war he was 79 years of age. Forty-four years of his life had been spent in the park which was as much a part of him as he was of it. He had established a unique record of dedication and total service to a high ideal. To choose a replacement for such a man was singularly difficult, and once the successor had been selected, the task which confronted him would be awesome.

The choice was Colonel J. A. B. Sandenburg of the South African Air Force, an administrative officer of high reputation with a background of farming, hunting, and life in the Eastern Transvaal. Stevenson-Hamilton approved of him and on 30 April 1946, the heartsore warden left his beloved 'Cinderella' (as he like to call it) for retirement in White River, where so many others from the park have spent their last years. His book, *South African Eden,* will always remain the classic record of the early years of the park.

Thus the park was reopened to the public in 1946 under entirely new control. In his valediction, Stevenson-Hamilton had warned that whoever controlled the future should keep a sharp watch on glib ideals such as development, improvement and scientific research; these could simply be a camouflage for exploitation. Nor should the park ever be converted into a glorified zoo and botanical garden dotted with scientific experimental stations, hotels and public recreation grounds; such developments would initiate the liquidation of all wildlife.

Reflecting on his years in the park, Stevenson-Hamilton had even regretted the period of predator control which, for a while, had been carried out with the good intention of rapidly replenishing the antelope population. To him, everything had its place in nature which could quite happily function without the management of man. If things were left alone the balance would be restored. Man's interference only deformed nature, the tides of which would still inexorably take their course. A national park was essentially a place where man could stand apart and watch the creative force of nature at work and to study and compare its changes to those made by himself in the outside world. The comparison, whether good or bad, would always be instructive.

Sandenburg did not completely agree with Stevenson-Hamilton. He reintroduced predator control but banned controlled burning which has always been a subject of great controversy. To an airman flying the length of Africa, the characteristic scene below him is not (as some would have it) the glint of sunshine on empty bottles, but one of columns of smoke rising to the heavens from the incessant fires of the shifting cultivation of peasant farmers, or the wanton destruction of accidental conflagration. In a continent where rainfall is generally confined to a few months of the year, leaving the land so dry that any spark is enough to start a fire, obvious dangers are always present. A particularly wet season produces long grass which cannot be disposed of by the insufficient animal population. It dies in the dry season and becomes a menace. Safety precautions are taken in the form of firebreaks burned into mountain sides and bush by foresters and rangers, leaving hideous geometric patterns. Deliberate burning is also practised in order to remove dead grass, stimulate shrubs and prevent vegetative changes. But fire is as ruthless a tool as the rifle of the veterinary. Mistakes are unremediable and the gross pollution of the atmosphere is offensive to all the senses. A great deal of research had still to be done on this subject, and one of the park's deficiencies was a lack of systematic information on which management could rely for the creation of policies.

A vast amount of study was waiting to be done. On the practical side, the park was also completely unfenced; tourist accommodation was very patchy; trading arrangements with the various private concessionaires left much to be desired; and the fact that 38 376 tourists visited the park in the first season of its reopening was a warning that there would soon be a human flood to control, shelter, supply and feed. The visit to the park in 1947 of the British Royal Family and their accommodation at Skukuza in specially built luxury cottages, gave the place tremendous post-war publicity. Every dignitary, touring sports team, and general tourist who visited South Africa, wanted to see the park. Obviously destined to rapidly become one of the great tourist attractions of the world, its management would require delicacy and skill.

Water supplies continued to cause serious problems. Sandenburg launched another 'water-for-game' fund which brought in money for a further 46 successful boreholes. Biological research was also commenced with the appointment in 1951 of a biologist and senior research officer.

Major changes in the entire administrative structure of the park were also imminent. The relatively easy, romantic years were over. In February 1952 a Pretoria firm of accountants, headed by Professor P.W. Hoek, was appointed by the Board to investigate the administration and to make recommendations for more efficient and economical handling. The so-called Hoek Report was submitted in August 1952 and, with a considerable portion of its contents

*Overleaf: A miracle of nature; a shallow pan formed by wild animals drinking and wallowing in water flavoured with lime brought to the surface by ants.*

being highly confidential, was for some years the subject of controversy. One of its recommendations was that the Board be reduced in size to six specialist members appointed by the Minister of Lands, and that this board – consisting of a naturalist, biologist, accountant, tourism expert, nominee of the Wild Life Protection Society and a practising civil engineer – should elect a chairman who would be the Director of National Parks. Directly responsible to him and his board would be a head of biological services, a controller and a head of tourism and development.

The Board, however, decided to appoint a full-time park director, to whom the departmental heads would be subordinate. This post was advertised in January 1953 and out of 80 applicants from all over the world, Mr Rocco Knobel was appointed to the post on 1 April 1953. The son of a missionary in Botswana, he had a background of administrative work in such positions as assistant director of the Johannesburg Municipal Welfare Department and as chief professional officer of the *Armesorgraad van die Witswatersrand* (Council for the Care of the Poor of the Witwatersrand). The warden of the park was from then on left purely in charge of conservation while control of tourists became the responsibility of a tourist manager in the person of H. C. van der Veen who had formerly been the principal officer in that department.

Colonel Sandenburg resigned at the end of 1953 and the then senior ranger, Louis Steyn, was appointed to succeed him. The following year experienced good rains after a long dry spell and was spent in a considerable exercise in management and organisation. Experiments were started in the various vegetational areas, with a vast network of 3 800 km of firebreak roads established and eventually completed to divide the park into 400 different blocks. The entire park – its administration, vegetation and wildlife – was to be brought under close control. Improvement work was also expedited on all camps and roads, with the entrance gate at Orpen (named after the husband and wife benefactors of the park) completed to replace the old gate on the farm *Rabelais,* named by the surveyor after the French satirical author.

Veld management by means of burning was a subject of continuous argument. In 1955 a three-year rotational burning programme was introduced, with a two-year rotational programme in the long grass area of Pretorius Kop. It was again a season of good rains. The park was looking superb and with the seasons remaining favourable for the next four years, it was, in fact, a good time to study the effects of burning during times of plenty.

The whole park – vegetation, birds, insects and mammals – seemed to be blossoming. Even tourist traffic in 1955 brought in over 100 000 visitors (101 058) for the first time. All facilities were under pressure, particularly the privately run trading stations and restaurants, which on 1 December, were taken over by the Board. From then on they became integral parts of national park management, a factor which was definitely to the advantage of tourists and the park. All the camps were growing at such a rate that some of them (notably Skukuza) were becoming vast, sprawling complexes of rondawels. Pretorius Kop received a swimming pool the following year, while houses for staff at the administrative centre of Skukuza were becoming so numerous, that the place began to look increasingly like a village.

Several new research programmes were launched, and considerable activity also commenced in the eradication of exotic plants. To cope with the proposed great developments in roads (over 2 000 km by 1972) and camps, a Department of Works was also established in 1958 under the direction of a qualified civil engineer. A major task involved the complete fencing of the park boundaries, the work on which commenced in 1959. The southern boundary along the Crocodile River was completed first. In 1960 the western and northern boundaries were fenced, and then the eastern frontier with Moçambique. Later, heavy cable, as it became available, was added in order to make the fence even elephant-proof.

The purpose of the fence in impeding the movement of game animals, was to curb the spread of diseases, facilitate boundary patrolling and inhibit the movement of poachers. The fence was breached in many places by wandering animals, but they gradually became used to being confined, although many of them, notably zebra, wildebeest, and elephant, showed a marked inclination towards east-west seasonal migrations. The years of good rain were providing excellent foodstuffs which lured across the frontier from Moçambique many elephants who were under pressure there from hunters and peasant farmers steadily burning off the bush to extend their lands. The first aerial census of elephants was conducted in 1959 and revealed the number of the animals in the park as being 986. As with most of the mammals (especially the browsing species), the elephants increased their numbers rapidly during the good years.

After considerable debate, carnivora control was terminated in December 1958. A new policy was introduced whereby control would only be imposed on a temporary and local basis where carnivora were endangering some declining prey population. Such a situation could periodically occur as it did, for example, in 1960 when there was an outbreak of anthrax, a disease to which kudu and roan antelope were particularly susceptible. The roan suffered severely in this outbreak with so many having died that their continued presence in the park was threatened. A state veterinary surgeon was appointed to the park in 1960 to study diseases of wild animals and to devise measures of control which, it was hoped, would be an improvement on the usual large-scale slaughtering which passed for veterinary treatment.

By then, Stevenson-Hamilton, aged 90, had died of a stroke on 10 December 1957. The warden, Louis Steyn, retired on 20 April 1961 and his departure marked the end of tradition where the patriarchal figure of the dedicated warden-conservationist was the head of the national park. He was replaced by the chief biologist, A.M. Brynard, who assumed the title of Nature Conservator, with the research and ranger sections united under his control into a single Nature Conservation Department. Dr. U. de V. Pienaar was promoted to Chief Biologist while Henry Wolhuter became Senior Ranger.

The new management was immediately confronted with two very dry years after the period of plenty. The erratic pattern of Africa has always been a major problem to all forms of life. To any management where dependability of supply is essential to stability and future planning, this unpredictable pattern is disconcerting. The original African population sought to counter capricious weather with the magic of rainmaking whereby a good weaver of spells could make a fortune. The few tribal groups which formerly inhabited the area of the park all practised rainmaking. Close to the Punda Malia camp for visitors there is a well-forested and most handsome hill known as Gumbandevu, after a headman who once lived there. His daughter Khama practised rainmaking and to her came supplicants, bringing presents of snuff, hoes and livestock. At the foot of the mountain a goat would be sacrificed in such a way that its prolonged death cries would summon the spirits. Taking some of the animal's bones as well as her magic ingredients, Khama would then climb the hill and in a secret bower she would weave the spells until clouds appeared and rain fell. Whether this occurred in the homeland of her clients is unknown, but certainly the area around the hill was always green and the summit covered in a fine stand of ironwood trees. The hill is taboo and it is said that the sound of ghostly drums and singing may sometimes still be heard in the quietest hour of the night.

Modern management did not possess the magic resources of a Khama, so an emergency drilling programme had to be launched with the park acquiring its own boring machine. A long period of creating artificial watering holes ensued. The tourist camps were also very thirsty places; with ever-increasing tourist traffic there would obviously soon be many more people visiting the park each year than there were game animals. The existing camps were expanding. New camps such as Olifants (opened in 1960) perched on a high cliff, and Balule camp, were being developed and several others planned. Additional roads were being constructed; at the same time, dust caused by the traffic resulted in a decision to tarmac the surface of all arterial roads. Picnic spots were provided, such as the one on the Lower Sabi road under the great Mkuhlu tree in 1959, and at Hlangulene and Manzene in 1963. With better roads, more of the park was opened throughout the year: Skukuza from 1962; Lower Sabi, Crocodile Bridge and as far north as the picnic spot at Tshokwane in 1963; and the whole area as far as the Letaba River in 1964. Also in that year, the number of visitors reached 216 680 exceeding the 200 000-a-year mark for the first time, with 56 686 motor vehicles using the roads.

The wildlife population too, was increasing, and a programme commenced whereby species which had been shot out in former years were reintroduced. On 13 October 1961 the first batch of square-lipped (white) rhino were translocated from Zululand. As a result of the success of this operation, over 300 of these interesting animals were introduced by 1972.

A less happy event in 1964 was the shooting of 104 hippos in the Letaba River which had become very dry and its remaining pools overcrowded. These were the first herbivorous animals to be destroyed in the park for reasons of overpopulation. The entire subject of the wild animal population – its increases and decreases – was a matter of considerable interest and study. In August 1964 the first aerial census of elephant and buffalo was conducted by means of a chartered helicopter. A total of 2 374 elephant and 10 514 buffalo were counted. A fine veterinary laboratory and office block was opened in Skukuza and several additional veterinary and research officers appointed, with comprehensive programmes of study involving the participation of visiting students and scientists whose papers, on completion, could be expected to throw considerable light on many aspects of wild animal behaviour.

The rains returned in 1965, but the year was more notable for the Board's convening in Pretoria of a conference on the theme of the overprotection of nature, a rather surprising subject for a conservation body. The conference, held on 30 November, adopted a resolution advising the Board to cull those herbivorous animals whose population levels were thought to be increasing beyond natural controls. In the park, such species were considered to be elephant, buffalo, zebra, wildebeest, impala and hippo. Culling quotas were determined in 1966 and it was the intention that the results of the operation would be checked each year by aerial census, while the effects on vegetation would be observed through transect points. Meat and animal products would be disposed of to best advantage, a plant for which purpose, known as the byproducts depot, was constructed at Skukuza. Biltong, bone meal, canned and cooked meat, skin, ivory and trophies were to be produced.

With the aid of immobilisation drugs, the animals could be destroyed from helicopters in the most modern, humane manner. The capture, translocation and sale of live animals was also commenced. A game capture official was stationed at Tshokwane, with holding pens erected to corral the animals before they were redistributed to other less populated areas of the park, or translocated to outside places. The ingenious plastic-and-net corral method of capture devised by Jan Oelofse of the Natal Parks Board was introduced and this allowed entire herds to be caught with a minimum chance of injury. The year 1968 saw the whole operation fully launched with the sale of products amounting to R37 077, mainly the proceeds of the shooting of 1 242 impala, 237 wildebeest, 390 buffalo, 355 elephant and the killing or capture for sale of 276 zebra.

The public was slightly puzzled at the news of these developments, for they were not visually aware of any overpopulation of wild animals and would be likely to regard the establishment of a meat industry as aesthetically offensive in the setting of a game reserve. The reason for such a necessity and the fact that veterinary restrictions made it impossible to build the factory outside the park, would have to be explained. As it was, the popularity of the park with tourists grew each year; in 1968, 306 346 people visited the park (exceeding 300 000 a year for the first time). Facilities also were expanding and improving at an equal rate. Electric power from Escom was fed into the park to light the camps while strenuous efforts were made to solve the water problem. Each year more boreholes were drilled. The mining magnate, Charles Engelhard, donated R120 000 for the construction of a dam in the Letaba River and work was started in 1971 on a pipeline from the Olifants River to Satara camp, with 15 branch pipes along its length leading to drinking water sites for wild animals.

The park was enlarged in 1968, with the addition of the wild and hitherto remote area between the Limpopo and Luvuvhu rivers (the so-called Pafuri Game Reserve). The few people living there were resettled in land excised from the park between Shangani and Punda Malia gate while the rugged area of the old Crooks Corner became the site of a new ranger post. Although the population of game animals there was very slight, it would certainly improve under protection. Also, this area was historically and scenically one of the most interesting in the park.

Further changes in management occurred on 13 March 1970 when Nature Conservator A. M. Brynard, was promoted to the Pretoria head office to replace R. J. Labuschagne, who had resigned as Deputy Director of National Parks. Chief Biologist Dr U. de V. Pienaar was promoted to the position of Nature Conservator, with P. van Wyk appointed as Chief Research Officer and Don Lowe as Senior Ranger. Further reorganisation in May 1974, resulted in Rocco Knobel becoming Chief Director of National Parks, with A. M. Brynard as his deputy. In 1979 Rocco Knobel retired and Mr A. M. Brynard became Chief Director.

The year 1970 was the driest ever known in the park. Every river – even the Sabi – stopped flowing. Animal mortality throughout the park was dreadful with hundreds of dead hippos befouling what little water remained in the rivers. Fortunately, the year ended with rains so heavy that the African cycle of drought to flood see-sawed to completion. Chocolate brown water gushed down the dry river courses causing the rivers to reach their highest known flood levels. The new Engelhard Dam spilled over for the first time on 9 January 1971.

The extent of some of the downpours may be gauged from the fact that in one night, Punda Malia received 219 mm. The ghost of old Khama, on her mountain, must have been working overtime! The park soon looked its best. Vegetation revives so rapidly after rain that its stirring and growth is almost audible. Unfortunately for the game animals, not only was culling in full swing with the byproducts depot in working order, but anthrax broke out in the northern areas in September and October 1971. The already small population of roan antelope was nearly wiped out while kudu were also very badly affected. Animals such as impala, wildebeest, buffalo, elephant, and zebra were already being systematically culled, but to supplement the wild animal population a programme commenced whereby cheetahs were imported from South West Africa in order to increase the present small numbers. Also, on 17 May 1971 the first two black rhino were reintroduced to the park after their kind had become extinct in the 1930s. A further 18 black rhino were sent up from Natal and 12 from the Zambezi Valley of Zimbabwe in 1972. Resettlement schemes were also under way in the park for such rare antelope as eland, tsessebe, oribi and roan. A prophylactic protection against anthrax was developed in 1971 and the remaining roan population was immunised by dart syringes fired from a helicopter. The future of this species in the park now seems to be more secure.

Boreholes (362 in the park by the end of 1979) as well as 316 windpumps, were steadily stabilising drinking water supplies and plans were made for many more watering places. The tarring of main roads was also progressing well, the completion date scheduled for 1980.

At the end of 1979 there were 13 tourist camps in the park, each of which contained varying numbers of huts and rondavels: Skukuza, 200; Pretorius Kop, 148; Satara, 110; Olifants, 103; Lower Sabi, 102; Shingwidzi, 95; Letaba, 93; Malalane, 35; Punda Malia, 26; Crocodile Bridge, 20; Orpen, 12; Balule, four; and Nwanedzi, one. Restaurants and trading stores in all the main camps had reached a very high standard with a trading turnover of R2 500 000. The byproducts depot, in the interval 1972 to 1978, sold products worth R840 200, while in that year, 372 988 tourists visited the park. The most recent aerial census of larger wild animals revealed the population figures of impala as being 162 000; buffalo 27 977; zebra 16 328; wildebeest 4 569; elephant 7 715; kudu 2 126; giraffe 2 124; warthog 4 500-plus; waterbuck 3 300; hippo 2 039; lion 1 300; sable antelope 1 320; reedbuck 1 000-plus; leopard 900-plus; tsessebe 622; eland 286; wild dog 350; roan antelope 286; cheetah 250 – a total of 243 817 of the larger game animals.

The Kruger National Park of today, 1 948 528 ha in extent, differs considerably from the vision cherished by Stevenson-Hamilton, but this was largely inevitable. Relentless pressure from the public has resulted in the development of a tourist resort and vacation area in the setting of a park. Tourist facilities are of a high standard with accommodation ranging from camping grounds to luxury chalets. Restaurants and shops are well run and stocked with a great variety of goods. Tarmac roads make the whole park accessible in all seasons.

With more humans visiting the park in the course of a year than there are wild animal inhabitants, it is difficult for the average tourist, who undoubtedly experiences a great deal of pleasure there, to assess the park according to its original intent; that it be a sanctuary of the wild, where mammals, birds, insects, reptiles and plant life would be left undisturbed to pursue their own destiny in complete contrast to the developments and onslaught of man on nature outside. This is not the case today, however. The park is, in fact intensely managed, with controls imposed on most things, including vegetation – culling extends even to trees, specifically mopane.

Over-management has, at times, had unfortunate effects, including a drastic reduction in the population of blue wildebeest and zebra. The byproducts depot in Skukuza represents a substantial profitmaking vested interest which needs to be regularly supplied with raw materials – such raw materials can only be carcasses.

The question of culling is delicate and controversial. If it has to be carried out, the decisions should be made known to the public, with reasons accessible to all. For it is the public who own the Kruger National Park,not the officials, the Board, or any single poohbah, private club, party or society. The public are entitled to ask questions, to argue, and to secure valid proof that the park, in fact, cannot carry more wildlife than it does, and that man with his rifle, box of matches and poison is, in fact, better qualified to manage the wilderness than nature itself.

The northern part of the park has been badly disfigured by the construction of pylons carrying high-tension cables from the Cabora Bassa hydro-electric station in Moçambique. Electrical engineers and post office telecommunications technicians are notorious for ruining the landscape by insensitive planning, callously justified solely by mechanical convenience and so-called 'national need'. An even worse threat to this area is the fact that prospectors from the Iron and Steel Corporation have found deposits of coking coal in the area. Railways, slag heaps, mining townships, complete with amenities such as drive-ins, supermarkets, and assorted hideosities are on the drawing boards for this piece of wilderness. Very sharp watch has to be kept on the 'lunatechs' and 'idiotechs' (lunatic and idiot technicians) – the organisational men, chartered accountants and graduate masters of business administration – lest they destroy with glibly vociferous scientific persuasions, the entire concept of a national park, carve it into a moneymaking area, and perfectly fulfill Stevenson-Hamilton's most pessimistic vision. Perhaps one or two elderly lions will be left, chained to stakes near the roads, trained to occasionally snarl at tourists in exchange for being pelted with an empty beer can.

A visit to the Kruger National Park, notwithstanding the problems of the place, is an extraordinary experience. With the bulk of the park open throughout the year it is possible for the tourist to see the wonderful changes of vegetation from season to season; the migratory birds that come and go; the periods of love and courtship between animals with innumerable duels in the sun. During spring and early summer when the birds are nesting, baby elephants stumble around on rubbery legs; zebra foals are so dainty as to be unreal; little giraffes stretch their necks even further to take a snack; impala fawns gambol about their graceful parents.

Numbi Gate is the principal entrance to the park through which 58 per cent of all visitors pass. It lies 8 km from the main north-south tarmac road of the Eastern Transvaal linking Nelspruit to the north across the Eastern Transvaal lowveld. An unforgettable travel experience is provided by journeying one way through the full length of the Kruger National Park and returning along the scenic drive of the Eastern Transvaal road.

The Pretorius Kop camp is situated 9 km from Numbi Gate. The road passes through the ridge of rocky hillocks which, in previous years, represented welcome landmarks to the transport riders bringing wagons through the tsetse areas of the lowlands. Shabeni is the imposing height to the north of the road. To the south looms the rather insignificant hillock of Pretorius Kop. By the roadside may be seen the restored grave of the hunter, said to have been the original Pretorius, who had the misfortune of dying there.

In summer this area is normally luxuriantly grassed and the tall forest trees beautifully green. Game animals are far more numerous in summer than in winter, but throughout the year there is always something interesting to be spotted in the bush. The reintroduced rhino population is largely concentrated in this area while sable antelope may often be seen. Trees are particularly impressive and in spring the forest is adorned with the blossoms of species such as the white pear tree which produces masses of white flowers. Acacias scent the air with the sweet perfume of their yellow or white blossoms, and the camp of Pretorius Kop is notable for its spectacular red-flowering kaffirboom trees (*Erythrina* species) in spring.

The camp itself, the second largest in the park, has excellent facilities and is pleasant, relaxed and informal. A swimming pool provides a very welcome asset during the warm summer months. The caravan park, as with most others in the Kruger Park, has been tacked on to the bungalow accommodation in recent years as an afterthought since caravanning increased in popularity. Facilities are shared with the bungalows but in time the park will no doubt develop separate caravan parks on level, shady ground.

The Pretorius Kop area has always been extremely popular with tourists, with several drives – short and long – radiating from it. A perceptible atmosphere of the pioneer days lingers about the place.

The main tarmac road, known as Naphe road (from Naphi hill) leads eastwards from Pretorius Kop to Skukuza, 47 km away. The gravel Hippo Pools road and the parallel Doispanne road, provides an alternate 61-km drive to Skukuza, revealing many pleasant views of the Sabi River, its hippos and riverside forests. The Doispanne road is said to have received its name from a game guard nicknamed 'Dustpan', who was once stationed in those parts. Near the junction of the Doispanne and Hippo Pools roads, a short turnoff leads westwards to a few mounds covered in bush – all that remains of the buildings where the safari trader, João Albasini, had his depot. This turnoff is closed to the public.

The most interesting of all the roads radiating from Pretorius Kop is the original transport trail which leads south-eastwards and is known as the Voortrekker road. Marked with stone beacons in memory of Jock, the hero of the most famous dog story every written, *Jock of the Bushveld*, it passes on the way many well-known landmarks of the transport days, including (at 14 km) Ship Mountain, a rocky hillock which resembles the battered hull of a ship which had the misfortune (during the Stone Age perhaps?) of turning turtle. Most of the game animals of the park may be seen along this road, especially numerous giraffe. Klipspringer and sable antelope are also always present.

After 40 km the old transport road (now well surfaced with gravel) joins the road from Skukuza to Malalane. Turning southwards along the road, the tourist reaches after 19 km, the pretty little camp and entrance gate known as *Malalane*, from the lala palms which flourish in those parts. The camp is notable for its bougainvillaea and spring flowers. The Crocodile River, the southern boundary of the park, flows near by the camp. There is an interesting 16-km drive up the left bank of this river to the western boundary of the park, an area to which wild dogs seem partial.

Retracing the route for 11 km on the Skukuza road, a turnoff is reached which leads eastwards for 43 km to Crocodile Bridge. Buffalo, impala, elephant and kudu are generally seen along this road and the trees such as fine canopied acacias are handsome. The ground is carpeted with the sweet grazing beloved by most herbivorous animals. Towards the end of the drive there is a turnoff stretching for 3 km to a viewsite overlooking the Crocodile River.

where hippos laze in a pool and very faded Bushman paintings may be seen in a rock shelter covered with flowering aloes in June.

Crocodile Bridge is a small but very pleasant camp situated on the banks of the river known to the Swazi as the *Mgwenya* (crocodile). The railway bridge of the now disused Selati Line which runs through the park, crosses the river at this point and there is also a low-level bridge for motor vehicles. It is the third most popular entrance gate to the park through which 10,8 per cent of visitors pass. Facilities include a small store, some neat bungalows and a pleasant caravan park. The area has always been a great resort of buffalo, while the sweet grass on the flats beneath the Lubombo range attracts herds of zebra and wildebeest. Kudu, waterbuck and impala are also very fond of the area.

From Crocodile Bridge the main tarmac arterial road leads northwards through an interesting landscape of flat parkland, with many fine trees and well populated with game. At 13 km the road reaches a gravel turnoff known as the Randspruit road which provides an alternate way to Skukuza. At the turnoff point a stand of old bluegum trees marks the site of a former trading station run by a Greek by the name of Sardelli. Just beyond the turnoff, at the stream named after the petty chief Gomondwane, the tarmac road passes a small memorial to the Dutch exploration party which, in 1725, before being driven back, reached this point after journeying from the little fort at the bay of Lourenço Marques.

After 22 km (35 km from Crocodile Bridge) the tarmac road enters the camp of Lower Sabie, one of the larger camps in the park, where there is a fine restaurant and store and the facilities are excellent. Many of the bungalows and huts overlook the Sabi River and since the camp is situated in some of the best game country in the park (lion are especially numerous) it is particularly popular with visitors from overseas. Without being picturesque, the camp is a pleasant and convenient centre from which to explore several very interesting drives.

From Lower Sabie the main tarmac road continues up the right bank of the Sabi River in one of the most rewarding drives in the entire park. The riverine trees are imposing and the luxuriant, sweet grazing and perennial water attracts considerable numbers of wild animals, making the area popular with many tourists. Impala are particularly partial to this area where warmth, food and water is available. Since they, in their turn, constitute 25,5 per cent of food for lions (with zebra 17,6 per cent; wildebeest 16,6 per cent; and buffalo 14,8 per cent as an alternate choice of menu!) it follows that the area is well populated with predators of all species. Bushbuck, waterbuck and kudu are also very partial to the thickets on the banks of the Sabi, while hippos and crocodiles are common in the river itself.

At 43 km from the Lower Sabie camp, the tarmac road reaches Skukuza, the administrative centre and largest camp in the park. Built in a pleasant situation on the banks of the Sabi River, Skukuza has had the misfortune of 'just growing' (like the famous Topsy) into a gangling, unplanned array of tourist accommodation, a restaurant, shop, post office, open-air cinema, museum and the Stevenson-Hamilton Memorial Library, built in 1960 by the Wild Life Protection Society. Staff are accommodated in 125 houses; there is a school, clinic, club, staff golf course and some other sports facilities. Skukuza is actually a growing village, which, certain field staff have suggested with sardonic humour, should be deproclaimed, excised from the park, fenced off, given municipal status and its colony of officials required to pay normal tourist admission fees to see the wild animals.

Skukuza was in previous years renowned for its hyenas. Vast colonies lived around the camp feeding on garbage and tourist handouts, sleeping and breeding in such places as stormwater drains. At night they sounded like a craze of lunatics at their annual picnic benefit for which type of jollification Skukuza was certainly a world winner. The hyenas roamed around the camp freely, contributing to visitors memories of night sounds and sights. Unfortunately the inevitable happened. In 1966 two tourists in Olifants rest camp were severely bitten by hyenas and this necessitated the erection of game-proof fences around all camps. The hyena population of Skukuza was banned, purged and packed off to the graveyard. The nights are now dull, respectable and silent, which is a pity. Every tourist longs at night to hear the voice of Africa – the roar of a lion, the sound of drums, or the lunatic cackle of a hyena. Hyenas make a great variety of sounds, but the unforgettable giggle (really a sound of excitement and rage) is something to hear. Any management with imagination would leave a garbage pile within earshot of each tourist camp.

A tarmac road 12 km long connects Skukuza to the Paul Kruger Gate, opened on 21 March 1973, which provides a convenient entrance and exit for officials and tourists.

The main arterial tarmac road leaves Skukuza, crosses the Sabi River and stretches north-eastwards into the central portion of the park, an area of sweet grazing where the highest density of game animals live. Impala, giraffe, kudu, wildebeest and zebra frequent this area throughout the year. After 11 km a tarmac turnoff south links up with the Lower Sabie road, and the Salitje gravel road leading eastwards into fine game country.

At 19 km the main tarmac road reaches a gravel turnoff north which traverses excellent game country, passing the picnic sites of Hlangulene (28 km ), Mzanzene (57 km) and at 68 km, joining the road linking Orpen Gate to Satara. Just beyond this gravel turnoff there are tablets set into a large granite boulder commemorating the proclamation in 1898 of the original Sabi Game Reserve, and then the Kruger National Park in 1926. The memorial was unveiled in September 1933 by Mrs Stevenson-Hamilton and is today a picnic spot.

Fourteen kilometres beyond this memorial (33 km from Skukuza) the tarmac road reaches the picnic spot and tearoom of Tshokwane, famous for its perky population of those comic characters of the bird community, the hornbills, and the lovely blue-coloured glossy starlings. The Shangane name for these cheeky little birds is *Makwezi* and it compares them to the colour of a shooting star. As far as wild animals are concerned, this is one of the most lively areas in the entire park. It is here that game capturing operations and corrals are centred. Interesting drives along gravel roads branch out in several directions: south to join the Salitje road; west on the Hutomi road and east to the finely situated Eileen Orpen Dam built in 1969, where there is a lookout allowing visitors the chance of watching the wild animals.

Beyond the dam, the gravel road continues north for 19 km and then joins the Louis Trichardt road. On the way it is worthwhile taking a short turnoff east which climbs to the summit of the flat-topped hill known as Nwamuriwa, from where there is a tremendous view over the vast savanna plains of the park, with Tshokwane clearly visible in the middle distance. Beyond this turnoff, the road passes the Lindanda Memorial erected on the site of Harry Wolhuter's celebrated adventure with the lions.

The main tarmac road, meanwhile, continues its interesting journey northwards. After 15 km it reaches a memorial to the Voortrekker, Louis Trichardt, erected at the spot where his pioneer trail crosses the modern road. This old trail has been developed into a good gravel road for tourists. To the west it winds for 19 km through a parkland of big game, frequented by giraffe, impala, wildebeest and zebra. It then joins the road leading through Hlangulene picnic site to the Orpen-Satara road. To the east, the Louis Trichardt road stretches for 13 km to join the Lindanda road from Tshokwane.

Keeping close to the frontier line with Moçambique, the gravel road swings northwards and continues for a further 24 km to reach a pleasant picnic site situated in the shade of trees on the banks of the Nwanedzi River. From there the road continues across a grassy savanna (where steenbok are particularly common) until, after a further 47 km, it reaches a junction. Continuing north for 13 km, the road terminates at the picnic place enhanced by an impressive view of the gorge carved out by the Olifants River as it penetrates the Lubombo range. Back at the junction, the turn westwards also leads for 13 km and then reaches a causeway across the Olifants River at the hippo pools and bungalows of the small Balule rest camp. Across the river, the traveller has the choice of swinging west to join the main tarmac road of the park or turning north-eastwards and driving for 10 km through good game country before reaching the spectacularly situated Olifants camp.

The main tarmac road, meanwhile, beyond the crossing with the Louis Trichardt road, continues northwards across a vast, grassy, level parkland. Elephant, giraffe, waterbuck, zebra, wildebeest, impala, buffalo and lion are often seen. At 35 km from the Louis Trichardt road (50 km from Tshokwane), the road reaches the large modern camp of Satara, with little claim to atmosphere or beauty, but possessing a fine restaurant and shop. However, it does lie in the centre of some of the best game viewing country in the park and as such it is a convenience. The presence of lion and hyena often enliven the nights.

From Satara a gravel road leads westwards to the Orpen Gate through a lovely parkland of bush-willow and acacia trees, where a great variety of game may be seen. After 6 km the road reaches a turnoff to the picnic site on the river known as the *Timbavati* on account of the numerous bushbuck living in the splendid riverine forest. The Timbavati River is essentially a series of pools linked together by a surface flow brought on only during the rainy season. Nevertheless, the pools are permanent and provide water for one of the largest concentrations of game in the park. From the picnic spot a gravel road continues northwards for 37 km along the right bank of the river and then rejoins the Satara-Orpen road. Both of these rivierside drives are very worthwhile.

The road from Satara to Orpen, after the turnoff to Timbavati at 6 km, leads westwards for a further 11 km, reaching the road which turns up the right bank of the river, and then carries on southwards to eventually enter Skukuza. The Orpen-Satara road continues from this crossroads for a further 26 km to reach the entrance gate of Orpen, 43 km from Satara. The drive is splendid throughout, revealing views of elephant, zebra, wildebeest, giraffe, lion and wild dog.

Orpen is a very pleasant little rest camp with a small shop. Near by on the banks of the Timbavati River is the separate (* ® ) caravan park of Maroela, a very attractive little place where caravanners can be close to nature in the form of lion, leopard, elephant and other game who frequently wander around the outskirts (and inskirts!).

From Satara camp, the main tarmac road continues northwards across the grassy plain populated with herds of impala, wildebeest and zebra, and many giraffe, waterbuck, and kudu. Crossing the Olifants River by means of the high-level bridge opened in 1972, the road skirts the left bank of the river for a few kilometres and then, 46 km from Satara, reaches the tarmac turnoff to the camp of Olifants 11 km away.

Olifants, perched on top of a high cliff overlooking the Olifants River is the most spectacularly situated camp in the park. Opened on 3 June 1960 it is also modern in its design and has a fine restaurant, shop and observation point which looks out on a superb and as wild a piece of Africa as the heart could desire. Game watching could not be easier: from a comfortable seat, or the window of a bungalow, an eagle's-eye view may be had of many kilometres of river, lined with handsome trees and the resort of elephant and many different antelope. Sunsets and dawns are glorious.

From the Olifants camp an interesting drive may be followed for 48 km along a gravel road up the right bank of the Letaba River to Letaba camp, with the Engelhard Dam spread out in a spacious sheet of water where it holds back the river. Elephant, bushbuck, buffalo and waterbuck frequent the verges of the river.

The main tarmac road, after the turnoff to Olifants camp, continues north for 19 km (65 km from Satara), reaching what is considered by many to be the prettiest camp in the Kruger National Park. Letaba camp is shaded by beautiful trees on the high right bank of the Letaba River. A fine restaurant and store provide amenities, while the bungalows are informally arranged around a central garden brimming with flowers and interesting plants. Monkeys play incessantly in the trees, elephant feed in the reeds and wander around outside the camp; leopard have always been common, and hippos and crocodiles find a home in the river. Bird life is especially rich. The atmosphere is redolent of Africa, of big game, interesting characters and old adventures.

Several worthwhile drives radiate from Letaba. A gravel road leads westwards for 50 km and a tarmac road south-westwards for 48 km, both of them ending at Phalaborwa Gate, opened in 1961 to replace the old Malapene Gate and nowadays the second most frequented entrance to the park, with 16,6 per cent of all visitors passing through it. The border area there is watched over by a ranger stationed at *Mahlangeni* (the place of reeds).

The main tarmac road continues northwards from Letaba. Crossing the river, it enters a more arid area dominated by mopane trees, a favourite haunt of elephant, eland, roan and tsessebe. After 39 km the road reaches the picnic and resting place named Shawo. After stretching his legs at this point, the traveller has a choice of three roads all leading northwards and ending at Shingwidzi camp. Via the main road, the journey is 63 km from Shawo past the ranger post of Tsende. The more easterly road is 69 km long and closely follows the frontier of Moçambique. Game animals are not numerous in this arid, hot area of vast mopane wood-land, where baobab trees dominate the landscape.

Shingwidzi camp is a pleasantly informal place notable for its trees, brilliantly flowering impala lilies *(Adenium multiflorum),* bougainvillaea and bird life. There is a good restaurant and store, and the place is tinged with an atmosphere of the wilderness. Leopards stalk baboons through the tall trees; monkeys and the loveliest of birds move through the branches; elephant, impala, waterbuck, buffalo, kudu, zebra and wildebeest wander along the banks of the Shingwidzi River. A fine 56-km drive leads to the Tshange lookout point where an immense view may be had over the great mopane parklands, stretching westwards to the ranger post named after the old chief Shangoni.

The Shingwidzi area straddles the Tropic of Capricorn. North of the Olifants River, the soil rests on a limestone base, as opposed to the granite of the south. The grazing is good, but lack of dependable surface water has inhibited any dense population of wild animals. The climate is warm to hot and the tourist finds himself in a world which differs from the other parts of the park.

The main road travels north-westwards across a level plain of grass and mopane trees. After 32 km the road reaches the picnic and resting place of Babalala, built around a large wild fig tree. A further 16 km (48 km from Shingwidzi) takes the road to a parting of the ways. Continuing northwards the right-hand branch of the road leads for 35 km to the banks of the Luvuvhu River. The left-hand road swings north-westwards and after 21 km reaches the camp of Punda Malia, with the Punda Malia Gate 8 km to the west.

Punda Malia is picturesquely (if rather awkwardly) situated on the steep slopes of a hill. Although one of the older camps, it is comfortable, informal and pleasant, and has a small restaurant and shop.

The story has already been told of Khama the rainmaker who practised on the nearby hill of Gumbandevu. About 48 km north of the camp, overlooking the Luvuvhu River, lies another hill with a notable history. On this hill a group of early people, the Lembethu, had built a stronghold and stone-walled settlement. Their local chief, whose dynastic title was Makahane, was the last of his line to rule on the hill and had a reputation for insanity and cruelty. Many atrocities were committed on this hilltop with people being thrown over the cliffs. Today, the stone ruins seem to abound with ghosts (especially at night).

Makahane's cruelty was eventually his undoing. The Paramount Chief received so many complaints that he sent his son (Makahane's brother) to kill the madman. In a dance of welcome to his brother, Makahane was stabbed to death. He lies buried in front of his throne, a seat built into one of the stone walls. The hilltop was afterwards abandoned and the old settlement now forms an interesting ruin.

The whole area north of Punda Malia is a densely forested and most rugged extent of sandveld. The Luvuvhu River is a handsome stream, typically African – sulky, erratic and enigmatic. Some large crocodiles (uncommonly fat) live in its pools, hippos are numerous and elephant and buffalo like the area. Baobab, seringa, ironwood, mahogany, ebony and

677

sycamore fig trees cover a landscape of deep valleys and red-coloured mountains. In the heart of this lovely wilderness, little trodden by man, is a touch of humour. Surrounded by huge sycamore fig trees lies a waterhole the name of which is *Siyafa* (we are dying). It refers to one of the famous old-timers of the park – the well-digger, dam maker, ranger and hard case, Bill Lamont – who, because he persisted in working through the heat of the day, was given this name by his workers as they claimed they were all dying.

Punda Malia, as previously mentioned, was built as a ranger post to block the famous Ivory Trail. Following this romantic old trail of poachers and blackbirders, the tourist makes a romantic journey to the northern end of the park. The road leads north-westwards for the first 17 km past the slopes of Gumbandevu and then joins the direct road coming up from Shingwidzi. Near the junction is a short loop road passing the waterhole known to the Africans as *Shikuwa* (the fig tree) but to Europeans as *Kloppersfontein* after Hans Kloppers, a hunter who often camped there.

The road now swings northwards and leads through an undulating wilderness of mopane and baobab trees. A famous landmark on the way is Baobab Hill, on top of which a solitary baobab stands sentinel. On its western side could be found drinking water, on its eastern side a camping site often used by the great poacher *Bvekenya*. The road continues until 42 km from Punda Malia, it reaches the deep riverine forests on the banks of the Luvuvhu.

From here a side road turns west up the river for 3 km to a hippo pool, revealing a fine view of the tree-girt river and a glimpse of the Valley of Giants, where a whole community of baobab trees flourish like the living relics of a lost world.

Turning east, the main road continues down the southern bank of the Luvuvhu past the turnoff leading to the old ford across the river (now an army bridge, built in 1974) and for a further 13 km through the riverside forest of fever trees and sycamore figs.

Elephant, the lovely nyala, bushbuck, impala, zebra, hippos, crocodiles and pythons flourish in this tropical setting. A fine picnic and resting place is situated beside the river and there is a turnoff along which the actual junction of the Luvuvhu with the Limpopo River may be viewed. The point of land projecting between the two converging rivers was originally the notorious Crooks Corner. The whole area, once so celebrated for its tough characters and their adventures, is now part of the park.

The road being followed passes through a magnificent forest of fever trees and then ends at the police border post of Pafuri, where the genial Harold Mockford for many years managed the depot of the Witwatersrand Native Labour Association (Wenela). From this oasis in the wilderness, a sandy road enters Moçambique, while another road returns in a westerly direction and after 11 km joins the main road already followed from Punda Malia and throughout the park. In this most pleasant place then, the journey regrettably ends, leaving with the traveller a longing to return, to once again feed the cheeky glossy starlings; to breathe in the air, touched perhaps with the earthy smell of newly cut potatoes from the fruits of the *Phyllanthus* shrubs; to meet interesting people; to feel close to nature for just a little while before civilisation envelops him once more in its depressing rush.

The Kruger National Park is open throughout the year. Travel in the park is limited to daylight hours and the rules thereafter are very simple: stay in your car, keep to the road and observe speed restrictions (50 km depending on the road).

## Accommodation
Family cottages with kitchenette (4 persons), R27 D.
Huts with shower and toilet (2 persons) R15 D.
Ordinary huts (2 persons), R10 D. In Nwanedzi, there is one hut for 10 people, R50 D.

## Caravans and camping
Caravans R4 D up to 4 people, 50c each additional person.

Chapter Thirty-four

# THE WESTERN TRANSVAAL

Several roads penetrate the seemingly endless plains of the Western Transvaal, providing travellers with the chance to explore a portion of Southern Africa which contains a surprising number of scenic wonders both natural and unnatural.

From Krugersdorp on the edge of the Witwatersrand, 32 km from Johannesburg, the main tarmac road to Mafeking leads westwards past many smallholdings and nurseries. After 5,5 km a turnoff to the Krugersdorp Game reserve (page 587) is reached, a very worthwhile project whereby a portion of the Witwatersrand has been preserved as it was before the advent of man.

The road loses altitude as it continues westwards, passing the rural area of Tarlton (11,5 km from Krugersdorp) and, at 21,5 km, the Orient Hills where fresh trout are sold from wayside stalls. At 29 km the road reaches the village of . . .

## MAGALIESBURG

Magali was chief of the Po tribe who lived in the area of the village and the handsome mountain ridge known as the *Magaliesberg*. Tobacco and citrus are produced here and the warm climate and scenic beauty has resulted in the establishment of several holiday resorts much frequented by people seeking an escape from the cold winters of the Witwatersrand. A branch railway connects Magaliesburg to Pretoria and along this line runs what is known as the Potato Express, a mixed train drawn by a puffer, making a daily return journey which provides train lovers with a pleasant outing.

### Accommodation
* Happy Valley Hotel, 46 rooms, all with baths. R8,50 B/B. Phone 1.
* Magaliesburg Hotel, 10 rooms, 5 with baths. R9,32 B/B. Phone 26.

## THE MAGALIESBERG

Consisting of a flat-topped ridge of quartzite and red-coloured sediments of the Transvaal System, the Magaliesberg looms up like a wall of rock 120 km long, its highest point 1 852 m above sea level. The slopes and summit are richly wooded and numerous streams have their source on the ridge. In former years this area was renowned for big game, including elephant.

The ledges on the precipice faces have always provided good roosts for vultures and about 250 breeding pairs of the species *Gyps coprotheres* have their nests there. Thermal air currents rising from the heated rocks of the mountain facilitate the lazy, spiralling flight of vultures who may usually be seen circling the sky. An amusing spectacle occurs when gliders are flown in the area. The vultures seem to regard them as bigger birds and fly along with the gliders, turning and manoeuvring in perfect unison.

From the village of Magaliesburg, a tarmac road branches off from the main Johannesburg-Mafeking road, and leading into the foothills of the Magaliesberg, eventually reaches Rustenburg. This road provides access to the various holiday resorts in the area.

From Magaliesburg the road follows a green and most pleasant valley. By the shady wayside are situated nurseries and resorts such as the Wicker Tea Garden and Lovers Rock Pleasure Resort; Boys Town run by the Roman Catholic Church; and Camp Caplan of the United Progressive Jewish Congregation.

## Caravans and camping
★® Lovers Rock Pleasure Resort, 150 sites. R3 D plus 30c D per person.

After 7,5 km a turnoff leads to the hamlet of Hekpoort and from there to Pretoria or, by means of a turnoff right, through the actual *Hekpoort* (passage of the gateway). This is a fine natural pass, by means of which the road climbs the Witwatersrand, passing the turnoff to the Sterkfontein Caves and then continuing to Krugersdorp. The distance is a total of 44 km from the Magaliesburg-Rustenburg road which meanwhile proceeds westwards along the length of the Magaliesberg, passing many farms where citrus, subtropical fruit, flowers and vegetables are produced. After 8 km from the turnoff to Hekpoort, the road reaches the hamlet of Doornkloof, from where a gravel road leads northwards to climb the Magaliesberg by means of Breedtsnek. This drive is very worthwhile, revealing grand views and interesting scenery.

After 13 km of climbing this well-maintained gravel road, a turnoff stretches for 4,5 km to the Utopia Holiday Resort overlooking the dam of Buffelspoort, a fine area for swimming and general sporting activities. Opposite the turnoff to this resort, there is another turnoff leading for 3,5 km to the Sparkling Waters Hotel, beyond which the road continues for 13 km, passing *Parrots Paradise* where John Brown Rough founded his exotic parrot-breeding farm in 1968. After descending a handsome pass down the cliffs of the Magaliesberg, the road joins the main tarmac road to Rustenburg.

## Accommodation
★★® Sparkling Waters Hotel, 40 rooms, all with baths. R13 – R15 D/B/B. Phone Rustenburg 9-3240.
★Utopia Holiday Resort, 110 chalets. R16,21 D.

From Doornkloof, where the road turns off to the top of the Magaliesberg, the main tarmac road continues westwards along the mountain wall. Peach orchards, maize fields and shady indigenous trees line the route. From here the Magaliesberg is revealed at its best. In Retief's Kloof, a favourite resort for nature lovers and mountaineers, sequences have been shot for feature films on themes such as the Voortrekkers descending the Drakensberg. The streams are crystal clear and there are fine waterfalls and deep pools. Adding to the spectacle is the Olifantsnek Dam, built in 1928 where the Hex River finds a way through the mountain wall by means of a narrow pass. The concrete wall of the dam – 24 m high and 134 m long – impounds enough water to irrigate 2 428 ha of farmland where citrus, tobacco and other crops are cultivated on the northern side of the range.

## Accommodation
★ Olifantsnek Hotel, 31 rooms, all with baths. R10 B/B. Phone 9-2208.

The road skirts the verges of the lake, revealing fine views of the mountains across the water. Elephants found their way through this pass in former years and the modern road, following their old trail, emerges without difficulty on the northern side on to the vast plains of the Northern Transvaal bushveld.

Just below the pass, 33 km from Doornkloof, the road passes the citrus farm of *Boschfontein,* once the home of George Rex, grandson of the founder of Knysna, who settled there to hunt and farm. The modern resort of Hunters Rest now stands amongst the citrus groves.

**Accommodation**
★★® Hunters Rest Hotel, 83 rooms, all with baths. R15,50 B/B. Phone Rustenburg 9-2140.

**Caravans and camping**
★★® Caravan park (at above hotel), 40 sites. R5 D. 15 cottages, 61 rooms, R16,50 D.

From Hunters Rest the tarmac road continues westwards through a veritable garden of indigenous trees, orchards, tobacco fields and citrus groves. Wayside stalls offer a variety of fruits, honey, nuts and other produce for sale. After 1,5 km the road passes a turnoff which joins the Rustenburg-Pretoria road and at 4,5 km a turnoff leading to Kroondal. The road proceeds past the Waterkloof Holiday Resort with its bungalows and restaurant and, at 8 km, the Tambuti Inn, on the outskirts of the town of Rustenburg, reached 14 km from Hunters Rest.

# RUSTENBURG

The rapidly growing town of Rustenburg lies in a real garden setting of luxuriant vegetation and warmth backed by the superb Magaliesberg range, whose forest-covered slopes and ravines give rise to hiking trails and many pleasant recreational possibilities. Jacaranda and poinciana trees enhance the streets with their shade and flowers. Gardens are notable for hibiscus, frangipani, poinsettias and bougainvillaea of many different colours.

The town was founded in April 1851, when a church was established there and a town laid out in September of the same year. The Reverend D.E. Faure named the place *Rustenburg* (town of rest) after Rustenburg in the Cape.

For some years the town was a frontier post, a resort of hunters, explorers and prospectors who used it as their base for ventures into the far interior, the Kalahari and the world of trees and granite hills north of the Limpopo River. Men such as Henry Hartley the hunter and Karl Mauch the geologist, equipped their expeditions from the trading stores of Rustenburg. Paul Kruger grew up in the area on the farm *Buffelsfontein,* owned by his father, Casper Kruger and in 1863, at the age of 16, acquired a farm of his own called *Boekenhoutfontein*. This farm, north-west of Rustenburg, now contains a museum, the earliest surviving pioneer cottage (built in 1841) and the Kruger homestead built in the 1870s. In front of the civic centre in Rustenburg stands a fine bronze of President Kruger, the work of the French sculptor Jean Jaques Achard.

Rustenburg was the scene of several important events in the history of the South African Republic. It was there, on 16 March 1852, that a momentous meeting ended the almost fatal rivalry of the two great Voortrekker leaders, Andries Hendrik Potgieter and Andries Pretorius, ushering in a period of peace in the stormy story of the Transvaal by the acceptance of the Sand River Convention with the British. The reunion between the two rivals took place in the grounds of the Hervormde Kerk. The cornerstone of the original church on this square has been preserved.

In Kerk Street stands a marble replica of the stump of the original syringa tree under which the Reformed Church was founded in 1859 as a separate body from the Dutch Reformed Church.

During the Anglo-Transvaal War of 1881, a small British garrison was besieged in the town but survived without any major attack or casualty. Several small British forts were built on the overlooking hills during the Anglo-Boer War.

Rustenburg became a municipality in April 1918 and has a population of 32 919. It is the centre of a magnificent farming area, the home of the Magaliesberg Co-operative Tobacco Growers Association, the Rustenburg Co-operative Packhouse Company Ltd, where Outspan oranges are packed, the United Tobacco Co. with its large factory and the Tobacco Research Institute.

Also the centre for a considerable mining industry, the two largest platinum mines in the world are situated on the outskirts of Rustenburg. The workings of Rustenburg Platinum Mines Ltd comprise the world's largest underground mining operation. The source of platinum is the Merensky Reef, discovered in 1924 in the Lydenburg district by A.F. Lombard. It was traced and proved into the Rustenburg and other areas of the Transvaal by the geologist Hans Merensky.

The town is situated on the verge of the remarkable geological feature known as the Bushveld Igneous Complex, notable for its high mineralisation. Asbestos, chrome, granite, lead, marble, slate and tin are mined in the district.

South-west of the town lies the Rustenburg Nature Reserve, an area of 2 898 ha proclaimed a nature reserve in 1967 and situated on the summit and northern slopes of the Magaliesberg. The vegetation on the summit, 400 m above the level of the plain, is extremely varied and the views are superb. The Waterkloof River also has its source here and flows through a large reed swamp in a basin contained between two arms of the Magaliesberg. Game animals such as sable, waterbuck, zebra, kudu, red hartebeest, oribi, klipspringer, mountain reedbuck, grey duiker, and reedbuck thrive in the area as do about 140 species of birds. Leopard, caracal, aardwolf, black-backed jackal and the rare brown hyena hunt in the area. Oddly shaped boulders combine with rich vegetation to form what appears to be a huge rock garden. Trees such as syringa and boekenhout and several acacia species are numerous. A two-day hiking trail in the reserve may be followed and there is a place at which to stop overnight.

Overlooking the town is the small Kwaggapan Reserve with its stone lookout tower from where Rustenburg and its surroundings may be viewed. Giraffe, kudu and other antelope live in the reserve. The Paul Budenstein Park contains aviaries and a collection of bronze animals, part of which is the bronze *Punt in die Wind,* by Coert Steynberg.

The Nederduitsch-Gereformeerde Kerk, built in 1850, is a national monument. During the Anglo-Boer War it was transformed into a hospital by the British. Six of the British soldiers who died here were recipients of the Victoria Cross and the graves of five of them lie next to the rebuilt Anglican Church in the small military cemetery. This pretty little church, built in 1811, is also a national monument. It was rebuilt on its present site in Van Staden Street in 1907 when township development threatened its original position.

Rustenburg Kloof in the Magaliesberg has been developed by the municipality into a fine recreational area with places for swimming, picnic sites, hiking trails, bungalows, caravan and camping sites. There are several excellent privately run resorts in this amiable setting of green trees, blue skies and red-coloured mountains. From the Ananda Hotel there are two excellent hiking trails which lead into the Magaliesberg.

## Accommodation

★® Ananda Holiday Resort, 47 rooms, all with baths. R12 B/B. Phone 2-2332.
★★ Rustenburg Hotel, 50 rooms, all with baths. R11 B/B. Phone 2-2160.
★★® Safari Hotel, 64 rooms, all with baths. R12,50 B/B. Phone 2-2234.
★ Tambuti Inn, 52 rooms, all with baths. R10 B/B. Phone 9-2361.
★ Tourist Hotel, 14 rooms, 5 with baths. R8,50 – R9,50 B/B. Phone 2-2470.
★ Transvaal Hotel, 12 rooms, 2 with baths. R8,50 B/B. Phone 2-2478.

## Caravans and camping

★★★® Ananda Caravan Park, 60 sites. R3,50 D plus 10c D per person.
★★® Rustenburg Kloof Caravan Park, 200 sites. R4 D. 31 cottages and 37 rondawels, R6– R18 D.

# RUSTENBURG TO THE EAST

From Rustenburg the tarmac road to Pretoria stretches eastwards along the northern side of the Magaliesberg, in which verdant area several resorts are situated. The Omaramba Caravan Park lies 4,5 km from Rustenburg, the Bergheim Pleasure Resort 12 km, and near by, the Wigwam Holiday Resort, set in superb grounds and built in a very novel manner. The Rondalia-owned Buffelspoort Holiday Resort is situated at Marikana, 30 km from Rustenburg and 2 km further away, is the Mountain Sanctuary Park. From the Buffelspoort Resort a gravel turnoff leads to the Buffelspoort Dam where the fishing is good, and there are facilities for watersports, and picnic and camping grounds on the lake verges. This gravel road joins the road previously described which climbs the southern side of the Magaliesberg from Doornkloof (page 680).

## Accommodation
★ Marikana Hotel, 7 rooms, 3 with baths. R6,25 – R7,25 D/B/B. Phone Marikana 2.
★ Rondalia-Buffelspoort Hotel, 19 rooms, all with baths. R10 B/B. Phone Pretoria 48-2664.
★★® Wigwam Hotel, 110 rooms, all with baths. R16 – R18 D. Phone Rustenburg 9-2147.

## Caravans and camping
★★ Bergheim Holiday Resort, 80 sites. R4 D plus 20c D per person. 6 rondawels, R7,50 – R12,50 D.
★★ Buffelspoort Holiday Resort, 100 sites. R3,50 D. 140 rondawels, R8,25 D.
★★ Mountain Sanctuary Park, 28 sites. R4 D plus 60c D per person. 6 cottages, R11 – R20 D.
★★ Omaramba Caravan Park, 200 sites. R3 D plus 40c D per person.

# RUSTENBURG TO PILANESBERG

From Rustenburg, the main tarmac road to Swartruggens leaves the town, travelling north-westwards for 6 km and then reaching a tarmac turnoff to Derdepoort and the Pilanesberg. This turnoff passes through the Tswana residential area of Phokeng, largely inhabited by workers of the Bafokeng Platinum Mine, and at 17 km reaches a turnoff to Paul Kruger's old homestead of *Boekenhoutfontein,* now a national monument and museum open Tuesdays to Fridays from 09h00 to 16h00; on Saturdays and Sundays from 10h30 to 17h30. Beyond this turnoff the road continues through a part of *BophuthaTswana* (that which binds the Tswana), the homeland of several of the 59 different Tswana tribes of South Africa.

At 38 km a tarmac turnoff stretches for 9 km to the interesting geological occurrence and recreational area of the . . .

# PILANESBERG

Phalane was a Tswana chief whose followers settled in the area of the subconical volcanic mass of rock (1 682 m high) subsequently named by Europeans the *Pilanesberg.* The Pilanesberg is one of the largest and most interesting examples in the world of alkaline rock. It is 27 km in diameter, almost circular in shape, and looks like a bushy cluster of six rings of high hills composed of volcanic rock and syenites.

In the centre of this rock wilderness, the Southern Sun hotel group have, in co-operation with the BophuthaTswana administration, created a vast resort known as Sun City where practically every known facility for entertainment, gambling, sport and recreation may be found. In the hills around this resort, a wildlife sanctuary has been established and, with its game viewing trails and waterholes, provides a remarkable contrast between primeval nature and the sophisticated glitter of the hotel (a very plush, large-scale cash register of a place!).

Four restaurants provide an interesting range of foods, there is a superb swimming pool and an 18-hole golf course.

## Accommodation

★★★★★® Sun City Hotel, 340 rooms, all with baths. Single rates Sun/Thurs, R26 room only. Fri/Sat, R36 room only. Double rates (per person) Sun/Thurs, R17,50 room only. Fri/Sat, R22,50 room only.
Suites, R50 – R100. Phone 014220 21-000.

The tarmac road from Rustenburg to Swartruggens, after the turnoff to Derdepoort and the Pilanesberg, continues through well-wooded country, gently climbing the eastern slopes of the Magaliesberg. At 8 km there is a turnoff leading to the Ananda Holiday Resort and back to Rustenburg, passing the turnoff to Rustenburg Kloof.

Citrus groves line both sides of the road, bearing their golden fruit around the month of June. Roadside stalls offer fruit and other produce for sale. The famous Magaliesberg vultures circle overhead and the colours of earth, sky and vegetation are vivid. The road descends the northern side of the Magaliesberg on to a great plain, densely covered in low bush. At 21,5 km a turnoff leads to Vlaklaagte and the farm *Shylock* on which stand the ruins of one of the substantial towns of stone huts, canals and passageways built by Tswana people in former years.

Across the Koster River, 32 km from Rustenburg, the road passes the Oom Paul School and then continues westwards until 58 km from Rustenburg, it reaches the town of Swartruggens, where it joins the main tarmac road from the Witwatersrand to Mafeking from which the road to Rustenburg turned off at Magaliesburg.

## MAGALIESBURG TO MAFEKING

From Magaliesburg the main tarmac road proceeds westwards across plains covered in maize fields. Small railway and commercial centres line the route, each with a tall maize silo as their principal landmark. From Derby, 53 km from Magaliesburg, a road leads to some interesting caves 27 km away, on the road to Ventersdorp.

At 69 km from Magaliesburg, the road reaches the town of . . .

## KOSTER

When the railway was opened to Mafeking in 1910, Koster was established as a lowly siding consisting of one tin shanty. The siding lay on the farm *Kleinfontein,* owned by Bastiaan Hendricus Koster, who named the place after himself. It became a village in 1913 and a municipality in 1930 and is now an agricultural, slate and diamond mining centre. Near here, on 11 November 1970, 167 diggers raced to stake their claims in one of the last diamond rushes to take place in South Africa.

The Koster Dam provides recreational opportunities for the inhabitants of the town.

## Accommodation
★ Koster Hotel, 11 rooms, 3 with baths. R7,75 B/B. Phone 9904.

## Caravans and camping
★★ Wonderbaar Rest Camp, 50 sites. R3,50 D.

From Koster the tarmac road continues eastwards for 34 km and at the town of Swartruggens, joins the road previously described which leads from Rustenburg.

# SWARTRUGGENS

Also known as Rodeon, *Swartruggens* (the black ridge) is a rural and railway centre situated at the foot of a low, bush-covered ridge. The town originated in 1907 when the railway line was built from Krugersdorp to Mafeking and Swartruggens station was built on the farm *Brakfontein*. A scattering of stores, a church and school grew up near the station. A township was eventually proclaimed there and given the name of Rodeon.

Accommodation
* Swartruggens Hotel, 10 rooms, 5 with baths. R9,50 – R10,50 B/B. Phone 82.

Caravans and camping
* Municipal caravan park, 50 sites. R1 D. 9 rondawels, R3 D.

From Swartruggens the tarmac road continues westwards over acacia-covered hills and finds its way into the fertile valley of the Groot Marico River where many beautiful lucerne, orange, tobacco and cattle farms flourish in the warm climate and fertile soil. At 29 km from Swartruggens the road passes through the small rural centre of Groot Marico, laid out on the farm *Wonderfontein,* owned by Francois Joubert, and granted its first health committee in 1927. The Marico River, after which the place is named, contributes to the agricultural prosperity of the town and is crossed 1,5 km west of the town. The name of the river is a corrupted form of the Tswana name, *Maligwa* (the erratic river).

Accommodation
* Groot-Marico Hotel, 22 rooms, 12 with baths. R9,50 – R10 B/B. Phone 88.

Thirty-three kilometres from Groot Marico the tarmac road reaches the Klein Marico Poort Dam, built across a passage through a ridge of acacia-covered hills. Three kilometres beyond the dam, the road passes the marked grave of Diederik Coetzee and 3 km further on (39 km from Groot Marico) reaches the town named after his brother-in-law . . .

# ZEERUST

In its early days, *Zeerust* (Coetzee's rest) had the reputation of being wild and woolly and it is still easy to imagine a rugged crowd of hunters and prospectors bound for the far interior, heading down its one main street and enjoying a final fling in the old hostelries. Today it is a pleasant enough little rural town in a green and fertile setting of trees and long grass, backed by a high ridge of hills.
The town originated in 1864 when an itinerant builder named Walter Seymore, was engaged to erect a church and fortification on the farm *Hazenjacht,* owned by Casper Coetzee. Coetzee died before the church was finished but his brother-in-law, Diederik Coetzee, continued the work, laid out a town and named it in memory of old Casper who was buried there. The first erven in the town were sold on 20 March 1867. Zeerust became a municipality on 18 March 1937 and today the population numbers 11 325.
The town is a centre for cattle ranching, sheep, corn, tobacco, fruit and vegetables. A museum, housed in the civic centre, is devoted to local history and is open from 08h00 to 17h00 weekdays.

Accommodation
* Transvaal Hotel, 17 rooms, 11 with baths. R8,11 – R9,41 B/B. Phone 120.

*Overleaf: Deep underground in the Sterkfontein Caves; a wonderful curtain of dripstone close to the subterranean lake with its strange medicinal properties.*

**Caravans and camping**
* Krans Holiday Resort, 19 sites. R3,50 D. 10 rondawels, R7,80 – R8,84 D.

From Zeerust a tarmac road leads north to the centre of Nietverdiend (60 km) and from there for 40 km to the border with Botswana at Kopfontein. The Botswana post is named Tlokweng from where it is 20 km to Gaborone.

From Zeerust, the tarmac road to Mafeking swings south-westwards, passing through the fertile valley of the *Mosega* (the divider) River. After 14 km the road reaches the railway siding of *Sendelingspos* (missionary's post), in the midst of the shallow valley. This fine agricultural area has been amply fertilised by the blood of mankind. In former years it was the home of the Hurutshe tribe who (in the custom of the Tswana-speaking people) erected two substantial towns known as *Tshwenyane* and *Kaditshwene*. These towns consisted of thousands of mud huts, the inhabitants of which prospered on agriculture, mining and working iron and trading. Good fortune, unfortunately, has always attracted envy; the Ndebele, then living near the site of modern Pretoria, started to raid them.

In May 1831, in the midst of an ominously developing situation, two French missionaries, Prosper Lemue and Samuel Rollard, arrived in the area and secured permission from the Hurutshe chief to establish a mission close to the site of the present railway siding of Sendelingspos. In February 1832 the missionaries effected their settlement, building the first European house in the Transvaal, and laying out an irrigated garden. Within a few months however, the Ndebele invaded the area. The missionaries fled to Kuruman for safety and the Hurutshe tribe was practically destroyed. Having overthrown them, the Ndebele settled in the fertile valley of the Mosega.

A second party of missionaries, this time American, arrived and with the permission of Mzilikazi, chief of the Ndebele, rebuilt the former French station at Sendelingspos, settling there in 1836 to commence work among the wild followers of Mzilikazi who lived in the river valley with their great herds of cattle.

Both the Zulu and the Voortrekkers then appeared on the scene. The Ndebele fought the advancing Voortrekkers south of the Vaal River in 1836; were raided by the Zulu in July of that year and, in November, in the 'Nine Days Battle' with the Boers were soundly defeated and driven north on a refugee trail which eventually took them to the highlands north of the Limpopo. In the face of this upheaval, the missionaries fled and all that remains of their venture is the simple railside monument marking the site of their pioneer settlement.

Beyond Sendelingspos the road gradually leads out of the valley into more open, level and lightly bushed country. The hills recede into the east. At 13 km from Sendelingspos (29 km from Zeerust) there is a turnoff north to Ottoshoop and south to Lichtenburg. *Ottoshoop,* named after Cornelius Otto, a former magistrate of Zeerust, is now little more than a railway station but, around 1895, it was the scene of a gold rush after Michael Kelly made a discovery in the vicinity. A proper town was laid out, but unfortunately the rush proved abortive. The tarmac road now traverses a fine open grass- and parkland, where handsome karee and acacia trees flourish. At 43 km from Zeerust there is a turnoff south to the huge cement factory at Slurry (1,5 km). A further 6 km brings the road to the border of the Cape Province with the town of Mafeking 14,5 km further west (64 km from Zeerust).

The factory of the Pretoria Portland Cement Company at Slurry was established in 1916 on the farm *Rietvallei* where a huge limestone deposit reached the surface. It was called Slurry on account of the name applied to the raw materials used in cement manufacture when the wet process is used. Managed by a famous character in the cement business, an American, Ezekiel Davidson, this factory was skilfully developed into one of the biggest and most efficient in the world. At present consumption, the limestone deposit there is estimated to be sufficient for the next hundred years.

The road branching to Lichtenburg from the railway station of Ottoshoop, 14 km before

Slurry, leads southwards over a high grassland seemingly so boundless and smooth that the traveller is distinctly aware of the gentle curvature of the earth. After 1,5 km a turnoff stretches to the source of the Molopo River, with another road to the same remarkable spring turning off at 21 km from Ottoshoop. A well-developed holiday resort has been created at this gigantic spring, where swimming and boating may be enjoyed in superbly clear water.

### Caravans and camping
★ Molopo Eye Holiday Resort, 60 sites. R4 D. 26 rondawels, R10,50 – R16,50 D.

South of the turnoff to the source of the Molopo, the road enters the diamond mining area where patches of the landscape resemble the site of a large-scale war. The human industry and energy expended in the massive disruption of this landscape are almost beyond description. The local place names such as Elandsputte, Bakerville and Grasfontein, are legendary in the history of diamonds. There is a turnoff to Bakerville at 30 km and at 50,5 km the road reaches the diamond centre of . . .

# LICHTENBURG

Commencing its development in conventional fashion, Lichtenburg then experienced some of the most hectic events in the entire history of Southern Africa.

In 1859 Hendrik Greef settled on the farms *Elandsfontein* and the copiously watered *Doornfontein*. On 25 July 1873 a town was proclaimed on portions of these farms which President Burgers named *Lichtenburg* (the town of light) in the hope that it would give rise to progress on the western plains. It was some time, however, before the light could be lit, for the place was remote, progress was slow and the village only attained the status of a health committee in 1902.

Maize farming was the principal occupation in a district which remained half asleep until the year 1926 when there came a change, shattering in its suddenness. On 13 March of that year, Jacobus Voorendyk (son of the postmaster of Lichtenburg) with an African labourer named Jan, was digging holes for stakes on his farm *Elandsputte*. As they dug the last hole of a series, Jan suddenly exclaimed 'Master, here is a diamond!' Jacobus looked at the 0,75 carat chip in disbelief. He washed it in a bucket of water, realising that it could be glass for all he knew about diamonds.

He saddled a horse and rode with the chip to see his father in Lichtenburg. The two men took the stone to Mr Bosman the science master of the Lichtenburg High School. 'It looks like a piece of bottle to me,' he said dubiously.

'Try it in acid,' said Voorendyk. The little chip was placed in a bottle of acid and left on a shelf. That weekend the men almost tiptoed back to see it, but there it lay, sparkling in the bottle of acid. There was no doubt about it; this was the first diamond of Lichtenburg.

The story of the rush that followed is beyond the scope of short description. Nowhere in the world has there been a wilder or more frenzied scramble for fortune. Within 12 months there were 108 000 people on the diggings. In many of the great claim-pegging races organised by the authorities, over 30 000 men – some hired athletes, others even on crutches – raced one another over the veld in an avalanche of diamond-crazed humanity, each man hoping to peg a claim on a fancied portion of newly proclaimed mining area.

On *Elandsputte* farm, the scene of the first discovery, were 32 000 diggers. With Voorendyk taking 15 per cent on all diamond finds, 50 per cent on claim fees, and selling water at 5c for a 50-ℓ barrel, he made £4 000 in the first month and £45 000 in three months. He eventually made a fortune. His farm resembled a fairground, with butcher's, baker's, tearooms and boarding houses springing up like weeds. Pagel's circus arrived, as did merry-go-rounds and a prayer of four Dutch Reformed parsons who were intent on supervising the morals of the diggers. Schools were started, social workers appeared and so did doctors and midwives. Shrouding the entire scene was a permanent cloud of red dust so appalling that it was like a London fog. Motorists had to switch on their headlights in the daytime; at night it settled on the cool faces of sleepers. It was said that when a true Lichtenburg digger breathed, a cloud of dust moved in and out of his mouth!

Many magnificent diamonds were found. The rush which had started at *Elandsputte* swept like a tornado over the veld, following the run of diamonds apparently buried in the gravels of an antique river course. Bakerville, Grasfontein, Carliesonia, Skelm Koppie and many other places became areas of digging. It is worth taking the road to Zeerust just to see these fields, mainly clustered 15 km north of Lichtenburg. The road leads for kilometres across a landscape which has been uprooted on a large scale. An atomic bomb could not have caused more prodigious a disturbance. The great rush has long since been over, petering out in about 1935 when a few minor discoveries were made in isolated potholes and pockets. Today, a few hopefuls still root around amid the rubble hoping to find that for which so many others have sought in the selfsame place, but have perhaps overlooked.

A total of 17 975 people live in Lichtenburg today, which has settled down to become a sober, prosperous and attractive little town. A commercial centre has been built around a magnificent square, the lawns and fountains of which are shaded by a most elegant collection of karee trees, and where a superb equestrian statue of General De la Rey, the renowned leader in the Anglo-Boer War, stands. Maize, sheep and cement (produced in the substantial White's Cement Works established in 1950) .contribute to the town a prosperity which, although not as meteoric as the diamond fields, is far more lasting. There is a fine library in the town and a museum devoted to the history of the diamond fields and the life of General Jacobus de la Rey. The museum in the civic centre is open on weekdays from 09h00 to 12h00 and from 14h00 to 16h00; on Saturday from 09h00 to 12h00.

## Accommodation

★★ Elgro Hotel, 38 rooms, all with baths. R15 B/B. Phone 3051.
★ Langrish Hotel, 46 rooms, 30 with baths. R10 – R12 B/B. Phone 5041.

## Caravans and camping

★★® Municipal caravan park, 100 sites. R2 D plus 50c D per person.

From Lichtenburg, the tarmac road leads south-westwards over a vast, level plain covered in maize and sunflower fields interspersed with plantations of gum trees. Here the mealie and sunflower are king and queen of the earth and the small rural centres passed along the way are all made prominent by tall grain silos standing next to their railway stations.

The road, 40 km from Lichtenburg, reaches Biesiesvlei and after a further 19 km enters *Sannieshof,* named after Sannie Voorendyk, wife of the Lichtenburg postmaster of diamond discovery fame.

## Accommodation

★ Sannieshof Hotel, 19 rooms, 9 with baths. R10 – R11 B/B. Phone 104.

Twenty-one kilometres from Sannieshof (80 km from Lichtenburg) the road reaches a short turnoff of 1,5 km leading to . . .

# BARBERSPAN

A natural freshwater lake 25 square kilometres in extent, Barberspan is known to the Africans as *Leghadighadi* (the deep waterhole) and is fed by flood spill from the Harts River (known to the Africans as *Kollong,* the place of the flowing water). It is a proclaimed bird and fish reserve, frequented by immense numbers of birds such as flamingos. Shaped like a basin with a hard, flat bottom, the depth reaches up to 8 m, depending on the water level and the rains. Although the water is brackish, it is well liked by cattle who flourish there. Carp, yellowfish, mudfish and the barber (barbel) which gives the lake its name, thrive in the waters, the record carp weighing 24,5 kg. Freedom from bilharzia or mosquitoes make this a favourite pleasure resort where swimming, boating, aquaplaning and fishing are favourite pastimes. No shooting is allowed. It is a great place for organised fishing competitions which attract a considerable crowd of enthusiasts. A fishing licence for Barberspan may be bought from any magistrate, at a cost of R1 a year.

## Accommodation
★ Barberspan Hotel, 9 rooms, 5 with baths. R7,50 – R8 B/B. Phone 1811.

## Caravans and camping
Caravan park, 50 sites. R2 D. 16 bungalows, R4 D.

From Barberspan the tarmac road continues south-westwards. After 5 km the road passes the Barberspan station, dominated by the usual tall grain silo. After a further 14 km (100 km from Lichtenburg) the road reaches the town of . . .

# DELAREYVILLE

This place is situated in a slight hollow in the centre of which is a lakelet (actually a pan). These pans occur frequently on this flat landscape since there is no run-off of rainwater which then tends to collect in the slightest depression. Most of these pans are saline and salt is recovered from them. The two principal pans near Delareyville produce about 70 000 sacks of salt a year.

*Delareyville* was founded in 1914 when the first erven were sold and the town named after the famous General De la Rey of the Anglo-Boer War. The population now numbers 8 160.

## Accommodation
★ Elgro Hotel, 23 rooms, 9 with baths. R9,50 – R10,50 B/B. Phone 25.

From Delareyville the tarmac road swings south and, in company with the railway line, continues across the flat maize and sunflower lands. After 5 km a turnoff east to Ottosdal is reached and a further 19 km takes the road past the rural centre and grain silo of Migdol. For a further 19 km the maize lands stretch without a break, then begin to peter out into stonier soil covered in grass, where flocks of sheep and herds of cattle graze. Low hills appear and the road, 30,5 km from Migdol, passes the substantial Wentzel Dam in the Harts River, where fine camping, caravan and picnic sites are shaded by numerous trees. Three kilometres further on, sheltered by a ridge of bush-covered hills, lies the pleasant little town of . . .

# SCHWEIZER-RENEKE

The town lies on the banks of the Harts River, at the foot of the hillock known as Mamusa, used as a stronghold in former years by the Korana chief, David Massouw. In the year 1885 the cattle rustling activities of these people provoked a small-scale war with the Transvaal Republic. The hill stronghold was captured with ten Europeans killed, and the Korana driven away. The stone fortifications of David Massouw may still be seen on top of the hill, which yields an excellent view of the town, laid out in 1886 and named after two of the Europeans killed in the punitive attack, Captain C.A. Schweizer and Field-Cornet G.N. Reneke. In a fertile valley shaded by handsome acacia trees, the town has flourished on the production of maize, sunflowers, groundnuts, cattle and sheep. The population is 9 448.

## Accommodation
★ Therese Hotel, 18 rooms, 13 with baths. R10 – R11 B/B. Phone 5.

## Caravans and camping
★® Wentzel Dam (municipal), 150 sites. R2,50 D plus 10c D per person.

From Schweizer-Reneke, the tarmac road leads south-westwards across a level, open parkland of acacia and karee trees, where substantial maize and mixed farms flourish on rich, dark-red coloured soil. One and a half kilometres from the town lies a turnoff south to Bloemhof (56 km) while 90 km from Schweizer-Reneke, the road reaches the town of Christiana and joins the Diamond Way from the Cape to Johannesburg (page 213). Alternatively, from Schweizer-Reneke, the tarmac road may be taken leading for 29 km to the small rural centre of *Amalia*. Named after Mrs Amalia Faustmann, a well-known church personality in Schweizer-Reneke, this little farming centre was founded as a church community on 23 April 1927. From there a good gravel road crosses the Cape border and after 8 km reaches a junction with the main tarmac road linking Kimberley to Mafeking.

---

The main tarmac road from the Cape to the Witwatersrand – sometimes known as the Diamond Way – branches off from the Kimberley-Mafeking road at Warrenton on the Vaal River. During the low water winter season alluvial diggers may generally be seen here searching for diamonds in the gravels left by the receding water. The road leads under the main railway line, passing the station of Fourteen Streams and (4 km from the bridge) a turnoff south to the diversionary weir in the Vaal River which supplies water to the Vaal-Harts irrigation scheme. This great weir was completed in 1935 and diverts water from the Vaal to the valley of the Harts River in the Cape Province where 1 200 smallholdings produce rich crops from irrigated lands. At the weir, the impounded Vaal provides fine boating and fishing opportunities and there is a free camping ground with simple facilities and a small shop.

At 2,5 km from the turnoff to the weir, the road reaches the Cape-Transvaal border. The landscape consists of a vast plain covered in grass and a scattering of acacia trees, inclined to be bleak in the dry, cold, winter months but green and pleasant in summer. In the midst of this plain, lying in the shade of trees growing on the right bank of the Vaal River, 34,5 km from Warrenton, is the town of . . .

# CHRISTIANA

A straggling little place where the houses stand in plots so large that they could be miniature farms, Christiana is essentially a rural centre, with towering maize storage silos being the principle landmark.

The town was the offspring of the diamond mania during the late 1860s. In *Lost Trails of the Transvaal* it is revealed that during the unseemly and bitter arguments concerning possession of the diamondiferous reaches of the Vaal River, President Pretorius of the Transvaal laid claim to the area. In order to emphasise ownership of this portion of the Transvaal, a town was hurriedly laid out on the banks of the Vaal and the first erven sold on 25 November 1870. To this place was applied the name of *Christiana* in honour of the daughter of President Pretorius.

In 1872 diamonds were found in the river gravels at Christiana and the subsequent rush to the area stimulated the growth of a digger's town, inhabited by some notably rough and tough characters.

A few diggers still work the Christiana fields and occasionally a good diamond is found. The town, however, is nowadays the home of a far more sober-minded crowd of people whose excitement is derived from the pleasures of good fishing and boating on the river, a sulphur bath 6 km out of town, camping and caravan sites beneath the riverine willows, numerous islands on the river and some interesting prehistoric engravings on the rocks. The population has reached 7 109.

### Accommodation
* Karee Hotel, 15 rooms, 5 with baths. R9,50 B/B. Phone 81.

From Christiana, the main tarmac road continues north-eastwards over flat, lightly bushed country. The diamond diggings lie to the left of the road. After 6 km there is a turnoff to the sulphur baths, well developed by the Transvaal Provincial Council for Public Resorts. The sulphur springs are tepid (36,7° C) but highly mineralised. The holiday resort (known as the Rob Ferreira Mineral Baths, after the Chairman of the Mineral Baths Board of Trustees) comprises warmed private baths; a fine open-air swimming bath (filled with filtered water from the adjacent Vaal River); a restaurant; and numerous recreational facilities. A game reserve adjoins the resort.

### Caravans and camping
***® Rob Fereirra Mineral Baths, 200 sites. R4,50 D. 86 rondawels, 14 rooms, R6,80 – R16,20 D.

Beyond the resort the road passes the scene of another of the old diamond rushes where countless pits and gravel dumps provide the sole reminder of the feverish activity which once took place there.

Twenty-four kilometres from Christiana the road passes a large salt pan, one of the peculiar depressions which form the principal feature of this otherwise level country.

At 55 km from Christiana the road reaches the town of . . .

# BLOEMHOF

This town, the name of which means 'the garden of flowers', is a maize centre, dominated by tall storage silos. Dairy products, salt and malt are also produced there.

The town had its origin in March 1866 when James Barkly laid out a town on his farm and named it after a little garden of flowers cultivated there by his daughter. In those days a pontoon known as the North Star provided a ferry service across the Vaal River adjoining the town. The great storage dam of Oppermansdrift has now been built on the site. The town is now inhabited by 6 236 people.

### Accommodation
* Commercial Hotel, 19 rooms, all with baths. R9,50 B/B. Phone 87.

From Bloemhof the Diamond Way continues across the flat, grassy plain, notable for its brown-red coloured soil, maize lands, sheep runs and scattered acacia bush. After 39 km the road passes the scene of another of the chaotic old diamond rushes. Here the landscape is rather reminiscent of a world war battlefield carved by innumerable holes, trenches and cuts and stacked with piles of rubble. This rush took place along the course of the Bamboesspruit and its tributaries. An occasional digger still searches through this narrow, 64-km-long jumble hoping to find by modern means what the old-timers overlooked in their first frenzy.

Five kilometres further on there is a turnoff east leading to the railway junction and small town of Makwassie, and 64,5 km from Bloemhof the road reaches the town of . . .

# WOLMARANSSTAD

The town lies in the shallow valley of the *Makwasi* stream, so named on account of the number of wild spearmint bushes growing along its banks. In 1876 a trader, Thomas Leask, established a store on this site and on 16 February 1891, a town was established there by proclamation, and named after J.M.A. Wolmarans, a member of the Executive Council of the South African Republic.

The town was planned as a centre for the farming community, with maize as the principal local product. The population numbers 9 295.

### Accommodation
★ Wolmaransstad Hotel, 20 rooms, 16 with baths. R9,50 – R11 B/B. Phone 272.

### Caravans and camping
★ Municipal caravan park, 28 sites. R3 D.

From Wolmaransstad the main road continues over gently undulating grassy plains, covered with maize fields and patches of acacia bush. At 37 km from Wolmaransstad there occurs an especially dense thicket of these acacia thorn trees, known as the *Leeuwdoorns* (lion thorns), a great stronghold for predators in the days when the plains were alive with herds of game. The small town of Leeuwdoringstad lies to the south.

After 51,5 km the road reaches a turnoff north to the Dominion Reefs mining area, the first sign of gold mining activity on what has so far been entirely a diamond region.

After a further 21 km a turnoff leads to Hartbeesfontein while 6 km further on (81 km from Wolmaransstad) the road reaches the substantial mining town of . . .

# KLERKSDORP

With a population of 85 350, *Klerksdorp* originated with the arrival in the Transvaal of the first Voortrekkers. Early in 1838, an intrepid character, C.M. du Plooy, settled on the banks of the Schoonspruit (clean stream) and set himself up as master of a 16 187-ha farm named *Elandsheuvel*. Other trekkers joined him and, in exchange for the construction of a dam and water furrow, received rights to half of the huge farm. There they settled and the collection of rough dwellings which they erected, subsequently received the name of *Klerksdorp*, from Barend le Clerq, the patriarch of the early settlement.

For some years Klerksdorp remained a quiet little rural village, its principal buildings consisting of a church and store run by James Taylor and Thomas Leask which contained under one roof practically every possible commercial activity.

Then in August 1886, A.P. Roos found gold on the town commonage. A tremendous boom started, with what was named the Schoonspruit Gold Field being regarded as a new Barberton. Over 4 000 diggers drew lots for rights to mine the town lands in July, 1888, and the shacks they erected caused the town to sprawl in an untidy and unlovely manner, as if it was composed of corrugated iron and dust.

By the beginning of 1889 there were 200 commercial buildings, including 69 canteens and one stock exchange. At the end of the year the boom suddenly collapsed. There was no doubt about the presence of gold in the area but, compared to the spectacular finds on the Witwatersrand, the discoveries all consisted of low-grade ore. Most of the companies floated

692

to exploit the Klerksdorp reefs were too over-capitalised to ever show a profit on such grades. Many went bankrupt. Those that remained drastically reduced their capital, and their continuing activities, combined with agriculture (principally maize production) brought the area to its present state of prosperity.

Gold and uranium are largely mined in the area today. The Central Western Co-operative Company (the largest grain co-operative in the Southern Hemisphere and second largest in the world) has its headquarters in the town. Numerous mills, silos and elevators demonstrate that Klerksdorp is one of the leading grain towns of the world. Sussex cattle are bred to perfection in the area. The town is a bustling, modern place with an impressive commercial and civic centre.

## Accommodation
** Constantia Hotel, 24 rooms, all with baths. R13,50 B/B. Phone 2-4501.
** Klerksdorp Hotel, 42 rooms, 29 with baths. R14,50 B/B. Phone 2-3521.
* Tivoli Hotel, 84 rooms, 25 with baths. R12,50 – R14,50 B/B. Phone 2-3737.
** Van Riebeeck Hotel, 16 rooms, all with baths. R14,50 – R15,50 B/B. Phone 2-8571.

## Caravans and camping
** Water Paradise Caravan Park, 75 sites. R5,20 D.

From Klerksdorp the main road, now a double carriageway, continues north-eastwards over open grassy plains, covered with maize fields, plantations of gum trees, and cattle farms. After 10 km the road passes the mining township of . . .

# STILFONTEIN

Laid out in 1949 and now serving four important mines – Stilfontein, Hartbeesfontein, Buffelsfontein and Zandpan – the township of *Stilfontein* (quiet fountain) has grown rapidly into a modern and vigorous mining town which is worth turning aside to visit. The parks are handsome and a shopping centre has been built around a garden and fountain. An attractive building houses the health committee which administrates the place. Generally the town is neat, well laid out, thoroughly modern and functional. A total of 28 500 people live there.

## Accommodation
** Three Fountains Hotel, 26 rooms, 20 with baths. R14,50 B/B. Phone 4-1771.

From Stilfontein the double carriageway continues north-eastwards, passing, after 3 km, the Hartbeesfontein Gold Mining Company's complex of dumps, shafts and works.

The country is becoming increasingly wooded with indigenous acacias and plantations of gum trees flourishing. Past the turnoff south to Orkney (24 km from Klerksdorp) the road proceeds over this landscape of bush and low hills. At 46,6 km from Klerksdorp the road reaches the attractive town of . . .

# POTCHEFSTROOM

Founded by the Voortrekkers as their first town north of the Vaal River, Potchefstroom was once the capital of the original South African Republic. It was in November 1837, after the defeat of the Ndebele in the famous Nine Days' Battle, that Andries Hendrik Potgieter, leading his men back to their wagons in the south, forded the river they named the *Mooi* (beautiful) on account of its green and pleasant banks. Potgieter decided then that a town should be established at the site of the crossing and a weeping willow tree was planted to mark the spot.

693

At the end of 1838 the town was laid out on a site about 11 km upstream from modern Potchefstroom. The wet season of 1840 revealed that the reason for the site being so vividly green was that it was actually a marsh. A new town was hurriedly laid out downstream, this time on a well-chosen site. Planned on a spacious scale, with broad, straight streets running in the direction of the compass points, lined each side with water furrows, erven of 1,2 ha each, and three vast squares for a church, market and outspan, the town received the name of *Potchefstroom* (stream of chief Potgieter) while the original site is only recorded by history as being the *Oudedorp* (old town).

Potchefstroom experienced a stormy political period during its position as capital of the Republic. Even after 1860, when Pretoria became the state capital, Potchefstroom still remained a place of political and cultural importance. During the curious Boer 'Civil War' of 1862-1864, Potchefstroom changed hands several times after siege and countersiege during which the vicious sound of rifle fire often echoed down the streets.

It was in Potchefstroom that the first glimmer was seen of the future gold wealth of Southern Africa. On 20 March 1867 the first agricultural show in the Transvaal was held in Potchefstroom. Among the displays was a collection of 100 mixed mineral specimens recently gathered in the country by the German geologist, Karl Mauch. Mauch received a prize of £5 for his collection, the variety of his samples impressing on many people the possibilities of the as yet untouched mining resources of the country.

In November of the same year, Mauch returned to Potchefstroom from a prospecting journey to the north accompanied by the famous hunter, Henry Hartley. To the Potchefstroom newspaper, the *Transvaal Argus,* fell the excitement of publishing the first news of Mauch's claim to have found a goldfield of enormous wealth on the Tati River in Botswana. This story, reprinted all over the world, started the first rush to Southern Africa, attracting a stream of adventurers to Potchefstroom where they completed their outfits and prepared for ventures into the interior in search of gold and game.

The Anglo-Transvaal War of 1880-1881 saw a British garrison besieged in the Potchefstroom fort, where the soldiers remained securely bottled up for the duration of the disturbance. All these alarms and excursions now belong to the past, but they have left with Potchefstroom an atmosphere and a character peculiarly its own.

The town lies in one of the most fertile and well-watered areas of Southern Africa. The springs of the Mooi River are powerful and Potchefstroom is one of the few remaining places in Southern Africa to retain the amiable old luxury of having irrigation water gurgling down the furrows on either side of the streets for use by gardeners.

With a cold, dry, frosty highveld winter and a warm summer with a good rainfall of 609 mm, the valley of the Mooi River is a healthy and productive place in which to live. Irrigation is largely practised and fruit, vegetables and maize are produced. Grain silos dominate the town, while more day-old chicks are hatched and marketed here than from anywhere else in the country. Culturally, Potchefstroom retains considerable importance for it is a university town and the schools of both language mediums are numerous. It is also the headquarters of the Western Transvaal Command of the Department of Defence, with its substantial military camp and one of the world's most famous artillery ranges.

Industries such as organ-building and sausagemaking are carried out locally and the largest salt factory in the world and the principal chalk and crayon factory in Southern Africa are situated outside the town.

A museum exhibits (amongst other things) the President Pretorius Collection and there is a handsome conservatoire of music, as well as a theological seminary, the Potchefstroom Agricultural College and Research Institute and a fine library. There are numerous churches in the town and splendid recreational facilities for swimming, boating and angling at the pleasure resort created among the willow trees growing on the banks of the Mooi River Dam.

The population of the town of Potchefstroom is 66 000.

## Accommodation

★★ Elgro Hotel, 45 rooms, all with baths. R15,75 B/B. Phone 5304.
★ Impala Hotel, 33 rooms, 18 with baths. R8,50 – R11 B/B. Phone 2-3954.
★ Kings Hotel, 34 rooms, 8 with baths. R9 B/B. Phone 3241.
★ Royal Hotel, 40 rooms, 20 with baths. R8 – R9 B/B. Phone 4219.
★ Scandinavia Bridge Hotel, 5 rooms, all with baths. R8 B/B. Phone 9-1595.

## Caravans and camping

★★★® Lakeside Recreational Resort, 300 sites. R3,60 D. 17 cottages, 35 rondawels, R9,68 – R10,40 D.

Beyond Potchefstroom the main road crosses the Mooi River and leaves the town in an easterly direction, winding and climbing through low hills. Plantations of gum trees alternate with maize fields and clumps of acacia bush. This pleasant rural landscape scattered with many fine farms is particularly green in summer.

Roads branch off at 10 km to Vereeniging and at 40 km to Fochville, at which latter point the road climbs over a long ridge of acacia-covered hills. High on these hills, 47 km from Potchefstroom, may be seen to the south the monument to Danie Theron, a renowned figure in the Anglo-Boer War and the scourge of the British army. He was eventually killed while scouting British positions from the top of this hill. The site of his death is marked by a tall monument which appears rather odd from a distance but is worth closer inspection. The metal sculpture on top of the plinth symbolises the flame of liberty. A path leads to the summit of the hill where some interesting ruins remain of the defensive stone walls built by prehistoric African tribes. Similar walls can be found on the summits of many hills in the Transvaal. The settlements they protected were nearly all abandoned when the Ndebele destroyed the tribal structure of the area.

The signs of considerable mining activity are now visible, for the road is traversing what is, in fact, one of the world's richest gold mining areas. At 50 km from Potchefstroom, where the road reaches an important crossroads with branches leading to Fochville (south), and Carletonville (north), it is interesting to learn some of the history of this wealthy mining area.

## THE FAR WEST WITWATERSRAND MINING AREA

The Mooi River (on the banks of which stands the town of Potchefstroom) has its birthplace in a series of magnificent springs which gush out of dolomite formations. One of its principal tributaries, the Mooirivierloop, flows down a long, shallow grassy valley stretching up the high ridge of the Witwatersrand. Among the springs of this tributary is the famous *Wonderfontein* (wonderful fountain), which rises out of the dolomite near the railway station of Bank, flowing from a great cave in a perennial stream of the clearest water imaginable.

The splendid water of the valley captivated the attention of the Voortrekkers and as early as 1842 they started to settle there on farms such as *Buffelsdoorn,* owned by the Harmse family; *Wonderfontein* owned by the Oberholzers; and *Welverdiend* (well deserved), whose pleasant name is said to have derived from its first owner, F.G. Wolmarans. Searching for new grazing and weary after a long ride, he off-saddled there and rested in the shade of a bush. He fell asleep so peacefully that when he awoke he was gratified to think that he had enjoyed such a 'well deserved' rest.

Notwithstanding its copious water, the dolomite soil of the area was not rich agriculturally. As early as 1895, however, the area was prospected and there was a general feeling amongst geologists that the Main Reef of the Witwatersrand extended under the dolomites to the west. In the period 1898 to 1899, D.J. Pullinger sank a series of boreholes in the area and one of these, on *Gemsbokfontein,* struck gold.

The Anglo-Boer War retarded development, but when peace came, the Western Rand Estates Ltd was formed to work the area, and the Main Reef was found on farms such as *Libanon* and *Venterspost*. In 1910 the first shaft, known as the Pullinger Shaft, was sunk on *Gemsbokfontein*, but water flooded in from the dolomite when it was only 29,5 m deep. Several other equally abortive efforts were made but there was no technical answer to the flooding problem and the work petered out. It is ironic that nowadays the Pullinger Shaft is used to supply domestic water to the Venterspost mine on whose property it lies.

Several years passed during which time the cementation process was perfected as a means of overcoming underground water problems. Modern geophysicists also entered the picture. Dr Rudolf Krahmann, a German geophysicist, studied the area with the aid of a magnetometer, a delicate instrument which allowed him to trace the magnetic shales known to occur in relation with the Main Reef group. The results were so remarkable that the New Consolidated Gold Fields Co. became interested. Options were taken up on the whole valley and in 1932, Western Witwatersrand Areas Ltd was formed for the specialised task of proving and developing the area.

Immense activity ensued in the vicinity of Wonderfontein. In the space of a few short years the barren valley was transformed by tarmac roads, townships and enormous new working gold mines. Of these, the one on the aptly named farm *Blyvooruitzicht* (joyful prospect), registered on 10 June 1937, and the nearby West Driefontein Mine are two of the richest gold mines in the world. In 1965 their yield in penny-weights of gold per ton of ore was 12,5 dwt and 16,4 dwt respectively, compared to an average of 7,5 dwt for the industry.

The fact that these mines produce at all is a miracle of applied science, for the technical difficulties of working through dolomite are immense. When the first Blyvooruitzicht shaft was sunk in 1938, water burst from a fissure at a depth of 430 m, flooding the shaft at the rate of 1 818 400 l an hour.

Some 917 cubic metres of broken brick and 14 438 packets of cement were tipped into the shaft to form an underground concrete plug, through which the shaft was continued. It was completed in June 1941, reaching a depth of 1 536 m. Milling operations started in February 1942 and by December 1950, 2 615 028 oz of gold had been produced. The principal town in this remarkable mining area is . . . .

## CARLETONVILLE

Named after Mr Carleton Jones, the resident director of the New Consolidated Gold Fields Ltd, *Carletonville* with its population of 108 040, was proclaimed in 1948 and on 1 July 1959 became a municipality. In its area are included the townships of Carletonville and extensions, Oberholzer and extensions, Welverdiend, Blyvooruitzicht, Bank, Blybank, West Wits and Water's Edge.

### Accommodation
* Carletonville Hotel, 24 rooms, 14 with baths. R8 B/B. Phone 3305.
* Oberholzer Hotel, 15 rooms, 4 with baths. R9,50 B/B. Phone 6011.
* President Hotel, 23 rooms, 11 with baths. R7,50 – R8 B/B. Phone 6771.

### Caravans and camping
* Safari Garage (Welverdiend), a complimentary overnight convenience. ⁻

From the Fochville-Carletonville crossroads (50 km from Potchefstroom) the main road continues north-eastwards, passing the wayside Kraalkop Hotel (53 km) and then climbing over a ridge of hills to descend into the Wonderfontein mining valley. At 63 km the road passes the Kloof Gold Mining Company; at 66 km there is a turnoff north to Carletonville; and a further

1,5 km brings the road to a turnoff to the mining areas and townships of Libanon, Westonaria and Venterspos.

Ahead to the north and east, the long ridge of the Witwatersrand may now be seen; a continuous complex of mines, factories and built-up areas. Turnoffs are numerous: at 72 km to Randfontein (16 km); at 74 km to Western Areas Gold Mining Co; at 87 km to Lawley (south) and Randfontein (north).

The main road now passes the Johannesburg municipal waterworks at Zuurbekom and then traverses the city's principal complex of African residential areas built around Nancefield (96,5 km). At 98 km from Potchefstroom this road passes the Kliptown turnoff (100 km), climbs through plantations of wattle and gum trees and, 106 km from Potchefstroom, joins the great trunk road of Africa, coming in from the Cape on its way to the far north. This is the terminus of the Diamond Way and the entrance to the city of Johannesburg the civic centre of which lies 10 km away (116 km from Potchefstroom).

# Chapter Thirty-Five

# NAMIBIA

## THE NORTHERN AREAS

The south-western part of the African continent, the area lying between the Orange River in the south and the Kunene River in the north, is a sunbaked confection of rocky hillocks, rugged mountains, seas of sand dunes and plains so vast that a traveller halfway across them feels he is in the midst of eternity. It is these plains, some of them deserts, other prairielands of grass and still others savanna parklands covered in trees, that give the country its modern name of Namibia. In the language of the people who inhabit the southern part of the area, *Namib* means a large plain and the people of this part of the country are generally known as the *Namaqua* (people of the plains).

The total area of Namibia is 824 269 square kilometres, where live 853 000 people whose origins and cultures range from the Latter Stone Age to the age of nuclear power. The largest section of the population (45,5 per cent) consists of a group of related tribes who live in the north-eastern section of the country and are collectively known as the Ovambo. The second largest group (14 per cent) consists of people of European origin. Of this group, 66,3 per cent are Afrikaans-speaking, 23,9 per cent are German-speaking and 8,3 per cent are English-speaking. The members of this European group are scattered throughout the country. The third largest group of people (8,4 per cent) is the Damara who live mainly in the north-western part of the country. The fourth largest group (6,72 per cent) is the Herero who inhabit the central portion of the country. The fifth largest (6,62 per cent) is made up of the various tribes collectively known as the Nama, who are related to the Hottentot people of the Cape. The sixth largest group (2,24 per cent) is the Bushmen. The balance of the population consists of several minor groups.

With a population so small living in a country of such vastness, silence and solitude predominate and there is a sense of emptiness and isolation. This widespread stillness subtly combines with a landscape which is singular in its colours, full of contrasts of light and shade. Fertility confronts the harshest aridity, and mountains rise so abruptly from the plains that they seem like jagged islands in a sea of grass or sand. Travelling through this part of Africa is an experience so full of novelty of scene and in an atmosphere so different from any other part of the world that the visitor might well imagine himself to have landed on a distant planet faced with the prospect of discovering all manner of natural and unnatural wonders.

Exploring this south-western part of Africa is made easy by a magnificent network of roads of which the construction and maintenance absorbs no less than 36 per cent of the total administrative budget of the country. The investment of this money and a prodigious amount of hard work on the part of the engineering and maintenance staff has given the country more kilometres of road per head of population than any other part of Africa, including South Africa. There are over 15 km of constructed roads in the country for every person. Those who explore this expanding network of roads, at present consisting of 12 800 km of trunk and main roads, (3 000 km of which are tarred), can find themselves on long stretches so completely empty that the road seems to have been built for their use alone. These roads find their way over the plains and far away and sometimes the only other vehicle encountered on a long journey is a road scraper patiently at work, as though maintaining a smooth surface for ghost vehicles which are seldom seen to pass.

This vast network of roads was not simply constructed as a cosmetic luxury for the country. Roads can either follow progress, providing comfort for the pioneer and support to enterprise, or they can stretch ahead into untouched spaces, tempting the explorer onwards to new farms, mines and projects made accessible by road. The vast per capita expenditure on such roads in a developing country is therefore an investment and a sign of confidence in the future. It is to the credit of any country's administration that so large a portion of its revenue is used on such a worthwhile asset, rather than squandered on military lethal devices and lunatic ambitions of changing the world.

The complete tarring of the main north, south, east and west trunk roads stretching from the capital, Windhoek, has made all-weather travelling possible to every main centre in the country and from the southern to the northern frontiers. The main district roads are so well maintained that, apart from dust, the traveller has no real difficulty in penetrating the smaller towns, villages and rural areas. It is these untarred roads which, in fact, lead the visitor to the discovery of many remarkable places and scenes. No tourist should be reluctant to venture along these byways for they lead to experiences and sensations which are quite enchanting.

The maintenance of these byways is the responsibility of a famous breed of man, the so-called *padjapie* (road rustic), as he is nicknamed. They are the suntanned, dehydrated, dusty-looking individuals who spend their lives living in lonely camps by the wayside, maintaining about 58 000 km of by-roads and sometimes not seeing a town or village for months on end. There are 1 400 *padjapies* working on the roads of the country, operating about 800 pieces of heavy machinery with 155 grader units and several specialised work forces.

The labours of these individuals have resulted in many notable achievements, not least of which are the unique salt roads built along the desert coast. All roads on this coast, and the streets of town such as Swakopmund, are built of gypsum and salt. Gypsum which is found in the desert, is laid down and soaked with brine extracted from brine springs far saltier than the sea. The brine compounds the gypsum into a hard surface as smooth as any tarmac which is perfectly harmonious and suited to a climate without rain but which is misty and salty and where the wind blows incessantly.

To build and maintain roads over sand dunes, the *padjapies* use special 'sand-spoor' equipment and a technique devised by the Roads Division. A type of sleigh is used which traverses the dunes and creates tracks in the sand which motor vehicles can follow. To keep the coastal road between Swakopmund and Walvis Bay clear of drifting sand, a special four-wheel-drive vehicle is used with hydraulically operated blades mounted in front of the vehicle to remove sand drifts up to a metre high which are carried across the road by the winds.

One problem concerning the roads in this south-western part of Africa is the presence throughout the territory of a vast population of game animals, especially antelope such as kudu. These handsome creatures, like the kangaroo of Australia, unfortunately have very poor traffic sense. Signs urging travellers to be cautious of kudu are very common along the roadsides and should be heeded. Kudu are large antelope who like to keep together in groups. They find the grazing on the road verges attractive and if one runs across a road, others will certainly follow without the slightest concern for oncoming traffic. Slow speeds are essential especially at night, as the animals are dazzled by headlights. Other antelope, attracted by the salt used in road construction, come to such roads to lick the salt and frequently collide with vehicles. Their presence at the roadside proves delightful to travellers, but they need to be carefully watched.

Along the roadsides, engineers have constructed lay-bys and rest places at suitable points beneath shady trees. In arid areas small thatched shelters with cement tables and seats have been erected. Such rest places are provided with litter bins. In such a way travellers can rest or relax for a while, and have the chance of taking their eyes off long distances and refreshing themselves with a drink, a snack or a snooze. The roadmakers must be commended for leaving many beautiful trees standing, and occasionally tolerating a bend in the road when straightening it would destroy some interesting rock or feature of the landscape.

The nature conservation and tourist department has been responsible for many splendid features of this part of Africa. Their resorts, game sanctuaries and reserves are notable for imaginative and excellent management. The accommodation they provide is of an impeccable standard at rates which make a holiday still possible for the family man, when hotels have become beyond the reach of all save those travelling on professional expense accounts. The atmosphere of informal comfort and cleanliness, and the courtesy of their staff is a credit to the country and the author of this book, visiting them all without special privilege or facility, found them to be of an exceptional standard. For the tourist and the traveller, the discovery of Namibia – the south-western part of Africa – is an experience which is exciting, novel, delightful and unique, a venture into a different world which should not be missed by any visitor. The country will certainly not ever be forgotten for its scenes, atmosphere and people.

# WINDHOEK

Handsomely situated 1 654 m above sea level in the cul-de-sac at the head of the valley formed by a tributary of the upper Swakop River, Windhoek is surrounded by clusters of high hills and mountains well covered in trees and grass. A group of hot springs (23,9 °C to 26,7 °C) reaches the surface in several places in the cul-de-sac of the valley, giving the area a perennial greenness and attracting to the site, game animals and man.

The Herero named the area *oTjomwuse* (the place of steam), while the Nama called it */Ai/gams* (fire water). Several early tribes settled temporarily at the springs and at the end of 1840, Jonker Afrikaner, the renowned Nama chieftain established himself there with his followers. He named the place *Winterhoek,* in memory of his birthplace in the Cape and built his home near the site where the most powerful spring reached the surface and the Berg Hotel was later constructed, (now the South African diplomatic headquarters).

In December 1842 the Rhenish missionaries, Hans Kleinschmidt and Carl Hahn established a church and school on the site of the future city. At that time there were about 1 000 of Jonker Afrikaner's followers living in the valley. More people were being attracted to the site by the chief who wanted to increase his following in preparation for continuing the brutal sequence of wars and outrages which had passed for the history of the south-western part of Africa over a considerable period of time.

One group of Jonker Afrikaner's followers were attached to the Wesleyan Church and these people brought with them to the valley two missionaries, Joseph Tindall and Richard Haddy who were invited by the chief to commence work in the area. The Rhenish mission was then moved down the valley to oTjikango, the site of another hot spring, where they founded the station named Neu-Barmen, for the benefit of the Herero people.

Traders were drawn to the valley and the first wagon trails were blazed from the coast by vehicles loaded with alcohol, guns and gunpowder – the commodities most wanted in the country. The traders who brought these goods into the country required cattle as payment and this barter trade had already degraded most of the south-western part of Africa. To pay for guns and booze the tribes fought one another with insensate brutality, looting, killing and rustling. Nobody ever seems to learn a lesson from the past. To settle his own debts, Jonker Afrikaner began raiding the herds of the Herero. One raid simply provoked retaliation with barbarism so appalling that an account of that period of history makes gruesome reading.

The end of the settlement of Winterhoek came on 25 August 1880. Five days previously, Jonker Afrikaner's men had rustled 1 500 special oxen carefully bred by the Herero for religious rites and sacrifice. The Herero responded with a full-scale attack on Winterhoek. Jonker Afrikaner and his people fled southwards and the disheartened missionaries withdrew down the valley. The abandoned settlement of Winterhoek was left for the Herero to destroy totally and for some time only a few renegades and bandits frequented the place.

After ten years, the Germans arrived. At the beginning of October 1890 Major Curt von Francois occupied the site of Jonker Afrikaner's former settlement and renamed it *Windhoek* (sometimes spelt Windhuk), either as a corruption of the original Winterhoek or because the Germans found the glen to be windy on their arrival. On 18 October 1890, Von Francois started building a fort on a hill commanding the upper valley. This fort survives as a handsome 'Beau Geste' type of stronghold turreted with white walls and shadowy verandas, courtyard and passages. This *Alte Feste* (old fort) as it is called, was completed in 1892 and became the headquarters of the *Deutsche Schutztruppe* (German Colonial Troops) and of German administration which steadily expanded control over the country.

A town grew under the protection of the fort. A narrow-gauge railway from the coast at Swakopmund reached the place in June 1902 and by 1906 Windhuk had grown sufficiently to be granted civil administration. It received a town council in 1909 and in 1910 became the seat of the newly constituted Legislative Assembly, thus confirming its position as the capital of German South West Africa.

After the invasion of the country by South African forces in 1914, Windhuk (with the spelling of its name then established as Windhoek), became the seat of the new administration when the country as a mandate of the League of Nations was placed under the trusteeship of South Africa. Under the new regime it developed as a centre for government, communications, trade, education and culture. On 19 October 1965, as part of the celebrations on the 75th anniversary of its establishment, Windhoek became a city and now has 76 000 inhabitants.

Built on the floor and up the slopes of foothills and the sides of the valley, Windhoek has a pleasant range of elevation. There are fine viewsites and the variety of suburban locations gives the city an attractive diversity of appearance.

The principal street, running north to south is Kaiser Street, lined with modern commercial buildings and a few pleasing survivors of German colonial architecture. The municipal building is an impressive structure which faces on to this street and in the flower beds in front of it stands a statue of Major Curt von Francois, sculpted by a South African artist, Hennie Potgieter. This statue dedicated to the father of modern Windhoek, was unveiled on 19 October 1965 during the city's 75th anniversary celebrations.

Further north along Kaiser Street lies the Hendrik Verwoerd Gardens, formely the zoo gardens. This is a pleasant area of lawns, trees and flowers in the centre of the city. In this garden stands a memorial erected on 5 April 1897 in memory of members of the Deutsche Schutztruppe killed during the war with the Hottentots under Hendrik Witbooi. Also in the garden is a display of elephant fossils recovered from the mud around one of the hot springs and a collection of fragments of a meteorite found on the site.

The Alte Feste still stands on its hill site overlooking the city. The building is now a museum housing an interesting collection of photographs and items related to the days of German administration. Outside the museum stands a real gem of interest to railway enthusiasts – a narrow-gauge train complete with locomotive and coaches seemingly about to set off on the return trip through the wild mountains and across the Namib Desert to Swakopmund, a journey which this little train made many times during its years of service.

In front of the Alte Feste stands the Rider memorial, a fine equestrian statue sculpted by Adolf Kürle of Berlin and unveiled on 27 January 1912 at a military parade in honour of the Kaiser's birthday. The statue is a memorial to the men of the German Colonial Force who died during the Herero and Nama wars between 1904 and 1908. The Alte Feste museum is open to the public Mondays to Fridays 09h00 to 18h00, Saturdays 10h00 to 12h45, and 14h00 to 18h00. Holidays and Sundays 11h00 to 12h30 and 15h00 to 18h00.

Close to the Alte Feste stands the imposing building of the German Evangelical Lutheran Church with its tall steeple which provides the city with a striking landmark. There is a garden notable for its flowering trees and an avenue of olive trees behind the church. Overlooking this garden is the administrative building erected by the German administration. Popularly known as the *Tintenpalast* (palace of ink) it is still in use. Adjoining it is the modern building erected to house the Legislative Assembly, and which contains numerous works of art and a superb mural decorating the front wall inside. Visitors are allowed on conducted tours Mondays to Fridays 09h00, 10h00, 11h00, 14h00 and 15h00. A small game park is situated behind the administrative buildings.

In the centre of the city, facing Leutwein Street, is the Art Gallery, Public Library, State Museum, Archives and the theatre used by SWAPAC (South West African Performing Arts Council) and other producers in the staging of drama, ballet and opera. The library has an excellent collection of books and periodicals, including many rare works dealing with this part of Africa since its early days. The State Museum has social and nature science exhibits and is open Mondays to Fridays 09h00 to 18h00, Saturdays 10h00 to 12h45 and 14h00 to 18h00. Holidays and Sundays 11h00 to 12h30 and 15h00 to 18h00.

Outside the Windhoek railway station is displayed one of the narrow-gauge locomotives which worked the old line to Swakopmund. Near this locomotive is a garden and monument commemorating the lives lost in the 1916 revolt by Chief Mandume and a section of the Ovambo people. Another memorial in Windhoek is the Cross of Sacrifice erected at the southern end of Leutwein Street opposite the military cemetery. Each year on 11 November an interdenominational service is held here, conducted in Afrikaans, English and German, commemorating the war dead of both sides in the two world wars. The Oudstryders Memorial stands in Bismarck Street in memory of the Boer 'Bittereinders' who refused to accept the terms of the peace of Vereeniging at the end of the Anglo-Boer War and who moved to German South West Africa in order to avoid British rule.

The suburbs of Windhoek contain many fine homes and gardens. On the heights above Heinitzburg Road in the suburb of Klein Windhoek, may be seen three interesting castle-like residences which were constructed in 1890. During the wars with the tribes, Captain von Francois built a rough fortress on the site of the present government hostel. A second fortification was built on a hill overlooking the valley. An architect named Wilhelm Sander arrived in Windhoek shortly afterwards and set up practice designing many of the buildings of the German period, including the famous Tintenpalast.

The fortifications built by Von Francois captivated the architect. When the war was over he secured one of the abandoned fortresses and developed it into a picturesque ruin, a 'folly' which he named *Sperlingslust* (sparrow's longing). It was bought by Rudolf Moeller and turned into a tavern with an arched beer room filled with enormous vats of cold beer for thirsty people.

In 1894, when Governor Von Leutwein took office, he had a private secretary, the young Graf Schwerin. This young nobleman took a liking to the inn, bought it and commissioned Sander to complete it as a castle. Timber was imported from Germany and the finished place was named *Schwerinburg* after its owner. It became an outpost of German aristocracy in Africa with its tapestries, chests and crystal chandeliers.

In 1908 Sander created a second castle which was also bought by the Graf Schwerin and named *Heinitzburg* after his wife's family name. This castle was built on the same hill as Schwerinburg but on a lower level. It was fitted with a children's nursery decorated with a quaint frieze of nursery rhyme characters. The Graf lived in one castle and his family in the other. A path linked the two castles along which a special messenger tramped backwards and forwards conveying messages. At the bottom of the gateway of Heinitzburg stands an oddly designed beehive-shaped construction with windows for eyes and a nose built above a mouth which serves as an entrance.

In 1911 Sander built the third castle in Windhoek as a home for himself and named it *Sanderburg*. Like the other two castles it has several odd touches: a fierce-looking bulldog is

702

painted on the wall; there are pillars without purpose, useless niches and towers with unapproachable rooms. It also has living rooms with absolutely breathtaking views out over the mighty sweep of hills and mountains surrounding Windhoek.

Suburbs such as Avis, Khomasdal and Pioneers Park are residential areas. Eros (named after a fruit-bearing shrub which grows wild there), is a light industrial area and the site of the caravan park and the airfield for private and light planes. *Ausspannplatz* (outspan place) was the original main staging post for ox wagons. The J. G. Strydom international airport is situated in a place with the weird name of *oNdekaremba* (the fly on the cow) and the name of the industrial area and township built for Non-Europeans is *Katutura.*

Windhoek is a clean, healthy and well-ordered city. The shops are amply stocked with the necessities and luxuries of living. Tourists will find the gemstone and curio shops exceptionally good. Fur shops are amply stocked with local karakul skins. Books and photographic shops are of a high standard as one would expect in a place with German influence. Meat is good but bread indifferent; fruit and dairy products come mainly from South Africa. There are some good eating places but traditional German cooking is difficult to find. Locally made chocolate is delicious.

Entertainment is on the quiet side, as must be expected in a small city, but it has some bright features, especially during the last week of April and the first week of May and also during the first week of October. These are carnival times in Windhoek, when masked balls, general jollifications and parades take place and a great deal of beer is drunk.

The April-May period is especially pleasant. The rains are over, the country is green and the air cool. October is the hottest month although the altitude of Windhoek prevents the temperature from becoming excessively hot and there is no humidity. The maximum temperature in summer is 36° C and 360 mm of rain falls each year.

Windhoek is pleasant to visit at all seasons with its novel scenes, atmospheres and activities. Not least of these is the cosmopolitan crowd in the streets – sophisticated European women being curiously upstaged by majestic Herero ladies who promenade the town in their colourful 'missionary's wife' costumes dating from the previous century. They move with a stately gait resulting from a combination of their own weight and from the effects of a custom in past years when their feet were burdened by the heavy bangles which were fashionable. The Herero menfolk, unfortunately, are birds of far drabber plumage. It is their ladies who dominate the passing show of Windhoek! Even the local cemetery is worth visiting as it is extremely green and beautiful. Visitors might be tempted to book a plot for future use!

## Accommodation
** Continental Hotel, 69 rooms, 57 with baths. R11 – R28 B/B. Phone 22681.
** Fürstenhof Hotel, 18 rooms, all with baths. R12 – R18 room only. Phone 29202.
*** Grand Hotel, 79 rooms, all with baths. R16 – R26 B/B. Phone 25471.
* Grossherzog Hotel, 39 rooms, 9 with baths. R7,50 – R9 B/B. Phone 22631.
* Hansa Hotel, 10 rooms, 5 with baths. R10 – R13 B/B. Phone 23249.
* Kaiserkrone Hotel, 26 rooms, 10 with baths. R9 – R12 B/B. Phone 26369.
*** Kalahari Sands Hotel, 186 rooms, all with baths. R23 room only. Phone 25511.
* Kapps Farm Hotel, 5 rooms, 2 with baths. R6 – R7 B/B. Phone 29713.
** Thüringer-Hof Hotel, 42 rooms, 40 with baths. R11 – R19 B/B. Phone 26031.
** ® Safari Motel, 105 rooms, 79 with baths. R14 – R26 room only. Phone 26591.
* South West Star Hotel, 10 rooms, 6 with baths. R5,50 – R7,50 room only. Phone 24689.

## Caravans and camping
** ® Safari Motel, 50 sites. R2,20 D plus 80c D per person. 7 caravans for hire, R8 – R14 D plus 80c D per person.

*Overleaf: A fantasy of some of the strange ores found in the Tsumeb mine, the world's greatest single mineral locality.*

# DAAN VILJOEN GAME PARK

The Daan Viljoen Game Park lies 21 km from the city, in the hills overlooking Windhoek from the west along a first-class tarmac road which leads to the Khomas Hochland. The 3 953-ha park was proclaimed in 1962 and named after the administrator of South West Africa, the Honourable D. T. du P. Viljoen. The park lies 2 000 m above sea level and has a spectacular view over the great valley containing the city of Windhoek. The scene on a night when the moon is full, is particularly lovely. The picture is unforgettable as the moon, large and reddish in colour, rises directly behind the city. The lights of Windhoek glitter below surrounded by the dark shapes of the mountains and hills.

The park carries an interesting population of wildlife. There are about 200 different species of birds and numerous kudu, blue wildebeest, mountain zebra, oryx, eland, springbok and hartebeest. The Augeigas River is dammed in the park providing opportunity for fishing, with pleasant picnic facilities around its verges. There is a circular drive 6,4 km in length, wilderness trails for walkers, a restaurant, some bungalows and a caravan park. Admission is R1,20 D. Adults 60c D, children half price if accommodation is used.

## Accommodation
★★★ ® Bungalows (3 beds) R5,20 D. Bungalows (2 beds), R4,20 D. Caravan sites, R3 D. Tents and picnic sites, R2 D.

# THE ROAD TO BOTSWANA

From Windhoek a tarmac road leads eastwards through the hills and the valley containing the suburb of Klein Windhoek. From there, the road crosses a spacious, acacia-covered plain, passing the roadside hotel of Kapps Farm and the international airport 46 km from the capital.

Beyond the airport the tarmac road continues for a total of 224 km, traversing rather dull, dry, scrub and parkland country, passing small hotels at Omitara and Witvlei, where the beer is at least wet and cold, and thereafter reaching the town of . . .

# GOBABIS

A place which might aptly be described as a modern cow town, *Gobabis* (drinking place of the elephants), lies on the banks of the *Nossob* (large) River. It is the centre of a vast ranching district bordering Botswana, with the Kalahari just over the eastern horizon, where dawns and sunsets are rich with the colours of a dusty land.

A sunbaked little town, Gobabis had its origin in 1856 as the site of a Rhenish mission station. In 1894 the Germans established a military post there to guard the eastern frontier. On 6 November 1930, a railway line was opened connecting it to Windhoek which stimulated a considerable local industry in the despatch of beef cattle to many distant markets.

Gobabis received its first village management board in 1934 and in 1944 it became a municipality. The population has now reached 5 432. Today it is the site of a creamery, a point of departure for trading and hunting trips into Botswana and a major despatch station for cattle.

## Accommodation
★ Central Hotel, 12 rooms, 6 with baths. R8 – R9 B/B. Phone 2412.
★ Gobabis Hotel, 12 rooms, all with baths. R8 – R9 room only. Phone 2041.

## Caravans and camping
Municipal caravan park, free.

From Gobabis a gravel road continues for 125 km to the border of Botswana and beyond that point, four-wheel-drive vehicles are recommended.

## THE ROAD TO THE NORTH

From Windhoek, the main tarmac road to the north travels down the valley between the Eros and Khomas ranges, through a well-wooded parkland. This is a pleasant journey with many views of the mountains and numerous trees of a most graceful shape. The Swakop River is bridged after 64 km. Although it has only an intermittent flow, this is one of the most important watercourses in the territory and its broad, tree-lined course can carry turbulent floods during the rainy seasons.

Three kilometres beyond the bridge there is a turnoff eastwards leading circuitously to Gobabis and (10 km away) the Fritz Gaerdes Nature Park, created by Fritz Gaerdes, a nature lover. The park contains a fine collection of indigenous plants. One kilometre beyond this turnoff is a turnoff stretching westwards to the hot springs of Gross-Barmen. A further kilometre (69 km from Windhoek) takes the road into the town of . . .

## OKAHANDJA

This little place is pleasantly situated on the banks of a tributary of the Swakop River. The stream is known (because of its sandy bed), as the *oKahandja* (large sand flats), from which the town receives its name.

The site of the town has always been attractive to man and it has played an important part in the stormy history of this part of Africa. The Herero made the place their tribal centre and the graves of their early chiefs – Tjamuaha Maharero, Samuel Maharero and Friedrich Maharero – may be seen beneath the trees in the municipal gardens.

In 1872 the Rhenish Missionary Society established a station at Okahandja and the church still stands, an attractive and interesting building. Traders were drawn to the area and in 1894 the Germans established a garrison there, building a fort. It is accepted that the town was founded on that date.

On 21 December 1901 the narrow-gauge railway from Swakopmund on the coast to Okahandja was opened. The original railway station building is still in use. In January 1904 the war with the Herero people broke out and the inhabitants of Okahandja sheltered in the fort while shops and homes were looted and destroyed. They were besieged until 27 January 1904 when a relief force reached the town. The Herero were defeated in a battle on the slopes of Kaiserkop and driven away from Okahandja.

Today Okahandja is a prosperous centre for ranching with a population of 7 084. A large creamery and meat-packing plant is situated in the town as well as other industries. Biltong locally produced by the Closwa factory is particularly renowned and most travellers pause long enough in Okahandja to at least stock up with supplies of this delicacy. The town, set in a natural parkland, is a pleasant staging post for travellers. A privately run zoo and tearoom situated on the northern outskirts of the town on the main road to Otjiwarongo, is open to the public daily from 8h00 to 17h30. Admission is R1 adults and 50c children.

Each year on the last Sunday in August, the Herero people stage a memorial service dedicated to their former chiefs. Visitors are welcome to watch the procession, with the women superbly dressed in their Victorian-style dresses and the men mainly in uniform. Each grave is visited and the people take turns to touch the tombstones while prayers are said to the great leaders of the past.

### Accommodation
★ Wilhelmshof Hotel, 13 rooms, 7 with baths. R8,50 – R10,50 B/B. Phone 2203.

### Caravans and camping
★ Municipal caravan park, sites R1 – R2 D. Bungalows R1,75 – R10,50 D.

# GROSS-BARMEN

The hot springs and holiday resort at Gross-Barmen lies 24 km along a tarmac road which turns off 1 km from Okahandja on the main Windhoek road. Originally this was a Rhenish mission station established in 1844 on a site known to the Herero as oTjikarongo but renamed Barmen by the missionaries, after the headquarters of their society in Germany. The mission was eventually abandoned in 1904 and after lying in ruin for many years was taken over by the South West African administration. It has been developed into a major recreational resort with bungalows, a caravan park, shop, restaurant, an outdoor tepid swimming pool and an enclosed thermal pool with private baths for invalids.

The spring, rising from a depth of 2 500 m, reaches the surface at the rate of 6 700 ℓ an hour at 65° C. The water has a high fluoride content and also contains half a gram of Glauber salts in every 500 ml, the effect of which is the same as epsom salts. The chemical contents of the spring consists of sodium, 363 mg per litre; sulphate, 357 mg per litre; chloride, 127 mg per litre; silica, 100 mg per litre; potassium, 22 mg per litre and fluoride, 8,5 mg per litre. The water is extremely clear and smells of hydrogen sulphide. The temperature of the water in the thermal bath is cooled to 41 °C. An earth dam filled with fish is the home of a multitude of birds. Palm trees, graves and ruins are all that remain of the original mission. Yellow, orange and red varieties of *Aloe hereroensis* flourish in the area. Admission is R1,20 D. Adults 60c D, children half price if accommodation is paid for.

### Accommodation
Bungalows (5 beds) R10,90 D. Bungalows (3 beds), R7,30 D. Dormitory (4 beds), R5,50 D.

### Caravans and camping
★★★★ ® Caravan sites and tents, R3,70 D.

From Okahandja the main road continues northwards. The road leading westwards to the coast branches off on the outskirts of the town (see page 716). The north road passes the municipal rest camp and the zoo and then proceeds across an immense, flat plain covered in light bush, where an occasional hill rises island-like from what is superb ranching country.

After 47 km there is a gravel turnoff to the west which stretches 121 km to Kalkfeld, passing on the way (after 91 km), a turnoff leading to some dinosaur footprints, and 10 km further on, a turnoff leading 15 km to the private game reserve of the well-known professional hunter and conservationist, Jan Oelofse, whose clients secure their trophies in a spacious shooting area stocked with a considerable variety of game.

The main road continues northwards past the turnoff to Kalkfeld. The road passes the rural centre of Sukses, 104 km from Okahandja. To the west of this rural centre looms a landmark likely to attract the male eye – remarkable twin heights resembling a well-shaped bosom. The mounds actually suggest another shape to the Herero who know them as *omaTako* (the buttocks). Having travelled 168 km from Okahandja, the road reaches the town of . . .

# OTJIWARONGO

An important rail and road junction, *Otjiwarongo* (the pleasant place) is the centre for a considerable ranching area. Built on a gentle slope amid undulating plains, with the Water-berg range to the east, Otjiwarongo is a modern and pleasant town of 8 590 people which had its beginning after the Herero War in 1904. In that year the police post was established on the site of the town. Two years later the narrow-gauge railway from the coast to the Otavi copper mine reached Otjiwarongo and it became a staging post and transhipment station for goods destined for Outjo and Damaraland.

In 1907 a town was laid out around the railway station and police post. On 26 June 1915, South African troops occupied the town. Under the new administration it became the seat of a magistrate and on 1 May 1939, Otjiwarongo became a municipality.

### Accommodation
★ Brumme Hotel, 20 rooms, 12 with baths. R8,50 – R12 B/B. Phone 2420.
★ Hamburger Hof Hotel, 25 rooms, 16 with baths. R9,90 – R17,70 B/B. Phone 2520.

### Caravans and camping
Municipal, in public park. Free.

## THE WATERBERG

Lying 80 km east of Otjiwarongo, the Waterberg is a flat-topped ridge, a relic of a once higher plain. Well watered with its slopes covered in trees, the ridge is renowned for its species of plants, many of which are found nowhere else in the territory. There are also rock paintings and engravings and the summit of the plateau has been proclaimed a national park. It was on this high ridge that the Herero and the Germans fought a bitter battle on 11 August 1904. The Herero were defeated and suffered such grievous losses that their nation was almost annihilated, with a mere 16 000 people surviving out of a population originally estimated at 80 000. It took many years for the Herero to recover from the shock of this massive destruction. The Battle of Waterberg was the climax of a dismal sequence of repression, revolt, murder and outrage followed by vengence and fresh repression even more vicious than the original barbarisms occuring on both sides.

## OUTJO AND THE ROAD TO ETOSHA

From Otjiwarongo a tarmac road leads in a north-westerly direction over gently undulating savanna ranching country. After 69 km the road reaches the town of . . .

## OUTJO

This little place was named by the Herero, *oHutjo* (little hills), for it lies in a cluster of low hillocks. It is a clean and modern rural centre of 4 500 people, the terminus of a branch railway built from Otjiwarongo in 1915 and a staging post for tourists travelling to the Etosha National Park and exploring the remarkable scenery west of the town, in Damaraland and past Khorixas (see page 735).

### Accommodation
★★ Onduri Hotel, 25 rooms, 15 with baths. R7,50 – R16 B/B. Phone 14.
★ Etosha Hotel, 10 rooms, 4 with baths. R6 – R8 B/B. Phone 26.

### Caravans and camping
★ Municipal Tourist Camp, caravan sites, R2 D. Bungalows (2 beds) R3 D. Bungalows (4 beds) R5 D.

From Outjo, the tarmac road continues north-westwards. After 1,5 km there is a gravel turnoff to Khorixas and the Skeleton Coast (see page 731) and after 10 km a tarmac turn to Kamanjab. For a further 85 km the road continues through savanna ranching country and 95 km from Outjo, it reaches the Andersson Gate entrance to the Etosha National Park (see page 712).

## OTJIWARONGO TO THE NORTH

The main tarmac north road continues out of the town in a slightly easterly direction and, keeping close to the railway line, makes its way across savanna ranching country with the trees becoming taller and denser to the north. To the east may be seen the ridge of the Waterberg where many fine farms – citrus, cattle and general – prosper on the ample supplies of water from mountain streams. After 115 km the road reaches the railway junction of . . .

## OTAVI

The little town of *Otavi* (the gushing water), with its population of 1 750, is overlooked by the 2 149-m-high Otavi mountains. Well watered and fertile with a rich and varied mineralisation the area has always been desirable to man. Ovambo, Bushmen and Herero contended for the area over a long period with many barbarous conflicts and murders taking place. A pile of stones close to the railway line at Ondjora is still pointed out as being the grave of the Herero chief, Nandavetu, who was killed by a poisoned arrow during a fight over the possession of one of the copper outcrops in the area.

Copper, lead, zinc, cadmium, vanadium and germanium are found in this area. Active mining in Otavi itself is no longer carried out and the town is slightly decayed although it remains the shopping centre for outlying mines.

**Accommodation**
★ Otavi Hotel, 12 rooms, 6 with baths. R5 – R7 B/B. Phone 5.

From Otavi a tarmac road branches off eastwards and runs through a beautiful parkland with the high ridges of the rocky and richly coloured Otavi mountains lying on either side. After 40 km the road passes the copper mine of Kombat (*oKombahe Tjinene*, the large drinking place of the giraffe). Jacarandas and poinciana trees grow well in the valley and spring and early summer are made particularly beautiful by their blossoms. There is a gravel turnoff to Rietfontein after 58 km and the Uitkomst Research Station of the Department of Agricultural and Technical Services lies beside the road 72 km from Otavi. At 86 km there is a gravel turnoff which leads to the remarkable Hoba meteorite (see page 709), and after 92 km the road reaches the town of . . .

## GROOTFONTEIN

This place takes its name from the Afrikaans translation of the original Bushman name, *Gei-ous* (great fountain). *Grootfontein* lies on the slope of a hill and is shaded by magnificent avenues of flowering trees such as jacarandas. Bougainvilleae grow prolifically and a vivid display of colour may be seen in September and October.

European prospectors and explorers such as Sir Francis Galton and Charles Andersson observed the African people mining and trading for copper in the area as early as 1842 and several outcrops of ore were found in the area of the Otavi mountains. Farmers were also attracted by the fertile ground, plentiful water and ranching possibilities. In 1892 the Thirst-land Trekkers – families who had crossed the Kalahari from the Transvaal – planned to create in this area a republic named Upingtonia, but nothing was established.

708

In 1892 the South West Africa Company was floated in London to work several concessions in the territory and it was decided to create a town to serve the mines and ranching country around the Otavi mountains. The site of Grootfontein was selected where a small German military garrison had already been established at a place known as oTjivanda Tongwe (place of the leopard). The town grew up around this stronghold.

Grootfontein was laid out in 1907 and a narrow-gauge railway was built to it from Otavi in April 1908. The place expanded into a shopping, educational and administrative centre, with social life made lively by the presence of an official distillery on the farm Gemsboklaagte, producing an alcoholic spirit from makalani and mealies. This drink became famous amongst the miners and ranchers.

In 1933 Grootfontein elected its first village management board and in September 1947 it became a municipality. Its present population is 6 025.

### Accommodation
★ Meteor Hotel, 20 rooms, 18 with baths. R8 – R10,50 B/B. Phone 2078.
★ Nord Hotel, 11 rooms, 3 with baths. R8 – R9,50 B/B. Phone 2049.

### Caravans and camping
Municipal camping ground, 25c D.

From Grootfontein a road leads north-eastwards for 264 km to Rundu, the administrative centre of Kavango. Travellers are not allowed on this road without permission. The permit gate is 132 km from Grootfontein. The Berg Aukas vanadium mine is reached from a turnoff 30 km along the road from Grootfontein. After 68 km there is another turnoff (open to the public), leading eastwards for 222 km to Tsumkwe, administrative centre in an area of Bushmen.

## GROOTFONTEIN TO TSUMEB AND THE HOBA METEORITE

From Grootfontein a tarmac road stretches north-westwards for 64 km to Tsumeb. The journey traverses a fine parkland of trees and grass with high hills. Seven kilometres from Grootfontein is a gravel turnoff to the south-west which leads to the Hoba meteorite 21 km away. This meteorite, containing 93 per cent iron and 7 per cent nickel, with slight traces of cobalt, copper and chromium, was found in the early 1920s by Mr J. H. Brits, owner of the farm Hoba. It was proclaimed a national monument in 1955 and is said to be the largest metal meteorite ever found.

## OTAVI TO TSUMEB

The main road to the north from Otavi climbs and twists through a jumble of hills covered with a varied collection of trees, tall and elegant of shape. After 64 km of pleasant travel through this parkland, the road reaches one of the most famous mines in the world . . .

## TSUMEB

The town of Tsumeb has grown on the site of the extraordinary mine known to the Herero as oTjisume (place of algae) because the surface outcrops of highly coloured copper ore reminded them of the algae covering stagnant pools. Bushmen converted this name into Sumeb and Europeans made it Tsumeb.

Tsumeb, with its population of 14 477, is a real garden town. Jacaranda, poinciana, bougainvillaea and other flowering trees, shrubs and creepers grow to perfection in the area

709

and the streets are shaded and beautified by them. The visitor is recommended to explore the side streets in the residential part of the town. Spring in Tsumeb is something to see and experience.

The town is dominated by the mine and its headgear which towers over the main street. The mine produces large quantities of copper, zinc and lead and has been properly described by the American *Mineralogical Record* as the world's greatest mineral locality. From the one mine, over 184 different mineral species are found and to collectors all over the world, Tsumeb is the source of innumerable beautiful and almost unreal specimens of rocks, crystals and gemstones.

This diverse mineralisation originates in a volcanic pipe or throat which is filled to the brim with an astonishing richness of material. The pipe was first discovered in prehistoric times and worked by several different ethnic groups. When first located, the ore body protruded above the surface in the form of a low hill composed of minerals rather than rock and of brilliantly variegated colours.

European explorers and prospectors were informed of this dazzling outcrop. On 12 January 1893 a prospector, Mathew Rogers, working for the South West Africa Company, reached the outcrop and in a report to his company, stated ' . . . in the whole of my experience I have never seen such a sight as was presented before my view at Tsumeb, and I very much doubt that I shall ever see such another in any other locality.'

Rogers negotiated with the local tribe for rights to the outcrop and began a detailed assessment of the quantity of ore, its nature and the viability of a mine in so remote a place. Financing and planning of the mine took several years. In 1900 the company formed to work concessions over the area, the Otavi Mining and Railroad Company, sent a party of 33 miners under Christopher James to commence mining. Two shafts were sunk into the hill of copper and a hint of the wonders lying beneath the surface was revealed. In the first cross-cut, a vein of pure chalcocite was encountered running through rich galena. Such was the pattern of ore in the volcanic pipe. As the miners worked into the pipe they constantly encountered astonishing mixtures, rich veins and unexpected 'jewellery boxes' of sensationally beautiful rarities.

On 28 December 1900 the first shipment of ore was sent by ox wagon to Swakopmund. The mine was developed in the teeth of tremendous difficulties with transport, while a narrow-gauge railway was constructed from the coast. The railway reached Tsumeb on 24 August 1906 and within 12 months the little narrow-gauge trains had carried 25 700 tons of ore to the coast.

Over the years, with setbacks caused by World War I, depressions and political troubles, the Tsumeb mine continued its operations. In 1946, at the end of World War II the mine and other assets of the Otavi Company were put up for sale by the Custodian of Enemy Property. A syndicate (the Tsumeb Corporation) was formed to buy the mine. It consisted of the Newmont Mining Corporation; American Metal Co.; Selection Trust; British South Africa Co.; Union Corporation; South West African Co.; and the O'Kiep Copper Co. The purchase price was a little over £1 000 000. The new management recommissioned the mine and developed it to its present state of high productivity with levels being worked below 1 000 m. There are reserves of ore sufficient to maintain production at its present output until at least the end of 1987. The end of the pipe has not yet been reached.

Drilling and testing have revealed the extraordinary geology of the mine. It is a classic example of an ore pipe. Such pipes or 'throats' have, at various times in the earth's relatively not too distant geological past, been blown up from the depths, probably as escape vents for gases under enormous pressure. Along with the gases, molten matter also surged upwards, as though taking the opportunity to escape from the infernal regions at the core of earth. This molten material cooled and solidified in the throat.

As it happens in the strange lottery of creation, among the contents of this throat was a phenomenal proportion of economic minerals: copper, lead, zinc, cadmium, silver and germanium. During the past 70 years about R700 million worth of these minerals have been extracted from the throat. If the Tsumeb mine produced only these economic minerals it would be considered wonderful, and fully equal to the celebrated Comstock lode in America. But added to the already varied economic minerals is a dazzling variety of secondary minerals created as a result of the infiltration of water and several different gases into the solid body of the throat.

The infiltrations, in a manner quite unpredictable, reacted upon the complex mother lode in the throat and, at different levels, produced some of the most startling and beautiful crystals and oxides ever found in the earth. Some of these minerals are found in quantity, others in such minute amounts that they are just sufficient to be identified. Collectors of mineral specimens throughout the world regard Tsumeb as the single principal source of so vast a range of gorgeous and unusual rocks that anything near a complete collection would be a prize of incalculable value. Tsumeb can be justifiably listed among the greatest natural wonders on earth. Of the 184 different minerals so far identified from the Tsumeb mine, ten of them occur nowhere else in the world.

Probably the most complete collection of Tsumeb mineral specimens is in the Museum of Natural History of the Smithsonian Institute in Washington. A fine collection of specimens is also exhibited in the museum in Tsumeb along with photographs and records of the mine since its beginning. The museum is open on Wednesdays and Sundays 17h00 to 19h00. Admission is 30c adults and 20c children.

Fifteen kilometres west of Tsumeb stand the masts and buildings of the Jonathan Zenneck Research Station of the Max-Planck Institute for Aeronomy of Göttingen in Germany. The research station is named in honour of one of the great pioneers of radiophysics.

## Accommodation
★ Eckleben Hotel, 15 rooms, 9 with baths. R11,95 – R13,55 B/B. Phone 3051.
★★ Minen Hotel, 37 rooms, 33 with baths. R10 – R18,50 B/B. Phone 3041.

## Caravans and camping
Municipal camping ground, free.

From Tsumeb the main tarmac road continues north-eastwards across a tree-covered plain on which the Tsumeb Corporation operates a considerable agricultural industry, producing citrus, timber, vegetables, meat and dairy products to feed the workers of the mine and the residents of Tsumeb. A herd of 200 Swiss and Simmentaler cows provides milk while 7 000 head of cattle are ranched to provide meat.

Much of the water for this agriculture, and for use in Tsumeb, comes from a great sinkhole in the dolomite which is passed by the main road 20 km from Tsumeb. This sinkhole is known as Lake Otjikoto and was formed when the ceiling of a huge cavity in the dolomite rock collapsed. The lake was originally plumbed in 1851 to a depth of 55 m by the first Europeans to visit it, Sir Francis Galton and Charles Andersson. Pumping operations have reduced this depth to 36 m. The water is clear and well populated by fish of the *Tilapia guinasana* species. These fish were introduced to the lake in the 1930s and were brought from Lake Guinas 15 km away. Their origin in that lake is uncertain but they were possibly deposited there by an ancient flood spreading over the plain. The fish are derived from the common *Tilapia* or *Vleikurper*. Another fish found in the lake is an odd little mouth breeder with a name considerably larger than itself, *Pseudocrenoolabrus philander dispersus!* This dwarf bream was resident in the lake before the Tilapias were introduced. It has a habit of protectively carrying its eggs and fry in its mouth. The dwarf bream live at the bottom of the lake while the Tilapia live near the surface.

During the 1914 war the Germans dumped a number of artillery pieces and transport vehicles into Lake Otjikoto which were later retrieved by the South African forces. One of these vehicles, an ammunition wagon, is on display in the Alte Feste museum in Windhoek. In 1927 the postmaster of Tsumeb, Johannes Cook, drowned while swimming in the lake. His body was never recovered, giving rise to a story that there was a treacherous whirlpool in the lake. This has never been proved.

A little over 6 km north-west of Lake Otjikoto, the main tarmac road passes a gravel turnoff leading for 24 km through ranching country to the sinkhole lake known as Otjiguinas. This sinkhole is notable for its beautiful setting, with the rock faces around it covered in aloes which flower in May. The water is used to irrigate the adjoining farmlands. The sinkhole is said to be about 200 m deep and the water is clear and fresh. It is populated by many *Tilapia guinasana* species of fish.

At 49 km north-east of the turnoff to Otjiguinas (75 km from Tsumeb) there is a turnoff from the main tarmac road leading for 24 km to the Von Lindequist Gate entrance to the Etosha National Park. Beyond this turnoff, the main road continues for 185 km to Ondangwa in Ovamboland. From there it is 36 km to Oshakati and 61 km to the border of Angola. A permit to use this road is required.

## THE ETOSHA NATIONAL PARK

The Etosha National Park conserves 22 270 square kilometres of savanna country, including the Etosha Pan itself – a vast, shallow depression 130 km by 50 km in extent – which gives the park its name. This is one of the grandest and most important of all the national parks and game sanctuaries in Africa. The pan alone would be worth conserving as a classic example of its kind; a great, white, ghostly lake, dazzling with heatwaves and mirages for most of the year, filling from December to April with (at the most), a metre of slushy, muddy, algae-rich goo. This annual inundation, fed by the overflow of flooding rivers which carry the run-off of rains in Angola to the sea, and supported by 400 mm of local rainfall in the same period, attracts to the pan countless waterfowl, including pelicans and flamingos of both greater and lesser species. Depending on the extent of the floods, the pan dries out about March, leaving a hard floor, white with salt, soda and other chemicals. As the Ovambo name *Etosha* indicates, it becomes once again, the great ghostly, white 'lake of mirages'.

The verges of the lake are well treed and grassed, with several perennial springs providing water for game animals. The game animals who live permanently around the pan number approximately 30 000 blue wildebeest, 25 000 springbok, 23 000 zebra, 5 000 kudu, 3 000 hartebeest, 3 000 oryx, 2 600 eland, 450 giraffe, 2 000 elephant, 260 lions, 20 black rhino and numerous smaller creatures. During the dry winter season considerable herds of game animals move into the area, attracted by the water and grazing.

Bird life is prodigious with 325 species identified so far, including many lovely little creatures such as the crimson-breasted shrike (the bird emblem of the territory), sometimes known as the 'German flag' because of its black, red and white colouring.

The Etosha National Park lies on approximately the same latitude as the Wankie National Park in Zimbabwe and is its twin in atmosphere and in the magic of its game watering pans and springs which, flavoured by various mineral salts such as lime, are very palatable to wild animals. The wise tourist simply settles himself comfortably at a shady site overlooking one of these watering places and there, fortified by assorted refreshments and a good book with which to occupy any dull moments (there are not likely to be many), waits for the action to come to him, as it surely will. This strategy is preferable to bumping about on long, hot and dusty roads, endlessly searching for some excitement which can be as elusive as the mirages on the pan.

Among the most famous of the watering places in the Etosha National Park is the Ombika waterhole near the Andersson Gate and Rietfontein, near Halali, where the Thirstland Trekkers camped and hunted for a while in 1876. They left a few graves behind them there, including that of Mrs J. E. M. Alberts, wife of the trek leader Gert Alberts. Other waterholes include Goas and Okevi near Namutoni, and Andoni on the extreme north-eastern side of Etosha Pan. This waterhole is fed by a powerful fountain, said to have been opened by a prospector searching for oil. It attracts vast numbers of zebra, oryx, wildebeest and springbok.

There are three tourist camps in the park. The camp at which the headquarters is stationed is called Okaukuejo and is 18 km north of the Andersson Gate entrance. Dominated by a castle-like water tower which serves as an observation point, this is a substantial camp with a well laid out complex of bungalows, caravans and camping sites, garage, restaurant, shop, community rooms, museum, swimming pool and a floodlit waterhole enabling visitors to view the game from the comfort of the camp. Okaukuejo started as a veterinary post created by the Germans during a rinderpest epidemic in 1897. In 1901 a small fort was built there as a military stronghold but has long since vanished. From Okaukuejo the south-western side of the park may be conveniently explored, including the strangely localised *Sprokieswoud* (enchanted forest) of *Moringa ovafolia* trees. These are the 'upside down' trees which fable says were weeds thrown out of the garden of paradise. They fell to earth upside down and, embedded in the ground, simply continued to grow with their roots pointing towards the sky.

Seventy-seven kilometres east of Okaukuejo lies the central camp of *Halali*, said to have taken its name from a German hunting camp positioned on the site in former years. At the end of each hunting season the Germans blew a traditional end-of-season *halala* on their bugle and this sound, denoting the end of all hunts and declaring peace between man and wild animals, is surely an apt name for a camp in a game sanctuary. Halali is a magnificent, modern camp, shaded by mopane trees, with bungalows, a restaurant, shop, garage and swimming pool.

There is an excellent viewsite on the shores of the Etosha Pan north of Halali camp, where a road is constructed for a short distance on to the floor of the pan. The turning point reveals a tremendous panorama over the pan and its shores. The surface of the pan is a remarkable spectacle when it is dry and patterned into innumerable fragments.

The third tourist camp in the Etosha National Park is Namutoni, 74 km east of Halali. This is the classic camp of the park, made famous by the presence of the beautiful 'Beau Geste'-type fort built by the Germans as a police outpost.

The history of Namutoni is well displayed in the museum, which is housed in part of the building. Initially, only a strong spring bubbled up there from a swampy, reed-grown morass in a limestone basin. This spring was known to the Ovambo as *oMutjamatunda* and travellers regularly stopped there. The first Europeans known to visit it were Charles Andersson and Sir Francis Galton. Others followed and the Ovambo name of the place began to be distorted as the various visitors mispronounced and misspelt it until it became the *Namutoni* of today.

In 1897 the rinderpest livestock disease broke out. A veterinary cordon was established along the northern border of German territory with Namutoni and Okaukuejo both becoming posts. At the end of the outbreak, Namutoni was maintained as a police outpost and customs post from which trade with Ovamboland was supervised. In 1903 a small fort was built at Namutoni consisting of a rectangular building of unbaked bricks, 10 m by 24 m in extent, with battlemented walls and towers erected on its eastern and western corners.

At the outbreak of the Herero rebellion on 11 January 1904, the Ovambo chief, Netshale, joined the uprising. He sent 500 warriors under the command of Shivute, to attack Namutoni. The garrison of the fort was not very considerable; there was a sergeant, a medical orderly and two privates, one down with rheumatic fever. Three local ranchers were also at the post, seeking sanctuary for their livestock.

On 28 January 1904 at 06h00, two Ovambo spies arrived at the waterhole to reconnoitre. An hour later three messengers approached the fort and announced that Shivute was on a hunting trip with his warriors and intended to visit the fort. At 09h30 the 'hunting party' arrived, well armed with Martini-Henry rifles plus five horses and about 30 riding oxen. While the main party rested at the watering place, Shivute and a companion approached the fort and offered to exchange a riding ox for a sack of rice. The German sergeant agreed to the barter but the ox was not produced and the warriors gradually drew nearer to the fort. Inside the fort, the Germans prepared their weapons and made arrangements for a stout defence.

At 11h00, with a stentorian shout, the warriors suddenly jumped up and rushed at the fort. They stormed into the storeroom under the western tower and started looting the place, while others tried to shoot the defenders who were positioned on the battlements. The Germans opened fire on their attackers and the Ovambo, not wishing to be shot, retreated, carrying their loot with them and driving away the cattle and horses belonging to the three ranchers.

Retreating into cover, the Ovambo began firing at the defenders and a long shooting duel ensued, lasting until 15h30 that afternoon. The Ovambo then retired northwards into the bush leaving behind about 80 dead and wounded men. By that time the defenders had a mere 150 rounds of ammunition left and their position was grave. With the Ovambo out of firing range, they descended to the ground and abandoned the fort, retreating southwards.

The Ovambo spent the night taking potshots at the deserted fort. On discovering at dawn that the place was empty, they looted it, set it on fire and set off for home without attempting to pursue the Germans. The seven Germans, half carrying their sick comrade, made their way southwards for 14 hours until they reached the farmhouse of *Sandhup,* which had been abandoned by two of the ranchers. The building had been looted by Bushmen but it at least provided shelter. From there, the Germans sent messengers to Grootfontein with news of what had taken place. A relief force reached them on 1 February 1904.

After the defeat of the Herero on 11 August 1904 in the Battle of Waterberg, a new garrison of 30 men was sent to Namutoni. They reached the place on 29 November 1904 and found it in total ruin. The surroundings were littered with the bones of the Ovambo, broken up by various scavengers. The garrison included several marines, who hoisted the flag of the Imperial navy to the top of a tree. The marines remained until February 1905 when they were relieved by a military garrison which shortly afterwards was placed under the command of a wealthy Silesian nobleman, Count Wilhelm von Saurma-Jettsch.

It was this nobleman who dreamed up the idea of a gleaming white fort in the wilderness. Aided by his little garrison in whose ranks there were masons, carpenters and other artisans, he designed and built the new Namutoni. They laboured in the sun, making air-dried bricks and bringing building materials by wagon through the bush from Karibib.

The Count designed the fort as an irregular quadrangle, 60 m by 68 m, with four towers and three gates. Accommodation for officers and men were provided inside. There was a kitchen, coolroom for provisions, some sheds, a bakery, smithy's, gunsmith's workshop, joinery, wheelwright's and even a swimming bath outside the fort.

On 1 February 1906 Namutoni became the administrative centre for a new district and the Count was appointed as the first District Commissioner. Later that year, however, when the fort was almost complete, he returned to Germany on leave. He was replaced by Lieutenant Hans Kaufman who in turn was replaced by First Lieutenant Adolf Fischer, author of the book *Menschen und Tiere in Südwest Afrika* (People and Animals in South West Africa) and a well-known figure in the history of conservation in Africa.

Fischer led a very happy life in Namutoni. His garrison, known as Machine Gun Platoon No. 1, was connected by heliograph to the outside world. It was almost self-sufficient, having a mixed batch of artisans and gardeners, dairymen and transport men. The fort dominated one of the principal routes into Ovamboland controlling customs, immigration, and the movement of Ovambo labourers travelling south to work on farms and mines.

On 22 March 1907, Lieutenant Fischer really came into his own. The government estab-lished a nature reserve around the Etosha Pan and Lieutenant Fischer became the first game warden, with his garrison acting as rangers. For three years Fischer busied himself in a study of the area and escorted visiting parties of scientists, hunters and tourists. In July 1910 Fischer was transferred to Koes, in the Kalahari. Fischer Pan, a real metropolis of birds close to Namutoni is named after him. Namutoni itself was transferred to the police but on 1 April 1912 was completely abandoned for economic reasons. Only on 6 July 1915 was Namutoni reoccupied, this time by South African troops after the Germans were defeated.

From then on the fort was only occupied occasionally and gradually became dilapidated. On 1 February 1938, lightning destroyed one of the towers and the whole place became so ramshackle that it was eventually decided to demolish it. Several organisations and individuals intervened to save the fort. Dr A. Pienaar (well known as an author under the pseudonym of *Sangiro*) was appointed game warden of Etosha after the First World War. He and Dr Lemmer, founder of the South West African Historical Monuments Commission and other influential individuals campaigned to raise public support while G. Kraft, a well-known architect, inspected the place and made recommendations for its reconstruction.

On 15 February 1950, Namutoni was declared a historical monument. Funds were allocated by the government to rehabilitate it and to convert it into a tourist camp. In 1957 the reconstructed building was opened to tourists and in the following year handed over to the Department of Nature Conservation and Tourism. Immaculately maintained, Namutoni is a delight to visitors and a unique showpiece in Southern Africa. Additional accommodation, a shop, garage, caravan park and swimming pool have been built outside the fort. The original spring still surfaces next to the fort and the reed beds and surrounding trees are roosts for countless birds. Sunset at Namutoni is a superb spectacle of colour enlivened by the excitement of the birds drinking, squabbling and enjoying a last flight around the waters before settling down for the night. Each dawn and sunset, a flag-raising and lowering ceremony is carried out on the fort, complete with bugle calls and national anthem.

Namutoni is situated 11 km from the Von Lindequist Gate which is connected to the main Tsumeb-Ovamboland road. Admission to the Etosha National Park is R1,20 D for adults and 60c D for children (half price if accommodation is used). The park is open from the second Friday in March to 31 October.

## Accommodation
Note: The three camps differ in their accommodation but are all of ★★★ ® grading. Namutoni is the oldest and Halali the newest. The restaurants vary depending on chefs.

### Okaukuejo
Bungalows: 2 rooms (5 beds), R8,30 D. 1 room (6 beds), R7,80 D. 1 room (3 beds), R4,70 D. Room with 8 beds, R7,30 D. Tents with 4 beds, R4,20 D.

### Halali
Bungalows: 2 rooms (5 beds), R8,30 D. 1 room (3 beds), R4,20 D. Room with 10 beds, R9,90 D. Room with 2 beds, R3,50 D. Tents with 4 beds, R4 D.

### Namutoni
Room with 2 beds, R3,10 D. Room with 3 beds, R4,20 D. Room with 4 beds, R4,70 D. Room with 6 beds, R5,70 D. Room with 12 beds, R7,80 D. 'Ski-cabins' (2 beds), R2,60 D.

### Caravans and camping
Sites, R3,10 D for all camps.

## Chapter Thirty-Six

# NAMIBIA

## THE CENTRAL AREAS

From Okahandja, 68 km from Windhoek up the north road, the all-tarmac west road to the coast branches off immediately outside the commercial centre. It leads due west over undulating savanna country, a great place for kudu. Numerous signs along the way warn travellers to beware of these antelope whose road sense is notably poor. After 62 km there is a turn leading southwards for 70 km to the old mission station with the pleasant name of *oTjimbingwe* (the place of refreshing water). This was one of the first places in the interior of the territory to be settled by Europeans. The original powder tower, built in 1872 by the Rhenish missionaries for defence purposes and still standing after being attacked on at least two dozen occasions, is an historical monument.

One kilometre beyond the turnoff to oTjimbingwe, is a gravel turnoff north-west leading to Omaruru (see page 736). The main tarmac road to this town branches off a further 46 km down the west road. Three kilometres further on (112 km from Okahandja), the west road reaches the town of . . .

## KARIBIB

This little place, whose name means 'place of gari plants', had its start as a narrow-gauge railway station built in 1900 on the farm owned by Otto Hälbich. A mission station was established there two years later and the town developed as a ranching and mining centre. Marble of excellent quality is found in the district. Lithium and mica are also mined there while gemstones such as aquamarines, citrines (golden topaz) and tourmalines are found in the pegmatites. Sydney Pieters, one of the world's leading authorities and dealers in gemstones, extracts superb tourmalines from a mine located near the town. These gems find their way into collections and jewellery shops all over the world.

Growing in the area is the medicinal plant, *Harpagophytum procumbens* D.C., locally known as the *Teufels Kralle* (devil's paw) because of its strange shape. A herbal tea brewed from this plant is very beneficial to sufferers of arthritis, rheumatism, liver and gall bladder complaints and various stomach malfunctions. The plant is exported to many countries.

Karibib became a municipality in 1909. Today it is a rather atmospheric little place housing 1 867 people. There is a tall German-style church and one long main street lined with various shops (including a good gemstone shop run by the Henckert family), several buildings dating from German times and a marble works. Two tall chimneys and the abandoned buildings of a meat cannery and creamery are situated off the main street.

The climate of Karibib hardly makes the place a holiday resort. Hot and dry, washed by brilliant sunshine rather than rain, it is nevertheless, an interesting little place to explore, with gardens full of unusual plants and tress.

### Accommodation
★ Laszig Hotel, 10 rooms, 5 with baths. R7 – R9 B/B. Phone 81.

From Karibib, the tarmac road continues west for 29 km, then reaches the town of . . .

# USAKOS

The name of this sunbaked little town situated in the valley of the Khan River, is said to mean 'touch the forehead', but the reason for this is obscure. The town had its origin as a station on the old narrow-gauge railway which was built in 1900. Several buildings date from this German period, including a delightful municipal office. The railway station, with an old puffer mounted outside, is also worth seeing. The population of the town is 2 690.

The handsome mountains known as the *Erongo* (a watering place in the midst of a plain) lie to the north of the town. This massif is renowned for the rock art found in caves such as the Philipp Cave, named after Emil Philipp who owned the farm *Ameib*, on which it was found. This rock shelter is 50 m long by 20 m deep. The famous Abbé Breuil visited it in 1950 and wrote the book *Philipp Cave*, which deals with its prehistoric art and is considered by authorities to be of major importance. The Philipp Cave is 32 km from Usakos along a gravel road. Apart from the rock art which includes a great painting of a white elephant, there is a pile of stones known as the Bull's Party. Also situated there is a picnic place with shade and water. Admission is 25c per person. Phone Usakos 1111 before visiting, to obtain owner's permission.

## Accommodation
★ Bahnhof Hotel, 10 rooms, 4 with baths. R8,50 – R9 B/B. Phone 4.
★ Usakos Hotel, 17 rooms, 10 with baths. R6,50 – R8,50 B/B. Phone 8.

## Caravans and camping
Municipal caravan park, on banks of Khan River under shady trees. Free.

From Usakos, the tarmac road to the west continues over a grass-covered prairie which becomes increasingly arid. The Erongo mountains, whose highest point is the 2 350-m Bockberg, and the extraordinary, much-photographed Spitzkoppe (1 829 m high), dominate the plain like rocky islands looming out of a dried-up sea. At 23,5 km from Usakos, a turnoff north leads to Henties Bay, with a turnoff 1 km along this branch road which leads to the tin mine of Uis 101 km away (see page 737). This road provides access to the Spitzkoppe where there are several Bushman caves and deposits of artefacts and gemstones such as topaz.

The main tarmac road continues westwards across the plain, where the prairie grassland gradually gives way to the gravel plains of the Namib. After 77,5 km a turnoff south leads to the Rio Tinto Mine and at 88,5 km a turnoff takes the traveller to the uranium mine at . . .

# RÖSSING

When the Germans built the narrow-gauge railway from Swakopmund to the interior, they created a station in the Namib Desert and named it in honour of Nonus von Rössing, commander of the Railway Brigade in Berlin. Traces found of several minerals and gem-stones, such as the rare *heliodor* (gold of the sun), suggested that the area was richly mineralised. Heliodor is a topaz coloured golden by the traces of uranium present in the stone. In 1928 Captain Peter (Taffy) Louw, who had come to South West Africa with the Imperial Light Horse during World War I, and had remained to become a very active prospector, found strange dark-coloured rock in the Rössing area. He and his wife, Margery, suspected that the rock was pitchblende, which carried what was known in those days as radium. Margery, who had been a radiographer in Guys Hospital, London, confirmed this identification in a darkroom in Swakopmund, by placing a sample of the ore on a sensitive photographic plate. From the fogging which resulted on the plate, it was evident that the rock was radio-active.

Captain Louw formed a company to prospect the area of his find. Other prospectors became interested, although no one anticipated the energy crisis of the 1970s when uranium came into its own as a highly valuable mineral.

A second prospecting company found another area of uranium mineralisation about 20 km from Captain Louw's first discovery. The deposit was large, but of low grade, so it was not developed any further. Captain Louw tried to interest mining houses in his finds and eventually the Rio Tinto-Zinc Corporation became interested. They took an option on the Rössing uranium area and began a four-year programme of testing and evaluation. As a result of this programme, the company in 1973 decided to proceed with the establishment of what was planned to be the largest uranium mine in the world.

The uranium ore of Rössing occurs in granite as opposed to other major deposits in the rest of the world which are found in sedimentary material. The ore is recovered from an open-cast working which, it is estimated, will eventually cover about 5 square kilometres. About 900 000 tons of ore and waste are removed, and about 360 tons of explosives are used in a six-day week. After complex treatment, about 5 000 tons of uranium oxide are produced each year and exported for further processing and use as nuclear fuel.

Radio-activity levels in the mine are carefully monitored and the workers are safeguarded and under constant check to ensure that they are not exposed to harmful radiation. Employees of the mine are housed at Swakopmund and in a special township created at the railway junction with the odd name of *Arandis* (place where the people get upset).

Beyond the turnoff to Rössing, the tarmac road to the west continues across the Namib gravel plain, which in these parts, is often shrouded in heavy coastal fog. After 33 km (121,5 km from Usakos) there is a turnoff to the Deblin Mining Co. A further 19 km sees a turnoff south to the Namib Desert Park (see page 726) and half a kilometre further on, stands the interesting historical monument known as Martin Luther.

'Martin Luther' consists of the remains of a steam tractor which was brought to South West Africa in 1896 by Lieutenant Edmund Troost who hoped it would prove the solution to the problem of transporting goods from the coast across the Namib to the interior. The tractor towed a train of three wagons loaded with freight but it never seems to have had much liking for its work, for after a few journeys and having carried a total of 13 605 kg, it came to a standstill so resolute, that Martin Luther's celebrated statement was brought to mind:

*'Here I stand; God help me, I cannot do otherwise.'*

Boiler upsets (resulting from the salty water of the Namib) were the undoing of the poor thing. Completely out of sorts, it was abandoned to the wind and sands of the desert. The tractor almost rusted away until interested parties in recent times handsomely restored it and mounted it on a pedestal next to the modern tarmac west road where it was proclaimed an historical monument.

Three kilometres west of Martin Luther (144 km from Usakos), the main road to the west reaches the holiday resort (formerly a port) and most interesting little town of . . .

## SWAKOPMUND

The name of *Swakopmund* is rather an unfortunate one, but it is certainly unique. The Topnaar Hottentots who live in the valley of the Swakop River (at whose mouth the town lies) gave the river its name on account of the evil-looking mud, flotsam and general detritus washed down during its infrequent floods, which reminded them of a very loose evacuation of the bowels, or diarrhoea!

Notwithstanding its name, the Swakop is one of the most important rivers in the south-western part of Africa. It formed the traditional boundary betwen the various Hottentot tribes and the Herero people and was the scene of many brutal conflicts. Like most of the other rivers in the territory, the Swakop has an extremely erratic flow. However, when it floods during seasons of exceptional rainfall in the interior, it carries such a vast quantity of sand to the sea that the entire coastline is changed until wave action partially restores the original shore and the surplus sand is blown inland, increasing still further the size of the great dunes of the Namib. Water remains below the surface of the riverbed long after the river has ceased to flow. Trees and shrubs grow in the bed and on the riverbanks and farmers make the most of the vegetation and water to carry out limited agricultural activity.

Swakopmund had its start through necessity. The Germans, in the process of expanding their colony of South West Africa, needed a port, but the only natural harbour on this part of the coast was Walvis Bay, which was already annexed to the Cape. The roadstead off the mouth of the Swakop offers little shelter to ships but at least the anchorage is good. The Germans decided to make the best of the place, creating an artificial harbour there and building a narrow-gauge railway to convey goods across the Namib to the interior.

In 1892 Captain Curt von Francois built a military post on the site of the present town and this was the beginning of Swakopmund. Soon, several trading and forwarding firms established themselves there. In 1896 the building of the narrow-gauge railway began and in the following year the town was properly laid out by a surveyor. For various reasons Swakopmund only became a town in 1909 when it was well established as an entry port for the German colony.

In 1899, when goods were first being landed, a mole was built to provide a small breakwater. From the limited shelter of this structure, Kru-boys, specially brought from West Africa for their skill in handling surfboats, landed freight and passengers. The protected basin soon silted up, however, and a wooden pier was built in 1909, thereafter being replaced by a metal pier in 1911. The new pier, originally planned to be 640 m long, had only been built 262 m into the sea when World War I broke out. South West Africa was taken over by South Africa and Walvis Bay automatically displaced Swakopmund as the harbour. The old wooden pier was demolished after the war but the metal pier remains, a solid piece of engineering which has survived the battering of many storms. Today it is a promenade and vantage point for fishermen.

There are several other interesting reminders of pre-war German days in Swakopmund – the lighthouse built in 1902 and several houses below it built in the same period, including the *Kabelmesse* (seat of the Eastern and South African Telegraph Company) and the building which housed the *Bezirksgericht* (District Court). This building was reconstructed after the First World War and became the holiday residence of the administrator of South West Africa, who, in an official capacity, spent six weeks of each year in Swakopmund.

In Bismarck Street stand the castle-like barracks which housed the German soldiers. In the same street is the beautiful Woermann House and its Damara Tower, built in 1905 as the quarters for crews of the largest German shipping line serving South West Africa. The tower acted as a lookout to control shipping movements. The building later became the Hofmeyr Hostel, then fell into disuse but has now been restored and declared a national monument.

In Post Street stands the original post office, built in 1908 and now the municipal offices. In the same street may be found the Antonius Hospital, built in 1908; the Schröder House, constructed in 1904; the adjoining façade of the original Hansa Hotel (now rebuilt on another site); the Lutheran Church erected in 1910; the adjoining parsonage built in 1911 and, opposite the church, the school built in 1913.

The railway station, built in 1901 as the terminus of the narrow-gauge line, is an architectural gem of its kind, complete with a 'witch's hat' turret. The original courthouse (*Amtsgericht*), built in 1905, stands in Garnisen Street, while the prison (*Gefängnis*), also built in 1905, is one of the most remarkable buildings of its kind in the world. The façade resembles at the least, the sumptuous home of some German nobleman. It is built in a beautiful half-timbered style. The accommodation inside is not quite as elegant!

The so-called *Ritter Castle*, named after its original owner, Mr Th. Ritter, a director of a shipping agency, was built in 1905 and is now the local office of the Department of Tourism. Altona House, also of 1902 vintage, was the office of the Woermann Line of ships. Opposite it stand the half-timbered remains of the office of the German Colonial Company. The old Adler Apotheke, built in 1909, is still a pharmacy and near it stands a nostalgic fragment of the once grand Bismarck Hotel, in its day the premier hotel of the territory but insolvent in 1974.

Amongst other interesting buildings dating from the German period are the Kazerne, built in 1904 to house railway construction workers; Hohenzollern House, a former hotel, now a block of flats; the Prinzessin Rupprecht-Heim, once a military hospital but now a private hotel; the Standard Bank building, once a hotel; Barclays Bank, once the building of the German Afrika Bank; and next to it the half-timbered former building of the Damara Bank. Several private homes dating from the German period also survive, especially in the southern part of the town.

The Swakopmund Museum is excellent, crammed with well displayed exhibits on themes such as the Namib Desert, the ocean, and Swakopmund. It is housed in the original German customs post and is open daily from 10h30 to 12h30 and from 16h00 to 18h00. Admission is 30c. It should not be missed by visitors to Swakopmund.

The museum looks out across a pleasant garden to the modern building opposite, which encloses an Olympic-sized, freshwater swimming bath heated to 27°C throughout the year. It is open weekdays from 08h00 to 10h00 and from 14h30 to 20h00. Sundays from 12h00 to 19h00. Admission is adults 30c, children 15c.

The beach in front of the enclosed pool is pleasant for sunbathing and there is swimming in the sea in the area protected by the old mole. The sea temperatures, averaging 12°C in winter and 22°C in summer, are likely to appeal only to hardy swimmers! The ocean currents are tricky in the area beyond the protection of the mole.

A promenade stretches beneath a line of palm trees from the bathing beach to the pier. At the entrance to the garden there is a monument to marines killed in action during the Herero War of 1904.

There is a public library and reading room in the town, and the Sam Cohen Memorial Library houses a fine collection of books, periodicals and papers dealing with all aspects of the territory. For the researcher, this library is one of the best sources of information.

Swakopmund has increased considerably in size with the development of the uranium mine at Rössing. About 1 500 people connected with this mine live in Swakopmund in two residential suburbs, *Tamariskia,* named after the wild tamarisk trees, and *Vineta,* named after the mystic underwater town in the Oder River. The total population of Swakopmund is now 16 800.

As the principal holiday resort of the territory, Swakopmund has a variety of hotels and bungalows and one of the largest caravan parks in Africa. There are several restaurants, including an exceptional Wienerwald, the Bayern Stübchen, and the Café Anton, famous for its pastries. The shopping centre is good, with a variety of food, clothing and other shops including curio and gemstone shops of a high standard. There is also a good bookshop.

Legend has it that a commercial traveller representing a firm making traffic control lights was once stranded in the town and couldn't pay his hotel bills, so his range of sample traffic lights was dumped on Swakopmund in lieu of payment. The same thing seems to have happened to a few other towns in the territory, which are equally hag-ridden by traffic lights. A salesman selling four-way stop signs would have been more welcome. Incidentally, many of the street signs in Swakopmund date from German times.

### Accommodation
★ Atlanta Hotel, 10 rooms, 5 with baths. R10 – R13 B/B. Phone 2360.
★ Eggers Hotel, 12 rooms, 3 with baths. R7,50 – R8,50 B/B Phone 2321.
★★ Europahof Hotel, 16 rooms, 15 with baths. R8 – R12 B/B. Phone 2503.
★★★ Hansa Hotel, 32 rooms, all with baths. R10 – R14,50 B/B. Phone 311.
★ Prinzessin Rupprecht-Heim, 26 rooms, 6 with baths. R7 – R11 B/B. Phone 2231.
★ Rapmund Pension, 15 rooms, 11 with baths. R8,50 – R10 B/B. Phone 2035.
★ Schweizerhaus Pension, 18 rooms, all with baths. R9 – R11 B/B. Phone 2419.

★ Schütze Hotel, 12 rooms, 5 with baths. R6,50 – R7,50 B/B. Phone 2718.
★★ Strand Hotel, 24 rooms, 14 with baths. R9,50 – R14,50 B/B. Phone 315.
★★ Zum Grünen Kranz Hotel, 14 rooms, 12 with baths. R12 B/B. Phone 2039.

### Caravans and camping
★★★Administration Holiday Resort, bungalows: 2 rooms (6 beds), R9 – R10,90 D. 1 room (2 beds), R4,40 D. 2 rooms (4 beds), R4,50 D.
★★★ Mile Four Caravan Park, 500 sites. R3,10 D.

From Swakopmund the coastal road to Walvis Bay stretches southwards from the town. The Swakop River is crossed by means of the longest road bridge in the territory, which is 688 m long, with its foundations penetrating 30 m of sand to rest on the essential bed rock. South of the river, the road runs into dune country and the 34-km journey along the coast to Walvis Bay can be quite an experience during a sandstorm.

The drive along a fine tarmac road, is interesting at all seasons. A strange contrast is drawn between the cold, mist-stricken waters of the South Atlantic – rich in marine life – pounding the shores of one of the most arid deserts in the world. Gigantic sand dunes move sluggishly with the winds which seem to blow incessantly, bringing with them a touch of the Antarctic if they are southerly, and the breath of a fiery dragon if they blow from the north-east. The railway maintains its right of way by means of gangs of labourers who, armed with shovels, trudge along the railway track clearing sand off the line and, leaning into the wind, they remind one of the famous painting *In the Steppes of Central Asia*.

In the midst of this desolation lies a bleak little railway siding which nevertheless can claim singular international renown. On 15 November 1962, a misguided Russian representative to the United Nations, Mr A. K. Gren, made a fool of himself by reading to the august assembly, an extract from the ebullient little twice-a-week local newspaper, published in Walvis Bay and called the *Namib Times*. In this paper, the editor features an occasional column devoted to the doings of the Rand Rifles Town Council. Mr Gren quoted an interesting passage:

'The Municipality of Rand Rifles has issued the following directive. It has come to the attention of the council that employees have been dying on their jobs and refusing or neglecting to fall down. Any employee found dead on the job in an upright position will be dismissed.'

The reluctance of its employees to move, had apparently given the Rand Rifles Council grounds for previous concern. It had even been suggested since it was becoming increasingly difficult to distinguish between the death and natural movement of some council men, that foremen should investigate if no movement was noticed in any two-hour spell. To hold a pay packet in front of the nose was a good test. There should at least be some involuntary effort made to grab the packet.

Mr Gren was not amused when it was pointed out to the United Nations that the Rand Rifles Municipality was a figment of the lively imagination of Paul Vincent, editor of the *Namib Times,* who used this means to poke fun at local council politics in general. The 'mayor' of Rand Rifles was a Mr Meyer, who had once been stationed in the place as a ganger. He had long since left and Rand Rifles was simply a place of wind, sand, fog and sunshine. The name is derived from the Rand Rifles regiment who had camped there during the First World War.

A camping ground at Dolfynstrand lies 18 km from Swakopmund. At 22 km the road passes the guano platform built in 1939 by Adolf Winter over a small, rocky islet which was a favourite resting place for sea birds such as cormorants. This platform provides a level surface for the birds, 548 m long and 274 m wide and is mounted on stainless steel pillars. Mr Winter's platform is not only convenient for the birds; it is also profitable to man. Each year after the nesting season, about 1 000 tons of guano is removed from the platform and sold as fertilizer.

Twelve kilometres beyond the guano platform (34 km from Swakopmund), lies . . .

*Overleaf: Welwitschia plants shun each other's company on the gravel plains of the Namib,*
*with mist their only source of moisture.*

# WALVIS BAY

The principal port on the south-western side of Africa, *Walvis Bay* (whale bay) lies in a superb natural harbour created as part of the delta of the Kuiseb River. These days, this extraordinary river has a flow of water which very seldom reaches the sea on the surface of its bed. After the river has received a copious amount of rainwater from the interior, it reaches the coastal plain of the Namib and simply soaks into a layer of sand about 61 m deep. This mass of sand acts as a natural reservoir, retaining a prodigious amount of water estimated at about 67,5 million kilolitres. Water that does eventually manage to filter to the sea is considered to take about 70 years to journey from the inland watershed to the buried mouth of the river.

Walvis Bay harbour consists of a deepwater bay sheltered from the open sea by a long, low, narrow spit of land running northwards, parallel to the coast and ending at Pelican Point. The bay shallows in the south where the spit is attached to the mainland and this area is the home of countless aquatic birds, particularly flamingos and pelicans. For the bird lover, this area of sandbanks and shallows is an overwhelming spectacle, especially at sunset when the birds return from their day's hunt for food and settle down for the night.

The first ship known to venture into the harbour of Walvis Bay was that of Bartholomew Dias during the course of his voyage to discover the end of Africa and the sea route to the East. On 8 December 1487, Dias entered the bay and named it the Bay of Our Lady Immaculate. The entire coast looked so barren and uninhabited that he named it the Sands of Hell. Apart from the shelter of the bay the Portuguese found the area unattractive. There was not even any surface water to drink. Heat and sand were not tradable commodities. However, the riches of the sea were well observed by the Portuguese. The first chart of the coast, produced in 1489 from the discoveries of Bartholemew Dias, called the area around Walvis Bay the *Praia dos Sardinha* (coast of sardines). By the middle of the next century the Portuguese maps were marked with the name *Bahia das Bahleas* (bay of whales) and, after being distorted in various ways, this name was taken up by visitors of other nationalities, becoming the *Walvis Bay* of today.

American and British sailors paid particular attention to the area. The rich nitrogen content of the Benguela Current supported such a wealth of plankton that it has been aptly described as a meadow of the ocean in which whales and vast shoals of pelagic fish – pilchards and anchovies – feed, moving about like flocks of sheep, with sea birds and seals in turn, devouring them.

Whales, seals and guano attracted many ships to the coast of south-western Africa in the 17th century. Walvis Bay and Sandwich Harbour lying to the south of it (another remnant of the sand-buried delta of the Kuiseb River) both came into irregular use as harbours for these ships. This shipping activity and rumours of possible wealth from copper and cattle in the interior of the territory, attracted the attention of the Dutch at the Cape. The ship *Meermin*, under Captain F. R. Duminy, was sent to inspect the coast and on 26 February 1793, Walvis Bay (as the captain called it) was annexed to Holland.

When the British occupied the Cape in 1795, Captain Alexander was sent up the coast where he hoisted the British flag in Walvis Bay. Apart from the visits of whalers and a little trade with the Topnaar Hottentots who lived in the valley of the Kuiseb and Swakop rivers, nothing official resulted from these annexations. Exploration of the interior and the first actual settlement were effected essentially by private enterprise.

In April 1837, Sir James Alexander, on a scientific expedition of discovery for the Royal Geographical Society, reached Walvis Bay after journeying overland from Cape Town. This was an epic trip by ox wagon through totally unknown country. He found the shores of the bay well littered with the spoils of whaling and a few Topnaar Hottentots in residence, living on whale meat, fish and nara melons.

The first European settlers reached the bay in June 1844 when two traders, Peter Dixon and Thomas Morris, together with their families, arrived by wagon after a tedious eight-month journey from Cape Town. They opened a store and started business by exporting cattle bartered from the inland tribes. In the following year (1845), the first missionaries arrived; first the Wesleyan Joseph Tindall, on a reconnaissance and then the Rhenish missionary, H. Scheppmann, who in that year established a station at Rooibank in the valley of the Kuiseb to serve the Topnaar Hottentots. The Rhenish Missionary Society also built the first church in Walvis Bay in 1880. The building still stands as a national monument, but the early Rooibank mission has long since vanished.

Walvis Bay prospered on the cattle trade and the development of copper mines in the interior. The first road in the territory was constructed in 1844 by the Nama chieftain, Jan Jonker Afrikaner. Known as the Bay Road, it connected Walvis Bay to the Matchless Mine and Jonker's capital of Windhoek.

The interior of south-western Africa was in a sad state of uproar during the 1870s. Rival tribes, factions, bandits and cattle rustlers were all involved in an almost lunatic series of killings and outrages. There was no supreme control of the country and many people appealed to the British Government at the Cape, to intervene. A commissioner, W. Coates Palgrave, was sent to the territory to investigate. As a result of his findings, the British decided that some intervention was necessary but the apparent poverty of the area made the prospect of adding it to the British Empire unattractive. Tentatively, the British decided to repeat their early annexation of Walvis Bay, delineate the area properly and establish a representative there who, by controlling imports, exports and immigration, might be able to influence the chaotic political events in the interior.

To fulfil this intention, the naval vessel *Industry* arrived in Walvis Bay on 6 March 1878 and on 12 March, Commander R. C. Dyer formally annexed the area demarcated by him as being 'on the south by a line from a point on the coast fifteen miles south of Pelican Point to Scheppmansdorf; on the east by a line from Scheppmansdorf to the Rooibank, including the Plateau, and thence to ten miles inland from the mouth of the Swakop River; on the north by the last ten miles of the course of the said Swakop River.' Rooibank, in the valley of the Kuiseb, was the nearest place to Walvis Bay where there was grass, trees and fresh water. The total area of this odd little enclave in the desert amounted to 750 square kilometres.

In January 1880, W. Coates Palgrave was established as the first magistrate of Walvis Bay and this was the start of British administration. Unfortunately, this date also marked the beginning of a major disturbance in the interior between the Herero and Nama people. For the next eight years, trade and mining in the interior were severely disrupted and Walvis Bay experienced little of the prosperity anticipated after the British annexation.

The arrival of the Germans in 1889 quietened down the disturbances in the interior. However, it was awkward that a German colony in south-western Africa should be dependent on a British-owned port for its trade. The Germans found this a difficult problem to solve but until they managed to develop the roadstead at Swakopmund as a port, they were forced to use Walvis Bay. A short boom followed, with the first wharf being erected in 1898 to allow ships to unload cargo directly on to the shore rather than into lighters. The wooden wharf only had a draught of 3 m at low tide with the result that large vessels still had to remain anchored further out and unload into lighters.

The conveyance of goods across the coastal belt of sand dunes was a great problem, which was eventually solved by the construction of a narrow-gauge railway stretching for 17,7 km to a terminus named Plum, near Rooikop on the German border. Mules and donkeys hauled 3-ton trucks along the line, but in 1899 a steam locomotive named Hope was sent up by sea from the Cape and this little puffer, weighing 7 tons, worked the line until 1906 when the growth of the rival port of Swakopmund lured most of the traffic away. The line fell into disuse, became covered in sand and Hope ran out of steam. Today the locomotive is mounted outside the Walvis Bay railway station as an interesting reminder of former days at the port.

The outbreak of World War I transformed Walvis Bay. It became the base for the South

African forces invading German territory. In 1915 a railway was hurriedly built to connect Walvis Bay to the German line from Swakopmund to the interior. Virtually overnight, Swakopmund fell into disuse as a port and Walvis Bay came into its own as the principal harbour of the territory.

A second wooden wharf was erected in 1922 and in 1924 work began on the dredging and construction of a first-class harbour which was opened in August 1927 by the Earl of Athlone, Governor-General of South Africa. This harbour has been still further developed and today consists of a concrete quay 1 400 m long with eight berths and a separate tanker berth 192 m long. The draught is 11 m at low water.

Water problems in Walvis Bay provide an interesting study. There is a celebrated tale of an American visiting the place, who wanted to send a postcard home to show his folks something of the local scene. Caught in a sandstorm he wandered into a hardware shop instead of a stationer and not finding any postcards available, bought a piece of sandpaper, cut it to size, stamped and addressed it and posted it off with a terse message scrawled on the back, 'Aerial view of Walvis Bay'.

In August 1874, the hunter, Gerald McKiernan, visited the port and described it in these words:

> 'No water has flowed over the bed of the Kuiseb into the bay for twelve years, so you can imagine that water is not one of the obstacles to be met with. Sand Fountain is a pit dug in the bed of the river, and yields a scant supply of very brak water. It has not rained at the bay for 18 years but fogs are common and fleas more than common. I have never seen their equal in numbers or appetite. The only known disease at the bay is intoxication. Drinking water is brought from Cape Town, and they will give you a bottle of English ale worth 25 cents sooner than a drink of water.'

In 1899 a sea water condensing plant was built by the government, consisting of a cluster of low glass buildings resembling cucumber frames. Shallow depressions in the ground were filled with sea water. The sun heated the water, the moisture condensed on the glass and was caught in gutters, yielding a supply of fresh water which was perfectly drinkable but considered to be about the most expensive in the world, selling for about R10,50 per 1 000 gallons (4 546 l).

The growth of the town and the demands of ships and thirsty steam locomotives soon outstripped the output of the condensation plant. The answer to the problem, however, was there, waiting for man to discover it. William MacDonald, who visited the place in 1914 and wrote a book called *Destiny of Walvis Bay*, made the matter very clear when he wrote:

> 'In my childhood days I was told the story of a vessel sailing in the mighty Amazon, while the crew lay dying of thirst, thinking they were still out in the open sea. At last, another ship hove in sight. The suffering crew signalled a message of distress. A moment later the amazing answer flashed back "dip down". This matter I leave with the authorities of Walvis Bay.'

Nine years passed before the hint was taken. Eventually, on the advice of Professor R. H. Charters, the government sank test boreholes into the bed of the Kuiseb upstream from Rooibank. The results were exciting and in 1927 Walvis Bay received from this source in the sandy bed of the Kuiseb, 4 500 000 l of fresh water a day and the cost dropped to R1 per 4 546 l. Today the Rooibank water scheme supplies Walvis Bay, Swakopmund and the uranium mine at Rössing with ample amounts of fresh water and it is estimated that the potential yield is sufficient to maintain the area for a considerable time to come.

This generous supply of water has transformed the desert towns. Waterborne sewerage systems have been introduced and Walvis Bay and Swakopmund are now noted for their flowers, trees (especially palms), lawns and gardens. Gardeners have a special problem in that the water table in Walvis Bay and Swakopmund is only a little over 3 m below the surface. This water is brine with a salt content about four and a half times that of sea water. Any plant or tree foolhardy enough to sink its roots into this liquid simply withers overnight. Consequently, everything cultivated has to be of the type which lives very close to the surface. Hardy, salt-tolerant trees and plants such as casuarinas, Port Jackson and pittosporum have been successfully cultivated and a park such as the one in Walvis Bay, named after the ex-mayor Mr J. C. Harries, is a splended example of skilled work, largely carried out by Mr K. H. Daehne, the first municipal gardener who was appointed in 1961.

Walvis Bay received a health committee in 1922, a village management board in 1925 and then achieved full municipal status on 16 March 1931.

Today, it is a modern little desert town of 23 000 inhabitants, flooded with brilliant sunshine and pestered by winds, drifting sand and an occasional strong whiff of sulphur caused by submarine disturbances in the bay, but at least cooled by the cold sea and its mists. The port is the coastal terminus for the railway system of the territory and the harbour is capable of handling substantial traffic. An outstanding building in the town is the civic centre.

Fishing, particularly for pilchards, developed as a major industry in the town with the first factory, the Walvis Bay Canning Company Ltd, being established in 1943 and managed by R. Ovenstone. The success of the cannery attracted a further nine factories, also canning pilchards and processing fish such as snoek for export. Large fleets of foreign fishing boats accompanied by factory ships also exploit the pilchard and anchovy shoals of the Benguela Current. Consequently, this massive onslaught has sadly depleted the natural resources of pilchards. Fishing – like mining – is essentially parasitic. It takes out but puts nothing back and the result is inevitable as man incessantly wants more and finds every excuse to avoid conservation or control.

The shopping centre of Walvis Bay is second only to Windhoek in size. There are numerous sporting facilities, including such novelties as sliding down the dunes. The bay is a fine area for yachts and waterskiers while anglers find great sport all along the coast. Fifty-six kilometres south of Walvis Bay, along a sandy track open to four-wheel-drive vehicles only, lies the great bird and angling resort of Sandwich Harbour. There are no facilities and overnight stays are not permitted. The area is also closed on Sundays but a visit during weekdays is a unique experience for bird lovers and fishermen.

The pertinent little trilingual local newspaper, *The Namib Times,* first published on 5 December 1958 by a then very youthful editor, Paul Vincent, perhaps sums up perfectly the irrepressible nature of Walvis Bay despite its setbacks, booms, peculiar difficulties and hardships which are always tempered by a commendable sense of humour and an ability to see the funny side of its own predicaments. In the issue of 16 November 1962, appeared this fruity little item:

'Walvis Bay is not commonly regarded as the "Garden City of South West Africa" and it is certainly not "The Garden of Eden". However, on Monday a European man got his facts a bit mixed and was found strolling down at the lagoon end of 7th Street completely naked.

'The police were immediately summoned after the man had surprised several passers-by and housewives who happened to notice him walking down the street.

'It is understood he since has been committed to an institution.'

## Accommodation
★★ Atlantic Hotel, 16 rooms, 7 with baths. R7 – R9,50 B/B. Phone 2811.
★ Flamingo Hotel, 39 rooms, 14 with baths. R8 – R13 B/B. Phone 3012.
★ Mermaid Hotel, 24 rooms, 18 with baths. R10 – R19 B/B. Phone 2542.
★ Casa-Mia Hotel, 11 rooms, 4 with baths. R10,50 – R16 B/B. Phone 3455.

## Caravans and camping
★★ ® Municipal, 25 sites. R1,50 D.

# THE NAMIB DESERT PARK

For the connoisseur of scenery, atmosphere and the unusual, there is nothing quite like the Namib. As a wilderness it is superb. A vast, solitary place, harsh and primeval, it is said by geologists to be the oldest desert on earth. Yet for all its severity, it is a place where life has discovered that even in its most austere mood, nature still has compassion.

In creating a landscape entirely without water, nature has relented and with a subtle alchemy, has provided mists with which to sustain an astonishing amount and variety of life. Even in so desolate a place, ruthlessness is softened by the winds which carry fragments of vegetation into the desert, providing the sustenance which enables a chain of life to begin. The brooding stillness is somehow relieved by strange harmonies murmured by the breezes as they frolic amongst the sand dunes, or play a melody, using as an instrument any chance rock, stick or rusting debris left by man. Even though the solitude of the place is immeasurable, man cannot feel alone, for something intangible, indefinable and reflective reaches out to stir his thoughts and touch his soul. At night, through the crystal clearness of the air, the dome of the sky may be seen to blaze with light and the milky way gleams like a rift in the mystery of space, through which may be glimpsed the shining lights of paradise.

In the language of the Nama people, *Namib* means a vast, open, desolate plain, a desert wilderness seemingly without end. In modern geographical terms, the name is applied to the entire arid coastal belt which varies in width from 80 km to 140 km, and extends from the sandveld at the northern end of the winter rainfall region of the Cape, as far north as the area just past Mossamedes in Angola. This expanse has been conveniently divided by geographers into three parts: in the south lies the transitional Namib, extending to approximately the line formed by the main road from Aus to Lüderitz; north of this road lies the middle Namib which the Nama themselves call the *Gobaba* – the dune country, the sea of sand, the grandest part of the desert – 400 km long and 140 km wide, which ends abruptly at the valley of the Kuiseb River; north of the river lies the northern Namib, the area of arid, seemingly endless gravel plains.

The dune sea of the middle Namib is the supreme desert. The dunes reach 275 m in height, with their nearest rivals in the empty quarter of Arabia only reaching 200 m. The Namib dunes are not only gigantic, but they are extremely beautiful, the older ones being tinted red by iron oxidisation and the younger ones more grey in colour.

Where has all the sand which makes these mighty dunes come from? The birth date of the Namib was somewhere between Oligocene and Pleistocene times, about 80 million years ago. This is considered old for a desert, but not old as far as geological ages are concerned. Something happened during that time to alter the weather – perhaps the earth received a nudge from outer space – resulting in a sudden change in the sea along the south-western coast of Africa.

A powerful ocean current, a regular 'river' of cold water originating in the Antarctic, started to flow northwards up the coast. This cold stream (10°C to 20°C) is about 150 km wide and travels at about 15 km an hour. The presence of this cold 'river' flowing close to the shoreline of South West Africa, isolates the coast from the outer warm ocean. The prevailing westerly winds pick up moisture from the warm water but in crossing the cold current, they are cooled. The winds are therefore unable to take up further moisture from such cold water and the moisture they already carry is turned into a clammy mist by the sudden drop in temperature.

The mists roll over the coast and cover the Namib, causing some dampness due to condensation, but no proper rain. Any rain which does fall on the desert comes from the east coast – a long way off. Most of the moisture contained in such easterly winds is precipitated on the highlands of the interior. As these winds drop over the escarpment to the coastal regions, they warm up to an unpleasant extent, precipitation decreases and they have a searing, dehydrating effect.

Both directions, therefore, yield little rain for the Namib, but exceptions can be caused by freak conditions. In 1934, 153 mm of rain fell in Swakopmund, a place which normally only gets 14 mm of rain a year. The flood waters of the Swakop River transported an estimated 35 million cubic metres of sediment downriver which extended the coastline more than 1 km into the sea. Walvis Bay, in addition to its numerous troubles, was inundated for several months, most of the town actually being below sea level. The Kuiseb River flooded the town, pushing the sand dunes at its mouth out to sea. The sea then flowed in as the river receded and fresh water was replaced by salt water. From January until May 1934 the only means of transportation was by boat. Snakes, washed down by the river, clambered into houses to escape drowning. Sharks swam in with the sea in search of take-aways and quick snacks. Mosquitoes bred, the supply of drinking water was disrupted and sanitary pails had to be collected by boat with the result that the town could at least claim to have waterborne sewerage!

Between 30 and 31 March 1976, in the space of 36 hours, Walvis Bay which normally receives 18 mm of rain a year, received a total of 66 mm, the equivalent of a four-year supply. The place was more than half drowned and it is said that some of its children still looked relatively clean, 12 months after the event!

The Namib can obviously be capricious and, perhaps understandably, the Nama Hottentots sometimes refer to the desert as a female. It is at its most contrary in its support of life. By all the accepted norms of deserts, nothing should live there. A desert is usually defined as an area where potential evaporation is at least twice as great as the average precipitation. In the Namib it is approximately 200 times greater, as the potential evaporation averages 3 500 mm per year, while the average precipitation is only about 18 mm. Any liquid falling on the desert surface is therefore more than promptly snatched away like air into a vacuum. How then do so many creatures live there? The answer to most questions asked in the Namib is whispered by the winds.

Winds and the cold Benguela Current were the parents of the Namib. Hills and mountains have been steadily reduced to dust by the incessant winds which wear down the rock, already weakened by expansion and contraction due to hot days and cold nights. Flooding rivers carry sand to the sea where waves wash it back on to the beach and the wind returns it to the desert. The dune sea lies in the area of greatest wind and, consequently, it has the most sand. The huge dunes are blown into parallel ridges and valleys which run in a north-south direction, totally covering a vast plain dissected by the dried-up remains of ancient stream valleys and marked by the skeletons of island-like hills.

Even though the winds perform this work of destruction and transformation, they also bring the means of life. The east wind carries on its hot breath fragments of vegetation from the escarpment. This detritus, desiccated and seemingly unappetising, is the staff of life to primitive creatures such as silverfish, who feed on this matter where it is caught at the foot of the dunes. About 200 different species of beetles also feed on this substance and on the silverfish. Scorpions, spiders, geckos, chameleons, crickets, wasps and lizards devour the silverfish, beetles and one another. The strange little 5-cm golden moles consume everything they can catch. Side-winder snakes hunt through the sand, climbing the dunes with their peculiar sideways movement. Snake-eating eagles prey on the snakes and jackals eat everything. So much for their eating habits, but from where do they all get water?

Some of the creatures make their own water by means of a complex process of synthesis from the provisions of dry vegetable matter. Most of the creatures, however, depend on the fog which extends about 110 km inland and is present on an average of 102 days a year. It precipitates from 35 to 45 mm of moisture a year, which is condensed by the desert insects, reptiles and mammals according to their own methods. The side-winder snakes simply lie in the mist and steadily lick their own bodies. Three of the nocturnal beetle species belonging to the genus *Lepidochora*, construct their own fog-collecting structures. As soon as they realise that fog is approaching, they trench up two parallel ridges in the sand. The height and orientation of these ridges traps the passing mist. The mist condenses into water along the ridges of the trench. The beetles wait until the ridges are nicely damp, then move along the trench between the ridges and take up the trapped moisture.

Amongst the specialised drinkers, perhaps the most remarkable is the beetle *Onymacris unguiculanis*, the celebrated 'fog-basking' beetle. This bustling little creature spends its days foraging the slip faces of the dunes and feeding on windblown seeds and other detritus. At sunset the beetle normally burrows into the sand to a level where the temperature is to its liking and goes to sleep in security. Creatures from many other different species do the same thing, each one finding its own level with the required 'air conditioning'. A big dune is like an apartment building, with many levels providing desirable living quarters where some occupants sleep during the day, others at night.

If the fog comes, however, there is a great stirring among the beetles. They emerge from their sleeping quarters and eagerly scramble to the knife-edged crests of the dunes. There they stand heads down, facing into the wind in order to present the maximum surface of their 20-mm-long bodies to the fog. The fog condenses on their bodies and down grooves that nature has ingeniously provided the drops of water move, straight into the mouths of the beetles. Research shows that the beetle can increase its body weight by as much as 34 per cent from moisture obtained in a single fog.

The Namib has so many unique features that it deserves much study. To aid this work, the Namib Desert Research Station was founded in 1962 at Gobabeb, with Dr Charles Koch as its guiding spirit. Dr Koch was an outstanding entomologist and the world authority on the *Tenebrionidae* (the 'tok-tokkie' beetles) who live in the Namib. He was an Austrian who became an entomologist at Vienna University, developed an interest in the *Tenebrionid* beetles and in order to study them, visited the deserts of Arabia and North Africa. In 1949 he transferred his interests to South Africa with a research grant from the South African Council for Industrial and Scientific Research. In 1953 he was appointed Curator of Coleoptera in the Transvaal Museum. The Namib, with its 200 *Tenebrionid* species of beetles, always fascinated him and the idea of establishing a research station was his brainchild. To raise funds, the Namib Desert Research Association was formed. After considerable effort, enough finance was found and the South West African Administration granted a site. Building commenced in 1962 and research in a number of fields began, with many interesting and rapid results. In October 1963, the historic rediscovery of the golden mole occurred. This strange little mammal, living only in the sand dunes of the Namib, had not been seen for 125 years and was thought to be extinct. It has no visible external eyes or ears and by some freak evolutionary process, is able to breathe and live in the sand. It 'swims' rather than burrows through the loose sand.

In 1966 the South African Council for Industrial and Scientific Research established a Desert Ecological Research Unit based on the Namib Desert Research Station. Dr Koch was appointed its first director. In 1970 the Division of Nature Conservation and Tourism of the South West African Administration assumed full responsibility for the buildings and material development. Unfortunately, Dr Koch died shortly afterwards on 23 February 1970, and was not destined to see the fine development of the Namib Station, funded by the Administration.

The South African Council for Industrial and Scientific Research continues to fund and control research activities which involves two main objectives. The first is to establish a basis for understanding the unique aspects of the Namib. Why is it that only in this desert, a fauna has developed in vegetationless areas of the dunes, using windblown detritus and fog as food and moisture? While work is being done on this problem, information is being compiled to provide a sound background for those authorities regulating the economic development now taking place in the Namib, largely resulting from the discoveries of economic minerals such as uranium. The staff consists of a director (at present Dr Mary Seely) and four permanent staff members. Various visiting scientists also carry out research at the station.

Gobabeb was selected as the site for the research station because it provides direct access to three main desert biotypes or natural divisions. These consist of the dune sea of shifting sand (the *Cobaba*), which lies south of the station; the flat, gravel plain, the Namib proper, lying to the north; and the extraordinary river which effectively divides these two divisions, the Kuiseb, with its subterranean water, vegetation, wildlife and human inhabitants, the Topnaar people.

It is said that in the Nama language, *Kuiseb* means a gorge. The name appears to describe the steep canyon through which the river finds its way from the interior highlands to the coastal terrace of the Namib. There is no other river in the world quite like the Kuiseb, for nature has allocated to it several important tasks, each of considerable interest to man.

The Kuiseb only flows very intermittently on the surface. However, this occasional surface flow is of vast importance, for the river constantly has to confront the great sand dunes of the south. The dunes inexorably attempt to cross the river and their inclination is to press northwards on to the gravel plains but the river stubbornly blocks their march. The periodic surface floods carry the encroaching sand down towards the sea. Only at the delta of the river, where surface water seldom reaches the sea except during uncommon floods (15 recorded times between 1837 and 1963), do the dunes make progress. Through this one weak spot in the Kuiseb, they force a passage and advance triumphantly up the coast until they reach the Swakop River, which finally blocks them.

The spectacle of these great, red dunes towering over the meandering valley of the Kuiseb, is awesome. The sand constantly infiltrates, furtively trickling over edges or suddenly tumbling down like a minor landslide from a more aggressive and pushful dune. It seems inevitable that the dry river course must be overwhelmed. Only rains in the interior can provide it with the strength to resist and sweep away the forceful sands.

The Kuiseb has been aptly described as a linear oasis. In complete contrast to the dunes of the south and the plains of the north, its banks and course are covered in handsome trees and rich plant life. Giraffe acacias, wild figs, ana and tamarisk trees flourish along the Kuiseb and it is a great home for the nara melon. These cucumber-like little melons provide most forms of life with food. The Topnaar people, a mini nation about 200 strong under a chief named Esau Kooitjie, live along the Kuiseb with their flocks of goats. They harvest the melons from November to April, put them on the roofs of their huts to ripen, and then boil them. The seeds float to the top and are scooped off, dried and eaten or sold in Walvis Bay. As well as being nutritious, they are claimed to be aphrodisiacs! The pulp is simply thrown on to the sand where it dries and is then rolled up like felt and stored. It can be boiled with water and eaten at any time. It is almost the only vegetable known to the Topnaars and they value the nara so highly that clumps of the shrub are claimed by inheritance. They make no effort to cultivate the plant.

Wild animals such as oryx, springbok, baboons, jackals, hyenas and other creatures also depend on the Kuiseb for their livelihood. The Topnaars dig wells into the sand of the riverbed as there is always water very near the surface. Wild animals also make shallow excavations in order to find water.

An important research duty of the Namib scientists is to monitor the level of the subterranean water. With vast quantities now being pumped out to supply Walvis Bay, Swakopmund and the mining areas such as Rössing, the possible depletion of the water could cause a lowering of the established water table with several diasastrous consequences. Apart from the withering of trees and vegetation and life becoming insupportable in the valley, the river's struggle with the sand dunes could be drastically weakened. Once across the Kuiseb they would inexorably invade the gravel plains and the consequences of such a change are difficult to visualise. It is vital that a balance be maintained and only as much water removed as can be replenished by the inland rains.

The Namib requires careful conservation as it is a curiously fragile landscape, easily damaged. Visitors driving motor vehicles at random over its gravel plain leave tracks which can scar the surface almost indefinitely. The presence of uranium and other minerals means exploitation by man, and as a result it must be understood and protected as much as possible. Too many of its plants and animals are unique. One of the very first discoveries made by the research station, along with the golden mole, was that of a new species of spider, *Leucorchestris spes,* popularly named the 'dancing spider' or the 'desert call girl' because of its habit of leaping about in a grotesque, excited dance when captured.

The strange *Welwitschia mirabilis* plants are also indigenous to the Namib. Welwitschia is a dwarf tree which simply flourishes on the moisture provided by fog. It belongs to a single species without any close relatives but curiously enough, it is very distantly related to pine and fir trees. The plant produces a turnip-like stem which can reach a width of over 1 m but which seldom projects more than a cautious few centimetres above the ground. The stem tapers off into a taproot, probing down as deep as 20 m. Two leaves are developed on opposite sides of the surface stem. The leaves are the same width as the stem and are about 3 m long, constantly growing outwards but dying at the tips where they touch the ground. Welwitschia plants always seem bedraggled, like women who always have their hair in curlers. In the harsh conditions of wind, daytime heat and night-time cold, the leaves fray into long ribbons, giving the impression that there are several, rather dilapidated leaves.

After about 20 years the welwitschia produces its first flowers, with the tenebrionid beetles providing the romantic touch of fertilisation. The lifespan of the plant is estimated at over 1 000 years. They were first discovered by Dr Friedrich Martin Welwitsch, an Austrian botanist appointed by the Portuguese Government in 1852 to carry out research on the flora of its then colony of Angola. During the following nine years, Dr Welwitsch classified 3 227 plants, including many new species, but none more bizarre than the extraordinary *Welwitschia mirabilis* which bears his name. It was known to the Angola tribes as the *ntumbo.*

Dr Welwitsch found his first specimen of this plant 1,5 km inland from Cape Negro on the south coast of Angola. Almost simultaneously, Thomas Baines found and sketched the plant in the Namib south of the Kunene River where it had, in fact, been noticed but not appreciated by early hunters in the area.

The north-eastern corner of the Namib Desert Park is the home of many welwitschias, including several exceptionally large specimens. The landscape in which they live is almost surrealistic – a vast, eerie gravel plain in a setting of sharply etched pegmatite hills. There is hardly any vegetation but in such an improbable setting the welwitschias flourish. One specimen growing there, is estimated at over 1 500 years of age. To find it, enter the park from the entrance 3,5 km from Swakopmund on the main tarmac road to Windhoek. The gravel road through the park runs for 40 km. Then, near the site of an old iron mine, there is a turnoff leading for 24 km on to a high plain where many welwitschias grow. The giant specimen lives 2 km along a signposted side track, in an enclosure protected by some rusty metal posts with holes bored through them to support wires. Quite by accident, when the wind blows in the right direction through these holes, a flute-like sound is produced, rising, falling and changing tone, creating a strange harmony of the desert, a serenade to an ancient plant.

Exploring the Namib Desert Park is a vintage experience for the connoisseur of travel, colour, atmosphere and scenery. The gravel roads are adequate and signposted. The tourist must simply guard against running out of petrol and must carry a supply of drinking water and food. There are a number of camping places but facilities are limited to pit toilets. Nights in these camps are fascinating: jackals sing; the wind and the mist wander over the face of the desert; springbok, oryx and ostriches somehow find enough to eat and drink. The silence can almost be felt.

Among the camps, Bloedkoppies, Kuiseb Canyon and Homeb are particularly attractive. The Namib Desert Research Station may only be visited by special permission. It lies 85 km from the Walvis Bay entrance to the park with the camp at Homeb 20 km further on. The research station and the Homeb camp both lie on the banks of the Kuiseb. To the north lie the gravel plains with all their remarkable contrasts of light-coloured pegmatites and dark-coloured dolerite, and in the south is the red dune country. The beautifully wooded river course, a unique world of its own, provides the division between two vastly different landscapes and biotypes.

Permits to enter the Namib Desert Park must be obtained at Swakopmund from the office of the Division of Nature Conservation and Tourism. Admission is 60c for adults and 30c for children. Camping sites cost 50c per night for up to eight people.

## THE SKELETON COAST

The name 'Skeleton Coast' or the 'Coast of Death' is applied specifically to the desolate coast stretching for 400 km between Swakopmund in the south and the Kunene River in the north. The Portuguese called this area the Coast of Hell. The Skeleton Coast was given its name in 1933 by Sam Davis, newspaperman and writer, who was reporting on the futile search for a Swiss airman, Carl Nauer, who disappeared somewhere along the coast while attempting to break the Cape Town to London solo air record.

It is an apt name, for many people have lost their lives on this formidable coast with its mists, powerful currents, cold sea and almost totally bare gravel plains, where no rain falls and there is no surface water other than a few salty springs. Modern road construction, using the ingenious technique of soaking gypsum in brine, has opened up almost the whole coast and it is now a great resort for fishermen who find the cold, misty air a tonic, after the heat and dehydration of the interior. At several points up the coast, the administration has created resorts for anglers, with toilets and camping sites. Today the Skeleton Coast is not nearly as forbidding as it used to be. Wrecks of ships, run-down mines and abandoned prospectors' claims still remain as relics of former hardships and the lost hopes of vast deposits of diamonds and precious minerals.

From Swakopmund, the salt road travels up the coast past the suburbs of Vineta and Tamariskia and after 5 km, passes the turnoff to the Mile 4 Caravan Park (see Swakopmund). At 9 km the road passes the salt works of the South West Africa Salt Company. Permits to visit these works may be obtained from the operating company in Swakopmund. The salt produced is largely used in the manufacture of plastics, synthetic materials and explosives.

At 16 km the salt road reaches the fishing site of Mile 8 and 7 km further on, the Mile 14 Caravan Park where camping sites are available at R1 D. After a further 7 km the salt road reaches a rather haphazard collection of seaside shacks and bungalows erected at the place known as *Wlotzkasbaken*, after Paul Wlotzka, a transport rider in Swakopmund and a keen fisherman, who built a hut and guided visitors here to an excellent fishing ground.

At 42,5 km from Swakopmund, the road reaches the fishing site of Mile 30 with its facilities of toilets and parking bays but where no camping is allowed. The next turnoff, after 13,5 km, leads 4 km to the camping and caravan park of Jakkalsputz, with sites available at R1 D, and 13 km beyond this camp, to the coastal resort of . . .

## HENTIES BAY

Named after Major Hentie van der Merwe who started recreational fishing there in 1929, *Henties Bay* consists of shops, tearooms, garages, a number of bungalows, and a hotel. There is a sandy, dark-coloured beach situated at the choked-up mouth of the Omaruru River. The river valley now serves as a golf course. Fishing and swimming (in cold water), and some amusing social life are the seasonal activities of the resort. Anglers secure good catches of such fish as galjoen, kabeljou, steenbras and stompneus, all of which provide excellent eating. Rock lobsters are numerous and the quality of their flesh makes them world renowned. Pilchards and anchovies have always frequented these waters in vast shoals.

## Accommodation

★ Hotel de Duine, 10 rooms, 4 with baths. R7 – R8 B/B. Phone 1.

From Henties Bay the branch road leads inland for 2 km to rejoin the main coastal salt road. The landscape is pure Namib gravel plain – hard surface, no dunes and a few shrubs. At the junction of the Henties Bay road with the main coastal road, another road continues eastwards for 118 km to join the main tarmac Swakopmund-Windhoek road.

The coastal road continues northwards. After 5,5 km a turnoff leads inland for 158 km, past the Brandberg, to the Uis Mine (see page 737) and thence to Khorixas or Omaruru. After 25 km the coastal road passes a cluster of pans and salt works with a turnoff 3,5 km further on leading to the Strathmore Tin Mine. The area is notable for its mirages, salt pans, black basalt reefs along the coast and eroded dolerite, rutile and ilmenite gravel which covers the lighter coloured sand.

One kilometre north of the turnoff to the Strathmore Mine is the Mile 72 Caravan Park with camping sites at R1 D. It was while staying in this caravan park in 1972, that Sydney Pieters, the gemstone authority from Windhoek, tired of unproductive fishing and turned his attention to some interesting looking geological indications close to the camp. He found several aquamarines at first, and then a strange, slender, hexagonal, light-blue coloured crystal, 3 cm in length which he did not recognise. He kept the crystal for a year and then sent it to the Smithsonian Institute in Washington for identification. He might not have caught any fish on his coastal outing but what he had found shook the mineralogists of the Smithsonian Institute. The crystal was Jeremejebite, a rarity discovered in Siberia 80 years previously, in the form of two crystals and some fragments the size of sugar grains. One crystal found its way to the British Museum but the other vanished and no further samples of the gemstone had ever been found.

Jeremejebite is a boron mineral with a hardness of 7. The deposit at Mile 72 is blue in colour while the original Siberian crystals were white. The Russian name, pronounced with a soft 'j', is derived from a nobleman concerned with the first discovery. The crystals found at Mile 72 are in a boron-rich setting and are associated with tourmaline, muscovite and appatite deposits which occur in a weird 'lost world' landscape of dry salt pans and dark, gravel-covered hillocks looming out of the Namib plain. Ten kilometres from the caravan park (129 km from Swakopmund) the road reaches a turnoff to . . . .

# THE CAPE CROSS SEAL RESERVE

In the year 1485 the Portuguese navigator, Diego Cão, was the first European to reach as far south down the coast of Africa as Cape Cross. In terrible isolation on a rocky crag, with the cold grey-green Atlantic to the west and the desert wilderness of the Namib behind him, he erected a cross on which was inscribed in Latin and Portuguese:

'Since the creation of the world 6 684 years have passed and since the birth of Christ 1 484 years and so the Illustrious Don John has ordered this pillar to be erected here by Diego Cão, his knight.'

Diego Cão paid with his life for daring to sail as far as this desolate spot. He died there of some unknown cause and was buried at the height named the *Serra Parda* near Cape Cross. His dust remains in that place but the cross was later removed to the Oceanographical Museum in Berlin and a granite replica now stands on the original site.

A prodigious number of Cape fur seals (about 150 000) flourish in the cold water of the Benguela Current on the south-western coast of Africa. Along this coast are numerous islets and isolated parts of the shore which they use as nurseries for their young. Although the area is described as a seal sanctuary (6 000 ha in extent), the unfortunate mammals are much hunted in the usual, brutal manner. The cows produce one pup each year and it is the pelts of these offspring which yield the best fur for the making of sealskin coats. The earliest commercial exploitation of any part of South West Africa was by sealers from Europe and America who discovered the seal colonies, killing each year many thousands of the animals. Sealskins have remained in constant demand and each year pelts, salted and graded according to size and quality, are packed in large barrels and shipped overseas. The carcasses are processed into bonemeal, liver oil, meat meal and fat. The fat is utilised in perfume and margarine industries.

Breeding takes place during October and November, at which time a large seal rookery is the scene of great activity. The bulls, weighing up to 360 kg, fight for territorial rights in one of the nurseries. After many bloody battles, a bull establishes his territory but can seldom risk leaving it for fear of a competitor invading his harem. The bulls fast for about six weeks, living on their accumulated fat. Pups are born in the rookery, and mating takes place usually within five days after the birth, the gestation period being 361 days. A bull in his prime can have a substantial harem of cows, but the day he weakens, either through ill-health, injury or the onset of old age, a younger bull will invade his territory and take over his cows.

The diet of seals consists of cephalopods, crustaceans and fish with an adult seal consuming about 5 kg of food a day. They hunt individually, there being no evidence of concerted planning by groups of seals. They frequent the shallows, searching the kelp beds for octopus, crab or crayfish, but they can also dive to depths of 80 m. A curious, and as yet unexplained habit of seals is their swallowing of stones. It has been suggested that these stones act as ballast and as many as 70 have been found in the stomach of a seal. Young seals seem to swallow more stones than the adults.

The sealing industry is an important asset to the economy of South West Africa as about 50 000 pelts are exported every year. Despite wild accusations against these creatures on the part of fishermen (who regard seals as voracious competitors), their presence signifies the existence of ample fish and owing to the wide range and tastes of seals, only a portion of their diet in fact brings them into competition with man.

Sleek and beautiful, seals are playful and friendly with swimmers and there is no record of one attacking a human being. They are hunted by sharks and have no defence against them other than flight.

Visitors are allowed into the area from 16 December to 28 February, and during the April and September school holidays from 08h00 to 17h00 daily. Weekends only from 1 March to 30 June at the same time. Admission is 60c for adults, 30c for children.

Beyond the turnoff to Cape Cross, the main coastal salt road continues for a further 24,5 km, passing (153,5 km from Swakopmund) the fishing site at Honingbaai which has toilets and parking bays. The road continues past several large pans. Numerous claim pegs and beacons reveal intense prospecting activity for a variety of precious things – somewhat surprising in a landscape which, from its dark gravel surface and black sea sand, seems to be in mourning – a real coast of death.

At 161,5 km a turnoff leads to the Brandbergwes copper mine while a further 43,5 km brings the salt road to the Ugab River and the Skeleton Coast Park entrance gate on its south bank, 205 km from Swakopmund.

## THE SKELETON COAST PARK

The Skeleton Coast Park covers an area of 1 636 000 ha conserving a very strange landscape of fog-bound coast, gravel plains, dunes in the north, sand, persistent wind, mirages and a singularly eerie atmosphere. From the entrance gate, which closes at 15h00 each day, the salt road closely follows the shoreline, passing the remains of ships such as the *South West Sea* wrecked in 1976, and the derelict diamond mine known as Toscanini (51 km from the entrance gate), remnants of the *Luanda,* wrecked in 1969, and fragments of several other forgotten shipping disasters which still litter the shoreline.

A turnoff, 103 km from the entrance gate, leads inland to Khorixas (see page 735). Pinkish-coloured sand dunes now reappear in the Namib, the first since the Swakop River, and the salt road runs northwards between them and the sea. At 10 km from the Khorixas turnoff, the road reaches the seasonal fishermen's resort of Torra Bay, said to be named after the outcrop of dolerite boulders which the Damara people call *Torra*. This resort is only open during the summer holiday season with camping sites available at 50c D each, tents for hire with 3 beds at R2,50 D. Admission is 60c for adults and 30c for children.

At 12 km north of Torra Bay the road crosses the reed-grown course of the Unjab River, with the remains of the *Atlantic*, wrecked in 1977 lying at its mouth. Springbok, oryx and other wild creatures graze in the river valley and it is a fertile example of a linear oasis in a desert. Beyond the river the salt road continues for a further 36 km and then 161 km from the entrance gate (366 km from Swakopmund), reaches the camp and administrative centre of the Skeleton Coast Park situated at the old mine of the Desert Diamond Mining Company at Terrace Bay.

The Terrace Bay camp consists of bungalows, offices, a restaurant, shop, landing strip and a jumble of debris left behind after the spectacular R42 million bankruptcy of the celebrated Mr Ben du Preez, whose name will always be associated with lost hopes on the Skeleton Coast. From the camp the road continues for a further 80 km up the coast, ending at *Möwe Bay*, named after a German warship of former years. A special permit is needed to visit Möwe Bay, the administrative centre for the northern part of the Skeleton Coast Park, which lies between the Hoanib and Kunene rivers.

The northern portion of the park is maintained as a pure wilderness area. It was on this coast, on 30 November 1942, that the *Dunedin Star* was wrecked, followed by the tug *Sir Charles Elliott* which had been sent to rescue survivors. Later a Ventura aircraft sent to drop supplies landed in a rescue attempt and stuck fast in the sand. Remnants of these wrecks still remain.

Amethysts and agates are found in this area, especially at Sarusas. There are also signs of some prehistoric settlement; mysterious circles of stones built by unknown people for unknown purposes. River courses act as linear oases and game animals are numerous, especially in the Hoarusib Canyon. Cape Frio has a large colony of fur seals and Rocky Point is the home of many sea birds.

Fishing is good all along the Skeleton Coast, where kabeljou, steenbras, galjoen, dassie and other species may be caught. Summer is a popular season as the cold sea and mists always keep the temperature cool along the coast, providing a complete contrast to the interior. Wind is the main problem, with the cold south-westerly prevailing. It occasionally retreats, however, especially in June and July, giving way to the hot easterly wind, known (because of its moaning sound) as the *Soo-Oop-Wa*.

### Accommodation
Bungalows, with inclusive restaurant meals. Single, R10,90 – R13 D, seasonal.
Double, R19,80 D, seasonal.

Reservations must be made in advance through the offices of Nature Conservation in Windhoek or Swakopmund.

## TORRA BAY TO OUTJO

The gravel road from Torra Bay to Khorixas provides a very spectacular and unusual travel experience which is at times dusty, but quite within the capability of any good driver in a normal vehicle. The turnoff to Khorixas is 9,5 km south of Torra Bay. The road is sandy at first but soon climbs on to a hard dolerite, gravel-covered plain. The temperature increases abruptly as soon as the road leaves the area influenced by coastal mists. Welwitschia plants appear, thriving in a setting abhorrent to most other plants. After travelling 25 km from the junction with the coastal salt road, the gravel road climbs a ridge of dark brown rock with the overlooking hillocks a pronounced purple colour.

Once over the ridge, the road reaches the shallow valley of the Koichab River. The valley is covered in shrubs and a few trees which offer shade and some convenience for man and dog. At 35 km from the coastal road, the inland boundary of the Skeleton Coast Park is passed. The road climbs up a wild-looking escarpment, where the air becomes considerably cooler

At 90 km from the coastal road, the main gravel road linking Khorixas with Kamanjab is reached. Turning to Khorixas, the traveller is faced with a spectacular drive through a rugged mass of strangely shaped, vividly coloured hills, where many interesting rocks may be found at the roadside. The geology is complex and interesting. There is a confusion of sedimentary and igneous rocks whose combination produces remarkable mixtures, metamorphoses, intrusions, changes and colours. Some of the hills are actually composed of volcanic ash, spewed out from ancient eruptions and accumulated as vast heaps of debris.

At 132 km from the coast, the road reaches a turnoff running 20 km through well-wooded mopane tree country to the slopes of the vividly coloured ridge of hills known as the Verbrande Berg or Burnt Mountain. At the 20-km point is a turnoff leading to Twyfelfontein (see below). The road continues for a further 5,5 km, passing an odd rock formation known as the Organ Pipes and then ends at the foot of the remarkable Burnt Mountain. The mountain is a flat-topped remnant of an old plateau, extensive in size. The colours of its cliffs are almost unbelievable, with dark reds and purples predominating. The road ends where there are piles of black, cinder-like rock, resembling slag raked out from furnaces beneath the Burnt Mountain. The place gives one the uncanny impression of being a vast, phantom brickfield or pottery where various demons are employed in the baking of building materials, ceramics and large beer mugs. The Burnt Mountain is the kiln, still red hot, out of which the cinders are regularly raked, forming a pile at its foot.

# TWYFELFONTEIN

On the road to the Burnt Mountain, there is a 5,5-km turnoff to Twyfelfontein and its world-famous collection of rock engravings. The road ends at the ruins of a farmhouse in a valley at the foot of the Burnt Mountain plateau. The position of the engravings indicated by arrows, is in the rocks of a steeply sloping ravine east of the farmhouse.

The valley is known in the Damara language as Uais (one fountain). This fountain, when it flows, has greatly attracted game animals and man. Since its nature has always been erratic, Europeans have named it Twyfelfontein (doubtful fountain).

There are numerous, well-preserved rock engravings here. Their origin is uncertain, but they are probably the work of Bushman or Hottentot artists and estimated by some to be about 5 000 years old. Engraving on rock is difficult, with no chance of erasing errors. The engravings at Twyfelfontein are so skilfully done that they must have been the work of an artist or artists who had previously learned the skill on waste rock and who had made no amateurish mistakes. The engravings suggest that the artist experienced keen intellectual pleasure in executing them.

The main road from the Skeleton Coast to Khorixas passes the turnoff to the Burnt Mountain and Twyfelfontein, and traverses a mopane tree parkland dotted with isolated hills and ridges. After 28,5 km (160,5 km from the coastal road), a turnoff leads for half a kilometre to the Petrified Forest where a considerable number of petrified tree trunks can be seen lying on the ground. No one is certain where they come from and why they are so well preserved.

The main road continues for a further 42 km, then reaches a junction with a left turn leading for 1,5 km to the fine tourist camp of Khorixas, a real haven in the wilderness, with accommodation, a restaurant, swimming pool and shop.

### Accommodation
★★★ ® Khorixas Rest Camp, bungalows: luxury (4 beds), R15 D. Ordinary (4 beds), R12 D. Ordinary (2 beds), R8 D. Rondawels (2 beds), R6 D.

### Caravans and camping
Per site, R3 D up to 4 people.

From the turnoff to the Khorixas Rest Camp, the main road continues for 2,5 km and then reaches the village of Khorixas, formerly known as Welwitschia. *Khorixas* is a corruption of the Damara name *Gôrigas,* a species of water bush which flourishes in the area. The reason for the misspelling is not known as Gôrigas is the correct pronunciation of the name. The village is growing considerably as the administrative centre for Damaraland. It is 202 km from the salt road up the Skeleton Coast.

From Khorixas the main gravel road continues eastwards through the mopane parkland. After 8 km there is a crossroads with a turn north to Kamanjab and south to Uis. A further 23 km brings the road to a turnoff leading southwards for 18 km to the oft-photographed rock known as *Vingerklip* (finger stone). This is one of several detached pinnacles of rock remaining in the area after the erosion of an ancient landscape and is about 18 m high. Vingerklip stands on a private farm whose owner charges an admission fee of 40c per car.

From the turnoff to Vingerklip, the main road continues eastwards for 5,5 km then passes a turnoff to the ★★★Bambatsi Holiday Ranch and Restaurant, a popular resort with accommodation available at R15 D/B/B.

After the turnoff to Bambatsi, the main road stretches 72 km, then reaches the town of Outjo (see page 707) 310 km from the Skeleton Coast salt road.

## KALKFELD, OMARURU, UIS AND THE BRANDBERG

From Otjiwarongo, a fine tarmac road leads south-westwards over an undulating plain covered with acacia and other trees. This is superb ranching country where fine herds of beef stock, mainly of zebu varieties, graze on the grass and leaves. Occasional hillocks rise abruptly from the bush. After 70 km, the road passes through the small rail centre of Kalkfeld, with its cluster of stores and houses watching the trains go by. After 64 km of pleasant travelling, the tarmac road reaches the town of . . . .

## OMARURU

This little place, with its population of 3 712, has a Herero name meaning 'the bitters' after the bitter tasting water of the area which affected the milk of the tribal cattle herds.

The Omaruru River, on whose banks the town stands, is dry for most of the year but is formidable during its occasional floods. The riverbanks are lined with magnificent trees and the town, with its long main street running parallel to the river, is well shaded and pleasant. The town is a rail, ranching and dairy centre, with a pretty tourist camp situated beneath the trees to accommodate travellers exploring the country.

The town was originally a German police post and during the 1904 Herero War, had a few hectic experiences. The Herero laid siege to the post and the officer commanding, Captain Victor Franke, had a rough time quelling an upheaval that cost the lives of 123 German civilians and eventually, many thousands of Herero. The war is commemorated in Omaruru by the Franke Tower, a fortification erected in 1907 which now houses a museum.

On 4 August 1905, the narrow-gauge railway reached Omaruru from the coast. Now being linked to the outside world, the town started to grow, receiving its first municipal council on 22

July 1909. The narrow-gauge railway was eventually replaced by a wide-gauge line in 1961. A creamery opened there in 1928 was the first to be registered in the territory.

## Accommodation
★ Central Hotel, 10 rooms, 5 with baths. R8 – R12 B/B. Phone 30.
★ Staebe Hotel, 17 rooms, 14 with baths. R7 – R9 B/B. Phone 35.

## Caravans and camping
★ ® Municipal caravan park, R2 D per site. Bungalows: 2 beds, R2,50 – R6 D. 3 beds, R4 D.

From Omaruru, the main tarmac road continues south-westwards. After 3 km a gravel turnoff leads to the Kranzberg Mine and Paula's Cave. At 60,5 km from Omaruru the road joins the main tarmac Windhoek-Swakopmund road.

Another interesting drive from Omaruru leads westwards to the tin mine at Uis and also to the Brandberg. This gravel road crosses a vast plain covered with shrubs and acacia trees. The imposing heights of the Brandberg lie on the western horizon and to the south is the massive bulk of the Erongo mountains. The landscape becomes increasingly arid towards the west. After 30 km there is a turnoff south leading to the Bushman caves and tourist resort of Etemba where accommodation is available at R11 B/B in a ★ranch-style private hotel. At 115 km there is a turnoff which passes the Spitzkoppe on its way to Usakos and after a further 1,5 km (116,5 km from Omaruru), the road reaches the tin mine of . . .

# UIS

It is said that *Uis* simply means 'bitter water' in the Damara language. The landscape is composed of many interesting varieties of pegmatites containing tin intrusions which appear as black-coloured streaks and blobs. In 1911, Dr Paul, while journeying by horse from Otjimboyo to the Brandberg, observed these signs of tin. He was an employee of the Deutsche Kolonialgesellschaft and the company pegged a number of claims in the area. A local farmer, Etemba Schmidt, also pegged a substantial block.

Mining commenced, but conditions were primitive and there was a serious shortage of water. The pioneers persisted, using donkeys to drag rolling barrels of water obtained from a spring known as Uis Water, 13 km away. In 1923, August Stauch, who had started the diamond rush at Kolmanskop, bought up all the tin claims and consolidated them into Namib Tin Mines Ltd. This company, unfortunately, went bankrupt in 1930 and the claims passed through various hands with a German mining engineer, E. Vaatz, working them from 1934. With the outbreak of World War II, he was interned, and after hostilities, in 1948, the Custodian of Enemy Property sold the tin claims for £13 000 to a partnership headed by a Mr Munro. After diligent work in the area, Mr Munro and his wife were killed in an air crash in 1949 but as a result of his labours, the Uis Tin Mining Company (S.W.A.) Ltd was formed in 1951 and the first large-scale mining commenced. In 1958, Industrial Minerals Exploration (Pty) Ltd, a subsidiary of the South African Iron and Steel Industrial Corporation (Iscor), acquired the mineral rights of the Uis Mine and associated properties and claims scattered over the Namib Desert.

After investigating the various prospects, the company decided to concentrate on the Uis Mine and in 1966 the Industrial Minerals Mining Corporation was formed to exploit this property. This company is a wholly-owned subsidiary of Iscor which set out to develop a major mine in the area. To achieve this, the problem of water had to be solved. Adequate supplies were eventually obtained through a pipeline running all the way from the Omaruru River where considerable quantities are stored in natural reservoirs beneath the sand.

In the vicinity of Uis there are eight major outcrops of pegmatite dykes containing fairly low concentrations of tin. They vary in width from a few centimetres to about 60 m and lengths of over 900 m are exposed on the surface. Mining is by open-cast quarry. The tin is processed to a concentrate which is sent to Swakopmund where it is loaded on to trains for the long ride to a reduction plant at Vanderbijlpark in the Transvaal.

A small town has been built west of the mine to house the workers. The mine lies in the Damara oKombahe Reserve.

From Uis the gravel road continues westwards towards the Brandberg and after 28 km joins the gravel road from Khorixas (127 km) to Henties Bay (120 km). This is a road which yields magnificent views of the Brandberg, the highest massif in the territory and its principal peak, Köningstein (2 579 m high). This range of mountains is impressive from any direction. Thirteen kilometres down the road towards Henties Bay there is a turnoff leading to the Brandberg West Mine. This road is worth exploring for those who wish to photograph the Brandberg.

Fifteen kilometres up the road towards Khorixas, from the junction with the road from Uis, there is a turnoff leading for 30 km to the Tsisab gorge in the Brandberg where may be seen one of the most celebrated of all examples of rock art.

## THE WHITE LADY OF THE BRANDBERG

The rock shelter containing this famous painting lies in a superb setting. The Tsisab gorge is named after the leopards who live in the area. It is a wild and beautiful place where a vast jumble of rocks, remnants of many ancient landslides, choke up the gorge. When it rains, a stream somehow finds its way through this wilderness of stone. Pools of water remain well into the dry season before they sink beneath the sand to hide from the heat of the sun.

It was in 1918 that the surveyor and painter, Reinhard Maack, first found the rock shelter in this gorge and drew the attention of the world to the gallery of paintings it contained. The Abbé Breuil visited the site in 1948 and brought out a book in which the rock art of the shelter was reproduced. The book also established the fame of the central figure, named by the Abbé Breuil the White Lady of the Brandberg, who speculated that she was of Phoenician or other exotic origin.

These days, the impression is that the good Abbé was possibly romantically inclined. The painting of the figure in question is intriguing, beautiful and most interesting, but the depiction is almost certainly that of a male – probably a youth daubed in white clay for some ceremony or dance. In fact, it would be more precise to call 'her' the White Knight of the Brandberg! Whatever the identification of the central figure – and it is still controversial – this gallery of prehistoric rock art in the Maack Cave has fascinated innumerable visitors. A walk up the valley to the shelter (well marked with arrows) is an exciting experience. Please do not throw liquids of any kind over the paintings to make them clearer. Such drenchings have greatly harmed the gallery, causing the paintings to fade and decay.

Chapter Thirty-Seven

# NAMIBIA

## THE SOUTHERN AREAS

From Windhoek the main tarmac road and railway to the south has a lengthy, steady climb from the 1 655-m altitude at which the capital is situated, to the siding of Kruin (1 922 m). The scenery comprises a rugged mass of bronze-coloured, bush-covered hills and the journey is attractive either by rail or road.

Once over the ridge, the railway and road commence a winding descent, passing the station, store and ★ hotel of *Aris* (place of the steenbok) 24 km from Windhoek. From this point, the road traverses a parkland of handsome trees, many of which support the unwieldy community nests of the social weaver birds. Long grass, high hills and graceful trees combine to produce a pleasant landscape. After 89 km the road reaches the town of . . .

## REHOBOTH

This is the centre for the 11 257-strong tribe of *Basters* (half-breeds) whose origin can be traced back to about 30 European renegades and adventurers who settled in the mountains south of the Orange River, married Hottentot girls and fathered numerous offspring. In 1868, about 90 Baster families moved to the site of Rehoboth where an abandoned mission station stood. They settled in this beautifully wooded area and developed into the present community, with a handsome church watching over the village built among the trees.

South of Rehoboth, the main tarmac road leads through fine park-like country, made doubly attractive by a varied collection of mountains and hills lying to the north and east. As the road continues south, through good ranching and livestock country, the trees dwindle into a well-grassed savanna, with low acacia thornbush. At 97 km the road passes through the small rail and trading centre of *Kalkrand* (chalk ridge) with accommodation provided by the ★ Kalkrand Hotel.

For a further 52 km the tarmac road travels south across the savanna, then reaches a point where the landscape changes notably. The road suddenly loses more than 100 m in altitude, descending an escarpment into the broad and level valley of the Fish River. At the bottom of this turnoff, 58 km from Kalkrand, a tarmac turnoff leads for 12 km to the . . .

## HARDAP DAM

Completed in 1963, this dam is one of the showpieces of the territory and a major recreational asset to a thirsty land. The 39,2-m-high dam wall contains a lake holding 232 million cubic metres of water, covering an area of 25 square kilometres. The dam irrigates an extensive agricultural settlement producing a considerable variety of products, including table grapes and vegetables.

The administration has developed the lake and its verges into a superb recreational area with water sports and fishing. Bungalows, a caravan park, restaurant and shop have been built on a viewsite. The area surrounding the lake is a nature reserve, sheltering a good population of oryx, mountain zebra, eland, springbok, hartebeest, kudu and other antelope, while bird life is prolific.

*Overleaf: Mukurob, the finger of God; perhaps a reminder to the Creator of one forgotten essential in this wilderness – water?*

The lake projects 30 km upriver and contains vast quantities of fish such as large and small-mouth yellowfish, blue kurper, carp, barbel, mud mullet and mudfish. There is an aquarium in the main office block and excellent fish dishes are served in the restaurant.

The origin of the name Hardap is controversial, but is thought to derive from a Nama name originally applied to a big pool now flooded by the waters of the manmade lake. This pool was known as *!Narob,* meaning an iron hook used by the Nama for fishing.

## Caravans and camping

★★★®100 sites, R3,10 D. Bungalows: 5 beds, R9,40 D. 3 beds, R7,30 D. Rooms (2 beds), R3,60 D.

Admission: Day visitors R1,20 adults, 60c children. Overnight visitors: 60c adults, 30c children.

From the turnoff to the Hardap Dam, the main tarmac road continues south for a further 16 km, then reaches the town of . . .

# MARIENTAL

Named after Marie Brandt, wife of H. Brandt, the pioneer settler in the area, *Mariental* is the principal town of the Gibeon magisterial district and the rail and trading centre for a considerable industry in the breeding of karakul sheep. There are 6 430 people living there.

## Accommodation

★ Mariental Hotel, 20 rooms, 9 with baths. R6 – R11 B/B. Phone 856.
★ Sandberg Hotel, 23 rooms, 17 with baths. R7,50 – R9 B/B. Phone 2291.

From Mariental, the main tarmac road proceeds southwards along the level, increasingly arid floor of the broad Fish River Valley. To the east lies the extraordinary flat-topped escarpment of the Weissrand, while to the west, the country rises towards the Schwarzrand, 95 km away. The vegetation is notably more sparse than it is in the north.

After 52 km of travel the road passes the railway station of Gibeon, where a turnoff to the west leads to the old mission station of the same name, originally founded in 1863 for the benefit of the Witbooi tribe of Hottentots.

The tarmac road now traverses a vast, arid plain with only a glimpse of mountain in the west. The dullness of this landscape, however, is relieved by several features of considerable interest, one of which is a height so dominant, that for 80 km of travel it provides a constant landmark on the western side of the road. This is the extinct volcanic crater known as *Mount Brukkaros,* 1 586 m high. Its strange name, meaning 'skin trousers', derives from a Hottentot tribe once living on its slopes, who affected that garment. The deep crater of this volcano, over 2 000 m in diameter, has a flat, rubble-filled floor and it was from here, in 1930, that the Smithsonian Institute studied the surface of the sun in detail.

At 96 km from Mariental the road reaches the small railway centre of *Asab* (the new place). From this point, a turnoff stretches eastwards for 23 km to the much-photographed and remarkable natural feature known as *Mukurob* (the finger of God). This formation consists of a steep cone of slate, topped with a 34-m-high pillar of rock which points towards the heavens like a gigantic admonishing finger. A small dried-out pan at the foot of the pillar, and the remnant of a table-topped plateau nearby are also of interest. Mukurob is so precariously balanced that, in geological terms, it won't last for very much longer. God must have had a touch of humour when He made it. Maybe He had forgotten something and had left the finger as a reminder?

Beyond the turnoff to Mukurob, the main tarmac road continues south. At a distance of

144 km from Mariental the road passes the railway station, mission and administrative centre known as *Tses,* the name of which means a travelling stage of a day's journey.

A further 78 km (222 km from Mariental) brings the road to a gravel turnoff leading eastwards for 13 km to Koes and the farm *Gariganus,* where a forest of kokerbooms (*Aloe dichotoma*) may be seen growing. These are trees which normally do not seem to like one another, therefore they grow apart. At this place, however, about 300 of them – fat, thin, short, tall, old and young – do manage to grow in close proximity. They are protected as a national monument. The name of *kokerboom* (quiver tree) comes from the Bushman practice of hollowing out the pithy interiors of the branches and using the tough outer casings of bark as quivers in which to keep their weapons.

Three kilometres south of the turnoff to the kokerboom forest (225 km from Mariental) lies the town of . . .

# KEETMANSHOOP

This place was named after a wealthy German industrialist, Johan Keetman, who actually never visited the town. He provided funds for the establishment there in 1866 of a mission station for the benefit of Hendrik Zeib's section of the Nama people. The mission flourished, despite a fiendish succession of droughts, violent floods from the usually dry Swartmodder River, and murderous disturbances among the surrounding population of primitive tribes-people. The substantial stone mission church, built in 1895, still dominates the town and its clock continues to sound the hours with a pleasant chime. The building now houses a museum which is open on Wednesdays and Saturdays.

A school and hostel were attached to the mission and traders arrived. In 1894, after the German annexation of the territory, a garrison established itself there in a fort, later moving to what is now the rather picturesque castle-like police station and administrative building. Settlers began farming (largely the breeding of karakul sheep) and the town started to develop as the principal centre in the southern part of the territory.

In a climate as thirsty as this, a brewery inevitably followed, while four hotels did a roaring trade. In 1908 a narrow-gauge line was completed to the town from Lüderitzbucht on the coast. With an imposing German colonial-type railway station, Keetmanshoop became established as a trading, administrative and commercial centre for a prosperous karakul-breeding district. Political changes after the First World War did not impede the town's growth and today it remains a flourishing and busy little centre of 13 050 people, in the heart of the surrounding thirstlands. It is a neat, clean and friendly place, with several interesting buildings surviving from the German days.

### Accommodation
★★★ Canyon Hotel, 47 rooms, all with baths. R12 – R25 room only. Phone 361.
★ Union Hotel, 26 rooms, 7 with baths. R10 – R11 B/B. Phone 331.

### Caravans and camping
★ Municipal caravan park, 30 sites. R1,50 D.

# THE KARAKUL SHEEP INDUSTRY

This industry in the southern portion of the land of Namibia originated in 1902 when a German fur trader, Paul Thorer, visited Bukhara (in Uzbekistan, Russia) during the course of his business. As an experiment he decided to buy some of the fur-producing sheep known as the *Karakul* (black lake), or Persian sheep. A total of 69 sheep were shipped to Germany on his behalf but conditions in Europe were totally unsuitable for them.

It was subsequently suggested that climatic conditions in South West Africa, then a German colony, would be similar to those of the arid natural home of the karakul in Asiatic Russia. Friedrich von Lindequist, Governor of South West Africa at the time, received the idea with enthusiasm. Twelve karakuls were sent from Germany in 1907 and results were so encouraging that two years later Thorer shipped out 278 more sheep. An experimental farm, *Fuerstenwalde*, was established by the government, forming the basis of the present prosperous industry.

After the First World War, the South African administration continued research in karakul breeding and a new experimental farm was established at *Neudam*, near Windhoek. The standard of sheep was systematically improved. In 1919 the Karakul Breeders' Association was formed and a karakul stud book opened. As a means of identification, photographs of lambs were taken and negotations with international furriers were started to place the industry on a sound commercial basis.

The value of pelts steadily increased. In 1937 the industry genuinely came of age when, for the first time, over one million pelts were exported (1 190 212), fetching £1 222 629. In 1941, over two million pelts were exported and in 1976 the figure reached 2,8 million, valued at R50 million. The United States and Canada are the largest markets for the pelts.

---

From Keetmanshoop, the main tarmac road continues southwards across savanna country, through the range of the *Karas* (sharp) Mountains. This is a landscape of bronze and burnished colours, sunbaked to such an extent, that it seems never to have quite cooled since its creation. Acacia thorn trees flourish in the area, however, and in their boughs the social weaver birds have built many communal nests where vast flocks live in a strange society of dissident chirps, whistles, scandals and gossips associated with bird life.

After 159 km the road reaches the small rail centre of *Grünau* (green meadow) rather incongruously named after one of the suburbs of Berlin, somewhat remote from the situation of this little place: It forms the junction of a tarmac road to Karasburg (52 km away) and Upington in South Africa, and of a gravel road to the Fish River Canyon. From Grünau with its shops, garage and ★ hotel, the main tarmac road crosses the railway and continues southwards over a spacious, sandy plain dotted with isolated hills, several of which have interesting shapes. After 30 km there is a turnoff to Ai-Ais (see page 743), and another turnoff to the same place, 99 km from Grünau. The main tarmac road then traverses a lunar-like plain with weirdly shaped hillocks and ridges of saw-toothed peaks.

There are turnoffs to several mines such as the Seven Pillar Mines, and a long steady descent into the valley of the Orange River. Having come 140 km from Grünau, the main road reaches . . .

## NOORDOEWER

This small centre, whose name means 'north bank', lies at the southern end of the vast, sparsely populated south-west African land of Namibia. Four kilometres south of it the road reaches the border of South Africa on the Orange River and the bridge at Vioolsdrif which connects the two countries.

**Accommodation**
★ Suidwes Motel, 24 rooms, 20 with baths. R6,90 – R7,90 room only. Phone 13.

**Caravans and camping**
Sites, R2,50 D.

# THE FISH RIVER CANYON AND AI-AIS

The Fish River Canyon is one of the most staggering scenic spectacles in Africa and reputedly second only in size to the Grand Canyon of America. The canyon is 161 km long, 27 km wide at maximum, and 457 m to 549 m deep. It is revealed with startling abruptness in an arid landscape covered with pebbles, euphorbias and small succulents.

These days, the Fish River, whose energy caused this vast gash in the landscape, flows intermittently only, but water is always contained in a succession of deep pools which are full of fish such as barbel and yellowfish. Four pluvials (wet periods) seem to have occurred in the south-western part of Africa during the last million years, resulting in the powerful run-off of water which eroded this canyon.

Several springs occur on the floor of the canyon, the most notable being *Ai-Ais*, a Nama name meaning 'very hot'. This spring has a temperature of 60 °C and is rich in fluorides, sulphates and chlorides which are reputedly beneficial to people suffering from rheumatic and nervous disorders. The spring has been developed by the administration into a first-class resort.

Hikers are fond of walking through the canyon, following the route which is 86 km long and normally takes four days to complete. Permits are issued each day to one group only, comprising three to 40 people and then only between 1 May and the end of August. A medical certificate of fitness must be produced when applying for permission.

Ai-Ais is open from the second Friday in March to the end of October, the rest of the year being too hot for visitors.

From the main tarmac road stretching from Noordoewer to Grünau, there are two gravel turnoffs leading to Ai-Ais. The first turnoff starts 30 km south of Grünau from where it is 62,5 km to Ai-Ais. The road descends into the Fish River Valley through a jagged mass of rocks rich in rose quartz and the natural habitat of the strange plant *Pachypodium namaquanum*, popularly known from their shape as 'Elephant's Trunk' or 'Halfmens'.

At 12,5 km prior to reaching Ai-Ais, this road from Grünau is joined by another gravel road leading for 82,5 km to the main tarmac north-south road, which it joins 41 km from Noordoewer.

At a point 22,5 km from Ai-Ais on the road to Grünau, there is a turnoff which leads northwards for 55 km to the viewsites overlooking the grandest part of the canyon. There are toilets and resting places at these viewsites, and paths down to the floor of the canyon take hikers to the starting points of the walk to Ai-Ais. From the main viewsite there is a road along the eastern edge of the canyon which ends in a cul-de-sac after 18 km. This road reveals many magnificent views of the canyon. From the main viewsite a road stretches eastwards for 48 km to join the Grünau-Seeheim road, 37 km from Grünau.

Monitor lizards, numerous birds, snakes, baboons and mountain zebra inhabit the canyon which, scenically, is awesome; a brutal scar, the unhealed wound from several lashings inflicted by nature's rage. The impression is grand, sombre and immensely powerful.

## Caravans and camping

★★★® Ai-Ais Hot Springs: caravan and camping sites, R2,10 D.

Caravans (4 beds), R5,20 D. Tents (4 beds), R4,20 D. Flats (4 beds), R7,30 D.

Admission to the hot springs is: day visitors, R1,20 for adults, 60c for children. Overnight visitors, 60c for adults, 30c for children.

# KEETMANSHOOP TO LÜDERITZ

Two kilometres out of Keetmanshoop on the main tarmac road to South Africa, a turnoff to the west leads to Lüderitz and the coast of diamonds. The tarmac road traverses a well-grassed plain covered with kokerbooms and various trees. At 32,5 km there is a gravel turnoff to the Naute Dam and at 44 km a turn to Seeheim, the Fish River Canyon and Grünau.

The road crosses the Fish River 1,5 km further on. At this stage in its course, the river flows intermittently down a broad, shallow valley where there is no hint of the canyon soon to start. Forts were erected by the Germans to guard the river crossings along this road and there are turnoffs to these historical monuments, of which nothing much remains. Many flat-topped hillocks may be seen in this area, with the dolerite 'umbrellas' which protect their summits.

At 105,5 km the road reaches the small railway centre known as *Goageb,* whose name indicates that it is at the junction of two rivers. A ⋆ hotel and a few shops comprise the commercial area. From Goageb a tarmac road stretches for 30 km to the old mission station of Bethanie, established in 1814 by the Reverend Heinrich Schmelen for the benefit of the Hottentots resident in the area. The original house belonging to the missionary and the house of Captain Fredericks, chief of the Orlam Hottentot tribe, are preserved as historical monuments. The village comprises a ⋆ hotel and shops. From Bethanie (sometimes spelt Bethanien), the road continues for 82 km to the small rural centre named after the village of Helmeringhausen in Westfalia.

From Goageb (pronounced *Gwageb),* the main road to Lüderitz continues over undulating savanna country. After 20 km there is a gravel turnoff to Bethanie; at 102 km a turnoff to Helmeringhausen, and after another kilometre (193 km from Goageb), a turnoff leading southwards for 163 km to the zinc mine of . . .

# ROSH PINAH

This mine was discovered by one of the most renowned prospectors of the south-western part of Africa, Mose Eli Kahan, a Prussian Jew who immigrated to South Africa in order to escape Nazi persecution, and who eventually became a prospector. Rumours of vast mineral riches in the south-west African wilderness attracted him to the territory and in the valley of the lower Orange he discovered a copper deposit which he pegged and named *Lorelei.* The deposit was situated in remote and extremely difficult mountain country, although there was a track leading from Aus down to the Orange River at *Sendelingsdrif* (missionaries' ford). This track was used by a few farmers and in order to guard Sendelingsdrif, the Germans had erected a police post and camel patrol station on the north bank of the river.

Mose Kahan, by dint of vast exertion, improved the track and commenced mining for copper. In 1930, the price of copper fell below working costs and Kahan turned his attentions to diamonds. Although his eyesight was failing and he had to use a monocle, persistence spurred him on to make several rich discoveries along the diamond coast north of Lüderitz. He found a fortune in the sands of the Namib coast but he never forgot the mountains north of Lorelei.

In 1968, in *Namasklufd* (cleft of the Namas), where the track from Sendelingsdrif passed through the mountains, he found the deposit of zinc to which he gave the Hebrew name *Rosh Pinah* (the cornerstone), because he considered the discovery to be the most important one of his life and the cornerstone of his mining endeavours. He died shortly after the discovery but his son George successfully concluded negotiations started by his father with the South African Iron and Steel Corporation for a joint venture in bringing the mine into production.

Rosh Pinah is now a major producer of zinc. The old track from Aus has been developed into a first-class gravel road, with an extension 22 km long, leading to the Orange River from where the mine draws its water. The Octha Diamond Mine lies on the south bank of the river, the South African side, where Oscar Thanning found diamonds in a concession area of the O'Kiep Copper Company. The name *Octha* is a combination of the company name and that of the prospector. A village has been created at Rosh Pinah to house the mine workers. The area is renowned for its succulents.

From the turnoff to Rosh Pinah the main road to Lüderitz continues for a further 2,5 km and then, 105,5 km from Goageb, it reaches the village and railway centre of *Aus* (place of snakes) with its ★ hotel, shops, garages and residences.

Beyond Aus, a first-class tarmac road takes the traveller on a fascinating journey, smoothly descending the escarpment into the magic world of the Namib Desert and the *Sperrgebiet* (prohibited area). After 23 km the road crosses the wire fence which marks the eastern boundary of Diamond Area No. 1 and from this point, travellers are restricted to the tarmac main road and its immediate verges.

The surface of the Namib is gravel, forming the transitional area to the great dune country whose start can be seen to the north. At first clumps of shrub occur, but these peter out as the road continues westwards next to the railway line. Oddly shaped rock islands loom up abruptly from the plateau while patches of pink-coloured sand creep in from different directions. This is a gorgeous stretch of desert wilderness, rich in subtle colours and forms, with wide views of vast space.

At 86,5 km there is a turnoff northwards to Koichab Pan, and after 13,5 km a turnoff to the south where the road to the river of diamonds begins (see page 747). At 110 km the road passes the Lüderitz airport and after another kilometre, the turnoff to the ghost town of Kolmanskop which may be visited by a permit obtainable from the Consolidated Diamond Mines office in Lüderitz. For a further 10 km, the road winds its way through a mass of rock and then, 121 km from Aus, reaches the port of . . .

# LÜDERITZ

Populated by 7 250, this is an atmospheric, faded little place, whose early bustle is a past dream, and where there are now almost as many empty shops and houses as those that are occupied. There still lingers, however, an intangible feeling of the glamour and excitement of past events; a history rich with stories of prospectors and diamonds; of fortunes made and hopes lost; of fishing and guano; strange rumours of schemes, intrigues, projects; and the adventures of a colourful company of human beings.

In January 1488, the pioneer explorer, Bartholomew Dias, sailed down the coast he called the Sands of Hell and found his way into the sheltered harbour the Portuguese named *Angra Pequena* (little bay). For five days, bad weather detained Dias in the bay. On Pedestal Point he erected a stone pillar dedicated to St James and when he sailed, he left a solitary negress standing forlornly on the beach. She was one of four unfortunate women kidnapped from their home on the coast of Guinea by the Portuguese and dumped down on selected spots along the coast in order to spread the fame of Portugal to any local inhabitants who might be inclined to listen rather than run.

The Portuguese, as well as subsequent visitors, all recognised Angra Pequena as the finest natural harbour on the entire coast of south-west Africa but its setting was repellent. Nature could not have been in a particularly good mood when the area was created. The wind blows cold, with a nasty persistence; the situation is a rock wilderness denuded in appearance, a mixture of dark-coloured dolerite and light-coloured granite.

The shoreline is inhospitable for most of its length. Rocky cliffs, stark and sharp, rear out of the cold sea like packs of predatory animals snarling hungrily at passing ships. Mist rolls in almost daily, particularly around Dias Point where a rather battered looking lighthouse stands in defence of the land, a small clenched first holding the mist at bay, with a foghorn next to it growling like a defiant watchdog.

A number of dried-out pans lie among the rocks and there are some beaches of grey-coloured dolerite sand, such as *Grosse Bucht* (great bay). Halifax Island provides a sheltered lee for Guano Bay, while Agate Beach is well protected by three islets: Flamingo, Sea and Penguin. Shark Island, connected to the mainland by a causeway, provides shelter for the

745

Robert Harbour and its yacht basin. The presence of gypsum in the sand at many places yields the strange crystals known as 'desert roses', while agates can be found on the beaches.

Sealers, whalers, fishermen and guano collectors were the first people to use the harbour, but the total absence of drinking water was the ultimate disadvantage to life in a difficult, moody part of the world.

The man who was destined to influence the area was Adolf Lüderitz, a German trader who, searching for some new field, encountered a 20-year-old man named Heinrich Vogelsang. Vogelsang had worked for a Cape trader and was enthusiastic about prospects in south-western Africa. At the same time, an out-of-work sea captain, Carl Timpe, whose experience included the south-western coast of Africa, applied to Lüderitz for employment.

Lüderitz decided on a venture. He bought the brig Tilly and loaded it with assorted merchandise, sending Vogelsang ahead to scout conditions. In Cape Town, while posing as the globe-trotting son of wealthy parents, he met the missionary Dr Theophilus Hahn who drew up a report for him on the possibilities of buying Angra Pequena from the Bethanie Hottentots who claimed to own the place. Vogelsang decided that Angra Pequena was a good base for trade. When the Tilly arrived in Cape Town at the end of March, supplies were loaded, a false declaration given to the harbour authorities and the ship sneaked off up the coast, arriving at Angra Pequena on 10 April.

At the harbour, the Germans found a number of guano collectors and a man named Radford who had lived there since 1862. The Germans landed their stores and built a prefabricated hut which they named Fort Vogelsang. Vogelsang then travelled across the Namib to Bethanie. On 1 May 1883, Captain Josef Fredericks ceded the bay of Angra Pequena and the adjoining territory for 8 km in all directions, to the firm of Adolf Lüderitz for the equivalent of R200 and 200 rifles.

Vogelsang returned to Angra Pequena in triumph. On 12 May, the German flag was hoisted and Lüderitz was informed of events by means of a terse telegraph from the ship, 'Land bought from the chief with a single payment.' On 25 August 1883, Vogelsang concluded a second agreement with Captain Fredericks in which he acquired the whole coastal area from the Orange River to the 26 degrees of south latitude extending 32 km inland. This was in exchange for another amount equivalent to R200 and 60 Wesley-Richard rifles. The area was named Lüderitzland.

British interest was stirred at news of this cession of land. Lüderitz arrived in Cape Town on 13 September 1883 and had to deal with complaints, especially from the guano-collecting company of De Pass, Spence & Co. who claimed that they had bought the same area from the same Hottentots 20 years previously. Lüderitz bustled around arguing and negotiating. His government gave him support by sending the gunboat Nautilus to what was now being called Lüderitz Bay, and Vogelsang commenced a booming trade by flooding the southern part of the territory with cheap guns.

Lüderitz returned to Germany and found official sympathy for his projects. The intent in Germany was to belatedly enter the current scramble for empires, therefore Lüderitz was regarded as a pioneer. In the Cape, the colonial administration was horrified at the prospect of the Germans taking over an area which it had for years been begging the British Government to annex. However, the British were prepared to do a deal with the Germans. In exchange for favours elsewhere, notably in Egypt, they obliged the Germans at Angra Pequena and in other places. Two German corvettes were then sent to Angra Pequena and at 08h00 on 7 August 1884, the German flag was hoisted on shore, followed by a parade and everybody, particularly Captain Josef Fredericks, becoming very merry on good beer and schnapps. This was the Germans' first colony and the beginning of their annexation of the whole of what was called South West Africa.

Lüderitz never profited from his venture. He was forced to sell his interests to a company formed in Germany and in 1886, while prospecting down the coast in two canvas boats, he and a companion vanished without trace.

The settlement which bore his name grew slowly, with a narrow-gauge railway surveyed in 1905 to cross the Namib and to provide a trade link with the interior. Construction started in 1906 and the line reached Keetmanshoop on 21 June 1908. It was at that time that diamonds were discovered by railway workers (see page 748) and the fortunes of Lüderitz Bay really boomed. In 1909 it became a municipality and was the centre of a succession of diamond finds, a port for the shipment of supplies, and the scene of great activity in shore trading and fortune-seeking. Fishing, canning, and the processing of rock lobsters for export also developed into a major industry.

An excellent museum in Lüderitz contains many interesting exhibits, photographs and records of the diamond rush days, and displays of the natural history of the area. It is open on Tuesdays, Thursdays and Saturdays from 16h00 to 18h00. Many buildings survive from the German period, notably the magistracy, the old post office and numerous private homes. The scenic road to Dias Point (20 km) and thereafter down the coast to Grosse Bucht (12 km) and back to Lüderitz (15 km), is filled with interesting scenes and places.

## Accommodation
* Kapps Hotel, 24 rooms, 6 with baths. R8 – R11 B/B. Phone 2916.
* Bogenfels Hotel, 10 rooms, 4 with baths. R6 – R7 B/B. Phone 2533.

## Caravans and camping
** Administrative resort, bungalows (2 beds), R3,10 D. Beach house (4 beds), R5 – R5,50 D. Caravan sites, R2 D.

# THE ROAD TO THE RIVER OF DIAMONDS

The story of the road to the river of diamonds, of the prohibited area, of the diamond discoveries, rushes and ghost towns of the south-western part of Africa, is bitter-sweet. The sands of the Namib inter the skeletons of many men who died of privation in the great loneliness of that wilderness. For them, no one shed a tear or even wondered for a while what had become of them.

The road to the river of diamonds, extending from Lüderitz to Oranjemund, was blazed by many feet, and paved with broken hopes and the bones of forgotten men. The elusive spirit of fortune wanders along this road and her siren call is softly carried by the winds.

Why should this spirit be feminine? Prospectors and gamblers speak about 'lady luck'. Only a woman could be so capricious, inconsistent, unpredictable, superficial, erratic, enigmatic, desirable and cruel. And of the prospectors who pursue this personification of chance? Only a man could be so lunatic, foolish, romantic, fanatical, idealistic and persistent in folly to pursue this phantom long after all hope should have been abandoned, and even then, sick or dying, alone or afraid, still try to reach out and grasp the cold elusive spirit and to whisper something as foolish as saying 'I love you' to a dream.

It was strange how long it took men to find the desert diamonds. Many prospectors must have slipped on a diamond in the desert while their eyes were far away on something else. It was pure chance which started the whole remarkable sequence of events.

One day in April 1908, a labourer, Zacharias Lewala, while clearing sand off the track near Kolmanskop, picked up a diamond. He had worked in Kimberley and therefore knew what diamonds looked like. He took it to his foreman, August Stauch, a German ganger who had immigrated to Lüderitz during the previous year in the hope that the dry climate would relieve his asthma. He was no prospector, but he was interested in collecting stones and knew how to identify a diamond. He tested the stone on the glass of his wristwatch and it left a scratch.

Stauch took the discovery to two of the directors of the railway firm. They financed him whereupon he abandoned his job as a ganger and started to prospect. He was quickly rewarded and on 20 June 1908 he exhibited his findings in the offices of the Deutsche Kolonial-Gesellschaft. His discoveries caused a sensation. Nearly every able-bodied man in Lüderitz rushed out to find diamonds. All of a sudden they were located in many places so obvious that people were baffled that they had failed to notice them before. It was almost as though it had rained diamonds there overnight.

In the Pomona area, Stauch went prospecting with a Dr Scheibe. While Stauch plotted his position on a map, he told his servants to look for diamonds. One of them simply went down on his knees, filled both hands with diamonds, and even stuffed some into his mouth. The stones lay on the ground as thick as plums fallen from a tree. Dr Scheibe stared at the scene in amazement, repeating over and over again, *'Ein marchen, ein marchen'* ('a fairy tale, a fairy tale'). Stauch named the field *Idatal* (Ida's Valley) after his wife.

The pioneer discovery at *Kolmanskop*, a hill named after a transport rider, Kolman, who habitually rested his draught animals there, consisted of a rich deposit lying in the gravel bed of a dry river. A substantial mine was developed there with a village built to house the staff on the slopes of Kolmanskop. This village survives as a perfect example of a ghost town.

The operating company built and maintained the village. There was a bakery, butchery, general dealer's store, ice factory, lemonade and soda water factory, a fine community centre with a hall, a theatre with a stage, massive kitchen and storage rooms, a hospital with the first X-Ray machine in the territory, four skittle alleys, single quarters, married quarters, and magnificent homes for the manager and senior staff.

Each household received a block of ice and a free supply of soda water and lemonade each day. The hospital was surely unique in that it had its own wine cellar. Dr Kraenzle, who was in charge, believed that every patient on the way to recovery should receive wine or champagne and caviar sandwiches. Another doctor with unusual ideas was Dr V. Lossow, who enthusiastically ate raw onions. He was a familiar sight, walking about whistling and chewing onions.

There was also a school, a furniture factory and a paint shop. An orchestra played for tea dances on Saturday and Sunday afternoons, and the theatre, the acoustics of which were superb, was used for performances by companies brought out from Europe.

There was a children's playground and a large swimming pool continuously fed by sea water pumped from Elizabeth Bay, 35 km away. Drinking water was brought by train from Garub and there was enough to allow for the cultivation of gardens. Dances and parties were nightly events, while Christmas involved a large celebration. The Kirchoff family possessed a tame ostrich which was trained to draw a sleigh over the sand. Father Christmas always came to Kolmanskop in this sleigh, while at Easter it was used to convey the Easter bunny.

Kolmanskop was conveniently situated next to the railway line from Lüderitz to Keetmans-hoop. From this line, the mining people built a private 60-cm-gauge railway running down the coast to serve a whole series of working diamond mines. There were so many of these mines that it was sometimes said that this was the only railway in the world with stations almost as long as its total length of 95 km, for each mine had its own private platform. Petrol electric locomotives worked the line and it was in the process of being electrified when the 1914 war broke out.

The line ended at the great 26-m-high *Bogenfels* (arched rock), where a large mine worked a diamond deposit found by Georg Klinghardt, one of the most renowned of the prospectors. Other large mines were located at Pomona and Elizabeth Bay and there were smaller workings in many remote places.

To control the activity and to market the diamonds in such a way that prices would be reasonably maintained, the German Government, in September 1908, declared the whole area to be the *Sperrgebiet* (prohibited area), with licensing and disciplines imposed on individuals and companies. Thousands of claims had already been pegged, with five million carats of diamonds having been recovered between 1908 and 1914.

The 1914-1918 war totally disrupted mining. When hostilities were over, Ernest Oppenheimer went to Germany and obtained options on the various mining groups. Ten of the largest of the former companies were amalgamated into the Consolidated Diamond Mines of South West Africa and this concern obtained exclusive diamond rights for 50 years over the area stretching 350 km north of the mouth of the Orange River and 95 km inland from the coast.

The surface of the Namib will, for a long time, retain the footprints and vehicle tracks of its prospectors. The gravel surface is particularly retentive of such trails and the footprints of men such as Georg Klinghardt, who knew the area better than any other human being, might still be followed into the most inaccessible places.

The indomitable Mose Eli Kahan was also industriously prospecting for diamonds. He found a deposit 95 km north of Lüderitz, in Diamond Area No. 2. He registered these claims under the names of Ophir and Atlantis and started to work them. His difficulties were typical of those encountered in mining in the Namib dune country. He tried to service the mine by boat but the coast was dangerous and one ship was wrecked. He then organised mule trains, following the beach, but the animals took 20 days to complete the journey and most of their carrying capacity was exhausted in their having to convey their own drinking water.

Kahan was irrespressible. He bought war surplus Centurion tanks but even these machines stuck in the sand. He took their tracks off and fitted war surplus tyres made for Dakota aircraft. The tanks travelled much better but were still foiled by windstorms which made the dunes too steep. So Kahan obtained long steel cables and auxiliary motors to haul the tanks up the dunes.

Throughout this period there was great controversy surrounding the origin of the diamonds. They lay scattered on or very near the surface, especially in ancient watercourses. Their distribution was quite unpredictable and seemed entirely erratic. Apart from Kolmanskop, all major finds were along the coast and there was a feeling that perhaps the mother lode was somewhere beneath the sea and that the diamonds had been washed up on the beach. For the diamonds to have originated in the interior, they would have required a major river to carry them down to the coast, but there was no sign of such a river being present, even in distant geological times.

Prospectors worked down the coast as far as the mouth of the Orange, blazing the trail of the future road with immense difficulty. They found diamonds as far south as *Chamais* (lion) Bay, but south of that there seemed to be nothing. One prospector, F. W. Martens, wandered down the trail from Aus to Sendelingsdrif in 1909 and from there to the mouth of the Orange where he found several small diamonds on the South African side. He pegged claims but the area was too remote and he never developed them.

In 1910, F. C. Cornell also prospected the lower Orange but found nothing. The Orange being a possible source of the diamonds was dismissed by prospectors and it was left alone. In solitude near the river mouth, in 1909, the Germans built a police station and camel patrol post, perched on a cliff. It was named *Hohenfels* (high rock) and regarded by its garrison as the very end of the world where nothing ever happened save the silent flow of the river day and night, sweeping steadily past the police post with a brooding, sullen disregard of man and his attempts to fathom the mystery of the diamonds.

Why was the mystery so elusive? Luck was really feminine to be so persistent a tease. It was all there to see but the keenest eyes seemed to be blind. Dr E. Reuning, a geologist for the German Government, blazed a trail all the way down from Kolmanskop and reached the Orange River mouth. There he met a farmer, Geel Louw of *Sandkraal* farm, on the north bank of the river near the present bridge. Reuning asked Louw to dig a series of exploratory pits in the gravels of the river. Nothing was found. The pits still lie there filled with pebbles and flotsam. A mere 40 m away, subsequent prospectors found the fabulous diamond treasure chest in the marine gravels.

In February 1926 at Port Nolloth, F. C. Carstens found the first diamond south (60 km) of the Orange River, in the township reserve. The site appeared to be an ancient course of the Kamma River. A rush to the area ensued, with Dr Hans Merensky arriving on the scene from the Transvaal. He was joined by Dr Reuning and I. B. Celliers, who acted as assistants. Merensky noticed that, up until now, the diamonds had been found, oddly enough, in association with the shells of an extinct oyster. Oysters certainly do not produce diamonds in place of pearls, but whatever had killed the oysters had also dumped diamonds along the beach, possibly some change of current or temperature. Geologists were thus reminded that nothing is permanent; vast colonies of rock lobsters live in the cold Benguela Current which flows up the south-west African coast, but sudden fluxes of warmer water in modern times have temporarily caused such a disturbance in this creepy community, that the lobsters have been seen to clamber out in countless numbers on to rocks and beaches in an effort to escape the warmth. A three-week blow from the warm north wind at Walvis Bay has been enough to drive the whole lobster population out of the water.

Merensky was persuaded to use the presence of oyster shells as an indication of the possible presence of diamonds. On the south bank at the mouth of the Orange, two prospectors, Victor Gordon and a Mr Kaplan, were already prospecting. Near the ruins of a stone storehouse built by Sir James Alexander as a place of shipment for copper, Merensky found shingle which looked promising. He put Dr Reuning to work there, assisted by the two brothers Coetzee. They soon found diamonds and this was the start of Alexander Bay. By February 1927, the whole area was covered in claim pegs right up the Orange as far as Sendelingsdrif. In 1928, on the north side of the river mouth, Dr Werner Beetz, consulting geologist for De Beers, found the first diamonds in a marine terrace, an ancient raised beach composed of pebbles and oyster shells buried under a 10-m-thick layer of sand and extending for at least 40 km up the coast. It was estimated that this strip alone contained many million carats of diamonds. Soon, other similar terraces were found all the way up the coast as far as Bogenfels. Dr Scheibe had called it 'a fairy tale, a fairy tale'. This was certainly a strange and eerie sort of fairyland.

In the midst of the excitement, the Wall Street crash occurred and there was a disastrous collapse in the sale of diamonds. All at once there were far too many of them and too few people with money enough to buy such jewels, no matter how glittering. During this crisis, Ernest Oppenheimer succeeded to the chairmanship of the Consolidated Diamond Mines and with great skill, steered the industry through a very difficult period. The Diamond Corporation was formed as the central selling organisation. The vast over-production of diamonds was bought up, stored away, and future sales so carefully regulated that prices were controlled, gradually restored and maintained at a worthwhile level.

With marketing problems solved and the world returning to prosperity, diamond producing was resumed. Work on the marine terraces was commenced in January 1935 and the township of *Oranjemund* (orange mouth) was established in 1936 to house the workers and to replace Kolmanskop as the principal centre of the diamond industry in the Sperrgebiet. The headquarters of the company were moved to Oranjemund in 1943. Kolmanskop was slowly phased out of production after 1939, although it was not until 1956 that the last inhabitants were transferred elsewhere. Now the place is committed to memory and the visits of tourists. The road to the river of diamonds was built south of Kolmanskop, stretching for 288 km over the Namib gravel plain. It is perhaps the longest private road in the world, ending at Oranjemund. It carries workers and supplies to the new fairyland of gemstones. Perhaps it also carries a whispered warning from the dying Kolmanskop that the sands of the Namib alone are eternal.

Kolmanskop and the chain of other diamond mines had been relatively unsophisticated in their method of recovering diamonds from the desert. Oranjemund and its terraces at the southern end of the road were a different proposition from the start. The most advanced techniques in mechanisation were introduced. Even though there were few problems in mining the marine deposits, the sheer volume of material handled eventually made the recovery process one of the largest earthmoving operations in the world. On a normal 24-hour working day, six days a week, the marine terrace resembles a battlefield of giant earthmoving machines (the biggest fleet in Africa), including a huge bucket wheel excavator, resembling a monstrous thing from outer space. All are busy stripping overburden, loading and hauling, supported by an ant-like army of men who clean the bedrock with brushes so that not a single diamond remains. All the diamonds are conveyed in a mixture of rocks and shells to one of several conglomerate plants. Here the rock is crushed into gravel and fed to a recovery plant which identifies and sorts the diamonds by means of X-Rays, optical sorters and keen-eyed humans who spot the last diamond in an annual output which, in 1977, reached 2 001 217 carats.

To provide the mine with a second link to the outside world, a bridge 1 km long was built over the Orange River in 1949 and replaced with a new structure in 1960. By the convenience of this bridge and a road link to the Cape to augment traffic on the old road from Kolmanskop to the river of diamonds, the scope of mining operations was increased and Oranjemund, as the dormitory for the workers, grew rapidly into an attractive and surprising garden town conjured out of the desert by the pure magic of diamonds.

In a strange way Oranjemund, in its desert fairyland, has become a classic example in a setting of capitalism at its most glittering, of a town without private ownership by its residents. It is well cared for, beautified and maintained without municipality or politics, without slums, poverty or obvious extremes of wealth. It has efficient social services, minimal crime and a superb supply of fresh vegetables, dairy products, fruit and meat produced on a vast company-run, ingeniously integrated farm named *Beauvallon* situated on the alluvial banks of the Orange. There are recreational facilities and entertainments all dispensed by a form of benevolent company paternalism, motivated, certainly, by the need to keep employees contented in so remote a place, but revealing in the success of its application, that Utopian ideals of orderly life without want or greed, can be achieved by sensible organisation rather than violent confrontation. The consequence of so amiable an arrangement is obviously profitable to workers and management.

The gemstone fairyland of the Namib is the contrary setting for many surprising things. As prospectors have explored and scientists have interpreted, so the nature of the mystery of the diamonds has become better understood but the ultimate secret has still not finally been solved. Persistent exploration has shown that the diamonds only occur along the coast, not inland. On the coast they are found in a series of ancient beaches raised above the sea and usually buried under layers of windblown sand. These diamondiferous beaches extend north and south of the mouth of the Orange, with the beaches furthest away containing the smaller stones.

Diamonds also lie beneath the sea and have been recovered in significant quantities by concerns such as the Marine Diamond Corporation, launched by S. C. Collins in 1961, and the Terra Marina Company who in 1966, commissioned a dredger to work the submarine gravels around Sinclair and Plumpudding islands. The effort and hazards of such recovery in the storms, mists, winds and currents of the coast made work exceedingly costly. As a result, two recovery barges were wrecked.

The largest diamond recovered so far in the coastal area weighed 230 carats and occasionally the odd gem of over 100 carats turns up. The majority are small, however, but are of superb quality and occur in a great variety of colours.

Careful study on diamond size distribution, indicates that the mouth of the Orange River is the point of origin. Bartholomew Dias called this area the *Terra dos Bramidos* (the land of roarings) but did not leave any explanation for the name. It would seem that over a considerable period of time, and during successive cycles of erosion and prodigious flood, the Orange carried diamonds to the sea. The prevailing currents and winds gradually carried the diamonds up and down the coast, washing them on to the beaches. Eroding and rebuilding the shoreline, constantly changing in the unpredictable moodiness of creation, these currents and winds reached as far inland as Kolmanskop, but for most of the forgotten years, remained close to the present shoreline.

The river then, brought the diamonds from some secret mother lodes far in the interior. Diamonds of similar type and quality are found in the river gravels but these are simply remnants left behind. The river seemed obsessed with taking the diamonds to the sea. The sea and wind received them, played with them along the beaches and lost them like the toys of children left scattered in a nursery.

Still the great river flows, moody and enigmatic, its ultimate mysteries still concealed. Over the face of the Namib the winds sculpt and model the dunes and the sun dazzles the gravel plains with brilliant light. The sea, cold and relentless, surges in upon beaches which sometimes seem as thin, scraggly and despondent as a woman ill-used by a brutish man. The mists roll in, sometimes slowly, sometimes with unexpected speed and unpleasant effect. At night, the river of diamonds is a river of stars, its surface a mirror which reflects the countless diamonds of the heavens. The ruins of the old police post look upon the water in silence; the camel corral is empty; the pathway stretches off into the shadows past many graves. Is it only fancy that makes one hear a call to follow, to seek and adventure, to wander into the unknown; a call inviting one to reach out, to try and seize the hand of the elusive spirit of fortune and touch her cold lips?

752

# Chapter Thirty-eight

# BOTSWANA

In the extraordinary patchwork quilt of climatic zones, vegetational regions and landscapes which comprise Southern Africa, the area of windblown sands which makes up Botswana is so unique as to be one of the natural wonders of the world. This mantle of sand covers an area of 1,2 million square kilometres of central Southern Africa. Of this sandy region, Botswana occupies 570 000 square kilometres.

The sand mantle, the largest in the world, forms a shallow saucer, tilted downwards to the north. The entire geological receptacle is a thirsty trap, a beggar's pan held out towards the north in supplication. Rainfall over the mantle of sand is erratic and skimpy; at best, about 700 mm a year may fall in favoured areas, and only 200 mm or less over half of Botswana. Rainfull occurs, as in most of Africa, in the short 'wet' seasons of December and January, with some spit and promise in November, petering out into scattered thunderstorms in February, March and April. From May to October there is no rain.

No water remains on the surface of the sand mantle and there is no run-off. For short periods, water gathers in depressions and hollows forming shallow lakelets or pans, most of them well mineralised with natural salts and lime. Without constant replenishment however, the parched sand and atmosphere simply absorbs the water, which soaks down and evaporates rapidly until nothing is left. The vegetation which has blossomed amazingly with the rains, reverts to a drab appearance.

The supplicating pan, however, reaches northwards hopefully and finds nature to be compassionate in a very ingenious way. Far to the north, in the highlands of Angola, heavy rainfall of up to 2 500 mm a year finds a run-off in the form of the Okavango River, one of the principal drainers of these floodwaters. Nature has caused the river to flow due south but it is under the wrong impression if it presumes its destination is the seaside. The river drops down from the highlands in cascades and waterfalls and about June each year its floodwaters are confronted by the saucer of sand.

There is no escape for the Okavango. Disconcerted, it spreads out in a cone-like shape over the northern portion of the sand mantle, forming 16 000 square kilometres of swampland. Depending on the amount of rainfall in the highlands, the water pushes southwards despairingly, infiltrating every hollow and rill, groping on in the hope of finding a sudden drop in altitude to restore its flow. It becomes sluggish as it is impeded by the seemingly endless saucer of sand, which eventually rises towards the southern rim. The river finally gives up; it even starts to flow in reverse as the pressure of the floods ends. The furthest points that the river reaches are Lake Ngami and the great shallow depression of Makgadikgadi, with its two main pans of Ntwetwe and Sua. This depression terminates the flow once and for all, filling with about 250 mm of sludgy water which covers an area over 1 000 km in circumference. For a couple of months the morass remains, a smelly mix of natural salts, soda and plankton which attracts prodigious quantities of aquatic birds. *Ngami* (the big water) is about 2 m deep during a good season, but in a poor season it too becomes a swampy puddle and in a bad season can be completely dry. Its variations have baffled many visitors who, lured there by reports of a great lake teeming with fish, arrive to see nothing more than mirages playing on a hard floor. They leave, certain that all the descriptions of a blue-water lake so vast it is impossible to see across to its furthest shore, have simply been fabrications.

The interplay of sand and water in Botswana is a very wonderful thing to see. The vegetation and wildlife of Botswana is also magnificent for the sand mantle is dissimilar to the face of a desert such as the dune country of the Namib or the Sahara. The annual rainfall is quite sufficient to stimulate a generous growth of vegetation. A great variety of grasses, flowering plants (especially lilies), trees – mainly of the thorny type such as various acacia species – cover the sand and provide rich grazing for antelope. Predators live on these herds of game as do the earliest known human inhabitants of the area, the nomadic Bushman (or Sarwa) hunters. About 10 000 pure-blooded and 20 000 mixed descendants of these pioneer people continue to roam this wilderness and regard it as their own.

African Iron Age tribes also found the area attractive and excellent for grazing cattle. The first of these people to migrate into the sand wilderness were the *Kgalagadi,* the name of whom Europeans corrupted to *Kalahari* and brought into use as a geographical name, the Kalahari Desert. About 25 000 of these people still live in the area.

The great Karanga tribe whose main homeland lay to the north-east also overlapped into the sand area. Their ancient skills in mining were exercised considerably when they found surface outcrops of gold on the high rim of the saucer. As with modern prospectors, the prehistoric workers were baffled by the covering of sand, a recent geological creation blanketing the same rock formations common to the rest of Southern Africa and which could be expected to contain similar deposits of minerals, coal and other valuable treasures. However, the sand mantle made the landscape as enigmatic as a masked human face. What lay beneath it was a tantalising mystery. About 45 000 of the Karanga (or Kalaka) people live in Botswana today.

In about the 16th century a new human element migrated into the area from the north. These people spoke the language now known as *seTswana* and tradition says that they were led by a chief named Masilo. This chief had two sons, Mohurutshe and Malope, who after their father's death, divided his following between them. Most of the descendants of Mohurutshe's section live in South Africa today, but 7 000 stay in their original homeland.

Malope's section remained, and on his death, three of his sons divided his following between them, the descendants of whom are the dominent people of modern Botswana. These three related tribal groups bear the names of the three sons – Kwena, Ngwato and Ngwaketse. In later years a section of the Ngwato, under a chief named Tawana, broke away and settled in the Okavango where they now number about 45 000. The Kwena tribe number 75 000; the Ngwato 201 000; and the Ngwaketse 72 000.

Other minor tribal elements wandered into the sandy wilderness at different times, settled there and became subservient to one or other of the descendant groups of Masilo's people. Besides the Bushmen and the Kalaka, about 30 separate tribal groups speak the same language but know themselves only by their tribal names. The present total population is 700 000, a population density of just over 1 person per square kilometre in a country 570 000 square kilometres in extent.

The generic name of Tswana was applied by foreigners to these various tribal groups, but the meaning and origin is obscure. It was convenient for the people to accept this name, originally spelt (among other ways) Chuana. In its modern application *seTswana* is the language; *baTswana* the people; *moTswana* an individual; and *boTswana* (Botswana) the country.

The people of Botswana have by nature always been peaceful. They were raided in past years by such martial tribes as the Ndebele, but invariably beat them off, or retired into the wilderness to hide until the trouble passed. They have always been agriculturalists and breeders of cattle, and prefer to live close together in large settlements built adjacent to water supplies.

Botswana became a British protectorate in 1884 and was known by the hopelessly misspelt name of Bechuanaland. The country was at first ruled directly by a High Commissioner who, strangely enough, had his headquarters in Mafeking in the Cape Province. It was therefore one of the few states whose capital was situated in a foreign country. In 1960 Botswana received a representative Legislative Council and in 1965 the centre of government was moved to Botswana itself, to Gaborone which became the capital of the country. On 30 September 1966 Botswana became an independent republic with Sir Seretse Khama as President.

Meat is the principal agricultural product of the country with a considerable export trade in livestock and carcasses based at Lobatse. Diamonds are mined in a great pipe at Orapa, west of Francistown. A smaller mine is situated at Letlhakane and the opening of a new mine is intended at Jwaneng. Coal has been found at places such as Mamabula and Morupule; low-grade iron ore is mined at Chadibe; and there is a copper-nickel deposit at Selebi-Phikwe. Salt, soda ash, potash and bromides are obtained from pans such as Sua Pan, while agates are found at Bobonong, among them a rose-coloured variety peculiar to Botswana.

A prodigious wealth of wildlife is the greatest natural treasure of Botswana. Vast numbers of game animals roam across the wilderness, especially in the northern areas of Ngamiland, along the banks of the Chobe River upstream from Kasane, and in the delta of the Okavango.

Controlled hunting takes place under licence in most parts of Botswana. The country is divided into 36 controlled hunting areas, of which 14 are conceded to professional safari companies, 20 are open to private hunters, two are closed, and one is under private concession.

The hunting season for most of Botswana, covers the period 15 March to 15 November. At least a dozen professional companies conduct hunting or photographic safaris into the country, which is today one of the principal areas in Africa for this form of sport and recreation. A variety of hunting licences are available embracing an assortment of game animals. Licences for individual animals range from R150 for an elephant; R80 for a crocodile, tsessebe, waterbuck or zebra; R20 for a buffalo, bushbuck, hartebeest, reedbuck, or wildebeest; R15 for an impala or springbok; R10 for an ostrich or wild pig; and R4 for a duiker, steenbok or warthog. Animals such as giraffe, rhino, hippo, cheetah, antbear, brown hyena, badger, klipspringer, oribi, otter, pangolin, puku, and yellow-spotted dassie, are totally protected. The world record gemsbok, hartebeest, and black wildebeest have been shot in Botswana. Elephants are average in stature but moderate in ivory, the Botswana record being 59,5 kg compared to the world record of 102,5 kg, taken in Kenya.

Francistown and Maun are the two principal depots for hunting safaris in Botswana, which, under the auspices of professional organisations, usually last 21 days and cost from R100 to R150 a day per person inclusive of food, staff and camping kit. Hunting licences, arms, alcohol and photographic materials are separate.

Game birds occur in immense numbers in Botswana and may be shot under licence at a cost ranging from R3 for seven days, to R15 for one year. Fishing is unrestricted and provides tremendous sport in the Chobe River and the Okavango where tiger fish abound.

Photographic and sightseeing safaris are conducted into Botswana by the professional companies at a cost of around R30 a day per person inclusive of everything other than photographic material, liquor and personal requirements.

There are no restrictions on private travel in Botswana except in specific game areas, but discretion and caution is recommended. This is wild and arid country: four-wheel-drive or heavy transport vehicles are essential if the traveller intends leaving the one north-south tarmac road, or the branch to Maun from Francistown.


# GABORONE

A small section of the Tlokwa tribe, most of whom now live in South Africa, moved westwards into the sand wilderness. After wandering about for some years, they settled at a place called

Mosaweng during the 1890s. Their leader was named Gaborone, a man who only succeeded his father in power at the age of about 60, but who remained a very well-loved chief until his death in 1932 at the estimated age of 106.

The building of the railway from Vryburg in the Cape to Bulawayo in 1896-1897, established Gaborone as a place name on the map for the first time. A crossing point for trains was created there, and adjoining it a tin shanty shimmering in the heat on a rough platform of cinders. The railway was built in the record time of 645 km in 400 days with the erection of luxuries like stations and conveniences simply left for more relaxed times.

The strip of ground on which the railway was constructed from north to south was actually transferred by the various chiefs to the construction company of Cecil Rhodes. Gaborone and his people, who were living there by permission of the Kwena chief, overnight found themselves considered squatters on a railway reservation. They stayed there under tolerance until 1905 when the tract of land was transferred to the British South Africa Company. The Tlokwa were supposed to move but instead payed the company a rental of £150 (R300) a year and were allowed to remain as tenants. In 1933, after the death of Gaborone, the homeland of his little tribe was proclaimed the Batlokwa Native Reserve, small and congested, but at least allowing the Tlokwa to retain their identity as one of the smallest tribal units in Botswana.

Under the British Protectorate administration, Botswana was at first very simply divided into two districts: northern and southern. Palapye was selected as the administrative centre of the northern district and what was then called Gaborones (i.e. Gaborone's place) as the centre of the southern region. William Surmon was stationed there as Assistant Commissioner, responsible to the Resident Commissioner in Mafeking.

A 'camp' was erected at Gaborone with a small fort serving as police post and government offices. Conditions were very primitive and the camp was hemmed in by thick bush. A well was dug for water and a couple of shacks were erected but even these simple amenities disappeared at the outbreak of the Anglo-Boer War. The police and other officials were ordered to retire north to Mahalapye and to destroy Gaborone. Everything of value was removed, including a small safe which was laboriously conveyed to Bulawayo and when opened, was found to contain nothing more than a few small coins to the value of 45 cents. Another safe which was far too heavy to move in the general rush, was abandoned. When the Boers occupied the place they found this safe, blew it open and discovered inside it only a piece of paper containing the words 'sold again'!

At the end of the war the administrative camp at Gaborone was rebuilt; a few traders arrived and the place took on a more substantial appearance. The big change came in 1965 when Gaborone was selected as capital of Botswana instead of Mafeking. An entire new town was planned west of the original Gaborone, at the railway station. There being no shortage of level ground covered in trees, the new Gaborone was laid out on spacious lines, with a central pedestrian mall overlooked by a double row of commercial buildings. A government enclave is situated at the head of the mall and the buildings of Parliament, the splendid National Museum and art gallery, the library and university are all handsome new buildings. The museum contains a collection of superbly mounted wild animals of Botswana and the painted dioramas are masterpieces. The museum and art gallery are open daily from 09h00 to 18h00.

A national stadium and airport are situated on the western outskirts of the town as well as a substantial dam which provides the town with water and recreational opportunities such as boating and fishing. Gaborone is well spread out with plenty of open areas planted with bush and trees. The population is 45 000.

## Accommodation
★ Gaborone Hotel, 17 rooms, 5 with baths. P11,50 room only. Phone 4226.
★★★ Holiday Inn, 159 rooms, all with baths. P24 room only. Phone 5-111.
★★ President Hotel, 24 rooms, all with baths or showers. P15 – P16 room only. Phone 2216.

From Gaborone a tarmac road leads eastwards for 20 km to the border post of *Tlokweng* (place of the Tlokwa tribe) with the South African border post of Kopfontein facing it across the frontier. The posts are open from 07h00 to 20h00. A tarmac road 93 km long links Kopfontein to Zeerust and the main road to Johannesburg.

---

South of Gaborone, a tarmac road stretches for 73 km through well-bushed, hilly country to reach . . .

# LOBATSE

The situation of Lobatse – a valley surrounded by rocky hills – is pleasant. With a population of 19 000, the place has a similar atmosphere to a rather slovenly but animated cow town of the wild west. Lobatse is also the seat of the High Court of Botswana. The abattoir of the Botswana Meat Commission is situated here, as well as a large canned meat factory. Cattle on the hoof are constantly being driven into the town from the ranching areas and the shops do a roaring trade with the cowboy types who ride the herds on their last long journey to the abattoir. Meat is sent by train to South Africa and exported to several countries.

Two caves containing dripstone formations and plenty of bats, are situated in the vicinity of the town. However, they are difficult to enter and are therefore more suited to serious cave explorers than casual visitors. Their full length has yet to be explored.

### Accommodation
★★ Cumberland Hotel, 18 rooms, all with baths. P18,50 B/B. Phone 281.
★ Lobatse Hotel, 19 rooms, all with baths. P12,50 B/B. Phone 319.

Beyond Lobatse a tarmac road leads eastward for 8 km to the border post of Pioneer Gate and the South African post of Skilpadshek across the frontier line from where the tarmac road continues for 50 km to Zeerust in the Transvaal. The two posts are open daily from 07h00 to 20h00.

---

From Lobatse the tarmac road continues southwards. After 5 km a turnoff west to Kanye is reached while the main road continues close to the railway line to Pitsane (30 km from Lobatse) and from there to the border of South Africa at Ramatlabama (50 km from Lobatse). The Botswana and South African posts of Ramatlabama are open daily from 07h00 to 20h00. Mafeking is 25 km south of Ramatlabama on the tarmac road.

---

From the main road 5 km south of Lobatse, a tarmac turnoff leads westwards for 47 km to . . .

# KANYE

The flat-topped hill of Kanye, a natural fortress of the kind much favoured by the Tswana people, dominates a fertile and relatively well-watered extent of the wilderness. The Ngwaketse tribe established it as the principal centre of their tribal area. Nearly 200 years ago, under the chief Makaba, a substantial town was created there which today has a population of 22 000.

As originally created, Kanye was a fortified settlement built on top of the hill. Stone

*Overleaf: Rust-coloured sand, turquoise skies, prodigious space; the wilderness of the Central Kalahari, home of the Bushmen.*

defensive walls were constructed to reinforce the hill, and piles of rocks kept as missiles to be used against enemies attempting to climb the slopes. The place was attacked on several occasions by people such as the Ndebele of Mzilikazi, the outlaw Jan Bloem and others. At times the Ngwaketse were driven away but they always returned and the old town still stands on the summit of the hill, with modern extensions built on the lower slopes.

The town is an interesting place to explore – a maze of pathways and passages. Most of the habitations consist of the traditional thatched huts – generally a cluster comprising residence, cornhouse and workhouse built around a neat courtyard, with walls and floors of clay and dung. The walls are usually tastefully decorated by the women with various designs and patterns. The residence of the chief and the *kgotla* (meeting place) is situated at Kgoseng on top of the hill. The town is still provided with water from a deep gorge known as Pharing although there are now modern amenities such as pipes, boreholes and taps. From Kanye a track leads north to Ghanzi in the form of a cattle trail, suitable only for heavy or four-wheel-drive vehicles.

---

From Gaborone a tarmac road stretches over level country for 66 km to Molepolole, the principal centre of the Kwena people. This is a large, sprawling village without any very notable feature but an interesting place to visit. The village of huts, shacks and commercial buildings is scattered in a natural parkland of acacias. The tarmac road ends at the entrance to the Scottish Livingstone Hospital.

Aloes grow in great profusion around the village and a local legend says that these plants once saved Molepolole from attack. A party of Boers – always the bogeymen of the Tswana – stole upon the place one night in 1850. In the light of the half moon they mistook the aloes for an army of warriors waiting on the defensive. The attack was abandoned!

It is said that the name *Molepolole* originates from a curse placed on the site by a wizard. When the Kwena chief decided to build his capital on the site, the wizard was ordered to relieve the place of the curse. Hence the name, which means 'Let him undo it'.

### Accommodation

★ Mafenya Tlala Hotel, 10 chalets. P9,25 D Sundays - Thursdays. P7,50 D Fridays - Saturdays. Phone 032-394.

From Molepolole a track leads north-west for 72 km to *Letlhakeng* (place of reeds), a settlement on the banks of a fossil river. From this place the track deteriorates and can only be used by four-wheel-drive vehicles. For 72 km the track winds across the face of the wilderness and then reaches the . . .

## KHUTSE GAME RESERVE

This reserve, 2 500 square kilometres in extent, is an area of tree-covered sand plains littered with pans which hold water only during and after good rains. Hartebeest, kudu, springbok and wildebeest live in the area but tend to migrate with the rains, being able to sense where water is available or where some thunderstorm has benefited the grazing. A permanent population of smaller animals always remains around the pans and the area is populated by Bushmen and Kgalagadi. A Department of Wildlife and Tourism camp is situated at Golalabadimo Pan but no accommodation is provided. Guides may be obtained; otherwise the visitor must rely on his own resources. There are tracks leading to most parts of the reserve which was proclaimed in 1971. The best months to visit it are July, August and September.

# CENTRAL KALAHARI GAME RESERVE

This vast game reserve, 51 800 square kilometres in extent and the largest in the world, is a complete wilderness. There are no roads and it is closed to the public unless special permission is obtained for research purposes. Nomadic Bushman hunting groups wander through this wilderness of sandy, savanna plains where innumerable pans occasionally retain water from wet seasons.

Vast herds of antelope migrate through the reserve but their movements are unpredictable and completely dependent on the caprice of the weather. Eland, gemsbok, hartebeest and springbok sometimes form herds of 100 000; at other times they disperse as effectively as water evaporating in the heat, to be remembered as though simply a mirage. In the thirstland of the central Kgaligadi, life and water are so tightly interwoven that the number of inhabitants increases or decreases according to the frequency of thunderstorms and the accessibility of the scattered drinking places.

Vegetation consists of a considerable variety of grass species, acacia thorn trees, and a surprising number of flowering plants, especially lilies.

----

# GABORONE TO FRANCISTOWN

The road from Gaborone to Francistown used to be purgatory for travellers, but it has now received a tarmac surface, making the experience of exploring Botswana a pleasure.

The road leaves Gaborone, passing after 1 km, the turnoff to Molepolole, the Botswana Agricultural College at 9,5 km and the Morwa rural centre, 31 km from Gaborone. Just beyond this centre (34,5 km from Gaborone), a tarmac turnoff leads for 6 km to the village of . . .

# MOCHUDI

The Kgatla tribe established a capital for themselves in 1871 when they moved from the Transvaal, choosing a pleasant site on which the village developed around the base of a cluster of low hills. The village was named *Motshodi,* after an individual who lived there prior to the arrival of the Kgatla. The name, inevitably, has been corrupted to *Mochudi.*

The village, although straggling, has scattered in it several homes built in the traditional Kgatla style with superbly thatched roofs of considerable size. Entrances are finely decorated and many interesting architectural features abound. Two baobab trees growing in the village are the most southerly of their kind in Botswana.

From the turnoff to Mochudi, the main tarmac road continues north over a flat, acacia-covered plain unmarked by any prominent features for 162 km until it reaches . . .

# MAHALAPYE

Correctly known as *Mhalatswe,* this village derives its name from the impala antelope which once frequented the area in large numbers. It is a railway and agricultural centre. West of the village, 45 km away on a gravel road, lies the old Ngwato capital of Shoshong, now much smaller in size but containing relics of stone walls and signs of mining and smelting.

**Accommodation**
★ Chase-me Inn, 16 rooms, P7 – P9 D/B/B. Phone 200.

From Mahalapye the main tarmac road continues north for 73 km and then reaches a crossroads. To the west, 43,5 km away, lies Serowe. To the east, 5 km away, is the village of . . .

# PALAPYE

As with Mahalapye, this village receives its name (correctly spelt *Phalatswe*) from the number of impala antelope which once lived in the area. A railway and agricultural centre, it is situated near the coal mine at Morupule, 6 km to the west.

## Accommodation
★Palapye Hotel, 12 rooms. P5,20 B/B. Phone 277.

From the crossroads at Palapye, a turn to the west crosses a level savanna. After 6 km there is a turnoff to the Moropule Colliery and 43 km further on, the road reaches the Ngwato tribal capital of . . .

# SEROWE

In 1902 the Ngwato tribe moved their principal centre from the old Palapye (east of Palapye) to an area known as *Serowe* form the small bulbs which grow there and are relished for their sweet flavour. A new tribal capital was created around a central, tree-covered hill which serves as the burial ground of the Khama family. The grave of Khama III is marked by a fine bronze duiker sculpted by the South African artist, Anton von Wouw. The duiker is the emblem of the Ngwato tribe.

Serowe is a large, straggling village built in a natural parkland where, to its advantage, several hillocks provide variety of landscape and excellent viewsites for photographers. An interesting mixture of old and new may be seen in the domestic architecture, several stores, garages, public buildings, and the Sekgoma Memorial Hospital which lies at the end of the tarmac road.

The graves of the Khama family may be visited with the permission of the District Chief whose home and offices are situated at the foot of the hill. Thathaganyana hill is also worth climbing. On its flat summit may be seen the ruins of an 11th century settlement, where there are numerous engraved holes and slides in the rocks.

Of all the Tswana villages, Serowe is probably the most photogenic.

## Accommodation
★ Serowe Hotel, 6 rooms with showers. P10 B/B. Phone 234.
★ Tswaragana Hotel, 5 rondawels with showers. P5 room only. Phone 377.

———

From the turnoffs to Serowe and Palapye at the crossroads, the main tarmac road from Gaborone continues north across the level savanna, with mopane steadily taking over from acacia as the tree typical of the area.

At 78 km there is a tarmac turnoff leading eastwards for 56 km to the mining centre of . . .

# SELEBI-PHIKWE

The name of the modern mining town of Selebi-Phikwe is derived from two places, *Selebi* (place of waterholes) and *Phikwe* (a mound of sticks left after clearing land). As a result of routine geological explorations by Roan Selection Trust, a deposit of nickel was found at Selebi in 1963, and at Phikwe in 1966. Copper was found shortly afterwards at Phikwe where there are signs of ancient workings in surface outcrops. Mining commenced at Phikwe in 1974 and it is planned to develop a second mine at Selebi.

A township to serve the two mining areas was created in a parkland between the two deposits and given the combined name of Selebi-Phikwe. A dam was built in the Shashe River to supply water to the mines. The town is a bright, sundrenched, modern little place and mining operations are considerable, notwithstanding many technical difficulties and financial problems resulting from fluctuations in the price of base metals.

## Accommodation
★★ Bosele Hotel, 22 rooms, all with baths. P20 room only, single. P26 room only, double. Phone 676.

From the turnoff to Selebi-Phikwe, the main tarmac road from Gaborone continues north through a mopane-covered plain – flat, hot and featureless. After 60 km the road passes the small trading centre of Shashe, with the Shashe Dam situated to the west of the railway line. A further 27 km brings the tarmac road to . . .

# FRANCISTOWN

Situated in a cluster of hillocks, with the Tati River flowing on the south side, Francistown originated after the discovery of gold in the area and the development of the Monarch Mine. A considerable mining industry had flourished in the area in prehistoric times. Innumerable ancient workings – shafts, adits and trenches – were sunk by early miners, presumably of the Karanga tribe. These early workers extracted a considerable amount of gold from such surface workings, but without pumps or haulage gear, they were forced to abandon work as soon as they reached the water level.

European hunters such as Henry Hartley observed the signs of this early mining and in 1866 he showed the old goldfield to the German geologist, Karl Mauch. The reports made by Mauch stimulated the first gold rush in Southern Africa by European miners who were attracted to the area in the hope of fortune. Among the cosmopolitan crowd of diggers was Daniel Francis, namesake of Francistown.

The field never matched the expectations of the European diggers; popular fancy had converted the place into the Ophir of the Bible and men rushed there expecting to find vast riches. The early miners, however, had skilfully extracted most of the surface gold, the remainder being at some depth. Nevertheless, mining for gold continued in the area until 1964 when the Monarch Mine closed down. Nickel and copper deposits have been found in the area but have so far not been exploited.

Francistown started as a typical mining town with a street of stores and pubs facing the railway line. The 1890s saw the place at its rowdiest and most opulent. After the mines closed down the town went into a decline, but slowly revived as a trading, rail, administrative and communications centre for the northern district of Botswana.

It is still a boisterous little place where the nights are filled with the din of trains shunting and the volcanic eruption of noise from such establishments as the Sisters and Brothers open-air disco. The climate is hot and thirsty.

On the railway station stands an interesting old locomotive, a type 15 Garratt, a leviathan number 352 which has seen several million kilometres of hard labour, pulling heavy trains through the heat of Botswana and Zimbabwe. Cattle, coal, copper, gold, freight, passengers – all were heaved along by this willing old puffer. Now it has been honourably retired, watching with some disdain as the modern 'growlers' – the diesels – carry out the chores of transport.

## Accommodation
★★ Grand Hotel, 28 rooms, with showers. P18,80 D. Phone 300.
★ Tati Hotel, 8 rooms, all with showers. P10 single, P18 double B/B. Phone 321.

**Caravans and camping**

★ Municipal camping ground, P1,50 D.

Francistown is situated at a major junction on the main road from Gaborone. To the north, the road continues across the savanna until, 86 km from Francistown, it reaches the border of Zimbabwe at Ramokgwebane. The border post is open daily from 07h00 to 20h00.

To the west of Francistown, a tarmac road leads across the savanna, a level parkland that seems endless. After 7,5 km there is a turnoff south-west leading for 260 km to the diamond mine at Orapa. This rich diamond-bearing volcanic pipe (the second largest in the world) was found in 1967 by prospectors of De Beers. Production started in 1971. A second, slightly smaller pipe was located 40 km south-east of Orapa at Letlhakane where production started in 1976. Both mines are worked by De Beers Botswana Mining Company (Pty) Ltd of which the Botswana Government and De Beers are equal shareholders.

From the turnoff to Orapa, the tarmac road continues westwards through thickly bushed savanna country. Mopane and baobab trees dominate the flat, sandy plains and cattle posts and patches of farmland nestle amongst the trees.

At 122 km from Francistown a veterinary cordon fence is reached where vehicles and travellers pass through a dip – a precaution against the spread of foot-and-mouth livestock disease. Numerous sellers of curios make and offer for sale their wares at the roadside.

After a further 10 km the road reaches a turnoff to the verge of Sua Pan, one of the two main pans of the Makgadikgadi system. This sandy turnoff is negotiable by 4-wheel-drive vehicles only. Beyond this turnoff the trees start to dwindle into stunted mopane. At 30 km from the Sua turnoff, to the south of the road, stands a giant baobab tree, a favourite camping spot for many travellers. The tree stands on the verge of the huge depression, an open grassy area containing in its centre the Makgadikgadi basin.

Beyond the baobab tree, the tarmac road continues west into an area of grass and tall vegetable ivory palms *(Hyphaena ventricosa)*. At 17 km from the baobab tree (18 km from Francistown) the road reaches the Nata River with the fairly large settlement of Nata situated on its banks. The *Nata* (black) River flows from the east and is one of the principal sources of water for Sua Pan, part of the . . .

# MAKGADIKGADI BASIN

In the Bushman language, *sua* means salt. For generations these people have extracted salt from this shallow depression and they still use it as an article of trade with the Tswana tribes. The pan, connected to Ntwetwe Pan like a Siamese twin, is one of the natural wonders of Africa. These are the two main pans contained by the Makgadikgadi basin.

The entire surface of Sua Pan is only occasionally filled with water, but in the north the Nata River provides a fairly reliable flow and the delta, where this river enters the pan, is a resort for vast numbers of aquatic birds such as flamingos, especially in autumn and winter.

In the south, Sua Pan is overlooked by an escarpment, from where there are wide views over the whole shimmering white surface. In the south-west lies a rocky elevation 10 m high on which stands the ruin of a prehistoric stone settlement.

Ntwetwe Pan comprises a complex of islands, small depressions, large depressions containing deep water, grassy peninsulas and vast plains covered in grass and palm trees. These plains are favoured by antelope such as zebra and wildebeest who migrate there during the dry months of winter, spending their summers at Nxai Pan in the north. Both Nxai Pan and the grass plains north and west of Ntwetwe are national parks. Four-wheel-drive vehicles are essential for their exploration.

At Nata, the main road divides. To the north, a gravel road continues to Kazungula and Kasane on the border of Zambia. Kazungula, where grows a famous old muzungula tree, is connected by pont to Zambia across the Zambezi River. The border post is open daily from 06h00 to 18h00. Kasane is the gateway to the . . .

# CHOBE NATIONAL PARK

The 1 160-square kilometre extent of the Chobe National Park contains one of the largest concentrations of wild animals in Africa. May to September – the dry months – is the best time of year to visit this fascinating national park. Vast herds of buffalo feed in the marshes. Elephant, eland, giraffe, impala, kudu, lechwe, oribi, puku, roan, tsessebe, waterbuck, wildebeest and zebra are very numerous. Predators – lion and leopard – and scavengers roam the whole area. Hippos and crocodiles inhabit the waterways and bird life is magnificent. Rhino have been reintroduced. Warthog, wild pigs, baboon and monkeys abound.

The park was created in 1968 and named after the Chobe River which forms its northern boundary. The higher reaches of this river are known as the Linyanti. A fair gravel road skirts the southern side of the river for 120 km as far as Kachikau. Beyond this place the tracks are suited to four-wheel-drive vehicles only. The visitor is well served by scenic loop roads branching off from the river road and in this area may be seen some of the largest concentrations of game animals. The riverine vegetation is luxuriant. There is a public campsite at Serondella.

South of the river lies an area of mopane forest where there are numerous large pans. These pans contain water and provide drinking places for an interesting variety of wild animals, including gemsbok, oribi, reedbuck and roan. There is a campsite in this area at Nogatsau.

The south-western portion of the park consists of the Mababe Depression, which appears to have once been a lake. Now only enough water reaches it in time of flood from the Chobe River through the Savuti channel to maintain it as a marsh. Buffalo and various antelope graze around the verges of the marsh and there is a camping ground at Savuti. Interesting rock paintings may be seen in the area on a hill near the channel. The Magwikhwe Sand Ridge stretches like a disintegrating wall along the western side of the depression.

## Accommodation

★★® Chobe Safari Lodge, 27 rooms, all with baths. P12 single, room only. P21 double, room only. Rondawels, P7 single, room only. P12 double, room only. Phone Kasane 26.

★★★® Chobe Game Lodge. Phone Kasane 6.

Apart from the camping grounds of the National Park authorities, several private concerns have tented camps in the Chobe area. These camps act as bases for conducted tours to view game, and where professional guides, boats, fishing tackle and four-wheel-drive vehicles may be hired. Prices range from about P60 to P70 daily.

Both Gametrackers (Pvt) Ltd, Carlton Centre, Johannesburg, and Safari South, Box 40, Maun, have camps at Savuti. Hunters Africa (Pty) Ltd, Box 11, Kasane, have various camps in the area and Linyanti Explorations, Box 11, Kasane, have one camp.

Visitors to the area need to take sensible health precautions. Tsetse flies carry sleeping sickness, mosquitoes carry malaria, and the lakes and rivers are infected with bilharzia.

---

From the Mababe Gate at the south-western end of the Chobe National Park, a track suitable only for four-wheel-drive vehicles leads south for 30 km and then reaches a division: to the south the track continues for 120 km to Maun, to the west a branch leads for 22 km to the . . .

# MOREMI WILDLIFE RESERVE

This spectacular 1 800-square kilometre wildlife reserve was created by the Tawana tribe in 1968. It is a pure wilderness area of great beauty with water lily-covered lagoons, palm-covered islands, rich green vegetation and a vast population of wild animals. Bird life is magnificent. The heronries at Cakanaca and Gcodikwe are impressive towards evening and the lagoons are always resorts for duck, geese, ibis, jacanas, spoonbills, storks and waders.

Only very rough tracks penetrate this reserve and visitors are allowed on foot at their own risk. Game viewing, bird watching and photographic possiblilities are tremendous but the area is hot, with tsetse flies and mosquitoes being present. The wet season, December to April, reduces the tracks to deep mud, therefore visits in this season are not recommended. August and September are the best months.

### Accommodation
** Khwai River Lodge, 16 rondawels, all with baths. Phone Maun 211.
** San-Ta-Wani Lodge, 6 double rooms. P70 D. Phone Johannesburg 211-456.


# NATA TO MAUN

From the settlement on the Nata River, with its two garages and stores, where the main tarmac road from Francistown divides, the left hand branch leads west. At present this road is gravel but the surface is excellent except in heavy rains. The landscape is completely flat, a plain covered in grass, clumps of palm trees and patches of mopane bush dominated by occasional baobab trees. The road skirts the northern end of the Magkadikgadi depression, crossing several outlying pans and extensions of the main pan, some filled with shallow water, others dry and hard.

A few cattle posts are passed at the beginning of the drive but the country is sparsely populated. After 40 km there is a road camp at Zorongosa and at 97 km a turn to Gweta. The road then traverses the game utilisation corridor between the . . .


# MAKGADIKGADI PANS GAME RESERVE AND NXAI PAN NATIONAL PARK

These two associated wildlife sanctuaries cover over 10 000 square kilometres of country, penetrable by tracks only in four-wheel-drive vehicles. No accommodation facilities are provided. The main track leading for 43 km to Nxai Pan branches north from the road to Maun at a point 164 km west of Nata.

The game population of this area is essentially migratory. From December to March a tremendous amount of wildlife is concentrated at Nxai Pan (originally an ancient lake bed), and the nearby grass plains at Kanyu. Gemsbok, giraffe, impala, springbok, wildebeest and zebra are especially numerous. Eland and sable are less prolific while buffalo and elephant only appear during very wet seasons. Cheetah, lion, hyenas, jackals, wild dogs and bat-eared foxes are plentiful.

There are several other pans in the vicinity such as Kgamakgama, where wildlife concentrates and the entire area is fascinating to explore. On the east shores of Kudiakam Pan grow a group of baobab trees known as the Sleeping Sisters. Originally painted by Thomas Baines, they still look the same after more than 100 years.

At the end of the rainy season, about May, the game animals migrate south from Nxai Pan across the main road to Maun and south into the Makgadikgadi depression where they disperse over the grassy plains on the verge of Ntwetwe Pan. As the small pans dry up, the wildlife converges more on the Botletli (or Boteti) River, which links the Makgadikgadi depression to the Okavango Swamps and supplies them with drinking water during the dry months.

From the turnoff to Nxai Pan, the main road to Maun continues west. After 49 km (213 km from Nata) the road passes a turnoff to Motopi. At 243 km a foot-and-mouth veterinary gate and dip is reached at Makalamobedi. A further 56 km (299 km from Nata) brings the road to the banks of the beautiful Thamalakane River. Across it lies the town of . . .

# MAUN

The atmospheric, amiable and informal little town of Maun (correctly spelt *Maung* – the place of short reeds) is remote but cheerful, and a surprising oasis to find in the wilderness of the Kgaligadi. Lying on the banks of the Thamalakane River, the sundrenched little place is provided with shade and is beautified by the tall, riverine forest. The surrounding area is a proclaimed wildlife sanctuary and it is delightful to find a river in so arid a setting, with its clear water providing a home for numerous fish, aquatic birds, hippos and crocodiles. Water lilies ornament the calm surface and mirrored on it· are reflections of trees and clouds. For the fisherman and canoeist this river is fascinating and exploring its languid, sinuous course upstream to the Okavango Swamps or downstream until it loses itself in the sand of the Kgaligadi, is a unique experience in travel.

   Maun is the main gateway to the wilderness areas of sand and water of Botswana. Safari companies such as Ker, Downey and Selby; Moremi Safaris; and Safari South, are based there from where they conduct parties north into the swamps, south into the wilderness of the central Kgaligadi and west to Lake Ngami, Ghanzi and the sand areas along the border with Namibia.

   The town is served by shops, garages, curio and handicraft sellers, tanneries specialising in game skins, a hotel, various riverside lodges and administrative buildings. The town is the principal centre for Ngamiland, the home of the Tawana tribe and several smaller tribal troups such as the Teti and the Herero. The majority of tourists visit Maun during the winter months (mainly August and September) when the weather is cool. October and November are extremely hot prior to the rainy months of January and February, when the country is at its best, especially for photography. The area is then green and cloud formations are superb. The summer months are also the best for fishing.

## Accommodation
★® Crocodile Camp, 8 chalets (25 beds). P15,25 D/B/B. Phone 265.
★★® Island Safari Lodge, 12 bungalows. P27 D/B/B. Phone 300.
★® Okavango River Lodge, 5 bungalows with shower. P19 D/B/B. Phone 298.
★® Rileys Hotel, 16 rooms. P10,50 – P13 B/B. Phone 204.

## Caravans and camping
★ Crocodile Camp, 50 sites. P1 D per person.
★★ Island Safari Lodge, 50 sites. P1 D per person.
★ Okavango River Lodge, 30 sites. P1 D per person.

The Thamalakane River is normally in flood from early June until October when the river drops. However, local rains can cause it to flood slightly during the wet season of December and March. The safari companies provide boat trips up the river to camps in the Okavango Swamps. Canoes and boats can be hired from the lodges. A delightful short trip follows the

Boro tributary of the Thamalakane. Longer trips of seven to 14 days, allow for exploration of the wonders of the swamplands and the delta of the Okavango, an area 15 000 square kilometres in extent. The Thamalakane is well populated with fish, notably bream, barbel, and vundu. Tiger fish are found higher up in the actual course of the Okavango River and in the delta.

The Thamalakane River is the southern drain of the Okavango swampworld, carrying away the water which manages to penetrate the vast morass. South-west of Maun, the river divides: one branch continues south-west as the Nxhabe, to feed Lake Ngami; the other branch swings east as the Botletli (or Boteti) to feed the Makgadikgadi pans. The entire complex pattern of waterways in a sea of sand is one of the natural wonders of the world, not simply of Africa.

―――――――――

At present, Maun forms the terminus of good roads in Botswana. Beyond lies the pure safari country although it is possible to reach Lake Ngami in a normal vehicle, 71 km along a rough but fairly firm road.

## LAKE NGAMI

Ngami has always been one of the mysterious lakes of Africa. Its very existence is dependent entirely on the extent of rains in Angola and the penetration of water through the swamps to the Thamalakane River and from there through the Nxhabe to the lake. This process is quite unpredictable: if no water reaches the lake, it dries up completely; during heavy floods it becomes an inland sea. Descriptions of the lake by olden-day travellers are understandably very varied.

The name *Ngami* apparently means 'big'. The Bushmen called it *Nxhabe* (place of giraffes); the Yei called it *Ncame* (place of reeds). During a good season it can fill to a depth of almost 2 m. A prodigious fish population, particularly barbel, appears with the water, feeding on rich nutrients and attracting to the lake countless aquatic birds. When the lake dries up nothing remains save a flat floor, several mirages and the bones of unfortunate creatures who have died of thirst.

The road from Maun reaches the village of Toteng after 64 km. From here a left turn 3 km out of the village crosses the plain to the Nxhabe River on the bank of which is a campsite at a point where the river reaches the lake. From Toteng the track to Sehithwa may be followed for 20 km, after which various turnoffs lead to the lake and a fishing camp on a promontory. Bird life is impressive and views of the lake are grand at this point.

From Sehithwa a track leads northwards for 310 km to Shakawe, the border post with the Caprivi Strip of Namibia. This track is only suited to four-wheel-drive or heavy vehicles. From it turnoffs stretch to several interesting places. From the village of Tsau, 50 km north of Sehithwa, a turnoff proceeds west for 195 km to Cwihaba where, inside a rocky valley, are situated what are known as Drotsky's Caves, a series of connected caverns containing many stalactites but few stalagmites. The main cavern is about 15 m high by 50 m long. Many bats inhabit the caves, the exploration of which is as yet, incomplete. The caves are named after Marthinus Drotsky, a farmer from Ghanzi, who was led to them by a Bushman in June 1932. They were declared a national monument in 1934.

Beyond the turnoff to these caves at .Tsau, the road continues to the north over sandy savanna country. Villages such as Nokaneng and Gomare are passed. At Sepopa village there is a crossing of tracks: to the east a track leads to the Okavango Fishing Lodge; to the west a track stretches for 40 km to the hills called *Tsodilo* (steep). These hills are situated in clusters known to the Bushmen as 'Man', 'Woman' and 'Child'. The highest hill rises about

420 m above the savanna. These hills were occupied by man from an early period and numerous signs of early villages are visible. Mining for iron ore was evidently quite a local industry. On suitable rock faces in the hills, over 1 700 paintings may be seen in over 200 galleries. The paintings appear to be of divided origin: red paintings were probably done by the Bushmen and black paintings by the Iron Age people who displaced the Bushmen. Some paintings include several colours.

Local Bushmen act as guides for visits to the paintings but do not know anything about their origin. An Historic Monuments officer, stationed at Mbukushu village just south of the largest hill, will direct visitors and arrange guides. Pleasant camping sites are situated in the hills and water may be obtained from springs. A landing strip close to the hills enables aircraft to land. The hills, reputedly haunted, are atmospheric and eerie.

---

From Sehithwa the sandy track to the west continues for 192 km to reach the village of . . .

## GHANZI

This isolated little ranching centre is said to derive its name from the word *gantshi* (place of flies). The surrounding area offers fine pasturage for cattle. Hottentot pastoralists moved into the region in prehistoric times and dug many wells there. In 1874 six families of Transvaal Boers, led by Hendrik van Zyl, settled there with the permission of the Tawana chief. Incessant brawls erupted with the local tribes and the extreme isolation made life very difficult. Van Zyl was eventually killed in one of the fights by other whites who had settled in the area which became known as a staging post for Thirstland Trekkers – different groups of people wandering away from the Transvaal in search of some promised land of milk and honey in the west.

In 1898, 37 families made their homes in the area, each family being allocated a substantial ranch. The village of Ghanzi was founded as their centre. In the 1950s, 130 additional ranches were granted and Ghanzi developed into a village with several stores administrative buildings and a hotel.

### Accommodation
★ Kalahari Arms Hotel, 17 rooms, 8 with baths. P10,50 B/B. Phone 1.

From Ghanzi the track to the west continues for 98 km to Kalkfontein and from there for a further 97 km to Mamuno, the border post with Namibia. The post is open daily from 08h00 to 16h00.

South of Ghanzi lies a track frequently used by cattle men taking livestock to the abattoirs at Lobatse. This track leads for 271 km to Kang, and for 317 km to Kanye, where it joins the tarmac road to Lobatse (see page 757). From Kang a track branches off west for 109 km to Tshane and from there swings southwards for 246 km to Tshabong, close to the border with South Africa. This track passes through the . . .

## MABWASEHUBE GAME RESERVE (AND GEMSBOK NATIONAL PARK)

*Mabwasehube* (red sands) takes its name from a dried-out pan in the northern part of the reserve. The reserve is actually an eastern extension of the Kalahari Gemsbok Park, a 9 000-square kilometre wilderness which is completely undeveloped and best seen from the portion on the South African side west of the Nossob River which acts as the frontier line.

Eland, gemsbok, hartebeest, springbok and other drought-resistant wild animals frequent the area, the pans in the Mabwasehube Reserve attracting large numbers of these inhabitants of the wilderness. Predators are numerous, comprising lion, cheetah, wild dog, leopard, brown hyenas and various small wild cats.

Bushman groups wander through the area among the great dunes of red-coloured sand. The hardy vegetation and the surprising number of living creatures who have adapted to the harsh conditions all make fascinating study. The area is difficult to explore and demands the use of four-wheel-drive vehicles. Water and self-reliance is essential. For such visitors, Botswana in its entirety is a world of its own, a wonderful wilderness where it is still possible, for a little while at least, to leave civilisation behind and to lose oneself in a primeval landscape, to hear the sound of sweet silence, to breathe air that knows no pollution, and to see the stars at night, so vividly above a camp that one is tempted to reach upwards to touch them and to learn whether they are hot or cold.

# Chapter Thirty-Nine

# LESOTHO

Into the 30 300 square kilometres that is the diminutive state of Lesotho, is concentrated some of the most spectacular scenery to be found on the continent of Africa. A full 85 per cent of the landscape consists of a mass of mountains, while the remaining 15 per cent is comprised of lower level viewsites from which to admire the heights. Lesotho is a delight to artists and photographers, and notable for the vividness of its scenic colours: yellow, orange and red sandstone cliffs; intensely blue skies in summer with towering banks of white clouds; green grass, turning brown in winter; and the transparent blueness of high basalt mountains shrouded in mantles of snow.

In addition to these rich colours the rocks have been modelled into fantastic shapes by massive natural and unnatural erosion, giving the place the appearance of the abandoned toyroom belonging to an untidy nursery of giants. Balancing rocks, table-topped mountains, pinnacles, spires, deep ravines, dongas, cliffs, caves and almost every geological formation imaginable are littered over this landscape. The effect is bizarre, eerie and surprising.

The 1 200 000 people living in Lesotho are collectively known as *baSotho* while an individual is *moSotho;* the language is *seSotho;* and the country is correctly known as *leSotho.* As with many other African people the name was applied to them by foreigners. Research indicates that the name of *Sotho* or *Suthu* was given to them by the Nguni people (Zulu and Swazi), since the first people the Nguni encountered who spoke the Sotho language, happened to live along the banks of the *uSuthu* (dark brown) River in Swaziland. They were, from that time on, referred to as the *baSuthu* and, for want of a collective name of their own, retained this appellation. The Zulu spelling, incidentally, gives English readers a correct pronunciation. The orthography of the modern Sotho language is not particularly satisfactory. With rather peculiar consequences for English readers, the language was originally reduced to the written word by French-speaking missionaries while modern orthographers have further complicated it.

The language and customs of the Sotho are substantially the same as those of the inhabitants of Botswana. Tradition states that during the 18th century, sections of the same people who had occupied Botswana wandered over the highveld plains. The men drove cattle and the women carried on their heads supplies of seeds for the cultivation of pumpkins, sorghum, beans and later, maize, the great staple crop, which was introduced by Europeans.

These migrants, belonging to several quite independent clans, stumbled by chance into the beautifully fertile valley of the river they knew as the *Mohokare* (river of willow trees) but which Lieutenant-Colonel Richard Collins, in 1809, subsequently named the *Caledon* in honour of the Governor of the Cape, the Earl of Caledon who had sent him north to explore the interior of Southern Africa.

Originally resident in this area were several Bushman clans; as a result, the numerous sandstone caves of Lesotho shelter some of the finest galleries of polychrome rock art in the world. These cave galleries remain one of the great treasures of the country, although many are sadly mutilated by the scrawlings of vandals, the soot of fires lit by herdboys, or by the corroding effect of water, thrown on to them by people trying to temporarily revive their colours.

The newcomers to the valley of the Caledon, with their cattle and agricultural activity, soon drove away the herds of game animals and the Bushman hunters who lived on them. The immigrants themselves were not left in peace for long, for in Zululand the human upheaval which resulted in the rise to power of Shaka and his Zulu people was developing. The shock waves of this disturbance spread all over Southern Africa in the form of raiding bands and refugees trying to find new homes for themselves as far from Shaka as possible.

Several of these refugee clans and raiders fled over the Drakensberg and found their way into the valley of the Caledon. Then began a dismal chapter in the human story in Southern Africa. This was the time of the *Lifaqane* (migratory wars) where murder, brutality, raids, fights, and cannibalism became the lot in life for many once peaceful people. It was during this troubled period, however, that the Sotho nation came into being.

The flat-topped sandstone hills which are so remarkable a feature of the Caledon Valley, made superb natural fortresses. These hills are the remnants – like the pieces of a scattered jigsaw puzzle – of a higher plain which has been destroyed by natural erosion. The summit of the original, fragmented plain remains in the form of small plateaus supported by almost unscalable cliffs. Springs surface on some of the plateau summits, and there is sufficient grazing to support livestock. The surrounding cliff faces have restricted and easily defensible lines of approach, and these sandstone hills were the Sotho equivalent of a feudal castle. Any chieftain possessing a natural stronghold such as this, could survive attack, and at the same time, use his hill as a base from which to raid others.

Living on one of these hills in the northern end of the Caledon Valley was the young chief of the section of the Kwena people known as the baMokoteli. This chief, named Lepoqo, was nicknamed *Moshoeshoe* (the shaver) on account of his skill in rustling the livestock of his neighbours. To Europeans he was known as *Moshesh*.

Moshoeshoe and his people had as their stronghold the hill called *Botha-Bothe* (the lair, a place of lying down), now known as Butha-Buthe. On this stronghold Moshoeshoe found himself having to withstand a succession of sieges by various raiding bands wandering in from Zululand, as well as from Sotho tribes such as the Tlokwa who, unsettled by the invaders from the coast, were themselves roaming about looting for a living, led by an amazon-like chieftainess named Mantatisi and her juvenile son Sigonyela.

Moshoeshoe found life increasingly precarious. The Botha-Bothe stronghold was not invulnerable and so many people were fleeing to him for protection that there was not enough room to accommodate them. At the height of his dilemma, however, one of his followers who had been hunting further south, managed to reach him, giving an enthusiastic description of a sandstone hill fortress he had found and considered absolutely impregnable.

Moshoeshoe decided to move to this new stronghold. Exploiting the distraction of a Zulu attack on the Tlokwa, Moshoeshoe and his followers abandoned Botha-Bothe and made a forced march southwards. On the way they ran the gauntlet of a host of thugs, bandits, renegades and cannibals who infested the mountains. There are many accounts of adventures, escapes, and tragedies which occurred on this march.

Tradition has it that on an afternoon in July 1824, Moshoeshoe and his followers reached the new stronghold. Moshoeshoe was at first somewhat unimpressed but as evening approached the hill seemed to gain in strength. He named it *Thaba Bosiho* (mountain of the night). Finding it unoccupied, they scrambled to the top and were delighted at the new discovery. Of all natural fortresses in the world, this is in fact, one of the most remarkable.

To the undiscerning eye, Thaba Bosiho (or Bosiu) simply resembles a rather inconspicuous fragment of the original plateau at the foot of the Maluti range. However, prodigious natural erosion which shattered the plateau into pieces, left this fragment with a fairly level top which was grassy, fed by several springs and made nearly impregnable by sharp precipice cliffs of irregular shape. It was almost impossible for a primitive army to scale these heights up the few practical paths and to be able to dislodge any resolute defenders.

Thus established, Moshoeshoe built a village above the main route of access (the Khubelu

Pass), with the nearby Ramasali Pass (the back entrance, so to speak) being very convenient for secret comings and goings. From these heights Moshoeshoe – intelligent and kindly but resolute by nature – defied all attacks and personally saw to it that the members of the future Sotho nation were protected.

In 1827 the Ngwaneni people from Natal attacked the mountain but were driven off. In 1830 the Korana made an abortive attempt and in 1831 the Ndebele also tried and were defeated. The reputation of Moshoeshoe and his invincible mountain spread far and wide and his following grew. Europeans arrived: traders, the French Protestant missionaries, Casalis and Arbousset, and individuals such as David Webber (a deserter from the British army) who settled on the mountain. Being a good mason, he built Moshoeshoe a stone house while another deserter, John Wilks, an armourer, took charge of Moshoeshoe's artillery of odd-sized cannons obtained from various gun runners or cast locally.

In 1852 the British under General Cathcart attacked the Sotho but, although approaching Thaba Bosiho, they retired without attempting to storm the place.

In 1858 the Orange Free State tried to terminate Moshoeshoe's hold when Commandant Senekal led a thousand men to attack Thaba Bosiho. From their camp at the bottom they assessed the impregnable place and its garrison of 10 000 warriors, and quietly went home again!

The reputation of Moshoeshoe increased steadily. More followers, including Europeans, rallied to his rule; gunsmiths, horse traders, artisans and missionaries, including Allard and Gerard, the Roman Catholics who established Roma.

In 1865 another war broke out with the Orange Free State and the mountain was besieged for two months by Commandant General Fick at the head of a resolute little army of 2 000 men, supported by President Brand. On 8 August the Free Staters set out to take Thaba Bosiho by storm. Eight men managed to reach the summit, to the consternation of the defenders, but the charge was repulsed.

On 15 August, the Free Staters tried again, attacking up the Khubelu Pass. They forced a passage half way up the pass but their commander, Louw Wepener, was killed and the men retreated. The Free Staters then laid determined siege to the mountain, hoping to starve Moshoeshoe into submission.

Conditions became dismal on the summit; there were too many cattle, thousands of which died of hunger, thirst, or by falling over the cliffs. However, Moshoeshoe and his men remained in command of the mountain and the siege eventually dwindled. In April 1866 the so-called Peace of the Kaffircorn was arranged at a meeting held beneath the mountain, as the Sotho wanted the chance to harvest their crops. With food in the larder they resumed fighting but without notable success. The Free Staters controlled almost the whole of Lesotho apart from Thaba Bosiho itself. In March 1868, at the request of the now aged and weary Moshoeshoe, the British declared the country a protectorate and the war ended. The Sotho lost all territory west of the Caledon River (the so-called 'conquered territory') but at least were allowed independent control of the strip of plains between the river and the slopes of the Maluti, as well as the mountain mass itself, hitherto uninhabited but which became increasingly settled from then on.

Moshoeshoe died in 1870 and was buried on Thaba Bosiho. There is a legend that his spirit lingers about the place in a perceptible atmosphere of serenity and strength. A strange dune of red sand on the summit is blown by the winds but like Moshoeshoe, never leaves it. It is said that even though a sample of this sand may be taken away as a souvenir, it will somehow contrive to return to Thaba Bosiho.

After the death of Moshoeshoe, his son Letsie succeeded him and moved the seat of government to Matsieng, near the French mission centre of Morija. Thaba Bosiho was retained by Masupha, another of Moshoeshoe's sons, who strengthened its defences. But the days of its military importance were over; Masupha, after leading a truculent life, was eventually defeated in a civil war in 1897 by Lerotholi (son of Letsie), the new Paramount Chief. Thus Thaba Bosiho was abandoned to memory. It is a fascinating place to visit. Near by stands the impressive *Qiloane* (the pinnacle), looming up like a gigantic rock sentinel, guarding Moshoeshoe's mountain.

Lesotho (at that time known to Europeans as Basutoland) remained a British protectorate for nearly 100 years and was administered by a Resident Commissioner with the descendants of Moshoeshoe as the heads of state. In 1903 the country received a National Council, an advisory body of nominated members and in 1959 a Legislative Council, with half the members elected while the rest were chiefs and nominated members. In 1964 this council became an elected National Assembly of 60 members with the Paramount Chief or king as head of state. The incumbent is Motlotlehi, also known as Moshoeshoe II. On 4 October 1966, Lesotho finally emerged as a fully independent state, the Kingdom of Lesotho, having seSotho and English as the two official languages.

## MASERU

The capital and largest town in the Kingdom of Lesotho, *Maseru* (the place of red sandstone), has a population of about 30 000. It originated in 1869 when the newly established British administration of the Protectorate of Basutoland required a site for their headquarters. Moshoeshoe selected Maseru and Commandant James Bowker, appointed as High Commissioner's Agent, established his camp there. The British always referred to the administrative posts of Basutoland as 'camps', since it was never really expected that they would grow into towns and as a result, they did not have the benefit of proper planning or layout.

In its early years, Maseru was a completely informal place. Commandant Bowker had his camp on the rocky height of red sandstone where the new Lesotho National Museum has since been built. The first trader, Richard Trower, built a store in 1869 on the most convenient level spot, the site of the present Lancers Inn. Other traders followed, such as Irvine, Holden & Co. who built a store at Hobson's Square, named after one of their managers, George Hobson; and the Fraser brothers who opened a store in 1880 on the site of their present retail shop in Maseru.

The site of the 'camp' was uneven and awkward, dominated on the south side by three rocky hillocks named the World, the Flesh, and the Devil, and hemmed in by the Caledon River on the northern and western sides. The Caledon was crossed at a fording place from where a wagon trail led westwards into the Orange Free State. In 1880 a pont was built at the ford by an Italian, Stefano Massa, which provided the principal link with the outside world.

The years 1880 and 1881 saw the camp of Maseru under heavy attack during the Gun War. On 10 October 1880 Masupha invaded the place and destroyed several buildings. Another attack, on 18 October, ended in a pitched battle, before the defenders held firm near the site of the present China Garden Restaurant. The three overlooking hillocks, which were named by the garrison at this time, were occupied on different occasions by the attackers, with the World often used by snipers to fire at the defenders. The present site on this hillock of the Hilton Hotel, was a strongpoint for the attackers.

On 18 December 1905 the pont across the Caledon was replaced by a rail and road bridge. As a result, Maseru grew considerably and the camp changed into a village where several notable buildings were built out of the sandstone common to the area. The principal street, Kingsway, became the first stretch of tarmac road in Lesotho. Fronting it were buildings such as the sandstone headquarters of the British Resident Commissioner, now the office of the Prime Minister of Lesotho, and, at the eastern end the twin-towered sandstone Catholic Cathedral of Our Lady of Victories, overlooking Cathedral Circle where Kingsway divides into the northern and southern highways of Lesotho. Stores, banks, offices and other places of business were erected along Kingsway which have either been added to or replaced by modern structures. Side streets such as Palace Road lead to the royal palace, and Parliament Road leads to the Houses of Parliament. The original site of the first camp of Maseru is in Griffith Hill Road, behind the Standard Bank.

Two notable modern buildings on Kingsway, one shaped like a large Sotho hat, the other in the form of a Sotho shield, display for sale the handicrafts of the Sotho people. There are also displays of traditional dancing on Saturday mornings. The Khotso Gift Shop further up Kingsway is the retail outlet for the Roma Valley Co-operative Society. The Public Library and the office of the Lesotho Tourist Corporation are also situated on Kingsway. The Royal Lesotho Tapestry Weavers, Afrotique (Afro Rugs Boutique), and Thorkild Handweaving have outlets on Moshoeshoe Road; Basotho Sheepskin Products and Royal Crown Jewellers are both in Mohlomi Road. Thaba Bosiho Ceramics can be found in Motsoene Road.

Modern Maseru could hardly be described as beautiful but it is certainly an animated place. Traffic along Kingsway must be sharply watched, for driving standards in Lesotho are generally not of the best. The old camp is now very much an adolescent town, having grown up all by itself and now regretting its lack of early civic 'education' when the legacy of town planning might have saved it a few problems.

Despite its unconventionality, Maseru is atmospheric. The numerous international aid organisations which have established their headquarters in the town provide quite a cosmopolitan population. Several of these groups help by training and stimulating the Sotho people to develop their arts, crafts and home industries, the result of which has been the production of much original and worthwhile work, which is not only displayed in the various shops already mentioned but is exported to many foreign countries where it compares and competes with international products.

South African holidaymakers find Maseru attractive on account of the slight touch of salacity present in its nightlife. With censorship being less rigorous than in South Africa, cinema shows of very devious artistic merit abound, as well as literature of the lurid type, strip and cabaret shows (sometimes good, sometimes tatty), and the inevitable casino with its one-armed bandits and gambling tables. Harmless fun is available for those who do not take things too seriously; an occasional win against impossible odds is just a bonanza, and the losses one can afford should be regarded as payment for entertainment.

A word of caution to visitors: Maseru is notorious for a complaint known as 'Maseru Guts', a problem seemingly caused by the drinking water. Local doctors profit from the malady but not visitors. The wise traveller brings his own anti-dysentery tablets, sticks to mineral water and regards with caution some of the food in hotels whose menus are pretentious and beyond the technical skill of their chefs.

The Caledon Bridge border post is open daily from 06h00 to 22h00.

## Accommodation
★ Airport Hotel, 16 rooms, all with baths. R13,20 – R16,50 D, room only. Phone 2081.
★★★★ Lesotho Hilton, 240 rooms, all with baths. R18 – R45 D, room only. Phone 23111.
★★★ Holiday Inn, 238 rooms, all with baths. R18 – R25 D, room only. Phone 2434.
★ Lakeside Hotel, 36 rooms, all with baths. R10 – R11,50 D, room only. Phone 3646.
★ Lancers Inn, 61 rooms, all with baths. R11 – R16,50 D, room only. Phone 2114.
★ Maseru Hotel, 6 rooms. R8,50 – R11,50 B/B. Phone 22150.
★ Sea Point Hotel, 6 rooms. R8,80 – R9,90 D, room only. Phone 2052.
★★★ Victoria Hotel, 102 rooms, all with baths. R16 – R21 D, room only. Phone 2002.

## Caravans and camping
There is no caravan park in Maseru but many visitors stay in the park at Ladybrand, 16 km from Maseru in the Orange Free State (see page 535), or at the caravan park 40 km from Maseru on the mountain road (see page 777).

The traveller should leave Maseru as soon as possible to explore the beautiful countryside of Lesotho. The delights of Maseru can safely be exhausted in one night but the wonders of Lesotho are endless.

The principal feature in the vicinity of Maseru is the renowned natural stronghold of *Thaba Bosiho* (the mountain of the night) which will forever be associated with the name of Moshoeshoe. To reach this interesting place, drive out from Maseru on the tarmac road to Mafeteng in the south. After 4 km there is a gravel turnoff marked Thaba Bosiho. This is the old road which can be rough for 16,5 km until a better gravel road is joined, which is known as the new Thaba Bosiho road. The new road is reached by continuing for 9,5 km on the tarmac Mafeteng road, past the old turnoff to Thaba Bosiho, and by taking the tarmac turnoff to Roma. At 6 km along this road (20 km from Maseru) the new Thaba Bosiho gravel road branches off, joining the old road after 6,5 km. Thaba Bosiho is 2,5 km beyond the junction of the two roads.

Both roads include interesting features. The old road passes the strangely shaped Pack Saddle Hill and the turnoff to the Botsabelo Leper Settlement. The substantial village of Ha Mahkoathi, 14 km from Maseru, is overlooked by an isolated pile of sandstone known as Bogate, a fragment of the massive Berea plateau summit to the north of the road. Bogate is worth visiting for in its rock shelters are some fine Bushman paintings.

At 16 km from Maseru the road crosses, by means of a causeway, the *Phuthiatsana* (little Duiker River) also known as the Little Caledon River. About 200 m downstream from the causeway there is a confluence with a small tributary. Up this tributary (about 55 m) on the left side of a fork are numerous footprints of prehistoric creatures preserved in the stone.

Where the new road passes the school run by the Church of Lesotho, a track leads for about 1 km to the strange cave houses of *Ntlo Kholo* (the great hut), the ruins of which stand underneath a sandstone overhang. The huts, whose architecture is interesting and unusual, were still occupied in the 1950s.

## THABA BOSIHO

At 24 km from Maseru on the old road (29 km via the new road) lies the village of Ha Rafutho at the foot of the Khubelu Pass, the main route to the summit of Thaba Bosiho. The caretaker of the mountain lives in this village and guides are available to conduct visitors to the several places of interest on the summit which is reached after a moderately strenuous walk. Defensive piles of stones used as missiles by the Sotho may still be seen, as well as a luck heap of pebbles deposited there by various African visitors going to interview Moshoeshoe (dropping a pebble on the heap was reputed to bring luck).

The ruins of Moshoeshoe's village may be seen, including the partly restored residence of the renowned chief, and the cemetery contains the graves of Moshoeshoe and many of his descendants and their families. There are some pieces of cannon and the outline of a foot, a memorial to a son of Moshoeshoe, named Maleleko, who was denied permission to marry his true love. Before jumping to his death, it is said that he carved his footprint into the rock. A delightful little spring of clear water reaches the surface where Moshoeshoe took his refreshment and there is, of course, the strange red-coloured sand dune which, folklore says, contains the spirit of Moshoeshoe. The views from the summit are superb.

From the foot of the Khubelu Pass, the road continues past the Thaba Bosiho Mission and up the valley of the Phuthiatsana River. A good view may be had of the rock known as *Qiloane* (the pinnacle) which stands like a giant sentry guarding Thaba Bosiho. The road then fords the river by means of a causeway and climbs to the summit of a plateau, eventually reaching the main Maseru-Teyateyaneng road via a winding scenic route.

---

# ROMA

The principal centre of the Roman Catholic Church in Lesotho and the site of the University of Lesotho is to be found at Roma. To reach it from Maseru, follow the tarmac road south towards Mafeteng. After 13 km there is a tarmac turnoff leading for 19 km to Roma.

Roma was founded in 1862 when Moshoeshoe granted the site to Bishop J. S. Allard and Father Joseph Gerard. These two pioneers were joined by sisters of the Holy Family of Bordeaux and the mission was named *Motse-oa-ma-Jesu* (village of the mother of Jesus). The mission flourished and in 1870 Father Francois Le Behan built the attractive burnt-brick chapel and a double-storeyed building to house the members of the mission. Primary and secondary schools, teachers' training college, seminaries, hospital and library were added.

The church serves as a cathedral while in 1945 the Catholic University College, the Pius XII College, was founded with six students under Father Paul Beaule. The university college was at first linked to the University of South Africa but grew rapidly, becoming the University of Basutoland, Botswana and Swaziland. In 1964 it became fully autonomous and is now the National University of Lesotho.

# THE ROAD TO RAMABANTA

Along the road to Roma, 3 km beyond the turnoff to the new road to Thaba Bosiho, a gravel turnoff provides a spectacular drive to the trading station of Ramabanta and the start of the bridle path and four-wheel-drive track to Semonkong, an interesting route into the verges of the mountain heart of Lesotho.

For 7,5 km this road crosses maize fields and then joins the Koro-Koro-Maseru road which has branched off from the main Maseru-Mafeteng road 16 km from Maseru. The combined roads continue eastwards towards the mountains with the 2 533-m-high *Thaba Telle* (tall mountain) dominating the horizon. The journey is exceedingly picturesque, lined with villages, fields of maize, herds of cattle and flocks of sheep. Exotic American aloes (agaves) have been planted to form fences around the cattle corrals and villages; cosmos flower in March; and yellow peach trees flourish, quite uncared for, after pips thrown down have taken root by chance.

Caves with Bushman paintings may be seen at places such as Ha Mphotu village. This area is a great producer of reeds used for thatching and the principal stream here is called *Malehlakana* (mother of reeds). Just across the river, a track turns south for 6 km to Mofoka's village, and thence on into the upper valley of the Koro-Koro stream where vast expanses of reeds grow. The *Koro-Koro* stream takes its onomatopoeic name from a curiously shaped cave near its source. Rocks dropped into this cave cause an echo to reverberate, which sounds like a gradually dwindling series of 'koro-koro' sounds.

The road crosses the wall of the dam in the Koro-Koro River (a great place for aquatic birds), and swings southwards up the valley of the Koro-Koro. After 3 km there is a branch stretching due south to St Joseph's Mission (3 km) at the village of Mapeshoane. From here, there is a path to the fine Bushman cave of Halekokoane with its extensive gallery of paintings. The permission of the village headman and a guide should be obtained before visiting the cave from Mapeshoane.

The road to Ramabanta bears eastwards into the mountains after the turnoff to St Joseph's. After 3 km there is a track branching eastwards up the gorge of Raboshabane. There is an interesting tradition about this wild area and a walk up the gorge is rewarding.

The track leads up a very rugged ravine, choked with sandstone fragments. Keeping to the left bank of the stream, the track passes (3 km) the great cave of Mohomeng. After 1,5 km, just above the confluence of the Popa tributary stream, there looms the famed *lefika la Raboshabane* (the rock of Raboshabane).

*Overleaf: The gorge (left) in the rainy roof of Lesotho where the Maletsunyane River (right) falls headlong into a pool of many legends, 193 m below.*

# THE ROCK OF RABOSHABANE

This great rock rears up 200 m and can only be climbed on its northern side. A Sotho proverb says: 'The rock of Raboshabane is slippery', a variant of the old 'There's many a slip twix cup and lip'. This is the story:

During the days of war and cannibalism in the first quarter of the 19th century, a racketeer named Raboshabane established himself on top of this rock, where he built a cluster of huts. To the much harassed peasantry of the district he announced that he would provide a protection service, defending them from evil, on payment of regular tributes. He also offered to store their harvests on top of his rock, supplying them on demand against payment of commission.

By intimidation and the offer of some security for harvests, Raboshabane accumulated during that time of famine, a vast store of food on top of his rock, growing fat and increasingly avaricious in the process. The peasants were starving and disgruntled, but had no counter to the bully. At last one of them, a scarecrow of a man named Sofeng, found the answer.

Trusting for safety on his thinness, he made his way to the stronghold of a notorious brotherhood of 28 cannibals led by a tough ruffian named Motleyoa. Sofeng pretended to be lost and appeared innocent of their reputation. He craved their hospitality for a night and regaled them with gossip very acceptable to individuals normally shunned by their fellow men. Sofeng included an account of Raboshabane, describing his fat shape so lusciously that the mouths of the cannibals watered as they repeated his name and address!

And so it happened that one dark night the 28 cannibals, each carrying a club and dragging behind them a huge cooking pot, silently scaled the rock of Raboshabane. A wild fight ensued on the summit. While the peasantry watched and listened, they heard first a sudden uproar, and then sounds of jollification. The glow of a great cooking fire was seen on the top of the rock, and in the morning the head of Raboshabane was thrown down to the waiting peasants. From this occurrence stems the proverb and tradition of the downfall of Raboshabane.

---

From the turnoff to this notable rock, the road to Ramabanta starts to climb steeply, reaches the top of the sandstone and continues over a grassy plateau, where views of the mountains and the gorge of Raboshabane and the rock may be seen.

The road passes over a ridge, with Motlepu's village lying immediately beyond. From Motlepu's village, mountaineers leave the road to climb the spectacular Thaba Telle, 2 533 m high and no easy achievement. The road now loses altitude, surrounded by handsome scenery. At 30 km from the start of this gravel road, on the Roma road, a junction is reached with a track coming from the Thabana li Mele pottery works and Roma, via a very rough route.

The road continues southwards, dominated to the east by the twin summits of *Thabana Dimele* (hills like breasts). Passing the trading station of Thabana Dimele the road descends to cross the *Makhalaneng* (place of little crabs) River by means of a causeway at the 36-km point. The road climbs steadily to the top of Nkesi's Pass (2 012 m) from where a superb view of the 3 096-m-high *Thaba Putsoa* (blue-grey mountain) and its associate range may be seen.

The road descends, revealing below the cul-de-sac at Ramabanta's store, the mission station of Fatima and the site of the Catholic National Shrine of Lesotho, a scene of pilgrimage which owes its origin to events surrounding the conversion in May 1946 of the local chieftainess, Makopi Api. The road ends at Ramabanta's store 45 km from the turnoff on the Maseru-Roma road.

The end of this road, close to the banks of the river known as the *Makhaleng* (place of crabs), is the starting point for the bridle path and four-wheel-drive track to Semonkong and the 193-m-high waterfall in the river known as the Maletsunyane, from a Bushman who once lived there. This is an exhilarating two-day ride over the summit of the Thaba Putsoa range via Makheka's Pass and across the basalt moorland roof of Southern Africa to the trading station at *Semonkong* (the place of smoke). In a gorge on the banks of the Maletsunyane River, Messrs Fraser maintain some bungalows to accommodate people viewing the falls. The charge is R2,75 per person a night. Food must be taken but bedding is provided. From here there is a short ride to the prodigious gorge of the Maletsunyane where the river thunders down as one of the great waterfalls of the world. An eerie atmosphere and strange confusion of sounds pervades this almost enchanted place. The journey to it is unforgettable, revealing superb views of a world of green and blue mountains. Dense masses of red-hot pokers (*Kniphofia* species) flower around the month of March, giving the slopes a bloodstained appearance.

In winter, when most of the waterfalls in Lesotho are frozen, the Maletsunyane Falls are a fantastic sight, with towers of ice rising up from the ground to meet spirals of ice suspended from above.

From Thabana Dimele (15 km from Ramabanta) it is possible, in a four-wheel-drive vehicle, to return to Maseru via the alternate route through Roma. This route branches off northwards past the pottery works, continues up the valley of the Makhalaneng River and then climbs steeply through rugged mountain country. Dominating the west are the high mountains of Popa and Popanyane, Thabana Dimele, the flat-topped Qaba and Qabanyane peaks, Furumela, on whose slopes grow the famous spiral aloes (*Aloe lattifolias*), and *Thaba Tjhitja* (round mountain) from whose 2 499-m-high summit – reached by a relatively easy climb – there is a stunningly beautiful view.

After 9 km the road reaches Nyakasuba village, where there is a turnoff to the east over Black Nek (the starting point for climbs to Thaba Tjhitja) to the store at Makhaleng. From this junction the road bears north-westwards, crossing the Makhaleng River after 1,5 km and traversing a plateau. After a further 1,5 km, the descent of Ngakana's Pass commences. At the bottom of this pass the road stretches north-westwards, passing the Roma Mission Station and from there, back to Maseru. The round trip comprising 136 km is a drive – rough and steep – that will never be forgotten by those who have completed it.

## THE MOUNTAIN ROAD

The famous mountain road of Lesotho takes the traveller 124 km from Maseru over the roof of Southern Africa to the trading station at the Mantsonyane River. From there the road is under construction and, to be named the trans-Maluti highway, it will one day continue to the valley of the Orange, to Qacha's Nek and out to Matatiele in the Cape.

The road to Mantsonyane is perfectly usable for normal vehicles except in rainy weather. In winter it is also blocked by snow for periods, and must always be negotiated with maximum caution. Scenically, the road provides a majestic and exciting experience. For mountaineers, fishermen, hikers, campers, artists and photographers, it is the key to a high world of sport and wonderful scenery hitherto only accessible by laborious walking or riding on horseback.

The mountain road branches eastwards from the main Maseru-Roma road at a point 24,5 km south of Maseru, from where it proceeds slightly north-eastwards, climbing sandstone cliffs to reach the level of the grassy plateau at the foot of the Maluti range. On the summit of this plateau the traveller is treated to a majestic view of the great massif of the Maluti, and the handsome bulk of the 2 884-m-high Machache immediately ahead. To the south are views into the valley where the Roma mission, pro-cathedral, and the campus of the university are clearly visible.

After losing altitude the road proceeds eastwards across an undulating plateau covered in maize, sorghum and grain. At 34 km from Maseru, the road reaches the village of Ha Ntsi, with its stores and petrol supply. Immediately beyond this village, the road crosses a stream which drains the *Mohlaka-oa-Tuka* (the marsh which burns), a place where underground peat fires burn incessantly.

Immediately across this stream there is a turnoff leading northwards for 3 km to Ha Khotso village. From here, a track continues for a further 3 km to the gorge of the Liphiring River where, in the rock shelter known as *Ha Baroana* (place of the little Bushmen), may be seen one of the finest galleries of rock art in the world. A caretaker is stationed at the rock shelter and there is an admission charge of 30c per person. Visitors to these and other Bushman caves should discourage guides from throwing water over the paintings. This may brighten the colours temporarily, but causes permanent damage.

The main gravel road, meanwhile, after crossing the river from the marsh, continues towards the great mountain wall. After 5 km the road passes two rondawels and a wayside tearoom originally erected there as toll houses for the mountain road. This is now the ★★ Maluti Caravan Park with sites available at R2,50 daily. The bungalow is R5 for two people and R2 for each additional person. Beyond the caravan park, passing the Machache Agricultural Station, the road arrives at the foot of the mountains and starts to climb the slopes of *Thaba Tseka* (mountain with a white mark) by means of the *Lekhalo la Baroa* (Bushman's Pass).

The road climbs steeply for 6 km and then (46,5 km from Maseru) reaches the summit 2 268 m above sea level. A sweeping panorama is revealed over the original zigzag bridle path which, before the road was made, was the sole means of access to this mountain world. Until 1890 nobody lived there at all other than Bushmen in the valleys. Cattle posts were established and eventually, from about 1912, the pressure of population in the lowlands drove people to seek new homes in the valleys of the inner mountains. All the provisions and exports of these people were carried on the backs of pack animals and the famous Basuto ponies made nimble, sturdy and shaggy as a result of hard usage, open-air life, and the treatment meted out to them by owners who were horse users rather than horse lovers.

A complex network of bridle paths was made over the mountains and in 1948, the Government Surveyor, W. K. Hudson, located this remarkable road following the route of one of the main bridle paths.

From the summit of Bushman's Pass, the road descends steeply into the valley of the *Makhaleng* (place of crabs) River. After 5 km the road crosses the river, and continues up the river valley. There are fine pools in which to swim and fish and pleasant camping sites. If a guide is obtained from one of the villages, the energetic hiker, by following the course of the Makhaleng, will eventually reach the lovely cascades of Quiloane, at whose foot is a magnificent swimming pool. It is a half day return trip and the going is steep.

The road soon leaves the Makhaleng: At 53 km from Maseru a road camp is passed where there is a pretty waterfall, natural swimming pool, fine picnic spot and a most attractive little hotel, known as *Molimo Nthuse* (God help me) from the mountain pass above it. This ★★ hotel offers snug accommodation in the high mountains at R8 per person room only and R12 on weekends. There is an à la carte restaurant. From the hotel the road starts to climb and after 1,5 km passes the Setibing trading station. A further 1,5 km of ascent takes it through the pass (2 318 m) known as Molimo Nthuse.

The road continues up the valley of a stream abounding with crystal pools and rushing cascades. At the top of the valley (64 km from Maseru) the road reaches the summit – 2 621 m above sea level – of the Blue Mountain Pass, named after the 2 902-m-high *Thaba Putsoa* (blue-grey mountain) which dominates the range 1,5 km to the north.

For 9 km the road curves along the contour slopes of the range. Descending steeply, it passes a road camp in the upper reaches of the valley of the Likalaneng, 80 km from Maseru. At 1,5 km beyond the camp there is a turnoff leading down the valley for 2 km to the Likalaneng trading station from where horses and guides may be hired for a visit to the beautiful Senqunyane Falls, about 6 km away at *Semonkong* (place of mist or smoke).

The main gravel road passes the turnoff to Likalaneng store and starts to climb and twist up the slopes from where sweeping views and spectacular patches of red-hot pokers flowering around March may be seen.

At 90 km from Maseru, the road reaches the top of this pass, 2 621 m above sea level. The view is superb and the panorama is forever changing as the road makes a long, curving descent into the fertile, well populated valley of the Senqunyane River where, at 99 km from Maseru, the road passes the trading station and police post of Marakabei, named after a former chief of the area. After a further 2 km the road bridges across the Senqunyane River, where the pleasant tourist lodge of Messrs Fraser shelters in a grove of trees on its banks. Accommodation at the Senqunyane Lodge (R2,75 daily) should be booked at Frasers Store in Maseru. Guests must take their own food, but a cook and also bedding is provided.

Fishing, riding and climbing are pleasant pursuits along this crystal clear river. Immediately across the bridge a turnoff leads down the riverbank for 1,5 km to a water gauge. Camping, swimming and fishing spots are numerous: many a fat trout has been grilled hereabouts, in happy camps beneath the stars.

The Senqunyane is also known as the Little Orange, for it is one of the principal upper tributaries of the great Orange, the draining river of Lesotho. Beyond the river, the road climbs steeply for 9 km until it reaches the summit of the Cheche Pass, nearly 762 m above the river. The road is now at the 2 560 m level. It immediately starts to descend through a narrow valley and then emerges into the cultivated valley of the *Mantsonyane* (small black) River where, 124 km from Maseru, the road ends at the store of Messrs Collier & Yeats, a short distance above the river. Beyond this point the road is still under construction.

Unless a four-wheel-drive vehicle is used the traveller has to turn back. A lasting vision remains of the wild jumble of dark, basalt mountains covered with snow in winter and laced with rivers and streams, cascades of ice, ski slopes and toboggan runs. Impressions of the scarlet red-hot pokers linger vividly as do those of deep valleys, stupendous views and lonely cattle posts; the herdboys and the shepherds on the mountain slopes, the gentle sound of their *lesibas* floating in the wind; flags waving at the village huts where beer is available; the isolated stores; the horsemen in their colourful blankets on shaggy little ponies; the sheer loveliness and airy spaciousness of the high hills.

## THE NORTH-SOUTH ROAD OF LESOTHO

The main road of Lesotho is the north-south highway stretching down the valley of the Caledon River. Branches lead from this road into the mountains and it is constantly being improved, with substantial lengths now under tarmac. The beginning of the road in the north is the border post of Caledon Poort Bridge, 9 km from the town of Fouriesburg in the Orange Free State. The border post is open from 08h00 to 16h00. A most majestic entrance to Lesotho is made as the road makes its way past towering, flat-topped sandstone hills, the romantic 'castles' of the Sotho, and then reaches the border post where the Caledon River flows through an impressive gorge beneath high sandstone cliffs. Through this gigantic natural gateway may be seen the beautiful Maluti range, very blue in the eastern distance.

After crossing the river and passing through the border post into Lesotho, the road leads along badly eroded hill slopes for 9 km, entering the township of . . .

## BUTHA-BUTHE

Named after Moshoeshoe's old mountain stronghold of *Botha-Bothe* (the lair) which dominates it from the north-east, *Butha-Buthe* consists of a rather untidy and straggling collection of administrative buildings and Indian-owned trading stores. There is a small market place where a government-run shop sells Sotho handicrafts and is built in the form of a characteristic Sotho straw hat. The situation of the place, as with all the early administrative posts, is picturesque, surrounded by sandstone 'castles'. The pioneer British administrative officials also had enough sense to plant trees. Consequently, the place is shady, pleasant, and a sharp contrast to the surroundings which are almost totally devoid of trees.

## Accommodation
★ Crocodile Inn, 10 rooms, all with baths. R6,50 D room only.

# THE BUTHA-BUTHE DISTRICT

From Butha-Buthe, a road stretches north-eastwards to the border post of Joel's Drift. From this road branches lead to several places of interest, one of which is the colossal series of rock shelters known as *Sekubu* (like the hippopotamus) on account of a curious similarity in the shape of the rocks to the teats of a hippo. These caves were first occupied by Bushmen and afterwards became the lair of cannibals during the *Lifaqane*. Moshoeshoe's followers subsequently built houses in them, and finally they became stables for livestock.

To reach these caves, take the turnoff 7 km from Butha-Buthe village on the road to Joel's Drift, just after it passes Botha-Bothe summit. The turnoff leads up the left bank of the Serutle River and takes the traveller to the Sekubu Mission (4,5 km) from where guides take visitors along a 3-km footpath to the caves.

The main road to Joel's Drift, from the turnoff to the Sekubu caves, continues north-eastwards across the Serutle River. After 5 km a turnoff west of 1 km reaches the border post at Joel's Drift.

From this turn to Joel's Drift, a gravel road continues up the valley of the Caledon. After 2 km (15 km from Butha-Buthe) there is a fork where one branch swings eastwards to Oxbow while the other continues northwards and, although rough in parts, rewards the traveller with some spectacular scenery. At 25 km from Butha-Buthe there is a turnoff to Hendrik's Drift, crossing the Caledon into South Africa.

The main road, deteriorating from this point, continues up the left bank of the Caledon, traversing some delightful scenery and serving a string of trading stations, missions and villages. At 34 km, the road passes Thakabana's store and then starts to climb, yielding fine views of mountains and across the plains to points such as Rheboks Kop (2 803 m high), the highest peak in the Orange Free State. At 50 km from Butha-Buthe the road descends to Libono store and police post where (at present) it terminates with a glimpse ahead of the great Drakensberg escarpment.

# OXBOW AND MOKHOTLONG

At 15 km from Butha-Buthe, on the road to Libono (just described), there is a junction: the road to Libono goes northwards; a branch leads south-eastwards for 12 km to Tsime; and the Oxbow branch stretches eastwards up the valley of the Hololo River. This is the beginning of one of the most spectacular road journeys in Africa. However, it is not a road to be taken by faint-hearted motorists; at 8 km from the turnoff on to the road, at Khukhune store (23 km from Butha-Buthe), a notice warns that the track ahead is used at the driver's own risk.

Dominated by the handsome Khatibe mountain (2 743 m high), the track bridges across the Khukhune River tributary of the Hololo. Continuing up the valley of the latter river, the road passes a number of spectacular sandstone overhangs and the countryside becomes increasingly rugged. At 34 km from Butha-Buthe there is an especially notable sandstone rock shelter known as Liphofung, with another overhang lying under the road. These shelters, watered by a fine cascade, were used by Bushmen whose gallery of polychrome paintings may be seen in the cave under the road.

780

The road rises steadily and approaches the main wall of the Maluti range of mountains. At 46 km from Butha-Buthe the foot of the spectacular Moteng Pass is reached. For the next 9 km the road, twisting and climbing, rises about 762 m, reaching at the summit (56 km from Butha-Buthe), the highest point attained by normal two-wheel-drive vehicles on a public road in Southern Africa (2 834,6 m above sea level).

This is the basalt roof of Southern Africa: a world of winter snows, frozen waterfalls and cascades of ice; lonely cattle posts; crisp, clear air, and crystal streams where fat trout dart like glints of light through deep and tranquil pools.

The road descends from the summit of the pass to the Tsehlanyane River (60 km from Butha-Buthe), climbs a ridge and from its summit looks down on the valley of the *Malibamatso* (river of dark pools) where, just below the confluence of that river and the Tsehlanyane, the construction of the great Oxbow Dam is planned. At the proposed site, the river meanders in the shape of an oxbow, hence the name. The stored water would be fed by tunnels through the mountains into the Hololo Valley to drive hydro-electric stations, irrigate the lowlands, and supply South Africa with about 1 000 million litres a day, possibly increasing to 3 600 million litres a day.

The road descends from the spur and at 65 km from Butha-Buthe reaches the Oxbow Camp, a great centre for trout fishermen, ski enthusiasts and pony treks through the mountains.

Just beyond the camp, the road crosses the Malibamatso River from where the road becomes a rugged track really only suitable for four-wheel-drive vehicles and horsemen. This track continues over the heights for a further 46 km to the diamond fields of Letseng la Terae, and for a further 72 km (184 km from Butha-Buthe) to the isolated administrative post of *Mokhotlong* (place of the bald-headed ibis). At Mokhotlong there are trading stations, a police post and a small government guest house which provides accommodation at 50c per person a night. A mountaineer's chalet with five rooms at R4,50 D, is also available.

The little settlement (or 'camp') of Mokhotlong has always enjoyed some renown as one of the loneliest villages in Southern Africa. For many years it could only be reached by horse and all goods were carried in by pack animals (including one 317,5-kg flywheel for a mill at Tlokoeng). The 56-km-long track from *Sani* (Bushman) Pass down to Natal, has since October 1948, when the first vehicle did the journey, been improved into a route for four-wheel-drive vehicles and is a great tourist attraction. A mountaineer's chalet (the highest licensed hotel in Southern Africa) is situated at the head of the Sani Pass, from where there are fine rides, climbs and ski-runs in winter, and bridle paths which lead to places such as the summit of the 3 482-m-high *Thabana Ntlenyana*. Notwithstanding its incongruous name (meaning 'the nice little mountain'), it is the highest point in Southern Africa. The mountaineer's chalet has six rooms accommodating 22 people at a charge of R3 per person a night.

## BUTHA-BUTHE TO MASERU

Beyond Butha-Buthe, the main trunk road of Lesotho runs south-westwards through rugged, sandstone country which is densely inhabited. Climbing up to Rampai's Nek (4,5 km), the road traverses a ridge and then descends through Levi's Nek into a valley dominated on the southern and eastern side by the sandstone heights of the extensive plateau hillock known as *Leribe* from a rock shaped like the forehead of a baboon. Strange, richly coloured rock shapes may be seen on all sides, creating the effect of a vast assembly of weird, petrified figures.

At 17 km, the road passes the Roman Catholic mission of Maryland with its handsome sandstone church built close to the village of the chief, Jonathan. Colourful towering sandstone cliffs look down from the Leribe heights around which the road swings southwards. At 23 km there is a turnoff to the Leribe Mission of the Lesotho Evangelical Church, nestling against the cliffs, where there is also a great rock overhang under which are the ruins of a village built by unknown people. Bushman paintings may be seen in several rock shelters.

A further 2 km (24 km from Butha-Buthe) sees a track turning off westwards just beyond the bridge over the Subeng stream, leading to the original causeway across the stream. Thirty metres downstream from this ruined causeway, may be clearly seen 24 five-toed footprints of dinosaurs, well preserved in the sandstone.

The main road, now running southwards, passes the Leribe Farmers' Training Centre run by the Oxford Committee for Famine Relief and, 1,5 km further on (32 km from Butha-Buthe), reaches the village of . . .

# HLOTSE

The administrative centre of the Leribe District, Hlotse had its start in 1876 when Canon J. Widdicombe established a mission there and built the little church which is still standing. A residency for a magistrate, Major Bell, was also built in 1877 and the following year, the small watch tower which protected the place during the Gun War of 1880. Several attacks were made on Hlotse during this disturbance: the residency was sacked and the church damaged, but the little fort held out. During these troubles, the renowned General 'Chinese' Gordon stayed in the place for three days trying to negotiate peace, but without any success.

*Hlotse* (dead meat) receives its name from the river which flows around the heights on which the mission and government camp were erected. It is said that the name refers to the practice of travellers who, before fording rivers, threw meat into the water in order to lure away crocodiles.

## Accommodation
* Mountain View Hotel, 23 rooms, R8 – R9 B/B.

# THE LERIBE DISTRICT

From Hlotse village a drive approaches the mountains, ending after 26 km at the trading centre of Pitseng. On the way (16 km from Hlotse) there is a turnoff to the store at Seetsa, and from there a track leads to the mine at Kao, where the prospector Ken Carlstein found diamonds at a point 41 km from the turnoff on the Pitseng Road. Fine views of the mountain country may be had from Pitseng.

Another interesting drive stretching towards the mountains in the Leribe District, begins with a turnoff eastwards 15 km from Hlotse on the main road to Teyateyaneng. After 4,5 km there is a turnoff southwards to the mission station of the Immaculate Conception and to trading stations such as Mapoteng. Just before the road reaches the mission (25 km from Hlotse), an extraordinary mushroom-shaped balancing rock may be seen on the slope of an overlooking height on the eastern side of the road.

The main road, from the turnoff to this rock and the mission, meanwhile continues south-eastwards, passing the Corn Exchange (38 km from Hlotse) and branching to serve various trading stations close to the mountains, as well as the mission station of Santa Thérèse (48 km from Hlotse), near which may be seen some superb Bushman paintings. Guides for the short walk may be found at the mission.

This mission was the scene of one of the most extraordinary poltergeist manifestations ever to occur in Southern Africa. It all started on 11 October 1947 after the priest then in charge of the station, Father Hamel, had delivered a stiff sermon on the evils of black magic. During the course of this sermon he made some pointed comments about an individual who happened to be a member of his church. The person concerned immediately walked out of the church exclaiming loudly that she would send her *tokoloshe* (poltergeist) to break the Father's neck.

And so the game commenced: a shower of stones and other missiles regularly disrupted the work of the mission. Each sunset saw a start to proceedings with the principal target being the private quarters of Father Hamel. Items were removed from the priest's study, letters were mixed up in locked postbags, and everybody was hit by stones. As with similar manifestations, these stones, although fist-sized, did not travel through the air with speed; there was a curious deliberation about their movement as though they were being carried by an invisible hand, and not being thrown. When they reached the ground they neither bounced nor rolled.

The school was greatly disturbed by stones falling on the roof all night and the clothes of the boarders being spirited away in the dark hours, only to be found at dawn, festooned so high in the branches of trees that sticks and ladders had to be used to recover them.

Several investigators and senior members of the Catholic Church went to the mission to examine this strange occurrence. The conclusion was reached that the centre of the disturbance was a hut occupied by three young Sotho, one of whom, Johannes, aged 12, was suspected of being host to the poltergeist. He stated that a curious-tasting sweet had been given to him by the person accused of raising the poltergeist; this magic mixture was therefore suspected of having attached the playful spirit to his person.

As an experiment, Johannes was sent away from the mission with two adult Sotho being detailed to escort the boy home. Being prudent souls, the escorts presented themselves for duty wearing miners' steel helmets, souvenirs of work on the goldfields! This was apparently too much for the poltergeist's sense of humour: the two steel helmets became targets for an accurate attack of stone-throwing. The escorts ended their duties by galloping over the hills amid stones plonking down unerringly on their helmets.

Among the investigators of the manifestation were Father Pageau (the Provincial for Lesotho), Father Hebert (the Administrator), and Father Laydevant, from Saint Rose Mission, who specialised in such disturbances. He was not a man to exaggerate and his description of events, as given to the author, is fascinating.

'The stones usually fell in the open bare places where it would have been easy to notice if they had been thrown by some human being. One of them, while we were in Father Hamel's office, left his sleeping room, passed quickly through the office in a horizontal line about three feet from the ground, and dropped softly in front of the door.

'Near the mission dispensary one evening after sunset, seven or eight of us were standing talking. We heard a heavy thud, as though of somebody falling to the ground. We looked towards the dispensary and all the witnesses, except myself, saw a man in a kind of kaross, walking slowly and disappearing in the Sisters' garden. We rushed at once to the spot where the man had disappeared, but there was no trace of anybody and the gate was locked.'

On 3 November at 15h00, a rock weighing about 7 kg fell with a colossal crash on to the iron roof of a shed where about ten girls were washing clothes. After the squeals of terror had subsided, Father Laydevant examined the heavy stone and the roof, but there was no sign of the damage one might have expected from such a missile.

Similar manifestations continued for some time. Fathers Laydevant and Hamel read exorcism prayers, sprinkled holy water and resorted to everything they knew. The manifestations gradually diminished and finally, after a special service of exorcism, they vanished altogether. But there was a strange sequel . . .

In December 1947 Maria Makhetha lodged a complaint with the District Commissioner of Teyateyaneng. She stated that Father Hamel had in public accused her of being the witch responsible for the hauntings, a claim to which she objected. She sued Father Hamel for damages and although summoned, he refused to appear in court.

The complainant arrived but without her witnesses. She complained that Father Hamel had openly stated that any individual helping her with evidence or money, would be expelled from church. Father Hamel was charged with conspiring to defeat the ends of justice and, forced to appear in court, he was fined £20, while Maria Makhetha was awarded £20 damages with costs for defamation. This ended a very curious matter!

## HLOTSE TO TEYATEYANENG

From Hlotse, the main trunk road of Lesotho descends the ridge on which the village stands, crosses the Hlotse River, and continues westwards. After 10 km there is a turnoff leading westwards across the Caledon to Ficksburg (8 km away). The border post is open from 07h00 to 20h00. The main road continues south-westwards down the Caledon Valley and after 3 km reaches the turnoff east to the Corn Exchange and Santa Thérèse Mission.

The road proceeds over the widest portion of the Lesotho plains lying between the Caledon and the Maluti range where there are a few isolated hills; otherwise, the landscape comprises open, undulating fields of maize. At 32 km from Hlotse, the road passes through the village of Peka and then swings southwards, continuing across the open plains. After a further 23 km a turnoff east leads for 32 km to Mamathes and Mapoteng. Half a kilometre beyond this turnoff (56 km from Hlotse), the road reaches the village of . . .

## TEYATEYANENG

The odd-sounding name of *Teyateyaneng* is taken from the river, so called on account of the 'shifting or quick sands' in its bed. The village was founded in 1886 as the seat of the magistrate, Lagden. An Anglican mission station was also founded there and for nearly 50 years the well-known Father William Wrenford was in charge of the place. The thatched building in which he lived and worked remains a picturesque feature in the modern village.

Teyateyaneng is nowadays a busy trading and administrative centre for the Berea District. There is considerable local industry in weaving, while tourists find several fine galleries of Bushman paintings in the numerous caves and rock shelters of the area.

### Accommodation
★ Blue Mountain Inn, 15 rooms, 10 with baths. R10 B/B.

### Caravans and camping
★ Blue Mountain Inn Caravan Park, 25 sites. R1 D.

From Teyateyaneng, the main trunk road of Lesotho descends the ridge on which the village stands, and after 1 km crosses the river which gives the village its name. High sandstone cliffs, containing many interesting caves, overlook the river.

The tarmac road climbs a ridge, passes beneath sandstone cliffs and descends again to continue south-westwards. At 35 km there is a turnoff east to Lancers Gap, and, 4,5 km further on (40 km from Teyateyaneng), the road reaches Maseru, the capital of Lesotho, already described (pages 772 to 773).

## MAFETENG, MOHALE'S HOEK AND QUTHING

The tarmac main highway of Lesotho leads southwards from Maseru across a classic landscape of gigantic natural and unnatural erosion. The central mountain mass (the *Luting* or place of mountains) recedes eastwards and the road traverses a sunny plain of maizelands, cattle herds, villages, watercourses, and 'Sotho castles', the sandstone jigsaw-puzzle remnants of a once higher plateau now eroded into fragments.

At 5 km from Maseru there is a turnoff east to Thaba Bosiho and at 15 km a turnoff east to Roma and the famous mountain road. The Roman Catholic mission named after Bishop Eugene de Mazenod stands just beyond the turnoff. One kilometre south of this mission lies another turnoff to the east leading to Ramabanta and one of the finest scenic drives in Lesotho (already described).

Yet another turnoff, 24 km further on (40 km from Maseru) stretches east to *Morija* (named after the Mount Morija of the Bible), the chief station of the pioneer French Protestant missions, and also to *Matsieng* (place of Letsie), the heir of Moshoeshoe, who was established there in order to be near the missionaries. Since then, this area has been the seat of the Paramount Chiefs of Lesotho.

A further 9 km sees a turnoff east to Makhakes, and 30 km further south (75 km from Maseru), the road passes through . . .

## MAFETENG

A straggling little trading and administrative centre built on a high, open plateau, *Mafeteng* (place of the fat, unmarried women) has the appearance of an American cow town, with its horsemen, trading stations, dusty streets and unmade pavements. A market place offers oddments for sale, but there is nothing else of note.

During the Gun War of 1880, Mafeteng was attacked on several occasions but the small government force held its own in the 'camp'.

Notwithstanding its nondescript appearance (and derogatory name), Mafeteng has always been one of the principal trading centres of Lesotho. Traders such as William Scott, W. Wilkinson, Fred and Sydney Collier, and Donald and Douglas Fraser (whose first store was close to Mafeteng, at *Liphiring* – the place of horses) all started business in this district.

From Mafeteng, the main road continues south-eastwards across the open, rocky plains. After 11 km there is a turnoff westwards to Sephapo's Gate (8 km) on the border of South Africa, while a further 10 km sees a turnoff eastwards to Lifateng. After 11 km (40 km from Mafeteng) the road crosses the Makhaleng River (known to Europeans as the Cornet Spruit), flowing from the mountains down a handsome valley. Overlooking the bridge across the Makhaleng River from the east is *Thaba Tsoeu* (white mountain) notable for the petrified wood near its upper layer of white sandstone.

Five kilometres beyond this river, there is a turnoff leading eastwards for 32 km into the foothills of the Maluti range, to a trading station with the odd name of *Masemouse*, derived, it is said, from a Bushman known as Masmous. This road allows access to some fine mountain scenery, with panoramic views of the Makhaleng Valley. Dominating the mountains here is the impressive *Pedlar's Peak* (2 908 m), the highest point of this part of the range. To the Sotho it is known by the common name of *Thaba Putsoa* (blue-grey mountain), but Europeans have named it *Pedlar* in the mistaken conclusion that Masemouse (which lies at its foot) is itself derived from the Afrikaans *smous* (pedlar). The mountain is climbed from Khaphe's village near the end of the road. It is a day-long scramble, with a stunning view the ultimate reward.

From the turnoff to Masemouse, the main road continues southwards for 5 km and then (49 km from Mafeteng) reaches the pleasantly situated administrative centre of . . .

## MOHALE'S HOEK

This little place had its start in 1884 when the chief Mohale, brother of Moshoeshoe, presented to the government the beautifully situated and well-watered site, for the establishment of an administrative post. The original government 'camp' grew into a busy trading centre. With ample trees planted by thoughtful people in the past, it is today one of the most pleasant of all the Lesotho villages.

Overlooking Mohale's Hoek is a fine example of a 'Sotho castle' with crumbling buttresses, known as Castle Rock, which looms over the golf course. About 2 km south of Mohale's Hoek is the cave stronghold used by the notorious cannibal band led by Motlejoa during the bad years of the 1820s. The cave, the atmosphere of which is sinister, is worth visiting.

### Accommodation
★ Mount Maluti, 14 rooms, 6 with baths. R7 room only. Phone 224.

The main road leaves Mohale's Hoek, travelling first westwards and then swinging to the south from the point 5 km away where a road leads for 4 km to the border post at Makhaleng Gate, and from there to Zastron, 47 km away.

The main Lesotho highway continues southwards through increasingly rugged scenery, and climbs steadily up a ridge to the top of the pass known as *Mesitsaneng* (place of wild beans), from where may be seen handsome views of a rugged, sundrenched landscape. At 9 km from Mohale's Hoek, the road reaches the summit with a branch stretching eastwards to Maphutseng (10 km) and the Bethesda Mission founded by the French Protestants in 1843, close to the then residence of the renowned chief Moorosi. Near the Bethesda Mission are many tracks and relics of dinosaurs. Guides are obtainable at the mission or store.

From the summit of the Mesitsaneng Pass the main road descends into the great valley of the Maphutseng River, revealing fine views of the central mountain massif.

At 23 km from Mohale's Hoek the road crosses the Maphutseng River where it flows through a deep gorge. A further 6 km takes the road across the Mekaling River while 16 km further on (42 km from Mohale's Hoek) the road reaches the Seako Bridge across the Orange River.

The Seako Bridge is the longest in Lesotho, extending for 191 m. Made in England in the 1880s, it was carried by wagon to Commissiedrif in the Orange Free State on the road from Smithfield to Rouxville. Retired from this position, it was sent piecemeal to Lesotho and erected across the Orange River in 1959 to replace a pontoon that had been washed away ten years earlier.

Across the Orange (known to the Sotho by the Bushman name of *Senqu*) the road continues for 6 km reaching a turnoff leading westwards for 10 km to the border post of Telle Bridge which is open from 08h00 to 16h00. A further 3 km sees a turnoff south to the Masitise Mission of the French Protestants, with its cave house and Bushman paintings. The cave was first used by Bushmen, followed by the Phuthi headman Mazitizi (after whom the mission is named), and in 1867, converted into a home by the Reverend D. F. Ellenberger, who raised a family there.

Passing the Villa Maria Roman Catholic Mission, with its training school for young priests and, just beyond it, the industrial school of *Leloaleng* (place of the mill) run by the Paris Mission, the road twists into the ravine of the Qomoqomong River. At 56 km from Mohale's Hoek there is a turnoff north-eastwards leading to Moorosi's Mountain. The road climbs up to a shoulder of the overlooking heights and, after 3 km (58 km from Mohale's Hoek) leads into the administrative centre for the Quthing District, the 'camp' or village of . . .

# MOYENI (QUTHING)

This little village, whose name *Moyeni* means 'the windy place', was established in 1877 on the site of the present Leloaleng Industrial School. Abandoned during the Gun War of 1880, the camp was re-established in 1889 and built on the present site with its commanding views. The original buildings were then presented to the Paris Evangelical Mission for their industrial school, and a watermill was built there which gave the place its name.

Quthing is the name of the district, although the name is also often applied to Moyeni village. The Orange River in its upper reaches is known as the *Senqu* (literally, great river of the

Bushmen). The Quthing is one of its tributaries, reaching the great river under the northern slopes of Mount Moorosi, therefore the name seems to suggest a Sotho locative, meaning 'at the great river'.

Moyeni camp was pleasantly laid out and planted with many handsome trees whose healthy growth indicates the afforestation possiblities of the countryside.

The whole of the great valley of the upper Orange was a favourite resort for Bushmen and their paintings may be seen in many rock shelters in the Quthing District. Beneath Moyeni village there is one gallery situated in a snug little shelter in the cliffs. More paintings comprising several galleries, may conveniently be seen in the grounds of the Masitise Mission. Particularly magnificent rock art may be found 8 km from Moyeni on the road to the Qomoqomong store, where a small gorge of the Ratlali stream is situated 1 km before the store.

### Accommodation
* Orange River Hotel, 4 rooms, all with baths. R10 B/B. Phone 228.

## MOUNT MOOROSI AND QACHAS NEK

Three kilometres from the centre of Moyeni, on the road to Mohale's Hoek, a turnoff leads north-eastwards to the famous stronghold of Moorosi's Mountain and thence to Qachas Nek. The road is quite practical for normal vehicles, but requires careful driving.

The road crosses the Qomoqomong River immediately after the turnoff, and 250 m further on a fenced area protects some dinosaur tracks. The road descends in an easterly direction to the Orange River 5 km from the turnoff. The road now leads up the left bank of the Orange surrounded by many picturesque scenes of villages, ferry boats, and the high mountains overlooking the sinuous course of the great river.

At 12 km the road passes the store at *Fort Hartley,* the base camp of the Cape Mounted Rifles, named after Major Hartley, their medical officer during the assault on Moorosi's Mountain. The graves of five soldiers lie near by. Overlooking Fort Hartley is the village of Pokane from where it is possible to reach a magnificent gallery of rock art 1 km away in the valley of the Pokane River. This is one of the finest Bushman caves in Southern Africa.

In 1967, scientists of the British Museum found fragments of the most ancient mammal discovered so far, close to Fort Hartley. Lesotho seems to have been a favourite resort for these creatures of the past.

The road climbs further up the slopes of the deep valley of the Orange. At 24 km there is a turnoff south leading to St Gabriels Roman Catholic Mission. The main road continues along the valley slopes negotiating numerous climbs and curves. At 32 km it crosses the important Sebapala tributary of the Orange and after a further 4 km of climbing, reaches a junction. The southern branch stretches for 12 km to Tosing store, beyond which a bridle path leads to the southern border of Lesotho at Lehana's Pass.

The main road continues. At 40 km the Mount Moorosi store is reached and at 48 km the road reaches the village of Mogalo, dominated by Mokotjomelo mountain, a great landmark in this area. Immediately ahead looms the great height of Moorosi's Mountain, looking down on the Orange River like a tollkeeper waiting for travellers.

Moorosi was the chief of the Phuthi people (a section of the Zizi tribe) who settled along this stretch of the upper Orange after migrating from Natal. They were not Sotho, but allied themselves with Moshoeshoe's followers. Moorosi was a veritable prince of cattle thieves and horse rustlers; a resolute, truculent man, courageous and stubborn. Attached to Moorosi's people were many Bushmen and the result of the combined talents in rustling was formidable.

About the year 1850 Moorosi first discovered this grim, sullen-looking mountain and recognised it as a stronghold of superlative strength. He settled on the summit and over a period of ten years fortified the mountain with stone walls and protected vantage points. At the same time, his followers raided and plundered far and wide.

In 1877, the British established a government post at Moyeni and tried to impose law and to collect taxes in the area of the great river. Moorosi had a son named Dodo who was hardly as placid a bird as his name suggests. He was arrested by the British and incarcerated in the ramshackle gaol in Moyeni. During the night, Dodo's followers broke down the gaol and fled with him to the mountain stronghold.

The British authorities mustered what strength they could, marched to the mountain, and C. D. Griffiths, the local magistrate, sent up a demand for the surrender of Dodo. The reply was insulting. Accordingly, on the night of 8 April 1879, 250 men of the tough, professional Cape Mounted Rifles, supported by volunteer yeomanry, assembled silently in a rock shelter known as the Commandant's Cave at the foot of the southern side of the mountain, and from there launched a resolute assault on Moorosi's stronghold.

Precipitous rock faces, showers of missiles, and gallingly accurate rifle fire, kept the attackers at bay. Dodging from rock to rock, the troopers attempted to escalade, but they had no proper ladders and Moorosi's men were entrenched behind a series of parallel, fortified stone walls known as shanzen. Thirty-four of the troopers died before the attack petered out.

Dawn came wretchedly for the troopers. There was disappointment, chagrin and angry recrimination over the parts played by the regulars and volunteers. Comrades were missing. The wounded, cruelly injured by the homemade soft lead bullets of Moorosi's men, were screaming with pain under primitive surgical treatment. Up on the mountain top could be heard the hilarity of the rustlers as they celebrated victory with a colossal beer-drink. Two Victoria Crosses were awarded to men for valour in this attack.

For two months there was a stalemate situation, with raids, sniping, counter-raids and innumerable fights as the rustlers continued their activities. On the night of 29 May, the rustlers surprised a piquet post overlooking the Quthing River. They poured over the protective stone wall and shot 21 of the sleeping soldiers. On another night, a patrol of yeomanry was ambushed and one prisoner captured. The next morning the rustlers decapitated him in full view on the mountain top, threw his body over the cliffs, and mounted his head on a pole.

Tempers reached boiling point. The British gathered reinforcements and on the night of 5 June they launched a long-planned second attack. It failed totally, with 14 more casualties littering the mountain slopes. The surgeon, Major Hartley, had to crawl from one man to the other at such risk to his life that he received the Victoria Cross.

Winter came. The mountains slept beneath their blanket of snow, and the Orange dwindled into a sluggish, shallow flow. The opposing sides warmed themselves as best they could, and waited. Sir Gordon Sprigg, Prime Minister of the Cape, came to the mountain and parleyed with Moorosi, half way up the slopes, but the fight continued throughout an icy winter.

In October the weather warmed up. Colonel Bayly arrived as a new commander. He reconnoitred the mountain in great detail, and commenced a persistent bombardment of its rock defences, using round 7-kg shells with delayed fuses to allow them to roll behind defence works before they exploded. In reply, Moorosi's men, and in particular an individual nicknamed Captain Jonas by the troopers, sniped with deadly accuracy.

Bayly mustered 400 regulars of the Cape Mounted Rifles for his planned attack. They were as mixed a crowd as the French Foreign Legion: remittance men, adventurers, mercenaries; all bound together in a military unit renowned for its rugged courage and comradeship. To spur the men on, rewards of £200 were offered for Moorosi or Dodo, dead or alive, and £25 for the first man to reach the mountain top.

For four days prior to the grand attack, the artillery lobbed one shell every ten minutes at the mountain. Then, at 22h00 on 19 November 1879, the troopers paraded in dark clothes, with their guns and bayonets blackened. At midnight the bombardment suddenly ended and three gaudy skyrockets rent the air above the mountain and died amid a shower of hissing stars in the water of the Orange. The big show was on.

All through the dark hours the men fought their way upwards. The false dawn was already lightening the sky when the scaling ladders were placed against the final cliff at a place on the eastern slopes known as Bourne's Crack.

Lieutenant Springer climbed up the first ladder. He was near the top when one of Moorosi's men looked over the edge into his face. 'Don't come up here, boss,' said the man considerately in English. 'I'll shoot you.'

'Go to hell!' replied Springer, and raising his revolver, he shot the man dead, sending the body hurtling down into the darkness past the ladder. On all sides of the mountain arose a great clamour of combat as different approaches were tried, some determinedly, others as a diversion.

Springer clambered to the top, followed by his men. Forming into a line, they swept the summit. For a few minutes it was hand to hand, but the defenders were cut down or shot where they stood. Some dived directly over the precipices. The few that escaped did so by a miracle of rolling down the slopes, and diving into the water of the Orange.

The mountain summit was a shambles, littered with the bodies of 200 of Moorosi's men and most of their women. Moorosi's body was also found among the dead. Captain Jonas was discovered with 14 bullets in his body but with his rifle still gripped in his hands. At 05h30, Moorosi's head was mounted on the selfsame pole which had carried the remains of the unfortunate patrolman. Dodo had vanished but was later found in a cave beyond the Orange, dying of wounds and a thigh broken during his wild escape down the mountain.

Moorosi's gunpowder storehouse on the summit, containing 6 247 kg of ammunition, was exploded and the fortifications partly destroyed. The troopers went away. Forty-three Europeans had been killed and 84 wounded in that battle. Five hundred of Moorosi's men, the cream of his rustlers and all his sons, had died. The rest scattered into the innermost ranges of Lesotho and there the matter ended.

Only the brooding old mountain is left, with its slopes still littered with cartridge cases and the bric-à-brac of battle. Beneath it, the great river sweeps silently past on its way to the sea. In a way, this river and the rugged mountain, are characteristic of Southern Africa itself: every inch richly storied with legends and tradition, shrouded by an atmosphere of incredible romance.

It is fairly easy to scramble to the summit of Moorosi's Mountain. On the way is passed a small rock shelter, the walls of which are engraved with initials and other graffiti dating from the attack. On the summit may be seen the ruins of stone buildings, a natural reservoir in the rock which stored drinking water, and the remains of defensive walls. A panoramic view reveals sheer cliffs falling away abruptly to the Orange and the confluence where the Quthing River joins it as a tributary. Guides are always obtainable from the village where the road passes over the saddle of land connecting Moorosi's Mountain to the high ground south of the Orange. At this point the road is 4 km from the village of Mogale and 44 km from the turnoff on the main tarmac road from Maseru to Moyeni.

From this saddle, the road descends into the valley of the Quthing River. On the right-hand side of the road, 2 km below the summit of the saddle, a cluster of three cyprus trees shades the common grave of soldiers killed in the attack on Mount Moorosi.

The road finds a complex way up the gorge containing the Quthing River. The area is wild, rocky and famous for its aloes. There are many delightful places in which to camp. At 18 km from Mogale village there is a particularly beautiful site in a deep sandstone gorge with a level, grassy floor overlooked by cliffs covered in aloes which flower in October and November and also in winter.

The road continues up a valley of great scenic variety, opening up into fertile, alluvial stretches, closing again between narrow sandstone cliffs. Another fine camping site 21 km further along the road is situated next to a concrete causeway which carries the road across the strongly flowing river.

Beyond the causeway, the road commences a zigzag climb to the top of a mountain ridge. For 20 km the road makes an involved ascent, descends again, and immediately starts to climb a second pass. At 86 km from Mogale (at Moorosi's Mountain) the road passes the Mopeli trading station with the mission of Christ the King 19 km further along the road. A further 8 km takes the road past the Sekake trading store and after 21 km the White Hill trading station is reached (134 km from Moorosi's Mountain).

Nineteen kilometres beyond White Hill is situated a turnoff to Tsoelike and Ramatseliso Gate, and a further 10 km sees the road enter the small centre of Qachas Nek. The entire journey of 203 km from Qachas Nek to the junction with the tarmac Maseru road 3 km north of Moyeni village is dramatised by magnificent mountain scenery. The road demands a full day's travelling and should not be attempted in rainy weather. Winter snows transform the landscape while the flowers of spring are unforgettable.

# QACHAS NEK

The village of Qachas Nek lies 2,5 km from the border post with Transkei. The border is open daily from 06h45 to 16h00. From this post the road descends the Drakensberg escarpment to Matatiele 32 km away. The name *Qacha* is a hopelessly misspelt version of the name of Ncatya, a son of the famed Moorosi, who established himself there as chief of a group of rather mixed people, engaged mainly in cattle rustling into the low country below the Drakensberg. The Orange River (the *Senqu*) twists into a great bend at this point. Flowing southwards from its source north of Mokhotlong, it swings westwards and sets out on its long journey to the Atlantic Ocean.

From Qachas Nek, bridle paths follow the valley of the great river and lead to places such as the Sehlabathebe National Park with its strange rock formations and 65 square kilometres of mountain scenery. Wheat and corn are grown in the valley of the Orange while goats and sheep live on the rocky slopes. The village consists of a cluster of stores, administrative and police buildings, one hotel and a couple of churches, notably the Roman Catholic Church of the Most Holy Redeemer.

### Accommodation
★Qachas Nek Hotel, 6 rooms, 4 with baths. R8 – R11 room only. Phone 24.

# Chapter Forty

# SWAZILAND

A mere 17 000 square kilometres in extent; Swaziland is one of the smallest self-contained sovereign states in the world. Despite its diminutive size, however, the country possesses a remarkable variety of scenery, climate and atmosphere. Its inhabitants, the Swazi, are colourful and amiable and amongst a substantial population of Europeans (known as Swazilanders), there are also a number of very picturesque characters.

The best way to gain an overall impression of Swaziland (for those who are energetic enough) is to climb to the rounded summit of the highest mountain, *mLembe* (place of the spider), which rises 1 862 m above sea level. From this vantage point, by no means difficult to reach, may be seen practically the entire country.

The mLembe mountain forms part of the range known as *Khahlamba* (the barrier) which lies along the western border of Swaziland, separating it from the Transvaal. The range consists of a jumble of mountains marking the end of the South African highveld. The scenery here is romantically beautiful and the road from Barberton to Piggs Peak, climbing and twisting high around the slopes of mLembe, provides the most spectacular entrance to Swaziland.

Several rivers of considerable size make their way through these mountains from sources on the South African highveld. In addition, their flow is increased by over 1 000 mm of rain a year, falling on the Swaziland peaks. The combination of rivers and rainfall make Swaziland one of the best watered parts of Africa. The mountain slopes are beautifully green and crisply cool. This mountain area is known as the *Nkhangala* (treeless country) although modern afforestation has blanketed it with trees.

East of the mountains the territory falls away into a hilly belt of middleveld – foothill country with rich alluvial soil in the valleys such as that of the principal river, the uSuthu. This river, always regarded as the heart of Swaziland, is the site of most of the principal settlements of the Swazi people.

Beyond the middleveld, the country subsides still further into what is known as the *Hlanzeni* (place of trees), a stretch of typical savanna bushveld linking the warm Eastern Transvaal lowveld to the bush country of northern Zululand. Considerable numbers of game animals once roamed this area. Only a few remain today, but they may still be seen and are protected in certain parts.

On the eastern side of Swaziland, 145 km from the western boundary on the top of mLembe, lies another mountain range, running north to south and rising as sharply as a garden wall out of the tangled greenery of the bushveld. This range, the *Lubombo* (ridge), provides a natural boundary with Moçambique on the east, and the wide plateau which forms its level summit is a cool and pleasant home for considerable numbers of people.

The people known as the Swazi first arrived in what is now called Swaziland in about the year 1750. According to tradition these people were part of a migratory mass known as the Nguni who moved down the coastal belt of Moçambique from an original home far in the north. Some disturbance caused this mass to disintegrate and a small section, led by a chief named Ngwane, wandered into modern Swaziland, settling there while the rest of their fellows moved further south into Zululand.

Ngwane's followers gave themselves the same name as their chief and the country in which they had settled became known as *kuNgwane*.

These early settlers made their homes in the southern portion of the country. Ngwane died there and was buried in a taboo forest known as *emBilaneni* (the hallowed place). Under the rule of his descendants, his people steadily increased in number and spread northwards. In this way they eventually penetrated the fertile valley of the great river which they named *uSuthu* (dark brown), on account of its muddy appearance. Living on the banks of this river were a number of fragments of the people the newcomers named *baSuthu* (people of the dark brown river). This name has become generally applied to all related tribal groups scattered over the South African interior (the Sotho).

The new settlers (led by a grandson of Ngwane named Sobhuza) ejected the early inhabitants and made their homes in the valley of the uSuthu River. Sobhuza's heir was Mswazi, who succeeded to power in 1836. It was during his rule that Europeans first entered the country as traders and hunters. They were the first to call the people the Swazi, after their chief, a name which soon became generally accepted.

The Swazi flourished in their new home. They were raided by the Zulu people but the mountains yielded many hiding places – caves and secret valleys – and they survived with few losses. However, during the reign of Mswazi's son Mbhandeni, the Swazi experienced their most trying times. Gold was discovered at Piggs Peak and Forbes Reef, resulting in a flood of Europeans in search of fortune. Thus began the famous 'concession rush' in Swaziland. It seemed certain that the country was destined for a great boom and a regular mania developed in the negotiation of concessions from Mbhandeni which granted exclusive rights for the establishment of all manner of enterprises. Mbhandeni secured considerable amounts of money from the annual fees paid to him by these concessionaires. Practically every known form of human industry was covered by these concessions, many of them idiotic enough to provide the ingredients for a grotesque comic opera.

Among the concessionaires and the gold diggers was a picturesque crowd of bandits, renegades, highwaymen and runaways from justice, who had also found sanctuary in Swaziland. There were individualists such as Bob MacNab and Charlie Dupont whose escapades provide Swaziland with some of its more lurid memories. The details are recorded in *Lost Trails of the Transvaal*.

The concession rush suddenly petered out as the concessionaires realised that they had made fools of themselves. The gold finds were limited and fortune-seekers moved out of Swaziland even more quickly than they had entered.

At the height of the chaos during the concession rush in 1895, the South African Republic (Transvaal), took over the administration of Swaziland. At the end of the Anglo-Boer War the British assumed control and were confronted by the absurd situation where practically the entire country was claimed by the absentee owners of various concessions. If the concessions were recognised as being at all valid, then as far as land was concerned the Swazi had been reduced to a nation of squatters living on other people's property. The Swazi claimed that the concessions were merely temporary leases, but a government commission, established to investigate the matter, found otherwise. The concessions were recognised as valid as long as their owners paid their dues. However, in 1907 a third of the area of each land concession was expropriated in order to provide a home for the Swazi. Title to the remaining two-thirds of Swaziland was granted to the holders of the various concessions or leases.

It was then the great desire of the Swazi to win back the rest of their country by purchase or peaceful negotiation. Sobhuza II, grandson of Mbhandeni, who was installed as Paramount Chief in 1921, dedicated himself to this great objective. As a result of persistant effort by the Swazi nation, land has been steadily bought back and today over 60 per cent of the country is in the possession of the Swazi.

Under the British, Swaziland was ruled by a Resident Commissioner, and informal discussion was held with the Paramount Chief (known as *iNgwenyama* or the lion), who wielded considerable power over his own people. In 1944 the Ngwenyama-in-Council was recognised as the native authority by means of the Native Administration Proclamation. In 1950 this proclamation was replaced by one recognising still wider powers.

In 1974 elections took place for the first Legislative Council, and in 1967, for the first House of Assembly. At midnight on 5 September 1968 Swaziland became fully sovereign, with Sobhuza II being acknowledged as King. A kindly, intelligent and likeable man, Sobhuza's popularity among his people was such that in the election for the first House of Assembly in 1967, the Mbokodvo Party (Royalists) won 79,4 per cent of the votes.

Swaziland has always basically been a prosperous little country, richly endowed with good soil, fine grazing, plenty of water, a healthy climate, a variety of minerals, and an agreeable, happy and law-abiding population. Sugar, citrus, cotton, rice, pineapples, tobacco, cattle and timber are produced. Iron, asbestos and coal are mined.

From a tourist point of view, the country has delightful scenery and atmosphere. The Swazi are tasteful woodcarvers and potters. Many of their curios are of superlative quality and they are developing an industry which will bring them considerable renown. They are also justly proud of their national dress and consequently are among the best looking people in Africa.

The architecture of their huts is interesting, and the big centres, such as Lobamba, the seat of the Queen Mother (known as *iNhlopukhati* or the she elephant), which is also the legislative capital of the country, is a fascinating place to visit.

Each year, two remarkable ceremonies take place in Lobamba in the great enclosure used as a cattle corral. In August-September *uMhlango* (the reed dance) is performed. A great gathering takes place of girls superbly dressed in tribal costume. Divided into age groups, they collect reeds with which to repair (as a sign of homage) the windbreaks around the residence of the Queen Mother.

For four days the girls gather these reeds. On the fifth day they prepare their costumes of bead skirts, anklets, bracelets and necklaces. On the morning of the sixth day, the girls bathe and dress. In the early afternoon they carry their bundles of reeds to the Queen Mother's residence and throwing the bundles into the air, they begin to dance in a gorgeous pattern of colour and energy. At night they stop, resuming the dance the following afternoon and completing the entertainment that night with singing and feasting.

A great spectacle occurs in Swaziland at the beginning of each year when the moon is new (end of December and into January). This is the magnificent sacred ceremony known as *iNcwala,* a complex ritual of kingship, a reinforcement for the coming year of the national spirit, and a celebration of the harvesting of the first fruits.

At the preceding new moon, officials known as *bemanti,* fetch samples of water from all the major rivers of Swaziland, as well as from the sea. When they return to Lobamba, what is known as the Little Incwala commences, where ceremonies and songs continue until the moon is full. At this time the next phase begins.

On the first day, youths and warriors from Lobamba march to join the men of the King's residence at Lositha. The combined force sings ritual songs and towards evening, the King sends the youths off to gather branches of the *lusekwane* trees growing at Gunundwini. In this test of endurance, the youths have to march 40 km before midnight. As the full moon appears over the horizon each boy cuts the largest branch he thinks he can carry. They then march all the way back to Lobamba singing through the night. In the morning, they deposit their branches in the cattle corral and only then do they really rest. This ends the second day.

At dawn on the third day the boys who were too young to do the 80-km walk to fetch the lusekwane boughs, set off to collect branches of the *mbondvo* shrub, which are also deposited in the cattle corral. Using the lusekwane and mbondvo branches, the elders build an *nhlambelo* (bower) for the King at the western end of this great enclosure.

At about 15h00 the bemanti and the various officials of the ceremony arrive and are joined by the King. The warriors muster, dressed in their special iNcwala costumes of skins. Ritual songs (taboo for the remainder of the year) are sung and a black ox is driven into the

793

*Overleaf: The patient skill of a Swazi woodcarver in the creation of a bowl to grace some table in a far off land.*

nhlambelo and doctored. The youths have meanwhile gathered outside and excitement mounts. The black ox is suddenly driven out and is overpowered by the surging crowd who carry the dying animal back into the bower where parts of it are used in the ritual. Outside, the warriors, drawn up into a great crescent, dance backwards and forwards like the surging sea, singing the strange-sounding ritual songs. Another black ox is caught by the youths and taken into the bower, for use in certain ceremonies. It is later released.

The fourth day sees iNcwala reach its climax in the afternoon ceremony. The Swazi army, in full costume, is mustered in the enclosure. Official guests arrive and take their seats in a special grandstand. If a guest of honour is present, he is escorted by the King to inspect the warriors. The King then joins his warriors and a great dance begins, in which the Queen Mother, her ladies, and many citizens participate. Guests drink traditional beer and then depart, saying farewell to the King who, escorted by members of his royal clan, enters his bower.

The warriors dance to and fro, singing their ritual songs and pleading with the King to return to them for a further year of rule. The King, with some show of reluctance, leaves his bower, symbolically tasting the first fruits of the harvests from which time the crops may be reaped and eaten.

The fifth day is a sacred day of seclusion and is taboo. No work is done.

On the sixth and last day the warriors march into the hills behind Lobamba to collect firewood for a huge bonfire in the centre of the cattle corral. In the afternoon this pyre is set alight and on to it the warriors place items of their old costume. Dancing and singing around the fire, they beg the ancestral spirits to send rain to douse the fire as a sign of favour for the coming year. Rain actually falls on most occasions and the ceremony ends with a general celebration of feasting, dancing and singing. If no rain falls, certain ceremonies must be repeated until ancestral approval is revealed by means of rain.

Incwala is one of the most impressive traditional ceremonies practised in the world today. Visitors are welcome for most of the ceremony, but must comply when asked to leave during taboo sections. No attempt should be made to photograph or sound record such parts of the ritual, the penalty of which is to have equipment broken.

## TRANSVAAL TO THE MOÇAMBIQUE BORDER

The principal entrance to Swaziland from the west is through the South African border post of *Oshoek* (ox glen), with the Swazi border post of Ngwenya facing it. The posts are handsomely situated at the edge of the Transvaal highveld, with deep valleys and the grassy range of the *Ngwenya* (crocodile) mountains stretching northwards along the border. Both posts are open daily from 07h00 to 22h00.

The tarmac road leads eastwards and after 1,5 km passes a beautifully constructed cluster of Swazi huts containing an interesting stock of curios and expertly made local handicrafts.

Three kilometres beyond this handicrafts shop, the road passes the Ngwenya mine of the Swaziland Iron Ore Development Company. From the mine a railway was built in 1964 to transport iron ore for 219 km to the Moçambique border at Goba. The railhead is called *kaDake*, the Swazi name for Grosvenor Darke who once traded near there. From there the iron ore is taken on to Maputo and shipped mainly to Japan. Coal is also loaded for export by Swaziland Colliers, at Mpaka station further down the line.

The Ngwenya mountains were mined by prehistoric people at least as far back as 36 000 B.C. and several of these ancient mines may still be seen. The miners worked oxides and earth colouring such as red haematite, presumably with which to paint themselves. Lion Cavern, a 10-m excavation, is probably the oldest mine in the world and may be visited by permission of the Swaziland Iron Ore Development Company in Mbabane. Also in the area are ruins of ancient Sotho stone buildings.

Beyond the Ngwenya mine, the road (10 km from Oshoek) passes the trading centre of *Darketon,* named after Grosvenor Darke, one of the pioneer traders of Swaziland. The road traverses a fine, grassy bowl contained by the mountains, where several outcrops of granite loom up in the form of huge domes.

At Motsane, 12,5 km from Oshoek, there is a tarmac turnoff north to Piggs Peak (see page 800). The road starts to climb through ancient, weathered hills. After 3 km the summit is reached, where plantations of wattle trees flourish in the mist belt. The road soon begins to descend and 27 km from Oshoek, enters the pleasantly situated little town of . . .

# MBABANE

Originally the British administrative capital of Swaziland and still the principal seat of government, Mbabane had its start as a trading station established by a man known as Bombardier Wells. His establishment was built on the banks of a stream watering the grazing lands of the chief Mbabane Khunene. The site of the town is green, fertile, and surrounded by a jumble of high granite hills.

In 1902 the new British administration set up its headquarters on the site, and Mbabane soon developed into a village. Endowed with a pleasant climate and handsome scenery, the village grew without much attention being given to town planning. Today it is a straggling, easygoing little place with pretty gardens, shady trees, and a bustling market where all manner of attractive Swazi handicrafts may be obtained, as well as locally-grown fruit and other products. The long main street, Allister Miller Street, is lined with an assortment of shops. Contained in the modern shopping centre is a large supermarket and there is a government area of administrative buildings, a hospital and some transmitters of the radio and television service.

## Accommodation
⋆ Jabula Inn, 23 rooms, E8,50 – E10 room only. Phone 42406
⋆⋆ Tavern Hotel, 32 rooms, E13 – E16 B/B. Phone 4231.

From Mbabane, the main tarmac road climbs out of the valley of the Mbabane stream. Passing a turnoff to the Highlands View Hotel, the road, after 2 km, reaches the summit of the rise from where the traveller is presented with a magnificent view of what is known as *eZulwini* (the place of heaven) and the great valley of the uSuthu River. This is the heart of Swaziland – the site of the royal residences and Parliament, the Mlilwane Game Reserve, and a cluster of hotels, casino, caravan park, curio and craft shops, a hot spring and other places of entertainment. Dominating the valley is the well-known mountain landmark of *Lugogo* (skin of a cow), known to Europeans as Shebas Breasts, on account of their rather knobbly resemblance to those interesting features.

The road descends steeply into the valley and is flanked by signs warning travellers about the number of fatal accidents and the need for extreme caution, especially in misty, wet conditions.

At 3,5 km from Mbabane the road passes the Swazi Inn, attractive in its garden setting with a panoramic view. At the foot of the descent, 9 km from Mbabane, lies Diamonds Valley Motel and 1 km further on the *Timbali* (place of flowers) Caravan Park. Another 1 km takes the road past the hot magnesium spring known locally as the 'Cuddle Puddle', maintained by the Royal Swazi Spa where there are changing rooms, saunas, facilities for massage and beauty treatments and a pleasant warm water swimming pool. The springs are open daily from 09h00 to 20h00. In former years this was a favourite moonlight resort for Swazilanders, the name of the Cuddle Puddle dating from the halcyon days when the place was always open, without people being barred from entering at night and being charged to go in during the day.

The Cuddle Puddle now lies in the grounds of the Royal Swazi Spa Hotel, the entrance of which is 5 km further along the road. This hotel forms the centrepiece of the string of hotels built in the Ezulwini Valley and much frequented by South Africans in search of fun. The hotel has a fine 18-hole golf course and is situated in a beautiful garden. There is a theatre, used mostly for the screening of the usual pornographic movies, and where live shows are occasionally presented. The casino contains a bright assortment of one-armed bandits and a gambling room presided over by the sort of staff to be seen in similar establishments all over the world; rather thumb-marked-looking females and bored, pasty-faced male supervisors who sit around like zombies in evening suits.

Situated immediately down the road from the entrance to the Royal Swazi Spa are two Holiday Inns and after another kilometre, the Yen Saan Hotel with its Chinese architecture and cuisine.

Immediately beyond is a turnoff to the Mantenga Falls near which is a fine crafts shop, a hotel further along the turnoff, the Smokey Mountain Village, and a 3-km drive to a parking spot at the foot of the waterfall in the uSutshwana River. This beautiful waterfall is reputedly named after a man, Mantenga, about whom there is a legend that he used to lower himself down the face of the waterfall to retrieve some treasure from the pool. A jealous rival is said to have cut the rope, causing Mantenga to fall to his death. It is believed that his ghost haunts the waterfall.

At 10 km along the road from Mbabane a turnoff leads to the tea-growing area, revealing views of the Mdzimba mountain. The last hotel in the series lining the main road is the Happy Valley Motel, 15 km from Mbabane. From this point there is a turnoff to the Mlilwane Game Reserve and to Mantenga Crafts.

## Accommodation

★★ Diamonds Valley Motel, 50 rooms, all with baths. E10 – E15 room only. Phone Mbabane 61041

★★ Happy Valley Motel, 32 rooms, all with baths. E8,50 – E11 B/B. Phone Mbabane 61061

★ Highland View Hotel, 70 rooms, all with baths. E9 – E13 room only. Phone Mbabane 42461.

★★ Holiday Inn (Ezulwini), 120 rooms, all with baths. E17 – E24 room only. Phone Mbabane 61201.

★★ Holiday Inn (Lugogo), 204 rooms, all with baths. E17 – E24 room only. Phone Mbabane 61101.

★ Mantenga Falls Hotel, 9 rooms, all with baths. E10 B/B. Phone Mbabane 61049.

★★★★ Royal Swazi Spa Hotel, 158 rooms, all with baths. E22 – E38 room only. Phone Mbabane 61001.

★★ Smokey Mountain Village, 14 chalets (3-6 beds), E24,80 – E36,80. Phone Mbabane 61291.

★★★® Swazi Inn, 42 rooms, all with baths. E15 – E17 B/B. Phone Mbabane 42235.

★★★® Yen Saan Hotel, 32 rooms, all with baths. E12 – E18 room only. Phone Mbabane 61051.

## Caravans and camping

★★★® Timbali Caravan Park, 50 sites. E2 D plus E1 D per person. Rondawels (2 beds) E8,50. Rondawels (4 beds), E11. Caravans E8,50 – E11,50. All prices include an additional 20 per cent during school holidays.

## THE MLILWANE WILDLIFE SANCTUARY

Reached via a turnoff from the main Mbabane-Manzini road, 15 km from Mbabane, this sanctuary was the creation of Terence Reilly whose personal enthusiasm for conservation has been the means by which at least a few of Swaziland's original wild animal inhabitants have been preserved.

Mlilwane is 4 450 ha in extent, covering an expanse of varied country that is bushy, grassy and overlooked by the mountain known as *Nyonyane* (place of the small bird) on the summit of which stand the ruins of stone buildings erected by early Sotho people. The name *Mlilwane* (embers) refers to the glow of fires on the mountains.

The mountain slopes needed protection as much as the remaining wildlife after a tin mining company had secured a concession to mine the area using hydraulic sluicing. The damage done to the landscape was a fearsome example of totally uncontrolled parasitic operations – the mountain slopes were literally slashed into ghastly dongas and deep ruts. With the venality of a few individuals being the only motive, such an industry can be a curse to any country, since the miners eventually quit the scene leaving behind slag heaps, rusted machinery, corrugated iron and open excavations.

The present rejuvenation of an area once considered totally ruined is the reward of conservation. In his endeavours, Reilly secured the all-powerful support of His Majesty, Sobhuza II of Swaziland, and sponsors such as the Swaziland Iron Ore Development Co., the Usutu Pulp Co. and others.

On 12 July 1964 the Mlilwane Wildlife Sanctuary was opened by Mrs Hilda Stevenson-Hamilton, widow of the revered warden of the Kruger National Park. The sanctuary was then only 500 ha in extent but with the support of King Sobhuza, who became patron, it was extended to its present size and the King started a second reserve at Hlane in the lowveld. Over 20 000 wire snares have so far been removed from the two reserves. This is far more than the total number of surviving game animals in Swaziland. Man is therefore resolute in his destruction of wildlife and as a result, a conservationist has to be very determined in his intentions, otherwise he will simply be overwhelmed by the bloodlust. Terence Reilly and his royal patron persisted and the two sanctuaries are now well protected.

A delightful little rest camp was created and gravel roads made to allow visitors easy access to many interesting parts of the sanctuary where a good number of most of the birds and mammals indigenous to Swaziland may be seen. Maintained in the camp is the Gilbert Reynolds Memorial Garden containing a collection of aloes, originally the possession of the late Mr Reynolds, the great authority and standard author on aloes. The collection was presented to the sanctuary by Mr Reynolds's widow. July is the best time to see the aloes in flower.

A friendly crowd of tame birds and mammals wanders through the camp. Facilities include chalets, large huts and a caravan park for accommodation; a hall for lectures and film shows; and a shop. A campfire is lit at night and the atmosphere is informal and pleasant. Guided tours of the sanctuary are undertaken on horseback or in vehicles. Mlilwane is a fine asset to Swaziland and should not be missed by visitors.

### Caravans and camping

★® E1,50 per adult, 50c per child. 13 chalets and huts. E5 D per adult, E3 D for persons under 16. Phone Mbabane 61037.

From the turnoff to the Mlilwane Wild Life Sanctuary, the main tarmac road continues down the broad alluvial floor of the uSutshwana (little uSuthu) River. Crossing the river the road passes after 1 km the National Stadium and the buildings of the Houses of Parliament near which is a small museum. After another kilometre, there is a turnoff to the royal residential villages of Lositha and Lobamba. There is a second turnoff to Mlilwane after a further 1,5 km and 22 km from Mbabane, a tarmac turnoff to Malkerns, Bunya and Mankayane (page 803).

The main road continues south-eastwards down the valley. After 3 km there is another turnoff to Malkerns. The road then swings eastwards, crosses the railway and the uSutshwana River and, after a further 10 km (42 km from Mbabane), reaches the principal industrial centre of Swaziland . . . .

# MANZINI

Named after the chieftain Manzini Motha, who lived there, *Manzini* had its start in 1885 as a trading station housed in a tent and run by a trader named Bob Rogers. This flourishing enterprise was bought by Albert Bremer who erected on the site a permanent store and hotel which became a bustling centre during the concession rush for Mbhekelweni, the then royal kraal of the Swazi king, Mbhandeni, situated near by.

To Europeans the place became known as *Bremersdorp*. The Swazi, however, know the area as Manzini and since 1960 this has become the official name of the town.

Manzini and its industrial township of Matsapha is the scene of considerable commerce and trade. There is a cotton ginnery, meat processing works, brewery, an electronics industry and other factories. The principal airport of Swaziland is also situated at Matsapha. Curios and handicrafts may be bought at a market in town.

The streets of Manzini are shaded with jacaranda, poinciana and African flame trees which flower in spring and early summer. On the walls of the lounge in what is now the Uncle Charlie Hotel (once the Manzini Arms), there is a frieze with a central African theme painted by the wandering artist, Conrad Genal. The same artist painted on the wall of the bar an amusing monochrome frieze depicting a medieval scene, but this has unfortunately vanished. Such work belonged to the hotel during its more elegant days and served as a reminder of the coming and going of many colourful characters.

## Accommodation

★★ George Hotel, 52 rooms, all with baths. E9,50 room only. Phone 52061.
★★ Highway Motel, 10 rooms, all with baths. E9,50 room only. Phone 50-6113.
★ Uncle Charlie Hotel, 22 rooms, 8 with baths. E7,85 – E11,60. Phone 52297.

## Caravans and camping

★ Paradise Rest Camp, 50 sites. E10 plus E0,75D per person. 29 huts, E5 D.

From Manzini, the main road to the east climbs gently through a fine avenue of flowering trees. At the time of the concession rush, this was known as the 'Gin Road', a highway of adventurers, cattle rustlers, smugglers and renegades such as the famed Bob MacNab, one of the classic horse thieves of Southern Africa.

At 8 km from Manzini there is a tarmac turnoff south to Sipofaneni and Natal. A further 8 km sees a turnoff north to Bhalekane and Tshaneni. The main road continues eastwards, descending gently into the natural parkland of the bushveld, a plain covered in long grass and stunted acacia trees. The great ridge of the Lubombo lies to the east, the wall bordering on Moçambique. At 25 km from Manzini the road passes the store known as *Ngogolo* (the reedbuck ram), the name given by the Swazi to Bob MacNab who traded here for several years.

The bush thickens into great ranching country with rich grazing on sweet grass, acacia leaves and seed pods. Situated 38,5 km from Manzini is the Mpaka Mine of Swaziland Colliers and 13 km further on the road divides into two important branches. The main road swings northwards while a tarmac turnoff continues eastwards directly towards the mountain wall of the Lubombo. Just before the road begins the ascent, a turnoff stretches south to Big Bend. The road climbs steeply up the Lubombo, with views over the bushveld becoming increasingly spacious as the road gains altitude. At 63 km from Manzini the road reaches . . .

# SITEKI

Situated in a parkland of jacaranda and tulip trees and lined with fine avenues of tall eucalyptus, the village of Siteki is a straggling little trading and administrative centre for the pleasantly cool and fertile plateau summit of the Lubombo. Removed from the rest of the world, it experiences a very different climate from the hot bushveld in the west and the sandy lowlands of Moçambique in the east.

In former years, renegades used the area as a hideaway. Conveniently close to the border, it offered the facility whereby these adventurers could slip backwards and forwards if the police on either side made any attempt to apprehend them. The atmosphere of bygone days still lingers about the modern village. The name *Siteki* (the place of much marrying) conjures up some interesting possibilities as to its origin, which as yet, remains elusive.

The Mhlumeni border post between Moçambique and Swaziland is 30 km away. It is open from 07h00 to 08h00; from 08h30 to 12h00 and from 13h00 to 20h00. The Moçambique border post is Goba from where it is 115 km to Maputo. A rural road leads south along the top of the Lubombo for 30,5 km to Tikuba and then on to a dead end at Nkonjane. The views over the lowveld are tremendous. A track continues from Nkonjane to Abercorn on the uSuthu River.

### Accommodation
* Bamboo Inn, 31 rooms, 11 with showers. E12 B/B. Phone 18.
* Siteki Hotel, 10 rooms, 6 with baths. E11 B/B. Phone 26.

From the turnoff to Siteki and Big Bend, the main road from Manzini continues northwards through savanna country along the foot of the Lubombo range. After crossing the railway line the road passes the Hlane Game Sanctuary on the western side. At 15 km from the turn to Siteki, the road passes the entrance to the sanctuary. Camping facilities are simple and there is no other accommodation. The name *Hlane,* means uninhabited place or wilderness.

The road now approaches the valley of the *Mbuluzi* (iguana) River where sugar cane is under intense cultivation. The road crosses the river and reaches a division. Straight ahead the road continues for 19,5 km to the Swazi border post of Lomahasha, and the Moçambique post known as Namaacha, both variants of the name of a man who once lived there. The posts are open to travellers from 08h30 to 12h00 and from 13h00 to 20h00.

From the division at the Mbuluzi bridge, a tarmac road leads westwards through extensive sugar and citrus plantations. At 21,5 km from the bridge, the road reaches *Mhlume,* named after the *Adina galpini* trees which grow near by. This centre comprises a sugarmill and residences for employees on the extensive irrigation scheme of the Colonial Development Corporation.

After a further 7,5 km of travel across the cane fields, a crossroads is reached. To the north, 5 km away, is the Mananga border post and the South African post simply known as Border Gate. The posts are open to travellers from 08h00 to 18h00. Ahead stretch the Tunzini citrus orchards. Rice is also extensively cultivated in this area. A turnoff south from the crossroads leads through a 2-km-long avenue of poinciana trees to . . .

# TSHANENI

This little place, the name of which means 'at the small stone', is a centre for the extensive irrigation projects undertaken by the Colonial Development Corporation. The Sand River Dam near by and the Khomati and Mbuluzi rivers, provide water for this large-scale industry which produces sugar, rice and citrus. The Sand River Dam is the largest stretch of water in Swaziland and is used for boating. All water in Swaziland, however, is infected with bilharzia and direct contact – swimming or paddling – should be avoided.

### Accommodation
* Impala Arms Hotel, 18 rooms, E10,50 B/B. Phone 11.

From Tshaneni a gravel road leads south-westwards through the rural centre of *Bhalekane* named after the chief Bhalekane Vilakani, where there is a clinic and after 34 km, reaches a junction with the road descending the mountains from Piggs Peak. The road proceeds southwards for 32 km and then joins the main tarmac road from Manzini to Siteki. Turning up the road from Piggs Peak, the traveller is confronted with an involved but scenically exciting drive. This road crosses the Khomati River, passes through a superb grove of acacia trees and, after 7 km, reaches a turnoff connecting the Transvaal to Piggs Peak (page 801).

The road at present being followed climbs steadily up bush-covered hill slopes. After a further 16 km the road arrives at a magnificent viewsite overlooking the lowveld to the east. Six kilometres further on the Endingeni store and mission is passed. Dense plantations of saligna trees stretch on either side of the road. After 10 km the road passes a large sawmill and a further 7 km brings it into Piggs Peak, 76 km from Tshaneni. The drive is extremely pleasant but although the gravel surface is fair, it should not be attempted in wet weather.

## MBABANE TO PIGGS PEAK AND HAVELOCK

The all-tarmac road from Mbabane to Piggs Peak is a splendid scenic route, revealing some of the beautiful hill country of Africa. The road starts at the trading centre of Motjane, 14,5 km from Mbabane on the main tarmac road to the South African border at Ngwenya (Oshoek). The Piggs Peak road leads northwards over a rolling stretch of grass country with rocky hills and the ranges of the Ngwenya and Silotwane mountains visible to the west.

After 10 km the road reaches the site of the old Forbes Reef gold mine, a gold bearing reef discovered in November 1884 by Alex Forbes and C. I. Swears. It was worked until 1896 and yielded a rich output of gold. Ruins of the mining village, including the hotel, may still be seen. The area is now overgrown with wattle trees.

Beyond Forbes Reef, the tarmac road continues northwards across a well-watered and, in summer, intensely green landscape, with numerous streams, patches of wattle trees and lovely tree ferns. The road crosses the Mbuluzi River. At 5 km from Forbes Reef a track branches off westwards. After 2 km of driving and 4 km of walking along this track, the highest waterfall in Swaziland is reached, occurring in the Maloloja tributary of the Khomati River. The waterfall is well worth the effort of a walk which is in itself pleasant.

The tarmac road passes the small market place of Nkaba with its handicraft stall and at 12 km from Forbes Reef, reaches the edge of the valley of the Khomati River. The scenery is on a vast scale, superbly photogenic in form and colour.

The road finds a tortuous descent for 10 km to the floor of the valley. Swazi handicraftsmen offer their products for sale at the side of the road and the scenery is attractive. The Khomati River is said to take its name from the number of cows grazing along its banks. It is a strong, rushing flow of water, particularly impressive when viewed from the bridge.

The road climbs the northern side of the valley, passing through the plantations of Swazi-land Plantations Ltd with a timbermill 12 km from the river crossing. A further 5 km (49 km from the turnoff to the Mbabane-Oshoek road) brings the road into the village of . . .

## PIGGS PEAK

In 1884, a prospector, William Pigg, found the Devils Reef of payable gold near the site of the village named after him. The mine enjoyed a long life producing gold but has since been exhausted. Piggs Peak has become the centre for a great industry in timber production based on afforestation started in the late 1940s by Peak Timbers.

The village is beautifully situated, with a grand view. Its one long street is shaded by an avenue of tall eucalyptus trees and is lined with stores, administrative buildings and a handicraft market. In 1958 Mrs Coral Stephens started a school of weaving in Piggs Peak. As a result, the industrious students have become internationally acknowledged masters of their craft, producing curtains for use in theatres and public and private buildings in many parts of the world.

## Accommodation
★ Highlands Inn, 18 rooms, E10,50 B/B. Phone 12.

From Piggs Peak, a gravel road leads eastwards to join the Tshaneni-Manzini road in the lowveld (page 799). The main tarmac road continues north through plantations, past the forestry workers' residential township of Rocklands and down to the lowveld. At 13 km from Piggs Peak the road passes near the waterfall in the Phophonyane River. This lovely waterfall is often photographed and has been used as a location in the production of motion pictures such as *The Flame of Africa*.

The tarmac road continues northwards down the valley of the Lumati River and after 42 km reaches the customs post of Matsamo, with the South African post of Jeppes Reef just across the border. The posts are open daily from 08h00 to 16h00.

---

Beyond Piggs Peak a gravel road stretches westwards for 21 km through plantations, past the disused mine workings of the Devils Reef and, after considerable twisting, turning, rising and falling reaches Bulembu, the site of . . .

## THE HAVELOCK SWAZILAND ASBESTOS MINE

This is one of the five largest asbestos mines in the world. The mine had its start in about 1923, when Gowran Fitzpatrick, caretaker of the Piggs Peak mine, employed some Swazi prospectors to search the mountains for mineral samples. One of them brought him five samples of asbestos fibre found on the banks of the Tutusi stream in the old mining concession area named after Sir Arthur Havelock, a former Governor of Natal.

Fitzpatrick formed a syndicate and endeavoured to interest the Canadian asbestos mining firm of Turner and Newall in the find, but they considered the area to be too remote and the find too patchy. As a result, Fitzpatrick abandoned his scheme.

Then, in 1928, a prospector named Izaak Holthausen rediscovered the outcrop. With his partner, Herbert Castle, he proved the deposit and this time Turner and Newall showed interest. In 1930 they paid £240 000 for the 100 claims of the mine, and began a complex process of preparation for production.

The mine lay in completely isolated mountain country. Only a bridle path wandered over the hills from Barberton. Curving around the slopes of mLembe, it crossed a great gorge by means of a natural bridge of rock (the Devils Gorge) known to the Swazi as the *esiKhaleni sebuLembu* (pass of the spider's web), and found a difficult way to the mine at Piggs Peak. This path was, however, quite useless for transport.

To solve the problem, the company built a spectacular aerial ropeway which stretches directly over the mountains for 20 km to Barberton. The operation consists of 52 pylons and 11 stations varying in height from 4,5 m to 5,41 m to carry the cables; a 25-mm carrying cable and a 15-mm traction cable. In places the ropeway hangs 190 m above the ground, while the longest span extends 1 207 m across a deep valley.

From Havelock Mine (1 134 m above sea level) the ropeway climbs to Angle Station, 10,5 km away, the highest point at 1 607 m. There the ropeway is deflected 4 degrees 1 193 mm and then continues to Barberton railhead, 827 m above sea level. Two hundred and twenty-four carriers of various types ride the ropeway at a time, each carrier being spaced roughly 182 m apart and carrying 170 kg of bagged asbestos fibre. Two small electric motors of 60 horse power, one at Havelock and one at Barberton, drive the ropeway at a steady 10,5 km an hour.

The ropeway was built by the German firm of Bleichert and Company and is a most efficient carrier. A ride on the ropeway (the author has enjoyed that rare privilege) is an unforgettable experience, as it conquers the mountains with its slow, steady, giant strides.

The Havelock Mine is a model of its kind in Africa, with a neat town to house its workers laid out in a setting of tremendous scenic beauty. It produces over R5 million worth of chrysotile asbestos each year.

One kilometre beyond the Havelock Mine, the road crosses into South Africa at the customs post of Josefdal. The posts are open from 08h00 to 16h00. After a kilometre there is a turnoff leading down to the Diepgeziet mine of African Chrysotile Asbestos Ltd. Past this turn the road curves around the towering slopes of mLembe. The views of the mountain country at the edge of the South African highveld are superb.

Passing through the Welgelegen Plantation (24 km from Havelock) and the Highlands Plantation, with its turnoff to the Shiwa-lo-Ngubu dam (31 km from Havelock), the road makes a most spectacular descent into the mighty Kaap Valley. At the bottom the road passes the sites of the training camps of various regiments in the Second World War and then reaches the romantically situated old mining town of Barberton, 42 km from Havelock. This is a wonderful drive, not easily forgotten.

## MBABANE TO BUNYA

From Mbabane, a rather dusty road leads west and then southwards through spectacular granite hills into the timber country of the Usutu Pulp Company. Their plantations (mainly pine) are amongst the largest manmade forests in the world with the mill at Bunya having an output in excess of 100 000 tons of pulp each year.

The road climbs out of Mbabane revealing along the way, grand views into the upper reaches of the Ezulwini Valley. After 15,5 km there is a turnoff to Meikles Mount where Murray and Nora Meikle own a holiday resort in a setting of high hills. The views are impressive and there are riding and hiking trails and fishing in the uSutshwana River.

### Accommodation
★★® Meikles Mount, 8 cottages, E20 – E40 D. Phone Mhlambanyati 740-110.

Beyond the turn to Meikles Mount, the gravel road continues for 8,5 km and then reaches . . .

## MHLAMBANYATSI

Founded as a residential township for workers in the Usutu plantations, *Mhlambanyatsi* (the swimming place of the buffaloes) is surrounded by many hectares of trees and provides a cool, pleasant retreat for people from the warmer lowlands.

### Accommodation
★★® Foresters Arms Hotel, 24 rooms, all with baths. E18 D/B/B. Phone 740-77.

The road continues through the plantations, descending to the valley of the uSuthu River where, after 14,5 km, the pulp mill at Bunya is reached. At Bunya the road joins a tarmac road which has come up the valley of the uSuthu for 23 km, passing Malkerns (page 803) on its way from the main Mbabane-Manzini road. This road provides an interesting return route, flanked by the river flowing through a series of rapids and pools on the floor of a valley settled by peasant farmers. From Bunya, this tarmac road climbs steeply out of the valley of the uSuthu and after 32 km of passing granite boulders and plantations of trees, reaches the customs post of Sandlane and the South African post of Nerston. Both posts are open daily from 08h00 to 16h00.

## MBABANE TO LUVE

The road from Mbabane to Luve, where it joins the Tshaneni-Manzini road, provides a fascinating 63-km-long scenic excursion (in dry weather). The road starts from the upper (northern) end of Allister Miller Street in Mbabane and follows Pine Valley Road. The road climbs into the Dlangeni hills, with a turnoff to Fonteyn leading to the radio masts and a magnificent view of Mbabane.

The road to Luve follows the valley of the Mbuluzi River whose flow is broken by several cascades, waterfalls and deep pools. This is superb walking and riding country, cool in summer and enhanced by lovely scenery.

## MALKERNS TO NHLANGANO

At 22 km from Mbabane on the main tarmac road to Manzini, a tarmac turnoff leads through an intensive agricultural area where crops such as pineapples, citrus, sugar and cotton are grown. At 1,5 km from the turnoff stands the Tishweshwe farm stall and cottage crafts. The cannery of Libbys lies just ahead, with its residential township and country club.

At 6 km from the turnoff lies the rural centre of *Malkerns*, named after a trader, Malcolm Kerns Stuart, who ran a trading station there at the beginning of this century. At Malkerns the road joins another tarmac road which has travelled 7 km from the Mbabane-Manzini road. Five kilometres down this road stands the wayside shop of Nyanza Gemstones (Pty) Ltd, offering an interesting collection of locally made jewellery, curios and artwork. Voi Nyanza Kingsley (Mrs Williams) is the brain and the name behind the enterprise. Her mother, known to Swazilanders as 'Lady Lil', was the blonde bombshell of the Lichtenburg diamond diggings, where, as Miss Lily Clayton, a young schoolmistress, she dug for diamonds and had a whirlwind romance with another digger, Fred Kingsley.

From the junction at Malkerns, the tarmac road continues southwards past large pineries, the Malkerns Research Station, the Swaziland Agricultural College and the University Centre of Elangeni, built in 1966. At 5,5 km from Malkerns there is a turnoff to Mankayane. The main tarmac road carries on for 20 km up the valley of the uSuthu to Bunya (page 802).

The gravel turnoff to Mankayane is a scenic switchback railway type journey, climbing the hills on the southern side of the valley of the uSuthu. After 9 km from the turnoff, the road passes the Ngabeni Mission with its handicrafts industry. After a further 11 km of climbing and turning, the road reaches the Mtimani Forest, from where the panorama of the uSuthu valley may be viewed. The road tops a high ridge and then descends through the trees, reaching, 25 km from the turnoff . . .

## MANKAYANE

A Swazi chief by the name of Mankayane Sodho had his residence near the site of the present village – a cluster of shops, administrative buildings and hotel shaded by a grove of jacaranda, silver oak, eucalyptus and other trees.

**Accommodation**
★ Inyatsi Inn, 5 rooms, E11,50 D/B/B. Phone 12.

From Mankayane the gravel road proceeds southwards over hill and dale through pleasant rural countryside. At 28 km there is a junction with a road leading for 5 km to the customs post at Sicunusa, and on the other side, the South African post of Houtkop. The posts are open daily from 08h00 to 18h00.

The combined roads veer south-eastwards through a densely settled area of small farms interspersed with patches of wattle trees. At 15 km from the junction, the rural centre of Gege is reached from where a road leads for 5 km to the Gege customs post and the South African post of Bothashoop across the border. The posts are open daily from 08h00 to 16h00.

The main road continues south-eastwards through cattle and sheep country and rolling, grassy hills patched with trees. The Shiselweni plantations extend for many hectares on each side of the road. At 23 km from Gege a road branches westwards for 12 km to the customs post of Mahamba and the South African post of the same name across the border. The posts are open daily from 07h00 to 22h00. At 3,5 km beyond this turnoff to the border lies the village of . . .

# NHLANGANO

Once known as Goedgegun, this village, the name of which means 'a meeting place', was founded in 1921 as a centre for an important agricultural and timber area. Hemmed in by trees, the village experiences a pleasantly cool climate and the air is clear. A handicraft market offers goods for sale and there are two hotels, one with a small casino and a cinema showing the usual pornographic fare.

## Accommodation
*** Nhlangano Hotel, 48 chalets, all with baths. E14 – E21 room only. Phone 157.
* Robin Inn, 6 rooms, E8,40 B/B. Phone 160.

Nhlangano is the principal centre for a part of Swaziland, the historical importance of which is equal to that of its economy. In 1750, when the ancestors of the Swazi people first migrated to what is now Swaziland, they settled in this southern part of the country, burying their early chiefs here in graves which are taboo. Nzama, Mlokojwa and Shiselweni are the sites of these graves.

Beyond Nhlangano the road to the east passes through this area. Small trading centres are situated at places such as Mthosheni and Hluti. After 92 km this road reaches the customs post at Lavumisa and the South African post of Golela across the border. The posts are open daily from 07h00 to 22h00. There is a handicraft market at Lavumisa, the name of which indicates a hot place – a claim fully justifiable in summer.

## Accommodation
* Lavumisa Hotel, 40 rooms, E7,35 B/B. Phone 7.

From Nhlangano a road stretches northwards, passing after 6,5 km the King's residence of emBangweni. The road finds a complex way through seemingly endless hills covered in saligna and pine trees, and with many exciting views revealed. At 26,5 km the road reaches . . .

# HLATIKHULU

Perched high on a ridge, this little rural centre consists of a street of shops, a hotel and a few houses, all enjoying a fine view to the north-west of what is known as Grand Valley. The name *Hlatikhulu* means 'big bush'. The village was founded as an administrative centre for the southern hill country of Swaziland.

## Accommodation
★ Assegai Inn, 6 rooms, 2 with baths. E7,80 D/B/B. Phone 16.

Five kilometres north of Hlatikhulu, the road divides. The left-hand division continues north-wards, descending into the valley of the Mkhondvo River and providing a fine drive for 64 km to Sidvokodvo and from there for 23 km to Manzini. The right-hand division of the road makes a winding descent through the hills for 32 km to the trading station of Kubuta, with banana plantations covering the hill slopes. A further 14 km takes the road to Sitobela where there is a turnoff south to Maloma. The road continues northwards for 26,5 km, reaching the uSuthu River at *Siphofaneni* (tawny coloured place) where there are hot saline chloride springs and a camping ground on the banks of what is the largest river in Swaziland. Fishing is good here and the river crossing picturesque with tall wild fig trees growing on the banks. Immediately across the river the road joins the tarmac road linking Manzini (43 km away) to Big Bend, 37 km to the east.

# BIG BEND

The uSuthu River, confronted by the barrier of the Lubombo mountains, experienced a phase of uncertainty as to how to continue its journey. This indecision resulted in 'Big Bend', yielding ideal opportunities for the irrigation of a large area of lowveld. The village of Big Bend is the centre for sugar production, the mill there being the first (in 1960) to produce sugar in Swaziland. The gorge through which the uSuthu River penetrates the Lubombo is wildly beautiful, frequented by rich bird life, hippos, crocodiles and tiger fish. The gorge may be reached from Big Bend, either on horseback or on foot. The summers are very hot.

## Accommodation
★★® The Bend Inn, 26 rooms, all with baths or showers. E13,50 – E20 B/B. Phone 6.

From Big Bend the main road to the south crosses the uSuthu River after 3,5 km, finding a way through the cane fields and acacia bush with the Lubombo range towering up immediately to the east. At 31,5 km from Big Bend the road passes the trading centre of Nsoko, and after a further 2,5 km, crosses the Ngwavuma River, its banks lined with magnificent fever trees. At 31,5 km beyond the river, the road reaches the border post of Lavumisa at the southern tip of Swaziland (page 804). This is the second most important entrance to Swaziland after Oshoek-Ngwenya and the main link to Natal.

# Chapter Forty-one

# ZIMBABWE

Between the river systems of the Zambezi in the north and the Limpopo in the south there lies a superb natural parkland 375 830 square kilometres in extent. Trees in vast numbers and considerable variety flourish in this parkland while flowering shrubs and creepers grow in such profusion that the whole area is a garden of infinite colour and form.

Running east to west through the centre of the country is a ridge which acts as a divide between the two river systems. The summit of this ridge forms a narrow linear plateau, less thickly treed, more richly grassed and cooler than the low country to the north and south and providing a fine residential area for human beings, with deep soil, a good rainfall during warm summers, cool winters, and freedom from tropical pests such as malarial mosquitoes.

Scattered throughout the area between the two great river systems are some of the most imposing geological features to be seen anywhere on earth: gigantic domes and whalebacks of granite, surging upwards as though they were petrified bubbles of an ancient sea of molten magma. Their age – well over 3 000 million years – makes them the oldest dateable rocks found on earth, in addition to being one of the principal natural wonders on this planet.

Animal life of great variety and profusion finds a congenial home in this parkland. Man made his appearance at a very early period and artefacts, relics and galleries of rock art provide prehistorians with an inexhaustable field of study.

Bushmen hunted through the forests and savannas from ancient times. During the period of Christ, Iron Age people immigrated to the area from the north, displacing the Bushmen and creating a unique culture which embraced activities such as mining for surface metals (copper and gold), trading with the Arabs who sailed down the east coast of Africa, and erecting stone walls for defensive purposes around their habitations, the conventional African mud and thatch huts.

These settlers from the north formed powerful related tribal groups – the Karanga, Rozvi, and others. Their kings were known as *mambo* or *mwana mutapa* (lord conqueror), the royal residences of whom were surrounded by elaborate walls often skilfully decorated with various patterns. They neither learned how to roof these stone constructions nor did they ever devise any form of cement. Stone units of roughly the same size secured from the natural flaking of granite, were simply placed one on top of the other. The work was almost certainly carried out by the women and the results, although crude, are singularly impressive and harmonise perfectly with the vast environment of Africa. Nothing similar may be seen anywhere else in the world.

Portuguese traders entered the area during the 16th century, by which time the dominant Karanga-Rozvi people seem to have passed the peak of their power and fragmented into rival groups. Invasions by various Nguni groups from the south – the Ndebele, Shangane and other people – reduced the early inhabitants to a state of poverty, with their walled residences being overrun and their mining operations abandoned.

European ivory hunters from the south crossed the Limpopo during the early 19th century. In the western part of the central ridge they found the chief Mzilikazi established with a heterogeneous following of Zulu and Sotho who had fled with him from troubles in South Africa. These people were collectively named by the Sotho *maTebele* (people who hide) and in the Zulu language this name became *Ndebele*. Europeans converted it into *Matabele*. The original Karanga-Rozvi who inhabited the land between the two rivers, were leading a harried existence, being raided by the Ndebele and the Shangane people from Moçambique. To the Karanga-Rozvi the Ndebele gave the derogatory name of *maShona* (bankrupt people).

The early European hunters and traders noticed the numerous signs of mining, which they called 'ancient workings'. Stories spread that this must have been the Ophir of the Bible. Highly exaggerated reports of immense riches simply waiting to be exploited, were published in Europe. Cecil Rhodes, then at the height of his remarkable career as mining magnate, financier and politician, utilised the confused tribal situation in the country. He sent agents to see Mzilikazi's son and successor, Lobengula, obtaining an exclusive concession covering mining rights to all minerals and metals in his domain. In exchange, Lobengula was offered £100 a month; one thousand Martini-Henry rifles; one hundred thousand rounds of ammunition; and a steam gunboat on the Zambezi River. The concession was signed by Lobengula on 30 October 1888.

Rhodes used this mining concession as an excuse to occupy the entire eastern portion of the country. In Cape Town he persuaded Frank Johnson, a young director of the Bechuanaland Explorations Company, to organise a column of men, lead them across the Limpopo, avoid a clash with the Ndebele, construct a road and to occupy the country of the Shona people. While the Shona would certainly be surprised at the occupation of their country on the strength of mining concessions granted by the Ndebele, they would be powerless to do anything about it.

This Pioneer Column, as it was called, reached the site of Salisbury, the capital of Rhodesia, on 12 September 1890. The name *Fort Salisbury* was given to the place in honour of Lord Salisbury, the Prime Minister of Great Britain. The Union Jack was run up, a fort constructed and, on 30 September 1890, the 180 men of the Pioneer Column were disbanded and rewarded with rights to prospect mining claims and select farms for themselves.

Although gold was found in many places, it did not match up to hopelessly exaggerated expectations of vast wealth. Stories then spread that the real Ophir was, after all, in the Ndebele part of the country. In 1893 the British South Africa Company of Cecil Rhodes invaded the Ndebele area, occupying Lobengula's capital of Bulawayo and taking possession of the whole of what was named Rhodesia. Lobengula fled to the north, pursued by a section of the Company's men. The subsequent events do not provide pleasant reading. In the hope of ending the war Lobengula sent messengers carrying a thousand gold sovereigns as a peace offering to the Company. The messengers were intercepted by two policemen who embezzled the money.

The pursuit of Lobengula continued and ended in disaster. On the Shangani River, an advance patrol led by Allan Wilson made a dash to secure Lobengula but were instead completely annihilated by the chief's bodyguard. Lobengula fled further north and committed suicide. He is buried in the cave in which he died. As in the Shona portion of the country, gold was found in the Ndebele area but not in the extravagant amount anticipated.

Rhodesia was run by the British South Africa Company as a Royal Charter until 1922 when it was annexed to Britain. In the following year it was given responsible government after having rejected a proposal of joining South Africa as a fifth province. Subsequent to the Second World War the idea of a union of Rhodesia, Northern Rhodesia and Nyasaland was discussed. The result was the creation of a Federation with the first joint parliament holding session in Salisbury in 1954.

The Federation never settled down. Riots occurred in 1959 in Nyasaland and in 1963 in Northern Rhodesia. The three countries separated, becoming Malawi, Zambia and Rhodesia. The Rhodesian Front party, led by Ian Smith, which held power in Rhodesia, repudiated British attempts to liberalise the regime. African leaders such as Robert Mugabe, Joshua Nkomo and Ndabaningi Sithole were detained and on 11 November 1965 Ian Smith declared a UDI (Unilateral Declaration of Independence).

In 1969 Rhodesia became a Republic but did not receive world recognition. Trade embargoes were imposed. Several attempts were made by the British Government to find solutions to the various problems but the situation deteriorated. On 21 December 1972 the first attack on a farm was made by African guerilla fighters. From then on, civil war commenced between supporters of the white government, and the blacks led by the African National Congress.

Despite several attempts at peace made by such concerned people as the South African Prime Minister, John Vorster, and President Kaunda of Zambia, and as a conciliatory gesture, the release from detention of Robert Mugabe and Joshua Nkomo in 1974, the war continued. In 1976 Mugabe and Nkomo formed the Patriotic Front, two separate armies of which fought against the government forces; Nkomo in the west and Mugabe in the east. Casualties were heavy.

In 1978 an 'internal settlement' was arranged between the Rhodesian Government and various African leaders such as Bishop Abel Muzorewa, Ndabaningi Sithole and Chief Chirau. In 1979 a general election was held and Bishop Abel Muzorewa became Prime Minister. The Patriotic Front ignored the new regime and the civil war intensified. The British Government of Mrs Margaret Thatcher then intervened in a situation that was fast becoming disastrous. After a great deal of hard talking in Lancaster House, London, the rival groups at last reached a settlement. The government of Bishop Abel Muzorewa resigned and Rhodesia once again became a colony with Lord Soames sent from London as Governor.

In 1980 a general election was held in which Robert Mugabe won 57 seats; Joshua Nkomo 20; and Bishop Muzorewa three. Twenty seats were reserved for Europeans and these were all won by the Rhodesian Front. On 1 April 1980 the government of Robert Mugabe took office in a fully independent state named Zimbabwe.

## SALISBURY (HARARE)

With a population of 566 000, Salisbury is the capital of Zimbabwe. Situated 1 471 m above sea level, the city lies in the centre of some of the most fertile and beautiful parkland in Zimbabwe and as a result is a real garden of trees and flowers, enhanced by rich soil and a summer rainfall (November to March) of 700 mm a year.

A view of the place from the toposcope on top of the overlooking Salisbury Koppie, reveals the exact manner in which this clean and pleasant city has grown in the midst of the surrounding parkland of tall, elegantly shaped brachystegia trees. The forest has been pushed aside to make room for the city and its suburbs, but in such a situation the trees and plants are irrepressible, reclaiming their own and spreading back into the city which as a result has shaded pavements, beautiful public parks, private gardens, and flowers blooming in every possible situation.

Salisbury Koppie is known to the local Zezuru tribe as *Neharare Tshikomo* (the hillock of Neharare). Neharare was one of their chiefs who was buried on this hillock. Consequently, the Zezuru call Salisbury *Harare*, after this chief.

Salisbury had its start as a European city on 13 September 1890 when the Pioneer Column sent by Rhodes to occupy Mashonaland, halted its journey, hoisted the Union Jack on the site of the present memorial flagstaff in Cecil Square, and commenced the building of a fort named *Salisbury* in honour of Lord Salisbury, the Prime Minister of Great Britain. It was there, on 30 September 1890, before the earth walls of the fort, on the square named after Cecil Rhodes, that the men of the Pioneer Column completed their contracts and were dismissed to commence the search for gold, or to settle on farms. This then, was the beginning of what was named Rhodesia. On each anniversary of the founding of Salisbury, descendants of the Pioneers gathered in Cecil Square to once again raise the flag on the tall post standing on the site of the Pioneers' flagpole.

Salisbury was built on the banks of a small stream with the ingenious name of *Mutyisambizi* (the river where the zebra is frightened). When the city was founded this stream divided the place into two parts which were linked by a causeway (hence the name Causeway being applied to the portion of the modern city containing most of the administrative buildings). The stream now flows underground through large drains and its former course is today the busy thoroughfare of Kingsway.

The wide, straight streets of Salisbury are the result of the pioneers' requirements for manoeuvring ox wagon transport. Basking in brilliant sunlight and with clear air unpolluted by industry, the city is clean, crisp, well scrubbed and well heeled befitting its population of traders, professional men and civil servants. The number of bicycles in use, especially by the African population, make the place notable: during rush hours, when there is an influx and exodus of these vehicles between the city and its residential suburbs, the impressive picture provided is one of massed pedal power.

Apart from its wide streets and modern buildings, Salisbury has several features of interest. As the capital of Zimbabwe, it is the seat of Parliament and the resort of diplomats, politicians and lobbyists, with numerous buildings housing civil service departments. A visit to Parliament while it is in session is interesting, for Zimbabwe has always made world news and its past, preserved in a handsome and extremely well-kept National Archives, makes fascinating study. The Strangers' Gallery in Parliament is open to the public during sittings. When Parliament is not in session visitors may be shown over the building by arrangement with the Sergeant-at-Arms or Chief Messenger. The National Archives are open Mondays to Fridays from 08h00 to 16h00 and on Saturdays from 08h00 to 13h00.

The Town House, situated in Kingsway, contains several treasures such as the Blakeway Marine Shell Collection and the original medals and decorations of Frank Johnson (who led the Pioneer Column to Salisbury). Framed in the walls are the names of the men who accompanied him on his adventurous journey. Outside the Town House there is an ingenious floral clock installed in 1950 on the occasion of the Diamond Jubilee of the city. The fine modern buildings of the university, and the National Gallery, also grace the city. The Queen Victoria Museum is well known for its collection of Bushman paintings, relics from the various ancient ruins of Zimbabwe, and a good representative collection of the ornithology of Central Africa. The National Gallery is open daily except Mondays, from 09h00 to 17h00, 1 April to 30 September, and from 10h00 to 18h00, 1 October to 31 March. The Queen Victoria Museum is open Mondays to Saturdays from 10h00 to 17h00, Sundays from 14h30 to 17h00.

Salisbury is the largest tobacco market in the world. Sales are held on the tobacco auction floors every morning, Mondays to Fridays between March and September. Visitors are welcome. The sing-song calling of the auctioneers must be heard to be believed.

Salisbury's greatest beauty and principal asset, however, is its magnificent park-like setting. The main Salisbury Public Gardens literally extend over the entire city in the form of innumerable carefully planned avenues and streets of flowering trees. The trees planted have been specially selected to ensure that there is always something in flower somewhere in the city. These trees not only beautify Salisbury, but provide a living link with the arboreal countryside and, notwithstanding the contrast of modern buildings, enable the city to harmonise with its surroundings.

Salisbury Public Gardens stand on a portion of land set aside by Cecil Rhodes for public use when he planned the city. The garden is famous for its spring displays of sweet peas and stocks, while zinnias and marigolds seem to catch fire with colour in the summer months.

A fine collection of water lilies may be seen in the pond built in 1937 to celebrate the coronation of George VI. A great variety of trees also flourish in the gardens. There is one enormous Indian toon tree, planted little over 30 years ago by the Duke of Connaught, which now provides shade for garden parties held for visiting dignitaries.

Another interesting tree is the *Ficus religiosa,* regarded as being so sacred in India that no metal is allowed to came into contact with it. The father of all the Mexican feather duster trees

(Schizolobiem excelsum) in Salisbury, also grows in the garden. From this prolific specimen have sprung all the feather duster trees in the city, including the one in Cecil Square. The popular name of these trees is very apt; they comprise a tall, clean trunk topped with a bunch of feathery leaves.

In the children's section of the gardens stands a Himalayan cyprus tree which is annually decorated as a Christmas tree with lights of changing colour. During the month of December a Father Christmas postbox is placed near the tree into which children post their letters to Father Christmas. The local Toc H organisation answers the letters.

There are several memorials in the garden commemorating the rebellion of 1896, and the two world wars. An interesting attraction is provided by a miniature Victoria Falls, built by a former superintendent of the park, Mr G. W. McGuffog. The falls are made to scale, including the gorge and the famous railway bridge. Even the rainbow may be seen in the morning sun.

Cecil Square in the centre of Salisbury is also the home of many beautiful trees and flowering plants. To symbolise the fact that Salisbury was the brainchild of Cecil Rhodes, then living in Cape Town, the plants in the section of the garden around the feather duster tree have all come from the grounds of Rhodes's cottage at Muizenberg in the Cape Peninsula.

The major feature of Cecil Square, however, is its fountain. This most effective, varying, automatic display of water patterns and coloured lights was built by municipal departments in Salisbury and commenced playing its merry water game during the Diamond Jubilee in 1950. The fountain is particularly beautiful at night.

Spring and early summer – September, October and November – are the most spectacular seasons in Salisbury. At that time the jacarandas are in full blossom. Bauhinias in two varieties (pink and white, and white and purple) are also in flower, as well as the Australian flame trees and the lovely yellow cassias. Bougainvillaea glow with colours of many different shades.

From January to July the African flame trees display their beauty, while in August and September the flamboyants make a magnificent show. More sedate, but interesting, are the tall palms in Kingsway, Phoenix reclinata and Washingtonia robusta, presented to the city in the 1920s by Pickstones, the famous nursery in the Cape closely associated with Rhodes. The graceful indigenous musasa trees grow to perfection in this their natural habitat.

## Accommodation

- ★★★ Ambassador Hotel, 85 rooms, all with baths. $10 B/B. Phone 708121.
- ★★ Courtney Hotel, 50 rooms, all with baths. $8,50 single – $12 double B/B. Phone 706411.
- ★ Elizabeth Hotel, 28 rooms, 12 with showers. $5,10 – $6,10 B/B. Phone 708591.
- ★★ Feathers Hotel, 17 rooms, 9 with baths. $6 room only. Phone 36612.
- ★ Federal Hotel, 6 rooms, $3,50 B/B. Phone 706118.
- ★★ George Hotel, 35 rooms, all with baths. $6,50 B/B. Phone 36677.
- ★ International Hotel, 42 rooms, $4,50 room only. Phone 700333.
- ★★★★ Jameson Hotel, 125 rooms, all with baths. $14 single – $20 double B/B. Phone 794641.
- ★ Kamfinsa Park Hotel, 20 rooms, 12 with baths. $4,50 room only. Phone 45890.
- ★★ Kentucky Hotel, 34 rooms, all with baths. $6 B/B. Phone 50655.
- ★★★★ Meikles Hotel, 113 rooms, all with baths. $11,50 – $16,75 single, room only. $19 – $28 double, room only. Phone 707721.
- ★★★★ Monomatapa Hotel, 200 rooms, all with baths. $16 single – $25 double, room only. Phone 704501.
- ★★ Mount Hampden Motel, 14 rooms, 12 with baths. $8 B/B. Phone 32947.
- ★★ Oasis Motel, 88 rooms, all with baths. $6,50 – $8,50 room only. Phone 704217.
- ★ Observatory Country Inn, 8 rooms, all with baths. $5 B/B. Phone 32995.
- ★★★ Park Lane Hotel, 36 rooms, all with baths. $6,75 single, $10,50 double, room only. Phone 707631.
- ★ Queens Hotel, 42 rooms, 24 with baths. $6 B/B. Phone 700877.

★★ Red Fox Hotel, 7 rooms, all with baths. $7,50 single – $12 double B/B. Phone 45466.
★ Salisbury Motel, 24 rooms, all with baths. $6,75 B/B. Phone 24223.
★ Seven Miles Hotel, 15 rooms, $5 single – $8 double B/B. Phone 67587.
★ Skyline Motel, 14 rooms, all with baths. $5,50 single, $7,50 double, room only. Phone 67588.
★★ Spaniards Hotel, 20 rooms, all with baths. $5,50 B/B. Phone 39510.
★ Terreskane Hotel, 87 rooms, 20 with baths. $4,75 – $5,25 room only. Phone 707031.
★ Windmill Park, 8 chalets, 5 rooms, $6 B/B. Phone 394017.
★★ Windsor Hotel, 32 rooms, 11 with baths. $5 – $6 room only. Phone 706475.

### Caravans and camping
★★★® Coronation Park (municipal), 400 sites, $1,50 D.
Youth hostel: members, $1 room only. Non-members, $1,50 room only. Phone 26990.


## LAKE McILWAINE AND THE SALISBURY COUNTRYSIDE

The citizens of Salisbury are fortunate in being surrounded by a green and pleasant countryside with many interesting features all made easily accessible by means of excellent roads. Lake McIlwaine, 32 km from the city, is a major recreational area as well as being the principal water supply for the city. Named after Sir Robert McIlwaine, first chairman of the Natural Resources Board, the great dam was created in 1952, with the completion of a massive earth wall 36,5 m high, 85,3 m long and 274,3 m wide, blocking the Hunyani River in a narrow pass through a range of hills. The summer rains normally fill the dam and the overflow, pouring down the spillway of the wall, provides a spectacular sight.

The surroundings of Lake McIlwaine – a brachystegian parkland dominated by rocky hillocks – has become a national park and the recreational attractions it possesses are numerous. The northern shore has been developed with resorts, tearooms, and the club buildings of yachting, aquaplaning and boating enthusiasts. The numerous picnic, barbecue, caravan and camping sites are pleasant and launches take sightseers on tours around the lake.

The southern shore of the lake consists of a game reserve, open daily from 07h00 to 18h00. Here a considerable variety of antelope live in their natural habitat and are perfectly agreeable to being admired and photographed. Bushman paintings in the rock shelters of the overlooking granite hills vividly reveal that in prehistoric times, this area was a favourite resort for game animals and man. Remnants of Karanga walled settlements and agricultural activity may also be seen. The lake is full of tiger fish, bream, yellowfish, barbel and Hunyani salmon. As a result, anglers find their time pleasantly occupied. Swimming – as in most inland waters in the warmer parts of Africa – is not to be recommended on account of bilharzia.

Rides may be taken on the longest miniature railway in Southern Africa along the lake shore on Sundays and public holidays. An aquarium exhibiting the largest variety of freshwater fish in Africa, is open to the public daily from 08h00 to 17h00. It is situated beside the restaurant at the dam wall.

### Accommodation
★★ Hunyani Hills Hotel, 14 rooms, all with baths. $7,25 B/B. Phone 2642683.

### Caravans and camping
★★® National Park, 50 sites. $1,50 D.
21 chalets, furnished but no bedding, $3 – $5 D.
3 lodges, furnished, with bedding. 4 people, $6,50 – $8,50 D.

*Overleaf: A strip road in Zimbabwe leads invitingly on for many kilometres through the green parkland of the Kalahari sand country.*

# EWANRIGG NATIONAL PARK

This beautiful garden, lying to the east of Salisbury, was the private creation of Basil Christian, owner of the farm *Ewanrigg,* which he named after his elder brother, Ewan, killed in the First World War. The name he combined with *rigg,* the Welsh word for a ridge. An enthusiastic gardener, he acquired aloes and cycads from many parts of Africa, as well as trees, cacti and shrubs from all over the world. This tremendous assembly (the largest aloe collection in Southern Africa) is admirably displayed around a stream full of aquatic and marsh-loving plants. The collection is well documented and a resident curator is in charge. Mr Christian bequeathed his farm to the country on his death.

Ewanrigg is at its best during the winter months, June to August, but there is always something to be seen there. To reach the garden take the Mtoko road for 8 km to the Shamva turnoff. This road should be followed for a further 18 km, after which a turnoff to the garden is reached. There are picnic sites at Ewanrigg but no facilities for refreshments or camping are provided.


# THE BALANCING ROCKS NEAR EPWORTH MISSION

As a whole, Zimbabwe is something of a gigantic rockery. All manner of weird and wonderfully shaped fragments (mainly granite) of hillocks long disintegrated by the action of sun and rain, have been scattered around by nature with all the abandon of an untidy children's playroom. Seventeen kilometres from Salisbury, past the Epworth Mission, lies a particularly wonderful collection of these rocks, some balancing on each other, others of such bizarre shape that one is reminded of the strange totems and idols of long-forgotten religions. This strange area was named after Tshirembe, a renowned witchdoctor who once had his home here.


# MAZOE AND THE MERMAID'S POOL

An extremely interesting 200-km-long circular drive leaves Salisbury, passing through the handsome northern suburbs of the city and continuing along what is known as the Golden Stairs Road, across a fertile rural area where maize and dairy farms flourish in beautiful surroundings. The tarmac road descends easily into a bushy valley and, 39 km from Salisbury, reaches the Mazoe Dam which was created in 1920 by the British South Africa Company. A concrete wall blocks the passage of the *Mazowe* (river of elephants) as it passes through the Iron Mask range of hills. The impounded water is used to irrigate the Mazoe Citrus Estate. The Mazoe Dam is famous for the size of its carp and is a popular fishing resort.

The road passes through the Iron Mask range next to the dam wall and after 1 km reaches the small centre of Mazoe where there is one hotel. One kilometre further on the tarmac road joins the road from Concession (15 km), where H. C. Moore once held a mining concession. The road then swings eastwards down the valley of the Mazowe River through spacious groves of citrus trees which are in full bearing during May and June. Five kilometres from the junction the road passes the Citrus Estates office, beyond which the groves give way to maize and then to brachystegia bush. Numerous signs of mining activity, both ancient and modern, are visible. Forty-six kilometres from the junction (84 km from Salisbury), the tarmac road passes through the village of Bindura, built on the slope of a hill of that name. From here a turnoff leads north for 52 km to the administrative post of Mount Darwin.

### Accommodation
★★ Coach House Inn, 20 rooms, all with baths. $9,50 single, $15 double B/B. Phone Bindura 777.

* Kimberley Reef Hotel, 30 rooms, 9 with baths. $7 B/B. Phone Bindura 351.
* Mazoe Inn, 8 rooms, $4,75 – $5,25 B/B. Phone Mazoe 443.

**Caravans and camping**
* Bindura Caravan Park, 25 sites. $1,50 D.

The main road continues eastward through fields of maize and cotton, passing a cotton-packing depot at Tafuna siding 21 km from Bindura. The road has now dwindled to a narrow mat, but the tarmac surface is perfectly good and leads through interesting and rugged scenery until 27 km from Bindura it reaches the picturesque old mining centre of *Shamva,* named after the tsamvi trees (a variety of wild fig) which flourish there. The gold mine is no longer worked, but the signs of its former activity will long remain in the shape of an enormous open-cast working on top of the hill, a substantial rubble dump and a huddle of houses. Shamva remains the terminus of the branch line from Salisbury and is now the centre for the local Grain Marketing Board.

At Shamva the road from Bindura joins a wide tarmac road coming from Mount Darwin (77 km north) and the combined roads swing southwards back to Salisbury. Fields of cotton stretch on either side. The picking season in May and June is beautiful. The tarmac road climbs out of the valley through hills covered in acacia and brachystegia trees. African villages and odd little mines may be seen by the wayside. The drive, along a fine, modern road, is altogether diverting and worthwhile.

At 25 km from Shamva, the road passes the impressive granite mass of Lion's Head, with a path leading to some interesting Bushman paintings. A further 25 km takes the road past a turnoff of 1 km leading to the Mermaid's Pool, a popular weekend resort with a restaurant and a variety of accommodation clustered around a natural pool (50 m across and 5 m deep), situated at the bottom of a rock slide formed by a perennial stream.

Three kilometres beyond the Mermaid's Pool turnoff, the tarmac road reaches the turnoff to the Ewanrigg National Park with its famous garden (see page 812). The road now narrows for 20 km and then reaches a junction with the main road leading east to Mrewa (66 km) and Mtoko (130 km). Turning west along this main road, the traveller is taken through the suburb of Highlands and back to Salisbury (15 km from the junction with the Mtoko road). It is altogether a magnificent drive, filled with the scenic novelty and beautiful wilderness which only Africa can offer.

## SALISBURY TO THE ZAMBEZI

From Salisbury, the great north-south road of Africa stretches north as Route A1. For the first 10 km after leaving the city centre the road penetrates the outlying suburbs, and then leads north-westwards through a lovely, grassy parkland, where great maize lands are cultivated among the trees. Sixteen kilometres from the city, to the north of the road, may be seen the landmark of Mount Hampden, a hillock originally intended as the destination of the Pioneer Column on its march into Rhodesia.

Eleven kilometres further on the tarmac road passes the Gwebi Agricultural College, with its model fields immaculately cultivated around the banks of the small stream whose name, *Gwivi* (hairless), from the worn-out grass along its banks, has been corrupted into the European form of Gwebi.

For a further 20 km the road continues across level parkland, after which it reaches a long, flat-topped ridge, well covered in trees and running north to south. This ridge is actually a surface outcrop of the Great Dyke of Zimbabwe, one of the most extraordinary geological features of Southern Africa. The Great Dyke contains an immense variety of minerals, especially chrome and asbestos, and the signs of mining and prospecting may be seen throughout its length. About 700 million years ago an enormous subterranean eruption resulted in the intrusion of a molten mass of material between the sedimentary layers of parts of the Transvaal and Zimbabwe. In the Transvaal this disturbance resulted in the Bushveld Igneous Complex while in Zimbabwe it produced a gigantic trough up to 7 km wide and 500 km long running south to north almost the full length of the country, and known as the Great Dyke.

The road climbs over the ridge (known to Europeans as the Mvukwe range) by means of an attractive pass called the Great Dyke Pass, and descends easily on the western side to another tree-covered but less fertile looking plain. At 66 km from Salisbury there is a turnoff north leading to the Vanab Mine (48 km) and Mtoroshanga (38 km). Twenty-five kilometres further on the road passes through the village of Banket, a mining and agricultural centre on the branch railway from Salisbury.

Accommodation
★ Blue Jay Inn, 17 rooms, 3 with baths. $4,75 – $6,75 B/B. Phone 24.

A further 20 km brings the road to the bridge over the Hunyani River and 1 km beyond this lies the village of Sinoia, a typical Zimbabwean rural centre – clean, well kept and orderly, with a fountain playing in the garden square and a line of commercial enterprises hoping to attract patronage from traffic on the main through road.

It is 8 km beyond Sinoia village that the Great North Road (route A1) reaches the famous feature which gives the area its name . . .

## THE SINOIA CAVES

Comprising a national park the Sinoia Caves lie at the foot of the long ridge of the range of tree-covered hills known to Europeans as the *Hunyani* (correctly *Mhanyami,* meaning 'high land'). In level ground the earth has collapsed into an enormous circular sinkhole. Looking down from the top the viewer sees, 50 m below, the mirror-like surface of a pool over 100 m in depth – the 'sleeping pool' containing crystal clear water of a remarkable blue colour. A natural sloping passage leads underground to the verge of this strange pool, while a whole complex of galleries and caverns honeycombs the dolomite rock around it.

Tradition tells of an outlaw named Nyamakwere who used these caves as his stronghold and who executed many victims by throwing them down to the sleeping pool. He was eventually killed there himself and the chief of the area gave the caves to his own daughter who was married to a headman named Tshinoyi. It is his name, corrupted to *Sinoia,* which is used by Europeans today. Tshinoyi used the caves as a sanctuary during times of raids, maintained stores of food there, and fortified the entrances. To the Africans, the caves are known as *Tshirodziva* (the fallen pool).

Accommodation
★ Caves Motel, 14 rooms, all with baths. $8 B/B. Phone 2340.
★★ Orange Grove Motel, 24 rooms, all with baths. $8,95 B/B. Phone 2785.
★ Sinoia Hotel, 27 rooms, all with baths. $7,50 B/B. Phone 2313.

Caravans and camping
★ Sinoia Caves National Park, 50 sites. $1,50 D.

Past the Sinoia Caves, the Great North Road (A1) finds an easy pass over the Hunyani ridge and continues north-westwards across a savanna plain of tobacco, maize and cattle farms. After 16 km the road crosses the railway at the station of Lions Den, from where there is a turnoff north to Zawi (7 km), the terminus of the branch railway, and to Mangula (47 km), with its great chrome mine.

The main tarmac road continues north-westwards across a plain densely covered with musasa trees and long grass. After 5 km the road crosses the Angwa River and a further 56 km of travelling brings the road to the village of Karoi (200 km from Salisbury). Tradition has it that in former years a *muroyi* (witch) was punished for her spells by being drowned in the river which was thenceforth known as the *Karoyi*. The modern European village which has taken its name from this event, is a centre for the mining of mica and for tobacco farming.

### Accommodation
* Karoi Hotel, 33 rooms, 18 with baths. $4,25 – $5,50 room only. Phone 317.
* Twin River Inn, 18 chalets, $6,50 B/B. Phone 411.

The Great North Road (A1) continues north-westwards from Karoi across extensive tobacco fields, with the drying sheds visible on every farm. After 11 km there is a turnoff north-east to Miami (18 km). The main road continues through country which becomes increasingly rugged and wild, densely covered in bush and a great variety of trees. Twenty-four kilometres from the Miami turnoff there is a pleasant resting and barbecue site in the shade of tall wayside trees. A further 20 km brings the tarmac road to a wayside drinking waterpump.

The country is now notably devoid of human habitation. After a further 16 km, another shady resting place with a drinking water supply is reached. Signs warning against wild animals appear on the road and 9 km further on, there is a tsetse fly traffic control for vehicles coming south which might have picked up some of the pestilential fly from the valley of the Zambezi River. Southbound vehicles are driven into a shed and treated to copious draughts of chemical spray.

One kilometre north-west of the tsetse control point the Great North Road reaches the Makuti Motel and a turnoff (79 km) to Lake Kariba (see page 816).

### Accommodation
* Makuti Motel, 20 rooms, all with baths. $4,75 room only. Phone Makuti 526.

The main tarmac road proceeds north-westwards and approaches the edge of the Zambezi escarpment. The journey now becomes extremely dramatic, the superbly located tarmac road making its way through a most lovely wilderness, enhanced by magnificent trees and tremendous views. Sunset is the best time to make this journey. Daytime in the great Zambezi Valley can be sultry, but at sunset the air starts to cool, the far-off hills are painted in pastel shades which are indescribably lovely while, when darkness comes, the headlights of passing traffic reveal many game animals – a leopard on the hunt or a heard of elephants heading for some special place. This is indeed a wonderful portion of the diverse continent of Africa, and one of the most dramatic sections of the entire Great North Road.

At 16 km from Makuti the tarmac road reaches the office of the Department of Parks and Wild Life at Marangora. Six kilometres further along the road, there is a turnoff east leading for 73 km through a magnificent piece of wilderness down into the Zambezi Valley, to the game reserve of . . . .

# MANA POOLS

This game reserve (375 square kilometres in extent) on the banks of the Zambezi River, is one of the most fascinating in Africa. The actual pools consist of a cluster of lakelets on the flood plain of the Zambezi. Bird life and game animals live around these lakes in considerable numbers, while elephant, buffalo, zebra, sable, waterbuck, impala, eland, rhino, lion, leopard, wild dog, hippo and crocodile all abound in the area. The pools and the river are full of fish. Anglers find considerable sport in catching tiger fish.

The only restrictions in the Mana Pools Game Reserve are placed on shooting. Visitors may walk or drive anywhere they please, remembering only that the wild animals are dangerous. Mosquitoes, tsetse fly and heat are always present, against which precautions must be taken. All food, bedding etc. must be taken into the reserve. There is a fine 4-ha camping and caravan site and the Mana Tree Lodge offers luxurious accommodation. The Mana Pools Game Reserve is open from 1 May to 31 October.

## Accommodation

Mana Tree Lodge, 7 rooms, $9,50 D, inclusive of meals and morning and evening game-
viewing drives. Book at Makuti Motel.

## Caravans and camping

Vundu Camp, 2 huts (4 beds in each), $5 D.

---

From Marangora, the tarmac Great North Road (A1) descends steeply into the valley of the Zambezi River. Majestic views are revealed, and a magnificent collection of trees grows along the escarpment and on the broad alluvial floor of the valley. The very body fragrance of Africa itself seems to reach out from the valley (especially in May) and embrace the traveller with the earthy, warm new-cut potato odour of the *Phyllanthus reticulatus* shrubs which are then in fruit. Mopane trees cover the valley floor in a dense and sultry forest, with great baobab trees rearing up their sinuous branches like petrified land-octopuses from a weird past.

At 6 km from Marangora the main road reaches the floor of the valley and the turnoff to the Mana Pools Game Reserve. Magnificent baobabs line the road, which leads due north-west across the level floor of the valley. After a further 6 km the road crosses the Nyakasanga River. Twenty-eight kilometres of travel through this wilderness brings the tarmac road to a turnoff leading north for 3 km to the Chirundu Sugar Estate. Half a kilometre ahead there is another tsetse fly control point and the cluster of buildings belonging to the Valley Services – garage, restaurant and chalets. Half a kilometre further on (58 km from Makuti and 344 km from Salisbury), the great north-south trunk road of Africa reaches the banks of the Zambezi, the frontier between Zimbabwe and Zambia. At this point, known as *Chirundu,* from an overlooking eminence on which a man named Tshirundu once built his home in an effort to escape the relentless heat of the valley, the end of the journey up the Great North Road (A1) is reached, as far as this book is concerned. Ahead, beyond the customs barrier, looms the 320-m-long silver arch of the Otto Beit Bridge which spans the turbulent waters of the Zambezi and carries the road on into Zambia. The customs and immigration post at Chirundu is open continuously, day and night.

# KARIBA

The second largest manmade lake in the world, Kariba is reached via the turnoff from the Great North Road (A1) at Makuti (283 km from Salisbury). The road descends steeply into the valley of the Zambezi through heavily wooded, rugged hill country, where many magnificent baobab trees may be seen. As the road descends, so the stifling heat of the valley reaches up to envelop the traveller; consequently, summer is not the time for the average tourist to make the journey. For those who do, drinking water is obtainable 20 km from Makuti and wildlife is visible at all seasons, particularly the many elephants living on the floor of the valley. A tsetse fly control point is situated 20 km further on, and the road reaches the dam wall after a total distance of 76 km from Makuti. The dam wall, spanning the Zambezi River border with Zambia, acts as a bridge between the two countries and there are customs posts on either side. The customs and immigration post at Kariba is open April to September, from 06h00 to 18h00 and October to March from 06h00 to 19h00.

The dam wall of Kariba was completed in 1959 and consists of a double curvature concrete arch with a crest length of 579 m and a height of 128 m. On top of this structure runs a 12-m-wide road. The six flood gates, each 9 m by 9,5 m, have a discharge capacity of 336 000 cusecs. The capacity of the dam is 865 million cubic metres (40 837 000 million gallons) and the surface area is 510 000 ha. Six 100 000-kw turbo-generators on the Zimbabwe side of the dam feed their power through a 1 430-km-long transmission system to various points in Zimbabwe and Zambia. The original project visualised a second set of turbo-generators to be installed on the Zambian side of the dam, with a capacity of 900 000 kw. During normal seasons the spillway gates are open from about mid-December to the end of January. This lowers the level of the dam in order to prepare it for the seasonal influx of floodwaters. Further spillway discharge depends on the scale of flood influx but normal influx is handled by the steady flow of water through the turbines. The average annual inflow to the dam is 49 000 million cubic metres from all sources. Of this, 16 400 million cubic metres is used to drive the turbines; 20 097 million cubic metres is discharged through the spillways and 8 600 million cubic metres is lost through evaporation. The residue is used in increase of storage, lost or discharged through the spillways. Tours of the underground hydro-electric power station of Kariba are conducted at 10h00 and 11h00 on Mondays, Tuesdays, Fridays, Saturdays and Sundays.

The dam was built at the entrance to what the Africans call a *kariba* (rocky gorge). A township for the construction workers was built on a hilltop overlooking the dam and this housed a population of 10 000 workers at the peak of building operations. The total construction cost of the whole project was £78 million. The principal contractors were Impresit Kariba (Pvt) Ltd, of Italy.

The lake, 280 km long by 32 km wide at its maximum width, covers 5 000 square kilometres and has been developed into a major recreational asset for Zimbabwe. Fishing for tiger fish, bream and a variety of other species, provides great sport, while cruising on the dam (more like an inland sea) is popular. Swimming is inadvisable on account of bilharzia and crocodiles, but most of the hotels and camps have swimming pools. Temperature must be taken into account (especially in summer) by those susceptible to heat and the effects of excessive sunburn. April to September are the coolest months, while October and November are the hottest. Boats of many types are available for hire and there is a considerable variety of accommodation available, ranging from air-conditioned luxury to picturesque fishermen's camps.

## Accommodation
★★★ Bumi Hills Safari Lodge, 34 rooms, all with baths. $12,50 – $19 D/B/B. Phone 353.
★ Caribbea Bay Hotel, 42 chalets. $12 – $15 per person. Phone 454.
★★ Cutty Sark Hotel, 65 rooms, all with baths. $11,50 B/B. Phone 322.
★ Kariba Breezes Hotel, 30 rooms, all with baths. $7,50 B/B. Phone 433.
★ Kariba Heights Hotel, 19 rooms, all with baths, or showers. $7,50 B/B. Phone 364.
★ Lake View Inn, 56 rooms, all with baths. $11 – $14 B/B. Phone 411.

## Caravans and camping
★★ Caribbea Bay, 25 sites. $2 D plus 50c D per person.
★ Msuna By the Lake, 30 sites. 75c D per person. 12 chalets, $3,25 D per person.
★★ Mopani Bay Caravan Park, 30 sites. $2 D.

# SALISBURY TO BEIT BRIDGE

From Salisbury the main tarmac road (A4) to the south, leads through park-like country, the grass beautifully green during summer. After 54 km the road passes the small rural centre of *Beatrice* (named after the sister of the pioneer, Henry Barrow), comprising a small motel, garage and store. After a further 46 km the road passes the rural centre of Featherstone and a further 40 km (140 km from Salisbury) brings the road to the village of . . .

# ENKELDOORN

The first European settlers in this area found growing on the site of the village a particularly fine *Acacia robusta* tree, known in Afrikaans as an *enkeldoorn*. From this tree is derived the name of the village which grew as the centre for a prosperous agricultural community.

**Accommodation**
* Enkeldoorn Hotel, 16 rooms, 5 with baths. $6,20 – $7,20 D/B/B. Phone 26.

**Caravans and camping**
Enkeldoorn Town Board Caravan Park, 15 sites. $1 D.

Fifty-one kilometres south of Enkeldoorn, across the grassy savanna, the main road reaches the old mining and railway centre of . . .

# UMVUMA

At Umvuma, the Falcon gold mine flourished for years, working a profitable but very recalcitrant ore. Extracting the gold required a complex chemical recovery plant and noxious fumes were carried out of harm's way up a tall smokestack which still provides a landmark although the mine is no longer working.

Umvuma lies on a river known to the Africans as *Mumvumi* (the place of magic singing). Legend has it that there was a pool there, from which could be heard emanating the sound of singing, drumming and the lowing of cattle.

**Accommodation**
* Falcon Hotel, 12 rooms, 1 with bath. $3,75 – $4,50 room only. Phone 29.

The tarmac road continues from Umvuma, losing altitude gently and passing the rural centre of Chilimazi after 40 km. After a further 60 km the road reaches the town of . . .

# FORT VICTORIA

The oldest European town in Zimbabwe, Fort Victoria has a population of 20 300. When the Pioneer Column made its way up Providential Pass on 13 March 1890, the men were exhilarated by the change of climate and altitude from the low country to the middleveld or intermediate plateau. They made a fortified camp on the site they named *Fort Victoria* in honour of the Queen, and for a few days they marshalled their resources and prepared for the next move forward. The scene, as related by Captain Sir John Willoughby, was reminiscent of an English village fair, with its tents, wagons, flags, and everybody being very jolly and relaxed, playing games and holding contests.

The main Pioneer force moved on after six days, but the men left behind strongly garrisoned the earthwork Fort Victoria and it remained a major staging post on the Pioneer Road to the south. A neat little fort was built to act as a stronghold, parts of which still stand in the centre of the town.

Apart from its importance as an administrative and communications centre, Fort Victoria flourishes on a rich mineral and agricultural industry. In the district, asbestos, beryl, chrome, gold, copper and lithium are worked, while ranches produce slaughter animals which are processed in the town and prepared for railage in a large cold-storage plant. Vast sugar-producing developments in the lowveld have also added to the prosperity of Fort Victoria while the great Kyle Dam, built in the district to provide irrigation water for the sugar project, has added an extra recreational facility to an already important tourist area.

Fort Victoria became a municipality on 6 November 1953 and is a clean, sunny little town, the terminus of the branch railway from Gwelo, and the centre for the famed Zimbabwe Ruins. Spring in Fort Victoria (September and October) sees a vivid display of poinsettias, jacarandas and bougainvillaea.

## Accommodation
** Chevron Hotel, 42 rooms, all with baths. $10,75 B/B. Phone 2054.
** Flamboyant Motel, 46 rooms, all with baths. $9,50 B/B. Phone 2005.

## Caravans and camping
**® Fort Victoria Caravan Park, 30 sites. $1,25 D.

## THE ZIMBABWE RUINS

Twenty-eight kilometres south-east of Fort Victoria lies Great Zimbabwe, one of the most famous ruins in the world. A great deal of nonsense has been written about this most impressive and beautiful complex of ruins. It is therefore necessary to make it quite clear that, apart from in the imagination of numerous writers, journalists and publicity men, not the slightest evidence has ever been found to substantiate any claims that these ruins were built by people other than the same Africans – fragments of the once great Karanga-Rozvi tribal group – who live in the area today. Archaeologists have excavated, prehistorians, historians and ethnologists have researched but, although all of them would have dearly loved to have unearthed a find as glamorous as, for example, the Queen of Sheba's brass brassiere, no such interesting item has ever been found, only the relics – pots, huts and beads – of African people who lived on the site even before the ruins were built.

These ruins are essentially a complex of elaborate stone walls, without mortar or foundation and built to widely different standards of workmanship during the course of several generations of occupants. Within these protective stone walls the inhabitants lived in the conventional mud and thatch huts of Africa, the foundations of which may still be seen. No part of the stone walls was ever roofed or ever built or designed to serve any purpose other than that of a solid, impressive, defensive enclosure. No other similar structures have been found anywhere else in the world outside Zimbabwe and the Northern Transvaal. They represent the primitive Iron Age culture of the Karanga-Rozvi people who entered Zimbabwe from the north sometime after A.D. 500. Developing over the years an industry in the mining of iron and gold, and the architecture of wall building from granite fragments littering the country, they reached a height of power and affluence in the 10th century, and then were toppled during the 19th century when, already weakened by civil strife, they were successfully invaded by powerful tribal groups from the south.

The Karanga-Rozvi people built in Zimbabwe many walled settlements known as *madzim-bahwe* (great stone buildings). The most imposing of these walled structures surrounded the residences of chiefs, while what is known to Europeans as Great Zimbabwe was the residence of the *mambo* (king), the supreme ruler whose title of *Mwana Mutapa* (the lord conquerer) became known to the early Portuguese as the Monomotapa. His kingdom and its gold mines were considered by medieval scholars to be the Ophir of the Bible, and enjoyed a romantic renown.

The site of Great Zimbabwe is one of the finest in Zimbabwe. Standing at the head of the valley of the *Mutirikwi* (the gatherer), a river so named because it gathers to itself many tributaries, Great Zimbabwe was built on a site selected as one of the most delectable of all residences for a monarch in Africa: well watered, always green, fertile soil, a magnificent view, commanding position, and cool, equable climate from the moisture-laden winds whispering up the valley from the Indian Ocean. To the wilderness-dwelling people of Africa the site could only be fit for a king. Proof of his claims to be able to control the rains was verified by the obvious fertility surrounding his residence.

The great hill of Zimbabwe had attracted human settlement from early times. Bushmen had found shelter in its caves, and successive black tribes found this hill to possess remarkable characteristics. Apart from greenness and security, its natural structure made it easy to fortify. Innumerable terraces, passageways, granite boulders and natural platforms suggested a style of architecture. As the population on the hill increased, so men found more room on it by building up additional platforms from the loose rubble lying at its base. When the rubble was exhausted, some primitive genius found that by lighting fires on top of granite, and then pouring cold water over the heated rock, flakes could be obtained of ideal and remarkably uniform size for use in building. These flakes, dressed into size by hammering and piled one on top of the other, produced the walls of Zimbabwe, with over 900 000 of them used in the construction of what Europeans call the Temple.

The so-called Temple ruins of Zimbabwe actually enclosed what was apparently the residence of the king. The chevron pattern on the walls (an emblem of water) indicated his presence as the great national rainmaker. The powerfully impressive conical towers were also probably emblems of the king's masculinity and presence. The ruins on the hill, known to Europeans as the Acropolis, were likely to have been the military stronghold. It was from there also, in a small cave with a singular natural acoustic shape, that the voice of *Mwari* (the Karanga name for God) spoke as an oracle. To supplicants, standing trembling in the valley below, the great booming voice projecting from this cave must have sounded like the voice of doom itself.

The beauty and impressiveness of Great Zimbabwe and the other ruins of Zimbabwe are very vivid. The primeval crudity of their construction imparts a tremendous power. It is strikingly lovely how perfectly they blend with the environment: not only were the granite units once part of the actual landscape, but the close relationship is perpetuated by the builders who, unable to remove obstructions such as isolated boulders, simply incorporated them bodily into the walls. In this way, the entire hill of Zimbabwe becomes part of the construction with odd stairways, passages and walls simply serving to link one natural enclosure or terrace with another.

A visit to Great Zimbabwe is one of the wold's major travel experiences, for there are few places with a more impressive atmosphere. The entire area is splendidly maintained as a national park, with a site museum, and a variety of convenient accommodation, such as bungalows and a caravan park, which allow the visitor the unique opportunity of wandering through the ruins at night – a remarkable experience – and sleeping in the actual area of this colossal wreck of an antique African state.

## Accommodation
★ Great Zimbabwe Ruins Hotel, 35 rooms, all with baths. $8 B/B. Phone Fort Victoria 2274.

## Caravans and camping
★★® Zimbabwe National Park, 100 sites. S1,50 D. Rondawels and chalets, $4 – $5 D.

820

# THE KYLE DAM

Situated at the confluence of the Mutirikwi and Mshangashi rivers, 32 km from Fort Victoria, the Kyle Dam was built to supply irrigation water for the sugar and citrus estates in the lowveld of Zimbabwe. The concrete dam wall, 62 m high and 311 m long, was completed in 1961 and blocks the passage of the united rivers through a narrow gorge between granite hills. The dam is named after a farm which was inundated by the waters (kyle being a Scottish word meaning 'a channel of water').

The 'Y'-shaped lake covers an area of 56 square kilometres with a shoreline about 257 km in circumference.

The dam lies in an attractive park-like setting of hills and forest. A 6 480-ha game reserve is situated on a large peninsula on the northern side of the dam which has been stocked by translocating such game animals as square-lipped rhino (from Zululand), buffalo, kudu, waterbuck, giraffe, sable, zebra, eland and other smaller antelope. Hippos are also present in Lake Kyle. A fish research centre in the game reserve contains an aquaruim and is presided over by a resident biologist.

The dam has been developed into a recreational area with boating, fishing and camping in picturesque surroundings. The granite country of Zimbabwe is one of the chief scenic glories of Africa and the environment of the Kyle Dam is a fine example of this type of landscape. A magnificent variety of trees and plants grow around the verges of the dam, while the whole area is ornamented with piles of granite, balancing rocks and many fanciful stone shapes.

Bushmen were fond of this area and immediately above the rest camp may be seen a perfect example of their rock shelter homes. On top of a granite dome there stands a pile of odd-shaped rocks carefully arranged by nature and bound by the powerful roots of a wild fig tree to make a remarkable shelter. Giant euphorbias stand near by, perhaps (as they do in Zululand) to guard the graves of forgotten chiefs. On the walls of the shelter there is a gallery of paintings. The atmosphere is so tranquil and perfect that it seems as though the Bushmen are just out visiting and will return at any moment, instead of having vanished forever.

Another of these rock shelters is situated a few kilometres away, above the boat club, under cool, shady trees surrounded by a collection of flowering aloes, resurrection plants and ferns. Through the trees the blue waters of the manmade lake may be seen twinkling. Around the old Bushman home all is still, with only the wind and the birds providing life.

## Caravans and camping
★★® Kyle View Caravan and Camping sites, 100 sites. 60c D per person.
Kyle View Chalets, 8 furnished cottages (2 – 5 beds), $4 D per adult.
★★® Kyle Recreational Reserve, 50 sites. 60c D. Chalets, $4 – $5 D.

# THE MUSHANDIKE NATIONAL PARK

Lying 32 km west of Fort Victoria on the road to Shabani, this park covers 12 960 ha around the Mushandike Dam. The dam, renowned for black bass, bream and barbel, provides good fishing. The park is thickly wooded and is inhabited by sable, kudu, waterbuck and numerous smaller antelope. In addition, a fine Bushman rock shelter crowned by a majestic wild fig tree whose roots festoon the rocks, may be seen in this park.

## Caravans and camping
★★® Mushandike Sanctuary, 50 sites. 50c D. Chalets, $4 – $5 D.

Fort Victoria lies on an intermediate terrace plateau, one step in altitude above the low country, one step below the central ridge. Eleven kilometres south of the town, the main tarmac road reaches a small wayside monument marking the top of Providential Pass, so named in August 1890 when Frederick Selous, the renowned hunter who was guiding the Pioneer Column, found by chance this easy natural gateway to the highlands. It is a beautifully wooded pass and the verges of the road have been ornamented with poinsettias and bougainvillaea in many lovely shades.

The road descends the pass and leads for 92 km through a parkland of trees. Turnoffs lead to the Mushandike National Park, Lake Kyle and the Zimbabwe Ruins. After 30 km the road crosses the Tokwe or Tugwi River, the name meaning a river that sweeps away when in flood. A further 30 km brings the road to a turnoff leading eastwards to the sugar cane growing areas of Triangle (82 km); Hippo Valley (113 km) and the Chipinda Pools (161 km). Triangle was the creation of Tom McDougall whose first experimental plantations of sugar cane were planted in the shape of a triangle. He proved the irrigation possiblilities of this part of the low country and commenced a large-scale agricultural industry.

Scenically, this is one of the most spectacular areas of the low country. Huge granite domes surge out of the parkland and in spring the musasa trees provide a lovely spectacle. The Lundi River meanders through the trees and granites. The name *Lundi* is a European corruption of *Runde,* meaning a river subject to great floods. In the dry winter months this river is simply a succession of pools contained in a bed of sand and giant granite boulders. Reeds and handsome trees line the banks, and the scene resembles a still life, with hippos lazing and hardly a sign of movement in the warm air. With the arrival of summer rains, between December and March, the scene is often transformed when the river awakes in sullen fury at being disturbed out of its sleep by the thunder. Great surges of chocolate-coloured water sweep down with a menace and power capable of immense damage.

The road reaches this river 104 km from Fort Victoria. In former years a low-level bridge crossed the river and was frequently inundated by the floods. A pretty little hotel, known as the Rhino Hotel, was built on the banks to shelter travellers caught by the storms and when a river crossing was often delayed for days by the floods. Now a fine high-level bridge spans the river well above the floods. The bridge is named after Stuart Chandler, the pioneer road builder of the country. Down the Lundi River lies the . . .

## GONA RE ZHOU NATIONAL PARK

This national park was created in 1967, largely as the result of the enthusiasm of Allan Wright, who served as District Commissioner of the Nuanetsi area from 1958 to 1968. The name *Gona re Zhou* means 'refuge of the elephant'. The park covers 4 964 square kilometres of very wild country and provides a home for nyala antelope, the very rare King Cheetah (the striped cheetah) and many elephants. *Bvekenya* (Cecil Barnard), the renowned poacher, often hunted in this area and the famous giant elephant known as *Dhlulamithi* (taller than the trees) who features in the book on Barnard's life, *The Ivory Trail,* was shot on the borders of the park in August 1967. Its tusks are rated as the largest ever secured south of the Zambezi. The left tusk weighed 62 kg and the right tusk 48 kg. The park is open from 1 May to 31 October.

### Caravans and camping
Camping sites at Chipinda Pools, Chinguili, Chilojo and Swimuwini, $1,50 D.
Chalets at Swimuwini, $4 – $5 D.

---

From the Lundi River, the main tarmac road continues south through the trees. After 41 km the road crosses the railway line leading to Moçambique near Rutenga station. After a further 20 km the road crosses the Nuanetsi River with a turnoff on the north bank leading for 3 km to the administrative post of Nuanetsi. A further 38 km brings the road to the Bubye or Bubi River, another great hazard to travel in the days of low-level bridges. In the riverine forest on the riverbanks stands the Lion and Elephant Motel.

### Accommodation
★® Lion and Elephant Motel, 22 rooms, all with baths. $7,50 B/B. Phone Nuanetsi 0-1502.

### Caravans and camping
★★® Lion and Elephant Caravan Park, 20 sites. $1,50 D.

---

South of the Bubye River the road stretches through a hot and arid area of mopane trees. Rainfall is a scant 200 mm a year and the heat of summer is relentless. Baobab trees thrive in these harsh conditions, however, and there are many gigantic specimens visible from the road. This is ranching country, where a few game animals may still be seen.

At 76 km from the Bubye River the road joins the main road coming south from Bulawayo and the combined roads then lead for a further 4 km to enter the border village of . . .

## BEIT BRIDGE

This is the principal southern gateway into Zimbabwe from South Africa and consists of a cluster of hotels, garages, stores, administrative and customs buildings standing on the northern side of the Limpopo River. A 475-m-long, 14 span combined road and rail bridge crosses the river into South Africa. Alfred Beit, the mining financier and colleague of Rhodes, on his death on 16 July 1906, bequeathed the bulk of his immense personal fortune to the welfare of Southern Africa. The Beit Bridge, opened in 1929, was built with funds from the estate. The tower on the central pier carries a bronze plaque commemorating Alfred Beit. The customs post is open daily from 06h00 to 20h00.

### Accommodation
★ Beit Bridge Hotel, 21 rooms, $6,60 B/B. Phone 14.
★★® Peter's Motel, 39 rooms, all with baths. $8,35 B/B. Phone 21.

### Caravans and camping
★★® Doorstop Caravan Park, 15 sites. $1,50 D.

## Chapter Forty-two

# THE NDEBELE COUNTRY

### BULAWAYO

With a population of 335 900, Bulawayo is the administrative centre of Matabeleland, home of the Ndebele people. The country's principal railway junction and marshalling yard, the city is a spacious, sunny and friendly place, lying 1 356 m above sea level on the plateau summit of the central ridge of Zimbabwe.

The romantic history of Bulawayo began in November 1837, at the famous Nine Day Battle in the Transvaal, when the Voortrekkers under Hendrik Potgieter defeated Mzilikazi and his following, who were known to the Sotho people as *maTebele* (refugees or runaways). Mzilikazi, already a runaway from Zululand, led his people northwards in search of a new home. After a long period of wandering in the wilderness, the maTebele or *Ndebele* as they called themselves in their own Zulu language, found their way to the western end of the central ridge forming the watershed between the Limpopo and Zambezi rivers. There they settled, flourishing in the cool, healthy air, and accumulating great herds of cattle by raiding the earlier inhabitants who were contemptuously referred to by the Ndebele as *maShona* (bankrupt people).

Mzilikazi built his capital, *Hlahlandlela* (where the pathway is cut), close to the site of modern Bulawayo. On his death in 1868 his son Lobengula, after some argument, succeeded to the leadership of the Ndebele. In 1872 the young king built a new capital for himself which he named *kwaBulawayo* (place of the man who was killed), in the sense that he considered himself as having been 'killed' or persecuted by the opposition of some of the tribe to his succession to power. In Zululand the renowned chief, Shaka, had also given his capital this name, for the same reason.

This was the beginning of the modern city. The original Bulawayo of African-type huts was dynamited and set on fire by the Ndebele in 1893 when they were conquered by the Europeans. A new Bulawayo was laid out on the site by Dr Jameson, and it grew with phenomenal speed as a boom town of prospectors and land speculators rushing to explore the riches of what they called Matabeleland. For a while it was hoped that the place would prove to be a second Johannesburg. The bubble burst in 1895, however, but sufficient gold had been found in the area, and the pastoral and agricultural richness of the locality had been proved to such an extent that the future of the town was secure.

The Matabele Rebellion of 1896 caused a setback, with Bulawayo in the centre of the uprising. The market square was hastily converted into a fortified area in which the 800 women and children of the town were concentrated. Some gruesome murders occurred in the surrounding countryside, resulting in the deaths of 146 Europeans and the disappearance of a further 58, but Bulawayo itself was never attacked. A relief force from South Africa soon reached it and the little town was jammed with a crowd of men whose characters were often as picturesque as their choice of uniform: Cecil Rhodes; Baden-Powell (of Boy Scout fame); Johan Colenbrander, the renowned frontiersman; prospectors such as Frank Lewis and Orlando Baragwanath; and innumerable other individuals who have played a not insignificant part in the stormy story of Southern Africa, all rallied to the subjugation of the Ndebele.

The most spectacular fighting took place in the granite wilderness of the Matobo Hills outside Bulawayo, where the rebels took refuge so successfully that the whole disturbance was only effectively ended after Cecil Rhodes held his four famous *indabas* (conferences) with the leaders of the Ndebele and agreed to several improvements in their administration and treatment.

The termination of the rebellion saw Bulawayo once again experiencing a surge of progress. The railway line from South Africa across Botswana, built during the rebellion at the record speed of 640 km in 400 days, reached Bulawayo on 19 October 1897, and from there was extended east to Salisbury and north to the great coalfields at Wankie, and on to the Zambezi River. Cattle ranching developed at the same time and especially after the Anglo-Boer War, mining activity expanded considerably when the British South Africa Company (which at the time had a controlling charter over Rhodesia) relaxed its demands for 50 per cent of the profits of any mines and allowed small workers a chance of exploiting the innumerable reef outcrops, and the ancient workings of early African miners.

Substantial industrial development has in recent years also come to Bulawayo. Becoming a city in 1943, it is today a busy place as well as a centre for communications and tourism. Government House, north of the city, occupies the original site of Lobengula's country residence. The tree which shaded indabas in the royal cattle corral, still stands.

The city is notable for its wide streets and spacious planning. Amenities include two adjoining parks covering 45 ha. One of them, Centenary Park, contains a modern theatre and the fine Colosseum-style building of the National Museum which is open Mondays to Saturdays from 10h00 to 17h00; on Sundays from 14h30 to 17h00.

The adjoining Central Park, apart from being graced by a handsome variety of trees and magnificent flowers, contains one of the finest caravan parks in Southern Africa. The Borrow Street swimming bath, one of four in Bulawayo, is situated close to the caravan park. In Central Park stands one of the finest illuminated fountains in Southern Africa, inaugurated on 4 November 1968 to mark the 75th anniversary of the city. The fountain is a skilfully designed, constantly changing pattern of water and colour, a notable feature being a rainbow which appears in the morning light.

The civic centre of Bulawayo, built on the site in the market square which was used as a stronghold during the rebellion, contains among other things, the original of the often copied painting of Wilson's last stand. The well which supplied water to the market square stronghold is preserved in the garden and was overlooked by a fine statue of Sir Charles Coghlan, the first Premier of what was then Rhodesia. Another particularly impressive statue, that of Rhodes, modelled from life, stood at the intersection of Eighth Avenue and Main Street.

At Hillside Dam, 6 km south of Bulawayo, there is a nature reserve, aviary and picnic site while the dam itself offers fishing and boating opportunities.

Bulawayo is a spacious, sunny city surrounded by plenty of open land to allow for expansion. The atmosphere is reminiscent of a large agricultural centre which occasionally comes to life, but normally experiences long spells of quiet. Handsome trees and gardens are an admirable feature with the months of September and October being particularly lovely when jacarandas and bougainvillaea are in full bloom.

## Accommodation
* Bee Gee Hotel, 26 rooms, 6 with baths. $4 – $5. B/B. Phone 35452.
** Cecil Hotel, 55 rooms, 47 with baths. $8,67  B/B. Phone 60295.
*** Holiday Inn, 152 rooms, all with baths. $15 single, room only. $17 double, room only. Phone 72464.
* Lido Hotel, 10 rooms, $4,50. B/B. Phone 26806.
* Palace Hotel, 26 rooms, 12 with baths. $6,50 – $7,50 B/B. Phone 64294.
* Plaza Hotel, 26 rooms, 4 with baths. $5,75 – $7,50 B/B. Phone 64281.
* Rhodes Matopos Hotel, 10 rooms, $4,50 – $6 B/B. Phone 883435.
** Rio Hotel, 24 rooms, all with baths or showers. $7,50 B/B. Phone 881384.

**Caravans and camping**

## THE KHAMI RUINS AND THE MATOBO HILLS

The bush-covered countryside around Bulawayo is a spacious wilderness containing many features of considerable interest. The beauty of this area culminates in the great stronghold of granite domes – one of the most impressive landscapes to be seen anywhere on earth – known to the Africans as the *Matobo* (corrupted by Europeans into the Matopos).

Twenty-two kilometres west of Bulawayo, on a hillock overlooking the Khami River, lies the fascinating pile of ancient stone walls and terraces known as the Khami Ruins. This picturesque complex of ruins is all that remains of one of the most considerable stone-walled settlements of prehistoric Rhodesia.

Whoever selected the site for this settlement had excellent taste: surrounded by a lovely parkland, the settlement looks out over a particularly pleasant stretch of the Khami River. According to tradition, this walled settlement was one of the last to be inhabited in Rhodesia. The Rozvi section of the Karanga tribe were reputed to have built it and many interesting relics of their occupation have been found, including indications of the presence of a Portuguese missionary. The ruins are extensive, and a day's exploration and picnicking in so remarkable and agreeable a place, is not wasted.

There are several magnificent drives, many fine walks, and numerous recreational possibilities for visitors around the complex of granite domes known as the Matobo. The road from Bulawayo leads directly over an acacia-covered plain so level that, from the city, the traveller is surprised to see the first signs of the range looming up ahead. At this point the tarmac road passes the Matobo Dam, where there is a hotel, and boating and fishing opportunities. A further 3 km takes the road past a turnoff to the Matobo Agricultural Research Station. Three kilometres (32 km from Bulawayo) brings the road to the entrance of . . .

## THE MATOBO NATIONAL PARK

This national park covers an area of 928 ha and contains some of the most majestic granite scenery to be seen anywhere on earth. It is here that natural erosion has stripped away the central ridge of Zimbabwe and revealed an 80-km-long concentration of outcrops of granite masses estimated from the disintegration of radio-active elements as being over 3 000 million years old. These old granites, surging up from the secret depths of the earth, are part of the Fundamental or Basement Complex, the earliest of all geological systems.

The extraordinary shapes – domes, whalebacks, rock castles and weird fragments – which constitute the complex, as well as the beauty and unique atmosphere of the area, are so fascinating that the human imagination cannot avoid being deeply impressed. Mzilikazi, the Ndebele ruler, is said to have been particularly fond of the area. With a degree of humour and perspicacity he likened the granites to an assembly of elders, devising the apt name of *Matobo* (the bald heads). The earlier Karanga tribespeople had also sensed the primeval power of the ancient granites. Their priests practised there the worship of *Mwari* (God), presiding over an oracle in one of the great caves.

At the end of the rebellion of 1896, Rhodes also found himself fascinated by the wonderful granites. Riding in the area at the time of the last great indaba with the Ndebele, he found by chance the colossal dome named *Marindidzimu* (the haunt of the ancestral spirits). The view from the top and the serene atmosphere of forgotten ages stretching back to the very birth of the earth, gave him tremendous intellectual excitement.

'The peacefulness of it,' he said to his companions. 'The chaotic grandeur of it all. I call this one of the world's views. It brings home to me how very small we all are.'

He sat down in the shadow of a boulder, and added simply: 'I shall be buried here, looking in that direction.' (He pointed north).

After his death at Muizenberg in the Cape on 26 March 1902, he was buried on the summit of this gigantic rock mass, looking out, as expressed by his friend Kipling, in his poem *The Burial*:

'*Across the world he won,*
*The granite of the ancient north,*
*Great spaces washed with sun.*'

Rhodes had already acquired a considerable personal landholding on the verge of the Matobo which he bequeathed to the people of Zimbabwe. The British South Africa Company added to this the area including Rhodes's burial hill of Marindidzimu (World's View): in this way the present national park had its beginning.

Close to Rhodes's grave, on top of the hill, lie the graves of his stormy petrel colleague Sir Leander Starr Jameson (who died in London on 26 November 1917), and Sir Charles Coghlan, first Prime Minister of Rhodesia, who died on 14 August 1930. A slightly incongruous monument of Grecian design contains the remains of Major Allan Wilson and his men who lost their lives in the persuit of Lobengula when the latter's country was occupied in December 1893.

Many of the caves in the Matobo contain superb galleries of Bushman paintings. Especially notable are the caves named Silozwane, Bambata, Gulubahwe, Nswatugi, Pomongwe, Amadizimba, and the rock shelter known as the White Rhino Shelter. All are accessible and thoroughly worth visiting, not only for their prehistoric art (mainly Latter Stone Age), but also for the singular beauty of their situations, each being different from the other in the setting of the granite wilderness.

The fauna of the area includes sable antelope, baboons, monkeys, and numerous small antelope and other animals. A 1 012-ha game park has been created in the western portion of the Matobo around the Chintampa Dam and this contains white and black rhino, giraffe, eland, wildebeest, zebra, kudu, sable and buffalo, as well as many varieties of smaller game. Bird life throughout the national park is rich in variety and quantity. Lizards and reptiles also flourish in the area and all visitors to Rhodes's grave notice the brilliantly coloured rock lizards *(Platysaurus capensis)* which abound there and are extremely tame. They are, incidentally, quite harmless. The game park is open daily from sunrise to sunset.

Many handsome trees grow in the area. Especially notable are the musasas *(Brachystegia speciformis)*, brilliantly coloured in spring; the kaffirbooms *(Erythrina caffra)* whose blossoms are a gorgeous blood-red; the paper trees *(Commiphora marlothi)* with their peeling bark; the candelabras *(Euphorbia ingens);* the wild figs, and many others. Ground orchids, ferns and flowering plants make the Matobo a garden of infinite variety of shape and colour.

This wonderful national park is well served with roads, paths, picnic sites and rest camps.

## Caravans and camping
National Park Authority (Maleme Dam), 20 chalets, $3 – $5 D. 2-ha caravan and camping site, $1,50 D.

Mpopoma Dam, 2-ha caravan and camping site, $1,50 D.
Mtshelele Dam, 4-ha caravan and camping site, $1,50 D.
Toghwana Dam, 2-ha caravan and camping site, $1,50 D.

# BULAWAYO TO BEIT BRIDGE

From Bulawayo, the road known as A6 leads south-east for 27 km over the grassy summit of the central plateau ridge of Zimbabwe. Reaching the edge of the escarpment, it makes a steady descent over 6 km from the 1 370-m level of the plateau to the 1 160-m level of the acacia-covered middleveld.

Eight kilometres from the bottom of the pass, the road passes through the small rural and railway centre of Essexvale (41 km from Bulawayo) pleasantly situated in rugged country, with the Ncema Dam (headquarters of the Bulawayo Power Boat Club) 15 km away, and the popular picnic area of the Nyankuni Dam, 27 km away.

### Accommodation
★ Essexvale Hotel, 4 chalets, 6 rooms, 2 with baths. $10 – $14 room only. Phone 303.

Fifteen kilometres south of Essexvale there is a turnoff west leading to the Rhodes indaba site (16 km), and the picnic site of *Diana's Pool* (18 km), named after Diana Richardson, wife of a former district commissioner. The main tarmac road continues south, gradually losing altitude through well-wooded country dominated by handsome granite domes and whalebacks. Twenty-three kilometres from Essexvale (64 km from Bulawayo) the road reaches a prominent specimen of these granite domes, known as *Balla Balla,* from the colour and stripes on its slopes resembling those of the antelope of that name (the greater kudu). From here a main road (A9) stretches east for 33 km to Filabusi, an old gold mining centre, to the asbestos mining centre of Shabani, and to Fort Victoria (224 km).

### Accommodation
★ Balla Balla Hotel, 10 rooms, $7,50 D/B/B. Phone 25525.

The main tarmac road (A6) continues southwards through impressively beautiful granite dome country, where many fine trees grow and the views are picturesque. At 62 km from Balla Balla the road reaches the village of *Gwanda,* named after a thorny type of grassy shrub growing there. Gwanda lies 985 m above sea level (375 m below Bulawayo), on a warm, densely bushed plain. From here, a scenic gravel road, practical only in dry weather, leads for 120 km through the Matobo area to Bulawayo. Another gravel road, branching off south from Gwanda, leads for 140 km to the site of the old Pioneer fort at Tuli.

### Accommodation
★ Hardy's Inn, 14 rooms, 8 with baths. $10,50 D/B/B. Phone 476.

### Caravans and camping
★ Gwanda Caravan Park, 12 sites. $1,50 D.

The main tarmac road (A6) swings eastwards from Gwanda and traverses a granite land-scape considerably marked by the signs – active and extinct – of mining, for this has always been a great area for the famous Rhodesian type of enterprise known as a 'small working'. Innumerable little gold mines have flourished here, where many hardy and interesting characters have either made small fortunes, or quietly gone bankrupt, labouring beneath the sun.

Twenty-five kilometres from Gwanda the road reaches Colleen Bawn, where the large cement works of the United Portland Cement Company are situated. In Gaelic, *colleen bawn* means 'white girl'. The name was given to the limestone claims registered by John Daly on 28 March 1895.

The main tarmac road continues through hilly country, swinging south past the rail siding of Jessie with its hotel (100 km from Bulawayo), and the halfway beacon to Beit Bridge. The bric-à-brac of mining lies scattered among the hills. One kilometre south of the hotel lie the workings of the Lanninhurst Mine, while a further 7 km brings the road to the terminus of the branch railway from Bulawayo at *West Nicholson,* where the buildings of Messrs Liebigs Meat Factory dominate the scene and the memory of Andy Nicholson, an old-time prospector, is preserved by the name.

### Accommodation
* Halfway Hotel (Jessie), 7 rooms, $4,50 B/B. Phone 00822.
* Tod's Hotel (West Nicholson), 15 rooms, 6 with baths. $6 – $7,50 B/B. Phone 0-1912.

The road is now 169 km from Bulawayo. It crosses the Mzingwani River by means of a fine bridge stretching high above the tremendous floods which sweep down during the rainy season. In winter, however, the river is almost dry and little more than a chain of pools. The road leads on southwards, gradually losing altitude through mopane bush country. After 28 km the road passes Tod's Hotel. An interesting point is reached 20 km further south when the road crosses the route of the original trail blazed by the Pioneers on their way to occupy Mashonaland in 1890. The trail has long since been overgrown, but the crossing place is marked.

The modern road continues southwards through a hot wilderness of mopane trees – ranching and game country, where signs warn of the presence of wild animals. At 98 km (320 km from Bulawayo) the road reaches Beit Bridge, 500 m above sea level, on the Limpopo River frontier with South Africa. Here the customs and immigration authorities provide a service daily from 06h00 to 20h00. Beit Bridge is described on page 823.

## BULAWAYO TO PLUMTREE

From Bulawayo, the main tarmac road (A7) leading west to the Botswana border at Plumtree, makes its way out of the city through the industrial suburb of Belmont, and the residential suburbs of Donnington and Bellevue. After 6 km the road leaves the built-up area and continues across the acacia-bush plateau.

At 26 km from the city a turnoff south leads to the Matobo area and the Cyrene Mission (3 km), famous as a centre for African art. Nine kilometres further on (39 km from Bulawayo), the road passes the small railway centre of Figtree.

### Accommodation
* Figree Hotel, 4 rooms, $6,50 B/B. Phone 1511.

Keeping company with the railway line, the main road proceeds westwards for a further 32 km reaching the rural and railway centre of Marula. From here a turnoff leads south for 26 km through attractively rugged bush and granite country to the Mangwe Pass, the original main route of entry for travellers in the adventurous days when Mzilikazi and his son Lobengula ruled the Ndebele country.

A further 9 km of travel west brings the main road to a turnoff south to a place with the rather resonant name of Mphoeings. A further 24 km to the west, the road reaches the village of Plumtree with its cluster of shops, hotel, school, and railway buildings. From here the road leads for a further 2 km, reaching the customs and immigration post on the border with

*Overleaf: The queen of all waterfalls and one of nature's greatest wonders;* Mosi o a Thunya, *the smoke that rises.*

Botswana (105 km from Bulawayo). The customs post is open daily from 06h00 to 13h00; 14h00 to 18h30 and 19h00 to 20h00.

**Accommodation**
* ★ Plumtree Hotel, 10 rooms, $6,60 B/B. Phone 16.

# BULAWAYO TO SALISBURY

From Bulawayo, the main all-tarmac road (A5) leads north-east across the acacia-covered summit of the central plateau ridge of Zimbabwe. Twelve kilometres from the city, the road passes the factory of the United Portland Cement Company, and 3 km beyond it, the turnoff to the Llewellyn Barracks of the Zimbabwe army.

Immediately to the north of the road may be seen the low, flat-topped hill known as *Ntaba yezinDuna* (the hill of the headmen). It was there, according to tradition, that Mzilikazi settled accounts with a group of headmen who had revealed a tendency to repudiate his rule. All of them were killed there, except one, Dambisamahubo, who escaped to the east and cursed the Ndebele. Even today, when the dry east wind blows away the sorely needed rain clouds, the curse of Dambisamahubo is said to be the cause.

The main tarmac road continues north-eastwards across a grassy savanna, scattered with trees and clumps of bush. The road and railway keep close company, for the central ridge is narrow and falls away sharply to the low country on the north and south.

At 48 km from Bulawayo a turnoff leads south-eastwards for 40 km to the Dhlo-Dhlo Ruins, one of the most beautifully constructed ancient ruins of Zimbabwe. The interesting Regina Ruins at Zinjanja may also be reached from this road, as well as the remnants of Fort Rixon, built on the farm of Theodore Rixon during the rebellion. The main tarmac road (A5) continues north-eastwards. At 82 km from Bulawayo it passes the small rail centre of Insiza and after a further 17 km reaches the small rail centre of Shangani, where another turnoff leads to the Dhlo-Dhlo Ruins (20 km). The Shangani River is crossed 8 km further on. At an ill-fated point about 192 km downstream, Allan Wilson and his men, pursuing Lobengula in 1893, came to a most unfortunate end.

A further 9 km brings the main road to a turnoff leading for 18 km to the beautifully situated ruins known as Nalatale. These ruins of a walled settlement, together with the nearby Dhlo-Dhlo Ruins, are probably the most attractive in Zimbabwe and although small and considerably damaged by treasure-seeking vandals, are thoroughly worth seeing.

Forty-eight kilometres north-east of the turnoff to Nalatale, the main tarmac road (A5), 168 km from Bulawayo reaches the city of . . .

# GWELO

The principal centre of the midlands of Zimbabwe, Gwelo became a city on 1 October 1971 and has a population of 68 200. It is a clean and neatly laid out place built around Gwelo Koppie, a long, low hill, on top of which stands a tall radio mast. The name Gwelo originates from the *Gweru* (dry) River which flows through the centre of the town. Lying 320 m above sea level the place enjoys a pleasantly warm summer and a winter cold enough to waken anyone who might have gone to sleep during the sultry days.

Gwelo is an army and air force training centre, as well as an important railway junction, with branch lines to Fort Victoria and Selukwe. A variety of industries operate in the city which is a busy place, with a modern shopping area and such amenities as a handsome public park. Gardens and flowers flourish in the area, and the attractive little municipal office block boasts a notable garden of roses.

Twenty-eight kilometres south of Gwelo, on the edge of the escarpment, lies the chrome mining centre of Selukwe. A drive to this picturesque mining town is strongly recommended, especially in spring. The musasa trees growing in that part of Zimbabwe attain such brilliance of colour – red, plum, yellow – and occur in such profusion, that the spectacle is overwhelming. May is the month for poinsettias, when an immense variety of colours may be seen. In November the poincianas or flamboyant trees are in full bloom; in September and October, roses, bougainvillaea and jacarandas reach perfection.

## Accommodation
★★ Cecil Hotel, 46 rooms, 40 with baths. $9,50 B/B. Phone 2863.
★ Grand Hotel, 15 rooms, $4,75 B/B. Phone Selukwe 372.
★★★ Midlands Hotel, 52 rooms, 44 with baths. $9 – $11 B/B. Phone 2581.

## Caravans and camping
★® Ferny Creek (Selukwe), a pretty recreational area with a natural swimming pool. 3 rondawels (2 beds in each), $2 D. 75 caravan sites, $1,50 D.
★ Gwelo Caravan Park, 15 sites. $1,50 D.

From Gwelo, the main tarmac road (A5) leads northwards through dense bush country, gently losing altitude. Thirty-two kilometres from Gwelo the road passes the workings of the Connemara gold mine and 3 km further on, the small rural centre of Hunters Road. The area known as *Battlefields* was named after the number of mining claims in the vicinity, all of which were named after famous battles.

The main road continues north. At 48 km from Gwelo it bridges over the river pleasantly known to the Africans as the *Hwe Hwe* (or *Kwe Kwe),* from the sound made there at night by a multitude of frogs. A further 8 km brings the road to the turnoff west leading for 6 km to the works of *Riscom* (Rhodesian Iron and Steel Commission). Eight kilometres further on (63 km from Gwelo) the road reaches the town of . . .

# QUE QUE

The name of *Que Que* is a European corruption of the name of the *Hwe Hwe* River which the road crosses 16 km before the town.

A centre for a long established mining industry in gold, chrome, iron and lime, Que Que had its start in 1890 when a prospector, E. T. Pearson, pegged an ancient gold working shown to him by a local African. Pearson named the outcrop the Phoenix Reef. A second prospector, Schakula by name, pegged a second outcrop 450 m away, which he named the Globe Reef. The two blocks of claims were bought in 1894 by L. G. Phillips, and combined into what became one of the best known and most profitable gold mines in what was then Rhodesia, the Globe and Phoenix Mine, which yielded 28 g of gold for every ton of ore mined.

Que Que was the offspring of the two mines in the form of a commercial and administrative centre. It is a compact little town of 51 500 people and its streets are attractively planted with flame trees and bougainvillaea of numerous colour and variety.

Recreational areas for the town are situated at the dam known as Dutchman's Pool, on the Sebakwe River; the oft-photographed Sebakwe Poort; and on the Umvuma road, where the 9 000-ha Sebakwe National Park has been developed around the Sebakwe Dam. Facilities include boating, fishing, bungalows and a caravan and camping site.

## Accommodation
★ Phoenix Hotel, 22 rooms, $6,45 B/B. Phone 2141.
★★ Que Que Hotel, 48 rooms, all with baths. $9,75 B/B. Phone 2387.
★ Sebakwe Hotel, 27 rooms, 9 with baths. $7,75 – $8,80 B/B. Phone 2981.

### Caravan and camping
★★ Que Que Municipal Caravan Park, 30 sites. $1,50 D.

From Que Que, the main tarmac road (A5) continues northwards. Nine kilometres from the town the road crosses the river known as the *Sebakwe* (from *Tshibagwe,* a place of maize). The landscape is a densely wooded plain, the impression of a parkland being heightened by the consideration of the roads department in planting along the wayside, patches of such flowering shrubs as poinsettia and bougainvillaea, the vivid colours of which provide a contrast to the green of the forest.

Thirty-one kilometres from Que Que, the road crosses the Umniati River (a corruption from *Munyati,* meaning 'the river of buffaloes'). This river has always played an important part in the history of Zimbabwe. The great basin which forms its watershed is not only scarred with the signs of considerable prehistoric mining activity, but is also the site of many of the richest mines in modern Zimbabwe. One kilometre downriver from the road bridge, stands the 140 000 kw Umniati Power Station of the Electricity Supply Commission which draws its water from the river.

Eight kilometres further on a turnoff east leads for 67 km to the Ngezi National Park, a 10 125-ha recreational area created around a dam on the Ngezi River. Zebra, sable, water-buck, kudu, and other antelope inhabit the park, as well as hippos. Fishing and boating are pleasant. Accommodation is provided in cottages ($6,75 D) and there is a caravan park ($1,50 D).

---

Eighteen kilometres beyond this turnoff the main tarmac road (A5) crosses the Msweswe River (from *Muzvezve,* meaning 'a narrow river') and 16 km beyond this point (73 km from Que Que) reaches the town of . . .

## GATOOMA

With a population of 48 500, Gatooma is a mining and textile centre. Deposits of nickel, chrome, magnesite and iron are found in the area, while gold production amounts to nearly 50 per cent of the total output of Zimbabwe, with the largest mine in the country, the Cam and Motor, situated 5 km east of the town. The town, whose name derives from a Tonka chief, Kaduma, who once lived there, had its start in 1906 when a Mr Godwin built a hut alongside the Bulawayo-Salisbury railway line and set up business as a forwarding agent. The following year the place acquired a village management board, and in 1917 became a municipality.

Gatooma is a busy agricultural centre, where some notably fine bulls are bred. The Cotton Industries Board spinning mill is situated there, with 42 000 spindles producing cotton and rayon yarns, and cotton wool. An agricultural research station stands on the town common-age.

A recreational area for the people of Gatooma has been created around the Pasi Dam, 15 km away, where there are picnic sites, and fishing opportunities for a variety of indigenous fish.

### Accommodation
★★ Gatooma Motel, 57 rooms, 24 with baths. $9,31 – $10,31 B/B. Phone 2604.
★ Specks Hotel, 24 rooms, 12 with baths. $6,50 – $7,75 B/B. Phone 2003.

### Caravans and camping
★ Hippo Caravan Park (John Mack Lake), 50 sites. $1,75 D.

From Gatooma the main tarmac road (A5) continues north-eastwards, passing the factory of Messrs Gatooma Textiles Ltd, and after 16 km, a turnoff east, leading to the mining centre of Eiffel Flats (12 km).

The main tarmac road crosses flat savanna, maize, cotton and cattle country. At 33 km from Gatooma the road passes through the small rural centre of Hartley, with a turnoff north leading to Sinoia (94 km). The main road then veers eastwards, traversing level agricultural and savanna country, and crossing the Mfuli River (from *Mumvuri,* a river of shade), after 8 km. At 67 km from Gatooma, the small rural centre named after the famous hunter, Frederick Selous, is passed.

### Accommodation
* Hartley Hotel, 18 rooms, 7 with baths. $6,10 – $6,60 B/B. Phone 223.
* Halfway Hotel (Selous), 4 rooms, 2 with baths. $4,50 – $5,50 B/B. Phone 291.

The fine thick, red-coloured soil, combined with the green foliage, maize fields, and deep blue skies of this part of Zimbabwe, provide a scene of vivid colour. At 35 km from Selous the main road passes the industrial township of Norton, where paper and agricultural machinery is produced. *Norton* was named after Joseph Norton, first owner of the farm, who was murdered in the Mashona Rebellion.

The road now finds a way alongside a ridge of hills lying to the south and east. After 7 km the Hunyani River (from *Mhanyami,* meaning 'a place of high land') is crossed, and a turnoff south is passed which leads to the wall of the Lake McIlwaine Dam and the Robert McIlwaine National Park (see page 811). Five kilometres further on there is another turn, to Lake McIlwaine and the Hunyani Hills Hotel. A third turnoff, close to the Salisbury Motel, 11 km further on, also leads to Lake McIlwaine, the tarmac road is now approaching the capital city of Zimbabwe and, passing through the area of the Warren Hills (attractive park-like country), enters the city of Salisbury, 144 km from Gatooma.

## WANKIE AND THE FALLS

The finely made all-tarmac road known as A8 leads through the northern suburbs of Bulawayo and gradually begins to descend from the central ridge of the country on to the flat, forest-covered world of Kalahari sands. The road stretches north through this great primeval parkland, with few features to be seen save an occasional watercourse, but the trees, tall and varied, provide many a pleasant view down green and silent aisles.

Signs periodically warn the traveller to beware of wild animals, but these creatures normally keep away from the road. Human beings also are seldom seen in what is essentially a world of trees: mopane, acacia, teak, brachystegia, and many more. Small trading centres at places such as the Bubi River (175 km) and Halfway House (225 km) provide landmarks. At 249 km from Bulawayo, the road reaches the atmospheric and pleasant Gwaai River Hotel.

### Accommodation
* Gwaai River Hotel, 23 rooms, all with baths or showers. $5,75 B/B. Phone Dett 00-104.

Eight kilometres beyond this hotel there is a tarmac turnoff leading for 24 km to the entrance of . . .

## THE WANKIE NATIONAL PARK

This great national park, 15 000 square kilometres is extent, is unsurpassed by any other game sanctuary in the world. Nowhere else may a larger variety of animal life be seen, and in numbers which make it impossible for visitors, even on the shortest stay, to be disappointed. Pleasant camps, good roads, congenial atmosphere, an intelligent and courteous staff, and game-viewing platforms at several waterholes, all contribute to the success of the park.

It was in 1928 that the Rhodesian Government, spurred on by the enthusiasm of such members of the Legislative Assembly as Major W. J. Boggie, declared as a reserve what was the last principal retreat of game animals left in Rhodesia not under pressure from human population. In September 1928, Ted Davison, a 22-year-old official employed at the time on tsetse fly control, was offered the appointment as first warden. He accepted with alacrity and, in the 33 years he remained in charge of the reserve, Ted Davison developed it to its full grandeur as a great national park. His name will forever be identified with it.

Davison found the reserve in a completely wild state, without roads or pathways, and only occasionally penetrated by hunting parties of Bushmen and Europeans. Visually it was an enormous parkland, exceedingly flat and sandy for most of its area, but hilly and stony in the north. In this part an odd recluse by the name of H. G. Robins had made his home, complete with an astronomical telescope mounted on a tower. On his death he bequeathed his block of farms to the national park and *Robins Camp* now houses visitors around his original home and observation tower.

The most remarkable physical features of the park are the shallow pans (lakelets), and the number of natural salt licks (sodium and lime), which attract the game animals from the heart of the adjoining Kalahari wilderness.

The pans comprise one of the natural wonders of Southern Africa. Most of them are 20 m to 30 m in diameter and, when full after the rainy season, reach a depth of up to 1 m. Strangely enough, they have been created by ants and the wildlife itself. Ants, building ant heaps, began the process by bringing to the surface the mineral salts such as lime, which in turn attracted the wild animals (especially elephants) who have a particular craving for these salts. Eating the ant heaps to obtain the salts, the wild animals form depressions into which the rain water collects. The depressions are constantly expanded by the animals eating more of the lime-flavoured soil, drinking the water churned into mud, and carrying the mud away on their hides after wallowing in it.

The largest pans have formed in the area of richest lime deposit such as at Main Camp, Kennedy, Ngwashli and Ngamo and the lime-flavoured water attracts heavy concentrations of wildlife. Observation platforms built at some of the pans (Nyamandlovu and Guvulala) allow visitors the pleasure of watching on moonlit nights an endless procession of game coming to drink, bath, and occasionally ambush one another in bitter dramas of life and death.

The original Wankie Game Reserve was proclaimed a national park on 27 January 1950, and from that time on it was developed as a major conservation and tourist asset. Today, three camps – Main, Robins and Sinamatela – provide a variety of accommodation. Good roads lead to most of the interesting places in the park, and the population of game animals, protected and supplied with reliable permanent watering places by means of boreholes augmenting the natural supply in some of the pans, has increased to a spectacular extent.

Elephant (about 7 000) as well as buffalo are particularly numerous in the park, tremendous herds of which may be seen, especially at the pans during their habitual drinking time between 16h00 and 21h00. Eland also drink at this time while zebra, giraffe and sable drink from 16h00 to 19h00, and wildebeest at night and in the morning. Roan, sable and kudu frequent the pans during the daytime and carnivora – lion, leopard and cheetah – drink in the early morning.

Herds of 3 000 or more buffalo and several hundred elephant may often be seen in Wankie. The superb sable antelope and the kudu, surely the most handsomely horned of all game animals, are numerous. Gemsbok (oryx), impala, numerous smaller antelope varieties, warthogs, baboons, wild dogs, jackals, hyenas (spotted and brown), black rhino, and many smaller animals, may also be seen. Tsessebe and hartebeest are also present but are rare.

The pans attract a great concentration of varied bird life, especially duck species, during the rainy seasons.

Main Camp, Sinamatela Camp, and the north-eastern part of the park, are open throughout the year. The rest of the park and the camp at Robins, is open from 1 June to 31 October. The gates are open from sunrise to sunset. Caravans must be left in the camps, which are individually accessible by separate approach roads from the main Bulawayo-Falls road. Winter is the best season to visit the park when the wild animals concentrate around the waterholes and pans. In summer the park is beautifully green but very hot and seasonal rains allow the wild animals to scatter, as a result of which they are not easily seen.

An excellent road leads for 145 km through the park from Main Camp to Robin's Camp, and thence out of the park for 68 km to the main Bulawayo-Falls road at Matetsi. Apart from this main road, there are at present about 400 km of game-viewing roads open to the public. Only the northern portion of the park has so far been developed for tourists. The western border of the park lies on the frontier with Botswana, where an enormous wilderness area continues deep into the Kalahari, providing safari parties with a field of unparalleled adventure, game viewing and sport. Controlled hunting during the period May to September is also permitted in areas north and east of the Wankie National Park.

## Accommodation
★★★® Main, Nantwich, Robins and Sinamatela camps: Chalets, cottages and lodges, $3 – $8,50 D.

## Caravans and camping
Sites, $1,50 D.

On the approach road to the Wankie National Park from the main Bulawayo-Falls road is situated the Wankie Safari Lodge and, in the small rail centre of Dett, the Game Reserve Hotel.

## Accommodation
★ Game Reserve Hotel, 12 rooms, 7 with baths. $7 – $8,50 B/B. Phone Dett 30.
★★★ Wankie Safari Lodge, 100 rooms, all with baths. $14 – $25 B/B. Phone Dett 72.

The tarmac Bulawayo-Falls road (A8) continues north-westwards from the turnoff to the Wankie National Park. After 25 km the road reaches a petrol and trading point at a junction, from where a turnoff leads westwards for 16 km to the railway station and village of Dett. A turnoff north stretches for 28 km to the tin mining centre of Kamativi and thence to Mlibizi (98 km) and Binga (161 km), situated on the western shores of Lake Kariba and much resorted to by fishermen.

## Accommodation
★ Binga Rest Camp, 3 chalets and 6 rooms, $7 B/B. Caravan and camping sites, 60c D per person. Phone Binga 11.
★ Mlibizi Hotel, $15 D. Phone Zeb 25 Bulawayo.

Beyond the turnoff to these resorts, the main Bulawayo-Falls road continues in a north-westerly direction through the mopane forest. After 25 km (310 km from Bulawayo) the road crosses the Inyantye River. Baobab trees begin to make their appearance and the presence of huts reveal a human population more numerous than has been seen so far along the road. At 325 km the road crosses the Likazi River, where a substantial mission station looks down at the bridge from an overlooking hillock.

The road is now in the homeland of the Nambya section of the Rozvi tribe. Their ruler, whose dynastic name was Hwange, provided Europeans with the corrupted name of Wankie and, 11 km beyond the Lukazi bridge, a turnoff leads to the railway and mining centre of that name.

## WANKIE

Early in 1893 a German, Albert Giese, while on a hunting trip, met an African who told him that in Hwange's country there could be found a great marvel – black stones that burned. Giese realised what this meant and eventually managed to reach the area where he found on the surface an enormous outcrop of high-grade coal. This discovery was the basis of the Wankie (Rhodesia) Coal, Railway and Exploration Company, formed in 1899 to exploit the deposit and today one of the biggest coal mines in Africa. A large village grew up to house the mine workers and provide them with facilities for trade and recreation.

### Accommodation
** Baobab Hotel, 50 rooms, all with baths. $8,50 – $9,50 B/B. Phone 493.

---

From the turnoff to Wankie, the tarmac Bulawayo-Falls road continues through increasingly rugged country, with rocky hillocks covered in mopane trees. The signs and odours of a substantial activity in coal mining are evident all around. The heat is so heavy and oppressive, especially around October and November, that the stranger may be forgiven for wondering whether the countryside, being so substantially made of coal, may not perhaps have caught fire!

A point on the road is reached 342 km from Bulawayo, where a turnoff leads north for 48 km to the fishing resort at the confluence of the Deka and Zambezi rivers.

### Accommodation
* Deka Drum Fishing Resort, 12 cabins, $4 – $5,50 B/B. Caravan and camping sites, $2 D.

The main tarmac road (A8) continues in a north-westerly direction past Thomson Junction, and across the Deka and Matetsi rivers. At 464 km from Bulawayo, a turnoff west leads for 65 km to the border of Botswana at Panda-ma-Tenga and to Robin's Camp (67 km) in the Wankie National Park.

The country becomes increasingly densely wooded. After a further 27 km (426 km from Bulawayo), the road passes the Falls airport and 6 km further on, straight ahead, the traveller can generally see the spray rising from the great waterfall. A further 5 km brings the road to the entrance of the Victoria Falls National Park with the journey ending 11 km further on (449 km from Bulawayo), at what is surely one of the most spectacularly situated frontiers between any two countries on earth: the customs and immigration posts of Zimbabwe and Zambia on either side of the great bridge which spans the gorge of the Zambezi within reach of the spray of the thundering waterfall. The customs and immigration posts are open 24 hours a day.

## THE VICTORIA FALLS NATIONAL PARK

Not only is the Victoria Falls the undisputed monarch of all waterfalls, but it is without doubt one of the greatest and most unforgettable scenic spectacles. The physical nature of the waterfall is in itself astonishing, for it occurs in country that is perfectly level. From its source in a lonely grove of trees on the borders of Zaire, the Zambezi River meanders for 1 300 km across the wooded plateau of Zambia, eroding for itself a shallow valley in the great sheet of lava which forms the surface of this part of Africa. A few minor rapids and the small Gonye Falls alone provide some flurry of activity to the otherwise easy going flow of the river.

Nature, however, has set a trap for the Zambezi. A series of faults in the lava sheet, in the form of vertical cracks, crosses the course of the river. These cracks, filled with relatively soft matter, have literally tripped up the river in its course. Finding the lowest crack, the river scooped out the contents, tumbled into what was now a trench, and promptly had to tumble out again on the far side. The river eventually found a weak spot on the lower lip of the trench and forced a passage which was steadily deepened into an exit gorge. A tremendous waterfall spectacle had now been created where the river fell headlong across the full width of an enormous trench filled with mist and thundering echoes, and then boiled out through the narrow gap.

During the last half million years the Zambezi has scoured out no less than eight of these cracks across its bed, and there is every indication that there are a number of others situated higher up. In its day, each trench must have provided successively a magnificent waterfall display, for the lower lip running the full length of the fall, and broken only by the narrow escape gorge forced by the river, has always served as an ideal observation platform. So it is today, with the river falling into a scoured-out crack, the earlier cracks being completely washed out to form 'legs' for the zigzag gorge, and the powerful flow of the river forcing its way out of the present crack through the Boiling Pot and the eight successive gorges.

The Victoria Falls, at present occuring where the river is 1 900 m wide, presents the spectacle of an average maximum of 550 million litres (120 million gallons) of water a minute tumbling over the upper lip of the trench in five main falls – the Devil's Cataract, Main Falls, Horseshoe Falls, Rainbow Falls, and the Eastern Cataract – each separated from the other only by slightly elevated islands of rock on the lip of the fall. The highest fall is Rainbow Falls, on an average, 100 m high. A peak flood sees 750 million litres of water hurtling over the falls every minute.

Below the falls, what is known as the middle Zambezi flows for 800 km through some of the wildest scenery in Africa. Through the gorge of Kariba (where the great dam wall has been built), and other gorges, it eventually shoulders its way through the last barrier of the Cabora Bassa, and then for a final 500 km (the lower Zambezi) meanders across the coastal flats of Moçambique before losing itself in the Indian Ocean. It is altogether an impressive river.

At its lowest in October, the river attains its peak at the end of April; it is then that the falls are staggering to see but the spray tends to obscure the view and make photography difficult. June to September is the period of medium flow when conditions are ideal for sightseeing. In October and November the area is excessively hot.

Rainbows are always visible at the falls: full moon produces a lunar rainbow, especially clear as the moon rises in the early evening.

The banks of the Zambezi above the falls are beautifully wooded with riverine forest. Spray, ceaselessly falling on the opposite side of the trough, has given rise to a gorgeous forest. The path leading through this forest, along the edge of the trough, is one of the world's most famous tourist promenades. Suitably attired in raincoats, countless visitors from many countries have walked along this path, spellbound by the gigantic spectacle of the falling waters revealed to them through the dripping leaves of the rain forest.

Eventually leaving the rain forest, the path traverses an open area sodden with spray, and ends abruptly at Danger Point, looking down into the great gap in the trough through which the river makes its escape into the gorge. A spectacular view may be had across the gap to the Eastern Cataract. A curious indentation in the rocks at Danger Point is called Eve's Footprint.

To the Africans, the waterfall is known by several names: the Kololo people of the upper reaches of the river gave it the well-known name of *Mosi o a Thunya* (smoke that rises), while the Ndebele called it *aManza Thunqayo* (the water that rises like smoke).

Dr Livingstone, the first European to visit the falls (on 16 November 1885), reached them from upstream. Travelling down in the canoes of the friendly Kololo people, he had reached the brink of the falls, first viewing them from Kazeruka (or Livingstone) Island which separates Main Falls from Rainbow Falls. To peer directly into the prodigious chasm must have been a staggering experience. Livingstone's African companions told him that the Tonka people who lived along the middle reaches of the river offered sacrifices to their ancestors at the fall, in three places, each within sight of the rainbow, which they considered marked the presence of God.

Livingstone named the falls after Queen Victoria. On the island he planted a few peach and apricot stones, and carved his initials and the date in a tree, before setting out on the long walk to the mouth of the Zambezi, where he was picked up by HM brig *Frolic* on 12 July 1856. A most impressive statue of Dr Livingstone (sculpted by Sir William Reid-Dick), stands on the western side of the chasm immediately overlooking the Devil's Cataract where the river, when in flood, rages past at a speed of 160 km an hour.

The combined road-rail bridge over the gorge, 200 m long and 106 m high, was opened on 12 September 1905, the construction having been stimulated by the discovery of copper in the north. The precise site of the bridge was selected at the express wish of Cecil Rhodes, so that the spray of the waterfall would fall upon the passing trains. The centre of the bridge now marks the boundary between Zimbabwe and Zambia.

There are several most interesting walks, drives, flights, canoe and launch trips in the vicinity of the waterfall. Paths lead from the front of the Victoria Falls Hotel to the second and third gorges. From Livingstone's statue visitors may follow, with the aid of chains, a path descending one-third of the way down the gorge to a spectacular viewsite from where the full length of the great trough of the waterfall is revealed. Another path from the statue finds an interesting way through the trees up the right bank of the river and leads to, among other things, an enormous baobab tree 20 m in circumference.

From the falls, the road follows the right bank of the river for 8 km and then enters the Victoria Falls National Park. Across this 53 000 ha park, the road known as the Zambezi Drive continues for 48 km to the Sominungwa turnabout. Apart from fine riverine scenery all the way, the road passes through densely inhabited game country especially noted for its herds of sable antelope, elephant and buffalo. A second road into the park, known as the Chamabonda Drive, penetrates the southern portion of the area for 24 km and provides particularly fine game-viewing opportunities, especially between September and December. The entrance is reached via a turnoff on the main Bulawayo road, 11 km south of Victoria Falls. The park is open from May to December.

The village of Victoria Falls is the northern frontier village of Southern Africa and is a relaxed and picturesque little holiday resort in a park-like setting. Hotels, stores, garages, curio shops, a rest camp, some bungalows and a caravan park, cluster within the shadow of the mist cloud of the waterfall. Launch cruises up the river, airflips and game-viewing flights are available.

## Accommodation
★★★★ Makasa Sun Hotel, 102 rooms, all with baths. $13 – $18 B/B. Phone 275.
★★★ Victoria Falls Hotel, 143 rooms, all with baths. $17 B/B. Phone 204.
★★ Victoria Falls Motel, 49 rooms, all with baths. $8 B/B. Phone 345.

## Caravans and camping
★★ Victoria Falls Rest Camp, 34 chalets, $3 – $5 D. 60 caravan sites, S2 D.
★★ Zambezi and Victoria Falls National Park, 20 lodges, $4,50 – $8,50 D.

# Chapter Forty-three

# MANICALAND

From Salisbury, the main tarmac road (A3) to the beautiful Eastern Districts leaves the city past the suburb of Eastlea and the municipal caravan park and then off into open country consisting of a lightly bushed plain scattered with granite boulders. The countryside is immaculately kept, spanned by a finely made road and beautified with trees and wayside patches of flowers and shrubs. There are numerous resting places along the way where the weary traveller may pause and once refreshed, find the journey as pleasant as it should be.

Twenty-five kilometres from Salisbury, the road passes the Ruwa Country Club, with a turnoff north to the administrative centre of Goromanzi (12 km), and the beautiful Norah Valley. Nine kilometres further on the road passes the Jamaica Inn, with the rural centre of *Bromley* (named after Bromley, on the shores of Loch Lomond) ahead. The road and railway keep close company on this journey eastwards along the 1 525-m-high plateau summit of the central ridge of Zimbabwe, so narrow at this point that on either side may be seen the descent to the surrounding low country. The plateau summit is a lovely, entirely rural landscape covered with hectares of rich farmland and impressive granite domes (ornamented with lichens) which loom up along the verges of the plateau, as though guarding it from the encroaching valleys of the low country.

## Accommodation
★★ Beverley Rocks Motel, 38 rooms, all with baths. $5,80 B/B. Phone Salisbury 46056.
★ Jamaica Inn, 10 rooms, 6 with baths. $5 B/B. Phone Bromley 27.

At 60 km from Salisbury a turnoff south leads to the administrative centre of Wedza (70 km). Plantations of gum and fir trees line the road like rigid soldiers on parade, while 9,5 km further on the road passes the Grasslands Research Station. A further 3 km (72 km from Salisbury) brings the tarmac road (A3) to the rural town of . . .

## MARANDELLAS

With a population of 21 000, *Marandellas* takes its name from Maronera, a chief of the Zezuru people who once lived there. It is a neat agricultural town built around a large central square. Timber, cattle, grain and tobacco and dairy products provide the town with its prosperity. The Borradaile Trust homes for the aged situated in the midst of a garden, may be seen as the road enters the town.

## Accommodation
★ Marandellas Hotel, 27 rooms, 4 with baths. $6,50 – $7,50 B/B. Phone 4006.
★ Three Monkeys Inn, 14 rooms, 10 with baths. $7 – $7,50 B/B. Phone 3247.

From Marandellas, the main tarmac road A3 continues eastwards through plantations of tall gum trees and across handsome farmlands, with graceful musasa trees ornamenting the slopes of the plateau. At 9 km from Marandellas the road passes Peterhouse school and a further 22 km brings it to the rural centre of Macheke, situated in a natural rockery of granite.

## Accommodation
* Macheke Hotel, 12 rooms, 3 with baths. $5,50 – $6 B/B. Phone 49.

The main road continues eastwards through gum and pine plantations. At 17 km from Macheke the road tops a rise and, from what is known as Eagles Nest, the first good view may be seen ahead of the beautiful eastern mountains of Zimbabwe.

At 59 km from Marandellas, the road passes the rural centre of Headlands and begins to lose altitude through a picturesque natural rockery of granite boulders and rock fragments of various odd shapes. At 91 km from Marandellas, the road crosses the Rusape River, with the Crocodile Motel on its banks and, 1 km further on, enters the small town of . . .

# RUSAPE

Receiving its name from the river, named on account of its erratic flow as being 'sparing of its waters', *Rusape* is a quiet agricultural town, the streets of which are shaded with flowering trees.

## Accommodation
* Balfour Hotel, 16 rooms, 11 with baths. $6,70 B/B. Phone 410.
* Crocodile Motel, 14 rooms, 8 with baths. $6,40 – $7,40 B/B. Phone 404.

## Caravans and camping
* Lake Rusape Caravan Park, 20 sites. $1 D.
* Makoni Caravan Park, 15 sites. $1 D.

From Rusape a turnoff east leads through rugged granite country for 104 km to Inyanga. The main tarmac road A3 continues in a southerly direction through granite country covered in musasa trees, which becomes increasingly wild in appearance. After 3 km the road crosses the Inyazura River and 35 km further on reaches the Odzi River, with a small rural centre situated on its right bank.

## Accommodation
* Inyazura Hotel, 10 rooms, $4,50 B/B. Phone 4.
* Odzi Hotel, 6 rooms, $5,25 – $6,25 B/B. Phone 6.
* Travel Lodge Motel, 8 rooms, 4 with baths $4 – $5 B/B. Phone 0-3312.

The main tarmac road has in the meanwhile swung eastwards and stretches directly into the foothills of the eastern mountains of Zimbabwe. Thick bush covers the slopes and valleys, and the climate, with the road now at a lower altitude (1 100 m), is warm and tropical. The road traverses an old gold mining area. Ten kilometres from the Odzi River the road crosses Battery Spruit, and after a further 9 km, reaches a turnoff north leading to Inyanga, and the site of Old Umtali. Another kilometre through this most impressive mountain mass brings the road (81 km from Rusape) to the turnoff north leading to Penhalonga (9 km). The main tarmac road A3 now starts to climb a mountain slope far more beautifully overgrown with wild flowers, shrubs and trees, than any manmade garden. *Christmas Pass* was so named by the surveyor of the original road, F. W. Bruce, who found himself camped there over Christmas 1891.

## Accommodation
Christmas Pass Hotel, 19 rooms, 7 chalets $5 B/B. Phone Umtali 63818.

The summit of Christmas Pass yields a superb view over the great valley in which shelters the town of Umtali, and deep into the mass of granite mountains to the east and south. Two short scenic roads branch off east and west from the main road at the summit of the pass. Both lead to viewsites, the east road climbing steeply to what is known as Umtali Heights, a vantage point nearly 1 740 m above sea level which reveals a breathtaking panorama of mountains and valley.

The main tarmac road commences a steady descent past the handsomely situated Umtali Municipal Caravan Park, down through a green forest of beautiful trees and past a nature reserve on Murahwa's Hill. Six kilometres from the summit (89 km from Rusape and 250 km from Salisbury), the road reaches the city of . . .

## UMTALI

With a population of 61 300, Umtali is one of the most beautifully situated cities in Southern Africa. Lying in the valley of the stream known as the *Sakubva* from the *Vitex payos* shrubs which grow on its banks, the town is completely dominated by a concentration of some of the most massive granite mountains in Southern Africa. The valley in which it lies forms a natural gateway between the coastal lowlands of Moçambique and the interior of Zimbabwe.

Umtali is a frontier town and railway marshalling yard on the road and rail route to Beira and lying 1 220 m above sea level, experiences a warm climate, which is, however, cooler than the heat and humidity of the lowlands of Moçambique.

Umtali has been described as the town that moved. The first Umtali (what is known as Old Umtali) had a very lively birth in 1891, as the rough and ready mining settlement built on the banks of the river known as the *Mutare* (river of ore). The inhabitants of this roaring camp were more interested in gold and strong drink than in linguistics and they named their town *Umtali*, as a corruption of the name of the river. Some 160 mines came into operation around the town and Old Umtali experienced a hectic social life, a renowned part of which were wild parties, and the use of the main street (about the only part of the country then cleared of bush) as a playing field for a variety of sports.

In March 1896 this boisterous little town received a sad blow: a narrow-gauge railway was being built to Zimbabwe from the port of Beira. Cecil Rhodes visited Old Umtali and informed its dismayed inhabitants that the construction engineers understandably wanted to bring the railway through the mountain barrier by means of the easiest possible natural pass, namely the valley of the Sakubva stream, 17 km away and separated from Old Umtali by a high granite ridge. Rhodes was the supreme businessman. It would cost a fortune to bring the railway to Old Umtali, therefore it would be far cheaper to move the town to the railway!

Rhodes literally bought Old Umtali and distributed £50 000 in cash to the residents, laying out a duplicate town on the site of the present Umtali next to the railway line in the valley of the Sakubva. Each property owner in Old Umtali was entitled to a plot in the new town, and to these sites they removed piecemeal their houses, shacks and huts. In this way, in 1896, the new Umtali was born, and Old Umtali was abandoned to the bush.

The new Umtali was a beautifully laid out town, spaciously planned by its surveyor, Rhys Fairbridge, to fully exploit the superb setting with broad, flamboyant-lined streets. Rhodes always regarded the new town of Umtali as being peculiarly his own. He supervised the establishment of a spacious park and, inevitably, a stock exchange and race track where he could relax on his visits to the area. Flowering trees in considerable quantity were planted, gardens laid out, and new Umtali was planned from the beginning to be what it is now – an altogether pleasant place and a friendly gateway to welcome travellers into Zimbabwe from the east coast ports of Moçambique.

Umtali became a city on 1 October 1971. Today it is lively and prosperous, with a fine theatre, concert hall, a superb civic centre, and first-class sporting amenities, including a magnificent swimming pool. Several industries have established themselves there, such as a refinery, an assembly plant of the British Motor Corporation, various coffee and tea packing and blending factories, canning, plywood, board and paper mills, and other enterprises.

Christmas time sees the flame trees of Umtali at their peak of brilliance. In winter, aloes and cycads are in flower, while September and October are the months for jacarandas and bougainvillaea.

The Umtali Museum houses an interesting collection of the fauna and flora of the Eastern Districts and the collection of antique firearms and transport vehicles, including Cecil Rhodes's coach, and early locomotives, is worth seeing. The museum is open daily from 10h00 to 17h00 and from 14h30 to 17h00 on Sundays.

### Accommodation
★★ Manica Hotel, 85 rooms, all with baths. $12 single, $18 double. Phone 64431.
★ Little Swallow Inn, 15 rooms, all with baths. $6,50 room only. Phone 62441.
★★★ Wise Owl Motel, 69 rooms, all with baths. $7,50 single – $12 double B/B. Phone 64643.

### Caravans and camping
★★ Municipal caravan park (Christmas Pass), 50 sites. $1 D.

From Umtali, the main tarmac road A3 continues eastwards down a heavily wooded valley hemmed in by high hills, and forming a picturesque and beautiful gateway between Zimbabwe and Moçambique. After 6 km the road reaches the customs and immigration post, where a restaurant, The Little Swallow, offers refreshment to travellers before they commence the 280-km run to the coast at Beira. The customs and immigration post (Forbe's Post) is open daily from 06h00 to 23h30.

## THE VUMBA

One of the most spectacular mountain drives in Africa leads from Umtali to the heights of what is known as the *Vumba* (from *Mubvumbi,* meaning 'the mountains of drizzle'), an enormous ridge of granite overlooking Umtali from the south-east.

The tarmac road leaves Umtali and climbs steeply, revealing superb views of the valley below which allows the road and railway to pass through the mountains to Moçambique. At 6 km the road reaches the Impala Arms Hotel and 3 km further on a gravel turnoff south provides a circular drive of 75 km around the Vumba, past the Nyachowa Falls, and through the densely wooded Burma Valley, before rejoining the main Vumba road.

Ahead now looms a magnificent mass of granite mountains, the slopes of which are densely wooded with musasa trees, providing in spring one of the most brilliant botanical displays to be seen anywhere. Leopards, wild pigs, bush buck and samango monkeys frequent the forests of the Vumba. At 11 km from Umtali there is a turnoff (the Vumba North Road) leading to the White Horse Inn (2 km) and several handsome private residences built on viewsites.

The main tarmac road now begins a steep climb, with superb views visible through gaps in the forest which blankets the slopes. After 3 km (15 km from Umtali) the road reaches the summit of the climb at what is known as *Cloudlands,* the farm of the well-known Lionel and Mary Cripps, 1 585 m above sea level. A gravel turnoff leads eastwards from here for 75 km through the scenic Circular Drive back to the main tarmac road (5 km down the road towards Umtali). At 24 km along the Circular Drive, accommodation is provided at the Vumba Chalets.

At the turnoff to the Circular Drive, the tarmac surface of the main Vumba road ends and is replaced by an all-weather gravel surface. The road winds on over the summit of the ridge, reaching after 1 km (16 km from Umtali), a turnoff south to the Eagle Preparatory School, perched on the slopes and overlooking a romantic view of hills and valleys.

A further 5 km takes the road past the Vumba Heights Children's Hostel and School, built among the trees and overlooked by the 1 910-m (the highest) point of the Vumba, Castle Beacon, a giant granite dome topped by the mast of a radio communication station. The main road twists around the slopes of this dome, tunnelling through patches of lovely indigenous forest and plantation, with panoramic views to the north-east far over the lowlands of Moçambique.

The main Vumba road, at 24 km from Umtali, enters the 24-ha *Binga* (dense forest) and after 1 km a turnoff is reached leading northwards for 4 km to the Vumba National Park (see further on). The Binga Forest was presented to the Rhodesian nation on 25 February 1946 by the Honourable Lionel Cripps. A fine, representative section of the original Vumba forest, it is particularly rich in ferns (about 250 varieties).

The main road continues along the summit ridge, past the Woodlands Store and Curio Shop. The summit ridge narrows sharply at this point and at 27 km from Umtali a superlative view to the south and north may be seen, with a footpath branching off and providing walkers with a route down to the Leopard Rock Hotel. Ahead (28 km from Umtali), the road passes the Mountain Lodge Hotel and then terminates at the African school named *Mutore,* after a local headman.

The two hotels mentioned above have both been built on superlative sites. The Mountain Lodge is a thatched reproduction of an old English country inn, the windows of which look towards the south at a tremendous view of the mountains lying along the eastern border. The Leopard Rock Hotel can only be described as a magnificent and most imaginative development on what is one of the supreme hotel sites of the world.

The hotel had its beginning in 1936 when Leslie Seymour Smith visited the Eastern Districts on holiday. Smith was of that happy (but rare) breed of man – an affluent small worker. Examples of non-affluent small workers are numerous in the land of El Dorado, but Smith had a profitable little mine, the Patsy Mine, in Matabeleland, at a hill named *Mbigo* (the lookout). Drought had brought work to a temporary halt. While waiting for rain, Smith took a holiday, during which he discovered the perennial greenness and beauty of the Vumba. He decided to buy property there. A retired bank manager named Rutherford, who was something of an amiable crank, with the habit of taking the hindquarters of leopards down to the Umtali Club to feed his friends, owned an overgrown farm named *Scandinavia* on the slopes of the Vumba. Leslie Smith bought a portion of this farm and named it *Mbigo,* after the hill overlooking his mine.

The area was a real African dreamland: a superb view; the rich greenness resulting from the misty rain and perennial water supply; magnificent trees; a unique atmosphere, and a romantic past, all contributed to make the place perfect. The mountain overlooking the farm was known to the Africans as *Tshinyakweremba* (the place of tired feet). Legend has it that a village of the Jindwi people once flourished on the slopes of this peak. An ancestral spirit in the guise of a decrepit old man is said to have visited the place. He found the drunken inhabitants so rude and inhospitable that he destroyed the village with a landslide that night, sparing only one person who had been kind to him. The village still lies buried under the huge pile of boulders and the scar on the mountain from where the landslide originated, stands out in the form of a 180-m-high precipice.

The scene of this legendary disaster is today a place of haunting beauty submerged beneath lovely trees, filled with the whisper of the wind and the drowsy murmuring of rock pigeons and lowries. A family of leopards for a long time made their home among the fallen boulders and were often seen sunning themselves on a particular vantage point. This was the site which Leslie Smith selected for his home and there he built one of the most individualistic of houses. Visitors think of it as a pseudo-castle but it is simply a development of a leopard's lair. No architect would have designed such a place – a client requesting a plan of this nature would have been referred to a lunatic asylum. But if this is the result of lunacy, would that it were catching. Designed by Leslie Smith, the house is a projection of the fallen rock which buries the village. Using the same rock for material, the house has been built over boulders and into fissures.

The original rock on which the leopards sunned themselves is now enclosed in a colossal toilet, the seat of which is actually cut into the stone. There is no other W.C. like it: a privy where anyone would be happy to spend a dollar rather than a cent! When the British Royal Family visited the place, it is said that the Queen Mother, on retiring to the privy and just before latching the door, popped her head out and observed innocently, 'Mr Seymour Smith, I see you have a throne as well.'

The view from the house is overwhelming and the grounds of the whole estate are superbly landscaped. Huge wild fig trees, tree ferns, arum lilies, moonflowers, hydrangeas and some particularly magnificent *Albizia gummiflora* trees, are notable features of the garden.

The hotel building was also designed by Leslie Smith, at the suggestion of a Salisbury architect that it would be an interesting experiment to try a building involving double-storied rondawels. The castle effect is incidental. The unique atmosphere of this 'rondawel castle' is the result of a very great deal of thought. There is a fern room containing a grotto fountain; a lounge with a remarkable floor comprising a variety of indigenous timber, and a central fireplace; a children's room with a slide designed as a miniature castle. It is altogether one of the most remarkable hotels in the world and proof of a considerable creative imagination hidden behind the rough-hewn exterior of Mr Leslie Seymour Smith. The hotel was opened in June 1946.

## THE VUMBA NATIONAL PARK

This 183-ha national park is a general botanical garden containing flora of both exotic and indigenous origin. The climate and conditions on the Vumba ridge are such that almost anything seems to grow to perfection there, from Namaqualand daisies of the arid west coast, to tree ferns and cycads from tropical rain forests.

The garden originated in 1917 when Edgar Evans, who (like Leslie Smith of Leopard Rock) had made money by working a small mine, decided to retire to the cool heights of the Vumba. His mine had been named the Kent Mine and he was jocularly called the 'Duke of Kent'. He bought the undeveloped farm *Manchester Park,* so named by its original owner, a Mr Robert Magden from Manchester. To this farm Evans built a road from Cloudlands and started development. Then, in 1926, Frederick John Taylor, who had emigrated from Devonshire in 1901 to work for the Meikles organisation in Rhodesia, bought the farm and with his wife Helen, started the wonderful garden. In 1943 he retired there and worked full time on the garden. In 1958 he sold it to the Rhodesian Government for £23 000 and the right to continue residence there for life. He died on 21 November 1961. As a national park it has been developed to its present stage of magnificence and is especially notable for its gladioli, azaleas, begonias, lilies and hydrangeas. There is a tearoom, swimming pool, artificial lake, and a 3-ha caravan and camping site.

### Accommodation
* Impala Arms Hotel, 20 rooms, 8 with baths. $5,60 – $6,60 B/B. Phone Umtali 60722.
** Leopard Rock Hotel, 36 rooms, all with baths. $11,50 – $13 D. Phone Umtali 2103-25.
** Mountain Lodge Hotel, 17 rooms, 10 with baths. $9,50 – $10,50 D. Phone Umtali 2185-20.
** White Horse Inn, 8 rooms, all with baths. $6,50 – $7,50 B/B. Phone Umtali 216612.

### Caravans and camping
*** ®Vumba National Park, 50 sites. $1,50 D.

# UMTALI TO INYANGA

Two roads lead north from Umtali into the mountain massif along the border and up to Inyanga. The longer (and rougher) road is the scenic route, which will be followed first. It is a most picturesque drive, especially notable for the magnificent trees growing by the wayside.

This road branches off north from the main Umtali-Salisbury road (A3) opposite the Christmas Pass Hotel, 8 km west of Umtali. The road immediately enters a beautifully wooded area where fine specimens of wild fig and acacia trees may be seen. After 5 km a turnoff is reached leading eastwards into the Imbeza Valley to the Imbeza Forest Estates Sawmill. Tree lovers will find this short diversion worth exploring, for the valley floor shelters some of the most gracefully shaped acacia trees to be seen in Africa, and several beautiful homesteads.

Three kilometres beyond this turnoff stands a small memorial to the pioneer nurses who walked from Beira in 1891 to establish on this hillside site the first hospital in the Eastern Districts. The signs of old mining activity are visible in many places and 1 km from the memorial, the road enters the one-time boom mining village of Penhalonga, now dilapidated and with most of the 22 commercial enterprises lining its one street, bankrupt and abandoned.

In its day, Penhalonga (together with Old Umtali) acted as the centre for some 160 gold mines. From it a road branches eastwards and for 8 km finds its way up a once busy mining valley in the mountains, past the Imbeza Forest Estates, and on until it reaches a small border post on the divide where the international frontier line runs. This was the original entry point into what was then Rhodesia, and it was from here that Rhodes, in 1891, first entered the country named after him and saw ahead that long view of bush and mountain.

Most of the gold mines are now exhausted but what slight activity there is, at least sustains a glimmer of life in Penhalonga. There is no hotel in the village but an excellent caravan park provides a base for the exploration of an interesting area. Penhalonga was named after Count Penhalonga of the Moçambique company.

From the village, the main road climbs up the valley of the Mutare River, with a fine cascade to the east. The road passes several handsome estates and many graceful trees. At 12 km from Penhalonga, the road reaches a crossroads leading to Stapleford Forest (17 km east), and the Odzani Dam (6 km west) where there is a caravan and camping site. The road continues its climb into the granite hills where may be seen growing some of the most gorgeously coloured musasa trees whose spring colours have a particularly vivid glow on account of the situation and climate.

On top of this rise, 16 km from Penhalonga, a 1-km turnoff leads west to the waterfall on the Odzani River, which the main road crosses further on. A further 3 km brings the tarmac road to an end at a turnoff east to Odzani. The main road (now gravel) continues north through lovely patches of musasa trees, passing many tribal villages and viewsites east into the Honde Valley. At 28 km from Penhalonga, the road reaches the rural centre of Tzonso, situated on a high grassy plateau, and there joins the main tarmac road leading from Umtali to Inyanga.

This main tarmac road branches off from the Umtali-Salisbury road (A3), 9 km west of Umtali (1 km west of the turnoff to the scenic route). The road stretches north across the bushy valley of the Mutare River, with clusters of African huts enhancing the picturesque appearance of the area. After 5 km a gravel turnoff leads westwards to the site of Old Umtali, where a Methodist church centre has been established.

An odd-shaped assembly of granite peaks looms ahead. The road climbs and twists towards them penetrating a real garden of Pan, with masses of wild flowers blooming by the roadside. After 25 km the road finds a way through a natural passage in one of the granite spurs and emerges on a plateau well populated by African tribespeople. At 28 km the road reaches the small trading centre of Tzonso, where the alternate road joins it from Umtali (48 km) through Penhalonga. Ahead lie more granite masses and there are fine views west and east into the colossal Honde Valley (from *Muhonde*, river of euphorbia trees) where the extraordinary outcrops known as *Masimiki* (rocks that stand upright) occur.

The road climbs steadily into an area of wattle plantations. At 46 km there is a turnoff west to the mission station of Bonda. At 49 km a turnoff east follows what is known as the Scenic Road, which leads to Inyanga (44 km) in a spectacular (but rough) alternate route described further on.

The main tarmac road continues northwards through the plantations of the Rhodesian Wattle Company. At 56 km the road reaches the beautiful cascade in the Odzi River. Huge plantations of pine and wattle trees blanket the granite slopes while innumerable streams rush downwards from the heights.

At 72 km (80 km from Umtali) a junction with the road coming from Rusape is reached. Five kilometres along this road is the Pine Lodge Hotel. The main route turns east (right) and after 1 km reaches Juliasdale, with its store, garage and hotel. The road leads on revealing fine views over a deep valley, with the high granite peaks reaching off into the dim northern horizon. At 3 km from Juliasdale there is a turnoff east to the Scenic Road and 6 km further on (81 km from the start of the road and 89 km from Umtali), the road enters the Inyanga National Park. It is opportune at this point, before exploring the park, to examine the charms of . . .

## THE SCENIC ROAD

This route branches off from the main road to Inyanga 48 km from the start of the road (57 km from Umtali). The road is gravel and steep in places. The surface is occasionally poor and made tedious by corrugations and potholes caused by heavy vehicles engaged in the transport of timber. Caution is therefore necessary and the road is not suitable for caravans. Scenically, however, this alternative route to Inyanga possesses several notable features.

After 1 km there is a turnoff east into the Honde Valley and the tea estates 50 km down the valley – a drive which passes through wild and rugged country. One kilometre further on a viewsite is situated just off the road, looking down into the Honde Valley, a view worth seeing, and very photogenic on a clear day.

A further 12 km brings the road to a rough turnoff leading for 9 km to the Mutarazi Falls, where the stream known as the *Mutarazi* (the sound of its water falling) makes a tremendous leap.

Three kilometres further on, a short loop leads to a famous view and picnic site overlooking the valley of the *Pungwe* (an ideophone denoting the closing in and clearing of mists). From here a majestic view may be had of the oft-photographed cascade, the deep gorge, and to the north-east, the great bulk of the 2 593-m Inyangani, the highest mountain in Zimbabwe.

Beyond this viewsite, the road continues for 12 km rewarding the traveller with many handsome views as compensation for the bumps, and then joins a major gravel road which links up (to the west) with the main tarmac road at Juliasdale (9 km). To the east, after 8 km, the road enters the . . .

## INYANGA NATIONAL PARK

This magnificent mountain national park (40 500 ha in extent) is situated at an altitude of 1 982 m in the bracing air of an extensive mountain-top plateau. The park owes its origin to the magnanimity of Cecil Rhodes. In 1896, while arranging for the removal of Umtali to its new site, Rhodes heard of the beauty of this area. He bought a large block of farms there, where he established experimental plantations of fruit and trees. The stone farmhouse on *Fruitfield* farm became a mountain retreat for Rhodes and, preserved in much of its original state, is now the Rhodes Inyanga Hotel.

On the death of Rhodes, the estate was bequeathed to the nation, and is today a magnificent recreation area; cool, green, close to nature and relaxing to all who seek a release from the nervous tensions of city life.

The history of the Inyanga area is particularly fascinating. The name *Inyanga* comes from a famous witchdoctor, Sanyanga, who ruled over the mountain lands – a fitting domain for so great a magician – in the first half of the 19th century. Scattered over some 4 000 square kilometres of these mountain lands is a concentration of ruins of stone walls, enclosures, irrigation furrows and terraces occurring in such numbers that they must be seen to be believed.

The area of the Inyanga National Park contains a vast assortment of these ruins, apparently built by primitive people when times of stress drove them from their normal homes in the warmer lowlands. Resorting to the cold heights for security they dug curious, stonelined pits, presumably in which to shelter their livestock, while on the aloe-grown summit of the hill known as *Nyangwe* (place of the leopard), stands a fort, crudely built, but impressive in its power, glowering out over the surrounding moorlands like a watchdog.

The spectacle of these strange ruins left behind by a vanished people provides a curious touch of melancholy to an enchanted landscape. Exactly who the builders were, remains a mystery. No relics of any exotic people have been found, and the buildings were most probably the work of the same African people (a section of the Karanga) who live in the warmer lowlands today, whence they doubtless removed to escape the upland cold as soon as political conditions allowed them to do so in safety. Europeans like to refer to the pits as 'slave pits', but this is romanticism; the African name for them, *Matanga epasi* (underground cattle enclosures), is probably more appropriate, their small size being suited to the dwarf cattle of the Karanga.

The Inyanga National Park offers many fine walks and drives with what is known as the Circular Drive providing a grand tour of the whole area. It is quite a drive, following the slopes of the great fortress-like Inyangani mountain: rising, falling, twisting and turning. There is an immense variety of flora (much of it reminiscent of the Cape) such as proteas, everlastings and ericas. Over and above this, however, looms the unique landscape – the strange and most ancient granite mountains, each with its own peculiar shape, name, legend and character. The peaks loom up through the mists like petrified giants, forgotten gods of an antique world whose brooding memory haunts this land as surely as the winds whisper through the tussock grass.

It is from the Circular Drive that the walker may easily reach the summit of Inyangani, from where is revealed a panorama of mountain and moorland. In spring, the patches of colourful musasa trees – brown, orange, magenta and crimson – may be seen splashing the granite slopes like the stains of sacrifices made on altars of the past.

The many other pleasant features of this park include the handsome Inyangombe Falls and fishing for trout (brown and rainbow), with 85 km of streams in ideal surroundings. There are fine walks, and accommodation facilities comprise bungalows and caravan and camping sites. The trout fishing season at Mare Dam (where there is also a trout hatchery) is from 1 September to 31 May and in the streams from 1 November to 31 May. It is altogether a delightful national park.

## Accommodation
★★★ Brondesbury Park Hotel, 41 rooms, 33 with baths. $5 – $9 room only. Phone Juliasdale 242.
★★★★ Montclair Hotel, 56 rooms, all with baths. $10 B/B. Phone Juliasdale 232.
★ Rhodes Inyanga Hotel, 20 rooms, 7 with baths. $7 – $9 D. Phone Inyanga 377.

## Caravans and camping
Numerous cottages, chalets and lodges maintained by the National Park Authority, $4 – $8,50 D. Caravan and camping sites, $1,50 D.

*Overleaf: The ancient ruins of a vanished civilisation; baobabs grow where forgotten people once worked and lived at Matendere, near the Save River.*

Just across the northern border of the national park lies the village of Inyanga. The post office, shops, two hotels, caravan and camping sites and government administrative offices of this informal little place are all so spreadeagled over a vast area with considerable amounts of wilderness in between each building that it seems as though the village was laid out by people who didn't like one another!

Five kilometres beyond the north-eastern boundary of the Inyanga National Park (20 km from the Rhodes Hotel and warden's office) lies the interesting and extensive area known as the . . .

## INYANGA DOWNS AND TROUTBECK

The inhabitants of Zimbabwe have always been notable individualists, the consequences of which characteristic are often interesting. In the story of the Vumba area it has been seen how individuals created such places as Leopard Rock and the original Manchester Gardens. A very similar situation occurred in relation to the Inyanga Downs.

In 1926 an artilleryman, Colonel Alfred McIlwaine, left the regular British army and took possession of a farm at Marandellas, intending to grow tobacco under a land settlement scheme. An international rugby player (representing England twice and many times captain of the British army team), he was a versatile and purposeful character. The slump in 1930 proved ruinous to many settlers and reduced the Colonel to living on mealie porridge (with sausage on Sundays!), and selling eggs at 6d a dozen – his sole means of livelihood.

In this sad situation he received a letter from Charles Hanmin which contained some interesting news. Up in the highlands of the Eastern District the Anglo-French Matabeleland Company had originally acquired 27 200 ha of completely virgin and uninhabited land. Finding no use for the land the company, in 1930, sold part of it to Charles Hanmin and his brother William, who named their purchase *Inyanga Downs*. The remainder of the estate, lying east of the Inyangani mountain, was procured by a syndicate who named it the Inyangani Estates.

The Hanmins built a house and started afforestation on their estate, but their discerning eyes observed many other possibilities in the area. It was as a result of this that they wrote to Colonel McIlwaine. Although the Hanmins were not fishermen themselves to their mind the Inyanga Downs, with its multitude of clear streams fed by over 1 000 mm of rain a year, looked ideal fishing country. Colonel McIlwaine, a renowned trout fisherman, was therefore asked to advise on the prospects. Together with his wife he visited the area.

They were delighted with what they saw. Everything seemed perfect: the stream temperatures were ideal for trout; there was plenty of food in the water; and the only indigenous fish were small mountain barbel. The Hanmins asked McIlwaine to develop the fishing, offering him his choice of 200 acres (80 ha) at 4/- an acre and a kilometre stretch of any of the streams. McIlwaine was still broke, but this was a fantastic opportunity. He selected a kilometre of the stream named *Tsanga* (reedy), and on his land built a cottage which he named *Troutbeck*, after the village in Cumberland, the surroundings of which were similar to the Inyanga Downs.

The first task was to plant trees – wattle and pine – for the Inyanga Downs were devoid of indigenous trees to the point of bleakness. Transport problems made fuel excessively expensive, therefore wood was needed for fires. In 1934 the first trout ova were introduced from the Cape, taking with ease to the mountain streams. Two years later fishermen were throwing back everything weighing less than half a kilogram.

The McIlwaines lent their cottage to friends and many of these visitors liked the area so much that they obtained plots for themselves. Eventually, a settlement grew up around Troutbeck. After the Second World War, Colonel McIlwaine bought more land and built a dam across the Tsanga stream. This enormous addition to the trout waters suggested the building of a hotel. No contractor during that time of post-war building boom was interested in working in so remote a situation, so the Colonel built the place himself. It took four and a half years of effort to complete, with a minimum of technical aid, but on 1 March 1951 Troutbeck Inn was opened, a spacious and atmospheric place that is one of Southern Africa's best hotels.

Freed from these building chores, the Colonel next bought 815 ha of land high above Troutbeck – scenically dramatic, cloud-covered, windswept and having staggering views of the lowland world of bush and granite hillock. In the basin-like depression on these heights, the Colonel constructed three dams: Loch Maree, Loch Con and Loch Corrib; named the area Little Connemara; made a circular drive and started selling 2-ha 'pocket estates', each with unlimited water rights, fishing rights, fresh air, sunsets and prodigious views. The principal viewsite – known as World's View – is 2 380 m above sea level and, with the red-flowering aloes of winter covering the foreground, this is one of Zimbabwe's most memorable outlooks. Some very individualistic people have settled in the area, including the Whirley-Birch family and the artist, Channing Renton.

### Accommodation
★★★ Troutbeck Inn, 75 rooms, all with baths. $12 – $18 D/B/B. Phone Inyanga 305.

## NYAHOKWE AND THE VAN NIEKERK RUINS

From the village of Inyanga, a gravel road descends into the low country, reaching after 15 km, the Nyahokwe Field Museum and Ancient Village Site. Here relics may be seen of human activity in the area from Stone Age man (40 000 years ago) to the ancestors of the present African people resident in the vicinity. Interesting reconstructions have been made of an ancient smelting furnace. Ruins of substantial villages and pit structures have been well preserved and there is a complex terracing on the hill known as *Nyahokwe,* from a former headman (Hokwe) of the Nyama people who live there today.

The Field Museum acts as an excellent introduction to the prodigious expanse of ruins which lie ahead for the next 17 km. These are the famous *Van Niekerk Ruins,* named after Major P. van Niekerk who, in 1905, guided the archaeologist, Professor D. Randall Maciver to them. This truly staggering complex of ruins covers an area of 80 square kilometres, dominated by a 1 745-m-high granite peak nowadays known as *Ziwa* (from a headman named Saziwa who lived there in recent times), and two minor satellite peaks.

In similar manner to Great Zimbabwe, this settlement seems to have been dominated by and built around an imposing mountain. On the southern slopes of the peak stand the ruins of several substantial complexes approached by walled passageways. Here the politico-religious head is most likely to have had his abode, and to have used the caves of the mountain as an oracle from which issued the voice of *Mwari* (God).

The area around the slopes of Ziwa is completely covered with terraces, parallel walls and circular enclosures, so well preserved that in them may still be seen the grinding stones of women and the seats of men. The peak period of the building of these ruins seems to have been around the 17th century, and the builders appear to have been the Rwe people, who still live in the eastern mountains today. What exactly possessed them to build so involved a residential area, remains unknown. The amount of labour expended in piling stones one on top of the other is beyond estimation. In true African fashion, it is doubtless the women and children did the work, while the lordly men occupied themselves with debates and wars. Implicitly obeying the instruction to build, the drudges simply went on piling rock after rock with scant design or planning.

Perhaps these structures were built under the delusion of security, but in the 19th century, the area was invaded by raiding Shangane and Nguni people, who simply overran the walls.

The survivors (their delusions of safety shattered), probably fled the blood-drenched place in horror and abandoned forever their peculiar culture of building endless stone walls.

Whatever the speculation, today all is silent and nothing moves through these vast ruins. The sophisticated visitor can only be reminded of the difficulties and dangers which beset his own primitive ancestors the world over when, with many a stumble and mistake, they contended with nature and their own ruthless fellows for even the most miserable and precarious existence.

---

From the Van Niekerk Ruins, the gravel road leads westwards for 85 km to join the main Umtali-Salisbury road (A3) at Baddeley. This road passes, among other features, the gigantic granite dome of Domba. In spring, when the musasa trees are in full colour, the pass around this mass of rock has rewarded the author with some of the most wonderful botanical spectacles he has seen anywhere in the world. This area is a paradise for brachystegia trees.

## UMTALI TO FORT VICTORIA

From Umtali, the main tarmac road to the south leads out of the town, past the African township of Sakubu, and along a hot, densely bushed valley. After 8 km a turn east leads to the Fern Valley smallholdings. A further 8 km takes the tarmac road past a turnoff east to the Ximunya township, and after a further 12 km the road reaches a turnoff to the Clydesdale North road.

At 40 km from Umtali, the tarmac road crosses the *Mpudzi* (pumpkin) River and 3 km further on reaches a turnoff east leading to what is known as . . .

## HIMALAYA

The gravel road to what some surveyor named Himalaya, climbs to the summit ridge of the mountains, 2 220 m above sea level, from where a tremendous view is revealed to the north across the Burma Valley to the ridge of the Vumba. This is, in fact, the area which confronts the Vumba and provides that mountain land with its superb view. The Vumba fully returns the compliment to Himalaya and provides an equally fine view of itself.

The gravel road winds and climbs through rugged granite mountain country, following the valley of the river known as the *Tshitora* (the taker away), on account of the damage it causes during its floods. Musasa trees thickly blanket the valley where seed potatoes are grown and Romney Marsh sheep flourish. Yellow arum lilies, everlastings, proteas, yellowwood and cedar trees cover the heights. In former times a footpath wandered up this valley, finding a tortuous way across the mountains. This path was known to early travellers as *Tsetsera* (hurry on), for the cold and rainswept heights caused the death of many people caught by storms. This African name still applies to the heights of the Himalaya where many skeletons have been found of unfortunate travellers who died of exposure while making the journey.

As in the Vumba, several individualists have made their homes on these heights. Many fine farms such as *Butler North, Helvetia, Engwe* (the place of the leopard) and others, line the wayside. At 48 km from its start, the road reaches the summit plateau where, lying on the boundary line of Moçambique, half lost in the clouds, the traveller finds the dream-like *Tsetsera* farm established by Senhor Victor Machado de Carvalho which stands in an exquisite forest of yellowwood trees. The timber of 400 yellowwood trees was used in the construction of the homestead. Superbly furnished, romantic in design, and overlooking a most serene view of the Chimanimani Mountains, this is a paradise in the wilderness of Africa. The story of the farm is fascinating . . .

In 1946 Senhor de Carvalho and his wife found the site of the farm. Wearying of big business in Lourenço Marques (now Maputo), they were searching for a farm on which to retire.

Travelling through the hot lowlands of Moçambique, they looked up at the cool mountains on the frontier with Zimbabwe and saw the lovely waterfalls tumbling down from the heights. Delighted at the sight, they found their way to the summit, an area proclaimed a Native Reserve, but which was uninhabited. For the African tribesman, the mountain summits were altogether too cold, bleak and damp. With 1 000 mm of rain a year, any person residing there needed to command resources of warmth, shelter, transport and agricultural technique, if he was to survive and make a living.

Senhor de Carvalho negotiated for the Tsetsera Heights, securing it in 1948. From the Zimbabwean side he built an involved and steeply graded road which provided the first practicable vehicle access to the heights. Only in 1958 was the spectacular road constructed up the face of the mountains from the Moçambique side. Meanwhile, Senhor de Carvalho had commenced farming on the heights, finding that the area was ideal for seed potatoes and cattle, being high above the level of African 'coast fever'. The farm became a major agricultural enterprise, producing dairy products for Beira and seed potatoes for the whole of Moçambique. The border gate on Tsetsera is locked and the road is not a route of entry between Zimbabwe and Moçambique.

---

Back on the main tarmac road where the Himalaya road branches off, 43 km south of Umtali, the journey continues through a landscape of hillocks, odd-shaped rocks and baobab trees. After 3 km the road crosses White Waters stream, passes the turnoff to Inyarapura and then, 17 km further on, reaches the Junction Tearoom, where a road turns off eastwards to Cashel (25 km) and Melsetter (81 km). For details of this celebrated scenic drive, see further on.

The tarmac road continues southwards through a landscape increasingly dominated by baobab trees. After 3 km the road crosses the pleasantly named *Mvumvumvu* (river of plenty), and traverses a densely populated tribal area where government irrigation projects have serviced numerous fertile smallholdings. Bananas, tropical fruit, vegetables and baskets are offered for sale at the roadside. At the end of this settled area (81 km from Umtali) the road passes the popular resort known as Hot Springs, where a copious outpouring of warm mineral water attracts many visitors for the pleasure and health of swimming in the large bath or taking the waters in private.

Twelve kilometres beyond Hot Springs, the tarmac road reaches another substantial irrigation settlement at *Nyanyadzi* named after the *Munyanyadzi* (the disappearer) stream, so called because of its eroding effects on crops when in flood. Here the road leads through a handsome avenue of acacias in whose shade the peasant farmers sell bananas, farm produce and finely made baskets. Green fields stretch down to the course of the river known as the *Odzi* (the rotter) from the damage caused by its floods. The agricultural settlement was started in 1933 for the benefit of the Ndawu tribe, who produce cotton, maize, beans, wheat and fruit.

The tarmac road leads on through a most picturesque wilderness of trees, with giant baobabs clustered in such numbers that this warm valley with its rocky soil is obviously their ideal home. At 120 km from Umtali the road reaches a junction. Straight ahead the road continues to Chipinga (56 km); Melsetter (98 km); and Mount Selinda (88 km). The tarmac road at present being followed swings sharp right. In this hot wilderness (one of the most concentrated baobab forest areas in Africa) may be seen ahead the astonishing sight of the soaring, steel arch of a gigantic bridge. After 8 km of travelling through the trees the road reaches the banks of the Save River and the famous bridge which spans it . . .

# THE BIRCHENOUGH BRIDGE AND THE SAVE RIVER

For some reason the European pioneers in Zimbabwe confused the name of the Save with that of the Sabi in the Transvaal. The proper name of this true river of the wilderness – Save – refers to its perennial flow. Meandering down the huge valley it has washed for itself, the river always provides an impressive sight, especially as its floods can reach gigantic proportions. Along its banks grow one of the greatest concentrations of baobab trees to be seen in Africa. Many other interesting species of flora flourish in the river valley, including the curious and beautifully flowered Star of the Sabi *(Adenuim multiflorem)*.

The Birchenough Bridge, opened in 1935, was built at a cost of £152 000 by the Beit Trust. The single span arch is 330 m long and 88 m at its highest point, with the total length of the bridge being 378 m. The road is carried 18,25 m above the river. Designed by Ralph Freeman, who designed the Sydney Harbour Bridge, it was named after Sir Henry Birchenough, at that time chairman of the Beit Trust. His ashes, together with those of his wife, are deposited in the abutment on the east side of the river.

On the right (west) bank of the river there stands a small hotel, notable for the variety and brilliance of the bougainvillaea growing in its grounds. The road leads westwards past this hotel, climbing steadily out of the baobab-covered valley floor and into a world of mopane trees growing on the higher land. The strong fragrance of new-cut potatoes issuing from the minute fruits of the *Pyllanthus reticulatos* shrubs, is characteristic of this area.

Nine kilometres from the bridge, the road crosses the river known as *Devure* (the spiller) from its habit of flooding its banks. A further 15 km takes the road past a turnoff south leading for 23 km to the headquarters of the great *Devuli* ranch.

The road, still steadily climbing out of the valley of the Save River, now passes through a range of granite hills, where baobab and mopane trees dominate the vegetation, and strangely shaped rocks lie scattered over the slopes like misshapen sculptures. The scenery here could only be seen in Africa: a wilderness of bush and rocky hillocks, with the huts of the tribespeople built on granite outcrops as a protection against termites.

At 50 km from the Birchenough Bridge there is a turnoff south to the substantial copper deposit worked by the mine known as *Umkondo* (the spear) from the ancient iron workings there, where many of these weapons were made. Jim Bentley found these abandoned prehistoric workings in 1906. After numerous problems involving transport and recovery, the mine is today a major producer.

The road now finds a way through a series of great granite domes by means of *Moodies Pass,* so named after the Moodie family who led the pioneer trek to settle the Melsetter area in 1892, and blazed the trail through this passage in the hills.

At 84 km from Birchenough Bridge there is a turnoff leading south to the administrative and mining centre of Bikita (10 km). Seventeen kilometres further on the road reaches the tin mining area around Glen Clova. The road has now ascended to the middleveld of Zimbabwe, an undulating, lightly bushed plain. At 136 km there is a turnoff to the administrative centre of Zaka (50 km south); at 142 km to the Zimbabwe circular drive; at 144 km to Glenlivet and Lake Kyle; at 152 km to Gutu; and at 158 km to the Kyle Game Reserve (18 km).

At 169 km from Birchenough Bridge (a total of 329 km from Umtali), the road reaches the town of Fort Victoria (see page 818).


# MELSETTER TO MOUNT SELINDA

Sixty-four kilometres south of Umtali, on the road to Birchenough Bridge, a small tearoom stands at the junction point of the wonderful scenic route to Melsetter and the southern section of the eastern mountains of Zimbabwe. The road leads eastwards, directly into the mountains, following the valley of the Mvumvumvu River, fertile and densely settled by peasant farmers.

The river itself is a rushing, gushing, bustling type of mountain torrent liberally supplied with water from the rainfall on the heights.

After 10 km of interesting travelling, the tarmac road reaches a junction. The main road turns sharp south, in a steady climb into the heights, past waterfalls and valleys, providing the shortest route to Melsetter (72 km). The old and scenically famous road continues east up the valley. At 24 km from the Umtali road, it passes through the rural centre of *Cashel,* so named after Lieutenant-Colonel E. Cashel who was a pioneer settler of those parts.

Beyond Cashel the road reaches a junction. Straight ahead the road continues past several fine farms such as *Thom's Hope* owned by George Heynes and eventually, after 8 km, reaches the border of Moçambique, revealing a fine view down into the low country. The road deteriorates at this point, and is not a public route of entry into Moçambique. At the junction outside Cashel, the main road swings sharp south to Melsetter, and this is the scenic route.

The road (gravel) climbs steadily up the valley of the Tandayi stream. Cascades and waterfalls are seen, while the reason for the name of the stream *(Tandayi* meaning 'the encircled one'), is apparent when the road reaches its headwaters in a basin completely hemmed in by mountains.

The Tandayi basin is a rural area where cattle, barley and fruit are produced on such farms as *Everest Orchards,* owned by an amiable couple named James. A small community centre named Tandaai, lies beside the road 9 km from Cashel. From here a track leads for 12 km up the mountains to one of the most spectacular viewsites imaginable which is thoroughly worth a bumpy ride. It overlooks not only the lowlands of Moçambique, but also the full length of the sparkling quartzite Chimanimani Mountains – a breathtaking sight. This track actually leads to another mountain farm once owned by the enterprising Senhor Victor de Carvalho of Tset-sera. This farm is named *Tandara* and occupies the plateau summit of a great mountain buttress situated just on the Moçambique side of the watershed boundary line. The plateau is ideal for the growing of seed potatoes and projects into one outlying peak on which stands a trigonometrical beacon. The panoramic view beyond the beacon is staggering. From the plateau a lovely waterfall leaps down to the lowlands of Moçambique. Standing guard on the verge of this fall is a solitary cedar tree, while down below a gorgeous rain forest flourishes on the spray from the falling water.

The main road leaves from the community centre of Tandaai and continues south, climbing steadily, passing (after 6 km) what is known as Steyn's Bank. There are so many members of the Steyn family living in these mountains that a local riddle asks: why is the area like a table cloth? To which the answer is: because there are so many Steyns on it!

The original coach road finds its way up the slopes on the eastern side of the modern road. At 27 km from Tandaai the road passes over a saddle of land known as Musapas Pass (2 135 m above sea level) and reveals ahead one of the classic views of Africa. Below and to the east stretches a long valley to the slopes of the beautiful Chimanimani range. The road makes a twisting descent into the valley past such farms as *Constantia,* owned by the Steyn family, and *Umsapa,* belonging to Philip Cremer and named after Musapa, a headman of the Ndawu people who once lived there.

For fifty-four kilometres after leaving Tandaai (95 km from the junction point on the main Umtali road), the road follows a route of superlative views, eventually reaching the village of *Melsetter* (so named by the Moody family of pioneers, who came from Melsetter in the Orkney Islands). A pleasantly rural little place and the centre of a timber, cattle, and vegetable industry, Melsetter is built on a terrace on the mountains with a sweeping view of the Chimanimani. The surroundings are green, and the flora richly varied. A notable feature is the Bridal Veil Falls (known to the Africans as *Mutsarara,* from the sound of the water falling).

## Accommodation
★★ Melsetter Hotel, 36 rooms, 24 with baths. $4,25 – $6 room only. Phone 11.

A short drive from the village of Melsetter leads to the entrance of the . . .

# CHIMANIMANI NATIONAL PARK

The mountain range known to the Africans as *Mawenje* (the rocky mountains), is called by Europeans *Chimanimani* from the ideophone *Tshimanimani* (to be squeezed together), which describes the narrow passage of the Musapa River through the range. Only about 50 km in length, it is singularly beautiful and in a granite world of grey-blue rock this range, with its jagged 2 240-m-high peaks made of a sugary-white quartzite sparkling in the brilliant sunshine, is a unique remnant of the water-deposited Frontier System. It presents one of the most spectacular scenes in Africa.

From Melsetter a gravel road leads to a parking and camping site (known as Dead Cow Camp) situated in a grove of wattle trees at the foot of the range. From this point a pathway provides the sole access up the mountain slopes.

It is an ancient pathway, almost as old as man himself in Africa, and a traditional route from the coast to the interior followed by countless travellers. It is a delight to the recreational hiker, but to the primitive African travellers it suddenly brought them from the warm lowlands to the heights where, exposed to driving rain and bitter cold, death awaited many of them.

A walk through the Chimanimani along this path rewards the energetic with many unforgettable sights and scenes. From the start, the main pathway climbs steadily through a beautifully wooded gorge, shady for most of the way and with plenty of clean mountain water to drink. There are so many interesting flowers and plants to see, and so many handsome vistas unfolding on the ascent, that the walker is diverted from any weariness he may feel.

To the botanist, the journey is a joy on account of the diverse and lovely flora. In many respects the Chimanimani resembles the Western Cape. The quartzite erodes into sand as fine and white as salt. In this rather unlikely looking soil flourish cedar and yellowwood trees; half a dozen different varieties of protea (some endemic to the area); golden everlastings; erica and leucospermum, all of which serve to make the visitor from the Cape feel at home until he notices that interspersed with these families are innumerable lovely things which belong to the island continent of Madagascar which lies at the same latitude. Ferns, orchids and aloes occur in great numbers and variety. One of the prides of the Chimanimani is the *Disa ornithantha* with its gorgeous red blooms to be seen in the marshlands during January and February.

The pathway being followed reaches the top of its climb and emerges on to a grassy plateau covered with odd-shaped rocks. Through this weird garden of rock the path meanders, with the traveller left to imagine at will all manner of petrified creatures – dwarfs, giants, demons.

All of a sudden the path tops a rise and the traveller is startled by a superb view of the inner valley of the mountains. Here, in a deep, thickly grassed valley, the Bundi River with its many crystal pools in which the watching peaks are reflected, finds its source in a great natural sponge.

Looking down upon this scene, 9 km (two hours' walk) from the start of the path, is a prince of mountain huts known as *Ball's Hotel,* from a mountain enthusiast named John Ball, who for 18 months devoted his weekends to its construction, completing the task in 1955. It shelters 24 people in two big dormitories and has a communal central room, a fine fireplace, a kitchen, and the luxury, in so remote a place, of waterborne sewerage and gas lighting. Hikers and climbers use this place as a base camp the like of which there is no better in Africa. Tariff for the use of Ball's Hotel is 75c per adult, including the use of sleeping bag. Camping is free anywhere in the park. The whole area (and the hut) is managed by the Department of National Parks and Wild Life. Trout fishing is permitted in the Bundi River from 1 October to 30 April. There is no bilharzia and swimming in the pools is fine.

Several paths radiate from Ball's Hotel. The main pathway descends to the floor of the valley, meanders across the grass and passes a strange pool known as *Mtseritseri* (the boiling place), where a powerful spring, as though boiling, churns up a permanent flurry of white sand from its bottom.

Herds of sable and eland may often be seen grazing in the valley, while baboons and leopards roam the heights. The pathway starts to climb the far side of the valley around the slopes of the highest peak of the range (2 240 m). This pass is known as Skeleton Pass and here the pathway reaches its highest altitude. Along the wayside the bones of several African travellers have been found where they have fallen by the way.

The summit reveals a sweeping view deep into Moçambique. Now on the frontier line, the single main path disperses into several branches. If one sat waiting at this point one would see many travellers passing by from distant tribal areas: Lawi from the north, Ndawu from the east, Shangane from the south; all intent on trudging somewhere, all making use of this natural passage in the mountains. The author wrote this as he sat resting there, and while doing so, three Ndawu came along, one bearing on his head a heavy load of homegrown tobacco to trade in Zimbabwe, one transporting a couple of fowls in a wickerwork basket and the third carrying a skimpy looking roll of blankets which must have provided scant cover for the three men if caught for the night on these heights. They had been walking for five days from some remote village in the bushlands, and they looked rather surprised to find a white man sitting there, wishing them a pleasant journey on their way.

From Skeleton Pass, the path veers south along the eastern slopes of the mountains, and finds a way through a dramatic landscape beneath towering cliffs. Many a stream comes cascading down and crosses the path. Clumps of evergreen forest shelter in the hollows; *shoma* (the bushbuck) barks an alarm from the thickets; in the sand of the path may be seen the track of *khamba* (the leopard) and *nungu* (the porcupine). The droppings of baboons and the cuds and shavings of wild sugar cane – the most popular food of the road for all African wayfarers – reveal the presence of many a traveller.

Presently the path climbs on to a broad, grassy ridge which acts as a watershed. South of it the streams unite to form a handsome river, the Mubvumodzi, filled with deep pools in a grassy valley. At the end of the high-lying valley this river suddenly rushes through a barrier of rock and tumbles in a fine, double leap 140 m down what is known as *Martin's Falls* (named after Gideon Martin, a pioneer of Melsetter and the first European to see them). It is a beautiful waterfall, complete with rainbow, and below it the river flows off on its involved way to the sea.

This is only one of the many lovely features of these handsome mountains and the walker and climber can be assured of infinite pleasure by a visit to this national park.

---

From Melsetter, the main road climbs steeply to what is known as Skyline Junction (17 km), where it joins with the new main road from Cashel and Umtali. Turning south at this junction the road ascends the undulating hills through kilometres of wattle plantations belonging to the Rhodesian Wattle Company, which has a factory 19 km from the junction.

Suddenly, the country changes. The road twists down after 16 km (52 km from Melsetter) to the head of the valley of the *Tanganda* (the flooding river). This was the site of *Waterfall*, the pioneer farm belonging to Thomas Moodie, who first settled in the eastern mountains in 1893 after an epic trek. His grave lies close to the road and here a branch leads west down the valley past the tea estates, to Birchenough Bridge, 48 km away.

The Tanganda Valley, steep and bush covered, was the route followed by the pioneer settlers in reaching the summit ridge of the eastern mountains. The magnificent estate *New Year's Gift*, marks the camp which the doughty Thomas Moodie and his followers erected on New Year's Day of 1893, after a fearsome journey dragging their wagons through the wilderness. This estate eventually passed into the hands of Arthur Wood, a retired tea planter from Assam. A pioneer of the enterprise of Thomas Moodie, he was of the opinion that tea could be grown in the eastern districts.

Arthur Wood persuaded Grafton Phillips, another tea planter from Assam, to migrate to Zimbabwe in 1925, and the two men established on *New Year's Gift* a nursery of tea plants imported from Assam. To their consternation they then discovered that the rainfall was totally inadequate. Tea requires at least 1 200 mm of rain a year, and if the two men had really studied local records they would never have started the venture. Now they were too involved to withdraw, but their precipitant action certainly paid dividends. They decided to irrigate from the Tanganda stream. Such cultivation was unique in tea growing but it worked: in 1929 they picked their first crop of 517 kg of tea. By 1945 they had passed 453 818 kg a year, and today the Rhodesia Tea Estates (Pvt) Ltd makes a significant contribution to the economy of Southern Africa with its Tanganda and Stella teas.

The head of the Tanganda Valley marks the end of the really high country of the eastern mountains. South of it, the main road continues at a lower level, through thickening bush. Nine kilometres from the turnoff down the valley, the road passes a turnoff east leading to the Eastern Border Road and the Ratelshoek Tea Estates. The main road continues south for 3 km and then reaches the village named *Chipinga* (the impeder) from a high buttress which blocked the early pathway there. This is a picturesque, half tropical little place – simply one street lined with shops and a few government buildings – but it is neat and clean, and beautified with plenty of flowers.

## Accommodation
* Chipinga Hotel, 17 rooms, 9 with baths. $6,50 – $7,50 B/B. Phone 226.

## Caravans and camping
* ®Chipinga Caravan Park, 40 sites. $1 D.

From Chipinga the road continues south over the middleveld type of bush country, scattered with cattle ranches and tea and coffee plantations. This is the administrative area known as Gazaland. After 32 km the road reaches the end of the eastern mountains and, right on the edge of the escarpment, facing east, is the beautiful 1 000-ha indigenous forest known as *Tshirinda* (the refuge). With its ironwoods, wild figs and red mahogany trees (one 65 m high and over 15 m in circumference), this lovely forest provides a fitting end to the scenic beauties seen so far. Butterflies and moths in prodigious numbers feed on the rotting vegetation and in spring, the Tshirinda Forest is a dazzling sight with the ironwood trees covered in snow-white blossoms.

In the forest stands the impressively well-built Mount Selinda Mission Station and next to the forest the government forestry plantation of Gungunyana. The hills peter out into the low country. There is a border gate through which the road continues into Moçambique to the tiny administrative post of *eSpungabera* (wood of the rock rabbits), with its one street of nondescript shops, police post, and astonishingly powerful electric lighting which makes the place literally glow at night, as though the village was a city in this solitary wilderness which sweeps up to the cool mountains in a restless sea of bush.

# Index

# INDEX

*Compiled by Nicole Monro*